W9-CNV-065

Programming
Microsoft® SQL Server™ 2008

Leonard Lobel
Andrew J. Brust
Stephen Forte

PUBLISHED BY
Microsoft Press
A Division of Microsoft Corporation
One Microsoft Way
Redmond, Washington 98052-6399

Library of Congress Control Number: 2008935426

Printed and bound in the United States of America.

1 2 3 4 5 6 7 8 9   QWT   3 2 1 0 9 8

Distributed in Canada by H.B. Fenn and Company Ltd.

A CIP catalogue record for this book is available from the British Library.

Microsoft Press books are available through booksellers and distributors worldwide. For further information about international editions, contact your local Microsoft Corporation office or contact Microsoft Press International directly at fax (425) 936-7329. Visit our Web site at www.microsoft.com/mspress. Send comments to mspinput@microsoft.com.

Microsoft, Microsoft Press, ActiveX, BizTalk, Excel, Expression Blend, IntelliSense, Internet Explorer, MS, MSDN, MSN, Outlook, PerformancePoint, PivotChart, PivotTable, ProClarity, SharePoint, Silverlight, SQL Server, Virtual Earth, Visio, Visual Basic, Visual C#, Visual Studio, Win32, Windows, Windows Live, Windows Mobile, Windows Server, Windows Server System, and Windows Vista are either registered trademarks or trademarks of the Microsoft group of companies. Other product and company names mentioned herein may be the trademarks of their respective owners.

The example companies, organizations, products, domain names, e-mail addresses, logos, people, places, and events depicted herein are fictitious. No association with any real company, organization, product, domain name, e-mail address, logo, person, place, or event is intended or should be inferred.

Acquisitions Editor: Ken Jones
Developmental Editor: Sally Stickney
Project Editor: Kathleen Atkins
Editorial Production: Waypoint Press
Technical Reviewer: Kenn Scribner; Technical Review services provided by Content Master, a member of CM Group, Ltd.
Cover: Tom Draper Design

Body Part No. X15-12263

To my partner, Mark, and our children, Adam, Jacqueline, and Joshua, for standing by me through every one of life's turns.

—Leonard Lobel

To my wife, Lauren, and my sons, Sean and Miles. Thank you for your love, your support, and your accommodation of the unreasonable.

—Andrew Brust

To Kathleen, thanks for your support and making me run marathons, which are more painful than book writing and building beta machines.

—Stephen Forte

Contents at a Glance

Part I **Core Fundamentals**
   1 Overview 3
   2 T-SQL Enhancements 13
   3 Exploring SQL CLR 111
   4 Server Management 161
   5 Security in SQL Server 2008 189

Part II **Beyond Relational**
   6 XML and the Relational Database 231
   7 Hierarchical Dataand the Relational Database 281
   8 Using FILESTREAM for Unstructured Data Storage 307
   9 Geospatial Data Types 341

Part III **Reach Technologies**
   10 The Microsoft Data Access Machine 377
   11 The Many Facets of .NET Data Binding 419
   12 Transactions 449
   13 Developing Occasionally Connected Systems 491

Part IV **Business Intelligence**
   14 Data Warehousing 563
   15 Basic OLAP 611
   16 Advanced OLAP 639
   17 OLAP Queries, Tools, and Application Development 717
   18 Expanding Your Business Intelligence with Data Mining 793
   19 Reporting Services 879

Table of Contents

Acknowledgments xxi

Introduction xxv

Part I   Core Fundamentals

1   Overview 3

Just How Big Is It?. 3

A Book *for* Developers 5

A Book *by* Developers. 6

A Book to Show You the Way. 6

Core Technologies. 7

Beyond Relational 8

Reaching Out 9

Business Intelligence Strategies. 10

Summary 12

2   T-SQL Enhancements 13

Common Table Expressions 14

Creating Recursive Queries with CTEs 18

The *PIVOT* and *UNPIVOT* Operators. 21

Using *UNPIVOT* 22

Dynamically Pivoting Columns 23

The *APPLY* Operator 25

TOP Enhancements 26

Ranking Functions 28

The *ROW_NUMBER* Function 28

The *RANK* Function 32

The *DENSE_RANK* and *NTILE* Functions 34

What do you think of this book? We want to hear from you!

Microsoft is interested in hearing your feedback so we can continually improve our books and learning resources for you. To participate in a brief online survey, please visit:

www.microsoft.com/learning/booksurvey

Using All the Ranking Functions Together 36

Ranking over Groups Using *PARTITION BY*. 37

Exception Handling in Transactions 40

The varchar(max) Data Type. 42

The *WAITFOR* Statement 43

DDL Triggers 43

SNAPSHOT Isolation 45

Table-Valued Parameters 45

More than Just Another Temporary Table Solution. 46

Working with a Multiple-Row Set. 48

Using TVPs for Bulk Inserts and Updates. 49

Working with a Single Row of Data 51

Creating Dictionary-Style TVPs 54

Passing TVPs Using ADO.NET 56

TVP Limitations 59

New Date and Time Data Types 59

Separation of Dates and Times 59

More Portable Dates and Times 60

Time Zone Awareness. 61

Date and Time Accuracy, Storage, and Format. 62

New and Changed Functions. 65

The *MERGE* Statement 68

Defining the Merge Source and Target 70

The *WHEN MATCHED* Clause 71

The *WHEN NOT MATCHED BY TARGET* Clause 72

Using *MERGE* for Table Replication 73

The *WHEN NOT MATCHED BY SOURCE* Clause 74

MERGE Output. 76

Choosing a Join Method. 78

MERGE DML Behavior. 79

Doing the "Upsert" 81

The INSERT OVER DML Syntax. 90

Extending *OUTPUT...INTO* 90

Consuming *CHANGES*. 94

The *GROUPING SETS* Operator 97

Rolling Up by Level 99

Rolling Up All Level Combinations 101

Returning Just the Top Level 103

Mixing and Matching 104
Handling *NULL* Values. 105
New T-SQL Shorthand Syntax 109
Summary 110

3   Exploring SQL CLR **111**
Getting Started: Enabling CLR Integration. 112
Visual Studio/SQL Server Integration 113
SQL Server Projects in Visual Studio. 114
Automated Deployment. 117
SQL CLR Code Attributes 117
Your First SQL CLR Stored Procedure 118
CLR Stored Procedures and Server-Side Data Access 120
Piping Data with *SqlDataRecord* and *SqlMetaData* 123
Deployment 125
Deploying Your Assembly 125
Deploying Your Stored Procedures. 127
Testing Your Stored Procedures 129
CLR Functions 131
CLR Triggers 136
CLR Aggregates 140
SQL CLR Types. 145
Security 150
Examining and Managing SQL CLR Types in a Database 152
Best Practices for SQL CLR Usage 159
Summary 160

4   Server Management **161**
What Is SMO? 161
What About SQL-DMO? 162
Latest Features in SMO 166
Working with SMO in Microsoft Visual Studio 167
Iterating Through Available Servers 169
Retrieving Server Settings 171
Creating Backup-and-Restore Applications 175
Performing Programmatic DBCC Functions with SMO 181
Policy-Based Management. 183
A Simple Policy. 184
Summary 188

5   Security in SQL Server 2008 .... **189**

Four Themes of the Security Framework 189

Secure by Design 189

Secure by Default. 190

Secure by Deployment 190

Secure Communications. 190

SQL Server 2008 Security Overview 191

SQL Server Logins 192

Database Users. 193

The *guest* User Account 194

Authentication and Authorization. 195

How Clients Establish a Connection 195

Password Policies. 197

User-Schema Separation. 198

Execution Context 200

Encryption Support in SQL Server. 203

Encrypting Data on the Move 204

Encrypting Data at Rest 206

Transparent Data Encryption in SQL Server 2008. 211

Creating Keys and Certificates. 211

Enabling TDE. 213

Querying TDE Views 213

Backing Up the Certificate 214

Restoring an Encrypted Database. 215

SQL Server Audit 216

Creating an Audit Object 216

Auditing Options 217

Recording Audits to the File System. 219

Recording Audits to the Windows Event Log 220

Auditing Server Events 220

Auditing Database Events. 221

Viewing Audited Events 222

Querying Audit Catalog Views 224

How Hackers Attack SQL Server 225

Direct Connection to the Internet. 225

Weak System Administrator Account Passwords 226

SQL Server Browser Service 226

       SQL Injection. 226

       Intelligent Observation. 227

    Summary 228

Part II **Beyond Relational**

6 **XML and the Relational Database** **231**

    XML in SQL Server 2000 233

    XML in SQL Server 2008—the *xml* Data Type. 234

       Working with the *xml* Data Type as a Variable. 234

       Working with XML in Tables. 235

       XML Schemas 237

       XML Indexes 244

    FOR XML Commands. 247

       FOR XML RAW 248

       FOR XML AUTO 248

       FOR XML EXPLICIT. 250

       FOR XML Enhancements. 253

       OPENXML Enhancements in SQL Server 2008 .261

       XML Bulk Load 262

    Querying XML Data Using XQuery. 263

       Understanding XQuery Expressions and XPath 263

       SQL Server 2008 XQuery in Action. 266

       SQL Server XQuery Extensions 275

       XML DML. 276

       Converting a Column to XML 278

    Summary 280

7 **Hierarchical Data and the Relational Database** **281**

    The *hierarchyid* Data Type 282

    Creating a Hierarchical Table. 283

       The *GetLevel* Method 284

    Populating the Hierarchy 285

       The *GetRoot* Method. 286

       The *GetDescendant* Method 286

       The *ToString* Method. 288

       The *GetAncestor* Method 293

Hierarchical Table Indexing Strategies 296
    Depth-First Indexing 297
    Breadth-First Indexing 298
Querying Hierarchical Tables...................................299
    The *IsDescendantOf* Method 299
Reordering Nodes Within the Hierarchy 301
    The *GetReparentedValue* Method...............................301
    Transplanting Subtrees 303
More *hierarchyid* Methods...................................305
Summary 306

8   Using FILESTREAM for Unstructured Data Storage 307
BLOBs in the Database 307
BLOBs in the File System...............................309
What's in an Attribute? 309
Enabling FILESTREAM 310
    Enabling FILESTREAM for the Machine 311
    Enabling FILESTREAM for the Server Instance 312
    Creating a FILESTREAM-Enabled Database.......................313
    Creating a Table with FILESTREAM Columns.....................315
The *OpenSqlFilestream* Native Client API...........................318
    File-Streaming in .NET......................................319
    Understanding FILESTREAM Data Access 321
    The Payoff...331
    Creating a Streaming HTTP Service 333
    Building the WPF Client 338
Summary 340

9   Geospatial Data Types 341
SQL Server 2008 Spaces Out 341
Spatial Models 342
    Planar (Flat-Earth) Model 342
    Geodetic (Round-Earth) Model................................343
Spatial Data Types 344
Defining Space with Well-Known Text 344
Working with *geometry*................................345
    The *Parse* Method 346
    The *STIntersects* Method 347

The *ToString* Method. 349

The *STIntersection* Method. 350

The *STDimension* Method 350

Working with *geography*. 351

On Your Mark …. 352

The *STArea* and *STLength* Methods 355

Spatial Reference IDs. 355

Building Out the *EventLibrary* Database 355

Creating the Event Media Client Application 357

The *STDistance* Method 363

Integrating *geography* with Microsoft Virtual Earth 364

Summary 374

Part III **Reach Technologies**

10 **The Microsoft Data Access Machine** **377**

ADO.NET and Typed *DataSet*s. 378

Typed *DataSet* Basics. 378

TableAdapter Objects 380

Connection String Management. 381

Using the TableAdapter Configuration Wizard. 382

More on Queries and Parameters. 385

DBDirect Methods and Connected Use of Typed *DataSet* Objects . . .387

"Pure" ADO.NET: Working in Code 387

Querying 101 388

LINQ: A New Syntactic Approach to Data Access. 392

LINQ to DataSet. 392

LINQ Syntax, Deconstructed 393

LINQ to SQL and the ADO.NET Entity Framework: ORM Comes to .NET. . . .395

Why Not Stick with ADO.NET? 396

Building an L2S Model 397

The Entity Framework: Doing ORM the ADO.NET Way 402

XML Behind the Scenes. 405

Querying the L2S and EF Models 406

Adding Custom Validation Code. 410

Web Services for Data: Using ADO.NET Data Services Against EF Models . .411

Creating the Service 412

Testing the Service. 414

Building the User Interface. 414

Data as a Hosted Service: SQL Server Data Services 415

Summary: So Many Tools, So Little Time. 417

11   The Many Facets of .NET Data Binding **419**

Windows Forms Data Binding: The Gold Standard 420

Getting Ready. 420

Generating the UI 421

Examining the Output. 423

Converting to LINQ to SQL 424

Converting to Entity Framework. 425

Converting to ADO.NET Data Services. 426

Data Binding on the Web with ASP.NET. 427

L2S and EF Are Easy. 428

Beyond Mere Grids 429

Data Binding Using Markup. 430

Using AJAX for Easy Data Access 430

ASP.NET Dynamic Data. 435

Data Binding for Windows Presentation Foundation 438

Design Time Quandary. 439

Examining the XAML. 441

Grand Finale: Silverlight. 445

Summary 447

12   Transactions. **449**

What Is a Transaction?. 450

Understanding the ACID Properties. 450

Local Transaction Support in SQL Server 2008. 453

Autocommit Transaction Mode. 453

Explicit Transaction Mode 453

Implicit Transaction Mode 456

Batch-Scoped Transaction Mode 457

Using Local Transactions in ADO.NET 459

Transaction Terminology. 461

Isolation Levels 462

Isolation Levels in SQL Server 2008 462

Isolation Levels in ADO.NET. 467

Distributed Transactions 468
    Distributed Transaction Terminology 469
    Rules and Methods of Enlistment 470
    Distributed Transactions in SQL Server 2008 472
    Distributed Transactions in the .NET Framework 473
    Writing Your Own Resource Manager 477
    Using a Resource Manager in a Successful Transaction 481
Transactions in SQL CLR (CLR Integration) 485
Putting It All Together 489
Summary 490

13   Developing Occasionally Connected Systems 491
Comparing Sync Services with Merge Replication 492
Components of an Occasionally Connected System .493
Merge Replication 494
    Getting Familiar with Merge Replication 494
    Creating an Occasionally Connected Application with
    Merge Replication 496
    Configuring Merge Replication 499
    Creating a Mobile Application Using Microsoft Visual Studio 2008 . . .520
Sync Services for ADO.NET 533
    Sync Services Object Model 534
    Capturing Changes for Synchronization 538
    Creating an Application Using Sync Services 543
    Additional Considerations 557
Summary 560

Part IV Business Intelligence

14   Data Warehousing 563
Data Warehousing Defined 563
The Importance of Data Warehousing 564
What Preceded Data Warehousing 566
    Lack of Integration Across the Enterprise 567
    Little or No Standardized Reference Data 568
    Lack of History 568
    Data Not Optimized for Analysis 568
    As a Result... 569
Data Warehouse Design 570

The Top-Down Approach of Inmon 572

The Bottom-Up Approach of Kimball 574

What Data Warehousing Is Not. 580

OLAP 580

Data Mining 581

Business Intelligence 582

Dashboards and Scorecards. 583

Performance Management 585

Practical Advice About Data Warehousing 585

Anticipating and Rewarding Operational Process Change. 586

Rewarding Giving Up Control 586

A Prototype Might Not Work to Sell the Vision 586

Surrogate Key Issues 587

Currency Conversion Issues 587

Events vs. Snapshots 588

SQL Server 2008 and Data Warehousing. 589

T-SQL *MERGE* Statement 589

Change Data Capture 592

Partitioned Table Parallelism 600

Star-Join Query Optimization 603

SPARSE Columns 604

Data Compression and Backup Compression. 605

Learning More 610

Summary 610

15   Basic OLAP 611

Wherefore BI? 611

OLAP 101 613

OLAP Vocabulary. 614

Dimensions, Axes, Stars, and Snowflakes. 615

Building Your First Cube 617

Preparing Star Schema Objects. 617

A Tool by Any Other Name 618

Creating the Project. 619

Adding a Data Source View 621

Creating a Cube with the Cube Wizard 625

Using the Cube Designer 626

Using the Dimension Wizard 629

Using the Dimension Designer 632

Working with the Properties Window and Solution Explorer 634

Processing the Cube 635

Running Queries. 636

Summary 637

16 Advanced OLAP **639**

What We'll Cover in This Chapter 640

MDX in Context 640

And Now a Word from Our Sponsor... 640

Advanced Dimensions and Measures. 641

Keys and Names. 641

Changing the *All* Member 644

Adding a Named Query to a Data Source View. 645

Parent/Child Dimensions 647

Member Grouping. 651

User Table Time Dimensions, Attribute Relationships,
Best Practice Alerts, and Dimension/Attribute Typing 652

Server Time Dimensions 660

Fact Dimensions. 661

Role-Playing Dimensions 664

Advanced Measures 665

Calculations. 667

Calculated Members 668

Named Sets. 673

More on Script View 674

Key Performance Indicators 677

KPI Visualization: Status and Trend. 678

A Concrete KPI 679

Testing KPIs in Browser View 681

KPI Queries in Management Studio 683

Other BI Tricks in Management Studio 688

Actions 689

Actions Simply Defined. 690

Designing Actions 690

Testing Actions. 692

Partitions, Storage Settings, and Proactive Caching 693

Editing and Creating Partitions 694

Partition Storage Options 696
Proactive Caching 697
Additional Features and Tips 699
Aggregations 700
Algorithmic Aggregation Design 700
Usage-Based Aggregation Design 701
Manual Aggregation Design (and Modification) 702
Aggregation Design Management 704
Aggregation Design and Management Studio .705
Perspectives 705
Translations 707
Roles 712
Summary 715

17   OLAP Queries, Tools, and Application Development **717**
Using Excel 719
Connecting to Analysis Services 719
Building the PivotTable 723
Exploring PivotTable Data 725
Scorecards 727
Creating and Configuring Charts 729
In-Formula Querying of Cubes 732
Visual Studio Tools for Office and Excel Add-Ins 737
Excel Services 738
Beyond Excel: Custom OLAP Development with .NET 743
MDX and Analysis Services APIs 744
Moving to MDX 744
Management Studio as an MDX Client 745
OLAP Development with ADO MD.NET 758
Using Analysis Management Objects 769
XMLA at Your (Analysis) Service 771
Analysis Services CLR Support: Server-Side ADO MD.NET 782
Summary 792

18   Expanding Your Business Intelligence with Data Mining **793**
Why Mine Your Data? 793
SQL Server 2008 Data Mining Enhancements 797
Getting Started 798
Preparing Your Source Data 798

Creating an Analysis Services Project. 800
Using the Data Mining Wizard and Data Mining Structure Designer. 802
Creating a Mining Structure. 804
Creating a Mining Model 805
Editing and Adding Mining Models 810
Deploying and Processing Data Mining Objects 816
Viewing Mining Models 818
Validating and Comparing Mining Models. 827
Nested Tables 830
Using Data Mining Extensions. 836
Data Mining Modeling Using DMX 837
Data Mining Predictions Using DMX 848
DMX Templates 856
Data Mining Applied 856
Data Mining and API Programming. 857
Using the Windows Forms Model Content Browser Controls 858
Executing Prediction Queries with ADO MD.NET 860
Model Content Queries 860
ADO MD.NET and ASP.NET 861
Using the Data Mining Web Controls. 862
Developing Managed Stored Procedures 863
XMLA and Data Mining 865
Data Mining Add-ins for Excel 2007. 866
Summary 877

19   Reporting Services **879**
Using the Report Designer 880
Creating a Basic Report. 883
Applying Report Formatting 887
Adding a Report Group 890
Working with Parameters 892
Writing Custom Report Code 897
Creating an OLAP Report. 900
Creating a Report with a Matrix Data Region. 906
Tablix Explained 910
Adding a Chart Data Region 915
Making a Report Interactive 917
Delivering Reports. 919
Deploying to the Report Server 919

Accessing Reports Programmatically 928

Administering Reporting Services 937

Using Reporting Services Configuration Manager 937

Using Report Manager and Management Studio 940

Integrating with SharePoint 949

Summary 951

Index 953

What do you think of this book? We want to hear from you!

Microsoft is interested in hearing your feedback so we can continually improve our books and learning resources for you. To participate in a brief online survey, please visit:

www.microsoft.com/learning/booksurvey

Acknowledgments

Working on this book has truly been the most rewarding experience of my professional career thus far, and I need to thank a great many people who have made it possible.

I first met Andrew Brust about 10 years ago, and we've enjoyed a close working relationship and growing friendship for the past 7 of those. I can't count the number of times Andrew has opened doors for me with project, writing, and speaking opportunities—and now, of course, this book. Andrew introduced me to Stephen Forte back in 2004, and after 30 years in the industry, I've learned to find new appreciation for the art of software development through Stephen's enthusiastic (that is, wacky and wild) personality. Andrew and Stephen both made this project significantly easier by producing the original edition of this book—an excellent treatment of Microsoft SQL Server 2005 that set the starting point for this new 2008 edition. It's been an absolute thrill and honor that they invited me to join them this time around and to assume the role of lead author for the new edition. Thanks to you both for entrusting me with that responsibility, as well as for your own hard work on this edition.

We could never have produced a book so broad and deep in scope without the additional aid of the other guest authors. Elsie Pan, Paul Delcogliano, Mark Frawley, and Jeff Bolton each did an outstanding job writing brand-new chapters, and Elsie also revised material from the last edition. Heartfelt thanks go out as well to Kenn Scribner, who performed an incredibly detail-oriented tech review of the entire book, and especially for helping out with updating important material at the bottom of the ninth with two men out and three men on. I'm very grateful for their contributions and professionalism, and I feel privileged to have worked with each of them. I'd also like to thank Jay Rabin, and all the wonderful folks at twentysix New York, for their continuous stream of support and encouragement throughout this whole project.

I was very lucky to have worked closely with Kathleen Atkins, Sally Stickney, and Ken Jones of Microsoft Press; Steve Sagman from Waypoint Press; and copy editor Jennifer Harris. Their superb editorial contributions, project planning, and overall guidance were vital to the production of this book. Double thanks go to Sally, who was always available to me (weekends too) for much-needed guidance as I entered the world of book writing. And the assistance provided by a number of people from various Microsoft product teams helped tackle the challenge of writing about new software as it evolved through several beta releases. So thank you to Steve Lasker, for support with Compact and Sync Services, and to Roger Doherty and Isaac Kunen for support with the "beyond relational" features. In particular, Roger inspired several of the FILESTREAM and geospatial demos found in those chapters. George Sobhy was also a great help with geospatial—he even arranged for a shared desktop demo between New York and Cairo (and thanks to Stephen Forte too, for the introduction).

This would all be moot, of course, without the love and support of my family. Almost all of my spare time over the past year was spent working on this project in one form or another—researching and writing new material, editing the whole book, and coordinating its production—which at times transformed me into an absentee partner and father. I owe an enormous debt of gratitude to my wonderful partner, Mark, and my awesome kids, Adam, Jacqueline, and Josh, for putting up with it all. So thanks, gang, I'm back home now! And thanks most of all to dear Mom, bless her soul, for always encouraging me to write with "expression" since the first grade.

—*Leonard Lobel*

Writing a book is hard, especially for the people in the authors' lives who lend heroic support. Revising a book is hard too, especially for the people in the authors' lives who lend that support *again*.

With that in mind, I'd like to thank my wife, Lauren (who endured this project while at the same time earning her master's degree and being an amazing mom to our two boys). And I thank our boys as well: Miles (who, though only four years old, is nonetheless a veteran of both editions of this book) and Sean (who, at age 18 months, has endured yet another thing that his older brother experienced first). All three have tolerated my intolerable absences from their events and their lives. Each one has my gratitude for the patience and understanding shown to me.

I'd also like to thank everyone at twentysix New York, especially Jay Rabin, for granting me a period of calm, with unprecedented duration, to get the work on this edition done.

Finally, but certainly not least of all, I'd like to thank Leonard Lobel for "taking the wheel" on this edition of the book. Had he not done so, we simply would not *have* this edition of the book. Lenni is prone to thanking me for exposing him to opportunity. What he fails to understand is that by repeatedly succeeding, he makes me look good simply for having the good taste to recommend him.

—*Andrew Brust*

It's nice to have your name on the cover of a book, but without help from various people, this book never would have happened. I'll start with Andrew and Lenni, my wonderful co-authors, both easy to work with, dedicated, and also very patient with me. The folks at Microsoft Press were all great to work with and had considerable energy and flexibility.

I would not have been able to take on this project if I did not have the support of the folks at Telerik, Triton Works, and Dash Soft, three companies that I work very closely with. I would like to give special thanks to the leaders of those firms, Vassil Terziev, Mark Storen, and Remon "FGD" Zakaria, for their understanding and support when deadlines for the book loomed.

We have also had tons of great reviewers. I was blessed to have folks like Kimberly Tripp, Peter DeBetta, and Roman Rehak help out with reading my chapters, as well as Kevin Collins, Remi Caron, Joel Semeniuk, Eileen Rumwell, Steve Lasker, Kirk Haselden, Ted Lee, Sergei Ivanov, Richard Campbell, Goksin Bakir, Malek Kemmou, Jason Gideon, Julie Lerman, Bill Ramos, Tom Halligan, and finally Jack Prilook—who looked at my manuscript 13 times.

I started this book on the first day of classes of my second year of my MBA education. Some days I had to choose whether to write on Policy-Based Management or macroeconomic trends in China and India. I'd like to thank all my group members at EMBA 26, most especially Dr. Ian Miller, Rosa Alvarado, Jason Nocco, Dmitriy Malinovskiy, and Cyrus Kazi. As fate would have it, I type these words on my last day of school. How fitting to finish a book and an MBA in the same weekend.

—Stephen Forte

Introduction

Welcome, developer!

The book you are holding, much like Microsoft SQL Server 2008 itself, builds on a great "previous release." SQL Server 2005 was—architecturally speaking—a groundbreaking upgrade from earlier versions of the product, and the 2005 edition of this book was a new printed resource that provided comprehensive coverage of the revamped platform. This new edition includes thoroughly updated coverage of the most important topics from the past edition, plus brand-new coverage of all the new exciting and powerful features for developers in SQL Server 2008. As with the 2005 edition, we set out to produce the best book for developers who need to program SQL Server 2008 in the many ways that it can be programmed.

To best understand our approach, we ask that you consider likening SQL Server 2008 to, of all things, a Sunday newspaper. A Sunday newspaper is made up of multiple sections, each of which is written separately and appeals to a distinct audience. The sections do have overlapping content and share some readership, of course, but most people don't read the whole paper, and they don't need to. Meanwhile, the entire paper is considered a single publication, and those who read it think of themselves as readers of the paper rather than of one or more of its sections. Likewise, SQL Server has many pieces to it: few people will use them all, and people will need to learn about them gradually, over time, as their business needs dictate.

Our book reflects this reality and in many ways replicates the structure of a Sunday newspaper. For one thing, a great number of authors have been involved in producing the book, drawing on their expertise in their chapters' specific subject matter. For another, the context of certain chapters differs markedly from those of other chapters. Some chapters cover specific subject matter deeply. Others cover a broader range of material, and do so at a higher level. That's an approach we didn't anticipate when we authored the 2005 edition of this book. But it's the approach we found most effective by the time we finished it, and one which we continue to follow in this new edition for SQL Server 2008. We have found that it makes an otherwise overwhelming set of technologies much more approachable and makes the learning process much more modular.

Make no mistake, though—the overall vision for the book is a cohesive one: to explore the numerous programmability points of SQL Server 2008 and, in so doing, provide widespread coverage of the great majority of the product's features, in a voice that caters to developers' interests. Whether you read every chapter in the book or just some of them and whether you read the book in or out of order, our goal has been to provide you with practical information, numerous useful samples, and a combination of high-level coverage and detailed discussion, depending on how deep we thought developers would want to go.

Just as the Sunday newspaper doesn't cover everything that's going on in the world, this book won't teach you everything about SQL Server. For example, we don't cover high-availability/fault tolerance features such as replication, clustering, or mirroring. We don't discuss query plans and optimization, nor do we investigate SQL Server Profiler, SQL Trace, or the Database Engine Tuning Advisor. Some features covered in the 2005 edition have not changed significantly in SQL Server 2008, such as native XML Web Services, Service Broker, Integration Services, and cross-tier debugging. These topics are also not covered, in order to make room for new SQL Server 2008 features. (The 2005 edition chapters that cover those topics are available for you to download from this book's companion Web site, which we explain toward the end of this introduction.)

We discovered as we wrote the book that covering *everything* in the product would result in a book unwieldy in size and unapproachable in style. We hope we struck the right balance, providing a *digestible* amount of information with enough developer detail and enough pointers to other material to help you become a seasoned SQL Server professional.

Who This Book Is For

Now that we have established *what* the book does and does not cover, we'd like to clarify just *who* we believe will be most interested in it and best served by it. In a nutshell, this book is for .NET and SQL Server developers who work with databases and data access, at the business logic/middle-tier layer as well as the application level.

In our perhaps self-centered view of the development world, we think this actually describes *most* .NET developers, but clearly some developers are more interested in database programming in general, and SQL Server specifically, than others, and it is this more interested group we want to reach.

We assume that you have basic, working knowledge of .NET programming on the client and Transact-SQL (T-SQL) on the server, although SQL experience on any platform can easily substitute. We also assume that you are comfortable with the basics of creating tables, views, and stored procedures on the server. On the client tools side, we assume that you are familiar with the prior generation of SQL Server and .NET development tools. If you've already been working with SQL Server Management Studio in SQL Server 2005, you'll feel right at home with the 2008 version, which has been extended to support new server features (and now even includes IntelliSense for T-SQL!). If you're still running SQL Server 2000 or earlier, you'll definitely appreciate SQL Server Management Studio as a vast improvement over the two primary tools that preceded it—Enterprise Manager and Query Analyzer. SQL Server Management Studio essentially represents the fusion of those two tools, packaged in a modern user interface (UI) shell very similar to that provided by Microsoft Visual Studio—complete with customizable menus and toolbars, floatable and dockable panes, solutions, and projects. The primary tool for .NET development is, of course, Visual Studio 2008, and experience with any version will also be beneficial for you to have.

Having said all that, we have a fairly liberal policy regarding these prerequisites. For example, if you've only dabbled with SQL and .NET, that's OK, as long as you're willing to try and pick up on things as you read along. Most of our code samples are not that complex. However, our explanations do assume some basic knowledge on your part, and you might need to do a little research if you lack the experience.

> **Note** For the sake of consistency, all the .NET code in this book is written in C#. (The only exceptions to this rule will be found in Chapter 19 for Reporting Services, since only Visual Basic .NET is supported for scripting report expressions and deployments.) However, this book is in no way C#-oriented, and there is certainly nothing C#-specific in the .NET code provided. As we just stated, the code samples are not very complex, and if you are more experienced with Visual Basic .NET than you are with C#, you should have no trouble translating the C# code to Visual Basic .NET on the fly as you read it.

In addition to covering the SQL Server core relational engine, its latest breed of "beyond relational" capabilities, and its ancillary services, this book also provides in-depth coverage of SQL Server's business intelligence (BI) features, including Reporting Services, and the online analytical processing (OLAP) and data mining components of Analysis Services. Although ours is not a BI book per se, it is a database developer's book, and we feel strongly that all these features should be understood by mainstream database developers. BI is really one of the cornerstone features of SQL Server 2008, so the time is right for traditional database developers to "cross over" to the world of BI.

Realizing that these technologies, especially OLAP and data mining, will be new territory for many readers, we assume no knowledge of them on your part. Any reader who meets the prerequisites already discussed should feel comfortable reading about these BI features and, more than likely, feel ready and excited to start working with BI after reading the BI-focused chapters.

How This Book Is Organized

This book is broken down into four parts. Each part follows a specific SQL Server "theme," if you will.

Part I begins with an overview that gives you a succinct breakdown of the chapters in all four parts of the book. Then it dives right in to core SQL Server technologies. We explore the many powerful enhancements made to Transact-SQL (T-SQL), both in SQL Server 2005 and 2008 (in that order). We also introduce you to SQL Server's .NET Common Language Runtime (CLR) integration features, which cut across our discussions of data types and server-side programming. You'll learn how to programmatically administer the server using Server Management Objects (SMO), which were introduced in SQL Server 2005, and how to use the new administrative framework called Policy-Based Management (PBM) in SQL Server 2008. Then we tackle security. After quickly covering basic SQL Server security concepts, we show how to encrypt your data both while in transit (traveling across the network) and at rest (on disk). We'll also teach the latest security features in SQL Server 2008, including Transparent Data Encryption (TDE) and SQL Server Audit, which you will find extremely useful in today's world of regulatory compliance.

Part II is dedicated to the SQL Server 2008 "beyond relational" release theme, which is all about working with semistructured and unstructured data. This is a concept that broadens our traditional view of relational databases by getting us to think more "outside the box" in terms of all the different types of data that SQL Server can be used to manage, query, and manipulate. We begin with a chapter on XML support (which was spearheaded in SQL Server 2005), and provide detailed coverage that includes the recent XML enhancements made in SQL Server 2008. All the remaining chapters in Part II cover nonrelational features that are brand new in SQL Server 2008. These include hierarchical tables, native file streaming, and geospatial capabilities. These features are designed to enrich the native database engine by bringing unprecedented intelligence and programming convenience down to the database level.

In Part III, we move away from the server and discuss concepts relating to actual database software development, be it in the middle tier or at the application level. This includes data access using "traditional" ADO.NET, language-integrated query (LINQ), the ADO.NET Entity Framework, and the latest innovations, ADO.NET Data Services and SQL Server Data Services. After you succeed in accessing your data, you'll need to deliver that data to your users, and that means data binding. We'll dig in to data binding for Microsoft Windows and ASP.NET Web applications, as well as the newest UI platforms, Windows Presentation Foundation (WPF) and Silverlight. We also cover transactions and various other topics relevant to extending your databases' reach with technologies such as merge replication, Sync Services for ADO.NET, and mobile database application development with SQL Server Compact 3.5.

Part IV is our BI section. In it, we provide efficient, practical coverage of SQL Server Analysis Services and Reporting Services. We are particularly proud of this section because we assume virtually no BI or OLAP knowledge on your part and yet provide truly deep coverage of SQL Server BI concepts, features, and programming. We have a chapter dedicated to the topic of data warehousing. In it, you'll see how to use a new SQL Server 2008 feature called Change Data Capture (CDC) to facilitate incremental updating of large data warehouses. Furthermore, we cover all the new important BI features in SQL Server 2008, expanded to include the latest data mining add-ins for Microsoft Office Excel 2007. The Reporting Services chapter has been written from scratch for the completely reworked and enhanced Report Designer, and also teaches you the many ways that Reporting Services can be programmed and managed.

Together, the four parts of the book provide you with a broad inventory of a slew of SQL Server 2008 developer-relevant features and the conceptual material necessary to understand them. We don't cover everything in SQL Server 2008, but we will arm you with a significant amount of core knowledge and give you the frame of reference necessary to research the product further and learn even more. Where appropriate, we refer you to SQL Server Books Online, which is the complete documentation library for SQL Server 2008 (available from the Start Menu under Programs, Microsoft SQL Server 2008, Documentation And Tutorials).

Code Samples and the Book's Companion Web Site

All the code samples discussed in this book can be downloaded from the book's companion Web site at the following address:

http://www.microsoft.com/mspress/companion/9780735625990/

 Important This book and its sample code were written for, and tested against, the Release Candidate (RC0) version of SQL Server 2008 Developer edition, released in June 2008. If and when we discover any incompatibilities with the Release To Manufacturer (RTM) version, or any further service packs that are later released, our intent is to update the sample code and post errata notes on the book's companion Web site, available at *http://www.microsoft.com/mspress/ companion/9780735625990/.* Please monitor that site for new code updates and errata postings.

In addition to all the code samples, the book's companion Web site also contains several chapters from the 2005 edition of this book that were not updated for the 2008 edition. These include the chapters on native XML Web Services and Service Broker, which are features that have not been widely adopted since they were introduced in SQL Server 2005 but that continue to be supported in SQL Server 2008. The 2005 edition chapters covering SQL Server Management Studio (the primary graphical tool you'll use for most of your database development work), SQL Server 2005 Express edition, Integration Services, and debugging are posted on the companion Web site as well. With the inclusion of all the new SQL Server 2008 coverage, space constraints simply did not permit us to include these topics (which have not changed significantly in SQL Server 2008) in this new edition. And while we provide completely new coverage on the latest data binding techniques, the 2005 edition covers ADO.NET programming techniques against then-new SQL Server features, and so it is posted on the companion Web site as well. This book's chapter on OLAP Application development has also been revised to include Excel 2007 coverage, and the 2005 edition is available on the companion Web site for those developers who are still working with Excel 2003 against Analysis Service OLAP cubes.

Because this is a developer book, we often include one or more Visual Studio projects as part of the sample code, in addition to SQL Server Management Studio projects containing T-SQL or Analysis Services script files. Within the companion materials parent folder is a child folder for each chapter. Each chapter's folder, in turn, contains either or both of the following two folders: SSMS and VS. The former contains a SQL Server Management Studio solution (.ssmssln file), the latter contains a Visual Studio solution (.sln file). Some chapters might have multiple Visual Studio solutions. After you've installed the companion files, double-click a solution file to open the sample scripts or code in the appropriate integrated development environment (IDE).

Because most of the code is explained in the text, you might prefer to create it from scratch rather than open the finished version supplied in the companion sample code. However, the finished version will still prove useful if you make a small error along the way or if you want to run the code quickly before reading through the narrative that describes it.

Some of the SQL Server Management Studio projects contain embedded connections that are configured to point to a default instance of SQL Server running on your local machine. Similarly, some of the Visual Studio source code contains connections or default connection strings (sometimes in code, sometimes in settings or configuration files, and other times in the *Text* property of controls on the forms in the sample projects) that are configured like-wise. If you have SQL Server 2008 installed as the default instance on your local machine with Windows-integrated security and the *AdventureWorks2008* sample database, the majority of the sample code should run without modification. If not, you'll need to modify the server name, instance name, or user credentials accordingly to suit your environment. You'll also need to install *AdventureWorks2008* if you have not already done so. (Download instructions for all the sample databases are given in the sections ahead.)

A number of chapters rely on various popular sample databases available for SQL Server. These include the *Northwind* and just-mentioned *AdventureWorks2008* sample transactional databases, the *AdventureWorksDW2008* sample data warehouse database, and the *Adventure Works DW 2008* Analysis Services sample database. None of our examples use the *pubs* database, which has been around since long before SQL Server 2000.

Using the Sample *Northwind* Database

You can use the version of *Northwind* that came with SQL Server 2000, if you have it, and attach it to your SQL Server 2008 server. Microsoft has also published a Windows Installer file (.msi) that will install the *Northwind* sample database on your server (even the older *pubs* sample database is included). The installer provides both the primary database file and the log file that can be directly attached, as well as T-SQL scripts, which can be executed to create the databases from scratch. At press time, the download page for the *Northwind* installer file is *http://www.microsoft.com/downloads/details.aspx?FamilyID=06616212-0356-46a0-8da2-eebc53a68034&DisplayLang=en*. An Internet shortcut to this URL is included with this chapter's sample code. If the link does not work for you, try running a Web search on "Northwind and pubs Sample Databases for SQL Server 2000."

Using the Sample *AdventureWorks2008* Databases

As of SQL Server 2005, and updated for SQL Server 2008, Microsoft provides the *AdventureWorks* family of databases. You can download these sample databases from CodePlex, which is Microsoft's open source Web site (in fact, all of Microsoft's official product code samples are hosted on CodePlex). This book uses the *AdventureWorks2008* relational online transaction processing (OLTP) database, the *AdventureWorksDW2008* relational data warehouse database, and the *AdventureWorksAS2008* Analysis Services database. The latest version of these sample databases are designed for use only with SQL Server 2008 and will not work with SQL Server 2005. (The older *AdventureWorks* databases for SQL Server 2005 are still available on CodePlex at the time of this writing, however.)

At press time, the download location for all sample *AdventureWorks2008* databases is *http://www.codeplex.com/MSFTDBProdSamples*. Click the Releases tab on this page to select any of the sample databases for downloading to your machine. An Internet shortcut to this URL is included on the book's companion Web site. If the link does not work for you, try running a Web search on "SQL Server 2008 product sample databases."

The *AdventureWorks2008* OLTP database uses the new FILESTREAM feature in SQL Server 2008, and therefore requires that FILESTREAM be enabled for the instance on which *AdventureWorks2008* is installed. Chapter 8 is devoted to FILESTREAM, and you should refer to the "Enabling FILESTREAM" section in that chapter, which shows how to enable FILESTREAM in order to support *AdventureWorks2008*.

> **Important** The samples for this book are based on the 32-bit version of the sample *AdventureWorks2008* databases, which is almost—but not exactly—identical to the 64-bit version. If you are using the 64-bit version of these sample databases, some of your query results might vary slightly from those shown in the book's examples.

System Requirements

To follow along with the book's text and run its code samples successfully, we recommend that you install the Developer edition of SQL Server 2008, which is available to a great number of developers through Microsoft's MSDN Premium subscription, on your PC. You will also need Visual Studio 2008; we recommend that you use the Professional edition or one of the Team edition releases, each of which is also available with the corresponding edition of the MSDN Premium subscription product.

Important To cover the widest range of features, this book is based on the Developer edition of SQL Server 2008. The Developer edition possesses the same feature set as the Enterprise edition of the product, although Developer edition licensing terms preclude production use. Both editions are high-end platforms that offer a superset of the features available in other editions (Standard, Workgroup, Web, and Express). We believe that it is in the best interest of developers for us to cover the full range of developer features in SQL Server 2008, including those available only in the Enterprise and Developer editions.

Most programmability features covered in this book are available in every edition of SQL Server 2008. One notable exception is the lack of Analysis Services support in the Workgroup, Web, and Express editions. Users of production editions other than the Enterprise edition should consult the SQL Server 2008 Features Comparison page at *http://msdn.microsoft.com/en-us/library/cc645993.aspx* for a comprehensive list of features available in each edition, in order to understand which features covered in the book are available to them in production.

To run these editions of SQL Server and Visual Studio, and thus the samples in this book, you'll need the following 32-bit hardware and software. (The 64-bit hardware and software requirements are not listed here but are very similar.)

- 600-MHz Pentium III–compatible or faster processor (1-GHz minimum, but 2GHz or faster processor recommended).

- Microsoft Windows 2000 Server with Service Pack (SP) 4 or later; Windows 2000 Professional Edition with SP4 or later; Windows XP with SP2 or later; Windows Server 2003 (any edition) with SP1 or later; Windows Small Business Server 2003 with SP1 or later; or Windows Server 2008 (any edition).

- For SQL Server 2008, at least 512 MB of RAM (1 GB or more recommended).

- For Visual Studio 2008, 192 MB (256 MB recommended).

- For SQL Server 2008, approximately 1460 MB of available hard disk space for the recommended installation. Approximately 200 MB of additional available hard disk space for SQL Server Books Online.

- For Visual Studio 2008, maximum of 20 GB of available space required on installation drive. This includes space for the installation of the full set of MSDN documentation.

- Internet connection required to download the code samples for each chapter from the companion Web site. A few of the code samples require an Internet connection to run as well.

- CD-ROM or DVD-ROM drive recommended.

- Super VGA (1024 × 768) or higher resolution video adapter and monitor recommended.

- Microsoft Mouse or compatible pointing device recommended.

- Microsoft Internet Explorer 6.0 SP1 or later. Microsoft Internet Explorer 7.0 recommended.

- For SQL Server Reporting Services, Microsoft Internet Information Services (IIS) 6.0 or later and ASP.NET 2.0 or later.

Support for This Book

Every effort has been made to ensure the accuracy of this book and the companion content. As corrections or changes are collected, they will be added to a Microsoft Knowledge Base article.

Microsoft Press provides support for books and companion content at the following Web site:

http://www.microsoft.com/learning/support/books/

Questions and Comments

If you have comments, questions, or ideas regarding the book or the companion content, or questions that are not answered by visiting the preceding sites, please send them to Microsoft Press via e-mail to:

mspinput@microsoft.com

Or send them via postal mail to

Microsoft Press
Attn: Programming Microsoft SQL Server 2008 Editor
One Microsoft Way
Redmond, WA 98052-6399

Please note that Microsoft software product support is not offered through the preceding addresses.

Part I
Core Fundamentals

In this part:

Chapter 1   Overview 3

Chapter 2   T-SQL Enhancements. 13

Chapter 3   Exploring SQL CLR 111

Chapter 4   Server Management 161

Chapter 5   Security in SQL Server 2008 189

Chapter 1
Overview

—Leonard Lobel

This is a book about Microsoft SQL Server 2008, written specifically with the developer in mind.

Microsoft's latest release of SQL Server improves upon its predecessors—SQL Server 2005 and earlier—in every key area, just as you would expect of any new version. There are many enhancements and new features in the product that yield important benefits across the board. Collectively, of course, these product enhancements and new features continue to bolster SQL Server's competitive position as an industry-strength database platform capable of handling the most demanding workloads. In this book, our particular focus is on *program-mability for database development*—a space in which the product continues to advance in new and powerful ways with the release of SQL Server 2008, the most programmable version of SQL Server to date.

Features like clustering, mirroring, and the ability to add new RAM and CPUs on the fly with zero downtime—just to name a few—are certainly important in any serious enterprise-level system. But to reiterate, this is a database book that targets developers, not administrators (although we do have an entire chapter dedicated to programmatically administering SQL Server). Reliability, availability, and scalability features that contribute toward making SQL Server a rock-solid platform are quite impressive and significant in their own right, but they are not particularly programmable and so they are not covered in this book.

If you're a developer, however, then welcome! This book is just for you. Whether you're programming against SQL Server 2008 natively at the database tier or further up the stack using .NET, this book shows you the way. Within these chapters, you'll find detailed coverage of the newest and most important SQL Server programming features. Together, we'll explore the plethora of ways in which SQL Server 2008 can be programmed—empowering you to rapidly develop rich database applications for your end users, while having fun in the process.

Just How Big Is It?

With each version of SQL Server, we tend to ask the same set of questions about the new release. Is it big? How many features have been added, what are they, and how relevant are they to my needs? What previous barriers have been removed? Has the product at its core changed radically since the last version? What's no longer supported? After probing like this for a while, we typically arrive at the ultimate question: Should I upgrade?

Let's be clear about this. SQL Server 2008 is *not* the watershed release that its predecessor SQL Server 2005 was roughly three years ago. At that time, SQL Server 2005 really redefined the product beyond just a relational database engine—which was already quite matured in SQL Server 2000 nearly six years prior. In SQL Server 2000 (and earlier versions), the relational database engine *was* the product. New advances beyond the relational database engine—in particular, business intelligence (BI) services for extraction, transformation, and loading (ETL) and for reporting and analysis—began appearing as early as 1999 and continued to steadily emerge after the arrival of SQL Server 2000. These capabilities were integrated into the product sporadically as a patchwork of add-ons, wizards, and management consoles. Over time, the result was a relational database system loosely bundled with a collection of value-added features supported by a somewhat inconsistent toolset.

Microsoft changed all that with SQL Server 2005, by giving the platform a complete structural overhaul that revolutionized the product. Disruptive change in the software industry—resulting from the distributed nature of a growing Internet for business-to-business (B2B) integration, as well as a growing market for BI, including online analytical processing (OLAP), data mining, and reporting—was the driving force behind the product's radical makeover. As of SQL Server 2005, the relational database engine no longer takes center stage. Rather, it is positioned alongside a series of core services that together comprise the overall product. The result is a broader, richer, and more consistent set of features and services that are built into—rather than bolted onto—the platform.

SQL Server 2008, in turn, represents a natural evolution of this model, building on and extending this new and improved architecture established in SQL Server 2005. Thus, upgrading from SQL Server 2000 (or earlier) to either 2005 or 2008 are both "leaps forward" in terms of platform architecture, whereas upgrading from 2005 to 2008 is more of an incremental step in that regard. By that comparison, the 2008 release isn't really all "that big."

On the flip side, SQL Server 2008 can definitely be viewed as a major product release in its own right. Microsoft has loaded SQL Server 2008 with many exciting new features that bring unprecedented intelligence, convenience, and programming power down to the database level. SQL Server 2008 builds on the Common Language Runtime (CLR) integration introduced in SQL Server 2005 to usher in a new breed of native data types based on rich CLR user-defined types (UDTs), enabling hierarchical and geospatial capabilities in the database.

Many significant enhancements to Transact-SQL (T-SQL) have been added as well. Backup compression, data compression, and Change Data Capture (CDC) help us cope with rapidly growing data warehouses. New security features such as Transparent Data Encryption (TDE) and SQL Server Audit make it easier to meet the demands of increasingly stringent requirements for regulatory compliance. We also get native streaming capabilities between the database and the file system for enhanced binary large object (BLOB) storage and a new synchronization model for replication between occasionally connected client systems. There are also new BI features for analysis and reporting. Consider as well improvements in reliability, availability, and scalability, and one could arguably maintain that SQL Server 2008 is in fact quite a big release. Our job isn't to convince you one way or the other—it's simply to help you understand and program the features you need to get the most out of Microsoft SQL Server 2008.

> **Note** Recent survey polls continue to indicate that many sites are still running SQL Server 2000. To aid in the upgrade process for these sites, Microsoft supports a direct migration path from SQL Server 2000 to SQL Server 2008 (that is, without requiring an intermediate upgrade to SQL Server 2005 along the way).

> **Important** Notification Services, which was available for SQL Server 2000 as a separate add-on and then later integrated into the core product in SQL Server 2005, has been discontinued in SQL Server 2008. (This is the only SQL Server 2005 component dropped by Microsoft in SQL Server 2008.)
>
> According to Microsoft, Notification Services will continue to be supported as part of the SQL Server 2005 product support life cycle. Moving forward however, support for key notification scenarios will be incorporated into SQL Server Reporting Services. Some notification require-ments are already addressed by existing Reporting Services features, such as standard and data driven subscriptions (discussed in Chapter 19). Features to support additional notification scenarios can be expected in future releases.

A Book *for* Developers

If you've gotten this far, we've already established that you're a developer (or, at least, that's one of the hats you wear). In tailoring the content of this book, there are a few other assump-tions that we make about you as well.

First, we expect that you're already knowledgeable in relational database concepts—whether that experience is with SQL Server or non-Microsoft platforms. As such, you already know about tables, views, primary and foreign key relationships, stored procedures, functions, and triggers. These essentials are assumed knowledge and are not covered in this book. Similarly, we don't discuss proper relational design with respect to the rules of data normalization, strategic indexing practices, and other relational fundamentals. We also assume that you have at least basic familiarity with SQL statement syntax—again, either T-SQL in SQL Server or SQL dialects in other platforms.

With that baseline established, what do we assume that you want to learn about? Well, that would be just about everything else that a developer could want to learn about Microsoft SQL Server 2008! It starts with the most powerful extensions to T-SQL and the relational database engine. We also assume that you're thirsty for knowledge in wider spaces beyond relational technologies, such as unstructured and semistructured data, client data access, security, and BI with data warehousing, analysis, and reporting.

As we began explaining, SQL Server 2005 was actually the groundbreaking release that redefined the product by incorporating a litany of features and services into the platform, while earlier versions had traditionally been focused on just the relational database engine. With respect to that fact, this book includes updated coverage of SQL Server 2005 enhancements as well as the very latest new features in SQL Server 2008. This makes it an ideal resource whether you are upgrading to SQL Server 2008 from any earlier version of SQL Server or from another relational database platform.

A Book *by* Developers

We, the authors and coauthors of this book, are first and foremost developers just like you. All of us have built careers in the pursuit of writing code that powers our applications, especially database applications. We've committed ourselves to building quality solutions that work with data and deliver that data in the most compelling ways to our businesses, partners, and customers. And, we love SQL Server!

Like SQL Server 2008 itself, this book builds on a previous edition written for SQL Server 2005, and it is the cumulative result of many years of work put in by many authors. We were fortunate enough to have a product manager from the Microsoft SQL Server product team contribute to the chapter on security. Our chapters on data mining, data warehousing, reporting, replication, and transactions were written by experts on those subjects as well.

Our approach has been to add value to the product's documentation by providing a developer-oriented investigation of the new and improved features and services in SQL Server 2008. As such, this book features an abundance of sample code, including a library of Visual Studio and SQL Server Management Studio sample projects that you can download from the book's companion Web site. (See the Introduction for details on downloading and using the sample code.)

A Book to Show You the Way

This book was carefully organized to present a potentially overwhelming array of new developer-oriented SQL Server 2008 features in the most coherent manner possible. To best achieve that, the chapters have been categorized into four primary sections, which are summarized at a high level in this overview.

Core Technologies

In Part I, we focus on core SQL Server technologies. These include enhancements to T-SQL, extended programmability with SQL CLR code in .NET languages such as Microsoft Visual Basic .NET and C#, server management, and security.

In Chapter 2, we explore the significant enhancements made to Transact-SQL (T-SQL)—which still remains the best programming tool for exploiting many new and old SQL Server features alike. We start with SQL Server 2005 enhancements, covering the ins and outs of writing re-cursive queries with common table expressions (CTEs) and examining scalar functions that provide the basis of ranking. We then go on to learn about exception handling and data definition language (DDL) triggers.

Then the chapter digs into the powerful extensions to T-SQL added in SQL Server 2008. Table-valued parameters (TVPs) allow entire result sets to be passed between stored pro-cedures and functions on the server, as well as between client and server using Microsoft ADO.NET. New date and time features are then explored, including separate data types for dates and times, time zone awareness, and improvements in date and time range, storage, and precision. We then show many ways to use *MERGE*, a new data manipulation language (DML) statement that encapsulates all the individual operations typically involved in any merge scenario. From there, you'll learn about INSERT OVER DML, which enhances our abil-ity to capture change data from the *OUTPUT* clause of any DML statement. Last, we look at *GROUPING SETS*, an extension to the traditional *GROUP BY* clause that increases our options for slicing and dicing data in aggregation queries.

Chapter 3 provides thorough coverage of SQL CLR programming—which lets you run com-piled .NET code on SQL Server—as well as guidance on when and where you should put it to use. We go beyond mere stored procedures, triggers, and functions to explain and dem-onstrate the creation of CLR types and aggregates—entities that cannot be created *at all* in T-SQL. We also cover the different methods of creating SQL CLR objects in Microsoft Visual Studio 2008 and how to manage their deployment, both from Visual Studio and from T-SQL scripts in SQL Server Management Studio and elsewhere.

In Chapter 4, we show you how to conduct administrative tasks programmatically, using Server Management Objects (SMO) introduced in SQL Server 2005. You'll learn how to use SMO to perform database backups and restores, execute Database Consistency Check (DBCC) runs, and more, all from your own code. We'll also learn about the Policy-Based Management (PBM) feature, new in SQL Server 2008, which helps developers work with administrators to ensure that development and production machines comply with the same configuration defined through custom policies.

Chapter 5 discusses SQL Server security at length and examines your choices for keeping data safe and secure from prying eyes. We begin with the basic security concepts concerning log-ins, users, roles, authentication, and authorization. You then go on to learn about key-based encryption support added in SQL Server 2005, which protects your data both while in transit and at rest. Important new security features added in SQL Server 2008 are then examined, which include Transparent Data Encryption (TDE) and SQL Server Audit. TDE allows you to encrypt entire databases in the background without special coding requirements. With SQL Server Audit, virtually any action taken by any user can be recorded for auditing in either the file system or the Windows event log. The chapter concludes by providing crucial guidance for adhering to best practices and avoiding common security pitfalls.

Beyond Relational

With the release of SQL Server 2008, Microsoft continues to redefine how we think of and use nonrelational data in the relational database world. One of the key release themes in SQL Server 2008 is "beyond relational," and by the time you complete Part II, you'll understand and appreciate the major strides Microsoft has made in this arena.

SQL Server 2005 embraced semistructured data by introducing the *xml* data type and a lot of rich XML support to go along with it. That innovation was an immeasurable improvement over the use of plain *varchar* or *text* columns to hold strings of XML (which was common practice in earlier versions of SQL Server), and thus revolutionized the storage of XML in the relational database. It empowered the development of database applications that work with hierarchical XML data *natively*—within the environment of the relational database system— something not previously possible using ordinary string columns. In Chapter 6, we cover the *xml* data type, XQuery extensions to T-SQL, server-side XML Schema Definition (XSD) collections, XML column indexing, XML enhancements in SQL Server 2008, and many other XML features available in SQL Server.

But native XML support was only the first step in a venture that Microsoft has pursued much more aggressively in SQL Server 2008, with new features added for handling a wider variety of nonrelational types, including unstructured data and spatial types. In the rest of Part II, we explore these new features and show how you can use them to build modern applications that demand unified services for storing and manipulating structured, semistructured, and unstructured data in the database.

As of SQL Server 2008, XML is no longer our only option for working with hierarchical data in the database. In Chapter 7, we explore the new *hierarchyid* data type that enables you to cast a hierarchical structure over any relational table. This data type is implemented as a "system CLR" type, which is nothing more really than a SQL CLR user-defined type (UDT), just like the ones we learned how to create for ourselves in Chapter 3 (except that you don't need to en-able SQL CLR on the server in order to use *hierarchyid*). The value stored in a *hierarchyid* data type encodes the complete path of any given node in the tree structure, from the root down to the specific ordinal position among other sibling nodes sharing the same parent. Using methods provided by this new type, you can now efficiently build, query, and manipulate tree-structured data in your relational tables.

In Chapter 8, you'll learn all about the new FILESTREAM feature in SQL Server 2008, which greatly enhances the storage of unstructured BLOB data in the database—an increasingly common scenario given the accelerating data explosion of our times. Previously, we've had to choose between storing BLOB data in the database using *varbinary(max)* columns or outside the database as unstructured binary streams (typically, as files in the file system). Neither approach is without significant drawbacks—which is where FILESTREAM comes in. This highly efficient abstraction layer allows you to logically treat BLOB data as an integral part of the database, while SQL Server 2008 stores the BLOB data physically separate from the database in the NTFS file system behind the scenes. It will even seamlessly integrate database transactions with NTFS file system transactions against your BLOB data. Following the walkthroughs in this chapter, you'll learn how to leverage this powerful new feature from your .NET applications by building Windows, Web, and Windows Presentation Foundation (WPF) applications that use FILESTREAM for BLOB data storage.

Chapter 9 explores the new *geometry* and *geography* data types. These new system CLR types in SQL Server 2008 provide geospatial capabilities at the database level that make it easy for you to integrate location-awareness into your applications. Respectively, *geometry* and *geography* support spatial computations against the two basic geospatial surface models: planar (flat) and geodetic (round-earth). With geographical data (represented by coordinates) stored in these data types, you can easily determine intersections and calculate length, area, and distance measurements against that data. This chapter first quickly covers the basics and then provides walkthroughs in which we build several geospatial database applications, including one that integrates with Microsoft Virtual Earth. While this is a vast topic that could fill its own book, our chapter covers the fundamentals you'll need for working with geospatial data.

Reaching Out

After we've covered so much material about what you can do on the server and in your database, we move to Part III of the book, where we cover technologies and techniques more relevant to building applications that work with your databases and extend their reach.

We start with Chapter 10, which first covers Microsoft ADO.NET and the data access features of Microsoft Visual Studio, including typed *DataSet* objects. After this core coverage of ADO.NET, we provide an overview of new data access technologies, including the concepts and syntax of language-integrated query (LINQ). We'll look at LINQ To SQL and ADO.NET Entity Framework Object Relational Mapping (ORM) technologies, ADO.NET Data Services, and SQL Server Data Services.

In Chapter 11, we cover data binding, in *droves*. We start with Windows Forms using Visual Studio drag-and-drop binding. Next we look at ASP.NET data binding using designers, code, and markup techniques. We then move on to using ASP.NET Asynchronous JavaScript and

XML (AJAX) for data presentation, and we introduce the new ASP.NET Dynamic Data feature set. We finish with data binding in WPF and Silverlight 2.0, showing you how they compare to each other and to the other data binding models too. Regardless of your application type, we'll help you manage your data with ease.

No matter how you write and package your code—whether it be in T-SQL or a .NET language; exposed as a conventional stored procedure, function, or Web service; or deployed to the client or the server—you must keep your data consistent to ensure its integrity. The key to consistency is transactions, and as with other SQL Server programmability features, transactions can be managed from a variety of places. If you're writing T-SQL code or you're writing client code using the ADO.NET *SqlClient* provider or *System.Transactions*, you need to be aware of the various transaction isolation levels supported by SQL Server, the appropriate scope of your transactions, and best practices for writing transactional code. In Chapter 12, we get you there.

We couldn't round out the reach story without covering merge replication and synchronization between distributed database environments. We start Chapter 13 with a walk-through for creating a synchronized client/server database application using conventional SQL Server Merge Replication. We then examine a new feature in SQL Server 2008 called Change Tracking, designed to work in tandem with the new Sync Services for ADO.NET—features that together enhance SQL Server Compact 3.5 applications running on an ever-increasing number of Windows-based mobile devices. These devices are used not just by consumers, but also by the mobile workforce—people who need ready access to their data no matter where they are, in both wireless online and offline settings. Mobile applications frequently alternate between connected and disconnected states. You'll learn how Merge Replication and Change Tracking with Sync Services for ADO.NET make it possible to implement mobile client and Windows desktop applications that work in offline mode, and seamlessly synchronize their data whenever a connection to the server is made available.

Business Intelligence Strategies

In Part IV of this book, we help you take your broad-based but tactical database management and programming knowledge and extend it to the realm of strategic analysis. Specifically, we teach you how to build a true data warehouse and then capitalize on your data warehouse through OLAP, data mining, and reporting.

In Chapter 14, we show you the ropes of data warehousing and explain how to use several new important SQL Server 2008 features designed specifically to help you work better with the data warehouses that will back your business intelligence (BI). The chapter begins by providing some important background, design guidance, and practical advice for building data warehouses. We then move on to provide hands-on coverage of new and improved SQL Server features that facilitate the process. These include applied use of the *MERGE* statement (which we also cover in Chapter 2), Change Data Capture (CDC), data and backup compression, and more—all of which are new in SQL Server 2008. CDC allows you to capture change data on CDC-enabled tables without resorting to triggers or code changes. This in turn facilitates the ETL processes that bring large data warehouses up-to-date incrementally. And as data warehouses continue to grow larger than ever before, data and backup compression are vital and welcome indeed. Other new and advanced data warehousing features covered in this chapter include partitioned table parallelism, star-join query optimization, and sparse columns.

In the remaining chapters, we show you how to use these transformed data repositories as the basis for sophisticated SQL Server Analysis Services databases that support cutting-edge BI features. Many books on SQL Server exclude coverage of Analysis Services on the grounds that it is a "specialized" subject, but we respectfully disagree with that notion. The very premise of SQL Server 2008 Analysis Services and its unified dimensional model paradigm is the *mainstream* appeal and accessibility of BI. We show you how easy BI programming can be and how powerfully it complements conventional relational databases and conventional database programming.

In Chapter 15, we take you through the basics of designing OLAP cubes using the Analysis Services project designers in Visual Studio. We show you how to build, deploy, and query OLAP cubes that support actionable, drill-down analysis of your data. We kept this chapter fairly short to provide a sort of "quick start" approach to BI for busy developers.

In Chapter 16, we take the basic cube we built in Chapter 15 and use Visual Studio designers to implement an array of new OLAP features brought to you by Analysis Services 2008. By the end of the chapter, your cube will have a number of the features underlying Microsoft's unified dimensional model. The chapter is long, but you can read it at your own pace, immediately mastering new features as you read each section.

In Chapter 17, we provide comprehensive coverage of a host of OLAP application development techniques. We cover the creation of OLAP user interfaces (UIs) in Microsoft Office Excel 2007, using PivotTables, charts, and new in-cell *CUBE* formulas. We then cover how to publish these assets to Web dashboards using Excel Services, a component of Microsoft Office SharePoint Server.

We provide a basic tutorial on multidimensional expression language (MDX) queries and show you how to run MDX queries from the SQL Server Management Studio MDX query window. We also show you how to run MDX queries from your own applications through application programming interface (API)–level programming with ADO MD.NET. We cover management of Analysis Services databases, both interactively using SQL Server Management Studio and programmatically using Analysis Management Objects (AMO). We introduce you to the Web Services–based XML for Analysis (XMLA) standard on which both ADO MD.NET and AMO are built, showing you how to create XMLA scripts in Management Studio and manipulate XMLA programmatically in .NET code. We also introduce you to Analysis Services' own .NET CLR integration, and show you how to create managed stored procedures in .NET using AMO and server-side ADO MD.NET.

Chapter 18 is all about data mining, and it provides a self-contained, end-to-end treatment of the topic, including the newest data mining features added in SQL Server 2008. We start with a conceptual introduction, and then we provide a tutorial on designing, training, browsing, and deploying your mining structures and models in Visual Studio. We then switch to SQL Server Management Studio, showing you how to manage your mining structures and models interactively, using the graphical user interface (GUI) tools provided, and programmatically, through SQL Data Mining Extensions (DMX) scripts. We then head back to .NET programming, showing you how to embed the Analysis Services Data Mining Model Browsers into your applications; how to use DMX, ADO.NET, and data binding together to build compelling Windows Forms and ASP.NET data mining applications; and how to use server-side ADO MD.NET to build DMX stored procedures. We finish by showing you how to leverage the powerful new data mining add-ins for Excel 2007.

Chapter 19 covers Reporting Services, which has been enhanced significantly in SQL Server 2008. We start with a tutorial on the new Report Designer in Visual Studio 2008 and then show you how to use Reporting Services to quickly and easily build sophisticated reports against both relational and OLAP databases. You'll see how to create full-scale reporting information systems that expose all the information in the feature-packed databases you've learned to build, maintain, extend, and develop against in the rest of the book. We'll show you how to deliver reports with the flexible layouts users want by using the new *tablix* data region (a hybrid of *table* and *matrix*) in your reports. Next we give you an overview of the report server configuration and administration tools, and we teach you how to deploy the reports for your users and how to embed reports into your Windows Forms and ASP.NET client applications. We also show you how to use the management and execution Web Services exposed by Reporting Services to programmatically integrate reporting and report administration into your custom applications and deployment scripts.

Summary

In this opening chapter, we compared the Microsoft SQL Server 2008 release with earlier product versions, and we discussed the wide range of programmability features at our disposal. In the process, we outlined the various chapters and how they are organized, accompanied with an overview of the extensive SQL Server 2008 product feature set for developers that you'll learn about throughout the rest of this book. Given the broad range of capabilities in that feature set, by no means does this book need to be read in any particular order. Read it from start to finish if you want, or jump right to the chapters that are most relevant for your needs. Either way, you'll find the practical guidance and information you need to get your job done.

Chapter 2
T-SQL Enhancements

—Stephen Forte and Leonard Lobel

By now, you must have heard that you can write Microsoft SQL Server stored procedures in any language that uses the common language runtime (CLR), such as Microsoft Visual C# or Microsoft Visual Basic .NET. This is great news if you've never mastered Transact-SQL (T-SQL), right? We hate to be the bearer of bad news, but CLR stored procedures are not a cure-all for your SQL Server programming challenges. As you'll see in Chapter 3, writing a stored procedure in a language that uses the CLR is useful for a number of database programming dilemmas—for instance, CLR stored procedures are often a good replacement for extended stored procedures in earlier versions of SQL Server. For almost everything else, you will want to use T-SQL.

In fact, reports of T-SQL's death have been greatly exaggerated. In most cases, using T-SQL for your queries and stored procedures is more efficient than writing CLR stored procedures.

Given that T-SQL is alive and well, let's look at how it has changed since SQL Server 2000. T-SQL has been improved in many ways. In this chapter, we'll begin by exploring the most notable changes in T-SQL introduced in SQL Server 2005, including the following:

- Common table expressions (CTEs)
- The *PIVOT* and *UNPIVOT* operators
- The *APPLY* operator
- Enhancements to the *TOP* parameter
- Ranking functions
- Exception handling using *TRY* and *CATCH* blocks
- The *varchar(max)* data type
- The *WAITFOR* statement
- Data definition language (DDL) triggers
- The SNAPSHOT isolation level

We'll continue with an in-depth look at these significant T-SQL features, which are new in SQL Server 2008:

- Table-valued parameters (TVPs)
- New date and time data types

- The *MERGE* statement

- The INSERT OVER DML syntax

- The *GROUPING SETS* operator

- New T-SQL shorthand syntax

T-SQL provides several important "beyond relational" data types as well, such as the *xml*, *hierarchyid*, *varbinary(max) FILESTREAM*, *geography*, and *geometry* data types. Chapters 6 though 9 in Part II provide in-depth coverage of these special SQL Server 2008 data types.

Common Table Expressions

A common table expression (CTE) closely resembles a nonpersistent view. It is a temporary named result set that you define in your query and that will be used by the *FROM* clause of the query. Each CTE is defined only once (but can be referred to as many times as necessary while still in scope) and lives for as long as the query lives. You can use CTEs to perform recursive operations. Here is the syntax to create a CTE:

```
WITH <name of your CTE>(<column names>)
AS
(
<actual query>
)

SELECT * FROM <name of your CTE>
```

Note Many of our examples in this chapter use the *AdventureWorks2008* sample database. To run these examples, you will need to download and install the sample database on your machine. The book's Introduction provides details and instructions for obtaining the *AdventureWorks2008* sample database.

An example of a simple CTE using *AdventureWorks2008* is shown in Listing 2-1.

LISTING 2-1 A simple CTE

```
USE AdventureWorks2008
GO
WITH AllMRContacts
AS
(
  SELECT * FROM Person.Person WHERE Title = 'Mr.'
)
SELECT LastName + ', ' + FirstName AS Contact
  FROM AllMRContacts
  ORDER BY LastName
```

The results are shown here:

```
Contact
-------------------
Abbas, Syed
Achong, Gustavo
Adams, Jay
Adams, Ben
Adina, Ronald
Agcaoili, Samuel
  ...
```

The following example gets a count of all the sales a salesperson made in the *AdventureWorks2008* orders system as a CTE and then executes a simple inner join with the *SalesPerson* table to return more information about the salesperson, such as his or her quota. This demonstrates how a CTE is joined to your calling query. You can do this without a CTE, but think about all the times you have created a temp table or a throwaway view and joined back to it—now you can use a CTE instead and keep the complexity of aggregating in the CTE only, thereby simplifying your code. The code is shown in Listing 2-2.

LISTING 2-2 CTE-to-query join

```
WITH OrderCountCTE(SalesPersonID, OrderCount)
AS
(
  SELECT SalesPersonID, COUNT(*)
    FROM  Sales.SalesOrderHeader
   WHERE SalesPersonID IS NOT NULL
   GROUP BY SalesPersonID
)
SELECT
  sp.BusinessEntityID,
  FirstName + ' ' + LastName as SalesPerson,
  oc.OrderCount,
  sp.SalesYTD
 FROM Sales.vSalesPerson AS sp
  INNER JOIN OrderCountCTE AS oc ON oc.SalesPersonID = sp.BusinessEntityID
 ORDER BY oc.OrderCount DESC
```

The results look like this:

BusinessEntityID	SalesPerson	OrderCount	SalesYTD
277	Jillian Carson	473	3857163.6332
275	Michael Blythe	450	4557045.0459
279	Tsvi Reiter	429	2811012.7151
276	Linda Mitchell	418	5200475.2313
289	Jae Pak	348	5015682.3752
282	José Saraiva	271	3189356.2465
281	Shu Ito	242	3018725.4858
278	Garrett Vargas	234	1764938.9859

283	David Campbell	189	3587378.4257
290	Ranjit Varkey Chudukatil	175	3827950.238
284	Tete Mensa-Annan	140	1931620.1835
288	Rachel Valdez	130	2241204.0424
286	Lynn Tsoflias	109	1758385.926
280	Pamela Ansman-Wolfe	95	0.00
274	Stephen Jiang	48	677558.4653
287	Amy Alberts	39	636440.251
285	Syed Abbas	16	219088.8836
:			

CTEs can also eliminate self-joins in some of your queries. Take a look at the example in Listing 2-3. We will create a table named *Products* and insert duplicates into the *ProductName* column.

LISTING 2-3 Inserting duplicates into the *AdventureWorks2008 ProductName* column

```
CREATE TABLE Products
 (ProductID int NOT NULL,
  ProductName varchar(25),
  Price money NULL,
  CONSTRAINT PK_Products PRIMARY KEY NONCLUSTERED (ProductID)
 )
GO
INSERT INTO Products VALUES (1, 'Widgets', 25)
INSERT INTO Products VALUES (2, 'Gadgets', 50)
INSERT INTO Products VALUES (3, 'Thingies', 75)
INSERT INTO Products VALUES (4, 'Whoozits', 90)
INSERT INTO Products VALUES (5, 'Whatzits', 5)
INSERT INTO Products VALUES (6, 'Gizmos', 15)
INSERT INTO Products VALUES (7, 'Widgets', 24)
INSERT INTO Products VALUES (8, 'Gizmos', 36)
INSERT INTO Products VALUES (9, 'Gizmos', 36)
```

One common problem found in databases is having duplicate product names with different product IDs. If you run a duplicate-finding query, that query will return all the records (the duplicates and the good values). This increases the difficulty of automatically deleting duplicates. If you want to find the *ProductName* duplicates without also including the first instance of the name in the table, you can use a self-join, as shown in Listing 2-4.

LISTING 2-4 Self-join without CTE

```
SELECT * FROM Products WHERE ProductID NOT IN
(SELECT MIN(ProductID) FROM Products AS P
 WHERE Products.ProductName = P.ProductName)
```

The self-join returns data like this:

```
ProductID ProductName Price
--------- ----------- -----------
8         Gizmos      36.00
9         Gizmos      36.00
7         Widgets     24.00
```

You can also rewrite your query using a CTE to eliminate the confusing-looking self-join and get the same results. This technique does not offer a performance gain over self-joins; it is just a convenience for code maintainability. The preceding self-join example is rewritten in Listing 2-5 as a CTE and yields the same results; notice that we are joining our CTE with the *Products* table.

LISTING 2-5 Self-join as a CTE

```
WITH MinProductRecords AS
(
  SELECT MIN(ProductID) AS ProductID, ProductName
    FROM Products
    GROUP BY ProductName
    HAVING COUNT(*) > 1
)
SELECT P.*
 FROM Products AS P
  INNER JOIN MinProductRecords AS MP
  ON P.ProductName = MP.ProductName AND P.ProductID > MP.ProductID
```

After you investigate your duplicates using the preceding CTE, you might want to delete the duplicate data. You might also want to update any foreign keys in related tables to use the original *ProductID* value. If your duplicate data does not have any related child rows in another table, or if you have updated them to the correct *ProductID*, you can delete the duplicate data by just rewriting the CTE, as shown in Listing 2-6, replacing the *SELECT* * with a *DELETE*.

LISTING 2-6 Deleting duplicates in a CTE

```
WITH MinProductRecords AS
(
  SELECT MIN(ProductID) AS ProductID, ProductName
    FROM Products
    GROUP BY ProductName
    HAVING COUNT(*) > 1
)
DELETE Products
 FROM Products AS P
  INNER JOIN MinProductRecords AS MP
  ON P.ProductName = MP.ProductName AND P.ProductID > MP.ProductID
```

Creating Recursive Queries with CTEs

The true power of CTEs emerges when you use them recursively to perform hierarchical queries on tree-structured data. In fact, this was a major reason that Microsoft built CTEs, in addition to ANSI SQL-92 compliance. A recursive CTE is constructed from a minimum of two queries. The first, the anchor member, is a nonrecursive query; the second, the recursive member, is the recursive query. Within your CTE's parentheses (after the *AS* clause), you define queries that are independent or refer back to the same CTE. The anchor and recursive members are separated by a *UNION ALL* statement. Anchor members are invoked only once; recursive members are invoked repeatedly until the query returns no rows. You can append multiple anchor members to one another using a *UNION* or *UNION ALL* operator, depending on whether you want to eliminate duplicates. (You must append recursive members using a *UNION ALL* operator.) Here is the syntax:

```
WITH SimpleRecursive(field names)
AS
(
    <Select Statement for the Anchor Member>

    UNION ALL

    <Select Statement for the Recursive Member>
)

SELECT * FROM SimpleRecursive
```

The example in Listing 2-7 demonstrates this feature. We'll create a table of employees and a self-referencing field back to *EmployeeID* named *ReportsTo*. We'll then write a query that returns all the employees who report to Stephen (*EmployeeID=2*) and all the employees who report to Stephen's subordinates.

LISTING 2-7 Example table for recursive CTE queries

```
CREATE TABLE EmployeeTree
  (EmployeeID int PRIMARY KEY,
   EmployeeName nvarchar(50),
   ReportsTo int)
GO

--insert some data, build a reporting tree
INSERT INTO EmployeeTree VALUES(1, 'Richard', NULL)
INSERT INTO EmployeeTree VALUES(2, 'Stephen', 1)
INSERT INTO EmployeeTree VALUES(3, 'Clemens', 2)
INSERT INTO EmployeeTree VALUES(4, 'Malek', 2)
INSERT INTO EmployeeTree VALUES(5, 'Goksin', 4)
INSERT INTO EmployeeTree VALUES(6, 'Kimberly', 1)
INSERT INTO EmployeeTree VALUES(7, 'Ramesh', 5)
```

Listing 2-8 shows the recursive query to determine which employees report to Stephen.

LISTING 2-8 Recursive CTE query

```
WITH SimpleRecursive(EmployeeID, EmployeeName, ReportsTo)
AS
(
  SELECT EmployeeID, EmployeeName, ReportsTo
   FROM EmployeeTree WHERE EmployeeID = 2
  UNION ALL
  SELECT p.EmployeeID, p.EmployeeName, p.ReportsTo
   FROM EmployeeTree AS P
    INNER JOIN SimpleRecursive A ON A.EmployeeID = P.ReportsTo
)
SELECT sr.EmployeeName AS Employee, et.EmployeeName AS Boss
 FROM SimpleRecursive AS sr
  INNER JOIN EmployeeTree AS et ON sr.ReportsTo = et.EmployeeID
```

Here are the results:

```
Employee    Boss
----------- ------------
Stephen     Richard
Clemens     Stephen
Malek       Stephen
Goksin      Malek
Ramesh      Goskin
```

This recursion starts where *EmployeeID = 2* (the anchor member or the first *SELECT*). It picks up that record and then, using the recursive member (the *SELECT* after the *UNION ALL*), picks up all the records that report to Stephen and that record's children. (Goksin reports to Malek, and Malek reports to Stephen.) Each subsequent recursion tries to find more children that have as parents the employees found by the previous recursion. Eventually, the recursion returns no results, and that is what causes the recursion to stop (the reason why Kimberly is not returned). If the anchor member is changed to *EmployeeID = 1*, Kimberly will also be returned in the results.

By design, the recursive member keeps looking for children and can cycle on indefinitely. If you suspect many cycles will occur and want to limit the number of recursive invocations, you can specify the *MAXRECURSION* option right after the outer query using the *OPTION* clause.

```
OPTION(MAXRECURSION 25)
```

This option causes SQL Server to raise an error when the CTE exceeds the specified limit. By default, the limit is 100 (if you've omitted the option). To specify no option, you must set *MAXRECURSION* to *0*. You can also run the same query to find direct reports and subordinates only one level deep (including direct reports Clemens and Malek and Malek's subordinate Goksin but skipping Ramesh, who is three levels deep), as shown in Listing 2-9.

LISTING 2-9 Recursive query with *MAXRECURSION*

```
WITH SimpleRecursive(EmployeeID, EmployeeName, ReportsTo)
AS
(
  SELECT EmployeeID, EmployeeName, ReportsTo
   FROM EmployeeTree WHERE EmployeeID = 2
  UNION ALL
  SELECT p.EmployeeID, p.EmployeeName, p.ReportsTo
   FROM EmployeeTree AS P
    INNER JOIN SimpleRecursive A ON A.EmployeeID = P.ReportsTo
)
SELECT sr.EmployeeName AS Employee, et.EmployeeName AS Boss
 FROM SimpleRecursive AS sr
  INNER JOIN EmployeeTree AS et ON sr.ReportsTo = et.EmployeeID
OPTION(MAXRECURSION 2)
```

Here are the results:

```
Employee    Boss
----------  ------------
Stephen     Richard
Clemens     Stephen
Malek       Stephen
Goksin      Malek
```

You will also see that the query raises the following error message:

```
Msg 530, Level 16, State 1, Line 2
The statement terminated. The maximum recursion 2 has been exhausted
before statement completion.
```

One way to avoid the exception is to use a generated column to keep track of the level you are on and include that in the *WHERE* clause instead of using *MAXRECURSION*. The revised example in Listing 2-10 returns the same data as the preceding example but without the error.

LISTING 2-10 Controlling recursion without *MAXRECURSION*

```
WITH SimpleRecursive(EmployeeID, EmployeeName, ReportsTo, SubLevel)
AS
(
  SELECT EmployeeID, EmployeeName, ReportsTo, 0
   FROM EmployeeTree WHERE EmployeeID = 2
  UNION ALL
  SELECT p.EmployeeID, p.EmployeeName, p.ReportsTo, SubLevel + 1
   FROM EmployeeTree AS P
    INNER JOIN SimpleRecursive A ON A.EmployeeID = P.ReportsTo
    WHERE SubLevel <= 2
)
SELECT sr.EmployeeName AS Employee, et.EmployeeName AS Boss
 FROM SimpleRecursive sr
  INNER JOIN EmployeeTree AS et ON sr.ReportsTo = et.EmployeeID
```

> **Note** SQL Server 2008 introduces a new *hierarchyid* data type that can implement a more ro-
> bust tree structure over a recursive self-joining table than the example we've shown here. The
> *hierarchyid* data type is covered in Chapter 7.

The *PIVOT* and *UNPIVOT* Operators

Let's face it—users usually want to see data in tabular format, which is a bit of a challenge given that data in SQL Server is most often stored in a highly relational form. *PIVOT* is a T-SQL operator that you can specify in your *FROM* clause to rotate rows into columns and create a traditional crosstab query.

Using *PIVOT* is easy. In your *SELECT* statement, you specify the values you want to pivot on. The following example in the *AdventureWorks2008* database uses the order years (calculated using the *DatePart* function) as the columns. The *FROM* clause looks normal except for the *PIVOT* statement. This statement creates the value you want to show in the rows of the newly created columns. This example uses the aggregate *SUM* of *TotalDue* (a calculated field in the *FROM* clause). Then we use the *FOR* operator to list the values we want to pivot on in the *OrderYear* column. The example is shown in Listing 2-11.

LISTING 2-11 Creating tabular results with the *PIVOT* operator

```
SELECT
  CustomerID,
  [2001] AS Y2001, [2002] AS Y2002, [2003] AS Y2003, [2004] AS Y2004
  FROM
  (
    SELECT CustomerID, DATEPART(yyyy, OrderDate) AS OrderYear, TotalDue
      FROM Sales.SalesOrderHeader
  ) AS piv
PIVOT
  (
    SUM(TotalDue) FOR OrderYear IN([2001], [2002], [2003], [2004])
  ) AS child
ORDER BY CustomerID
```

Here are the results:

```
CustomerID  Y2001        Y2002        Y2003        Y2004
----------- ----------   -----------  ------------ ------------
1           40732.6067   72366.1284   NULL         NULL
2           NULL1        5653.6715    12118.0275   4962.2705
3           39752.8421   168393.7021  219434.4265  51925.3549
4           NULL         263025.3113  373484.299   143525.6018
5           NULL         33370.6901   60206.9999   20641.1106
6           NULL         NULL         668.4861     2979.3473
```

7	NULL	6651.036	3718.7804	NULL
8	NULL	NULL	19439.2466	10900.0347
9	NULL	320.6283	11401.5975	5282.8652
10	NULL	96701.7401	291472.2172	204525.9634

. . .

That's all there is to it. Of course, this example is simplified to show you the concept; other, more sophisticated, aggregates are possible, and you can even use CTEs in the *FROM* clause. In any case, using *PIVOT* is simple.

Using *UNPIVOT*

You can use the *UNPIVOT* operator to normalize data that is already pivoted. For example, suppose you obtain pivoted data that shows, for each vendor, the number of orders placed by each employee. The code in Listing 2-12 creates such a table.

LISTING 2-12 Example table containing pivoted data

```
CREATE TABLE VendorEmployee
  (VendorID int,
   Emp1Orders int,
   Emp2Orders int,
   Emp3Orders int,
   Emp4Orders int,
   Emp5Orders int)
GO

INSERT INTO VendorEmployee VALUES(1, 4, 3, 5, 4, 4)
INSERT INTO VendorEmployee VALUES(2, 4, 1, 5, 5, 5)
INSERT INTO VendorEmployee VALUES(3, 4, 3, 5, 4, 4)
INSERT INTO VendorEmployee VALUES(4, 4, 2, 5, 4, 4)
INSERT INTO VendorEmployee VALUES(5, 5, 1, 5, 5, 5)
```

Our table looks like this:

VendorID	Emp1Orders	Emp2Orders	Emp3Orders	Emp4Orders	Emp5Orders
1	4	3	5	4	4
2	4	1	5	5	5
3	4	3	5	4	4
4	4	2	5	4	4
5	5	1	5	5	5

You might want to unpivot the data to display columns for vendor ID, employee, and number of orders. Listing 2-13 shows how to use the *UNPIVOT* operator to achieve this goal.

LISTING 2-13 Using the *UNPIVOT* operator

```
SELECT VendorId, Employee, Orders AS NumberOfOrders
  FROM
   (SELECT VendorId, Emp1Orders, Emp2Orders, Emp3Orders, Emp4Orders, Emp5Orders
     FROM VendorEmployee
   ) AS p
UNPIVOT
(
  Orders FOR Employee IN
   (Emp1Orders, Emp2Orders, Emp3Orders, Emp4Orders, Emp5Orders)
) AS unpvt
```

Here are the results:

```
VendorID  Employee      NumberOfOrders
--------- ------------  ----------------------
1         Emp1Orders    4
1         Emp2Orders    3
1         Emp3Orders    5
1         Emp4Orders    4
1         Emp5Orders    4
2         Emp1Orders    4
...
```

Dynamically Pivoting Columns

The problem with *PIVOT* is the same problem with *CASE* and other methods: you have to specify the columns. Consider the code in Listing 2-14.

LISTING 2-14 Statically driven *PIVOT*

```
SELECT *
  FROM (SELECT CustomerID, YEAR(OrderDate) AS OrderYear, TotalDue
         FROM Sales.SalesOrderHeader) AS header
PIVOT
(
  SUM(TotalDue) FOR orderyear IN([2002],[2003],[2004])
) AS piv
```

The results show us a nice crosstab query with the years displayed as columns:

```
CustomerID  2002       2003       2004
----------- ---------- ---------- -----------
14324       NULL       2264.2536  3394.9247
22814       NULL       5.514      NULL
11407       NULL       59.659     NULL
28387       NULL       NULL       645.2869
19897       NULL       NULL       659.6408
15675       2699.9018  2682.9953  2580.1529
24165       NULL       2699.9018  666.8565
...
```

Because this data goes only up to 2004, what happens when you add 2005 to the data? Do you want to go into all your queries and add the current year to the *IN* clause? We can accommodate new years in the data by dynamically building the *IN* clause and then pro-grammatically writing the entire SQL statement. Once you have dynamically written the SQL statement, you can execute it using *sp_executesql*, as shown in Listing 2-15. Since all we have to do is generate dynamically the *IN* clause, creating a dynamic *PIVOT* in SQL Server is much easier than creating a dynamic *CASE* statement. The results are exactly the same as those shown following Listing 2-14, except that as new yearly data is added to the table, the query dynamically adds the column for it. Remember that your reporting engine will most likely not accommodate the new dynamic columns, but data-bound controls will.

LISTING 2-15 Dynamically driven *PIVOT*

```
DECLARE @tblOrderDate AS TABLE(y int NOT NULL PRIMARY KEY)
INSERT INTO @tblOrderDate
 SELECT DISTINCT YEAR(OrderDate) FROM Sales.SalesOrderHeader

DECLARE @cols AS nvarchar(max)
DECLARE @years AS int
SET @years = (SELECT MIN(y) FROM @tblOrderDate)
SET @cols = N''
WHILE @years IS NOT NULL BEGIN
  SET @cols = @cols + N',[' + CAST(@years AS nvarchar(max)) + N']'
  SET @years = (SELECT MIN(y) FROM @tblOrderDate WHERE y > @years)
END
SET @cols = SUBSTRING(@cols, 2, LEN(@cols))
DECLARE @sql AS nvarchar(max)
SET @sql = '
  SELECT *
  FROM
    (SELECT CustomerId, YEAR(OrderDate) AS OrderYear, TotalDue
      FROM Sales.SalesOrderHeader
    ) AS a
    PIVOT
    (
      SUM(TotalDue) FOR OrderYear IN(' + @cols + N')
    ) AS b
  '
PRINT @sql -- for debugging
EXEC sp_executesql @sql
```

You can accomplish the same results using the newer CTE syntax instead of using the *table* variable, as shown in Listing 2-16.

LISTING 2-16 Dynamically driven *PIVOT* using a CTE

```
DECLARE @cols AS nvarchar(MAX)

WITH YearsCTE AS
 (SELECT DISTINCT YEAR(OrderDate) as [Year] FROM Sales.SalesOrderHeader)

SELECT @cols = ISNULL(@cols + ',[', '[') + CAST([YEAR] AS nvarchar(10)) + ']'
 FROM YearsCTE
 ORDER BY [YEAR]

-- Construct the full T-SQL statement and execute it dynamically.
DECLARE @sql AS nvarchar(MAX)
SET @sql = '
  SELECT *
  FROM
    (SELECT CustomerId, YEAR(OrderDate) AS OrderYear, TotalDue
      FROM Sales.SalesOrderHeader
    ) AS a
    PIVOT
    (
      SUM(TotalDue) FOR OrderYear IN(' + @cols + N')
    ) AS b
'
PRINT @sql -- for debugging
EXEC sp_executesql @sql
```

The *APPLY* Operator

APPLY is an operator that you specify in the *FROM* clause of a query. It enables you to invoke a table-valued function (TVF) for each row of an outer table. The flexibility of *APPLY* is evident when you use the outer table's columns as your function's arguments. The *APPLY* operator has two forms: *CROSS APPLY* and *OUTER APPLY*. *CROSS APPLY* doesn't return the outer table's row if the TVF returns an empty set for it; the *OUTER APPLY* returns a row with *NULL* values instead of the function's columns.

To see how *APPLY* works, we'll first create a TVF that returns a table. Listing 2-17 shows a simple function that returns as a table the top *n* rows for a customer from the *SalesOrderHeader* table.

LISTING 2-17 Returning a table

```
CREATE FUNCTION fnGetCustomerOrders(@CustomerID int, @TopRecords bigint)
RETURNS TABLE
 AS RETURN
  SELECT TOP (@TopRecords) *
   FROM Sales.SalesOrderHeader
   WHERE CustomerID = @CustomerID
   ORDER BY OrderDate DESC
```

After creating the *fnGetCustomerOrders* TVF, we call it from the query, as shown in Listing 2-18.

LISTING 2-18 Executing a query with *APPLY*

```
SELECT * FROM Sales.Customer cust
 CROSS APPLY fnGetCustomerOrders(CustomerID, 100)
```

This query returns all the records from the *Customers* table and then, as additional fields, the records from the *Orders* table (by way of the *fnGetCustomerOrders* function) that match for the customer ID because that's what's being passed in dynamically as the first argument to *fnGetCustomerOrders*. Because we passed the value 100 for the second parameter, rows for up to the first 100 orders per customer are generated and returned by this query.

TOP Enhancements

In SQL Server 2000 and earlier versions, *TOP* allows you to limit the number of rows returned as a number or a percentage in *SELECT* queries. As of SQL Server 2005, you can use *TOP* in *DELETE*, *UPDATE*, and *INSERT* queries and can also specify the number (or percentage) of rows by using variables or any valid numeric returning expression (such as a subquery). The main reason for allowing *TOP* with *DELETE*, *UPDATE*, and *INSERT* was to replace the *SET ROWCOUNT* option, which SQL Server traditionally didn't optimize very well.

You can specify the *TOP* limit as a literal number or an expression. If you're using an expression, you must enclose it in parentheses. The expression should be of the *bigint* data type when you are not using the *PERCENT* option and a *float* value in the range 0 through 100 when you are using the *PERCENT* option. You might find it useful to create an expression for *TOP* and make it a parameter that you pass in to a stored procedure, as shown in Listing 2-19.

LISTING 2-19 Using *TOP* enhancements in a stored procedure

```
CREATE PROCEDURE uspReturnTopOrders(@NumberOfRows bigint)
AS
  SELECT TOP (@NumberOfRows) SalesOrderID
   FROM Sales.SalesOrderHeader
   ORDER BY SalesOrderID
```

Executing the stored procedure is easy. Just pass in the number of records you want (in this case, 100), as shown here:

```
EXEC uspReturnTopOrders @NumberOfRows = 100
```

Here are the results:

```
SalesOrderID
------------
43659
43660
43661
43662
43663
  :

(100 row(s) affected)
```

Using a subquery can be powerful when you're doing things on the fly. The following example shows how to get the *TOP n* orders based on how many rows are in the *SalesPerson* table:

```sql
SELECT TOP (SELECT COUNT(*) FROM Sales.SalesPerson)
  SalesOrderID, RevisionNumber, OrderDate
 FROM Sales.SalesOrderHeader
 ORDER BY SalesOrderID
```

Because there are 17 rows in the *SalesPerson* table, the query returns only the top 17 rows from the *SalesOrderHeader* table:

```
SalesOrderID  Revision  NumberOrderDate
------------  --------  -------------------------
43659         1         2001-07-01 00:00:00.000
43660         1         2001-07-01 00:00:00.000
43661         1         2001-07-01 00:00:00.000
43662         1         2001-07-01 00:00:00.000
43663         1         2001-07-01 00:00:00.000
43664         1         2001-07-01 00:00:00.000
43665         1         2001-07-01 00:00:00.000
43666         1         2001-07-01 00:00:00.000
43667         1         2001-07-01 00:00:00.000
43668         1         2001-07-01 00:00:00.000
43669         1         2001-07-01 00:00:00.000
43670         1         2001-07-01 00:00:00.000
43671         1         2001-07-01 00:00:00.000
43672         1         2001-07-01 00:00:00.000
43673         1         2001-07-01 00:00:00.000
43674         1         2001-07-01 00:00:00.000
43675         1         2001-07-01 00:00:00.000

(17 row(s) affected)
```

Using the *PERCENT* option is just as easy. Just add the *PERCENT* keyword, and make sure that your variable is a *float*. In Listing 2-20, we're asking for the top 10 percent, so we'll get back 3,147 records because the *AdventureWorks2008 SalesOrderHeader* table has approximately 31,465 records in it.

LISTING 2-20 Returning *TOP* percentages

```
DECLARE @NumberOfRows AS float
SET @NumberOfRows = 10

SELECT TOP (@NumberOfRows) PERCENT *
 FROM Sales.SalesOrderHeader
 ORDER BY OrderDate
```

Ranking Functions

Databases hold data. Users sometimes want to perform simple calculations or algorithms on that data to rank the results in a specific order—like gold, silver, and bronze medals in the Olympics or the top 10 customers by region. Starting with SQL Server 2005, functionality is provided for using ranking expressions with your result set. You can select a number of ranking algorithms, which are then applied to a column that you specify and applied in the scope of the executing query. If the data changes, your ranking algorithm will return different data the next time it is run. This comes in handy in Microsoft .NET Framework applications for paging and sorting in a grid, as well as in many other scenarios.

The *ROW_NUMBER* Function

The most basic ranking function is *ROW_NUMBER*. It returns a column as an expression that contains the row's number in the result set. This number is used only in the context of the result set; if the result changes, the *ROW_NUMBER* changes. The *ROW_NUMBER* expression takes an *ORDER BY* statement with the column you want to use for the row count and the *OVER* operator, which links the *ORDER BY* to the specific ranking function you are using. The *ORDER BY* in the *OVER* clause replaces an *ORDER BY* at the end of the SQL statement.

The simple example in Listing 2-21 gives a row number to each row in the result set, ordering by *SalesOrderID*.

LISTING 2-21 Row number ranking

```
SELECT
  SalesOrderID,
  CustomerID,
  ROW_NUMBER() OVER (ORDER BY SalesOrderID) AS RowNumber
 FROM Sales.SalesOrderHeader
```

The results are shown here:

```
SalesOrderID    CustomerID    RowNumber
---------------  -------------  ---------------
43659            676            1
43660            117            2
43661            442            3
43662            227            4
43663            510            5
43664            397            6
43665            146            7
43666            511            8
43667            646            9
  :
```

ORDER BY Options

The ranking functions order your result set by the fields specified in the *ORDER BY* statement contained in the *OVER* clause. Alternatively, you can include an additional *ORDER BY* statement in your result set; this optional statement is distinct from the *ORDER BY* clause in the *OVER* expression. SQL Server allows this, but if you choose this option, the *ROW_NUMBER* function's results are displayed in the order in which they are determined in the additional *ORDER BY* statement, *not* by the *ORDER BY* statement contained within the *OVER* clause. The results can, therefore, be confusing. To illustrate, if we provide an additional *ORDER BY CustomerID* clause to the very same query we just ran, we get these "jumbled" results:

```
SalesOrderID    CustomerID    RowNumber
---------------  -------------  ---------------
43860            1              202
44501            1              843
45283            1              1625
46042            1              2384
46976            2              3318
47997            2              4339
49054            2              5396
50216            2              6558
51728            2              8070
57044            2              13386
63198            2              19540
69488            2              25830
65310            3              21652
71889            3              28231
53616            3              9958
  :
```

As you can see, if you expect the results to be sorted by the *OVER* clause's *ORDER BY* statement, you'd expect results ranked by *SalesOrderID*, when in fact they're ordered by *CustomerID*.

If you choose the *ROW_NUMBER* function to run against a nonunique column that contains multiple copies of the same value (also known as "ties," such as the same amount of items sold and the same time in a race), *ROW_NUMBER* breaks the tie and still produces a running count so that no rows have the same number. In Listing 2-22, for example, *CustomerID* can repeat, which will generate several ties; SQL Server simply increases the running count for each row, regardless of how many ties exist.

LISTING 2-22 Row number ranking with ties

```
SELECT
  SalesOrderID,
  CustomerID,
  ROW_NUMBER() OVER (ORDER BY CustomerID) AS RowNumber
  FROM Sales.SalesOrderHeader
```

The results are shown here:

```
SalesOrderID    CustomerID      RowNumber
-------------   -------------   ----------------
43860           1               1
44501           1               2
45283           1               3
46042           1               4
46976           2               5
47997           2               6
49054           2               7
50216           2               8
51728           2               9
57044           2               10
63198           2               11
69488           2               12
44124           3               13
  :
```

Grouping and Filtering with *ROW_NUMBER*

When you want to include a *GROUP BY* function in your query, ranking functions do not work. The easy way around this limitation is to create your *GROUP BY* in a CTE and then perform your ranking on the results, as shown in Listing 2-23.

LISTING 2-23 Grouping by row number

```
WITH CustomerSum
AS
(
  SELECT CustomerID, SUM(TotalDue) AS TotalAmt
  FROM Sales.SalesOrderHeader
  GROUP BY CustomerID
)
```

```
--this appends a row number to the end of the result set
SELECT
  *,
  ROW_NUMBER() OVER (ORDER BY TotalAmt DESC) AS RowNumber
 FROM CustomerSum
```

Here are the results:

```
CustomerID    TotalAmt          RowNumber
------------- ---------------   ---------------
678           1179857.4657      1
697           1179475.8399      2
170           1134747.4413      3
328           1084439.0265      4
514           1074154.3035      5
155           1045197.0498      6
72            1005539.7181      7
 :
```

To filter by a *ROW_NUMBER*, you have to put the *ROW_NUMBER* function in a CTE, as shown in Listing 2-24.

LISTING 2-24 Filtering by row number

```
WITH NumberedRows AS
(
  SELECT
    SalesOrderID,
    CustomerID,
    ROW_NUMBER() OVER (ORDER BY SalesOrderID) AS RowNumber
   FROM Sales.SalesOrderHeader
)

SELECT * FROM NumberedRows
 WHERE RowNumber BETWEEN 100 AND 200
```

Here are the results:

```
SalesOrderID    CustomerID      RowNumber
--------------- -------------   --------------
43759           13257           100
43760           16352           101
43761           16493           102
 :
43857           533             199
43858           36              200
```

The *RANK* Function

The ranking function you will probably use the most is *RANK*, which ranks the data in the *ORDER BY* clause in the order you specify. *RANK* is syntactically exactly like *ROW_NUMBER* but with true ranking results. It works just like in the Olympics, when two people tie for the gold medal—the next rank is bronze. For example, with the *RANK* function, if four rows are tied with the value *1*, the next row value for the rank column will be *5*. Consider the code in Listing 2-25.

LISTING 2-25 The *RANK* function

```
SELECT
  SalesOrderID,
  CustomerID,
  RANK() OVER (ORDER BY CustomerID) AS Rank
  FROM Sales.SalesOrderHeader
```

Here are the results:

```
SalesOrderID    CustomerID    Rank
---------------  -------------  ----------------
43860           1             1
44501           1             1
45283           1             1
46042           1             1
46976           2             5
47997           2             5
49054           2             5
50216           2             5
51728           2             5
57044           2             5
63198           2             5
69488           2             5
44124           3             13
  :
```

Just as with the other ranking functions, *RANK* needs the aid of a CTE to work with aggregates. Consider this query that ranks the customers from highest to lowest by total sales. We have to use a CTE to perform the aggregate first and then rank over the newly created aggregate expression, as shown in Listing 2-26.

LISTING 2-26 Ranked aggregates

```
WITH CustomerSum AS
(
  SELECT CustomerID, SUM(TotalDue) AS TotalAmt
    FROM Sales.SalesOrderHeader
    GROUP BY CustomerID
)
SELECT
  *,
  RANK() OVER (ORDER BY TotalAmt DESC) AS Rank
  FROM CustomerSum
```

The results are shown here. Notice that customer 678 is in first place:

```
CustomerID  TotalAmt                Rank
----------- ---------------------   --------------------
678         1179857.4657            1
697         1179475.8399            2
170         1134747.4413            3
328         1084439.0265            4
514         1074154.3035            5
  :
```

As stated earlier, it is important to remember that the ranking functions provided by SQL Server are valid only for the scope of the running query. If the underlying data changes and then you run the same query again, you will get different results. In Listing 2-27, for example, let's modify a record from customer 697. By changing one of the detail rows for an order placed by customer 697 and increasing the order quantity, we place customer 697 as our top customer.

LISTING 2-27 Changing *RANK* results with underlying data changes

```
UPDATE Sales.SalesOrderDetail
  SET OrderQty = 50  -- the original value was 2
  WHERE SalesOrderDetailID = 535
```

Now rerun the same query. Notice that customer 697 has now surpassed customer 678 as the top customer:

```
CustomerID  TotalAmt                Rank
----------- ---------------------   --------------------
697         1272595.5474            1
678         1179857.4657            2
170         1134747.4413            3
328         1084439.0265            4
514         1074154.3035            5
  :
```

The *DENSE_RANK* and *NTILE* Functions

The last two ranking functions we will cover are *DENSE_RANK* and *NTILE*. *DENSE_RANK* works exactly like *RANK* except that it increments only on distinct rank changes—in other words, unlike in the Olympics, it awards a silver medal when there are two gold medals. Listing 2-28 shows an example.

LISTING 2-28 Ranking with *DENSE_RANK*

```
SELECT
  SalesOrderID,
  CustomerID,
  DENSE_RANK() OVER (ORDER BY CustomerID) AS DenseRank
  FROM Sales.SalesOrderHeader
  WHERE CustomerID > 100
```

The results are shown here:

```
SalesOrderID CustomerID  DenseRank
------------ ----------- --------------------
46950        101         1
47979        101         1
49048        101         1
50200        101         1
51700        101         1
57022        101         1
63138        101         1
69400        101         1
43855        102         2
44498        102         2
45280        102         2
46038        102         2
46951        102         2
47978        102         2
49103        102         2
50199        102         2
51733        103         3
57058        103         3
  :
```

The following example shows the difference between *RANK* and *DENSE_RANK*. We will round the customers' sales to the nearest hundred (because managers always like to look at whole numbers in their reports!) and look at the difference when we run into a tie. The code is shown in Listing 2-29.

LISTING 2-29 *RANK* versus *DENSE_RANK*

```
WITH CustomerSum AS
(
  SELECT
    CustomerID,
    ROUND(CONVERT(int, SUM(TotalDue)) / 100, 8) * 100 AS TotalAmt
  FROM Sales.SalesOrderHeader
  GROUP BY CustomerID
)
SELECT *,
  RANK() OVER (ORDER BY TotalAmt DESC) AS Rank,
  DENSE_RANK() OVER (ORDER BY TotalAmt DESC) AS DenseRank
FROM CustomerSum
```

And here are the results:

```
CustomerID  TotalAmt    Rank    DenseRank
----------- ----------- ------- --------------------
697         1272500     1       1
678         1179800     2       2
170         1134700     3       3
328         1084400     4       4
  :
87          213300      170     170
667         210600      171     171
196         207700      172     172
451         206100      173     173
672         206100      173     173
27          205200      175     174
687         205200      175     174
163         204000      177     175
102         203900      178     176
  :
```

Notice that customers 451 and 672 are tied, with the same total sales amount. They are ranked 173 by both the *RANK* and the *DENSE_RANK* functions. What happens next is where the difference between the two functions comes into play. Customers 27 and 687 are tied for the next position, and they are both assigned 175 by *RANK* and 174 by *DENSE_RANK*. Customer 163 is the next nontie, and it is assigned 177 by *RANK* and 175 by *DENSE_RANK*.

NTILE divides the returned rows into approximately evenly sized groups, the number of which you specify as a parameter to the function. It assigns each member of a group the same number in the result set. A perfect example of this is the percentile ranking in a college examination or a road race. Listing 2-30 shows an example of using *NTILE*.

LISTING 2-30 Ranking with *NTILE*

```
SELECT
  SalesOrderID,
  CustomerID,
  NTILE(10000) OVER (ORDER BY CustomerID) AS NTile
  FROM Sales.SalesOrderHeader
```

The results are shown here:

```
SalesOrderID    CustomerID    NTile
---------------  -------------  ----------------
43860           1             1
44501           1             1
45283           1             1
46042           1             1
46976           2             2
47997           2             2
49054           2             2
50216           2             2
51728           2             3
57044           2             3
63198           2             3
69488           2             3
44124           3             4
   :
45024           29475         9998
45199           29476         9998
60449           29477         9998
60955           29478         9999
49617           29479         9999
62341           29480         9999
45427           29481         10000
49746           29482         10000
49665           29483         10000

(31465 row(s) affected)
```

Using All the Ranking Functions Together

So far, we have looked at the ranking functions in isolation. The ranking functions are just regular SQL Server expressions, so you can have as many of them as you want in a single *SELECT* statement. We'll look at one last example in Listing 2-31 that brings these all together into one SQL statement and shows the differences between the four ranking functions.

LISTING 2-31 Contrasting SQL Server ranking functions

```
SELECT
  SalesOrderID AS OrderID,
  CustomerID,
  ROW_NUMBER() OVER (ORDER BY CustomerID) AS RowNumber,
  RANK() OVER (ORDER BY CustomerID) AS Rank,
  DENSE_RANK() OVER (ORDER BY CustomerID) AS DenseRank,
  NTILE(10000) OVER (ORDER BY CustomerID) AS NTile
FROM Sales.SalesOrderHeader
```

The results are shown here:

```
OrderID  CustomerID     RowNumber  Rank    DenseRank NTile
-------- -------------- ---------- ------- --------- --------
43860    1              1          1       1         1
44501    1              2          1       1         1
45283    1              3          1       1         1
46042    1              4          1       1         1
46976    2              5          5       2         2
47997    2              6          5       2         2
49054    2              7          5       2         2
50216    2              8          5       2         2
51728    2              9          5       2         3
57044    2              10         5       2         3
63198    2              11         5       2         3
69488    2              12         5       2         3
44124    3              13         13      3         4
44791    3              14         13      3         4
  :
```

Ranking over Groups Using *PARTITION BY*

The ranking functions can also be combined with *windowing functions*. A windowing function divides a result set into equal partitions based on the values of your *PARTITION BY* statement in conjunction with the *OVER* clause in your ranking function. This is like applying a *GROUP BY* to your ranking function—you get a separate ranking for each partition. The example in Listing 2-32 uses *ROW_NUMBER* with *PARTITION BY* to count the number of orders by order date by salesperson. We do this by using *PARTITION BY SalesPersonID ORDER BY OrderDate*. You can do this with any of the four ranking functions.

LISTING 2-32 Ranking over groups with *PARTITION BY*

```
SELECT
  SalesOrderID,
  SalesPersonID,
  OrderDate,
  ROW_NUMBER() OVER (PARTITION BY SalesPersonID ORDER BY OrderDate) AS OrderRank
FROM Sales.SalesOrderHeader
WHERE SalesPersonID IS NOT NULL
```

The results are shown here. You might find that the order of your rows varies slightly from the results shown.

```
SalesOrderID    SalesPersonID    OrderDate       OrderRank
---------------  ----------------  ------------  --------------
    :
43659           279              2001-07-01 00:00:00.000  1
43660           279              2001-07-01 00:00:00.000  2
43681           279              2001-07-01 00:00:00.000  3
43684           279              2001-07-01 00:00:00.000  4
43685           279              2001-07-01 00:00:00.000  5
43694           279              2001-07-01 00:00:00.000  6
43695           279              2001-07-01 00:00:00.000  7
43696           279              2001-07-01 00:00:00.000  8
43845           279              2001-08-01 00:00:00.000  9
43861           279              2001-08-01 00:00:00.000  10
    :
48079           287              2002-11-01 00:00:00.000  1
48064           287              2002-11-01 00:00:00.000  2
48057           287              2002-11-01 00:00:00.000  3
47998           287              2002-11-01 00:00:00.000  4
48001           287              2002-11-01 00:00:00.000  5
48014           287              2002-11-01 00:00:00.000  6
47982           287              2002-11-01 00:00:00.000  7
47992           287              2002-11-01 00:00:00.000  8
48390           287              2002-12-01 00:00:00.000  9
48308           287              2002-12-01 00:00:00.000  10
    :
```

Let's partition our ranking function by country, as shown in Listing 2-33. We'll create a CTE to aggregate the sales by customer and by country. Then we'll apply the ranking function over the *TotalAmt* field and the *CustomerID* field, partitioned by the *CountryName* field.

LISTING 2-33 Aggregates with *PARTITION BY*

```
WITH CTETerritory AS
(
  SELECT
    cr.Name AS CountryName,
    CustomerID,
    SUM(TotalDue) AS TotalAmt
  FROM
    Sales.SalesOrderHeader AS soh
    INNER JOIN Sales.SalesTerritory AS ter ON soh.TerritoryID = ter.TerritoryID
    INNER JOIN Person.CountryRegion AS cr ON cr.CountryRegionCode = ter.
CountryRegionCode
  GROUP BY
    cr.Name, CustomerID
)
SELECT
  *,
  RANK() OVER(PARTITION BY CountryName ORDER BY TotalAmt, CustomerID DESC) AS Rank
  FROM CTETerritory
```

The results look like this:

```
CountryName    CustomerID    TotalAmt    Rank
-------------  ------------  ----------  --------------
Australia      29083         4.409       1
Australia      29061         4.409       2
Australia      29290         5.514       3
Australia      29287         5.514       4
Australia      28924         5.514       5
   :
Canada         29267         5.514       1
Canada         29230         5.514       2
Canada         28248         5.514       3
Canada         27628         5.514       4
Canada         27414         5.514       5
   :
France         24538         4.409       1
France         24535         4.409       2
France         23623         4.409       3
France         23611         4.409       4
France         20961         4.409       5
   :
```

PARTITION BY supports other SQL Server aggregate functions, including *MIN* and *MAX* as well as your own scalar functions. You can apply your aggregate function in the same way that you apply the ranking functions, with a *PARTITION BY* statement. Let's apply this technique to the current sample by adding a column to our result set using the *AVG* function, as shown in Listing 2-34. We will get the same results but with an additional column showing the average by country.

LISTING 2-34 Using *AVG* with *PARTITION BY*

```
WITH CTETerritory AS
(
  SELECT
    cr.Name AS CountryName,
    CustomerID,
    SUM(TotalDue) AS TotalAmt
  FROM
    Sales.SalesOrderHeader AS soh
    INNER JOIN Sales.SalesTerritory AS ter ON soh.TerritoryID = ter.TerritoryID
    INNER JOIN Person.CountryRegion AS cr ON cr.CountryRegionCode = ter.
CountryRegionCode
  GROUP BY
    cr.Name, CustomerID
)
SELECT
  *,
  RANK() OVER (PARTITION BY CountryName ORDER BY TotalAmt, CustomerID DESC) AS Rank,
  AVG(TotalAmt) OVER(PARTITION BY CountryName) AS Average
  FROM CTETerritory
```

Here are the results:

```
CountryName     CustomerID    TotalAmt    Rank    Average
-------------   -----------   ---------   ------  -----------------
Australia       29083         4.409       1       3364.8318
Australia       29061         4.409       2       3364.8318
Australia       29290         5.514       3       3364.8318
  :
Canada          29267         5.514       1       12824.756
Canada          29230         5.514       2       12824.756
Canada          28248         5.514       3       12824.756
  :
```

Exception Handling in Transactions

SQL Server offers major improvements in error handling inside T-SQL transactions. As of SQL Server 2005, you can catch T-SQL and transaction abort errors using the *TRY/CATCH* model without any loss of the transaction context. The only types of errors that the *TRY/CATCH* construct can't handle are those that cause the termination of your session (usually errors with severity 21 and above, such as hardware errors). The syntax is shown here:

```
BEGIN TRY
  --sql statements
END TRY
BEGIN CATCH
  --sql statements for catching your errors
END CATCH
```

If an error within an explicit transaction occurs inside a *TRY* block, control is passed to the *CATCH* block that immediately follows. If no error occurs, the *CATCH* block is completely skipped.

You can investigate the type of error that was raised and react accordingly. To do so, you can use the *ERROR_xxx* functions to return error information in the *CATCH* block, as shown in Listing 2-35.

LISTING 2-35 T-SQL exception handling example

```
BEGIN TRY
  SELECT 5/0
END TRY
BEGIN CATCH
  SELECT
    ERROR_NUMBER()    AS ErrNumber,
    ERROR_SEVERITY()  AS ErrSeverity,
    ERROR_STATE()     AS ErrState,
    ERROR_PROCEDURE() AS ErrProc,
    ERROR_LINE()      AS ErrLine,
    ERROR_MESSAGE()   AS ErrMessage
END CATCH
```

You can examine the value reported by any of the various *ERROR_xxx* functions to decide what to do with the control flow of your procedure and whether to abort any transactions. In our example in Listing 2-35, which attempts to divide by zero, here are the values returned by the error functions. (The *ERROR_PROCEDURE* function returns *NULL* in this example because the exception did not occur within a stored procedure.)

```
ErrNumber  ErrSeverity  ErrState  ErrProc  ErrLine  ErrMessage
---------- ------------ --------- -------- -------- --------------------------------
8134       16           1         NULL     2        Divide by zero error encountered.
```

When you experience a transaction abort error inside a transaction located in the *TRY* block, control is passed to the *CATCH* block. The transaction then enters a failed state in which locks are not released and persisted work is not reversed until you explicitly issue a *ROLLBACK* statement. You're not allowed to initiate any activity that requires opening an implicit or explicit transaction until you issue a *ROLLBACK*.

Certain types of errors are not detected by the *TRY/CATCH* block, and you end up with an unhandled exception even though the error occurred inside your *TRY* block. If this happens, the *CATCH* block is not executed. This is because *CATCH* blocks are invoked by errors that take place in actual executing code, not by compile or syntax errors. Two examples of such errors are syntax errors and statement-level recompile errors (for example, selecting from a nonexistent table). These errors are not caught at the same execution level as the *TRY* block, but at the lower level of execution—when you execute dynamic SQL or when you call a stored procedure from the *TRY* block. For example, if you have a syntax error inside a *TRY* block, you get a compile error and your *CATCH* block will not run, as shown here:

```
-- Syntax error doesn't get caught
BEGIN TRY
   SELECT * * FROM Customer
END TRY
BEGIN CATCH
   PRINT 'Error'
END CATCH
```

The result is an error from SQL Server, not from your *CATCH* block, as follows:

```
Msg 102, Level 15, State 1, Line 2
Incorrect syntax near '*'.
```

Statement-level recompilation errors also don't get caught by *CATCH* blocks. For example, using a nonexistent object in a *SELECT* statement in the *TRY* block forces an error from SQL Server, but your *CATCH* block will not execute, as shown here:

```
-- Statement level recompilation doesn't get caught
BEGIN TRY
  SELECT * FROM NonExistentTable
END TRY
BEGIN CATCH
  PRINT 'Error'
END CATCH
```

The result is an error from SQL Server, as follows:

```
Msg 208, Level 16, State 1, Line 3
Invalid object name 'NonExistentTable'.
```

When you use dynamic SQL or a stored procedure, these types of compile errors do get caught because they are part of the current level of execution. Each of the SQL blocks shown in Listing 2-36 will execute the *CATCH* block.

LISTING 2-36 Catching syntax and recompilation errors in dynamic SQL and stored procedure calls with exception handlers

```
-- Dynamic SQL Example
BEGIN TRY
  EXEC sp_executesql 'SELECT * * FROM Customer'
END TRY
BEGIN CATCH
  PRINT 'Error'
END CATCH
GO

-- Stored Procedure Example
CREATE PROCEDURE MyErrorProc
AS
  SELECT * FROM NonExistentTable
GO

BEGIN TRY
  EXEC MyErrorProc
END TRY
BEGIN CATCH
  PRINT 'Error'
END CATCH
```

The varchar(max) Data Type

The *varchar(max)*, *nvarchar(max)*, and *varbinary(max)* data types are extensions of the *varchar*, *nvarchar*, and *varbinary* data types that can store up to 2 gigabytes (GB) of data. They are alternatives to *text*, *ntext*, and *image* and use the *max* size specifier. Using one of these data types is easy—you just specify it in your *CREATE TABLE* statement (or in any variable declaration) with a *(max)* identifier, as in this example:

```
CREATE TABLE TableWithMaxColumn
  (Customer_Id int, CustomerLifeStory varchar(max))
```

All the standard T-SQL string functions operate on *varchar(max)*, including concatenation functions *SUBSTRING*, *LEN*, and *CONVERT*. For example, you can use the T-SQL *SUBSTRING* function to read parts of the string (*chunks*), and the *UPDATE* statement has also been enhanced to support the updating of chunks.

This is a vast improvement over the limitations in SQL Server 2000 and earlier, where *text* and *image* fields were used to store this type of data. These data types are not allowed as stored procedure parameters and cannot be updated directly, and many of the string manipulation functions don't work on the *text* data type.

The *WAITFOR* Statement

In SQL Server 2000, *WAITFOR* waited for a specified duration or a supplied *datetime* value. Starting with SQL Server 2005, as with the *TOP* enhancements, you can use *WAITFOR* with a SQL expression. You can essentially use the *WAITFOR* function to wait for a T-SQL statement to affect at least one row. (You can also set a time-out on that SQL expression.) You can specify *WAITFOR* to wait not only in *SELECT* statements but also in *INSERT*, *UPDATE*, *DELETE*, and *RECEIVE* statements. In essence, *SELECT* statements won't complete until at least one row is produced, and data manipulation language (DML) statements won't complete until at least one row is affected.

Here is the syntax:

```
WAITFOR(<statement>) [,TIMEOUT <timeout_value>]
```

This feature provides an alternative to polling. For example, you can use *WAITFOR* to select all the records in a log or a queue table, as shown here:

```
WAITFOR (SELECT * FROM MyQueue)
```

DDL Triggers

SQL Server supports data definitin language (DDL) triggers, allowing you to trap DDL operations and react to them. You can thus roll back the DDL activity. DDL triggers work synchronously, immediately after the triggering event, similar to the way that DML triggers work. DDL triggers can be database-wide and can react to certain types of DDLs or all DDLs.

The cool thing about DDL triggers is that you can get context information from querying the *EVENTDATA* function. Event data is an XML payload of data about what was happening when your DDL trigger ran (including information about the time, connection, and user), the type of event that was fired, and other useful data. To get at *EVENTDATA* data, you have to use the *EVENTDATA* function in your trigger code. If you issue a *ROLLBACK* statement in the trigger, the *EVENTDATA* function will no longer return information. In this situation, you must store the information in a variable before issuing the *ROLLBACK* statement to be accessed later.

> **Note** SQL Server 2008 introduces new security features that allow you to audit DDL actions, as an alternative to using DDL triggers for auditing the same information. We cover SQL Server Audit in Chapter 5.

The *AdventureWorks2008* trigger, shown in Listing 2-37, is created at the database level and will capture *DROP TABLE* attempts. First we'll create a log table to log all our event data using an XML column, and then we'll create a dummy table that we will attempt to delete for testing our trigger on. Our trigger will issue a *ROLLBACK* (which effectively cancels the attempted *DROP TABLE* operation) and then write the event data to this table.

LISTING 2-37 Catching *DROP TABLE* attempts with a trigger

```
-- Create a log table
CREATE TABLE TriggerLog (LogInfo xml)

-- Create a dummy table to delete later on
CREATE TABLE TableToDelete (Id int PRIMARY KEY)

-- Add some dummy data
INSERT INTO TableToDelete VALUES(1)
GO

-- Create a trigger that will prevent the table from being deleted
CREATE TRIGGER StopTableDrop ON DATABASE AFTER DROP_TABLE
AS
  DECLARE @EventData AS xml
  SET @EventData = EVENTDATA() -- must be captured *before* rollback
  ROLLBACK
  PRINT 'DROP TABLE attempt in database ' + DB_NAME() + '.'
  INSERT INTO TriggerLog VALUES(@EventData)
```

The following example attempts to drop a table (which will fail because of our DDL trigger) and then queries the *TriggerLog* table to examine the details of the attempt:

```
-- The trigger in action...
DROP TABLE TableToDelete
SELECT * FROM TriggerLog
```

The results look like this:

```
DROP TABLE attempt in database AdventureWorks2008.

(1 row(s) affected)
Msg 3609, Level 16, State 2, Line 2
The transaction ended in the trigger. The batch has been aborted.
```

The *EventData* XML recorded to the *TriggerLog* table at the time we ran the script in Listing 2-37 on our system looks like this:

```
<EVENT_INSTANCE>
  <EventType>DROP_TABLE</EventType>
  <PostTime>2008-06-11T22:07:42.910</PostTime>
  <SPID>55</SPID>
  <ServerName>SQL08DEV</ServerName>
  <LoginName>SQL08DEV\Administrator</LoginName>
  <UserName>dbo</UserName>
  <DatabaseName>AdventureWorks2008</DatabaseName>
  <SchemaName>dbo</SchemaName>
  <ObjectName>TableToDelete</ObjectName>
  <ObjectType>TABLE</ObjectType>
  <TSQLCommand>
    <SetOptions ANSI_NULLS="ON" ANSI_NULL_DEFAULT="ON" ANSI_PADDING="ON" QUOTED_
IDENTIFIER="ON" ENCRYPTED="FALSE" />
    <CommandText>DROP TABLE TableToDelete</CommandText>
  </TSQLCommand>
</EVENT_INSTANCE>
```

SNAPSHOT Isolation

For working with T-SQL transactions, SQL Server 2005 introduced a new isolation level called SNAPSHOT that allows you to work in a mode in which writers don't block readers. Readers thus read from a previously committed version of the data they request, rather than being blocked during write transactions. SNAPSHOT isolation works by SQL Server maintaining a linked list in *tempdb* that tracks changes to rows and constructs an older, committed version of data for readers to access. This isolation level is useful for optimistic locking, in which *UPDATE* conflicts are uncommon. For example, if process 1 retrieves data and later attempts to modify it, and if process 2 has modified the same data between the retrieval and modification belonging to process 1, SQL Server produces an error when process 1 attempts to modify data because of the conflict. Process 1 can then try to reissue the transaction. This mode can be efficient in situations where *UPDATE* conflicts are not common.

Look for a more thorough discussion of SQL Server isolation levels and transactions in Chapter 12.

Table-Valued Parameters

We explored common table expressions (CTEs) at the beginning of this chapter and saw how, in SQL Server 2005, they provided a new alternative to using temporary tables and table variables, which have been around for a long time in SQL Server. Table-valued parameters (TVPs) in SQL Server 2008 give us yet another choice for treating a set of rows as a single entity that you can query or join against. It is now also remarkably easy to send an entire set of rows from our .NET client applications to SQL Server with just one server roundtrip using Microsoft ADO.NET, as you'll see close up toward the end of our discussion of TVPs.

> **Note** TVPs and all the remaining topics in this chapter are all-new features available only in SQL Server 2008.

More than Just Another Temporary Table Solution

A TVP is based on a new user-defined table type in SQL Server 2008 that describes the schema for a set of rows that can be passed to stored procedures or user-defined functions (UDFs). It's helpful to understand TVPs by first comparing them with table variables, temp tables, and CTEs and then contrasting their similarities and differences. All of these techniques provide a different way of querying or joining against a typed temporary result set, enabling you to treat a TVP, table variable, temporary table, or CTE just as you would an ordinary table or view in many scenarios.

Both CTEs and table variables store their row data in memory, assuming reasonably sized sets that don't overflow the RAM cache allocated for them (in which case, they do get pushed into *tempdb*). In contrast, the new TVPs in SQL Server 2008 are always stored in *tempdb*. This means that they incur disk I/O just as regular temp tables do, which is a performance hit evaded by (reasonably sized) memory-resident CTEs and table variables, and a consideration for you to bear in mind when using TVPs. Conversely, this also means that TVPs are better suited than CTEs and table variables when dealing with larger numbers of rows, since TVPs can be indexed but CTEs and table variables cannot.

The real power of TVPs in SQL Server 2008 lies in the ability to pass an entire table (a set of rows) as a single parameter from client to server and between your T-SQL stored procedures and user-defined functions. Table variables and temporary tables, on the other hand, cannot be passed as parameters. CTEs are limited in scope to the statement following their creation (as mentioned at the beginning of this chapter) and are therefore inherently incapable of being passed as parameters.

Reusability is another side benefit of TVPs. The schema of a TVP is centrally maintained, which is not the case with table variables, temporary tables, and CTEs. You define the schema once by creating a new user-defined type (UDT) of type *table*, which you do by applying the new *AS TABLE* clause to the *CREATE TYPE* statement, as shown in Listing 2-38.

LISTING 2-38 Defining the schema for a user-defined table type

```
CREATE TYPE CustomerUdt AS TABLE
  (Id int,
   CustomerName nvarchar(50),
   PostalCode nvarchar(50))
```

This statement creates a new user-defined table type named *CustomerUdt* with three columns. TVP variables of type *CustomerUdt* can now be declared and populated with rows of data that fit this schema, which SQL Server will store in *tempdb* behind the scenes. These variables can be passed freely between stored procedures—unlike regular table variables, which are stored in RAM behind the scenes and cannot be passed as parameters. When TVP variables declared as *CustomerUdt* fall out of scope and are no longer referenced, the underlying data in *tempdb* supporting the TVP is deleted automatically by SQL Server.

> **Tip** The schema of this *CustomerUdt* table type is now embedded in the database (just like any other UDT), which makes it easily reusable throughout your T-SQL code. Even if you don't necessarily need the parameter-passing capability of a TVP, defining one makes it easy to instantly declare a variable of the table type without declaring the entire schema. Compare that with table variables and temporary tables, where you can find yourself duplicating the same schema in your code.

So although it's called a table-valued *parameter*, in fact, we see that a TVP is essentially a new user-defined table *type*. This new table type earns its name by allowing populated instances of itself to be passed on as parameters to stored procedures and user-defined functions (UDFs)—something you still can't do with a regular table variable. In a sense, you can think of TVPs as table variables on steroids: they provide similar functionality (temporary row set storage), add new capabilities (can be passed as parameters), and carry more overhead (use disk storage versus RAM).

> **Note** In this text, the terms *table-valued parameter (TVP)* and *user-defined table type* are used interchangeably.

Once the table type is defined, you can create stored procedures with parameters of that type to pass an entire set of rows using TVPs.

TVP types are displayed in Management Studio Object Explorer in the new *User-Defined Table Types* node beneath *Programmability, Types*, as shown in Figure 2-1.

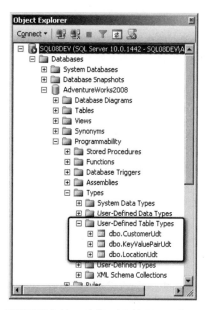

FIGURE 2-1 User-defined table types that can be used for TVPs displayed in Management Studio Object Explorer

There are many practical applications for this newly acquired ability to pass entire sets of data around as parameters, and we'll explore a number of them in the rest of this section. You will be sure to discover more good uses for TVPs on your own, just by setting your imagination loose on your requirements.

Working with a Multiple-Row Set

One common scenario in which TVPs can be applied is a typical order entry system. When a customer places an order, a new order row and any number of new order detail rows must be created in the database. Traditionally, this might be accomplished by creating two stored procedures—one for inserting an order row and one for inserting an order detail row. The application would invoke a stored procedure call for each individual row, so for an order with 20 details, there would be a total of 21 stored procedure calls (1 for the order and 20 for the details). There could of course be even larger orders with many more than 20 details. As a result, numerous roundtrips are made between the application and the database, each one carrying only a single row of data. Additional programming would also be required to wrap the entire set of insert operations within a single atomic transaction. The transaction would be needed to ensure that an order is completely inserted into the database—or not inserted at all—in the event that an error occurs at any point during the process.

Enter TVPs. Now you can create a single stored procedure with just two TVPs, one for the order row and one for the order details row. The client can now issue a single call to this stored procedure, passing to it both the order and all of the order details at one time, as shown in

Listing 2-39. Furthermore, the entire operation is guaranteed to succeed or fail as a whole, eliminating the need to program a transaction around the process.

LISTING 2-39 Creating a stored procedure that accepts TVPs

```
CREATE PROCEDURE uspInsertNewOrder
  (@OrderTvp AS OrderUdt READONLY,
   @OrderDetailsTvp AS OrderDetailUdt READONLY)
AS
    INSERT INTO [Order]
     SELECT * FROM @OrderTvp

    INSERT INTO [OrderDetail]
     SELECT * FROM @OrderDetailsTvp
```

As you can see, this code is inserted into the *Order* and *OrderDetail* tables directly from the rows passed in through the two TVPs. We have essentially performed a bulk insert with a single call, rather than individual inserts across multiple calls wrapped in a transaction. (Note that the code in Listing 2-39 assumes that the *Order* and *OrderDetail* tables already exist and that the *OrderUdt* and *OrderDetailUdt* table types have already been created with a column schema that matches the tables.)

We'll now take a closer look at the bulk insert possibilities for TVPs and how to create, declare, populate, and pass TVPs in T-SQL. Then we'll look at how TVPs can be used as a powerful T-SQL parameter-passing mechanism. In the last part of this section, we'll demonstrate how to populate TVPs and pass them across the network from .NET client application code to stored procedures using ADO.NET.

Using TVPs for Bulk Inserts and Updates

Here's an example of a stored procedure that you can create in the *AdventureWorks2008* database that accepts a TVP and inserts all of the rows that get passed in through it into the *Product.Location* table. By creating a user-defined table type named *LocationUdt* that describes the schema for each row passed to the stored procedure, any code can call the stored procedure and pass to it a set of rows for insertion into *Product.Location* using a single parameter typed as *LocationUdt*.

First we'll create the user-defined table data type *LocationUdt*, as shown in Listing 2-40.

LISTING 2-40 Creating the *LocationUdt* table type to be used for bulk operations with TVPs

```
CREATE TYPE LocationUdt AS TABLE(
  LocationName varchar(50),
  CostRate int)
```

Now a TVP variable of this type can be declared to hold a set of rows with the two columns *LocationName* and *CostRate*. These rows can be fed to a stored procedure by passing the TVP variable into it. The stored procedure can then select from the TVP just like a regular table or view and thus use it as the source for an *INSERT INTO...SELECT* statement that appends each row to the *Product.Location* table.

Rows added to *Product.Location* require more than just the two fields for the location name and cost rate. The table also needs values for the availability and modified date fields, so we'll let the stored procedure handle that. What we're doing here is defining a schema that can provide a *subset* of the required *Product.Location* fields (*Name* and *CostRate*), for passing multiple rows of data to a stored procedure that provides values for the remaining required fields (*Availability* and *ModifiedDate*). In our example, the stored procedure sets *Availability* to *0* and *ModifiedDate* to the *GETDATE* function on each row of data inserted from the TVP (passed in as the only parameter) that provides the values for *Name* and *CostRate*, as shown in Listing 2-41.

LISTING 2-41 Creating a stored procedure to perform a bulk insert using a TVP declared as the *LocationUdt* table type

```
CREATE PROCEDURE uspInsertProductionLocation
  (@TVP LocationUdt READONLY)
AS
    INSERT INTO [Production].[Location]
      ([Name], [CostRate], [Availability], [ModifiedDate])
    SELECT *, 0, GETDATE() FROM @TVP
```

We now have a stored procedure that can accept a TVP containing a set of rows with location names and cost rates to be inserted into the *Production.Location* table and that sets the availability quantity and modified date on each inserted row—all achieved with a single parameter and a single *INSERT INTO...SELECT* statement! The procedure doesn't know or care *how* the caller populates the TVP before it is used as the source for the *INSERT INTO...SELECT* statement. For example, the caller could manually add one row at a time, as follows:

```
DECLARE @LocationTvp AS LocationUdt

INSERT INTO @LocationTvp VALUES('UK', 122.4)
INSERT INTO @LocationTvp VALUES('Paris', 359.73)

EXEC uspInsertProductionLocation @LocationTvp
```

Or the caller could bulk insert into the TVP from another source table using *INSERT INTO... SELECT*, as in our next example. We will fill the TVP from the existing *Person.StateProvince* table using the table's *Name* column for *LocationName* and the value *0* for *CostRate*. Passing this TVP to our stored procedure will result in a new set of rows added to *Production.Location* with their *Name* fields set according to the names in the *Person.StateProvince* table, their

CostRate and *Availability* values set to *0*, and their *ModifiedDate* values set by *GETDATE*, as shown here:

```
DECLARE @LocationTVP AS LocationUdt

INSERT INTO @LocationTVP
 SELECT [Name], 0.00 FROM [Person].[StateProvince]

EXEC uspInsertProductionLocation @LocationTVP
```

The TVP could also be populated on the client using ADO.NET, which we cover at the end of this section.

Bulk updates (and deletes) using TVPs are possible as well. You can create an *UPDATE* statement by joining a TVP (which you must alias) to the table you want to update. The rows updated in the table are determined by the matches joined to by the TVP and can be set to new values that are also contained in the TVP. For example, you can pass a TVP populated with category IDs and names for updating the *Categories* table in the database, as shown in Listing 2-42. By joining the TVP to the *Categories* table on the category ID, all the matching rows in the *Categories* table can be updated with the new category names in the TVP.

LISTING 2-42 Bulk updates using TVPs

```
UPDATE Category
  SET Category.Name = ec.Name
  FROM Category INNER JOIN @EditedCategoriesTVP AS ec ON Category.Id = ec.Id
```

Working with a Single Row of Data

You don't need to be working with multiple rows of data in a set to derive benefit from TVPs. Because they encapsulate a schema, TVPs can come in handy even when dealing with only a single row that holds a collection of column values to be used as a typed parameter list.

It is now easy to pass these multiple values along from one stored procedure to another by using a single parameter rather than by authoring and maintaining duplicate signatures with multiple parameters in your T-SQL code. As you've seen, the schema of a TVP is defined just once, using the *CREATE TYPE...AS TABLE* statement shown earlier, and is thus maintained centrally in one location for the entire database. This makes TVPs easy to reuse as structures for wrapping a typed parameter list passed around as a single parameter in code.

By creating the preceding *CustomerUdt* TVP that encapsulates three columns, we can now pass the three values from one stored procedure to another using one TVP, rather than using three separate parameters for each column. For longer parameter lists, of course, this can mean the difference between one parameter versus a dozen of more. So without using the TVP, our stored procedure might look like the code in Listing 2-43.

LISTING 2-43 Creating a stored procedure with a typical parameter list

```
CREATE PROCEDURE uspPassWithoutUdt(
  @Id int,
  @CustomerName nvarchar(50),
  @PostalCode nvarchar(50))
AS
  BEGIN
    -- Use the parameters
    SELECT @Id, @CustomerName, @PostalCode
  END
```

A call to this stored procedure would typically look like this:

```
EXEC uspPassWithoutUdt 1, 'Christian Hess', '23911'
```

Now imagine many more stored procedures with the same parameter list. These would all have the same three parameters, which would lead you to copy and paste, duplicating and maintaining them in each stored procedure. Using a TVP instead alleviates this burden, since the schema is centrally defined only once in the definition of the user-defined table type (see Listing 2-38).

With this table type defined, our stored procedures now have a much simplified signature that no longer requires us to duplicate the parameter list. The same stored procedure can now be implemented as shown in Listing 2-44.

LISTING 2-44 Creating a stored procedure with parameter values embedded in a TVP

```
CREATE PROCEDURE uspPassWithUdt(@CustomerTvp CustomerUdt READONLY)
AS
  BEGIN
    -- Extract values from the TVP
    SELECT Id, CustomerName, PostalCode FROM @CustomerTvp
  END
```

To call this stored procedure, we declare a TVP variable of type *CustomerUdt*, insert into it a single row of data containing the three values, and then pass just the single variable on to the stored procedure, as shown here:

```
DECLARE @CustomerTvp CustomerUdt

INSERT INTO @CustomerTvp(Id, CustomerName, PostalCode)
 VALUES(1, 'Christian Hess', '23911')

EXEC uspPassWithUdt @CustomerTvp
```

This is logically analogous in the .NET world to creating a class or struct instance, populating its properties or fields, and passing the instance on to a method call that then retrieves the values it wants from those properties or fields. A "package the parameters" approach such as this usually results in neater and more maintainable code—whether that code is written in .NET or T-SQL—particularly for lengthy and frequently reused parameter lists.

If you take proper care up front, you can design these parameter lists to tolerate the addition of new columns to the schema of the user-defined table type in the future without disturbing existing T-SQL code that references preexisting columns. To completely insulate code from extensions to the parameter list schema, you'll need to pay some special attention to your coding style when populating values—namely, avoiding *INSERT* statements that have no explicit column list. *INSERT* statements that populate a TVP should always use an explicit column list so that new columns added in the future do not affect their behavior and cause errors.

> **Tip** In general, it is best practice to use explicit column lists in your *INSERT* statements.

INSERT statements with no explicit column list adapt dynamically with respect to the schema of the table being inserted into. As the result of adding new columns to the table, an *INSERT* statement without an explicit column list that worked before will now certainly fail because the number of values specified in its *VALUES* clause will no longer match the number of columns in the table. To ensure that these statements continue to function despite future extensions to the schema, they *must* provide an explicit column list for mapping the specified *VALUES*. This will allow you to insert new columns anywhere in the schema (not just appended to the end), since providing an explicit column list means that you are not tied to the number (or order) of the columns in the table type. You'll also need to make sure that new columns added to the schema are either nullable or have default values assigned to them so that existing *INSERT* statements will continue to work properly without the concern of providing values for newly added columns.

This strategy puts you in the best position, since you are now in control and can make your own decisions about how, when, and where to use the values newly added to your typed parameter lists. You can choose to use the newer values only in new T-SQL code that needs to support them, without ever revisiting or modifying existing code that continues to work just fine. You can also incrementally and selectively update any existing code as you need or want to.

If you've coded defensively as we've just discussed, you're ready to safely extend the *CustomerUdt* table definition by adding a fourth column. There is no *ALTER TYPE...AS TABLE* statement available, so the table type must be dropped and then re-created. Because SQL Server tracks and enforces integrity on object dependencies in the database, it will also be necessary to first drop all the stored procedures that reference the table type, drop the table type itself, re-create the table type with the new schema, and then re-create the dropped stored procedures. This might (and perhaps should) discourage you from too frequently extending the parameter lists in your TVP schemas, although the burden is alleviated by the ability to easily generate all the necessary scripts that re-create all the programmability objects (stored procedures, TVPs, and so on) in the database. The code in Listing 2-45 drops and re-creates the table type and stored procedure.

LISTING 2-45 Revising the schema of the *CustomerUdt* table type

```
DROP PROCEDURE uspPassWithUdt
DROP TYPE CustomerUdt
GO

CREATE TYPE CustomerUdt AS TABLE
  (Id int,
   CustomerName nvarchar(50),
   HomePhone nvarchar(50), -- inserted new column
   PostalCode nvarchar(50))
GO

CREATE PROCEDURE uspPassWithUdt(@CustomerTvp CustomerUdt READONLY)
AS
BEGIN
    -- Extract values from the TVP
    SELECT Id, CustomerName, PostalCode FROM @CustomerTvp
  END
```

The *SELECT* statement in the stored procedure has not been modified and therefore continues to use only the original three columns. Had the *SELECT* statement been coded instead as *SELECT* * (that is, without an explicit column list), it would now be selecting the new *HomePhone* column as well, without any modification on your part. Understanding this, it's up to you to determine on a case-by-case basis whether to use *SELECT* * or *SELECT* with an explicit column list against your TVPs (although *SELECT* * is generally regarded as poor practice in production code). For *INSERT* statements, as we've explained, you should always use an explicit column list to code defensively against extensions to the TVP schema.

Creating Dictionary-Style TVPs

You can use TVPs to implement a generic dictionary-like structure to use as another flexible parameter-passing mechanism. This technique is roughly analogous to populating a *Dictionary* object in .NET that uses a string for the key and an object (which can hold any data type) for the value and then passing the dictionary object to another method. Achieving this with T-SQL in the past would typically require composing a string containing all of the data, with one delimiter separating each pair and another delimiter separating the key and value within each pair. The stored procedure would accept this string and then decompose it by parsing the delimiters to extract the values and casting them to their appropriate types. Using the intrinsic T-SQL string manipulation functions to implement this is both tedious and awkward. With SQL Server 2005, the situation could be improved marginally by leveraging the *xml* data type and composing an "array" in XML to be passed on to a stored procedure, which could then decompose the XML using XQuery. Here too, TVPs can provide a much easier solution natively.

First create a simple user-defined table type named *KeyValuePairUdt*, as shown in Listing 2-46.

LISTING 2-46 Creating a table type to be used for storing and passing key-value pairs

```
CREATE TYPE KeyValuePairUdt AS TABLE
  (K nvarchar(50),
   V sql_variant)
```

This table type defines the two columns *K* and *V*, which can hold a string key and a value of any data type. (The *sql_variant* data type is a "one size fits all" type that can hold almost any SQL Server data type.) Then declare a TVP, populate it with several key-value pairs, and pass it on to your stored procedure, as shown here:

```
DECLARE @Username AS nvarchar(50)
DECLARE @DOB AS date
DECLARE @IsActive AS bit
SET @Username = 'Admin'
SET @DOB = '1/2/2006'
SET @IsActive = 1

DECLARE @ParamsPackage AS KeyValuePairUdt

INSERT INTO @ParamsPackage(K, V) VALUES('Username', @Username)
INSERT INTO @ParamsPackage(K, V) VALUES('DOB', @DOB)
INSERT INTO @ParamsPackage(K, V) VALUES('IsActive', @IsActive)

EXEC uspProcessEntry 392, @ParamsPackage
```

Here we have three values assigned into variables for username, date of birth, and an active flag, of types *nvarchar(50)*, *date*, and *bit*. We then declare a TVP named *@ParamsPackage* typed as our new *KeyValuePairUdt* table type, into which we insert each of the three differently typed values with the corresponding string keys *Username*, *DOB*, and *IsActive*. Because the key column (*K*) in *KeyValuePairUdt* is *nvarchar*, the keys must be strings. However, by declaring the value column (*V*) as *sql_variant*, we are able to store a mix of data types as values in each row of our *@ParamsPackage* TVP.

We then call the *uspProcessEntry* stored procedure, as shown in Listing 2-47, passing two parameters: a regular integer for *EntryId* and the TVP holding our dictionary of key-value pairs. The stored procedure picks up the first parameter as a normal integer value. To extract elements from the dictionary passed in by the second parameter, the stored procedure selects them one at a time from the TVP by the string keys it expects the caller to have set (*Username*, *DOB*, and *IsActive*). Again, because of the *sql_variant* data type, the stored procedure is able to extract the values in their various different native data types.

LISTING 2-47 Creating a stored procedure that accepts a dictionary of values using a TVP

```
CREATE PROCEDURE uspProcessEntry(
 @EntryId AS int,
 @KeyValuePairTvp AS KeyValuePairUdt READONLY)
AS
 BEGIN
   SET NOCOUNT ON
   DECLARE @Username AS nvarchar(max)
   DECLARE @DOB AS date
   DECLARE @IsActive AS bit

   SELECT @Username = CONVERT(nvarchar, V)
    FROM @KeyValuePairTvp WHERE K = 'Username'

   SELECT @DOB = CONVERT(date, V)
    FROM @KeyValuePairTvp WHERE K = 'DOB'

   SELECT @IsActive = CONVERT(bit, V)
    FROM @KeyValuePairTvp WHERE K = 'IsActive'

   PRINT 'EntryId: ' + CAST(@EntryId AS nvarchar)
   PRINT 'Username: ' + @Username
   PRINT 'DOB: ' + CAST(@DOB AS nvarchar)
   PRINT 'IsActive: ' + CAST(@IsActive as nvarchar)

 END
```

Passing TVPs Using ADO.NET

Arguably the most compelling facet of TVPs is the ability to marshal multiple rows of data from a client application to SQL Server 2008 without requiring multiple roundtrips or implementing special logic on the server for processing the data. We'll conclude our discussion of TVPs with the new *SqlDbType.Structured* enumeration in ADO.NET, which makes doing this both possible and easy.

Simply prepare a *SqlCommand* object as you did in the past, setting its *CommandType* property to *CommandType.StoredProcedure* and populating its *Parameters* collection with *SqlParameter* objects. All you do to mark a *SqlParameter* as a TVP is to set its *SqlDbType* property to *SqlDbType.Structured*. You will then be able to specify any *DataTable*, *DbDataReader*, or *IList<SqlDataRecord>* object as the parameter value to be passed to the stored procedure in a single call to the server.

In Listing 2-48, a new customer order is stored in separate *Order* and *OrderDetail DataTable* objects within a *DataSet*. The two tables are passed to the SQL Server stored procedure we saw earlier, which accepts them as TVPs for insertion into the *Order* and *OrderDetail* database tables.

LISTING 2-48 Passing TVPs to a SQL Server stored procedure from ADO.NET

```
// Assumes conn is an open SqlConnection object and ds is
// a DataSet with an Order and OrderDetails table
using(conn)
{
    // Create the command object to call the stored procedure
    SqlCommand cmd = new SqlCommand("uspInsertNewOrder", conn);
    cmd.CommandType = CommandType.StoredProcedure;

    // Create the parameter for passing the Order TVP
    SqlParameter headerParam = cmd.Parameters.AddWithValue
      ("@OrderTvp", ds.Tables["Order"]);

    // Create the parameter for passing the OrderDetails TVP
    SqlParameter detailsParam = cmd.Parameters.AddWithValue
      ("@OrderDetailsTvp", ds.Tables["OrderDetail"]);

    // Set the SqlDbType of the parameters to Structured
    headerParam.SqlDbType = SqlDbType.Structured;
    detailsParam.SqlDbType = SqlDbType.Structured;

    // Execute the stored procedure
    cmd.ExecuteNonQuery();
}
```

This code calls a SQL Server 2008 stored procedure and passes to it an order header and the complete set of order details with a single roundtrip in a single implicit transaction. Remarkably, it's just as simple as that.

You can also send a set of rows directly to a parameterized SQL statement without creating a stored procedure. Because the SQL statement is dynamically constructed on the client, there is no stored procedure signature that specifies the name of the user-defined table type for the TVP. Therefore, you need to tell ADO.NET what the type is by setting the *TypeName* property to the name of the table type defined on the server. For example, the code in Listing 2-49 passes a *DataTable* to a parameterized SQL statement.

LISTING 2-49 Passing TVPs to a parameterized SQL statement from ADO.NET

```
// Define the INSERT INTO...SELECT statement to insert into Categories
const string TSqlStatement =
  "INSERT INTO Categories (CategoryID, CategoryName)" +
  " SELECT nc.CategoryID, nc.CategoryName" +
  " FROM @NewCategoriesTvp AS nc";

// Assumes conn is an open SqlConnection object and ds is
// a DataSet with a Category table
using(conn)
{
    // Set up the command object for the statement
    SqlCommand cmd = new SqlCommand(TSqlStatement, conn);
```

```
        // Add a TVP specifying the DataTable as the parameter value
        SqlParameter catParam = cmd.Parameters.AddWithValue
          ("@NewCategoriesTvp", ds.Tables["Category"]);

        catParam.SqlDbType = SqlDbType.Structured;
        catParam.TypeName = "dbo.CategoriesUdt";

        // Execute the command
        cmd.ExecuteNonQuery();
    }
```

Setting the *TypeName* property to *dbo.CategoriesUdt* in this code means that you have a user-defined table type by that name on the server, created using the *CREATE TYPE...AS TABLE* statement that defines the *CategoryID* and *CategoryName* columns.

You can also use any object derived from *DbDataReader* to stream rows of data to a TVP. In the example shown in Listing 2-50, we first call an Oracle stored procedure to select from an Oracle database into a connected *OracleDataReader*. The reader object gets passed as a single table-valued input parameter to a SQL Server 2008 stored procedure, which can then use the Oracle data in the reader as the source for adding new rows into the *Category* table in the SQL Server database.

LISTING 2-50 Passing a connected *OracleDataReader* source as a TVP to SQL Server

```
    // Set up command object to select from Oracle
    OracleCommand selCmd = new OracleCommand
      ("SELECT CategoryID, CategoryName FROM Categories;", oracleConn);

    // Execute the command and return the results in a connected
    // reader that will automatically close the connection when done
    OracleDataReader rdr = selCmd.ExecuteReader
      (CommandBehavior.CloseConnection);

    // Set up command object to insert into SQL Server
    SqlCommand insCmd = new SqlCommand
      ("uspInsertCategories", connection);

    insCmd.CommandType = CommandType.StoredProcedure;

    // Add a TVP specifying the reader as the parameter value
    SqlParameter catParam = cmd.Parameters.AddWithValue
      ("@NewCategoriesTvp", rdr);

    catParam.SqlDbType = SqlDbType.Structured;

    // Execute the stored procedure
    insertCommand.ExecuteNonQuery();
```

TVP Limitations

There are a number of limitations to TVPs that you should be aware of. First and foremost, TVPs are read-only after they are initially populated and passed; they cannot be used to return data. The *READONLY* keyword must be applied to TVPs in the signatures of your stored procedures, or they will not compile. Similarly, the *OUTPUT* keyword cannot be used. You cannot update the column values in the rows of a TVP, and you cannot insert or delete rows. If you must modify the data in a TVP, one workaround is to insert the data from the TVP into a temporary table or into a table variable to which you can then apply changes.

There is no *ALTER TABLE...AS TYPE* statement that supports changing the schema of a TVP table type. Instead, you must first drop all stored procedures that reference the type before dropping the type, re-creating it with a new schema, and then re-creating the stored procedures. Indexing is limited as well, with support only for *PRIMARY KEY* and *UNIQUE* constraints. Also, statistics on TVPs are not maintained by SQL Server.

New Date and Time Data Types

The *date*, *time*, *datetime2*, and *datetimeoffset* types are four new data types in SQL Server 2008 for storing dates and times, which you should now begin using for new database development in lieu of the traditional *datetime* and *smalldatetime* data types. The new types are now much better aligned with the .NET Framework, Microsoft Windows, and the SQL standard—unlike *datetime* and *smalldatetime*—and have important advantages over those types, including improvements in range, precision, and storage.

In addition, SQL Server 2008 delivers full Open Database Connectivity (ODBC), OLE-DB, and ADO.NET client provider support for all four data types. They are compatible for use across all other SQL Server components, including client tools, Integration Services, Replication, Reporting Services, and Analysis Services.

Separation of Dates and Times

We'll begin by looking at the new *date* and *time* types. Database developers have long been clamoring for the ability to store dates and times as separate types, and SQL Server 2008 now finally delivers it to us with these two new types. If you need to store only a date value (for example, a date of birth), use the new *date* type. Similarly, use the new *time* type for storing just a time value (for example, a daily medication time), as shown here:

```
DECLARE @DOB date
DECLARE @MedsAt time
```

The *datetime* and *smalldatetime* types, which were the only previously available options, each include both a date and a time portion. In cases where only the date or only the time is needed, the extraneous portion consumes storage needlessly, which results in wasted space in the database. In addition to saving storage, using *date* rather than *datetime* yields better performance for date-only manipulations and calculations, since there is no time portion to be handled or considered.

> **Note** Separate *date* and *time* data types are planned for a future version of the .NET Framework. Until then, the .NET data types that map to the newly separated SQL Server 2008 *date* and *time* types are *System.DateTime* and *System.TimeSpan*.

More Portable Dates and Times

To continue storing both a date and a time as a single value, use the new *datetime2* data type. This new type supports the same range of values as the *DateTime* data type in the .NET Framework, so it can store dates from 1/1/0001 (*DateTime.MinValue* in .NET) to 12/31/9999 (*DateTime.MaxValue* in .NET) in the Gregorian calendar. Contrast this with the allowable date values for the regular *datetime* type, which range only from 1/1/1753 to 12/31/9999. This means that dates in .NET from 1/1/0001 through 12/31/1752 can't be stored at all in SQL Server's *datetime* type, a problem solved by using either the *date*, *datetime2*, or *datetimeoffset* type in SQL Server 2008. Since the supported range of dates is now the same in both .NET and SQL Server, any date can be safely passed between these client and server platforms with no special considerations. You are strongly encouraged to discontinue using the older *datetime* and *smalldatetime* data types and to use only *date* and *datetime2* types for new development (or the new *datetimeoffset* type for time zone awareness, which is discussed next).

> **Note** The SQL standard calls the *datetime2* data type a *timestamp*. Unfortunately, Microsoft has already used the name *timestamp* for a special data type that generates unique binary values often used for row versioning but does not, in fact, represent either a date or a time. For this reason, SQL Server 2008 again deviates from the SQL standard by naming this new type *datetime2* and simultaneously introduces a new synonym for the poorly chosen *timestamp* type, now more aptly named *rowversion*. This discourages continued use of the name *timestamp* as originally defined by Microsoft.
>
> You're not alone if you feel that *datetime2* was yet another poor naming choice for this new type designed as a replacement for *datetime*. Being unable to use the name *timestamp*, Microsoft clearly had a difficult time coming up with a new name and finally just settled on *datetime2*. Don't be surprised to see a new synonym for this type appear in the future, when someone in Redmond finally has better luck at choosing good names!

There has also been a need for greater precision of fractional seconds in time values. The *datetime* type is accurate only within roughly 3.33 milliseconds, whereas time values in Windows and .NET have a significantly greater, 100-nanosecond (10-millionth of a second), accuracy. (The *smalldatetime* type doesn't even support seconds and is accurate only to the minute.) Storing times in the database therefore results in a loss of precision.

Like the expanded range of supported dates, the new *time*, *datetime2*, and *datetimeoffset* types are now more aligned with .NET and other platforms by also providing the same 100-nanosecond accuracy. As a result, we no longer incur any data loss of fractional second accuracy between platforms when recording time values to the database. Of course, there are storage implications that come with greater time precision, and we'll discuss those momentarily.

Time Zone Awareness

The fourth and last new data type in this category introduced in SQL Server 2008 is *datetimeoffset*. This type defines a date and time with the same range and precision that *datetime2* provides but also includes an offset value with a range of –14:00 to +14:00 that identifies the time zone. In the past, the only practical approach for globalization of dates and times in the database has been to store them in Coordinated Universal Time (UTC) format. Doing this requires back-and-forth conversion between UTC and local time that must be handled at the application level, and that means writing code.

Using the new *datetimeoffset* type, you can now store values that represent the local date and time in different regions of the world and include the appropriate time zone offset for the region in each value. Because the time zone offset embedded in the date and time value is specific to a particular locale, SQL Server is able to perform date and time comparisons between different locales without any conversion efforts required on your part. While *datetimeoffset* values appear to go in and come out as dates and times local to a particular region, they are internally converted, stored, and treated in UTC format for comparisons, sorting, and indexing.

Calculations and comparisons are therefore performed correctly and consistently across all dates and times in the database regardless of the different time zones in various regions. By simply appending the time zone offset to *datetimeoffset* values, SQL Server handles the conversions to and from UTC for you automatically in the background. Even better, you can obtain a *datetimeoffset* value either as UTC or local time. For those of us building databases that need to store various local times (or even just dates) in different regions of the world, this is welcomed as an extremely convenient new feature in SQL Server 2008. The database now handles all the details, so the application developer doesn't have to. Time zone functionality is now simply available for free right at the database level.

For example, the database knows that 9:15 AM in New York is in fact later than 10:30 AM in Los Angeles if you store the values in a *datetimeoffset* data type with appropriate time zone offsets. Because the New York time specifies a time zone offset of –5:00 and the Los Angeles time has an offset of –8:00, SQL Server is aware of the three-hour difference between the

two time zones and accounts for that difference in all date/time manipulations and calculations. This behavior is demonstrated by the code in Listing 2-51.

LISTING 2-51 Time zone calculations using *datetimeoffset*

```
DECLARE @Time1 datetimeoffset
DECLARE @Time2 datetimeoffset
DECLARE @MinutesDiff int

SET @Time1 = '2007-11-10 09:15:00-05:00'  -- NY time is UTC -05:00
SET @Time2 = '2007-11-10 10:30:00-08:00'  -- LA time is UTC -08:00

SET @MinutesDiff = DATEDIFF(minute, @Time1, @Time2)

SELECT @MinutesDiff
```

The output result from this code is:

```
-----------
255

(1 row(s) affected)
```

SQL Server was clearly able to account for the three-hour difference in time zones. Because
10:30 AM in Los Angeles is actually 1:30 PM in New York, a difference of 255 minutes (4 hours
and 15 minutes) between that time and 9:15 AM New York time was calculated correctly.

> **Note** Time zone *names* are not supported, nor is there support for daylight savings time.
> Unfortunately, these features did not make it into the final release of the product, but they are
> on the list for the next version of SQL Server. Time zones can be expressed only by hour/minute
> offsets, and you must continue to handle daylight savings time considerations on your own.

The .NET Framework also now provides the same functionality in a new type by the same
name, *System.DateTimeOffset*. This means that .NET client applications and SQL Server can
seamlessly pass time zone–aware values back and forth to each other.

> **Note** SQL Server 2008 also provides time zone support for the *xsd:dateTime* type. We cover this
> Extensible Schema Definition (XSD) enhancement in Chapter 6.

Date and Time Accuracy, Storage, and Format

Date values stored in *date*, *datetime2*, and *datetimeoffset* types are compacted into a fixed
storage space of 3 bytes. They use an optimized format that is 1 byte less than the 4 bytes

consumed by the date portion of the older *datetime* type (supporting a greater range in a smaller space).

Time values stored in *time*, *datetime2*, and *datetimeoffset* types, by default, consume five bytes of storage to support the same 100-nanosecond accuracy as Windows and .NET. However, the folks at Microsoft did not cast aside the storage concerns of developers and database administrators who don't require the highest degree of fractional-second precision. You can specify a lower degree of precision in order to benefit from further compacted storage by providing an optional scale parameter when declaring *time*, *datetime2*, and *datetimeoffset* variables. The scale can range from 0 to 7, with 0 offering no fractional-second precision at all being contained in the smallest space (3 bytes) and 7 (the default) offering the greatest fractional-second precision (100 nanoseconds) in the largest space (5 bytes). The scale essentially dictates the number of digits supported after the decimal point of the seconds value, where a scale value of 7 supports a fractional precision of 100 nanoseconds (each 100 nanoseconds being 0.0000001 second).

Table 2-1 shows the storage requirement and precision of *time*, *datetime2*, and *datetimeoffset* values for the different scale values from 0 through 7. The value in the precision column refers to the number of characters contained in an International Organization for Standardization (ISO)–formatted string representation of the three types for each possible scale value.

TABLE 2-1 Storage Requirements and Precision of the New Date and Time Data Types

	time		*datetime2*		*datetimeoffset*	
Scale Value	Bytes	Precision	Bytes	Precision	Bytes	Precision
0	3	8	6	19	8	26
1	3	10	6	21	8	28
2	3	11	6	22	8	29
3	4	12	7	23	9	30
4	4	13	7	24	9	31
5	5	14	8	25	10	32
6	5	15	8	26	10	33
7	5	16	8	27	10	34

The default scale is 7, which offers the greatest precision (to 100 nanoseconds) in the largest space. This means that declaring a variable as *time*, *datetime2*, or *datetimeoffset* is the same as declaring it as *time(7)*, *datetime2(7)*, or *datetimeoffset(7)*, making the following two statements equivalent:

```
DECLARE @StartDateTime datetime2
DECLARE @StartDateTime datetime2(7)
```

If you don't require any fractional precision at all, use a scale of 0, as in this example:

```
DECLARE @FeedingTime time(0)
```

As shown in the preceding table, only 3 bytes are required to store a time in *@FeedingTime*, which is accurate only to the second.

Two time values with differing scales are perfectly compatible with each other for comparison. SQL Server automatically converts the value with the lower scale to match the value with the greater scale and compares the two safely.

Almost all industry-standard string literal formats are supported for conveniently representing dates and times. For example, the date May 15, 2008, can be expressed in any of the formats shown in Table 2-2.

TABLE 2-2 Common Valid Date and Time String Literal Formats

Format	Example
Numeric	5/15/2008, 15-05-2008, 05.15.2008
Alphabetical	May 15, 2008
ISO8601	2008-05-15, 200805153
ODBC	{d'2008-05-15'}
W3C XML	2008-05-15Z

You have similar flexibility for representing times. For example, the same time value can be expressed as 23:30, 23:30:00, 23:30:00.0000, or 11:30:00 PM. Time zone offsets are expressed merely by appending a plus or minus sign followed by the UTC hours and minutes for the zone—for example, +02:00 for Jerusalem.

> **Note** There are even more possible formatting variations than those we've indicated here. The purpose of Table 2-2 is to convey how accommodating SQL Server is with respect to variations in date and time syntax. Refer to SQL Server Books Online for a complete specification of supported date and time literal formats.

You can use *CAST* or *CONVERT* to extract just the date or time portion of a *datetime2* column for searching. When you perform such a conversion on a *datetime2* column that is indexed, SQL Server does not need to resort to a sequential table scan and is able to perform the much faster index seek to locate the specific date or time. For example, the following code defines a table with a *datetime2* type that has a clustered index. Selecting by date or time only can be achieved using *CONVERT*, while still using the clustered index for efficient searching, as shown in Listing 2-52.

LISTING 2-52 Using *CONVERT* to extract the date and time portion from a *datetime2* column

```
CREATE TABLE DateList(MyDate datetime2)
CREATE CLUSTERED INDEX idx1 ON DateList (MyDate);

-- Insert some rows into DateList...

SELECT MyDate FROM DateList WHERE CONVERT(date, MyDate) = '2005-04-07';
SELECT MyDate FROM DateList WHERE CONVERT(time(0), MyDate) = '09:00:00';
```

New and Changed Functions

All of the traditional date-related and time-related functions, including *DATEADD*, *DATEDIFF*, *DATEPART*, and *DATENAME* now of course fully support the new date and time data types introduced in SQL Server 2008, and several new functions have been added as well. We conclude our discussion of the new date and time data types by exploring the T-SQL extensions added to support them.

The new *SYSDATETIME* and *SYSUTCDATETIME* functions return the date and time on the server as *datetime2* types (with full seven-scale precision accuracy within 100 nanoseconds), just as the *GETDATE* and *GETUTCDATE* functions continue to return the current date and time as *datetime* types. Another new function, *SYSDATETIMEOFFSET*, returns the date and time on the server as a *datetimeoffset* type, with a time zone offset reflecting the regional settings established on the server, which includes awareness of local daylight savings time. The code in Listing 2-53 shows the contrast between the various similar server date and time functions.

LISTING 2-53 Comparing server date and time functions

```
SET NOCOUNT ON
SELECT GETDATE() AS 'GETDATE() datetime'
SELECT GETUTCDATE() AS 'GETUTCDATE() datetime'
SELECT SYSDATETIME() AS 'SYSDATETIME() datetime2'
SELECT SYSUTCDATETIME() AS 'SYSUTCDATETIME() datetime2'
SELECT SYSDATETIMEOFFSET() AS 'SYSDATETIMEOFFSET() datetimeoffset'
```

Running this code just after 8:20 PM on November 10, 2007, in New York results in the following output:

```
GETDATE() datetime
----------------------
2007-11-10 20:21:19.380

GETUTCDATE() datetime
----------------------
2007-11-11 01:21:19.380
```

```
SYSDATETIME() datetime2
---------------------------
2007-11-10 20:21:19.3807984

SYSUTCDATETIME() datetime2
---------------------------
2007-11-11 01:21:19.3807984

SYSDATETIMEOFFSET() datetimeoffset
----------------------------------
2007-11-10 20:21:19.3807984 -05:00
```

There are also new *TODATETIMEOFFSET* and *SWITCHOFFSET* functions that allow you to perform time zone offset manipulations. *TODATETIMEOFFSET* will convert any date or time type (that has no time zone offset) to a *datetimeoffset* type by applying whatever time zone offset you provide. *SWITCHOFFSET* makes it easy to find out what the same time is in two different time zones. You provide the *datetimeoffset* for a source location and a time zone offset for a target location, and *SWITCHOFFSET* returns a *datetimeoffset* representing the equivalent date and time in the target location, as shown in Listing 2-54.

LISTING 2-54 Performing time zone offset manipulations using *TODATETIMEOFFSET* and *SWITCHOFFSET*

```
DECLARE @TheTime datetime2
DECLARE @TheTimeInNY datetimeoffset
DECLARE @TheTimeInLA datetimeoffset

-- Hold a time that doesn't specify a time zone
SET @TheTime = '2007-11-10 7:35PM'

-- Convert it to one that specifies time zone for New York
SET @TheTimeInNY = TODATETIMEOFFSET(@TheTime, '-05:00')

-- Calculate the equivalent time in Los Angeles
SET @TheTimeInLA = SWITCHOFFSET(@TheTimeInNY , '-08:00')

SELECT @TheTime AS 'Any Time'
SELECT @TheTimeInNY AS 'NY Time'
SELECT @TheTimeInLA AS 'LA Time'
```

Here is the output result:

```
Any Time
---------------------------
2007-11-10 19:35:00.0000000

NY Time
----------------------------------
2007-11-10 19:35:00.0000000 -05:00

LA Time
----------------------------------
2007-11-10 16:35:00.0000000 -08:00
```

You can use *TODATETIMEOFFSET* with *INSERT INTO...SELECT* to bulk-insert date and time values with no time zone information from a source table into a target table and to apply a time zone offset to produce *datetimeoffset* values in the target table. For example, the following code copies all the row values from the *dt2* column in table *test1* (of type *datetime2*, which has no time zone information) into the *dto* column in *test2* (of type *datetimeoffset*) and applies a time zone offset of –05:00 to each copied value:

```
INSERT INTO test2(dto)
 SELECT TODATETIMEOFFSET(dt2, '-05:00') FROM test1
```

The next example retrieves all the *datetimeoffset* values from the *dto* column in the *test2* table, which can include values across a variety of different time zones. Using a *SWITCHOFFSET* function that specifies an offset of –05:00, the values are automatically converted to New York time from whatever time zone is stored in the *test2* table:

```
SELECT SWITCHOFFSET(dto, '-05:00') FROM test2
```

Last, both the existing *DATEPART* and *DATENAME* functions have been extended to add support for microseconds (*mcs*), nanoseconds (*ns*), and time zone offsets (*tz*) in the new types, as shown in Listing 2-55.

LISTING 2-55 Using the new date portions in SQL Server 2008 with *DATEPART* and *DATENAME*

```
SET NOCOUNT ON
DECLARE @TimeInNY datetimeoffset
SET @TimeInNY = SYSDATETIMEOFFSET()

-- Show the current time in NY
SELECT @TimeInNY AS 'Time in NY'

-- DATEPART with tz gets the time zone value
SELECT DATEPART(tz, @TimeInNY) AS 'NY Time Zone Value'

-- DATENAME with tz gets the time zone string
SELECT DATENAME(tz, @TimeInNY) AS 'NY Time Zone String'

-- Both DATEPART and DATENAME with mcs gets the microseconds
SELECT DATEPART(mcs, @TimeInNY) AS 'NY Time Microseconds'

-- Both DATEPART and DATENAME with ns gets the nanoseconds
SELECT DATEPART(ns, @TimeInNY) AS 'NY Time Nanoseconds'
```

Running this code returns the following output:

```
Time in NY
---------------------------------
2007-11-10 20:50:55.7851424 -05:00
```

```
NY Time Zone Value
------------------
-300

NY Time Zone String
------------------------------
-05:00

NY Time Microseconds
--------------------
785142

NY Time Nanoseconds
-------------------
785142400
```

The *MERGE* Statement

The new *MERGE* statement in SQL Server 2008 does just what its name says. It combines the normal insert, update, and delete operations involved in a typical merge scenario, along with the select operation that provides the source and target data for the merge. That's right—it combines four statements into one. In fact, you can combine *five* statements into one using the *OUTPUT* clause, and even more than that with INSERT OVER DML (a new T-SQL feature), as you'll see later in this chapter.

In earlier versions of SQL Server, separate multiple statements were required to achieve what can now be accomplished with a single *MERGE* statement. This new statement has a flexible syntax that allows us to exercise fine control over source and target matching, as well as the various set-based DML actions carried out on the target. The result is simpler code that's easier to write and maintain (and also runs faster) than the equivalent code using separate statements to achieve the same result.

More Info We cover the most pertinent *MERGE* statement keywords in our discussions. You can and should refer to Books Online for the complete *MERGE* syntax.

More Info The *MERGE* statement is particularly suited to data warehousing scenarios. We cover the concepts and techniques behind data warehousing in Chapter 14.

Let's look at our first example, which uses *MERGE* to efficiently manage our stocks and trades. We begin by creating the two tables to hold stocks that we own and daily trades that we make, as shown in Listing 2-56.

LISTING 2-56 Creating the *Stock* and *Trade* tables

```
CREATE TABLE Stock(Symbol varchar(10) PRIMARY KEY, Qty int CHECK (Qty > 0))
CREATE TABLE Trade(Symbol varchar(10) PRIMARY KEY, Delta int CHECK (Delta <> 0))
```

We start off with 10 shares of Adventure Works stock and 5 shares of Blue Yonder Airlines stock. These are stored in our *Stock* table:

```
INSERT INTO Stock VALUES ('ADVW', 10)
INSERT INTO Stock VALUES ('BYA', 5)
```

During the day, we conduct three trades. We buy 5 new shares for Adventure Works, sell 5 shares of Blue Yonder Airlines, and buy 3 shares for our new investment in Northwind Traders. These are stored in our *Trade* table, as follows:

```
INSERT INTO Trade VALUES('ADVW', 5)
INSERT INTO Trade VALUES('BYA', -5)
INSERT INTO Trade VALUES('NWT', 3)
```

Here are the contents of the two tables:

```
SELECT * FROM Stock
GO

Symbol     Qty
---------- -----------
ADVW       10
BYA        5

(2 row(s) affected)


SELECT * FROM Trade
GO

Symbol     Delta
---------- -----------
ADVW       5
BYA        -5
NWT        3

(3 row(s) affected)
```

At the closing of the day, we want to update the quantities in our *Stock* table to reflect the trades of the day we recorded in the *Trade* table. Our Adventure Works stock quantity has risen to 15, we no longer own any Blue Yonder Airlines (having sold the only 5 shares we owned), and we now own 3 new shares of Northwind Traders stock. That's going to involve joining the *Stock* and *Trade* tables to detect changes in stock quantities resulting from our trades, as well as insert, update, and delete operations to apply those changes back to the

Stock table. For the first time in SQL Server, all this logic and manipulation can now be performed with a single statement using *MERGE*, as shown in Listing 2-57.

LISTING 2-57 Applying trades to stocks using *MERGE*

```
MERGE Stock
 USING Trade
 ON Stock.Symbol = Trade.Symbol
 WHEN MATCHED AND (Stock.Qty + Trade.Delta = 0) THEN
   -- delete stock if entirely sold
   DELETE
 WHEN MATCHED THEN
   -- update stock quantity (delete takes precedence over update)
   UPDATE SET Stock.Qty += Trade.Delta
 WHEN NOT MATCHED BY TARGET THEN
   -- add newly purchased stock
  INSERT VALUES (Trade.Symbol, Trade.Delta);
```

Let's dissect this statement. It begins of course with the *MERGE* keyword itself, followed by *USING* and *ON* keywords that respectively identify the *target* and *source* of the merge operation, and the *joining keys* used to relate the source and target to each other for the merge. Three *merge clauses* then follow with the *WHEN...THEN* syntax, and the statement is then finally terminated with a semicolon (;).

> **Important** The terminating semicolon (part of the SQL standard) is rarely necessary in SQL Server. However, the new *MERGE* statement in SQL Server 2008 absolutely requires it, and you will receive an error if you omit it.

Defining the Merge Source and Target

MERGE has an elegant implementation in SQL Server 2008. At its core, it operates on a join between the source and target of the merge no differently than the way any standard *JOIN* predicate in the *FROM* clause of any *SELECT* statement operates. As you'll see shortly when we examine SQL Server's query plan for *MERGE*, the source, the target, and the join between them are handled internally in exactly the same manner as for a regular *SELECT*. The parts of the *MERGE* syntax that express this select operation include the *MERGE* keyword itself along with *USING* and *ON*, which respectively specify the target, source, and join predicate, as shown here:

```
MERGE Stock
 USING Trade
 ON Stock.Symbol = Trade.Symbol
```

The target can be any table or updatable view and is specified immediately following the *MERGE* keyword. It is the recipient of the changes resulting from the merge, which can include combinations of new, changed, and deleted rows. This is the *Stock* table in our example, which receives changes merged into it from its source of daily trade information.

The source is the provider of the data, which is the *Trade* table in our example, and is specified with the *USING* keyword right after the target. Anything you can reference in the *FROM* clause of an ordinary *SELECT* statement is supported as the source for *MERGE*. This includes not only regular tables and views, but subqueries, text files accessed with *OPENROWSETBYTES*, remote tables, CTEs, table variables, and TVPs as well. If you can put it in the *FROM* clause of a *SELECT* statement, you can put it in the *USING* clause of a *MERGE* statement. (Later in this section, you'll see an example of using an embedded *SELECT* to perform a subquery that generates source data on the fly.)

The join predicate specified by the *ON* keyword that follows defines the column key or keys relating the source and target to each other, no differently than a standard table join. Again, anything you can put in a *SELECT* join can be specified for a *MERGE* join with *ON*—nothing more, nothing less. The join defines which records are considered matching or nonmatching between the source and target. This is the *Symbol* column relating stocks to trades in our current example. It tells SQL Server what stocks exist and don't exist in both tables so that we can insert, update, and delete data in the target table accordingly. The *type* of join (inner, left outer, right outer, or full outer) is determined by which of the various merge clauses are then applied next in the *MERGE* statement.

The *WHEN MATCHED* Clause

Our example uses three merge clauses: two *WHEN MATCHED* clauses and one *WHEN NOT MATCHED BY TARGET* clause. Let's look at each of them closely.

The first *WHEN MATCHED* clause executes when a matching stock symbol is found in both the *Stock* and the *Trade* tables, as shown here:

```
WHEN MATCHED AND (Stock.Qty + Trade.Delta = 0) THEN
    -- delete stock if entirely sold
    DELETE
```

A match would normally mean updating the quantity value in the *Stock* table by the delta value (amount bought or sold) in the *Trade* table. However, in our scenario, we want to physically delete the row in the *Stock* table if its updated value results in *0*, since that means we don't really own that particular stock at all anymore (as is the case with Blue Yonder Airlines). We can code for that scenario by qualifying the *WHEN MATCHED* clause with an additional predicate that tests whether the stock quantity resulting from the trade yields *0*. You get tremendous flexibility by being able to provide your own criteria as predicates to your merge clauses in this way, because you can then apply custom business logic to the various matching conditions. In this particular case, we want to remove a row from the *Stock* table using the *DELETE* statement rather than changing its value to *0*.

The next merge clause is another *WHEN MATCHED* clause, but this second one has no predicate qualifying the match condition, as shown here:

```
WHEN MATCHED THEN
  -- update stock quantity (delete takes precedence over update)
  UPDATE SET Stock.Qty += Trade.Delta
```

This second clause handles all the other trades of preexisting stock that have not resulted in *0* and changes the stock quantity accordingly using the *UPDATE* statement (that is, the *Stock.Qty* values will go up or down depending on the positive or negative number in *Trade.Delta*). In our example, we want the Adventure Works stock quantity to go up to 15, reflecting the 5 shares purchased on top of the 10 we already owned.

> **Note** An error would occur if we tried to sell more than we owned. In fact, an error would also occur if we tried to sell *everything* that we owned without first catching that condition by deleting the stock in the earlier merge clause. That's because we instructed the database to enforce such rules and not to tolerate any zero or negative *Qty* values by defining a check constraint on the *Qty* column when we created the *Stock* table at the beginning of our example.

SQL Server 2008 has very particular rules governing the use of multiple merge clauses. You are permitted to have one or two *WHEN MATCHED* clauses—but no more. If there are two *WHEN MATCHED* clauses, the first one must be qualified with an *AND* condition. Furthermore, one clause must specify an *UPDATE*, and the other must specify a *DELETE*. As demonstrated in our current example, *MERGE* will choose one of the two *WHEN MATCHED* clauses to execute based on whether the *AND* condition evaluates to *true* for any given row.

The *WHEN NOT MATCHED BY TARGET* Clause

Our last merge clause is *WHEN NOT MATCHED BY TARGET*, as shown here:

```
WHEN NOT MATCHED BY TARGET THEN
  -- add newly owned stock
 INSERT VALUES (Trade.Symbol, Trade.Delta);
```

This clause handles rows found in the source but not in the target. In our example, this refers to stocks that are being traded for the first time, which is the new Northwind Trader stock that doesn't yet exist in the target *Stock* table. The clause has no predicate (although it could), and so there are no additional conditions for the clause. Here, we simply add the new data found in the *Trade* table to the *Stock* table using the *INSERT* statement.

> **Note** The *BY TARGET* keywords are optional for this clause. *WHEN NOT MATCHED* is equivalent to *WHEN NOT MATCHED BY TARGET*.

Only one *WHEN NOT MATCHED BY TARGET* clause is permitted in a single *MERGE* statement. It can be qualified with an *AND* condition, as we saw earlier with *WHEN MATCHED*. (There is no purpose for an *AND* condition on the *WHEN NOT MATCHED BY TARGET* clause in this example.)

After executing the *MERGE* statement, the *Stock* table is updated to reflect all the trades of the day merged into it, as shown here:

```
SELECT * FROM Stock
GO

Symbol     Qty
---------- -----------
ADVW       15
NWT        3

(2 row(s) affected)
```

Just as we wanted and expected, Blue Yonder Airlines is gone, Northwind Traders has been added, and Adventure Works has been updated. This is a rather impressive result for just one statement! It took less code to write and will take less effort to maintain than the equivalent operations written as separate statements would, and it also runs faster because it is compiled and executed as a single statement. No additional overhead is incurred for the simple reason that this statement operates on the same fundamental principles as your basic *SELECT* statement's *FROM* and *JOIN* clauses.

Using *MERGE* for Table Replication

Let's move on to another example that shows how *MERGE* can be used as a tool for achieving simple replication between tables. We first define two tables with identical schemas named *Original* and *Replica*. Then we create a stored procedure that has a *MERGE* statement that will replicate changes made in the *Original* table over to the *Replica* table, as shown in Listing 2-58.

LISTING 2-58 Creating two tables and a stored procedure that uses *MERGE* to synchronize them

```
CREATE TABLE Original(PK int primary key, FName varchar(10), Number int)
CREATE TABLE Replica(PK int primary key, FName varchar(10), Number int)
GO

CREATE PROCEDURE uspSyncReplica AS
 MERGE Replica AS R
  USING Original AS O ON O.PK = R.PK
  WHEN MATCHED AND (O.FName != R.FName OR O.Number != R.Number) THEN
    UPDATE SET R.FName = O.FName, R.Number = O.Number
  WHEN NOT MATCHED THEN
    INSERT VALUES(O.PK, O.FName, O.Number)
  WHEN NOT MATCHED BY SOURCE THEN
    DELETE;
```

The *MERGE* statement in this stored procedure handles the replication task by joining the two tables on their primary keys (*PK*) and providing three merge clauses. The first clause processes updates, as shown here:

```
WHEN MATCHED AND (O.FName != R.FName OR O.Number != R.Number) THEN
  UPDATE SET R.FName = O.FName, R.Number = O.Number
```

Here we use *WHEN MATCHED* to find all the records that exist in both the original and the replica, and then we update the matching rows on the replica side with the latest original data using the *UPDATE* statement. Performing such an update when no data has actually changed is wasteful, so we apply a predicate that qualifies the merge clause to apply only when a row change is detected in any of the nonkey values between the original and the replica.

The second merge clause handles insertions, as follows:

```
WHEN NOT MATCHED THEN
  INSERT VALUES(O.PK, O.FName, O.Number)
```

As mentioned earlier, *WHEN NOT MATCHED* is equivalent to *WHEN NOT MATCHED BY TARGET*, which returns all the original rows not found in the replica table. These records represent new rows added to the original table since the last merge, which are now added to the replica as well using the *INSERT* statement in this clause.

The *WHEN NOT MATCHED BY SOURCE* Clause

The third and last merge clause handles deletions, as shown here, followed by the required semicolon terminator:

```
WHEN NOT MATCHED BY SOURCE THEN
  DELETE;
```

The *WHEN NOT MATCHED BY SOURCE* clause serves as the exact reverse of *WHEN NOT MATCHED BY TARGET* and returns target (replica) rows not found in the source (original) table. This scenario would occur as the result of removing rows from the original table after they have been replicated. Rows removed from the original table need to be removed from the replica table as well, which is done by the simple *DELETE* statement in this clause.

WHEN NOT MATCHED BY SOURCE has the very same rules as *WHEN MATCHED* concerning multiple clauses. You are permitted up to two *WHEN NOT MATCHED BY SOURCE* clauses. If you have two, the first one must be qualified with an *AND* condition. Furthermore, one clause must specify an *UPDATE*, and the other must specify a *DELETE*. If two *WHEN NOT MATCHED BY SOURCE* clauses are specified, *MERGE* will choose one of them to execute for any given row based on whether the *AND* condition evaluates to *true*.

Let's get started with some data. Both tables are empty at this point (which does in fact mean that they are already in sync), so we'll first fill the original table with a few rows, as shown here:

```
INSERT Original VALUES(1, 'Sara', 10)
INSERT Original VALUES(2, 'Steven', 20)
```

Now let's call our *uspSyncReplica* stored procedure to bring the replica table up to date. The first time we call the stored procedure, only the *WHEN NOT MATCHED* clause will execute. It will execute twice, actually, once for each of the two rows to be added to the replica table from the original table. The rows affected count displayed after running the stored procedure conveys this, as shown here:

```
EXEC uspSyncReplica
GO
```

```
(2 row(s) affected)
```

Examining both tables now verifies that the replica is synchronized with the original, as shown here:

```
SELECT * FROM Original
SELECT * FROM Replica
GO
```

```
PK           FName       Number
-----------  ----------  -----------
1            Sara        10
2            Steven      20
```

```
(2 row(s) affected)
```

```
PK           FName       Number
-----------  ----------  -----------
1            Sara        10
2            Steven      20
```

```
(2 row(s) affected)
```

Now we perform some more changes to the original table. A mix of insert, update, and delete operations brings the two tables out of sync again:

```
INSERT INTO Original VALUES(3, 'Andrew', 100)
UPDATE Original SET FName = 'Stephen', Number += 10 WHERE PK = 2
DELETE FROM Original WHERE PK = 1
GO

SELECT * FROM Original
SELECT * FROM Replica
GO
```

```
PK            FName       Number
-----------   ---------   -----------
2             Stephen     30
3             Andrew      100

(2 row(s) affected)

PK            FName       Number
-----------   ---------   -----------
1             Sara        10
2             Steven      20

(2 row(s) affected)
```

Invoking the stored procedure once again brings the two tables back in sync by replicating changes from the original table to the replica, as follows:

```
EXEC uspSyncReplica
GO

(3 row(s) affected)
```

This time, we see that three rows were affected as the result of one insert (Andrew), one update (Stephen), and one delete (Sara). Examining both tables verifies that the replica is once again synchronized with the original, as shown here:

```
SELECT * FROM Original
SELECT * FROM Replica
GO

PK            FName       Number
-----------   ---------   -----------
2             Stephen     30
3             Andrew      100

(2 row(s) affected)

PK            FName       Number
-----------   ---------   -----------
2             Stephen     30
3             Andrew      100

(2 row(s) affected)
```

MERGE Output

The *MERGE* statement also supports the same *OUTPUT* clause introduced in SQL Server 2005 for the *INSERT*, *UPDATE*, and *DELETE* statements. This clause returns change information from each row affected by DML operations in the same *INSERTED* and *DELETED* pseudo-tables exposed by triggers. Being able to capture this information in the *OUTPUT* clause is a much better choice than capturing it in triggers, since triggers introduce nondeterministic behavior—that is, you cannot guarantee that multiple triggers on the same table will consistently fire in the same order every time, and that is often the cause of subtle bugs that are very difficult to track down. (Triggers should therefore generally be avoided if at all possible.)

In addition to *INSERTED* and *DELETED* pseudo-table columns, a new virtual column named *$action* has been introduced for *OUTPUT* when used with the *MERGE* statement. The *$action* column will return one of the three string values—'INSERT', 'UPDATE', or 'DELETE'—depending on the action taken for each row. Listing 2-59 shows a slightly modified version of our *uspSyncReplica* stored procedure that includes an *OUTPUT* clause on the *MERGE* statement. The *OUTPUT* clause selects the virtual *$action* column and all the columns of the *INSERTED* and *DELETED* pseudo-tables so that the *MERGE* statement can provide a detailed report of every DML operation it performs.

LISTING 2-59 Using the *OUTPUT* clause and *$action* virtual column with *MERGE*

```
CREATE PROCEDURE uspSyncReplica AS

MERGE Replica AS R
  USING Original AS O ON O.PK = R.PK
  WHEN MATCHED AND (O.FName != R.FName OR O.Number != R.Number) THEN
    UPDATE SET R.FName = O.FName, R.Number = O.Number
  WHEN NOT MATCHED THEN
    INSERT VALUES(O.PK, O.FName, O.Number)
  WHEN NOT MATCHED BY SOURCE THEN
    DELETE
  OUTPUT $action, INSERTED.*, DELETED.*;
```

Running this modified version of the *MERGE* statement for the last set of changes in our replication example produces the following output:

```
$action PK     FName   Number PK     FName   Number
------- -----  ------- ------ -----  ------- ------
DELETE  NULL   NULL    NULL   1      Sara    10
UPDATE  2      Stephen 30     2      Steven  20
INSERT  3      Andrew  100    NULL   NULL    NULL

(3 row(s) affected)
```

This output shows all the actions taken by the merge and all the before-and-after data involved. Of course, you can use *OUTPUT...INTO* just as you can with the *INSERT, UPDATE*, and *DELETE* statements to send this information to another table or table variable for history logging or additional processing. And SQL Server 2008 introduces an extension of this feature that gives us even more flexibility called INSERT OVER DML, which we'll learn about right after we conclude our treatment of *MERGE*.

Choosing a Join Method

SQL Server is very smart about examining *MERGE* statements with different combinations of merge clauses and automatically performs the appropriate type of join to return the source and target data needed on both sides. There are four types of joins, and SQL Server cleverly picks the right one for the job, based on the merge clauses that it finds in the *MERGE* statement, as shown in Table 2-3.

TABLE 2-3 Source-to-Target Table Join Types Chosen by SQL Server Based on Your Merge Clause(s)

Merge Clause	Join Type	Returns	Valid Actions
WHEN MATCHED	Inner	Matching data in both source and target	Update, delete
WHEN NOT MATCHED [BY TARGET]	Left outer	Source data not found in target	Insert
WHEN NOT MATCHED BY SOURCE	Right outer	Target data not found in source	Update, delete
WHEN NOT MATCHED [BY TARGET] combined with any other clause	Full outer	Source data not found in target, and other matching or nonmatching target data	Insert, update, delete

The *WHEN MATCHED* clause returns rows that are found in both tables (that is, rows in both tables with matching values in the joining key columns defined with *ON*). The query processor treats this as an inner join, because we are retrieving only rows that exist on both sides. Either an *UPDATE* or a *DELETE* operation on matching target rows is permitted in the *WHEN MATCHED* clause.

WHEN NOT MATCHED [BY TARGET] is treated as a left outer join, since it retrieves only source rows that do not exist in the target. Therefore, only an *INSERT* can be performed in the *WHEN NOT MATCHED [BY TARGET]* clause to "fill the hole" in the target with the missing source data.

The *WHEN NOT MATCHED BY SOURCE* clause is the complement to *WHEN NOT MATCHED [BY TARGET]* and results in a right outer join to retrieve only target rows that do not exist in the source. As with *WHEN MATCHED*, you can perform an *UPDATE* or a *DELETE* operation on those target rows missing from the source.

Last, combining *WHEN NOT MATCHED [BY TARGET]* with either or both of the other two clauses retrieves source data not found in the target as well as target data found or not found in the source. In this case, a full outer join is performed between the two tables. You can perform an *INSERT* in the *WHEN NOT MATCHED [BY TARGET]* clause to add source data missing from the target and an *UPDATE* or *DELETE* in the other clause(s) to modify or remove target data.

Warning Be very careful of *NULL* values in the key columns you join on. As with any regular join, they will never match, and you might therefore end up inserting rows into the target that you don't intend to.

Important The only valid statement in *WHEN MATCHED* or *WHEN NOT MATCHED BY SOURCE* is *UPDATE* or *DELETE*, and the only valid statement in *WHEN NOT MATCHED [BY TARGET]* is *INSERT*. No other T-SQL statements (including stored procedure calls) are allowed in any of these merge clauses. However, the *INSERT* and *UPDATE* statements in a merge clause are permitted to reference user-defined functions (UDFs).

MERGE DML Behavior

As you've just learned, the *MERGE* statement combines the four separate DML statements (*SELECT*, *INSERT*, *UPDATE*, and *DELETE*) involved in a merge operation. The actual internal implementation of *MERGE* is the very same as the distinct DML statements it encapsulates. This was a good call by Microsoft, since it means that developers can begin using *MERGE* right away to leverage its improved performance and reduced maintenance benefits, without concern for breaking any existing code.

All *AFTER* and *INSTEAD OF* triggers that have already been defined in existing tables or updateable views continue to fire when those tables or updatable views are designated as the target of a *MERGE* statement. For example, the *WHEN NOT MATCHED THEN...INSERT* clause fires any insert triggers defined for the target; similarly, the *WHEN MATCHED THEN...DELETE* clause fires delete triggers. There is no new concept of a "merge trigger," and this means that you simply have no concerns before starting to use *MERGE* in your T-SQL code. The end result is that triggers are fired just the same as they would be using separate statements instead of *MERGE*. Existing business logic, constraints, and rules all continue to function as they did before.

The same options and features you are accustomed to using with the separate DML statements are also available with *MERGE*. For example, you can use a CTE for the source of a merge by defining it using the *WITH* clause before the *MERGE* statement and then referencing it with the *USING* clause. The *TOP* clause is similarly supported, as are traditional query hints. And of course, both source and target tables can be aliased with *AS* just as tables in regular queries can.

We can see how SQL Server internally implements the *MERGE* statement we wrote for our stored procedure that handles table replication by examining the database engine's query execution plan, shown in Figure 2-2.

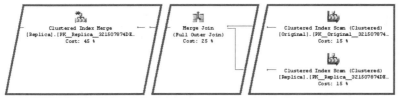

FIGURE 2-2 Query plan for a *MERGE* operation to synchronize a replica with an original (screen image has been cropped to fit the printed page)

If you are not already familiar with query plans, the first thing you should know is that you read them from right to left. (Books Online provides an explanation of graphical query execution plans in SQL Server Management Studio.) The work begins by scanning the source and target tables.

In Figure 2-3, we see the advantage of having created indexes on the columns joining the *Original* and *Replica* tables for the merge. Because the join predicate uses the primary keys of both tables, the query optimizer uses a clustered index scan for the best possible read performance. You should therefore always create an index (possibly clustered and ideally unique) on the joined columns used for merging two tables.

FIGURE 2-3 Clustered index scans performed on both source and target tables for *MERGE*

The plan also reveals that a full outer join is performed between the two tables, as shown in Figure 2-4.

FIGURE 2-4 Full outer join selected by the query plan for *MERGE*

As mentioned earlier, the type of join used depends on which *WHEN...THEN* merge clauses are (or aren't) specified in the *MERGE* statement. In this case, SQL Server performs a full outer join because our *MERGE* statement uses all three of the possible merge clauses. The filter operation that follows (see Figure 2-5) implements the predicate on our first merge clause that selects matching rows only if any of the nonkey columns have changed between the original and replica tables.

```
            ▒▒▒
      Clustered Index Merge        ←
[Replica].[PK__Replica__321507874DE...
           Cost: 45 %
```

FIGURE 2-5 Clustered index merge operation that processes updates, inserts, and deletes for *MERGE*

The clustered index merge is a new operation that basically consumes the stream delivered by the full outer join and decides on a row-by-row basis whether the row being passed to this operation should be processed as an update, an insert, or a delete, based on the syntax of the *MERGE* statement and the data in the source and target tables.

Doing the "Upsert"

The *MERGE* statement is certainly intended to be used for the types of set-based operations (processing of multiple rows at a time) that we've been performing thus far. However, it also comes in handy for the typical maintenance task of inserting or updating a single row, where an update is performed if the row already exists in the target and an insert is performed otherwise. This operation (commonly referred to as an "upsert," because it performs either an update or an insert) involves testing for the existence of a row to determine whether an update or an insert is needed.

We'll take a look at two stored procedure implementations of the upsert using *MERGE*. The first is a simple version that doesn't support output parameters, identity values, or concurrency checking. Once you understand how it works, we'll move on to the second version, which supports all three of those elements and is far more likely to be required in any real-world application.

As promised earlier, we will also demonstrate how to use a subquery to construct a source table on the fly for the merge operation. Both versions of our stored procedure create the source table dynamically using an embedded *SELECT* statement. The source table holds a single row built from the stored procedure input parameters to be inserted or updated in the target. Let's dive in.

First we'll create the *Customer* table, as shown in Listing 2-60.

LISTING 2-60 Creating the *Customer* table

```
CREATE TABLE Customer(
  CustomerId  int PRIMARY KEY,
  FirstName   varchar(30),
  LastName    varchar(30),
  Balance     decimal)
```

Next we'll create the stored procedure that we can call to insert a new customer or update an existing customer, as shown in Listing 2-61.

LISTING 2-61 Simple "upsert" stored procedure using *MERGE*

```
CREATE PROCEDURE uspUpsertCustomer(
  @CustomerId int,
  @FirstName varchar(30),
  @LastName varchar(30),
  @Balance decimal)
AS
BEGIN

  MERGE Customer AS tbl
   USING (SELECT
             @CustomerId AS CustomerId,
             @FirstName AS FirstName,
             @LastName AS LastName,
             @Balance AS Balance) AS row
    ON tbl.CustomerId = row.CustomerId
  WHEN NOT MATCHED THEN
    INSERT(CustomerId, FirstName, LastName, Balance)
     VALUES(row.CustomerId, row.FirstName, row.LastName, row.Balance)
  WHEN MATCHED THEN
    UPDATE SET
       tbl.FirstName = row.FirstName,
       tbl.LastName = row.LastName,
       tbl.Balance = row.Balance
  ;
END
```

This *MERGE* statement is very straightforward. First the *Customer* table is declared as the target for the merge and aliased as *tbl*. The source for the merge is then declared with the *USING* clause as a single row built from the incoming parameter values with an embedded *SELECT* statement and aliased as *row*. The table and the row are then joined for the merge on the *CustomerId* column with the *ON* clause.

Two merge clauses then follow: one to handle the insert and the other for the update. The *WHEN NOT MATCHED* clause runs if the *CustomerId* passed in for the row cannot be found in the *Customer* table. In this case, the new row is added with the values in the source that were populated by the other parameters passed in. The *WHEN MATCHED* clause runs if the *CustomerId* passed in for the row already exists in the *Customer* table, in which case, the existing row is updated with the values in the source table.

Let's now call this stored procedure to add two new customers with credit balances, as shown here:

```
-- Add Customer 1
EXEC uspUpsertCustomer 1, 'Mark', 'Boyer', 100

-- Add Customer 2
EXEC uspUpsertCustomer 2, 'Ted', 'Bremer', 120
```

```
SELECT * FROM Customer
GO

CustomerId FirstName LastName  Balance
---------- --------- --------- -------
1          Mark      Boyer     100
2          Ted       Bremer    120
```

As expected, the stored procedure inserted both customers as new rows because the customer ID values *1* and *2* did not previously exist, which triggered the *WHEN NOT MATCHED* clause of the *MERGE* statement.

The next time customer 1 visits our store, he makes a $10 purchase on credit, which raises his balance from $100 to $110. He also brings it to the cashier's attention that the person who originally entered his data misspelled his first name as Mark, when the correct spelling is actually Marc. The customer can be updated in the database using the exact same stored procedure call that was made for the original insert, as shown here:

```
-- Change Customer 1's first name and balance
EXEC uspUpsertCustomer 1, 'Marc', 'Boyer', 110

SELECT * FROM Customer
GO

CustomerId FirstName LastName  Balance
---------- --------- --------- -------
1          Marc      Boyer     110
2          Ted       Bremer    120
```

This time around, the stored procedure performed an update because customer ID 1 already exists, triggering the *WHEN MATCHED* clause of the MERGE statement.

Now let's get more realistic. We very often allow SQL Server to automatically generate new integer primary keys using *IDENTITY* values. In this scenario, the customer ID is determined by the database and not by the application. We would therefore need *@CustomerId* to be implemented as an input/output parameter so that *NULL* could be passed in for a new customer and the *IDENTITY* value assigned to the newly added customer row could be passed back out. In the case of an update, an existing customer ID would be passed in, and its value would not be changed (that is, the same value passed in for *@CustomerId* would be passed back out).

For auditing purposes, it is also common to use the server's date and time to store creation and modification times in each row. As with *@CustomerId*, we would want *@Created* and *@Modified* parameters added to our stored procedure that can return these server-assigned values. Unlike *@CustomerId*, however, these would be output-only parameters because the client can never provide values for them. Our auditing requirements don't demand fractional-second precision, so we will use a *datetime2(0)* data type for compact storage of the creation and modification times.

> **Note** Fractional-second precision and the *datetime2* data type are described in detail earlier in this chapter.

Last, we'll need to deal with row versioning if we want to enforce *optimistic concurrency checks* on updates. Such a strategy is often implemented using a *rowversion* column. (Remember, the *rowversion* type was previously called *timestamp*, which is now a deprecated term from earlier versions of SQL Server.) When you define a *rowversion* column on a table, SQL Server stores a unique 8-byte binary value that can be used to track row-changed conditions for optimistic concurrency checks. This requires clients to retrieve the current *rowversion* value when they first select a row for changes and to then provide the value back again when they attempt to update the row. The update can then be rejected if the *rowversion* passed back in for the update is different from the current *rowversion* value in the table, as that would be an indication that another user or process has modified the row since this client originally retrieved its data.

To support this functionality in our stored procedure, we will add *@Version* as an input/output *rowversion* parameter. To perform an update, the client will pass in the original *rowversion* value that was retrieved when the row was initially selected. The stored procedure will then use that value to enforce the concurrency check before updating the row in the table. If the update succeeds, the new *rowversion* value is passed back out to the client through the *@Version* parameter. For an insert, there is no concurrency check. In this case, the client would pass in *NULL* for *@Version* and receive back the *rowversion* value assigned to the newly added row.

Our enhanced version of the *uspUpsertCustomer* stored procedure supports all of these requirements. But first we need to revise the *Customer* table schema. We want to enable *IDENTITY* values for the *CustomerId* primary key, add two *datetime2* columns for auditing creation and modification times, and add a *rowversion* column for concurrency, as shown in Listing 2-62.

LISTING 2-62 Creating a new version of the *Customer* table to support enhanced upsert capabilities

```
CREATE TABLE Customer(
  CustomerId int IDENTITY(1, 1) PRIMARY KEY,
  FirstName varchar(30),
  LastName varchar(30),
  Balance decimal,
  Created datetime2(0),
  Modified datetime2(0),
  Version rowversion)

ALTER TABLE Customer ADD CONSTRAINT
 DF_Customer_Created DEFAULT (SYSDATETIME()) FOR Created

ALTER TABLE Customer ADD CONSTRAINT
 DF_Customer_Modified DEFAULT (SYSDATETIME()) FOR Modified
```

Notice that we've also established default values for *Created* and *Modified* as the current server date and time returned by the *SYSDATETIME* function. As you'll see, doing so will make it unnecessary to provide *Created* and *Modified* values for newly inserted customers—SQL Server will just automatically set them to the current date and time by default.

Now let's revise the *uspUpsertCustomer* stored procedure itself to support all of our new requirements, as shown in Listing 2-63.

LISTING 2-63 Advanced upsert stored procedure using *MERGE*

```
CREATE PROCEDURE uspUpsertCustomer(
  @CustomerId int OUTPUT,   -- Passed in as NULL for new customer
  @FirstName varchar(30),
  @LastName varchar(30),
  @Balance decimal,
  @Created datetime2(0) OUTPUT,
  @Modified datetime2(0) OUTPUT,
  @Version rowversion OUTPUT)
AS
  BEGIN

    -- Merge single-row source built from params into Customer table
    MERGE Customer AS tbl
     USING (SELECT
              @CustomerId AS CustomerId,
              @FirstName AS FirstName,
              @LastName AS LastName,
              @Balance AS Balance) AS row
      ON tbl.CustomerId = row.CustomerId
    -- Insert new row if not found (@CustomerId was passed in as NULL)
    WHEN NOT MATCHED THEN
      INSERT(FirstName, LastName, Balance)
      VALUES(row.FirstName, row.LastName, row.Balance)
    -- Update existing row if found, but *only* if the rowversions match
    WHEN MATCHED AND tbl.Version = @Version THEN
      UPDATE SET
        tbl.FirstName = row.FirstName,
        tbl.LastName = row.LastName,
        tbl.Balance = row.Balance,
        tbl.Modified = SYSDATETIME()
    ;

    -- If no rows were affected by an update, the rowversion changed
    IF @@ROWCOUNT = 0 AND @CustomerId IS NOT NULL
      RAISERROR('Optimistic concurrency violation', 18, 1)

    -- If this was an insert, return the newly assigned identity value
    IF @CustomerId IS NULL
      SET @CustomerId = SCOPE_IDENTITY()
```

```
-- Return 'read-only' creation/modification times and new rowversion
SELECT @Created = Created, @Modified = Modified, @Version = Version
 FROM Customer
 WHERE CustomerId = @CustomerId

END
```

There's a bit more going on here than before, so let's examine the stored procedure piece by piece.

Starting with the signature, notice that *@CustomerId* is now declared as an output parameter. For a new customer, this will be passed in as *NULL* and passed out as the newly assigned primary key value for the customer generated by the database using *IDENTITY*. For an existing customer, the same value used to identify the customer being updated is passed in to and out of *@CustomerId*.

We have also added the *@Created* and *@Modified datetime2(0)* output parameters. For a new customer, these will both be returned with the same date and time that the customer row is inserted. For an existing customer, the original creation time and the updated modification time are returned through these parameters.

Last, we have added the *@Version rowversion* output parameter. For a new customer, this will be passed in as *NULL*. For an existing customer, this will be passed in as the original *rowversion* value retrieved when the customer was initially selected from the database to be used for the optimistic concurrency check. For both new and existing customers, the updated *rowversion* value is passed back out through this parameter.

The target, source, and join predicates for the *MERGE* statement are implemented exactly the same way as in our first version of the stored procedure. Once again, the target is specified as the *Customer* table, the source is built as a single-row table from an embedded *SELECT* subquery of the input parameters, and the join predicate matches the source row to the target table on the *CustomerId* column.

The *WHEN NOT MATCHED* merge clause is virtually identical to the first version of the stored procedure except that the customer ID is not specified for the *INSERT* statement. By defining *CustomerId* as an *IDENTITY* column, we put SQL Server in charge of assigning new ID values, so we couldn't specify a primary key value for the insert even if we wanted to. (We'll receive an error if we try.) This means that the client does not know what the ID will be for a new customer until after the row is added to the table. The client therefore passes in *NULL* for *@CustomerId*, which of course will not be found in the table, causing the *WHEN NOT MATCHED* clause to insert a new row for the customer. The newly assigned *CustomerId* primary key value will be retrieved using the *SCOPE_IDENTITY* function following the *MERGE* statement. Notice too that the insert also doesn't provide *Created* or *Modified* values and relies instead on the *SYSDATETIME* defaults we established earlier for these two columns to use the current server date and time. (Although the *Modified* column will be changed when existing rows are updated, we implement the *Created* column as an immutable value that reliably reflects the original time of insertion for the lifetime of the row.)

For existing rows, the *WHEN MATCHED* merge clause is now qualified with a predicate that prevents updating data that has been modified by another user or process since the time this client originally retrieved the earlier version of it. This is accomplished by testing that the current *rowversion* value in the table matches the *rowversion* passed in by the client. A different value for the same customer indicates definitively that the data in the table has been changed in the interim and should therefore not be overwritten by a second update based on a previous version of the data. The merge clause evaluates to *true* only if this concurrency check is satisfied, which will then allow the *UPDATE* statement to execute. This update is almost identical to the first version of the stored procedure except that it also changes the *Modified* column.

After the *MERGE* statement, the stored procedure generates an error if it perceives that no rows were affected by the update in the *WHEN MATCHED* clause. This condition is detected by testing the SQL Server built-in *@@ROWCOUNT* variable for *0*. This variable would normally report the value of *1* as the result of a successful row insert or update. If it returns *0* and *@CustomerId* wasn't passed in as NULL (meaning that an update was requested by the client), the *WHEN MATCHED* predicate detected different *rowversion* values (or another user has deleted the customer) that suppressed the update operation, and we want an error to be raised in that case, as shown here:

```
IF @@ROWCOUNT = 0 AND @CustomerId IS NOT NULL
  RAISERROR('Optimistic concurrency violation', 18, 1)
```

> **Note** If you're thinking that the *RAISERROR* statement would be better placed in a *WHEN MATCHED AND tbl.Version <> @Version THEN* clause, you're absolutely right. Unfortunately, however, absolutely no T-SQL statements other than the permitted *INSERT, UPDATE*, and *DELETE* are valid in any merge clause.

If *@CustomerId* was passed in as *NULL* (meaning that an insert was requested by the client), we store the newly assigned *IDENTITY* value generated by SQL Server and exposed through its *SCOPE_IDENTITY* function back into the *@CustomerId* output parameter returned back to the client, as shown here:

```
IF @CustomerId IS NULL
  SET @CustomerId = SCOPE_IDENTITY()
```

Last, the creation/modification time and *rowversion* values are retrieved from the customer row into the *@Created*, *@Modified*, and *@Version* output parameters for returning to the client, as shown here:

```
SELECT @Created = Created, @Modified = Modified, @Version = Version
 FROM Customer
 WHERE CustomerId = @CustomerId
```

Let's now see this new implementation at work. We will write some T-SQL code that simulates the same client operations we performed for the first version of this stored procedure, which involves two inserts and an update. We'll need to declare a few local variables first to hold the values returned by output parameters in the new version of this stored procedure, as follows:

```
DECLARE @C1Id int
DECLARE @C2Id int
DECLARE @Crt datetime2(0)
DECLARE @Mod datetime2(0)
DECLARE @C1Ver rowversion
DECLARE @C2Ver rowversion
```

Because the first two customers are new, we assign *NULL* to the variables holding their customer ID values, as shown here:

```
SET @C1Id = NULL
SET @C2Id = NULL
```

We then call the stored procedure once per customer. For each call, we pass in the customer ID variables (which we've just assigned as *NULL*) and receive back the newly assigned *IDENTITY* primary key values via the first input/output parameter. The first name, last name, and balance values are passed in as normal input parameters just as before. We also return the creation time, modification time, and *rowversion* via three additional output parameters and store them in other local variables declared previously. After each stored procedure call, we select the output parameters so that we can see their values. For simulation purposes, we also add a delay to wait one second between each call, as shown here:

```
-- Add Customer 1
EXEC uspUpsertCustomer
 @C1Id OUTPUT, 'Mark', 'Boyer', 100, @Crt OUTPUT, @Mod OUTPUT, @C1Ver OUTPUT

SELECT @C1Id AS C1Id, @Crt AS Crt, @Mod AS Mod, @C1Ver AS C1Ver
WAITFOR DELAY '00:00:01'

-- Add Customer 2
EXEC uspUpsertCustomer
 @C2Id OUTPUT, 'Ted', 'Bremer', 120, @Crt OUTPUT, @Mod OUTPUT, @C2Ver OUTPUT

SELECT @C2Id AS C2Id, @Crt AS Crt, @Mod AS Mod, @C2Ver AS C2Ver
WAITFOR DELAY '00:00:01'
```

When we execute this code, we can see the values assigned by SQL Server that were returned in the output parameters of each stored procedure call. The two customers have been assigned the ID values of *1* and *2* as the result of the *IDENTITY* values generated for their primary keys. The creation and modification times are the same because these two customers have just been inserted. Because of the *WAITFOR DELAY*, the two customers have creation times that are one second apart. Last, we receive the unique *rowversion* values assigned to each of the two customers, as shown here:

```
C1Id        Crt                 Mod                 C1Ver
----------- ------------------- ------------------- ------------------
1           2007-11-22 14:14:21 2007-11-22 14:14:21 0x0000000000001026

C2Id        Crt                 Mod                 C2Ver
----------- ------------------- ------------------- ------------------
2           2007-11-22 14:14:22 2007-11-22 14:14:22 0x0000000000001027
```

The same scenario we described earlier then ensues, with customer 1 raising his balance from $100 to $110 and changing the spelling of his name from Mark to Marc. As before, the customer can be updated in the database by using exactly the same stored procedure call that was made for the original insert; only this time, the original *rowversion* value included in the call must match the current value in the database to guard against concurrency violations. Recall that we have stored that original *rowversion* value in our *@C1Ver* local variable as we received it from the original insert two seconds earlier. We can therefore use the same *@C1Ver* variable to pass in the original *rowversion* and to receive back again the new *rowversion* after the update, as shown here:

```
-- Change Customer 1's first name and balance, passing in the
--  rowversion from the original insert
EXEC uspUpsertCustomer
 @C1Id OUTPUT, 'Marc', 'Boyer', 110,
 @Crt OUTPUT, @Mod OUTPUT, @C1Ver OUTPUT

SELECT @C1Id AS C1Id, @Crt AS Crt, @Mod AS Mod, @C1Ver AS C1Ver
```

This time around, the customer ID passed in via *@C1Id* has a value of *1*, which was assigned by the original insert. (The *OUTPUT* keyword is still required, however, even though the value will never change on an update.) The *rowversion* passed in via *@C1Ver* in this example has a value of *0x1026*, which was also assigned by the original insert. Assuming that no other user or process modified this customer during the last two seconds, the update will succeed and the new *rowversion* value will be returned back out into *@C1Ver*, as follows:

```
C1Id        Crt                 Mod                 C1Ver
----------- ------------------- ------------------- ------------------
1           2007-11-22 14:14:21 2007-11-22 14:14:23 0x0000000000001028
```

This result confirms that the update ran successfully as expected. Although the creation time of 14:14:21 hasn't changed (and never will), the modification time of 14:14:23 shows our update that ran two seconds later. We can also see that the *rowversion* value has been changed from *0x1026* to *0x1028*.

If another user or process had changed the row during the two seconds between the time that this customer is created at 14:14:21 and the time we attempted the update at 14:14:23, its *rowversion* value would no longer be *0x1026*. In that event, our update attempt would fail with the *RAISERROR* statement that we coded in the stored procedure, as follows:

```
Msg 50000, Level 18, State 1, Procedure uspUpsertCustomer, Line 36
Optimistic concurrency violation
```

The INSERT OVER DML Syntax

SQL Server 2005 introduced the *OUTPUT* clause for *INSERT*, *UPDATE*, and *DELETE* statements as a way of capturing changed data resulting from those DML actions. Before and after snapshots of the changed data are exposed through the special *INSERTED* and *DELETED* pseudo-tables normally associated with triggers, so we don't actually need to resort to triggers (which are best avoided, if possible) anymore to capture this information. As you saw in the preceding section, the new *MERGE* statement in SQL Server 2008 also supports the *OUTPUT* clause for this purpose. When used with *MERGE*, the *OUTPUT* clause can select from the *INSERTED* and *DELETED* pseudo-tables and also from a special virtual *$action* column of type *nvarchar(10)* that returns a value of 'INSERT', 'UPDATE', or 'DELETE' according to the action performed for each row processed by the merge operation.

The results generated by the *OUTPUT* clause can be captured in another table or table variable using *OUTPUT...INTO*, making it possible to easily maintain historical records of changes in the database. In SQL Server 2008, we now have much greater flexibility in how we handle the captured data than before—specifically with regard to filtering. Because using *OUTPUT...INTO* dumps *every* row captured by the clause into the destination table or table variable, it is not possible to filter on this data.

Extending *OUTPUT...INTO*

This inability to filter *OUTPUT...INTO* change data has been removed in SQL Server 2008—but not by supporting a new *WHERE* clause for *OUTPUT...INTO*, as one might expect. Instead, a new feature named INSERT OVER DML provides a special syntax in which you wrap an *INSERT INTO...SELECT* statement around any DML statement (*INSERT, UPDATE, DELETE,* or *MERGE*) that has an *OUTPUT* clause, rather than using *OUTPUT...INTO* on the DML statement itself. The subtle but crucial difference here is that *OUTPUT...INTO captures* the changes, while the new INSERT OVER DML syntax *consumes* the changes captured by *OUTPUT*. By treating the *OUTPUT* changes as the source for a standard *INSERT INTO...SELECT* statement, we can obviously apply any *WHERE* clause to the *INSERT INTO...SELECT* statement that we want.

Note *INSERT OVER DML* is the term given by Microsoft to the new capability in SQL Server 2008 to consume and filter data changes captured by the *OUTPUT* clause of any DML statement. There is no actual *INSERT OVER DML* statement in T-SQL. Instead, you use the special new syntax described here to use the feature that's called INSERT OVER DML.

Beyond that, there isn't anything more you can do with INSERT OVER DML than you could by using *OUTPUT...INTO*. But to casually overlook or dismiss the significance of being able to filter on change data is to miss the point of INSERT OVER DML entirely. By being able to filter with a *WHERE* clause, you can now apply custom business logic for deciding which data changes captured are shipped to the destination table and which aren't. There are many practical use cases for this capability, including extract, transform, and load (ETL) processes for data warehousing, history tracking of slowly changing dimensions, or any other scenario in which you want to filter the changes streamed by DML output that are dumped into a secondary table for processing.

Here's a simple example that maintains an audit of all changes that are posted from one table to another. We maintain a master list of book prices and shelf locations in the *Book* table, and each book is identified by its ISBN number. Every week, we receive a new table named *WeeklyChanges* that contains updates to the book data, also keyed by ISBN number. In addition to price and shelf changes for existing books, the weekly update table can also include new books. You learned already that *MERGE* can handle this scenario (it was *made* to, in fact) and can effectively apply the appropriate updates and inserts from the *WeeklyChanges* table to the *Book* table by joining on *ISBN* and using the *WHEN MATCHED* and *WHEN NOT MATCHED* clauses. We also know that we can use the *OUTPUT...INTO* clause to capture and store all data changes performed by the merge into a history table. So let's first start by using *OUTPUT...INTO* to dump these changes to the *BookHistory* table. We'll then modify our approach to use the new INSERT OVER DML feature instead and see how that enhances our control over the process of archiving data changes.

Let's start by creating the *Book* and *WeeklyChange* tables, which both have the same schema, as shown in Listing 2-64.

LISTING 2-64 Creating the *Book* and *WeeklyChange* tables

```
CREATE TABLE Book(
  ISBN varchar(20) PRIMARY KEY,
  Price decimal,
  Shelf int)

CREATE TABLE WeeklyChange(
  ISBN varchar(20) PRIMARY KEY,
  Price decimal,
  Shelf int)
```

Next we create the *BookHistory* table, which will be the recipient of the changes captured by the *OUTPUT INTO* clause of our *MERGE* statement, as shown in Listing 2-65.

LISTING 2-65 Creating the *BookHistory* table

```
CREATE TABLE BookHistory(
  Action nvarchar(10),
  NewISBN varchar(20),
  NewPrice decimal,
  NewShelf int,
  OldISBN varchar(20),
  OldPrice decimal,
  OldShelf int,
  ArchivedAt datetime2)
```

We can now create our *uspUpdateBooks* stored procedure that performs the weekly update merge operation and records all data changes to the *BookHistory* table, as shown in Listing 2-66.

LISTING 2-66 Using *OUTPUT...INTO* with *MERGE*

```
CREATE PROCEDURE uspUpdateBooks AS
 BEGIN

  MERGE Book AS B
   USING WeeklyChange AS WC
   ON B.ISBN = WC.ISBN
   WHEN MATCHED AND (B.Price <> WC.Price OR B.Shelf <> WC.Shelf) THEN
    UPDATE SET B.Price = WC.Price, B.Shelf = WC.Shelf
   WHEN NOT MATCHED THEN
    INSERT VALUES(WC.ISBN, WC.Price, WC.Shelf)
   OUTPUT $action, inserted.*, deleted.*, SYSDATETIME()
    INTO BookHistory;

 END
```

This code requires no detailed explanation, as we covered *MERGE* thoroughly earlier in this chapter. What you should notice, however, is the *OUTPUT...INTO* clause. This clause records the action, new values, old values, and current server date and time in the *BookHistory* table, from the *$action* virtual column, *INSERTED* pseudo-table columns, *DELETED* pseudo-table columns, and *SYSDATETIME* function. In our particular scenario, *$action* can return only the string *'INSERT'* or *'UPDATE'*, since we are not processing deletions.

We now populate the *Book* and *WeeklyChange* tables to set the stage for our update, as shown here:

```
INSERT INTO Book VALUES('A', 100, 1)
INSERT INTO Book VALUES('B', 200, 2)
INSERT INTO WeeklyChange VALUES('A', 101, 1)
INSERT INTO WeeklyChange VALUES('C', 300, 3)
```

The *WeeklyChange* table shows a change in price for book A from $100 to $101 and also adds a new book C priced at $300 on shelf 3. When we run the *uspUpdateBooks* stored procedure, those two operations take place as we'd expect and as indicated by the number of rows affected message, as shown here:

```
EXEC uspUpdateBooks
GO

(2 row(s) affected)
```

In addition, the actions and data changes made by those insert and update operations (and the dates and times that they occurred) have been saved to the *BookHistory* table as the result of the *OUTPUT...INTO* clause, as shown here:

```
SELECT * FROM BookHistory
GO

Action NewISBN NewPrice NewShelf OldISBN OldPrice OldShelf ArchivedAt
------ ------- -------- -------- ------- -------- -------- --------------------------
UPDATE A       101      1        A       100      1        2007-11-25 14:47:23.9907552
INSERT C       300      3        NULL    NULL     NULL     2007-11-25 14:47:23.9907552
```

So far, so good, right? But what happens now if our requirements change slightly? After further consideration, we realize that an unacceptable amount of storage is going to be required for capturing the inserts that have no old values and that therefore don't provide any meaningful historical value beyond the creation date and time (which we could store in the *Book* table if we wanted to). Given that every book must be inserted but most books are not typically updated, the result will be a disproportionate amount of inserts over updates in the *BookHistory* table. That's a lot of storage to hold data that has little or no value. Unfortunately, there's simply no way to filter out the inserts and save just the updates using *OUTPUT...INTO*.

With SQL Server 2008, using INSERT OVER DML now provides just the solution needed to solve this problem. In our modified scenario, we are interested in capturing only updates and not inserts. Just to make things interesting, and also to show you that we can, we will append the historical data to the *Book* table itself rather than to a separate *BookHistory* table. (This is possible as well, coincidentally, using *OUTPUT...INTO*.) We'll add a new column to the *Book* table named *ArchivedAt* that will contain the server date and time for history records added when books are updated. There will always be one unique row containing the current values for each book with a *NULL* value in the *ArchivedAt* column.

We start as we did the last time by creating our tables, as shown in Listing 2-67.

LISTING 2-67 Creating new versions of the *Book* and *WeeklyChange* tables for use with INSERT OVER DML

```
CREATE TABLE Book(
  ISBN varchar(20),
  Price decimal,
  Shelf int,
  ArchivedAt datetime2)

CREATE UNIQUE CLUSTERED INDEX
 UI_Book ON Book(ISBN, ArchivedAt)

CREATE TABLE WeeklyChange(
  ISBN varchar(20) PRIMARY KEY,
  Price decimal,
  Shelf int)
```

Notice this time that we created a unique index on the combined *ISBN* and *ArchivedAt* columns. We can no longer create a primary key on just the *ISBN* column as we did before, since the *Book* table will now contain multiple records with the same ISBN number because the table holds historical change data as well as current data. Only one row per ISBN number will have a *NULL* value in the *ArchivedAt* column, which is the row that contains the current values for a book. All other rows with the same ISBN number will have non-*NULL* values in *ArchivedAt,* which serves as the time stamp of a previous update and will contain the historical values archived for that book at that time. By ensuring uniqueness between both *ISBN* and *ArchivedAt,* we are guaranteed that only one *current* row for each book is ever stored in the *Book* table, since the table will not tolerate two rows with the same ISBN numbers and *NULL* values for *ArchivedAt.*

Consuming *CHANGES*

We now implement a modified version of the *uspUpdateBooks* in Listing 2-68 that uses the new INSERT OVER DML syntax to capture and store historical data for updates that are appended to the *Book* table.

LISTING 2-68 Using *MERGE* with INSERT OVER DML

```
CREATE PROCEDURE uspUpdateBooks AS
BEGIN
 INSERT INTO Book(ISBN, Price, Shelf, ArchivedAt)
  SELECT ISBN, Price, Shelf, GETDATE() FROM
  (MERGE Book AS B
    USING WeeklyChange AS WC
     ON B.ISBN = WC.ISBN AND B.ArchivedAt IS NULL
    WHEN MATCHED AND (B.Price <> WC.Price OR B.Shelf <> WC.Shelf) THEN
     UPDATE SET Price = WC.Price, Shelf = WC.Shelf
```

```
    WHEN NOT MATCHED THEN
      INSERT VALUES(WC.ISBN, WC.Price, WC.Shelf, NULL)
      OUTPUT $action, WC.ISBN, Deleted.Price, Deleted.Shelf
    ) CHANGES(Action, ISBN, Price, Shelf)
     WHERE Action = 'UPDATE';
  END
```

Because we have historical data in the *Book* table that should not be considered relevant for the merge operation, we have added criteria to the join predicate after the *ON* keyword that tests for *NULL* values in the *ArchivedAt* column. This tells *MERGE* to consider only *current* books as matching target rows against the source of weekly changes and to completely ignore all the archive records.

The *CHANGES* keyword is the enabler here and is really what makes INSERT OVER DML possible. It exposes the columns of the *OUTPUT* clause defined on the inner *MERGE* statement to the *WHERE* clause of the outer *INSERT INTO...SELECT* statement. In our example, this includes the virtual *$action* column, the ISBN number, and the old values for price and shelf being replaced by the update operation.

By exposing the virtual *$action* through the *CHANGES* keyword as *Action*, the *INSERT INTO... SELECT* statement can apply a *WHERE* clause to filter out the actions of newly inserted books and append only the actions of *changed* books back into the *Book* table. This is something that cannot be achieved using the *OUTPUT...INTO* clause on the *MERGE* statement itself but that is possible with INSERT OVER DML using this very specific syntax.

In our case, we filter out insert actions with the simple criteria *WHERE Action = 'UPDATE'*. We could of course apply even more sophisticated logic than that if we wanted to, by examining any of the changed data columns returned by the *OUTPUT* clause and exposed by the *CHANGES* keyword. And that's exactly the key to the power of INSERT OVER DML.

Let's walk through our scenario step by step. We'll start with two books (A and B) and one price change (book A from $100 to $110), as shown here:

```
INSERT INTO Book VALUES('A', 100, 1, NULL)
INSERT INTO Book VALUES('B', 200, 2, NULL)
INSERT INTO WeeklyChange VALUES('A', 110, 1)

SELECT * FROM Book
SELECT * FROM WeeklyChange
GO

ISBN Price Shelf ArchivedAt
---- ----- ----- ----------------------
A    100   1     NULL
B    200   2     NULL

(2 row(s) affected)
```

```
ISBN Price Shelf
---- ----- -----
A    110   1
```

(1 row(s) affected)

When we now execute *uspUpdateBooks*, the inner *MERGE* statement will update the price for book A in the *Book* table and send its original values to the *OUTPUT* clause. The *OUTPUT* clause values are then consumed by the outer *INSERT INTO...SELECT* statement via the *CHANGES* keyword. The outer statement can therefore use those original book values for inserting historical data back into the *Book* table with an *ArchivedAt* value set to the current server date and time (just before 5:00 PM on 11/25/2007, in this example), as follows:

```
EXEC uspUpdateBooks
SELECT * FROM Book
GO

ISBN Price Shelf ArchivedAt
---- ----- ----- -------------------------
A    110   1     NULL
A    100   1     2007-11-25 16:57:19.8600000
B    200   2     NULL
```

(3 row(s) affected)

We can see the current data for book A (the row with an *ArchivedAt* date of *NULL*) at $110, and we also see the previous data for book A, which was changed from $100 at about 5:00 PM on November 25, 2007. Sometime later, we receive a new set of changes. This time, book A has changed from shelf 1 to shelf 6, and a new book C has been added, as shown here:

```
DELETE FROM WeeklyChange
INSERT INTO WeeklyChange VALUES('A', 110, 6)
INSERT INTO WeeklyChange VALUES('C', 300, 3)
GO
```

Just like the first time we ran the stored procedure, the current row for book A is updated, and a snapshot of the previous contents of the row is added to the table with the current server date and time, as shown here:

```
EXEC uspUpdateBooks
SELECT * FROM Book
GO

ISBN Price Shelf ArchivedAt
---- ----- ----- -------------------------
A    110   6     NULL
A    100   1     2007-11-25 16:57:19.8600000
A    110   1     2007-11-25 16:58:36.1900000
B    200   2     NULL
C    300   3     NULL
```

(5 row(s) affected)

Now book A has two history records showing the values saved from two earlier updates identified by date and time values in the *ArchivedAt* column. We also see a new row for book C, which was inserted by the *WHEN NOT MATCHED* clause of the MERGE statement.

However, notice that there is no history row for book C, since the insert action that was actually captured by the *MERGE* statement's *OUTPUT* clause was subsequently filtered out in the *WHERE* clause of the outer *INSERT INTO…SELECT* statement. Had we not filtered out insert actions in that *WHERE* clause, another history record would have also been added to the table for book C with meaningless NULL values for both *Price* and *Shelf*. We therefore evade the proliferation of such history rows that would occur as the result of each new book by filtering *OUTPUT* actions by using INSERT OVER DML. We also eliminated the extra columns for the new values that we used in the previous example's *BookHistory* table, as they are simply stored in each updated version archived in the *Book* table itself. And we eliminated the need to store an *Action* column, since we are capturing only update actions. In the end, we gained a lot of benefit by eliminating a lot of needless storage and using a single INSERT OVER DML statement.

As you can see, the combination of the new *MERGE* and INSERT OVER DML features in SQL Server 2008 is a very powerful addition to T-SQL. A fully loaded *MERGE* (handling inserts, updates, and deletes) wrapped up using INSERT OVER DML delivers an enormous amount of functionality in a single manageable statement. We recommend using these new features in lieu of the traditional multistatement approaches in whatever future development scenarios you find it possible to do so. In addition to improved performance, you'll appreciate the greater manageability that results from consolidating multiple statements into one.

The *GROUPING SETS* Operator

The *GROUP BY* clause has been part of the *SELECT* statement syntax since the earliest dialects of T-SQL. We use *GROUP BY* to create queries that collapse multiple rows belonging to the same group into a single summary row and perform aggregate calculations (such as *SUM* and *AVG*) across the individual rows of each group. SQL Server 6.5 later extended the *GROUP BY* clause by adding the *WITH CUBE* and *WITH ROLLUP* operators. These operators perform additional grouping and aggregation of data in standard relational queries, similar to what is provided by online analytical processing (OLAP) queries that slice and dice your data into Analysis Services cubes, but without ever leaving the relational database world. SQL Server 2008 now also adds a new operator named *GROUPING SETS* that further extends the capabilities of the *GROUP BY* clause for summarizing and analyzing your data.

In this section, we will examine *GROUP BY* in many of its variant forms. We'll start with the basic *GROUP BY* clause, and then you'll learn how the *WITH CUBE* and *WITH ROLLUP* operators can be used to enhance those summary results. Then we'll explore the *GROUPING SETS* operator, new in SQL Server 2008.

We start with a simple inventory table that contains quantities for various items in diverse colors that are available at different store locations, as shown in Listing 2-69.

LISTING 2-69 Creating the *Inventory* table

```
CREATE TABLE Inventory(
  Store varchar(2),
  Item varchar(20),
  Color varchar(10),
  Quantity decimal)
```

Next we'll add some inventory data. We have 13 rows that contain inventory for tables, chairs, and sofas available in blue, red, and green at NY, NJ, and PA locations, as shown in Listing 2-70.

LISTING 2-70 Populating the *Inventory* table

```
INSERT INTO Inventory VALUES('NY', 'Table', 'Blue', 124)
INSERT INTO Inventory VALUES('NJ', 'Table', 'Blue', 100)
INSERT INTO Inventory VALUES('NY', 'Table', 'Red', 29)
INSERT INTO Inventory VALUES('NJ', 'Table', 'Red', 56)
INSERT INTO Inventory VALUES('PA', 'Table', 'Red', 138)
INSERT INTO Inventory VALUES('NY', 'Table', 'Green', 229)
INSERT INTO Inventory VALUES('PA', 'Table', 'Green', 304)
INSERT INTO Inventory VALUES('NY', 'Chair', 'Blue', 101)
INSERT INTO Inventory VALUES('NJ', 'Chair', 'Blue', 22)
INSERT INTO Inventory VALUES('NY', 'Chair', 'Red', 21)
INSERT INTO Inventory VALUES('NJ', 'Chair', 'Red', 10)
INSERT INTO Inventory VALUES('PA', 'Chair', 'Red', 136)
INSERT INTO Inventory VALUES('NJ', 'Sofa', 'Green', 2)
```

Let's now look at how a basic *GROUP BY* clause operates on this data:

```
SELECT Item, Color, SUM(Quantity) AS TotalQty, COUNT(Store) AS Stores
 FROM Inventory
 GROUP BY Item, Color
 ORDER BY Item, Color
```

As indicated clearly by its syntax, this query will group all the inventory records by item and then by color within each item. The result set will therefore include one summary row for each unique combination of items and colors. The store location is not included in the grouping, so the results returned by the query apply to all stores. Each summary row includes a *TotalQty* column calculated by the *SUM* aggregate function as the total quantity for all rows of the same item and color across all stores. The last column *Stores* is calculated by the

COUNT aggregate function as the number of store locations at which each unique combination of items and colors is available, as shown here:

```
Item                  Color       TotalQty                      Stores
--------------------  ----------  ----------------------------  ------
Chair                 Blue        123                           2
Chair                 Red         167                           3
Sofa                  Green       2                             1
Table                 Blue        224                           2
Table                 Green       533                           2
Table                 Red         223                           3

(6 row(s) affected)
```

These results show that SQL Server grouped the inventory records sharing the same item and color into a single summary row. The store location is not included in the breakdown, since we did not group by it, so each summary row applies to all stores. For each item, the total quantity is calculated as the sum of the individual quantity values for the item and color combinations in each group, and the store count is calculated as the number of store locations at which each item and color combination is available. With *GROUP BY*, every column returned by the query must either be one of the columns actually being grouped by (such as the *Store*, *Item*, and *Color* columns) or be an aggregate function that operates across all the combined member rows for the group (such as the *SUM(Quantity)* and *COUNT(Store)* functions).

Rolling Up by Level

This query demonstrates the most basic application of the *GROUP BY* clause, which simply groups and aggregates. It answers the question "How many items per color are in each store location?" by grouping items and colors. The *WITH ROLLUP* and *WITH CUBE* operators (which were introduced in SQL Server 6.5) can be used to answer more questions than that. Each of these operators supplements the results of an ordinary *GROUP BY* clause with additional summary aggregations on the underlying data. Here is exactly the same query we ran before, only this time using *WITH ROLLUP*:

```
SELECT Item, Color, SUM(Quantity) AS TotalQty, COUNT(Store) AS Stores
  FROM Inventory
  GROUP BY Item, Color WITH ROLLUP
  ORDER BY Item, Color
GO
```

```
Item                  Color       TotalQty                      Stores
--------------------  ----------  ----------------------------  ------
```

NULL	**NULL**	**1272**	**13**
Chair	**NULL**	**290**	**5**
Chair	Blue	123	2
Chair	Red	167	3
Sofa	**NULL**	**2**	**1**
Sofa	Green	2	1
Table	**NULL**	**980**	**7**
Table	Blue	224	2
Table	Green	533	2
Table	Red	223	3

```
(10 row(s) affected)
```

This time, we receive the same six grouped results as before, supplemented with four additional *rollup* rows (the ones with *NULL* values for *Item* or *Color*, highlighted here in bold). Rollup rows contain additional higher-level summary information that essentially "groups the groups" of the query results. Any row with *NULL* values in it is a rollup row, and the *NULL* should be thought of as "all values" in this context.

In these results, the first row is the top-level rollup, as indicated by *NULL* values for both *Item* and *Color*. This top-level rollup reports a grand total quantity of 1,272 for the entire set (all items in all colors) in all store locations (where the entire set consists of the 13 unique item/color combinations across all locations).

The next result is an item-level rollup for chairs. It reports a total quantity of 290 for chairs in all colors across 5 store locations. The two results that follow are the same summary rows for chairs returned by our first "plain" *GROUP BY* query and that were just rolled up. They show 123 blue chairs in 2 locations and 167 red chairs in 3 locations. The next result is an item-level rollup for sofas. Only one store location carries sofas, and they're available only in green. The sofa rollup therefore contains the same values as the one and only summary row for 2 green sofas available in 1 location. The last set of rows report on tables in the same way that the chair and sofa data was returned. This includes an item-level rollup showing 980 tables across 7 locations followed by the summary rows showing 224 blue tables in 2 locations, 533 green tables in 2 locations, and 223 red tables in 3 locations returned.

So by simply adding *WITH ROLLUP*, we can answer a second question that our first ordinary *GROUP BY* query couldn't: "How many chairs, tables. and sofas are in stock, *regardless* of color?"

Rolling Up All Level Combinations

Using *WITH CUBE* now instead of *WITH ROLLUP* takes this result set to the next level, as shown here:

```
SELECT Item, Color, SUM(Quantity) AS TotalQty, COUNT(Store) AS Stores
 FROM Inventory
 GROUP BY Item, Color WITH CUBE
 ORDER BY Item, Color
GO
```

Item	Color	TotalQty	Stores
NULL	NULL	1272	13
NULL	**Blue**	**347**	**4**
NULL	**Green**	**535**	**3**
NULL	**Red**	**390**	**6**
Chair	NULL	290	5
Chair	Blue	123	2
Chair	Red	167	3
Sofa	NULL	2	1
Sofa	Green	2	1
Table	NULL	980	7
Table	Blue	224	2
Table	Green	533	2
Table	Red	223	3

```
(13 row(s) affected)
```

We now have the same result set returned by *WITH ROLLUP*, only this time three more rollup rows have been added (again, indicated in bold here). Let's look at exactly what SQL Server did here. By applying *WITH CUBE*, we instructed the database engine to create a multidimensional representation of the data on the fly, which is referred to as a *cube*. The number of dimensions in the cube is based on the number of grouping columns. Our inventory example therefore has only two dimensions, but a query could have many more dimensions, as dictated by the number of grouping columns it specifies. A cube contains rollups for all the possible permutations of dimension values, not just the combinations of one value *within* another, as per the nesting levels defined by grouping columns listed in the *GROUP BY* clause.

So *WITH CUBE* returns the same rollups returned by *WITH ROLLUP*—which includes all items regardless of color—plus additional rollups for all colors regardless of item. As a result, we can now answer a third question that our earlier *GROUP BY* queries couldn't: "How many items of *any* type in a particular color are in stock?" That means that we can now also see how many blue, green, or red items we have in inventory regardless of whether they are chairs, sofas, or tables.

Because a cube rolls up every possible combination of dimension values independent of the order of levels expressed with *GROUP BY*, each additional grouping level increases the size of the result set exponentially. For example, if we modify our query to group by store location as well, SQL Server returns 44 rows including rollups for every possible combination of values across the three grouping columns *Store*, *Item*, and *Color*, as follows:

```
SELECT Store, Item, Color, SUM(Quantity) AS TotalQty
 FROM Inventory
 GROUP BY Store, Item, Color WITH CUBE
 ORDER BY Store, Item, Color
GO
```

Store	Item	Color	TotalQty
NULL	NULL	NULL	1272
NULL	NULL	Blue	347
NULL	NULL	Green	535
NULL	NULL	Red	390
NULL	Chair	NULL	290
NULL	Chair	Blue	123
NULL	Chair	Red	167
NULL	Sofa	NULL	2
NULL	Sofa	Green	2
NULL	Table	NULL	980
NULL	Table	Blue	224
NULL	Table	Green	533
NULL	Table	Red	223
NJ	NULL	NULL	190
NJ	NULL	Blue	122
NJ	NULL	Green	2
NJ	NULL	Red	66
NJ	Chair	NULL	32
NJ	Chair	Blue	22
NJ	Chair	Red	10
NJ	Sofa	NULL	2
NJ	Sofa	Green	2
NJ	Table	NULL	156
NJ	Table	Blue	100
NJ	Table	Red	56
NY	NULL	NULL	504
NY	NULL	Blue	225
NY	NULL	Green	229
NY	NULL	Red	50
NY	Chair	NULL	122
NY	Chair	Blue	101
NY	Chair	Red	21
NY	Table	NULL	382
NY	Table	Blue	124
NY	Table	Green	229
NY	Table	Red	29
PA	NULL	NULL	578
PA	NULL	Green	304

```
PA    NULL              Red        274
PA    Chair             NULL       136
PA    Chair             Red        136
PA    Table             NULL       442
PA    Table             Green      304
PA    Table             Red        138
```

```
(44 row(s) affected)
```

These results can now answer questions about our inventory for every conceivable combination of grouping levels. For example, across all locations, there are 347 blue items (tables, chairs, and sofas), 290 chairs (all colors), and 533 green tables, whereas in NY specifically, there are 50 red items, 382 tables, and 124 blue tables, and so on. Every permutation of store location, item, and color—and their rollups—are returned by this single query.

Returning Just the Top Level

The last variation on *GROUP BY* is the *GROUPING SETS* operator, new in SQL Server 2008. This operator returns *just* the top-level rollup rows for each grouping level and does not include the actual group level summary information that was returned by our earlier versions of the query, as follows:

```
SELECT Store, Item, Color, SUM(Quantity) AS TotalQty
 FROM Inventory
 GROUP BY GROUPING SETS (Store, Item, Color)
 ORDER BY Store, Item, Color
GO
```

```
Store Item                 Color      TotalQty
----- -------------------- ---------- ------------------------------
NULL  NULL                 Blue       347
NULL  NULL                 Green      535
NULL  NULL                 Red        390
NULL  Chair                NULL       290
NULL  Sofa                 NULL       2
NULL  Table                NULL       980
NJ    NULL                 NULL       190
NY    NULL                 NULL       504
PA    NULL                 NULL       578
```

```
(9 row(s) affected)
```

GROUPING SETS is merely another variation on *GROUP BY* that you can use when you require only top-level rollups for each of your grouping levels (that is, one set of group rollups per level). In this case, we get a total quantity report for all colors, all items, and all store locations without including the summary rows for each of the combinations of grouping levels, as the earlier versions of our query did.

Mixing and Matching

But the *GROUPING SETS* story doesn't end here, of course. Unlike *WITH ROLLUP* and *WITH CUBE*, which are mutually exclusive in the same query, rollup and cube operations can now be used together and with *GROUPING SETS* in any combination. This means that you can compose one query that returns only top-level rollups for certain grouping levels and also returns the lower-level rollups and summary rows for other grouping levels, just as you get by using *WITH ROLLUP* or *WITH CUBE* in separate queries.

To achieve this, SQL Server 2008 introduces a new alternative syntax for *WITH ROLLUP* and *WITH CUBE* that makes these operators capable of being expressed together in the same *GROUP BY* clause. This newer syntax is actually quite simple: drop the *WITH* keyword, place the *ROLLUP* or *CUBE* keyword before the grouping columns rather than after, and enclose the grouping columns in parentheses.

For example, the following two *GROUP BY* clauses are interchangeable:

```
GROUP BY Item, Color WITH ROLLUP
GROUP BY ROLLUP(Item, Color)
```

Similarly, these two clauses are also equivalent:

```
GROUP BY Item, Color WITH CUBE
GROUP BY CUBE(Item, Color)
```

Although the two versions are interchangeable when used on their own, you *must* use the newer syntax if you want to combine them with one another or with *GROUPING SETS* in a single query. Here is another version of our inventory query that does just that:

```
SELECT Store, Item, Color, SUM(Quantity) AS TotalQty
  FROM Inventory
  GROUP BY GROUPING SETS(Store), CUBE(Item, Color)
  ORDER BY Store, Item, Color
```

The *GROUP BY* clause in this query includes both a *GROUPING SETS* operator on *Store* and a *CUBE* operator on *Item* and *Color*. This tells SQL Server to return top-level rollups only on the *Store* column and full summaries with multidimensional rollups on the *Item* and *Color* columns. Here are the results:

```
Store Item                Color       TotalQty
----- ------------------- ----------  ------------------------------
NJ    NULL                NULL        190
NJ    NULL                Blue        122
NJ    NULL                Green       2
NJ    NULL                Red         66
NJ    Chair               NULL        32
NJ    Chair               Blue        22
NJ    Chair               Red         10
NJ    Sofa                NULL        2
```

NJ	Sofa	Green	2
NJ	Table	NULL	156
NJ	Table	Blue	100
NJ	Table	Red	56
NY	**NULL**	**NULL**	**504**
NY	NULL	Blue	225
NY	NULL	Green	229
NY	NULL	Red	50
NY	Chair	NULL	122
NY	Chair	Blue	101
NY	Chair	Red	21
NY	Table	NULL	382
NY	Table	Blue	124
NY	Table	Green	229
NY	Table	Red	29
PA	**NULL**	**NULL**	**578**
PA	NULL	Green	304
PA	NULL	Red	274
PA	Chair	NULL	136
PA	Chair	Red	136
PA	Table	NULL	442
PA	Table	Green	304
PA	Table	Red	138

```
(31 row(s) affected)
```

The rows with *NULL* values for both *Item* and *Color* (highlighted here in bold) are the top-level rollups for *Store* returned by the *GROUPING SETS(Store)* operator. These rows report just the totals for each store (all items, all colors). All of the other rows are the multidimensional rollup and summary results returned by *CUBE(Item, Color)*. These rows report aggregations for every combination of *Item* and *Color*. Because *Store* is returned by *GROUPING SETS* and not by *CUBE*, we don't see combinations that include all stores.

You can use *GROUPING SETS*, *ROLLUP*, and *CUBE* in any combination you want with the *GROUP BY* clause. As a result, you gain tremendous flexibility for grouping, aggregating, and analyzing your data just the way you need to. The only restriction in usage is the same one that applies when using *GROUP BY* on its own: columns returned by the query must be specified either in the *GROUP BY* clause (in any of the *GROUPING SETS*, *ROLLUP*, or *CUBE* operators) or in an aggregate function that operates across all the combined rows for the group (such as *SUM*, *COUNT*, *MIN*, and *MAX*).

Handling *NULL* Values

We'll end our treatment of *GROUPING SETS* by discussing *NULL* values. As you've seen, SQL Server returns *NULL* values to represent all values in high-level rollup rows. If you're fortunate enough to be working with data that is guaranteed not to contain *NULL* values, life is good for you. Otherwise, a problem arises distinguishing between "real" *NULL* values and the *NULL* values representing "all values" in rollup rows.

To demonstrate, let's add two more rows to our *Inventory* table for lamps that have no color association. These rows store *NULL* values in the *Color* column, as shown in Listing 2-71.

LISTING 2-71 Introducing *NULL* values into the *Inventory* table

```
INSERT INTO Inventory VALUES('NY', 'Lamp', NULL, 36)
INSERT INTO Inventory VALUES('NJ', 'Lamp', NULL, 8)
```

Now let's run exactly the same query we ran before:

```
SELECT Store, Item, Color, SUM(Quantity) AS TotalQty
 FROM Inventory
 GROUP BY GROUPING SETS(Store), CUBE(Item, Color)
 ORDER BY Store, Item, Color
GO
```

```
Store Item                 Color      TotalQty
----- -------------------- ---------- -----------------------------
NJ    NULL                 NULL       8
NJ    NULL                 NULL       198
NJ    NULL                 Blue       122
NJ    NULL                 Green      2
 :
NJ    Table                Blue       100
NJ    Table                Red        56
NY    NULL                 NULL       36
NY    NULL                 NULL       540
NY    NULL                 Blue       225
NY    NULL                 Green      229
 :
PA    Table                Green      304
PA    Table                Red        138
```

(37 row(s) affected)

These are very confusing results. Because both the "all colors" rollup columns and the lamp columns with "no color" have a *NULL* value for *Color*, it is impossible to distinguish between the two when analyzing the query results. For example, the first row returns the rollup for all items with *no* color in NJ (that's the 8 lamps), and the second row returns the rollup for all items in *all* colors in NJ, but there is no way to discern that difference because *NULL* is used to represent both "no color" and "all colors." The same problem occurs again further down in the results for NY, where there are also colorless lamps in stock. Once again, because "no color" and "all colors" are both represented by *NULL* values, the results are nothing short of perplexing.

The solution to this problem is to use the *GROUPING* function in our query. The *GROUPING* function returns a bit value of *1* (true) if the column passed to it represents an "all values" rollup, and it returns *0* (false) otherwise. It is therefore possible to distinguish between "all values" rollup columns (which are always *NULL*) and regular data (which *might* be *NULL*, as is the case for the lamps, which have no color values). Here is a revised version of our query that uses the *GROUPING* function in conjunction with *CASE* to produce a better result set that clears up the confusion between "all values" and "no value":

```
SELECT
  CASE WHEN GROUPING(Store) = 1 THEN '(all)' ELSE Store END AS Store,
  CASE WHEN GROUPING(Item) = 1  THEN '(all)' ELSE Item  END AS Item,
  CASE WHEN GROUPING(Color) = 1 THEN '(all)' ELSE Color END AS Color,
  SUM(Quantity) AS TotalQty
 FROM Inventory
 GROUP BY GROUPING SETS(Store), CUBE(Item, Color)
 ORDER BY Store, Item, Color
```

The *CASE* construct tests each grouping column returned by the query using the *GROUPING* function. If it returns *1* (true), that means that the column represents an "all values" rollup. In this case, we return the string *(all)*, rather than the *NULL* value that would have otherwise been returned. If it returns *0* (false), the column contains regular data, which might or might not be *NULL*. Although we have only *NULL* values for the *Color* column (as is the case for the lamps), we apply the same *CASE* and *GROUPING* to the *Store* and *Item* columns as well. This is a defensive coding measure against the possibility of the *Store* or *Item* column also containing *NULL* values in the future. Taking this approach now resolves the confusion with respect to *NULL* values and rollups in the query results, as shown here:

```
Store Item                 Color       TotalQty
----- -------------------- ----------  -------------------------------
NJ    (all)                NULL        8
NJ    (all)                (all)       198
NJ    (all)                Blue        122
NJ    (all)                Green       2
  :
NJ    Table                Blue        100
NJ    Table                Red         56
NY    (all)                NULL        36
NY    (all)                (all)       540
NY    (all)                Blue        225
NY    (all)                Green       229
  :
PA    Table                Green       304
PA    Table                Red         138

(37 row(s) affected)
```

It's perfectly understandable now that the first row returns the rollup for all items with no color in NJ, whereas the second row returns the rollup for all items in all colors (including no color) in NJ. The same is true farther down in the NY results, where there are also colorless lamps in stock. Therefore, to avoid any potential confusion concerning *NULL* values in your grouping queries, you should always use the *GROUPING* function in this manner to translate the *NULL* values that mean "all values" for the user.

As long as we're modifying our query to produce more readable results, let's enhance it one more time. In the same way that we translated the *NULL* for "all values" to the text *(all)*, we would like to translate the *NULL* values for our regular missing data to *(n/a)*. This is easily achieved by adding an *ELSE* clause to the *CASE* construct that uses the *ISNULL* function on the column, as shown here:

```
SELECT
  CASE WHEN GROUPING(Store) = 1 THEN '(all)'
    ELSE ISNULL(Store, '(n/a)') END AS Store,
  CASE WHEN GROUPING(Item) = 1  THEN '(all)'
    ELSE ISNULL(Item,  '(n/a)') END AS Item,
  CASE WHEN GROUPING(Color) = 1 THEN '(all)'
    ELSE ISNULL(Color, '(n/a)') END AS Color,
  SUM(Quantity) AS TotalQty
FROM Inventory
GROUP BY GROUPING SETS(Store), CUBE(Item, Color)
ORDER BY Store, Item, Color
```

The *ELSE* clause in each *CASE* construct runs if the *GROUPING* function returns *0* (false). This means that the column is not an "all values" rollup, but regular column data. We want our regular column data to be returned as is except for *NULL* values that should be returned as the string *(n/a)*. The *ISNULL* function tests for *NULL* values and performs the translation on them, as shown in the results returned by the query:

```
Store Item                  Color       TotalQty
----- --------------------  ----------  -----------------------------
NJ    (all)                 (all)       198
NJ    (all)                 (n/a)       8
NJ    (all)                 Blue        122
NJ    (all)                 Green       2
   :
NJ    Sofa                  Green       2
NJ    Stool                 (all)       8
NJ    Stool                 (n/a)       8
NJ    Table                 (all)       156
NJ    Table                 Blue        100
NJ    Table                 Red         56
NY    (all)                 (all)       540
NY    (all)                 (n/a)       36
NY    (all)                 Blue        225
   :
NY    Chair                 Red         21
NY    Stool                 (all)       36
NY    Stool                 (n/a)       36
NY    Table                 (all)       382
NY    Table                 Blue        124
   :
PA    Table                 Green       304
PA    Table                 Red         138

(37 row(s) affected)
```

The query now returns no *NULL* values at all, which is much better for our users, who don't really know or care exactly what *NULL* means anyway. By translating these values appropriately to *(all)* and *(n/a)*, we have produced a far more usable report for them.

New T-SQL Shorthand Syntax

If you write a lot of T-SQL code, you will definitely appreciate these minor (but extremely handy) enhancements to the language syntax. These features may pale in the face of everything else new in SQL Server 2008, but they are welcome timesavers just the same and further demonstrate Microsoft's continued investment and innovation in T-SQL.

We can finally declare and initialize variables with a single statement, and compound assignment operators are supported as well. Plus, row constructors allow you to build multiple rows of data inline. For example, you can now insert multiple rows of data with a single *INSERT* statement that wraps the operation in an implicit transaction. Listing 2-72 shows the applied use of all of these T-SQL shortcuts with a simple example.

LISTING 2-72 Using the new T-SQL shorthand syntax in SQL Server 2008

```
CREATE TABLE StateList(StateId int, StateName char(2))
GO

-- Declare variable and assign a value in a single statement
DECLARE @Id int = 5

-- Insert multiple rows in a single statement with IDs 5, 6, and 7
INSERT INTO StateList VALUES(@Id, 'WA'), (@Id + 1, 'FL'), (@Id + 2, 'NY')

-- Use compound assignment operator to increment ID values to 6, 7, and 8
UPDATE StateList
 SET StateId += 1

-- View the results
SELECT * FROM StateList
```

And here is the output:

```
StateId StateName
------- ---------
6       WA
7       FL
8       NY

(3 row(s) affected)
```

Summary

We covered a lot of ground in this chapter. SQL Server 2005 and 2008 introduce many great enhancements to the T-SQL engine. You can see that Microsoft has continued its investment in T-SQL and that it offers many powerful new ways to query complex data using T-SQL, including *PIVOT, UNPIVOT, APPLY*, ranking functions, *TOP* enhancements, *GROUPING SETS*, and recursive operations through common table expressions (CTEs). You've learned how to use table-valued parameters (TVPs) to pass sets of rows across client, server, stored proce- dures, and user-defined functions (UDFs). New date and time data types have also been added for your programming use, and new DML possibilities are enabled with *MERGE* and INSERT OVER DML.

T-SQL is still the main way you will interact with data. When your operations require you to interact with the operating system or use the .NET Framework, you can use the CLR to write your queries in Visual Basic .NET or Visual C#. In the next chapter, you'll learn how.

Chapter 3
Exploring SQL CLR

—Andrew Brust

The banner headline for Microsoft SQL Server 2005 was its integration of the Microsoft .NET Common Language Runtime (CLR). This architectural enhancement gave SQL Server the ability to use certain .NET classes as basic data types as well as accommodate the use of .NET languages for the creation of stored procedures, triggers, functions, and even user-defined aggregates. This capability is carried forward and enhanced in SQL Server 2008. It also is the underlying enabler of various new SQL Server 2008 data types, including *geometry* and *geography*, covered in Chapter 9.

> **Note** Throughout this chapter, we will refer to the CLR integration in SQL Server as SQL CLR features, functionality, or integration, and we will refer to SQL CLR stored procedures, triggers, functions, aggregates, and user-defined types (UDTs) as the five basic SQL CLR entities.

Let's face facts: Transact SQL (T-SQL) is essentially a hack. Back when SQL Server was first developed, Microsoft and Sybase took SQL—a declarative, set-based language—and added variable declaration, conditional branching, looping, and parameterized subroutine logic to make it into a quasi-procedural language. Although extremely clever and useful, T-SQL lacked, and still lacks, many of the niceties of a full-fledged procedural programming language.

This shortcoming has forced some people to write T-SQL stored procedures that are overly complex and difficult to read. It has forced others to put logic in their middle-tier code that they would prefer to implement on the database. And it's even forced some people to abandon stored procedures altogether and use dynamic SQL in their applications, a practice that we do not endorse. Because of these workarounds to address T-SQL's procedural limitations, CLR integration is a welcome feature in SQL Server, and it has caught the market's attention.

Meanwhile, T-SQL—and, one might argue, SQL itself—is vastly superior to procedural languages for querying and manipulating data. Its set-based syntax and implementation simply transcend the approach of procedurally iterating through rows of data. This is no less true in SQL Server 2005 and 2008 than in earlier versions of the product, and T-SQL has been greatly enhanced in this release (as detailed in Chapter 2), making it more valuable still.

Although the euphoria over SQL CLR died down considerably after the release of SQL Server 2005, it is still an important technology and, as we said, is being used by Microsoft to enable new data types in SQL Server 2008. So SQL CLR *still* places database application developers at a crossroads. We must simultaneously learn how the SQL CLR features work and develop a sophisticated, judicious sense of when to use T-SQL instead of the SQL CLR feature set. We must resist the temptation to completely ".NET-ify" our databases but learn to take advantage of the SQL CLR feature set where and when prudent. This chapter aims to help you learn to use SQL CLR features and to develop an instinct for their appropriate application.

In this chapter, you will learn:

- How to enable (or disable) SQL CLR integration on your SQL Server.
- How SQL Server accommodates CLR code through the loading of .NET assemblies.
- How to use SQL Server 2008 and Microsoft Visual Studio 2008 together to write SQL CLR code and deploy it, simply and quickly.
- How to deploy SQL CLR code independently of Visual Studio, using T-SQL statements, with or without the help of SQL Server Management Studio.
- How to create simple CLR stored procedures, triggers, functions, aggregates, and UDTs, use them in your databases, and utilize them from T-SQL.
- How both the standard SQL Server client provider and the new server-side library can be combined to implement SQL CLR functionality.
- How SQL CLR security works and how to configure security permissions for your assemblies.
- When to use SQL CLR functionality and when to opt to use T-SQL instead.

Getting Started: Enabling CLR Integration

Before you can learn how to use SQL CLR features, you need to know how to enable them. As with many new products in the Microsoft Windows Server System family, most advanced features of SQL Server 2008 are disabled by default. The reasoning behind this is sound: each additional feature that is enabled provides extra "surface area" for attacks on security or integrity of the product, and the added exposure is simply not justified if the feature goes unused.

The SQL CLR features of SQL Server 2008 are sophisticated and can be very useful, but they are also, technically, nonessential. It is possible to build high-performance databases and server-side programming logic without SQL CLR integration, so it is turned off by default.

Don't be discouraged, though: turning on the feature is easy. Microsoft provides a system stored procedure for enabling or disabling SQL CLR integration. You can also enable SQL CLR integration by using Policy-Based Management (PBM), using the steps illustrated in an example in Chapter 4. In this chapter, we cover just the T-SQL approach.

Open SQL Server Management Studio, and then connect to the server you want to configure. Then, from a query window, type the following statements, and click the Execute button on the Management Studio SQL Editor toolbar:

```
sp_configure 'clr enabled', 1
GO

RECONFIGURE
GO
```

That's all there is to it! To disable SQL CLR integration, just use the value *0* instead of *1* as the second parameter value in the *sp_configure* call.

> **Tip** Don't forget that this will work from any tool that can connect to SQL Server, not just Management Studio. In fact, you could issue the preceding command text from your own code using the ADO.NET *SqlCommand* object's *ExecuteNonQuery* method as long as your code can connect to your server and your server can authenticate you as a user in the *sysadmin* server role.

With SQL CLR integration enabled, you're ready to get started writing SQL CLR code. Before we dive in, we need to discuss Visual Studio/SQL Server integration and when to use it.

Visual Studio/SQL Server Integration

Visual Studio 2008 and SQL Server 2008 integrate tightly in a number of ways. It's important to realize, however, that the use of Visual Studio integration is completely optional and the use of T-SQL is a sufficient substitute. With the release of SQL Server 2005, T-SQL was enhanced with new data definition language (DDL) commands for maintaining CLR assemblies, types, and aggregates, and its existing commands for stored procedures, triggers, and functions have been enhanced to recognize code within deployed assemblies. Visual Studio can execute those commands on your behalf. It can also make writing individual SQL CLR classes and functions easier.

Ultimately, we think all developers should be aware of both Visual Studio–assisted and more manual coding and deployment methods. You might decide to use one method most of the time, but in some situations, you'll probably need the other, so we want to prepare you. As we cover each major area of SQL CLR programming, we will discuss deployment from both points of view. We'll cover some general points about Visual Studio integration now, and then we'll move on to cover SQL CLR development.

SQL Server Projects in Visual Studio

Visual Studio 2008 provides a special SQL Server Project type and, within projects of that type, defined templates for the five basic SQL CLR entities. These templates inject specific code attributes and function stubs that allow you to create SQL CLR code easily. The attributes are used by Visual Studio to deploy your assembly and its stored procedures, triggers, and so on to your database. Some of them are also used by SQL Server to acknowledge and properly use your functions, UDTs, and aggregates.

To test out the new project type and templates, start Visual Studio 2008, and then create a new project by choosing File, New, Project, clicking New Project on the toolbar, pressing Ctrl+Shift+N, or clicking the Create: Project link on the Visual Studio Start Page. In the New Project dialog box, shown in Figure 3-1, select Database from the Project Types tree view on the left (the Database node appears under the parent node for your programming language of choice; in Figure 3-1, the language is C#), and then click the SQL Server Project icon in the Templates list on the right. Enter your own project name if you want, and then click OK.

Tip If you are using Visual Studio Team Edition for Database Professionals or Visual Studio Team Suite, you can also create a SQL CLR project by selecting the Database Projects\Microsoft SQL Server\SQL-CLR node from the Project Types tree view and then clicking the Visual Basic or C# SQL Server Project item in the Templates list on the right.

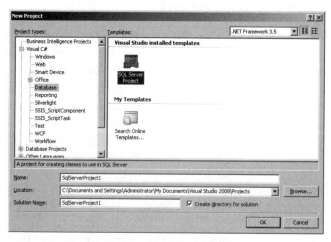

FIGURE 3-1 The Visual Studio 2008 New Project dialog box with the SQL Server project type selected

The Add Database Reference dialog box will appear, as shown in Figure 3-2.

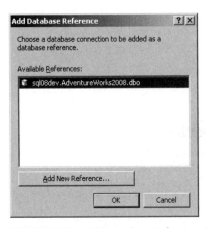

FIGURE 3-2 The Add Database Reference dialog box

Because Visual Studio provides automated deployment of your SQL CLR code, it must associate your project with a specific server and database via a database reference (connection). Any database connections that have already been defined in the Server Explorer window appear in this window, as does an Add New Reference button that allows you to define a new connection if necessary. Select an existing connection or define a new one, and then click OK. The project opens.

Note If no data connections have already been defined in the Server Explorer window, the New Database Reference dialog box will appear in place of the Add Database Reference dialog box. In the New Database Reference dialog box, you can specify server, login, and database details for a new database connection that will be used by your project as its database reference and added to Server Explorer as a new data connection.

Tip After clicking OK in the Add Database Reference dialog box, you might be prompted by Visual Studio to enable SQL CLR debugging for the connection. If this happens, click Yes in the two successive message boxes that appear.

You can easily add preconfigured classes for the five basic SQL CLR entities to your project. You can do this in a number of ways: directly from the main menu's Project option or from the Add submenu on the project's Solution Explorer shortcut menu, as shown in Figure 3-3.

FIGURE 3-3 The Solution Explorer project node shortcut menu and its Add submenu

You can also add the preconfigured classes from the Add New Item dialog box, shown in Figure 3-4, which is displayed by clicking Project, Add New Item or by choosing Add, New Item using the project's Solution Explorer shortcut menu.

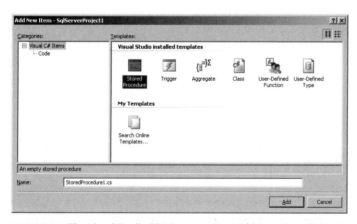

FIGURE 3-4 The Visual Studio SQL Server project Add New Item dialog box

Automated Deployment

Once opened, SQL Server projects add Deploy options to the Build option of the Visual Studio main menu. In addition, the Play (Start Debugging) button and the Start Debugging, Start Without Debugging, and Step Over options on the Debug menu (and their keyboard shortcuts F5, Ctrl+F5, and F10, respectively) all deploy the project assembly in addition to performing their indicated functions.

Visual Studio can do a lot of deployment work for you. But as you'll learn, you can perform the same tasks on your own and, in certain circumstances, have more precise control over the deployment process when you do so.

SQL CLR Code Attributes

A number of .NET code attributes are provided for SQL CLR developers; these are contained in the *Microsoft.SqlServer.Server* namespace. Many of them are inserted in your code when you use the various templates in the SQL Server project type, as is a *using* statement to alias the *Microsoft.SqlServer.Server* namespace itself. If you choose to develop code without these templates, you must add the appropriate attributes, and optionally the *using* statement, yourself. Although all these attributes are provided in the same namespace, some are used exclusively by Visual Studio and others are used by both Visual Studio and SQL Server.

There are more SQL CLR attributes available for you to use than we will be able to cover in this chapter. Specifically, we will provide coverage of the *SqlProcedure*, *SqlFunction*, *SqlTrigger*, *SqlUserDefinedAggregate*, and *SqlUserDefinedType* attributes. We will not cover the *SqlFacet* and *SqlMethod* attributes.

Just as certain attributes are not covered here, we cover only some of the parameters accepted by the attributes that we do cover. And in some cases, we cover only certain of the possible values that can be passed to these attributes. For example, *SqlFunction* accepts several parameters, but the only ones we will cover are *Name*, *FillRowMethodName*, and *TableDefinition*. For *SqlUserDefinedAggregate* and *SqlUserDefinedType*, we will cover only a single value setting for the *Format* parameter and will not cover the several other parameters those two attributes accept.

The coverage we provide will be more than sufficient for you to implement basic, intermediate, and certain advanced functionality with all of the five basic SQL CLR entities. The attributes and parameters that we won't cover are useful mostly for optimizing your SQL CLR code, and they are well documented in SQL Server Books Online and articles on MSDN.

About the Sample Code

The sample .NET code for this chapter is provided on the book's companion Web site in two versions. The primary material is supplied as a Visual Studio SQL Server project, accessible by opening the solution file Chapter03.sln in the Chapter03 subfolder of this chapter's VS sample code folder. We also supply the code as a standard Class Library project, accessible by opening the solution file Chapter03Manual.sln in the Chapter03Manual subfolder. The code in each project is virtually identical, although the Class Library project does not autodeploy when the various Build and Debug commands are invoked in Visual Studio 2008. As we cover each SQL CLR feature, we'll discuss how automated deployment takes place from the SQL Server project and how command-driven deployment should be performed for the Class Library project.

We'll also discuss executing test scripts from within Visual Studio for the SQL Server project and from SQL Server Management Studio for the Class Library project. As a companion to those discussions, we provide a Management Studio project, accessible by opening Chapter03.ssmssln in this chapter's SSMS folder. This project consists of a number of SQL scripts used for testing the sample SQL CLR code and a script for cleaning up everything in the database created by the sample code and tests. The project also contains a script file named CreateObjects.sql, which deploys the Class Library assembly and the SQL CLR entities within it.

Your First SQL CLR Stored Procedure

Although SQL CLR programming can get quite complex and involved, it offers in reality a simple model that any .NET developer can use with high productivity in relatively short order. That's because the crux of SQL CLR functionality is nothing more than the ability of SQL Server 2008 to load .NET assemblies into your database and then to allow you to use the functions and types within those assemblies as you define your columns, views, stored procedures, triggers, and functions.

To give you a good understanding of SQL CLR integration, we must examine its features and techniques carefully. Before doing so, however, let's quickly walk through an end-to-end scenario for creating and executing a SQL CLR stored procedure. This will make it easier for you to understand the individual features as we describe them.

Strictly speaking, any .NET class library assembly (in certain cases, using appropriate .NET code attributes in its classes and functions) can be loaded into your database with a simple T-SQL statement. To see how easily this works, start Management Studio, and then open a query window using a connection to the *AdventureWorks2008* sample database. In the sample code folder for this chapter, confirm that the file Chapter03.dll is located in the VS\ Chapter03Manual\Chapter03\bin\Debug subfolder. If the parent folder were C:\Projects\ Chapter03, you would load the assembly into the *AdventureWorks2008* database with the following T-SQL command:

```
CREATE ASSEMBLY Chapter03
  FROM 'C:\Projects\Chapter03\VS\Chapter03Manual\Chapter03\bin\Debug\Chapter03.dll'
```

There are other syntax options for the *CREATE ASSEMBLY* command, but for now we'll focus on the preceding limited usage.

Functions in an assembly that reside within a class and perform local computational tasks and certain types of data access can be easily exposed as SQL Server stored procedures, triggers, or functions. As with conventional stored procedures, triggers, and functions, all it takes is a simple T-SQL *CREATE PROCEDURE, CREATE TRIGGER*, or *CREATE FUNCTION* statement to make this happen. We'll go through each of these options in this chapter, but for now let's create a simple CLR stored procedure.

You can view the source code for the *Chapter03* assembly by opening the solution file VS\ Chapter03Manual\Chapter03Manual.sln in this chapter's sample code folder. Within the project, the file Sprocs.cs contains the following code:

```
using System.Data.SqlClient;
using Microsoft.SqlServer.Server;

public partial class Sprocs
{
  public static void spContactsQuick()
  {
    SqlContext.Pipe.ExecuteAndSend(new SqlCommand("SELECT * FROM Person.Person"));
  }
}
```

The *spContactsQuick* method is designed to connect to the database in which its assembly has been loaded (*AdventureWorks2008*), perform a *SELECT* * against the *Person.Person* table, and then use special server-side objects to send the data back to the client application. To make this CLR code available via SQL Server as a stored procedure, also named *spContacts-Quick*, you simply execute the following command from the Management Studio query window you opened earlier:

```
CREATE PROCEDURE spContactsQuick
  AS EXTERNAL NAME Chapter03.Sprocs.spContactsQuick
```

 Important Be sure to enter the *Sprocs.spContactsQuick* portion of the command verbatim. This phrase is case sensitive.

To test the SQL CLR stored procedure, run it from a Management Studio query window as you would any conventional stored procedure, as shown here:

```
EXEC spContactsQuick
```

Or simply:

```
spContactsQuick
```

Management Studio should respond by displaying the contents of the *Person.Person* table in the Results tab of the query window.

As you can see from this rather trivial example, writing a CLR stored procedure can be very easy and is a lot like writing client-side or middle-tier code that performs data access using ADO.NET. The biggest differences involve the provision of a database connection and the fact that the data must be piped back to the client rather than loaded into a *SqlDataReader* and returned, manipulated, or displayed through a user interface (UI). The presence of the *SqlContext* object also differentiates SQL CLR code from conventional ADO.NET data access code. We'll cover the use of the *SqlContext* object and its *Pipe* property in the next section.

The bits of T-SQL and C# code just shown certainly don't tell the whole SQL CLR story. The use of the *ExecuteAndSend* method allowed us to skip over a number of otherwise important concepts. There are three ways to deploy assemblies, and you've seen only a simplified version of one of those ways. Security considerations must be taken into account, and we haven't even begun to look at triggers, functions, aggregates, or UDTs. So although the example showed how easy SQL CLR programming can be, we'll now take our time and show you the nooks and crannies.

CLR Stored Procedures and Server-Side Data Access

Our previous "quick and dirty" sample looked at CLR stored procedure development, but we need to cover that topic more thoroughly now. We've already covered the mechanics of writing and deploying a stored procedure, but let's back up a bit to try and understand how CLR stored procedures work from a conceptual standpoint.

SQL CLR stored procedure code runs in an instance of the .NET CLR that is hosted by SQL Server itself; it is not called as an external process, as Component Object Model (COM)–based extended stored procedures (XPs) would be. Because SQL CLR code runs in the context of the server, it treats objects in the database as native, *local* objects, more or less. As such, it must treat the client that calls it as *remote*. This contextual environment is, in effect, the opposite of that under which client and middle-tier ADO.NET code runs. There, communicating with the database requires a remote connection (even if the database is physically on the same computer), and the ADO.NET code runs locally. The SQL CLR reversal of this takes a little getting used to, but once you've mastered thinking about things this way, SQL CLR code becomes easy to write and understand.

Meanwhile, as .NET has no intrinsic way of accessing local objects on the server or transmitting data and messages to the client, you must use a special set of classes to perform these tasks. These classes are contained in the *Microsoft.SqlServer.Server* namespace.

> **Note** As an aside, it is interesting and important to note that the *Microsoft.SqlServer.Server* namespace is actually supplied by the *System.Data.dll* .NET Framework assembly. This means that you don't need to worry about adding a reference to your project to use this namespace. The namespace's location within *System.Data.dll* also further emphasizes the tight integration between .NET and SQL Server.

If you want, you can think of *Microsoft.SqlServer.Server* as a helper library for *System.Data.SqlClient*. It supplies the SQL CLR code attributes we already mentioned, a few enumerations, an exception class, an interface, and five other classes: *SqlContext*, *SqlPipe*, *SqlTriggerContext*, *SqlMetaData*, and *SqlDataRecord*. We'll cover *SqlMetaData* and *SqlDataRecord* at the end of this section, and we'll cover *SqlTriggerContext* when we discuss CLR triggers later in this chapter. We'll cover the *SqlContext* and *SqlPipe* objects right now.

At a high level, the *SqlContext* object, which is *static*, provides a handle to the server-side context in which your code runs. It also has a channel to the client through which you can return data and text: its *Pipe* property, which in turn provides access to a properly opened and initialized *SqlPipe* object.

A *SqlPipe* object can send data and messages to the calling client though several methods: *Send*, *SendResultsStart*, *SendResultsRow*, *SendResultsEnd*, and *ExecuteAndSend*. In the preceding code sample, we used the *SqlPipe* object's *ExecuteAndSend* method to implicitly open a connection, call *ExecuteReader* on a *SqlCommand* object that uses that connection, and transmit the contents of the resulting *SqlDataReader* back to the client. Although the implicit work done by *ExecuteAndSend* might have been convenient for us to get started quickly, it's important to avoid such shortcuts in our detailed discussion of SQL CLR programming.

In general, SQL CLR stored procedure code that queries tables in the database must open a connection to that database, use the *SqlCommand* object's *ExecuteReader* method to query the data, and then use one or a combination of the *Send* methods to send it back. The *Send* methods do not accept *DataSet* objects; they accept only *SqlDataReader* objects, strings, and special *SqlDataRecord* objects. Listing 3-1, which shows the implementation of the function *spContacts* from spTest.cs in the sample project, is a representative example of how this is done.

LISTING 3-1 *spContacts* from spTest.cs

```
[SqlProcedure()]
public static void spContacts()
{
    SqlConnection conn = new SqlConnection("context connection=true");
    SqlCommand cm = new SqlCommand("SELECT * FROM Person.Person", conn);

    conn.Open();
    SqlDataReader dr = cm.ExecuteReader();
    SqlContext.Pipe.Send("Starting data dump");
    SqlContext.Pipe.Send(dr);
    SqlContext.Pipe.Send("Data dump complete");
    dr.Close();
    conn.Close();
}
```

Note Because the *Person.Person* table includes *xml* columns, and because such columns can cause a slowdown in SQL CLR stored procedures, the query in the sample code for *spContacts* uses a column list (which excludes the *xml* columns) in the *SELECT* clause rather than the * wildcard. We retained the *SELECT* * syntax in the printed code, for simplicity and terseness.

For this code to work, we need to use both the *Microsoft.SqlServer.Server* and *System.Data.SqlClient* namespaces (and if you look in the chapter's sample project rather than Listing 3-1, you'll see that we have aliased both of those namespaces with *using* statements). This is because any conventional ADO.NET objects we might use, such as *SqlConnection*, *SqlCommand*, and *SqlDataReader*, are supplied to us from *System.Data.SqlClient*, just as they would be in a conventional client application or middle-tier assembly. And as already discussed, we need the *Microsoft.SqlServer.Server* namespace in order to use objects such as *SqlContext* and *SqlPipe*. The stored procedure template in Visual Studio SQL Server projects includes the *using* statement for *Microsoft.SqlServer.Server* and *System.Data.SqlClient* automatically.

Although server-side code uses *SqlClient* objects, it does so in a specialized way. For example, notice that the *context connection=true* connection string is passed to the *SqlConnection* object's constructor. This essentially instructs ADO.NET to open a new connection to the database in which the CLR assembly resides. Notice also the second call to the *SqlContext.Pipe* object's *Send* method. Here, the *SqlDataReader* parameter overload of the *SqlPipe* object's *Send* method is used to push the contents of the *SqlDataReader* back to the client. You can think of this method as performing a *while (dr.Read())* loop through the *SqlDataReader* and returning the values of each column for each iteration of the loop. But instead of your having to do that work yourself, the *Send* method does it for you.

Before and after the *SqlDataReader* is *piped* (returned to the consumer), we use the *String* parameter overload of the *Send* method to send status messages to the client. When this stored procedure is run in Management Studio, the piped text appears on the Results tab of the query window when you use the Management Studio Results To Text option and on the Messages tab when you use the Results To Grid option.

The rest of the listing contains typical ADO.NET code, all of it using objects from the *SqlClient* provider. And that illustrates well the overall theme of SQL CLR programming: do what you'd normally do from the client or middle tier, and use a few special helper objects to work within the context of SQL Server as you do so.

Piping Data with *SqlDataRecord* and *SqlMetaData*

We mentioned that the *SqlPipe* object's *Send* method can accept an object of type *SqlDataRecord*, and we mentioned previously that *Microsoft.SqlServer.Server* provides this object as well as an object named *SqlMetaData*. You can use these two objects together in a CLR stored procedure to return a result set one row at a time instead of having to supply the *SqlPipe* object's *Send* method with a *SqlDataReader*. This allows (but does not require) you to inspect the data before sending it back to the client. Sending *SqlDataReader* objects prevents inspection of the data within the stored procedure because *SqlDataReader* objects are forward-only result set structures. Using the *ExecuteAndSend* method and a *SqlCommand* object has the same limitation.

The *SqlDataRecord* object permits .NET code to create an individual row to be returned to the calling client. Its constructor accepts an array of *SqlMetaData* objects, which in turn describe the metadata for each column in the row.

Listing 3-2, which shows the implementation of the *spContactCount* function from spTest. cs in the sample project, illustrates how to use *SqlPipe.Send* together with *SqlDataRecord* and *SqlMetaData* objects to return a single-column, single-row result set from a stored procedure.

LISTING 3-2 *spContactCount* from spTest.cs

```
[SqlProcedure()]
public static void spContactCount()
{
  SqlConnection conn = new SqlConnection("context connection=true");
  SqlCommand cm = new SqlCommand("SELECT COUNT(*) FROM Person.Person", conn);
  SqlDataRecord drc = new SqlDataRecord(new SqlMetaData("ContactCount", SqlDbType.Int));

  conn.Open();
  drc.SetInt32(0, (Int32)cm.ExecuteScalar());
  SqlContext.Pipe.Send(drc);
  conn.Close();
}
```

The code declares variable *drc* as a *SqlDataRecord* object and passes its constructor a single *SqlMetaData* object. (Passing a single object rather than an array is permissible if the

SqlDataRecord object will have only a single column.) The *SqlMetaData* object describes a column named *ContactCount* of type *SqlDbType.Int*.

> **Note** The *SqlDbType* enumeration is contained within the *System.Data.SqlTypes* namespace. The SQL Server Stored Procedure template inserts a *using* statement for this namespace. If you are creating SQL CLR code without using this template, you will need to add the *using* statement yourself.

The rest of the code is rather straightforward. First, a context connection and command are opened and a *SELECT COUNT(*)* query is performed against the *Person.Person* table. Because the query returns a single scalar value, it is run using the *SqlCommand* object's *ExecuteScalar* method. Next, the value returned by *ExecuteScalar* is cast into an *Int32*, and that value is loaded into column 0 (the only returned column) of the *SqlDataRecord* object using its *SetInt32* method. The *SqlDataRecord* is then piped back to the client using the *SqlPipe* object's *Send* method.

> **Note** If we wanted to send back multiple *SqlDataRecord* objects, we would send the first object using the *SqlContext* object's *SendResultsStart* method and then send all subsequent *SqlDataRecord* objects using the *SendResultsRow* method. We would call the *SendResultsEnd* method after all *SqlDataRecord*s had been sent.

Once the stored procedure has been deployed (the techniques for which we will discuss shortly), you can execute it from SQL Server Management Studio just as you would any other stored procedure. Although the result is a single value, it is presented as a column, and the column name *ContactCount* is shown on the Results tab of the query window. Keep in mind that this *COUNT(*)* query result could have been returned without using the *SqlMetaData* and *SqlDataRecord* objects; the sample is provided to demonstrate the use of these objects as an alternative to piping *SqlDataReader* objects and text to the client.

CLR Stored Procedure Usage Guidelines

It's important to understand how to perform data access and retrieval in CLR stored procedures. As a .NET developer, you already know how to perform computational tasks within your code, so our samples illustrate server-side data access more than anything else. As proof-of-concept code, these samples are completely adequate.

Meanwhile, you should avoid writing CLR stored procedures that merely perform simple "CRUD" (Create, Read, Update, and Delete) operations. Such tasks are better left to conventional T-SQL stored procedures, which typically perform these operations more efficiently than ADO.NET can. CLR stored procedures work well when you need to perform computations on or using your data and you require the expressiveness of a .NET language or the rich functionality provided by the .NET base class libraries to do so (where such expressiveness and base class library support is missing from T-SQL).

For example, implementing a "fuzzy search" using business logic embedded in .NET assemblies to determine which data has an affinity to other data is a good use of SQL CLR stored procedures. Regular-expression-based data validation in an update or insert stored procedure is another good application of SQL CLR integration. As a general rule, straight data access should be left to T-SQL. "Higher-valued" computations are good candidates for SQL CLR integration. We'll revisit the SQL CLR usage question at various points in this chapter.

Deployment

Before you can test your SQL CLR code, you must deploy the assembly containing it and register the individual functions that you want recognized as stored procedures. A number of deployment methods are at your disposal; we will pause to cover them now, before discussing testing of your stored procedures and the other four basic SQL CLR entities.

Deploying Your Assembly

As mentioned earlier, Visual Studio deploys the SQL Server project version of the sample code when you build, start, or step through the project, or you can use the Build, Deploy option you'll find on Visual Studio's main menu. If you're working with the SQL Server project version of the samples, go ahead and use the Deploy option or one of the Start or Build options in Visual Studio now.

For deploying the Class Library project version, assuming C:\Projects\Chapter03 as this chapter's sample code parent directory, you can execute the following T-SQL statement from within Management Studio:

```
CREATE ASSEMBLY Chapter03
 AUTHORIZATION dbo
 FROM 'C:\Projects\Chapter03\VS\Chapter03Manual\Chapter03\bin\Debug\Chapter03.dll'
 WITH PERMISSION_SET = SAFE

GO
```

The *AUTHORIZATION* clause allows you to specify a name or role to which ownership of the assembly is assigned. The default authorization is that of the current user, and because you are most likely logged in as *dbo* for *AdventureWorks2008*, in this case the clause is unnecessary (which is why we omitted it from our previous example).

The meaning and effect of the *WITH PERMISSION_SET* clause are discussed at the end of this chapter. For now, just note that this clause allows you to specify the security permissions with which your assembly runs. Like the *AUTHORIZATION* clause, in this case the *WITH PERMISSION_SET* clause is technically unnecessary because *SAFE* is the default *PERMISSION_SET* value used when a *CREATE ASSEMBLY* command is executed. Regardless, it's a good practice to include both clauses.

If your assembly has dependencies on other assemblies, SQL Server looks to see whether those assemblies have already been loaded into the database and, if so, confirms that their ownership is the same as that of the specified assembly. If the dependent assemblies have not yet been loaded into the database, SQL Server looks for them in the same folder as the specified assembly. If it finds all dependent assemblies in that location, it loads them and assigns them the same ownership as the primary assembly. If it does not find the dependent assemblies in that folder or in the global assembly cache (GAC), the *CREATE ASSEMBLY* command will fail.

You can supply a string expression instead of a literal in the *FROM* clause, allowing for some interesting data-driven possibilities. For example, you could fetch an assembly path reference from a table in your database. It is also possible to supply an assembly directly inline by providing a binary stream in the *FROM* clause instead of a file specification. You do this by specifying a *varbinary* literal value or expression (or a comma-delimited list of *varbinary* values or expressions, when dependent assemblies must be specified) that contains the actual binary content of your assembly (or assemblies). This allows the creation of a database, including any CLR assemblies it contains, to be completely scripted, without requiring distribution of actual assembly files. The binary stream can be embedded in the script itself or, using an expression, it could be fetched from a table in a database.

> **More Info** See SQL Server Books Online for more information about this advanced SQL CLR assembly deployment technique.

In addition to using Visual Studio deployment and the T-SQL *CREATE ASSEMBLY* statement, you can upload the assembly into your database interactively from Management Studio. Simply right-click the *servername*\Databases\AdventureWorks2008\Programmability\ Assemblies node in the Object Explorer window (where *servername* is the name of your server), and then choose New Assembly from the shortcut menu. The New Assembly dialog box, shown in Figure 3-5, appears.

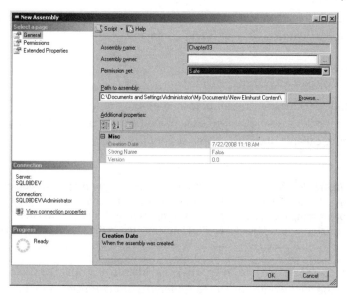

FIGURE 3-5 The Management Studio New Assembly dialog box

Type the assembly path and file name in the Path To Assembly text box, or use the Browse button to specify it interactively. You can specify *AUTHORIZATION* and *WITH PERMISSION_SET* details in the Assembly Owner text box (using the ellipsis button, if necessary) and the Permission Set combo box, respectively.

Regardless of the deployment method you use, once your assembly has been added to your database, it becomes an integral part of that database and its underlying .mdf file. This means that if your database is backed up and restored, or deployed, any assemblies within it move along with the data itself and need not be manually added as a subsequent step.

Deploying Your Stored Procedures

In the SQL Server project version of the sample code, deployment of all the stored procedures is handled by Visual Studio when the assembly itself is deployed. This is due to the application of the *SqlProcedure* attribute to the methods in the *StoredProcedures* class (found in the spTest.cs file). The *SqlProcedure* attribute accepts an optional *Name* parameter, the value of which is the actual callable stored procedure name. If you do not supply a value for the *Name* parameter, the name of the .NET method is used as the stored procedure name.

The *SqlProcedure* attribute is used only by Visual Studio in SQL Server projects. Therefore, it has been removed from the source code in the Class Library project. Deploying the stored procedures from that version of the source code requires issuing a *CREATE PROCEDURE* T-SQL command using the *EXTERNAL NAME* clause to specify the assembly, the fully qualified class name specifier, and the method name. For example, to load the Class Library version of *spContacts*, you would issue the following command:

```
CREATE PROCEDURE spContacts
 AS EXTERNAL NAME Chapter03.StoredProcedures.spContacts
```

The preceding command specifies that the *spContacts* method, found in the class named *StoredProcedures*, in the loaded assembly with T-SQL name *Chapter03*, should be registered as a CLR stored procedure callable under the name *spContacts*.

> **Note** All necessary *CREATE PROCEDURE* commands for the Class Library project version of the sample code are contained in the CreateObjects.sql script in the Management Studio project supplied with the chapter's sample code on the book's companion Web site. You will need to run that script in order to use the various SQL CLR entities implemented in the Class Library project.

Note that if the CLR stored procedure had been written in Microsoft Visual Basic .NET rather than C#, the class name specifier would change to *Chapter03.StoredProcedures*. This would necessitate a change to the deployment T-SQL code as follows:

```
CREATE PROCEDURE spContacts
 AS EXTERNAL NAME Chapter03.[Chapter03.StoredProcedures].spContacts
```

In Visual Basic projects, the default namespace for a project itself defaults to the project name, as does the assembly name. The class within the project must be referenced using the default namespace as a prefix. Because the class specifier is a multipart dot-separated name, it must be enclosed within square brackets so that SQL Server can identify it as a single indivisible name. Because C# projects handle the default namespace setting a little differently, the namespace prefix is not used in the class specifier for C# assemblies.

One last point before we discuss how to test your now-deployed CLR stored procedures. It is important to realize that the class specifier and method name in the *EXTERNAL NAME* clause are *case sensitive* and that this is true *even for assemblies developed in Visual Basic .NET*. Although this point might seem perplexing at first, it does make sense. SQL Server searches for your methods within your assemblies, not within your source code. In other words, it's looking within Microsoft Intermediate Language (MSIL) code, not Visual Basic .NET or C# source code. Because MSIL is case sensitive (it has to be, to support case-sensitive languages like C#), SQL Server must be as well as it searches within an assembly for a specific class and method.

The fact that SQL Server is not case sensitive by default (even though it once was) and that Visual Basic .NET is not a case-sensitive language is of no import! If you attempt to register a method and you receive an error that it cannot be found within the assembly, double-check that the case usage in your command matches that of your source code.

Testing Your Stored Procedures

With your assembly and stored procedures now deployed, you're ready to run and test them. Typically, you should do this from Management Studio; however, Visual Studio SQL Server projects allow you to test your SQL CLR code from inside Visual Studio itself. When you create a Visual Studio SQL Server project, a folder named Test Scripts is created as a subdirectory in your source code directory. Within that subdirectory, Visual Studio creates a script file named Test.sql. If you look at that file, you'll see a number of commented T-SQL code examples for testing CLR stored procedures, user-defined functions (UDFs), UDTs, and aggregates. It also contains an uncommented *SELECT* command that echoes a text literal to the caller explaining that the test script must be edited.

Visual Studio connects to your database and runs this script immediately after your assembly is deployed, and the output from the script appears in Visual Studio's Output window. This allows you to execute any number of T-SQL commands directly from Visual Studio without having to switch to another tool. Although this approach is much less interactive than a Management Studio query window, it allows you to run quick tests against your code. It is especially useful for regression testing—that is, confirming that a new version of your assembly does not break older, critical functionality.

The file name extension of the script must be .sql, but otherwise the name of the file is inconsequential. You can have multiple script files in the Test Scripts folder. To add a new one, right-click the Test Scripts folder node or the project node in the Solution Explorer window, and then choose the Add Test Script option from the shortcut menu. Only one script can be active at one time, and as soon as you have more than one script, you must specify which one is active. To make a script active, simply right-click its node in the Solution Explorer window and then choose the Set As Default Debug Script option from its shortcut menu. When you do so, the node is displayed in bold. You can run or debug a script even if it is not the active script. To do so, right-click its node in the Solution Explorer window, and then choose the Debug Script option from its shortcut menu.

If you're working with the Class Library version of the sample code, you must test the stored procedures from Management Studio or another SQL Server query tool. And even if you are working with the SQL Server project version, you'll find that testing your SQL CLR code in Management Studio provides a richer experience and more flexibility.

 Note If you are using Visual Studio Team Edition for Database Professionals or Visual Studio Team Suite, you could add a Team System Database project to your solution and create SQL scripts from there that would work against even a Class Library project's SQL CLR code.

The TestStoredProcs.sql script file in the Management Studio project supplied with the sample code will run both of our CLR stored procedures (*spContactCount* and *spContacts*). Open the file in Management Studio, and then click the Execute button on the SQL Editor toolbar, choose Execute from the Query menu, press F5, or press Ctrl+E. (You can also right-click anywhere inside the query window and select Execute from the shortcut menu.)

When the script runs, you should see the single-valued result of the *spContactCount* stored procedure appear first, as shown in Figure 3-6. Notice that the column name *ContactCount* appears on the Results tab, and recall that this is a direct result of your using the *SqlMetaData* object in the CLR code. Below the *spContactCount* result, you will see the results from the *spContacts* stored procedure come in. Because the *Person.Person* table has almost 20,000 rows, these results might take some time to retrieve.

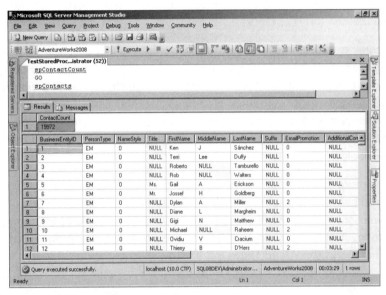

FIGURE 3-6 TestStoredProcs.sql script code and results

Even while the results are coming in, the "Starting data dump" status message should be visible on the Messages tab (or on the Results tab if you're using Management Studio's Results To Text option). After all the rows have been fetched, you should see the "Data dump complete" message appear as well. If you get impatient and want to abort the query before all rows have been fetched, you can use the Cancel Executing Query button on the SQL Editor toolbar or the Query, Cancel Executing Query option on the main menu; you can also use the Alt+Break keyboard shortcut.

We have yet to cover CLR functions, triggers, aggregates, and UDTs, but you have already learned most of the skills you need to develop SQL CLR code. You have learned how to create Visual Studio SQL Server projects and use its autodeployment and test script features. You have also learned how to develop SQL CLR code in standard Class Library projects and to use T-SQL commands and Management Studio to deploy the code for you. You've learned about the subtle differences between deploying C# code and Visual Basic .NET code, and we've covered the case-sensitive requirements of T-SQL–based deployment.

With all this under your belt, we can cover the remaining four basic SQL CLR entities relatively quickly.

CLR Functions

Let's take everything we've discussed about SQL CLR stored procedures and deployment and apply it to SQL CLR functions. As any programmer knows, a *function* is a procedure that returns a value (or an object). Mainstream .NET functions typically return .NET types. SQL CLR functions, on the other hand, must return a *SqlType*. So to start with, we need to make sure that our classes that implement SQL CLR functions import the *System.Data.SqlTypes* namespace with a *using* statement. The SQL Server Project template for User-Defined Functions contains the appropriate *using* statement by default; you will need to add the statement manually to standard Class Library class code.

Once the namespace is imported, you can write the functions themselves. In Visual Studio SQL Server Projects, they should be decorated with the *SqlFunction* attribute; this attribute accepts an optional name parameter that works identically to its *SqlProcedure* counterpart. In our sample code, we will not supply a value for this parameter. *SqlFunction* is used by Visual Studio SQL Server projects for deployment of your SQL CLR functions, but for scalar-valued functions in Class Library projects, the *SqlFunction* attribute is optional, so it appears in the Class Library sample code only for our table-valued function (TVF; described later in this section).

Listing 3-3, which shows the code for function *fnHelloWorld* from fnTest.cs in the sample code, implements a simple "Hello World" function that returns a value of type *SqlString*.

LISTING 3-3 *fnHelloWorld* from fnTest.cs

```
[SqlFunction()]
public static SqlString fnHelloWorld()
{
    return new SqlString("Hello World");
}
```

Notice that *SqlType* objects (such as *SqlString*) require explicit instantiation and constructor value passing; you cannot simply declare and assign values to them. The code in Listing 3-3 instantiates a *SqlString* object inline within the *return* statement to avoid variable declaration.

A function that accepts no parameters and returns a hard-coded value is of little practical use. Typically, functions are passed values and perform calculations with those values, and they are often used from within T-SQL statements, in effect as extensions to the functions built into the T-SQL language itself. Listing 3-4, which shows the code for function *fnToCelsius* in fnTest.cs in the sample project, implements a Fahrenheit-to-Celsius conversion function.

LISTING 3-4 *fnToCelsius* from fnTest.cs

```
[SqlFunction()]
public static SqlDecimal fnToCelsius(SqlInt16 fahrenheit)
{
    return new SqlDecimal(((((Int16)fahrenheit) - 32) / 1.8);
}
```

The function accepts a Fahrenheit temperature (as a *SqlInt16*), converts it to Celsius, and re-turns it (as a *SqlDecimal*). Notice that the code casts the input parameter from a *SqlInt16* to a .NET *Int16*, applies a Fahrenheit-to-Celsius conversion formula, and then passes the result to the constructor of a new *SqlDecimal* object.

Deployment of these functions is automatic in the Visual Studio SQL Server project version of our sample code. For the Class Library version, use the T-SQL *CREATE FUNCTION* statement in a similar fashion to our use of the *CREATE PROCEDURE* statement in the preceding section, but include a data type specification for the return value. For example, to deploy the *fnHelloWorld* function, you would use this statement:

```
CREATE FUNCTION fnHelloWorld()
 RETURNS nvarchar(4000) WITH EXECUTE AS CALLER
 AS EXTERNAL NAME Chapter03.UserDefinedFunctions.fnHelloWorld
```

Notice the use of data type *nvarchar(4000)* to correspond with the *SqlString* type used in the function's implementation. The *WITH EXECUTE AS CALLER* clause specifies that the SQL CLR function should execute under the caller's identity.

> **Tip** You can enter the *CREATE FUNCTION* command yourself, but note that all such necessary commands for the sample code SQL CLR functions are available in the CreateObjects.sql script file in the Management Studio project supplied with this chapter's sample code on the book's companion Web site.

You can test these functions using the Visual Studio SQL Server project test script or in Management Studio. Use the following query in your test script or a Management Studio query window to test the two functions. (You can also run the TestScalarFunctions.sql script file in the Management Studio sample project.)

```
SELECT
  dbo.fnHelloWorld() AS HelloWorld,
  dbo.fnToCelsius(212) AS CelsiusTemp
```

T-SQL functions can return result sets as well as scalar values. Functions which return result sets are called *table-valued functions* (TVFs). Writing SQL CLR TVFs is possible, although you do so differently than you would SQL CLR scalar-valued functions or SQL CLR stored proce-dures. SQL CLR TVFs must return a type that implements the .NET interface *IEnumerable*, and they must also provide a "fill row" method that interprets that type and converts an instance of the type to a table row.

Listing 3-5, which shows the code for functions *fnPortfolioTable* and *FillTickerRow* in fnTest.cs in the sample project, implements a TVF named *fnPortfolioTable*.

LISTING 3-5 *fnPortfolioTable* and *FillTickerRow* from fnTest.cs

```
[SqlFunction(
    FillRowMethodName="FillTickerRow",
    TableDefinition="TickerSymbol nvarchar(5), Value decimal")]
public static System.Collections.IEnumerable fnPortfolioTable(SqlString tickersPacked)
{
    string[] tickerSymbols;
    object[] rowArray = new object[2];
    object[] compoundArray = new object[3];
    char[] parms = new char[1];

    parms[0] = ';';
    tickerSymbols = tickersPacked.Value.Split(parms);

    rowArray[0] = tickerSymbols[0];
    rowArray[1] = 1;
    compoundArray[0] = rowArray;

    rowArray = new object[2];
    rowArray[0] = tickerSymbols[1];
    rowArray[1] = 2;
    compoundArray[1] = rowArray;

    rowArray = new object[2];
    rowArray[0] = tickerSymbols[2];
    rowArray[1] = 3;
    compoundArray[2] = rowArray;

    return compoundArray;
}
public static void FillTickerRow(object row, ref SqlString tickerSymbol,
ref SqlDecimal value)
{
    object[] rowArray = (object[])row;
    tickerSymbol = new SqlString((string)rowArray[0]);
    value = new SqlDecimal(decimal.Parse(rowArray[1].ToString()));
}
```

Rather than implementing its own *IEnumerable*-compatible type, *fnPortfolioTable* uses an array. This is perfectly legal because arrays in .NET implement *IEnumerable*. The *fnPortfolioTable* function accepts a semicolon-delimited list of stock ticker symbols and returns a table with each ticker symbol appearing in a separate row as column *TickerSymbol* and a value for the ticker as column *Value*. The structure of the returned table is declared in the *TableDefinition* parameter of the *SqlFunction* attribute in SQL Server projects and in the *CREATE FUNCTION* T-SQL command for Class Library projects. The assigned values are hard-coded, and only three rows are returned, regardless of how many ticker symbols are passed in. As with our other samples, this one is more useful as a teaching tool than as a practical application of TVFs.

Arrays are the name of the game here. First the *Split* method is used to crack the delimited ticker list into an array of single ticker strings. Then the TVF structures the data so that each element in the return value array (*compoundArray*) is itself a two-element array storing a single ticker symbol and its value. The function code itself needs only to return *compoundArray*. Next the *FillTickerRow* function (named in the *FillRowMethodName* parameter of the *SqlFunction* attribute) takes each two-element array (passed in as the first parameter) and converts its members to individual scalars. These scalars are then returned via *ref* parameters that start in the second parameter position; the parameter names are not significant, but their positions must correspond to those of the columns in the *TableDefinition* argument of the *SqlFunction* attribute.

Because the *FillRowMethodName* parameter of the *SqlFunction* attribute is required by SQL Server, we have decorated the Class Library version of the *fnPortfolioTable* function with that attribute, supplying a value for that one parameter. In the SQL Server project version, we also supply a value for the *TableDefinition* parameter to enable autodeployment of the TVF.

As with the other functions, deployment of this function is performed by Visual Studio in the SQL Server project sample code. For the Class Library version, you can deploy the function using the following T-SQL command (also contained in the CreateObjects.sql script file):

```
CREATE FUNCTION fnPortfolioTable(@TickersPacked nvarchar(4000))
 RETURNS table (
  TickerSymbol nvarchar(5),
  Value decimal
 )
 WITH EXECUTE AS CALLER
 AS EXTERNAL NAME Chapter03.UserDefinedFunctions.fnPortfolioTable
```

As with *fnHelloWorld*, we have mapped the *SqlString* data type to an *nvarchar(4000)*, this time for one of the input parameters. Because *fnPortfolioTable* is a TVF, its return type is declared as *table*, with inline specifications for the table's definition.

Use the following query in your Visual Studio test script or a Management Studio query window to test the TVF (or run the TestTableValuedFunction.sql script file in the Management Studio sample project):

```
SELECT * FROM fnPortfolioTable('IBM;MSFT;SUNW')
 ORDER BY TickerSymbol
```

The following data should be returned:

```
TickerSymbol Value
------------ ------
IBM          1
MSFT         2
SUNW         3
```

Note that as of SQL Server 2008, it is possible to provide a "hint" to the database that your TVF returns data in a particular order. This can optimize queries or creation of indexes ordered on the same expression. To take advantage of this, you must first ensure that logic in your CLR TVF code returns data in a specific order and, second, ensure that you specify that order in an *ORDER* clause in the *CREATE FUNCTION* T-SQL command. For example, imagine that our SQL CLR TVF code ordered its results by the *TickerSymbol* column. In that case, we could modify the T-SQL code that creates the function as follows:

```
CREATE FUNCTION fnPortfolioTable(@TickersPacked nvarchar(4000))
 RETURNS table (
  TickerSymbol nvarchar(5),
  Value decimal
 )
 WITH EXECUTE AS CALLER
 ORDER (TickerSymbol)
 AS EXTERNAL NAME Chapter03.UserDefinedFunctions.fnPortfolioTable
```

Although our code does not *actually* return data in *TickerSymbol* order, you can still use the preceding T-SQL command for the Class Library version of the TVF. If you reexecute the query in the TestTableValuedFunction.sql script file, everything will work correctly, because the input data is coincidentally supplied in *TickerSymbol* order (*'IBM;MSFT;SUNW'*). If, however, you modify the input string to, for example, *'IBM;SUNW;MSFT'*, you will receive the following error:

```
The order of the data in the stream does not conform to the ORDER hint specified for the CLR
TVF 'fnPortfolioTable'. The order of the data must match the order specified in the ORDER
hint for a CLR TVF. Update the ORDER hint to reflect the order in which the input data is
ordered, or update the CLR TVF to match the order specified by the ORDER hint.
```

We point out this error text because it is really the only outward proof (other than analysis of query execution plans) that this new ordered SQL CLR TVF feature is in fact supported, and we assume that you would prefer not take this information on mere faith. Please note that this feature can be taken advantage of, practically speaking, only when registering a SQL CLR TVF using one's own T-SQL code. That is because there is no parameter in the *SqlFunction* attribute for specifying an *ORDER* clause, so Visual Studio automated deployment cannot emit that clause. This means that you must use the *ORDER* clause only with a class library project or else omit the *SqlFunction* attribute from your SQL CLR TVF code in a SQL Server project and register the TVF "manually," either from an external script or by using special predeployment and postdeployment scripts in Visual Studio. These special scripts are discussed in the next section.

CLR Triggers

T-SQL triggers are really just stored procedures that are called by SQL Server at specific times and that can query values in the *DELETED* and *INSERTED* pseudo-tables (which expose "before and after" snapshots of data changed by the statement that fired the trigger). SQL CLR triggers are similar to SQL CLR stored procedures, and they too can be created for all data manipulation language (DML) actions (updates, inserts, and deletes).

SQL Server 2005 introduced the concept of data definition language (DDL) triggers, which can intercept and handle actions such as *CREATE TABLE* and *ALTER PROCEDURE*. (DDL triggers are covered in Chapter 2.) Like DML triggers, DDL triggers can be implemented in T-SQL or SQL CLR code. We will cover both SQL CLR DML and DDL triggers in this section.

SQL CLR DML triggers, like their T-SQL counterparts, have access to the *DELETED* and *INSERTED* pseudo-tables and must be declared as handling one or more specific events for a specific table or, under certain circumstances, a specific view. Also, they can make use of the *SqlTriggerContext* object (through the *SqlContext* object's *TriggerContext* property) to determine which particular event (update, insert, or delete) caused them to fire and which columns were updated.

Once you understand these concepts, writing SQL CLR DML triggers is really quite simple. Listing 3-6, which shows the code for the *trgUpdatePerson* function from trgTest.cs in the sample project, shows the SQL CLR code for the *trgUpdatePerson* DML trigger, which is designed to function as a *FOR UPDATE* trigger on the *Person.Person* table in the *AdventureWorks2008* database.

LISTING 3-6 *trgUpdatePerson* from trgTest.cs

```
//[SqlTrigger(Target="Person.Person", Event="for UPDATE")]
public static void trgUpdatePerson()
{
    SqlTriggerContext context = SqlContext.TriggerContext;
    string oldName = string.Empty;
    string newName = string.Empty;
    SqlConnection conn = new SqlConnection("context connection=true");
    SqlCommand cmOld = new SqlCommand(
                    "SELECT FirstName FROM DELETED", conn);
    SqlCommand cmNew = new SqlCommand(
                    "SELECT FirstName FROM INSERTED", conn);
    conn.Open();
    SqlDataReader drOld = cmOld.ExecuteReader();
    if (drOld.Read())
    {
        oldName = (string)drOld[0];
    }
    drOld.Close();
    SqlDataReader drNew = cmNew.ExecuteReader();
    if (drNew.Read())
```

```
    {
        newName = (string)drNew[0];
    }
    drNew.Close();
    conn.Close();
    SqlContext.Pipe.Send("Old Value of FirstName:" + oldName);
    SqlContext.Pipe.Send("New Value of FirstName:" + newName);
    for (int i = 0; i <= context.ColumnCount - 1; i++)
    {
        SqlContext.Pipe.Send("Column " + i.ToString() + ": " +
            context.IsUpdatedColumn(i).ToString());
    }
}
```

This CLR DML trigger queries the *DELETED* and *INSERTED* pseudo-tables and echoes back the "before and after" values (respectively) for the *FirstName* column when a row is updated. It does so not by piping back *SqlDataReader* objects but by fetching values from the pseudo-tables and echoing back the values as text using the *SqlPipe* object's *Send* method. The trigger code also uses the *TriggerContext.IsUpdatedColumn* method to return a list of all columns in the *Person.Person* table and whether each was updated.

To deploy the trigger automatically, you would normally configure a *SqlTrigger* attribute and apply it to the .NET function that implements the trigger. Because DML triggers are applied to a target object (a table or a view) and an event (for example, "for UPDATE" or "instead of INSERT"), the *SqlTrigger* attribute has parameters for each of these pieces of information and you must supply values for both. The *SqlTrigger* attribute deploys only a single copy of the trigger, but you can use T-SQL to deploy the same code as a separate trigger for a different event and table. Each separate deployment of the same code must be assigned a unique trigger name.

Unfortunately, a bug in Visual Studio prevents the *SqlTrigger* attribute from being used for target objects not in the *dbo* schema. (For example, our table, *Person.Person*, is in the *Person* schema rather than the *dbo* schema.) This is because the value for the *Target* parameter is surrounded by square brackets when Visual Studio generates its T-SQL code (generating, for example, *[Person.Person]*, which will cause an error). It is for this reason that the *SqlTrigger* attribute code is commented out in Listing 3-6. A workaround to this problem is available through the use of predeployment and postdeployment scripts, which we will discuss shortly.

> **Important** Although you might be tempted to work around the Visual Studio schema bug by supplying a *Target* value of *Person].[Person* instead of *Person.Person*, this will also fail to work. You can initiate a trace in SQL Server Profiler to observe the erroneous T-SQL generated by Visual Studio in either scenario.

Although Listing 3-6 does not demonstrate it, you can create a single piece of code that functions as both the update and the insert trigger for a given table. You can then use the *TriggerContext* object's *TriggerAction* property to determine exactly what event caused the trigger to fire, and you can execute slightly different code accordingly. Should you want to deploy such a CLR trigger using the *SqlTrigger* attribute, you would set its *Event* parameter to *FOR UPDATE, INSERT*.

The T-SQL command to register a .NET function as a SQL CLR trigger (for the update event only) is as follows:

```
CREATE TRIGGER trgUpdatePerson
 ON Person.Person
 FOR UPDATE
 AS EXTERNAL NAME Chapter03.Triggers.trgUpdatePerson
```

Note All necessary *CREATE TRIGGER* commands for the Class Library project version of the sample code are contained in the CreateObjects.sql script in the Management Studio project supplied with the chapter's sample code available on the book's companion Web site.

Beyond using such T-SQL code in Management Studio, there is a way to execute this T-SQL command from Visual Studio and thus work around the *SqlTrigger* non-*dbo* schema bug. An essentially undocumented feature of Visual Studio SQL Server projects is that they allow you to create two special T-SQL scripts that will run immediately before and immediately after the deployment of your assembly. To use this feature, simply create two scripts, named PreDeployScript.sql and PostDeployScript.sql, in the root folder (not the Test Scripts folder) of your project. Although not case sensitive, the file names themselves must match verbatim.

Tip You can create the PreDeployScript.sql and PostDeployScript.sql scripts outside Visual Studio and then add them to your project using the Visual Studio Add Existing Item feature. You can also add them directly by right-clicking the project node or Test Scripts folder node in Solution Explorer, choosing the Add Test Script option from the shortcut menu, renaming the new scripts, and then dragging them out of the Test Scripts folder into the root folder of your project.

To use this feature to work around the *SqlTrigger* non-*dbo* schema bug, insert the preceding *CREATE TRIGGER* code in your PostDeployScript.sql file, and then insert the following T-SQL code into your PreDeployScript.sql file:

```
IF EXISTS (SELECT * FROM sys.triggers WHERE object_id = OBJECT_ID(N'[Person].
[trgUpdatePerson]'))
 DROP TRIGGER Person.trgUpdatePerson
```

Regardless of deployment technique, you can use the following query in your Visual Studio test script or a Management Studio query window to test the trigger. (This T-SQL code can be found in the TestTriggers.sql script file in the Management Studio project.)

```
UPDATE Person.Person
 SET    FirstName = 'Gustavo'
 WHERE  BusinessEntityId = 1
```

If you place the *TriggerContext* object's *TriggerAction* property in a comparison statement, Microsoft IntelliSense will show you that there is a wide array of enumerated constants that the property can be equal to, and that a majority of these values correspond to DDL triggers. This demonstrates clearly that SQL CLR code can be used for DDL and DML triggers alike.

In the case of DDL triggers, a wide array of environmental information might be desirable to determine exactly what event caused the trigger to fire, what system process ID (SPID) invoked it, what time the event fired, and other information specific to the event type such as the T-SQL command that caused the event. The *SqlTriggerContext* object's *EventData* property can be queried to fetch this information. The *EventData* property is of type *SqlXml*; therefore it, in turn, has a *CreateReader* method and a *Value* property that you can use to fetch the XML-formatted event data as an *XmlReader* object or a string, respectively.

The code in Listing 3-7, taken from function *trgCreateTable* in trgTest.cs in the sample project, shows the SQL CLR code for the DDL trigger *trgCreateTable* registered to fire for any *CREATE TABLE* statement executed on the *AdventureWorks2008* database.

LISTING 3-7 *trgCreateTable* from trgTest.cs

```
[SqlTrigger(Target = "DATABASE", Event = "FOR CREATE_TABLE")]
public static void trgCreateTable()
{
  SqlTriggerContext context = SqlContext.TriggerContext;
  if (!(context.EventData == null))
  {
    SqlContext.Pipe.Send("Event Data: " + context.EventData.Value.ToString());
  }
}
```

The code interrogates the *Value* property of *SqlContext.TriggerContext.EventData*, converts it to a string, and pipes that string back to the client. Note that the *SqlTrigger* attribute is not commented out in this case because a schema prefix is not used in the *Target* parameter value. Thus, you can use attribute-based deployment in the SQL Server project or the following command for the Class Library version:

```
CREATE TRIGGER trgCreateTable
 ON DATABASE
 FOR CREATE_TABLE
 AS EXTERNAL NAME Chapter03.Triggers.trgCreateTable
```

Use the following T-SQL DDL command in your Visual Studio test script or a Management Studio query window to test the DDL trigger. (You can find this code in the TestTriggers.sql script file in the sample Management Studio project.)

```
CREATE TABLE Test (low int, high int)
DROP TABLE Test
```

Your result should appear similar to the following:

```
<EVENT_INSTANCE>
  <EventType>CREATE_TABLE</EventType>
  <PostTime>2008-07-21T11:12:35.720</PostTime>
  <SPID>58</SPID>
  <ServerName>SQL08DEV</ServerName>
  <LoginName>SQL08DEV\AndrewB</LoginName>
  <UserName>dbo</UserName>
  <DatabaseName>AdventureWorks2008</DatabaseName>
  <SchemaName>dbo</SchemaName>
  <ObjectName>Test</ObjectName>
  <ObjectType>TABLE</ObjectType>
  <TSQLCommand>
    <SetOptions ANSI_NULLS="ON" ANSI_NULL_DEFAULT="ON" ANSI_PADDING="ON"
      QUOTED_IDENTIFIER="ON" ENCRYPTED="FALSE" />
    <CommandText>CREATE TABLE Test (low int, high int)</CommandText>
  </TSQLCommand>
</EVENT_INSTANCE>
```

> **Note** The actual output would consist of continuous, unformatted text. Line breaks and indentation have been added here to make the *EventData* XML easier to read.

CLR Aggregates

T-SQL has a number of built-in aggregates, such as *SUM*, *AVG*, and *MAX*, but that set of built-in functions is not always sufficient. Luckily, the SQL CLR features in SQL Server 2008 allow us to implement user-defined aggregates in .NET code and use them from T-SQL. User-defined aggregates can be implemented only in SQL CLR code; they have no T-SQL equivalent. Because aggregates tend to perform computation only, they provide an excellent use case for SQL CLR code. As it turns out, they are also quite easy to build.

At first, aggregates look and feel like functions because they accept and return values. In fact, if you use an aggregate in a non-data-querying T-SQL call (for example, *SELECT SUM(8)*), you are actually treating the aggregate as if it were a function. The thing to remember is that the argument passed to an aggregate is typically a column, so each discrete value for that column—for whichever *WHERE, HAVING, ORDER BY,* and/or *GROUP BY* scope applies—gets passed in to the aggregate. It is the aggregate's job to update a variable, which eventually will be the return value, as each discrete value is passed to it.

CLR aggregates require you to apply the *SqlUserDefinedAggregate* attribute to them. The *SqlUserDefinedAggregate* attribute accepts a number of parameters, but all of them are optional except *Format*. In our example, we will use the value *Format.Native* for the *Format* parameter. For more advanced scenarios, you might want to study SQL Server Books Online to acquaint yourself with the other parameters this attribute accepts. Sticking with *Format.Native* for the *Format* parameter is sufficient for many scenarios.

> **Note** User-defined aggregates greater than 8,000 bytes in size are now supported in SQL Server 2008. However, they require use of the *Format.UserDefined* value for the *Format* parameter, rather than the *Format.Native* value used in our example.

Unlike the *SqlProcedure*, *SqlFunction*, and *SqlTrigger* attributes, the *SqlUserDefinedAggregate* attribute is required by SQL Server for your class to be eligible for use as an aggregate. Visual Studio SQL Server projects do use this attribute for deployment, and the attribute is included in the aggregate template, but it also must be used in generic Class Library project code for T-SQL registration of the aggregate to succeed.

Aggregate classes must have four methods: *Init*, *Accumulate*, *Merge*, and *Terminate*. The *Init* method is used to start a new aggregate computation. The *Accumulate* method accepts a SQL type for processing. The *Terminate* method returns a SQL type representing the result. And last, the *Merge* method accepts an object typed as the aggregate class itself so that it can be combined with the executing instance.

The *Accumulate* method handles the processing of a discrete value into the aggregate value, and the *Terminate* method returns the final aggregated value after all discrete values have been processed. The *Init* method provides startup code, typically initializing a class-level private variable that will be used by the *Accumulate* method. The *Merge* method is called in a specific multithreading scenario, which we will describe later in this section.

Just to be perfectly clear, your aggregate class will not implement an interface to supply these methods; you must create them to meet what we might term the "conventions" that are expected of SQL CLR aggregate classes (as opposed to a "contract" with which they must comply). When you develop your code in a Visual Studio 2008 SQL Server project, the Aggregate template includes stubs for these four methods as well as the proper application of the *SqlUserDefinedAggregate* attribute.

Creating your own aggregates is fairly straightforward, but thinking through aggregation logic can be a bit confusing at first. Imagine that you want to create a special aggregate named *BakersDozen* that increments its accumulated value by 1 for every discrete value's multiple of 12 (much as a baker, in simpler times, would throw in a free 13th donut when you ordered 12). By using what you now know about CLR aggregates and combining that with integer division, you can implement a *BakersDozen* aggregate quite easily. Listing 3-8, the

code from struct *BakersDozen* in aggTest.cs in the sample project, contains the entire implementation of the aggregate *BakersDozen*.

LISTING 3-8 *BakersDozen* struct from aggTest.cs

```
[Serializable]
[Microsoft.SqlServer.Server.SqlUserDefinedAggregate(Format.Native)]
public struct BakersDozen
{
    private SqlInt32 DonutCount;

    public void Init()
    {
        DonutCount = 0;
    }

    public void Accumulate(SqlInt32 Value)
    {
        DonutCount += Value + ((Int32)Value) / 12;
    }

    public void Merge(BakersDozen Group)
    {
        DonutCount += Group.DonutCount;
    }

    public SqlInt32 Terminate()
    {
        return DonutCount;
    }
}
```

The code here is fairly straightforward. The private variable *DonutCount* is used to track the
BakersDozen-adjusted sum of items ordered, adding the actual items ordered value and incrementing the running total by the integer quotient of the ordered value divided by 12. By
this logic, bonus items are added only when an individual value equals or exceeds a multiple
of 12. Twelve includes a full dozen, and so would 13. Twenty-four includes two dozen, and so
would 27. Two individual orders of 6 items each would not generate any bonus items because
a minimum of 12 items must be contained in a discrete value to qualify for a bonus.

To deploy the aggregate, use attribute-based deployment in the SQL Server project or the
following command for the Class Library version:

```
CREATE AGGREGATE BakersDozen (@input int)
 RETURNS int
 EXTERNAL NAME Chapter03.BakersDozen
```

Notice that no method name is specified because the aggregate is implemented by an entire class rather than an individual function. Notice also that the return value data type must be declared as the data type of the values this aggregate function will process. The @*input* parameter acts as a placeholder, and its name is inconsequential. Note that aggregates can be built on SQL CLR types (covered in the next section) as well as SQL scalar types.

> **Note** The preceding *CREATE AGGREGATE* statement for the Class Library project version of the sample code is contained in the CreateObjects.sql script in the Management Studio project supplied with the sample code on the book's companion Web site.

To see the aggregate work, first run the CreateTblAggregateTest.sql script file in the Management Studio sample project to create a table named *AggregateTest* with columns *OrderItemId*, *OrderId*, and *ItemsOrdered* and several rows of data, as shown here:

```
CREATE TABLE tblAggregateTest(
    [OrderItemId] [int] IDENTITY(1,1) NOT NULL,
    [OrderId] [int] NULL,
    [ItemsOrdered] [int] NOT NULL
)
GO

INSERT INTO tblAggregateTest VALUES (1,2)
INSERT INTO tblAggregateTest VALUES (1,4)
INSERT INTO tblAggregateTest VALUES (2,1)
INSERT INTO tblAggregateTest VALUES (2,12)
INSERT INTO tblAggregateTest VALUES (3,3)
INSERT INTO tblAggregateTest VALUES (3,2)
```

With such a table built, use the following T-SQL DDL statement in your Visual Studio test script or a Management Studio query window to test the aggregate function:

```
SELECT
  OrderId,
  SUM(ItemsOrdered) AS SUM,
  dbo.BakersDozen(ItemsOrdered) AS BakersDozen
FROM tblAggregateTest
GROUP BY OrderId
```

For each distinct value in the *OrderId* column, this query effectively uses our CLR code under the following algorithm:

1. Call *Init()*.

2. Call *Accumulate* once for each row with the same *OrderId* value, passing it that row's value of the *ItemsOrdered* column.

3. Call *Terminate* to retrieve the aggregated value that the query will return to the client.

The results should be as follows:

```
OrderId      SUM          BakersDozen
-----------  -----------  -----------
1            6            6
2            13           14
3            5            5
```

By including the built-in T-SQL aggregate *SUM* in our query, we can see how many bonus items were added. In this case, for *OrderId 2*, a single bonus item was added, due to one row in the table with the following values:

```
OrderItemId OrderId      ItemsOrdered
----------- -----------  ------------
4           2            12
```

All the other rows contain *ItemsOrdered* values of less than 12, so no bonus items were added for them.

Because SQL Server sometimes segments the work required to satisfy a query over multiple threads, the query processor might need to execute your aggregate function multiple times for a single query and then merge the results together. For your aggregate to work properly in this scenario, you must implement a *Merge* method.

The *Merge* method takes the result of one thread's aggregation and merges it into the current thread's aggregation. The calculation required to do this could be complicated for some aggregates; in our case, we simply added the *DonutCount* value from the secondary thread's aggregate (accessible via the *Group* input parameter) to our own. There is no need to add bonus items because they would have been added in the individual *Accumulate* calls on the secondary thread. Simple addition is all that's required. An aggregate that calculated some type of average, for example, would require more complex *Merge* code.

Don't forget that aggregates can be passed scalar values and can be used from T-SQL without referencing a row set. Your aggregate must accommodate this scenario, even if it seems impractical. In the case of *BakersDozen*, single scalar values are easily handled. To see for yourself, try executing the following table-less T-SQL query:

```
SELECT dbo.BakersDozen(13)
```

You will see that it returns the value *14*.

> **Note** The TestAggregate.sql script file in the Management Studio project contains both aggregate-testing queries.

Note A new feature in SQL Server 2008 provides support for aggregates that accept multiple input parameters. Implementing such aggregate functions involves accepting two or more parameters in the Accumulate method, processing them in your code, and then declaring them in the CREATE AGGREGATE T-SQL statement, if you are not using Visual Studio autodeployment. Aggregates that accept multiple input parameters still must, of course, return a single value.

Aggregates are an excellent use of SQL CLR programming. Because they are passed data values to be processed, they typically perform only computational tasks and no data access of their own. They consist of compiled CLR code, so they perform well, and unlike stored procedures, triggers, and functions, they cannot be implemented at all in T-SQL. That said, you must still make your aggregate code, especially in the *Accumulate* method, as "lean and mean" as possible. Injecting your own code into the query processor's stream of work is an honor, a privilege, and a significant responsibility. Take that responsibility seriously, and make sure that your code is as low-impact as possible.

SQL CLR Types

The last SQL CLR feature for us to explore is user-defined types (UDTs). This feature is perhaps the most interesting, yet also the most controversial. It's interesting because, technically, it allows for storage of objects in the database. It's controversial because it's prone to abuse. SQL CLR types were not implemented to allow developers to create object-oriented databases; they were created to allow multivalue or multibehavior data types to be stored, retrieved, and easily manipulated.

SQL CLR types have certain indexing limitations, and their entire value must be updated when any of their individual property/field values is updated.

More Info More information about SQL CLR UDTs is available in the MSDN article "Using CLR Integration in SQL Server 2005" by Rathakrishnan et al. You can find this article online at *http://msdn.microsoft.com/en-us/library/ms345136.aspx*. Although written for SQL Server 2005, it is nonetheless an excellent source of information that is applicable to SQL Server 2008 as well. When reading it, just be mindful of the small SQL CLR changes from SQL Server 2005 that are cataloged in this chapter.

SQL CLR type methods must be static. You cannot, therefore, call methods from T-SQL as instance methods; instead, you must use a special *TypeName::MethodName()* syntax. You can implement properties as you would in any conventional class and read from them or write to them from T-SQL using a standard *variable.property/column.property* dot-separated syntax.

Listing 3-9, the code from struct *typPoint* in typTest.cs in the sample project, shows the implementation of *typPoint*, a SQL CLR type that can be used to store Cartesian coordinates in the database.

LISTING 3-9 *typPoint* struct from typTest.cs

```
[Serializable]
[SqlUserDefinedType(Format.Native)]
public struct typPoint : INullable
{
    private bool m_Null;
    private double m_x;
    private double m_y;

    public override string ToString()
    {
        if (this.IsNull)
            return "NULL";
        else
            return this.m_x + ":" + this.m_y;
    }

    public bool IsNull
    {
        get
        {
            return m_Null;
        }
    }

    public static typPoint Null
    {
        get
        {
            typPoint pt = new typPoint();
            pt.m_Null = true;
            return pt;
        }
    }

    public static typPoint Parse(SqlString s)
    {
        if (s.IsNull)
            return Null;
        else
        {
            //Parse input string here to separate out points
            typPoint pt = new typPoint();
            char[] parms = new char[1];
            parms[0] = ':';
            string str = (string)s;
            string[] xy = str.Split(parms);
            pt.X = double.Parse(xy[0]);
```

```
            pt.Y = double.Parse(xy[1]);
            return pt;
        }
    }

    public static double Sum(typPoint p )
    {
        return p.X + p.Y;
    }

    public double X
    {
        get { return m_x; }
        set { m_x = value; }
    }

    public double Y
    {
        get { return m_y; }
        set { m_y = value; }
    }

}
```

Through the class's *X* and *Y* properties, you can process coordinates in a single database column or variable. You can assign coordinate values to an instance of the type as a colon-delimited string—for example, *3:4*, by using the *Parse* method (implicitly). You can then read them back in the same format by using the *ToString* method. Once a value has been assigned, you can individually read or modify its *X* or *Y* portion by using the separate *X* and *Y* properties. The class implements the *INullable* interface and its *IsNull* property. The *Sum* method demonstrates how to expose a static member and allow it to access instance properties by accepting an instance of the SQL CLR type of which it is a member.

Notice that the class is a *struct* and that the *Serializable* and *SqlUserDefinedType* attributes have been applied to it. Like the *SqlUserDefinedAggregate* attribute, *SqlUserDefinedType* is required by SQL Server and appears in the Class Library sample code as well as the SQL Server project version. As with the *SqlUserDefinedAggregate*, we simply assign the value *Format. Native* to the *Format* parameter and leave the other parameters unused.

> **Note** Like user-defined aggregates, CLR types greater than 8,000 bytes in size are permitted in SQL Server 2008, but code implementing them must use the *Format.UserDefined* value for the *Format* parameter of their special attribute (*SqlUserDefinedType*). You might want to study SQL Server Books Online for information about using other parameters for this attribute.

Listing 3-10, the code from struct *typBakersDozen* in typTest.cs in the sample project, re-implements the *BakersDozen* logic we used in our aggregate example, this time in a UDT.

LISTING 3-10 *typBakersDozen* struct from typTest.cs

```
[Serializable]
[SqlUserDefinedType(Format.Native)]
public struct typBakersDozen : INullable
{
    private bool m_Null;
    private double m_RealQty;

    public override string ToString()
    {
        return (m_RealQty + (long)m_RealQty / 12).ToString();
    }

    public bool IsNull
    {
        get
        {
            return m_Null;
        }
    }

    public static typBakersDozen Null
    {
        get
        {
            typBakersDozen h = new typBakersDozen();
            h.m_Null = true;
            return h;
        }
    }

    public static typBakersDozen Parse(SqlString s)
    {
        if (s.IsNull)
            return Null;
        else
        {
            typBakersDozen u = new typBakersDozen();
            u.RealQty = double.Parse((string)s);
            return u;
        }
    }

    public static typBakersDozen ParseDouble(SqlDouble d)
    {
        if (d.IsNull)
            return Null;
        else
        {
            typBakersDozen u = new typBakersDozen();
            u.RealQty = (double)d;
            return u;
        }
    }
```

```
    public double RealQty
    {
        get { return m_RealQty; }
        set { m_RealQty = value; }
    }

    public double AdjustedQty
    {
        get
        {
            return (m_RealQty + (long)m_RealQty / 12);
        }
        set
        {
            if (value % 12 == 0)
                m_RealQty = value;
            else
                m_RealQty = value - (long)value / 13;
        }
    }
}
```

The *RealQty* and *AdjustedQty* properties allow the ordered quantity to be assigned a value and the adjusted quantity to be automatically calculated, or vice versa. The real quantity is the default "input" value, the adjusted quantity is the default "output" value of the type, and the *Parse* and *ToString* methods work accordingly. If the *AdjustedQty* property is assigned a value that is an even multiple of 12 (which would be invalid), that value is assigned to the *RealQty* property, forcing the *AdjustedQty* to be set to its passed value plus its integer quotient when divided by 12.

To deploy the UDTs, use attribute-based deployment for the SQL Server project. The script file CreateObjects.sql in the Management Studio project supplied with the sample code contains the T-SQL code necessary to deploy the Class Library versions of the UDTs. Here's the command that deploys *typPoint*:

```
CREATE TYPE typPoint
 EXTERNAL NAME Chapter03.typPoint
```

The script file TestTypPoint.sql in the Management Studio project contains T-SQL code that tests *typPoint*. Run it, and then examine the results for an intimate understanding of how to work with the type. The script file CreateTblPoint.sql creates a table with a column that is typed based on *typPoint*. Run it, and then run the script file TestTblPoint.sql to see how to manipulate tables that use SQL CLR UDTs.

The script file TestTypBakersDozen.sql contains T-SQL code that tests *typBakersDozen*. The *ParseDouble* method demonstrates how to implement a non-*SqlString* parse method.

We named it *ParseDouble* because the *Parse* method itself cannot be overloaded. You must call *ParseDouble* explicitly as follows:

```
DECLARE @t AS dbo.typBakersDozen
SET @t = typBakersDozen::ParseDouble(12)
```

This is equivalent to using the default *Parse* method (implicitly) and assigning the string *12* as follows:

```
DECLARE @t AS dbo.typBakersDozen
SET @t = '12'
```

Notice that *typBakersDozen* essentially stores a value for the real quantity, and its properties are really just functions that accept or express that value in its native form or as an adjusted quantity. There is no backing variable for the *AdjustedQty* property; the *get* block of the *AdjustedQty* property merely applies a formula to the backing variable for *RealQty* and returns the result.

As both of these examples show, you should think of CLR UDTs less as objects stored in the database and more as classes that wrap one or a set of scalar values and provide services and conversion functions for manipulating them. This is why Microsoft itself implemented the *geometry* and *geography* data types as SQL CLR UDTs. These types don't store complex objects, but they do manage entities that cannot be thought of as simple, single values.

More specifically, you should not think of SQL CLR UDTs as object-relational entities. While it might seem counterintuitive, consider the use of (de)serialization and the *xml* data type as more appropriate vehicles for storing serialized .NET objects in the database.

We have now investigated all five SQL CLR entities. Before we finish up, we need to discuss assembly security and ongoing maintenance of SQL CLR objects in your databases.

Security

Depending on the deployment method, you have numerous ways to specify which security level to grant a CLR assembly. All of them demand that you specify one of three permission sets:

- *Safe*   Assembly can perform local data access and computational tasks only.
- *External_Access*   Assembly can perform local data access and computational tasks and also access the network, the file system, the registry, and environment variables. Although *External_Access* is less restrictive than *Safe*, it still safeguards server stability.

■ *Unsafe*   Assembly has unrestricted permissions and can even call unmanaged code. This setting can significantly compromise SQL Server security; only members of the *sysadmin* role can create (load) unsafe assemblies. Also note that the *TRUSTWORTHY* property must be set to *ON* for the database in which the unsafe assembly will be loaded and the *dbo* must have *UNSAFE ASSEMBLY* permission (or the assembly must be specially signed). There is commented code at the top of the CreateObjects.sql script that sets the *TRUSTWORTHY* property to *ON* for the *AdventureWorks2008* database.

When you deploy an assembly from Visual Studio, its security level is set to *Safe* by default. To change it, you can select the project node in the Solution Explorer window and set the Permission Level property in the Properties window by selecting Safe, External, or Unsafe from the combo box provided, as shown in Figure 3-7.

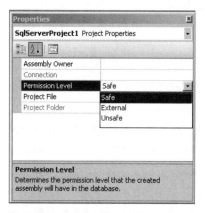

FIGURE 3-7 The Permission Level property and its options in the Visual Studio 2008 Properties window

Alternatively, you can right-click the project node in the Solution Explorer window and then select Properties from the shortcut menu. You can also double-click the Properties node (or the My Project node in Visual Basic projects). Either action opens the project proper- ties designer. Select the designer's Database tab, and then select a permission set from the *Permission Level* combo box, as shown in Figure 3-8. (The same three options are available here as in the Properties window.)

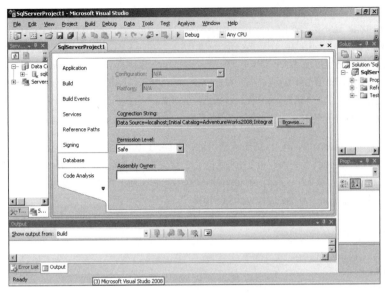

FIGURE 3-8 The Database tab of the Visual Studio project properties designer

To specify an assembly's permission set using T-SQL, simply specify *SAFE, EXTERNAL_ACCESS*, or *UNSAFE* within the *"WITH PERMISSION_SET"* clause of the *CREATE ASSEMBLY* statement, covered earlier in this chapter. Recall that our example used the default *SAFE* setting in this clause.

Last, in the Management Studio New Assembly dialog box (shown earlier in Figure 3-5) and the Assembly Properties dialog box, you can select Safe, External Access, or Unrestricted from the Permission Set combo box. The last of these three options is equivalent to selecting the Unsafe permission set in Visual Studio or T-SQL.

Examining and Managing SQL CLR Types in a Database

Once deployed, your SQL CLR stored procedures, functions, triggers, aggregates, and UDTs and their dependencies might become difficult to keep track of in your head. Luckily, you can easily perform discovery on deployed SQL CLR entities using the Management Studio UI. All SQL CLR objects in a database can be found in the Management Studio Object Explorer window. To find them within the Object Explorer window's tree view, first navigate to the *servername*\Databases*databasename* node (where *servername* and *databasename* are the names of your server and database, respectively). Refer to Table 3-1 for the subnodes of this node that contain each SQL CLR entity.

TABLE 3-1 Finding CLR Objects in Object Explorer

To View...	Look In...
Parent node for SQL CLR stored procedures, DDL triggers, functions, aggregates, and UDTs	Programmability (see Figure 3-9).
Assemblies	Programmability\Assemblies (see Figure 3-10).
Stored procedures	Programmability\Stored Procedures (see Figure 3-11).
Functions	Programmability\Functions\Scalar-Valued Functions and Programmability\Functions\Table-Valued Functions (see Figure 3-12).
Aggregates	Programmability\Functions\Aggregate Functions (see Figure 3-12).
DML triggers	Tables*tablename*\Triggers, where *tablename* is the name of the database table, including the schema name, on which the trigger is defined (see Figure 3-13).
DDL triggers	Programmability\Database Triggers (see Figure 3-14). (Also, for server-level triggers, *servername*\Server Objects\Triggers, where *servername* is the name of your server.)
UDTs	Programmability\Types\User-Defined Types (see Figure 3-15).

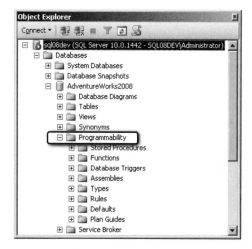

FIGURE 3-9 The SQL Server Management Studio Object Explorer window, with the Programmability node highlighted

FIGURE 3-10 The Object Explorer window, with the Assemblies node highlighted (note the presence of the *Microsoft.SqlServer.Types* assembly, which is Microsoft's SQL CLR assembly for new SQL 2008 data types)

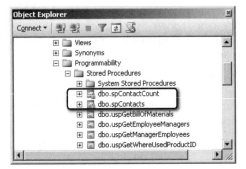

FIGURE 3-11 The Object Explorer window, with SQL CLR stored procedures highlighted

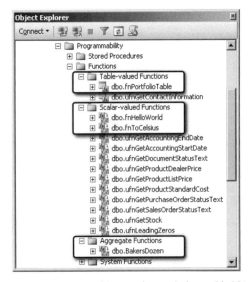

FIGURE 3-12 The Object Explorer window, with SQL CLR table-valued, scalar-valued, and aggregate functions highlighted

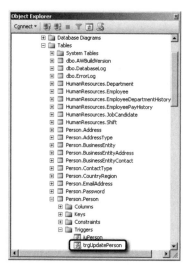

FIGURE 3-13 The Object Explorer window, with SQL CLR DML trigger highlighted

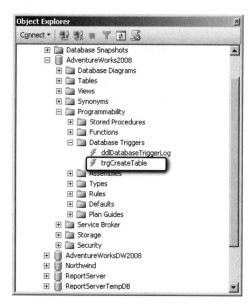

FIGURE 3-14 The Object Explorer window, with SQL CLR DDL trigger highlighted

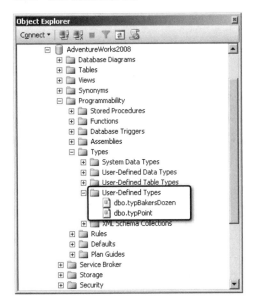

FIGURE 3-15 The Object Explorer window, with SQL CLR UDTs highlighted

Bear in mind that you might need to use the Refresh shortcut menu option on the nodes listed in the table to see your SQL CLR objects. If you've deployed or deleted any SQL CLR objects (as will be discussed shortly) since opening the Object Explorer connection to your database, the tree view will be out of date and will need to be refreshed. Notice that the tree view icons for SQL CLR stored procedures and SQL CLR DML triggers differ slightly from their T-SQL counterparts—they have a small yellow padlock on the lower-right corner.

Once you've located a SQL CLR entity in the Object Explorer window, you can right-click its tree view node and generate *CREATE*, *DROP*, and in some cases, *ALTER* scripts for it by selecting the Script *object type* As option from the shortcut menu (where *object type* is the SQL CLR object type selected). The script text can be inserted into a new query window, a file, or the clipboard, or it can be used to create a SQL Server Agent job.

For stored procedures, you can also generate *EXECUTE* scripts or, by selecting Execute Stored Procedure from the shortcut menu, execute interactively and generate the corresponding script via the Management Studio Execute Procedure dialog box. This dialog box explicitly prompts you for all input parameters defined for the selected stored procedure.

In addition to generating scripts for your SQL CLR entities, you can view their dependencies (either objects that are dependent on them or objects on which they depend). Just right-click the object, and then choose the View Dependencies option from the shortcut menu.

To remove your SQL CLR objects, either in preparation for loading a new version of your assembly or to delete the objects permanently, you have several options. For Visual Studio SQL Server projects, redeploying your assembly causes Visual Studio to drop it and any SQL

CLR objects within it that had been previously deployed by Visual Studio. This means that new versions can be deployed from Visual Studio without any preparatory steps.

For Class Library projects, you must issue T-SQL *DROP* commands for each of your SQL CLR objects and then for the assembly itself. You must drop any dependent objects before you drop the SQL CLR entity. For example, you must drop *tblPoint* before dropping *typPoint*. You can write these *DROP* scripts by hand or generate them by using the Script *object type* As, DROP To shortcut menu options in the Management Studio Object Explorer window.

You can also use the Delete shortcut menu option on any SQL CLR object in the Management Studio Object Explorer window to drop an object. This option displays the Delete Object dialog box, shown in Figure 3-16.

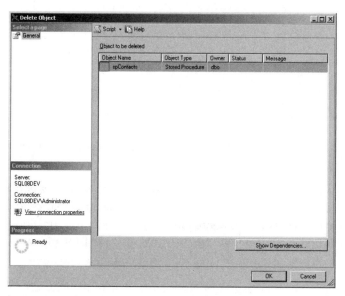

FIGURE 3-16 The Management Studio Delete Object dialog box

The script file Cleanup.sql in the Management Studio project provided with the sample code contains all the necessary *DROP* commands, in the proper order, for removing all traces of our Visual Studio SQL Server project or Class Library project from the *AdventureWorks2008* database. For the SQL Server project, you need to run this script only if you want to permanently remove the objects. For the Class Library project, run it before you deploy an updated version of your assembly or if you want to permanently remove these objects.

> **Note** Cleanup.sql also removes the tables *tblAggregateTest* and *tblPoint,* which are created by the scripts CreateTblAggregateTest.sql and CreateTblPoint.sql, respectively. If you ran CreateTblPoint.sql, you will need to drop *tblPoint,* either manually or by running Cleanup.sql, in order to drop *typPoint* and deploy the Visual Studio SQL Server project again.

SQL CLR objects, with the exception of DDL triggers, can also be viewed in the Visual Studio 2008 Server Explorer window, as shown in Figure 3-17.

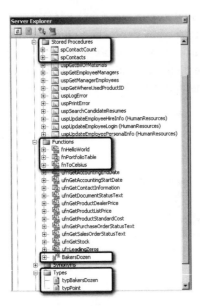

FIGURE 3-17 The Visual Studio Server Explorer window, with SQL CLR stored procedures, functions, aggregate, and UDTs highlighted

You'll find most of the objects under their appropriate parent nodes within the data connection parent node: SQL CLR stored procedures appear under the Stored Procedures node; scalar-valued functions and TVFs, as well as aggregates, appear under the Functions node; the Types and Assemblies nodes contain their namesake objects; and DML triggers appear under the node of the table to which they belong, following that table's columns.

You can also drill down on a particular assembly node and view a list of all its SQL CLR objects (with the exception of DDL triggers), as well as the source code files that make it up, as shown in Figure 3-18.

For assemblies created from Visual Studio 2008 SQL Server projects, you can double-click any SQL CLR object in the Server Explorer window to view its source code. (You can also do this by selecting the Open option from the SQL CLR object node's shortcut menu or the Data, Open option from Visual Studio's main menu while the node is selected.) If the assembly's project is open when you open the object's source, the code will be editable; if the project is not open, the source will be read-only.

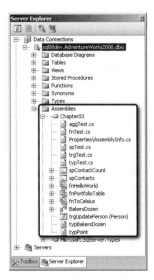

FIGURE 3-18 The Server Explorer window, with the Assemblies node and its child nodes highlighted

Caution Because *trgUpdatePerson*, our SQL CLR DML trigger, was deployed via T-SQL in the PostDeployScript.sql script and not via the *SqlTrigger* attribute, its source cannot be browsed through the Server Explorer window connection's Tables\Person (Person)\trgUpdatePerson node or its Assemblies\Chapter03\trgUpdatePerson (Person) node. You can, however, view its source through the Assemblies\Chapter03\trgTest.cs node.

Best Practices for SQL CLR Usage

Before we close this chapter, we'd like to summarize certain best practices for the appropriate use of SQL CLR programming.

The CLR integration in SQL Server 2008 is a powerful technology. In some cases, it allows you to do things you can't do practically in T-SQL (such as apply complex computational logic in stored procedures or triggers), and in other cases, it allows you to do things you can't do at all in T-SQL (such as create your own aggregate functions).

The fact remains, however, that set-based data selection and modification are much better handled by the declarative constructs in T-SQL than in the procedural constructs of .NET and the ADO.NET object model. SQL CLR functionality should be reserved for specific situations when the power of .NET as a calculation engine is required.

In general, functions and aggregates are great uses of SQL CLR integration. UDTs, if used to track complex *values*, rather than objects per se, make good use of SQL CLR integration as well.

For stored procedures and triggers, we recommend that you start with the assumption that these should be written in T-SQL and write them using SQL CLR code only if a case can be made that they cannot be reasonably written otherwise. And before you make such a case, consider that SQL CLR functions, aggregates, and UDTs can be used from within T-SQL stored procedures and triggers.

Summary

In this chapter, you've been exposed to the "mechanics" of developing the five basic SQL CLR entities and using them from T-SQL. You've seen how to take advantage of SQL Server 2008/Visual Studio 2008 integration as well as how to develop SQL CLR code in conventional Class Library assemblies and deploy them using T-SQL and SQL Server Management Studio. You've also been exposed to most of the SQL CLR .NET code attributes and their use in SQL Server projects and standard Class Library projects. You've gotten a sense of how to use Management Studio and the Visual Studio 2008 Server Explorer window as management tools for your SQL CLR objects, and we've discussed scenarios in which using SQL CLR integration is a good choice as well as scenarios in which T-SQL is the better choice.

Part I of this book essentially covers building databases, so in this chapter, we intentionally kept our focus on using SQL CLR objects from T-SQL and Management Studio. In the previous chapter, we highlighted a number of enhancements to T-SQL that you can use in your database development process. Part III of this book covers developing applications that use your databases. In Chapter 10's sample code, we demonstrate how to consume your SQL CLR objects in .NET applications. The sum total of the material from this chapter and the sample code from Chapter 10 provides a rich resource for diving into SQL CLR development.

Chapter 4
Server Management

—Stephen Forte

Working with Microsoft SQL Server requires that you perform many different management tasks. As a developer, you might think that management is the realm of the database administrator (DBA) and that you have to worry only about building applications by writing code. This is not always the case. You sometimes have to perform simple maintenance tasks such as attaching a database as part of an application or a setup program. For example, when you deploy an application, you might have to include an auxiliary program that attaches the application's database to an existing SQL Server installation. You might also make simple database security management part of your application. A contract developer or an independent software vendor (ISV) might be required to supply some automated backup-and-restore functionality that sits outside the realm of the SQL Server agent technology. A corporate developer might need to perform some simple administrative functions programmatically to verify that certain administrative tasks are completed or automate simple tasks such as performing a group of database attaches and detaches.

In the past, you performed these tasks using SQL Distributed Management Objects (SQL-DMO). You created an application, perhaps in Microsoft Visual Basic, that performed some basic routine maintenance or administrative tasks based on user input. If your customers or users did not have a full-time DBA, you might have used SQL-DMO to create an easy-to-use administrative tool that performed more advanced administrative functions behind the scenes.

Microsoft SQL Server 2005 introduced a new object model called SQL Server Management Objects (SMO). SMO allows you to do all the things you did with SQL-DMO, including managing SQL Server 2000, SQL Server 2005, and SQL Server 2008 database servers. SQL Server 2008 also introduces Policy-Based Management (PBM), a new framework that allows you to make sure that the configuration of your server or group of servers complies with a set policy that you define. Gone will be the days of "it works on my machine." In this chapter, we'll explore both SMO and PBM, and you'll learn how to leverage these features to help streamline server management.

What Is SMO?

SMO is a Microsoft .NET–based object model included with the SQL Server 2008 client tools in an assembly named *Microsoft.SqlServer.Smo.dll*. Other supporting assemblies are typically located in the Program Files\Microsoft SQL Server\100\SDK\Assemblies folder for a 32-bit

installation and in the Program Files (x86)\Microsoft SQL Server\100\SDK\Assemblies for a
64-bit installation. A handful of the SMO namespaces are shown in Table 4-1, along with their
assembly if it differs from *Microsoft.SqlServer.Smo.dll*.

TABLE 4-1 Partial SMO Namespace Map

Class	Function
Microsoft.SqlServer.Management.Smo	The core SMO namespace, which contains instance classes, utility classes, and enumerations that are used to programmatically manipulate SQL Server
Microsoft.SqlServer.Management.Common	Classes that are common to Replication Management Objects (RMO) and SMO (in *Microsoft.SqlServer.SqlWmiManagement.dll*)
Microsoft.SqlServer.Management.Smo.Agent	Classes for SQL Server Agent
Microsoft.SqlServer.Management.Smo.Wmi	Classes for the WMI Provider (in *Microsoft.SqlServer.SqlWmiManagement.dll*)
Microsoft.SqlServer.Management.Smo .RegisteredServers	Classes for identifying and working with registered servers (in *Microsoft.SqlServer. SmoExtended.dll*)
Microsoft.SqlServer.Management.Smo.Mail	Classes for Database Mail
Microsoft.SqlServer.Management.Smo.Broker	Classes for SQL Server Service Broker

SMO allows you to programmatically manipulate SQL Server versions 2008, 2005, 2000,
and 7.0. All the functionality in SQL Server Management Studio is available using SMO, but
features available only in SQL Server 2008 will not function in earlier versions of SQL Server.
Actually, SMO offers several more features than Management Studio, and the vast majority of all the features and functionality of SQL Server can be manipulated from SMO—much
more than with Management Studio. If you were so inclined, you could even create a
more feature-complete version of Management Studio using Windows Forms or Windows
Presentation Foundation (WPF) and SMO.

Developers who are accustomed to programmatically running Transact-SQL (T-SQL) scripts
during setup or on behalf of a user might never have looked at SQL-DMO and might wonder
why SMO would be of any use to them. One reason is security. Executing T-SQL scripts results
in a vulnerability to SQL injection attacks. SMO greatly reduces the attack surface because
the developer explicitly defines what functions to expose. A user cannot inject malicious code
into your custom *Backup* function using SMO and compiled C# code.

What About SQL-DMO?

Developers previously had to use the Component Object Model (COM)–based SQL-DMO
to perform programmatic administrative tasks. SMO is the logical evolution of SQL-DMO.

SMO has feature parity with SQL-DMO and even many of the same objects, but it has a number of additional features that supersede SQL-DMO. To account for new SQL Server 2005 and 2008 features and to achieve maximum data definition language (DDL) and administrative support for SQL Server 2008, SMO adds more than 150 new classes from SQL-DMO. SQL Server 2008 Books Online has a complete listing of the SQL-DMO–to–SMO object and functionality mapping as well as a rich SMO object model description.

The primary advantages of SMO are that it is a native .NET object model and that it provides increased performance and scalability over SQL-DMO. SMO has a cached object model, which allows you to change several properties of an object before applying the changes to SQL Server. This results in a significant benefit because SMO makes fewer roundtrips to the server. SMO also has optimized instantiation, which means that you can partially or fully instantiate objects. You can load many objects quickly by not instantiating all the properties of the objects. Compare this with SQL-DMO, which must load all the properties of the object when you load the object, thereby increasing network traffic and use of server resources.

With its object model, SMO is the preferred application programming interface (API) for programmatically managing and manipulating instances of SQL Server. SQL-DMO is shipped with SQL Server to provide backward compatibility. Because SQL-DMO is depreciated (should not be used), it is better to use SMO with .NET COM Interop in COM applications than to use SQL-DMO in order to reduce migration issues in the future and to guarantee future support from Microsoft. If you need to use SQL-DMO for any reason, keep in mind that SQL-DMO has a managed object that simplifies the interface to WMI to support WMI monitoring and server configuration through the SMO object interface. If you are considering a move to SMO, take a look at Table 4-2, adapted from Books Online, which shows the SQL-DMO–to–SMO mapping.

Table 4-2 **SQL-DMO–to–SMO Mapping**

SQL-DMO Object(s)	SMO Equivalent
Alert and *AlertSystem*	*Microsoft.SqlServer.Management.Agent* namespace
Application	Removed
BackupDevice, Backup, and *Backup2*	*Backup* and *BackupRestoreBase* objects
BulkCopy and *BulkCopy2*	Replaced by *Transfer* object
Category	Moved to *Microsoft.SqlServer.Management.Agent* namespace; replaced by *AlertCategory, OperatorCategory,* and *JobCategory* objects
Check	*Check* object
Column and *Column2*	*Column* object
Configuration	*Configuration* and *ConfigurationBase* objects

SQL-DMO Object(s)	SMO Equivalent
ConfigValue	*ConfigProperty* object
Database and *Database2*	*Database* object
DatabaseRole and *DatabaseRole2*	*DatabaseRole* object
DBFile object	*DataFile* object
DBOption and *DBOption2*	Moved into the *DatabaseOptions* object
Default and *Default2*	*Default* object
DistributionArticle and *DistributionArticle2*, *DistributionDatabase* and *DistributionDatabase2*, *DistributionPublication* and *DistributionPublication2*, *DistributionSubscription* and *DistributionSubscription2*, *Distributor* and *Distributor2*	Part of RMO, the *Microsoft.SqlServer.Replication* namespace
DRIDefault	Moved to *ScriptingOptions* object
FileGroup and *FileGroup2*	*FileGroup* object
FullTextCatalog and *FullTextCatalog2*	*FullTextCatalog* and *FullTextIndex* objects
Index and *Index2*	*Index* object
IntegratedSecurity	Functionality moved to *ServerConnection* object in *Microsoft.SqlServer.Management.Common* namespace
Job, JobFilter, JobHistoryFilter, JobSchedule, JobStep, JobServer and *JobServer2*, and *Operator*	Moved to *Microsoft.SqlServer.Management.Smo.Agent* namespace
Key	*ForeignKey* and *Index* objects
LinkedServer and *LinkedServer2*	*LinkedServer* object
LinkedServerLogin	*LinkedServerLogin* object
LogFile	*LogFile* object
Login and *Login2*	*Login* object
MergeArticle and *MergeArticle2*	*MergeArticle* object; moved to *Microsoft.SqlServer.Replication* namespace
MergeDynamicSnapshotJob	*Microsoft.SqlServer.Replication* namespace
MergePublication and *MergePublication2*	*MergePublication* object; moved to *Microsoft.SqlServer.Replication* namespace
MergePullSubscription and *MergePullSubscription2*	*MergePullSubscription* object; moved to *Microsoft.SqlServer.Replication* namespace

SQL-DMO Object(s)	SMO Equivalent
MergeSubscription	*MergeSubscription* object; moved to *Microsoft. SqlServer.Replication* namespace
MergeSubsetFilter	Moved to *Microsoft.SqlServer.Replication* namespace
NameList	Removed; similar functionality in *Scripter* object
Permission and *Permission2*	*ServerPermission, DatabasePermission, ApplicationRole*, and *ObjectPermission* objects
Property	*Property* object
Publisher and *Publisher2*	*ReplicationServer* object; moved to *Microsoft. SqlServer.Replication* namespace
QueryResults and *QueryResults2*	Replaced by *DataTable* or *DataSet* system object
RegisteredServer and *RegisteredSubscriber*	Moved to *Microsoft.SqlServer.Replication* namespace
Registry and *Registry2*	Removed
RemoteLogin	*ServerConnection* object; moved to *Common* namespace
RemoteServer and *RemoteServer2*	*ServerConnection* object; moved to *Microsoft. SqlServer.Management.Common* namespace
Replication, ReplicationDatabase, and *ReplicationDatabase2*	Moved to *Microsoft.SqlServer.Replication* namespace
ReplicationSecurity	*ServerConnection* object; moved to *Microsoft. SqlServer.Management.Common* namespace
ReplicationStoredProcedure and *ReplicationStoredProcedure2*	*ReplicationStoredProcedure* object; moved to *Microsoft.SqlServer.Replication* namespace
ReplicationTable and *ReplicationTable2*	*ReplicationTable* object; moved to *Microsoft. SqlServer.Replication* namespace
Restore and *Restore2*	*Restore* and *BackupRestoreBase* objects
Rule and *Rule2*	*Rule* object
Schedule	Moved to *Microsoft.SqlServer.Replication* namespace
ServerGroup	Removed
ServerRole	*ServerRole* object
SQLObjectList	*SqlSmoObject* array
SQLServer and *SQLServer2*	*Server* object
StoredProcedure and *StoredProcedure2*	*StoredProcedure* and *StoredProcedureParameter* objects

SQL-DMO Object(s)	SMO Equivalent
Subscriber and *Subscriber2*	*Subscriber* object; moved to *Microsoft.SqlServer .Replication* namespace
SystemDatatype and *SystemDataType2*	*DataType* object
Table and *Table2*	*Table* object
TargetServer and *TargetServerGroup*	Moved to *Microsoft.SqlServer.Management.Smo. Agent* namespace
TransactionLog	Functionality moved into the *Database* object
TransArticle and *TransArticle2*	*TransArticle* object; moved to *Microsoft.SqlServer. Replication* namespace
Transfer method and *Transfer2 object*	*Transfer* object
TransPublication and *TransPublication2*	*TransPublication* object; moved to *Microsoft. SqlServer.Replication* namespace
TransPullSubscription and *TransPullSubscription2*	*TransPullSubscription* object; moved to *Microsoft .SqlServer.Replication* namespace
Trigger and *Trigger2*	*Trigger* object
User and *User2*	*User* object
UserDefinedDatatype and *UserDefinedDataType2*	*UserDefinedType* object
UserDefinedFunction	*UserDefinedFunction* and *UserDefinedFunctionParameter* objects
View and *View2*	*View* object

Latest Features in SMO

To account for the new features in SQL Server 2005 and 2008, SMO includes the following functionality:

- Captures and batches the execution of T-SQL statements. Statements can be captured and sent as a batch to improve network performance.

- Manages SQL services using the WMI Provider. This means that SQL services can be started, stopped, and paused programmatically.

- Includes advanced scripting capabilities. T-SQL scripts can be generated to re-create SQL Server objects that describe relationships to other objects on the SQL Server instance.

- Data transfer leverages SQL Server Integration Services (SSIS).

- Uses unique resource names (URNs) for resolution of remote servers.

- Includes rich event handling model that allows you to insert code that will execute when a specific event occurs.

SMO also has a number of new objects and properties that correspond to new components in SQL Server 2005 and 2008. These include the following:

- Support for snapshot isolation and row-level versioning for increased concurrency

- Table and index partitioning for storage of data on a partition scheme

- Hypertext Transfer Protocol (HTTP) endpoints for managing Web Service requests

- Full support for XML technologies, including the XML data type, XML schema collection, and XML indexes

- The ability to create read-only copies of databases using viewpoint (snapshot) databases

- Full support for SQL Server Service Broker

- Facilitates management of Database Mail

- Allows programmatic management of registered servers

- Programmatic replay of SQL Server events and manipulation of SQL Trace

- Support for DDL triggers

Working with SMO in Microsoft Visual Studio

To get started working with SMO, you must first set a reference in the Visual Studio project to the SMO assembly by choosing Project, Add Reference and then selecting the *Microsoft. SqlServer.Smo, Microsoft.SqlServer.SmoExtended, Microsoft.SqlServer.Management.Sdk.Sfc,* and *Microsoft.SqlServer.ConnectionInfo* components, as shown in Figure 4-1.

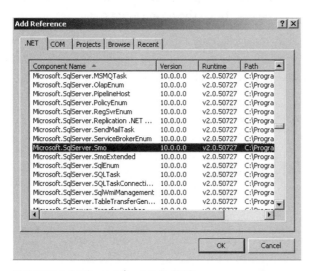

FIGURE 4-1 Setting a reference to SMO

You then add two *using* statements for the two namespaces that you will use most often, as shown here:

```
using Microsoft.SqlServer.Management.Common;
using Microsoft.SqlServer.Management.Smo;
```

Next you will want to work with SMO objects, the first being the *ServerConnection* object. This object represents a connection to a SQL Server instance. It lets you connect to a server and assign that connection to an SMO *Server* object. The *Server* object represents an actual SQL Server instance. The object allows you to retrieve the database server's properties and perform tasks such as attaching a database. To help you understand how to use these objects, we will create a simple application to connect to a SQL Server instance using the *ServerConnection* object and then use a *Server* object to retrieve the SQL Server version, edition, and name of the instance. This application will ask the user for a user ID and password or allow the use of integrated security, as shown in Figure 4-2.

FIGURE 4-2 Simple SMO application

The code in Listing 4-1 shows how to connect to a SQL Server instance using either integrated security or SQL Server security. The results are shown in Figure 4-3.

LISTING 4-1 Connecting to a SQL Server database via SMO

```
private void btnConnect_Click(object sender, EventArgs e)
{
  //ServerConnection object used to connect
  ServerConnection conn = new ServerConnection();
  //pass in the name of the server/instance
  conn.ServerInstance = this.txtServer.Text;

  //determine if integrated security is set
  if (!chkSSPI.Checked)
  {
    //using sql security
    conn.LoginSecure = false;
    conn.Login = this.txtUID.Text;
    conn.Password = this.txtPwd.Text;
  }
```

```
    //try to connect and return server information
    try
    {
      Server svrLocal = new Server(conn);
      //display the message box to the user here
      //get the info via the Information property
      MessageBox.Show(
        "You are now connected to: " + svrLocal.Name + System.Environment.NewLine +
        " Edition Info: " + svrLocal.Information.Edition + System.Environment.NewLine +
        " Version Info: " + svrLocal.Information.Version, "SMO Demos");
    }
    catch (SmoException exSMO)
    {
      //catch SMO-specific exceptions
      MessageBox.Show(exSMO.ToString());
    }
    catch (Exception ex)
    {
      MessageBox.Show(ex.ToString());
    }
}
```

FIGURE 4-3 Results of the simple SMO application

> **Tip** When you reference a local server with an instance name, you can use the syntax *(local)\\ instance_name* instead of the less flexible *server_name\instance_name*.

Iterating Through Available Servers

Depending on the type of functionality you need when performing your administrative tasks, you might have to programmatically enumerate a list of or iterate through available SQL Server instances. To perform this task in SMO, you can use the *SmoApplication* object's *EnumAvailableSqlServers* method, passing in a Boolean value to tell SMO whether to look only locally. The *EnumAvailableSqlServers* method returns a *DataTable* with the results of the enumeration filled with lots of properties. The following code calls a reusable method in a helper class named *ListAllKnownInstances*. *ListAllKnownInstances* searches the network for all the SQL Server instances it can "see" by using *EnumAvailableSqlServers* and returns the resulting *DataTable*. Our code then takes that *DataTable* and binds it to a *DataGridView*, as shown here:

```
private void button1_Click(object sender, EventArgs e)
{
  DataTable dtList = SMOUtilities.ListAllKnownInstances();
  dataGridView1.DataSource = dtList;
}
```

Listing 4-2 makes a call to the *EnumAvailableSqlServers* method and returns the results in a *DataTable*.

> **Warning** Be aware that the code in Listing 4-2 will sometimes take a long time to process. Microsoft uses similar code in the SQL Server Import And Export Wizard, and it takes a while to process the available servers. According to Books Online, "The computer running the instance SQL Server might not receive responses to the **EnumAvailableSqlServers** method in a timely manner. The returned list might not show all the available instances of SQL Server on the network. When you call the **EnumAvailableSqlServers** method in subsequent tries, more servers might become visible on the network."

LISTING 4-2 Enumerating available servers

```
public static DataTable ListAllKnownInstances()
{
  //this method will return a DataTable based on the all of the servers available
  //this method can take some time depending on your network
  //will also connect to SQL Server 2000 machines
  DataTable dtServers = new DataTable();
  try
  {
    // Obtain a list of all available SQL Server instances
    //this method returns a DataTable
    dtServers = SmoApplication.EnumAvailableSqlServers(false);
  }
  catch (SmoException exSMO)
  {
    MessageBox.Show(exSMO.ToString());
  }
  catch (Exception ex)
  {
    MessageBox.Show(ex.ToString());
  }

  return dtServers;
}
```

Figure 4-4 shows the results of running the code in Listing 4-2 when the *DataTable* filled with server information is bound to a *DataGridView*.

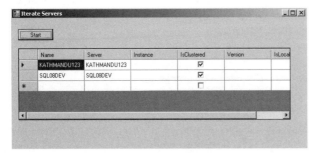

FIGURE 4-4 Simple enumeration of available servers

Retrieving Server Settings

A frequent task with SMO is retrieving the server settings of a particular SQL Server instance. You might have to create a Windows-based application like the one shown in Figure 4-5 or create a Web-based application to retrieve server settings and allow your users to modify them. You can choose which settings to allow users to change by simply deciding whether to show those settings in the application.

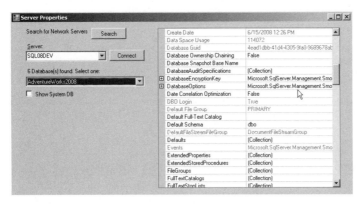

FIGURE 4-5 Retrieving server settings

The application in Figure 4-5, although complex-looking, is simple and builds on what you have learned so far. It allows you to iterate through all the available servers, select a server, and then select a database and display the server's settings.

We can list all the servers available to our application by reusing the *ListAllKnownInstances* method (which is part of the custom code shown earlier in Listing 4-2). *ListAllKnownInstances* returns a *DataTable* of all the servers that are available and visible to you. As shown in Listing 4-3, we then iterate through the *DataRow* collection for each row in the *DataTable*, verifying that the value is not null or blank and adding it to the combo box named *cboServers* using the *Items.Add* method. Last, after we have filled the combo box with all the available servers, we can select as the default value in the combo box the local SQL Server instance's name by using the *Server.Name* property.

LISTING 4-3 Enumerating available servers and filling the combo box

```
private void btnSearch_Click(object sender, EventArgs e)
{
  this.Cursor = Cursors.WaitCursor;

  //get a DataTable of the servers
  DataTable dtList = SMOUtilities.ListAllKnownInstances();

  foreach (DataRow dr in dtList.Rows)
  {
    string serverName = dr["Server"].ToString();

    if (!string.IsNullOrEmpty(dr["Instance"].ToString()))
    {
      serverName += @"\" + dr["Instance"].ToString();
    }

    if (this.cboServers.Items.IndexOf(serverName) < 0)
    {
      this.cboServers.Items.Add(serverName);
    }
  }

  //  By default, select the local server
  Server localServer = new Server();
  string localServerName = localServer.Name;

  if (!string.IsNullOrEmpty(LocalServer.InstanceName))
  {
    localServerName += @"\" + localServer.InstanceName;
  }

  int cboIndex = this.cboServers.FindStringExact(localServerName);
  if (cboIndex >= 0)
  {
    this.cboServers.SelectedIndex = cboIndex;
  }

  this.Cursor = Cursors.Default;
}
```

Next we need to connect to the selected server. We can do this by calling the *ConnectSMO* custom method described shortly in Listing 4-4. You call this method by passing in the name of the SQL Server instance you want to connect to and a Boolean value indicating whether you want to include system databases in the returned list of available databases. The applications form has a check box to indicate whether you want to include system databases. We can call *ConnectSMO* like this:

```
private void btnConnect_Click(object sender, EventArgs e)
{
  this.ConnectSMO(this.cboServers.Text, this.chkSystemDB.Checked);
}
```

The *ConnectSMO* method is responsible for adding each database to the *cboDatabase* combo box. It first calls a generic method named *FillComboWithDatabases*, which is located in the *SMOUtilities* class. Listing 4-4 shows the *ConnectSMO* method that calls *FillComboWithDatabases*. After the *FillComboWithDatabases* method is called, *ConnectSMO* cleans up the user interface and returns control to the user.

LISTING 4-4 The *ConnectSMO* custom method

```
private void ConnectSMO(string serverName, bool includeSystemDB)
{
  try
  {
    //use an hourglass
    this.Cursor = Cursors.WaitCursor;

    //clear out the items; if you don't do this, the combobox will have duplicates
    // when you click on the show system database box
    this.cboDatabase.Items.Clear();

    //this is a reusable function that fills the combobox with the available
    // databases on a particular server, passing in the combobox by ref
    //we will reuse this in a later example
    SMOUtilities.FillComboWithDatabases
      (serverName, includeSystemDB, ref this.cboDatabase);

    //now that the combobox is processed, we will manipulate the UI
    if (this.cboDatabase.Items.Count > 0)
    {
      this.lblDatabase.Text =
        this.cboDatabase.Items.Count.ToString() + " Database(s) found. Select one:";
      this.cboDatabase.Enabled = true;
    }
    else
    {
      this.lblDatabase.Text = "No Results";
    }

    this.chkSystemDB.Enabled = true;
  }
  catch (SmoException exSMO)
  {
    MessageBox.Show(exSMO.Message.ToString());
```

```
      //clear out the form's text boxes and comboboxes
      this.SetFormErrorParms();
   }
   catch (Exception ex)
   {
      MessageBox.Show(ex.ToString());
      this.SetFormErrorParms();
   }
   finally
   {
      this.Cursor = Cursors.Default;
   }
}
```

FillComboWithDatabases, shown in Listing 4-5, accepts a *ComboBox* object as well as the server name and a flag to indicate whether you should include system databases. *FillComboWithDatabases* obtains a reference to the SQL Server instance you want by using the *Server* object and then iterating through the *Databases* collection and adding each database to the *cboDatabase* combo box.

LISTING 4-5 Filling the combo box with the databases using the *FillComboWithDatabases* custom method

```
public static void FillComboWithDatabases
   (string serverName, bool includeSystemDB, ref ComboBox cbo)
{
   // Fill the database name combobox with databases from the selected server
   Server svr = new Server(serverName);

   foreach (Database db in svr.Databases)
   {
      //determine if the system database flag is set and include/exclude
      if ((includeSystemDB) || (!db.IsSystemObject))
      {
         cbo.Items.Add(db.Name);
      }
   }
}
```

Now that we have our SQL Server instance selected, it's time to select the database and then display all its properties. In this application, we will bind the properties of the database to a Windows Forms *PropertyGrid*. We'll do this in the combo box's *SelectedIndexChanged* event, which is shown in Listing 4-6. If you want to show only certain properties, you can iterate through the properties collection and display only the properties you want the user to be able to see.

LISTING 4-6 Reacting to the *SelectedIndexChanged* event

```csharp
private void cboDatabase_SelectedIndexChanged(object sender, EventArgs e)
{
  try
  {
    //This function gets the properties for the indicated database
    this.Cursor = Cursors.WaitCursor;

    Server selectedServer = new Server(this.cboServers.Text);
    Database selectedDatabase = selectedServer.Databases[this.cboDatabase.Text];

    this.propertyGrid1.SelectedObject = selectedDatabase;
  }
  catch (SmoException exSMO)
  {
    this.DBPropLabel.Text = string.Empty;
    MessageBox.Show(exSMO.ToString());
  }
  catch (Exception ex)
  {
    this.DBPropLabel.Text = string.Empty;
    MessageBox.Show(ex.ToString());
  }
  finally
  {
    this.Cursor = Cursors.Default;
  }
}
```

Creating Backup-and-Restore Applications

The most common application that developers created with SQL-DMO over the years was a backup-and-restore application—sometimes for customers who do not have security access to the database and cannot use Management Studio, and sometimes for customers who need remote administration and verification. These backup-and-restore applications eventually led to the creation of monitoring tools. SMO makes it easy to create an application for backup, verification, and restore. To demonstrate those capabilities, we will work with a simple backup-and-restore application created entirely in SMO, as shown in Figure 4-6.

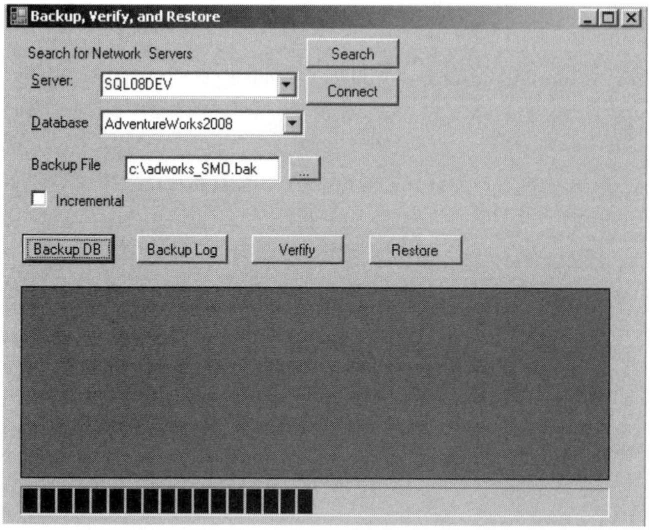

FIGURE 4-6 Backup-and-restore application

Backup

This application allows you to search for servers by reusing the code from prior examples. To obtain the list of servers, we will reuse our *ListAllKnownInstances* method as well as the *FillComboWithDatabases* method to list all the databases on the server. The application then allows you to select a backup file—c:\adworks_SMO.bak, for example. The application you see in Figure 4-6 is clearly a Windows Forms application that includes a button in the user interface for the user to run the backup. Alternatively, you could take the backup process code in this application and automate backups by using a console application, a WPF application, or even an ASP .NET Web page.

Once you have selected a server and a database, the backup code can be run. This code creates a *Server* and a *Backup* object and then assigns the *Action* property to *BackupActionType*. *Database* as the action to take for the backup. (Eventually, we will look at actions involving log files.) You have to add the device you want to back up to (most likely a file), but you can back up to tape and other standard SQL devices as well. You can use a *Boolean* flag to indicate whether to make only an incremental backup, as shown in Listing 4-7. The actual backup operation is performed by executing the *Backup.SqlBackup* method.

LISTING 4-7 Performing a backup programmatically using SMO

```
private void btnBackup_Click(object sender, EventArgs e)
{
  //use the server selected in the Server combobox
  //this server can be typed in the combobox as well
  Server svr = new Server(this.cboServers.Text);
  Backup bkp = new Backup();
```

```csharp
this.Cursor = Cursors.WaitCursor;
this.dataGridView1.DataSource = string.Empty;

//attempt the backup, and show a progress meter
//a lot can go wrong here, from file access to SQL issues, so it is important
//to handle all errors that may arise
try
{
  string fileName = this.txtFileName.Text;
  string databaseName = this.cboDatabase.Text;

  bkp.Action = BackupActionType.Database;
  bkp.Database = databaseName;

  //set the device: File, Tape, etc
  bkp.Devices.AddDevice(fileName, DeviceType.File);

  //set this when you want to do Incremental
  bkp.Incremental = chkIncremental.Checked;

  //progress meter stuff
  this.progressBar1.Value = 0;
  this.progressBar1.Maximum = 100;
  this.progressBar1.Value = 10;

  //this gives us the % complete by handling the event
  //provided by SMO on the percent complete, we will
  //update the progress meter in the event handler

  //set the progress meter to 10% by default
  bkp.PercentCompleteNotification = 10;
  //call to the event handler to increment the progress meter
  bkp.PercentComplete += new PercentCompleteEventHandler(ProgressEventHandler);

  //this does the backup
  bkp.SqlBackup(svr);

  //alert the user when it is all done
  MessageBox.Show("Database Backed Up To: " + fileName, "SMO Demos");
}
catch (SmoException exSMO)
{
  MessageBox.Show(exSMO.ToString());
}
catch (Exception ex)
{
  MessageBox.Show(ex.ToString());
}
finally
{
  this.Cursor = Cursors.Default;
  this.progressBar1.Value = 0;
}
}
```

Progress Meter

You might have noticed the progress meter at the bottom of the screen in the preceding example, which displays the progress of the backup operation being performed. You can implement this quite easily. The following code shows the event handler for the backup with the *PercentCompleteEventArgs* parameter, which contains the percent complete value as an integer between 0 and 100. We set the progress bar's *Value* property equal to that value.

```
public void ProgressEventHandler(object sender, PercentCompleteEventArgs e)
{
   //increase the progress bar by percent
   this.progressBar1.Value = e.Percent;
}
```

To handle progress events, simply assign an event handler to the *PercentComplete* event as shown earlier in Listing 4-7. You can set the *PercentCompleteNotification* value to any value you want; we set it to 10 percent. This is the starting value of your progress meter, so 10 will represent 10 percent of the progress meter getting filled.

> **Tip** For larger databases, you might want to set the percentage to a lower value because 10 percent of a large backup might take a long time. You also want the user to see that the application is still functioning correctly. Using a smaller value will cause the progress meter to change more frequently.

Log Backup

You do back up your log files, don't you? Backing up a log file requires exactly the same code shown in Listing 4-3 for backing up your database except that you set the *Action* property to *Log* instead of to *Database*:

```
bkp.Action = BackupActionType.Log;
```

Verify

After you perform a backup, it's prudent to verify that the backup was performed properly and that your backup device is not corrupt. (Or you might want to verify that your backup device is not corrupt before you perform the backup.) You can do this by using the *Restore* object's *SqlVerify* method, as shown in Listing 4-8.

LISTING 4-8 Verifying a backup via SMO

```csharp
private void btnVerify_Click(object sender, EventArgs e)
{
  Server svr = new Server();
  Restore rest = new Restore();
  string fileName = this.txtFileName.Text;

  this.Cursor = Cursors.WaitCursor;
  this.dataGridView1.DataSource = string.Empty;

  try
  {
    rest.Devices.AddDevice(fileName, DeviceType.File);
    bool verifySuccessful = rest.SqlVerify(svr);

    if (verifySuccessful)
    {
      MessageBox.Show("Backup Verified!", "SMO Demos");
      DataTable dt = rest.ReadFileList(svr);
      this.dataGridView1.DataSource = dt;
    }
    else
    {
      MessageBox.Show("Backup NOT Verified!", "SMO Demos");
    }
  }
  catch (SmoException exSMO)
  {
    MessageBox.Show(exSMO.ToString());
  }
  catch (Exception ex)
  {
    MessageBox.Show(ex.ToString());
  }
  finally
  {
    this.Cursor = Cursors.Default;
  }
}
```

SMO returns to you a *DataTable* filled with all the properties of the backup, which you can easily bind to a *DataGrid*, as shown in Figure 4-7. This is quite useful if you want to build a Web page to show the results of a backup (which you can even check using your cell phone).

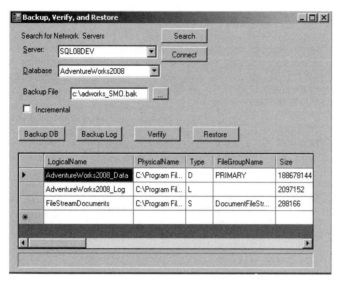

FIGURE 4-7 Backup verification

Restore

What good is a backup without a restore? As shown in Listing 4-9, you perform a restore operation by instantiating a *Server* object and a *Restore* object and providing the name of the backup file (or device) and the name of the database you are restoring to. Be sure to set the *Action* property of the *Restore* object to *RestoreActionType.Database* to restore your database. If you are going to restore the log, set the *Action* property of the *Restore* object to *RestoreActionType.Log*. Notice that we are using the same event handler for the progress meter as in the backup example, reusing as much code as possible.

LISTING 4-9 Performing a restore with SMO

```
private void btnRestore_Click(object sender, EventArgs e)
{
  Server svr = new Server(this.cboServers.Text);
  Restore res = new Restore();

  this.Cursor = Cursors.WaitCursor;
  this.dataGridView1.DataSource = string.Empty;

  try
  {
    string fileName = this.txtFileName.Text;
    string databaseName = this.cboDatabase.SelectedValue.ToString();

    res.Database = databaseName;
    res.Action = RestoreActionType.Database;
    //use for restore of the log
    //res.Action = RestoreActionType.Log;
    res.Devices.AddDevice(fileName, DeviceType.File);
```

```
        //progress meter stuff
        this.progressBar1.Value = 0;
        this.progressBar1.Maximum = 100;
        this.progressBar1.Value = 10;

        res.PercentCompleteNotification = 10;
        res.ReplaceDatabase = true;
        res.PercentComplete += new PercentCompleteEventHandler(ProgressEventHandler);

        //use the following if you want to relocate the mdf files
        //res.RelocateFiles.Add(new RelocateFile("aw_data", @"c:\aw_dat.mdf"));

        //perform the restore
        res.SqlRestore(svr);

        MessageBox.Show("Restore of " + databaseName + " Complete!", "SMO Demos");
    }
    catch (SmoException exSMO)
    {
        MessageBox.Show(exSMO.ToString());
    }
    catch (Exception ex)
    {
        MessageBox.Show(ex.ToString());
    }
    finally
    {
        this.Cursor = Cursors.Default;
        this.progressBar1.Value = 0;
    }
}
```

Restoring to a Different Location

The SMO backup and restore functionality has many other features—for example, changing the file location of your restore. SMO allows you to do this by simply using the *RelocateFiles. Add* method of the *Restore* object, as shown here:

```
res.RelocateFiles.Add
    (new RelocateFile("adventureworks1_data", @"c:\adventureworks1_dat.mdf"));
```

Performing Programmatic DBCC Functions with SMO

Another useful SMO feature is database integrity checks. You can perform just about all of the Database Consistency Check (DBCC) functions using SMO; Table 4-3 shows a subset of what is available. (DBCC can do many administrative checks in addition to integrity checks.)

TABLE 4-3 Integrity Checks with SMO

SMO Method	DBCC Function
CheckAllocations	*DBCC CHECKALLOC*
CheckAllocationsDataOnly	*DBCC CHECKALLOC('databasename', NOINDEX)*
CheckCatalog	*DBCC CHECKCATALOG*
CheckTables	*DBCC CHECKDB*
CheckTablesDataOnly	*DBCC CHECKDB('databasename', NOINDEX)*

The simple application shown in Listing 4-10 uses the DBCC commands shown in Figure 4-8. This application allows you to search for servers reusing code from prior examples and then list all the databases on that server. To obtain the list of servers, we will reuse our *ListAllKnownInstances* method as well as the *FillComboWithDatabases* method to list all the databases on the server. The example code uses only the *CheckCatalog* SMO method (which is the DBCC command); however, with minor code changes, you can use any of the DBCC commands listed earlier in Table 4-3 with similar code.

LISTING 4-10 Performing a Database Consistency Check (DBCC) with SMO

```
private void btnRunDBCC  (object sender, EventArgs e)
{
  Server svr = new Server(this.cboServers.Text);
  Database db = svr.Databases[this.cboDatabase.Text];

  StringCollection results = db.CheckCatalog(); //can also do most DBCC commands
  //clear the text box
  this.label1.Text = string.Empty;

  foreach (string result in results)
  {
    if (!string.IsNullOrEmpty(result))
    {
      this.lblResults.Text += result;
    }
  }
}
```

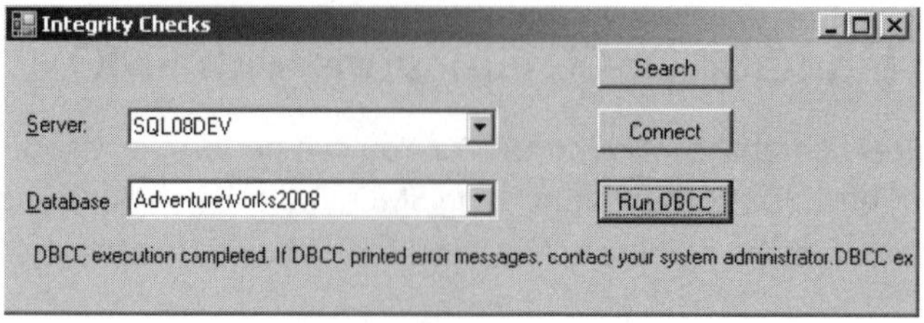

FIGURE 4-8 DBCC application via SMO

Important Books Online states that *CheckCatalog* performs various consistency checks between system metadata tables. In reality, if *DBCC CHECKCATALOG* reports back any errors, that means that someone manually added data to the system tables or edited or deleted data. We recommend regularly performing this check on your Web site's database because modified system tables are among the top symptoms of a SQL injection attack because of potential holes in your site's security model. You can run the code here every few hours and have the results e-mailed to you, or you can place the code in this section on a private administrative Web page that you can check anytime.

The *CheckCatalog* method, like all integrity-checking SMO methods, returns a *StringCollection* object filled with the results. As the code in Listing 4-10 shows, you can iterate through the results and then take the appropriate actions. If all is fine in your database, as it was in this example, you get the following ubiquitous message from DBCC: "DBCC execution completed. If DBCC printed error messages, contact your system administrator."

 Note The problem with running a DBCC check is that if you are not a SQL Server DBA, you most likely won't know what to do about an error. The administrative functions of DBCC are beyond the scope of the book, but you can consult a DBA for corrective action. If you are the developer and the DBA, this is an area where you should investigate further.

You can run many other DBCC functions. The code is exactly the same, but sometimes you have to pass in a table name or an index name. See Table 4-3 or Books Online for more examples.

Policy-Based Management

Quite often, developers spend a lot of time wondering why their application works properly on "their machine" and not on the target test or production server. Usually, this is caused by some difference between the two environments. For example, the developer might have written a new SQL common language runtime (CLR) stored procedure on his or her local machine where the SQL CLR is enabled, but the SQL CLR is disabled on the target server. With more and more features being built into each new release of SQL Server, it is becoming increasingly challenging to configure the database server exactly as you want. To help mitigate these issues, SQL Server 2008 introduces a new feature called Policy-Based Management (PBM) that focuses on server management. PBM allows a developer or DBA to set a desired server configuration (that is, a policy) and then check that system configuration for compliance with that policy. PBM will also enforce rules that you can create, such as "all new tables must be in either the *ssn* or *prw* schema." In addition, PBM will allow a developer or DBA to enforce that policy on remote servers.

Although PBM is mostly a DBA feature, we will take the point of view of a developer trying to enforce policies in a deployment scenario. Using PBM, a developer can ensure that a test server or a production server is in full compliance with his or her developer machine. Most likely, a developer will work with the DBA to make sure that the development machine is in compliance with the test and production machines.

Before we start on a simple demonstration, let's review some basic PBM terminology, shown here:

- **Target type**   The SQL Server entities that are managed by PBM—for example, database, table, index, stored procedure, and schema.

- **Management facet**   A logical set of predefined properties that will model the behavior or configuration for your target types. There are many facets that define most aspects of SQL Server behavior.

- **Condition**   The desired state or behavior of the facet set with a Boolean expression.

- **Policy**   The expected state or behavior of a given condition.

A Simple Policy

Now let's look at a simple example to demonstrate how PBM works. We want a policy that says that the SQL CLR must be enabled for the database, and then we want to enforce that policy by using PBM. To do that, we will create our own policy named *MyCLRPolicy*. This is the policy that will ensure that the condition of the Server Configuration facet's target type of *ClrIntegrationEnabled* is true. Table 4-4 shows the target type, management facet, and condition and policy values for this example.

TABLE 4-4 PBM CLR Policy Enforcement Parameters

Our Policy	PBM Values
MyCLRPolicy	Policy
True	Condition
Server Configuration	Management facet
ClrIntegrationEnabled	Target type

In Object Explorer, navigate from the server tree node to the Management, Policy Management, and Facets nodes, as shown in Figure 4-9. There you will see a list of all of the facets that come predefined in SQL Server 2008.

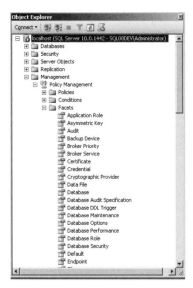

FIGURE 4-9 PBM interface in Object Explorer

To build our new policy that checks whether the SQL CLR is enabled, we have to first create a new condition. To do that, right-click the Conditions node under Policy Management, and then select New Condition. This displays the Create New Condition dialog box, as shown in Figure 4-10. Give the condition a name—for example, **MakeSureCLRIsEnabled**. In the Facet drop-down list, select Server Configuration, and then click in the Expression pane where you see the text "Click here to add a clause." Once you do, you can select @ClrIntegrationEnabled in the Field box and True in the Value box. After you have finished, click OK to create the new condition.

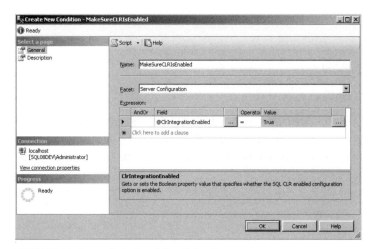

FIGURE 4-10 Create New Condition dialog box

Now that our condition is all set, we have to wire it up to a policy. To do so, right-click the Policies node in Object Explorer to display the Create New Policy dialog box, shown in Figure 4-11.

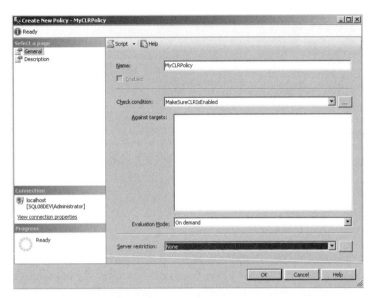

FIGURE 4-11 Create New Policy dialog box

Name the policy **MyCLRPolicy**, and in the Check Condition drop-down list, select the MakeSureCLRIsEnabled condition that we just created. The assigned targets are any remote servers that you are connected to—in this case, we are going to only run this policy locally, so you can leave this option blank. For execution mode, you have a choice of the following:

- On Demand
- On Schedule
- On Change—Log Only
- On Change—Prevent

For our example, choose On Demand (which is the default), and click OK to create the new policy. By selecting On Demand, you specify that the policy will run only when you manually execute it. On Schedule will run via SQL Server Agent at times that you set using the Agent Scheduling dialog box. Selecting On Change—Log Only runs the policy whenever the property in the management facet is changed and violations are sent to the Windows event log.

Selecting On Change—Prevent will run the policy whenever the property in the management facet is changed but will prevent the change via a DDL trigger. (Not all changes can be detected and rolled back by PBM, and this option is available only when it is possible to prevent the condition.)

Our last step is to run the policy. To do so, right-click the newly created policy, and then choose Evaluate from the shortcut menu to display the Evaluate Policies dialog box, as shown in Figure 4-12. Clicking the Evaluate menu item causes SQL Server to run the policy, evaluate the condition, and obtain the results. If you don't have SQL CLR enabled, the policy will fail. (This is indicated in Figure 4-12 by a circle with an *X* in the lists.)

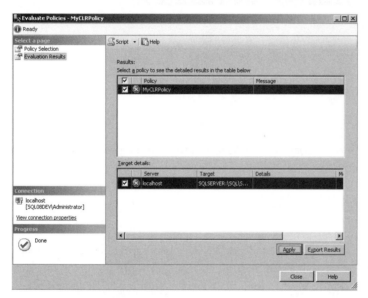

FIGURE 4-12 Evaluate Policies dialog box showing failed results

Now imagine that you want to enforce this policy for the set of servers the policy pertains to (from the Create New Policy dialog box, shown earlier in Figure 4-11). Policies are very easy to enforce with PBM. In the Evaluate Policies dialog box, select the condition, and then click the Apply button. This will enforce the policy by making the change—in our case, enabling the CLR. The results are shown in Figure 4-13. (Notice that the circle is then filled with a checkmark, replacing the *X*.) You can also export this condition as a T-SQL script to run offline.

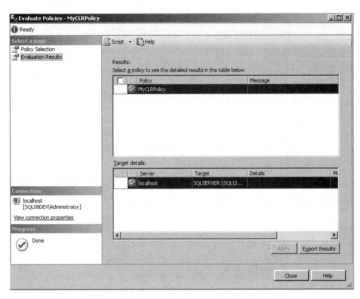

FIGURE 4-13 Evaluate Policy dialog box showing successful results after enforcing a policy

PBM is a great tool for developers and DBAs to use to align the configuration environment in which they are working.

Summary

We've only scratched the surface of SMO and PBM in this chapter because both SMO and PBM have tremendous capability and offer exceptionally rich programming features. Without a doubt, SMO is an exciting object model that covers everything SQL Server does—and in fact, even more than SQL Server Management Studio covers. As a developer, you might find yourself performing the same task over and over in Management Studio. If that's the case, consider writing an application using SMO. Also keep in mind that SMO is more feature-complete and performs better than the legacy SQL-DMO, and therefore, it can fulfill many of your administrative needs. PBM makes it easy to ensure that your development environment and the target test and production environments are identically configured. This enables developers to more successfully model test and production environments as they develop code designed to use SQL Server.

Chapter 5
Security in SQL Server 2008

—Rob Walters and Leonard Lobel

With the growing concern about personal data protection and the proliferation of computer viruses, developing a methodology for secure computing continues to be a vital task for Microsoft. Back in 2003, Microsoft created the Trustworthy Computing initiative, which described the advances that needed to be made for people to feel more comfortable using devices powered by computers and software. (The initiative can be found at *http://www.microsoft.com/mscorp/twc/twc_whitepaper.mspx.*) From this initiative, Microsoft SQL Server 2008 leverages what is known as the Security Framework, shown in Figure 5-1.

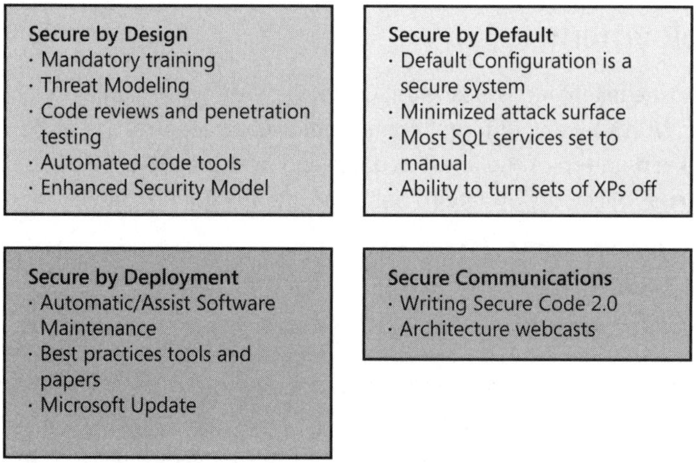

Secure by Design	**Secure by Default**
· Mandatory training · Threat Modeling · Code reviews and penetration testing · Automated code tools · Enhanced Security Model	· Default Configuration is a secure system · Minimized attack surface · Most SQL services set to manual · Ability to turn sets of XPs off
Secure by Deployment	**Secure Communications**
· Automatic/Assist Software Maintenance · Best practices tools and papers · Microsoft Update	· Writing Secure Code 2.0 · Architecture webcasts

FIGURE 5-1 Security Framework in SQL Server 2008

Four Themes of the Security Framework

SQL Server 2008 security is organized around four themes: Secure by Design, Secure by Default, Secure by Deployment, and Secure Communications.

Secure by Design

Security has been a design consideration in all earlier versions of SQL Server. As of SQL Server 2005, the product development group made sure that everyone was on the same page when it came to security. The entire product team went through mandatory security training, and threat models were written and reviewed for all components of all the features within the product. In addition, a massive effort was carried out to review code with respect to security for the entire product. Microsoft takes security very seriously, and designers of features within SQL Server have made security a top consideration in the final design.

Secure by Default

The Secure by Default approach is one of the most notable areas of the Security Framework that SQL Server users will experience. You can experience it by simply installing SQL Server with the default options. Users of SQL Server 2000 and earlier versions will notice that services such as SQL Server Agent are off by default. In addition, certain features such as *xp_cmdshell* and *OPENROWSET* queries are disabled. This "off by default" approach attempts to minimize the surface area for attack, and the effects of this can be seen throughout the product.

Secure by Deployment

Perhaps one of the most challenging issues with SQL Server is effective deployment in a production environment. With so many different configurations and features, it can be difficult for administrators to keep on top of the latest updates and best practices. SQL Server 2005 and 2008 are now part of Microsoft Update to help alleviate the pain of determining the latest update to apply.

Secure Communications

Even before SQL Server 2005 was released to the public, a plethora of technical information was already available in various forms. White papers, Webcasts, and active newsgroups educated and assisted beta customers with the product. Today, most of these Webcasts and white papers have been updated and provide rich educational content.

All editions of SQL Server 2008 include security features that help users protect their data. This chapter will cover the following aspects of SQL Server security:

- Overview of security, including authentication and authorization
- User-schema separation
- Encrypting data within the database and while in transit
- Auditing monitored server and database events
- Protecting SQL Server 2008

Reducing the Surface Area for Attack

The more doors you have in your house, the more opportunities an intruder has to break in. Even if those doors are made of solid steel, each with a nice shiny lock, they are still considered a surface area that is vulnerable to attack. One obvious way to eliminate this vulnerability is to not have a door where you don't need one. In a computer application, the equivalent solution is that if you are not using a particular feature, you should turn it off if possible.

Out of the box, SQL Server provides a reduced surface area for attack by automatically turning off features that are optional. These features include the SQL Server Agent service; the SQL Server Browser service; various server functions, including *xp_cmdshell*; Common Language Runtime (CLR) integration; and others.

In SQL Server 2005, a system stored procedure named *sp_configure* was introduced that could be used to turn many of these features on and off programmatically. SQL Server 2005 also introduced a graphical management utility named the SQL Server Surface Area Configuration Tool. This utility allowed administrators to turn these features on and off from a user interface. In SQL Server 2008, the *sp_configure* stored procedure still remains, but the Surface Area Configuration Tool has been discontinued (although some features are configurable using a graphical front end with the SQL Server Configuration Manager). Instead, administrators now use the Surface Area Configuration *facet* provided by the new Policy-Based Management (PBM) framework.

PBM is a new feature in SQL Server 2008 that allows you to declare and enforce different management policies against various target environments. Functionality formerly provided by the Surface Area Configuration Tool in SQL Server 2005 is now one of many PBM facets that can be configured in SQL Server 2008. We examine PBM in Chapter 4, including coverage of the Surface Area Configuration facet for enabling CLR integration.

SQL Server 2008 Security Overview

If you are already familiar with the concepts of *users* and *roles* and SQL Server *logins*, you can probably skip ahead to the next section of this chapter. But for those who aren't, we'll provide a quick explanation. The concepts of users and roles exist both in the Microsoft Windows world and in SQL Server. In an abstract sense, they are referred to as *principals*. Principals are entities that can request resources from the application or an operating system. In the case of Windows, principals are entities such as Domain Users and Groups and Local Users and Groups. In SQL Server, these entities are logins and server roles. Within a database, these entities are database users, database roles, and application roles, to name a few.

So what can we do with entities? Chances are, you have an object such as a file or a database table that you want to allow access to. These objects, or *securables*, are the resources to which the authorization system regulates access. Some securables can be contained within other securables, creating nested hierarchies called *scopes* that can themselves be secured. The securable scopes in the SQL Server database engine are *server*, *database*, and *schema*. Every securable in SQL Server has an associated permission that can be granted to a principal.

Figure 5-2 shows a graphical representation of the principal-securable-permission model.

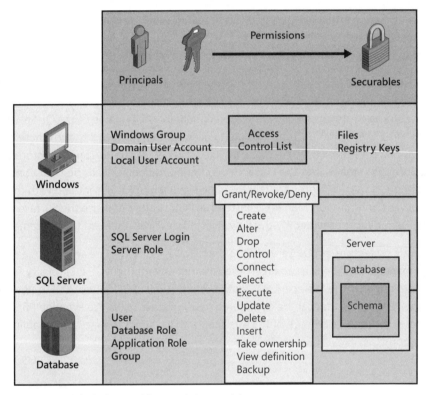

FIGURE 5-2 Principal-securable-permission model

SQL Server Logins

Now that we have a high-level understanding of SQL Server security and how it relates to Windows security, we can get into SQL Server–specific areas. To connect to SQL Server, you need a login. This login can be a combination of a custom user name (such as *Login1*) and a complex password. Alternatively, you can add an existing Windows account as a login to SQL Server and forego the creation of a separate user name and password. Thus, SQL Server supports two types of logins: Windows logins and SQL Server logins.

Logins themselves have no access to any specific database within SQL Server; they allow only for connection to SQL Server. Thus, logins are entities that can be granted server-wide permissions to perform certain actions. These actions are bundled into server roles such as *sysadmin*, *diskadmin*, and *dbcreator* (to name a few). Table 5-1 shows the list of server roles and their corresponding functions. Server roles are fixed—you cannot drop them or create new ones in addition to the set of nine fixed server roles.

TABLE 5-1 Fixed Server Roles

Server Role	Description
bulkadmin	Members can run the *BULK INSERT* statement. Membership in this role still requires that non-*sysadmin* users have access to the object being updated.
dbcreator	Members can create, alter, drop, and restore any database.
diskadmin	This role is used for managing disk files. Most of the capabilities relate to adding and removing backup devices.
processadmin	Members can terminate processes that are running in an instance of SQL Server. This role is useful if you want to give someone the ability to kill a long-running query or an orphaned connection.
public	All valid SQL Server logins are members of the public role.
securityadmin	Members can manage logins and their properties. They can *GRANT*, *DENY*, and *REVOKE* server-level permissions as well as database-level permissions. They can also reset passwords for SQL Server logins. This role has no rights to assign database permissions. If you want *securityadmin* members to be able to do this, you must make their logins part of the *db_accessadmin* fixed database role for the specific database.
serveradmin	Members can change server-wide configuration options and shut down the server.
setupadmin	Members can add and remove linked servers and also execute some system stored procedures.
sysadmin	Members can perform any activity on the server. By default, all members of the Windows *BUILTIN\Administrators* group, the local administrator's group, are members of the *sysadmin* fixed server role. The SQL Server service account is also a member of this role.

Database Users

Logins can be created using SQL Server Management Studio or via the Transact-SQL (T-SQL) statement *CREATE LOGIN*. After you create a login, you then grant it access to a particular database. Databases themselves have their own set of roles that define specific access and actions that users of these roles can take within a particular database. Before we can grant database access to a login, we must create a database user for the login. Again, you can cre-

ate a database user by using SQL Server Management Studio or via the T-SQL statement
CREATE USER.

Once you create a database user, you can optionally include it in one of the database roles.
Table 5-2 lists the roles that all databases have. Like server roles, these database roles are
fixed and cannot be modified. However, unlike server roles, additional database roles can be
defined as desired.

TABLE 5-2 Fixed Database Roles

Database Role	Description
db_accessadmin	Members can add or remove access for Windows logins, Windows groups, and SQL Server logins.
db_backupoperator	Members can back up the database.
db_datareader	Members can read all data from all user tables.
db_datawriter	Members can add, delete, or change data in all user tables.
db_ddladmin	Members can run any data definition language (DDL) command in a database.
db_denydatareader	Members cannot read any data in the user tables within a database.
db_denydatawriter	Members cannot add, modify, or delete any data in the user tables within a database.
db_owner	Members can perform all configuration and maintenance activities on the database, including dropping the database.
db_securityadmin	Members can modify role membership and manage permissions.

There is a special database role that *sysadmin* users cannot explicitly give other users
permissions to; it is known as the *public* role. All database users are implicitly included in
the *public* role. This role captures all default permissions for users in a particular database. It
cannot have users, groups, or roles assigned to it because everyone belongs to this role by
default. This role cannot be dropped. Thus, to protect against unauthorized data access, you
should minimize the permissions granted to the *public* role. Instead, grant permissions to
other database roles and to user accounts associated with logins.

The *guest* User Account

On the topic of unauthorized data access, it is important to note a special user account available in SQL Server called *guest*. This account is created by default on new user-defined databases but does exist in *master* and *tempdb*. However, the *guest* account is disabled by default,
which means that it does not have any access within the database. The *guest* account allows
a login without a user account to access a database. A login assumes the identity of the *guest*
account when all of the following conditions are met:

- The login has access to an instance of SQL Server but does not have access to the database through his or her own user account or via a Windows group membership.

- The database contains a *guest* account.

- The *guest* account is enabled in the database.

You can apply permissions to the *guest* account just as you can to any other user account. If possible, however, you should avoid using the *guest* account entirely, because all logins without their own database permissions obtain the database permissions granted to the *guest* account. If you absolutely must use the *guest* account, be sure to grant minimum permissions to it.

> **Note** Although we have discussed various aspects of server and database principals, a complete discussion of these topics is beyond the scope of this book. For in-depth information about user management within SQL Server, see SQL Server Books Online.

Authentication and Authorization

Before we dive into the concepts of authentication and authorization, it is important to discuss a feature added in SQL Server 2005 called *endpoints*. In earlier versions of SQL Server, clients could connect via Transport Control Protocol (TCP), named pipes, shared memory, and Virtual Interface Architecture (VIA). As long as one of these protocols was enabled on the server and the user had a valid login, the connection was accepted. SQL Server 2005 introduced a separation of this behavior via endpoints.

Endpoints can be considered a point of entry into SQL Server. Administrators can create an endpoint not only for TCP, named pipes, shared memory, and VIA, but also for Hypertext Transfer Protocol (HTTP). Once an endpoint is created, you can restrict access so that users can connect only via a certain endpoint type. For example, you might create a login named *Login1* and grant access to the HTTP endpoint while denying access to all other endpoints. In this case, *Login1* can access SQL Server only via the HTTP endpoint; it cannot directly connect to SQL Server via TCP or any of the other protocols. To see how this endpoint verification affects authentication, let's examine the process of making a client connection.

How Clients Establish a Connection

If a TCP client wants to make a connection to SQL Server, it must first know which port to connect to. Prior to SQL Server 2005, there was always a thread waiting on User Datagram Protocol (UDP) port 1434 whose purpose was to return details on all of the running instances of SQL Server as well as the port numbers of those instances. All a client had to do was make a UDP connection to port 1434 and then determine which port it wanted to connect to, given a specific instance of SQL Server. This process generally worked until hackers found a way to launch a Denial of Service (DoS) attack on SQL Server by continuously sending packets to this port requesting the enumeration. Because the enumeration process was part of the SQL Server service, the "SQL Slammer" worm virus created serious problems for SQL Server installations. As of SQL Server 2005, this functionality has been pulled out into a separate service named the SQL Server Browser service that can be turned on and off without touching the SQL Server service itself.

Note Of course, this means that the Browser service is now vulnerable to DoS attacks. You can mitigate this concern if you block port 1434 on your firewall. If you are concerned about intranet attacks from inside the firewall, you might want to consider not running the Browser service at all and explicitly pass port numbers on the connection strings instead.

After the network connection request and pre-login handshake have been made, SQL Server must authenticate the user to make sure that he or she has access to begin with. Figure 5-3 depicts the authentication process.

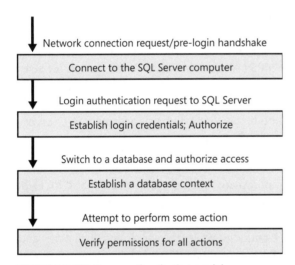

FIGURE 5-3 SQL Server authentication model

At this point, the service accepts the login credentials supplied by the user and attempts to validate them. If successful, the login is authorized against the endpoint corresponding to the type of connection made to SQL Server. In this example, the login is checked to see whether it has been granted *CONNECT* permissions to the TCP endpoint. If this is true, the authentication process proceeds; otherwise, the connection fails at this point.

Note By default, new logins are automatically granted *CONNECT* permissions to the TCP endpoint.

Once the login has passed the endpoint check, SQL Server switches to a database context (the default database specified for the login or specified in the connection string). It then attempts to authenticate the login as a user of that database. If the login can be authenticated, the connection succeeds; otherwise, it fails. When a database context has been established and the login has been authenticated, the user can perform work against the database on the server.

Password Policies

In the Windows world, administrators can set login expirations and enforce password policies (for example, requiring passwords to be a certain length and contain a mixture of special characters). Traditionally in SQL Server, SQL logins never respected these global policy settings. In SQL Server 2005 and 2008, both Windows-authenticated and SQL logins obey the group policy settings defined in the Windows domain.

> **Note** Password policy enforcement is available only in SQL Server running on Microsoft Windows Server 2003 and later.

To help illustrate password policies, let's define a minimum password length using the Local Security Settings applet located in the Administrative Tools folder of Control Panel. This tool is shown in Figure 5-4.

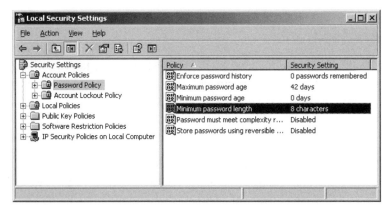

FIGURE 5-4 Password Policy node of Local Security Settings

Using this tool, we can change a variety of parameters. In the example shown in Figure 5-4, we've changed the minimum password length to eight characters. Once this change has been made, we can create our new login. Prior to SQL Server 2005, this was done by calling the system stored procedure *sp_addlogin*. In SQL Server 2005 and 2008, we create logins by using the DDL statement *CREATE LOGIN*, as shown here:

```
CREATE LOGIN foo WITH PASSWORD='123',
 CHECK_POLICY=ON,
 CHECK_EXPIRATION=ON
```

When this statement is executed, it fails because our password has only three characters and we specified a password policy that requires a minimum of eight characters, as follows:

```
Msg 15116, Level 16, State 1, Line 1
Password validation failed. The password does not meet policy requirements because it is too
short.
```

The system view *sys.sql_logins* returns information about logins, such as whether the policies and expirations are set. If you want additional information regarding a particular login, such as how many bad passwords were attempted, you can use the *LOGINPROPERTY* built-in function, as shown here:

```
DECLARE @name varchar(20)
SET @name='sa'
SELECT
 LOGINPROPERTY(@name, 'PasswordLastSetTime') AS PasswordLastSetTime,
 LOGINPROPERTY(@name, 'IsExpired') AS IsExpired,
 LOGINPROPERTY(@name, 'IsLocked') AS IsLocked,
 LOGINPROPERTY(@name, 'IsMustChange') AS IsMustChange,
 LOGINPROPERTY(@name, 'LockoutTime') AS LockoutTime,
 LOGINPROPERTY(@name, 'BadPasswordCount') AS BadPasswordCount,
 LOGINPROPERTY(@name, 'BadPasswordTime') AS BadPasswordTime,
 LOGINPROPERTY(@name, 'HistoryLength') AS HistoryLength,
 LOGINPROPERTY(@name, 'PasswordHash') AS PasswordHash
```

User-Schema Separation

Imagine that an employee in an organization who has created many tables and stored procedures leaves the company. As a database administrator, your task is to reassign ownership of all the objects that this former employee created and owned. Prior to SQL Server 2005, this was a tedious task. In SQL Server 2005 and 2008, the task is made a lot easier because of the schema feature.

SQL Server 2005 introduced a different concept of schemas than in earlier versions of SQL Server. In SQL Server 2000 (and earlier versions), database users and schemas were equivalent. Every database user was the owner of a schema that had the same name as the user. An owner of an object was effectively identical to the owner of the schema that contained the object. This one-to-one mapping behavior made it very tedious to reassign ownership.

As of SQL Server 2005, users and schemas are separate entities, and schemas are independent containers that can contain zero or more objects. Users can own one or more schemas and can be assigned a default schema. If a default schema is not specified, the user is defaulted to the *dbo* schema of the database. This default schema is used to resolve the names of securables that are referred to without using their fully qualified name. In SQL Server 2000, the location that is checked first is the schema owned by the calling database user, followed by the schema owned by *dbo*. In SQL Server 2005 and 2008, each user has a default schema, so when SQL Server resolves the names of securables, it checks the default schema.

You can thus transfer ownership of many securables, and a schema can contain securables owned by a database user other than the owner of the schema. This is important to note because if you leverage the old system views, such as *sysobjects*, the results returned in queries will not show up correctly. You must use a catalog view, such as *sys.objects*, instead.

The *CREATE SCHEMA* statement is used to create a new schema. It can also be used to create tables and views within the new schema and to set *GRANT*, *DENY*, or *REVOKE* permissions on those objects, as shown in the following example:

```
CREATE SCHEMA Sales AUTHORIZATION Rob
CREATE TABLE Leads (id int, name varchar(max),phone nvarchar(20))
GRANT SELECT ON Sales.Leads TO Tammie
DENY SELECT ON Sales.Leads TO Vince;
GO
```

This example creates the *Sales* schema and assigns it to Rob. A *Leads* table is created within the *Sales* schema, and Tammie is granted select access to the table, while Vince is denied select access.

For Tammie to access the table in versions of SQL Server prior to SQL Server 2005, she must use Rob for the schema name, as shown here:

```
SELECT * FROM Production.SalesReps.Rob.Leads
```

In SQL Server 2005 and 2008, she can use the *Sales* schema name instead:

```
SELECT * FROM Production.SalesReps.Sales.Leads
```

If Rob ever quits or gets fired, all the *sysadmin* user has to do to transfer ownership of the *Sales* schema to Tammie is the following:

```
ALTER AUTHORIZATION ON SCHEMA::Sales TO Tammie;
GO
```

The abstraction of database users from schemas provides many benefits to developers and administrators, including the following:

- Multiple users can own a single schema through membership in roles or Windows groups. This extends familiar functionality and allows roles and groups to own objects.

- Dropping database users is greatly simplified.

- Dropping a database user does not require renaming objects that are contained by the schema of that user. Therefore, you do not have to revise and test applications that refer explicitly to schema-contained securables after dropping the user who created them.

- Multiple users can share one default schema for uniform name resolution.

- Shared default schemas allow developers to store shared objects in a schema that was created specifically for a particular application, instead of in the *dbo* schema.

- Permissions on schemas and schema-contained securables can be managed with a greater degree of detail than in earlier releases.

- Fully qualified object names have four parts: *server.database.schema.object*.

Execution Context

Granting and managing permissions to non-*sysadmin* users has always been an interesting challenge, especially when it comes to users who own stored procedures that use tables and other objects that they do not own. In a typical example, suppose there are three users: User1, User2, and User3. User3 owns a table, *CustomerInformation*. User2 has written a stored procedure that enumerates only the customer name from this table. User1 needs to execute User2's stored procedure. Prior to SQL Server 2005, User1 not only needed *EXECUTE* permission on User2's stored procedure but also needed access to the underlying *CustomerInformation* table owned by User3. Now multiply this requirement across an enterprise, and you can appreciate the permission management nightmare that unfolded. As of SQL Server 2005, User2 can change the execution context of the stored procedure to any of the following:

- ***EXECUTE AS CALLER***   Executes under the credentials of the caller. This is the same default behavior as in earlier versions of SQL Server.

- ***EXECUTE AS SELF***   Executes under the credentials of the user who last modified the stored procedure.

- ***EXECUTE AS <insert name of login>***   Executes under the credentials of the login specified. For this to work, the user creating or modifying the stored procedure must be granted the *IMPERSONATE* permission for the specified login.

> **Note** *EXECUTE AS* also takes a database user name. If you use a login, the scope for the impersonation is server level. If you use a database user, the scope is for the database only.

- ***EXECUTE AS OWNER***   Executes under the credentials of the login who owns the stored procedure. If the owner changes after the object was created, the execution context is automatically mapped to the new owner.

Referring back to our example, let's script our original problem, as shown in Listing 5-1.

LISTING 5-1 Execution context example

```
--Create our logins
CREATE LOGIN User1 WITH PASSWORD='^*ahfn2@^(K'
GO
CREATE LOGIN User2 WITH PASSWORD='*HABa7s7aas'
GO
CREATE LOGIN User3 WITH PASSWORD='zxd837&^gqF'
GO

CREATE DATABASE MyDB
GO
USE MyDB
GO

--User3 will own a table
CREATE USER User3 WITH DEFAULT_SCHEMA=User3
GO
CREATE SCHEMA User3 AUTHORIZATION User3
GO

--User2 will have SELECT access and write a procedure to access
CREATE USER User2 WITH DEFAULT_SCHEMA=User2
GO
CREATE SCHEMA User2 AUTHORIZATION User2
GO

--User1 will have the right to exec the procedure
CREATE USER User1 WITH DEFAULT_SCHEMA=User1
GO
CREATE SCHEMA User1 AUTHORIZATION User1
GO

GRANT CREATE TABLE TO User3
GO
GRANT CREATE PROC TO User2
GO
EXECUTE AS LOGIN='User3'
GO

CREATE TABLE User3.CustomerInformation
  (CustomerName nvarchar(50))
GO
INSERT INTO CustomerInformation VALUES('Bryan''s Bowling Alley')
INSERT INTO CustomerInformation VALUES('Tammie''s Tavern')
INSERT INTO CustomerInformation VALUES('Frank''s Fresh Produce')
GO
GRANT SELECT ON CustomerInformation TO User2
GO
REVERT
GO
EXECUTE AS LOGIN='User2'
GO
```

```
--create a stored procedure that will return the rows in our table
CREATE PROC ViewCustomerNames
AS
 BEGIN
    SELECT * FROM User3.CustomerInformation
 END
GO
GRANT EXECUTE ON ViewCustomerNames TO User1
GO
REVERT
GO
```

Now that all of the users and objects have been created, let's log in as User1 and try to directly access the table and stored procedure, as shown here:

```
EXECUTE AS LOGIN='User1'

-- User1 cannot access table directly
SELECT * FROM User3.CustomerInformation

--User1 can execute the procedure but does not have permissions on the underlying table
EXEC User2.ViewCustomerNames
GO

REVERT
GO
```

At this point, in versions of SQL Server prior to SQL Server 2005, we would have to give User1 some form of access against User3's table. As of SQL Server 2005, User2 can change the execution context of the stored procedure so that User1 doesn't need to be granted access to User3's table. In our example, User2 will change the execution context to *EXECUTE AS OWNER*. This will cause the stored procedure to be executed as User2 because User2 is the owner of the stored procedure, as shown here:

```
EXECUTE AS LOGIN='User2'
GO

ALTER PROCEDURE ViewCustomerNames WITH EXECUTE AS OWNER
AS
 BEGIN
  SELECT * FROM User3.CustomerInformation
 END
GO

REVERT
GO
```

Now, when User1 executes User2's stored procedure, the stored procedure will be executing under the credentials of User2 and thus have access to User3's table. This access will be permitted only within the context of the stored procedure. Thus, User1 can execute User2's stored procedure without having explicit access to the underlying table, as follows:

```
EXECUTE AS LOGIN='User1'

--User1 still cannot access table directly
SELECT * from User3.CustomerInformation

--User1 can execute a procedure that uses the CustomerInformation table
EXEC User2.ViewCustomerNames
GO

REVERT
GO
```

Another form of execution context switching is used within the preceding example. As of SQL Server 2005, it is possible to change the execution context of the current connection without having to close and reopen the connection. The user must either be a *sysadmin* or have *IMPERSONATE* permission on the login for this to work. Alternatively, you can use this same statement to switch the user context for a database user. When used for switching the context on a database, the scope of impersonation is restricted to the current database. In a context switch to a database user, the server-level permissions of that user are not inherited. In addition, a user must either be a *sysadmin* or have *IMPERSONATE* permission on the user of the database.

Executing context switching is a powerful and efficient way to reduce the number of permissions to manage. For developers and administrators, it provides an easy way to test scripts and debug without having to log out and reconnect to SQL Server.

Encryption Support in SQL Server

Let's face it: data that is stored in databases is interesting not only to us as users but to many others in the world whom we might not know or trust. With the increased leverage of the power of relational databases by businesses and consumers, database vendors are under greater pressure to provide more security-related features.

Other than locking down access to SQL Server databases, administrators and developers can provide another layer of protection against the bad guys, and that is *encryption*. At a high level, encryption takes interesting information, such as your credit card number, and translates it into a binary representation that can be understood only by authorized parties. Data can be encrypted for use in transit, such as when you are sending your password back to a Web server, or it can be stored in an encrypted format (on the file system or in a database, for example). In SQL Server 2008 (Enterprise edition only), the entire database can be encrypted automatically using Transparent Data Encryption (TDE), which will be described in detail later in this chapter.

Data in SQL Server is encrypted using *encryption keys*. These keys can be either *symmetric* or *asymmetric*, and there are pros and cons to using either one. With symmetric key encryption, both the sender and the receiver of the data have the same key. The sender encrypts the data using the key and an encryption algorithm. When the data reaches the recipient, it is decrypted using the same encryption algorithm and key. The main benefit of this approach is better encryption and decryption performance compared with using asymmetric keys. The problem with symmetric key encryption comes into play when we consider what happens when someone else somehow gets hold of our symmetric key. Because we are encrypting with just one key, anyone who has that key can decrypt the data.

Asymmetric key encryption uses two keys, a public key and a private key. The sender encrypts the data using the recipient's public key, which is freely obtainable by anyone. The security comes in when the recipient receives the data; the recipient decrypts it via his or her private key. The public key in this case cannot decrypt the data. Thus, the private key is the valuable asset when using asymmetric encryption.

The other concept that arises in encryption discussions is *certificates*. Certificates are basically asymmetric keys that contain extra *metadata*. This metadata includes information such as an expiration period and the certificate authority that issued the certificate. Certificates can be created by anyone, and in some circumstances, you want to make sure that the sender or recipient of the data is actually who he or she says. This is where certificate authorities come into play. These companies act as a mediator between the sender and receiver. After you pay a nominal fee and they conduct an identity check, they provide you with a certificate that they have signed. When you use this signed certificate to send data, the recipient can validate the certificate with the certificate authority, and because both of you trust the certificate authority, it's safe to assume that the message was in fact signed by the sender.

There is another type of certificate called a *self-signed certificate,* which anyone can create. In some cases, it is acceptable to use a self-signed certificate. SQL Server automatically creates a self-signed certificate the first time it starts. This certificate is used to encrypt the connection during SQL Server authentication.

Encrypting Data on the Move

All connection login requests made to SQL Server are encrypted if the client is using the SQL Server Native Access Client application programming interfaces (APIs). This is a huge improvement, because in SQL Server 2000 and earlier versions, if a user wanted to authenticate using SQL Server Authentication, the user name and password were sent in clear text across the wire. SQL Server 2005 and 2008 can automatically encrypt the login packet information via the self-signed certificate it created the first time the service started.

Login packets are not all that's encrypted in the connection. The entire connection itself can optionally be encrypted for the lifetime of the connection. The request for an encrypted channel can be forced by the server (so that all connections are encrypted by default), or the request can be made by the client making the connection. It is recommended that administrators use a real certificate rather than the self-signed certification because of potential "man-in-the-middle" attacks.

To force encryption on the server, launch the SQL Server Configuration Manager tool (available in the Configuration Tools folder of the SQL Server 2008 Program Files menu item). This tool is used for managing the protocols and services of SQL Server. Expand SQL Server Network Configuration, right-click Protocols For MSSQLSERVER, and select Properties to open the Protocols For MSSQLSERVER Properties dialog box, shown in Figure 5-5.

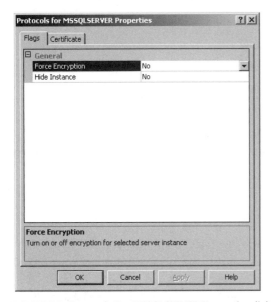

FIGURE 5-5 Protocols For MSSQLSERVER Properties dialog box

The dialog box has two tabs. The Flags tab allows you to force encryption on the server. The Certificate tab allows you to select a certificate that is already installed on the local machine to be used by SQL Server to encrypt the data. If you do not select a certificate and choose to force encryption, SQL Server uses its self-signed certificate to encrypt the data. Remember that SQL Server's self-signed certificate is not considered trusted by the client connections. For clients to be able to use SQL Server's self-signed certificate, they must set this option in the Properties dialog box of the SQL Native Client 10.0 Configuration node in the same Configuration Manager tool. This dialog box is shown in Figure 5-6.

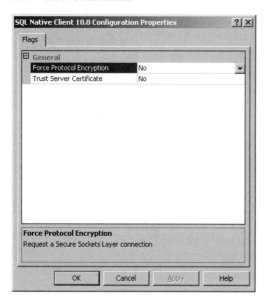

FIGURE 5-6 SQL Native Client 10.0 Configuration Properties dialog box

This dialog box offers two options: The Force Protocol Encryption option forces clients to always make encryption connections. The second option is what needs to be set if the client wants to make encrypted connections to SQL Server and have it leverage SQL Server's self-signed certificate.

Encrypting Data at Rest

Social Security or other government-issue identification numbers, credit card numbers, salary information, driver license numbers, passwords—the list of sensitive information just keeps going. Access to this information stored in the database has traditionally been secured by permissions. This is still the case, but another layer of protection is available natively in SQL Server 2005 and 2008. Sensitive data can now be encrypted by using symmetric keys, asymmetric keys, or certificates.

Before we jump in and encrypt data in a column, it is important to define the building blocks of encryption support within SQL Server. The first time SQL Server starts, it creates a special symmetric key called the Service Master Key (SMK). This key is used to encrypt all database master keys (DMKs) as well as all server-level secrets such as credential secrets or linked server login passwords. The key itself is a 128-bit 3DES key. The 3DES algorithm is used because of its availability on all Windows-based platforms supported by SQL Server.

> **Note** Encryption algorithm availability depends on the cryptographic service provider of the operating system that SQL Server is running on. For example, Microsoft Windows XP Service Pack 2 (SP2) supports DES, 3DES, RC2, RC4, and RSA, while Windows Server 2003 and 2008 support all those plus AES128, AES192, and AES256. An explanation of these algorithms is well beyond the scope of this book, but plenty of resources are available to help you choose an appropriate encryption algorithm. For more information, run a Web search on "Choosing an encryption algorithm for SQL Server."

The SMK is encrypted by using the Windows security API, the Data Protection API (DPAPI), and the credentials of the SQL Server service account. Because the SMK is used to encrypt all DMKs and other server-level secrets, it is very important and should be backed up regularly. You can back up and restore the SMK by using the *BACKUP SERVICE MASTER KEY* or *RESTORE SERVICE MASTER KEY* statement. In the event of a compromised SMK, or if you want to change the SMK as part of implementing a normal security best practice, you can regenerate it by using the *ALTER SERVICE MASTER KEY REGENERATE* statement.

With respect to encrypting data, the SMK is used by SQL Server to decrypt the DMK so that the DMK can in turn decrypt the requested data for the client. There is only one DMK per database, and none are created by default, because a DMK is used only for data encryption.

To create a DMK, we can use the new DDL statement as follows:

```
USE <user-defined database>
GO

CREATE MASTER KEY
 ENCRYPTION BY PASSWORD = '<password>'
```

When DMKs are created, they are encrypted by the SMK (so that SQL Server can decrypt the data for the client) and by a password. It is possible to remove the SMK encryption, but the password of the DMK would need to be specified by the user every time he or she accesses this key.

Now that we have discussed the main components of encryption, let's consider an example. This scenario will include a table named *SalaryInfo* that contains the name, department, and salary of employees at our company. There is a user named *HR_User* that needs to be able to insert and view data into this table.

Because a lot of steps are involved in setting up this example, it is best to walk through Listing 5-2 line by line and follow the inline comments included throughout the listing. The comments explain exactly what each T-SQL statement does and why.

LISTING 5-2 Encryption using *ENCRYPTBYKEY* and *DECRYPTBYKEY*

```
USE master
GO

CREATE LOGIN HR_Login WITH PASSWORD='SomeComplexPassword'
GO

USE MyDB
GO

CREATE USER HR_User FOR LOGIN HR_Login
GO

--Create the database master key for the ExampleDB database
CREATE MASTER KEY ENCRYPTION BY PASSWORD='AComplexPassword'
GO

--Create the table that will store sensitive information
--Notice we use a varbinary for our salary information
--This is because the ciphertext (encrypted data) is binary
CREATE TABLE SalaryInfo
(Employee nvarchar(50),
 Department nvarchar(50),
 Salary varbinary(60))
GO

--Give access to this table to HR_User so it can add data
GRANT SELECT,INSERT TO HR_User
GO

--Create a Symmetric Key
--Encrypt the key with a password
--Give access to the key to HR_User
CREATE SYMMETRIC KEY HR_User_Key
 AUTHORIZATION HR_User
 WITH ALGORITHM=TRIPLE_DES
 ENCRYPTION BY PASSWORD='CompensationPlansRule'
GO

--Now let's log in as HR_User and encrypt some data
EXECUTE AS LOGIN='HR_Login'
GO

--First, we need to open the key that will be used to encrypt data
--Notice we have to pass the password for the key
OPEN SYMMETRIC KEY HR_User_Key DECRYPTION BY PASSWORD='CompensationPlansRule'
GO

--This system view shows open keys that can be used for encryption
SELECT * FROM sys.openkeys

--Insert sensitive data into the table
--ENCRYPTBYKEY takes the GUID of the key and the text of the data
```

```
--Since remembering GUIDs is not easy, KEY_GUID is a function
--that does the lookup for us
INSERT INTO SalaryInfo VALUES
 ('Bryan', 'Sales', ENCRYPTBYKEY(KEY_GUID('HR_User_Key'), '125000'))
INSERT INTO SalaryInfo VALUES
 ('Tammie', 'Sales', ENCRYPTBYKEY(KEY_GUID('HR_User_Key'), '122000'))
INSERT INTO SalaryInfo VALUES
 ('Frank', 'Development', ENCRYPTBYKEY(KEY_GUID('HR_User_Key'), '97500'))
INSERT INTO SalaryInfo VALUES
 ('Fran', 'Marketing', ENCRYPTBYKEY(KEY_GUID('HR_User_Key'), '99500'))

--When we are done, always close all keys
CLOSE ALL SYMMETRIC KEYS
GO

--View the table as it lives in the database; notice the binary
SELECT * FROM SalaryInfo

--Now, let's decrypt and view the contents
--We use DECRYPTBYKEY and pass the column name
--We don't have to specify a key GUID because SQL will look
--at all your open keys and use the appropriate one automatically
OPEN SYMMETRIC KEY HR_User_Key DECRYPTION BY PASSWORD='CompensationPlansRule'
GO

SELECT Employee, Department, CONVERT(varchar, DECRYPTBYKEY(Salary))
 FROM SalaryInfo
GO

CLOSE ALL SYMMETRIC KEYS
GO

--Revert back to sysadmin
REVERT
GO

--When encrypting by password, need to know the password
--and pass it every time you encrypt something
--Alternatively you can create a certificate and give access to
--the HR User. With this, the user doesn't have to provide a password
--and you can easily revoke access to that encrypted data by simply
--removing the certificate for that user
CREATE CERTIFICATE HRCert1
 AUTHORIZATION HR_User
 WITH SUBJECT='Certificate used by the Human Resources person'

--Open the key so we can modify it
OPEN SYMMETRIC KEY HR_User_Key DECRYPTION BY PASSWORD='CompensationPlansRule'
GO

--We cannot remove the password because we would leave the key
--exposed without encryption so we need to add the certificate first
ALTER SYMMETRIC KEY HR_User_Key
ADD ENCRYPTION BY CERTIFICATE HRCert1
GO
```

```
--Now we can remove the password encryption from the key
ALTER SYMMETRIC KEY HR_User_Key
DROP ENCRYPTION BY PASSWORD= 'CompensationPlansRule'
GO
CLOSE ALL SYMMETRIC KEYS
GO

--Now change context to HR_Login to test our changes
EXECUTE AS LOGIN='HR_Login'
GO

--Notice we opened the key without a password!
--This is because we created the certificate and gave authorization
--on it explicitly to HR_User
OPEN SYMMETRIC KEY HR_User_Key DECRYPTION BY CERTIFICATE HRCert1
GO

SELECT Employee, Department, CONVERT(varchar, DECRYPTBYKEY(Salary))
  FROM SalaryInfo
GO
```

The preceding example described the basics of encrypting and decrypting in SQL Server. The amount of data in this example is trivial to encrypt and decrypt, even for old (slow) machines. Performance for encryption depends on two factors other than how big a server you are running on: the size of the data to encrypt and the algorithm used to encrypt the data. Using RSA2048 to encrypt a very large piece of data might take a bit longer than encrypting a Social Security number that has only 9 characters. It is difficult to give a nice graph of size versus time because it depends on so many factors. The best approach is set up a test environment that simulates your production environment and run some performance tests: encrypt and decrypt various data sizes in different algorithms, or at least in the algorithm you are planning to use.

Another interesting issue with encrypted columns is indexing and searching. To SQL Server itself, these are binary columns, so there is no effective way to create an index on them because we cannot predict a random stream of bytes. The best thing to do in this case is to create or use another unencrypted column to index on. The problem with this is that you might inadvertently give information about the data that is encrypted. Imagine we want to index on salaries and create a column named *range*. Anyone who has *SELECT* permission on the table can guess what the employee makes. If you must index or search encrypted data, be creative about your unencrypted columns.

> **More Info** Encryption is not a trivial undertaking, and a thorough discussion is outside the scope of this book. Resources are available online to help you understand more about encryption in SQL Server security. Laurentiu Cristofor, one of the Microsoft developers behind encryption in SQL Server, has a wealth of information on his blog site dedicated to encryption: *http://blogs.msdn.com/lcris*. Raul Garcia is also on the SQL Server Security team. His blog at *http://blogs.msdn.com/raulga/* has additional useful information, as does the dedicated SQL Server Security blog at *http://blogs.msdn.com/sqlsecurity/*.

Transparent Data Encryption in SQL Server 2008

SQL Server can now encrypt the entire database (both the data and the log files) automatically, and without requiring any programming or application changes on your part. This is achieved by using a new feature in SQL Server 2008, available only in the Enterprise edition, called Transparent Data Encryption (TDE). Data is encrypted on the fly as it is written to disk and decrypted when it is read back. Encryption is performed at the page level and does not increase the size of the database. Because the process is entirely transparent, it's extremely easy to use TDE in SQL Server 2008. Let's see how.

> **Note** The NTFS file system in Windows Server 2000 and later provides a feature called Encrypted File System (EFS). This feature also applies transparent encryption to any data stored on the hard drive, but it will not protect databases or backups that have been copied onto a CD or other media. TDE in SQL Server 2008 is based on a certificate that is needed to decrypt or restore any encrypted database, regardless of where the data is transferred.

Creating Keys and Certificates

To start using TDE, you need to create a certificate, and to create a certificate, you need to create a *master key*. You create the master key only once per server instance, and it can be created only in the *master* database. Although certificates in general can be created in any database, certificates used for TDE must be created in the *master* database as well, as shown here:

```
USE master
GO

CREATE MASTER KEY ENCRYPTION BY PASSWORD = 'Hrd2GessP@ssw0rd!'
CREATE CERTIFICATE MyEncryptionCert WITH SUBJECT = 'My Encryption Certificate'
```

You can query the *sys.certificates* view to confirm that the certificate has been created, as follows:

```
SELECT name, pvt_key_encryption_type_desc FROM sys.certificates
 WHERE name = 'MyEncryptionCert'
```

The output verifies that the certificate exists and that its private key is protected by the master key, as shown here:

```
name                            pvt_key_encryption_type_desc
------------------------------- ----------------------------------
MyEncryptionCert                ENCRYPTED_BY_MASTER_KEY

(1 row(s) affected)
```

Next, switch to the database you want to encrypt and create a *database encryption key* (DEK):

```
USE MyDB
GO

CREATE DATABASE ENCRYPTION KEY
 WITH ALGORITHM = AES_128
 ENCRYPTION BY SERVER CERTIFICATE MyEncryptionCert
```

> **Note** Because we have not yet backed up the server certificate, SQL Server issues a warning at this time alerting you to the fact that the certificate being used to encrypt the DEK has not been backed up. This warning should be taken seriously, since you will not be able to access any database encrypted by the DEK without the certificate. Should the certificate be lost or damaged, your encrypted databases will be completely inaccessible. Later in this section, you will learn how to back up and restore the certificate.

This statement creates a DEK for the *MyDB* database. Based on this DEK, SQL Server 2008 will encrypt *MyDB* using the *AES_128* algorithm. The *WITH ALGORITHM* clause can also specify *AES_192, AES_256,* or *TRIPLE_DES_3KEY* to be used for the encryption algorithm. The DEK itself is encrypted by using the *MyEncryptionCert* certificate we created in the *master* database. (A DEK can be encrypted only by a certificate; it cannot be encrypted with just a password.) The DEK will be used not only to encrypt the database but also to protect the database backups. Without the certificate used to encrypt the DEK, an encrypted database backup cannot be restored anywhere, end of story.

Enabling TDE

Once you've created a certificate-protected DEK for the database, you can start the encryption process. Encryption occurs in the background and does not interfere with applications
that are concurrently accessing the database. Use the *ALTER DATABASE* statement and
specify the *SET ENCRYPTION ON* clause to start encrypting the *MyDB* database, as follows:

```
ALTER DATABASE MyDB SET ENCRYPTION ON
```

That's all there is to it! From this point forward, the database and all of its backups will be
encrypted. If an unauthorized party somehow gains access to the physical media holding any
backups, the backups will be useless without the certificate protecting the DEK.

Querying TDE Views

You can query the catalog view *sys.databases* to see which databases are protected by TDE.
For example:

```
SELECT name, is_encrypted FROM sys.databases
```

The query results show that *MyDB* is the only encrypted database on the server:

```
name                          is_encrypted
----------------------------- ------------
master                        0
tempdb                        0
model                         0
msdb                          0
ReportServer                  0
ReportServerTempDB            0
AdventureWorks                0
AdventureWorksDW              0
MyDB                          1

(9 row(s) affected)
```

> **Note** Encrypting one or more databases results in the encryption of *tempdb* as well. This can
> have a performance impact for unencrypted databases on the same server instance. However,
> because the encryption in *tempdb* is implicit, *is_encrypted* is returned as *0* (false) by *sys.databases*
> for *tempdb*.

You can also query the dynamic management view *sys.dm_database_encryption_keys* to see all the DEKs and to monitor the progress of encryption (or decryption, when you disable TDE) running on background threads managed by SQL Server. This view returns the unique database ID that can be joined on *sys.databases* to see the actual database name. For example, if we run the following query after enabling TDE, we can obtain information about the DEK and background encryption process:

```
SELECT
    sys.databases.name,
    sys.dm_database_encryption_keys.encryption_state,
    sys.dm_database_encryption_keys.percent_complete,
    sys.dm_database_encryption_keys.key_algorithm,
    sys.dm_database_encryption_keys.key_length
 FROM
    sys.dm_database_encryption_keys INNER JOIN sys.databases
    ON sys.dm_database_encryption_keys.database_id = sys.databases.database_id
 WHERE
    sys.databases.name = 'MyDB'
```

If this query is executed after we enable TDE but before SQL Server has completed encrypting the entire database in the background, we get results similar to the following:

```
name        encryption_state percent_complete key_algorithm  key_length
----------  ---------------- ---------------- -------------- -----------
MyDB        2                78.86916         AES            128

(1 row(s) affected)
```

The value returned by *encryption_state* tells you the current status of encryption (or decryption), as follows:

- 1 = Unencrypted
- 2 = Encryption in progress
- 3 = Encrypted
- 4 = Key change in progress
- 5 = Decryption in progress (after *ALTER DATABASE...SET ENCRYPTION OFF*)

Certain database operations cannot be performed during any of the "in progress" states (2, 4, or 5). These include enabling or disabling encryption, dropping or detaching the database, dropping a file from a file group, taking the database offline, or transitioning the database (or any of its file groups) to a *READ ONLY* state.

Backing Up the Certificate

It is extremely important to back up the server certificates you use to encrypt your databases with TDE. Without the certificate, you will not be able to access the encrypted database or restore encrypted database backups (which, of course, is the point of TDE). Attempting to restore an encrypted database without the certificate will fail with an error similar to this from SQL Server:

```
Msg 33111, Level 16, State 3, Line 1
Cannot find server certificate with thumbprint '0x6B1FEEEE238847DE75D1850FA20D87CF94F71F33'.
Msg 3013, Level 16, State 1, Line 1
RESTORE DATABASE is terminating abnormally.
```

Use the following statement to back up the server certificate to a file. In addition to the certificate itself, the certificate's private key must also be saved to a file and protected with a password.

```
BACKUP CERTIFICATE MyEncryptionCert TO FILE='C:\MyEncryptionCert.certbak'
 WITH PRIVATE KEY (
  FILE='C:\MyEncryptionCert.pkbak',
  ENCRYPTION BY PASSWORD='Pr!vK3yP@ssw0rd')
```

This statement creates two files: *MyEncryptionCert.certbak* is a backup of the server certificate, and *MyEncryptionCert.pkbak* is a backup of the certificate's private key protected with the password *Pr!vK3yP@ssw0rd*. Password protection is absolutely required when backing up the certificate's private key. Both of these files and the password will be needed to restore an encrypted database backup onto another server or instance. At the risk of stating the obvious, these backup files and the private key password should be closely safeguarded.

Restoring an Encrypted Database

Before an encrypted database can be restored elsewhere, the server certificate that its DEK is encrypted by must be restored first. And if the target instance does not have a master key, one must be created for it before the server certificate can be restored, as shown here:

```
USE master
GO

CREATE MASTER KEY ENCRYPTION BY PASSWORD = 'An0thrHrd2GessP@ssw0rd!'
```

To restore the server certificate from the backup files we made earlier, use an alternative form of the *CREATE CERTIFICATE* statement, as follows:

```
CREATE CERTIFICATE MyEncryptionCert
 FROM FILE='C:\MyEncryptionCert.certbak'
 WITH PRIVATE KEY(
  FILE='C:\MyEncryptionCert.pkbak',
  DECRYPTION BY PASSWORD='Pr!vK3yP@ssw0rd')
```

This statement restores the *MyEncryptionCert* server certificate from the certificate backup file *MyEncryptionCert.certbak* and the certificate's private key backup file *MyEncryptionCert.pkbak*. Naturally, the password provided in the *DECRYPTION BY PASSWORD* clause must

match the one that was used when the certificate's private key was backed up, or the certificate will fail to restore. With a successfully restored certificate, you can then restore the
backup of any encrypted database whose DEK is based on the *MyEncryptionCert* certificate.

SQL Server Audit

SQL Server 2008 introduces SQL Server Audit—a powerful new security feature that can track
virtually any server or database action taken by users and log those activities to the file system or the Windows event log. Like TDE, SQL Server Audit is available only in the Enterprise
edition of SQL Server 2008. This feature helps meet the demands of regulatory compliance
standards, which typically require that our enterprise installations implement highly stringent
security tactics that often include some form of auditing. You can work with SQL Server Audit
either by using SQL Server Management Studio or in T-SQL by using a new set of DDL statements and catalog views.

> **Note** Here we cover only the T-SQL DDL auditing statements and catalog views except when
> showing how to view audit logs in SQL Server Management Studio. In SQL Server Management
> Studio, you'll find SQL Server Audit support beneath the Security nodes at both the server and
> database levels.

Creating an Audit Object

Our first step to using SQL Server Audit is to create an *audit object* with the *CREATE SERVER
AUDIT* statement. When we create an audit object, we are essentially defining a destination
to which SQL Server will record information about interesting events that occur. The specific
events to be monitored for are described by creating *audit specifications*, which we define
after creating one or more audit objects.

An audit object can capture monitored events to either the file system or to the Application
or Security event log. The desired destination is specified after the *TO* keyword in the *CREATE
SERVER AUDIT* statement. For example, the following statement creates an audit object
named *MyFileAudit* that records all monitored events that will be associated with this audit
object to files that SQL Server will create in the *C:\SqlAudits* directory (which must already
exist, or the statement will fail):

```
USE master
GO

CREATE SERVER AUDIT MyFileAudit TO FILE (FILEPATH='C:\SqlAudits')
```

Notice that it is necessary to first switch to the *master* database before you can create an audit object. If you don't switch away from a user database to the *master* database before running this DDL statement, SQL Server will return the following error:

```
Msg 33074, Level 16, State 1, Line 1
Cannot create a server audit from a user database. This operation must be performed in the
master database.
```

When an audit object is first created, it is in a disabled state and will not audit any events until it is explicitly enabled. You cannot create and enable an audit in a single step by using *CREATE SERVER AUDIT*, so the next step after creating an audit is to enable it by using *ALTER SERVICE AUDIT*. The following statement enables the *MyFileAudit* audit object we just created:

```
ALTER SERVER AUDIT MyFileAudit WITH (STATE=ON)
```

Just as when first creating an audit object, you must switch to the *master* database before you can execute an *ALTER SERVER AUDIT* statement (which is not necessary here, as we haven't yet switched away from *master* since creating the audit object).

The *ALTER SERVER AUDIT* statement can also be used with the *MODIFY NAME* clause to rename the audit object. The audit must be disabled before it can be renamed. For example, the following statements rename the audit object *MyFileAudit* to *SqlFileAudit*:

```
ALTER SERVER AUDIT MyFileAudit WITH (STATE=OFF)
ALTER SERVER AUDIT MyFileAudit MODIFY NAME = SqlFileAudit
ALTER SERVER AUDIT SqlFileAudit WITH (STATE=ON)
```

Once an audit object is created, you can define one or more audit specifications to monitor specific events of interest and associate those specifications with the audit object. Audited events captured by all audit specifications associated with an audit object are recorded to the destination defined by that audit object. We'll talk about audit specifications shortly, but first let's discuss some more general auditing options.

Auditing Options

You can specify several important options for your audit objects. These options, declared after the *WITH* keyword in either the *CREATE SERVER AUDIT* or *ALTER SERVER AUDIT* statement (or, in some cases, in both), are independent of the audit destination (that is, they are supported whether you're recording to the file system or to the event log).

QUEUE_DELAY

The *QUEUE_DELAY* option controls the synchronous or asynchronous behavior of audit processing. Specifying 0 for this option results in synchronous auditing. Otherwise, this option specifies any integer value of 1000 or higher to implement asynchronous processing for better auditing performance. The integer value for this option specifies the longest amount of time (in milliseconds) that is allowed to elapse before audit actions are forced to be processed in the background. The default value 1000 results in asynchronous processing in which monitored events are audited within 1 second from the time that they occur.

The *QUEUE_DELAY* setting can be specified when the audit object is created and then later changed as needed. To change this setting for a running audit object, you must first disable the audit object before making the change and then enable it again afterwards.

The following statements increase the time span for asynchronous processing of our *MyFileAudit* audit object by specifying the *QUEUE_DELAY* option with the value 60000 (60,000 milliseconds, or 1 minute). The audit object is temporarily disabled while the change is made.

```
ALTER SERVER AUDIT MyFileAudit WITH (STATE=OFF)
ALTER SERVER AUDIT MyFileAudit WITH (QUEUE_DELAY=60000)
ALTER SERVER AUDIT MyFileAudit WITH (STATE=ON)
```

ON_FAILURE

You can use the *ON_FAILURE* option to determine what course of action SQL Server should take if an error occurs while audited events are being recorded. The valid setting for this option is *CONTINUE* (which is the default) or *SHUTDOWN* (which requires that the login be granted the *SHUTDOWN* permission). This option can be specified when the audit object is created and then later changed as desired. As with *QUEUE_DELAY*, a running audit object must be temporarily disabled while the change is made.

Using *ON_FAILURE=SHUTDOWN* guarantees that the SQL Server instance brings itself down completely if it is unable to record security audits. For example, the following statements tell the running SQL Server instance to shut down if an error occurs while attempting to record to the *MyFileAudit* audit object.

```
ALTER SERVER AUDIT MyFileAudit WITH (STATE=OFF)
ALTER SERVER AUDIT MyFileAudit WITH (ON_FAILURE=SHUTDOWN)
ALTER SERVER AUDIT MyFileAudit WITH (STATE=ON)
```

AUDIT_GUID

By default, all audits are assigned an automatically generated unique globally unique identifier (GUID) value. In mirroring scenarios, you need to assign a specific GUID that matches the GUID contained in the mirrored database, and the *AUDIT_GUID* option allows you to do that. Once an audit object is created, its GUID value cannot be changed.

STATE

The *STATE* option is valid only with the *ALTER SERVER AUDIT* statement. It is used to enable or disable an audit object, using the keywords *ON* and *OFF*. (Recall that an audit object cannot be created in an enabled state.) As demonstrated earlier with the *QUEUE_DELAY* option, the *STATE* option cannot be combined with other audit options in an *ALTER SERVER AUDIT* statement.

When a running audit is disabled by using *STATE=OFF*, an audit entry is created indicating that the audit was stopped, when it was stopped, and which user stopped it.

Recording Audits to the File System

The *TO FILE* clause is used to record audits to the file system, as we've just specified for our *MyFileAudit* audit object. When you audit to the file system, you can specify several file options, as described here.

FILEPATH

Use the *FILEPATH* option to designate where in the file system SQL Server should create the files that record monitored events being audited. This can be either a local path or a remote location using a Universal Naming Convention (UNC) path to a network share. The directory specified by this path must exist, or an error will occur. Moreover, you need to make sure that the appropriate permissions are granted on each directory you'll be using, especially network shares. You cannot control the file names used for the files created by SQL Server Audit. Instead, the file names are generated automatically based on the audit name and audit GUID.

MAXSIZE

The *MAXSIZE* option specifies how large an audit file is permitted to grow before it is closed and a new one is opened (known as "rolling over"). The maximum size is expressed as an integer followed by *MB*, *GB*, or *TB* for megabytes, gigabytes, or terabytes. Note that you cannot specify a value less than 1 megabyte.

MAXSIZE can also be specified as *UNLIMITED* (which is the default value). In this case, the audit file can grow to any size before rolling over.

MAX_ROLLOVER_FILES

The *MAX_ROLLOVER_FILES* option can be used to automatically groom the file system as auditing data accumulates over time. The default value is 0, which means that no cleanup is performed as new audit files are created. (This will eventually, of course, fill the disk.) Alternatively, you can provide an integer value for this option that specifies how many audit files are retained in the file system as they roll over, whereas older audit files get deleted automatically.

RESERVE_DISK_SPACE

The default setting for the *RESERVE_DISK_SPACE* option is *OFF*, which means that disk space is dynamically allocated for the audit file as it expands to record more and more events. Performance can be improved (and disk fragmentation reduced) by preallocating disk space for the audit file at the time it is created. Setting this option to *ON* will allocate the amount of space specified by the *MAXSIZE* option when the audit file is created. *MAXSIZE* must be set to some value other than its default *UNLIMITED* setting to use *RESERVE_DISK_SPACE=ON*.

Recording Audits to the Windows Event Log

You can also create audit objects that record to the Windows event log. To send audit entries to either the Application or Security event log, specify *TO APPLICATION_LOG* or *TO SECURITY_LOG*. For example, this statement creates an audit object that records to the Application event log:

```
CREATE SERVER AUDIT MyEventLogAudit TO APPLICATION_LOG
```

Auditing Server Events

You create a *server audit specification* to monitor events that occur at the server level, such as failed login attempts or other actions not associated with any particular database. As already described, we associate our specifications with an audit object configured for recording to either the file system or the event log.

Use the *CREATE SERVER AUDIT SPECIFICATION* statement to create a specification that monitors one or more server-level events for auditing. The *FOR SERVER AUDIT* clause links the specification with an audit object that defines the destination, and *ADD* clauses list the server-level audit action groups to be monitored. Similarly, the *ALTER SERVER AUDIT SPECIFICATION* statement can be used to *ADD* more action groups to be monitored or *DROP* existing ones that should no longer be monitored.

Unlike audit objects, audit specifications can be created and enabled at the same time by using *CREATE SERVER AUDIT SPECIFICATION* with the *STATE=ON* option. The following statements create and enable a server audit specification that records all successful logins and failed login attempts to the file system (to the path *C:\SqlAudits*, as defined by the audit object *MyFileAudit* created earlier in this section):

```
CREATE SERVER AUDIT SPECIFICATION CaptureLoginsToFile
 FOR SERVER AUDIT MyFileAudit
  ADD (FAILED_LOGIN_GROUP),
  ADD (SUCCESSFUL_LOGIN_GROUP)
 WITH (STATE=ON)
GO
```

After executing this statement, all login attempts made against the server (whether or not they succeed) will be audited to the file system. If we later decide to also audit password changes and to stop auditing successful logins, we can alter the specification accordingly (as with audit objects, audit specifications must be disabled while they are being changed):

```
ALTER SERVER AUDIT SPECIFICATION CaptureLoginsToFile  WITH (STATE=OFF)
ALTER SERVER AUDIT SPECIFICATION CaptureLoginsToFile
 ADD (LOGIN_CHANGE_PASSWORD_GROUP),
 DROP (SUCCESSFUL_LOGIN_GROUP)
ALTER SERVER AUDIT SPECIFICATION CaptureLoginsToFile  WITH (STATE=ON)
GO
```

You'll find a complete list of server-level action groups that can be monitored for auditing in SQL Server Books Online. There are more than thirty-five action groups, including backup and restore operations; changes in database ownership; adding or removing logins from server and database roles; and creating, altering, or dropping any database object—just to name a few.

Auditing Database Events

A *database audit specification* is conceptually similar to a server audit specification. Both specify events to be monitored and directed to a designated audit object. The primary difference is that database audit specifications are associated with actions against a particular database rather than server-level actions.

 Note Database audit specifications reside in the database they are created for. You cannot audit database actions in *tempdb*.

The *CREATE DATABASE AUDIT SPECIFICATION* and *ALTER DATABASE AUDIT SPECIFICATION* statements work the same as their *CREATE* and *ALTER* counterparts for server audit specifications that we just examined. Like server audit specifications, database audit specifications can be created in an enabled state by including the clause *WITH (STATE=ON)*.

About fifteen database-level action groups can be monitored for auditing, such as changes in database ownership or permissions, for example. You can find the complete list in SQL Server Books Online. In addition, you can monitor for specific actions directly on database objects, such as schemas, tables, views, and stored procedures. The seven database-level audit actions are *SELECT, INSERT, UPDATE, DELETE, EXECUTE, RECEIVE*, and *REFERENCES*.

For example, the following statement creates and enables a database audit specification in the *MyDB* database named *CaptureDbActionsToEventLog*:

```
USE MyDB
GO

CREATE DATABASE AUDIT SPECIFICATION CaptureDbActionsToEventLog
 FOR SERVER AUDIT MyEventLogAudit
  ADD (DATABASE_OBJECT_CHANGE_GROUP),
  ADD (SELECT, INSERT, UPDATE, DELETE
        ON SCHEMA::dbo
        BY public)
WITH (STATE=ON)
```

The *FOR SERVER AUDIT* clause specifies that the monitored events should be directed to the server object *MyEventLogAudit*, which we created earlier to record audits to the application event log. The first *ADD* clause specifies *DATABASE_OBJECT_CHANGE_GROUP*, which watches for DDL changes made to any database object. This effectively audits any *CREATE*, *ALTER*, or *DROP* statement made against any object (table, view, and so on) in the database. The second *ADD* clause audits any DML action (*SELECT*, *INSERT*, *UPDATE*, or *DELETE*) made against any object in the *dbo* schema by any *public* user (which is every user).

> **Note** DDL triggers added in SQL Server 2005 provide another mechanism for capturing DDL events. See Chapter 2, in which we cover DDL triggers, for more information.

You get very fine-grained control with database audit specifications. The *ON* clause in the preceding statement causes every object in the *dbo* schema to be audited, but it could just as easily be written to audit DML operations on specific tables if desired. Similarly, rather than all users being audited by specifying the *public* role in the *BY* clause, individual users and roles can be listed so that only DML operations made by those particular users are audited.

Viewing Audited Events

After you enable your audit objects and audit specifications, SQL Server takes it from there. Audits for each monitored event declared in your audit specifications are recorded automatically to the destinations you've specified in your audit objects. After accumulating several audits, you'll want to view them, of course.

Audits recorded to the event log can be examined by using the Event Viewer (available from Administrative Tools in Control Panel). For example, Figure 5-7 shows the properties of an event recorded by a database audit for a *DELETE* statement against the *TestTable* table displayed by using the Event Viewer.

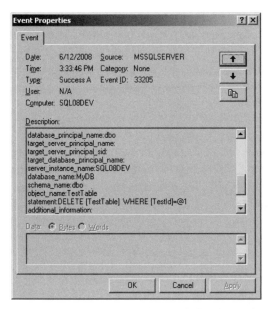

FIGURE 5-7 Displaying an audit recorded to the Application event log using the Event Viewer

Audits recorded to the file system are not stored in plain text files that can simply be viewed in Notepad. Instead, they are binary files that you can view in one of two ways. One way is from inside SQL Server Management Studio. Right-click the desired audit object beneath the Security node at the server instance level (not the Security node at the database level) in Object Explorer, and then choose View Audit Logs. This opens the Log File Viewer window, as shown in Figure 5-8.

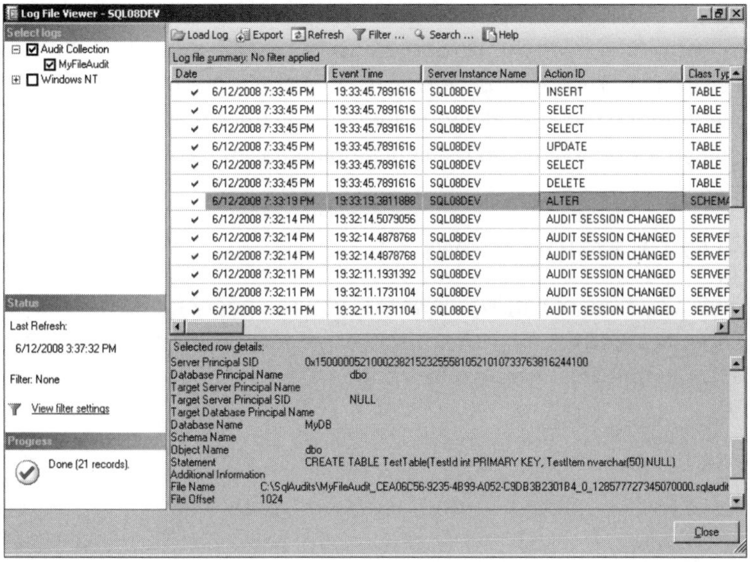

FIGURE 5-8 Displaying audits recorded to the file system using the Log File Viewer in Management Studio

Each audit entry contains a wealth of detailed information about the event that was captured and recorded. This includes date and time stamp, server instance, action, object type, success or failure, permissions, principal name and ID (that is, the user that performed the audited action), database name, schema name, object name, the actual statement that was executed (or attempted), and more.

Alternatively, you can use the new table-valued function (TVF) named *sys.fn_get_audit_file*. This function accepts a parameter that points to one or more audit files (using wildcard pattern matching). Two additional parameters allow you to specify the initial file to process and a known offset location to start reading audit records from. (Both of these parameters are optional but must still be specified by using the keyword *default*.) The function then reads the binary data from the file or files and formats the audit entries into an ordinary table that gets returned. For example:

```
SELECT event_time, database_name, schema_name, object_name, statement
 FROM sys.fn_get_audit_file('C:\SqlAudits\*.sqlaudit', default, default)
```

Here are some abbreviated results from this query:

```
event_time               database_name schema_name object_name statement
----------------------   ------------- ----------- ----------- ----------------------------
    :
2008-06-12 19:33:19.381 MyDB                       dbo         CREATE TABLE TestTable(TestId…
2008-06-12 19:33:45.789 MyDB          dbo          TestTable   INSERT INTO [TestTable] value…
2008-06-12 19:33:45.789 MyDB          dbo          TestTable   SELECT * FROM TestTable
2008-06-12 19:33:45.789 MyDB          dbo          TestTable   UPDATE [TestTable] set [TestI…
2008-06-12 19:33:45.789 MyDB          dbo          TestTable   UPDATE [TestTable] set [TestI…
2008-06-12 19:33:45.789 MyDB          dbo          TestTable   DELETE [TestTable]  WHERE [Te…
2008-06-12 19:33:45.789 MyDB          dbo          TestTable   DELETE [TestTable]  WHERE [Te…
    :
```

You can of course easily filter and sort this data by using *WHERE* and *ORDER BY*, as well as *INSERT* the data elsewhere. The *sys.fn_get_audit_file* function represents an advantage that auditing to the file system has over auditing to the Windows event log, as there is no equivalent function provided for querying and manipulating audits in the event logs.

Querying Audit Catalog Views

SQL Server provides a number of catalog views that you can query for information about the audits and audit specifications running on any server instance. These audit catalog views are listed in Table 5-3, accompanied by a brief description of each.

TABLE 5-3 Audit Catalog Views

Catalog View Name	Description
sys.server_file_audits	Returns all of the audit objects that are recorded to the file system
sys.server_audit_specifications	Returns all of the server-level audit specifications
sys.server_audit_specification_details	Returns detailed monitored event information for all of the server-level audit specifications
sys.database_audit_specifications	Returns all of the database-level audit specifications
sys.database_audit_specification_details	Returns detailed monitored event information for all of the database-level audit specifications
sys.dm_server_audit_status	Returns the status of each audit object
sys.dm_audit_actions	Returns every audit action that can be reported on and every audit action group that can be configured
sys.dm_audit_class_type_map	Returns a table that maps the class_type field in the audit log to the class_desc field in sys.dm_audit_actions

How Hackers Attack SQL Server

This section starts with a disclaimer: We do not cover every possible way that hackers can attempt to compromise SQL Server. Rather, we introduce the various methods of exploitation and try to get you thinking about security up front when you design database applications and configure your system. Let's start the discussion with topics related to how SQL Server is configured.

Direct Connection to the Internet

Exposing any operating system or application directly to the Internet without the use of a firewall is a bad thing—no matter whether you are using Linux, UNIX, Windows, or any other operating system. It's rather like the carnival game where someone sits on a platform above a pool of water waiting for someone else to throw a ball and hit the bull's-eye. When that happens, the person sitting on the platform is plunged into the water. Why expose your system, allowing anyone to take shots until you eventually get soaked? Microsoft has done a lot of work toward protecting its operating systems and applications out of the box. When an exploitation is discovered, they quickly address these problems and provide fixes.

This is only half of the battle, though. With all the switches and states of security for various products, it is not that difficult for an administrator or user to inadvertently misconfigure something and expose the systems to exploitation. To mitigate these issues, it is important that users isolate their systems from the Internet via firewalls and other isolation techniques.

Weak System Administrator Account Passwords

One of the easiest ways to give someone the keys to SQL Server is by providing a weak password for the system administrator (SA) account. In versions of SQL Server prior to SQL Server 2005, it was possible to give a blank password for the SA account without much complaint from SQL Server itself. As of SQL Server 2005, there is a lot more functionality around password policies and enforcement. Earlier in this chapter, we mentioned this topic in regard to SQL Server authentication accounts obeying the group policies of the Windows domain. Configuring a strong password length and account lockout in your domain will ensure that all users of SQL Server are supplying passwords that are more difficult to crack.

SQL Server Browser Service

SQL Server uses UDP port 1434 to return SQL Server instance names and port numbers to the requesting client. A few years back, this enumeration was the key to the "SQL Slammer" DoS virus. By consistently hitting the server with requests for enumeration, the virus left the server too busy to process other requests. Starting with SQL Server 2005, this enumeration functionality is in a separate service called the SQL Server Browser service. The functionality no longer runs in SQL Server's process space, and it can be turned on and off without affecting SQL Server. If you do not want to use the SQL Server Browser service, you can still connect to other instances on your server, but the connection string must contain additional information (such as a specific port number in the case of TCP connections). If you want to use the Browser service in your organization, you can mitigate additional attacks by blocking UDP port 1434 on your firewall.

SQL Injection

SQL injection is the process by which a malicious user enters SQL statements instead of valid input. For example, suppose a Web site is asking for a user name. Instead of actually typing in a user name, a malicious user could type *'blah'; DROP TABLE Sales;*. The Web server will happily take the user input and pass it along to the application layer, where it is executed in code as follows:

```
SqlCommand cmd = new SqlCommand
  ("SELECT * FROM Sales WHERE Name='" + customerName + "'", conn)
```

To SQL Server, it looks like the following:

```
SELECT * FROM Sales WHERE Name='blah'; DROP TABLE Sales;
```

When this statement executes, the sales table will be erased (which is not quite what the application developer had in mind!). You can see how easy it is for malicious users to cause problems and return potentially sensitive information via simple inputs to Web pages or applications that blindly accept user input to build dynamic SQL. To eliminate this potential, add the user input as a parameter to the *SqlCommand* rather than concatenating dynamic SQL strings, as shown here:

```
SqlCommand cmd = new SqlCommand("SELECT * FROM Sales WHERE Name=@CustomerName", conn));
cmd.Parameters.Add("@CustomerName", customerName);
```

By using the *Parameters* collection of the *SqlCommand* object, whatever the user types will be treated just as the value of the name part of the *WHERE* clause.

Intelligent Observation

With powerful search engines such as Google and MSN Search, finding things on the Web is relatively easy. Web crawlers from these search engines go off and fetch key words and place them into their own internal database. These key words are used within their own search algorithms so that when you type something to search on, the search engine can easily return a list of possible choices. These crawlers not only search for and store things like Web sites for pizza places, they also obtain various kinds of error information returned from Web servers. Error information is very valuable to hackers. For example, if a hacker types *invalid password access denied* into the search string in MSN, they'll get a list of various topics that are, in general, not that interesting. However, one item might show this string: *Warning: mysql_pconnect(): Access denied for user 'root'@'localhost' (using password: YES) in /home/vhosts/<<removed for legal reasons>>/docs/citeheader.inc.php on line 2*. Hackers know that this site is using MySQL and PHP, and they also learn some of the directory structure of the Web site */home/vhosts/<<removed for legal reasons>>/docs*. Now they can try to query that individual directory path using an ordinary browser to see whether they can uncover any additional goodies—a script file, perhaps. If they find a script file in this directory and the developer has hard-coded login credentials to the database, they are only one connection away from compromising the database.

The moral of the story is that search engines are very good hacker tools. Never hard-code passwords in script files, and always provide Web page redirects for errors within your Web application. In addition, always pay extra attention to any Web application that receives input. Make sure that these kinds of data are protected against SQL injection attacks.

Summary

Security is one of the most important considerations in any project, and the time you spend learning how to lock down SQL Server and your application is worthwhile in the long run. Microsoft has made efforts to increase the security of SQL Server 2008 out of the box by turning off features such as *xp_cmdshell*, the SQL Server Agent service, and many other optional features within the product. It has also extended the security feature set by adding the ability to easily encrypt data in transit and at rest within the database, by providing more granular permissions and allowing easy context switching, among other examples.

This chapter introduced some of the core concepts of security in SQL Server. You learned about logins, users, roles, and schemas, as well as authentication and authorization. We then went on to cover advanced new security features in SQL Server 2008 such as encryption and auditing. Many online resources (such as SQL Server Books Online) go through these and additional security topics in more detail. As you sit down to design your next application, never stop thinking of how someone might try to illegally gain access to your data or application. In today's world, a simple lock on the door to keep honest people honest is not enough. Everyone from IT professionals to developers needs to be diligent and must always be thinking about security.

Part II
Beyond Relational

In this part:

Chapter 6	XML and the Relational Database............................ 231
Chapter 7	Hierarchical Data and the Relational Database................. 281
Chapter 8	Using FILESTREAM for Unstructured Data Storage 307
Chapter 9	Geospatial Data Types...................................... 341

Chapter 6
XML and the Relational Database

—Stephen Forte

Since it appeared on the world scene in 1998, Extensible Markup Language (XML) has become quite a useful standard for exchanging data and documents between different systems. XML is a markup language (derived from Standard Generalized Markup Language, or SGML) for documents that contain structured information.

You might be wondering why you would want to store and work with XML in the database. Isn't that what XML parsers and applications are for? Until now, XML was usually derived from database tables and queries and then programmatically placed into a transport format (such as a physical document or a Web service), parsed, read on the receiving end, and then placed in another database.

Database purists might insist that you should never store XML in the database because it is a transfer mechanism, not a storage mechanism. They would argue that you should always use XML to transport data from one database or application to another, deconstruct the XML on import and store it in relational tables, and reconstruct it on export from the relational tables back to XML for transport. On the other end of the spectrum, XML junkies (especially bloggers) might argue that the database is dead—that you don't need databases anymore because XML provides a nice data storage mechanism with data integrity (XML Schema, also known as XML Schema Definition [XSD]) and a query engine (XQuery or even XPath). They view the world as just a bunch of XML files—they rarely use relational databases and instead use XML technologies to store and manipulate their data.

As with the most extreme viewpoints in any dispute, however, both camps are wrong. Each has a good argument and valid points. A relational database has features such as primary keys, indexes, and referential integrity that make it a far superior storage and querying mechanism for raw data. Some applications, or even databases themselves, shred XML data into relational data to store it in the database and compose XML when data is retrieved. At other times, the XML data is simply persisted as (unstructured) text in the database. When Microsoft SQL Server 2000 was introduced, it offered both of these options, yet neither is necessarily the desirable solution today. It would be much better if XML could be stored in a relational database in its native format.

So which do you use, a "pure" relational approach or a hybrid approach where you store XML in the database and work with it there? The answer, as with so much in SQL Server, is, "It depends." When you are architecting a highly transactional application system (tradition-ally referred to as an online transaction processing, or OLTP, system) where many simulta-neous reads and writes are performed by users, the most suitable choice is a full relational database technology that includes features such as primary keys, referential integrity, and transactions. Or if you have a massive data warehouse and want to provide users with access to trend analysis and data mining algorithms, you should probably use the traditional relational model in conjunction with the online analytical processing (OLAP) technology.

We will not try to convince you to convert all of your data to XML just for the sake of using a new technology, but sometimes you should definitely consider using XML in your database. One situation in which you might want to store and use XML in a relational database occurs when you are transforming data out of an OLTP database to another, "flatter" (less relational), database that is used for simple queries and for display on Web pages. For example, let's say you have a highly transactional real-time database with many users and highly normalized data. This data also powers your Web site, but the Web site can tolerate a level of latency in terms of the data being refreshed from the real-time application. (An example is a traditional banking application, which usually takes from 2 minutes to 1 day for an ATM transaction to appear on your online banking site, depending on the bank.) A good architecture choice is to transform on a regular basis (as your business needs require) the OLTP data to a more denormalized or flat model used for Web access and reports. Your data model is then tailored to the Web page access and queries that drive page content, and you can build an index strategy around this process. At this point, you might want to store some data for XML because you can easily transform it, bind it, or do whatever you want to it on the client side.

One such example from our experience involved architecting a large consumer destination Web site during the dot-com boom. This site was a well-known "brand name," and traffic was huge—more than a billion unique page views a month. We "published" a version of the OLTP database every four hours from production to the flat Web database. A few of the tables were for user search result functionality and contained all the detail of a record's data from our core business data in XML format in a *TEXT* column. The XML data was hierarchical and contained data from several sources, so it was a convenience to the Web developer to represent and store it as XML directly in the database. This approach was also advantageous because we had to support multiple clients: Netscape, Microsoft Internet Explorer, and Wireless Markup Language (WML) for mobile/cellular access. (This was pre–Microsoft ASP.NET.) Our client ASP page transformed the XML field based on what browser was detected, so different HTML was sent down for Internet Explorer and Netscape, and WML was created with the same page data for mobile browsers.

A negative result of this approach was that we could not use a lot of the XML technologies inside the database and we had to rely heavily on Extensible Stylesheet Language Transformations (XSLT) on the client tier. At the time, SQL Server 2000 did not support XML as much as we would have liked.

XML in SQL Server 2000

As mentioned in the preceding section, SQL Server 2000 offered two options for working with XML data: shred and compose, or store as text. While revolutionary at the time, today this capability is too limiting, and here's why. Let's assume that a developer decides to store XML data in a text data type in a SQL Server 2000 database. The first issue is validating the XML that is persisted (and by this, we mean validating the XML against an XSD schema). SQL Server 2000 has no means of performing such a validation, so the XML data can't be validated except by an outside application (a risky proposition—the true power of a relational database management system, or RDBMS, is applying rules at the server level).

The second issue is querying the data. Sure, you could look for data using character and pattern matching by using functions such as *CharIndex* or *PatIndex*, but these functions cannot efficiently or dependably find specific data in a structured XML document. In the consumer Web site in the preceding example, we had to put the search elements from the XML data column into regular SQL Server fields for querying. The developer could also implement full-text search, which could also index the text data, but this solution would make things only a little better. It would still be difficult to extract data from a specific attribute in a specific child element in the XML content, and it wouldn't be very efficient. You would not be able to write a query that said "Show me all data where the 'Author' attribute is set to 'John Smith'."

The third issue is modifying the XML data. The developer could simply replace the entire XML contents—which is not at all efficient—or use the *UpdateText* function to do in-place changes. However, *UpdateText* requires that you know the exact locations and length of data you are going to replace, which, as we just stated, would be difficult to do and slow.

Unless the XML is being persisted in the database as is and is being replaced as needed, it is difficult to implement an XML storage solution using text. Therefore, developers have taken the other route and have shredded and composed XML data as it is put in and retrieved from the database. SQL Server 2000 offered two features to facilitate these options: the *OPENXML* function for shredding XML data and the *FOR XML* clause of the *SELECT* statement for composing XML. However, *OPENXML* is not the most efficient mechanism for shredding XML data, and *FOR XML* has its own limitations that in moderately complex scenarios require the use of the *EXPLICIT* option. (As any developer who has used this option will tell you, it is not a pretty sight.) Consequently, developers would instead shred and compose XML outside the database and pass relational data to and from SQL Server.

The natural evolution of persisting native XML data in the database has been realized in SQL Server 2005 and SQL Server 2008, which allow XML to be stored in its native format in the database. Not only can SQL Server now persist native XML data in the database, but it can index the data, query it using XPath and XQuery, and even modify it efficiently.

XML in SQL Server 2008—the *xml* Data Type

SQL Server 2005 introduced a new data type, *xml*, for working with XML data, and SQL Server 2008 further enhances it. Using this new data type, you can store XML in its native format, query the data within the XML, efficiently and easily modify data within the XML without having to replace the entire contents, and index the data in the XML. You can use *xml* as any of the following:

- A variable

- A parameter in a stored procedure or a user-defined function (UDF)

- A return value from a UDF

- A column in a table

There are some limitations of the *xml* data type that you should be aware of. Although this data type can contain and be checked for null values, unlike other native types, you cannot directly compare an instance of an *xml* data type with another instance of an *xml* data type. (You can, however, convert that instance to a *TEXT* data type and then do a compare.) Any such equality comparisons require first casting the *xml* type to a character type. This limitation also means that you cannot use *ORDER BY* or *GROUP BY* with an *xml* data type. There are several other restrictions, which we will discuss in more detail later.

These might seem like fairly severe restrictions, but they don't really affect the *xml* data type when it is used appropriately. The *xml* data type also has a rich feature set that more than compensates for these limitations.

Working with the *xml* Data Type as a Variable

Let's start by writing some code that uses the new *xml* data type as a variable. As with any other Transact-SQL (T-SQL) variable, you simply declare it and assign data to it, as in the following example, which uses a generic piece of XML to represent a sales representative's data as XML:

```
DECLARE @xmlData AS XML
SET @xmlData='
<Customers>
   <CustomerID>TELRK</CustomerID>
   <CompanyName>Telerik, Inc</CompanyName>
   <ContactName>Stephen Forte</ContactName>
   <ContactTitle>Sales Representative</ContactTitle>
   <Address>5-9 Union Square West</Address>
   <City>New York</City>
   <PostalCode>10028</PostalCode>
   <Country>USA</Country>
   <Phone>030-0074321</Phone>
   <Fax>030-0076545</Fax>
   </Customers>'
SELECT @xmlData
```

This basic example shows an XML variable being declared like any other native SQL Server data type by using the *DECLARE* statement. The variable is then assigned a value. Oddly enough, a string of XML data is assigned to the *xml* data type, and the type parses it into XML. (Coincidentally, common language runtime [CLR]–based user-defined types [UDTs] also support and require this same parsing functionality.) The example also checks that the XML is well formed, such as by validating that an element's start and end tags match not only in name but also in case.

> **More Info** For more details on how to create well-formed XML, see Michael J. Young's book *XML Step by Step,* Second Edition (Microsoft Press, 2002).

The last statement returns the XML to the caller via a *SELECT* statement, and the results appear with the XML in a single column in a single row of data. Another benefit of having the database recognize that you are working with XML (rather than raw text that happens to be XML) is that XML results in SQL Server Management Studio are rendered as a hyperlink. Clicking the hyperlink then opens a new window displaying nicely formatted XML (using the Windows Internet Explorer XML Template) with color coding and collapsible/expandable nodes. If you then right-click on the XML result window's title bar, you'll see a shortcut menu with some useful options, such as the ability to save the XML to a file or to copy the full XML path.

Working with XML in Tables

As we stated earlier, you can also define a column in a table as XML, as shown in the following example:

```
USE AdventureWorks2008
GO
--create the table with the XML data type
CREATE TABLE OrdersXML
  (OrderDocID int PRIMARY KEY,
   xOrders xml NOT NULL)
```

As we also stated earlier, the *xml* data type has a few other restrictions—in this case, when it is used as a column in a table:

- It cannot be used as a primary key.
- It cannot be used as a foreign key.
- It cannot be declared with a UNIQUE constraint.
- It cannot be declared with the COLLATE keyword.

We stated earlier that you can't compare two instances of the *xml* data type. Primary keys, foreign keys, and unique constraints all require that you be able to compare any included data types; therefore, XML cannot be used in any of those situations. The SQL Server *COLLATE* statement is meaningless with the *xml* data type because SQL Server does not store the XML as text; rather, it uses a distinct type of encoding particular to XML.

Now let's get some data into the column. This example takes some simple static XML and inserts it into the *OrdersXML* table we just created, using the *xml* data type as a variable:

```
--Insert Static XML via a variable
DECLARE @xmlData AS XML
SET @xmlData = '
<Orders>
  <Order>
    <OrderID>5</OrderID>
    <CustomerID>65</CustomerID>
    <OrderAmount>25</OrderAmount>
  </Order>
</Orders>'
--insert into the table
INSERT INTO OrdersXML (OrderDocID, xOrders) Values (1, @xmlData)
```

You can insert XML into these columns in a variety of other ways: XML Bulk Load (which we will discuss later in this chapter), loading from an XML variable (as shown here), or loading from a *SELECT* statement using the *FOR XML TYPE* feature, which we will discuss shortly. Only well-formed XML (including fragments) can be inserted—any attempt to insert malformed XML will result in an exception, as shown in this fragment:

```
--Fails because of the malformed XML
INSERT INTO OrdersXML (OrderDocID, xOrders) VALUES (3, '<nm>steve</NM>')
```

The results produce the following error from SQL Server:

```
Msg 9436, Level 16, State 1, Line 1
XML parsing: line 1, character 14, end tag does not match start tag
```

Defaults and Constraints

The *xml* data type can, like other data types, conform to nullability, defaults, and constraints. If you want to make a field required (*NOT NULL*) and provide a default value on your XML column, just specify this as you would for any other column, as shown here:

```
CREATE TABLE OrdersXML
    (OrderDocID INT PRIMARY KEY,
    xOrders XML NOT NULL DEFAULT '<Orders/>')
```

The following insert works because it relies on the default:

```
INSERT INTO OrdersXML (OrderDocID, xOrders) VALUES (2, DEFAULT)
```

Adding a default does not enforce just *<Orders>* from being added. For example, we have specified an Orders node as the default but have not yet indicated any way to enforce that. The following insert works even if we want only *<Orders>* in our table because we have not declared a constraint or provided a column schema:

```
INSERT INTO OrdersXML (OrderDocID, xOrders) VALUES (3, '<blah>steve</blah>')
```

XML Schemas

One powerful feature of XML is its ability to strongly type the data in an XML document. XML Schema Definition (XSD) defines a standard set of data types that must be supported in all XML documents. You can use XSD to create an XML schema for your data, requiring that your data conform to a set of rules that you specify. This gives XML an advantage over just about all other data transfer/data description methods and is a major contributing factor to the success of the XML standard.

Without XML Schema, XML would just be a more modern, more verbose text-delimited format. An XML schema defines what your data should look like, what elements are required, and what data types those elements will have. Analogous to how a table definition in SQL Server provides structure and type validation for relational data, an XML schema provides structure and type validation for the XML data.

We won't fully describe all the features of XML Schema here—that would require a book of its own. You can find the XSD specifications at the World Wide Web Consortium (W3C), at *http://www.w3.org/2001/XMLSchema*. Several popular schemas are publicly available, including one for Really Simple Syndication (RSS), the protocol that powers weblogs, blogcasts, and other forms of binary and text syndication, and one for SOAP, which dictates how XML Web Services convey information.

You can choose how to structure your XSD. XSD can create required elements and set limits on what data types and ranges are allowed. It can even allow document fragments.

SQL Server Schema Collections

SQL Server 2005 gave you the ability to create your own schemas and store them in the database as database objects and to enforce a schema on any XML instance, including columns in tables and SQL Server variables. This gives you more control over the XML that is going into the database and also lets you strongly type your XML instance. SQL Server 2008 enhances this support with the following:

- Preserving time zones in *xsd:dateTime* values

- Lax validation

- Union and list types in schemas

Before we dive into these new enhancements, we will review how schemas work with SQL Server. To get started, you can create the following simple schema and add it to the *schemas* collection in *AdventureWorks2008*, as shown in Listing 6-1.

LISTING 6-1 Creating an XML schema collection

```
--syntax for adding a schema
--schema can disallow fragments if you say so
CREATE XML SCHEMA COLLECTION dbo.order_xsd
AS
'<xsd:schema xmlns:xsd="http://www.w3.org/2001/XMLSchema">
  <xsd:simpleType name="orderAmt" >
    <xsd:restriction base="xsd:int" >
      <xsd:maxExclusive value="5000" />
      <xsd:minInclusive value="1" />
    </xsd:restriction>
  </xsd:simpleType>
  <xsd:element name="Order">
  <xsd:complexType>
    <xsd:sequence>
    <xsd:element name="CustomerName" type="xsd:string" />
    <xsd:element name="OrderDate" type="xsd:dateTime"/>
    <xsd:element name="OrderAmt" type="orderAmt"/>
    </xsd:sequence>
  </xsd:complexType>
  </xsd:element>
</xsd:schema>'
GO
```

This schema is named *order_xsd*, and you can use it on any *xml* type, including variables, parameters, return values, and especially columns in tables. This schema defines elements named *CustomerName, OrderDate,* and *OrderAmt. OrderAmt* uses the *orderAmt* type, which is defined as an *int* data type whose minimum value is 1 or greater and whose maximum value is 4999. (We know that you will likely not model your data this way, but you might have to transform your relational data into XML for invoicing or display purposes, and restricting by an XSD type restriction is then very valuable.) Next create a simple table and apply the schema to the XML column by referring to the schema name in parentheses after your *xml* data type in the *CREATE TABLE* statement, as shown in Listing 6-2.

LISTING 6-2 Creating a table with a schema

```
--create table with xml column and use schema as a rule for a particular column
CREATE TABLE xml_schematest (
    Order_ID int PRIMARY KEY,
    Order_XML xml(order_xsd) --XML Schema Name
)
GO
```

As you can see in this example, the *Order_XML* column is defined not as simply *xml* but as *xml(order_xsd)*. The *xml* data type has an optional parameter that allows you to specify the bound schema. This same usage also applies if you want to bind a schema to another use of an *xml* data type, such as a variable or a parameter. SQL Server now allows only a strongly typed XML document in the *Order_XML* column. This is much better than a *CHECK* constraint (which you can still add to this column, but only with a function). An advantage of using an XML schema is that your data is validated against it and you can enforce XML data types (at the XML level) and make sure that only valid XML data is allowed into the particular elements. If you were using a *CHECK* constraint, for example, you would need a separate *CHECK* constraint for each validation you wanted to perform. In this example, without the schema created in Listing 6-1, a few *CHECK* constraints would be needed just to enforce the minimum and maximum values. You would need one constraint requiring the element and then another constraint to verify the allowed low end of the range (1) and another one to verify the high end of the allowed range (4999).

Note When you create an *xml* column, any defaults you define must be valid for and not conflict with the bound schema; otherwise, the default value will always fail. Also, be sure that any defined constraints are valid for and do not conflict with the bound schema; otherwise, all attempts to insert or update data will likely fail.

Let's take a look at the schema in action:

```
--This will work ok
INSERT INTO xml_schematest VALUES (1, '
<Order>
  <CustomerName>Bill Gates</CustomerName>
  <OrderDate>2008-10-10T14:22:27.25-05:00</OrderDate>
  <OrderAmt>100</OrderAmt>
</Order>')
```

```
--This will fail
INSERT INTO xml_schematest VALUES (2, '
<Order>
  <CustomerName>Steve Ballmer</CustomerName>
  <OrderDate>2008-10-10T14:22:27.25-05:00</OrderDate>
  <OrderAmt>10000</OrderAmt>
</Order>')
```

SQL Server enforces the schema on insert and updates, ensuring data integrity. The data we provided conforms to the schema, so the inserts work smoothly. If you attempt to insert or update an invalid piece of data, you will receive an error, as shown here:

```
UPDATE xml_schematest
SET Order_XML='
<Order>
  <CustomerName>Bill Gates</CustomerName>
  <OrderDate>2008-10-10T14:22:27.25-05:00</OrderDate>
  <OrderAmt>10000</OrderAmt>
</Order>'
WHERE Order_ID=1
```

SQL Server reports back the following error:

```
Msg 6926, Level 16, State 1, Line 1
XML Validation: Invalid simple type value: '10000'. Location: /*:Order[1]/*:OrderAmt[1]
```

xsd:dateTime Enhancements

The *xsd:dateTime* data type is now time zone aware in SQL Server 2008. In SQL Server 2005, you had to provide a time zone for *dateTime* data. SQL Server 2005 did not preserve the time zone information for your data for *dateTime* or *time* values; it normalized them to Coordinated Universal Time (UTC). Returning to our order example, we added a date and time of 2008-10-10T14:22:27.25-05:00 for 2:22 PM in the eastern time zone of the United States. (The –5:00 is Greenwich Mean Time [GMT] minus 5 hours.) Take a look at the XML from the database. SQL Server 2005 normalizes the time zone information to 2008-10-10T19:22:27.250Z, and notice the Z to indicate UTC (or Zulu) and that our –5 is gone.

```
SELECT * FROM xml_schematest

<Order>
  <CustomerName>Bill Gates</CustomerName>
  <OrderDate>2008-10-10T19:22:27.250Z</OrderDate>
  <OrderAmt>100</OrderAmt>
</Order>
```

Perform the same operation in SQL Server 2008, and SQL Server 2008 automatically preserves the time zone data for you. The same data would look like this:

```
<Order>
  <CustomerName>Bill Gates</CustomerName>
  <OrderDate>2008-10-10T14:22:27.25-05:00</OrderDate>
  <OrderAmt>100</OrderAmt>
</Order>
```

Lax Validation

SQL Server 2008 has added XSD support for *lax validation*. To describe lax validation, let's say that we want to add another element to our XML from the preceding example, after *<OrderAmt>*, that is not part of the same schema. In SQL Server 2005, schemas can use the *processContents* values *skip* and *strict* for *any* and *anyAttribute* declarations as a wildcard. (If you're unfamiliar with these schema attributes and values, they're used to dictate how the XML parser should deal with XML elements not found in the schema.) If *processContents* is set to *skip*, SQL Server will skip completely the validation of the additional element, even if a schema is available for it. If *processContents* is set to *strict*, SQL Server will require it to have an element or namespace defined in the current schema against which the element will be validated. The result is an "all or nothing" implementation. SQL Server 2008 adds support for an additional "in-between" validation option: lax. By setting the *processContents* attribute for this wildcard section to *lax*, you can enforce validation for any elements that have a schema associated with them but ignore any elements that are not defined in the schema. For example, the schema shown in Listing 6-3 will be used in SQL Server 2008. (If you are following along and added the previous order schema from Listing 6-1, you have to drop it before adding the one you see in Listing 6-3.)

LISTING 6-3 Schema with lax validation and *dateTime*

```
--Valid SQL Server 2008 Schema (lax validation and dateTime)
CREATE XML SCHEMA COLLECTION dbo.order_xsd
AS '
<xsd:schema xmlns:xsd="http://www.w3.org/2001/XMLSchema">
  <xsd:simpleType name="orderAmt" >
    <xsd:restriction base="xsd:int" >
      <xsd:maxInclusive value="5000" />
      <xsd:minExclusive value="1" />
    </xsd:restriction>
  </xsd:simpleType>
  <xsd:element name="Order">
    <xsd:complexType>
      <xsd:sequence>
        <xsd:element name="CustomerName" type="xsd:string" />
        <xsd:element name="OrderDate" type="xsd:dateTime"/>
```

```
            <xsd:element name="OrderAmt" type="orderAmt"/>
            <xsd:any namespace="##other" processContents="lax"/>
         </xsd:sequence>
      </xsd:complexType>
   </xsd:element>
</xsd:schema>'
GO
```

After we add this schema, arbitrary XML elements following *<OrderAmt>* will be allowed to be stored without failing the validation. To see this in action, notice the random *<Notes>* element in the following example. The (arbitrary) *<Notes>* element will not only be allowed by SQL Server 2008 but can also be a whole new element structure that is supported by an additional schema of its own (as indicated by the *xmlns* attribute).

```
DECLARE @xml XML(dbo.order_xsd)
SET @xml = '
<Order>
  <CustomerName>Bill Gates</CustomerName>
  <OrderDate>2008-10-10T14:22:27.25-05:00</OrderDate>
  <OrderAmt>100</OrderAmt>
  <Notes xmlns="sf">My Notes for this order</Notes>
</Order>'
SELECT @xml
```

Union and List Types

In SQL Server 2005, you could define a simple type of *xsd:list* with an enumeration to require items in a list for any element that inherits that type. With the new support for union of lists in SQL Server 2008 with *xsd:union*, you can combine multiple lists into one simple type. For example, in the following schema in Listing 6-4, we allow a *shiptypeList* of strings such as *FastShippers* but also allow numeric values:

LISTING 6-4 Union and list types

```
--union and list types
DROP XML SCHEMA COLLECTION dbo.order_xsd
GO

CREATE XML SCHEMA COLLECTION dbo.order_xsd AS
'<xsd:schema xmlns:xsd="http://www.w3.org/2001/XMLSchema">
  <xsd:simpleType name="orderAmt" >
    <xsd:restriction base="xsd:int" >
      <xsd:maxInclusive value="5000" />
      <xsd:minExclusive value="1" />
    </xsd:restriction>
  </xsd:simpleType>
  <xsd:simpleType name="shiptypeList">
    <xsd:union>
      <xsd:simpleType>
```

```
        <xsd:list>
          <xsd:simpleType>
            <xsd:restriction base="xsd:integer">
              <xsd:enumeration value="1"/>
              <xsd:enumeration value="2"/>
              <xsd:enumeration value="3"/>
            </xsd:restriction>
          </xsd:simpleType>
        </xsd:list>
      </xsd:simpleType>
      <xsd:simpleType>
        <xsd:list>
          <xsd:simpleType>
            <xsd:restriction base="xsd:string">
              <xsd:enumeration value="FastShippers"/>
              <xsd:enumeration value="SHL"/>
              <xsd:enumeration value="PSU"/>
            </xsd:restriction>
          </xsd:simpleType>
        </xsd:list>
      </xsd:simpleType>
    </xsd:union>
  </xsd:simpleType>

  <xsd:element name="Order">
    <xsd:complexType>
      <xsd:sequence>
        <xsd:element name="CustomerName" type="xsd:string" />
        <xsd:element name="OrderDate" type="xsd:dateTime"/>
        <xsd:element name="OrderAmt" type="orderAmt"/>
        <xsd:element name="ShipType" type="shiptypeList"/>
        <xsd:any namespace="##other" processContents="lax"/>
      </xsd:sequence>
    </xsd:complexType>
  </xsd:element>
</xsd:schema>'
GO
```

If you now validate an XML instance with either a numeric value or a string value in the enumerated list, it will validate as follows:

```
--works with 1 or FastShippers in ShipType
DECLARE @xml XML(dbo.order_xsd)
SET @xml = '
<Order>
  <CustomerName>Bill Gates</CustomerName>
  <OrderDate>2008-10-10T14:22:27.25-05:00</OrderDate>
  <OrderAmt>100</OrderAmt>
  <ShipType>1</ShipType>
  <Notes xmlns="sf">Steve Test 1</Notes>
</Order>'
GO
```

This example is fairly basic, but it is useful if you have more than one way to describe something and need two lists to do so. One such possibility is metric and English units of measurement. This technique is useful when you need to restrict items and are writing them from a database.

We have touched only the surface of using XML schemas in SQL Server 2008. These schemas can get quite complex, and further discussion is beyond the scope of this book. You can easily enforce sophisticated XML schemas in your database once you master the syntax. We believe that you should always use an XML schema with your XML data to guarantee consistency in your XML data.

XML Indexes

You can create an XML index on an XML column using almost the same syntax as for a standard SQL Server index. There are four types of XML indexes: a single *primary XML index* that must be created and three types of optional *secondary XML indexes* that are created over the primary index. An XML index is a little different from a standard SQL index—it is a clustered index on an internal table used by SQL Server to store XML data. This table is called the *node table* and cannot be accessed by programmers.

To get started with an XML index, you must first create the primary index of all the nodes. The primary index is a clustered index (over the node table, not the base table) that associates each node of your XML column with the SQL Primary Key column. It does this by indexing one row in its internal representation (a B+ tree structure) for each node in your XML column, generating an index usually about three times as large as your XML data. For your XML data to work properly, your table must have an ordinary clustered Primary Key column defined. That primary key is used in a join of the XQuery results with the base table. (XQuery is discussed later in this chapter.) To create a primary XML index, you first create a table with a primary key and an XML column, as shown in Listing 6-5.

LISTING 6-5 XML index creation

```
--XML index Examples

--Drop the table since we used it before
DROP TABLE OrdersXML

--Create the table with a PK and an XML column
CREATE TABLE OrdersXML
  (OrderDocID int PRIMARY KEY,
   xOrders xml NOT NULL)
```

Next we insert some data into our new table, as follows, so that we can try some sample queries once we've established some indexes and learned how to create XQuery queries:

```
--Insert some data into our new table
INSERT INTO OrdersXML VALUES (1, '
<Orders>
  <Order>
    <OrderID>5</OrderID>
    <CustomerName>Stephen Forte</CustomerName>
    <OrderAmount>25</OrderAmount>
  </Order>
</Orders>')

INSERT INTO OrdersXML VALUES (2, '
<Orders>
  <Order>
    <OrderID>7</OrderID>
    <CustomerName>Andrew Brust</CustomerName>
    <OrderAmount>45</OrderAmount>
  </Order>
</Orders>')

INSERT INTO OrdersXML  VALUES (3, '
<Orders>
  <Order>
    <OrderID>2</OrderID>
    <CustomerName>Bill Zack</CustomerName>
    <OrderAmount>65</OrderAmount>
  </Order>
</Orders>')
```

To create a primary XML index, we use the *CREATE PRIMARY XML INDEX* syntax on the table, as shown here:

```
CREATE PRIMARY XML INDEX idx_1
  ON OrdersXML (xOrders)
```

We have successfully created a new primary XML index named *idx_1* on the *OrdersXML* table's *xOrders* column. The primary XML index, *idx_1*, now has the node table populated. If you want to look at the node table's columns, run this piece of T-SQL:

```
-- display the columns in the node table
SELECT col.column_id, col.object_id, col.name, col.system_type_id
 FROM sys.columns AS col
   INNER JOIN sys.indexes AS idx
   ON idx.object_id = col.object_id
 WHERE idx.name = 'idx_1' AND idx.type = 1
 ORDER BY column_id
```

The results are shown in Table 6-1.

TABLE 6-1 Columns in a Typical Node Table

column_id	object_id	name	system_type_id
1	855674096	id	165
2	855674096	nid	56
3	855674096	tagname	231
4	855674096	taguri	231
5	855674096	tid	56
6	855674096	value	98
7	855674096	lvalue	231
8	855674096	lvaluebin	165
9	855674096	hid	167
10	855674096	xsinil	104
11	855674096	xsitype	104
12	855674096	pk1	56

The three types of secondary XML indexes are *path*, *value*, and *property*. You can implement a secondary XML index only after you have created a primary XML index because they are both actually indexes over the node table. These indexes further optimize XQuery statements made against the XML data.

A path index creates an index on the *Path ID* (*hid* in Table 6-1) and *Value* columns of the primary XML index, using the *FOR PATH* keyword. This type of index is best when you have a fairly complex document type and want to speed up XQuery XPath expressions that refer-ence a particular node in your XML data with an explicit value (as explained in the section "Understanding XQuery Expressions and XPath" later in this chapter). If you are more con-cerned about the values of the nodes queried with wildcards, you can create a value index using the *FOR VALUE* XML index. The *VALUE* index contains the same index columns as the *PATH* index, *Value*, and *Path ID* (*hid*), but in the reverse order (as shown in Table 6-1). Using the property type index with the *PROPERTY* keyword optimizes hierarchies of elements or attributes that are name/value pairs. The *PROPERTY* index contains the primary key of the base table, *Path ID* (*hid*), and *Value*, in that order. The syntax to create these indexes is shown in Listing 6-6; you must specify that you are using the primary XML index by using the *USING XML INDEX* syntax.

LISTING 6-6 XML index created over a primary index

```
--structural (Path)
CREATE XML INDEX idx_a ON OrdersXML (xOrders)
 USING XML INDEX idx_1 FOR PATH

--value
CREATE XML INDEX idx_b ON OrdersXML (xOrders)
 USING XML INDEX idx_1 FOR VALUE

--property
CREATE XML INDEX idx_c ON OrdersXML (xOrders)
 USING XML INDEX idx_1 FOR PROPERTY
```

Be aware of these additional restrictions:

- An XML index can contain only one XML column, so you cannot create a composite XML index (an index on more than one XML column).

- Using XML indexes requires that the primary key be clustered, and because you can have only one clustered index per table, you cannot create a clustered XML index.

SQL Server 2008 Management Studio allows you to view the indexes on a table by drilling down from the Database node to the table name and down to the Indexes node in Object Explorer. You can also create a new primary XML index by right-clicking on the Indexes node and clicking New Index.

Armed with this new index type, you can write some very efficient queries using XQuery. Before we get to XQuery, however, let's take a look at some other XML features that will help you get XML data in and out of the database.

FOR XML Commands

SQL Server 2000 introduced an enhancement to the T-SQL syntax that enables normal relational queries to output their result set as XML, using any of these three approaches:

- *FOR XML RAW*
- *FOR XML AUTO*
- *FOR XML EXPLICIT*

These three features are also supported in SQL Server 2005 and 2008. We'll first discuss the features common to all three versions and then look closely at the new and enhanced features available in SQL Server 2008.

FOR XML RAW

FOR XML RAW produces *attribute-based XML. FOR XML RAW* essentially creates a flat representation of the data in which each row returned becomes an element and the returned columns become the attributes of each element. *FOR XML RAW* also doesn't interpret joins in any special way. (Joins become relevant in *FOR XML AUTO*.) Here is an example of a simple query that retrieves customer and order header data:

```
SELECT TOP 10 -- limits the result rows for demo purposes
    Customer.CustomerID, OrderHeader.SalesOrderID, OrderHeader.OrderDate
  FROM Sales.Customer Customer
   INNER JOIN Sales.SalesOrderHeader OrderHeader
   ON OrderHeader.CustomerID = Customer.CustomerID
  ORDER BY Customer.CustomerID
FOR XML RAW
```

If you are using SQL Server 2000, this will be output as a stream of text to Query Analyzer. However, with SQL Server 2005 and 2008, you can click on the XML hyperlink in the returned results to see the output shown here:

```
<row CustomerID="11001" SalesOrderID="43860" OrderDate="2001-08-01T00:00:00" />
<row CustomerID="11001" SalesOrderID="44501" OrderDate="2001-11-01T00:00:00" />
<row CustomerID="11001" SalesOrderID="45283" OrderDate="2002-02-01T00:00:00" />
<row CustomerID="11001" SalesOrderID="46042" OrderDate="2002-05-01T00:00:00" />
<row CustomerID="11002" SalesOrderID="46976" OrderDate="2002-08-01T00:00:00" />
<row CustomerID="11002" SalesOrderID="47997" OrderDate="2002-11-01T00:00:00" />
<row CustomerID="11002" SalesOrderID="49054" OrderDate="2003-02-01T00:00:00" />
<row CustomerID="11002" SalesOrderID="50216" OrderDate="2003-05-01T00:00:00" />
<row CustomerID="11002" SalesOrderID="51728" OrderDate="2003-08-01T00:00:00" />
<row CustomerID="11002" SalesOrderID="57044" OrderDate="2003-11-01T00:00:00" />
```

As you can see, we get flat results in which each row returned from the query becomes a single element named *row* and all columns are output as attributes of that element. Odds are, however, that you will want more structured XML output, which leads us to *FOR XML AUTO*.

FOR XML AUTO

FOR XML AUTO also produces attribute-based XML (by default), but its output is hierarchical rather than flat—that is, it can create nested results based on the tables in the query's join clause. For example, using the same query just demonstrated, you can simply change the *FOR XML* clause to *FOR XML AUTO*, as shown here:

```
SELECT TOP 10 -- limits the result rows for demo purposes
    Customer.CustomerID, OrderHeader.SalesOrderID, OrderHeader.OrderDate
  FROM Sales.Customer Customer
   INNER JOIN Sales.SalesOrderHeader OrderHeader
   ON OrderHeader.CustomerID = Customer.CustomerID
  ORDER BY Customer.CustomerID
FOR XML AUTO
```

Execute this query and click the XML hyperlink in the results, and you will see the following output:

```
<Customer CustomerID="1">
  <OrderHeader SalesOrderID="43860" OrderDate="2001-08-01T00:00:00" />
  <OrderHeader SalesOrderID="44501" OrderDate="2001-11-01T00:00:00" />
  <OrderHeader SalesOrderID="45283" OrderDate="2002-02-01T00:00:00" />
  <OrderHeader SalesOrderID="46042" OrderDate="2002-05-01T00:00:00" />
</Customer>
<Customer CustomerID="2">
  <OrderHeader SalesOrderID="46976" OrderDate="2002-08-01T00:00:00" />
  <OrderHeader SalesOrderID="47997" OrderDate="2002-11-01T00:00:00" />
  <OrderHeader SalesOrderID="49054" OrderDate="2003-02-01T00:00:00" />
  <OrderHeader SalesOrderID="50216" OrderDate="2003-05-01T00:00:00" />
  <OrderHeader SalesOrderID="51728" OrderDate="2003-08-01T00:00:00" />
  <OrderHeader SalesOrderID="57044" OrderDate="2003-11-01T00:00:00" />
</Customer>
```

As you can see, the XML data has main elements named *Customer* (based on the alias assigned in the query) and child elements named *OrderHeader* (again from the alias). Note that *FOR XML AUTO* determines the element nesting order based on the order of the columns in the *SELECT* clause. You can rewrite the *SELECT* clause so that an *OrderHeader* column comes before a *Customer* column, as shown here:

```
SELECT TOP 10 -- limits the result rows for demo purposes
    OrderHeader.SalesOrderID, OrderHeader.OrderDate, Customer.CustomerID
```

The output (as viewed in the XML viewer) now looks like this:

```
<OrderHeader SalesOrderID="43860" OrderDate="2001-08-01T00:00:00">
  <Customer CustomerID="1" />
</OrderHeader>
<OrderHeader SalesOrderID="44501" OrderDate="2001-11-01T00:00:00">
  <Customer CustomerID="1" />
</OrderHeader>
<OrderHeader SalesOrderID="45283" OrderDate="2002-02-01T00:00:00">
  <Customer CustomerID="1" />
</OrderHeader>
<OrderHeader SalesOrderID="46042" OrderDate="2002-05-01T00:00:00">
  <Customer CustomerID="1" />
</OrderHeader>
<OrderHeader SalesOrderID="46976" OrderDate="2002-08-01T00:00:00">
  <Customer CustomerID="2" />
</OrderHeader>
<OrderHeader SalesOrderID="47997" OrderDate="2002-11-01T00:00:00">
  <Customer CustomerID="2" />
</OrderHeader>
<OrderHeader SalesOrderID="49054" OrderDate="2003-02-01T00:00:00">
  <Customer CustomerID="2" />
</OrderHeader>
<OrderHeader SalesOrderID="50216" OrderDate="2003-05-01T00:00:00">
  <Customer CustomerID="2" />
</OrderHeader>
```

```
<OrderHeader SalesOrderID="51728" OrderDate="2003-08-01T00:00:00">
  <Customer CustomerID="2" />
</OrderHeader>
<OrderHeader SalesOrderID="57044" OrderDate="2003-11-01T00:00:00">
  <Customer CustomerID="2" />
</OrderHeader>
```

These results are probably not what you wanted. To keep the XML hierarchy matching the table hierarchy, you must list at least one column from the parent table before any column from a child table. If there are three levels of tables, at least one other column from the child table must come before any from the grandchild table, and so on.

FOR XML EXPLICIT

FOR XML EXPLICIT is the most complex but also the most useful and flexible of the three *FOR XML* options. It produces XML by constructing a *UNION* query of the various levels of output elements. So, if again you have the *Customer* and *SalesOrderHeader* tables and you want to produce XML output, you must have two *SELECT* statements with a *UNION*. If you add the *SalesOrderDetail* table, you must add another *UNION* statement and *SELECT* statement.

As we said, *FOR XML EXPLICIT* is more complex than its predecessors. For starters, you are responsible for defining two additional columns that establish the hierarchical relationship of the XML: a *Tag* column that acts as a row's identifier and a *Parent* column that links child records to the parent record's *Tag* value (similar to *EmployeeID* and *ManagerID*). You must also alias all columns to indicate the element, *Tag*, and display name for the XML output, as shown here. Keep in mind that only the first *SELECT* statement must follow these rules; any aliases in subsequent *SELECT* statements in a *UNION* query are ignored.

```
SELECT TOP 2 -- limits the result rows for demo purposes
  1 AS Tag,
  NULL AS Parent,
  CustomerID AS [Customer!1!CustomerID],
  NULL AS [SalesOrder!2!SalesOrderID],
  NULL AS [SalesOrder!2!OrderDate]
 FROM Sales.Customer AS Customer
UNION ALL
SELECT TOP 10 -- limits the result rows for demo purposes
  2,
  1,
  Customer.CustomerID,
  OrderHeader.SalesOrderID,
  OrderHeader.OrderDate
 FROM Sales.Customer AS Customer
  INNER JOIN Sales.SalesOrderHeader AS OrderHeader    ON OrderHeader.CustomerID = Customer.
CustomerID
 ORDER BY [Customer!1!CustomerID], [SalesOrder!2!SalesOrderID]
FOR XML EXPLICIT
```

Execute this query, and click the XML hyperlink to see the following output:

```
<Customer CustomerID="1">
  <SalesOrder SalesOrderID="43860" OrderDate="2001-08-01T00:00:00" />
  <SalesOrder SalesOrderID="44501" OrderDate="2001-11-01T00:00:00" />
  <SalesOrder SalesOrderID="45283" OrderDate="2002-02-01T00:00:00" />
  <SalesOrder SalesOrderID="46042" OrderDate="2002-05-01T00:00:00" />
</Customer>
<Customer CustomerID="2">
  <SalesOrder SalesOrderID="46976" OrderDate="2002-08-01T00:00:00" />
  <SalesOrder SalesOrderID="47997" OrderDate="2002-11-01T00:00:00" />
  <SalesOrder SalesOrderID="49054" OrderDate="2003-02-01T00:00:00" />
  <SalesOrder SalesOrderID="50216" OrderDate="2003-05-01T00:00:00" />
  <SalesOrder SalesOrderID="51728" OrderDate="2003-08-01T00:00:00" />
  <SalesOrder SalesOrderID="57044" OrderDate="2003-11-01T00:00:00" />
</Customer>
```

This output happens to resemble the output generated by our *FOR XML AUTO* sample. So what have we gained by composing a more complex query with *FOR XML EXPLICIT*? Well, *FOR XML EXPLICIT* allows for some alternative outputs that are not achievable using *FOR XML AUTO*. For example, you can specify that certain values be composed as elements instead of attributes by appending *!ELEMENT* to the end of the aliased column, as shown here:

```
SELECT TOP 2 -- limits the result rows for demo purposes
  1 AS Tag,
  NULL AS Parent,
  CustomerID AS [Customer!1!CustomerID],
  NULL AS [SalesOrder!2!SalesOrderID],
  NULL AS [SalesOrder!2!OrderDate!ELEMENT] --Render as an element
 FROM Sales.Customer AS Customer
UNION ALL
SELECT TOP 10 -- limits the result rows for demo purposes
  2,
  1,
  Customer.CustomerID,
  OrderHeader.SalesOrderID,
  OrderHeader.OrderDate
 FROM Sales.Customer AS Customer
  INNER JOIN Sales.SalesOrderHeader AS OrderHeader
   ON OrderHeader.CustomerID = Customer.CustomerID
 ORDER BY [Customer!1!CustomerID], [SalesOrder!2!SalesOrderID]
FOR XML EXPLICIT
```

Only one minor change was made (we appended *!ELEMENT* to the *OrderDate* column). However, this change has a major effect on the final output, as shown here:

```
<Customer CustomerID="1">
  <SalesOrder SalesOrderID="43860">
    <OrderDate>2001-08-01T00:00:00</OrderDate>
  </SalesOrder>
  <SalesOrder SalesOrderID="44501">
    <OrderDate>2001-11-01T00:00:00</OrderDate>
  </SalesOrder>
```

```
          <SalesOrder SalesOrderID="45283">
            <OrderDate>2002-02-01T00:00:00</OrderDate>
          </SalesOrder>
          <SalesOrder SalesOrderID="46042">
            <OrderDate>2002-05-01T00:00:00</OrderDate>
          </SalesOrder>
        </Customer>
        <Customer CustomerID="2">
          <SalesOrder SalesOrderID="46976">
            <OrderDate>2002-08-01T00:00:00</OrderDate>
          </SalesOrder>
          <SalesOrder SalesOrderID="47997">
            <OrderDate>2002-11-01T00:00:00</OrderDate>
          </SalesOrder>
          <SalesOrder SalesOrderID="49054">
            <OrderDate>2003-02-01T00:00:00</OrderDate>
          </SalesOrder>
          <SalesOrder SalesOrderID="50216">
            <OrderDate>2003-05-01T00:00:00</OrderDate>
          </SalesOrder>
          <SalesOrder SalesOrderID="51728">
            <OrderDate>2003-08-01T00:00:00</OrderDate>
          </SalesOrder>
          <SalesOrder SalesOrderID="57044">
            <OrderDate>2003-11-01T00:00:00</OrderDate>
          </SalesOrder>
        </Customer>
```

Notice that the *OrderDate* is rendered as a child element of the *SalesOrder* element. Although *EXPLICIT* mode could create robust results, it also requires creating even more complex queries to get such results. For example, to add a few more fields from *OrderHeader* and to add some more fields from *OrderDetail*, you would have to write the query as follows:

```
--XML EXPLICIT
SELECT --TOP 2 -- limits the result rows for demo purposes
  1 AS Tag,
  NULL AS Parent,
  CustomerID AS [Customer!1!CustomerID],
  NULL AS [SalesOrder!2!SalesOrderID],
  NULL AS [SalesOrder!2!TotalDue],
  NULL AS [SalesOrder!2!OrderDate!ELEMENT],
  NULL AS [SalesOrder!2!ShipDate!ELEMENT],
  NULL AS [SalesDetail!3!ProductID],
  NULL AS [SalesDetail!3!OrderQty],
  NULL AS [SalesDetail!3!LineTotal]
 FROM Sales.Customer AS Customer
 WHERE Customer.CustomerID IN (11000, 11001)
UNION ALL
SELECT
  2,
  1,
  Customer.CustomerID,
  OrderHeader.SalesOrderID,
  OrderHeader.TotalDue,
```

```
  OrderHeader.OrderDate,
  OrderHeader.ShipDate,
  NULL,
  NULL,
  NULL
 FROM Sales.Customer AS Customer
  INNER JOIN Sales.SalesOrderHeader AS OrderHeader
   ON OrderHeader.CustomerID = Customer.CustomerID
 WHERE Customer.CustomerID IN (11000, 110012)
UNION ALL
SELECT
  3,
  2,
  Customer.CustomerID,
  OrderHeader.SalesOrderID,
  OrderHeader.TotalDue,
  OrderHeader.OrderDate,
  OrderHeader.ShipDate,
  OrderDetail.ProductID,
  OrderDetail.OrderQty,
  OrderDetail.LineTotal
 FROM Sales.Customer AS Customer
  INNER JOIN Sales.SalesOrderHeader AS OrderHeader
   ON OrderHeader.CustomerID = Customer.CustomerID
  INNER JOIN Sales.SalesOrderDetail AS OrderDetail
   ON OrderDetail.SalesOrderID = OrderHeader.SalesOrderID
 WHERE Customer.CustomerID IN (11000, 11001)
 ORDER BY [Customer!1!CustomerID], [SalesOrder!2!SalesOrderID]
FOR XML EXPLICIT
```

As you can see, the code has become quite complex and will become increasingly complex as you add data to the output. Although this query is perfectly valid, this solution is unacceptable, which leads us to the new and improved *FOR XML* statement.

FOR XML Enhancements

As you've seen, SQL Server 2000 has a lot of XML features (including some not mentioned here, such as viewing the results over HTTP). Just about all of the SQL Server 2000 XML support revolves around *FOR XML*, a feature that appears to be much underused by developers. Following are a few ways that *FOR XML* has been enhanced in SQL Server 2005 and 2008) :

- Using the *TYPE* option, *FOR XML* can output to an *xml* data type (as opposed to streamed results) from a *SELECT* statement using *FOR XML*, which in turn allows you to nest the results of *SELECT...FOR XML* into another *SELECT* statement.

- The new option *FOR XML PATH* allows you to more easily shape data and produce element-based XML than the *EXPLICIT* option.

- You can explicitly specify a *ROOT* element for your output.

- You can produce element-based XML with *FOR XML AUTO*.

- *FOR XML* can produce XML using a *schema*.

- Nesting, whitespace, and null handling have been improved.

The *TYPE* Option

XML is an intrinsic data type of SQL Server 2008, so we can now automatically cast the XML output from the *FOR XML* query into an *xml* data type instance, as opposed to streamed results. You accomplish this by using the *TYPE* keyword after your *FOR XML* statement, like this:

```
DECLARE @xmlData AS xml

SET @xmlData =
 (SELECT Customer.CustomerID, OrderDetail.SalesOrderID, OrderDetail.OrderDate
   FROM Sales.Customer Customer
    INNER JOIN Sales.SalesOrderHeader OrderDetail
    ON OrderDetail.CustomerID = Customer.CustomerID
   WHERE Customer.CustomerID < 11200
   ORDER BY Customer.CustomerID
   FOR XML AUTO, TYPE) --Casts to XML type

SELECT @xmlData
```

This example declares a variable of type *xml* and then sets that variable to a casted result of a *FOR XML* query using the *TYPE* statement. The results of this query are shown here for demonstration purposes. You can also use this new *xml* variable as part of an *INSERT* statement (to an XML column) or pass it to a stored procedure, for example.

```
<Customer CustomerID="1">
  <OrderDetail SalesOrderID="43860" OrderDate="2001-08-01T00:00:00" />
  <OrderDetail SalesOrderID="44501" OrderDate="2001-11-01T00:00:00" />
  <OrderDetail SalesOrderID="45283" OrderDate="2002-02-01T00:00:00" />
  <OrderDetail SalesOrderID="46042" OrderDate="2002-05-01T00:00:00" />
</Customer>
<Customer CustomerID="2">
  <OrderDetail SalesOrderID="46976" OrderDate="2002-08-01T00:00:00" />
  <OrderDetail SalesOrderID="47997" OrderDate="2002-11-01T00:00:00" />
  <OrderDetail SalesOrderID="49054" OrderDate="2003-02-01T00:00:00" />
  <OrderDetail SalesOrderID="50216" OrderDate="2003-05-01T00:00:00" />
  <OrderDetail SalesOrderID="51728" OrderDate="2003-08-01T00:00:00" />
  <OrderDetail SalesOrderID="57044" OrderDate="2003-11-01T00:00:00" />
  <OrderDetail SalesOrderID="63198" OrderDate="2004-02-01T00:00:00" />
  <OrderDetail SalesOrderID="69488" OrderDate="2004-05-01T00:00:00" />
</Customer>
```

You can use *FOR XML TYPE* in any valid SQL expression. The next example uses the *FOR XML TYPE* syntax as an expression in the *SELECT* statement:

```
SELECT
   CustomerID,
   (SELECT
      SalesOrderID,
      TotalDue,
      OrderDate,
      ShipDate
   FROM Sales.SalesOrderHeader AS OrderHeader
   WHERE CustomerID = Customer.CustomerID
   FOR XML AUTO, TYPE) AS OrderHeaders
 FROM Sales.Customer AS Customer
 WHERE CustomerID IN (11000, 11001)
 FOR XML AUTO
```

The results are shown here:

```
1 <OrderHeader SalesOrderID="43860" TotalDue="14603.7393" OrderDate="2001-08-
01T00:00:00" ShipDate="2001-08-08T00:00:00" />
<OrderHeader SalesOrderID="44501" TotalDue="26128.8674" OrderDate="2001-11-
01T00:00:00" ShipDate="2001-11-08T00:00:00" />
<OrderHeader SalesOrderID="45283" TotalDue="37643.1378" OrderDate="2002-02-
01T00:00:00" ShipDate="2002-02-08T00:00:00" />
<OrderHeader SalesOrderID="46042" TotalDue="34722.9906" OrderDate="2002-05-
01T00:00:00" ShipDate="2002-05-08T00:00:00" />
2 <OrderHeader SalesOrderID="46976" TotalDue="10184.0774" OrderDate="2002-08-
01T00:00:00" ShipDate="2002-08-08T00:00:00" />
<OrderHeader SalesOrderID="47997" TotalDue="5469.5941" OrderDate="2002-11-
01T00:00:00" ShipDate="2002-11-08T00:00:00" />
<OrderHeader SalesOrderID="49054" TotalDue="1739.4078" OrderDate="2003-02-
01T00:00:00" ShipDate="2003-02-08T00:00:00" />
<OrderHeader SalesOrderID="50216" TotalDue="1935.5166" OrderDate="2003-05-
01T00:00:00" ShipDate="2003-05-08T00:00:00" />
<OrderHeader SalesOrderID="51728" TotalDue="3905.2547" OrderDate="2003-08-
01T00:00:00" ShipDate="2003-08-08T00:00:00" />
<OrderHeader SalesOrderID="57044" TotalDue="4537.8484" OrderDate="2003-11-
01T00:00:00" ShipDate="2003-11-08T00:00:00" />
<OrderHeader SalesOrderID="63198" TotalDue="4053.9506" OrderDate="2004-02-
01T00:00:00" ShipDate="2004-02-08T00:00:00" />
<OrderHeader SalesOrderID="69488" TotalDue="908.3199" OrderDate="2004-05-
01T00:00:00" ShipDate="2004-05-08T00:00:00" />
```

FOR XML PATH

If you want to create element-based XML, you can use *FOR XML PATH* to specify column aliases that contain valid XPath expressions that will shape your XML output, as shown here:

```
SELECT TOP 2 --limits result rows for demo purposes
```

```
BusinessEntityID AS [@BusinessEntityID],
FirstName AS [ContactName/First],
LastName AS [ContactName/Last],
EmailAddress AS [ContactEmailAddress/EmailAddress1]
FROM HumanResources.vEmployee FOR XML PATH
```

The output looks like this:

```
<row BusinessEntityID="263">
  <ContactName>
    <First>Jean</First>
    <Last>Trenary</Last>
  </ContactName>
  <ContactEmailAddress>
    <EmailAddress1>jean0@adventure-works.com</EmailAddress1>
  </ContactEmailAddress>
</row>
<row BusinessEntityID="78">
  <ContactName>
    <First>Reuben</First>
    <Last>D'sa</Last>
  </ContactName>
  <ContactEmailAddress>
    <EmailAddress1>reuben0@adventure-works.com</EmailAddress1>
  </ContactEmailAddress>
</row>
```

Now let's revisit the last example we demonstrated with *FOR XML EXPLICIT*. Using the *TYPE* option in conjunction with *FOR XML PATH*, you can reproduce that awful and complex query with a much simpler version, as shown here:

```
SELECT
  CustomerID AS [@CustomerID],
  (SELECT SalesOrderID AS [@SalesOrderID],
          TotalDue AS [@TotalDue],
          OrderDate,
          ShipDate,
          (SELECT ProductID AS [@ProductID],
                  OrderQty AS [@OrderQty],
                  LineTotal AS [@LineTotal]
             FROM Sales.SalesOrderDetail
             WHERE SalesOrderID = OrderHeader.SalesOrderID
             FOR XML PATH('OrderDetail'), TYPE)
     FROM Sales.SalesOrderHeader AS OrderHeader
     WHERE CustomerID = Customer.CustomerID
     FOR XML PATH('OrderHeader'), TYPE)
FROM Sales.Customer AS Customer
WHERE CustomerID IN (11000, 11001)
FOR XML PATH ('Customer')
```

Isn't that much better? This statement uses subqueries with the *FOR XML PATH* statement in conjunction with *TYPE* to produce element-based XML nested inside a much larger *FOR XML PATH* statement. This returns each separate *Order* for the customer as a new child node of the *CustomerID* node; you can see this in the results of the following query:

```
<Customer CustomerID="1">
  <OrderHeader SalesOrderID="43860" TotalDue="14603.7393">
    <OrderDate>2001-08-01T00:00:00</OrderDate>
    <ShipDate>2001-08-08T00:00:00</ShipDate>
    <OrderDetail ProductID="761" OrderQty="2" LineTotal="838.917800" />
    <OrderDetail ProductID="770" OrderQty="1" LineTotal="419.458900" />
      :
  </OrderHeader>
  <OrderHeader SalesOrderID="44501" TotalDue="26128.8674">
    <OrderDate>2001-11-01T00:00:00</OrderDate>
    <ShipDate>2001-11-08T00:00:00</ShipDate>
    <OrderDetail ProductID="761" OrderQty="1" LineTotal="419.458900" />
    <OrderDetail ProductID="768" OrderQty="3" LineTotal="1258.376700" />
      :
  </OrderHeader>
  <OrderHeader SalesOrderID="45283" TotalDue="37643.1378">
    <OrderDate>2002-02-01T00:00:00</OrderDate>
    <ShipDate>2002-02-08T00:00:00</ShipDate>
    <OrderDetail ProductID="759" OrderQty="1" LineTotal="419.458900" />
    <OrderDetail ProductID="758" OrderQty="3" LineTotal="2624.382000" />
    <OrderDetail ProductID="750" OrderQty="2" LineTotal="4293.924000" />
      :
  </OrderHeader>
  <OrderHeader SalesOrderID="46042" TotalDue="34722.9906">
    <OrderDate>2002-05-01T00:00:00</OrderDate>
    <ShipDate>2002-05-08T00:00:00</ShipDate>
    <OrderDetail ProductID="763" OrderQty="2" LineTotal="838.917800" />
    <OrderDetail ProductID="757" OrderQty="4" LineTotal="3499.176000" />
      :
  </OrderHeader>
</Customer>
  :
```

If you are familiar and comfortable with XPath, you will appreciate some additional *FOR XML PATH* features. You can use the following XPath node test functions to further control the shape of your XML output:

- *data*

- *comment*

- *node*

- *text*

- *processing-instruction*

The following example uses the *data* and *comment* methods of XPath. The *data* method takes the results of the underlying query and places them all inside one element. The *comment* method takes data and transforms it into an XML comment, as shown here:

```
SELECT
  Customer.BusinessEntityID AS [@CustomerID],
  Customer.FirstName + ' ' + Customer.LastName AS [comment()],
```

```
   (SELECT SalesOrderID AS [@SalesOrderID],
       TotalDue AS [@TotalDue],
       OrderDate,
       ShipDate,
       (SELECT ProductID AS [data()]
        FROM Sales.SalesOrderDetail
        WHERE SalesOrderID = OrderHeader.SalesOrderID
        FOR XML PATH('')) AS [ProductIDs]
    FROM Sales.SalesOrderHeader AS OrderHeader
    WHERE CustomerID = Customer.BusinessEntityID
    FOR XML PATH('OrderHeader'), TYPE)
 FROM Sales.vIndividualCustomer AS Customer
 WHERE BusinessEntityID IN (11000, 11001)
 FOR XML PATH ('Customer')
```

As you can see from the results, the concatenated contact name becomes an XML comment, and the subquery of *Product IDs* is transformed into one element:

```
<Customer CustomerID="11000">
  <!--Jon Yang-->
  <OrderHeader SalesOrderID="43793" TotalDue="3756.9890">
    <OrderDate>2001-07-22T00:00:00</OrderDate>
    <ShipDate>2001-07-29T00:00:00</ShipDate>
    <ProductIDs> 966 934 923 707 881</ProductIDs>
  </OrderHeader>
     :
</Customer>
<Customer CustomerID="11001">
  <!--Eugene Huang-->
  <OrderHeader SalesOrderID="43767" TotalDue="3729.3640">
    <OrderDate>2001-07-18T00:00:00</OrderDate>
    <ShipDate>2001-07-25T00:00:00</ShipDate>
    <ProductIDs> 779 878 870 871 884 712</ProductIDs>
  </OrderHeader>
     :
</Customer>
```

Specifying a *ROOT* Element

The *ROOT* option allows you to add a main, or root, element to your *FOR XML* output. You can combine this with other *FOR XML* keywords, as shown here:

```
SELECT Customer.CustomerID, OrderDetail.SalesOrderID, OrderDetail.OrderDate
 FROM Sales.Customer AS Customer
  INNER JOIN Sales.SalesOrderHeader OrderDetail
  ON OrderDetail.customerid=Customer.customerid
 WHERE Customer.CustomerID<11005
 ORDER BY Customer.CustomerID
 FOR XML AUTO, ROOT('Orders')
```

The output looks like this:

```
<Orders>
  <Customer CustomerID="1">
    <OrderDetail SalesOrderID="43860" OrderDate="2001-08-01T00:00:00" />
```

```
      <OrderDetail SalesOrderID="44501" OrderDate="2001-11-01T00:00:00" />
      <OrderDetail SalesOrderID="45283" OrderDate="2002-02-01T00:00:00" />
      <OrderDetail SalesOrderID="46042" OrderDate="2002-05-01T00:00:00" />
  </Customer>
    :
</Orders>
```

The code output here is the same as any *FOR XML AUTO* output for this query, except that the *XML ROOT* we specified with the *ROOT* keyword now surrounds the data. In this example, we used *ROOT ('Orders')*, so our output is surrounded with an *<Orders>* XML element.

Producing an Inline XSD Schema

As you've seen, schemas provide an enforceable structure for your XML data. When you export data using the *FOR XML* syntax, you might want to include an inline XML schema for the recipient so that the recipient can enforce the rules on his or her end as well. When you use the *RAW* and *AUTO* modes, you can produce an inline XSD schema as part of the output by using the *XMLSCHEMA* keyword, as shown here:

```
SELECT Customer.CustomerID, OrderDetail.SalesOrderID, OrderDetail.OrderDate
 FROM Sales.Customer AS Customer
  INNER JOIN Sales.SalesOrderHeader AS OrderDetail
   ON OrderDetail.CustomerID = Customer.CustomerID
WHERE Customer.CustomerID < 11005
ORDER BY Customer.CustomerID
FOR XML AUTO, XMLSCHEMA
```

The output looks like this:

```
<xsd:schema targetNamespace="urn:schemas-microsoft-
com:sql:SqlRowSet1" xmlns:schema="urn:schemas-microsoft-
com:sql:SqlRowSet1" xmlns:xsd="http://www.w3.org/2001/XMLSchema" xmlns:sqltypes="http://
schemas.microsoft.com/sqlserver/2004/sqltypes" elementFormDefault="qualified">
  <xsd:import namespace="http://schemas.microsoft.com/sqlserver/2004/
sqltypes" schemaLocation="http://schemas.microsoft.com/sqlserver/2004/sqltypes/sqltypes.
xsd" />
  <xsd:element name="Customer">
    <xsd:complexType>
      <xsd:sequence>
        <xsd:element ref="schema:OrderDetail" minOccurs="0" maxOccurs="unbounded" />
      </xsd:sequence>
      <xsd:attribute name="CustomerID" type="sqltypes:int" use="required" />
    </xsd:complexType>
  </xsd:element>
  <xsd:element name="OrderDetail">
    <xsd:complexType>
      <xsd:attribute name="SalesOrderID" type="sqltypes:int" use="required" />
      <xsd:attribute name="OrderDate" type="sqltypes:datetime" use="required" />
    </xsd:complexType>
  </xsd:element>
</xsd:schema>
<Customer xmlns="urn:schemas-microsoft-com:sql:SqlRowSet1" CustomerID="1">
```

```
        <OrderDetail SalesOrderID="43860" OrderDate="2001-08-01T00:00:00" />
        <OrderDetail SalesOrderID="44501" OrderDate="2001-11-01T00:00:00" />
        <OrderDetail SalesOrderID="45283" OrderDate="2002-02-01T00:00:00" />
        <OrderDetail SalesOrderID="46042" OrderDate="2002-05-01T00:00:00" />
    </Customer>
```

SQL Server infers the schema based on the underlying data types of the result set. For example, the *SalesOrderID* field is set to an *int* and is a required field (as per the inline schema based on the properties of the field in the underlying SQL table).

Producing Element-Based XML

Many developers prefer element-based XML ("canonical" XML) over attribute-based XML. Element-based XML presents its data as individual elements, as opposed to individual attributes, for each data point. A welcome enhancement to *RAW* and *AUTO* is the ability to specify element-based XML as a result by using the *ELEMENTS* keyword, as shown here:

```
SELECT Customer.CustomerID, OrderDetail.SalesOrderID,OrderDetail.OrderDate
 FROM Sales.Customer Customer
  INNER JOIN Sales.SalesOrderHeader OrderDetail
   ON OrderDetail.CustomerID = Customer.CustomerID
 WHERE Customer.CustomerID = 11000
 ORDER BY Customer.CustomerID
 FOR XML AUTO, ELEMENTS
```

The results look like this:

```
<Customer>
  <CustomerID>11000</CustomerID>
  <OrderDetail>
    <SalesOrderID>43860</SalesOrderID>
    <OrderDate>2001-08-01T00:00:00</OrderDate>
  </OrderDetail>
  <OrderDetail>
    <SalesOrderID>44501</SalesOrderID>
    <OrderDate>2001-11-01T00:00:00</OrderDate>
  </OrderDetail>
  <OrderDetail>
    <SalesOrderID>45283</SalesOrderID>
    <OrderDate>2002-02-01T00:00:00</OrderDate>
  </OrderDetail>
  <OrderDetail>
    <SalesOrderID>46042</SalesOrderID>
    <OrderDate>2002-05-01T00:00:00</OrderDate>
  </OrderDetail>
</Customer>
```

As you can see, each column of the query becomes an element in the resulting XML, as opposed to an attribute of one row.

The *ELEMENTS* keyword used in conjunction with the *FOR XML* statement converts each column from your result set to an individual XML element; using *AUTO*, it also converts each row from a joined table to a new XML element. Note that element-based XML is more verbose than attribute-based XML but is usually easier to view and work with.

OPENXML Enhancements in SQL Server 2008

Up to now, we have been using *FOR XML* to compose XML from rows of data, but what if we already have XML data and we want to shred it back into relational data? SQL Server 2000 introduced a feature called *OPENXML* for this purpose. *OPENXML* is a system function that allows an XML document to be shredded into T-SQL rows. SQL Server 2005 and 2008 also support the *OPENXML* function—with some enhancements, of course.

To shred data into relational rows using *OPENXML*, you must first create an XML document handle using the system stored procedure *sp_xml_preparedocument*. This system stored procedure takes an XML document and creates a representation that is referenced via a handle, which it returns via an *OUTPUT* parameter. *OPENXML* uses this handle along with a specified path and behaves like a database view to the XML data, so you simply choose *SELECT* from the *OPENXML* function just as you would *SELECT* from a table or a view. The code in Listing 6-7 shows an example of *OPENXML* in action.

LISTING 6-7 Using *OPENXML*

```
DECLARE @handle int
DECLARE @xmlOrder varchar(1000)
SET @xmlOrder = '
<Root>
  <Customer CustomerID="BRU" ContactName="Andrew Brust">
    <Order CustomerID="BRU" EmployeeID="5" OrderDate="2005-11-04">
      <OrderDetail OrderID="10248" ProductID="16" Quantity="12"/>
      <OrderDetail OrderID="10248" ProductID="32" Quantity="10"/>
    </Order>
  </Customer>
  <Customer CustomerID="ZAC" ContactName="Bill Zack">
    <Order CustomerID="ZAc" EmployeeID="3" OrderDate="2005-11-16">
      <OrderDetail OrderID="10283" ProductID="99" Quantity="3"/>
    </Order>
  </Customer>
</Root>'

--Create an internal representation of the XML document
EXEC sp_xml_preparedocument @handle OUTPUT, @xmlOrder


-- OPENXML rowset provider.
```

```
SELECT *
FROM OPENXML (@handle, '/Root/Customer', 1)
WITH (CustomerID varchar(10), ContactName varchar(20))
```

This code allows you to query and work with the XML text as if it were relational data. The output looks like this:

```
CustomerID  ContactName
----------- ----------------
BRU         Andrew Brust
ZAC         Bill Zack

(2 row(s) affected)
```

You can optionally specify whether you want *OPENXML* to use element-based or attribute-based XML relational mapping between the rowset columns and the XML nodes. There are two ways to control the mapping. The first is to use the *flags* parameter, which assumes that the XML nodes will map to corresponding rowset columns with exactly the same name. You can also use the *ColPattern* parameter, an XPath expression that allows you to use a schema to perform the mapping as part of the *SchemaDeclaration* in the *WITH* clause. The mapping specified in *ColPattern* overwrites the mapping specified by the *flags* parameter.

SQL Server 2005 introduced two enhancements to *OPENXML*, both involving the new *xml* data type. First, the *xml* data type is supported as an output column or an overflow column with the *OPENXML* statement. Second, you can pass an *xml* data type variable directly into *sp_xml_preparedocument*. Both of these enhancements enable you to more easily work with existing XML data in an XML column or created data using *FOR XML TYPE*.

XML Bulk Load

In SQL Server 2000, XML Bulk Load allowed users to load large XML documents on the client side. XML Bulk Load works by reading the XML and producing SQL *INSERT* statements that run on the client in a batched fashion. SQL Server 2005 and 2008 greatly enhance XML Bulk Load by allowing it to run on the server and to load directly into an *xml* data type column.

Using the enhanced XML Bulk Load requires using the system rowset provider function *OPENROWSET* and specifying the *BULK* provider, as shown in Listing 6-8.

LISTING 6-8 Performing an XML Bulk Load

```
--create a table with an xml column
CREATE TABLE tblXmlCustomers
 (CustomerID int PRIMARY KEY IDENTITY,
```

```
    CustomerXML xml NOT NULL)

--this file will load 1 record in (SINGLE_CLOB); for more records use a format file
INSERT INTO tblXmlCustomers
 SELECT * FROM OPENROWSET(BULK 'C:\customer_01.xml', SINGLE_CLOB) AS XmlData
```

This example works by first creating a table that has an *xml* column and a primary key value. We then use an *INSERT* statement that selects all of the data from the XML file using *OPENROWSET*. *OPENROWSET* uses the *BULK* provider and loads into the *xml* column of the *tblXmlCustomers* table the entire contents of the *customer_01.xml* file.

Querying XML Data Using XQuery

Storing XML in the database is one thing; querying it efficiently is another. With SQL Server 2000, which has no *xml* data type, you had to deconstruct the XML and move element and attribute data into relational columns to perform a query on the XML data residing in the text column. You could also resort to some other searching mechanism, such as full-text search. In SQL Server 2005 and 2008, XQuery provides a native and elegant way to query XML data.

Understanding XQuery Expressions and XPath

XQuery is a language used to query and process XML data. XQuery is a W3C standard; its specification is located at *http://www.w3.org/TR/xquery/*. The XQuery specification contains several descriptions of requirements, use cases, and data models. We encourage you to go to the specification and read "XQuery 1.0, an XML Query Language" and "XQuery 1.0 and XPath 2.0 Functions and Operators" to get a full understanding of what XQuery is all about. For now, we will explain enough to cover the basics. After reading this section, you will be able to select, filter, and update XML data using XQuery.

Because XQuery is an XML language, all the rules of XML apply. XQuery uses lowercase element names (keywords), and because XML itself is case sensitive, you must take this into account when writing queries. While XQuery has some powerful formatting and processing commands, it is primarily a query language (as its name suggests), so we will focus here on writing queries. The body of a query consists of two parts: an XPath expression and a *FLWOR* (pronounced "flower") expression. (FLWOR is an acronym composed of the first letters of *for*, *let*, *where*, *order by*, and *return*.)

XPath Expressions

XPath, another W3C standard (*http://www.w3.org/TR/xpath*), uses path expressions to identify specific nodes in an XML document. These path expressions are similar to the syntax you see when you work with a computer file system (for example, c:\folder\myfile.doc). Take a look at the following XML document:

```
<catalog>
  <book category="ITPro">
    <title>Windows Step By Step</title>
    <author>Bill Zack</author>
    <price>49.99</price>
  </book>
  <book category="Developer">
    <title>Developing ADO .NET</title>
    <author>Andrew Brust</author>
    <price>39.93</price>
  </book>
  <book category="ITPro">
    <title>Windows Cluster Server</title>
    <author>Stephen Forte</author>
    <price>59.99</price>
  </book>
</catalog>
```

The following XPath expression selects the root element catalog:

```
/catalog
```

This XPath expression selects all the book elements of the catalog root element:

```
/catalog/book
```

And this XPath expression selects all the author elements of all the book elements of the catalog root element:

```
/catalog/book/author
```

XPath enables you to specify a subset of data within the XML (via its location within the XML structure) that you want to work with. XQuery is more robust and allows you to perform more complex queries against the XML data using *FLWOR* expressions combined with XPath.

FLWOR Expressions

Just as *SELECT, FROM, WHERE, GROUP BY,* and *ORDER BY* form the basis of the SQL selection logic, the *for, let, where, order by,* and *return* (*FLWOR*) keywords form the basis of every XQuery query you write. You use the *for* and *let* keywords to assign variables and iterate through the data within the context of the XQuery query. (The *let* keyword is not supported in the SQL Server 2005 implementation of XQuery but is in SQL Server 2008.) The *where* keyword works as a restriction and outputs the value of the variable. For example, the following basic XQuery query uses the XPath expression */catalog/book* to obtain a reference to all the *<book>* nodes, and the *for* keyword initiates a loop, but only of elements where the *category* attribute is equal to *"ITPro"*. This simple code snippet iterates through each */catalog/book* node using the *$b* variable with the *for* statement only where the category attribute is *"ITPro"* and returns as output the resulting information ordered by the author's name using the *order* keyword:

```
for $b in /catalog/book
 where $b/@category="ITPro"
 order by $b/author[1] descending
 return ($b)
```

Here is a simple example that uses this XQuery expression on an *xml* data type variable. We assign the XML to the variable and then use the preceding XQuery expression in the *query* method (explained in the next section) of the *xml* data type.

```
DECLARE @XML xml
SET @XML='
<catalog>
   <book category="ITPro">
     <title>Windows Step By Step</title>
     <author>Bill Zack</author>
     <price>49.99</price>
   </book>
   <book category="Developer">
     <title>Developing ADO .NET</title>
     <author>Andrew Brust</author>
     <price>39.93</price>
   </book>
   <book category="ITPro">
     <title>Windows Cluster Server</title>
     <author>Stephen Forte</author>
     <price>59.99</price>
   </book>
</catalog>'

SELECT @XML.query('
   for $b in /catalog/book
   where $b/@category="ITPro"
   order by $b/author[1] descending
   return ($b)')
```

The results are as follows. Notice that Stephen's record is first because our order is descending by the *author* element. Andrew's record is not in the output because we are restricting only for *"ITPro"* in the category element.

```
<book category="ITPro">
  <title>Windows Cluster Server</title>
  <author>Stephen Forte</author>
  <price>59.99</price>
</book>
```

```
<book category="ITPro">
  <title>Windows Step By Step</title>
  <author>Bill Zack</author>
  <price>49.99</price>
</book>
```

Now that you've seen the basics, let's look at using XQuery with our SQL Server data.

SQL Server 2008 XQuery in Action

SQL Server 2008 has a standards-based implementation of XQuery that directly supports XQuery functions on the *xml* data type by using five methods of the *xml* data type, as shown here:

- **xml.exist**   Uses XQuery input to return 0, 1, or *NULL*, depending on the result of the query. This method returns 0 if no elements match, 1 if there is a match, and *NULL* if there is no XML data on which to query. The *xml.exist* method is often used for query predicates.

- **xml.value**   Accepts an XQuery query that resolves to a single value as input and returns a SQL Server scalar type.

- **xml.query**   Accepts an XQuery query that resolves to multiple values as input and returns an xml data type stream as output.

- **xml.nodes**   Accepts an XQuery query as input and returns a single-column rowset from the XML document. In essence, this method shreds XML into multiple smaller XML results.

- **xml.modify**   Allows you to insert, delete, or modify nodes or sequences of nodes in an xml data type instance using an XQuery querydata manipulation language (DML).

We will discuss the methods of the *xml* data type shortly. But first we must create some sample data. We will create a simple table that contains speakers at a software developer conference and the corresponding classes they will teach. Usually, you normalize the data and have a one-to-many relationship between a speakers table and a classes table. Instead of using an additional normalized table, we will model this as one table with the speakers' information and one XML column with the speakers' classes. In the real world, you might encounter this scenario when you have a speaker and his or her classes represented in a series of one-to-many tables in a back-office database. Then, for the Web database, you might "publish" a database on a frequent time interval (like a reporting database) or transform normalized data and use the XML column for easy HTML display (or XSLT transformations).

We first create a schema (for reasons that will soon become clear) for our XML column. This schema, shown in Listing 6-9, will define the type of XML allowed in the column, including the *xml* data types and required properties for particular XML elements.

LISTING 6-9 XML schema creation

```
CREATE XML SCHEMA COLLECTION dbo.classes_xsd AS
'<?xml version="1.0" encoding="UTF-8" ?>
<xs:schema xmlns:xs="http://www.w3.org/2001/XMLSchema">
  <xs:element name="class">
    <xs:complexType>
     <xs:attribute name="name" type="xs:string" use="required" />
    </xs:complexType>
  </xs:element>
  <xs:element name="classes">
    <xs:complexType>
      <xs:sequence>
        <xs:element ref="class" maxOccurs="unbounded" />
      </xs:sequence>
    </xs:complexType>
  </xs:element>
</xs:schema>'
```

Next we create our table, *tblSpeakers* in Listing 6-10. Notice that the *xml* column, *Speaker_ XML*, uses the *classes_xsd* XSD schema we just created.

LISTING 6-10 Creating a table with a schema

```
CREATE TABLE tblSpeakers
( Speaker_ID int PRIMARY KEY IDENTITY,
  Speaker_NM nvarchar(50),
  Speaker_Country nvarchar(25),
  Speaker_XML xml (classes_xsd) NOT NULL)
```

XQuery runs more efficiently when there is an XML index on the XML column. As you learned earlier, an XML index works only if there is a primary key constraint on the table (which we have). The code here creates a primary and then a structural (*PATH*) index because our examples apply a lot of *where* restrictions on the values of particular elements:

```
--XML Index: Primary
CREATE Primary XML INDEX idx_1
   ON tblSpeakers (Speaker_XML)

--PATH
CREATE XML INDEX idx_a
   ON tblSpeakers (Speaker_XML)
   USING XML INDEX idx_1 FOR PATH
```

Now that we have our index, remember that XQuery works more efficiently if it is strongly typed, so you should always use a schema on your XML column for the best performance. Without a schema, the SQL Server XQuery engine assumes that everything is untyped and simply treats it as string data.

Last, we need to get data into the table by using some *INSERT* statements, as shown in Listing 6-11. The final *INSERT* statement in Listing 6-11, *'Bad Speaker'*, will fail because it does not contain a *<classes>* element as required by the *classes_xsd* schema. (Because XML is case sensitive, its *<CLASSES>* element is not a match for the *<classes>* element specified as required in the schema.)

LISTING 6-11 Inserting XML data

```
INSERT INTO tblSpeakers VALUES('Stephen Forte', 'USA', '
 <classes>
   <class name="Writing Secure Code for ASP .NET"/>
   <class name="Using XQuery to Query and Manipulate XML Data in SQL Server 2008"/>
   <class name="SQL Server and Oracle Working Together"/>
   <class name="Protecting against SQL Injection Attacks "/>
 </classes>')

INSERT INTO tblSpeakers VALUES('Richard Campbell', 'Canada', '
 <classes>
   <class name="SQL Server Profiler"/>
   <class name="Advanced SQL Querying Techniques"/>
   <class name="SQL Server and Oracle Working Together"/>
   <class name="T-SQL Error Handling in Yukon"/>
 </classes>')

INSERT INTO tblSpeakers VALUES('John Huckaby', 'USA', '
 <classes>
   <class name="Smart Client Stuff"/>
   <class name="More Smart Client Stuff"/>
 </classes>')

INSERT INTO tblSpeakers VALUES('Malek Kemmou', 'Morocco', '
 <classes>
   <class name="SmartPhone 2005"/>
   <class name="Office System 2003"/>
 </classes>')

INSERT INTO tblSpeakers VALUES('Goksin Bakir', 'Turkey', '
 <classes>
   <class name="SmartPhone 2007"/>
   <class name="Office System 2007"/>
 </classes>')

INSERT INTO tblSpeakers VALUES('Jan  Vasters', 'Germany', '
 <classes>
   <class name="SOA"/>
   <class name="Biz Talk Services"/>
 </classes>')

INSERT INTO tblSpeakers VALUES('Monica L. Tripp', 'USA', '
 <classes>
   <class name="SQL Server Index"/>
   <class name="SQL Precon"/>
 </classes>')
```

```
INSERT INTO tblSpeakers VALUES('Bad Speaker', 'France', '
 <CLASSES>
   <class name="SQL Server Index"/>
   <class name="SQL Precon"/>
 </CLASSES>')
```

Now that we have our data, it's time to start writing some XQuery expressions in SQL Server 2008. To do this, we will use the query-based methods of the *xml* data type described earlier inside a regular T-SQL query. (We'll see *xml.modify* in action later.)

xml.exist

Having XML in the database is almost useless unless you can query the elements and attributes of the XML data natively. XQuery becomes very useful when you can use it to search based on the values of a particular element or attribute. The *xml.exist* method accepts an XQuery query as input and returns *0*, *1*, or *NULL*, depending on the result of the query: *0* is returned if no elements match, *1* is returned if there is a match, and *NULL* is returned if there is no data to query on. For example, we will see whether a node exists in this particular XML string of classes:

```
DECLARE @XML xml
SET @XML = '
<classes>
    <class name="SQL Server Index"/>
    <class name="SQL Precon"/>
</classes>'

SELECT @XML.exist('/classes')
```

The code returns *1* because the *<classes>* element exists in the XML variable. If you change the XQuery expression to search for an XML node that does not exist (*SELECT @XML.exist('/dogs')*, for example), it will return *0*. If would be nice if you could use this as part of a *CHECK CONSTRAINT*. However, because SQL Server does not allow you to use *xml.exist* as part of a *CHECK CONSTRAINT* directly, you have to first create a user-defined function (UDF) to perform the action. This UDF accepts an XML field and returns the value of an *xml.exist* method looking for an instance of *<Orders>*, as shown in Listing 6-12.

LISTING 6-12 Creating a function to use in a *CHECK CONSTRAINT*

```
CREATE FUNCTION dbo.DoesOrderXMLDataExist(@XML xml)
 RETURNS bit
AS
 BEGIN
```

```
        RETURN @XML.exist('/Orders')
    END
  GO
```

To use this UDF from Listing 6-12 as a *CHECK CONSTRAINT*, just create a table and pass to the UDF you just created the column that you want to apply the constraint to, as shown here:

```
Use AdventureWorks2008

--create the table using the function
CREATE TABLE OrdersXMLCheck
    (OrderDocID int PRIMARY KEY,
     xOrders xml NOT NULL DEFAULT '<Orders/>'
 CONSTRAINT xml_orderconstraint
  CHECK(dbo.DoesOrderXMLDataExist(xOrders) = 1))
```

You will most likely use the return value of *xml.exist* (*0, 1*, or *NULL*) as part of a *WHERE* clause. Think about it: you can run a T-SQL query and restrict the query on a value of a particular XML element! Going back to our main example, let's look for the value of *"SQL Server and Oracle Working Together"* in the *<class>* element. Here is the XQuery expression to do this:

```
/classes/class[@name="SQL Server and Oracle Working Together"]
```

Here's how you put expression to work:

```
SELECT * FROM tblSpeakers
 WHERE
   Speaker_XML.exist('/classes/class[@name="SQL Server and Oracle Working Together"]') = 1
```

The results look like this:

```
1  Stephen Forte   USA   <classes>...</classes>
2  Richard Campbell  Canada  <classes/>...</classes>
```

The XML returned in these results look like this for Stephen:

```
<classes>
  <class name="Writing Secure Code for ASP .NET " />
  <class name="Using XQuery to Query and Manipulate XML Data in SQL Server 2008" />
  <class name="SQL Server and Oracle Working Together" />
  <class name="Protecting against SQL Injection Attacks " />
</classes>
```

xml.value

The *xml.value* method takes a valid XQuery expression and returns a SQL Server scalar value that you specify. Let's say that you have an XML column and you want to return some data from the XML as an intrinsic SQL data type inside a T-SQL query. You call the *xml.value* method on that column by passing in the XQuery expression and the data type you want to convert the output to. This requires you to know and understand the data in your XML column. Here's an example of the syntax against our current XML document in the database:

```
xml.value('/classes[1]/class[1]/@name', 'varchar(40)')
```

This XQuery contains an XPath expression that navigates the first class's name attribute and a cast to *varchar(40)*.

You must perform an XQuery expression on an *xml* column as part of a regular T-SQL query, as shown here. What is phenomenal about this is that SQL Server combines both relational queries and XQuery in one query because in this example we use a traditional T-SQL *WHERE* clause to show only speakers from the United States.

```
USE AdventureWorks2008
GO

SELECT
  Speaker_ID,
  Speaker_NM,
  Speaker_Country,
  Speaker_XML.value('/classes[1]/class[1]/@name', 'varchar(40)') as Sessions
 FROM tblSpeakers
 WHERE Speaker_Country = 'USA'
```

The results are shown here:

```
Speaker_ID  Speaker_NM      Speaker_Country  Session
----------  --------------  ---------------  ----------------------------------
1           Stephen Forte   USA              Writing Secure Code for ASP .NET
3           John Huckaby    USA              Smart Client Stuff
7           Monica  Tripp   USA              SQL Server Index

(3 row(s) affected)
```

Let's dissect the XQuery expression. As you'll recall from Listing 6-11, the XML for Stephen looks like this:

```
<classes>
    <class name="Writing Secure Code for ASP .NET "/>
    <class name="Using XQuery to Query and Manipulate XML Data in SQL Server 2008"/>
    <class name="SQL Server and Oracle Working Together"/>
    <class name="Protecting against SQL Injection Attacks "/>
</classes>
```

The following XQuery path expression returns the value of the first class's *name* attribute (*Writing Secure Code for ASP.NET*) as a *varchar(40)*. So in the preceding query, the XQuery expression is placed in the *value* method of the XML column *Speaker_XML*. The XQuery expression itself does all the work of getting the first class's name, as shown here:

```
/classes[1]/class[1]/@name
```

This approach is useful when you want to pull data out of the XML column and produce it as regular scalar SQL Server data.

xml.query

The *xml.query* method works much like the *xml.value* method, except it returns an *xml* data type value, so you have a lot more flexibility. This method is useful only if you want the end result of the column in the query to be XML; if you want scalar data, use *xml.value*.

If you want to return the same data as in the preceding example, but you want to present the summary column in XML format, run the same query except with the *xml.query*, as follows:

```
--xml.query
--returns XML data type
--same as previous example but returns XML
SELECT
    Speaker_ID,
    Speaker_NM,
    Speaker_Country,
    Speaker_XML.query('/classes[1]/class[1]') AS Sessions
 FROM tblSpeakers
 WHERE Speaker_Country = 'USA'
```

xml.query works by passing in an XQuery expression that will result in XML output. The XQuery expression can return a single element, return all the elements, or use a *return* (the *R* in *FLWOR*) expression to completely transform the results. In this example, the first instance of the class element is returned. The results of the *Sessions* column for Stephen's records are the same as in the preceding example, except that they are now formatted in XML:

```
<class name="Writing Secure Code for ASP .NET " />
```

Instead of using *xml.value*, you can return a larger XML result of many nodes by leaving out the *[1]* ordinal position indicators in your path expression, as follows:

```
--same as previous but returns all
SELECT
  Speaker_ID,
  Speaker_NM,
  Speaker_Country,
  Speaker_XML.query('/classes/class') AS Sessions
 FROM tblSpeakers
 WHERE Speaker_Country = 'USA'
```

The results are the same except for Stephen's classes; here, we get all of the XML results as an XML column:

```
<class name="Writing Secure Code for ASP .NET " />
<class name="Using XQuery to Query and Manipulate XML Data in SQL Server 2008" />
<class name="SQL Server and Oracle Working Together" />
<class name="Protecting Against SQL Injection Attacks" />
```

You can gain further control over your XQuery path expression by using *FLWOR* expressions. For example, you can write an expression like this:

```
for $b in /classes/class
return ($b)
```

The expression uses the *for* and *return* keywords to loop through all of the class elements and return the values, and it yields the same results as the preceding example, which has *'/classes/class'* as its XQuery expression. (Of course, you can come up with much more interesting examples.) You can incorporate this expression into your T-SQL query, as shown here:

```
SELECT
  Speaker_ID,
  Speaker_NM,
  Speaker_Country,
  Speaker_XML.query('
  for $b in /classes/class
  return ($b)
  ') AS Sessions
 FROM tblSpeakers
 WHERE Speaker_Country = 'USA'
```

Let's say that you want to have more control over the XML output using *xml.query* or *xml. value* as well as combining the XQuery and a traditional T-SQL *WHERE* clause to show only the speakers in the United States. You can use an XML method in both the *SELECT* and *WHERE* clauses of a single query, as follows:

```
SELECT
  Speaker_ID,
  Speaker_NM,
  Speaker_Country,
  Speaker_XML.query('/classes/class') AS Sessions
 FROM tblSpeakers
 WHERE Speaker_Country = 'USA' AND
  Speaker_XML.exist('/classes/class[@name="SQL Server and Oracle Working Together"]') = 1
```

The T-SQL *WHERE* clause restricts on the *Speaker_Country* column, and our XQuery expression filters only for the *<class>* element we are interested in:

```
<class name="Writing Secure Code for ASP .NET " />
<class name="Using XQuery to Query and Manipulate XML Data in SQL Server 2008" />
<class name="SQL Server and Oracle Working Together" />
<class name="Protecting against SQL Injection Attacks " />
```

SQL Server 2008 now has support for *let*, which is used to assign values to variables in an XQuery expression. For example, we'll use the following XML to count the number of sessions per speaker using the *count* XQuery expression and assign the number of sessions to a variable via *let*:

```
DECLARE @xml xml
SET @xml='
```

```
<Speakers>
  <Speaker name="Stephen Forte">
    <classes>
      <class name="Writing Secure Code for ASP .NET "/>
      <class name="Using XQuery in SQL Server 2008"/>
      <class name="SQL Server and Oracle Working Together"/>
    </classes>
  </Speaker>
  <Speaker name="Richard Campbell">
    <classes>
      <class name="SQL Server Profiler"/>
      <class name="Advanced SQL Querying Techniques"/>
      <class name="SQL Server and Oracle Working Together"/>
      <class name="From 1 Server to 2"/>
    </classes>
  </Speaker>
</Speakers>'

SELECT @xml.query(
'<Speakers>
{
for $Speaker in /Speakers/Speaker
let $count :=count($Speaker/classes/class)
order by $count descending
return
<Speaker>
{$Speaker/@name}
{$Speaker/count}
<SessionCount>{$count}</SessionCount>
</Speaker>
}
</Speakers>')
```

Here is the result:

```
<Speakers>
  <Speaker name="Richard Campbell">
    <SessionCount>4</SessionCount>
  </Speaker>
  <Speaker name="Stephen Forte">
    <SessionCount>3</SessionCount>
  </Speaker>
</Speakers>
```

Notice that Richard sorts on top because we sorted the output based on the session count in a descending fashion. For comparison purposes, the sort expression used the variable we assigned using *let*. This is very helpful if you are manipulating simple XML and need to do a mini-transform via XQuery. If you were using the *return* statement all the time to make slight manipulations to your XML, you will find *let* very helpful. While this is the only addition to XQuery in SQL Server 2008, it is a much needed and welcome one.

xml.nodes

The *xml.nodes* method takes an XQuery expression just like *exist*, *value*, and *query*. The *xml.nodes* method then returns instances of a special *xml* data type, each of which has its context set to a different node that the XQuery expression you supplied evaluates to. The special XML data type is used for subqueries of XML data in your result set.

SQL Server XQuery Extensions

Microsoft has made some extensions to the XQuery specification that are implemented in SQL Server 2008 to aid the developer in tasks such as referencing non-XML data inside XQuery expressions to XML data manipulation language (DML) statements.

sql:column

The *sql:column* function, which is specific to SQL Server XQuery, allows the XQuery expression to refer to a column in the current row of the dataset. The syntax is *{sql:column("Column Name")}*, as shown here:

```
for $b in /classes/class
where $b/@name="SQL Server and Oracle Working Together"
return (<Sessions>{$b}<Speaker id="{sql:column("Speaker_ID")}">
   {sql:column("Speaker_NM")}</Speaker></Sessions>)
```

Bringing it all together, let's create an attribute named *Speaker id* with the value from the *Speaker_ID* column for the current row. The *<Sessions>* node is a node constructor, which means that you can create a node as part of your *return* in your *for* expression, as shown here:

```
SELECT Speaker_ID, Speaker_NM, Speaker_Country, Speaker_XML.query('
   for $b in /classes/class
   where $b/@name="SQL Server and Oracle Working Together"
   return (<Sessions>{$b}<Speaker id="{sql:column("Speaker_ID")}">
      {sql:column("Speaker_NM")}</Speaker></Sessions>)
   ') AS Sessions
 FROM tblSpeakers
 WHERE Speaker_XML.exist('/classes/class[@name="SQL Server and Oracle Working Together"]')=1
```

In the XML result for Stephen's record, shown next, notice that our *xml.query* expression in our *SELECT* is in tune with our T-SQL XQuery *WHERE* clause, and we limit our results to show the same element as in our *WHERE* clause:

```
<Sessions>
  <class name="SQL Server and Oracle Working Together" />
  <Speaker id="1">Stephen Forte</Speaker>
</Sessions>
```

sql:variable

The *sql:variable* function is also unique to the SQL Server implementation of XQuery. It works exactly like *sql:column*, but it refers to the value of a variable rather than the value of a column in a row. You have only a single value for the current query, as shown here:

```
DECLARE @Conf varchar(20)
SET @Conf= 'NYC .NET User Group'

SELECT Speaker_ID, Speaker_NM, Speaker_XML.query('
   for $b in /classes/class
   where $b/@name="SQL Server and Oracle Working Together"
      return (<Sessions
      conference="{sql:variable("@Conf")}">
      {$b}<Speaker id="{sql:column("Speaker_ID")}">
         {sql:column("Speaker_NM")}</Speaker></Sessions>)
   ') AS Sessions
 FROM tblSpeakers
 WHERE Speaker_XML.exist('/classes/class[@name="SQL Server and Oracle Working Together"]')=1
```

The results look like this:

```
<Sessions conference="NYC .NET User Group">
  <class name="SQL Server and Oracle Working Together" />
  <Speaker id="1">Stephen Forte</Speaker>
</Sessions>
```

XML DML

The W3C XQuery specification does not provide a way for you to modify XML data as you can modify relational table data using the *INSERT*, *UPDATE*, and *DELETE* keywords in T-SQL. The W3C has a working draft, but it might be a few years before it becomes a standard, so Microsoft has created its own XML data manipulation language, XML DML, which is included in its own XQuery implementation. The Microsoft version conforms to the W3C working draft, but by no means do we know whether Microsoft's current implementation and the final draft of the standard will coincide.

XML DML gives you three ways to manipulate the XML data of a column via the *xml.modify* method that we mentioned earlier:

- **xml.modify(insert)**   Allows you to insert a node or sequence of nodes into the *xml* data type instance you are working with

- **xml.modify(delete)**   Allows you to delete zero or more nodes that are the result of the output sequence of the XQuery expression you specify

- **xml.modify(replace)**   Modifies the value of a single node

xml.modify(insert)

The *xml.modify(insert)* method allows you to insert a node or sequence of nodes into the *xml* data type instance you are working with. You use the *xml.modify* method in conjunction with a T-SQL *UPDATE* statement and, if necessary, a T-SQL or an XQuery *where* clause (or both). You can also specify the keyword *first* or *last* beside an ordinal position. Here's a simple example:

```
--insert an XML node
UPDATE tblSpeakers
 SET Speaker_XML.modify(
  'insert
    <class name="Ranking and Windowing Functions in SQL Server 2008"/>
    into /classes[1]')
 WHERE Speaker_ID=1
```

In SQL Server 2008, the *xml.modify* method has been enhanced so that you can substitute the XML element with a variable using *sql:variable* (described earlier). This will work exactly the same as the previous query; however, it is easier to use this variable syntax:

```
DECLARE @newElement xml
SET @newElement = '<class name="Using Linq to SQL"/>'

UPDATE tblSpeakers
 SET Speaker_XML.modify(
  'insert
    sql:variable("@newElement")
    into /classes[1]')
 WHERE Speaker_ID=1
```

xml.modify(delete)

The *xml.modify(delete)* method deletes zero or more nodes based on the criteria you specify. The following example deletes a specific node based on its ordinal position; you can also combine this with a T-SQL or XQuery *WHERE* clause.

```
UPDATE tblSpeakers
 SET Speaker_XML.modify('delete /classes/class[3]')
 WHERE Speaker_ID = 1
```

xml.modify(replace)

The *xml.modify(replace)* method allows you to replace XML data with new information. This example replaces the class name:

```
UPDATE tblSpeakers
 SET Speaker_XML.modify('
   replace value of
    /classes[1]/class[3]/@name[1]
   with "Protecting against SQL Injection Attacks: Hackers must die"')
```

```
WHERE Speaker_ID = 1
```

Converting a Column to XML

If you have existing *text* or *varchar* columns in SQL Server 2008 that contain XML data, you're probably excited about using the *xml* data type and XQuery. Because you can use the T-SQL *CONVERT* and *CAST* functions to convert those columns to full-fledged XML data, it's easy to write a simple upgrade script.

First we need a table. For this example, we'll create a simple table:

```
CREATE TABLE tblXMLUpgradeTest
(Field_ID int  PRIMARY KEY IDENTITY,
 Field_XMLData nvarchar(4000))
```

Next we insert some data, as shown here, but remember that it is stored as text, not XML:

```
--insert some data as txt but is XML
--remember no cool XQuery or anything allowed!
DECLARE @xmlData AS varchar(8000)

SET @xmlData =
 (SELECT Customer.CustomerID, OrderDetail.SalesOrderID, OrderDetail.OrderDate
   FROM Sales.Customer Customer
    INNER JOIN Sales.SalesOrderHeader OrderDetail
     ON OrderDetail.customerid=Customer.customerid
   WHERE Customer.CustomerID=11000
   ORDER BY Customer.CustomerID
   FOR XML AUTO, ROOT('Orders'))

--first insert into the table
INSERT INTO tblXMLUpgradeTest(Field_XMLData) VALUES (@xmlData)
```

You can now convert your data from a plain string to an XML column in a series of six steps:

1. In the table containing the string field holding the data to be converted to XML, add a *varchar(8000)* or *text* field, depending on what your original column is. This is a temporary column to store the preconverted data. (Later we'll drop this column.)

2. Append the data in your current production text-based column to the new temporary column.

3. Drop your original text-based column.

4. Add the original column name back in, but with an *xml* data type.

5. Insert the data from the temporary column, using the *CONVERT* statement to convert the data to an *xml* data type.

6. Drop the temporary column.

A code example of all six steps is shown in Listing 6-13.

LISTING 6-13 Converting text data to XML

```
--first, alter the table
ALTER TABLE tblXMLUpgradeTest ADD Field_XMLData_Temp varchar(8000)
GO

--second, update the Field_XMLData_Temp column
UPDATE tblXMLUpgradeTest SET Field_XMLData_Temp = Field_XMLData
GO

--third, drop the original text column (Field_XMLData)
ALTER TABLE tblXMLUpgradeTest DROP COLUMN Field_XMLData
GO

--fourth, add the same column(Field_XMLData) but as XML
ALTER TABLE tblXMLUpgradeTest ADD Field_XMLData XML
GO

--fifth, insert the XML into Field_XMLData and convert to XML data type
UPDATE tblXMLUpgradeTest SET Field_XMLData = CONVERT(xml, Field_XMLData_Temp)
GO

--sixth, drop the Field_XMLData_Temp column since it has text, not XML
ALTER TABLE tblXMLUpgradeTest DROP COLUMN Field_XMLData_Temp
GO
```

Summary

We have taken a fairly extensive tour of the *xml* data type and its data manipulation mechanisms, XQuery and XML DML. As you have seen, SQL Server 2008 provides a rich feature set of XML technologies. At times, you will want to store XML in the database, and the *xml* data type allows you to work with XML natively—a vast improvement over earlier versions of SQL Server. Armed with this data type and the ability to query it using XQuery, you can fully exploit the power of XML inside your SQL Server 2008 databases and build smart, XML-aware applications.

Chapter 7

Hierarchical Data
and the Relational Database

—Leonard Lobel

Hierarchical data is not relational. It is organized as a tree structure of parent and child elements rather than as flat lists of rows in related tables. The most common hierarchical data format in today's world is XML, and in Chapter 6, we covered the rich XML support that Microsoft SQL Server provides. There's no doubt that XML is the right database storage choice for hierarchical data in many scenarios. It can be particularly useful when that data is consumed in XML format by client applications or in circumstances where you need to store and retrieve the entire hierarchy at a single time.

But XML is the *wrong* choice when you'd prefer to keep your data stored relationally as normal rows with standard SQL Server data-typed columns and all you really want is hier-archical *linking* capabilities between the rows. Using the *xml* data type means abandoning the relational model and committing yourself instead to a completely hierarchical model, since your data is then encapsulated within a single XML document (or fragment) composed of elements and attributes. You don't necessarily want to go to that extreme just to achieve hierarchical capabilities in the database. You can instead continue to store your data as a flat list of rows and columns within a table—if that makes better sense for your application—and use the new *hierarchyid* data type to implement a tree-structured organization across the individual rows in the table.

Of course, we've been modeling hierarchies out of relational tables for a long time by establishing table relationships between parent and child entities (such as the one-to-many relationship from *Customer* to *Order*, or *Order* to *Order Detail*). This join approach imple-ments a rigid hierarchy that is limited to the defined table relationships and cannot accom-modate a truly flexible tree-structured organization with virtually unlimited breadth and depth. The kinds of storage scenarios we're talking about supporting here include forum and mailing list threads, business organization charts, content management categories, product categories, and file/folder management. These are just a few examples; the point is that they are all hierarchical in nature, potentially growing both broad and deep, and are typically iter-ated recursively.

One traditional solution for achieving a tree structure in a table has been the self-joining approach, where each row has a primary key as well as a foreign key to the primary key of its parent row elsewhere in the table. A classic example is the chain-of-command hierarchy in the employee structure of a business organization. A single table contains employees that have both an *EmployeeId* primary key and a *ManagerId* foreign key that points to the *EmployeeId* of each employee's manager. (Being at the top of the hierarchy, the CEO's *ManagerId* would be *NULL*.)

The self-joining approach has certainly worked over the years, but it requires you to handle much of the maintenance of the tree structure yourself. In Chapter 2, you saw how common table expressions (CTEs) support recursive queries against such a table that can "walk" up the hierarchy all the way to the root from any given node. That certainly helps for some queries, but there are other types of hierarchical queries that are more difficult to implement. Plus, it's still your job to manage the hierarchy for updates. You must maintain its structure across node manipulations involving insertions, modifications, and deletions of child, parent, and sibling rows in the table or even manipulations of entire subtrees at a time. Subtree manipulations could further involve complex transactions that you need to implement. There's also no inherent way to exercise fine control of the ordering of child entities. For example, you can't say "insert a new child node before, after, or between other existing siblings."

The *hierarchyid* Data Type

The new *hierarchyid* data type in SQL Server 2008 enables a robust hierarchical structure over a relational table that can relieve you of much of this maintenance burden. As with the self-joining approach, each row in the table represents a node in the tree. However, instead of encoding just the parent value in a foreign key column, each row now has a unique *hierarchyid* value that describes the full path all the way from the root of the tree down to that row's node position within the tree. The *hierarchyid* value in each row therefore identifies each node's location in the tree with respect to its parent, sibling, and child nodes (which are simply other rows in the table with their own *hierarchyid* value). In this manner, the *hierarchyid* values link rows to one another as nodes that form the tree structure.

Using new Transact-SQL (T-SQL) extensions that support the *hierarchyid* data type, you can invoke methods to arbitrarily insert, modify, and delete nodes at any point within the structure very efficiently. You can even reparent entire subtrees in a single update. SQL Server determines the nodes affected by the update and manages the changes to their *hierarchyid* values automatically. Plus, querying a tree-structured table based on the new *hierarchyid* data type is significantly faster than running recursive queries on a traditional self-joining table using CTEs.

SQL Server employs an algorithm that encodes the path information of a *hierarchyid* value into an extremely compact variable-length format. The average number of bits that are required to represent a node in a tree with n nodes depends on the average number of children of a node, known as the average *fanout*. For small fanouts (0 to 7), the size is about $6*\log_A n$ bits, where A is the average fanout. In practical terms, this means that one node in a hierarchy of 100,000 nodes with an average fanout of 6 takes about 38 bits, which gets rounded up to 40 bits (5 bytes) for storage. The encoded value has no meaningful display representation, of course, but the *ToString* method will translate a *hierarchyid* value into a human-readable form that expresses a delimited node path, as you'll see shortly.

The *hierarchyid* type is implemented as a SQL common language runtime (CLR) user-defined type (UDT), as opposed to a more primitive SQL Server data type (such as *int* or *date*). This means that *hierarchyid* is hosted internally by the CLR and not natively by SQL Server (and is also why functions invoked on it are called *methods*). However, due to its tight integration in SQL Server, it can be used even with SQL CLR disabled. In other words, you don't need to enable SQL CLR to use the new *hierarchyid* data type (or any of the other new system CLR types, such as *geometry* and *geography*, which we cover in Chapter 9). As we point out in Chapter 3, the SQL CLR feature increases your exposure to security risks by allowing Microsoft .NET Framework code to run on the server and should therefore be enabled only if you are creating your own SQL CLR objects (stored procedures, user-defined functions [UDFs], and so on).

> **More Info** The *hierarchyid* data type is available to CLR clients as the *SqlHierarchyId* data type in the *Microsoft.SqlServer.Types* namespace. This namespace is contained in the *Microsoft. SqlServer.Types.dll* assembly, which can be found on the .NET tab in the Microsoft Visual Studio Add Reference dialog box. In the database itself, the node information represented by a *hierarchyid* value is stored as a *varbinary* data type, which can support a virtually unlimited number of child nodes per parent.

Creating a Hierarchical Table

Let's begin by implementing the classic manager-employee tree scenario using the new *hierarchyid* data type. We start with the structure of the *Employee* table, as shown in Listing 7-1.

LISTING 7-1 Creating a hierarchical table

```
CREATE DATABASE MyDB
GO

USE MyDB
GO

CREATE TABLE Employee
(
    NodeId          hierarchyid PRIMARY KEY CLUSTERED,
    NodeLevel       AS NodeId.GetLevel(),
    EmployeeId      int UNIQUE NOT NULL,
    EmployeeName    varchar(20) NOT NULL,
    Title           varchar(20) NULL
)
GO
```

Notice that the *NodeId* column is declared as the new *hierarchyid* type and is also defined as the table's primary key using a clustered index. The primary key is important for two reasons, the first of which is that SQL Server doesn't guarantee uniqueness of *hierarchyid* values in the table. Don't view this as a limitation—this fact actually enables advanced scenarios that can support multiple distinct hierarchies within a single table. With the single hierarchy in our example, defining a primary key is one way to enforce unique *NodeId* values. Defining an ordinary unique constraint instead would be another way, and you can certainly do that if some column other than the *hierarchyid* is more suitable for the table's primary key. Another reason for the primary key index is to support *depth-first indexing*, which we'll talk about shortly.

As we've started explaining, the value in the *NodeId* column identifies each row's unique node position within the structure. It can serve as the table's primary key, and you don't technically need to have any other identifying columns in the table. Practically, however, you'll most likely still want to define another unique column to serve as a more conventional identifier, since values assigned into the *hierarchyid* column as rows are added to the table are based on their node positions within the tree. Those *hierarchyid* values are essentially nondeterministic and will also shift automatically as the tree's node structure is changed using the techniques that you'll start learning about just ahead. For example, if you relocate a node and all of its descendants to a new position within the tree (also known as *reparenting* a subtree), the *hierarchyid* values of those nodes are automatically updated by SQL Server to reflect their new positions within the hierarchy. We therefore define *EmployeeId* as a unique integer column assigned with values that we control and that won't change when the structure of nodes in the tree is manipulated in the future. So when we add employees, their ID values remain the same regardless of how their nodes get repositioned in the future.

> **Note** You can also use *IDENTITY* values for the *EmployeeId* column, which puts SQL Server in control of assigning key values by using incrementing integers, and which would also not change as the tree structure is altered. To stay focused on *hierarchyid*, our example here does not add the extra code for using *IDENTITY*, and we simply assign our own unique *EmployeeId* integer values explicitly.

The *GetLevel* Method

The second column defined in the *Employee* table is *NodeLevel*, which we've declared as a calculated column that returns the 16-bit integer result of the *GetLevel* method applied to the *hierarchyid* value in the *NodeId* column. This is optional and provides a read-only column that returns a number indicating the level position of its row (node), extracted and decoded from the compacted *hierarchyid* value in the *NodeId* column. One and only one root row exists in any hierarchy and is positioned at level zero. Its immediate child rows are positioned at level one, grandchild rows at level two, and so on. Defining the *NodeLevel* column that calls the *GetLevel* method provides a convenient, easy to read, and easy to query value for the level position from the *hierarchyid* value held in *NodeId*. In addition, our *NodeLevel* column will allow us to create a *breadth-first index* on the table. (We discuss depth-first and breadth-first indexes shortly.)

The *EmployeeId* column is defined with a unique constraint and doesn't permit *NULL* values. We can therefore treat its integer value as an "alternate primary key" for our employees, since the *hierarchyid* value in the *NodeId* column has already been defined as the table's actual primary key. As we mentioned, in many practical cases, you will want to define such an alternate key to be used as an identifier with a value that you are in control of and that doesn't change unpredictably as the result of node manipulations the way a *hierarchyid* value does. You'll definitely need such identifiers if you want to establish relationships for joining with other tables, or you might want them just for your own convenience. But it's important to understand that SQL Server itself requires no such identifier to implement the hierarchy and that you can certainly cast a hierarchical structure over a relational table with only the *hierarchyid* value as the primary key and no other unique columns.

Populating the Hierarchy

Let's visualize our organizational chart before we start populating the *Employee* table with hierarchical data. Figure 7-1 shows the hierarchy of employees in our organization.

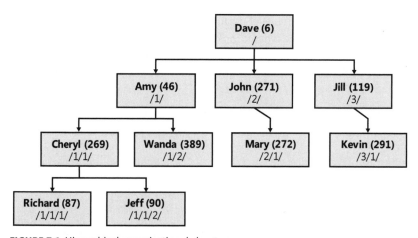

FIGURE 7-1 Hierarchical organizational chart

The first row added to a hierarchical table is always the root node of the tree, and there can be only one root. Additional rows beneath the root are then added as child and grandchild nodes, and so on. Nodes can be rearranged as needed by invoking methods on the *hierarchyid* values. The tree can grow both *broad* (with many siblings) and *deep* (with many descendants).

The *GetRoot* Method

We begin by inserting our first row for Dave, the marketing manager, at the top of the chart with an employee ID of 6, as shown in Listing 7-2.

LISTING 7-2 Inserting the root node row in the hierarchical *Employee* table

```
INSERT INTO Employee
  (NodeId, EmployeeId, EmployeeName, Title)
  VALUES
  (hierarchyid::GetRoot(), 6, 'Dave', 'Marketing Manager')
GO
```

Values can be assigned into *hierarchyid* columns by invoking methods that return *hierarchyid* values. When inserting the first row at the top of the chart, we call the *GetRoot* method on the *hierarchyid* type itself. The special double-colon (::) syntax is used when calling methods on the data type itself (akin to a static method call in object-oriented languages), rather than calling methods on *values* of the data type (akin to an instance method call), which uses the normal "dot" syntax (as we've already seen with the *GetLevel* method in Listing 7-1). Being the first row in our hierarchical table, the only valid *hierarchyid* value for *NodeId* is one that specifies the root, and that's exactly the value returned by *hierarchyid::GetRoot()*.

Also notice that we do not (and cannot) insert a value for *NodeLevel*, since that is a read-only calculated column that returns the level position of each row. Let's select the row back out from the table so that we can see what it looks like, as shown here:

```
SELECT * FROM Employee
GO

NodeId    NodeLevel EmployeeId EmployeeName   Title
--------- --------- ---------- -------------- --------------------
0x        0         6          Dave           Marketing Manager

(1 row(s) affected)
```

The *GetDescendant* Method

In the preceding output, we see Dave's record as the root node in our hierarchy at level zero. The *hierarchyid* value of *0x* for *NodeId* positions Dave as the top-level node, set by the *GetRoot* method when we inserted the row. Now it's time to add child nodes for the level-one employees who report directly to Dave. To set the *hierarchyid* values for these employees, we use the *GetDescendant* method on Dave's *hierarchyid* value. This method generates and returns a *hierarchyid* value that is a child of the *hierarchyid* it is invoked on and is a sibling positioned between the two *hierarchyid* values that get passed in as the method parameters.

Let's pause now before adding the employees beneath Dave so that we can further investigate and fully understand how to use the *GetDescendant* method. Suppose we want to construct a generic tree organized as shown in Figure 7-2.

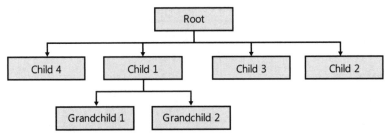

FIGURE 7-2 Sample hierarchy of nodes

The code in Listing 7-3 shows how to use *GetDescendant* to create child and grandchild nodes of the root node created by *GetRoot*.

LISTING 7-3 Using *GetDescendant* to construct a hierarchy

```
DECLARE @Root hierarchyid
DECLARE @Child1 hierarchyid
DECLARE @Child2 hierarchyid
DECLARE @Child3 hierarchyid
DECLARE @Child4 hierarchyid
DECLARE @Grandchild1 hierarchyid
DECLARE @Grandchild2 hierarchyid

SET @Root = hierarchyid::GetRoot()
SET @Child1 = @Root.GetDescendant(NULL, NULL)
SET @Child2 = @Root.GetDescendant(@Child1, NULL)
SET @Child3 = @Root.GetDescendant(@Child1, @Child2)
SET @Child4 = @Root.GetDescendant(NULL, @Child1)
SET @Grandchild1 = @Child1.GetDescendant(NULL, NULL)
SET @Grandchild2 = @Child1.GetDescendant(@Grandchild1, NULL)

SELECT
  @Root AS Root,
  @Child1 AS Child1,
  @Child2 AS Child2,
  @Child3 AS Child3,
  @Child4 AS Child4,
  @Grandchild1 AS Grandchild1,
  @Grandchild2 AS Grandchild2
```

The output appears as follows:

```
Root Child1 Child2 Child3 Child4 Grandchild1 Grandchild2
---- ------ ------ ------ ------ ----------- -----------
0x   0x58   0x68   0x62C0 0x48   0x5AC0      0x5B40

(1 row(s) affected)
```

The *ToString* Method

The preceding output shows the hexadecimal representation of each node's encoded *hierarchyid* value, which is hardly useful to us. To view this as human-readable text that conveys each node's path within the tree, change the *SELECT* statement in Listing 7-3 to call the *ToString* method on the *hierarchyid* values, as shown here:

```
SELECT
  @Root.ToString() AS Root,
  @Child1.ToString() AS Child1,
  @Child2.ToString() AS Child2,
  @Child3.ToString() AS Child3,
  @Child4.ToString() AS Child4,
  @Grandchild1.ToString() AS Grandchild1,
  @Grandchild2.ToString() AS Grandchild2
GO

Root Child1 Child2 Child3 Child4 Grandchild1 Grandchild2
---- ------ ------ ------ ------ ----------- -----------
/    /1/    /2/    /1.1/  /0/    /1/1/       /1/2/

(1 row(s) affected)
```

We can make several observations from this output. We can see that the *ToString* method decodes the *hierarchyid* value into a slash-delimited string. Each slash designates a level, so subtracting 1 from the number of slashes indicates what the zero-based level position of each node is (the same value that would be returned by the *GetLevel* method). *Root* is the only node with one slash, representing level zero. The *Child1*, *Child2*, *Child3*, and *Child4* nodes have two slashes, representing level one. The *Grandchild1* and *Grandchild2* nodes, naturally, have three slashes, representing level two.

We can also see how the two parameters that were passed to the *GetDescendant* method influenced the assignment of *hierarchyid* values. *Root* of course was assigned by *hierarchyid::GetRoot()* to get the tree started, as you saw in Listing 7-2. The *hierarchyid* for each of the four child nodes beneath the root parent was assigned by invoking the *GetDescendant* method on the root. And the ordinal position of each child node among siblings of the same parent was determined by the two parameters passed to *GetDescendant*.

Child1 is the first node defined beneath the root, as follows:

```
SET @Child1 = @Root.GetDescendant(NULL, NULL)
```

Because there are not yet any other child nodes beneath the root, there is no position relative to other child nodes that can be specified. We therefore pass *NULL* as both positional values to *GetDescendant*. The result is a *hierarchyid* represented as */1/,* which refers to the one and only child node beneath the root.

Child2 is created as the second node beneath the root, which we want to be placed after *Child1*. Think of this as inserting *Child2* between *Child1* and "the end," which we pass as the two parameters *Child1* and *NULL*, respectively, when calling *GetDescendant* for *Child2*:

```
SET @Child2 = @Root.GetDescendant(@Child1, NULL)
```

The result is a *hierarchyid* represented as */2/*, which refers to the second child node beneath the root, to the right of *Child1*. We then apply the same principle to create *Child3* as a third child node beneath the root, except that we want this child to be inserted between *Child1* and *Child2* rather than being appended as *Child2* was. We explicitly request such ordering when calling *GetDescendant* for *Child3*, as shown here:

```
SET @Child3 = @Root.GetDescendant(@Child1, @Child2)
```

This code assigns a *hierarchyid* value to *Child3* between *Child1* and *Child2*. Because we speci-fied a position between *Child1* and *Child2* with *hierarchyid* values of */1/* and */2/*, respectively, SQL Server assigns to *Child3* a *hierarchyid* value represented by *ToString* as */1.1/* (that is, after */1/* and before */2/*).

Last, we create *Child4* as another child beneath the root, this time inserted in front of all the other siblings (that is, before *Child1*). Think of this as inserting *Child4* between "the begin-ning" and *Child1*, which we pass as the two parameters *NULL* and *Child1*, respectively, when calling *GetDescendant* for *Child4*, as follows:

```
SET @Child4 = @Root.GetDescendant(NULL, @Child1)
```

The result is a *hierarchyid* represented as */0/* assigned for *Child4*, the last child node added beneath the root, to the left of *Child1*. If we continued adding more nodes to the left of *Child4*, their *ToString* representations would begin showing negative values, such as */–1/*, */–2/*, and so on.

Adding grandchild (level-two) nodes beneath *Child1* is achieved by using the very same approach:

```
SET @Grandchild1 = @Child1.GetDescendant(NULL, NULL)
```

This code assigns a *hierarchyid* value of */1/1/* to *Grandchild1*, the first child node beneath *Child1*. Once again, being the first child of a parent, there are no existing sibling nodes that we can refer to with respect to the position at which *Grandchild1* should be inserted, so the only possible values to pass as parameters to *GetDescendant* are *NULL* and *NULL*. Last, we add *Grandchild2* as a second child beneath *Child1*, positioned after its sibling node *Grandchild1*, as shown here:

```
SET @Grandchild2 = @Child1.GetDescendant(@Grandchild1, NULL)
```

Now let's get back to our real-world hierarchical employee table. After Dave has been added at the root, the level-one employee nodes that we will now add beneath him are assigned *hierarchyid* values returned by a call to *GetDescendant* on Dave. The first level-one employee we add is Amy, with the employee ID 46, as shown in Listing 7-4.

LISTING 7-4 Adding the first child node beneath the root of the hierarchy

```
DECLARE @Manager hierarchyid

SELECT @Manager = NodeId
 FROM Employee
 WHERE EmployeeId = 6

INSERT INTO Employee
  (NodeId, EmployeeId, EmployeeName, Title)
  VALUES
  (@Manager.GetDescendant(NULL, NULL), 46, 'Amy', 'Marketing Specialist')

GO
```

Let's examine this code closely. We first need to get the *hierarchyid* value of the parent (Dave, with employee ID 6), which we retrieve from the table and store in the *@Manager* variable (also declared as a *hierarchyid* data type, of course). Then we can insert Amy as the first child row by specifying a *hierarchyid* value returned by the *GetDescendant* method invoked on *@Manager*. Because there are no other child nodes yet beneath Dave, the only positional parameter values that can be passed to *GetDescendant* are *NULL* and *NULL*. Let's now view both rows in the table, including a *NodeIdPath* column that translates the encoded *hierarchyid* values using the *ToString* method:

```
SELECT NodeId.ToString() AS NodeIdPath, *
 FROM Employee
GO
```

```
NodeIdPath NodeId NodeLevel EmployeeId EmployeeName Title
---------- ------ --------- ---------- ------------ --------------------
/          0x     0         6          Dave         Marketing Manager
/1/        0x58   1         46         Amy          Marketing Specialist

(2 row(s) affected)
```

Sure enough, Amy has been added as the first level-one child node beneath Dave, as indicated by the *hierarchyid* value */1/* assigned to her by *GetDescendant*.

This demonstrates that adding a child node requires a *SELECT* to first obtain the *hierarchyid* value of the desired parent before performing an *INSERT* to actually add the new row. In this manner, the new row can be assigned a *hierarchyid* value based on the result of invoking *GetDescendant* on the *hierarchyid* value obtained from its parent. We wrote the code as two separate statements to make this process clear. However, we could have just as effectively written this as a single statement without requiring the temporary *@Manager* variable to hold the parent's *hierarchyid* by embedding the *SELECT* statement as a subquery within the *VALUES* clause of the *INSERT* statement, as follows:

```
INSERT INTO Employee
  (NodeId, EmployeeId, EmployeeName, Title)
 VALUES (
  (SELECT NodeId
    FROM Employee
    WHERE EmployeeId = 6).GetDescendant(NULL, NULL),
  46,
  'Amy',
  'Marketing Specialist')

GO
```

We want to simplify the process for adding more child and grandchild nodes to the hierarchy, so we'll create a stored procedure named *uspAddEmployee* that encapsulates the logic of retrieving the *hierarchyid* of any desired parent and invoking *GetDescendant* on it to obtain the appropriate *hierarchyid* for the new employee. The stored procedure code is shown in Listing 7-5.

LISTING 7-5 Creating a stored procedure to automatically insert child nodes in a hierarchy

```
CREATE PROCEDURE uspAddEmployee(
  @ManagerId int,
  @EmployeeId int,
  @EmployeeName varchar(20),
  @Title varchar(20))
AS
BEGIN

  DECLARE @ManagerNodeId hierarchyid
  DECLARE @LastManagerChild hierarchyid
  DECLARE @NewEmployeeNodeId hierarchyid

  -- Get the hierarchyid of the desired parent passed in to @ManagerId
  SELECT @ManagerNodeId = NodeId
   FROM  Employee
   WHERE EmployeeId = @ManagerId

  SET TRANSACTION ISOLATION LEVEL SERIALIZABLE

  BEGIN TRANSACTION

    -- Get the hierarchyid of the last existing child beneath the parent
    SELECT @LastManagerChild = MAX(NodeId)
     FROM  Employee
     WHERE NodeId.GetAncestor(1) = @ManagerNodeId

    -- Assign a new hierarchyid positioned at the end of any existing siblings
    SELECT @NewEmployeeNodeId =
     @ManagerNodeId.GetDescendant(@LastManagerChild, NULL)
```

```
    -- Add the row
    INSERT INTO Employee
      (NodeId, EmployeeId, EmployeeName, Title)
    VALUES
      (@NewEmployeeNodeId, @EmployeeId, @EmployeeName, @Title)

  COMMIT

END

GO
```

We can now use this stored procedure to easily insert new rows into the employee table at any level within the hierarchy (except the root). The stored procedure accepts a *@ManagerId* parameter that the caller provides as the employee ID of the parent that the newly added employee should be a child of. The remaining parameters (*@EmployeeId*, *@EmployeeName*, and *@Title*) simply provide values for the new employee.

After declaring a few local *hierarchyid* variables, the procedure retrieves the *hierarchyid* of the parent specified by the *@ManagerId* input parameter, just as we did earlier for Amy, and stores the result in the local *@ManagerNodeId* variable, as shown here:

```
-- Get the hierarchyid of the desired parent passed in to @ManagerId
SELECT @ManagerNodeId = NodeId
 FROM  Employee
 WHERE EmployeeId = @ManagerId
```

This is the value on which we now want to call *GetDescendant* in order to establish an appropriate *hierarchyid* value for the new employee. We don't particularly care about the order of siblings beneath each parent, so we want the procedure to simply append the new employee to the end of any siblings that might already exist. However, we still *must* provide the two positional parameters expected by *GetDescendant* that explicitly specify the point of insertion. Because we want new siblings to be appended to the end, we know that the second positional parameter should always be *NULL*. Our job therefore is to establish the appropriate value for the first positional parameter by ascertaining the *hierarchyid* value of the last existing sibling or using *NULL* if there are no siblings. We achieve this with the following *SELECT* statement:

```
-- Get the hierarchyid of the last existing child beneath the parent
SELECT @LastManagerChild = MAX(NodeId)
 FROM  Employee
 WHERE NodeId.GetAncestor(1) = @ManagerNodeId
```

The *GetAncestor* Method

The preceding code introduces a new *hierarchyid* method named *GetAncestor*. The *GetAncestor* method accepts an integer parameter that specifies how many levels to traverse up from the node it is invoked on to reach one of that node's ancestors and then returns the *hierarchyid* of the ancestor node. A value of *1*, as we are using here, returns the immediate parent of the node on which the *GetAncestor* method is invoked. By requesting all rows with *hierarchyid* values whose immediate parent is the same as the parent requested by the caller for the new employee, the preceding *WHERE* clause retrieves all the existing siblings of the employee about to be added. Since this can return multiple siblings, we apply the *MAX* aggregate function to retrieve the sibling with the highest-valued *hierarchyid* (which is the last sibling in the set) into the *@LastManagerChild* local variable. If there are no existing siblings, the *WHERE* clause will return no rows at all, and *NULL* will be assigned into *@LastManagerChild*. In either case, we have established the appropriate value in *@LastManagerChild* to be used as the first positional parameter for the call to *GetDescendant*, as shown here:

```
-- Assign a new hierarchyid positioned at the end of any existing siblings
SELECT @NewEmployeeNodeId =
 @ManagerNodeId.GetDescendant(@LastManagerChild, NULL)
```

We have now assigned an appropriate *hierarchyid* value for the new employee in *@NewEmployeeNodeId* by invoking *GetDescendant* on the parent (*@ManagerNodeId*). The two parameters passed to *GetDescendant* specify that the new employee should be inserted between the last sibling that exists (*@LastManagerChild*) and the end of the sibling list (*NULL*), which effectively means that it will be appended to the end. If *NULL* was assigned into *@LastManagerChild* because there were no previously existing siblings, *GetDescendant* is called with two *NULL* values, which (as you've already seen) is the correct way to call *GetDescendant* when adding the very first child beneath a parent.

All that's needed now is a straightforward *INSERT* statement that adds the new employee to the table at the correct node position beneath the parent specified by the caller, as shown here:

```
-- Add the row
INSERT INTO Employee
  (NodeId, EmployeeId, EmployeeName, Title)
 VALUES
  (@NewEmployeeNodeId, @EmployeeId, @EmployeeName, @Title)
```

The last part of this stored procedure that bears explanation is its use of a transaction surrounding the *SELECT* and *INSERT* statements. The purpose here is to guarantee that no other sibling nodes can be added by another user between the time the *hierarchyid* value of the last sibling is established and the time the new row is actually inserted. Without wrapping this logic inside a transaction, we have no such guarantee, and the *hierarchyid* value determined to be the last sibling in the set might no longer be the last sibling in the set at the time the new employee is added. A collision could therefore occur between two separate concurrent processes attempting to add two separate new employees beneath the same parent in the same position at the same time. Such an attempt would result in a primary key constraint violation, since both inserts would be attempting to store the same *hierarchyid* value in the *NodeId* column defined as the primary key. While the *SELECT* and *INSERT* statements could be combined into a single complex statement without using an explicit transaction (as you saw earlier when we added the employee row for Amy), the logic is much clearer (and thus more maintainable) when coding these as separate statements.

Now that we have created the *uspAddEmployee* stored procedure and understand how it works, adding the rest of the employees in our organizational chart is easy. All we need to do for each one is specify the employee ID of the new employee's parent, followed by the new employee's ID, name, and title, as shown here:

```
EXEC uspAddEmployee 6, 271, 'John', 'Marketing Specialist'
EXEC uspAddEmployee 6, 119, 'Jill', 'Marketing Specialist'
EXEC uspAddEmployee 46, 269, 'Cheryl', 'Marketing Assistant'
EXEC uspAddEmployee 46, 389, 'Wanda', 'Business Assistant'
EXEC uspAddEmployee 271, 272, 'Mary', 'Marketing Assistant'
EXEC uspAddEmployee 119, 291, 'Kevin', 'Marketing Intern'
EXEC uspAddEmployee 269, 87, 'Richard', 'Business Intern'
EXEC uspAddEmployee 269, 90, 'Jeff', 'Business Intern'
```

The *ToString* method on each row's *hierarchyid* value in *NodeId* confirms that the tree structure correctly represents our organizational chart:

```
SELECT NodeId.ToString() AS NodeIdPath, *
 FROM Employee
 ORDER BY NodeLevel, NodeId
GO


NodeIdPath NodeId NodeLevel EmployeeId  EmployeeName Title
---------- ------ --------- ----------- ------------ --------------------
/          0x     0         6           Dave         Marketing Manager
/1/        0x58   1         46          Amy          Marketing Specialist
/2/        0x68   1         271         John         Marketing Specialist
/3/        0x78   1         119         Jill         Marketing Specialist
/1/1/      0x5AC0 2         269         Cheryl       Marketing Assistant
/1/2/      0x5B40 2         389         Wanda        Business Assistant
/2/1/      0x6AC0 2         272         Mary         Marketing Assistant
/3/1/      0x7AC0 2         291         Kevin        Marketing Intern
/1/1/1/    0x5AD6 3         87          Richard      Business Intern
/1/1/2/    0x5ADA 3         90          Jeff         Business Intern

(10 row(s) affected)
```

The *ToString* method certainly displays a *hierarchyid* value in a more intelligible form than the raw internal *varbinary* value, but the string returned is still numeric and not descriptive. With a little code, we can create a user-defined function (UDF) that will accept any *NodeId* and return a more meaningful "breadcrumb-style" representation of the path leading up to that node. Listing 7-6 shows the code for the *fnGetFullDisplayPath* UDF that uses the *GetLevel* and *GetAncestor* methods together to do just that.

LISTING 7-6 Creating a UDF that builds a breadcrumb-style display path for a given node

```
CREATE FUNCTION dbo.fnGetFullDisplayPath(@EntityNodeId hierarchyid)
 RETURNS varchar(max)
AS
  BEGIN
    DECLARE @EntityLevelDepth smallint
    DECLARE @LevelCounter smallint
    DECLARE @DisplayPath varchar(max)
    DECLARE @ParentEmployeeName varchar(max)

    -- Start with the specified node
    SELECT @EntityLevelDepth = NodeId.GetLevel(),
           @DisplayPath = EmployeeName
     FROM  Employee
     WHERE NodeId = @EntityNodeId

    -- Loop through all its ancestors
    SET @LevelCounter = 0
    WHILE @LevelCounter < @EntityLevelDepth BEGIN

      SET @LevelCounter = @LevelCounter + 1

      SELECT @ParentEmployeeName = EmployeeName
       FROM  Employee
       WHERE NodeId = (
             SELECT NodeId.GetAncestor(@LevelCounter)
              FROM Employee
              WHERE NodeId = @EntityNodeId)

      -- Prepend the ancestor name to the display path
      SET @DisplayPath = @ParentEmployeeName + ' > ' + @DisplayPath

    END

    RETURN(@DisplayPath)
  END
```

After declaring a few local variables, the function starts by first selecting the employee name of the node passed in through the *@EntityNodeId* parameter (that is, the node's *hierarchyid* value). It obtains the level of the node by calling *GetLevel* and stores it in the *@EntityLevelDepth* variable. It also retrieves the employee name into the *@DisplayPath* variable, which will be the function's return value after it is prepended with all of the employee names of the node's ancestors, all the way up to the root.

The function then establishes a *@LevelCounter* integer variable, initialized to 0, and enters a loop that increments *@LevelCounter* and terminates the loop when its value reaches *@ EntityLevelDepth*. With each iteration, the incrementing *@LevelCounter* value is fed to the

GetAncestor method in order to retrieve the next employee name up the chain, which is then prepended to *@DisplayPath* along with the ' > ' level-separation string. In this manner, the code obtains the parent, grandparent, great-grandparent, and so on, all the way up to the root. When the loop terminates, *@DisplayPath* is returned to the caller. Here is the output from the *fnGetFullDisplayPath* function when run against our employee table:

```
SELECT
  NodeId,
  NodeId.ToString() AS NodeIdPath,
  dbo.fnGetFullDisplayPath(NodeId) AS NodeIdDisplayPath,
  EmployeeName
 FROM
  Employee
 ORDER BY
  NodeLevel, NodeId
GO
```

```
NodeId NodeIdPath NodeIdDisplayPath                    EmployeeName
------ ---------- ----------------------------------- ------------
0x     /          Dave                                 Dave
0x58   /1/        Dave > Amy                           Amy
0x68   /2/        Dave > John                          John
0x78   /3/        Dave > Jill                          Jill
0x5AC0 /1/1/      Dave > Amy > Cheryl                  Cheryl
0x5B40 /1/2/      Dave > Amy > Wanda                   Wanda
0x6AC0 /2/1/      Dave > John > Mary                   Mary
0x7AC0 /3/1/      Dave > Jill > Kevin                  Kevin
0x5AD6 /1/1/1/    Dave > Amy > Cheryl > Richard Richard
0x5ADA /1/1/2/    Dave > Amy > Cheryl > Jeff    Jeff
```

(10 row(s) affected)

The *NodeIdDisplayPath* in this result set shows the employee names along the hierarchical paths in each row.

Populating a hierarchical table does require some effort up front, as you've seen. However, once your data is in place, you can enjoy the real power of the *hierarchyid* data type by leveraging its methods for easily querying and rearranging the tree structure. We're almost ready to dive into that, but first let's take a moment to talk about the indexing schemes available for hierarchical tables that you need to know about.

Hierarchical Table Indexing Strategies

You can create a *depth-first* index or a *breadth-first* index (or both) on your hierarchical tables. These two types differ in how SQL Server physically stores node references in the index. Defining depth-first and breadth-first indexes can have a significant impact on performance for accessing data in hierarchical tables.

As their names imply, depth-first indexing stores parent and child node references near each other, while breadth-first indexing stores references for nodes at the same hierarchical level near each other. Therefore, you will choose the appropriate type of index based on an understanding of how your hierarchical data is shaped in the table, how it will grow, and how it will be typically queried by client applications. You can create both types of indexes as well, for efficient access both vertically and horizontally across the tree.

> **Note** Regardless of what indexing strategy you employ, *comparison* operations are *always* performed in depth-first order. Thus, *A < B* means that *A* always comes before *B* in a depth-first traversal of the tree (or *A* is to the left of *B* if they are both at the same level) even if breadth-first indexing is used.

Depth-First Indexing

Defining either a primary key index or a unique index on a *hierarchyid* column results in a depth-first index. Because we designated the *NodeId* column for the *hierarchyid* of our employee table as the primary key, we have already created a depth-first index on the table.

With depth-first indexing, which is depicted in Figure 7-3, SQL Server tries to physically store references to nodes in a subtree as near to one another as possible. By "near one another," we mean that SQL Server records them on disk on the same page, if possible—or in the same extent, if not, and so on—in order to improve query performance. This strategy yields high query performance if your hierarchy runs very deep with many levels. Creating a depth-first index for such a hierarchy will result in very fast vertical searching on the tree (that is, querying ancestors and descendants up and down a potentially long chain).

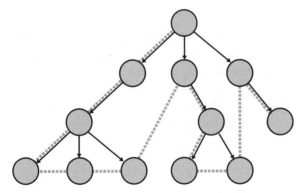

FIGURE 7-3 Physical row storage when optimized for depth-first searching

Breadth-First Indexing

With breadth-first indexing, illustrated in Figure 7-4, references to nodes at the same level of the hierarchy are physically stored as near to one another as possible. This type of index yields high query performance for trees that grow very broad. If there are many children beneath the parents in your hierarchy, you will want to create a breadth-first index to enable fast horizontal searching across a potentially large number of nodes at the same level.

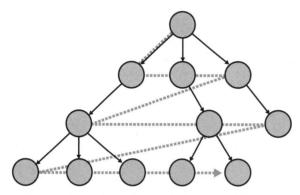

FIGURE 7-4 Physical row storage when optimized for breadth-first searching

To define a breadth-first index, you create a composite index on your hierarchical table that includes two columns: the integer column that holds the *level* of the node within the hierarchy (such as the *NodeLevel* column defined in our employee table that invokes the *GetLevel* method on the *NodeId* column) and the *hierarchyid* column itself (*NodeId*). So to create a breadth-first index, we run the following code:

```
CREATE UNIQUE INDEX IX_EmployeeBreadth
 ON Employee(NodeLevel, NodeId)
```

As we mentioned already, one table can have both depth-first and breadth-first indexes by creating one primary key or unique index on the *hierarchyid* column and another composite index on the node-level column and the *hierarchyid*. This will carry slightly more overhead for data manipulation language (DML) actions, since updates will need to be performed in both indexes; however, query performance will be very fast for both horizontal and vertical searching across large hierarchies that are both very broad and very deep.

Querying Hierarchical Tables

With our hierarchical table populated and indexed, we're ready to start writing efficient queries against it by using some more methods available on the *hierarchyid* type.

The *IsDescendantOf* Method

The *IsDescendantOf* method is invoked on one *hierarchyid* value and accepts another *hierarchyid* value as its parameter. It returns a *bit* (Boolean) value of *1* (true) if the *hierarchyid* that the method is invoked on is a descendant (either directly or indirectly) of the *hierarchyid* that is passed in as the parameter. Thus, this method essentially returns a subtree whose root is the node specified by the parameter. Because of its vertical traversal, it delivers very fast performance for tables that have a depth-first index.

We can easily query our employee table to return all the descendants (child rows, grandchild rows, and so on) of a particular employee using the *IsDescendantOf* method. For example, the following query lists all of Amy's descendants:

```
DECLARE @AmyNodeId hierarchyid

SELECT @AmyNodeId = NodeId
  FROM  Employee
 WHERE EmployeeId = 46

SELECT NodeId.ToString() AS NodeIdPath, *
  FROM  Employee
 WHERE NodeId.IsDescendantOf(@AmyNodeId) = 1
 ORDER BY NodeLevel, NodeId
```

This query selects all rows whose *NodeId* values are descendants of Amy (employee ID 46). Here is the result:

```
NodeIdPath NodeId NodeLevel EmployeeId EmployeeName Title
---------- ------ --------- ---------- ------------ --------------------
/1/        0x58   1         46         Amy          Marketing Specialist
/1/1/      0x5AC0 2         269        Cheryl       Marketing Assistant
/1/2/      0x5B40 2         389        Wanda        Business Assistant
/1/1/1/    0x5AD6 3         87         Richard      Business Intern
/1/1/2/    0x5ADA 3         90         Jeff         Business Intern

(5 row(s) affected)
```

Notice that the result includes Amy herself in addition to all of her descendants. Amy herself is returned because she is her "own descendant" at the 0 level of the subtree. Thus, we have selected a subtree that begins with Amy and includes all of her descendants, no matter how many levels deep they might exist beneath her.

To select *only* Amy's immediate child rows that are just one level beneath her, you can use the *GetAncestor* method. (We used this method earlier to create our *uspAddEmployee* stored procedure.) For example:

```
SELECT NodeId.ToString() AS NodeIdPath, *
  FROM  Employee
  WHERE NodeId.GetAncestor(1) =
    (SELECT NodeId
      FROM  Employee
      WHERE EmployeeId = 46)
  ORDER BY NodeLevel, NodeId
GO
```

```
NodeIdPath NodeId NodeLevel EmployeeId EmployeeName Title
---------- ------ --------- ---------- ------------ ----------------------
/1/1/      0x5AC0 2         269        Cheryl       Marketing Assistant
/1/2/      0x5B40 2         389        Wanda        Business Assistant
```

(2 row(s) affected)

This time, the results list only Cheryl and Wanda, but not Amy herself or any of Amy's deeper descendants. That's because we are requesting just the rows whose one-level-up ancestor is Amy (employee ID 46)—that is, just Amy's immediate children.

If we wanted to retrieve all the employees exactly *two* levels down from a particular manager, we could pass the value *2* to the *GetAncestor* method. For example, to select the employees that report to the employees beneath Dave (that is, to see all the employees two levels beneath him), we could request rows whose *grandparent* is Dave (employee ID 6; that is, just Dave's grandchildren), as shown here:

```
SELECT NodeId.ToString() AS NodeIdPath, *
  FROM  Employee
  WHERE NodeId.GetAncestor(2) =
    (SELECT NodeId
      FROM  Employee
      WHERE EmployeeId = 6)
  ORDER BY NodeLevel, NodeId
GO
```

```
NodeIdPath NodeId NodeLevel EmployeeId EmployeeName Title
---------- ------ --------- ---------- ------------ ----------------------
/1/1/      0x5AC0 2         269        Cheryl       Marketing Assistant
/1/2/      0x5B40 2         389        Wanda        Business Assistant
/2/1/      0x6AC0 2         272        Mary         Marketing Assistant
/3/1/      0x7AC0 2         291        Keven        Marketing Intern
```

(4 row(s) affected)

This query returned all employees that are two levels below Dave. The fact that some of them are cousins and not siblings (that is, some of them have different direct parents) is irrelevant. Being exactly two levels down beneath Dave qualifies them all for selection by this query. And because of the horizontal traversal of this query's index scan, it delivers very fast performance with a breadth-first index defined on the table.

To find the root node in the hierarchy, simply invoke the *GetRoot* method on the *hierarchyid* data type itself using the double-colon syntax, as shown in the following code. This is the same method we used to create the first employee at the top of our tree (Dave, as shown in Listing 7-2).

```
SELECT NodeId.ToString() AS NodeIdPath, *
 FROM   Employee
 WHERE NodeId = hierarchyid::GetRoot()
GO

NodeIdPath NodeId NodeLevel EmployeeId EmployeeName Title
---------- ------ --------- ---------- ------------ --------------------
/          0x     0         6          Dave         Marketing Manager

(1 row(s) affected)
```

Reordering Nodes Within the Hierarchy

Reorganizing a hierarchy is a common maintenance task. You might often need to alter the tree structure by changing the parent-child relationships within the hierarchy. The *hierarchyid* type provides a *GetReparentedValue* method that makes it easy to handle this kind of maintenance. We will start by first relocating just a single node without disturbing any other nodes in the hierarchy. Then we'll relocate an entire subtree (that is, all of a node's descendant nodes).

The *GetReparentedValue* Method

You invoke the *GetReparentedValue* method on the node you want to move, passing in two parameters. The first specifies the original parent (the source), and the second specifies the new parent (the target). Returning to our employee tree example, Wanda formerly reported to Amy but is now reporting to Jill instead (alongside Kevin). We therefore want to move Wanda's current position as a child of Amy to be a child of Jill instead. The following code uses the *GetReparentedValue* method to perform that change:

```
DECLARE @EmployeeToMove hierarchyid
DECLARE @OldParent hierarchyid
DECLARE @NewParent hierarchyid

SELECT @EmployeeToMove = NodeId
  FROM   Employee
  WHERE EmployeeId = 389 -- Wanda
```

```
SELECT @OldParent = NodeId
 FROM  Employee
 WHERE EmployeeId = 46 -- Amy

SELECT @NewParent = NodeId
 FROM  Employee
 WHERE EmployeeId = 119 -- Jill

-- Wanda now reports to Jill and no longer to Amy
UPDATE Employee
 SET   NodeId = @EmployeeToMove.GetReparentedValue(@OldParent, @NewParent)
 WHERE NodeId = @EmployeeToMove
GO
```

The hierarchy now looks like Figure 7-5.

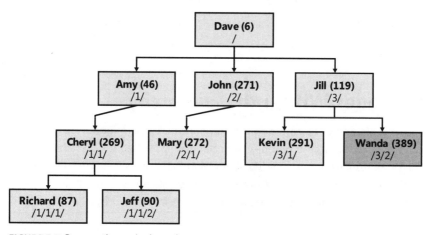

FIGURE 7-5 Reparenting a single node

Viewing the results of the following query confirms that Wanda's *NodeIdPath* has changed from */1/2/* (child of Amy) to */3/2/* (child of Jill):

```
SELECT
  NodeId,
  NodeId.ToString() AS NodeIdPath,
  NodeLevel,
  dbo.fnGetFullDisplayPath(NodeId) AS NodeIdDisplayPath,
  EmployeeName
 FROM
  Employee
 ORDER BY
  NodeLevel, NodeId
GO
```

```
NodeId NodeIdPath NodeLevel NodeIdDisplayPath                  EmployeeName
------ ---------- --------- -------------------------------    ------------
0x     /          0         Dave                               Dave
0x58   /1/        1         Dave > Amy                         Amy
0x68   /2/        1         Dave > John                        John
0x78   /3/        1         Dave > Jill                        Jill
0x5AC0 /1/1/      2         Dave > Amy > Cheryl                Cheryl
0x6AC0 /2/1/      2         Dave > John > Mary                 Mary
0x7AC0 /3/1/      2         Dave > Jill > Kevin                Kevin
0x7B40 /3/2/      2         Dave > Jill > Wanda                Wanda
0x5AD6 /1/1/1/    3         Dave > Amy > Cheryl > Richard      Richard
0x5ADA /1/1/2/    3         Dave > Amy > Cheryl > Jeff         Jeff

(10 row(s) affected)
```

Changing the position of a single node with the *GetReparentedValue* method as we just did does *not* affect any of that node's children. This means that if Wanda had any child nodes, not only would they not move along with Wanda as new descendants of Jill, they would also not move up one level in the hierarchy as direct descendants of Amy to occupy the position vacated by Wanda. The same would be true if Wanda were simply deleted rather than moved. Former child nodes of Wanda would therefore end up having no parent at all, but would rather have only a *grandparent* (which in this case would be Amy, Wanda's former parent). SQL Server 2008 will not enforce referential integrity on the hierarchy to catch this condition. Future versions of SQL Server might address this, but it's your job until then to handle orphaned nodes. In our example, you could simply move the orphaned nodes up one level in the hierarchy as direct descendants of Amy to close the gap left by Wanda by performing a subtree *transplant*, which you'll learn about next.

Transplanting Subtrees

We can easily move a larger number of people at one time by reparenting an entire subtree. Because we'll be moving all of a node's descendants as a single block, no orphaned nodes can result from this operation. In our next update, we will move all of Amy's subordinates to their new manager, Kevin. This is achieved by reparenting all nodes with *hierarchyid* values that begin with */1/* (Amy) to */3/1/* (Kevin), except for Amy herself. We use the *IsDescendantOf* method to return all of Amy's descendants for the update. Recall from our earlier discussion of the *IsDescendantOf* method that Amy is her own descendant at the 0 level (that is, she's the root of her own subtree). We must therefore exclude her (employee ID 46) from the rows to be updated, as shown in the following code:

```
DECLARE @OldParent hierarchyid
DECLARE @NewParent hierarchyid

SELECT @OldParent = NodeId
  FROM  Employee
  WHERE EmployeeId = 46 -- Amy
```

```
SELECT @NewParent = NodeId
 FROM   Employee
 WHERE  EmployeeId = 291 -- Kevin

UPDATE Employee
 SET    NodeId = NodeId.GetReparentedValue(@OldParent, @NewParent)
 WHERE  NodeId.IsDescendantOf(@OldParent) = 1
        AND EmployeeId <> 46 -- This excludes Amy from the move.
 GO
```

> **Note** The employee ID values are hard-coded for Amy and Kevin in this code. This was done for demonstration purposes. In a real-world implementation, this logic should be in a stored procedure that accepts any two nodes as input parameters and wraps the *SELECT* and *UPDATE* statements in a transaction.

Running this update moves all of Amy's descendants to be descendants of Kevin, as shown in Figure 7-6. Notice that the nodes have moved not only *across* the tree but *down* one level as well (since Kevin is one level deeper than Amy).

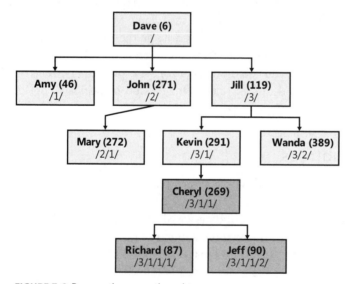

FIGURE 7-6 Reparenting an entire subtree

Selecting all the employees one more time shows how SQL Server updated the *hierarchyid* values in *NodeId* for Cheryl, Richard, and Jeff to reflect their new positions beneath Kevin. For the first time in our scenario, the hierarchy now runs five levels deep (counting from 0 to 4), as shown here:

```
SELECT
  NodeId,
  NodeId.ToString() AS NodeIdPath,
  NodeLevel,
  dbo.fnGetFullDisplayPath(NodeId) AS NodeIdDisplayPath,
  EmployeeName
 FROM
  Employee
GO
```

```
NodeId     NodeIdPath NodeLevel NodeIdDisplayPath                        EmployeeName
---------  ---------- --------- --------------------------------------- ------------
0x         /          0         Dave                                    Dave
0x58       /1/        1         Dave > Amy                              Amy
0x68       /2/        1         Dave > John                             John
0x78       /3/        1         Dave > Jill                             Jill
0x6AC0     /2/1/      2         Dave > John > Mary                      Mary
0x7AC0     /3/1/      2         Dave > Jill > Kevin                     Kevin
0x7B40     /3/2/      2         Dave > Jill > Wanda                     Wanda
0x7AD6     /3/1/1/    3         Dave > Jill > Kevin > Cheryl            Cheryl
0x7AD6B0   /3/1/1/1/  4         Dave > Jill > Kevin > Cheryl > Richard  Richard
0x7AD6D0   /3/1/1/2/  4         Dave > Jill > Kevin > Cheryl > Jeff     Jeff

(10 row(s) affected)
```

More *hierarchyid* Methods

Three more *hierarchyid* methods—*Parse*, *Read*, and *Write*—are provided by the *hierarchyid* data type, although they are less often used.

Parse is essentially the reverse of *ToString*. It accepts the same slash-delimited string representation that is returned by *ToString* and returns the equivalent compacted *varbinary hierarchyid* value that SQL Server uses internally to represent the nodes. This value could then be passed to *ToString*, in which case you'd get the original slash-delimited string back. It is the only other static method besides *GetRoot*, so it uses the double-colon syntax, as follows:

```
SELECT hierarchyid::Parse('/2/1/1/') AS NodeId
GO

NodeId
----------
0x6AD6

(1 row(s) affected)
```

Parse and *ToString* together enable serialization and deserialization to and from *hierarchyid* values and strings. Although you could manage the string representations on your own and use *Parse* to convert them for storage as *hierarchyid* values, the *hierarchyid* values are best assigned by calling the *GetDescendant* method, as we've demonstrated throughout our examples.

The last two methods, *Read* and *Write*, are the only methods not available in T-SQL. They can be used only in .NET code against the *Microsoft.SqlServer.Types.SqlHierarchyId* type. These two methods are used to pass *hierarchyid* values into and out of *BinaryReader* and *BinaryWriter* objects. They are also used internally by SQL Server as necessary, such as when reading from or writing to a *hierarchyid* column or for conversions between *varbinary* and *hierarchyid*. These methods are provided to enable such internal operations, as well as for integration with your own .NET code running under SQL CLR. They don't otherwise serve any real significant function in terms of the actual implementation of a hierarchical structure.

Summary

We can now work with hierarchical data that lives in normal relational tables. In this chapter, you learned how to use the new *hierarchyid* data type in SQL Server 2008 to cast a tree structure over data stored in everyday database tables, rows, and columns. The *hierarchyid* data type provides a set of methods and indexing strategies to enable efficient searching and manipulation of hierarchy nodes at the database level. This enables us to apply a hierarchical model to traditional table data rather than resorting to XML, in scenarios where it makes better sense to keep the data stored relationally than to refactor (revise) the data for XML storage.

Chapter 8
Using FILESTREAM for Unstructured Data Storage

—Leonard Lobel

Applications today commonly work with unstructured data much more frequently than they did in the past. The accelerating data explosion of our times—relentlessly driven by dropping storage costs and rising storage capacities—continues to generate more and more unstructured data for us to handle. While applications of the past required little more than mapping data entry screens into rows and columns in the database and being able to perform fairly simple queries, today you also have data like audio, video, and other multimedia-type files to cope with. You might have to store employee photos, surveillance videos, recorded conversations, e-mail messages (including embedded attachments), trend analysis spreadsheets, content in proprietary formats, or other related artifacts with your database records. These unstructured types hold binary streams of information, commonly referred to as binary large object (BLOB) data. This BLOB data needs to be associated with the structured data that lives in your relational database.

Traditionally, there have been two solutions for combining structured table data with unstructured BLOB data in Microsoft SQL Server: either keep BLOBs in the database with all your structured relational data or store them outside the database (in either the file system or a dedicated BLOB store) with path references in the database that link to their external locations. Each of these strategies has pros and cons with respect to storage, performance, manageability, and programming complexity that we'll talk about—but neither of them is intrinsically native to the core database engine.

FILESTREAM is a major new feature in SQL Server 2008 that provides native support for efficiently handling BLOBs in the database. By improving the way we can now store and manage BLOB data, FILESTREAM offers a more efficient solution over traditional strategies. First we'll examine the pros and cons of storing BLOB data inside or outside the database, and then you'll learn how to enhance the storage and manipulation of BLOB data by leveraging FILESTREAM in SQL Server 2008.

BLOBs in the Database

Your first option, of course, is to store BLOB data directly in the table columns of your database. Do this by declaring a column as a *varbinary(max)* data type, which can store a single BLOB up to 2 gigabytes (GB) in size.

> **Important** You should no longer use the *image* data type that was used to store BLOBs prior to SQL Server 2005. The *varbinary(max)* data type should now be used instead of *image*, which has been deprecated and may be removed from future versions of SQL Server.

Because BLOB data is stored inline with all the other structured table data, it is tightly integrated with the database. No effort is required on your part to link the relational data with its associated BLOB data. Management is therefore simplified, because everything is contained together within the file groups of a single database. Backup, restore, detach, copy, and attach operations on the database files encompass all structured and BLOB data together as a single entity. Transactional consistency is another important benefit of this approach. Because BLOB data is a physical part of the tables in the database, it is eligible to participate in transactions. If you begin a transaction, update some data, and then roll back the transaction, any BLOB data that was updated is also rolled back. Overall, the mixture of structured and BLOB data is handled quite seamlessly with this model.

Despite all these advantages, however, physically storing BLOBs in the database often results in a significant (and unacceptable) performance penalty. Because BLOB content (which tends to contain large amounts of data) is stored inline with structured data, it can consume a disproportionately large percentage of space in the database relative to the structured data. Query performance suffers greatly as a result, because the query processor needs to sift through much larger amounts of data in your tables that are holding inline BLOB content. The BLOBs also don't stream nearly as efficiently with *varbinary(max)* as they would if they were held externally in the file system or on a dedicated BLOB store. And last, *varbinary(max)* columns can store a maximum size of 2 GB. While this might not represent a limitation for handling typical documents, it can pose an obstacle for scenarios requiring much larger BLOB support (for example, where each row in a table of software products has a BLOB containing a distributable International Organization for Standardization [ISO] image of the software that can easily exceed 2 GB).

> **Note** If you have modest storage requirements for BLOBs, where they are each typically 1 megabyte (MB) or smaller, you should consider keeping them in the database using the *varbinary(max)* data type instead of using the file system. Matters are simplified by storing the BLOBs inline with your tables rather than externally, and doing so will typically not affect performance when you are working with very few or very small BLOBs. Furthermore, you should consider caching small, frequently accessed BLOBs rather than repeatedly retrieving them from the database.

BLOBs in the File System

To address these performance bottlenecks, you can instead store BLOBs outside the database as ordinary files in the file system. With this approach, structured data in your relational tables merely contains path information to the unstructured BLOB data held in the file system. Applications use this path information as a link reference for tracking and locating the BLOB content associated with rows in the database tables. Because they are physically held in the file system, any BLOB can exceed 2 GB. In fact, their size is limited only by the host file system and available disk space. They also deliver much better streaming performance, since the file system provides a native environment optimized for streaming unstructured data, whereas the *varbinary(max)* column in the database does not. And because the physical database is much smaller without the BLOBs inside it, the query processor can continue to deliver optimal performance.

While physically separating structured and unstructured content this way does address the performance concerns of BLOBs, it also raises new issues because the data is now separated not only physically but logically as well. That is, SQL Server has absolutely no awareness of the association between data in the database and files stored externally in the file system that are referenced by path information in the database tables. Their coupling exists solely at the application level. Backup, restore, detach, copy, and attach operations on the database files therefore include only structured table data without any of the BLOB data that's in the file system. The integrated management benefits you get when storing BLOBs in the database are lost, and the administrative burden is increased by having to manage the file system separately.

Application development against this model is also more complex because of the extra effort required for linking between the database and the file system. The database offers no assistance in establishing and maintaining the references between its structured data and the external BLOBs, so it's up to the database designer and application developer to manage all of that on their own. And last, although perhaps most significant, there is no unified transactional control across both the database and the file system.

What's in an Attribute?

Of course, this discussion has been leading toward the new FILESTREAM feature, which combines the best of both worlds (and then some) in SQL Server 2008. First, to be clear, this is *not* technically a new data type in SQL Server. Instead, FILESTREAM is implemented as an *attribute* that you apply to the *varbinary(max)* data type. It might look innocent enough, but merely applying this attribute unleashes the FILESTREAM feature—an extremely efficient storage abstraction layer for managing unstructured data in the database. With this attribute applied, we continue to treat the *varbinary(max)* column *as though* its contents were stored inline with our table data. Under the covers, however, the data is stored externally from the database in the server's NTFS file system.

With FILESTREAM, structured and unstructured data are logically connected but physically separated. The unstructured data is configured as just another file group in the database, so it participates in all logical database operations, including transactions and backup/restore. On disk, however, the BLOBs are stored as individual physical files in the NTFS file system that are created and managed automatically behind the scenes. SQL Server establishes and maintains the link references between the database and the file system. It knows about the unstructured BLOB data in the file system and considers the files holding BLOB data to be an integral part of the overall database. But the unstructured data doesn't impede query performance because it is not physically stored inline with table data. It's stored in the file system, which is highly optimized for streaming binary data. Logically, however, the database encompasses both the relational tables and the BLOB files in the file system. We therefore continue to treat BLOB data as though we were storing it inside the database itself, from both a development and an administrative perspective. For example, backing up the database includes all the BLOB data from the file system in the backup automatically.

> **Note** Because the BLOB data is contained in its own database file group, you can easily exclude it from backups if desired or as needed.

The end result is that SQL Server 2008 uses the appropriate storage for structured and unstructured data—storing relational (structured) data in tables and BLOB (unstructured) data in files—in order to deliver the best possible performance all around. Because it does this completely transparently, we enjoy integrated management benefits over the database. The database engine handles the link references between the relational tables and their associated BLOB data in the file system for us. So we also enjoy simplified application development because we don't need to worry about the additional complexities of manually associating the database with the file system and keeping the two in sync, as we did in the past. Last, by leveraging the transactional capabilities of the NTFS file system, BLOB updates participate seamlessly with database transactions. If you're starting to get excited by all this, that's the idea! We're ready to dive in to some real code now that puts FILESTREAM to work for us.

Enabling FILESTREAM

Like many other features, FILESTREAM is disabled by default in SQL Server 2008, and you must first enable it before the feature can be used. Enabling FILESTREAM is slightly more involved than configuring other SQL Server features because it requires two distinct steps. First the feature needs to be enabled for the machine (Microsoft Windows service), and then it needs to be enabled for the server instance. These two FILESTREAM configuration layers are by design, in order to draw a separation of security responsibilities between the roles of Windows administrator and SQL Server administrator.

Enabling FILESTREAM for the Machine

The first step is to enable FILESTREAM for the machine by setting an access level. This step can actually be performed at the time that SQL Server is initially installed by choosing a FILESTREAM access level during setup. The default access level, as already mentioned, is disabled. To enable FILESTREAM for the machine after SQL Server has been installed, the Windows administrator uses the SQL Server Configuration Manager to set the access level. (This tool can be launched from the Configuration Tools folder of the Microsoft SQL Server 2008 program group on the Start menu.)

The SQL Server Configuration Manager opens with a list of services displayed in the main panel. In the list of services, right-click the SQL Server instance that you want to en-able FILESTREAM for, and then choose Properties. In the Properties dialog box, select the FILESTREAM tab. The three check boxes on the FILESTREAM tab allow you to select the vari-ous levels of FILESTREAM access. Figure 8-1 shows the Properties dialog box with all three check boxes selected.

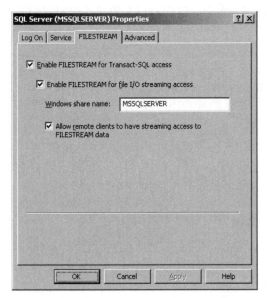

FIGURE 8-1 Enabling FILESTREAM for the machine to support file I/O streaming access by remote clients

When all three check boxes are cleared, FILESTREAM is completely disabled. Selecting the first check box enables FILESTREAM, but only for Transact-SQL (T-SQL) access. This provides a completely transparent FILESTREAM implementation, but it doesn't let you take advantage of streamed file access between the database and your client applications.

The real power of FILESTREAM comes into play when you enable direct file I/O streaming, which delivers the best possible performance for accessing BLOB data in the file system with SQL Server. You enable direct file I/O streaming access by selecting the second check box. Streamed file access also creates a Windows share name that is used to construct logical Universal Naming Convention (UNC) paths to BLOB data during FILESTREAM access, as we'll see further on when we use the *OpenSqlFilestream* function in our sample .NET applications. The share name is specified in a text box after the second check box and is set by default to the same name as the server instance (*MSSQLSERVER*, in this example).

In most cases, client applications will not be running on the same machine as SQL Server, so you will usually also need to select the third check box to enable FILESTREAM for remote client file I/O streaming access. One exception to this general practice might be when using Microsoft SQL Server 2008 Express edition as a local data store for a client application with everything running on the same machine. In this case, you would use the more secure setting and leave the third check box cleared. Doing so would enable file I/O streaming access for the local client application but deny such access to remote clients.

Throughout the rest of this chapter, we'll be building several sample .NET applications that work with FILESTREAM. These applications will demonstrate how to use *OpenSqlFilestream* for file I/O streaming access, so at least the first two check boxes must be selected for the sample code to work. If you are running the applications on a different machine than SQL Server, you will also need to select the third check box to allow remote access.

> **More Info**   There is no T-SQL equivalent script that can set the FILESTREAM access level for the machine. However, Microsoft posts a VBScript file available over the Internet that allows you to enable FILESTREAM from the command line as an alternative to using SQL Server Configuration Manager. At press time, the download page for this script is *http://www.codeplex.com/ SQLSrvEngine/Wiki/View.aspx?title=FileStreamEnable&referringTitle=Home*. An Internet short-cut to this URL is included with this chapter's sample code on the book's companion Web site. Alternatively, try running a Web search on "How to enable FILESTREAM from the command line."

Enabling FILESTREAM for the Server Instance

The second step is for the SQL Server administrator to enable FILESTREAM for the server in-stance. The concept here is similar to the first step in that varying levels of access are defined. FILESTREAM can be enabled for the server instance with a simple call to the *sp_configure* sys-tem stored procedure, as follows:

```
EXEC sp_configure filestream_access_level, n
RECONFIGURE
```

In the preceding code, replace *n* with a number from 0 to 2 to set the access level. The value *0* disables the FILESTREAM feature completely. Setting the access level to *1* enables

FILESTREAM for T-SQL access only, and setting it to *2* enables FILESTREAM for full access (which includes local or remote file I/O streaming access as enabled for the machine in the first step). To support our sample .NET applications that will demonstrate file I/O streaming access using *OpenSqlFilestream*, you'll need to select level 2 (full access).

> **Note** Naturally, the access level defined for the server instance must be supported by the access level defined for the machine. Typically, therefore, the access levels between the machine and the server instance should be set to match each other.

You can also set the FILESTREAM access level for the server instance in SQL Server Management Studio from the Advanced Server Properties dialog box. Right-click any server instance in Object Explorer, choose Properties, and then select the Advanced page. The various levels are available as choices in the Filestream Access Level drop-down list, as shown in Figure 8-2.

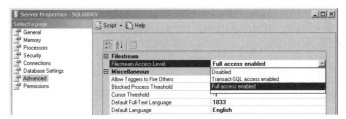

FIGURE 8-2 Selecting the FILESTREAM configuration level in SQL Server Management Studio

Creating a FILESTREAM-Enabled Database

Once FILESTREAM is enabled for both the machine and the server instance, any database running on the server instance can support unstructured data by defining a file group with the new *FILEGROUP...CONTAINS FILESTREAM* clause of the *CREATE DATABASE* statement. For example, the statement in Listing 8-1 creates a *PhotoLibrary* database that can store pictures using FILESTREAM.

LISTING 8-1 Creating a FILESTREAM-enabled catabase with *FILEGROUP...CONTAINS FILESTREAM*

```
CREATE DATABASE PhotoLibrary
 ON PRIMARY
  (NAME = PhotoLibrary_data,
   FILENAME = 'C:\PhotoLibrary\PhotoLibrary_data.mdf'),
 FILEGROUP FileStreamGroup1 CONTAINS FILESTREAM
  (NAME = PhotoLibrary_group2,
   FILENAME = 'C:\PhotoLibrary\Photos')
 LOG ON
  (NAME = PhotoLibrary_log,
   FILENAME = 'C:\PhotoLibrary\PhotoLibrary_log.ldf')
```

The *FILEGROUP...CONTAINS FILESTREAM* clause in this otherwise ordinary *CREATE DATABASE* statement enables the FILESTREAM feature for the *PhotoLibrary* database.

A few simple but important things warrant mention at this point. To begin, as when creating any database, the directory (or directories) specified for the primary and log file groups must exist at the time the database is created. In our example, the C:\PhotoLibrary directory specified by *FILENAME* in the *ON PRIMARY* and *LOG ON* clauses must exist, or the *CREATE DATABASE* statement will fail.

Interestingly, and somewhat oddly, the *FILENAME* specified in the new *FILEGROUP...* *CONTAINS FILESTREAM* clause does not actually specify the name of a file but instead specifies the name of a directory. And unlike the primary and log file group directories, this directory must *not* exist at the time that the database is created (although the path leading up to the final directory must exist), or the *CREATE DATABASE* statement will fail as well. Instead, SQL Server takes control of creating and managing this directory, much as it does for creating and managing the .mdf and .ldf files in the other file groups. In our example, SQL Server will automatically create the C:\PhotoLibrary\Photos folder when the *CREATE DATABASE* statement is executed and will then use that folder for storing all BLOB data—photos, in our example—in the *PhotoLibrary* database.

When we execute this *CREATE DATABASE* statement with an empty C:\PhotoLibrary directory, SQL Server creates the usual .mdf and .ldf files for us and also creates the Photos subdirectory for the FILESTREAM group, as shown in Figure 8-3.

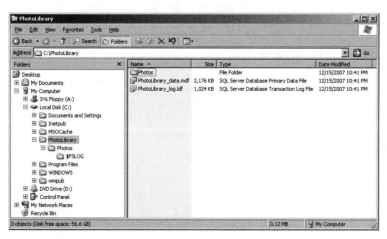

FIGURE 8-3 FILESTREAM storage in the file system

Behind the scenes, SQL Server will store all our pictures as files in the Photos subdirectory and track the references between those picture files and the relational tables that they logically belong to in database columns defined as *varbinary(max) FILESTREAM*. Unless we explicitly exclude the *FileStreamGroup1* file group from a backup or restore command, all our picture files in the *Photos* subdirectory will be included with the relational database in the backup or restore operation.

Creating a Table with FILESTREAM Columns

We're now ready to create the *PhotoAlbum* table. SQL Server requires that any table using FILESTREAM storage have a *uniqueidentifier* column that is not nullable and that specifies the *ROWGUIDCOL* attribute. You must also create a unique constraint on this column. Only one *ROWGUIDCOL* column can be defined in any given table, although defining one then allows you to declare any number of *varbinary(max) FILESTREAM* columns in the table that you want for storing BLOB data. The statement in Listing 8-2 creates the *PhotoAlbum* table with a *Photo* column declared as *varbinary(max) FILESTREAM*.

LISTING 8-2 Creating a FILESTREAM-enabled table

```
CREATE TABLE PhotoAlbum(
 PhotoId int PRIMARY KEY,
 RowId uniqueidentifier ROWGUIDCOL NOT NULL UNIQUE DEFAULT NEWSEQUENTIALID(),
 Description varchar(max),
 Photo varbinary(max) FILESTREAM DEFAULT(0x))
```

With this statement, we satisfy the FILESTREAM requirement for the *ROWGUIDCOL* column, yet we won't actually have to do anything to maintain that column. By declaring the *RowId* column with its *DEFAULT* value set to call the *NEWSEQUENTIALID* function, we can just pretend this column doesn't even exist—simply not providing values for it will cause SQL Server to automatically generate an arbitrary globally unique identifier (GUID) for the column that it needs to support FILESTREAM on the table. The column is set to not accept *NULL* values and is defined with the required unique constraint.

We have also declared an integer *PhotoId* column for the table's primary key value. We'll use the *PhotoId* column to identify individual photos in the album, and SQL Server will use the *RowId* column to track and cross-reference photos in the file system with rows in the *PhotoAlbum* table. The *Photo* column holds the actual BLOB itself, being defined as a *varbinary(max)* data type with the *FILESTREAM* attribute applied. This means that it gets treated like a regular *varbinary(max)* column, but we know that its BLOB is really being stored in the file system by SQL Server internally. For now, just take note that we've defined a default 0x binary value for the *Photo* column. This will come into play when we start streaming content with client code, but we're not there yet.

Manipulating BLOB data is not something that is easily or practically done in T-SQL. Of course, you can specify small binary streams inline directly in your T-SQL code, or embed and extract binary streams using byte arrays as you could with an ordinary *varbinary(max)* column. But the proper (and fastest) way to get data into and out of FILESTREAM columns is by using a native or managed client that calls the *OpenSqlFilestream* function provided by the SQL Server 2008 native client API.

With *OpenSqlFilestream*, native or managed code applications can use either the *ReadFile* and *WriteFile* Microsoft Win32 application programming interface (API) functions or the .NET *FileStream* class to deliver high-performance streaming of BLOB data. In the next section, you'll see exactly how to use the managed *FileStream* class in C# for storing and retrieving pictures in the *Photo* column. But right now, we're going to do something rather contrived instead and use T-SQL to cast string data into and out of the *varbinary(max)* data type in the *Photo* column. We're doing this so that you can come to understand FILESTREAM one step at a time, and the first thing we want to do is observe the effects on the NTFS file system as SQL Server uses it to store BLOB data in *varbinary(max)* FILESTREAM columns. So we'll begin modestly with the following *INSERT* statement that adds our first row to the *PhotoAlbum* table:

```
INSERT INTO PhotoAlbum(PhotoId, Description, Photo)
 VALUES(1, 'First pic', CAST('BLOB' As varbinary(max)))
```

This *INSERT* statement reads no differently than it would if we were using a regular *varbinary(max)* column for the *Photo* column without the *FILESTREAM* attribute. It appears to store the unstructured *Photo* column data inline with the rest of the relational columns, and it appears the same way when returning the data back with a *SELECT* query, as shown here:

```
SELECT *, CAST(Photo AS varchar) AS PhotoText FROM PhotoAlbum
GO

PhotoId RowId                               Description Photo      PhotoText
------- ----------------------------------- ----------- ---------- ---------
1       c04a7930-89ab-dc11-91e3-0003ff399330 First pic  0x424C4F42 BLOB

(1 row(s) affected)
```

However, if we peek beneath the covers, we can see that SQL Server is actually storing the *Photo* column outside the database in the file system. Because everything is tracked internally for us, we don't really need to understand the precise manner in which files and folders are named, organized, and cross-referenced back to the relational database. But just by drilling down and probing the subfolders beneath the *Photos* directory, we discover that there is in fact a new file stored in the file system created as a result of the *INSERT* statement that we can view by right-clicking the file name and then choosing Open, as shown in Figure 8-4.

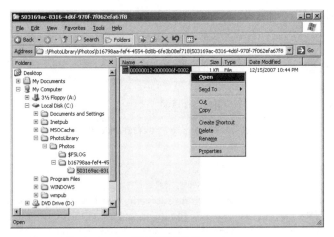

FIGURE 8-4 Exploring the FILESTREAM file system

If we select Notepad to open the file, we get proof positive that the unstructured content of the *Photo* column is stored outside the database and in the file system. In this example, the text *BLOB* that was inserted into the *Photo* column is stored in the file that we've just opened in Notepad, as shown in Figure 8-5.

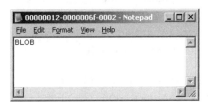

FIGURE 8-5 Examining unstructured FILESTREAM content in Notepad

This clearly demonstrates how FILESTREAM data is logically connected to—but physically separated from—the database. Because the unstructured data is stored entirely in the file system, we can easily alter its content by directly updating the file itself in Notepad without even involving the database. To prove the point further, let's change the text in the file from *BLOB* to *Cool* and save the changes back to the file system, as shown in Figure 8-6.

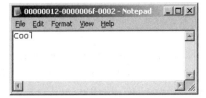

FIGURE 8-6 Changing FILESTREAM content directly in the file system

The changed FILESTREAM data is reflected in the same *SELECT* statement we ran earlier, as shown here:

```
SELECT *, CAST(Photo AS varchar) AS PhotoText FROM PhotoAlbum
GO

PhotoId RowId                                Description Photo      PhotoText
------- ------------------------------------ ----------- ---------- ---------
1       c04a7930-89ab-dc11-91e3-0003ff399330 First pic   0x436F6F6C Cool

(1 row(s) affected)
```

> **Important** We performed this exercise to demonstrate and verify that the file system is being used to store FILESTREAM data. Having said that, you should *never* tamper directly with files in the file system this way. With respect to FILESTREAM, consider the file system as part of the database file groups (.mdf and .ldf files); it gets managed by SQL Server exclusively.

The *OpenSqlFilestream* Native Client API

With an understanding and appreciation of how FILESTREAM is implemented internally by SQL Server, we're ready now to move forward and store real binary picture data in the *Photo* column. As we mentioned earlier, this is best achieved by writing client code that calls the *OpenSqlFilestream* function provided by the SQL Server native client API.

When you work with *OpenSqlFilestream*, you always work with transactions (even for read access). There is no way to avoid them, since FILESTREAM by design coordinates transactional integrity across structured and unstructured data access between SQL Server and the NTFS file system. (However, we should stress that you normally should try not to read while in a transaction when you're not working with *OpenSqlFilestream*.)

Here's how it works. We first start an ordinary database transaction, after which we perform any number of normal data manipulation language (DML) operations (such as inserts or updates) on the database. When we access a *varbinary(max) FILESTREAM* column, SQL Server automatically initiates an NTFS file system transaction and associates it with the database transaction. SQL Server also ensures that both the database transaction and the file system transaction will either commit or roll back together.

To then stream BLOBs in and out, there are two key pieces of information we need to obtain. First, we need the file system transaction context, which is returned by the *GET_FILESTREAM_TRANSACTION_CONTEXT* function. (This function returns *NULL* if a transaction has not yet been established.) Second, we need a logical UNC path to the file holding the BLOB on the server, which is returned by the *PathName* method invoked on a *varbinary(max) FILESTREAM* value instance. These two pieces of information are then passed as inputs to the *OpenSqlFilestream* function, which returns a file handle back to us that we can use to perform efficient streaming I/O operations directly against the BLOB data stored in the file system on the server. Only when the database transaction is committed does SQL Server permanently save changes both to the database (from the DML operations) and to the file system (from the streaming I/O operations). Similarly, rolling back the transaction undoes changes to both the database and the file system.

> **Note** The UNC reference returned by the *PathName* method is *not* a real path to the physical file system on the server. Rather, *PathName* returns a fabricated path to be used by *OpenSqlFilestream* to enable direct streaming between the file system and client applications. (The share name in this UNC path is based on the share name specified when FILESTREAM was enabled for the machine, as described earlier in this chapter.) The file system itself is secured on the server no differently than the data and transaction file groups (.mdf and .ldf files) are secured. Users should never be granted direct access to the file system on the server. Normal SQL Server column-level security permissions apply to *varbinary(max) FILESTREAM* columns.

The handle returned by *OpenSqlFilestream* can be used with the Win32 *ReadFile* and *WriteFile* API functions for client applications written in native code, such as C++. The handle can also be used by the *FileStream* class in .NET for client applications written in managed code, such as C# or Visual Basic .NET. Continuing with our photo library example, we'll proceed to create a Windows Forms application in C# that implements all of the key pieces that bring a FILESTREAM application together—nothing more, nothing less. Our application will allow the user to create a new photo in the database that streams the BLOB into the *Photo* column and to select a photo that streams the BLOB back out from the *Photo* column into a *PictureBox* control for display. *OpenSqlFilestream* will provide us with the handle we need to read and write the binary picture data using the ordinary *FileStream* class defined in the *System.IO* namespace.

File-Streaming in .NET

We'll begin with the Windows user interface (UI), which is very simple. Start Visual Studio 2008, and then create a new C# Windows Forms application. Design a form with two separate group boxes: one at the top of the form for inserting photos and another beneath it for selecting photos. Provide labels and text boxes for entering a photo ID, file name, and description in the top group box, along with a link label to invoke a save operation. In the bottom group box, provide a text box and label for entering a photo ID and a link label to invoke a load operation. Include a label to display the description returned from the database and a picture box to display the photo BLOB returned via FILESTREAM. After performing some aesthetic alignment and formatting, your form should appear something like the one shown in Figure 8-7.

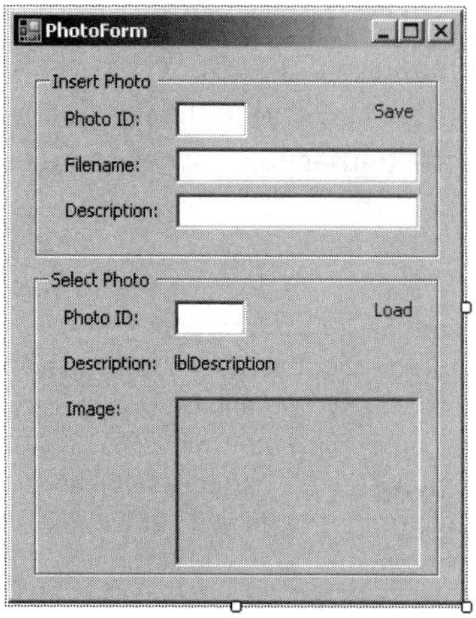

FIGURE 8-7 Simple FILESTREAM Windows UI form

We'll write only a very small amount of code behind this Windows form, and we'll implement the FILESTREAM logic in a separate data access class that can be reused across a variety of user interface technologies, including Windows Forms, ASP.NET, and Windows Presentation Foundation (WPF). Let's add the code behind the click events for this form's Save and Load link labels that hooks into the data access class named *PhotoData* (which we'll create right after the UI), as shown in Listing 8-3.

LISTING 8-3 UI calls into FILESTREAM data access class for saving and loading image files

```
private void lnkSave_LinkClicked(object sender, LinkLabelLinkClickedEventArgs e)
{
    int photoId = int.Parse(this.txtSavePhotoId.Text);
    string desc = this.txtDescription.Text;
    string filename = this.txtFilename.Text;

    PhotoData.InsertPhoto(photoId, desc, filename);
}

private void lnkLoad_LinkClicked(object sender, LinkLabelLinkClickedEventArgs e)
{
    int photoId = int.Parse(this.txtLoadPhotoId.Text);

    string desc;
    Image photo = PhotoData.SelectPhoto(photoId, out desc);

    this.lblDescription.Text = desc;
    this.picImage.Image = photo;
}
```

When the user clicks *Save*, the code retrieves the new photo ID, description, and file name from the three text boxes and passes them to the *InsertPhoto* method of the *PhotoData* class.

When the user specifies a photo ID and clicks Load, the code calls the *SelectPhoto* method of the *PhotoData* class to retrieve the requested description and image for display.

Understanding FILESTREAM Data Access

All the magic happens inside the *PhotoData* class, which is a UI-agnostic data access class. This design draws a clear separation between data access and the UI, with only a minimal amount of UI-specific code to maintain. Listing 8-4 shows the complete source code for the *PhotoData* class.

> **Note** The *PhotoData* class takes a minimalist approach for proof-of-concept purposes only. The connection string is defined as a hard-coded constant; a real-world application should encrypt and store the connection string elsewhere (such as a configuration settings file). The code also employs the *using* construct in C# to ensure that all objects that allocate unmanaged resources such as database connections and file handles are disposed of properly even if an exception occurs, without including any additional error handling logic. Once again, real-world applications should implement a robust and reliable exception handling strategy that includes the use of *try/catch/finally* blocks, error logging, and validation.

LISTING 8-4 Implementing a FILESTREAM data access managed client class

```
using System;
using System.Data;
using System.Data.SqlClient;
using System.Drawing;
using System.IO;

using Microsoft.Win32.SafeHandles;

namespace PhotoLibraryApp
{
  public class PhotoData
  {
    private const string ConnStr =
      "Data Source=.;Integrated Security=True;Initial Catalog=PhotoLibrary;";

    #region "Insert Photo"

    public static void InsertPhoto(int photoId, string desc, string filename)
    {
      const string InsertCmd =
        "INSERT INTO PhotoAlbum(PhotoId, Description)" +
        " VALUES(@PhotoId, @Description)";

      using (SqlConnection conn = new SqlConnection(ConnStr))
      {
        conn.Open();
```

```
      using (SqlTransaction txn = conn.BeginTransaction())
      {
        using (SqlCommand cmd = new SqlCommand(InsertCmd, conn, txn))
        {
          cmd.Parameters.Add("@PhotoId", SqlDbType.Int).Value = photoId;
          cmd.Parameters.Add("@Description", SqlDbType.VarChar).Value = desc;
          cmd.ExecuteNonQuery();
        }

        SavePhotoFile(photoId, filename, txn);
        txn.Commit();
      }

      conn.Close();
    }
  }

  private static void SavePhotoFile
   (int photoId, string filename, SqlTransaction txn)
  {
    const int BlockSize = 1024 * 512;

    FileStream source = new FileStream(filename, FileMode.Open, FileAccess.Read);

    SafeFileHandle handle = GetOutputFileHandle(photoId, txn);
    using (FileStream dest = new FileStream(handle, FileAccess.Write))
    {
      byte[] buffer = new byte[BlockSize];
      int bytesRead;
      while ((bytesRead = source.Read(buffer, 0, buffer.Length)) > 0)
      {
        dest.Write(buffer, 0, bytesRead);
        dest.Flush();
      }
      dest.Close();
    }

    source.Close();
  }

  private static SafeFileHandle GetOutputFileHandle
   (int photoId, SqlTransaction txn)
  {
    const string GetOutputFileInfoCmd =
      "SELECT Photo.PathName(), GET_FILESTREAM_TRANSACTION_CONTEXT()" +
      " FROM PhotoAlbum" +
      " WHERE PhotoId = @PhotoId";

    SqlCommand cmd = new SqlCommand(GetOutputFileInfoCmd, txn.Connection, txn);
    cmd.Parameters.Add("@PhotoId", SqlDbType.Int).Value = photoId;

    string filePath;
    byte[] txnToken;
```

```csharp
    using (SqlDataReader rdr = cmd.ExecuteReader(CommandBehavior.SingleRow))
    {
      rdr.Read();
      filePath = rdr.GetSqlString(0).Value;
      txnToken = rdr.GetSqlBinary(1).Value;
      rdr.Close();
    }

    SafeFileHandle handle =
      NativeSqlClient.GetSqlFilestreamHandle
        (filePath, NativeSqlClient.DesiredAccess.ReadWrite, txnToken);

    return handle;
}

#endregion

#region "Select Photo"

public static Image SelectPhoto(int photoId, out string desc)
{
  const string SelectCmd =
  "SELECT Description, Photo.PathName(), GET_FILESTREAM_TRANSACTION_CONTEXT()" +
  " FROM PhotoAlbum" +
  " WHERE PhotoId = @PhotoId";

  Image photo;

  using (SqlConnection conn = new SqlConnection(ConnStr))
  {
    conn.Open();

    using (SqlTransaction txn = conn.BeginTransaction())
    {
      string filePath;
      byte[] txnToken;

      using (SqlCommand cmd = new SqlCommand(SelectCmd, conn, txn))
      {
        cmd.Parameters.Add("@PhotoId", SqlDbType.Int).Value = photoId;

        using (SqlDataReader rdr = cmd.ExecuteReader(CommandBehavior.SingleRow))
        {
          rdr.Read();
          desc = rdr.GetSqlString(0).Value;
          filePath = rdr.GetSqlString(1).Value;
          txnToken = rdr.GetSqlBinary(2).Value;
          rdr.Close();
        }
      }
```

```
        photo = LoadPhotoImage(filePath, txnToken);

        txn.Commit();
      }

      conn.Close();
    }

    return photo;
  }

  private static Image LoadPhotoImage(string filePath, byte[] txnToken)
  {
    Image photo;

    SafeFileHandle handle =
      NativeSqlClient.GetSqlFilestreamHandle
        (filePath, NativeSqlClient.DesiredAccess.Read, txnToken);

    using (FileStream fs = new FileStream(handle, FileAccess.Read))
    {
      photo = Image.FromStream(fs);
      fs.Close();
    }

    return photo;
  }

  #endregion
 }
}
```

There is also a small source file in our application named *NativeSqlClient* that encapsulates the Component Object Model (COM) Interop and native code call interface details for invoking *OpenSqlFilestream* from our managed code. It's this *NativeSqlClient* class that actually calls *OpenSqlFilestream*, whereas our managed code client applications call into *NativeSqlClient* for issuing all *OpenSqlFilestream* requests. We'll begin our in-depth code coverage with the *PhotoData* class and then look at the supporting *NativeSqlClient* class at the point that we call into it.

We'll start at the top with some required namespace inclusions. The one to take notice of is *Microsoft.Win32.SafeHandles*, which defines the *SafeFileHandle* object returned by *OpenSqlFilestream* that we'll be using to stream BLOBs. (No special assembly reference is required to use the *Microsoft.Win32.SafeHandles.SafeFileHandle* class, because it is provided by the core .NET library assembly mscorlib.dll.) We also define a connection string as a hard-coded constant, which of course is for demonstration purposes only. A real-world application would encrypt and store the connection string elsewhere (such as a configuration settings file), but we're keeping our example simple.

The first method defined in the class is *InsertPhoto*, which accepts a new photo integer ID, string description, and full path to an image file to be saved to the database, as shown here:

```
public static void InsertPhoto(int photoId, string desc, string filename)
{
    const string InsertCmd =
        "INSERT INTO PhotoAlbum(PhotoId, Description)" +
        " VALUES(@PhotoId, @Description)";

    using(SqlConnection conn = new SqlConnection(ConnStr))
    {
        conn.Open();

        using(SqlTransaction txn = conn.BeginTransaction())
        {
            using(SqlCommand cmd = new SqlCommand(InsertCmd, conn, txn))
            {
                cmd.Parameters.Add("@PhotoId", SqlDbType.Int).Value = photoId;
                cmd.Parameters.Add("@Description", SqlDbType.VarChar).Value = desc;
                cmd.ExecuteNonQuery();
            }

            SavePhotoFile(photoId, filename, txn);
            txn.Commit();
        }

        conn.Close();
    }
}
```

The method first creates and opens a new *SqlConnection* and then initiates a database transaction using the *SqlTransaction* class against the open connection. Next it creates a *SqlCommand* object associated with the open connection and initiated transaction, and prepares its command text with an *INSERT* statement (defined in the *InsertCmd* string constant) that stores the photo ID and description values in a new *PhotoAlbum* record. Our *INSERT* statement does not provide a value for *RowId* and instead allows SQL Server to automatically generate and assign a new *uniqueidentifier ROWGUID* value by default just as before, when we used T-SQL to insert the first row. We also do not provide a value for the *Photo* column— and now is exactly when the default 0x value that we defined earlier for the *Photo* column comes into play. After executing the *INSERT* by invoking *ExecuteNonQuery*, the transaction is still pending. Although the row has been added, it will roll back (disappear) if a problem occurs before the transaction is committed. Because we didn't provide a BLOB value for the *Photo* column in the new row, SQL Server honors the default value 0x that we established for it in the *CREATE TABLE* statement for *PhotoAlbum*. Being a *varbinary(max)* column decorated with the *FILESTREAM* attribute, this results in an empty file being added to the file system that is linked to the new row. And like the new row, this new empty BLOB file will disappear if the database transaction does not commit successfully.

> **Important** You cannot open a file handle to a *NULL* column value. If you want to use *OpenSqlFilestream*, a binary 0x value should always be used with *varbinary(max) FILESTREAM* columns when inserting new rows. This will result in the creation of a zero-length file that can be streamed to (overwritten) by calling *OpenSqlFilestream*, as we're doing now.

It is precisely at this point that we call the *SavePhotoFile* method to stream the specified image file into the *Photo* column of the newly inserted *PhotoAlbum* row, overwriting the empty file just added by default. When control returns from *SavePhotoFile*, the transaction is finally committed and the connection is closed. This permanently updates both the database and the file system with the structured and unstructured content for a new *PhotoAlbum* row.

The *SavePhotoFile* method reads from the source file and writes to the database FILESTREAM storage in 512-KB chunks using an ordinary *FileStream* object, as shown here:

```
private static void SavePhotoFile(int photoId, string filename, SqlTransaction txn)
{
    const int BlockSize = 1024 * 512;

    FileStream source = new FileStream(filename, FileMode.Open, FileAccess.Read);

    SafeFileHandle handle = GetOutputFileHandle(photoId, txn);
    using(FileStream dest = new FileStream(handle, FileAccess.Write))
    {
        byte[] buffer = new byte[BlockSize];
        int bytesRead;
        while((bytesRead = source.Read(buffer, 0, buffer.Length)) > 0)
        {
            dest.Write(buffer, 0, bytesRead);
            dest.Flush();
        }
        dest.Close();
    }

    source.Close();
}
```

The method begins by defining a *BlockSize* integer constant that is set to a reasonable value of 512 KB. Picture files larger than this will be streamed to the server in 512-KB pieces. The local source image file is first opened on a read-only *FileStream*. In order to obtain a writable *FileStream* on the output file in SQL Server, we call the *GetOutputFileHandle* method, passing in the photo ID and pending transaction and receiving back a *SafeFileHandle* object (defined in the *Microsoft.Win32.SafeHandles* namespace imported with a *using* statement at the top of the source file). The *FileStream* class offers a constructor that accepts a *SafeFileHandle* object, which we use to gain write access to the destination BLOB on the database server's NTFS file system. Remember that this output file is enlisted in an NTFS transaction and will not be permanently saved until the database transaction is committed by the code that is calling *SavePhotoFile*.

The rest of the *SavePhotoFile* method implements a simple loop that reads from the source *FileStream* and writes to the destination *FileStream* until the entire source file is processed and then closes both streams.

Let's now examine the *GetOutputFileHandle* method, which is called by *SavePhotoFile* to obtain the destination handle for streaming to the BLOB file:

```
private static SafeFileHandle GetOutputFileHandle(int photoId, SqlTransaction txn)
{
    const string GetOutputFileInfoCmd =
        "SELECT GET_FILESTREAM_TRANSACTION_CONTEXT(), Photo.PathName()" +
        " FROM PhotoAlbum" +
        " WHERE PhotoId = @PhotoId";

    SqlCommand cmd = new SqlCommand(GetOutputFileInfoCmd, txn.Connection, txn);
    cmd.Parameters.Add("@PhotoId", SqlDbType.Int).Value = photoId;

    string filePath;
    byte[] txnToken;

    using(SqlDataReader rdr = cmd.ExecuteReader(CommandBehavior.SingleRow))
    {
        rdr.Read();
        txnToken = rdr.GetSqlBinary(0).Value;
        filePath = rdr.GetSqlString(1).Value;
        rdr.Close();
    }

    SafeFileHandle handle =
        NativeSqlClient.GetSqlFilestreamHandle
        (filePath, NativeSqlClient.DesiredAccess.ReadWrite, txnToken);

    return handle;
}
```

This code is the key to using FILESTREAM. To reiterate, it is called at a point in time after a new row has been added to the *PhotoAlbum* table and a new, empty related BLOB file has been added to the file system but before the transactions that those actions are enlisted on have been committed. This is precisely the time for us to hook into the process and stream BLOB data into the database using *OpenSqlFilestream*. Recall from our discussion earlier that in order to do that, we need two pieces of information: a transactional context token and a logical UNC path name to the file itself. We therefore obtain both these items in a single-row *SqlDataReader* using a *SELECT* statement that returns *GET_FILESTREAM_TRANSACTION_CONTEXT* and *Photo.PathName*.

Because we began the database transaction before running the *INSERT* statement, SQL Server initiated a file system transaction in NTFS over the FILESTREAM data in the new row's *Photo* column. The *GET_FILESTREAM_TRANSACTION_CONTEXT* function returns a handle to that NTFS transaction. SQL Server will automatically commit this NTFS transaction when we commit the database transaction or roll back the NTFS transaction if we roll back the database transaction. When we obtain the transaction context, which is a *SqlBinary* value, we store it in a byte array named *txnToken*.

The second value returned by our *SELECT* statement is *Photo.PathName*, which returns a fabricated path (in UNC format, including the file name) to the BLOB for the selected *PhotoId*. What we're essentially doing with the *WHERE* clause is reading back the same row we have just added (but not yet committed) to the *PhotoAlbum* table in order to get the full path name to the BLOB stored in the new file that was just created (also not yet committed) in the file system. We're then storing it in a string variable named *filePath*.

Armed with both the FILESTREAM transaction context and the full path name to the BLOB file, we have what we need to call the native *OpenSqlFilestream* SQL client function and obtain a handle to the output file for streaming our content. However, we don't actually call *OpenSqlFilestream* directly from our data access class (although we certainly could). Instead, we call *GetSqlFilestreamHandle*, defined in our supporting *NativeSqlClient* class, which in turn calls *OpenSqlFilestream*, as shown in Listing 8-5.

LISTING 8-5 Calling *OpenSqlFilestream*

```
using System;
using System.Runtime.InteropServices;

using Microsoft.Win32.SafeHandles;

namespace PhotoLibraryFilestreamDemo
{
    public class NativeSqlClient
    {
        public enum DesiredAccess : uint
        {
            Read,
            Write,
            ReadWrite,
        }

        [DllImport("sqlncli10.dll", SetLastError = true, CharSet = CharSet.Unicode)]
        private static extern SafeFileHandle OpenSqlFilestream(
            string path,
            uint access,
            uint options,
            byte[] txnToken,
            uint txnTokenLength,
            Sql64 allocationSize);
```

```
            [StructLayout(LayoutKind.Sequential)]
            private struct Sql64
            {
                public Int64 QuadPart;
                public Sql64(Int64 quadPart)
                {
                    this.QuadPart = quadPart;
                }
            }

            public static SafeFileHandle GetSqlFilestreamHandle
              (string filePath, DesiredAccess access, byte[] txnToken)
            {
                SafeFileHandle handle = OpenSqlFilestream(
                    filePath,
                    (uint)access,
                    0,
                    txnToken,
                    (uint)txnToken.Length,
                    new Sql64(0));

                return handle;
            }
        }
    }
```

As you can see, the *GetSqlFilestreamHandle* method merely wraps the native *OpenSqlFilestream* function, which is defined with an external reference to *sqlncli10.dll* (SQL Native Client version 10) by using the *DllImport* attribute. *GetSqlFilestreamHandle* accepts the transaction context token and the full path to the BLOB file obtained by the *GET_FILESTREAM_TRANSACTION_CONTEXT* function and the *PathName* method. It also accepts an enumeration value that specifies the desired access mode, which can be *Read*, *Write*, or *ReadWrite*. The *OpenSqlFilestream* function requires other parameters that are not generally applicable for standard FILESTREAM usage, such as the unsigned 32-bit options and 64-bit allocation size arguments. These simply get passed in as 0.

> **Tip** Of course, *PhotoData* could have called *OpenSqlFilestream* directly. The purpose of our *NativeSqlClient* client class is to keep the COM Interop and 64-bit SQL integers out of our data access code, drawing a separation between managed and native code concerns. The result is neater and more maintainable code. We are exposing a simple *GetSqlFilestreamHandle* managed code method wrapper around the native *OpenSqlFilestream* function, so our *PhotoData* class and any other managed code data access classes need no awareness of the native code details.

That covers inserting new photos. Returning now to the *PhotoData* class, the remaining methods query by *PhotoId* and stream the selected photo file content from the database into an *Image* object for display. If you've been following along so far, you'll find the rest of our code to be understandable and intuitive since it follows a very similar pattern.

The *SelectPhoto* method accepts a photo ID that is located in the database and returns the string description from the database in an output parameter. The method's return value is a *System.Drawing.Image* object that we will populate with the BLOB streamed in from the database server's NTFS file system using *OpenSqlFilestream*, as shown here:

```
public static Image SelectPhoto(int photoId, out string desc)
{
    const string SelectCmd =
        "SELECT Description, Photo.PathName(), GET_FILESTREAM_TRANSACTION_CONTEXT()" +
        " FROM PhotoAlbum" +
        " WHERE PhotoId = @PhotoId";

    Image photo;

    using(SqlConnection conn = new SqlConnection(ConnStr))
    {
        conn.Open();

        using(SqlTransaction txn = conn.BeginTransaction())
        {
            string filePath;
            byte[] txnToken;

            using(SqlCommand cmd = new SqlCommand(SelectCmd, conn, txn))
            {
                cmd.Parameters.Add("@PhotoId", SqlDbType.Int).Value = photoId;

                using(SqlDataReader rdr = cmd.ExecuteReader(CommandBehavior.SingleRow))
                {
                    rdr.Read();
                    desc = rdr.GetSqlString(0).Value;
                    filePath = rdr.GetSqlString(1).Value;
                    txnToken = rdr.GetSqlBinary(2).Value;
                    rdr.Close();
                }
            }

            photo = LoadPhotoImage(filePath, txnToken);

            txn.Commit();
        }

        conn.Close();
    }

    return photo;
}
```

Once again, we start things off by opening a connection and initiating a transaction. We then execute a simple *SELECT* statement that queries the *PhotoAlbum* table for the record speci- fied by the photo ID and returns the description and full path to the image BLOB, as well as the FILESTREAM transactional context token. And once again we use the path name and transactional context to tie into the server's file system in the *LoadPhotoImage* method, as shown here:

```
private static Image LoadPhotoImage(string filePath, byte[] txnToken)
{
    Image photo;

    SafeFileHandle handle =
        NativeSqlClient.GetSqlFilestreamHandle
        (filePath, NativeSqlClient.DesiredAccess.Read, txnToken);

    using(FileStream fs = new FileStream(handle, FileAccess.Read))
    {
        photo = Image.FromStream(fs);
        fs.Close();
    }

    return photo;
}
```

Just as we did in the *GetOutputFileHandle* method for inserting new photos (only this time using *DesiredAccess.Read* instead of *DesiredAccess.ReadWrite*), we get a *SafeFileHandle* ob- ject from our *GetSqlFilestreamHandle* method defined in *NativeSqlClient*. We just saw how this method merely wraps and calls the native SQL client *OpenSqlFilestream* function needed to get the handle for streaming our BLOBs. With this handle, we once again create a new *FileStream*, this time opened for read-only access.

Once we have our *FileStream*, we can deliver the highest streaming performance possible by fire-hosing the BLOB content directly from the NTFS file system on the server into a new *System.Drawing.Image* object by using the static *Image.FromStream* method. The populated image is then passed back up to the form, where it is displayed by using the *Image* property of the *PictureBox* control.

The Payoff

It's time to see all of this in action and give the application a run! To insert a new photo, specify a unique (unused) photo ID, an image file, and a description in the top group box in the PhotoForm window, as shown in Figure 8-8, and then click Save.

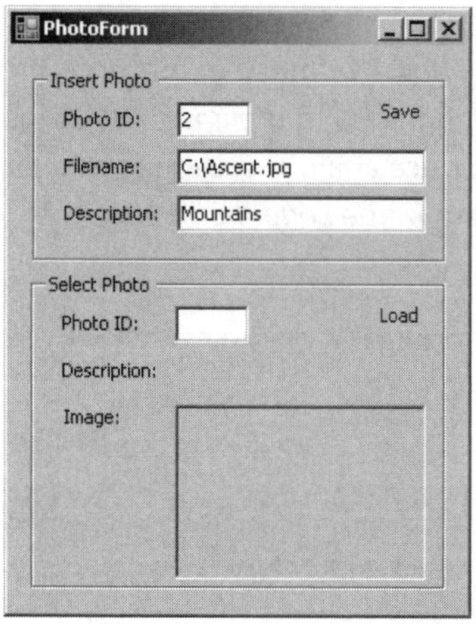

FIGURE 8-8 Inserting a new photo into FILESTREAM storage

To select and display the photo and its description back from the database, type its photo ID in the bottom group box, and then click Load. The photo is displayed, as shown in Figure 8-9.

FIGURE 8-9 Retrieving a photo from FILESTREAM storage

This simple application might be small, but it does demonstrate everything needed to leverage the power of FILESTREAM in your .NET client applications. The amount of code required is minimal, and the small amount of code that you do need to write implements fairly straightforward patterns that are easily adapted to various difference scenarios and UIs. For example, in our next FILESTREAM application, we'll stream content from a Hypertext Transfer Protocol (HTTP) service and consume it in a WPF client using the very same FILESTREAM principles that we applied in this Windows Forms application.

Creating a Streaming HTTP Service

We'll now build a simple service as a normal Microsoft ASP.NET Web Application project with a single PhotoService.aspx page. This page can be called by any HTTP client passing in a photo ID value appended to the URL query string; it will stream back the binary content for the specified photo from the database FILESTREAM storage in SQL Server to the client.

To build the service, follow these steps. Start Visual Studio, and then choose File, New, Project. Create a Microsoft Visual C# ASP.NET Web Application project named *PhotoLibraryHttpService* in a solution named *PhotoLibraryFileStreamDemo*, as shown in Figure 8-10.

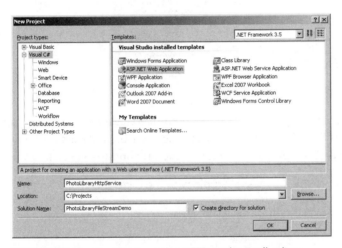

FIGURE 8-10 Creating the streaming HTTP service application

Delete the Default.aspx page created automatically by Visual Studio, and then add a new Web Form named PhotoService.aspx. Unlike a typical .aspx page, this page will not return HTML content. Instead, the page's code-behind class will stream out binary content from the database directly through the *Response* object. For this reason, we delete the HTML markup, leaving only the <@ *Page* %> directive that links the .aspx page with its code-behind class, as shown in Figure 8-11.

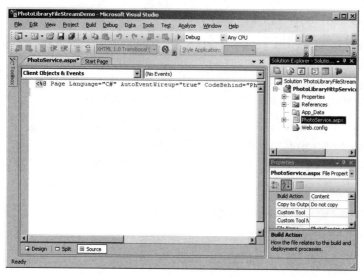

FIGURE 8-11 Creating the PhotoService.aspx page

Make this the default startup page by right-clicking PhotoService.aspx in Solution Explorer and then choosing Set As Start Page. Next, switch to the code-behind class file by right-clicking again on the PhotoService.aspx node in Solution Explorer and then choosing View Code.

Replace the starter code provided by Visual Studio with the code shown in Listing 8-6.

LISTING 8-6 Implementing code for the streaming photo service

```csharp
using System;
using System.Data;
using System.Data.SqlClient;
using System.Data.SqlTypes;
using System.IO;
using Microsoft.Win32.SafeHandles;

namespace PhotoLibraryHttpService
{
  public partial class PhotoService : System.Web.UI.Page
  {
    private const string ConnStr =
        "Data Source=.;Integrated Security=True;Initial Catalog=PhotoLibrary;";

    protected void Page_Load(object sender, EventArgs e)
    {
      int photoId = Convert.ToInt32(Request.QueryString["photoId"]);
      if (photoId == 0)
      {
        return;
      }
```

```csharp
        const string SelectCmd =
            "SELECT Photo.PathName(), GET_FILESTREAM_TRANSACTION_CONTEXT()" +
            " FROM PhotoAlbum" +
            " WHERE PhotoId = @PhotoId";

        using (SqlConnection conn = new SqlConnection(ConnStr))
        {
          conn.Open();

          using (SqlTransaction txn = conn.BeginTransaction())
          {
            string filePath;
            byte[] txnToken;

            using (SqlCommand cmd = new SqlCommand(SelectCmd, conn, txn))
            {
              cmd.Parameters.Add("@PhotoId", SqlDbType.Int).Value = photoId;

              using (SqlDataReader rdr = cmd.ExecuteReader(CommandBehavior.SingleRow))
              {
                rdr.Read();
                filePath = rdr.GetSqlString(0).Value;
                txnToken = rdr.GetSqlBinary(1).Value;
                rdr.Close();
              }
            }

            this.StreamPhotoImage(filePath, txnToken);

            txn.Commit();
          }

          conn.Close();
        }
      }

      private void StreamPhotoImage(string filePath, byte[] txnToken)
      {
        const int BlockSize = 1024 * 512;
        const string JpegContentType = "image/jpeg";

        SafeFileHandle handle =
            NativeSqlClient.GetSqlFilestreamHandle
            (filePath, NativeSqlClient.DesiredAccess.Read, txnToken);

        using (FileStream source = new FileStream(handle, FileAccess.Read))
        {
          byte[] buffer = new byte[BlockSize];
          int bytesRead;
          Response.BufferOutput = false;
          Response.ContentType = JpegContentType;
```

```
            while ((bytesRead = source.Read(buffer, 0, buffer.Length)) > 0)
            {
              Response.OutputStream.Write(buffer, 0, bytesRead);
              Response.Flush();
            }
            source.Close();
        }
      }
    }
  }
```

This code bears a strong resemblance to the code in our earlier Windows Forms application. The *Page_Load* method first retrieves the photo ID passed in via the *photoId* query string value. If no value is passed, the method returns without streaming anything back. Otherwise, as before, the photo file name and transaction context are obtained after establishing a connection and transaction on the database and invoking a *SELECT* statement calling the *PathName* method and the *GET_FILESTREAM_TRANSACTION_CONTEXT* function against the photo ID specified in the *WHERE* clause.

With these two key pieces of information in hand, the *StreamPhotoImage* method is called. The method begins by defining a *BlockSize* integer constant that is set to the reasonable value of 512 KB. As before, picture files larger than this will be streamed to the client in 512-KB pieces. Once again, an indirect call to *OpenSqlFilestream* is made through our *NativeSqlClient* wrapper class to obtain a *SafeFileHandle* that can be used to open an ordinary *FileStream* object and read the BLOB data from SQL Server. This means that you'll also need to create the *NativeSqlClient.cs* class file in this project as you did for the Windows application example (see Listing 8-5). Because this code is executing under the auspices of a Web server, you might also need to grant access to the photo storage directory for the account executing the Web page. This might be *ASPNET* or *NETWORK SERVICE* if you're using Internet Information Services (IIS) or your user account if you're executing the page using Visual Studio's development server.

Note As with all code in this book, the full FILESTREAM demo code in this chapter is available on the book's companion Web site.

Before streaming the binary photo content, we need to change two properties of the *Response* object. In an .aspx page, by default, the *Response* object's *BufferOutput* property is set to *true* and the *ContentType* is set to *text/html*. Here you'll change *BufferOutput* to *false* to deliver optimal streaming performance and inform the client that we're sending a JPEG image by changing the *ContentType* property to *image/jpeg*.

Using a *FileStream* object opened against *SafeFileHandle*, the code then reads from the database FILESTREAM storage in 512-KB chunks and streams to the client using the *Reponse. OutputStream.Write* and *Response.Flush* methods. This is implemented with a simple loop that reads content from the *FileStream* and sends it to the client via the *Response* object until the entire file is processed.

This completes our service application. Before moving on to build our WPF client, let's first test the service. Press F5 to start the application.

> **Note** Visual Studio may prompt that debugging is not enabled for the application and offer to modify the Web.config file to enable debugging. If this dialog box appears, click OK and allow Visual Studio to modify Web.config for server-side debugging. You might also receive a second dialog box informing you that script debugging is disabled in Internet Explorer. If this dialog box appears, click Yes to continue without client-side debugging enabled.

When Internet Explorer launches PhotoService.aspx, it displays an empty page because no photo ID is present in the URL's query string. In the Address bar, append *?photoId=2* to the URL and reload the page. The code-behind class retrieves photo ID 2 from the database and streams it back for display in the browser, as shown in Figure 8-12.

FIGURE 8-12 Streaming a photo over HTTP to Internet Explorer

We've created a functioning HTTP service application that streams pictures from the database to any HTTP client. It's now incredibly easy to build a small WPF client application that calls the service and displays photos. All that's needed is the proper URL with the desired photo ID specified in the query string, as you've just seen. We're using the ASP.NET Development Server provided by Visual Studio, which by default randomly assigns a port number on *localhost* (port 1045 was assigned this time, as indicated in Figure 8-12). We'll need to establish a fixed port number instead so that our WPF client can reliably construct a URL for calling the service. Any unused port number will suffice, so we'll just pick 22111 for this application. To set the port number, right-click the *PhotoLibraryHttpService* project in

Solution Explorer, and then choose Properties. Select the Web tab, select the Specific Port option, and then type **22111** for the port number, as shown in Figure 8-13.

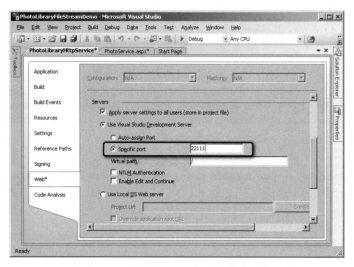

FIGURE 8-13 Setting a specific port number for the HTTP service application

Building the WPF Client

To build the WPF client, follow these steps. In Visual Studio, choose File, New, Project. Create a new Visual C# WPF Application project named *PhotoLibraryWpfClient*. Be sure to select Add To Solution in the Solution drop-down list, as shown in Figure 8-14, so that the project is added to the same *PhotoLibraryFileStreamDemo* solution that contains the *PhotoLibraryHttpService* project.

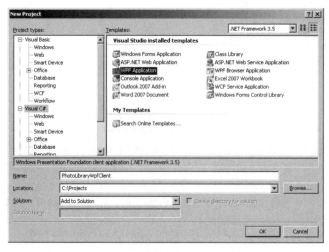

FIGURE 8-14 Creating the streaming WPF client application

Drag *Label*, *TextBox*, *Button*, and *MediaElement* controls from the toolbox, and drop them onto the Window1.xaml design surface. Adjust the control formatting and layout so that the window appears similar to that shown in Figure 8-15.

FIGURE 8-15 Simple FILESTREAM WPF UI window

The *MediaElement* control in WPF is a scaled-down media player that is capable of rendering a variety of multimedia types, including images and video, from any source. All we need to do is set its *Source* property to a URL that it can stream its content from. Double-click the *Button* control, and then insert the following code in the button's event handler:

```
private void btnDownload_Click(object sender, RoutedEventArgs e)
{
    string url =
        "http://localhost:22111/PhotoService.aspx?photoId=" +
        this.txtPhotoId.Text;

    this.mediaElement1.Source = new Uri(url);
}
```

This code simply constructs a URL to the PhotoService.aspx page that we know to be running on *localhost* port 22111, passing the desired photo ID in the query string. When the *MediaElement* control's *Source* property is set to that URL, the control automatically calls the service and renders the photo that is streamed from the database to the service and then from the service to the WPF client over HTTP.

To see it work, run the application, and request photo ID 2 for display, as shown in Figure 8-16.

FIGURE 8-16 Streaming a photo from the database over HTTP to a WPF client application

Summary

For applications that work with BLOB data, the new FILESTREAM feature in SQL Server 2008 greatly enhances the storage and performance of unstructured content in the database by leveraging the NTFS file system. It does this while maintaining logical integration between the database and file system that includes transactional support. As a result, we no longer need to make compromises in efficiency and complexity as we did in the past when making the choice between storing BLOB data inside or outside the database.

You also learned how to use the *OpenSqlFilestream* native client API function to deliver high-performance streaming of BLOB content between the file system managed by SQL Server and your Windows, Web, and WPF applications. You can apply the concepts you learned in this chapter across a wide range of applications that require integration between the relational database and a streaming file system.

Chapter 9
Geospatial Data Types

—Leonard Lobel

Geospatial support is a powerful new extension to the core database engine in Microsoft SQL Server 2008. Also referred to simply as *spatial*, this feature allows you to store and manipulate shapes, sizes, and locations using the new *geometry* and *geography* data types and to calculate areas, distances, and intersections over that spatial data. These capabilities enable location awareness for applications in which geographic data can be processed at the database level. In this chapter, we explore the concepts behind spatial data and how this new support in SQL Server 2008 can be used to integrate location intelligence into your database applications.

 Note We use the terms *spatial* and *geospatial* interchangeably throughout this chapter.

Geospatial capabilities are germane to a relatively small niche of database development projects, but we can reasonably expect business requirements for these capabilities to increase over time—even if only peripherally. Although Global Positioning System (GPS) and mapping applications such as Microsoft Virtual Earth and MapQuest are the most typical use cases that come to mind when one thinks geospatial, you don't need to be rendering graphical maps in order to make use of spatial data. Practical uses can also be found in traditional business applications. For example, customers that visit your e-commerce site can search for products and retrieve a list of branch locations stocking those products, ordered from nearest to farthest based on the customer's location.

SQL Server 2008 Spaces Out

By adding rich spatial support to SQL Server 2008, Microsoft keeps pace with other major vendors that have already been providing this feature for quite some time and now enables SQL Server developers to enjoy spatial capabilities at the database level. The database itself is now capable of understanding spatial data as a native data type and can efficiently store and process instances of these types for you. It is no longer necessary to perform spatial calculations at the application level, either through custom written code (which is far from trivial) or by using a third-party library (which is far from inexpensive).

The algorithms used in geospatial operations are very complex (to say the least), and a comprehensive treatment of the topic is well beyond the scope of our discussions here. At the same time, abstraction of complexity is a key aspect of these new spatial data types.

The geospatial support in SQL Server 2008 is designed specifically to enable the rapid development of spatial capabilities in your database without requiring deep knowledge of how to program spatial calculations. In this chapter, you'll learn how to quickly get started with basic spatial operations by first understanding the two basic spatial models and then walking through several code demonstrations that use the new *geometry* and *geography* data types in a variety of scenarios.

> **More Info** SQL Server 2008 supports the OpenGIS Simple Features for SQL standard, which is a specification published by an international regulatory body known as the Open Geospatial Consortium (OGC). More than 70 methods are provided for working with the new spatial types in SQL Server 2008, although we examine only the more common ones in our code demonstrations. You can download a PDF of the specification from *http://www.opengeospatial.org/standards/sfs*.

Spatial Models

Let's begin our discussion with an explanation of the two basic geospatial models: the *planar* and model *geodetic* model.

Planar (Flat-Earth) Model

The planar model is a flat surface where shapes are plotted using two-dimensional x- and y-coordinates. These coordinates are based on an arbitrary measurement system, so you can define any measurement unit you want (for example, centimeters, meters, kilometers, inches, feet, miles, pixels, and so on).

It makes sense to work with the planar model when dealing with relatively small areas (such as building floor plans), or even larger areas that are either conceptually flat or still small enough where the earth's curvature does not skew the outcome of area and distance calculations. Realize that projecting the earth onto a planar surface results in a spatial distortion that makes it impossible to accurately track measurements over large spaces across the globe. For example, if you draw a straight line from New York to Tel Aviv on the map shown in Figure 9-1, that line does not accurately represent the precise distance between those two cities. In reality, the actual flight path would be represented by that line being stretched and curved against the shape of the globe. Thus, the planar model is clearly inappropriate for calculating global long-distance trajectories.

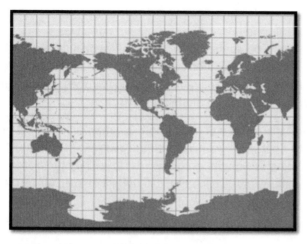

FIGURE 9-1 Planar spatial model (flat-earth projection)

Geodetic (Round-Earth) Model

If you need to perform spatial calculations that span large areas of the earth, your database application needs adopt the widely held belief that the world is round. To correctly plot and compute global shapes and intersections, the curvature of the earth must be taken into consideration. The geodetic model (depicted in Figure 9-2) represents locations on the planet using the earth's longitude and latitude coordinate system to support spatial capabilities on a planetary scale.

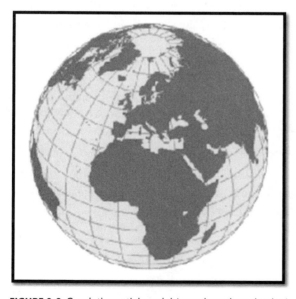

FIGURE 9-2 Geodetic spatial model (round-earth projection)

Spatial Data Types

SQL Server 2008 introduces two new data types for working with spatial data—one for each of the two spatial models (as you might have guessed). The *geometry* data type is provided to store and process spatial data using the planar (flat-earth) model, while its counterpart *geography* supports the geodetic (round-earth) model.

One nice thing about the new spatial types is that they both use many of the same methods for common spatial calculations. So if you're working with the geodetic model, you'll be using longitude and latitude coordinates with the *geography* data type. For the planar model, you'll be using x- and y-coordinates with the *geometry* data type. But in either case, you'll use many of the same methods for dealing with your spatial entities.

Defining Space with Well-Known Text

Shapes are projected onto spatial models using *vector objects*—which are collections of points, lines, and polygons (closed shapes). Both the *geometry* and *geography* data types support the same Well-Known Text (WKT) markup language, which is a convention that expresses the vector objects that you define using a syntax governed by the OGC.

Table 9-1 shows some examples of WKT strings.

TABLE 9-1 Examples of WKT Strings

WKT String	Description
POINT(6 10)	A single point at xy-coordinates 6, 10
POINT(-111.06687 45.01188)	A single point on the earth (longitude/latitude coordinates)
LINESTRING(3 4,10 50,20 25)	A two-part line, drawn between three points specified as xy-coordinates
POLYGON((*-75.17031 39.95601, -75.16786 39.95778,* *-75.17921 39.96874, -75.18441 39.96512,* *-75.17031 39.95601))*	An enclosed shape on the earth drawn between the points specified as longitude/latitude coordinates

As you can see, the same WKT syntax is used for expressing spatial elements using either the planar or the geodetic model. Also notice that geodetic coordinates are always expressed in WKT with the longitude value first, followed by the latitude value.

With this very basic understanding of geospatial concepts, we're ready to start working with spatial data in SQL Server 2008.

Working with *geometry*

Our first example shows how to define and store shapes representing town districts and avenues using the *geometry* data type and then demonstrates how to query this data to return a list of the avenues that run through each district. This little one-horse town has only three districts and two main avenues and is small enough to be expressed on a planar (flat) surface using the *geometry* data type. As we progress through the example, you'll learn how to use a number of common geospatial methods with this data type.

Figure 9-3 shows the shapes that map out the town and the xy-coordinates for the points of each shape. The three districts are polygons (closed shapes), and the two avenues are line strings. We will store these shapes in a SQL Server database using the *geometry* data type, expressing their coordinates in WKT syntax. Then we'll use the *STIntersects* and *STIntersection* methods to execute a query that returns the list of intersecting districts and avenues.

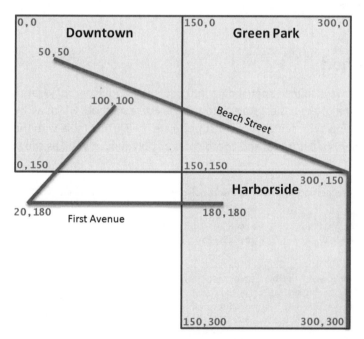

FIGURE 9-3 Small town map on a flat (planar) surface

> **Note** To simplify matters, our coordinate system in this example uses an arbitrary unit of measurement with square-shaped districts that are 150 by 150 in size. You might be surprised to learn that longitude and latitude coordinates can also be used with the *geometry* type. In that scenario, the coordinates are mapped to a flat projection of the earth just as with xy-coordinates. However, this does introduce spatial distortion that will result in errors for calculations over very large areas, as explained. Such distortion can be considered minuscule and insignificant for small areas, but for larger areas in which the discrepancy becomes unacceptable, the *geography* data type (which works only with longitude and latitude coordinates) must be used.

The first thing we need to do is create tables to hold the shapes that define our districts and avenues. The *District* table will store the polygons representing Downtown, Green Park, and Harborside in a *geometry* column named *DistrictGeo*. Similarly, we'll create a *Street* table to store the line strings representing Beach Street and First Avenue in a *geometry* column named *StreetGeo*, as shown in Listing 9-1.

LISTING 9-1 Creating the *District* and *Street* tables with *geometry* columns

```
CREATE TABLE District
  (DistrictId    int PRIMARY KEY,
   DistrictName  nvarchar(20),
   DistrictGeo   geometry)

CREATE TABLE Street
  (StreetId    int PRIMARY KEY,
   StreetName  nvarchar(20),
   StreetGeo   geometry)
```

The *Parse* Method

There are a number of ways to load spatial data into *geometry* and *geography* data type columns and variables. One of the easiest ways is to use the *Parse* method, which allows you to express your shapes using WKT syntax. We'll first populate the *District* table with the three districts along with their shapes, sizes, and coordinates as polygons in WKT, as shown in Listing 9-2.

LISTING 9-2 Using the *Parse* method with WKT to insert polygons into *geometry* columns

```
INSERT INTO District VALUES (1, 'Downtown',
  geometry::Parse('POLYGON ((0 0, 150 0, 150 150, 0 150, 0 0))'))

INSERT INTO District VALUES (2, 'Green Park',
  geometry::Parse('POLYGON ((300 0, 150 0, 150 150, 300 150, 300 0))'))

INSERT INTO District VALUES (3, 'Harborside',
  geometry::Parse('POLYGON ((150 150, 300 150, 300 300, 150 300, 150 150))'))
```

Notice how the square shapes representing each district are conveyed in WKT format as polygon elements. Each point connecting the lines of the polygon is expressed as an xy-coordinate. Unlike line strings (which we'll use shortly to define our streets), a polygon always represents a closed shape. In WKT, the coordinate for the final point in any polygon must be the same coordinate used for the starting point in the polygon in order to close the shape.

You can see how all of the district polygons in the preceding code close their shapes in this manner. If you attempt to express a polygon without closing the shape, you will receive a *FormatException*, as follows:

```
Msg 6522, Level 16, State 1, Line 1
A .NET Framework error occurred during execution of user-defined routine or aggregate
"geometry":
System.FormatException: 24306: The Polygon input is not valid because the start and end
points of the ring are not the same. Each ring of a polygon must have the same start and end
points.
```

This rather unfriendly error message also alludes to the fact that polygons can have multiple rings defined inside the exterior ring. This means that you can define complex polygons that have one or more "holes" inside them using WKT.

Now let's populate the *Street* table with line strings, as shown in Listing 9-3.

LISTING 9-3 Inserting line strings into *geometry* columns

```
INSERT INTO Street VALUES (1, 'First Avenue',
  geometry::Parse('LINESTRING (100 100, 20 180, 180 180)'))

INSERT INTO Street VALUES (2, 'Beach Street',
  geometry::Parse('LINESTRING (300 300, 300 150, 50 50)'))
```

The line string elements used to store the streets of the town specify the points that describe the paths of each street on the map. In this example, each street has three points expressing the two-part line strings for First Avenue and Beach Street.

The *STIntersects* Method

With our town data populated, we're ready to perform our first spatial query. We'd like to find out which streets intersect which districts, so we'll begin by composing a *CROSS JOIN* query that returns all possible combinations of districts and streets. Then we'll qualify the query with a *WHERE* clause that filters the results to report only those district and street combinations that actually intersect with one another. This is easily achieved by invoking the spatial method *STIntersects* on one *geometry* value, passing in a second *geometry* value as its parameter, and receiving back a *bit* (Boolean) value of 1 (true) or 0 (false) telling us whether the two *geometry* shapes intersect with each other, as follows:

```
-- Return all district/street intersections using STIntersects() method
SELECT
  S.StreetName,
  D.DistrictName
FROM     District AS D CROSS JOIN Street AS S
WHERE    S.StreetGeo.STIntersects(D.DistrictGeo) = 1
ORDER BY S.StreetName
```

When we run this query, the results indicate that Beach Street runs through all three of our districts, whereas First Avenue runs through only Downtown and Harborside but not Green Park, as shown here:

```
StreetName             DistrictName
--------------------   --------------------
Beach Street           Downtown
Beach Street           Green Park
Beach Street           Harborside
First Avenue           Downtown
First Avenue           Harborside

(5 row(s) affected)
```

Let's now select from the *District* and *Street* table so that we can see how SQL Server stores raw spatial data as a binary stream:

```
SELECT * FROM Street
SELECT * FROM District
```

Here are the results:

```
StreetId     StreetName            StreetGeo
-----------  --------------------  --------------------------------------------------------------------
1            First Avenue          0x0000000001040300000000000000000059400000000000000594000
00000000003440000000000008066400000000000080664000000000008066400100000001000000000100000
0FFFFFFFF0000000002
2            Beach Street          0000000001040300000000000000000C072400000000000C072400000
000000C072400000000000C062400000000000000049400000000000004940010000000100000000010000000FF
FFFFFF0000000002

(2 row(s) affected)

DistrictId   DistrictName          DistrictGeo
-----------  --------------------  --------------------------------------------------------------------

1            Downtown
0000000001040500000000000000000000000000000000000000000000000000000000000000000000C0624000000000
00C062400000000000C062400000000000C06240000000000000000000000000000000000000000000000000000000100
000002000000001000000FFFFFFFF0000000003
2            Green Park
0000000001040500000000000000000C07240000000000000000000000000000000C06240000000000000000000000000
00C062400000000000C062400000000000C072400000000000C062400000000000C07240000000000000000000000100
000002000000001000000FFFFFFFF0000000003
3            Harborside
0000000001040500000000000000000C062400000000000C062400000000000C072400000000000C0624000000000
00C072400000000000C072400000000000C062400000000000C072400000000000C062400000000000C062400100
000002000000001000000FFFFFFFF0000000003

(3 row(s) affected)
```

This output reveals that spatial data requires binary values that are quite large. Just look at the size of the *geometry* values representing the polygons in the *District* table, which are simple square-shaped polygons. In reality, the irregularly shaped polygons that express planetary shapes such as countries and cities have many sides, and thus the space requirement for storing such entities increases significantly. Because the *geometry* and *geography* types are system Common Language Runtime (CLR) types—which are nothing more really than SQL CLR user-defined types (UDTs)—eliminating the 8-KB limit on SQL CLR UDTs that existed in SQL Server 2005 was an absolute requirement for Microsoft in order for SQL Server 2008 to support geospatial data, since clearly complex shapes can easily exceed 8 KB.

Note SQL CLR and the elimination of the 8-KB maximum size constraint in SQL Server 2008 for SQL CLR UDTs are covered in Chapter 3.

The *ToString* Method

A common pattern for system CLR types is to provide a *ToString* method that can be used as a complement to the *Parse* method. In the same manner that *Parse* translates a WKT string into a raw binary value for internal storage, the *ToString* method translates any binary spatial value back into WKT for human readability.

The following query uses the *Parse* method to display the districts and streets as WKT strings:

```
SELECT StreetId, StreetName, StreetGeo.ToString() AS StreetGeo FROM Street
SELECT DistrictId, DistrictName, DistrictGeo.ToString() AS DistrictGeo FROM District
```

Here are the results:

```
StreetId     StreetName           StreetGeo

-----------  -------------------  -----------------------------------------------------------
1            First Avenue         LINESTRING (100 100, 20 180, 180 180)
2            Beach Street         LINESTRING (300 300, 300 150, 50 50)

(2 row(s) affected)

DistrictId   DistrictName         DistrictGeo
-----------  -------------------  -----------------------------------------------------------

1            Downtown             POLYGON ((0 0, 0 150, 150 150, 150 0, 0 0))
2            Green Park           POLYGON ((300 0, 150 0, 150 150, 300 150, 300 0))
3            Harborside           POLYGON ((150 150, 300 150, 300 300, 150 300, 150 150))

(3 row(s) affected)
```

The *STIntersection* Method

Earlier, we used the *STIntersects* method to tell us whether two spatial entities intersect with each another. But you can do more than just find out whether two entities intersect—you can actually obtain a shape that represents the overlapping area of intersection in a new spatial entity. The following is a modified version of the *STIntersects* query we ran earlier that also uses the *STIntersection* method to report which *pieces* of each road cut through each district:

```
-- Also show the road fragments that intersect each district using STIntersection()
SELECT
  S.StreetName,
  D.DistrictName,
  S.StreetGeo.STIntersection(D.DistrictGeo).ToString() AS Intersection
  FROM     District AS D CROSS JOIN Street AS S
  WHERE    S.StreetGeo.STIntersects(D.DistrictGeo) = 1
  ORDER BY S.StreetName
```

It's easy to read the road fragments as line strings by applying the *ToString* method to the result of the *geometry* value returned by *STIntersection*, as shown here:

```
StreetName            DistrictName          Intersection
--------------------  --------------------  -----------------------------------
Beach Street          Downtown              LINESTRING (150 90, 50 50)
Beach Street          Green Park            LINESTRING (300 150, 150 90)
Beach Street          Harborside            LINESTRING (300 300, 300 150)
First Avenue          Downtown              LINESTRING (50 150, 100 100)
First Avenue          Harborside            LINESTRING (180 180, 150 180)

(5 row(s) affected)
```

Notice that the portions of First Avenue that do not run through any of the three districts are excluded from the intersection shapes returned by the results.

The *STDimension* Method

The *STDimension* method accepts any *geometry* or *geography* data type instance and returns a number (0, 1, or 2) that indicates how many dimensions are defined by the shape in the instance. Single points have 0 dimensions, lines and line strings have 1 dimension, and polygons (closed shapes) have 2 dimensions. That means that all of the districts in our town are two-dimensional objects, while the avenues are one-dimensional objects. The following code displays the dimensions for the spatial objects currently stored in our database:

```
SELECT Street.StreetId, Street.StreetName, StreetGeo.STDimension() AS Dimensions FROM Street

SELECT District.DistrictId, District.DistrictName, DistrictGeo.STDimension() AS Dimensions
  FROM District
```

Here are the results:

```
StreetId    StreetName              Dimensions
----------- ----------------------- -----------
1           First Avenue            1
2           Beach Street            1

(2 row(s) affected)

DistrictId  DistrictName            Dimensions
----------- ----------------------- -----------
1           Downtown                2
2           Green Park              2
3           Harborside              2

(3 row(s) affected)
```

Working with *geography*

All of the methods we've covered for the *geometry* type work just the same for the *geography* type. The only real difference from our perspective is that we must use longitude and latitude values. Internally, as explained, SQL Server automatically compensates for the earth's curvature when performing calculations against our *geography* data. In the rest of our discussion of geospatial support in SQL Server 2008, we'll show applied use of the *geography* data type.

Another subtle but important difference to be aware of is that *geography* points must be defined in a counterclockwise fashion. You can load *geometry* points in either clockwise or counterclockwise order, but attempting to load a *geography* shape in clockwise order will result in a *GLArgumentException*, as follows (which essentially tells you that you're trying to turn the world inside out):

```
Msg 6522, Level 16, State 1, Line 1
A .NET Framework error occurred during execution of user-defined routine or aggregate
"geography":
Microsoft.SqlServer.Types.GLArgumentException: 24205: The specified input does not represent
a valid geography instance because it exceeds a single hemisphere. Each geography instance
must fit inside a single hemisphere. A common reason for this error is that a polygon has
the wrong ring orientation.
```

How do you get your hands on longitudes and latitudes? There are many ways. Coordinates for large cities and other major locations in the world can be easily obtained on the Web with a quick search. The old-fashioned way still works too—pilots can acquire them from sectional maps, for example. You can also use Microsoft Streets & Trips 2008, which has a "location sensor" tool that will tell you the longitude and latitude coordinates for any point or shape drawn on the map using the mouse. This Streets & Trips feature was used to obtain the coordinates for our next example.

On Your Mark ...

We'll use a real-life event to learn about spatial area, length, and distance calculations. In this application, we are mapping the Pro Cycling Tour held in Philadelphia (which entered its 24th year in 2008). Using coordinates obtained from Streets & Trips, we will build a database that stores different areas of the bike race. Then we'll see how to easily calculate the area and length of different regions using more new spatial methods.

The map for our application is shown in Figure 9-4. The entire race area is contained in one large 14-sided polygon. Within the race area, there are two popular locations where spectators gather and take pictures. One is the Parkway Area to the south, where the race starts and finishes, and the other is the Wall Area to the north.

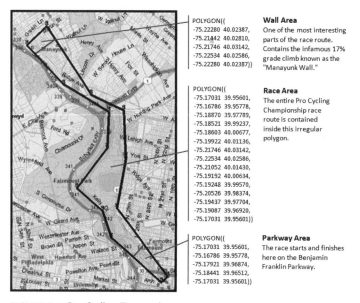

POLYGON((
-75.22280 40.02387,
-75.21442 40.02810,
-75.21746 40.03142,
-75.22534 40.02586,
-75.22280 40.02387))

Wall Area
One of the most interesting parts of the race route. Contains the infamous 17% grade climb known as the "Manayunk Wall."

POLYGON((
-75.17031 39.95601,
-75.16786 39.95778,
-75.18870 39.97789,
-75.18521 39.99237,
-75.18603 40.00677,
-75.19922 40.01136,
-75.21746 40.03142,
-75.22534 40.02586,
-75.21052 40.01430,
-75.19192 40.00634,
-75.19248 39.99570,
-75.20526 39.98374,
-75.19437 39.97704,
-75.19087 39.96920,
-75.17031 39.95601))

Race Area
The entire Pro Cycling Championship race route is contained inside this irregular polygon.

POLYGON((
-75.17031 39.95601,
-75.16786 39.95778,
-75.17921 39.96874,
-75.18441 39.96512,
-75.17031 39.95601))

Parkway Area
The race starts and finishes here on the Benjamin Franklin Parkway.

FIGURE 9-4 Pro Cycling Tour region map

In this application, we'll combine spatial features with FILESTREAM. Photos submitted by spectators will be stored in the database as binary large objects (BLOBs) in the file system using the techniques you learned earlier, during our FILESTREAM coverage in Chapter 8. Refer to the section "Enabling FILESTREAM for the Machine" in that chapter, which describes how to enable FILESTREAM using SQL Server Configuration Manager. Then execute the code in Listing 9-4 to create the FILESTREAM-enabled database for our application. (Note that the path to the database, C:\EventLibrary in this example, must exist before the database can be created.)

LISTING 9-4 Creating the *EventLibrary* database

```
USE master
GO

EXEC sp_configure filestream_access_level, 2
RECONFIGURE
GO

CREATE DATABASE EventLibrary
 ON PRIMARY
  (NAME = EventLibrary_data,
   FILENAME = 'C:\EventLibrary\EventLibrary_data.mdf'),
  FILEGROUP FileStreamGroup1 CONTAINS FILESTREAM
  (NAME = EventLibrary_group2,
   FILENAME = 'C:\EventLibrary\Events')
 LOG ON
  (NAME = EventLibrary_log,
   FILENAME = 'C:\EventLibrary\EventLibrary_log.ldf')
GO

USE EventLibrary
GO
```

Once the database is created, create the *EventRegion* table to hold the different map regions and then populate the table with the polygons representing the three regions being mapped, as shown in Listing 9-5.

LISTING 9-5 Creating the *EventRegion* table and populating it with geographical data

```
CREATE TABLE EventRegion
 (RegionId    int PRIMARY KEY,
  RegionName  nvarchar(32),
  MapShape    geography)

INSERT INTO EventRegion VALUES(1, 'Parkway Area', geography::Parse('POLYGON((
  -75.17031 39.95601, -75.16786 39.95778, -75.17921 39.96874,
  -75.18441 39.96512, -75.17031 39.95601 ))'))

INSERT INTO EventRegion VALUES(2, 'Wall Area', geography::Parse('POLYGON((
  -75.22280 40.02387, -75.21442 40.02810, -75.21746 40.03142,
  -75.22534 40.02586, -75.22280 40.02387))'))

INSERT INTO EventRegion VALUES(3, 'Race Area', geography::Parse('POLYGON((
  -75.17031 39.95601, -75.16786 39.95778, -75.18870 39.97789, -75.18521 39.99237,
  -75.18603 40.00677, -75.19922 40.01136, -75.21746 40.03142, -75.22534 40.02586,
  -75.21052 40.01430, -75.19192 40.00634, -75.19248 39.99570, -75.20526 39.98374,
  -75.19437 39.97704, -75.19087 39.96920, -75.17031 39.95601))'))
```

Now query for the list of regions you just created in the *EventRegion* table:

```
SELECT * FROM EventRegion
```

SQL Server Management Studio (SSMS) naturally executes this simple query and displays a result set with the three regions. The results are returned as plain text, which has always been the case with SQL Server—until now, that is. Because now SSMS recognizes that this result set contains spatial data, and so it adds a new tab named Spatial Results inconspicuously inserted between the familiar Results and Messages tabs. Click this tab, and you will be presented with a graphical rendering of the three regions in the new spatial results viewer, as shown in Figure 9-5.

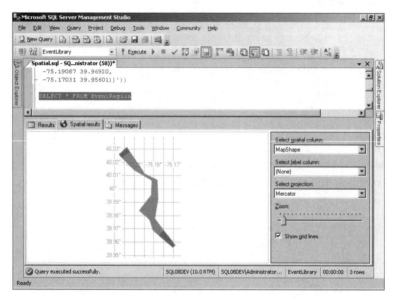

FIGURE 9-5 Viewing spatial data results in SQL Server Management Studio's new spatial viewer

A picture is worth a thousand words, as the old saying goes, and just a glance at this chart visually confirms that our *EventRegion* coordinates "look" correct. This simple yet awesome new feature in SSMS is a great benefit for spatial query development. (The spatial viewer in SSMS does, in fact, use the Dundas charting controls that Microsoft acquired in 2007.) If your result set includes multiple spatial data columns, you can graph any one of them using the first drop-down list to the right of the chart. You can add legend labels based on another column in the result set by using the second drop-down list. And with the third drop-down list, you can observe the different skewing effects that occur when flattening the globe using different flat-earth projection models. This drop-down list is applicable only to *geography* (geodetic) data and does not appear when you are viewing *geometry* (planar) data. You can also set the chart's magnification level and toggle the display of grid lines by using the slider and check box controls beneath the drop-down lists.

The *STArea* and *STLength* Methods

Area and length (perimeter) calculations are easily performed using the *STArea* and *STLength* methods. The following query displays the area and length of each region, sorted from largest to smallest:

```
SELECT
 RegionName,
 ROUND(MapShape.STArea(), 2) AS Area,
 ROUND(MapShape.STLength(), 2) AS Length
FROM
 EventRegion
ORDER BY
 MapShape.STArea() DESC
```

Here are the results:

```
RegionName                            Area                    Length
------------------------------------- ----------------------- -----------------------
Race Area                             6432902.35              22165.07
Parkway Area                          689476.79               4015.39
Wall Area                             334024.82               2529.11

(3 row(s) affected)
```

Spatial Reference IDs

The unit of measurement used to express these results is based on the Spatial Reference ID (SRID) of the spatial data type instance. By default, *geography* instances in SQL Server 2008 use an SRID value of 4326, which is based on the metric system. Therefore, the area and length results shown in the preceding code are given in square meters and meters, respectively.

You can execute the statement *SELECT * FROM sys.spatial_reference_systems* to obtain a list of all the SRIDs supported by SQL Server. Some of the SRIDs support different measurement systems, including foot, Clarke's foot, Indian foot, US survey foot, and German legal meter. Two *geography* instances with different SRIDs are incompatible with each other, and spatial calculations cannot be performed between them. See SQL Server Books Online or *http:// msdn.microsoft.com/en-us/library/bb964707(SQL.100).aspx* for more information about SRIDs.

Building Out the *EventLibrary* Database

Now it's time to create the *EventPhoto* table, as shown in Listing 9-6. The *RowId* and *Photo* columns respectively provide the *ROWGUIDCOL* and *varbinary(max) FILESTREAM* columns required for FILESTREAM storage and access to binary photo files, as we explored in depth in Chapter 8. The *Location* column stores the point (longitude and latitude) where the photo was taken in a *geography* data type. This table will be populated with several photos using the very same techniques we used in our earlier photo library FILESTREAM application from Chapter 8.

LISTING 9-6 Creating the *EventPhoto* table to hold photos and the locations where they were taken

```
CREATE TABLE EventPhoto (
 PhotoId int PRIMARY KEY,
 RowId uniqueidentifier ROWGUIDCOL NOT NULL UNIQUE DEFAULT NEWSEQUENTIALID(),
 Description varchar(max),
 Location geography,
 Photo varbinary(max) FILESTREAM DEFAULT(0x))
```

More Info   GPS devices for digital single-lens reflex (DSLR) cameras are available that provide real-time position (longitude and latitude) information to the camera, which is then recorded to each digital image file. This essentially "location-stamps" each photo you take, which would make it trivial to populate the *Location* column in the *EventPhoto* table. (In our demo code, of course, we'll hard-code the longitudes and latitudes of each photo.) Just run a Web search on "DSLR GPS" to get a list of readily available and reasonably priced products.

We'll create a Windows Forms application in C# that allows the user to select a region and re-trieve all the photos taken in that region. Once again, using the same FILESTREAM techniques we've already used for the *PhotoLibrary* application in Chapter 8, the user can then select a photo for display in a picture box control.

To support this application, we'll write several stored procedures, as shown in Listing 9-7. *GetRegions* is called to retrieve a list of all the region IDs and names, which gets bound to a combo box for the user to make a region selection. *GetRegionPhotos* accepts the ID of the region selected by the user and returns a list of all the photo IDs and descriptions of pictures taken in the selected region, which gets bound to a list box for the user to make a photo se-lection. The photo list is obtained by using the *STIntersects* method you learned about earlier in this chapter with the *geometry* type. Last, *GetPhotoForFilestream* returns the *PathName* and *GET_FILESTREAM_TRANSACTION_CONTEXT* values for calling *OpenSqlFilestream* to re-trieve and display the photo selected by the user.

LISTING 9-7 Creating the stored procedures for the sample event media application

```
CREATE PROCEDURE GetRegions AS
 BEGIN
     SELECT RegionId, RegionName FROM EventRegion
 END
GO
```

```
CREATE PROCEDURE GetRegionPhotos(@RegionId int) AS
  BEGIN

    DECLARE @MapShape geography

    -- Get the shape of the region
    SELECT   @MapShape = MapShape
     FROM     EventRegion
     WHERE    RegionId = @RegionId

    -- Get all photos taken in the region
    SELECT   PhotoId, Description
     FROM     EventPhoto
     WHERE    Location.STIntersects(@MapShape) = 1

  END
GO

CREATE PROCEDURE GetPhotoForFilestream(@PhotoId int) AS
  BEGIN

    -- Called by ADO.NET client during open transaction to get
    -- a SafeFileHandle from OpenSqlFilestream
    SELECT   Photo.PathName(), GET_FILESTREAM_TRANSACTION_CONTEXT()
     FROM     EventPhoto
     WHERE    PhotoId = @PhotoId

  END
GO
```

Creating the Event Media Client Application

To create the client application, start Microsoft Visual Studio 2008, and then create a
new C# Windows Forms application named *EventMediaSpatialApp*. Design a form named
PhotoSearchForm with a combo box for selecting a region, a link label to search for photos
by region, and a list box for displaying the results. Also include a picture box control for displaying the photo selected from the list box and a link label that we'll use to bulk load four
photo files into the *EventPhoto* table. After performing some aesthetic alignment and formatting, your form should appear something like the one shown in Figure 9-6.

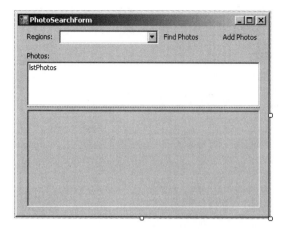

FIGURE 9-6 *EventMedia* Windows user interface (UI) form

Listing 9-8 contains the complete code behind the form, which requires no detailed explanation if you've read through our coverage of FILESTREAM in Chapter 8. As already mentioned, it calls the stored procedures we created earlier to populate the combo box with regions and to query for all photos taken in any region selected by the user. When a photo is selected, it streams the image from the FILESTREAM column in the database to the picture box control by using *OpenSqlFilestream*. As with our earlier FILESTREAM example in Chapter 8, the actual call to *OpenSqlFilestream* is encapsulated in a helper class that you'll need to add named *NativeSqlClient* (see Listing 8-5).

LISTING 9-8 *EventMedia* client application code

```
using System;
using System.Data;
using System.Data.SqlClient;
using System.Drawing;
using System.IO;
using System.Windows.Forms;

using Microsoft.Win32.SafeHandles;

namespace EventMediaSpatialApp
{
  public partial class PhotoSearchForm : Form
  {
    private const string ConnStr =
        "Data Source=.;Integrated Security=True;Initial Catalog=EventLibrary;";

    public PhotoSearchForm()
    {
      InitializeComponent();
    }
```

```csharp
protected override void OnLoad(EventArgs e)
{
  base.OnLoad(e);

  this.LoadRegions();
}

private void lnkAddPhotos_LinkClicked
 (object sender, LinkLabelLinkClickedEventArgs e)
{
  this.AddPhotos();
}

private void lnkSearch_LinkClicked
 (object sender, LinkLabelLinkClickedEventArgs e)
{
  this.FindRegionPhotos();
}

private void lstPhotos_SelectedIndexChanged(object sender, EventArgs e)
{
  this.DisplayPhoto();
}

private void LoadRegions()
{
  using (SqlDataAdapter adp = new SqlDataAdapter("GetRegions", ConnStr))
  {
    adp.SelectCommand.CommandType = CommandType.StoredProcedure;
    DataSet ds = new DataSet();
    adp.Fill(ds);
    this.cboRegions.DataSource = ds.Tables[0];
    this.cboRegions.ValueMember = "RegionId";
    this.cboRegions.DisplayMember = "RegionName";
  }
}

private void FindRegionPhotos()
{
  this.lstPhotos.SelectedIndexChanged -=
   new System.EventHandler(this.lstPhotos_SelectedIndexChanged);

  int regionId = (int)this.cboRegions.SelectedValue;

  using (SqlDataAdapter adp = new SqlDataAdapter("GetRegionPhotos", ConnStr))
  {
    adp.SelectCommand.CommandType = CommandType.StoredProcedure;
    adp.SelectCommand.Parameters.AddWithValue("@RegionId", regionId);
    DataSet ds = new DataSet();
    adp.Fill(ds);
    this.lstPhotos.DataSource = ds.Tables[0];
    this.lstPhotos.ValueMember = "PhotoId";
    this.lstPhotos.DisplayMember = "Description";
  }
```

```
    this.lstPhotos.SelectedIndexChanged +=
     new System.EventHandler(this.lstPhotos_SelectedIndexChanged);
    this.DisplayPhoto();
}

private void DisplayPhoto()
{
  int photoId = (int)this.lstPhotos.SelectedValue;
  this.picImage.Image = this.GetPhoto(photoId);
}

private Image GetPhoto(int photoId)
{
  Image photo;

  using (SqlConnection conn = new SqlConnection(ConnStr))
  {
    conn.Open();

    using (SqlTransaction txn = conn.BeginTransaction())
    {
      string filePath;
      byte[] txnToken;

      using (SqlCommand cmd =
       new SqlCommand("GetPhotoForFilestream", conn, txn))
      {
        cmd.CommandType = CommandType.StoredProcedure;
        cmd.Parameters.Add("@PhotoId", SqlDbType.Int).Value = photoId;

        using (SqlDataReader rdr = cmd.ExecuteReader(CommandBehavior.SingleRow))
        {
          rdr.Read();
          filePath = rdr.GetSqlString(0).Value;
          txnToken = rdr.GetSqlBinary(1).Value;
          rdr.Close();
        }
      }

      photo = this.LoadPhotoImage(filePath, txnToken);

      txn.Commit();
    }

    conn.Close();
  }

  return photo;
}

private Image LoadPhotoImage(string filePath, byte[] txnToken)
{
  Image photo;
```

```
    SafeFileHandle handle =
        NativeSqlClient.GetSqlFilestreamHandle
        (filePath, NativeSqlClient.DesiredAccess.Read, txnToken);

    using (FileStream fs = new FileStream(handle, FileAccess.Read))
    {
      photo = Image.FromStream(fs);
      fs.Close();
    }

    return photo;
  }

  private void AddPhotos()
  {
    this.InsertEventPhoto(1, "Taken from the Ben Franklin parkway near the finish
line", -75.17396, 39.96045, "bike9_2.jpg");
    this.InsertEventPhoto(2, "This shot was taken from the bottom of the Manayunk
Wall", -75.22457, 40.02593, "wall_race_2.jpg");
    this.InsertEventPhoto(3, "This shot was taken at the top of the Manayunk Wall.",
-75.21986, 40.02920, "wall_race2_2.jpg");
    this.InsertEventPhoto(4, "This is another shot from the Benjamin Franklin
Parkway.", -75.17052, 39.95813, "parkway_area2_2.jpg");
  }

  private void InsertEventPhoto(
   int photoId,
   string desc,
   double longitude,
   double latitude,
   string photoFile)
  {
    const string InsertCmd =
        "INSERT INTO EventPhoto(PhotoId, Description, Location)" +
        " VALUES(@PhotoId, @Description, geography::Parse(@Location))";

    const string PointMask = "POINT ({0} {1})";

    string location = string.Format(PointMask, longitude, latitude);

    using (SqlConnection conn = new SqlConnection(ConnStr))
    {
      conn.Open();

      using (SqlTransaction txn = conn.BeginTransaction())
      {
        using (SqlCommand cmd = new SqlCommand(InsertCmd, conn, txn))
        {
          cmd.Parameters.Add("@PhotoId", SqlDbType.Int).Value = photoId;
          cmd.Parameters.Add("@Description", SqlDbType.NVarChar).Value = desc;
          cmd.Parameters.Add("@Location", SqlDbType.NVarChar).Value = location;
          cmd.ExecuteNonQuery();
        }
```

```
          this.SavePhotoFile(photoId, photoFile, txn);
          txn.Commit();
      }

      conn.Close();
  }
}

private void SavePhotoFile(int photoId, string filename, SqlTransaction txn)
{
    const string LocalPath = @"..\..\Photos\";
    const int BlockSize = 1024 * 512;

    FileStream source =
     new FileStream(LocalPath + filename, FileMode.Open, FileAccess.Read);

    SafeFileHandle handle = GetOutputFileHandle(photoId, txn);
    using (FileStream dest = new FileStream(handle, FileAccess.Write))
    {
      byte[] buffer = new byte[BlockSize];
      int bytesRead;
      while ((bytesRead = source.Read(buffer, 0, buffer.Length)) > 0)
      {
        dest.Write(buffer, 0, bytesRead);
        dest.Flush();
      }
      dest.Close();
    }

    source.Close();
}

private static SafeFileHandle GetOutputFileHandle
 (int photoId, SqlTransaction txn)
{
    const string GetOutputFileInfoCmd =
        "SELECT Photo.PathName(), GET_FILESTREAM_TRANSACTION_CONTEXT()" +
        " FROM EventPhoto" +
        " WHERE PhotoId = @PhotoId";

    SqlCommand cmd = new SqlCommand(GetOutputFileInfoCmd, txn.Connection, txn);
    cmd.Parameters.Add("@PhotoId", SqlDbType.Int).Value = photoId;

    string filePath;
    byte[] txnToken;

    using (SqlDataReader rdr = cmd.ExecuteReader(CommandBehavior.SingleRow))
    {
      rdr.Read();
      filePath = rdr.GetSqlString(0).Value;
      txnToken = rdr.GetSqlBinary(1).Value;
      rdr.Close();
    }
```

```
        SafeFileHandle handle =
            NativeSqlClient.GetSqlFilestreamHandle
            (filePath, NativeSqlClient.DesiredAccess.ReadWrite, txnToken);

        return handle;
      }
    }
  }
```

The code behind the *Add Photos* link label click event inserts four photos and their longitude and latitude coordinates into the database. Two of the photos were taken in the Wall Area, and the other two were taken in the Parkway Area.

```
private void AddPhotos()
{
  this.InsertEventPhoto(1, "Taken from the Ben Franklin parkway near the finish line",
    -75.17396, 39.96045, "bike9_2.jpg");
  this.InsertEventPhoto(2, "This shot was taken from the bottom of the Manayunk Wall",
    -75.22457, 40.02593, "wall_race_2.jpg");
  this.InsertEventPhoto(3, "This shot was taken at the top of the Manayunk Wall.",
    -75.21986, 40.02920, "wall_race2_2.jpg");
  this.InsertEventPhoto(4, "This is another shot from the Benjamin Franklin Parkway.",
    -75.17052, 39.95813, "parkway_area2_2.jpg");
}
```

> **Note** As with all code in this book, the full *EventMedia* demo code in this chapter is available on the book's companion Web site. (See the Introduction for details.) Included with the code are the four photo files named bike9_2.jpg, wall_race_2.jpg, wall_race2_2.jpg, and parkway_area2_2.jpg. If you do not have access to these images, you can use any .jpg image files you want—doing so won't change the point of the demo.

Run the application, and click Add Photos to populate the *EventPhoto* table. Then select different regions from the drop-down list and test out the query. Based on the *STIntersects* method in the stored procedure, the application should list two of the pictures for the Wall Area, the other two pictures for the Parkway Area, and all four pictures for the Race Area (which encompasses both of the other regions). Selecting any photo streams the image from the database into the picture box.

The *STDistance* Method

You use the *STDistance* method for distance calculations. By joining the *EventPhoto* table to itself on *PhotoId*, we can invoke this method against every combination of any two pictures, as shown in the following code. The value returned by *STDistance* is the exact distance between the two pictures expressed in meters, so dividing that value by 1,000 converts the result to kilometers. (As mentioned earlier, the default SRID for the *geography* data type uses the metric system.)

```
SELECT
    P1.PhotoId AS Photo1,
    P2.PhotoId AS Photo2,
    ROUND(P1.Location.STDistance(P2.location) / 1000, 2) AS Km
 FROM
    EventPhoto AS P1 JOIN EventPhoto AS P2 ON P1.PhotoId < P2.PhotoId
ORDER BY
    P1.PhotoId
```

Here are the results:

```
Photo1        Photo2        Km
-----------   -----------   ----------------------
1             2             8.46
1             3             8.58
1             4             0.39
2             3             0.54
2             4             8.83
3             4             8.95

(6 row(s) affected)
```

Because the join is based on *P1.PhotoId < P2.PhotoId*, we don't get results for the distance between a photo and itself (which is always zero), and we also filter out duplicate "opposite direction" results. For example, the distance from photo 1 to photo 3 is the same as the distance from photo 3 to photo 1, so we don't need it to be repeated.

Integrating *geography* with Microsoft Virtual Earth

In our final geospatial application, we will use the *geography* type to store the location of all our customers (each as a single point on the earth). By selecting the customers and their locations and then extracting the longitude and latitude values from each location, we will construct a Microsoft Virtual Earth mash-up. The term *mash-up* is used to describe a scenario in which one set of data is overlaid on top of another—in our case, layering customer coordinates over a Virtual Earth map to produce an image that shows the location of our customers in the database as pushpin icons on the map.

First create an empty database named *MyDB*. Then create the *Customer* table with a *geography* column to hold customer locations and populate it with some sample data, as shown in Listing 9-9.

LISTING 9-9 Creating the *Customer* table and populating it with geographical data

```
CREATE DATABASE MyDB
GO

USE DATABASE MyDB
GO

CREATE TABLE Customer
 (CustomerId  int PRIMARY KEY,
  Name        varchar(50),
  Company     varchar(50),
  CustomerGeo geography)

INSERT INTO Customer VALUES (1, 'Adam', 'Coho Vineyard & Winery',
  geography::Parse('POINT(-111.06687 45.01188)'))

INSERT INTO Customer VALUES (2, 'John', 'ACME Corp.',
  geography::Parse('POINT(-104.06 41.01929)'))

INSERT INTO Customer VALUES (3, 'Paul', 'Litware, Inc.',
  geography::Parse('POINT(-111.05878 41.003)'))

INSERT INTO Customer VALUES (4, 'Joel', 'Tailspin Toys',
  geography::Parse('POINT(-121.05878 41.003)'))

INSERT INTO Customer VALUES (5, 'Martin', 'ABC Travel',
  geography::Parse('POINT(-110.05878 43.003)'))

INSERT INTO Customer VALUES (6, 'Remon', 'Wingtip Toys',
  geography::Parse('POINT(-113.05878 35.003)'))

INSERT INTO Customer VALUES (7, 'Jason', 'School of Fine Art',
  geography::Parse('POINT(-116.05878 34.003)'))

INSERT INTO Customer VALUES (8, 'Fred', 'Fourth Coffee',
  geography::Parse('POINT(-114.05878 43.003)'))
```

Now create a stored procedure to retrieve all the customers and their locations, as shown in Listing 9-10.

LISTING 9-10 Creating a stored procedure to retrieve customers and their locations

```
CREATE PROCEDURE GetCustomers
AS
 BEGIN
    SELECT  Name, Company, CustomerGeo
     FROM   Customer
 END
GO
```

With our database set up, we're ready to create our Virtual Earth mash-up. Start Visual Studio 2008, and then choose File, New, Project. Create a Visual C# ASP.NET Web Application project named *VirtualEarthSpatialApp*, as shown in Figure 9-7.

FIGURE 9-7 Creating the *VirtualEarthSpatialApp* project

In Default.aspx, replace the starter markup provided by Visual Studio with the code shown in Listing 9-11.

LISTING 9-11 Creating a Virtual Earth mash-up with geography data

```
<%@ Page Language="C#" AutoEventWireup="true" CodeBehind="Default.aspx.cs" Inherits="V
irtualEarthSpatialApp._Default" %>

<!DOCTYPE html PUBLIC "-//W3C//DTD XHTML 1.0 Transitional//EN" "http://www.w3.org/TR/
xhtml1/DTD/xhtml1-transitional.dtd">
<html xmlns="http://www.w3.org/1999/xhtml">
<head runat="server">
  <title>Untitled Page</title>
</head>
<body>
  <form id="form1" runat="server">
  <asp:ScriptManager ID="ScriptManager1" runat="server">
    <Services>
      <asp:ServiceReference Path="CustomerQueryService.asmx" />
    </Services>
    <Scripts>
      <asp:ScriptReference
        Path="http://dev.virtualearth.net/mapcontrol/mapcontrol.ashx?v=6" />
    </Scripts>
  </asp:ScriptManager>
  <div>
    <div id='divVirtualEarthMap'
      style="position: relative; width: 640px; height: 400px;" />
  </div>
```

```
    <input id="btnGetCustomers" type="button" value="Get Customers"
      onclick="btnGetCustomers_Click()" />
    <script type="text/javascript">

      var _map = null;

      function pageLoad()
      {
        _map = new VEMap('divVirtualEarthMap');
        _map.LoadMap();
      }

      function btnGetCustomers_Click()
      {
        VirtualEarthSpatialApp.CustomerQueryService.GetCustomers
          (OnDataRetrievalComplete);
      }

      function OnDataRetrievalComplete(results)
      {
        for (i = 0; i < results.length; i++)
        {
          var point = new VELatLong(results[i].Latitude, results[i].Longitude);
          var pin = new VEShape(VEShapeType.Pushpin, point);
          pin.SetTitle(results[i].Company);
          pin.SetDescription(results[i].Name);
          _map.AddShape(pin);
        }
      }
    </script>
    </form>
  </body>
</html>
```

This Web page uses Asynchronous JavaScript and XML (AJAX) to render a Virtual Earth map on which it draws pushpin icons for each of our customers. There are no page postbacks to the server; all the service calls are made directly from the client browser. Let's dissect this page carefully.

Every AJAX-enabled Web page requires a *ScriptManager* element, which is declared at the top of the form. Nested within the *ScriptManager* element, the page declares two service references. The first reference points to CustomerQueryService.asmx, which is a Web Service that we will create momentarily to call the stored procedure that retrieves customers and their locations. The second reference is to the Microsoft Virtual Earth Web Service, which exposes an application programming interface (API) that can be used to render an interactive map on any Web page. The Virtual Earth map provides controls that allow the user to zoom and pan by simply clicking and dragging the mouse.

After the *ScriptManager*, the page declares a *<div>* section that defines the rectangular area of the page (640 by 400 pixels in this example) in which the map should be displayed. The element is assigned an ID named *divVirtualEarthMap* that will be referenced later by a call into the Virtual Earth API when the map is created. Beneath the map, the page displays a button named *btnGetCustomers* that is wired to a client-side event handler named *btnGetCustomers_click()*. The rest of the page contains the JavaScript that interacts with the two services from the user's browser.

At the top of the script, a page-level variable named *_map* is declared. This variable will hold a reference to the *VEMap* (Virtual Earth map) object created in the *pageLoad* function, which fires on the client when the browser loads the page. The *pageLoad* function instantiates the *_map* variable by declaring it as a new *VEMap* object. This results in a call to the Virtual Earth Web Service that returns a *VEMap* object that gets stored in the *_map* variable. The object is bound to the *<div>* tag named *divVirtualEarthMap* (declared earlier in the markup) that was passed in as a parameter into the *VEMap* constructor. The result is that the map loads and displays itself in the *divVirtualEarthMap* section of the page when the page loads.

Next the button's click event handler is defined in the *btnGetCustomers_click()* function. The single line of code in this function calls our CustomerQueryService.asmx Web Service declared in the preceding *ScriptManager* section. This results in an asynchronous call to the service, which runs in the background to call our stored procedure and retrieve customers and their locations from the database. When the call is made, the page specifies the name of the callback function *OnDataRetrievalComplete* to be invoked when the results are returned by the service.

Last, the *OnDataRetrievalComplete* function is defined to receive and process the results of the customer query. In our case, this is a list of customers and their locations that is passed in to the function as a parameter named *results*. The list is processed as an array of objects iterated with a *for* loop. Each element in the array is an object with properties defined for the *Customer* class that we will create shortly. For each customer, the *Latitude* and *Longitude* properties are used to construct a *VELatLong* (Virtual Earth latitude/longitude) object stored in a variable named *point*. (Note that the *VELatLong* constructor requires the latitude value for the first parameter and the longitude value for the second parameter, unlike WKT, which uses the reverse order of longitude followed by latitude.) A new *VEShape* (Virtual Earth shape) object is then created for the point as a *VEShapeType.Pushpin* shape stored in the variable *pin*. The *Company* and *Name* properties are then used to set the pushpin's title and description using the *SetTitle* and *SetDescription* methods. The pushpin is then added to the map by invoking the *AddShape* method on the *_map* variable, which represents the map displayed in the *<div>* tag named *divVirtualEarthMap* on the page.

That completes the Web page. Our next step is to create the Web Service called by the page to retrieve our customers and their locations from the database. In Solution Explorer, right-click the *VirtualEarthSpatialApp* project, select Add, New Item, and then choose Web Service. Name the service **CustomerQueryService.asmx**, as shown in Figure 9-8.

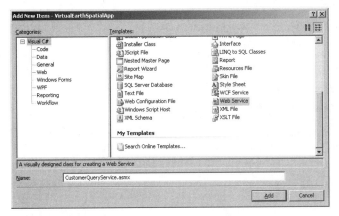

FIGURE 9-8 Creating the customer query Web Service

Then replace the starter code provided by Visual Studio with the code shown in Listing 9-12.

LISTING 9-12 Implementing the code for the customer query Web Service

```
using System;
using System.Collections.Generic;
using System.ComponentModel;
using System.Data;
using System.Data.SqlClient;
using System.Web.Script.Services;
using System.Web.Services;

using Microsoft.SqlServer.Types;

namespace VirtualEarthSpatialApp
{
  [WebService(Namespace = "http://tempuri.org/")]
  [WebServiceBinding(ConformsTo = WsiProfiles.BasicProfile1_1)]
  [ToolboxItem(false)]
  [ScriptService]
  public class CustomerQueryService : WebService
  {
    [WebMethod]
    public List<Customer> GetCustomers()
    {
      List<Customer> customers = new List<Customer>();

      using (SqlConnection conn = new SqlConnection
        ("Data Source=.;Initial Catalog=MyDb;Integrated Security=True;"))
      {
        conn.Open();

        using (SqlCommand cmd = new SqlCommand("GetCustomers", conn))
        {
          cmd.CommandType = CommandType.StoredProcedure;
```

```
    using (SqlDataReader rdr = cmd.ExecuteReader())
    {
      while (rdr.Read())
      {
        Customer customer = new Customer();
        customer.Name = rdr["Name"].ToString();
        customer.Company = rdr["Company"].ToString();

        SqlGeography geo = (SqlGeography)rdr["CustomerGeo"];
        customer.Latitude = (double)geo.Lat;
        customer.Longitude = (double)geo.Long;

        customers.Add(customer);
      }
      rdr.Close();
    }
  }

  conn.Close();

  return customers;
        }
      }
    }
  }
```

The *GetCustomers* method extracts the latitude and longitude values from the *geography*-typed *Location* column returned by the *GetCustomers* stored procedure that we created earlier. In Microsoft .NET, we can work with the new SQL Server 2008 system CLR types (such as *geography*) by using classes defined in the *Microsoft.SqlServer.Types* namespace. This namespace is declared by a *using* statement at the top of the code (highlighted in bold). The *SqlGeography* class in this namespace corresponds to the *geography* data type in SQL Server. The *Lat* and *Long* properties of a *SqlGeography* object expose the latitude and longitude values contained in the *geography* instance it encapsulates (as *double* data types).

Before using any types in this namespace, you must first establish a reference to its assembly. To do so, right-click the *VirtualEarthSpatialApp* project in Solution Explorer, and then select *Add Reference*. On the .NET tab, scroll down and select *Microsoft.SqlServer.Types*, as shown in Figure 9-9, and then click OK.

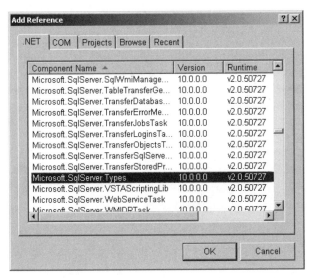

FIGURE 9-9 Adding a reference to the *Microsoft.SqlServer.Types* assembly

After opening a connection to the database, the *GetCustomers* method prepares a *SqlCommand* object to call the *GetCustomers* stored procedure in the database and then invokes the *ExecuteReader* method to obtain a *SqlDataReader* object that returns the results. The method loops through all the rows in the reader returned by the stored procedure and populates a generic *List<Customer>* object with the results. For each row, a *Customer* object is created and populated with the *Name* and *Company* columns. The *geography* value in the *CustomerGeo* column is cast to a *SqlGeography* object from which the customer's *Latitude* and *Longitude* properties are populated. The *Customer* object is then added to the generic *List<Customer>* object that is returned to the caller.

> **More Info** The generic *List<Customer>* object (and the *Customer* objects it contains) returned by the Web Service are automatically serialized and deserialized using JavaScript Object Notation (JSON) format. As a result, the asynchronous JavaScript callback function running on the page can easily access the results as an array of *Customer* objects on the client side. This functionality is provided by the AJAX support built into Microsoft ASP.NET so that the entire process is transparent to the developer and it all "just works."

The only thing that remains is the *Customer* class itself, which merely holds values for the *Name*, *Company*, *Latitude*, and *Longitude* properties of each customer. In Solution Explorer, right-click the *VirtualEarthSpatialApp* project, select Add, New Class, and then type the name **Customer.cs**, as shown in Figure 9-10.

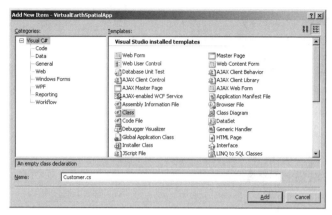

FIGURE 9-10 Creating the *Customer* class

Then replace the starter code provided by Visual Studio with the code shown in Listing 9-13.

LISTING 9-13 Implementing the *Customer* class properties

```csharp
using System;

public class Customer
{
  private string _name = null;
  private string _company = null;
  private double _latitude = double.MinValue;
  private double _longitude = double.MinValue;

  public string Name
  {
    get { return _name; }
    set { _name = value; }
  }

  public string Company
  {
    get { return _company; }
    set { _company = value; }
  }

  public double Latitude
  {
    get { return _latitude; }
    set { _latitude = value; }
  }
}
```

```
    public double Longitude
    {
      get { return _longitude; }
      set { _longitude = value; }
    }
  }
}
```

You can now give the application a run. To view the Web page, right-click Default.aspx in Solution Explorer, and then choose View In Browser. When the page loads, it runs the client-side JavaScript we wrote in the *pageLoad* function and displays the map in the browser. Click the Get Customers button to invoke the database query and display the pushpins corresponding to the locations of all the customers returned by the query, as shown in Figure 9-11.

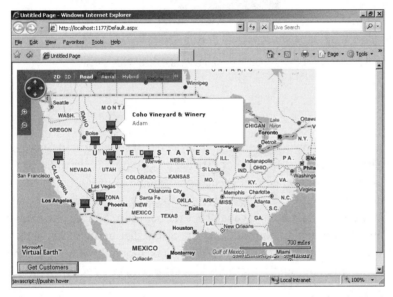

FIGURE 9-11 Running the Virtual Earth mash-up against *geography* data in SQL Server 2008

This page delivers full Virtual Earth capabilities to the user. Users can zoom, pan, and render aerial views of the map while the pushpins remain bound to your geographic data, as shown in Figure 9-12.

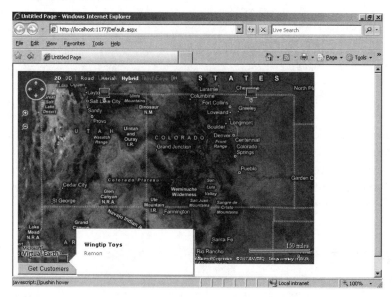

FIGURE 9-12 Zoom, pan, and aerial view capabilities of the Virtual Earth Web Service

Summary

No longer are geospatial capabilities limited to the domain of sophisticated Geographic Information System applications. The power of spatial processing is now readily available to all developers using the new *geometry* and *geography* data types in SQL Server 2008. In this chapter, you learned how to use these types by creating geospatial applications that integrate location intelligence and mapping capabilities for our users. You also saw how easy it is to express and project coordinates against either the planar (flat-earth) or geodetic (round-earth) spatial models using Well-Known Text (WKT) syntax. Along the way, we examined some of the most common geospatial methods for performing intersection, length, area, and distance calculations.

Part III
Reach Technologies

In this part:

Chapter 10   The Microsoft Data Access Machine. 377
Chapter 11   The Many Facets of .NET Data Binding 419
Chapter 12   Transactions 449
Chapter 13   Developing Occasionally Connected Systems 491

Chapter 10
The Microsoft Data Access Machine

—Andrew Brust

Anyone who's been working with Microsoft developer technologies for a long time knows that Microsoft comes out with new data access application programming interfaces (APIs) and tools on a fairly frequent basis. Going back to pre–.NET days, Microsoft Visual Basic programmers started with Data Access Objects (DAO) and then moved on to Remote Data Objects (RDO) before landing on ActiveX Data Objects (ADO). The last of these three provided the inspiration for Microsoft ADO.NET, which has, in successive versions, become a very sophisticated programming API for working with data (especially Microsoft SQL Server data) and, through typed *DataSet*s, a powerful rapid application development (RAD) tool with significant Visual Studio design time capabilities. But with the release first of Microsoft Visual Studio 2008 and Microsoft .NET Framework 3.5 in November of 2007 and the subsequent release of the Service Pack 1 (SP1) to those two products in August 2008, the array of new capabilities and options added to the .NET data access world is unprecedented, even for Microsoft.

The introduction of language-integrated query (LINQ) to C# and Visual Basic .NET, as well as the related LINQ to SQL technology and the ADO.NET Entity Framework, has brought about a generation of technology that raises the level of abstraction around data well beyond what ADO.NET provides, even with typed *DataSet*s. Meanwhile, LINQ as a language mechanism can be used against ADO.NET (with LINQ to DataSet), and ADO.NET can be used as an interface to the Entity Framework (using the EntityClient provider). So ADO.NET is not deprecated and still must be considered among other data access technology options. This has the potential to make a new world even more confusing.

But the choices don't stop there. ADO.NET Data Services, which marries the Entity Framework with representational state transfer (REST) Web Services technology, needs to be considered as well. And if the idea of a dedicated Web Service for data gets you excited, you'll likely be interested in the fully "cloud"–based option for this: SQL Server Data Services. Whew! That's a lot to digest, especially when you realize that ADO.NET and typed *DataSet*s themselves have been improved in .NET Framework 3.5 and that the old and new capabilities in ADO.NET need to be understood as well.

Our goal in this chapter is to give you a guided tour of each of these technologies, discussing the similarities and differences between them and the tradeoffs between each. While we can't dig deeply into all of them, we think that we can help you get your bearings and develop a certain literacy with each of them, as well as get a head start on learning the full details of the model(s) you find most appealing. This chapter will focus on using these technologies to serve up your data and some coding techniques for working with them.

We'll do some data binding in this chapter, but mostly in an incidental way. In the next chapter, we'll cover more deeply the host of technologies and the tools needed to consume the data: data binding in Windows Forms, ASP.NET (including ASP.NET Asynchronous Java and XML [AJAX]), Windows Presentation Foundation (WPF), and Silverlight. We'll also cover ASP.NET Dynamic Data, a technology that lets you generate entire Web sites for data management based on models constructed with either LINQ to SQL or the Entity Framework.

ADO.NET and Typed *DataSet*s

Accomplishing all of these goals is a tall order, so let's get started. It makes the most sense to begin with ADO.NET, the technology that most readers of this book likely know best. As discussed earlier, we need to cover the new features and review some longer-standing ones. But rather than cover the truly basic bits, let's gear our discussion toward the basics of working directly with tables and the extra steps required to work with stored procedures. Doing this will provide a nice baseline for appraising the other data access technologies that we'll cover in this chapter.

Typed *DataSet* Basics

In the transition from the Component Object Model (COM)–based ADO "classic" to ADO.NET 1.0, Microsoft introduced two radically new concepts. The first, contributed by ADO.NET itself, was the replacement of the (usually) connected single-result-set–oriented *Recordset* object with a disconnected, multiple-result-set relational object called the *DataSet*. The second new concept, contributed by Visual Studio .NET and based on .NET native support for inheritance, was the ability to create strongly typed *DataSet* objects (also known simply as typed *DataSet* objects).

Typed *DataSet* objects add schema-specific nested classes, methods, and properties to make data access from outside the database a more context-sensitive experience. One big benefit of typed *DataSet* objects is that their object models force column-level type fidelity in your code when you use their implemented properties. For example, a compiler error is generated if you try to store a string value into a column of a numeric data type. Likewise, the nested classes and properties, along with Visual Studio IntelliSense, prevent you from misspelling table or column names. The benefits go on and on.

Typed *DataSet* objects can be a great tool for your applications and middle-tier objects. Whether or not you want to take advantage of data binding technology, typed *DataSet* objects provide an elegant encapsulation layer for your data, its schema, and various queries on that data. As you will see, the convenience features added by typed *DataSet* objects have clearly inspired the various other data access technologies that we will explore in this chapter.

In Visual Studio 2008, as in earlier versions of Visual Studio, typed *DataSet* objects consist of one or more *DataTable* objects and, optionally, relations between those *DataTable* objects. In the Visual Studio typed *DataSet* designer, you specify the structure of the *DataTable* objects visually, and you can do so by designing them from scratch, by using the TableAdapter Configuration Wizard, or by using drag-and-drop techniques in concert with the Server Explorer window.

The Visual Studio sample solution for this chapter includes a C# Windows Application project named *Chapter10*. You can examine the typed *DataSet* object AW2008.xsd and forms in that project as you read this section of the chapter, or you can create a new C# Windows Application project and create the typed *DataSet* we'll discuss in this section.

> **Note** The Visual Studio sample solution for this chapter, as well as the sample code for this entire book, is available from the book's companion Web site. See the Introduction for the download location and more information.

Using the *DataSet* Designer

To begin, start Visual Studio 2008 and create a new Windows Forms project. Next, using the keyboard, menu options, or the appropriate Solution Explorer project node shortcut menu options, open the Visual Studio Add New Item dialog box. Select DataSet from the list of objects, and name your typed *DataSet* **AW2008.xsd**, as shown in Figure 10-1.

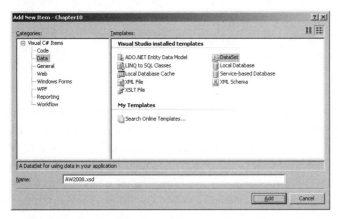

FIGURE 10-1 The Visual Studio Add New Item dialog box with the (typed) DataSet option selected

Click OK and observe that the *DataSet* opens in its own designer in the main tabbed document area of Visual Studio. For a new typed *DataSet*, the designer is displayed simply with an empty blue-and-white striped background and text that instructs you to add items using the DataSet tab of the Toolbox window or the Server Explorer window.

Get started by adding the *Sales.Currency* table to our new typed *DataSet*. Make sure that you define, or already have defined, a connection to the *AdventureWorks2008* database within the Server Explorer window. Once you have defined a connection, a node should appear within the Server Explorer window's Data Connections node that is configured to point to the *AdventureWorks2008* database. Expand the *AdventureWorks2008* database node, and then expand the Tables node within it. Last, locate the Currency (Sales) node, and drag and drop it onto the *DataSet* designer surface. Your *DataSet* should now contain fully specified *DataTable* and *TableAdapter* object definitions for the *Currency* table.

We'll cover how to add queries to a *TableAdapter* object, and we'll add more tables to the typed *DataSet*, but first let's take an inventory of what we have added so far. Notice that the large rectangle representing the *Sales.Currency* table is divided into two sections. The top section, labeled *Currency*, represents the actual ADO.NET *DataTable* within the *DataSet*. Click on one of the table's columns, and look at the Properties window. You'll see that the *DataColumn* object, which is a visual representation of an ADO.NET generic *DataColumn* object, has a number of editable properties. Notable among these is the *Caption* property. Changing the *Caption* property of a column causes all descriptive labels for subsequent data-bound controls for that column to reflect the caption rather than the name of the physical column in the database.

Other properties of interest include the *Expression* property, which allows you to configure the column to receive a computed value; the *ReadOnly* and *MaxLength* properties, which provide for declarative data validation rules independent of any constraints in the database; the *DefaultValue* property, which also operates independently of the physical table meta-data; and the *AllowDBNull* and *NullValue* properties, which govern handling of Nulls, also in a database-independent fashion.

TableAdapter Objects

The lower part of the rectangle, labeled *CurrencyTableAdapter*, represents the strongly typed *DataAdapter*, which manages the population of, and modifications to, the data in the *Currency DataTable*. Select it, and look at the Properties window. Several, but not all, standard *DataAdapter* properties are exposed, and a *Connection* property is provided, allowing you to specify a single *Connection* that will be used by the *TableAdapter* object's *SelectCommand*, *InsertCommand*, *UpdateCommand*, and *DeleteCommand* child object properties.

Just as the *DataTable* segment contains *Column* objects within it, the *TableAdapter* object contains *Query* objects within it. The *CurrencyTableAdapter* contains a single item by default—the line labeled *Fill,GetData ()*. Select it, and examine its properties in the Properties window; you will notice that a *Query* object has many of the properties of a simple ADO.NET *Command* object. We will discuss *Query* objects in more detail shortly.

Moving back to the *TableAdapter* object, notice that the *Connection* property itself has a number of child properties that can be independently configured. Rather than having to edit each one, you can select a named connection string from a drop-down list in the Value column of the parent *Connection* property, or you can enter it manually in the Value column of the *Connection.ConnectionString* child property. You might wonder where these named connections come from and how to maintain the list of them. Explaining this requires a brief detour out of the *DataSet* designer and into the Visual Studio 2008 Settings designer.

Connection String Management

To make the visual design of typed *DataSet* objects and both Windows Forms and Web data binding more straightforward than in the past, .NET provides a configuration file section explicitly for connection strings. You can thus reference connection strings by name and avoid the discouraged practice of hard-coding connection strings into application code. Visual Studio creates robust design-time support around this feature in several ways:

- For many Visual Studio project types, a special Settings designer allows you to create connection string entries in the application or Web configuration file, without editing the file directly, and to specify your connection string information using a Connection Properties dialog box.

- As you just saw, the Properties window, when used with *TableAdapter* objects inside the typed *DataSet* designer, permits selection of any configuration file–defined named connection string.

- The TableAdapter Configuration Wizard, which we will examine later in this chapter, allows selection of any configuration file–defined named connection string and saves any newly created connection strings into the configuration file if you ask it to.

- When you are writing code, IntelliSense prompts you with a full list of connection string entries as soon as you type the period after the expression *[ProjectName].Properties. Settings.Default*, where *[ProjectName]* is the name of your project's root namespace.

To test this out, open the Settings designer. In C# projects, you can get to the Settings designer by expanding the Properties node in the Solution Explorer window and then double-clicking its *Settings.settings* child node. You can also reach the Settings designer through the Settings tab of the Properties designer (and for some project types, you must use this technique to create the *Settings.settings* file to begin with).

Once you are in the Settings designer, you should see entries for any typed *DataSet*–derived connection strings. By observing how those connection strings are configured, you can easily see how to create your own. If you click within the Value cell, you can enter the connection string manually, but you can also click the ellipsis (...) button to the right of the cell to open the Connection Properties dialog box and define your connection string interactively.

Once you have finished, you can close the Settings designer/Properties designer and go back to the *DataSet* designer. If you now select the *CurrencyTableAdapter* object and, in the Properties window, click the drop-down arrow next to the *Connection* property, you should see in the drop-down list all the connection string entries that were in the Settings designer (make sure not to change the original setting of this property though).

Later in this chapter, you will encounter other contexts, as enumerated in the earlier list, in which the connection string setting entries are available. One of those is the TableAdapter Configuration Wizard, which we will examine now.

Using the TableAdapter Configuration Wizard

So far, we have used the Server Explorer drag-and-drop technique to place a table into a typed *DataSet*. Another, perhaps more flexible, technique is to use the TableAdapter Configuration Wizard. We will use this procedure to add an improved version of the *Currency DataTable* to our typed *DataSet* that uses only stored procedures to select, up-date, insert, and delete data. Create the stored procedures shown in Listing 10-1, which essentially encapsulate the dynamically generated Transact-SQL (T-SQL) code used by our initial *CurrencyTableAdapter*. Or download the chapter's SQL Server Management Studio solution (*Chapter10.ssmssln*) from the book's companion Web site, open it, and execute the CreateCurrencySprocs.sql script within it.

LISTING 10-1 Creating stored procedures for retrieving and modifying data using a *TableAdapter*

```
USE AdventureWorks2008
GO

CREATE PROCEDURE dbo.uspSelectCurrency
AS
    SET NOCOUNT ON;
SELECT      CurrencyCode, Name, ModifiedDate
FROM        Sales.Currency
GO

CREATE PROCEDURE dbo.uspInsertCurrency
(
    @CurrencyCode nchar(3),
    @Name Name,
    @ModifiedDate datetime
)
AS
    SET NOCOUNT OFF;
INSERT INTO [Sales].[Currency] ([CurrencyCode], [Name], [ModifiedDate]) VALUES (@
CurrencyCode, @Name, @ModifiedDate);

SELECT CurrencyCode, Name, ModifiedDate FROM Sales.Currency WHERE (CurrencyCode = @
CurrencyCode)
GO
```

```
CREATE PROCEDURE dbo.uspUpdateCurrency
(
    @CurrencyCode nchar(3),
    @Name Name,
    @ModifiedDate datetime,
    @Original_CurrencyCode nchar(3),
    @Original_Name Name,
    @Original_ModifiedDate datetime
)
AS
    SET NOCOUNT OFF;
UPDATE [Sales].[Currency] SET [CurrencyCode] = @CurrencyCode, [Name] = @Name,
[ModifiedDate] = @ModifiedDate WHERE (([CurrencyCode] = @Original_CurrencyCode) AND
([Name] = @Original_Name) AND ([ModifiedDate] = @Original_ModifiedDate));

SELECT CurrencyCode, Name, ModifiedDate FROM Sales.Currency WHERE (CurrencyCode = @
CurrencyCode)
GO

CREATE PROCEDURE dbo.uspDeleteCurrency
(
    @Original_CurrencyCode nchar(3),
    @Original_Name Name,
    @Original_ModifiedDate datetime
)
AS
    SET NOCOUNT OFF;
DELETE FROM [Sales].[Currency] WHERE (([CurrencyCode] = @Original_CurrencyCode) AND
([Name] = @Original_Name) AND ([ModifiedDate] = @Original_ModifiedDate))
GO
```

Once the stored procedures have been created, follow these steps:

1. Launch the wizard by right-clicking on a blank area of the *DataSet* designer surface
    and then choosing the Add, TableAdapter shortcut menu option. A blank *DataTable/
    TableAdapter* pair is added to the designer surface, and the TableAdapter Configuration
    Wizard appears after a brief pause.

2. On the first wizard page, the Choose Your Data Connection page, you specify a con-
    nection for the *DataTable/TableAdapter* pair you want to add to the *DataSet*. You will
    notice right away that the wizard allows the selection of any configuration file–based
    connection string, as well as those for Server Explorer window connections that are
    not represented in the configuration file. Just click the drop-down list, and if you
    want to know the underlying connection string, expand the Connection String node
    in the bottom half of the wizard page. Select the connection string pointing to the
    AdventureWorks2008 database that you used for the *CurrencyTableAdapter* object, and
    then click Next. If you selected a connection that was not present in the configura-
    tion file, the Save The Connection String To The Application Configuration File page of

the Wizard provides the option to save it to the file and allows you to define its name there. Accept the default settings, and then click next.

3. On the Choose A Command Type page, you specify whether the *TableAdapter* object's underlying *SelectCommand*, *InsertCommand*, *UpdateCommand*, and *DeleteCommand* should be based on dynamic SQL statements or calls to stored procedures. In the latter case, you have the choice of using existing stored procedures or having the wizard generate new ones. The existing stored procedures option actually allows you to select table-valued functions (TVFs) as well as stored procedures. Select the Use Existing Stored Procedures option, and then click Next.

4. On the Bind Commands To Existing Stored Procedure page, shown in Figure 10-2, you can specify the stored procedures to be used for each of the *TableAdapter*'s four commands. Go ahead and select uspSelectCurrency, uspInsertCurrency, uspUpdateCurrency, and uspDeleteCurrency from the Select, Insert, Update, and Delete drop-down lists now. For all but the Select query, you will notice that a grid to the right of the drop-down lists allows you to specify a mapping between the columns in the *DataTable* that we're creating (that is, those returned by the Select stored procedure) and the corresponding parameters in the stored procedure being configured. Accept the default assignments, and then click Next.

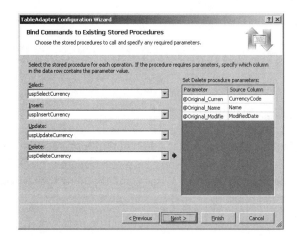

FIGURE 10-2 The TableAdapter Configuration Wizard Bind Commands To Existing Stored Procedures page

5. On the Choose Methods To Generate page, simply accept the default names by clicking Next.

6. On the Wizard Results page, you can review the tasks performed by the wizard and then click Finish to close the wizard.

You should now see your *DataTable* and *TableAdapter* on the *DataSet* designer surface. The *DataTable* should be named *uspSelectCurrency*, and the *TableAdapter* should be named *uspSelectCurrencyTableAdapter*. Delete the original *Currency* and *CurrencyTableAdapter* objects from the *DataSet*, and then rename the new objects **Currency** and **CurrencyTableAdapter**, respectively. Within the *TableAdapter* segment, you should see the *Fill* and *GetData* methods listed. In the wizard, had you assigned different names for these methods or chosen to generate only one of them, the method list would reflect your specific selections.

Before moving on, drag and drop the *ProductCategory (Production)*, *ProductSubcategory (Production)*, and *Product (Production)* tables and the *uspGetBillOfMaterials* stored procedure from the Server Explorer window onto your typed *DataSet*. Your typed *DataSet* should now appear as shown in Figure 10-3. Notice that a relation between the *ProductCategory* and *ProductSubcategory* tables, as well as one between the latter and the *Product* table are created automatically. This is because foreign key constraints between those tables already existed in the database.

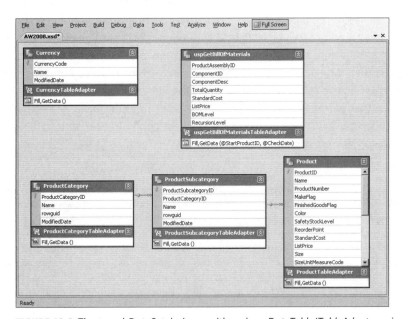

FIGURE 10-3 The typed *DataSet* designer with various *DataTable/TableAdapter* pairs defined

Keep in mind that you can modify an existing *TableAdapter* object through the TableAdapter Configuration Wizard at any time by right-clicking it and choosing the Configure option on the shortcut menu.

More on Queries and Parameters

Notice that the method list for the *Query* object within *uspGetBillOfMaterialsTableAdapter* includes parameters named *@StartProductId* and *@CheckDate*. These appear because the *uspGetBillOfMaterials* stored procedure itself has these parameters. Stored procedure or

SQL query parameters are together exposed as an ADO.NET parameter collection on the individual *Command* objects managed by your *TableAdapter* objects, and they are exposed as code-level parameters in the *TableAdapter* object's *Fill* and *GetData* methods.

The parameter(s) from your query as well as a stock *@RETURN_VALUE* parameter are represented in the *Parameters* collection property of the *Query* object and of the *TableAdapter* object's *SelectCommand*. See this for yourself by clicking in the Properties window value cell of either *Parameters* property and then clicking the ellipsis button. The wizard makes certain assumptions about the data type, scale, size, and direction of the parameters, as well as the existence of a return value. You can override any of these assumptions by changing the property values of individual parameters or by adding parameters to, or deleting parameters from, the collection properties.

Return to the *CurrencyTableAdapter* object, select the *UpdateCommand.Parameters* property, and then click the ellipsis button in its value cell. In the Parameters Collection Editor dialog box, notice that the last three parameters in the Members list all start with an *@Original_* prefix, because this stored procedure's *UPDATE* command specifies values for all columns in its *WHERE* clause, rather than just the primary key. Click any one of these parameters in the Members list, and then look at the *SourceVersion* property in the property grid to the right. You'll notice that its value is set to *Original*, whereas for all parameters not starting with the *@Original_* prefix, that property is set to *Current*. We point this out now in order to alert you to its importance so that you know to look for equivalent configuration options when we study some of the other data access models.

> **Note** We are not huge fans of update/delete stored procedures that parameterize each original column value. Typically, a primary key value (and possibly also an original *rowversion* value for concurrency) is all that is required, and in that case, there is typically no distinction between original and current values anyway. The supplied stored procedures for the *Currency* table were actually generated by the TableAdapter Configuration Wizard (and then reformatted and otherwise cleaned up), which is why they are structured this way. Regardless, having to work around original value parameters will ensure that you learn how to handle them, not just in the typed *DataSet* designer, but also in the LINQ to SQL and Entity Framework designers, which we will cover shortly.

You can easily add more queries to your existing *TableAdapter* objects. In essence, this adds methods, which can be parameterized, to your *TableAdapter* class; these in turn act as wrappers to SQL commands or stored procedures, which can also be parameterized. You can modify an existing *Query* object through the TableAdapter Configuration Wizard by right-clicking it and choosing the Configure option from its shortcut menu. You can add *Query* objects directly to a *DataSet*, rather than to a *TableAdapter* by right-clicking the *DataSet* designer surface and then choosing the Add, Query shortcut menu option.

DBDirect Methods and Connected Use of Typed *DataSet* Objects

TableAdapter objects act as strongly typed *DataAdapter* objects and are thus ideal for populating disconnected data sources. But *TableAdapter* objects have a special property, *GenerateDBDirectMethods*, that enables them to function as connected data sources as well. The *GenerateDBDirectMethods* property, a Boolean property whose default value is *True*, provides for autogeneration of three special methods (called DBDirect methods) on the *TableAdapter* class that handle immediate updates, inserts, and deletes, respectively, on the *DataTable* object's underlying physical database.

By using these three methods (which are automatically named *Update*, *Insert*, and *Delete*) along with the *GetData* method, developers can use the schemas and queries within typed *DataSet* objects without actually storing any data in their *DataTable* objects. Ironically, this allows you to use typed *DataSet* objects as if they were not *DataSet* objects at all. This usage is akin to setting up four separate ADO.NET *SqlCommand* objects and a *SqlConnection* object and using the *ExecuteReader* and *ExecuteNonQuery* methods of the *SqlCommand* objects to fetch and modify data, respectively.

The stored schemas that the *DataTable* objects contain facilitate design-time data binding, even when you use such connected techniques. You will put this to use in the next chapter, when we cover ASP.NET data binding.

Close the *DataSet* designer now, and then click Yes when asked whether you want to save your changes.

"Pure" ADO.NET: Working in Code

We've spent a lot of time covering the visual design features of typed *DataSet* objects. That information will help you to be a productive SQL Server 2008 developer, but many of the features in ADO.NET require at least some coding, without the use of Visual Studio designers. You can use coding techniques to manipulate or populate your typed *DataSet* objects, but for now, let's get down to some pure code development techniques that don't use typed *DataSet* objects at all. (We'll come back to designer-oriented features in the next chapter.)

We looked at the typed *DataSet* designer because it remains an important tool for most .NET developers (the emergence of so many new tools notwithstanding) and because understanding it well provides a context in which to discuss the other tools more easily. But now, let's take a moment to review the basic coding techniques used in ADO.NET for connected data access and for disconnected data access (using both typed and untyped *DataSet* objects).

Querying 101

We will look first at a simple query against the *AdventureWorks2008 Sales.Currency* table. To implement this query, add a new form to the project and name it **frmMain** (or just rename the *Form1* form added by default when you created the project). Next, drag a *DataGridView* control from the Toolbox window's Data tab onto the form, and name the control **dgvResults**. Drag a *Button* control from the Toolbox window's Common Controls tab onto the form, name it **btnLoadUntypedDS**, and set its *Text* property to **Untyped DataSet**. Resize the button as necessary so that its text shows fully.

Using ADO.NET against SQL Server requires the use of the *System.Data.SqlClient* ADO.NET provider, and it is a good idea to import that namespace in your code. So in the form's code-behind class, add the following line immediately after the existing lines of code that start with the *using* statement:

```
using System.Data.SqlClient;
```

Coding Against an Untyped *DataSet*

After you take care of the namespace housekeeping, you simply use a *SqlConnection*, a *SqlCommand*, and a *SqlDataAdapter*, along with a *DataSet* or *DataTable* object and a bound control, to query your database and display the result set.

It is possible to avoid creating and using the *SqlConnection* and *SqlCommand* objects because the *SqlDataAdapter* has a constructor overload that creates these objects for you implicitly. Nonetheless, we think it sensible to show you how to use the objects explicitly. The code in Listing 10-2, which contains the implementation of the *Click* event handler for the *Button* control, *btnLoadUntypedDS*, performs a simple query against the *Sales.Currency* table, populates a *DataTable* with the results, and binds that *DataTable* to the *DataGridView* control.

LISTING 10-2 Executing a SQL *SELECT* statement and binding the results to a *DataGridView* control

```
private string ConnString =
 Properties.Settings.Default.AdventureWorks2008ConnectionString;

private void btnLoadUntypedDS_Click(object sender, EventArgs e)
{
  SqlConnection cn = new SqlConnection(ConnString);
  SqlCommand cm = new SqlCommand
    ("SELECT CurrencyCode, Name, ModifiedDate FROM Sales.Currency", cn);
  SqlDataAdapter daUntyped = new SqlDataAdapter(cm);
  DataTable dt = new DataTable();
  daUntyped.Fill(dt);
  dgvResults.DataSource = dt;
}
```

Notice that the connection string that was added to the settings file earlier (which the preceding code assumes is named *AdventureWorks2008ConnectionString*) is stored into a class-level variable named *ConnString* that, in turn, is passed to the *SqlConnection* object's constructor; you can refer to the connection string by name using the *Properties.Settings* object's *Default* property. We could also pass a string literal, but the *Properties.Settings* technique is more sound because a change to the connection string in the settings file cascades out to this code without any additional effort on your part.

Passing a string literal or expression to the *SqlConnection* object's constructor has the effect of setting the object's *ConnectionString* property as the object is instantiated. Similar "constructor shortcuts" are used in the code listing. The *CommandText* and *Connection* properties of the *SqlCommand* object and the *SelectCommand* property of the *SqlDataAdapter* object are set by passing the corresponding string and objects to the constructors of objects *cm* and *daUntyped*. The *DataTable* object is instantiated using a default constructor and needs no specific initialization.

Once the objects are properly instantiated, we execute the query and populate our *DataTable* with its result set by simply calling the *SqlDataAdapter* object's *Fill* method and passing it our *DataTable* object. To display the results, we set our *DataGridView* control's *DataSource* property to *dt*—our *DataTable* object—and we've finished. Edit *program.cs* to make *frmMain* your startup form (unless you renamed the *Form1* form, in which case *program.cs* was updated automatically), run the application, and click the Untyped DataSet button to confirm that the *DataGridView* control is populated correctly.

Coding Against a Typed *DataSet*

Now add another button, name it **btnTypedDS,** and set its *Text* property to **Typed DataSet**. Listing 10-3 shows the code for the button's *Click* event, which populates the *Currency* table in our typed *DataSet* and binds it to *dgvResults*.

LISTING 10-3 Populating a typed *DataSet* and binding to one of its *DataTable* objects

```
private void btnTypedDS_Click(object sender, EventArgs e)
{
  AW2008TableAdapters.CurrencyTableAdapter da =
   new AW2008TableAdapters.CurrencyTableAdapter();
  AW2008 ds = new AW2008();
  da.Fill(ds.Currency);
  dgvResults.DataSource = ds.Currency;
}
```

Notice that in this version of the code, we need not explicitly declare *SqlConnection* or *SqlCommand* objects (since our *TableAdapter* object does so through its own *SelectCommand* and *Connection* properties), and we don't declare a *DataTable* object either (since our typed *DataSet* creates one through its *Currency* property). We've effectively reduced seven lines of real code to four; we've gained IntelliSense support for our typed *DataSet*, *TableAdapter*, and *DataTable* names; and we've avoided the need to write a SQL query in our code. Run the application, and then click the Typed DataSet button to test the code.

Coding with a Connected *DataReader*

Prefer to use the more basic ADO.NET objects for connected data access? Add an additional button, name it **btnConnected**, and set its text property to **Connected Reader**. Listing 10-4 has the *Click* event handler code you'll need.

LISTING 10-4 Populating a *DataGridView* control manually from a *DataReader* object

```
private void btnConnected_Click(object sender, EventArgs e)
{
  dgvResults.DataSource = null;
  dgvResults.Columns.Add("CurrencyCode", "CurrencyCode");
  dgvResults.Columns.Add("Name", "Name");
  dgvResults.Columns.Add("ModifiedDate", "ModifiedDate");

  SqlConnection cnSqlCli = new SqlConnection(ConnString);
  SqlCommand cmSqlCli = new SqlCommand
    ("SELECT CurrencyCode, Name, ModifiedDate FROM Sales.Currency", cnSqlCli);
    SqlDataReader drSqlCli;
    cnSqlCli.Open();
    drSqlCli = cmSqlCli.ExecuteReader(CommandBehavior.CloseConnection);
  while (drSqlCli.Read())
   dgvResults.Rows.Add(drSqlCli["CurrencyCode"], drSqlCli["Name"],
   drSqlCli["ModifiedDate"]);
  drSqlCli.Close();
}
```

In the preceding code, we use simple *SqlConnection*, *SqlCommand*, and *SqlDataReader* objects. We connect to the database, fetch our data, load it into the grid ourselves, and then disconnect, and we've finished. Because we're not *binding* the *SqlDataReader* object to the *DataGridView* control (in Windows Forms, you cannot do so), we need to add columns to the grid ourselves and then load each row's data. When we've finished, we can close the *DataReader*, and because it was instantiated using the *CommandBehavior.CloseConnection* enumerated constant, doing so closes our connection as well.

While this code is lengthier than the previous examples (and relies on the additional line of code that declares and assigns the value to the variable *ConnString* in our first example), it's arguably more efficient, especially if we don't intend to modify our data in any way. Note that before we add the columns to the grid, we clear out any preexisting data binding by setting its *DataSource* property to *null*. By the same token, if you want to be able to execute either of our *DataSet* examples after running the connected *DataReader* code, you'll need to insert in the other event handlers the following line of code immediately before the line that sets the grid's *DataSource* property:

```
dgvResults.Columns.Clear();
```

The sample application supplied with this chapter already includes this code.

Adding Validation Logic to a Typed *DataSet*

Let's look at one more coding technique that demonstrates the effectiveness of typed *DataSet* objects. We will add validation logic by supplementing the code generated by the typed *DataSet* designer with our own code. To do this, open the typed *DataSet* in its designer, and double-click the *Currency DataTable* object. This will open the typed *DataSet* object's code-behind file (but not the designer-generated code) and should place your cursor within the partial class code for the *CurrencyDataTable* class. Within that class, enter the code in Listing 10-5.

LISTING 10-5 Embedding custom validation logic into a typed *DataSet* using a partial class

```
protected override void OnColumnChanged(System.Data.DataColumnChangeEventArgs e)
{
  CurrencyRow row = (CurrencyRow)e.Row;
  if (row.Name == "Reserved")
  {
    row.SetColumnError(e.Column, "'Reserved' is an invalid name");
    row.RowError = "Errors have occurred";
  }
  else
  {
    row.ClearErrors();
  }
}
```

Now restart the application, click the Typed DataSet button, and type the string **Reserved** (verbatim, including capitalization) in the last row, within the Name column. Press Tab to move out of that cell (*but stay within the row*), and watch what happens. You should see a red exclamation point icon appear both within the *Name* cell and next to the row header as well.

Hover the mouse pointer over the exclamation point in the *Name* cell, and you'll see the column error message from our code appear in a tooltip. (Hover over the other, and you'll see the row error message from our code instead.) Return to the *Name* cell, and enter a different name; as soon as you type the first character, the red exclamation point will disappear from the cell. Press Tab to move out of the cell, and you'll see the red exclamation point disappear from the row header as well. Enter a unique code in the *CurrencyCode* column and a valid date in the *ModifiedDate* column, and you'll then be able to move to other rows in the grid. (If you don't do this, a rather large error message box will appear.)

If you click either of the other buttons on the form and try the same data entry steps, you'll see that this check will not occur. This validation behavior is embedded in our typed *DataSet* and will be automatically exhibited by any controls it is bound to; untyped *DataSet*s do not enjoy this benefit.

As you have seen, typed *DataSet* objects let us model the subset of our database that we want to work with, and they are highly compatible with stored procedures. They give us strongly typed IntelliSense support in code, allow that code to be terse, and even allow us to embed reusable validation logic and business rules in the typed *DataTable* classes them-selves. So while a host of new data access models has appeared and merits our attention, we'll need to keep in mind how useful ADO.NET is, both for quick and efficient pure-code techniques as well as for a rich design-time experience with great tool support in Visual Studio.

More Info The sample code contains many more examples of what you can do with ADO.NET directly in code, specifically programming against features that were introduced in SQL Server 2005. These include query notifications, asynchronous queries, *SqlClient* bulk copy operations, processing XML data, and retrieving Common Language Runtime (CLR) user-defined types (UDTs) as native CLR objects. These code samples are all contained in the form *frm2005Demos*, which can be opened by clicking the 2005 Demos button on the *Chapter10* project's main form, *frmMain*. Note that the scripts CreateTblBulkData.sql, CreateUspGetNames.sql, and EnableServiceBroker.sql in the *Chapter10.ssmssln* Management Studio solution must be run for the 2005 demo code to work properly. Detailed content on these code samples appeared in Chapter 8 of the previous edition of this book. For your convenience, an electronic copy of that chapter can be downloaded from this book's companion Web site.

Let's look at the other data access models now, but transition into that tour by exploring how we can use LINQ with *DataSet*s.

LINQ: A New Syntactic Approach to Data Access

To begin, let's address an issue that has certainly made the relatively new LINQ features in .NET harder to understand for the uninitiated: there is "brand confusion" around the name. That's because LINQ, which is actually just a new language feature in C# and Visual Basic .NET, is typically (but not always) used against LINQ to SQL data models and Entity Framework data models (the latter of which are queried using LINQ to Entities). Therefore, many people initially associate LINQ with one of these two Object Relational Mapping (ORM) tools.

LINQ to DataSet

To reiterate, however, LINQ itself is just a language feature and need not be used against models from either ORM tool. For example, LINQ can be used to query XML files (using LINQ to XML), and it can also be used to query an ADO.NET *DataSet* (using LINQ to DataSet). We will look at LINQ to SQL and the Entity Framework shortly, but since we've spent some time looking at ADO.NET, we'll first introduce you to the mechanics of LINQ by using LINQ to DataSet.

Unlike "native" ADO.NET, which requires you to supply a *Command* object's *CommandText* property with a string (either a T-SQL query or a stored procedure name), LINQ queries use actual language keywords and can thus be checked for correctness by the language compiler, rather than SQL Server. Add an additional button, name it **btnLinqToDataSet**, and set its text property to **LINQ To DataSet**. Listing 10-6 shows the *Click* event handler code you'll need. This code illustrates how to use LINQ to DataSet to execute the same select query we have illustrated in the prior listings.

LISTING 10-6 Populating a typed *DataSet* and binding to a LINQ to DataSet query against it

```
private void btnLinqToDataSet_Click(object sender, EventArgs e)
{
  AW2008TableAdapters.CurrencyTableAdapter daL2DS = new
   AW2008TableAdapters.CurrencyTableAdapter();
  AW2008 dsL2DS = new AW2008();
  daL2DS.Fill(dsL2DS.Currency);
  dgvResults.DataSource =
    (from currency in dsL2DS.Currency select currency).AsDataView();
}
```

Compare this to the code shown earlier in in Listing 10-3. Notice that the code is identical with the exception of the last line. Rather than simply binding to the entire *DataTable*, we instead run a query against it—specifically:

```
from currency in dsL2DS.Currency select currency
```

The result of this query, a collection of type *EnumerableRowCollection<AW2008. CurrencyRow>*, cannot be directly bound to the *DataGridView* control, so we convert it to a *LinqDataView* object using the *AsDataView* method.

LINQ Syntax, Deconstructed

What does this query actually do? It can look redundant and confusing upon first inspection. To understand how it works, it's helpful to compare it to a SQL query and then to alternate C# code. From a SQL point of view, the query is very similar to the following:

```
SELECT * FROM Currency
```

And since we know that the *DataTable* object's *SelectCommand* actually performs that query against the database, this makes sense, in a way. But looking at it that way masks a reality, and understanding that reality helps decipher why this code actually provides a benefit. The reality is that it's equivalent to the following, much more verbose C# code:

```
List<AW2008.CurrencyRow> myCollection = new List<AW2008.CurrencyRow>();
foreach(AW2008.CurrencyRow currency in dsL2DS.Currency)
{
  myCollection.Add(currency);
}
```

> **Note** A generic *List* containing typed *DataRow* objects actually results in certain *DataRow* prop-erties (which are not column values) being added as members. Those extra members can simply be suppressed in your user interface (UI), or the LINQ query could be altered to add just the true data column properties to each item in the list. For simplicity, the code samples in this section do not address this particular anomaly. Keep in mind that the *AsView* method avoids this issue entirely.

From here, the variable *myCollection* could be bound directly to the *DataGridView* control, since generic *List* objects are in fact bindable. But while the generic *List* might at first seem preferable to the *EnumerableRowCollection* object generated by the LINQ query, it turns out that the latter has numerous extremely useful methods like *Min, Max,* and *SelectMany,* that allow for further data manipulation without even needing to use the LINQ syntax.

Now that might still seem like redundant code, given that the *Currency DataTable* object itself already contains, in effect, the contents generated into the variable *myCollection*. And in fact, the last line of code in *btnLinqToDataSet_Click* could be replaced with the following, simpler version that just binds to the *Currency DataTable* as we did in our typed *DataSet* example:

```
dgvResults.DataSource = dsL2DS.Currency;
```

But we wanted to acquaint you with the full LINQ query syntax. To understand the utility of that syntax, consider the following variation of the LINQ query:

```
from currency in dsL2DS.Currency where !currency.CurrencyCode.StartsWith("A") select
currency
```

This one expression, when converted to a *List* and assigned to the *DataGridView* control's *DataSource* property, replaces what would otherwise need to be expressed as follows:

```
List<AW2008.CurrencyRow> myCollection = new List<AW2008.CurrencyRow>();
foreach (AW2008.CurrencyRow currency in dsL2DS.Currency)
{
  if (!currency.CurrencyCode.StartsWith("A"))
  {
    myCollection.Add(currency);
  }
}
dgvResults.DataSource = myCollection;
```

Even without counting braces, LINQ represents a 75-percent reduction in lines of code in this example! Moreover, it provides a SQL-like syntax (the *select* clause coming at the end of the query notwithstanding) for querying over collections in a set-based fashion that avoids the need to apply procedural logic. For example, LINQ also supports an *order by* clause—imagine having to implement *that* with procedural code! Even if you wrote a nicely factored function to perform a sort, the need to call it explicitly, as a separate step, would be less convenient and make the code less readable.

The preceding description of LINQ is not bad as a working definition: LINQ is an extension to the C# (and Visual Basic .NET) syntax that allows for set-based querying and generation of enumerable sets of objects. It is a "pluggable" facility in that providers can be built to permit LINQ queries over specific enumerable types. LINQ to DataSet does this for *System. Data* objects; LINQ to XML does it for *System.XML* objects; LINQ to Objects does it for generic C# objects; LINQ to SQL and LINQ to Entities do likewise for LINQ to SQL and Entity Framework data models. The last two of these are what we need to consider next.

LINQ to SQL and the ADO.NET Entity Framework: ORM Comes to .NET

We'll return to LINQ queries in a moment, but now it's time to focus on building models. While it is useful to compare LINQ itself to SQL and C# in order to better understand it, understanding a LINQ to SQL or Entity Framework (shortened to L2S and EF for the remainder of this discussion) *model*, and the corresponding designers, can be nicely accomplished by a comparison with a typed *DataSet* and the typed *DataSet* designer.

Our typed *DataSet* contained a model of a subset of our database and resulted in the generation of strongly typed classes to represent that *DataSet* and its *DataTable* and *TableAdapter* objects. L2S and EF models serve a similar purpose and produce similar results. Our typed *DataSet* could be configured to use stored procedures and, through the creation of a partial class, allow encapsulated data validation logic to be embedded within it. Guess what? To a greater or lesser degree, L2S and EF models do likewise. Typed *DataSet* objects support relations and one-to-many containment between *DataTable* objects. L2S and EF models do as well, with their own collection classes.

Database objects can be dragged from the Visual Studio Server Explorer window onto the typed *DataSet* designer surface, or they can be created manually. The L2S designer also supports Server Explorer window drag and drop, the EF designer supports addition of database objects through a wizard, and both the L2S and EF model designers support manual creation of classes.

The typed *DataSet* designer supports SQL Server first and foremost, although other databases, including Oracle, are supported as well, typically with tool support from the database vendor. L2S is SQL Server specific, whereas EF has a provider-based model that makes support of other databases possible. Out of the box, EF supports SQL Server; support for Oracle and IBM databases (DB2, Informix and UniVerse/UniData) is, at press time, under development.

Why Not Stick with ADO.NET?

With all these similarities between the models, and given that LINQ *can* be used against native ADO.NET objects, why bother with these new technologies? The justification stems mostly from the explicit ORM functionality provided by L2S and EF. While a typed *DataSet* generates classes mostly to aid in strong typing (and the IntelliSense and compile-time error checking support that comes with that), typed *DataSet* classes themselves are not designed to be used as true business entities.

But the classes in L2S and EF models are meant to be used directly as just that: classes. Just as you might create your own business entity classes as an encapsulation layer over your database, through whose properties and methods you might cease to think about the physical structure of your database tables and stored procedures, L2S and EF classes are designed to be used as a similar abstraction.

The typed *DataSet* designer doesn't allow for the creation of derived classes—that is, there is no built-in support for inheritance. But L2S does allow for simple inheritance, and EF models allow for very robust inheritance.

The correlation of *DataTable* objects and physical database tables and other objects is, essentially, one to one (although use of stored procedures and editing of a *TableAdapter* object's various *Command* properties provides a workaround for this). While L2S models also force a one-to-one correspondence with database objects, inheritance mitigates this restriction. And EF models easily allow a single entity (class) to map to multiple objects in the database.

While native ADO.NET supports the use of LINQ as an alternate syntax, the mainstream use of it will continue to be SQL-based. Meanwhile, L2S and EF will typically be used along with their LINQ implementations, making them more prone to implementation scenarios that are perhaps more modern.

Still not convinced? You don't have to be. And in reality, neither are we, at least not completely. The fact is that a typed *DataSet* provides a surprisingly extensive abstraction model, while at the same time giving you direct control over the SQL emitted when "CRUD" (create, retrieve, update, and delete) operations are executed and, as you will see in the next chapter, first-class data binding support. The option to use LINQ syntax is there if you want to use it, and at the same time, you can use untyped ADO.NET objects, including the low-overhead *Command* and *DataReader* objects, to perform any operation against the database. And because you are likely comfortable with T-SQL, relational theory, and so on, you are probably also comfortable with moving back and forth between that programming paradigm and the object-oriented mindset.

But the reality is that the ORM approach has its supporters, and the fact that Microsoft is adopting it means that there is direct support for it in the .NET Framework, mitigating the fragmentation that can occur when (numerous) third-party products provide the only way to implement a popular approach. Plus, Microsoft seems to have taken a liking to ORM and is building new technologies such as ADO.NET Data Services (which we will examine later in this chapter) on top of EF and ASP.NET Dynamic Data (which we will see in the next chapter) on top of both L2S and EF.

With all that in mind, it would behoove us to take a quick look at how to build L2S and EF models and then use them in code. We'll do this now by assembling models that mirror structurally the typed *DataSet* we created previously. At the end of this chapter, we'll address the question of whether L2S or EF (or one of the other data access options) is the best technology to use.

Building an L2S Model

Given what you've already learned about the typed *DataSet* designer and our conceptual introduction to L2S (and EF), we can cover the construction of an L2S model rather quickly.

Start by using one of the various menu, toolbar, or shortcut menu options to add a new item to your .NET project. When the Add New Item dialog box appears, select the LINQ To SQL Classes option from the Templates list on the right side of the dialog box. If you first click the Data option in the Categories tree view on the left, the number of options in the Templates list will be greatly reduced, thus allowing you to find the L2S template quickly. These selections are shown in Figure 10-4.

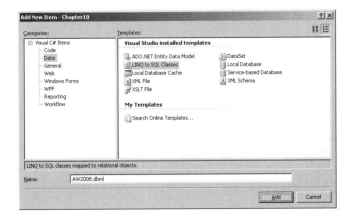

FIGURE 10-4 The Add New Item dialog box with the LINQ To SQL Classes template selected

Name your model **AW2008.dbml**, and then click the Add button. After a brief pause, the L2S model designer opens. The designer is divided into two panes: on the left, you can design your classes (from tables or views), and on the right, you can manage methods of the model (from stored procedures and database user-defined functions [UDFs]). We can quickly build out our model by dragging and dropping, from the Server Explorer window onto the data classes pane, the *Currency (Sales)*, *ProductCategory (Production)*, *ProductSubcategory (Production)*, and *Product (Production)* tables. Once you've done this, drag the following stored procedures onto the methods pane: *uspGetBillOfMaterials*, *uspDeleteCurrency*, *uspInsertCurrency*, *uspSelectCurrency*, and *uspUpdateCurrency*.

Note You can also drag stored procedures onto the data classes pane—they will be inserted into the methods pane regardless.

When you've completed these steps, the L2S model designer should be similar in appearance to the screen capture shown in Figure 10-5.

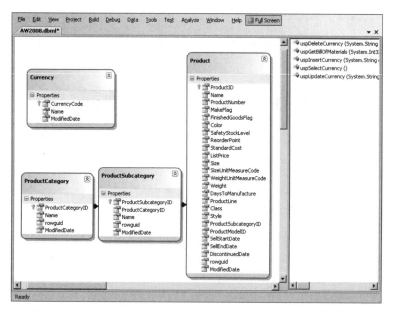

FIGURE 10-5 The L2S designer after adding our tables and stored procedures

Your model is already about 80-percent complete! With this in mind, go ahead and save it now.

Examining the Model

Before we further configure the model, let's look carefully at what was generated by our drag-and-drop actions. First, notice that each table that we dragged over has a corresponding class in the model. These really are classes, not tables—within each class shape in the diagram, you'll see, under the Properties heading, a list of properties, each of which corresponds to a column from the table on which the class is based. You can add an additional property manually by right-clicking the desired class and then selecting Add, Property from the shortcut menu.

Next, notice the arrow connecting the *ProductCategory* class to the *ProductSubcategory* class. (There is an analogous arrow between the latter and the *Product* class, but let's focus on the former arrow.) This arrow represents, as it is called in L2S parlance, an *association*.

Although this association was generated because of the existence of a foreign key constraint in the database, the association represents something a bit different. To understand this better, hover your mouse pointer over the association arrow. A tooltip will appear, displaying the following text:

ProductCategory.ProductSubcategories -> ProductSubcategory
ProductCategory <- ProductSubcategory.ProductCategory

What this tooltip is telling us is that the *ProductCategory* class contains an (unlisted) property, *ProductSubcategories*, that points to a collection of *ProductSubcategory* objects and that the *ProductSubcategory* class contains an (again unlisted) property, *ProductCategory*, that points to a single *ProductCategory* object. In other words, each parent object has a collection of child objects and a property pointing to that collection, while each child object has a property pointing to its (unique) parent object.

Makes sense, doesn't it? In an object-oriented world, one-to-many relationships are represented by child collections and parent/child properties. In L2S, these are called, intuitively enough, *association properties*. As you will see, in L2S, the collections and parent/child properties are populated and assigned for you automatically, when a parent object is instantiated.

If the Properties window is not visible, open it. Now carefully click each class, property, association, and method to view various (editable) aspects of the objects in the model. Last, select the model itself (that is, click on a blank area of the designer). Notice that the model's base class is *System.Data.Linq.DataContext* and its name is *AW2008DataContext*. Shortly, in code, we will need to reference this object in order to start querying the data in the model.

Hooking Up to Stored Procedures

Before we move to writing that code, however, we still need to configure the *Currency* class. Right now, despite the fact that the stored procedures for maintaining the table have been imported into the model as methods, this class is still configured to use plain-old dynamic T-SQL in response to CRUD operations performed on it. In order to connect the class to the stored procedures, right-click the light blue title area of the *Currency* class, and then choose Configure Behavior from the shortcut menu. This displays the Configure Behavior dialog box, as shown in Figure 10-6. (The screen in Figure 10-6 shows the Update behavior already customized for use with a stored procedure, as we'll do shortly.)

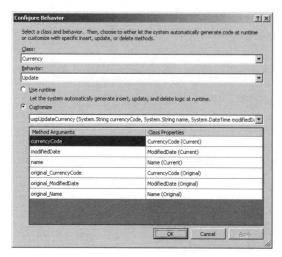

FIGURE 10-6 The Configure Behavior dialog box for the *Currency* class

A Class combo box appears at the top of the dialog box. Currency is selected by default, but all classes in the model appear in the drop-down portion of the combo box. Notice that the Behavior combo box contains selections for Insert, Update, and Delete, with Insert selected by default. For each of these options, you can select the Use Runtime or Customize option; Use Runtime is selected by default for each.

With Currency selected in the Class combo box and Insert selected in the Behavior combo box, go ahead and select the Customize option. A combo box beneath it is now enabled; from it, select uspInsertCurrency. You have now configured the model to use the *uspInsert-Currency* stored procedure, rather than dynamic SQL, to perform inserts in the *Currency* table in the database. Notice that the grid at the bottom of the dialog box is now populated with a list of the parameters in the method (corresponding to the underlying stored procedure's parameters) and the properties of the *Currency* class that have been mapped to each by default. This mapping is editable, but there is no need to change it. Click the Apply button.

Next select Update from the Behavior combo box, select the Customize option, and then select uspUpdateCurrency from the combo box beneath it. Observe the parameters grid. Notice that properties were assigned to the first three parameters, but not the last three. This is because default parameter mappings occur when (and only when) like-named properties exist. So for the *original_CurrencyCode*, *original_ModifiedDate*, and *original_Name* parameters, we must configure the parameter–property mappings ourselves.

Recall that the *UpdateCommand* property of the *CurrencyTableAdapter* object in our typed *DataSet* had its own parameters collection. You might remember that when we examined its contents in the Parameters Collection Editor dialog box, we noticed that the three parameters beginning with the *@Original_* prefix each had their *SourceVersion* property set to Original. We need to do the equivalent here for the three method parameters in question.

It turns out that this task is easy. Start by clicking in the cell in the Class Properties column for the *original_CurrencyCode* row. Click the drop-down arrow, and notice that options for both CurrencyCode (Current) and CurrencyCode (Original) appear in the drop-down list. The former was already assigned to the *CurrencyCode* property, so select the latter, and then do likewise for the remaining two parameters and their corresponding properties. Click Apply, and then select Delete from the Behavior combo box, assign the *uspDeleteCurrency* stored procedure to it, and configure its parameters in a similar fashion. When you've finished and you're certain that everything is configured correctly, click Apply, then click OK.

We've almost finished configuring our model, but we still never got the opportunity to assign the *uspSelectCurrency* method to anything! You might be surprised that no Select behavior option appeared in the Configure Behavior dialog box. Why is this? Well, given the use of LINQ with L2S models, there is, in effect, a default assumption that developers will prefer that their LINQ queries get converted to dynamic SQL and be executed directly against the table, even if stored procedures are being used for updates, inserts, and deletes. However, in many environments, direct access to tables will not exist for application users, and in any case, we believe that the use of stored procedures is better practice than the use of dynamic SQL.

The good news is that stored procedures *can* be used for select operations, but a few extra steps are required to make this work. First select the uspSelectCurrency method in the designer's methods pane, and then observe its Return Type property in the Properties window, which is set to (Auto-Generated Type). Click in the value cell for that property, and then click the drop-down arrow. A list of all classes in the model appears, from which you should select the Currency option (and click Yes when prompted with a warning message). This provides a hint to L2S that when this method is called, its result set should be used to populate the collection of *Currency* objects. As those objects are modified and the changes submitted to the database, the other three stored procedures will be used as appropriate.

This manual configuration step can be avoided, however. To do so, first select the *uspSelectCurrency* method and delete it. Next drag the *uspSelectCurrency* stored procedure again, but this time, drop it on the *Currency* class shape in the model, rather than directly onto the designer. Notice that the method appears in the designer once again; if you select it, you'll see that its return type was set to *Currency* automatically. As a last step, change the method's *Name* property value from *uspSelectCurrency* to simply **SelectCurrency**.

We've finished building our L2S model. Before we examine how to query it in code, save your work and now let's build the equivalent EF model.

The Entity Framework: Doing ORM the ADO.NET Way

Our concepts are really locked down now. This was true before we built our L2S model, but it's even more so after. You'll see as you build an EF model that many of the concepts *and* mechanics of building the model are patterned after the L2S designer. This includes configuration of stored procedures and their parameters.

Start by again opening the Add New Item dialog box, and this time, select the ADO.NET Entity Data Model option from the Template list. Name the model **AW2008.edmx**, and then click Add. The Entity Data Model Wizard will appear. On the Choose Model Contents page, Generate From Database is selected by default; the other option, Create Empty Model, allows you to exit the wizard and go directly to the EF model designer. Since the EF designer does not allow for drag-and-drop operations from the Server Explorer window, accept the default Generate From Database selection, and then click Next.

On the Choose Your Connection page, you will be presented with a drop-down list consisting of all the connections defined in the Settings designer as well as any additional connections defined in the Server Explorer window. The connection we created for our *DataSet*, *AdventureWorks2008ConnectionString*, will work perfectly; select it from the combo box at the top of the wizard page if it is not already selected.

The Entity Connection String multiline text box (which is disabled) shows you the EF connection string that will be used. Remember that EF is a provider-based model and one that builds on top of native ADO.NET. Notice that the EF connection string contains a *metadata=* clause that is unique to EF, but that the *provider connection string* section of the string is the standard ADO.NET connection string that was selected in the combo box above. At the bottom of the page is a check box, selected by default, that will allow you to save the entity connection string to the app.config file, and beneath the check box is a text box that allows you to specify the name of the entry.

> **More Info** The EF connection string's *metadata=* clause contains concatenated Uniform Resource Identifiers (URIs) terminating in .csdl, .ssdl, and .msl extensions. We will discuss the roles of these extensions at the end of this section.

Click Next to go to the Choose Your Database Objects page. After a brief pause, a tree view will appear with top-level nodes for Tables, Views, and Stored Procedures. Expand the Tables and Stored Procedures nodes, and then go ahead and select the check marks next to the nodes corresponding to the four tables and five stored procedures we used in our typed *DataSet* and our L2S model already. Notice the default value entered in the Model Namespace text box, *AdventureWorks2008Model*. We will need to import this namespace into our code in order to query the model. Now click Finish.

After another pause, your model will open in its designer. Because we're creating this model alongside a LINQ to SQL model of the same *AdventureWorks2008* database objects in the same project, numerous type name collisions result. (Try to build the solution now, and you'll see many "The type *x* already contains a definition for *y*" errors.) Correct this by scoping the generated code for the EF model in a separate namespace. Select the model AW2008.edmx in Solution Explorer, and then set the Custom Tool Namespace property to **AdventureWorks2008Model**. Build the solution now to confirm that it now compiles successfully.

Now that all of our objects are added, we'll need only to perform the stored procedure configuration steps equivalent to those we performed in the L2S model in order to bring the EF version to the same functional level.

Examining the EF Model

Before configuring our stored procedures, however, let's take review the objects in the generated model and the designer's user interface (UI). First, let's acknowledge the things in this model that appear equivalent to the L2S version. To start, each table is represented by classes that are named identically to table itself. Also, each database column has generated a corresponding property in the appropriate class; these appear under the heading Scalar Properties. Scalar properties can be added manually by right-clicking the title area or Scalar Properties heading and then selecting Add, Scalar Property from the shortcut menu. Arrows appear between the various product-related parent and child tables.

Meanwhile, there are some important differences. For example, the properties that point to child collections and parent objects are explicitly represented properties of their classes, under the heading Navigation Properties. We see, therefore, that EF *navigation properties* are the equivalent of *association properties* in L2S models. (The EF object connecting the two classes *is* called an association, however.) Notice that the child collection properties are named in the singular rather than the plural form used in L2S (for example, *ProductSubcategory* rather than *ProductSubcategories*). If you hover the mouse pointer over the association line, a tooltip appears indicating the multiplicity that the association represents between the two classes (that is, one-to-many or one-to-one).

A docked Model Browser window should appear. (By default, it will join the same tabbed, docked window grouping as the Solution Explorer window.) If it's not visible, right-click the model designer surface, and then select the Model Browser option from the shortcut menu. Notice that this window features a tree view with two top-level nodes: one with a diagram icon and labeled with the model's namespace, delineating the objects in the model, and the other with a database icon and labeled with the model's namespace and a suffix of *.Store,* showing the corresponding database objects. The model objects are then listed within child nodes labeled Entity Types (showing the classes), Associations, and Entity Container: (with the entity container name appended). Expand this last node to show the subnodes: Entity Sets (enumerating the collection classes for the entity *types* shown above them), Association Sets, and Function Imports (which we'll look at shortly).

Property Mapping and Stored Procedure Configuration

The mapping between scalar properties and database columns can be configured, by default, in the Mapping Details window. If this window is not visible, right-click one of the entity types (either its diagram shape or its node in the Model Browser window), and then select the Table Mapping option from the shortcut menu. The window should join the same tabbed, docked window grouping as the Output and Error List windows. The Mapping Details window for the *Currency* entity class is shown in Figure 10-7.

FIGURE 10-7 The Entity Framework designer Mapping Details window

The Mapping Details window contains a grid that allows you to map scalar properties (in the Value/Property column on the right) to database columns (in the column labeled Column on the left). As with L2S, columns are mapped to like-named properties by default. If you look at the mappings for the product-related tables, you'll see that some mappings appear to be missing. However, the mappings for these columns are addressed in the mappings for the associations themselves. (Look in the Mappings Details window with any of the associations selected to see this.)

Reselect one of the entity classes and notice that the last row in the grid contains the text *<Add A Table Or View>*. This placeholder allows you to map multiple tables to the same entity class. Whereas the wizard generated a one-to-one mapping, the fact remains that unlike L2S models, EF models can indeed vary from this pattern. For example, you could create a comprehensive class that mapped data from several of the tables in the *AdventureWorks2008 Person* schema; this can be a very effective way of making a highly normalized database simpler to program against.

You might have noticed that when you right-click an object in the model, a Stored Procedure Mapping option appears on the shortcut menu immediately after the Table Mapping option. You should also notice that at the left edge of the Mapping Details window, there are two (vertically oriented) toolbar buttons: Map Entity To Table/Views and Map Entity To Functions.

The latter includes both stored procedures and user-defined functions (UDFs). With the *Currency* entity class selected, use either UI option to look at the stored procedure mappings. Here, a grid allows you to map stored procedures to Insert, Update, and Delete functions; this is the equivalent of the L2S Configure Behavior dialog box.

Go ahead and assign the *uspInsertCurrency*, *uspUpdateCurrency*, and *uspDeleteCurrency* stored procedures to the *Insert*, *Update*, and *Delete* functions, respectively. Notice that the same default property–parameter mappings are generated, and that, for the Update function, a check box in the grid's Use Original Values column allows you to distinguish the original values from current values for the various *Original_*–prefixed parameters. Select the appropriate properties for the unmapped parameters now, and then select the Use Original Values check box for the *Update* function's *Original_* parameters. For the *Delete* function, despite the *Original_* prefix on the parameter names, the Original Values check box is not available, and so you should simply assign the properties and leave it at that. As we've almost finished, save your work.

The last step is to import the *uspSelectCurrency* stored procedure and identify it as returning *Currency* objects, in much the same way as we did in the L2S model. The stored procedure was already added to the model, but we still need to expose it as a function. We do this by creating a *function import*. Right-click the model designer surface, and then select the Add, Function Import option from the shortcut menu; this displays the Add Function Import dialog box.

Select uspSelectCurrency in the StoredProcedure Name combo box, enter **SelectCurrency** in the Function Import Name text box (as in the L2S model, this will be the name of the callable method, distinct from the name of the stored procedure), select the Entities option for Return Type, select Currency from the Entities combo box, and then click OK. In the Model Browser window, expand the AW2008.edmx/AdventureWorks2008Model/EntityContainer: AdventureWorks2008Entities/Function Imports node, and notice that the *SelectCurrency* "function" (method) now appears. If you select it, you'll see that the Properties window allows you to configure the function in a similar way to the Add Function Import dialog box.

If you want to add any database object to the model or update the model with changes to the physical structure of the database, you can do so by again running the Entity Data Model Wizard. To start the wizard, you can right-click just about anywhere in the EF designer or the Model Browser window and then select the Update Model From Database shortcut menu option. But our model is now complete, so close the designer, and then click Yes in the resulting dialog box to save your changes.

XML Behind the Scenes

Before we move on to coding techniques against both of our new ORM models, let's discuss what was actually generated by the EF designer. Right-click the EF model (AW2008.edmx) in

Solution Explorer, and then select Open With from the shortcut menu. In the resulting Open With dialog box, double-click the XML Editor option. As you can see, the EF designer merely provides a graphical editor for the management of a large XML document.

Collapse all nodes within the <edmx:Edmx>/<edmx:Runtime> element, and you'll notice three distinct sections following it: the store schema definition language (SSDL) content (containing the storage model—that is, the physical schema for the database objects), the conceptual schema definition language (CSDL) content (containing the conceptual model—that is, the EF object model), and the C-S Mapping content (containing the mappings between the conceptual model and the storage model). These three sections of the model correspond to the .ssdl, .csdl, and .msl URIs that we observed earlier in the EF connection string's *metadata=* clause.

Feel free to explore the XML structure of these sections and also feel free to read the numerous well-written articles and blog posts that document them. Going into such depth is beyond the scope of this book, and the EF designer is good enough that we don't really need to know these details. We haven't examined the internal XML schema definition (XSD) content of our typed *DataSet* either, and for exactly the same reason.

Close the XML Editor window, and then open the L2S model (AW2008.dbml) in its own XML Editor window. You will see that the structure of the latter is much flatter and more straightforward, with top-level sections for each class and function (that is, table/view and stored procedure), each containing its own mapping information. This simpler structure demonstrates well that L2S has more modest goals than EF: L2S provides just enough encapsulation to enable a LINQ interface to SQL Server objects, whereas EF allows for the construction of a full "conceptual" model that is quite separate from the physical model in the database, and a rich mapping layer to correlate the two. This separation of physical and conceptual allows for changes in the database to have minimal disruptive impact on the conceptual model.

With our L2S and EF models now built, it's time to write some code that uses them to query and update the database behind them. After that, we'll finish the chapter with a look at ADO.NET Data Services and SQL Server Data Services.

Querying the L2S and EF Models

Having already covered the details of querying our typed *DataSet* with a LINQ query, it's easy to understand how to query our new models, because the code is similar *and* less complex/verbose. Continuing with our sample Windows Form, add another button, name it **btnLinqToSql**, and set its text property to **LINQ To SQL**. Double-click the button, and then add its click event handler code, shown in Listing 10-7. This code queries against our L2S model and returns a similar result set to the various ADO.NET queries that we have looked at so far.

LISTING 10-7 Binding a LINQ to SQL query

```
private void btnLinqToSql_Click(object sender, EventArgs e)
{
  AW2008DataContext ctx = new AW2008DataContext();
  dgvResults.DataSource = from currency in ctx.Currencies select currency;
}
```

Recall that when we selected the L2S model's design surface and looked at its *Name* property in the Properties window, the value was AW2008DataContext. We mentioned then that the name would be significant. As you can see, the *Linq.DataContext* object acts in code somewhat like a typed *DataSet*. Note that the preceding query runs dynamic SQL directly against the *Currency* table in the database. (Compare that to a LINQ to DataSet query, which runs against a previously populated, memory-resident *DataSet*.) To use the *uspSelectCurrency* stored procedure rather than dynamic SQL, replace the second line of code with the following:

```
this.dgvResults.DataSource =
 (from currency in ctx.SelectCurrency() select currency).ToList();
```

This line of code queries our *SelectCurrency* method instead of the *Currencies* collection.

For the EF model, the code is nearly identical; the only major change required is, of course, the way we reference the data source itself. For EF, we reference the *AdventureWorks2008Entities* object within the *AdventureWorks2008Model* namespace. Add another button, name it **btnLinqToEF**, and set its text property to **LINQ To Entities**. Double-click the button, and then add its click event handler code, shown in Listing 10-8.

LISTING 10-8 Binding to a LINQ to Entities query

```
private void btnLinqToEF_Click(object sender, EventArgs e)
{
  AdventureWorks2008Model.AdventureWorks2008Entities ctx =
   new AdventureWorks2008Model.AdventureWorks2008Entities();
  dgvResults.DataSource = from currency in ctx.Currency select currency;
}
```

To shorten this code a bit, and to facilitate the other code that will likely follow it, it's a good idea to import the *AdventureWorks2008Model* namespace using the following line of code at the top of your source code file:

```
using AdventureWorks2008Model;
```

The EF code in Listing 10-8 also queries the *Currency* table directly (and notice that we do so by referencing a *Currency* collection rather than a *Currencies* collection, as was required by

L2S). To use the stored procedure instead, you can change the second line of code in a fashion identical to what we did for the L2S code.

Notice that in the preceding L2S and EF non–stored procedure queries, it was not necessary to convert the results of the LINQ queries to a *List* or other object type before binding them to our *DataGridView* control. That's because the *IQueryable* and *ObjectQuery* types returned by those L2S and EF LINQ queries, respectively, are directly bindable. For the stored procedure queries, conversion to a *List* object was required to force the L2S and EF models' *SelectCurrency* methods to execute.

As it happens, EF supports two additional ways to query its models: ADO.NET (using the EntityClient provider), and Object Services, EF's native API. In either of these two cases, we revert to supplying the query as a string, instead of using a LINQ expression. Interestingly, when doing so, we use neither T-SQL nor the LINQ syntax, but rather an EF-specific dialect of SQL called Entity SQL. Here's what the query text would be in our case:

```
SELECT VALUE c FROM Currency AS c
```

See the sample Windows Forms application, *Chapter10*, for the necessary Object Services and EntityClient code to make this query work.

What about modifying the data once we've queried it? Here's the code necessary to make a trivial update via L2S:

```
AW2008DataContext ctx = new AW2008DataContext();
var myCurrencies =
    from currencies in ctx.Currencies
    where currencies.CurrencyCode == "AED"
    select currencies;
myCurrencies.First().Name = "Emirati Dirham1";
ctx.SubmitChanges();
```

And here's the equivalent code for the EF model (assuming that the namespace import code shown previously has been inserted in the source code file):

```
AdventureWorks2008Entities ctx = new AdventureWorks2008Entities();
var myCurrencies =
    from currencies in ctx.Currency
    where currencies.CurrencyCode == "AED"
    select currencies;
myCurrencies.First().Name = "Emirati Dirham1";
ctx.SaveChanges();
```

Notice that only the first and last lines of code differ between the two examples. In both, we use the *First* method on the result set (*IQueryable* and *ObjectQuery*) objects to reference the actual objects returned by the queries. Since we know that these queries will return exactly one object each (*CurrencyCode* is unique), we also know that the *First* method will return the specific object we want to update. We can then reference that object's *Name* property and change its value and then submit our changes back to the database using the L2S *SubmitChanges* method or EF's *SaveChanges* method on the respective object context objects.

If you look at the IntelliSense list that pops up for the *myCurrencies* result set object (in either example), you'll see that there are a number of database query–sounding methods. Interesting examples of these include the *Select* and *Where* methods. Why are these methods present when that support is already provided for LINQ queries that use the *select* and *where* keywords? As it turns out, the LINQ expressions simply resolve to use these methods. To see this for yourself, in the L2S code, set a breakpoint on the line following the query and start the debugger. When you hit the breakpoint, open a QuickWatch watch window on the *myCurrencies* object. Drill down to the Non-Public Members/queryExpression node, and note that the object's value is:

```
{Table(Currency).Where(currencies => (currencies.CurrencyCode = "AED"))}
```

The preceding, a so-called *Lambda expression,* is the magic in .NET that makes LINQ possible. LINQ queries merely resolve to these more terse conditional expressions that are used to filter collections and project the results into new collection variables and properties. When you write LINQ code, you can feel free to combine use of the more verbose LINQ expressions and the helper methods on the collection objects themselves.

What about inserting and deleting rows/entities? The techniques differ slightly between the technologies. For L2S, each table/collection (for example, *AW2008DataContext.Currencies*) has *InsertOnSubmit* and *DeleteOnSubmit* methods to which an instance of that collection's type must be passed. The *InsertAllOnSubmit* and *DeleteAllOnSubmit* methods work similarly, but for entire collections rather than single instances. Inserts and deletes do not take effect until the *SubmitChanges* method is called.

For EF, the object context itself (for example, *AdventureWorks2008Entities*) has custom *AddToXxx* methods for each entity set, where *Xxx* is the entity set's name (for example, *AddToCurrency*), which accepts an instance of its entity class. There is also a generic *AddObject* method that requires you to specify the entity set as a string (for example, *"Currency"*) as well as the entity class instance. For deletion, a generic *DeleteObject* method can be used to delete the entity instance passed. Inserts and deletes do not take effect until the *SaveChanges* method is called.

The Windows Forms application included with this chapter's sample code, *Chapter10,* includes code samples that update, add, and delete rows from the *Sales.Currency* table, using both L2S and EF.

Adding Custom Validation Code

We've almost finished our L2S and EF coverage, but let's add a little polish and implement data validation logic for our models that mimics that which we added to our typed *DataSet*. We can do this through the creation of more partial classes. And since a single source code file can contain code for multiple classes, we can actually put all this validation code together in a single class file. To do this, add a new class file to your project and name it **Validation.cs**, and then replace its default code with the code shown in Listing 10-9.

LISTING 10-9 Custom validation code for our EF and L2S models

```
using System;
using System.Collections.Generic;
using System.Linq;
using System.Text;
using System.ComponentModel;

// L2S
namespace Chapter10
{
    public partial class Currency : INotifyPropertyChanging, INotifyPropertyChanged
    {
        partial void OnNameChanging(string value)
        {
            Validation.CheckForReserved(value);
        }
    }

    public class Validation
    {
        public static void CheckForReserved(string value)
        {
            if (value.Equals("Reserved"))
            {
                throw new Exception("'Reserved' is an invalid name");
            }
        }
    }
}

// EF
namespace AdventureWorks2008Model
{
    public partial class Currency : global::System.Data.Objects.DataClasses.
EntityObject
    {
        partial void OnNameChanging(string value)
        {
            Chapter10.Validation.CheckForReserved(value);
        }
    }
}
```

This code might look confusing at first, but it's actually very simple. Start at the top, in the *Chapter10* namespace. Here we have implemented both a partial class for the *Currency* class in our L2S model and a public class, *Validation*, containing a single static function, *CheckForReserved*, that contains our validation logic. The *OnNameChanging* handler (which fires whenever the value of a *Currency* object's *Name* property changes value) in the partial class calls the *CheckForReserved* method in the *Validation* class. The rest of the code contains identical handler code for the EF model. When this handler calls the *Validation.CheckForReserved* method, it prefixes it with its *Chapter10* namespace. The L2S handler code did not use the namespace prefix, since the L2S model exists within that namespace to begin with.

The only step left to do is handle the exception thrown by the validation code. To do this, create an event handler for our *DataGridView* control's *DataError* event and code it as shown in Listing 10-10.

LISTING 10-10 The *DataError* event handler for our *DataGridView* control

```
private void dgvResults_DataError(object sender, DataGridViewDataErrorEventArgs e)
{
    if (e.Exception != null)
    {
        MessageBox.Show(e.Exception.Message);
        e.Cancel = true;
    }
}
```

Now, for the LS2 and EF grid load routines, try going to the last row in the grid (the empty one) and typing **Reserved** in the name column. Press Tab to move out of the cell and see what happens. While not as robust as the typed *DataSet* validation logic (seen when you execute the typed *DataSet* and LINQ to DataSet code) with its red exclamation point UI niceties, the code in Listings 10-9 and 10-10 still add impressive capabilities to L2S, LINQ to Entities, and Object Services grid load routines.

Web Services for Data: Using ADO.NET Data Services Against EF Models

We have offered a fairly critical evaluation of both L2S and EF thus far, even while highlighting their features and pointing out their elegance. But we also mentioned that Microsoft seems to be taking a liking to ORM and is building new technologies on top of both L2S and EF. One of those technologies, ADO.NET Data Services (code-named "Astoria"), is very compelling indeed. It permits you to create a Web Service on top of your EF model, and do so with almost no code whatsoever.

> **Note** Out of the box, ADO.NET Data Services can work against L2S models as well, but only for read/select operations. In order to update models through the service, you must use EF.

While it has been possible since the release of the .NET Framework in 2002 to create an ASP. NET Web Service interface to ADO.NET *DataSet*s (both typed and untyped), such a Web Service is difficult to use from non-.NET platforms. And while you could solve that problem by returning POX (plain-old XML) instead of a *DataSet*, the work required to do so, and the necessary testing and debugging, is nontrivial.

ADO.NET Data Services solves this problem by returning an easily parsed XML result set rather than a *DataSet*. Given that EF entities are rather straightforward in their property structure, this is a logical approach. But the enlightened approach doesn't stop there: the ADO.NET Data Services team decided to use the REST standard instead of SOAP for implementing the generated services. A REST service is highly compatible with almost every platform that can work with XML and Hypertext Transfer Protocol (HTTP). Even a standard Web browser can fit those requirements, and as you will see, using an easy-to-follow URI scheme, you can in fact query an ADO.NET Data Services EF model from the browser.

Getting yourself all configured with ADO.NET Data Services involves four steps:

1. Create the service itself.

2. Test the service from the browser.

3. Add a Service Reference for it into your data-consumption application.

4. Write the application code to query the service.

Creating the Service

To begin, create a new ASP.NET Web Service Application project. (You can also add on to an existing solution, as we have done with the *Chapter10Service* project in the sample code for this chapter.) After the project is created, delete the Service1.asmx file that is added by default, and add a new ADO.NET Entity Data Model. Once again, name the model **AW2008** and build it identically to the model we created in our Windows Forms application, but this time leave its Custom Tool Namespace property blank.

Next open the Add New Item dialog box, and then select the ADO.NET Data Service template—it's available when either the root node or the Web option is selected in the Categories tree view on the left side of the dialog box. Name the file **AW2008Service.svc**, and then click Add. After a short pause, the service will open in code view, with a template consisting of a stubbed-out version of the *InitializeService* method and a set of helpful comments within it. Replace the *AW2008Service* class code within the namespace declaration with the code shown in Listing 10-11.

LISTING 10-11 Source code for our ADO.NET Data Service class

```
public class AW2008Service
  : DataService<AdventureWorks2008Entities>
{
    public static void InitializeService(IDataServiceConfiguration config)
    {
        config.SetEntitySetAccessRule("Currency", EntitySetRights.All);
        config.SetEntitySetAccessRule("Product", EntitySetRights.AllRead);
        config.SetEntitySetAccessRule("ProductSubcategory", EntitySetRights.AllRead);
        config.SetServiceOperationAccessRule("*", ServiceOperationRights.All);
    }

    [WebGet]
    public IQueryable<Currency> CurrenciesByLetter(string initialLetter)
    {
        return from c in this.CurrentDataSource.Currency
               where c.Name.StartsWith(initialLetter)
               select c;
    }

    [WebGet]
    public IQueryable<Currency> SelectCurrency()
    {
        return (this.CurrentDataSource.SelectCurrency()).AsQueryable();
    }
}
```

Let's discuss the code a little before moving on to test it. First, in the *public class* line, we have inserted our EF model class name (*AdventureWorks2008Entities*) to be the type on which AW2008Service is based. Next look at the code in the *InitializeService* method. This code exposes the *Currency* entity set from the model with all rights granted (that is, read and write operations are permitted) and the *Product* and *ProductSubcategory* entity sets for read access; all other entity sets are hidden. Also, by using the "*" wildcard expression, the service exposes *all* service operations (that is, Web methods) with all rights granted.

The *CurrenciesByLetter* function exposes a service operation that accepts a single-lettered string parameter and returns all members of the *Currency* entity set whose *Name* property begins with that letter. Notice that the returned data is sent as an *IQueryable<Currency>* and is generated using a LINQ to Entities query. Furthermore, instead of having to get an object context reference to the model, we can instead use the *this.CurrentDataSource* object to refer to the model on which the service is built.

The *SelectCurrency* service operation acts as a wrapper around our *SelectCurrency* method (which in turn wraps our *uspSelectCurrency* stored procedure). While it's unfortunate that we have to write our own service operation to expose a method that is already in our EF model, the fact remains that the code required to do this is rather trivial.

Testing the Service

Let's move on to testing the service from a browser. First, for testing purposes, go into the project properties sheet, and in the Web tab's Servers section, make sure that the Use Visual Studio Development Server option is selected and that the Specific Port option indented beneath it is selected as well. The port number is largely insignificant, but for the sake of consistency with the remaining code in this chapter, set the port number to **1328**. Now build the project. Assuming that the build was successful, try navigating to each of the following URIs:

http://localhost:1328/AW2008Service.svc
http://localhost:1328/AW2008Service.svc/Currency
http://localhost:1328/AW2008Service.svc/Currency('FRF')
http://localhost:1328/AW2008Service.svc/SelectCurrency('FRF')
http://localhost:1328/AW2008Service.svc/CurrenciesByLetter?initialLetter='B'
http://localhost:1328/AW2008Service.svc/ProductSubcategory(1)/Product
http://localhost:1328/AW2008Service.svc/Product?$filter=ListPrice gt 100&$orderby=Name

> **Tip** To view the data service's XML response content properly in Microsoft Internet Explorer 7, you might need to turn off Feed Reading View. To do this, click the Internet Options option on the Tools toolbar button's drop-down menu. Then, in the resulting Internet Options dialog box, click the Content tab, and in the Feeds section at bottom, click the Settings button. In the resulting Feed Settings dialog box, clear the Turn On Feed Reading View check box (second from bottom), and then click OK to close the Feed Settings dialog box and click OK again back in the Internet Options dialog box. When you've finished, exit and restart Internet Explorer.

The first of these URIs returns summary information about the service, including the entity sets it exposes. The second returns the contents of the entire *Currency* entity set. The third URI returns the data just for the entity whose key (that is, *CurrencyCode* value) is *FRF* (French franc). The next URI returns exactly the same result but does so by using the *SelectCurrency* service operation instead of querying the *Currency* entity set directly. The fifth URI calls our service operation and passes it *B* as a parameter value; the result is all currencies whose name (not code) starts with the letter *B*. The penultimate URI returns data for all products belonging to the subcategory whose key value (that is, *ProductSubcategoryID* value) is 1 (in other words, it returns product data for mountain bikes). The last URI returns all product entities whose *ListPrice* value is greater than 100, and orders the results by product name. As you can see, the URI syntax supported by ADO.NET Data Services is both rich and extremely logical.

Building the User Interface

Testing from the browser is nice, but we now must move on to building a .NET client application for the service. Before we can write the code, we will need access to its class definitions in the client project. Adding a service reference that points to the data service will do the trick. And adding the reference is easy. Start by right-clicking the References node for the Windows Forms project in the Solution Explorer window and selecting Add Service Reference from the shortcut menu. In the resulting Add Service Reference dialog box, type **http://localhost:1328/AW2008Service.svc** in the Address text box, type **AW2008Service** in the Namespace text box, and then click OK.

Next, in the the code-behind file for *frmMain*, add the following line at the end of the existing *using* statements to import a necessary namespace:

```
using System.Data.Services.Client;
```

You're now ready to put code in the Windows Forms application to query the service. Following is the code required to query the *Currency* entity set and bind the results to our *DataGridView* control:

```
AW2008Service.AdventureWorks2008Entities ctx =
 new AW2008Service.AdventureWorks2008Entities(new
 Uri("http://localhost:1328/AW2008Service.svc"));

dgvResults.DataSource = (from currency in ctx.Currency select currency).ToList();
```

Simple, isn't it? We just create a new instance of the service version of our EF model (passing the service's root URI as a .NET *Uri* object to the constructor) and then perform a LINQ query against it. As with some of our previous examples, we need to convert the results of the query to a *List* in order to force the query to execute and make the results bindable to the grid.

Data as a Hosted Service: SQL Server Data Services

Having looked at ADO.NET Data Services, do you find the idea of a Web Service built exclusively for data access compelling? Does the convenience and versatility of the REST standard and its ability to support direct queries from the browser strike you as elegant? Would you like to have such an interface to your data and have that data be hosted in Microsoft's own data centers without the need to host the database servers and Web servers yourself? If so, you might very well be interested in a "cloud"-based service from Microsoft: SQL Server Data Services.

At press time, this service is still in beta, making the intense study of code samples rather pointless (although the sample Windows Forms application *Chapter10* does include SQL Server Data Services sample code that we describe shortly). Also, in reality, despite the brand name of the service, the "experience" of using it is really nothing at all like working with SQL Server. But we think a brief description of the service is important to the goal of making this chapter a comprehensive examination of your data access options.

Using vocabulary similar to EF, SQL Server Data Services allows you to define *entities* and store them in *containers*. Multiple containers can be created within an *authority*, and you can create multiple authorities as well. An entity has both *static properties* (consisting of *ID*, *Kind*, and *Version*) and *dynamic properties* (in effect, the entities' columns) that can be of simple scalar data types. You can think of containers as databases, distinct *Kind* values as tables, and individual entities as rows. An authority can be thought of as a server, and in fact, all data within a given authority is guaranteed to be in the same physical location (whereas different authorities in the same SQL Server Data Services account *can* be distributed over geographically disparate facilities).

All of these objects are both created and queried via Web service calls, and SQL Server Data Services features both SOAP and REST interfaces. The URI syntax scheme for SQL Server Data Services's REST interface is (intentionally) similar to that used by ADO.NET Data Services, and it supports a LINQ-like syntax for querying its containers. While this might make SQL Server Data Services sound like a hosted version of ADO.NET Data Services, important differences remain.

Entities in SQL Server Data Services do *not* have defined schemas! The dynamic properties for each entity, even those of identical *Kind* value, might differ completely. This is because, in reality, the set of an entity's dynamic properties are collectively a single *static* property that functions like a .NET dictionary object (that is, a collection of name and value pairs). Each dynamic property is indexed, however, and you can (and probably will) create multiple entities whose dynamic "property bag" is identical in structure.

While entities of varying dynamic property structure or multiple *Kind* values can be queried together, there is no concept of a "join" when doing so. And because the query results can be entities of heterogeneous data structure, "binding" to a result set can be tricky.

If you're curious as to how SQL Server Data Services programming works, the sample code *Chapter10* Windows Forms application includes a Web reference configured for SQL Server Data Services and a form, *frmSSDS*, that demonstrates how to connect to SQL Server Data Services, create and delete its various object types, query its dictionaries, and perform update, insert, and delete operations with individual entities. The sample code uses the SQL Server Data Services SOAP interface, as that allows a Web reference to be set to it, and the proxy class generated by the Web reference allows easy programming against SQL Server Data Services and parsing/processing of the query results it returns.

Be aware of the risks of our including this code in the sample application! The code is based on an early beta and might not work correctly by the time you look at it. Also our UI is based on an assumption that all entities have the same dynamic property structure, which will normally be true only under specific circumstances. Still, the code can quickly acquaint you with the basic concepts and rather straightforward operations of SQL Server Data Services. We will be watching SQL Server Data Services carefully to see how it evolves. After reviewing the sample code, you might be inspired to do likewise.

Summary: So Many Tools, So Little Time

Although we explained at the beginning of this chapter that the number and variety of data access technologies available to Microsoft developers is great, you still might not have been prepared for just how many choices (and subchoices) there are. And the number of questions is greater still! Should you use ORM technology at all? If so, should it be LINQ to SQL or the Entity Framework? If the latter, should you use LINQ to Entities, EntityClient, or Object Services to query the models? Is conventional ADO.NET dead? Are the days of typed *DataSet*s numbered? And even if you are sticking with ADO.NET, should you start using LINQ to DataSet exclusively instead of staying with direct ADO.NET SQL queries?

The reality is that ADO.NET is still very much alive and well, and given EF's reliance on it, it's not likely to be going away. Conventional ADO.NET code will likely remain the most efficient way to perform data access. Even if Microsoft developers were to flock to ORM programming in droves, ADO.NET would likely remain in place and be at least the .NET data access analog to "native code."

Meanwhile, LINQ to SQL and the Entity Framework are so similar in approach and basic capabilities that we have some trouble imagining their continued equal coexistence. And in the battle between the two, we frankly see EF as the likely victor. It is brought to us by Microsoft's data team (as opposed to LINQ to SQL, which was developed by the language team); it is provider-based and already seeing adoption by other database vendors; and ADO. NET Data Services requires EF to perform updates to data. We can't guarantee the predicted outcome of EF as Microsoft's dominant ORM technology, but we can guarantee the sound logic in our forecast.

We see LINQ as a positive advance in filtering .NET enumerable object collections and interrogating their objects' property values. Used as a tool against XML and ADO.NET Data Services, for example, it provides a huge return on the small investment required to learn it and work with it. LINQ is also a very nice way of querying a stored procedure's result set on the client in ways that the stored procedure does not natively support. This provides for both ad hoc flexibility and adherence to the recommended practice of using stored procedures for database access. Used against actual database tables, however, we see LINQ having greatly reduced value. That's because nontrivial LINQ queries get translated to SQL queries that can be extremely complex and perhaps inefficient as well as difficult to monitor and optimize. For people who know SQL well, LINQ as a general database query tool adds a layer that is at best redundant and at worst harmful to productivity and performance.

You will see in the next chapter that this variety of data access tools combined with the numerous techniques for binding to and presenting their data and the emergence of WPF and Silverlight alongside Windows Forms and ASP.NET makes for a landscape of developer choice that is at once exciting and rather chaotic. We think that some shakeout is inevitable, if not for redundancy in the tools' capabilities then for developer fatigue in learning all of them.

In the future, we see WPF and Silverlight as increasingly dominant application platforms. We see an improved and optimized Entity Framework (along with ADO.NET Data Services and ASP.NET Dynamic Data technology), with more solid support for stored procedures and improved efficiency of generated SQL, as a popular and mainstream data access toolset. Conventional ADO.NET skills will likely remain useful and in-demand.

Typed *DataSets* might, in time, become more specialized in their use but will likely remain handy, productive, and important, especially in Windows Forms development. Windows Forms and ASP.NET will be around and will be popular for a long time. The collective skill set investments in these technologies, the productivity afforded by their designers and other development environment tools, not to mention the continuing need for HTML-based Web applications (as opposed to Rich Internet Applications [RIA]) virtually assures this.

While, again, we can't guarantee the accuracy of our predictions, we feel confident that our analysis is neither sloppy nor greatly counter to what others in the Microsoft developer world are anticipating. In the meantime, choose carefully where you invest your precious learning time. Our approach in this chapter has been to explain each technology in terms of the others so that what you've learned here will be useful regardless of how this friendly competition between tools resolves itself. And remember that while this "churn" in .NET data access technologies might pose some challenges, it is far preferable to stagnation and lack of innovation for the platform.

Chapter 11
The Many Facets of .NET Data Binding

—Andrew Brust

In Chapter 10, we looked at the multitude of data *access* technologies available to .NET developers building applications on top of Microsoft SQL Server 2008. Certainly, some work is required to make the right decision about how to get to your data. Once that decision is made, you still need to devise a strategy for displaying the data, and soliciting modifications to it, within your application's user interface (UI). Although you can certainly write your own code to load column values into controls and read them back, Microsoft has worked very hard to ensure that you don't have to. Whether you're developing for the Microsoft Windows Forms, ASP.NET, Windows Presentation Foundation (WPF), or Silverlight platforms, there are rich, sophisticated data binding technologies and techniques available to you to get this job done.

Data binding once carried a real stigma. That's because the data binding technologies found in older platforms—early versions of Microsoft Visual Basic for example—forced developers into a two-tier architecture that was more appropriate for demos and prototypes than production applications. But since the release of Windows Forms 1.0 in 2002 and ASP.NET 2.0 in 2005 (which introduced true two-way binding to .NET Web developers), data binding in the .NET world has been powerful, highly configurable, n-tier compatible, and extremely well supported by design time tools in Microsoft Visual Studio.

With the advent of WPF, Silverlight 2.0, LINQ to SQL (shortened to L2S for this discussion), the ADO.NET Entity Framework (shortened here to EF), and ADO.NET Data Services, .NET data binding has needed to evolve to accommodate the new platforms and options, and it has done so. In addition, a new technology, ASP.NET Dynamic Data, has emerged that practically extends data binding to an application platform in and of itself. So understanding data binding isn't just a viable option, it's now a downright necessity.

Our goal in this chapter is to familiarize you with all of these data binding technologies and the Visual Studio designer support around them. That might seem like another marathon mission for a single chapter. But it turns out that if you fully understand the fundamentals of Windows Forms and ASP.NET data binding for typed *DataSets*, understanding how to perform such data binding with L2S, EF, and ADO.NET Data Services involves only an incremental amount of learning. Furthermore, this understanding makes it easy to explain and understand the data binding models used by WPF and Silverlight as well. And you'll also see that ASP.NET Dynamic Data takes full advantage of the native ASP.NET data binding technology, so understanding the latter helps immensely in mastering the former.

Hold on tight—if you can open your mind to covering so much material in a short space, we can get to work right now on distilling these concepts sufficiently to make that practical.

> **Important**   The code presented in this chapter requires Visual Studio 2008 Service Pack 1 (SP1) and Silverlight 2.0. Also, some of the techniques discussed require Microsoft Expression Blend 2.5. At press time, Silverlight 2.0 was in beta and Expression Blend 2.5 was available only in a preview edition. By the time you read this, both of those products will likely be released in final form, or the release dates will be only a very short time away. Accordingly, some of what you read in this chapter, especially with respect to Silverlight, might differ slightly from the software you will be working with. However, we expect any such changes to be minimal.

Windows Forms Data Binding: The Gold Standard

With the initial release of Visual Studio .NET and the Microsoft .NET Framework, Windows Forms had a very good data binding story, but it took a little digging to learn it, and except for a wizard and some Properties window techniques, the designer support was weak. But with the release of Visual Studio 2005 and the .NET Framework 2.0, the flexibility, design time support, and ease of learning that Windows Forms data binding provided was simply fantastic. So much so, in fact, that little has changed (or has needed to change) in Visual Studio 2008 for Windows Forms data binding. Nonetheless, we need to cover how Windows Forms data binding and its tool support work, as the concepts are key to understanding the things that are new and different in other binding models.

The most expeditious way to demonstrate the largest cross section of power, features, and operational details of Windows Forms data binding is to use the design-time tools to build a three-level parent/child binding interface to the *AdventureWorks2008 ProductCategory*, *ProductSubcategory*, and *Product* tables in a typed *DataSet*. When we've finished, we'll deconstruct the various controls, components, property settings, and generated code produced by the designers, and then we'll modify the form to work with our L2S and EF models instead of with the typed *DataSet*.

Getting Ready

Use the *Chapter11* Windows Forms project included with this chapter's sample code, or create a new project and add a typed *DataSet* named **AW2008.xsd** with the previously specified tables. Edit the *DataSet* and rename the *Relation* object between the *ProductCategories* and *ProductSubcategories* tables **ProductSubcategories**, and rename the other *Relation* object **Products**. (This will ensure that the names of the *Relation* objects will be consistent with those of the association and navigation properties in the L2S and EF models that we will create subsequently.) Save and close the typed *DataSet*.

Next we need to use the Data Sources window. If the window is not visible, display it by selecting the Data, Show Data Sources option from the Visual Studio main menu. In the Data Sources window, you should see the typed *DataSet* and its constituent tables represented. (You might need to expand the *DataSet*'s node to see the tables.) If you expand any of the tables' nodes, you will see each of the table's columns represented as well. Now open the default *Form1* form if you're in a new project, or add a new form if you're in an existing project. With the form open in design mode, you'll see that the icons next to the table and column nodes in the Data Sources window will change, as shown in Figure 11-1.

FIGURE 11-1 The Visual Studio Data Sources window as it appears when a Windows Form is being designed

Essentially, each column node icon represents a default control type assigned to that column, and each table's icon represents either a grid view UI or a details view UI that will be generated if and when that node is dragged onto a form.

We're interested in creating a parent/child UI in which data for the product category is presented in a one-record-at-a-time details view and the category's child subcategories and products are presented in grids. To prepare for this, click the drop-down arrow on the *ProductCategory* table's node in the Data Sources window, and then select the Details option. Next expand the node to reveal the *ProductCategory* table's columns. Notice that the last "column" is actually a node representing the *ProductSubcategory* table; expand that node as well. Then notice that the last child node of the *ProductSubcategory* table's node represents the *Product* table; expand that too so that our entire three-table hierarchy is displayed.

Generating the UI

Now return to the node for the *ProductCategory* table and drag it to the form, carefully dropping it at the far left of the form's client area, about a quarter-inch from the top. When you let go of the mouse, a large number of controls and components will be placed on the form and in its component tray, as shown in Figure 11-2.

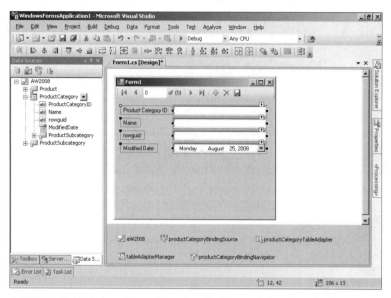

FIGURE 11-2 A Windows Form after a Details drag-and-drop data bind on the *ProductCategory* table has been performed

Before we inspect what has been generated, delete the label and text box corresponding to the *rowguid* column, and then grab the *ProductCategory* table's child node for the *ProductSubcategory* table and drop it to the right of all the generated text boxes, at a vertical location equal to the topmost label and text box currently on the form. Make certain that you drag the ProductSubcategory node that is indented underneath the ProductCategory node and *not* the top-level ProductSubcategory node below it.

Notice that a *DataGridView* control is generated to accommodate the subcategories. Although your mouse pointer was placed at the far right of the form, the form expanded horizontally to accommodate the new grid. As a last step, drag the "grandchild" node representing the *Product* table (and not the top-level node above it) and drop it just below the subcategory grid, at the same horizontal position.

You have now created a fully functional data maintenance form for product categories, complete with navigation and other necessary toolbar controls. The category data itself is presented one row/record at a time, with each column displayed in its own editable control. The grid on the upper right will display all subcategories belonging to the current category, and whichever row is selected in that grid will cause all of *its* products to be displayed in the grid on the lower right. The reason that only the child subcategory and product rows are displayed (rather than the entirety of each table's contents) is because we dragged and dropped the child nodes representing those tables, rather than the top-level nodes, from the Data Sources window.

Run the application (editing program.cs to make your new form the startup form, if necessary), and then view the results. You should find the functionality to be quite complete and impressive.

Examining the Output

The ease of drag-and-drop data binding is compelling, but most developers are uncomfortable with features they don't understand and can't control, no matter how powerful and convenient. With that in mind, here's a list of what was generated and how the objects' property settings are all connected:

- In the component tray, the *aW2008* object, which is an instance of our typed *DataSet*. Its *DataSetName property* is set to *AW2008*.

- Also in the component tray, a *BindingSource* component, *productCategoryBinding-Source*, that acts as the broker between the bound controls and the *ProductCategory* table in the typed *DataSet*. Notice that its *DataSource* property is set to *aW2008* and its *DataMember* property is set to *ProductCategory*.

- Still in the component tray, a *BindingNavigator* component (and its companion toolbar), *productCategoryBindingNavigator*. Notice that its *BindingSource* property is set to *productCategoryBindingSource*. Also various xxxItem properties (for example, *AddNewItem*, *MoveFirstItem*) are set to specific *ToolStripButton*, *ToolStripTextBox*, and *ToolStripLabel* controls within the *BindingNavigator* object's toolbar.

- On the form itself, two *TextBox* controls and a *DateTimePicker* control bound to the *ProductCategoryID*, *Name*, and *ModifiedDate* columns, respectively (as well as three companion *Label* controls). In the Properties window, if you select the *productCategoryIDTextBox* control's *(Data Bindings).Text* property and then click the drop-down arrow in its Values column, you will see that it is bound to the *ProductCategoryID* column of the *productCategoryBindingSource* component. Notice that similar property settings exist for the other two bound controls.

- Back in the component tray, an instance of our *TableAdapter* class for the *ProductCategory* table, *productCategoryTableAdapter*. If you look at the code-behind for the form, you'll notice that the *Fill* method of this object is called in the form's *Load* event handler function.

- In the component tray, additional *BindingSource* objects for the *ProductSubcategory* and *Product* tables (*productSubcategoryBindingSource* and *productBindingSource*, respectively). Notice that their *DataSource* properties are set to the parent *BindingSource* components (*productCategoryBindingSource* and *productSubcategoryBindingSource*, respectively) and that the *DataMember* categories are set to the parent *BindingSource* objects' child *Relation* objects (*ProductSubcategories* and *Products*, respectively). This is how the parent/child data binding is achieved—it is noteworthy that the child tables' *BindingSource* objects bind to other *BindingSource* objects and not to the typed *DataSet* object or any of its constituent objects.

- On the form, *DataGridView* controls, *productSubcategoryDataGridView* and *productDataGridView*, bound to the child *BindingSource* objects (via their *DataSource* properties).

- In the component tray, additional *TableAdapter* objects (*productSubcategoryTableAdapter* and *productTableAdapter*) for the child tables, whose *Fill* methods are also called in the form's *Load* event handler, and a *TableAdapterManager* object (*tableAdapterManager*), whose *UpdateAll* method is called in the *Click* event handler for the toolbar's Save button. To that method is passed the entire typed *DataSet* object, *aW2008*; the *productCategoryBindingSource* object's *EndEdit* method is called beforehand.

- In the designer-generated code (in *formname*.Designer.cs), lines of code that, for the simple bound controls (the *TextBox* and *DateTimePicker* controls) create new *Binding* objects and add them to the controls' *DataBindings* collections. For example, this line of code is generated for the *productCategoryIDTextBox* control:

```
this.productCategoryIDTextBox.DataBindings.Add(new
    System.Windows.Forms.Binding("Text", this.productCategoryBindingSource,
    "ProductCategoryID", true));
```

Notice that this code associates the *Text* property of the control with the *ProductCategoryID* property of the *productCategoryBindingSource* component. The "value" represented by the control's *(Data Bindings).Text* "property" in the Properties window is a simplified portrayal of this generated code.

These various generated controls, components, property assignments, and code might seem complex and elaborate, but once you have time to digest all of this, you'll see that there is a very logical hierarchical arrangement. The *BindingSource* brokers between the data source (a typed *DataSet* in this case) on the one hand and bound controls, a *BindingNavigator*, and optionally, child *BindingSource* components on the other hand. The *BindingNavigator* component effectively interfaces various toolbar elements with specific navigation and maintenance actions with the *BindingSource* control to which it is associated. Complex controls (like the *DataGridView* control) interface with *BindingSource* components via the former's *DataSource/DataMember* properties; simple controls (like the *TextBox* control) interface with *BindingSource* components through the former's *DataBindings* collection property. Instances of our typed *DataSet*, *TableAdapter*, and the special *TableAdapterManager* classes are added to the form to facilitate generated code for loading and saving data.

Converting to LINQ to SQL

That's really all there is to it, and the concepts are completely portable to other models. To show this, we can convert the form to use an L2S model instead of the typed *DataSet*. You can use the L2S model in the sample code's *Chapter11* project or add a new one. If you add a model yourself, be sure to name it **AW2008.dbml** and include the same three tables as in our typed *DataSet*, and then close the designer and save your changes.

Here are the steps required to convert our form to bind to the L2S model:

1. Delete from the form's component tray all items *except* the typed *DataSet* component, the three *BindingSource* components, and the *BindingNavigator* component. (Leaving the *DataSet* component allows the *DataGridView* controls to keep their *Columns* collections intact.)

2. Delete the code inside the form's *Load* event handler and the last line of code from the *BindingNavigator* Save button's *Click* event (that is, the line of code that calls the *UpdateAll* method on the *TableAdapterManager* component). Just delete the lines of code; do not delete the functions themselves.

3. Insert the following line of code at the beginning of the form's class declaration, immediately before its constructor:

```
AW2008DataContext dc = new AW2008DataContext();
```

4. Insert the following line of code in the form's *Load* event handler:

```
productCategoryBindingSource.DataSource = dc.ProductCategories;
```

5. Insert the following line at the end of the *BindingNavigator* Save button's *Click* event handler:

```
dc.SubmitChanges();
```

That's it! Now rerun the application, and notice that everything works as before.

Converting to Entity Framework

Similar changes can be made to convert the form to use our EF model. You can use the EF model in the sample code's *Chapter11* project or add a new one. If you add a model yourself, be sure to name it **AW2008.edmx**, include the same three tables as in our typed *DataSet* and L2S model, and then rename the *ProductCategory* class's *ProductSubcategory* navigation property (*not* its association) **ProductSubcategories** and the *ProductSubcategory* class's *Product* navigation property **Products**. Select the file AW2008.edmx in Solution Explorer, and then set the Custom Tool Namespace property to **AdventureWorks2008Model** and save your changes. Then make the following code changes:

1. Add the following line of code to the end of the using statements, before the class declaration:

```
using EF=AdventureWorks2008Model;
```

2. Use the following line of code at the beginning of the form's class declaration, immediately before its constructor (replacing the line placed there for the L2S sample):

```
EF.AdventureWorks2008Entities dc = new EF.AdventureWorks2008Entities();
```

3. Use the following line at the end of the *BindingNavigator* Save button's *Click* event handler (replacing the last line placed there for the L2S sample):

```
dc.SaveChanges();
```

4. And use the following block of code in the form's *Load* event handler (replacing the line that was placed there for L2S):

```
foreach (EF.ProductCategory cat in dc.ProductCategory)
{
    cat.ProductSubcategories.Load();
    foreach (EF.ProductSubcategory subcat in cat.ProductSubcategories)
    {
        subcat.Products.Load();
    }
}
productCategoryBindingSource.DataSource = dc.ProductCategory;
```

The nested *foreach* loops are necessary because EF does not automatically load child collections (as L2S does). Rerun the application, and confirm that everything works as before.

Note Against EF, our form will successfully select, update, and delete rows from the appropriate tables. However, because of specific properties of the *ProductCategory* table, inserts will not work properly without custom code. Against other tables, inserts would work fine with our data binding technique. Regardless, we chose to use the *ProductCategory* table because of its parent/child relationship to *ProductSubcategory* and *Product*. Also note that the ProductCategoryID column in the top-right *DataGridView* control is blank. That's because this property is implemented as a navigation property in the EF model and not as a scalar property.

Converting to ADO.NET Data Services

Binding to ADO.NET Data Services is easy as well. You can simply add a service reference to the URL *http://localhost:1863/AW2008Service.svc* (and set the namespace to AW2008Service), which points to the service in project *Chapter11Service* in this chapter's sample code.

Tip Note that the port number is the static port number that happens to be configured in the sample code's *Chapter11Service* project—change it if necessary, both in the service reference and in the following code. Also, if you've been working in your own Windows Forms project, make sure the service is running by including it in your solution. (That way, it will run when you press F5 in Visual Studio.)

Here are the code changes (replacing the corresponding changes made for the EF model) to make after that service reference is created:

1. Use the following line of code at the beginning of the form's class declaration, immediately before its constructor:

```
AW2008Service.AdventureWorks2008Entities dc =
new AW2008Service.AdventureWorks2008Entities(
  new Uri("http://localhost:1863/AW2008Service.svc"));
```

2. And use the following block of code in the form's *Load* event handler:

```
foreach (AW2008Service.ProductCategory cat in dc.ProductCategory)
{
    dc.LoadProperty(cat, "ProductSubcategories");
    foreach (AW2008Service.ProductSubcategory subcat in cat.ProductSubcategories)
    {
        dc.LoadProperty(subcat, "Products");
    }
}
productCategoryBindingSource.DataSource = dc.ProductCategory;
```

Again, nested *foreach* loops are necessary to load child collections, although the technique for doing so differs from that used for a local EF model.

 Note Although binding will work against ADO.NET Data Services for *displaying* data hierarchically, updates, inserts, and deletes require more work. Bound controls *will* properly update the underlying local entities, but those changes will not automatically update the server-side model when *SaveChanges* is called. Instead, the *AddObject* and *DeleteObject* methods of the data context object that we discussed in Chapter 10, along with its ADO.NET Data Services companion *UpdateObject* method, must be called explicitly on the entities in the various collections that have been added, deleted, or updated, respectively, before calling *SaveChanges*.

There's more to the Windows Forms data binding story than we've been able to cover in these examples, of course, but we have established a good overview of the technology and enough concepts to help you later understand WPF and Silverlight data binding. For now, however, let's move on to ASP.NET data binding.

Data Binding on the Web with ASP.NET

To see how easy it can be to bind an ASP.NET form to data, create a new ASP.NET Web Application project, and then create a typed *DataSet* named **AW2008.xsd**, add the *AdventureWorks2008 Currency* table to it, and build the project. (This is necessary in ASP.NET projects to make the *DataSet* and *TableAdapter* classes available to the designers.) Now open the project's Default.aspx form in Design view and perform the following steps:

1. From the Data tab of the Toolbox, add an *ObjectDataSource* control to the form. Set its (ID) property to **odsAW2008**.

2. Click the control's SmartTag (the arrow in the upper-right corner), and then select the Configure Data Source option from its ObjectDataSource Tasks menu.

3. On the Choose A Business Object page of the Configure Data Source Wizard that appears, select CurrencyTableAdapter, click Next, and then click Finish.

4. Now add a *GridView* control (also from the Data tab of the Toolbox) to the form. From its GridView Tasks menu, select odsAW2008 from the Choose Data Source drop-down list, and then select the Enable Editing check box as well. You might also want to use the Auto Format option to make the *GridView* control more attractive.

Now run the application, and confirm that the data is displayed correctly and allows editing in its columns.

L2S and EF Are Easy

Can we retrofit this form to work with L2S and EF? Absolutely. Just follow these steps:

1. Add an L2S model named **AW2008.dbml** and add the *Currency* table to it.

2. Build the project, and then return to the Default.aspx form.

3. Add a *LinqDataSource* control, and name it **ldsAW2008**.

4. Select the Configure Data Source option from the LinqDataSource Tasks menu. On the Choose A Context Object page of the Configure Data Source Wizard that appears, choose the AW2008DataContext object, click Next, and then click Finish.

5. Change the data source of the *GridView* control (using either the Choose Data Source GridView Tasks menu option or the DataSourceId property in the Properties window) from odsAW2008 to ldsAW2008, and then set the latter's EnableUpdate property to True. When prompted to refresh fields and keys, click No.

6. Run the application to confirm that its functionality is unchanged.

Converting the form to work with EF can be done easily by adding an equivalent EF model named **AW2008.edmx** (with no need to rename any object inside it), setting its Custom Tool Namespace property to **AdventureWorks2008Model,** building the project, and then adding an *EntityDataSource* control to the form named **edsAW2008.** As with the *ObjectDataSource* and *LinqDataSource* controls, you configure the *EntityDataSource* control using the Configure Data Source Wizard. Follow these steps:

1. On the wizard's Configure ObjectContext page, select the Named Connection option, select your model's connection (most likely AdventureWorks2008Entities) from the option's drop-down list, and then click Next.

2. On the Configure Data Selection page, select Currency from the EntitySetName drop-down list; select the Enable Automatic Inserts, Enable Automatic Updates, and Enable Automatic Deletes check boxes; and then click Finish.

3. Set the *GridView* control to use the new *EntityDataSource* control as its data source, and then run the application to confirm that all functionality is still present.

What about ADO.NET Data Services? It turns out there are a few ways of using Data Services from a Web application. One method is easy. First set a Service Reference to the service in the same fashion you just did for the Windows Form project. Next set the *GridView* control's *DataSourceId* property to (None), and click Yes when prompted to refresh fields and keys. Set the *AutoGenerateColumns* property to True, and then, in code, query the service, retrieve the desired result set, and set the *DataSource* property of the *GridView* control to the returned result set. Then call the control's *DataBind* method, as follows, and you've finished:

```
AW2008Service.AdventureWorks2008Entities dc = new
  AW2008Service.AdventureWorks2008Entities(new
  Uri("http://localhost:1863/AW2008Service.svc"));
GridView1.DataSource = dc.ProductCategory;
GridView1.DataBind();
```

You can also call ADO.NET Data Services from a special JavaScript library that we will discuss later in this chapter, in the section "Using AJAX for Easy Data Access".

Beyond Mere Grids

To finish our overview of ASP.NET data binding, let's look beyond the *GridView* control. For example, if you prefer to work in a details/one-row-at-a-time mode, you can use the *DetailsView* control instead. Although that control is displayed quite differently from a *GridView*, its use and configuration are so similar to that of the *GridView* control that we'll leave it as an exercise for you to get familiar with it. Instead, let's take a look at the *FormView* control and, with it, the ASP.NET data binding syntax.

Delete the *GridView* control from the form, and add a *FormView* control in its place. Auto-format the control if you want, and then set its data source to edsAW2008 (our *EntityDataSource* control). Enable paging in the SmartTag Form View Tasks list, and then in the Properties window, set the *PagerSettings.Mode* property to NextPreviousFirstLast. Comment out or delete any code in the page's *Load* event, run the application and explore.

Now close the browser, and once again select the *FormView* control in the Web form de-signer. Click its SmartTag, select the Edit Templates option from the FormView Tasks menu, and then select the EditItemTemplate option from the Display drop-down list that appears. Notice that an editable HTML region appears that displays the rendering design for the *FormView* control when in edit mode. You'll see that the *CurrencyCode* column is bound to a *Label* control, while the *Name* and *ModifiedDate* columns are bound to *TextBox* controls.

Click the *Label* control's SmartTag, and then select the Edit DataBindings option from the Label Tasks menu. The DataBindings dialog box appears with the Two-Way Databinding check box cleared and the grayed-out text *Eval("CurrencyCode")* displayed in the Code Expression text box. Now display the same dialog box for the Name *TextBox* control. You will see that the Two-Way Databinding check box is selected this time and the grayed-out text *Bind("Name")* is displayed in the Code Expression text box. Close the dialog box, click the *FormView* control's SmartTag, and select the End Template Editing option from the FormView Tasks menu.

Data Binding Using Markup

Now switch the form from Design view to Source view. Notice that for the *FormView* control's *EditItemTemplate*, the following markup is emitted for the *Label* control:

```
<asp:Label ID="CurrencyCodeLabel1" runat="server" Text='<%# Eval("CurrencyCode") %>' />
```

And the following for the *Name* column's *TextBox* control:

```
<asp:TextBox ID="NameTextBox" runat="server" Text='<%# Bind("Name") %>' />
```

The markup is not surprising given what we saw earlier in the dialog boxes. In both cases, the *Text* property (attribute) value is set to a binding expression in the form '<%# *action*("*col*") %>', where *col* is the column name the control is bound to and *action* is either *Eval* (for a one-way binding) or *Bind* (for a two-way binding).

Knowing this data binding syntax (and understanding that the Edit DataBindings dialog box merely provides a convenient UI to manage it) is very useful, as it enables you to take advantage of data binding even when designer support is not present—for example, with a stand-alone *TextBox* control (that is, without the use of a *FormView* control).

As you will also see, understanding the concept of a data binding markup syntax, including one-way and two-way binding, and combining that with the Windows Forms concepts of *BindingSource* and *Binding* objects is what will make it so easy to understand WPF and Silverlight data binding.

We won't examine the other data-bound controls, but we will mention here that the *ListView* control, new to ASP.NET 3.5, provides similar data-bound, templated functionality, with a repeating item pattern reminiscent of a *Repeater* control or even the *GridView* control. You should have enough knowledge now to work with this control and use it productively.

Using AJAX for Easy Data Access

We've looked in some detail at conventional ASP.NET. Meanwhile, using both generic AJAX techniques and using various parts of the ASP.NET AJAX framework for data access make for even more compelling applications. Collectively, these techniques allow your applications to provide dynamic data access (which everyone needs) without causing page refreshes (which everyone hates) when fetching data from the server. If you want your browser applications to look more like desktop clients and less like dumb terminal screens, AJAX is the way to go.

A comprehensive investigation of AJAX programming is beyond the scope of this book and would take us way beyond our allotted space. Meanwhile, giving you a sense of your options is very important to us, so let's take a look.

Essentially, your spectrum of choices ranges from the use of the ASP.NET AJAX *UpdatePanel* control as a simple option, to the use of various controls in the AJAX Control Toolkit as a somewhat more complex programming option, to the use of JavaScript coupled with the ADO.NET Data Services JavaScript Library as a more coding-intense option. In this section, we will cover all three.

Using the *UpdatePanel* Control

The premise of AJAX programming is that content in the browser page should be able to update itself, in place, without forcing the full page to be re-rendered entirely. Updating in place is less jarring to the user and also reduces the payload size that the server needs to send back. Wouldn't it be cool if there were a way to tell ASP.NET, declaratively, that certain portions of your page will be prone to frequent updates and you therefore want only that content to be re-rendered on the server side when a control on the page submits a postback?

The *UpdatePanel* control was designed with exactly that scenario in mind and provides for what is called a *partial page update*. Just add one or more *UpdatePanel* controls to your form and then place the controls that you know will be repeatedly re-rendered because of data refreshes, and the like, inside them. The content outside the *UpdatePanel* controls will not be re-rendered, making for more efficient client/server interaction and a better user experience.

> **Note** You can designate controls *outside* an *UpdatePanel* control as *update triggers* for the panel. For example, you could specify that a specific button's *Click* event should force a postback that updates the panel. By default, however, the *UpdatePanel* control's *ChildrenAsTriggers* property is set to *True*, and its *Triggers* collection is empty; in this configuration, postbacks from controls within the *UpdatePanel* (and only those postbacks) will trigger its re-rendering.

To see how easy this is, go to the AJAX Extensions tab of the Toolbox, drag from it a *ScriptManager* control (all AJAX operations require it) and an *UpdatePanel* onto our page, and then place the *FormView* control (but not the *DataSource* controls) within the *ScriptManager* control and rerun the application. Watch the status bar and other UI queues carefully as you navigate through the records/rows. You should see that the page does *not* refresh. If you want, return the page to its non-*UpdatePanel* state and retest; you'll see that the behavior is different, even when accessing your local Web server.

> **Note** The sample *Chapter11Web* project's UpdatePanel.aspx page contains the sample as we've described it so far.

> **Tip** If, from the Add New Item dialog box, you add an AJAX Web Form to your project, instead of a standard Web Form, the *ScriptManager* control will be inserted for you automatically. Adding an AJAX Master Page, with its own embedded *ScriptManager* control, is also possible.

The *UpdatePanel* control is one of those great tools in programming: it provides almost instant benefit and requires almost no work at all. But in reality, the controls within it are being served from the Web server, rather than simply having portions of themselves updated via client-side script. Arguably, the latter approach is what "real" AJAX programming is all about. So how can you take advantage of it, yet still not have to write a lot of script yourself? That's where the ASP.NET Control Toolkit comes in.

Adding AJAX Agility with the Control Toolkit

The AJAX Control Toolkit is not included with Visual Studio 2008 (unlike *ScriptManager*, *UpdatePanel*, and other core ASP.NET AJAX Extensions components, which are included); in fact, it is technically a community project and is available from Microsoft's CodePlex site. You can download the Toolkit from there if you want. (An Internet shortcut to the release download is included with this chapter's sample code.) On the other hand, the necessary assembly is already in our sample ASP.NET project *Chapter11Web*, so you can just use it from there.

And while you're there, open the page Accordion.aspx. This page (which is adapted from one of the ASP.NET AJAX samples from the excellent tutorials available at *http://www.asp.net*) combines the Toolkit's *Accordion* control with an *EntityDataSource* control to render the contents of the *Currency* table to the page. Run it and you'll see that the page initially displays all currency codes and the full name of the first currency. Click any other currency code, and its panel expands to show its full name while the first panel contracts to show only its code.

Here is the markup fragment for the *Accordion* control:

```
<ajaxtoolkit:Accordion ID="accCurrency" runat="server" HeaderCssClass="header"
ContentCssClass="content" Width="300px" DataSourceID="edsCurrency" FadeTransitions="true">
    <HeaderTemplate>
        <b>Currency <%#Eval("CurrencyCode")%></b>
    </HeaderTemplate>
    <ContentTemplate>
        <%#Eval("Name")%>
    </ContentTemplate>
</ajaxtoolkit:Accordion>
```

Does anything look familiar? You got it! The preceding markup uses the same data binding syntax that we studied earlier when observing the markup emitted by the *FormView* designer. The other aspect worth noting is that in order for this markup to function properly, your project requires a reference to the *AjaxControlToolkit.dll* assembly and the following line of markup at the top of the page:

```
<%@ Register Assembly="AjaxControlToolkit" Namespace="AjaxControlToolkit"
TagPrefix="ajaxtoolkit" %>
```

If you install the Toolkit on your system and add its controls to your toolbox, the preceding line will be added to your page automatically when you add a Toolkit control.

Looking at Extenders

In addition to controls, the Toolkit includes a number of *extenders* that add AJAX behavior to existing (standard) ASP.NET controls. An easy way to add these to a control on your page is to right-click the control and then choose Add Extender from the shortcut menu. The same option is also available from the control's Tasks menu by clicking its SmartTag. Another easy way to add an extender is to drag one from the toolbox and drop it on the control that it will extend.

Let's take a look at one such extender by examining the *Chapter11Web* project's *CascadingDropdown.aspx* page (which is adapted from the sample code in Joe Stagner's how-to video "Use ASP.NET AJAX Cascading Drop Down Control to Access a Database" available at *http://www.asp.net*). This page uses the Toolkit's *CascadingDropdown* control. This control, when combined with two standard ASP.NET *DropDownList* controls and an ASP.NET (.asmx) Web Service, can be used to populate one *DropDownList* control based on the selection made in the other.

By setting the control's *ServicePath* and *ServiceMethod* properties, you can direct it to a specific Web method that will be used to populate the control specified in its *TargetControlID* attribute. (The Web method in the service returns an array of *CascadingDropDownNameValue* objects.) The value of the selected item in the other *DropDownList* control (which is specified in the *ParentControlID* property) is determined within the Web method, thus allowing the returned data to be constrained by the selection.

On the CascadingDropdown.aspx page, a list of product categories is displayed in a *DropDownList* control; making a selection in this list causes the next *DropDownList* control to be populated with that category's subcategories. Selecting a subcategory then similarly populates a third *DropDownList* control with all products corresponding to the selection. The Web Service code is contained in CascadingDropdown.asmx, in the same project. (There's no reason the Web Service has to be on another server, or in a separate project.) Run the page, and then have a look at the code to see how it works.

> **Note** The Web method functions just happen to have parameters named *knownCategoryValues* and *category*. Do not confuse these with product categories in the *AdventureWorks2008* database—the similar names are mere coincidence.

> **Important** The Web Service class containing the Web methods called by the *CascadingDropDown* control must have the *System.Web.Script.Services.ScriptService* attribute applied.

There's a lot more to the ASP.NET AJAX Control Toolkit than what we've covered here. There are more techniques, more controls, and more extenders. But these two brief examples give a good introduction to the data access–oriented capabilities of the platform.

Using the AJAX Client Library for ADO.NET Data Services

The AJAX client for ADO.NET Data Services provides a script library that enables developers to call a data service from JavaScript in much the same way that the .NET client allows from .NET code. Using this library, it's possible for us to write code that calls in to AW2008Service. svc and updates even standard HTML controls on the fly, all with nothing but client-side code.

The ADONETDatSvcJS.aspx page (in the sample *Chapter11Service* project, not the *Chapter11Web* project) shows how this can be done. It features an HTML button that, when clicked, populates an HTML list box with product categories. Making a selection in that list box populates a set of text boxes with the column values for that category and an additional list box with all its subcategories.

Note that the JavaScript client library is distributed as two .js files (a debug version and a nondebug version), and one of these must be added to your project. The *Chapter11Service* project includes the debug version and can run without modification. However, you can download both .js files from CodePlex if you want. (An Internet shortcut to the release download is included with this chapter's sample code on the book's companion Web site.)

After you've included the library in your project, you can create a *Sys.Data.DataService* object in JavaScript code that can make an asynchronous call to your data service using the Uniform Resource Identifier (URI) syntax we discussed in Chapter 10. The call needs to reference two callback functions, which will handle both successful and unsuccessful queries. Here's the initial code used in ADONETDatSvcJS.aspx:

```
var ds = new Sys.Data.DataService("AW2008Service.svc");
ds.query("/ProductCategory", cbSuccess, cbFailure);
```

Because the page and the service are in the same project, we don't need a full (absolute) URI in the first line when we instantiate the *DataService* object—a relative URI does just fine. The second line fetches the *ProductCategory* collection and registers the functions *cbSuccess* and *cbFailure* as our callback functions.

The code in function *cbSuccess* takes three input parameters, and the first of them provides the results as an array of *ProductCategory* objects. The code can loop through the results array and use standard dynamic HTML (DHTML) code to populate the list box with the data. See the sample code for details, and look also at the code in the list box's *onchange* event to see how data for an individual category and its subcategories is loaded.

At this point, we have covered a variety of ways you can write code in ASP.NET to access your SQL Server data. We have just one more stop on our ASP.NET tour, and it is a technique that, ironically, doesn't require any code at all.

ASP.NET Dynamic Data

The elegance of *DataSource* and data-bound controls in ASP.NET speaks for itself. They're easy, they're declarative, and they're very flexible. Given that, wouldn't it make sense if we could use a templating technology to generate pages that can bind generically to any table in our database (or, more accurately, any class in our L2S or EF models)? ASP.NET Dynamic Data implements this approach, and does it very well. Sure, other template-driven development tools have existed for years, but when you have one that's built into Visual Studio 2008 and can generate entire sites, productivity soars. And when that tool allows you to customize the generated site, both through creation of your own templates and through declarative configuration, life as a developer is looking pretty good.

Getting this working on your own is straightforward. Simply create or add a new project in Visual Studio 2008, and then select either the Dynamic Data Web Application template (if you want to use L2S) or Dynamic Data Entities Web Application (if you want to use EF). The project template will generate a DynamicData folder, with several subfolders and files, in what is otherwise a conventional ASP.NET Web Application project. Once it does, you need to complete only two tasks to get it working: add a new, completed model (L2S or EF, as the case may be) to the project, and make two simple edits to the Global.asax file.

For our example, create a Dynamic Data Entities Web Application project, and then add an EF model to it named **AW2008.edmx** containing the *Currency*, *ProductCategory*, *ProductSubcategory*, and *Product* tables from the *AdventureWorks2008* database. Once that's done, edit the Global.asax page as shown in Listing 11-1. (Notice that the *using* statements have been omitted from this listing; those generated by default can be used.)

LISTING 11-1 The Global.asax file, in a Dynamic Data project, configured for our EF model

```
namespace Chapter11DynamicData
{
    public class Global : System.Web.HttpApplication
    {
        public static void RegisterRoutes(RouteCollection routes)
        {
            MetaModel model = new MetaModel();

            model.RegisterContext(typeof(AdventureWorks2008Entities), new
ContextConfiguration() { ScaffoldAllTables = true });

            routes.Add(new DynamicDataRoute("{table}/{action}.aspx")
            {
                Constraints = new RouteValueDictionary(new { action =
"List|Details|Edit|Insert" }),
                Model = model
            });
        }

        void Application_Start(object sender, EventArgs e)
        {
            RegisterRoutes(RouteTable.Routes);
        }

    }
}
```

Now run the application and take a look around! You'll first see a list of all your tables; click any one, and you'll be able to view the data in a *GridView* control (with the option to filter the displayed rows), delete any of the rows in place, and edit or add new rows in a *DetailsView* control. You can always return to the home page and edit a different table.

When you've finished, close the browser and look more closely at the Global.asax code. This code uses the routing facility from the ASP.NET model view controller (MVC) architecture to interpret any URI in the form *table/action*.aspx—where *table* is the name of the table to be edited, and *action* is List, Details, Edit, or Insert—and then route the client to List.aspx. Details.aspx, Edit.aspx, and so on in the project's DynamicData/PageTemplates folder. For example, the URI *http://localhost:20519/Currency/List.aspx* would route to the DynamicData/PageTemplates/List.aspx page and, in essence, pass *Currency* in as the table/entity to bind to.

Go ahead and open the DynamicData/PageTemplates/List.aspx page in Design view now. There you'll find many controls we've already examined: a *GridView*, an *EntityDataSource*, an *UpdatePanel*, and a *ScriptManager* (on the master page). Also present are a *Hyperlink* and a *ValidationSummary*, which are standard enough. Last, some ASP.NET Dynamic Data–specific controls are present. These include a *DynamicValidator*, a *FIlterRepeater*, and a *DynamicDataManager* (the first of which is available on the Validation tab of the Toolbox, and the last of which is available on the Data tab). Examining the page fully is beyond the scope of this book. But just by looking, we can see that many of the aspects of ASP.NET data source controls and AJAX that we've examined here are the same technologies that Microsoft used to create the Dynamic Data feature.

Likewise, we can't really show you all the tricks you can do with Dynamic Data, but one of these tricks is important, so let's cover it. Notice that in the DynamicData/PageTemplates folder, there is one page that Global.asax has not referenced yet: ListDetails.aspx. This page allows for in-place editing in a *GridView* control and provides a *DetailsView* control below it that allows for inserts (which a *GridView* control cannot accommodate) and also displays data for whichever row is selected in the *GridView*.

This means that ListDetails.aspx could actually accommodate all the List and Details operations and, through in-place editing, handle edits and inserts as well. We could, therefore, edit Global.asax to use this page for List and Details operations for all of our tables. But what if we want to let the *Currency* table be handled as before and only the other three tables to be routed to ListDetails.aspx? The solution is simple: in Global.asax, we just change the *RegisterRoutes* function as shown in Listing 11-2.

LISTING 11-2 The modified *RegisterRoutes* function in our Global.asax file

```
public static void RegisterRoutes(RouteCollection routes)
{
    MetaModel model = new MetaModel();

    model.RegisterContext(typeof(AdventureWorks2008Entities), new
ContextConfiguration() { ScaffoldAllTables = true });

    routes.Add(new DynamicDataRoute("Currency/{action}.aspx")
    {
        Constraints = new RouteValueDictionary(new { action =
"List|Details|Edit|Insert" }),
        Model = model,
        Table = "Currency"
    });

    routes.Add(new DynamicDataRoute("{table}/ListDetails.aspx")
    {
        Action = PageAction.List,
        ViewName = "ListDetails",
        Model = model
    });

    routes.Add(new DynamicDataRoute("{table}/ListDetails.aspx")
    {
        Action = PageAction.Details,
        ViewName = "ListDetails",
        Model = model
    });
}
```

Make and study the changes, and then run the application to see how nicely it works.

With what is now a very good grounding in Windows Forms and ASP.NET data binding, we can complete our work by looking at data binding in WPF and Silverlight.

Data Binding for Windows Presentation Foundation

Windows Presentation Foundation (WPF) is the chosen future platform for Windows desktop development. This might sound extreme, but WPF renders Windows Forms effectively obsolete. Moreover, WPF is not simply another forms package, and the transition from Windows Forms to WPF is much more disruptive and abrupt than was the switch from, say, Visual Basic 6.0 to Windows Forms. For one thing, WPF actually uses a markup language called Extensible Application Markup Language (XAML) to control the look and feel and the layout of controls on its forms. For another, the UI design for a typical WPF application is not just a "battleship gray" background and a bunch of standard input controls. Rather, it is design-intense, and aesthetic niceties are almost a mandatory part of the typical WPF application.

Meanwhile, the "tooling" (designer support) around WPF in Visual Studio is still rather rudimentary. This creates a problem and at the same time mitigates the disruption: inferior tooling makes the transition even harder, and it also slows down the transition. In other words, the Windows Forms development environment is still so much more productive than WPF's that the vast majority of client development is likely to remain in Windows Forms for some time to come. The fact remains, however, that Windows Forms will go away, and learning WPF should now be high on the priority list for .NET desktop developers. This gives us both motivation and time to start learning WPF.

In the realm of data access, the good news is that WPF has incorporated data binding capabilities into the very core of platform. And while it works differently from Windows Forms, it cleverly combines the latter's data binding concepts with those of ASP.NET. For the most part, doing data binding in WPF "feels" like it does in Windows Forms when you're working in a visual design environment and when you're working in code; however, when you're examining or modifying the markup behind the form, the binding experience is positively "ASP.NET-esque."

To a lesser degree, the same is true of Silverlight 2.0. Silverlight is, for all intents and purposes, the cross-platform, Web browser–based version of WPF. In fact, while Silverlight was in early development, it was referred to as WPF/e (the e standing for everywhere). The two are different but closely related: if they're not siblings, they're certainly cousins. The same goes for their data binding mechanisms. With that in mind, we'll look at WPF's data binding now and Silverlight's immediately after.

Design Time Quandary

One of the most challenging aspects of data access programming in WPF is that the Visual Studio 2008 visual designer provides *no support* for data binding. This leaves you with two options: perform all your data binding in XAML, or use Microsoft's visual design tool, Expression Blend (hereafter, Blend), which provides extensive data binding support, to do the data binding portion of your form design. What we'll do here is start in Blend, and then look at and modify the generated XAML so that we can understand WPF data binding from both perspectives.

If you don't have Blend, simply follow along with the text here, and then open the Main.xaml form, located in the sample code's *Chapter11WPF* project, in Visual Studio. Blend works with exactly the same solution, project, and file structure as does Visual Studio, so you can create your project in one, open it in the other, and then open it again in the first.

Start by creating a new WPF Application project in Visual Studio 2008. Add to it an EF model named **AW2008.edmx**, with just the tables *ProductCategory* and *ProductSubcategory*. Change the name of the *ProductCategory* class's *Name* property to **TheName**. (This is a bug workaround that might no longer be necessary by the time you read this.) Build your project and then close the project or solution. Open the project or solution in Blend, and then open the Window1.xaml file so that we can design the form. Display the Blend Data panel if necessary, and then click its +CLR Object button. In the resulting Add CLR Object Data Source dialog box, select the ProductCategory class (under the project's assembly and default namespace), and then click OK. The class should now appear in the Data panel; click the arrow to its left to expand the class and display its properties.

You should see the *ProductCategoryID* property displayed. Drag it onto the form, toward the upper left. A pop-up menu will appear asking you what type of control to bind the property to; click TextBox. Next the Create Data Binding dialog box will appear. In the middle of the dialog box is an expansion arrow (akin to the Details>> button you might see in some other dialog boxes); click the arrow, and the dialog box will expand as shown in Figure 11-3.

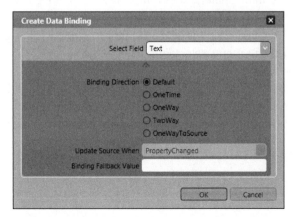

FIGURE 11-3 The Expression Blend Create Data Binding dialog box in expanded view

The Create Data Binding dialog box allows you to specify the field (which in this case really means property) of the control to which the value of the *ProductCategoryID* property will be bound, the binding direction, and a couple other attributes of the binding. Notice that in WPF, bindings can be one-way or two-way, and that the one-way binding can go in either direction (from the source or to the source). A one-time binding is also possible, and each control type has a default direction setting.

Accept the default selections of the Text field/property and Default binding direction and click OK. Last, size the text box vertically to be 25 pixels high, and then repeat the entire process for the *TheName* and *ModifiedDate* properties of the *ProductCategory* class. Next, locate the *ProductSubcategory* property in the Data panel, and notice that it is indicated as an array. Drag it onto the form, and then select ListBox as the control type to bind to. Notice in the Create Data Binding dialog box that the default binding property/field for a *ListBox* is *ItemsSource*—that is exactly what we want, so click OK.

At this point, the Create Data Template dialog box appears. Here's why: a *ListBox* in WPF can behave like a Windows Forms *ListBox*, but using a data template, it can also behave like an ASP.NET *Repeater* control (or perhaps more aptly, an ASP.NET *ListView* control) in that each item in the list box can be a container for a collection of constituent controls. The data template contains the XAML markup that is replicated once per list item.

So in our case, we want to create a data template with three data-bound text boxes, one for each *ProductSubcategory* property. The Create Data Template dialog box makes this fairly easy: first clear the ProductSubcategory item at the root of the fields list, and then select ProductSubcategoryId, Name, and ModifiedDate and, using the reorder arrows at the bottom-left of the dialog box, move these fields, in order, up to the top of the list. As a last step, from the combo boxes to the right of the fields list, select Grid as the control type for the ProductSubcategory parent item in the list, and then select TextBox (and not TextBlock) for each of the three selected properties. The dialog box should now appear as shown in Figure 11-4.

Click OK. We've almost finished, but unfortunately, Blend will default to creating a three-row by one-column grid for your data template, rather than the other way around (which is how we want it so that a gridlike UI will be created in the list box itself). To remedy this, right-click the *ListBox* control, and from its shortcut menu, select Edit Other Templates, Edit Generated Items (Item Template), Edit Template. This will set the designer to edit your data template rather than the host form. Here you'll need to resize the *Grid* to be wider (select the *Grid* itself by clicking it in the Objects And Timeline panel), create two new columns, move a text box into each column, and then delete the second and third rows. You'll need to become somewhat adept at using Blend to do this. If you're wary, you can skip this step and just use the data template's markup from the Main.xaml form in the *Chapter11WPF* sample code project.

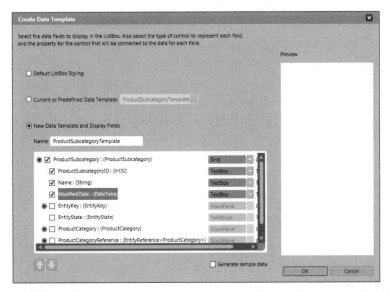

FIGURE 11-4 The Expression Blend Create Data Template dialog box, set up for child data in the *ProductSubcategory* table

> **Note** It would be infinitely more convenient to bind the *ProductSubcategory* property to some sort of data grid rather than a templated *ListBox*. Unfortunately, WPF, as of the release of the .NET Framework 3.5 SP1, does not have a native data grid. At press time, a WPF data grid is under development at Microsoft, but we chose not to use an early prerelease control in our sample. Our Silverlight sample does use a *DataGrid* control, so you might want to use that as guidance for the WPF control, once it's released.

To exit from editing the data template and return to the parent form, click the up arrow at the upper left of the Objects And Timeline panel. (The arrow has a tooltip that reads "Return scope to [Window].") Now save your work, close the project, and reopen it in Visual Studio.

Examining the XAML

Open the Window1.xaml form (if it's not open by default), and view the XAML markup. The markup should appear similar to that shown in Listing 11-3.

LISTING 11-3 Full XAML markup for our WPF form, including our defined data template

```
<Window x:Class="WpfApplication1.Window1"
    xmlns="http://schemas.microsoft.com/winfx/2006/xaml/presentation"
    xmlns:x="http://schemas.microsoft.com/winfx/2006/xaml"
    Title="Window1" Height="300" Width="429" xmlns:WpfApplication1="clr-
namespace:WpfApplication1" xmlns:d="http://schemas.microsoft.com/expression/
blend/2008" xmlns:mc="http://schemas.openxmlformats.org/markup-compatibility/2006"
mc:Ignorable="d">
  <Window.Resources>
    <ObjectDataProvider x:Key="ProductCategoryDS" ObjectType="{x:Type WpfApplication1:
ProductCategory}" d:IsDataSource="True"/>
    <DataTemplate x:Key="ProductSubcategoryTemplate">
      <Grid Width="207">
        <Grid.ColumnDefinitions>
          <ColumnDefinition Width="0.324*"/>
          <ColumnDefinition Width="0.357*"/>
          <ColumnDefinition Width="0.319*"/>
        </Grid.ColumnDefinitions>
        <Grid.RowDefinitions>
          <RowDefinition Height="*"/>
        </Grid.RowDefinitions>
        <TextBox HorizontalAlignment="Stretch" Margin="0,0,0,0" Grid.Row="0" Grid.
RowSpan="1" Text="{Binding Path=ProductSubcategoryID}"/>
        <TextBox Margin="0,0,0,0" Grid.Column="1" Grid.Row="0" Grid.RowSpan="1"
Text="{Binding Path=Name}"/>
        <TextBox Margin="0,0,0,0" Grid.Column="2" Grid.Row="0" Text="{Binding
Path=ModifiedDate}" Grid.RowSpan="1" VerticalAlignment="Stretch"/>
      </Grid>
    </DataTemplate>
  </Window.Resources>
  <Grid>

<TextBox HorizontalAlignment="Left" Margin="19,30,0,0" VerticalAlignment="Top"
Width="132" Height="23" Text="{Binding Path=ProductCategoryID, Mode=Default,
Source={StaticResource ProductCategoryDS}}"/>
    <TextBox HorizontalAlignment="Left" Margin="19,57,0,0" VerticalAlignment="Top"
Width="132" Height="25" Text="{Binding Path=TheName, Mode=Default,
Source={StaticResource ProductCategoryDS}}"/>
    <TextBox HorizontalAlignment="Left" Margin="19,86,0,0" VerticalAlignment="Top"
Width="132" Height="25" Text="{Binding Path=ModifiedDate, Mode=Default,
Source={StaticResource ProductCategoryDS}}"/>
    <ListBox Margin="176,30,45,43" ItemTemplate="{DynamicResource
ProductSubcategoryTemplate}" ItemsSource="{Binding Path=ProductSubcategory,
Mode=Default, Source={StaticResource ProductCategoryDS}}"/>
  </Grid>
</Window>
```

Let's deconstruct this markup a little, and then we'll modify it and add a little code to give ourselves a fully data-bound form.

First, at the top, in the *<Window.Resources>* section, is an *<ObjectDataProvider>* definition and the markup for our data template. By defining these as local resources, the markup within the form itself can reference these items in their own attribute settings. Notice, toward the bottom, three *<TextBox>* elements and one *<ListBox>* element, corresponding to our bound controls. Look at the first *TextBox* element and see that its *Text* attribute is set as follows:

```
Text="{Binding Path=ProductCategoryID, Mode=Default,
       Source={StaticResource ProductCategoryDS}}"/>
```

In other words, the *TextBox* control's *Text* property is bound to the *ProductCategoryID* property (via the *Path* attribute) of the current item coming from the *ProductCategoryDS ObjectDataProvider* resource defined above it (via the *Source* attribute), with the binding direction set to the default for the *TextBox* control type (via the *Mode* attribute). And this entire definition (contained in curly braces) creates a WPF *Binding* object implicitly. (This could be done in code as well, but by using the brace syntax, we can actually create objects in markup.)

The other two text boxes have similar markup, for their corresponding properties. The *ListBox* control's markup contains the following:

```
ItemTemplate="{DynamicResource ProductSubcategoryTemplate}"
ItemsSource="{Binding Path=ProductSubcategory, Mode=Default,
              Source={StaticResource ProductCategoryDS}}"
```

In other words, the *ListBox* control is bound to the *ProductSubcategory* field of the same *ObjectDataProvider* resource as the text boxes. This property is a collection/array; therefore, the control property it's bound to (*ItemsSource*) is as well, and the local resource *ProductSubcategoryTemplate* should be used as a data template to govern the rendering of each item. If you look at the template's definition, you'll see the details for the grid and the markup for the three *TextBox* controls, which is similar to that of the *TextBox* controls we just examined.

Notice, however, that the *TextBox* controls in the data template do not have a *Source* attribute in the *Binding* definitions for their *Text* properties. That's because they inherit their source from the containing *ListBox* control, which is, as we know, the *ProductSubcategory* array from *ProductCategoryDS*. WPF controls' data sources are always inherited from their parent control (going all the way up to the *Window* itself, if necessary).

With that in mind, let's actually remove the *Source* attribute from bindings of the *TextBox* controls and the *ListBox* control that have them. In effect, this says that these root-level controls will get their data from either the root layout control's *DataContext* property or that of the parent *Window* itself. That being the case, you can remove the entire *ObjectDataProvider* element from the markup as well.

Now all we have to do is set the *DataContext* property of the *Window* to a query of the *ProductCategory* entity set from our EF model and make sure that each entity's

ProductSubcategory collection is preloaded. To make that happen, create an event handler for the *Window* object's *Loaded* event (by double-clicking the form's client area in Design view). Code the handler as shown in Listing 11-4.

LISTING 11-4 The *Loaded* event handler for our WPF form

```
private void Window_Loaded(object sender, RoutedEventArgs e)
{
    AdventureWorks2008Entities ctx = new AdventureWorks2008Entities();
    var results =
        from cat in ctx.ProductCategory
        select cat;
    foreach (ProductCategory cat in results)
        cat.ProductSubcategory.Load();
    this.DataContext = results;
}
```

Notice a few things here:

- The *DataContext* property of the *Window* is much like the *DataSource* property of a Windows Forms *BindingSource* control.

- Child collections are handled in WPF data bindings in a similar fashion to the way they are in Windows Forms. The WPF *ListBox* control's *ItemsSource* property is set the same way that our *DataGridView* controls' *DataSource* properties were set (that is, to a child collection property). All child data is then displayed correctly.

- Although we've elected not to use one here, WPF *DataProvider* objects behave in a very similar way to ASP.NET *DataSource* controls (for example, the *EntityDataSource* control) and can allow for similar codeless data binding through markup.

Before you run the application, add a button, create a *Click* event handler for it, and insert the following code in it:

```
CollectionView cv = (CollectionView)CollectionViewSource.GetDefaultView(this.DataContext);
if (cv.CurrentPosition < cv.Count - 1)
    cv.MoveCurrentToNext();
```

This will create a button that will advance through the rows in the *ProductCategory* collection. For purposes of navigating through a collection, the WPF *CollectionView* object behaves similarly to a Windows Forms *BindingSource* object. The latter object has methods *MoveNext*, *MovePrevious*, *MoveFirst*, and *MoveLast* (although we didn't discuss them earlier). Similarly, the *CollectionView* object has methods *MoveCurrentToNext*, *MoveCurrentToPrevious*, *MoveCurrentToFirst*, and *MoveCurrentToLast*. You might want to add three more buttons to handle the remaining three navigation operations.

Now run the application! You should have full view into all product categories and each of their subcategories. If your code doesn't run on the first try, take a look at the Main.xaml form in the *Chapter11WPF* project. Not only does that form function fully, it also has nice WPF graphical elements and buttons to load data (no data is loaded initially) from L2S and a typed *DataSet* in addition to EF.

Grand Finale: Silverlight

Remember, Silverlight is the cross-platform version of WPF. Therefore, we can dive right into the markup (also XAML) for a Silverlight version of our WPF application (which we created by taking the WPF version's XAML, pasting it in, and modifying it). There are a few important differences in this version, however. First, there is no provision for doing local data access (meaning no ADO.NET, no EF, and no L2S) in Silverlight, so we have to create local class definitions for *ProductCategory* and *ProductSubcategory* as well as an XML file with the actual data. That means we'll need to use LINQ to XML to populate our object model, and then we'll bind to it. We'll also have to handle navigation differently since there's no *CollectionView* object to work with.

> **Note** Loading data into Silverlight from an ADO.NET Data Services service and binding to it *is* possible, even if loading from EF is not. The Main.xaml form in the *Chapter11Silverlight* project, included with this chapter's sample code, is written to load data using either LINQ to XML or ADO.NET Data Services (based on a radio button selection). We've explicated the LINQ to XML code here. See the sample application for details on the ADO.NET Data Services code. In order for the ADO.NET Data Services call to work correctly, you *must* start the Silverlight project by running its test project, *Chapter11SilverlightWeb*, rather than running the *Chapter11Silverlight* project directly.

Open the *Chapter11Silverlight* project's Main.xaml form and take a look. Let's start with the markup, an excerpt from which is shown in Listing 11-5.

LISTING 11-5 A XAML excerpt from our Silverlight page

```
<TextBox Text="{Binding ProductCategoryID}" Margin="153,166.157,0,0"
    Foreground="#FFFFCFD5" Background="Transparent" Height="24.843"
    VerticalAlignment="Top" Opacity="1" HorizontalAlignment="Left" Width="167"/>

<TextBox Text="{Binding Name}" Margin="153,200.493,0,0" Foreground="#FFFFCFD5"
    Background="Transparent" Height="27.507" VerticalAlignment="Top" Opacity="1"
    HorizontalAlignment="Left" Width="167"/>

<TextBox Text="{Binding ModifiedDate}" Margin="153,0,0,214.507"
    Foreground="#FFFFCFD5" Background="Transparent" Height="24.843"
    VerticalAlignment="Bottom" Opacity="1" HorizontalAlignment="Left" Width="167"/>

<my:DataGrid Name="dgSubcategories" Margin="353,164,10,194"
    ItemsSource="{Binding ProductSubcategory}" AutoGenerateColumns="True" />
```

Notice that there's no *Path* attribute for the Silverlight *Binding* object. Instead, the bound source property name is simply inserted in the object definition. Also, we have a *DataGrid* control in Silverlight, so we use that instead of a *ListBox* (and thus no data template is necessary). Also, there is no *DataProvider* object; Silverlight doesn't support them.

Now, on to code. Listing 11-6 has the data loading code for the Silverlight *Page*.

LISTING 11-6 Our Silverlight page's LINQ to XML data loading code

```
RecordNumber = 0;
Results = from r in XElement.Load("AW2008.xml").Elements("ProductCategory")
  select new ProductCategory
  {
    ProductCategoryID = r.Element("ProductCategoryID").Value,
    Name = r.Element("Name").Value,
    ModifiedDate = r.Element("ModifiedDate").Value,
    ProductSubcategory = from rr in r.Elements("ProductSubcategory")
      select new ProductSubcategory
      {
        SubcatID = rr.Element("ProductSubcategoryID").Value),
        Name = (rr.Element("Name").Value)
      }
  };
this.DataContext = Results.ElementAt(RecordNumber);
```

Notice the nested LINQ to XML query used to retrieve *ProductCategory* and subsidiary *ProductSubcategory* data from the file AW2008.xml. This query references the class definitions in the *Chapter11Silverlight* project's CategoryAndSubcategory.cs class file.

The query returns an *IEnumerable<ProductCategory>* collection into the variable *Results*, and we set the *Page* object's *DataContext* property not to that variable, but rather to a single member of it, which we fetch using its *ElementAt* method. Upon loading the data, we pass the latter method the variable *RecordNumber*, which is initialized in value to 0. Not shown here is code for the navigation buttons, where we increment the *RecordNumber* variable (to move to the next record), decrement it (to move to the previous record), set it to 0 (to move to the first record), or set it to *Results.Count()-1* (to move to the last record) and update the *DataContext* property using the *Results.ElementAt* method call again.

That's all there is to it. Run the application to see how well it works. Then take a deep breath, because we've finished!

Summary

You've seen enough data binding models and samples in this chapter to make your head spin. We know that this information can be confusing, especially when distilled into such a compact space. But our goal here was to show you that no matter which direction you take, be it Windows Forms, ASP.NET, ASP.NET AJAX, ASP.NET Dynamic Data, WPF, or Silverlight, data binding is there, and it works in conceptually similar ways, whether you're using ADO.NET, LINQ to SQL, the Entity Framework, or ADO.NET Data Services. Each binding model has borrowed from at least one other, and so by studying them together, you end up with the best qualifications for understanding them separately.

You might want to reread this chapter and dig into the samples carefully, even modifying them to test out related scenarios and make sure that you understand these concepts fully. If you do, you'll have the great reward of understanding how to build data-oriented applications in any .NET application platform, and above all, you'll know how to do so using the elegance and high productivity of concise data binding techniques rather than manual code.

Chapter 12
Transactions

—Updated by Leonard Lobel and Kenn Scribner

Have you ever developed an application with the intention of writing unreliable code? Of course not. It would be equally absurd for a customer to appreciate the system you wrote that completely corrupted the customer's data. Would you have much patience for a customer service representative who couldn't help you because the information on the service representative's computer wasn't correct?

As absurd and exaggerated as these scenarios might at first appear, the fact remains that many software professionals treat the idea of writing reliable software all too casually. They concentrate most of their effort on getting the logic right and pay too little attention to ensuring that the logic behaves correctly under all circumstances. At the same time, more and more tasks are becoming automated, which demands increasingly complex software, which in turn is made possible by increasingly powerful hardware. Just as the desktop machine you work on today is thousands of times more powerful than the microprocessors of 25 years ago, software has grown dramatically more complex over time. This increase in complexity demands much more reliability in our code, not less.

Despite this, most programmers continue to write unreliable software. Think of the last paycheck you received—the multitude of computer systems it went through and all the programmers who worked on that software. How would you feel if careless programming or inadequate testing resulted in a $100 reduction in your paycheck? Or what if a computer bug accidentally wiped out your retirement account, your Social Security number, or your identity?

Many programmers expect their careless mistakes to be caught in testing. But testing environments can rarely load-test applications appropriately and are for the most part incapable of reproducing various concurrent scenarios. The reality is that most software issues manifest themselves in the production environment, not in development or testing. Therefore, as developers, we must focus on making sure that our application logic is correct and behaves consistently in all scenarios. When application logic involves databases, those logical and data manipulation operations must conform to the *ACID* properties: *atomicity, consistency, isolation,* and *durability.* Generally, you ensure this by wrapping database operations in transactions. So we'll begin this chapter by exploring what a transaction is.

What Is a Transaction?

A *transaction* is a single operation or set of operations that succeed or fail together as a whole, thereby ensuring consistency of data should unforeseen circumstances arise. One scenario might be a financial transaction. For example, let's say you buy a car. The single transaction of buying a car consists of three distinct operations:

1. You select a car.

2. You pay for it.

3. You drive the car off the lot.

Skipping any of these steps could cause major angst to one or more of the parties involved. This is a simple example of a set of steps that must always occur together in a consistent manner.

Transactions allow us to ensure consistency in our data through four basic principles. These principles provide a set of rules that must be followed for our transaction to succeed. The four principles help ensure that the state of our data is atomic, consistent, isolated, and durable, regardless of the success or failure of the transaction. Let's examine these properties now.

> **Note** The discussion here centers around traditional two-phase commit ("XA-style") transactions. With the advent of Microsoft BizTalk and Web Services, long-running processes are common, so another type of transaction was created to handle those—the *compensated transaction*. We will not be covering compensated transactions in this chapter, preferring instead the traditional Microsoft SQL Server two-phase commit transaction.

Understanding the ACID Properties

Consider the transaction of going to an ATM and withdrawing $100 from your bank account. The data for this transaction can be easily represented in a database as a table with two columns, one holding your *AccountID* and the other holding your *AccountBalance*.

To begin with, your account balance is $100, so after withdrawing $100, your updated balance should be zero. Also, it makes logical sense that the system must ensure that you have the funds available in your account before the cash can be dispensed. What this means in database terms is that two database queries must be run in this transaction. The first query checks the account balance, as shown here:

```
SELECT AccountBalance FROM Account WHERE AccountID = @AccountID
```

If the query returns an *AccountBalance* value greater than or equal to the requested withdrawal, you can withdraw the cash.

After withdrawing the cash, you must update the account record with the updated balance. To do so, you run an *UPDATE* query:

```
UPDATE Account
 SET AccountBalance = AccountBalance - 100
 WHERE AccountID = @AccountID
```

The two distinct operations in this transaction are the two database queries that support the one operation of withdrawing cash. Both must succeed or fail together in an *atomic* manner, or the transaction should not be considered complete. *Atomicity* is the first ACID property.

Now let's change the nature of the transaction a bit. Let's say that the original account balance is $150 and that within the same transaction, the user requests to withdraw $100 and to transfer another $75 to a second account. The first update query will succeed, changing the account balance to $150 – $100 = $50. But the second operation will fail because there won't be enough money left in the account to transfer the $75. You therefore need a way to undo the cash withdrawal and return the database to its original state. You cannot leave the database midway through a transaction because it is in an *inconsistent state*. In a real-world scenario, you would not normally wrap a withdrawal and a transfer in the same transaction, but the point here is to show how data can end up in an inconsistent state between multiple operations. Rolling back operations that cannot be completed in this manner demonstrates the second ACID property, *consistency*.

Let's say now that the withdrawal and transfer operations are separated into two distinct transactions instead of one but that they happen to run simultaneously. Each transaction will have to check the current balance by attempting to execute a query like this:

```
SELECT AccountBalance FROM Account WHERE AccountID = @AccountID
```

Unless your system has explicit checks blocking concurrent reads, both transactions will get the same result: $150. Thus they will both assume that the account has enough funds for the transaction. One transaction will disburse $100, and the other will transfer $75. The result will be an overall deduction of $100 + $75 = $175, even though the account actually has only $150 available. In many systems, especially financial applications, such transactions must be isolated from each other to prevent what is known as a "dirty read." A dirty read happens when data is read at one point in a transition state and the result of the query doesn't reflect the data's true state at the end of the current operation. This brings us to the third ACID property, *isolation*.

Isolation means that other transactions attempting to request a common resource will be blocked. Blocking, in turn, seriously affects the response times of your application. As it turns out, you'll often want to relax this blocking behavior to suit your application architecture. You can do that by using *isolation levels*, which we'll discuss later in this chapter.

Last, when you have successfully completed all your operations within a transaction, you don't want to lose the changes made. In other words, system failures must not affect the transactional integrity of your operations. This brings us to the fourth ACID property, *durability*. Durability means that the systems involved with the transaction will faithfully retain the correct transacted state even if the system sustains catastrophic failure nanoseconds after the transaction completes. Conversely, if the transaction isn't completed because of system failure, it won't be allowed to complete (or be undone) until the system is reset and the application restarted. Transacted steps are retained, and the application can resume operations where it left off with no ill effects (at least from a data consistency perspective).

Let's summarize the four ACID properties before we continue:

- **Atomicity**   Operations succeed or fail together. Unless all steps succeed, the transaction cannot be considered complete.

- **Consistency**   Operations leave the database in a consistent state. The transaction takes the underlying database from one stable state to another, with no rules violated before the beginning or after the end of the transaction.

- **Isolation**   Every transaction is an independent entity. One transaction will not affect any other transaction that is running at the same time.

- **Durability**   Every transaction is persisted to a reliable medium that cannot be undone by system failures. Furthermore, if a system failure does occur in the middle of a transaction, either the completed steps must be undone or the uncompleted steps must be executed to finish the transaction. This typically happens by use of a log that can be played back to return the system to a consistent state.

> **Important** In our discussion of ACID transactional properties, we brushed over two other important concepts. The first refers to the actual process of disbursing cash as a part of the transaction. This alludes to the fact that transactions are not necessarily limited to database entities only. We will be examining more complex transactional situations later in this chapter when we discuss a namespace in the Microsoft .NET Framework named *System.Transactions*. The second refers to isolation levels that allow you to tweak the isolation behavior of a transaction to your specific needs, which we will also address later in this chapter.

A transaction can work with a single resource, such as a database, or multiple resources, such as multiple databases or message queues. Transactions limited to a single resource are referred to as *local transactions*, and transactions that span multiple resources are called *distributed transactions*. We'll first concentrate on local transaction support in Microsoft SQL Server 2008, and we'll talk about distributed transactions later in this chapter.

Local Transaction Support in SQL Server 2008

SQL Server, like any industrial-strength database engine, provides built-in support that enables you to wrap one or more queries inside a transaction. Local transactions (those that deal with only one physical database) operate in one of four transaction modes:

- Autocommit
- Explicit
- Implicit
- Batch-scoped

Let's explore each of these modes in turn.

Autocommit Transaction Mode

The *autocommit* transaction mode is the default transaction mode. Under this mode, SQL Server ensures data sanctity across the lifetime of the query execution, regardless of whether you requested a transaction. For example, if you execute a *SELECT* query, the data will not change over the execution lifetime of the query. On the other hand, if you execute a data manipulation language (DML) query (*UPDATE*, *INSERT*, or *DELETE*), the data will automatically be committed if no errors occur or *rolled back* (undone) otherwise. The execution of a single DML query will never result in a partial modification of records. The two notable exceptions to this rule are recursive common table expressions (CTEs), for which all of the returned data is not locked in advance, and situations where you explicitly request no transactional sanctity.

Explicit Transaction Mode

The autocommit transaction mode enables you to run single queries in a transactional manner, but frequently you'll want a batch of queries to operate within a single transaction. In that scenario, you use *explicit* transactions. Under the explicit transaction mode, you explicitly request the boundaries of a transaction. In other words, you specify precisely when the transaction begins and when it ends. SQL Server continues to work under the autocommit transaction mode until you request an exception to the rule, so if you want to execute a number of Transact-SQL (T-SQL) statements as a single batch, use the explicit transaction mode instead.

You specify when the transaction starts by using the *BEGIN TRANSACTION* statement. After you call *BEGIN TRANSACTION* on a database connection, the SQL Server Database

Engine attempts to enlist all ensuing operations within the same transaction. The *BEGIN TRANSACTION* statement uses the following syntax:

```
BEGIN { TRAN | TRANSACTION }
   [ { transaction_name | @tran_name_variable }
     [ WITH MARK [ 'description' ] ]
   ]
```

In this statement, you can specify a name for the transaction by using *transaction_name* or *@tran_name_variable*. You can also mark a transaction in the transaction log by specifying a description. This is useful if you want to restore the database to a named mark. (For more information about this feature, refer to SQL Server Books Online.)

Let's say that you have called *BEGIN TRANSACTION* and have been merrily executing a number of DML operations. When you've finished, you will want to end your transaction by saving (committing) your changes or undoing them (rolling back) in the event of an error. If you want to make the changes permanent, you execute a *COMMIT TRANSACTION* statement that uses the following syntax:

```
COMMIT { TRAN | TRANSACTION } [ transaction_name | @tran_name_variable ] ]
```

Here's an example that wraps two DML statements (an *UPDATE* and an *INSERT*) inside a single explicit transaction:

```
BEGIN TRANSACTION
   UPDATE Table1 SET Column1 = 'One'
   INSERT INTO Table2 (Column2) VALUES ('Two')
COMMIT
```

SQL Server maintains the transaction count, which returns the number of active transactions for the current connection. You can obtain the current transaction count by using the *@@TRANCOUNT* function. Every time you call *BEGIN TRANSACTION*, *@@TRANCOUNT* is incremented by 1. You can also call *BEGIN TRANSACTION* inside another *BEGIN TRANSACTION* block, which will increase the *@@TRANCOUNT* as well. Similarly, every time you call *COMMIT TRANSACTION*, SQL Server decrements *@@TRANCOUNT* by 1. Until *@@TRANCOUNT* drops back down to zero, the transaction remains active. When you call *BEGIN TRANSACTION* within a transaction block, you effectively create a *nested transaction*. But it isn't quite as simple as that. Before you can understand the nature of nested transactions in SQL Server 2008, we must also consider the scenario in which you want the changes to be undone (not saved permanently) when an error occurs within the transaction.

If you do not want the changes to be permanent and instead want to restore the database to its previous state, you can roll back the changes with the *ROLLBACK TRANSACTION* T-SQL statement, which uses the following syntax:

```
ROLLBACK { TRAN | TRANSACTION }
     [ transaction_name | @tran_name_variable
     | savepoint_name | @savepoint_variable ]
```

ROLLBACK is the opposite of *COMMIT*. Instead of saving, it undoes all changes made in the transaction. It is important to realize that SQL Server never assumes *COMMIT*. If you disconnect from SQL Server without explicitly issuing a *COMMIT*, SQL Server assumes a *ROLLBACK*. However, as a best practice, you should never leave that decision to SQL Server. You should explicitly tell SQL Server which of the two options you want. The reason for this is that connection pooling is implemented at various levels in any common data access application programming interface (API). Even if you close a connection, which would automatically cause the rollback if you didn't commit the transaction, it might take a while before an API such as Microsoft ADO.NET physically closes the connection. SQL Server might have to keep the transaction running and hence block valuable resources for longer than expected.

If a severe error occurs during the execution of a transaction, SQL Server rolls back the transaction. Unfortunately, SQL Server doesn't make clear its definition of a severe error. An error with a severity level of 11 or higher stops the execution of the current batch and rolls back the transaction. Errors with a severity level of 19 or greater go as far as to terminate the connection. Which one is more severe? In both cases, batch execution stops in some indeterminate state. Because of this ambiguity, it is a good idea to explicitly call *ROLLBACK* if an error occurs.

> **Tip** Always call *ROLLBACK* explicitly, and never rely on the API or SQL Server to issue a rollback for you.

Also note that *COMMIT TRANSACTION* decrements @@TRANCOUNT by 1, but *ROLLBACK TRANSACTION* always reduces @@TRANCOUNT to 0. What does this mean in terms of nested transactions? We'll explore this topic next.

Nested Transactions

What does all this talk of @@TRANCOUNT and nested transactions mean in practical terms? Let's look at the following code snippet:

```
BEGIN TRANSACTION OUTERTRAN
 INSERT INTO TEST (TestColumn) VALUES (1)
  BEGIN TRANSACTION INNERTRAN
   INSERT INTO TEST (TestColumn) VALUES (2)
  COMMIT TRANSACTION INNERTRAN
ROLLBACK
```

Interestingly, when you run this code (assuming that the *TEST* table exists), no rows are inserted into the database. This is because the *ROLLBACK* statement automatically rolls back the entire transaction to the outermost *BEGIN TRANSACTION* statement, reducing @@TRANCOUNT to 0. So the outer *ROLLBACK* overrides the inner *COMMIT*, even though *COMMIT* was called before *ROLLBACK*. This is a subtle but important transactional processing behavior that is specific to SQL Server.

Savepoints

Another important concept related to transactions is *savepoints*. Savepoints allow you to temporarily store portions of the transaction, allowing parts of the transaction to be rolled back instead of the entire transaction. They are defined using the *SAVE TRANSACTION* statement, which uses the following syntax:

```
SAVE { TRAN | TRANSACTION } { savepoint_name | @savepoint_variable }
```

By invoking *SAVE TRANSACTION* during a transaction, you mark a point within the transaction that you can roll back to without losing everything. Consider the following code:

```
BEGIN TRANSACTION
 INSERT INTO TEST (TestColumn) VALUES (1)
 SAVE TRANSACTION SAVEPOINT1
  INSERT INTO TEST (TestColumn) VALUES (2)
 ROLLBACK TRANSACTION SAVEPOINT1
COMMIT
```

This code inserts a row and sets a savepoint with the name *SAVEPOINT1*. It then performs another insert, but because you set a savepoint prior to this insert, you can roll back to the savepoint without losing your first insert. As you might have guessed, at the end of the code block, only one row is inserted with *TestColumn = 1*.

To get a better feel for how these features of transactions work, we suggest experimenting with various different combinations of *BEGIN TRANSACTION*, *SAVE*, *COMMIT*, *ROLLBACK*, and *@@TRANCOUNT* on a test table in your database.

Implicit Transaction Mode

When you connect to a database using SQL Server Management Studio and execute a DML query, the changes are automatically saved. This occurs because, by default, the connection is in autocommit transaction mode. If you don't want changes committed unless you explicitly ask them to be committed, set the connection to implicit transaction mode. You can set the database connection to implicit transaction mode (or unset it) by calling the *SET IMPLICIT_TRANSACTIONS* T-SQL statement, as shown here:

```
SET IMPLICIT_TRANSACTIONS {ON | OFF}
```

When a connection is set in the implicit transaction mode and the connection is not currently in a transaction, a transaction is automatically started for you when you issue any one of the following statements: *ALTER TABLE*, *CREATE*, *DELETE*, *DROP*, *FETCH*, *GRANT*, *INSERT*, *OPEN*, *REVOKE*, *SELECT*, *TRUNCATE TABLE*, or *UPDATE*.

With implicit transaction mode, the transaction is not committed or rolled back unless you explicitly request to do so. This means that if you issue an *UPDATE* statement, SQL Server will maintain a lock on the affected data until you issue a *COMMIT* or *ROLLBACK*. If you do not issue a *COMMIT* or *ROLLBACK* statement, the transaction is rolled back when the user disconnects.

> **Note** Don't be confused by the term *implicit*; this just means that a transaction is implicitly started (that is, without an explicit *BEGIN TRANSACTION* statement). As a result, it's necessary for you to explicitly commit the transaction afterward to save the changes.

In practical terms, you should avoid setting a connection to use implicit transaction mode on a highly concurrent database—for example, if while administering a database you will implicitly start transactions by issuing queries in an interactive mode through SQL Server Management Studio and might end up locking database resources, thus seriously affecting the performance of the system as a whole. One example for the appropriate use of implicit transaction mode is on a data warehouse where the reports need just read-only access to the data and can be run under isolation levels that avoid blocking (as we'll discuss shortly) and where you want to be very careful not to inadvertently modify the data.

Batch-Scoped Transaction Mode

SQL Server 2005 and 2008 connections can support multiple active result sets (MARS) on the same connection. Note that we said multiple active results, not parallel execution of commands. The command execution is still interleaved with strict rules that govern which statements can overstep which other statements.

Connections using MARS have an associated batch execution environment. The batch execution environment contains various components—such as *SET* options, security context, database context, and execution state variables—that define the environment under which commands execute. When MARS is enabled, you can have multiple interleaved batches executing at the same time, so all changes made to the execution environment are scoped to the specific batch until the execution of that batch is complete. Once the execution of the batch completes, the execution settings are copied to the default environment.

Thus, a connection is said to be using batch-scoped transaction mode if it is running a transaction, has MARS enabled on it, and has multiple interleaved batches running at the same time.

MARS and Transactions

MARS lets you execute multiple interleaved batches of commands. However, MARS does not let you have multiple transactions on the same connection, only multiple active result sets.

Transactions and MARS are an interesting mix, but to understand how transactions work in MARS, you must first understand what the command interleaving rules are.

In MARS, a command that reads results (such as *SELECT*, *FETCH*, or *READTEXT*) can, generally speaking, be interleaved freely or interrupted by a command that attempts to modify data (such as *UPDATE* or *INSERT*). Thus, a write operation can block a read operation, but a read operation cannot block a write operation. Read operations ensue once the write operation has finished. Also, if two writes show up together, they are serialized in the order of execution. Remember that command execution in SQL Server is always sequential, never parallel, even in multithreaded environments. Last, *BULK INSERT* statements block all other read and write operations.

So theoretically, *BULK INSERT* will block *INSERT*, *UPDATE*, and *DELETE*, which in turn will block all read operations. The problem, however, is that in most practical scenarios, you cannot accurately predict which command actually blocks which other command. This is because your read operation might have finished before the write operation interjected. You also cannot predict exactly when the read operation finished and the write operation started because the read operation depends on a number of factors—CPU speeds, network speeds, packet size, network traffic, and so on. It is thus impossible to predict whether the read data was "put on the wire" before the write operation was requested.

What this means in terms of transactions is that if you are running a transaction that inserts a row, which in turn fires a trigger, and there is a *SELECT* statement in the trigger, the MARS interleaving rules will dictate that your trigger's *SELECT* statement will be blocked by the original *INSERT* statement. Also, because of different command execution times, this behavior is impossible to predict reliably. If this ever happens, the SQL Server deadlock monitor will detect this condition and fail the *SELECT* statement. As a result, you might end up with a system that will work on a low-load developer's machine but fail in production where the load is greater. We know that these are the most difficult types of problems to troubleshoot. Thus, when you use MARS, you must consider interleaving rules and multiple batches in your design.

MARS and Savepoints

Because you have multiple interleaved commands all working in the same transaction, the commands that issue savepoints can easily confuse each other's logic. Imagine a situation in which two interleaved batches issue a rollback to a named savepoint, and it just happens that the savepoint name is the same in both batches. You cannot predict which rollback occurred first, so which savepoint should SQL Server roll back to? In addition, because you cannot accurately predict which statement ended up interleaving which other statement, you can't really be sure if the savepoint was ever created before you issued a rollback to it.

For these reasons, if multiple serialized commands are executing, MARS allows you to set a savepoint, but as soon as commands begin to get interleaved, any request to *BEGIN TRANSACTION* will fail. Because you cannot accurately predict the exact interleaving order of commands, you cannot know for certain whether your *BEGIN TRANSACTION* statement will succeed or fail. Considering this unpredictable behavior, it is best to stay away from savepoints on a MARS connection.

Using Local Transactions in ADO.NET

In ADO.NET, commands can be executed against a data source using a class that inherits from *DbCommand*. For SQL Server, this is a *SqlCommand* object. Let's say you have a table defined as follows:

```
CREATE TABLE TestTable
(
    TestID INT IDENTITY PRIMARY KEY,
    TestColumn INT
)
```

Now you need to execute this simple *INSERT* command on the table:

```
INSERT INTO TestTable (TestColumn) VALUES (100)
```

You can easily wrap this T-SQL command inside a *SqlCommand* instance, as shown in Listing 12-1.

LISTING 12-1 Using *SqlCommand* to execute a simple T-SQL command

```
using (SqlConnection conn = new SqlConnection(connectionString))
{
  SqlCommand cmd = conn.CreateCommand();
  cmd.CommandText = "INSERT INTO TestTable (TestColumn) VALUES (100)";
  try
  {
    conn.Open();
    cmd.ExecuteNonQuery();
  }
  finally
  {
    conn.Close();
  }
}
```

The *ExecuteNonQuery* method executes the command specified in the *CommandText* property against the database specified in the connection string property.

Now consider the following T-SQL code block, which includes two database queries in one transaction:

```
BEGIN TRANSACTION
  INSERT INTO TestTable (TestColumn) VALUES (100)
  INSERT INTO TestTable (TestColumn) VALUES (200)
COMMIT
```

The code block is actually made up of four distinct T-SQL commands. One straightforward approach would be to simply call the four lines of code as different command texts on a *SqlCommand* object. But that is hardly an elegant solution. It is good practice to ensure that a transaction be executed by wrapping the entire statement within one *SqlCommand* object. There are no guarantees that the same *SqlCommand* object will be available to your code when executing later commands. A much better implementation of the transactional code is to use two instances of the *SqlCommand* object and bind both of them in the same transaction, as shown in Listing 12-2.

LISTING 12-2 Binding two *SqlCommand* objects into one transaction

```
using (SqlConnection conn = new SqlConnection(connectionString))
{
  SqlCommand cmd1 = conn.CreateCommand();
  cmd1.CommandText = "INSERT INTO TestTable (TestColumn) VALUES (100)";
  SqlCommand cmd2 = conn.CreateCommand();
  cmd2.CommandText = "INSERT INTO TestTable (TestColumn) VALUES (200)";

  SqlTransaction tran = null;
  try
  {
    conn.Open();
    tran = conn.BeginTransaction();
    cmd1.Transaction = tran;
    cmd2.Transaction = tran;

    cmd1.ExecuteNonQuery();
    cmd2.ExecuteNonQuery();
    tran.Commit();
  }
  catch
  {
    if (tran != null)
    {
      tran.Rollback();
    }
    throw;
  }
  finally
  {
    conn.Close();
  }
}
```

As you can see, the code in Listing 12-2 is remarkably similar to the nontransactional code you saw earlier. The big difference, however, is that as soon as we open the connection, we begin the transaction on the connection by invoking the *BeginTransaction* method on the connection object. That method returns a *SqlTransaction* object that is assigned to the *Transaction* property of all *SqlCommand* objects that are intended to be run within the same transaction. In addition, we use the *try/catch/finally* construct to ensure a commit in the event of success or a rollback in the event of failure.

It is worth noting, however, that you need the connection to be open before you can call *BeginTransaction*, and once you have called *BeginTransaction* on a connection, all subsequent commands until a commit or rollback must lie within the same transaction. This is a bit of discipline that ADO.NET forces on you to keep your code clean.

Transaction Terminology

Before we go beyond the basics of transactions, let's review some terminology that is commonly used when talking about transactions:.

- **Beginning a transaction** Specifying that all subsequent operations that occur after a transaction begins are assumed to lie within the transaction.

- **Rolling back a transaction** Undoing operations that have occurred since a transaction began, thus restoring the affected data to its original state. This is done in the event of failure.

- **Committing a transaction** Making permanent all operations that have occurred since a transaction began. A transaction is committed in the event of success.

- **Dirty read** The operation of reading data that is yet to be committed. This occurs, for example, when transaction B is being blocked by transaction A, but because you have tweaked the isolation behavior, transaction B ends up reading transaction A's changes even though they have not been committed.

- **Nonrepeatable read** A condition where transaction B modifies the data that transaction A was working with, during the lifetime of transaction A. As a result, transaction A reads modified data, and the original read cannot be repeated.

- **Phantom read** Like a nonrepeatable read except that the number of rows changes between two reads within the same transaction. The rows that differ between the two reads are referred to as *phantom rows*.

Isolation Levels

As mentioned earlier in this chapter, the isolation behavior of a transaction can be tweaked to your application's needs. This is generally done by setting the isolation level of a transaction. Put simply, isolation levels determine how concurrent transactions behave. Do they block each other? Do they let each other step over themselves? Or do they present a snapshot of a previous stable state of data in the event of an overstepped condition?

You might find a slight mismatch between the isolation levels defined in ADO.NET compared with the isolation levels in SQL Server 2008 because ADO.NET was not written exclusively for SQL Server. We'll begin by looking at the isolation-level support in SQL Server 2008.

Isolation Levels in SQL Server 2008

You can set isolation levels in SQL Server by using the *SET TRANSACTION ISOLATION LEVEL* statement, which uses the following syntax:

```
SET TRANSACTION ISOLATION LEVEL
    { READ UNCOMMITTED
    | READ COMMITTED
    | REPEATABLE READ
    | SNAPSHOT
    | SERIALIZABLE
    }
```

A sample usage of this statement with the *BEGIN TRANSACTION* statement is shown here:

```
SET TRANSACTION ISOLATION LEVEL READ UNCOMMITTED
BEGIN TRANSACTION
 SELECT TestColumn FROM TestTable
COMMIT
```

As you can see from the syntax, SQL Server 2008 supports five isolation levels:

- Read uncommitted

- Read committed

- Repeatable read

- Snapshot

- Serializable

Read Uncommitted Isolation Level

By specifying the read uncommitted isolation level, you essentially tell the database to violate all locks and read the current immediate state of data. But by doing so, you might end up with a dirty read—reading data that is not yet committed. You should therefore avoid this isolation level if your application requires precise, committed data because transactions using this isolation level can return logically incorrect data.

Let's explore this isolation level by using an example:

1. Open two instances of SQL Server Management Studio. In each instance, use the database that contains the *TestTable* table created in the section "Using Local Transactions in ADO.NET" earlier in this chapter. These two instances will be used to simulate two users running two concurrent transactions.

2. In instance 1, execute an *UPDATE* on the row of data by running the following code block:

```
BEGIN TRANSACTION
UPDATE TestTable SET TestColumn=200 WHERE TestId=1
```

3. In instance 2 of Management Studio, execute the following query:

```
SELECT TestColumn FROM TestTable WHERE TestId=1
```

You will notice that your *SELECT* query is blocked. This makes sense because you are trying to read the same data that instance 1 is busy modifying. Unless instance 1 issues a *COMMIT* or a *ROLLBACK*, your query will remain blocked or will simply time out.

4. Cancel your blocked *SELECT* query by pressing Alt+Break or by clicking the Cancel button on the toolbar. Execute the following statement to set the isolation level of your *SELECT* query to read uncommitted on the connection held by instance 2:

```
SET TRANSACTION ISOLATION LEVEL READ UNCOMMITTED
```

5. Execute the *SELECT* query again, as follows:

```
SELECT TestColumn FROM TestTable WHERE TestId=1
```

You will find that the query isn't blocked; it produces *200* as a result.

6. Go back to instance 1, and issue a *ROLLBACK*.

7. Back in instance 2, execute the same *SELECT* query again. You should receive *100* as the result.

As you might have noticed, instance 2 returned different results for the same query at different times. As a matter of fact, the value *200* was never committed to the database, but because you explicitly requested a dirty read by specifying the *READ UNCOMMITTED* isolation level, you ended up reading data that was never meant to be final. So the downside is that you ended up reading logically incorrect data. On the upside, however, your query was not blocked.

Read Committed Isolation Level

Read committed is the default isolation level in SQL Server. As you will see shortly, this isolation level is the default because it strikes the best balance between data integrity and performance. This isolation level respects locks and prevents dirty reads from occurring. In the example you saw earlier, until we explicitly requested that the isolation level be changed to read uncommitted, the connection worked at the read committed isolation level. Therefore, our second transaction (the autocommit mode transaction in the *SELECT* query) was blocked by the transaction executing the *UPDATE* query.

A read committed isolation level prevents dirty reads, but phantom reads and nonrepeatable reads are still possible when using this isolation level. This is because the read committed isolation level does not prevent one transaction from changing the same data at the same time as another transaction is reading from it.

A phantom read can occur in the following type of situation:

1. Transaction 1 begins.

2. Transaction 1 reads a row.

3. Transaction 2 begins.

4. Transaction 2 deletes the row that was read by transaction 1.

5. Transaction 2 commits. Transaction 1 can no longer repeat its initial read because the row no longer exists, resulting in a phantom row.

A nonrepeatable read can occur in the following type of situation:

1. Transaction 1 begins.

2. Transaction 1 reads a row.

3. Transaction 2 begins.

4. Transaction 2 changes the value of the same row read by transaction 1.

5. Transaction 2 commits.

6. Transaction 1 reads the row again. Transaction 1 has inconsistent data because the row now contains different values from the previous read, all within the scope of transaction 1.

Repeatable Read Isolation Level

As the name suggests, the repeatable read isolation level prevents nonrepeatable reads. It does so by placing locks on the data that was used in a query within a transaction. As you might expect, you pay a higher price in terms of concurrent transactions blocking each other, so you should use this isolation level only when necessary. The good news, however, is that a concurrent transaction can add new data that matches the *WHERE* clause of the original transaction. This is because the first transaction will place a lock only on the rows it originally read into its result set. In other words, a transaction using this isolation level acquires read locks on all retrieved data but does not acquire range locks.

If you examine this pattern closely, you'll see that although nonrepeatable reads are avoided when using this isolation level, phantom reads can still occur. They can occur under the following circumstances:

1. Transaction 1 begins.

2. Transaction 1 reads all rows with, say, *TestColumn = 100*.

3. Transaction 2 begins.

4. Transaction 2 inserts a new row with *TestID = 2, TestColumn = 100*.

5. Transaction 2 commits.

6. Transaction 1 runs an *UPDATE* query and modifies *TestColumn* for the rows where *TestColumn = 100*. This also ends up updating the row that transaction 2 inserted.

7. Transaction 1 commits.

Because shared locks are not released until the end of the transaction, concurrency is lower than when using the read committed isolation level, so care must be taken to avoid unexpected results.

Serializable Isolation Level

A transaction running at the serializable isolation level will not permit dirty reads, phantom reads, or nonrepeatable reads. This isolation level places the most restrictive locks on the data being read or modified, keeping your data perfectly clean. This might sound like an isolation level that gives you perfect isolation behavior, but there is a good reason why you should seldom use this isolation level. In a sense, this is the perfect transaction, but transactions will block other running transactions, thereby affecting concurrent performance or even creating deadlocks. Thus, even if this transaction will keep your data perfectly clean, it will severely affect system performance. In most practical situations, you can get away with a lower isolation level.

Snapshot Isolation Level

In all of the isolation levels described earlier, we seem to be trading concurrent performance for logical sanctity of data. Because a transaction locks the data it is working on, other transactions that attempt to work with the same data are blocked until the first transaction commits or rolls back. Of course, the traditional way of getting around this problem is to allow dirty reads (and hence incorrect data) or to simply reduce the duration of transactions. But neither of these solutions allows you to read logically consistent data while offering non-blocking concurrent behavior.

Application architectures frequently present circumstances in which even the smallest transactions become a problem or transactions end up modifying so much data that their duration cannot be kept small. To get around this issue, a new isolation level was introduced in SQL Server 2005: the snapshot isolation level. This isolation level gives you consistent reads without blocking.

Transactions running under the snapshot isolation level do not create shared locks on the rows being read. In addition, repeated requests for the same data within a snapshot transaction guarantee the same results, thus ensuring repeatable reads without any blocking. This sounds like the best of both worlds—the responsiveness of read uncommitted combined with the consistency of repeatable read. However, you pay a price.

This nonblocking, repeatable read behavior is made possible by storing previously committed versions of rows in the *tempdb* database. As a result, other transactions that were started before the write in the current transaction and that have already read the previous version will continue to read that version. Because the previous version is being read from *tempdb*, the write can occur in a nonblocking fashion, and other transactions will see the new version. The obvious problem, of course, is the increased overhead on the *tempdb* database. For this reason, SQL Server requires you to enable the snapshot isolation level before you can use it. You shouldn't arbitrarily enable snapshot isolation on databases. But after testing, if you decide that your database needs this isolation level, you can enable it by using the following statement:

```
ALTER DATABASE MyDB
  SET ALLOW_SNAPSHOT_ISOLATION ON
```

As with all isolation levels, once you enable snapshot isolation for a database, you can use it on individual connections by using the *SET TRANSACTION ISOLATION LEVEL* statement, as follows:

```
SET TRANSACTION ISOLATION LEVEL SNAPSHOT
```

Read Committed Snapshot Isolation Level

Snapshot isolation prevents readers from being blocked by writers by providing readers with data from a previously committed version. Over the duration of the transaction, you are thus assured of repeatable reads. However, this method of ensuring a repeatable read incurs additional overhead and bookkeeping for the SQL Server Database Engine that might not be necessary in all situations. Thus, SQL Server offers a slight modification to the read committed isolation level that provides nonrepeatable reads over the duration of the transaction that are not blocked by transaction writers. This modification is called the read committed snapshot isolation level. This isolation level guarantees consistency of the data over the duration of a read query within a transaction but not over the entire transaction that holds the reader. The obvious advantage of read committed snapshot as compared with read committed is that your readers do not get blocked. When they request data, they are offered either a previous state of data (before any write operations) or the new state of data (after write operations), depending on the state of other concurrently running transactions, but they are never required to wait until other concurrent transactions release their locks on the data being requested.

To use the read committed snapshot isolation level, you must first enable it at the database level by using the following T-SQL command:

```
ALTER DATABASE MyDB
 SET READ_COMMITTED_SNAPSHOT ON
```

Once you have enabled the read committed snapshot isolation level on a database, all queries using the read committed isolation level will exhibit snapshot like behavior. Although this isolation level will give you snapshot like behavior, you will not be able to perform repeatable reads over the duration of a transaction.

> **Important** Neither the snapshot nor the read committed snapshot isolation level can be used with a database that supports the new FILESTREAM file group in SQL Server 2008 (covered in Chapter 8). The reason for this is, of course, that the database cannot snapshot the file system. If you try to enable either of these isolation levels for a database using FILESTREAM, the attempt will fail with the following error:
>
> ```
> Msg 5099, Level 16, State 3, Line 1
> ALTER DATABASE failed because the READ_COMMITTED_SNAPSHOT and the ALLOW_SNAPSHOT_
> ISOLATION
> options cannot be set to ON when a database has FILESTREAM filegroups.  To set
> READ_COMMITTED_SNAPSHOT or ALLOW_SNAPSHOT_ISOLATION to ON, you must remove the
> FILESTREAM
> filegroups from the database.
> ```

Isolation Levels in ADO.NET

As mentioned earlier, isolation levels in ADO.NET are slightly different from those in SQL Server. This is because ADO.NET is designed as a generic data access technology that supports other databases as well as SQL Server. The isolation levels defined in ADO.NET 2.0 under the *System.Data.IsolationLevel* enumeration are as follows:

- ■ *Chaos* Pending changes from more highly isolated transactions cannot be overwritten. This setting is not supported in SQL Server or Oracle.

- ■ *ReadUncommitted* Similar to read uncommitted in SQL Server, this level means that no shared locks are placed and no exclusive locks are honored.

- *ReadCommitted* As with read committed in SQL Server, shared locks are held while the data is being read by the transaction. This avoids dirty reads, but you might still get nonrepeatable reads and phantom reads.

- *RepeatableRead* Shared locks are placed on all data that is used in the predicate (criterion) of the query. Again, as with repeatable read in SQL Server, dirty reads and non-repeatable reads are not possible, but phantom reads are.

- *Snapshot* Similar to the snapshot isolation level in SQL Server, this isolation level provides a snapshot of earlier data while offering repeatable reads with nonblocking selects. Do not confuse this level with the read committed snapshot isolation level in SQL Server 2008, which must be enabled at the database level.

- *Serializable* This can be considered an ideal transaction type to use, in which exclusive locks are placed on data. This prevents other users from reading or modifying the data. Keep in mind that there are always tradeoffs, and exclusive locks should not be held for long periods of time.

- *Unspecified* This is a catchall isolation level for databases that support isolation levels not covered by the other choices or for scenarios in which the isolation level cannot be accurately determined.

You can specify an isolation level for a transaction as a parameter to the *BeginTransaction* method. For instance, in the following code snippet, we begin a transaction with the *ReadUncommitted* isolation level:

```
SqlTransaction tran = conn.BeginTransaction(IsolationLevel.ReadUncommitted) ;
```

In this example, any *SqlCommand* with its *Transaction* property set to *tran* will not honor any exclusive locks and will let you perform dirty reads on data being held by other transactions.

Distributed Transactions

Thus far, our discussion has been limited to transactions on a single database. What if more than one database is involved? What if more than one database server is involved? What if a nondatabase operation, such as modifying an in-memory cache, is involved? Can you use *BEGIN TRANSACTION* to bind other such operations within a single transaction? Unfortunately, you cannot. *BEGIN TRANSACTION* works only on local transactions dealing with data in a database. These transactions do not apply to an in-memory cache, since no transaction logging mechanism is available.

In this section, we'll look at a deeper theory of transactions and explore a namespace in the .NET Framework named *System.Transactions*. You'll also see why a transaction that is inherently expensive due to its overhead becomes even more expensive when it is being managed by an external entity—a transaction coordinator. This discussion addresses a scope broader than database-only transactions.

Distributed Transaction Terminology

You will frequently encounter the terms *resource manager*, *transaction manager*, *transaction coordinator*, and *two-phase commit* when working with distributed transactions. Let's look at those terms more closely.

Resource Manager

Transactions (database or otherwise) manage a resource. Any operation that needs to be made transactional is managed by a logical entity—a subroutine, a function, a dynamic-link library (DLL), an executable, a machine, or anything else that is capable of supporting transactions. Any such logical entity that is eventually responsible for managing the resource in a transactional manner is called a *resource manager* (RM).

Thus, an RM has the ability and responsibility to *enlist* itself in a current running transaction and thereby supports transactional capabilities.

Transaction Manager or Transaction Coordinator

If you have an RM that manages its resources in a transactional manner by enlisting in a current running transaction, by definition you need an external entity that manages the transaction itself. This external entity is responsible for listening to and coordinating between several RMs that are all enlisted within the same transaction. It acknowledges requests for new transactions and listens for and sends notifications in the event of success and failure. This entity is referred to as a *transaction manager* (TM), *transaction coordinator* (TC), or *distributed transaction coordinator* (DTC). Two common transaction coordinators that ship with Microsoft Windows are the Lightweight Transaction Manager (LTM) and the Microsoft Distributed Transaction Coordinator (MS DTC).

Do note that a TC is not necessarily a DTC. In fact, if the RM itself has transactional capabilities built in, it might not need a TC at all. For instance, in the case of SQL Server, if a transaction is limited to a single database, SQL Server 2008 is fully capable of managing the transaction on its own. Thus, for local transactions, SQL Server chooses not to consult the MS DTC. There are good reasons for this, which will become evident once you read about the typical implementation of a distributed transaction—namely, the two-phase commit process.

Two-Phase Commit

A distributed transaction can be implemented in a number of ways. One of the most common ways is through the two-phase commit process. Here is the typical flow of a two-phase transaction involving two RMs and a DTC:

1. The transaction initiator requests a transaction from the DTC. This transaction initiator can be the application that interacts with the two RMs, or it can be one of the RMs itself.

2. The transaction initiator requests that the RMs to do their work as a part of the same transaction. The RMs register themselves with the DTC as a part of the same transaction, thus expressing an interest in receiving notifications about the success or failure of the transaction as a whole. This process is referred to as *enlisting within a transaction*.

3. The RMs go ahead and do their work and notify the DTC of a success, while keeping a rollback mechanism in place. This is the first phase of a two-phase commit process, also called the *prepare phase*.

4. Once the DTC receives a success notification for the prepare phases from each of the enlisted RMs, the DTC issues a notification to go ahead and make the changes permanent. Upon receiving such a notification, all RMs make their changes permanent by committing their transient states. This is also known as the *commit phase*. The system has now gone from one stable state to another, and the distributed transaction is complete.

Rules and Methods of Enlistment

As you might have surmised, the DTC on a machine running Windows (MS DTC) engages in a lot of chatty communication with the various RMs involved in a transaction. Due to the network roundtrips involved, this chatting affects the performance of the application in general and might also be blocked by a firewall. In addition, RMs that enlist themselves in a distributed transaction often use the serializable isolation level. This architecture is the easiest to implement because when using the serializable isolation level, you have a perfect transaction—no dirty reads, no phantom reads, and no nonrepeatable reads. Of course, the downside is a serious performance impact.

But SQL Server 2008 itself is capable of managing transactions, so why should it have to escalate the isolation level to serializable in every circumstance? After all, depending on your logic, you might want to take advantage of an MS DTC–based transaction *if and only if* your transaction ends up involving more than one RM. But as long as only one database connection is involved, you shouldn't have to pay the extra cost of involving the DTC. As it turns out, the Microsoft engineers thought of this situation. And to rectify the situation, an RM can enlist within a transaction in different ways.

Volatile Enlistment

An RM that deals with resources that are volatile (not permanent) is a good candidate for volatile enlistment. Typically, in a volatile enlistment scenario, if the RM cannot perform the second (commit) phase of a distributed transaction for any reason, it doesn't explicitly need to recover the first (prepare) phase. This means that if an RM crashes in the middle of a transaction, the RM doesn't need to provide an explicit recovery contract to the TC. Volatile enlistment doesn't need the implementation of MS DTC, so it is usually managed by the LTM, which is a much lighter weight TC designed to work with volatile enlistment scenarios. An example of such an RM might be one that manages an in-memory cache. The cache data isn't meant to be permanent—it lasts only for a relatively short duration.

Durable Enlistment

Durable enlistment is necessary if the RM has permanent (durable) data that depends on the transaction for consistency. A good example is a transaction that involves disk I/O. Say you are writing to a file on disk. If the transaction fails, or if the RM crashes, the file that was written as a part of the prepare phase will need to be deleted. Thus the RM will need to prepare a transaction log and record the history of changes since the transaction was begun. In the event of a requested recovery, the RM needs sufficient information to perform a graceful rollback.

> **Note** SQL Server 2008 FILESTREAM implements a transparent coordination between database transactions and NTFS file system transactions. You will find detailed coverage of FILESTREAM in Chapter 8.

Promotable Single-Phase Enlistment

In many situations, the nature of a transaction can change as new RMs continue to enlist. For instance, a SQL Server 2008 database is perfectly capable of managing a transaction on its own, as long as the transaction is limited to one database. Or say, for instance, that an RM that manages an in-memory cache doesn't need the implementation of MS DTC because the cache by nature is temporary anyway. But if there is a transaction containing an in-memory cache RM or a SQL Server 2008 connection being managed by the LTM, and a second SQL Server 2008 connection enlists itself in the same transaction, the transaction will be promoted to MS DTC because the RMs are no longer capable of managing the transaction on their own.

It is important to note that along with the promotion comes what are sometimes considered (necessary) disadvantages of MS DTC—a higher isolation level and a more expensive and chatty transaction in general. Promotable single-phase enlistment (PSPE) offers a huge advantage in that as long as you don't really need MS DTC, you don't use it, so you don't pay the penalty for it. (However, when you truly need MS DTC, it's a great gift.)

There are well-defined rules for the promotion of a transaction from LTM to MS DTC. A transaction is escalated from LTM to MS DTC if any of the following happens:

- A durable resource that doesn't support single-phase notifications is enlisted in the transaction.

- Two durable resources that support single-phase notification enlist in the same transaction.

- The TC receives a request to marshal a transaction to a different .NET AppDomain or Windows process.

> **Note**   SQL Server 2000 connections are always promoted to MS DTC, and SQL common language runtime (CLR) connections inside a *System.Transactions.TransactionScope* are promoted to MS DTC even if only one of them is enlisted in the transaction scope.

With a good theory and a common terminology on our side, next we'll look at the support for distributed transactions in SQL Server 2008 and the .NET Framework in general.

Distributed Transactions in SQL Server 2008

SQL Server 2008 supports distributed transactions using the *BEGIN DISTRIBUTED TRANSACTION* statement. This statement requests the start of a T-SQL distributed transaction managed by the MS DTC. It uses the following syntax:

```
BEGIN DISTRIBUTED { TRAN | TRANSACTION }
    [ transaction_name | @tran_name_variable ]
```

The easiest way to enlist remote instances of the SQL Server Database Engine in a distributed transaction is to execute a distributed query that references a linked server. For instance, you can link *ServerB* and execute a query that looks like this:

```
DELETE FROM ServerB.TestDB.TestTable Where TestID = 1
```

Enlisting the preceding query in a distributed transaction is rather simple:

```
BEGIN DISTRIBUTED TRANSACTION
  DELETE TestDB.TestTable WHERE TestID = 1
  DELETE ServerB.TestDB.TestTable WHERE TestID = 1
COMMIT
```

The obvious shortcoming of this implementation is that the second query has no way to explicitly enlist. This might seem trivial, but if the second query is a stored procedure that calls *ServerC*, which in turn calls *ServerD*, all of them will be tied up in one really expensive transaction, all managed by the one MS DTC on the initiating server.

You can get around this issue by configuring the default behavior to not promote linked server queries to MS DTC. You can do this in two ways. First, you can do it at the server level, by using the following T-SQL command:

```
sp_configure remote proc trans 0
```

Or you can do it at the connection level, by using the following syntax:

```
SET REMOTE_PROC_TRANSACTIONS OFF
```

You can then use *BEGIN TRANSACTION* and have the SQL Server Database Engine manage the transactions for you. Conversely, if you use a setting of *1* or *ON*, a *BEGIN TRANSACTION* statement involving linked servers will then involve MS DTC—but this is an all-or-nothing approach.

Distributed Transactions in the .NET Framework

The concept of distributed transactions was not introduced with the .NET Framework. Prior to the .NET Framework, you could enlist in distributed transactions using third-party transactions coordinators such as COMTI or solutions such as COM+ or Microsoft Transaction Server (MTS) to enlist in distributed transactions. Starting with the .NET Framework 1.0, you could also use the *System.EnterpriseServices* namespace to enlist within a distributed transaction. *System.EnterpriseServices* essentially wraps the COM+ infrastructure.

The problem with *EnterpriseServices*-based solutions was that you had to implement your operation as a class library, decorate it with the *TransactionOption* attribute, strongly name it, and register it in the global assembly cache (GAC). This made debugging and deployment difficult. Also, the *TransactionOption* attribute hard-coded the transactional behavior of your operation to one of the following values:

- **Disabled**   Does not participate in transactions. This is the default value.
- **NotSupported**   Runs outside the context of a transaction.
- **Supported**   Participates in a transaction if one exists. If one doesn't exist, the operation will not request or create one.
- **Required**   Requires a transaction. If no transaction exists, one is created. If one exists, the operation enlists itself in the transaction.
- **RequiresNew**   Requires a transaction and creates a new transaction for itself.

You really couldn't enlist on demand in the .NET Framework 1.0, and debugging and deployment were difficult. The .NET Framework 1.1 offered a slightly better solution, which was made possible by the *ServiceConfig* class, as shown in Listing 12-3.

LISTING 12-3 Using the *ServiceConfig* class

```
ServiceConfig config = new ServiceConfig();
config.Transaction = TransactionOption.Required;
ServiceDomain.Enter(config);

try
{
    // SqlConnections will auto enlist in the transaction.
}
catch
{
    ContextUtil.SetAbort();
}
finally
{
    ServiceDomain.Leave();
}
```

This solution, known as "services without components," did not require you to register your assembly in the GAC or even strongly name it, but unfortunately it was at one time limited to Microsoft Windows 2003 and Windows XP with Service Pack 2, so it didn't gain a strong following. It has since been rolled out to other Windows-based operating systems but is still relatively unknown. Even so, you couldn't use concepts such as promotable enlistment. Thus, the .NET Framework 2.0 introduced a new namespace named *System.Transactions* to address all of these issues.

Let's look at the behavior of a *System.Transactions*-based transaction by creating an example. We will set up two databases and execute one query on each.

The following code creates the two databases and names them *Test1* and *Test2*. It then creates a table named *FromTable* in *Test1* and a table named *ToTable* in *Test2*, both of them with one *int* column named *Amount*. A row is then inserted into the *FromTable* table with the value *100*, and another row is inserted into the *ToTable* table with the value *0*.

```
CREATE DATABASE Test1
GO
USE Test1
GO
CREATE TABLE FromTable (Amount int)
GO
INSERT INTO FromTable(Amount) VALUES (100)
GO

CREATE DATABASE Test2
GO
USE Test2
GO
CREATE TABLE ToTable (Amount int)
GO
INSERT INTO ToTable(Amount) VALUES (0)
GO
```

Now we'll create a console application and name it *DistributedTrans*. Add the necessary reference to *System.Transactions*. Then add the necessary *using* statements to access the *System. Data*, *System.Data.SqlClient*, and *System.Transactions* namespaces, as follows:

```
using System.Data;
using System.Data.SqlClient;
using System.Transactions;
```

The aim of this example is to execute two queries, one on each database. One query will subtract 50 from *FromTable* in *Test1*, and the other will add 50 to *ToTable* in *Test2*. Both operations must be bound within the same transaction. We can do this easily by using the following code snippet, which you can just add to the static *Main* method. (Don't worry if you don't understand it just yet—we will explain the code shortly.)

```
const string ConnStr1 =
 "Data Source=(local);Initial Catalog=Test1;Integrated Security=SSPI;";
const string ConnStr2 =
 "Data Source=(local);Initial Catalog=Test2;Integrated Security=SSPI;";

const string CmdText1 = "UPDATE FromTable SET Amount = Amount - 50";
const string CmdText2 = "UPDATE ToTable SET Amount = Amount + 50";

using(TransactionScope tsc = new TransactionScope())
{
  using(SqlConnection conn1 = new SqlConnection(ConnStr1))
  {
    SqlCommand cmd1 = conn1.CreateCommand();
    cmd1.CommandText = CmdText1;
    conn1.Open();
    cmd1.ExecuteNonQuery();
  }

  // Operation #1 is done, going to Operation #2

  using(SqlConnection conn2 = new SqlConnection(ConnStr2))
  {
    SqlCommand cmd2 = conn2.CreateCommand();
    cmd2.CommandText = CmdText2;
    conn2.Open();
    cmd2.ExecuteNonQuery();
  }

  tsc.Complete();
}
```

Run the code. Notice that the two command objects *cmd1* and *cmd2* run in a distributed transaction. If the second query fails, the first one will automatically roll back. It's really just that simple. Of course, more complicated implementations are possible, but the basic process of implementing a distributed transaction using *System.Transaction* is really that easy. Now let's take a closer look at the code we just wrote.

At the beginning of the code snippet is a *using* block:

```
using (TransactionScope tsc = new TransactionScope())
{
  // ...Do transactional operations here...
}
```

The *using* block ensures that the *Dispose* method is always called on the *TransactionScope* instance *tsc* when the scope of the using statement ends. The instantiation of a *TransactionScope* starts a new transaction, and *Dispose* is called when the scope of the enclosing *using* block ends. By disposing *tsc*, the distributed transaction is committed. Thus, within the *using* block, any RM will attempt to enlist itself in the current running transaction and will commit the transaction assuming the *TransactionScope*'s *Complete* method is called prior to exiting the *using* block's scope and there is no exception within the block.

Also, as you might have noticed, the process of executing a query on the database is implemented in regular ADO.NET code, as follows:

```
using (SqlConnection conn1 = new SqlConnection(connStr1))
{
  SqlCommand cmd1 = conn1.CreateCommand();
  cmd1.CommandText = CmdText1;
  conn1.Open();
  cmd1.ExecuteNonQuery();
}
```

The magic here is that the *SqlConnection* instance *conn1* knows that it is working inside a *TransactionScope*. When the transaction scope is entered, it creates an *ambient transaction*. Since transactional code executing within the transaction scope now has an active transaction in which to enlist, it enlists itself with the appropriate TM.

Notice that we said "appropriate TM," not MS DTC. This is because when a *SqlConnection* instance is connected with a SQL Server 2008 database, it exhibits PSPE—that is, the transaction is managed by LTM and not MS DTC until the *conn2.Open* statement is called.

In the code snippet, where we invoke *conn2.Open*, set a breakpoint and run the application again. When the breakpoint is reached, examine the following value:

```
Transaction.Current.TransactionInformation.DistributedIdentifier.ToString()
```

While still in debug mode, execute the *conn2.Open* statement and check this value again. What do you see? You will see that right before *conn2* is opened, the value is a null globally unique identifier (GUID):

```
"00000000-0000-0000-0000-000000000000"
```

Right after *conn2.Open* is executed, this value changes to an actual GUID value, similar to the following:

```
"7b3ca1be-6c31-43b9-8fa8-fd759a1a8063"
```

If you immediately go to Control Panel, choose Administrative Tools, Component Services, and then navigate to the Transaction List, you will notice the very same GUID running there, as shown in Figure 12-1.

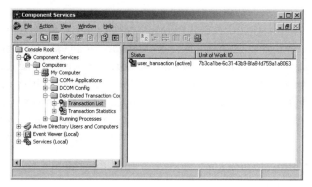

FIGURE 12-1 The current active transaction being managed by MS DTC

What this tells you is that right before *conn2.Open* was executed, the transaction was being managed by the LTM and hence didn't have a valid *DistributedIdentifier*. But as soon as the second RM enlisted in the transaction, the transaction was bumped up to MS DTC and got a valid *DistributedIdentifier*. If you were to run this same code sample against a SQL Server 2000 database, the *DistributedIdentifier* would have a valid value right after *conn1.Open* executes, thus proving that *SqlConnection* enlists durably when connecting with a SQL Server 2000 database yet exhibits PSPE when connecting with a SQL Server 2008 (or 2005) database.

It could be argued that you could easily achieve the same thing through the T-SQL statement *BEGIN DISTRIBUTED TRANSACTION*, without using the *System.Transactions* namespace. It is important to realize that *System.Transactions* provides a much more flexible architecture in which you can logically choose to enlist or not, and it deals with more than just database transactions. You can theoretically write an RM that encapsulates any operation in a transactional manner, as we'll do next.

Writing Your Own Resource Manager

It is only reasonable to expect that because databases are the most critical part of the architecture (at least to database developers and administrators!), they have had fantastic transactional support for a long time. But don't you want your other, nondatabase, operations to be transactional as well if they also could benefit from transactional behavior?

Let's consider the simple operation of setting a value to an integer and wrapping that as a part of a transaction, as shown in the following code snippet.

```
int myInt ;
myInt = 10;
```

The first question is, how do you set a value for an integer? Unfortunately, wrapping this code in a *TransactionScope* won't make it transactional. This is because *System.Int32* is not smart enough to understand that it is being wrapped inside a *TransactionScope* and that it should auto-enlist within a running transaction. This is probably a good thing, because in the event of a rollback, to perform a graceful recovery, *System.Int32* would have to maintain a previous version. You probably wouldn't want to pay this overhead for all your integers. So we need to write a class that allows us to maintain enough history in the event of a rollback. This class should also be able to interact with a TM and listen for various two-phase commit notifications. To do so, the RM you are writing must implement the *IEnlistmentNotification* interface. This interface requires you to implement certain methods that are called at the appropriate points in time by the TC during the two phases of a two-phase commit process.

Here are the methods that *IEnlistmentNotification* requires you to implement:

- **Commit**   Notifies the RM that the transaction has been committed. The RM then makes the changes permanent.

- **Rollback**   Notifies the RM that the transaction has been rolled back. The RM then reverts to the previous stable state.

- **Prepare**   Called during the first (prepare) phase of a distributed transaction—when the TM asks the participants whether they are ready to commit. If the TM receives a successful notification from each participating RM, it calls the *Commit* methods.

- **InDoubt**   Notifies the RMs if the TM loses contact with one or more participants in the transaction. In this situation, the status of the transaction is unknown, and the application logic must decide whether to revert to the previous consistent state or remain in an inconsistent state.

Listing 12-4 puts all of these concepts into actual code. It shows a full implementation of a volatile RM. You can also find this code in the *YourOwnRM* solution on the book's companion Web site.

LISTING 12-4 Implementing your own resource manager

```
public class VolatileRM : IEnlistmentNotification
{
    private string _whoAmI = "";
    public VolatileRM(string whoAmI)
    {
        this._whoAmI = whoAmI;
    }
```

```csharp
 private int _memberValue = 0;
private int _oldMemberValue = 0;
public int MemberValue
{
    get
    {
        return this._memberValue;
    }
    set
    {
        Transaction tran = Transaction.Current;
        if (tran != null)
        {
            Console.WriteLine(
              this._whoAmI + ": MemberValue setter - EnlistVolatile");
            tran.EnlistVolatile(this, EnlistmentOptions.None);
        }
        this._oldMemberValue = this._memberValue;
        this._memberValue = value;
    }
}

#region IEnlistmentNotification Members

public void Commit(Enlistment enlistment)
{
    Console.WriteLine(this._whoAmI + ": Commit");

    // Clear out _oldMemberValue
    this._oldMemberValue = 0;
    enlistment.Done();
}

public void InDoubt(Enlistment enlistment)
{
    Console.WriteLine(this._whoAmI + ": InDoubt");
    enlistment.Done();
}

public void Prepare(PreparingEnlistment preparingEnlistment)
{
    Console.WriteLine(this._whoAmI + ": Prepare");
    preparingEnlistment.Prepared();
}

public void Rollback(Enlistment enlistment)
{
    Console.WriteLine(this._whoAmI + ": Rollback");

    // Restore previous state
    this._memberValue = this._oldMemberValue;
    this._oldMemberValue = 0;
    enlistment.Done();
}

#endregion
}
```

Let's examine this code more closely. At the very top, we define a class that implements *IEnlistmentNotification*. This signifies that our RM will receive notifications from the current transaction manager:

```
public class VolatileRM : IEnlistmentNotification
```

We then define a constructor that accepts and stores a string variable named *_whoAmI*, as follows. This will be very valuable for our understanding of the chain of events via the trace, when we have more than one RM involved.

```
private string _whoAmI = "";
public VolatileRM(string whoAmI)
{
    this._whoAmI = whoAmI;
}
```

Next we have two class-level variables named *_memberValue* and *_oldMemberValue*, followed by a *MemberValue* property. The whole reason for writing this class is that *System. Int32* is unable to interact with an RM or maintain historical values to roll back integers. The *MemberValue* property's *get* accessor exposes *_memberValue*, and its *set* accessor assigns a new value to *_memberValue* and then enlists in the currently running transaction. The *_oldMemberValue* variable holds the historical value that we will use in the event of a rollback.

```
private int _memberValue = 0;
private int _oldMemberValue = 0;
public int MemberValue
{
    get { return _memberValue; }
    set
    {
        Transaction tran = Transaction.Current;
        if (tran != null)
        {
            Console.WriteLine(
              tran._whoAmI + ": MemberValue setter - EnlistVolatile");
            tran.EnlistVolatile(this, EnlistmentOptions.None);
        }
        this._oldMemberValue = this._memberValue;
        this._memberValue = value;
    }
}
```

As you can see, we first try to find the current transaction in the *Transaction.Current* variable, and then we use the *EnlistVolatile* method to enlist in the current transaction in a volatile manner. Volatile enlistment is sufficient for this example. If we were working with a durable resource, we would call the *EnlistDurable* method instead. Last, we perform the logic of assigning the new value and preserving the old value. With the class and its data set up, the rest of the details involve hooking up implementation so that we can enlist in a current running transaction with the RM and perform the appropriate actions based on the notifications received. This functionality is implemented in the four methods that the *IEnlistmentNotification* interface requires you to implement. The TM calls the appropriate methods (*Commit, Rollback, Prepare*, and *InDoubt*) for you and passes in a *System. Transactions.Enlistment* variable as a parameter. After successfully performing each step, you should call the *enlistment.Done()* method to indicate that this step has done its work.

The only exception to this rule is the *Prepare* method, which receives a special kind of *Enlistment*, a *System.Transactions.PreparingEnlistment* variable, as a parameter, which inherits from the *System.Transactions.Enlistment* class. *PreparingEnlistment* adds a few methods to *Enlistment*:

- *ForceRollBack()* or *ForceRollBack(Exception)*   Notifies the TM that an error has occurred and that the current participating RM wants to issue a rollback. You can specify your own exception if you want.

- *Prepared*   Notifies the TM that this RM has successfully finished doing its part of the transaction (the prepare phase of the two-phase commit process).

- *byte[] RecoveryInformation*   Used to specify information to the TM in the event of reenlistment to perform a graceful recovery (in situations such as the RM crashing). Alternatively, you can call the base class method *Done* to act as an innocent bystander and observe the transaction but not really participate in it. If you call *Done* in the prepare phase, the TM skips notifying the RM of the second (commit) phase of a two-phase notification process.

Using a Resource Manager in a Successful Transaction

Using the RM in transactional code is really simple. You just wrap it in a *TransactionScope*, as shown here:

```
VolatileRM vrm = new VolatileRM("RM1");
Console.WriteLine("Member Value:" + vrm.MemberValue);

using (TransactionScope tsc = new TransactionScope())
{
    vrm.MemberValue = 3;
    tsc.Complete();
}
Console.WriteLine("Member Value:" + vrm.MemberValue);
```

When you run this code, you should see the output shown in Figure 12-2.

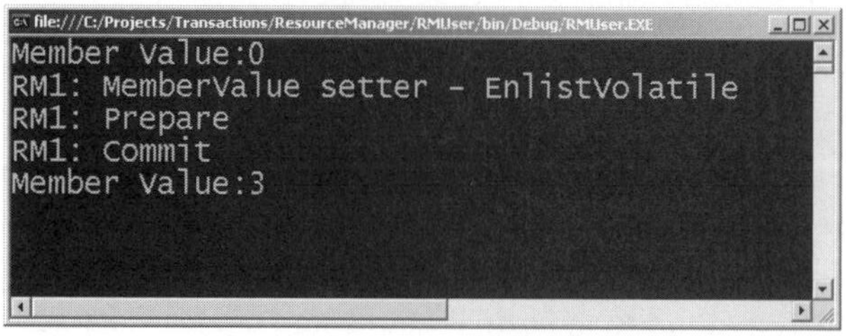

FIGURE 12-2 Our resource manager participating in a successful transaction

As you can see, our RM enlists in the prepare and commit phases of the two-phase commit process.

Using the Resource Manager When the Caller Issues a Rollback

Now we'll modify the code and comment out the *tsc.Complete()* statement and then run the application again. You should see the output shown in Figure 12-3.

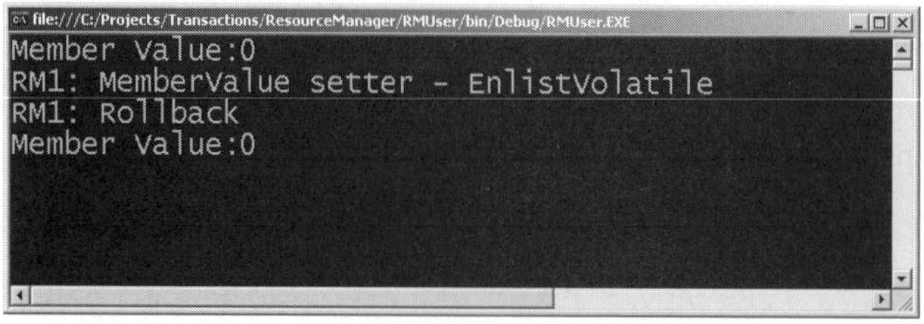

FIGURE 12-3 Our resource manager participating in a transaction when the caller issues a rollback

By commenting out the *tsc.Complete()* statement, we are simulating a circumstance in which the application that uses the RMs enforces a rollback. Instead of managing the prepare and commit phases, the code instead reacts to the rollback phase, and the final value of the member variable is unchanged from the original value.

Using the Resource Manager When It Issues a Rollback

Now we'll go ahead and put *tsc.Complete* back in the code and modify the *Prepare* method of the RM. Comment out the *Prepared* method call and put in a *ForceRollBack* call instead, as follows:

```
public void Prepare(PreparingEnlistment preparingEnlistment)
{
    Console.WriteLine(_whoAmI + ": Prepare");
    // preparingEnlistment.Prepared();
    preparingEnlistment.ForceRollback();
}
```

The RM now issues a rollback. When we execute the application with *tsc.Complete* in place, we should see an exception, as shown in Figure 12-4.

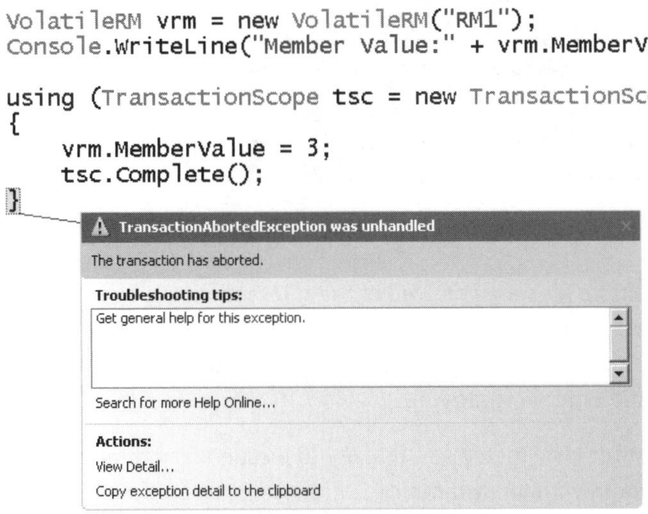

```
VolatileRM vrm = new VolatileRM("RM1");
Console.WriteLine("Member Value:" + vrm.MemberValue);

using (TransactionScope tsc = new TransactionScope())
{
    vrm.MemberValue = 3;
    tsc.Complete();
}
```

FIGURE 12-4 An exception caused because the resource manager itself issued a rollback

Using the Resource Manager with Another Resource Manager

Now we'll restore the *Prepare* method of our RM back to its original state so that a rollback isn't issued. Back in the host application, we'll modify the original code to include a second RM participating in the same transaction, as shown here:

```
VolatileRM vrm = new VolatileRM("RM1");
VolatileRM vrm2 = new VolatileRM("RM2");
Console.WriteLine("Member Value 1:" + vrm.MemberValue);
Console.WriteLine("Member Value 2:" + vrm2.MemberValue);

using (TransactionScope tsc = new TransactionScope())
{
    ...
    vrm.MemberValue = 3;
    vrm2.MemberValue = 5;
    tsc.Complete();
}

Console.WriteLine("Member Value 1:" + vrm.MemberValue);
Console.WriteLine("Member Value 2:" + vrm2.MemberValue);
```

As you can see, the code simply enlists another instance of the RM we wrote in the same transaction. When this code is executed, we get the output shown in Figure 12-5.

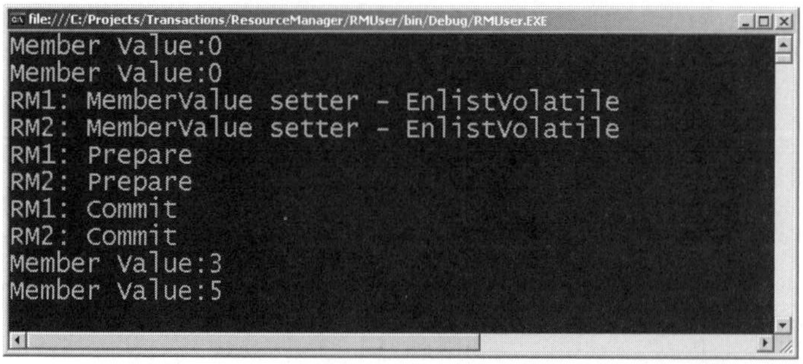

FIGURE 12-5 Two instances of our resource manager in a single transaction

As you can see, when multiple RMs are involved in the transaction, the appropriate prepare, commit, or rollback phases are called for each RM in succession. As an exercise, you could modify the RM code to include a *ForceRollBack* and see the succession of events if one of the RMs issues a rollback to the entire transaction.

We've saved the best part for last. Remember that *SqlConnection* is nothing but an RM, so you can retry this experiment with an instance of *SqlConnection*, a *SqlCommand*, and a database query executed within the same transaction that *VolatileRM* is enlisted in. To do so, modify the code to match this:

```
VolatileRM vrm = new VolatileRM("RM1");
Console.WriteLine("Member Value:" + vrm.MemberValue);

const string connStr =
  "Data Source=(local);Initial Catalog=Test1;Integrated Security=SSPI;";

const string cmdText = "UPDATE FromTable SET Amount = Amount - 50";

using (TransactionScope tsc = new TransactionScope())
{
    vrm.MemberValue = 3;

    using (SqlConnection conn1 = new SqlConnection(connStr))
    {
        SqlCommand cmd1 = conn1.CreateCommand();
        cmd1.CommandText = cmdText;
        conn1.Open();
        cmd1.ExecuteNonQuery();
    }
    tsc.Complete();
}

Console.WriteLine("Member Value:" + vrm.MemberValue);
```

By doing so, you would note that our *VolatileRM* now participates in the same transaction that a database query has enlisted itself in. This is something that *BEGIN DISTRIBUTED TRANSACTION* cannot do because by its very nature it talks to database queries, which cannot perform nondatabase operations (unless, of course, you are using SQL CLR, where things get a bit blurry).

Transactions in SQL CLR (CLR Integration)

No chapter on transactions is complete without a discussion of transactions in SQL CLR. Transactions behave so differently in the SQL CLR that this topic warrants its own section.

So far, we have discussed local transactions in SQL Server and ADO.NET, as well as distributed transactions in ADO.NET, SQL Server, and the .NET Framework in general. We noted that in PSPE, a distributed transaction might not be distributed. Thus, the boundaries of what is distributed and what is not are already blurry. Well, in SQL CLR, they are not only blurry, they are downright indistinct.

In Chapter 3, you learned about the basics of SQL CLR. We will build on the same concepts here and write a simple SQL CLR stored procedure to demonstrate the behavior of SQL CLR objects in a surrounding transaction. The stored procedure we will use is simplistic. It accepts no parameters and simply inserts a row in the *TestTable* table, as shown here:

```
[Microsoft.SqlServer.Server.SqlProcedure]
public static void InsertRow()
{
    using (SqlConnection contextConn =
        new SqlConnection("context connection = true"))
    {
        SqlCommand insertCmd = contextConn.CreateCommand();
        insertCmd.CommandText =
            "INSERT INTO TestTable(TestColumn) VALUES(100)";
        contextConn.Open();
        insertCmd.ExecuteNonQuery();
        contextConn.Close();
    }
}
```

As you can see, the code uses a context connection to execute a *SqlCommand*. The *SqlCommand* inserts a row into *TestTable* using a simple *INSERT* command. This SQL CLR stored procedure, once registered with SQL Server 2008, can be executed using the following T-SQL command:

```
EXEC InsertRow
```

As you can see, if you have a matching *TestTable* in the appropriate database, executing the stored procedure will indeed insert a row.

But what if we wrap this line of T-SQL code inside a *BEGIN TRANSACTION/ROLLBACK* block?

```
BEGIN TRANSACTION
  INSERT INTO TestTable(TestColumn) VALUES (200)
  EXEC InsertRow
ROLLBACK
```

Interestingly, the row that the *InsertRow* stored procedure would have inserted is rolled back. Thus, the *InsertRow* stored procedure can successfully enlist within a calling transaction.

> **Important** A SQL CLR object automatically enlists within a current running transaction.

You can easily issue a rollback from T-SQL by using the *ROLLBACK* command. Can you do the same from a SQL CLR stored procedure? Luckily, due to the fantastic integration of *System. Transactions* with SQL Server transactions, the answer is yes. You can access the current running transaction right from within SQL CLR by using the *Transaction.Current* property and, using the current transaction, issue a rollback, as shown here:

```
[Microsoft.SqlServer.Server.SqlProcedure]
public static void InsertRow()
{
    using (SqlConnection contextConn =
        new SqlConnection("context connection = true"))
    {
        SqlCommand insertCmd = contextConn.CreateCommand();
        insertCmd.CommandText =
            "INSERT INTO TestTable(TestColumn) VALUES(100)";
        contextConn.Open();
        insertCmd.ExecuteNonQuery();
        contextConn.Close();
    }
    Transaction.Current.Rollback();
}
```

Let's modify the T-SQL block so that it will attempt to commit, not roll back, as follows:

```
BEGIN TRANSACTION
    INSERT INTO TestTable(TestColumn) VALUES (200)
    EXEC InsertRow
COMMIT
```

Now, when we attempt to execute this T-SQL code block, we'll see an exception message, albeit an ambiguous one, something along the lines of "Transaction is not allowed to roll back inside a user-defined routine." However, the overall effect is that the transaction is rolled back. It would be nice if Microsoft would provide a better error message in this circumstance, but either way, the job gets accomplished. You would probably want to wrap such an error in a custom *BEGIN TRY...CATCH* or *try/catch/finally* block and throw a better error message.

> **Important** A SQL CLR object is able to roll back a current running transaction with the help of *System.Transactions* integration.

So far, we have been using a context connection to insert a row in the database. Instead, let's change the connection string to the one shown here:

```
Data Source=RemoteMachine;Initial Catalog=OtherDB;Integrated Security=SSPI;
```

A subtle difference is introduced in the preceding connection string. The T-SQL code we were executing connected to the local database (the *Test* database in the case of this chapter's sample code). In contrast, the new connection string connects to an entirely different database on an entirely different server. Now let's remove the *ROLLBACK* from the SQL CLR stored procedure and build and deploy it in the original database. Then we'll execute the following T-SQL code block:

```
BEGIN TRANSACTION
    INSERT INTO TestTable(TestColumn) VALUES (200)
    EXEC InsertRow
COMMIT
```

The transaction now spans two databases. In other words, SQL CLR was smart enough not only to understand that we were calling the SQL CLR object within a transaction but also to promote that transaction to a distributed transaction because an external resource is involved. In fact, if we tried connecting to an Oracle database, the SQL CLR function would still be enlisted within the same transaction. If you want to change this default behavior to not enlist within the same transaction, you can add *enlist=false* to the fully qualified connection string.

> **Important** SQL CLR will attempt to enlist any external connections within the same transaction.

We have seen how to use *System.Transactions.Transaction.Current* and obtain a handle to the current transaction. The obvious next question is, what else could we use? Could we use *SqlTransaction*? Yes, we could definitely use *SqlTransaction*, and in that case, we would use *SqlConnection.BeginTransaction* in a manner identical to non–SQL CLR ADO.NET. (We therefore won't cover it in depth here.)

The other approach, of course, is to use *System.Transactions.TransactionScope*. *TransactionScope* is great because you don't have to deal with the transaction—*Transaction-Scope* handles the details for you. In fact, in most scenarios, you probably don't want to deal with the current transaction using *Transaction.Current* directly. The only situations in which you'll want a direct handle on the transaction are the following:

- You want to roll back the external transaction by calling *Transaction.Current.Rollback*.

- You want to enlist resources that for some reason didn't auto-enlist. You can do so by using *Transaction.Current.EnlistVolatile* or *EnlistDurable*.

- You want to manually enlist in the current running transaction or modify the default behavior by explicitly listening for various callbacks in the two-phase commit process.

As mentioned, in all other cases, you probably want a more transparent method of writing transactional code, such as wrapping it in a *using* block so that everything is handled automatically or by using *TransactionScope*. This is easy to do by modifying your SQL CLR stored procedure code, as shown here:

```
[Microsoft.SqlServer.Server.SqlProcedure]
public static void InsertRow()
{
    using (TransactionScope tsc = new TransactionScope())
    {
        using (SqlConnection contextConn =
            new SqlConnection("context connection = true"))
        {
            SqlCommand insertCmd = contextConn.CreateCommand();
            insertCmd.CommandText =
                "INSERT INTO TestTable(TestColumn) VALUES(100)";
            contextConn.Open();
            insertCmd.ExecuteNonQuery();
            contextConn.Close();
        }
        tsc.Complete();
    }
}
```

Note that we are wrapping a context connection inside a *TransactionScope*. This is usually a bad practice, as you will find out soon. But if you have more than one database or RM involved in the transaction, *TransactionScope* will take care of enlisting everything in one transaction. The good part of this programming paradigm is that if there is already an active transaction, *TransactionScope* will take advantage of that transaction. If there is no active transaction, it will simply start a new transaction. This level of transparency helps you write more understandable and more manageable code.

Now let's comment out the *tsc.Complete()* statement from our SQL CLR stored procedure code and then build and deploy the stored procedure on the SQL Server 2008 database again. Then we'll try running it in the transactional T-SQL code. We'll get the following error:

```
Msg 8520, Level 16, State 1, Line 4
Internal Microsoft Distributed Transaction Coordinator (MS DTC) transaction failed to
commit: 0x8004d019(XACT_E_ABORTED).
```

This is as expected; we didn't mark the *TransactionScope* as complete, and the transaction aborted. What is surprising here, though, is that the message is coming from MS DTC. We had only one database connection, the context connection, and yet the transaction was promoted. This brings us to the next important point about SQL CLR transactions: when working inside SQL CLR in SQL Server 2008, the *TransactionScope* object will always cause the transaction to promote to MS DTC, even if you are using only context connections. For this reason, you should avoid using *TransactionScope* and stick with *SqlTransaction* or *System. Transactions.Transaction.Current* if you're using only context connections.

Putting It All Together

Let's end this chapter with one example that sums up the whole SQL CLR transaction story. We'll take the SQL CLR stored procedure we wrote and call it from a console application. Inside the console application, we will wrap the SQL CLR stored procedure and the RM we wrote earlier in this chapter in a single transaction, bound together with a single *System.Transactions. TransactionScope*.

Because we are using only a context connection in our SQL CLR stored procedure, let's follow the best practice of not using *TransactionScope* inside the SQL CLR stored procedure. The SQL CLR stored procedure should look like this:

```
[Microsoft.SqlServer.Server.SqlProcedure]
public static void InsertRow()
{
    using (SqlConnection contextConn =
        new SqlConnection("context connection = true"))
    {
        SqlCommand insertCmd = contextConn.CreateCommand();
        insertCmd.CommandText =
            "INSERT INTO TestTable(TestColumn) VALUES(100)";
        contextConn.Open();
        insertCmd.ExecuteNonQuery();
        contextConn.Close();
    }
}
```

Build and deploy the stored procedure to a SQL Server 2008 database. Create a console application named *BigBang* (you can find it on the companion Web site), and add references to *System.Transactions* and the RM project from the *YourOwnRM* solution we wrote earlier in this chapter.

Now modify the code of the *BigBang* console application's entry-point *Main* method, as shown here:

```
static void Main(string[] args)
{
    string connStr =
        "Data Source=(local);Initial Catalog=Test1;Integrated Security=SSPI;";
    string cmdText = "InsertRow";

    VolatileRM vrm = new VolatileRM("RM1");
    Console.WriteLine("Member Value:" + vrm.MemberValue);

    using (TransactionScope tsc = new TransactionScope())
    {
        using (SqlConnection conn1 = new SqlConnection(connStr))
        {
            SqlCommand cmd1 = conn1.CreateCommand();
            cmd1.CommandText = cmdText;
            cmd1.CommandType = CommandType.StoredProcedure;
```

```
            conn1.Open();
            cmd1.ExecuteNonQuery();
        }
        vrm.MemberValue = 3;

        tsc.Complete();
    }

    Console.WriteLine("Member Value:" + vrm.MemberValue);
}
```

When we execute this application, we'll see output similar to that shown in Figure 12-6.

FIGURE 12-6 The *BigBang* example running

Also note that our transaction is not promoted to MS DTC. As an exercise, you should try adding more RMs (say, another *SqlConnection*) or a noncontext connection inside the SQL CLR stored procedure, try to run the procedure, and observe the behavior of the code. *System.Transactions* transparently integrates all your operations between T-SQL, ADO.NET, and SQL CLR, and it promotes your transaction to MS DTC as necessary.

Summary

In this chapter, we covered the basic theory of transactions, which is probably one of the most important topics related to application architecture. You learned about transaction support in SQL Server 2008 and the supported isolation levels and their behavior. You also saw a side-by-side comparison with ADO.NET.

We also covered implementation of distributed transactions and the new support for writing transactional code that might have nothing to do with a database other than possibly enlisting in the same transaction as the database.

Last, you learned about the transaction support and implementation in SQL CLR. You saw how the *SqlConnection* object takes advantage of both local transaction implementation and distributed transaction implementation, as well as PSPE behavior when necessary.

Chapter 13
Developing Occasionally Connected Systems

—Paul Delcogliano

Today's business applications need to extend beyond the desktop. Users require access to pertinent data when they are not sitting at their desks. A company's "mobile workforce" needs access to data while on the road and on the go.

Salespeople visiting clients on site need access to inventory and product data. Their ability to process an order while away from the office could mean the difference between making and losing a sale. Delivery personnel need access to client addresses, driving directions, and delivery manifests. Having this information at a driver's fingertips improves efficiency and enables drivers to make more deliveries during the workday. Imagine how much time could be saved by eliminating the overhead of looking up directions on a map between deliveries or by electronically adjusting delivery quantities instead of using pen and paper.

More often than not, reliable, constant network connections won't be available to the mobile workforce—at least, not until ubiquitous WiFi access becomes a reality. Until that day arrives, applications need to provide data to users while they are not connected to the office network. Furthermore, data modifications made while a user is disconnected need to have the capability to be synchronized with a centralized database whenever a future connection is established. These types of applications that provide users the ability to work effectively while disconnected are commonly referred to as *occasionally connected systems*.

In this chapter, we'll take a close look at several replication technologies you can use to implement occasionally connected systems. These include traditional Microsoft SQL Server Merge Replication, as well as two exciting new features called Sync Services for ADO.NET and SQL Server Change Tracking.

> **More Info** This chapter helps get you started building occasionally connected systems quickly using Merge Replication and Sync Services for ADO.NET. You can learn more about these technologies by visiting the following Web sites and references:
>
> - Sync Services For ADO.NET Version 2 page on MSDN, available at *http://msdn.microsoft.com/en-us/library/bb726002(SQL.100).aspx*
> - "Microsoft Virtual Labs: Learn How to Build Occasionally Connected Applications," available at *http://download.microsoftvirtuallabs.com/download/8/a/7/8a71365b-4c80-4e60-8185-8f12f59bf1d4/LearnHowtoBuildOccasionallyConnectedApplication.pdf*

Merge Replication is a tried-and-true technology for replication and synchronization. It's known mostly as a tool for replicating databases as part of a disaster recovery plan. However, it also supports replication scenarios to support occasionally connected applications. Merge Replication offers lesser programmatic control when building such applications, but it still provides a lot of flexibility through its numerous configuration options.

Sync Services for ADO.NET is the new kid on the block. It gives you a subset of features from the Microsoft Sync Framework designed to handle database synchronization. This application programming interface (API) has roughly the same feature set as merge replication but is richer, and it gives you much more programmatic control than merge replication does.

 Note Sync Services for ADO.NET replaces an older mobile device synchronization technology named Remote Data Access (RDA).

The new SQL Server Change Tracking feature is designed to store and track information for modified data. Through Change Tracking, SQL Server maintains information about changes made to table rows, removing the burden of building a custom change tracking solution from you, the developer.

Comparing Sync Services with Merge Replication

Both Sync Services for ADO.NET and Merge Replication can be used to build occasionally connected systems. However, there are some differences between them that you need to be aware of when choosing which one to use. Depending on your requirements, you'll find one technology is better suited than the other. Table 13-1 lists some of the important differences between the two technologies.

TABLE 13-1 Comparison of Sync Services and Merge Replication Features

Feature	Sync Services	Merge Replication
Client database	SQL Server Compact 3.5	Any SQL Server version
Server database	Any relational database management system (RDBMS)	Any SQL Server version
Synchronize over n-tier or Web Services	Yes	No
Automatic schema change propagation	No	Yes
Programmatic synchronization control	Rich API, familiar ADO.NET *DataSet* model	Limited; wizard and stored procedure based

In short, if you are building an application whose synchronization requirements include having SQL Server clients synchronizing with non–SQL Server databases or if your application is built on top of an n-tier or service-oriented architecture, the choice is clear: Sync Services is your only option. For client/server applications or those where less programmatic control is required, you can choose to use either Sync Services or Merge Replication.

Components of an Occasionally Connected System

Many times, an occasionally connected system is an extension of a traditional desktop business application. Mobilizing an application requires some architectural redesign from the traditional application. The devices that run the client application are usually portable, are smaller, and have less processing power and memory than their desktop counterparts. They also need to store data locally since they are not always connected to the database via a local area network (LAN) connection. Having the data on the client device allows the mobile user to work while disconnected.

In an occasionally connected scenario, users receive copies of the data they need to perform their tasks. This data is retrieved from the central database while the mobile device is connected to the office network. This process is known as *synchronization*. While connected, a device synchronizes its local database with the data on the centralized server, thus allowing mobile workforce users to take the data with them on the road. Typical devices include laptops, Tablet PCs, and Microsoft Windows Mobile–based devices. For simplicity, we'll use the term *device* to refer to any of these.

The single biggest requirement of an occasionally connected application is to allow a user to work with application data without a network connection. Changes made while a user is disconnected are applied to the local database; usually this database is SQL Server Compact 3.5 for SmartPhone or Windows Mobile devices or SQL Server 2008 Express for laptops and Tablet PCs. Other requirements include the following:

- Ability to synchronize changes between client and server databases
- Capabilities to refresh the local data store
- Ability to resolve data conflicts that arise during synchronization
- Ability to handle transactional updates
- Capabilities to provide data expiration policies

Data synchronization can be either one-way, from server to client, or bidirectional, from server to client and back again. One-way synchronization is typically used for lookup data, like a list of products. In the case of one-way synchronization, the device does not update product data. From the device's perspective, the updated lookup data is read only.

Of course, bidirectional (two-way) synchronization requires that data can be updated on the client and sent back to the server. The updated data is then synchronized when a network connection is established. For instance, imagine a mobile application that downloads delivery manifests and stores the data locally. Throughout the day, a delivery person makes updates to each manifest by adding the delivery status to the manifest—in a similar manner to how many shipping companies deliver packages. The next time the mobile device connects to the office network, the changes stored locally in the device are synchronized with the centralized database.

In some cases, the data required by each member of the mobile workforce overlaps, like customer information. But in other cases, the data is very specific, like client addresses. For instance, different salespeople might need to share product data, but different delivery people might need only the client addresses relevant to those locations they are making deliveries to for the current day. Any conflicts can be handled and resolved by the synchronizing protocol.

With our basic premise established, let's hone in on the aforementioned technologies for building occasionally connected applications: Merge Replication and Sync Services for ADO. NET coupled with SQL Server Change Tracking.

Merge Replication

You might think of Merge Replication as a technology primarily used for replication and disaster recovery. While these are its more common uses, its replication capabilities make it a prime candidate for building the infrastructure of client applications that connect to the server only sporadically. Merge Replication provides several features that facilitate the synchronization process, including the ability to resolve data conflicts, control how often synchronization must occur, and clean up "stale" data.

Merge Replication works extremely well in situations where you don't need much programmatic control over the synchronization process and client/server–type applications. Setting up and configuring Merge Replication is mainly achieved using wizards.

Getting Familiar with Merge Replication

Our discussion of Merge Replication begins with a quick glossary of replication terms. Merge Replication uses a Publisher/Subscriber replication topology. Conceptually, it helps to think of this as analogous to publishing a newspaper. Merge Replication terminology consists of Publishers, Distributors, Subscribers, Articles, Publications, and Subscriptions.

> **More Info** Merge Replication is a huge topic in itself. In this chapter, we are limiting the discussion of Merge Replication to features specific to creating an occasionally connected application. For a more thorough description of Merge Replication, consult the SQL Server 2008 Books Online documentation.

Table 13-2 lists several definitions used throughout this chapter.

TABLE 13-2 Common Replication Terms

Term	Description
Publisher	The centralized database whose data is available to clients via replication. There can be multiple Publications available from a given Publisher, each making a different data set of data available to replicate.
Distributor	A database that stores replication metadata. The Distributor can store metadata for multiple Publishers. The distribution database stores information like replication status. The Distributor can reside in the same database instance as the Publisher—this is referred to as a *local Distribution*. If the Distributor is on a separate database instance from the Publisher, it is called a *remote Distributor*.
Subscriber	A client database that synchronizes with the Publisher. Subscribers can both receive and pass back data changes.
Article	A database object that is part of a Publication. The database object can be a table, view, or stored procedure. When the Article is a table, you can use filters to limit the data sent to a Subscriber.
Publication	A group of one or more Articles from a Publisher. A Publication allows related Articles to be replicated as a single unit.
Subscription	A copy of a Publication sent to a Subscriber. Merge Replication supports two types of Subscriptions: *push* and *pull*. A push Subscription is one where the Publisher sends changes to the Subscriber without the Subscriber making a request for changed data. A pull Subscription is one where the Subscriber is requesting changes. Typically, an occasionally connected system uses a pull Subscription.
Snapshot	A view of data as it exists in a specific moment in time. Snapshots are generated and sent to Subscribers. A snapshot "agent" is responsible for initializing and delivering Snapshots during synchronization. Snapshots can be generated according to a schedule.

Creating an Occasionally Connected Application with Merge Replication

The best way to learn about Merge Replication's synchronization features is through hands-on experience. In this section, we'll create a Pocket PC mobile application that simulates a company's order delivery process. The sample application uses a SQL Server Compact 3.5 database to record an order's delivery status. SQL Server Compact 3.5 is a lightweight database platform perfectly suited for single-user applications, such as those that run on a Pocket PC device.

Express or Compact?

You shouldn't consider SQL Server Compact 3.5 to be suitable only as a mobile database. Its lightweight, low-overhead design makes it a great solution for single-user laptop or desktop applications as well. Of course, SQL Server 2008 Express edition can also run on laptops and desktops, and both SQL Server editions are free. So which one should you use? Here is some practical advice for making an intelligent choice between the Express and Compact editions of SQL Server for database applications running on laptop or desktop computers.

First let's look at Express. Even though it's free, it supports all the features you (the developer) have come to know and love in SQL Server. It's a full implementation of the relational database engine limited only by scalability constraints on RAM, CPU, and database size. Express will use up to 1 gigabyte (GB) of RAM and one CPU (including multicore processors) and supports databases up to 4 GB in size. It can therefore easily handle light multiple-user environments such as small workgroups or departmental Web sites.

Because it lacks the enterprise features and business intelligence (BI) capabilities of the other editions, the Express deployment footprint is naturally also much smaller than the other editions. This means that you can certainly consider Express for single-user applications running on laptop or desktop machines. However, this is where you need to stop and think. For a local database store embedded in a single-user laptop or desktop application, your first consideration should be to use Compact rather than Express. Let's now examine Compact to understand why.

As small as SQL Server 2008 Express edition might be when compared with the upscale editions, it's still *huge* compared with Compact, which is *featherweight*—in terms of both size and run-time performance. Besides a dramatically reduced deployment footprint (only 1.5 MB), Compact also runs in process with your application. This means that there's no overhead of a full-blown service to affect your application's overall performance. For a single-user application—even those running on machines capable of hosting Express—a full implementation of SQL Server might very likely be overkill.

Do you really need a multiple-user service running in the background to support the basic data storage requirements of a typical single-user application? Very often, you probably don't. SQL Server Compact 3.5 presents a better choice when your single-user needs are simple and you don't want to incur all the overhead of a full-fledged Microsoft Windows Service—which Express edition is.

You've got to be prepared to give up some comfort and convenience if you want to travel light, however. With SQL Server Compact 3.5, we developers get a lot less to work with. It's extremely lean, and it supports only a very limited subset of Transact-SQL (T-SQL). Essentially, this means that only the basic data definition language (DDL) and data manipulation language (DML) statements are available for creating and managing tables and indexes and querying or updating data. Don't look for any fancy SQL Server features; you don't even get stored procedures. But you do get great performance for single-user applications—even those not running on mobile devices.

Of course, Express is not an option for mobile devices, just as Compact is not an option for multiple-user applications. But for single-user applications, running on laptop or desktop machines, you have a clear choice to make between Compact and Express editions. You should not view Compact as being limited to mobile devices. Microsoft makes this clear by no longer calling the product Mobile Edition as it once did. (It is also no longer called Everywhere Edition, as it was recently in SQL Server 2005.) You should have compelling reasons for using Express on a laptop or desktop machine to support a single-user application instead of using Compact, since doing so is very much like bringing out the snow blower to clear a small path when a plain shovel will suffice. Those reasons should include a real need for features that can be delivered only by Express and not by Compact—for example, XML, geospatial, or file streaming capabilities.

In our sample application, delivery personnel receive customer and order data when they synchronize their client devices with the server. Upon delivering an order, the delivery person updates the delivery status on a mobile device. The status is stored on the device until the delivery person synchronizes with the server, at which time the delivery status is updated on the server.

The sample database stores information you'd find in a typical database: customers, orders, and so on. (In a production database, we'd have many more tables and columns, but this subset of tables will suffice for our example.) First, we'll need to create a database in SQL Server 2008 to store customers and orders. Start SQL Server Management Studio, connect to your local SQL Server 2008 instance, and open a new query window. Then run the code shown in Listing 13-1 to create the application's database and tables.

LISTING 13-1 Creating the database and tables used in our examples

```
CREATE DATABASE SQL08SampleDB
GO

USE SQL08SampleDB
GO

CREATE TABLE [Customer] (
 CustomerID int NOT NULL IDENTITY(1,1),
 CustomerName varchar(100) NOT NULL,
 CONSTRAINT [PK_Customer]
   PRIMARY KEY CLUSTERED (CustomerID ASC)
)
GO

CREATE TABLE [Order] (
 OrderID int NOT NULL IDENTITY(1,1),
 CustomerID int NOT NULL,
 OrderDate datetime2(0) NOT NULL,
 IsDelivered bit NOT NULL DEFAULT(0),
 CONSTRAINT [PK_Order]
   PRIMARY KEY CLUSTERED (OrderID ASC)
)
GO

CREATE TABLE [Contact] (
   ContactID uniqueidentifier NOT NULL,
   CustomerID int NOT NULL,
   ContactName nvarchar(100),
   ContactPhone nvarchar(100),
   ContactEmail nvarchar(100),
   CONSTRAINT [PK_Contact]
     PRIMARY KEY CLUSTERED(ContactID ASC)
)
GO
```

Now run the code in Listing 13-2 to add sample data to the new database.

LISTING 13-2 Inserting sample data

```
INSERT INTO [Customer] (CustomerName) VALUES
  ('Johnson'), ('Smith'), ('Jones'), ('Davis'), ('Jefferson')

INSERT INTO [Order] (CustomerID, OrderDate, IsDelivered) VALUES
  (1, '01/15/2008', 0), (1, '02/14/2008', 1), (2, '02/13/2008', 0),
  (3, '03/17/2008', 1), (4, '04/12/2008', 0), (5, '04/01/2008', 0)
```

Note the use of row constructors in Listing 13-2. This is new T-SQL shorthand in SQL Server 2008 that allows you to insert multiple rows with a single *INSERT* statement. In our case, this code adds five customers and six orders.

Configuring Merge Replication

As we mentioned earlier, Merge Replication requires little code and is mostly configured through wizards and dialog options. There are five steps to implement Merge Replication, as follows:

1. Configure the Distribution.

2. Create a Publication.

3. Subscribe to a Publication.

4. Initialize a Subscription.

5. Synchronize data.

Each of these steps is made up of several smaller substeps.

Configuring the Distribution

The first task is to configure the *Distributor* database. Remember, the *Distributor* database contains all of the metadata required for replication. Keep the following issues in mind when designing and planning the *Distributor* database:

- Use a server with adequate resources. Like any other database, the *Distributor* database consumes disk space and processor resources.

- Carefully name the database and file locations. Once the Distributor is enabled on the database, you cannot rename the database. To rename it, you must disable and reconfigure the Distributor.

- Consider any and all Publishers who will be using the Distribution. Publishers not on the same server as the Distributor require passwords to make remote connections to the Distributor.

- The Replication Agent requires the SQL Server Agent to be configured to start automatically upon server startup.

For our sample application, we'll use the same server for the Distributor and the Publisher. Running the Distributor and Publisher together on the same server is referred to as a *local* Distribution.

The first of many wizards we'll be using here is the Configure Distribution Wizard. This wizard walks you through the process of setting up a Distributor in a few different configurations. For our example, we will be configuring the Distributor to be a Publisher that acts as its own Distributor. To start the wizard, navigate to the Replication node in SQL Server Management Studio Object Explorer. Right-click the Replication node, and then select Configure Distribution. Click Next on the wizard's start page to begin configuring the *Distributor* database. If it is not already selected, choose the option *<servername>* Will Act As Its Own Distributor, and then click Next.

> **Note** The Object Explorer connection in SQL Server Management Studio must be estab-
> lished against the actual server name in order to configure replication. If the connection was
> made against an IP address, server alias, *localhost*, or simply ".", you will receive an error mes-
> sage explaining this requirement when you try to start the Configure Distribution Wizard, and
> Management Studio will offer to reestablish the connection so that you can use the proper
> server name.

As we just mentioned, the replication agents used by Merge Replication require the SQL
Server Agent to be configured to run at startup. If the SQL Server Agent on your server is not
configured this way (which is the default, as per SQL Server's "secure by default" strategy),
you will see the dialog box shown in Figure 13-1. Select the Yes option, and then click Next.

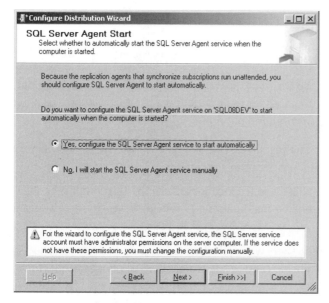

FIGURE 13-1 Configuring SQL Server Agent to start automatically for replication

Next you must specify the folder where SQL Server stores snapshot and schema files for
Subscribers to retrieve. Replication agents read and write data in this folder during synchro-
nization. By default, the local folder path C:\Program Files\Microsoft SQL Server\<*instance*>
\MSSQL\ReplData is specified. As indicated by the text in the dialog box (see Figure 13-2),
the snapshot folder must be a network share specified as a Universal Naming Convention
(UNC) path, in the form of *ComputerName**ShareName*, for applications that use a pull
Subscription or a remote Distributor.

A pull Subscription is defined as a Subscriber requesting (or pulling) changes from a
Publisher. This is different from a push Subscription, where a Publisher constantly pushes
changes to Subscribers. Because our sample application uses a pull Subscription, we'll use a
network share.

Create a network share for the snapshot folder by opening Windows Explorer and navigating to the C:\Program Files\Microsoft SQL Server\MSSQL10.MSSQLSERVER\MSSQL folder. Right-click the ReplData folder, and then choose the Sharing And Security option.

> **Note** For proper security in a production environment, you should assign specific accounts READ ACCESS to the snapshot directory share.

Choose the Share This Folder option, and then type the name **ReplicationSnapshots** for the share name.

> **Note** Different versions of Windows display this dialog box differently, especially depending on what service packs are installed.

After you have configured the folder to be shared, return to the wizard, enter the UNC path to the snapshot folder you just created (in this example, **\\SQL08DEV\ ReplicationSnapshots**), as shown in Figure 13-2, and then click Next.

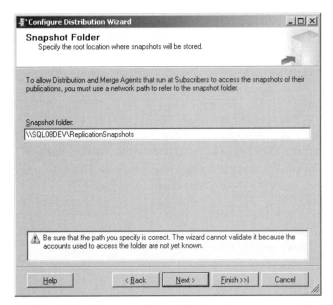

FIGURE 13-2 Setting the snapshot folder location

On the wizard's Distribution Database page, type **MyDistributor** for the Distribution database name. Accept the defaults for the data and transaction log folders, and then click Next.

The Publishers page, shown in Figure 13-3, establishes the Publishers that will use the new Distributor. By default, the local server is set up to act as both a Distributor and a Publisher. For our sample application, this is all we need, so go ahead and click Next.

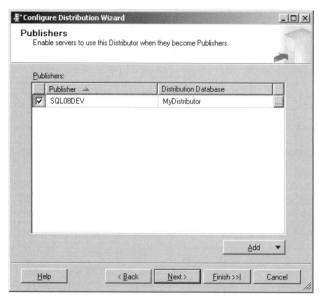

FIGURE 13-3 The local server set by default to act as both Distributor and Publisher

On the Wizard Actions page, shown in Figure 13-4, you specify the steps you want the wizard to execute when it is complete. Here you have the option of configuring the Distribution, creating a script that configures the Distribution, or both. Select the Configure Distribution check box, clear the Generate A Script File With Steps To Configure Distribution box, and then click Next. If you do decide to generate the script file, you will see an additional wizard step (not shown here) prompting you for a location where the script file is to be saved.

Last, the Complete The Wizard page displays a summary of the choices you made through the Configure Distribution Wizard. Click Finish to build and set up the Distributor. After the wizard is completed, you'll see a new database named *MyDistributor*. This database is created under the System Databases node in SQL Server Management Studio.

> **Note** You will receive an error if the SQL Server Agent Service is not running when you complete the wizard. If this occurs, rerun the wizard with the Agent Service started.

> **Note** You might have to refresh the System Databases node in Object Explorer in order to see the *MyDistributor* database after it is created.

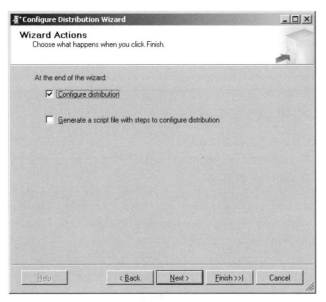

FIGURE 13-4 Instructing the wizard to configure distribution when Finish is clicked

A quick look at the Distribution Database Properties dialog box (displayed by right-clicking the Replication node, choosing the Distributor Properties menu item, and then clicking the ellipsis button to the right of the *MyDistributor* database) reveals several properties. The pertinent one in this discussion is the Transaction Retention property, shown in Figure 13-5. This property tells SQL Server the length of time to retain replication data. You can specify the minimum and maximum values by setting the At Least and But No More Than values.

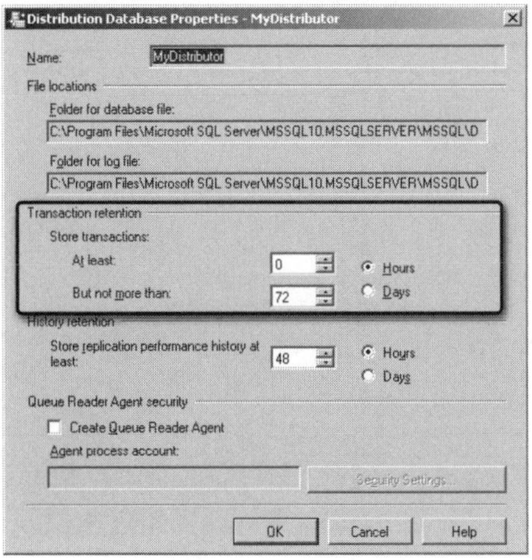

FIGURE 13-5 Viewing the Distributor properties

Creating a Publication

With the Distributor set up, we can now focus our efforts on setting up a Publication. For the sample application, we are publishing the *Customer* and *Order* tables. Open the Replication node in SQL Server Management Studio Object Explorer, right-click the Local Publications folder, and on the shortcut menu, choose the New Publication option. The New Publication Wizard appears; click Next to start the wizard.

The first page of the wizard is the Publication Database page. To create a Publication, choose the database containing the data you want to publish (in our scenario, that's the *SQL08SampleDB* database), and then click Next.

On the Publication Type page, shown in Figure 13-6, you specify the Publication type that best meets your application's requirements. For our sample application, the Publication type is Merge Publication. A Merge Publication is one where Subscribers are initialized with Publication data. After initialization, changes are synchronized occasionally when the client application is connected. Client applications like our sample, which uses SQL Server Compact 3.5, can subscribe only to merge Publications. Choose Merge Publication from the list, and then click Next.

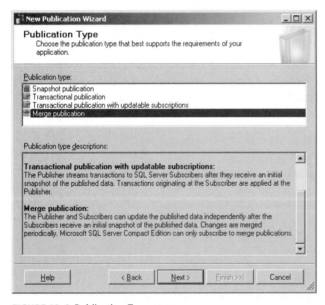

FIGURE 13-6 Publication Type page

Figure 13-7 shows the Subscriber Types page. Here you are basically picking the Subscriber's SQL Server version. The version you specify determines which features are available to a Publication. So if your Subscriber uses the SQL Server 2005 client database but you choose the SQL Server 2000 Subscriber type, your Publication will be limited to the SQL Server 2000 publication features.

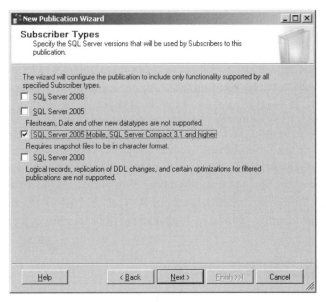

FIGURE 13-7 Subscriber Types page

We're using SQL Server Compact 3.5 for the sample application, so select the SQL Server 2005 Mobile, SQL Server Compact 3.1 And Higher check box, and then click Next to continue.

On the Articles page, shown in Figure 13-8, you specify which database tables to replicate. Here you'll choose which tables to synchronize and which will be tracked for all changes (including schema changes). You can also select specific columns to replicate. Select the Customer and Order tables.

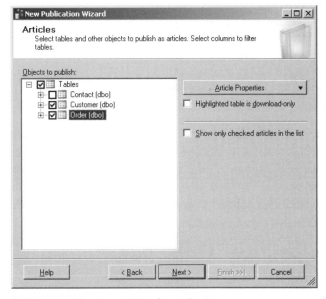

FIGURE 13-8 Choosing Articles for replication

If you select one of the tables in the tree view (Figure 13-8 shows the Order table selected), the Highlighted Table Is Download-Only check box will appear. If you select the Highlighted Table Is Download-Only check box, you are creating a one-way synchronization. The sample application uses two-way synchronization, so leave this check box cleared. Remember that in two-way synchronization, all DML changes that occur on the Subscription database are tracked and propagated back to the main SQL Server 2008 database. Click Next.

The Article Issues page, shown in Figure 13-9, presents a list of actions that will be taken on the Article after it is created. In the case of the *Customer* and *Order* tables, you are informed that the wizard will create *uniqueidentifier* columns in each table, along with corresponding unique indexes. Merge Replication uses the *uniqueidentifier* data type (GUIDs) to identify each row during replication. The wizard will also set the *ROWGUIDCOL* attribute, which will designate the globally unique identifier (GUID) value as a known identifier for every row inserted into the table.

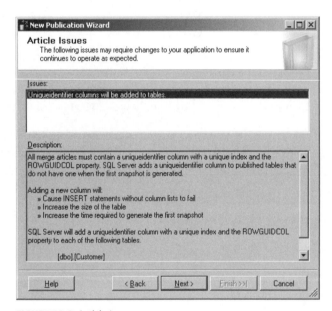

FIGURE 13-9 Article Issues page

To limit the amount of data transmitted during synchronization, we'll add a filter to the Publication using the wizard's Filter Table Rows page. Click the Add button, and then select Add Filter to open the Add Filter dialog box, shown in Figure 13-10. Select the *Order* table from the drop-down list, and then select the *IsDelivered* column and move it over to the filter statement text box. In the Filter Statement text box, add the text **= 0** to the end of the statement. The completed filter statement should read as follows:

```
SELECT <published_columns> FROM [dbo].[Order] WHERE IsDelivered = 0
```

The sample application uses a value of zero in the *IsDelivered* column to distinguish between delivered and undelivered orders. By establishing this filter, only those orders that haven't been delivered will be downloaded to the mobile device. Click OK to close the Add Filter dialog box.

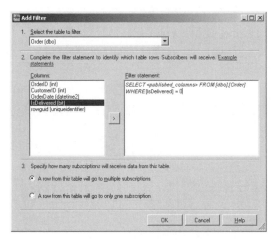

FIGURE 13-10 Establishing a row filter for replication

We're also going to add a join to the filter. The join further limits the data returned by retrieving only those customers who have undelivered orders. Select the *Order* table on the Filter Table Rows page, click the Add button, and this time, select Add Join To Extend The Selected Filter. In the Add Join dialog box, shown in Figure 13-11, select the *Customer* table from the Joined Table drop-down list. Next select the *CustomerID* value from the Filtered Table list and the *CustomerID* value from the Joined Table list, and then click OK.

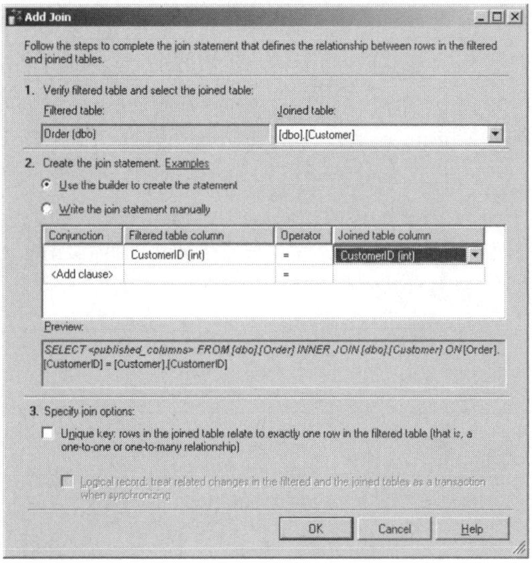

FIGURE 13-11 Adding a join to the filter

Click Next to advance the wizard to the Snapshot Agent page. On the Snapshot Agent page, shown in Figure 13-12, you can choose to run the agent immediately and set up a recurring schedule. For our sample application, click the Change button, and then set the agent to run every day at 4:30 PM. After setting the schedule, click OK to close the Job Schedule Properties dialog box, and then click Next.

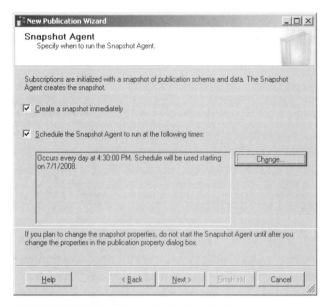

FIGURE 13-12 Setting the snapshot agent schedule

On the Snapshot Security page, you'll assign the security rights under which the snapshot agent runs. The snapshot agent is responsible for creating snapshot files that are used in the synchronization process.

Let's create a new Windows account that the snapshot agent will run under. We're going to leave SQL Server Management Studio for a moment and use one of the forms provided by Windows. Open the Computer Management applet from the Administrative Tools menu to add the new user. Create a new user named **SnapshotAgent**. Set the new account's password to **!Agent**. Add the new user to the local group named *SQLServerMSSQLUser$<MachineName>$<SQLServerInstanceName>*. In our example, the group is *SQLServerMSSQLUser$SQL08DEV$MSSQLSERVER*.

> **Note** There are various methods for adding user accounts, depending on the version of Windows you are running. Choose the method that is most familiar to you.

Our new Windows account needs login access to SQL Server. Create a new login for the *SQLServerMSSQLUser$SQL08DEV$MSSQLSERVER* group. This allows any users in the group to have login access to the server. Go back to SQL Server Management Studio, and run the script shown in Listing 13-3 to create the SQL Server login.

LISTING 13-3 Creating a SQL Server login for the local group

```
USE [master]
GO
CREATE LOGIN [SQL08DEV\SnapshotAgent] FROM WINDOWS WITH DEFAULT_DATABASE=[master]
GO
EXEC master..sp_addsrvrolemember @loginame = N'SQL08DEV\SnapshotAgent', @rolename =
N'sysadmin'
GO
```

Earlier, when we created the Distributor, we also created a UNC folder share named *ReplicationSnapshots*. Our new *SnapshotAgent* Windows account needs read and write access to that share. Open Windows Explorer. Navigate to the the ReplicationSnapshots folder, and then right-click the folder to display the shortcut menu. Choose Sharing and Security from the menu. To grant the *SnapshotAgent* account change/read access to the shared folder, click Permissions, and then click Add to add the SnapshotAgent account. After it is added, select the account and grant it Change and Read permissions. Click OK twice to close the Permissions and Properties dialog boxes. Close Windows Explorer.

Return now to the wizard, which should still be at the Agent Security page, and click the Security Settings button to open the Snapshot Agent Security dialog box, shown in Figure 13-13. Set the Snapshot Agent process to Run Under The Following Windows Account. Type the account *<**machine name**>***\SnapshotAgent** (be sure to include the domain or machine name) and the password **!Agent** in the Process Account and Password boxes. Make sure that the Connect To The Publisher option is set to By Impersonating The Process Account, and then click OK to return to the wizard.

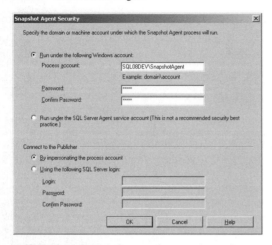

FIGURE 13-13 Setting the snapshot agent security

Click Next to advance the wizard. On the Wizard Actions page, you can specify whether you want to create the Publication now or script out all the options you just selected (or both). Select the Create The Publication option, and then click Next.

> **Important** Make sure that the SQL Server Agent service is running prior to completing the wizard. If it is not running, you might encounter errors or warnings when the wizard builds the Publication.

On the Complete The Wizard page, you provide a name for the new Publication. Type **MyPublication**, and then click Finish. The wizard builds and executes a script that creates the Publication. We are now ready to begin setting up synchronization.

To see the new *MyPublication* Publication in SQL Server Management Studio, drill down in the Replication node and expand the Local Publications node in Object Explorer.

We have to configure a couple more items manually for the Publication to be considered complete. Specifically, we need to set up a SQL Server user account that the Subscriber uses to synchronize with the Publication, and we have to grant that account access to the Publication.

Run the script shown in Listing 13-4 to create a new SQL Server login named *SubscriberAccount* with the password *account*. This script adds the new user to the *SQL08SampleDB* database and enrolls it as a member of the *MSmerge_PAL_role* role.

LISTING 13-4 Creating the *SubscriberAccount* SQL Server user account

```
USE [master]
GO
CREATE LOGIN [SubscriberAccount] WITH PASSWORD=N'account',
DEFAULT_DATABASE=[SQL08SampleDB], CHECK_EXPIRATION=OFF, CHECK_POLICY=OFF
GO

USE [SQL08SampleDB]
GO
CREATE USER [SubscriberAccount] FOR LOGIN [SubscriberAccount]
GO
USE [SQL08SampleDB]
GO
EXEC sp_addrolemember N'MSmerge_PAL_role', N'SubscriberAccount'
GO
```

After the script completes, open the *MyPublication* Publication Properties dialog box by right-clicking the Publication and then choosing Properties from the shortcut menu. Select the Publication Access List page, as shown in Figure 13-14, and then click Add.

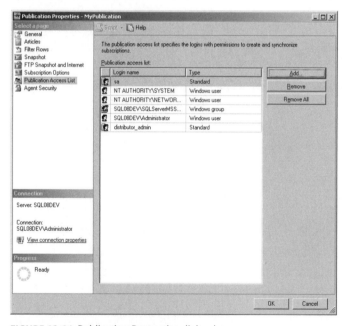

FIGURE 13-14 Publication Properties dialog box

The *SubscriberAccount* SQL Server account has to be added as an account with rights to access the Publication. Choose the *SubscriberAccount* account from the list, and then click OK. Click OK again in the Publication Properties dialog box to close it.

If everything is set up properly, the SQL Server 2008 Snapshot Agent runs immediately after creating the Publication. The agent's initial execution adds files to the Publication's network share. To initialize a snapshot or to execute the Snapshot Agent manually, open the View Snapshot Agent Status dialog box, shown in Figure 13-15, by right-clicking the *MyPublication* Publication and then choosing View Snapshot Agent Status from the shortcut menu. Click the Start button to start the agent.

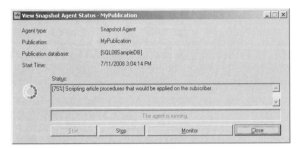

FIGURE 13-15 Monitoring the snapshot agent status

You can also monitor the agent's progress by clicking the Monitor button, which opens the Replication Monitor dialog box, shown in Figure 13-16. The Replication Monitor provides details about all of the Publications on the server, including Publication details, a list of Subscribers, a list of agent statuses, and so on.

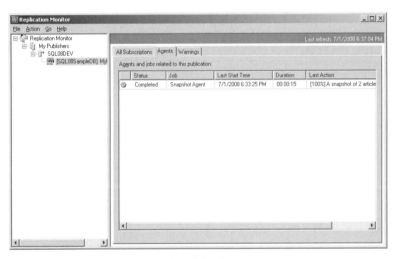

FIGURE 13-16 The Replication Monitor dialog box

We have now finished configuring the *MyPublication* Publication. Our next step is to configure the snapshot to be delivered over the Internet using Internet Information Services (IIS). Merge Replication supports the capability to deliver snapshots over the Internet using Hypertext Transfer Protocol (HTTP), referred to as *Web Synchronization*. Microsoft recommends using Web Synchronization, so our sample application uses Web Synchronization to synchronize the *Publisher* and *Subscriber* databases.

Web Synchronization for Merge Replication

Merge Replication supports a scalable architecture for Subscribers synchronizing data over the Internet. Web Synchronization is required when synchronizing mobile clients over the Web or through corporate firewalls. Using the HTTP/HTTPS protocol, Subscribers connect to a URL and transmit data as XML.

> **Note** Web Synchronization also supports the delivery of snapshots using FTP. To accomplish this, the Publication and Subscriptions must be set up to use FTP, and you'll need an FTP server, such as IIS. You should also be aware that FTP is less secure because the login password is sent unencrypted from the Subscriber to the FTP server during synchronization.

A Merge Agent running on the Subscriber's system packages and sends changes as XML to the server running IIS. The IIS server then converts the data to a binary format and forwards the data to the Publisher. The transmission between IIS and the Publisher is normally done using TCP/IP. Next the Publisher packages any updates as XML and sends them to back to the Subscriber via IIS.

> **Note** Web Synchronization is an option only for pull Subscriptions. All computers involved in the Web Synchronization process must be running SQL Server 2005 or later.

Web Synchronization can be configured with one, two, or more servers. For performance and security reasons, you'll want to configure Web Synchronization using at least two servers in your production environment. Some Web Synchronization best practices to keep in mind include the following:

- Use two separate servers: one for IIS and one for the *Publisher* and *Distributor* data-bases. Separate servers increase scalability and security.

- Use Secure Sockets Layer (SSL) to encrypt the transmission of data between the Subscriber and the IIS server. SQL Server Books Online notes that SSL is required for Web Synchronization—however, when building the sample application, you will find that it isn't. Nevertheless, SSL should always be used in a production environment.

- Use Basic Authentication on the Subscriber instead of Integrated Authentication. By using Basic Authentication, you avoid performance penalties associated with Kerberos delegation between IIS and the *Publisher* database.

- Configure all Windows accounts involved in Web Synchronization with the least amount of privileges possible.

> **Note** Review the information in SQL Server 2008 Books Online documentation for more advice on the best way to secure your production Web Synchronization environment.

Our sample application uses the single-server scenario, with anonymous access and unencrypted connections—an easy way to prototype the application, but certainly not the recommended approach for your production deployment.

The choices we made when setting up the *MyPublication* Publication earlier directly affect our ability to use Web Synchronization. Specifically, we created a Publication where the clients are running SQL Server Compact 3.1 and later and that uses the *Merge Publication* Publication type. Those choices allow us to configure Web Synchronization for the sample application.

Configuring IIS for Web Synchronization

There are three main steps involved in configuring Web Synchronization. The first step is to configure the Publication, which we've already done. The second step is to configure IIS for Web Synchronization. The third step is to configure the Subscriber. This section breaks down the individual steps involved with configuring IIS for our sample application.

> **Note** Web Synchronization is currently supported in IIS versions 5 and 6 but not version 7. Also, Web Synchronization requires Microsoft .NET Framework version 2.0 or later. It is recommended that versions of .NET earlier than 2.0 be removed from the IIS server. If multiple .NET Framework versions exist on your IIS server, your Web Synchronization implementation might throw exceptions.

IIS can be configured either manually or (you guessed it) via a wizard. We'll use the wizard method for our sample. To start the wizard, drill down to the Local Publications node under the Replication node in SQL Server Management Studio. Right-click the *MyPublication* Publication, and then select the Configure Web Synchronization option from the shortcut menu.

The wizard walks you through configuring several pieces of information, including virtual directory and security information. Click Next on the wizard's start page to begin.

The Subscriber Type page asks you to provide information about the version of SQL Server running the Subscriber database. The default is SQL Server. Select SQL Server Compact, and then click Next.

The Web Server page is where you provide information about the IIS server that is hosting Web Synchronization. Here you'll enter the server name and tell the wizard to create a new virtual directory in IIS.

> **Note** If you do not have the SQL Server Compact Server Tools installed, you will be prompted to install them during this step. If needed, go ahead and install the tools. The installer is the file SSCEServerTools-ENU.msi located in the C:\Program Files\Microsoft SQL Server Compact Edition \v3.5\Tools folder.

Select the Create A New Virtual Directory, and then select the Default Web Site node as the location where the new virtual directory should be created, as shown in Figure 13-17. Then click Next.

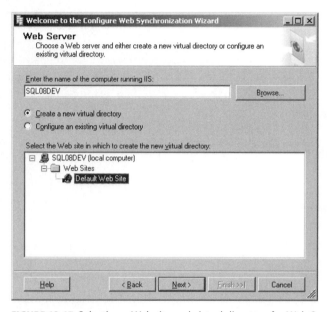

FIGURE 13-17 Selecting a Web site and virtual directory for Web Synchronization

On the Virtual Directory Information page, enter an alias for the new virtual directory. Use the value *MyWebSync* as the alias, and leave the virtual directory's path as the default.

> **Note** If the path does not exist, you will be prompted to create it. Additionally you might be prompted to "Copy and register the SQL Server Compact Server Agent" to this path. The SQL Server Compact Server Agent is the listener that waits for synchronization requests from Subscribers and fulfills those requests by communicating with the Publisher to replicate data. Click Yes to both of these prompts.

Once the virtual directory is created, its URL will be *http://<servername>/MyWebSync*—in our example, it is *http://SQL08DEV/MyWebSync*. Hold this URL in some storage location in short-term memory. We'll need it later when configuring Web Synchronization on the Subscriber. For now, click Next to continue.

On the Secure Communications page, you specify whether to use SSL to encrypt the data transmitted between the Subscriber and the IIS server. Choose the Do Not Require [SSL] option, and then click Next.

The Client Authentication page allows you to specify the method used to authenticate users connecting through the IIS server. Choose the Clients Will Connect Anonymously option, and then click Next.

Specify the Windows user account to be used when connecting anonymously. For the sample application, we'll use the default *IUSR_<MachineName>* account. Click Next.

The Snapshot Share Access page, shown in Figure 13-18, prompts you for the name of the network share containing the snapshot files. Enter the UNC path to the network share we created earlier in the form *ComputerName**ShareName*—in our example, the name is **\\ SQL08DEV\ReplicationSnapshots**.

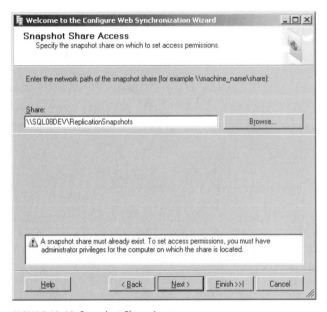

FIGURE 13-18 Snapshot Share Access page

Click Next, and then click Finish.

> **Note** If this is the first time you're setting up Merge Replication, you might be prompted with a message concerning an empty snapshot folder. Click Yes to continue through the wizard.

When you click Finish, the wizard configures Web Synchronization according to the parameters you entered.

> **Note** If you plan on replicating large amounts of data, you need to be mindful of the Merge Agent batch size limit. Web Synchronization transmits data between the Subscriber and IIS in chunks up to a maximum size of 25 MB. This limit includes the overhead associated with the XML tags that wrap the replica data. This limitation means that you cannot replicate any data in a single column that might be larger than 25 MB—for example, a binary file stored in a *varbinary(max)* column.

Configuring the Subscription Database for Web Synchronization

So far, we've completed two of the three steps needed to configure our application for Web Synchronization. The third and final step is to configure the Subscription Database. In this section, we'll set up a Subscription database running on SQL Server Compact 3.5. Before we complete this final configuration step, let's create our sample application's compact database.

From within SQL Server Management Studio, click the Connect button, and then choose the SQL Server Compact option. Click the Database file combo box, and then choose <New Database...> in the Connect To Server dialog box. In the Create New SQL Server Compact Database dialog box, shown in Figure 13-19, you enter information to create a new SQL Server Compact database. Type **C:\Projects\MergeRepSubscriber.sdf** for the database file name, and supply a password for your new database. You can use any password you want or none at all, although you will receive a warning (which you can ignore) if you supply an empty or weak password. In our case, we'll specify **password** as the password.

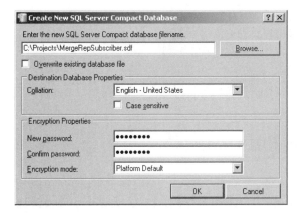

FIGURE 13-19 Creating a new SQL Server Compact database

Click OK to create the database and close the dialog box, and then answer Yes to ignore the weak password warning. (The password we chose lacks mixed-case and symbol characters, which is considered weak.)

Navigate to the new database in Object Explorer, and then expand the Replication node. Right-click the Subscriptions node, and then click New Subscriptions on the shortcut menu to open the New Subscription Wizard. Click Next to start the wizard.

Choose the *MyPublication* Publication from the Choose Publication wizard page, and then click Next.

> **Note** You might have to browse for the distribution server before you are able to select the Publication database.

On the Identify Subscription page, shown in Figure 13-20, type **OrderDeliverySubscription** for the Subscription name. The HOST_NAME value is used to segregate Subscriptions by workstation name. Our sample application does not segregate Subscriptions, so leave HOST_ NAME blank, and then click Next to continue.

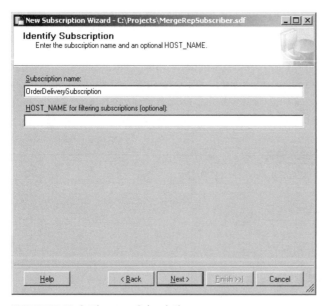

FIGURE 13-20 Setting up a Subscription

On the Web Server Authentication page, shown in Figure 13-21, you enter details about how the Subscriber connects to the Web server. Type the URL created earlier—in our example, **http://SQL08DEV/MyWebSync**. Select the option to allow the Subscriber to connect to the Web server anonymously, and then click Next.

On the SQL Server Authentication page, shown in Figure 13-22, select the option to use SQL Server authentication, and then type the user name **SubscriberAccount** and the password **account** (the SQL Account we created earlier).

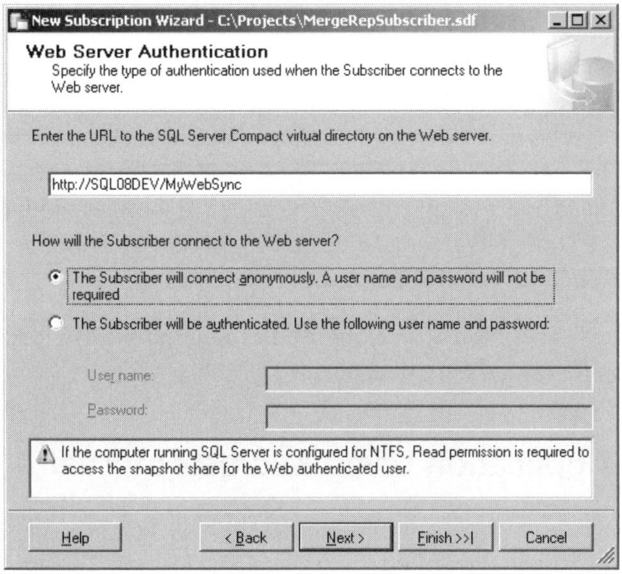

FIGURE 13-21 Configuring Web server authentication for the Subscription

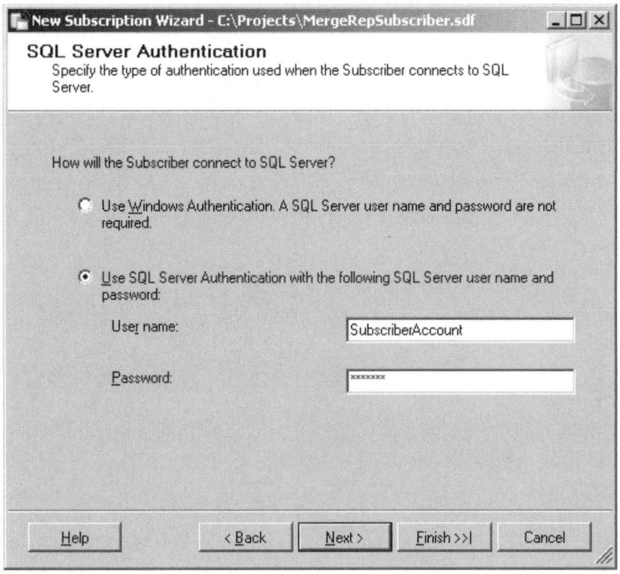

FIGURE 13-22 Configuring SQL Server authentication for the Subscriber

Click Next. The wizard generates and displays code for use in our client application. Copy the C# code from the Complete The Wizard page, starting just below the text *Code Sample (C#)* and ending just above the text *Code Sample (Visual Basic.NET)*. Open your favorite editor, and paste the code there. We'll refer to this code later. Click Finish to have the wizard configure the Subscriber.

Verifying the Subscription Using Management Studio

To verify that the Subscription has been created and synchronized, connect to the mobile database (MergeRepSubscriber.sdf) using SQL Server Management Studio. There you'll see that the *Customer* and *Order* tables have been pushed down through replication to the compact database. Additionally, if you execute a *SELECT* query against the *Order* table, you will now see data in the table. Notice how the only rows in the table are those where *IsDelivered* equals zero (false). Beyond the *Order* table's regular columns, you'll see the *rowguid* and other columns used by replication for tracking purposes.

Now that the distribution, Publication, and Subscription are configured, we can focus on creating a mobile application for our delivery people.

Creating a Mobile Application Using Microsoft Visual Studio 2008

Our sample is a Pocket PC application developed using Visual Studio 2008. The application synchronizes a SQL Server Compact 3.5 database with the SQL Server 2008 Publication we just created.

Start Visual Studio 2008. In the Server Explorer window, right-click Data Connections, and then choose Add Connection. In the Choose Data Source dialog box, select Microsoft SQL Server Compact 3.5, and then click Continue. The Add Connection dialog box appears, as shown in Figure 13-23. Type the path to the MergeRepSubscriber.sdf file (**C:\Projects\ MergeRepSubscriber.sdf** in our example) and the password (which we assigned earlier simply as **password**), and then click Test Connection to confirm the settings. Click OK to close the Add Connection dialog box.

FIGURE 13-23 Creating a SQL Server compact database connection in Visual Studio 2008

Next we'll create the Pocket PC project. Choose File, New, and then click Project. On the New Project form, expand the Visual C# node, and then click the Smart Device node. This exposes a series of templates. Choose Smart Device Project. Name the new project **MyPocketPCDemo**, and place it in the C:\Projects folder (or another folder of your choosing). Click OK to create the project. After the project is created, you'll have to select the target device platform, the Microsoft .NET Compact Framework version, and the project template. Choose Windows Mobile 5.0 Pocket PC SDK, .NET Compact Framework Version 3.5, and Device Application, as shown in Figure 13-24. Click OK to continue.

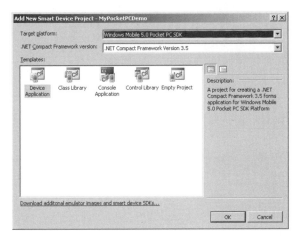

FIGURE 13-24 Creating a new Smart Device project for the .NET Compact Framework running on Windows Mobile Pocket PC in Visual Studio 2008

Let's change some of the project defaults. First, change the form name of *Form1* to *CustomerOrdersForm*. To do this, right-click Form1.cs in Solution Explorer, and then choose Rename. Change the name from Form1.cs to **CustomerOrdersForm.cs**. (Answer Yes when prompted to rename project code references.) Then set the form's *Text* property to *Customer Orders*.

Setting Up the Data Source

Now we'll create a data source. With a data source, you can drag and drop to create bound *DataGrid* objects on a form. Choose Add New Data Source from the Visual Studio 2008 Data menu to launch the Data Source Configuration Wizard. Click the Database icon, and then click Next.

By default, the correct data connection should appear. If it doesn't, select the SQL Server Compact 3.5 *MergeRepSubscriber* database. For simplicity, select the option to include sensitive information in the connection string, and then click Next.

Visual Studio prompts you to add the local data file to the project, as shown in Figure 13-25. Click Yes to copy the data file.

FIGURE 13-25 The Visual Studio prompt to add the local data file to the current project

On the Choose Your Database Objects page, shown in Figure 13-26, expand the Tables node to reveal the tables in the *MergeRepSubscriber* database.

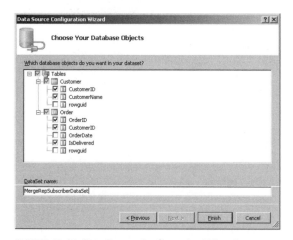

FIGURE 13-26 Data Source Configuration Wizard

Follow these steps to select the database objects used in the sample application:

1. Expand the Customer node.

2. Select the *CustomerID* and *CustomerName* columns. You'll notice the *rowguid* column added by SQL Server to keep track of replication; it is not needed when displaying data to the user, so don't select it.

3. Expand the Order node.

4. Select the *OrderID*, *CustomerID*, and *IsDelivered* columns.

5. Leave the DataSet Name as the default.

6. Click Finish.

The *DataSet* built from these database objects contains two tables. The Data Source Wizard does not pick up on the relationship between the *Customer* and *Order* tables, so we'll add it ourselves. Double-click the MergeRepSubscriberDataSet.xsd file in Solution Explorer to open the Dataset designer. Right-click any empty space, and then select Add and then Relation from the shortcut menu. Visual Studio infers the relationship by matching the column data types. In this case, it matches the *CustomerID* columns in the *Order* and *Customer* tables.

Click OK in the Relation dialog box, shown in Figure 13-27, to create the relation, and then save and close the Dataset designer window.

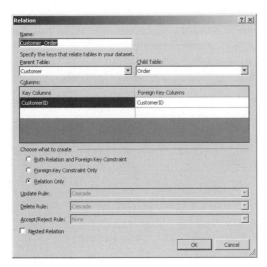

FIGURE 13-27 Defining the data set relationship between *Customer* and *Order*

Binding SQL Server Compact Data to a Pocket PC Form

Now we'll bind a couple of controls to our form by taking advantage of the drag-and-drop data binding features provided in Visual Studio 2008.

Return to the *CustomerOrdersForm* in the designer. Choose Show Data Sources from the Data menu. From the Data Sources window, select the *Customer* table; a drop-down button will appear. Select Details from the drop-down menu. Drill down on the *Customer* table by clicking on the plus sign to the left of the table. Select the *CustomerID* column, and set its control to None. Select the *CustomerName* column, and set its control to ComboBox. Drill down on the *Order* table (the one nested beneath the *Customer* table), and expand the node to see all of the fields. Set the controls for the *OrderID*, *CustomerID*, and *IsDelivered* columns to Label, None, and CheckBox, respectively, by using the smart tag next to each column.

Drag the *Customer* table and drop it somewhere near the upper-left area of the form. *Label* and *ComboBox* controls should appear on the form. Next drag the *Order* table onto the form (again, the one listed as a child node of the *Customer* table), and drop it on the form beneath the customer controls. A *DataGrid* control appears for displaying customer orders.

Next drop a button toward the lower right of the form. Name the button control **btnSync**, and set its *Text* property to **Sync**. When the application is running, clicking this button performs a manual synchronization between the device and the server.

Setting Control Properties

You'd think that by dragging the *Customer* table onto the form, all of the proper data binding properties would be set up for you. But this is not so. You need to set several properties on your own. View the *ComboBox* control's properties, and make the changes listed in Table 13-3.

TABLE 13-3 Property Values for the *customerNameComboBox* Control

Property Name	Property Value
DataSource	customerBindingSource
DisplayMember	CustomerName
ValueMember	CustomerID
DropDownStyle	DropDownList
(DataBindings), Text	Remove the data binding on the *Text* property.

Now let's focus on the *DataGrid* control. The first thing we need to do is change its *DataSource* property. By default, the *DataSource* is set to the table itself. However, we want to use our new relation as the grid's data source. By using the relation, rows in the grid will change as the user navigates through the customers in the drop-down list, without requiring us to write any code to make that happen. Select the grid, and then click its smart tag to display the DataGrid Tasks shortcut menu. Verify that the value specified in the Choose Data Source drop-down list is *customer_OrderBindingSource*, as shown in Figure 13-28.

FIGURE 13-28 Binding the grid to the *Customer_Order* relationship, resulting in automatic filtering of orders by customer as the user navigates from one customer to the next

*DataGrid*s in a Pocket PC form are read only. To edit the data in the grid, you'll need to add more forms to the application. Again, click the data grid's smart tag, reopen the DataGrid Tasks shortcut menu, and then click Generate Data Forms. Visual Studio adds two new forms to the project, one for creating new orders and one for editing existing orders. Code to navigate to these new forms from *CustomerOrdersForm* is also added. For our sample application, we're interested only in editing existing orders, so we're going to modify these forms a bit. As part of generating the forms, Visual Studio also adds a New button to the main menu of *CustomerOrdersForm* for navigation. By default, this button adds new orders. We're going to change the behavior of this button so that clicking it takes us directly to the edit page.

Save all the generated forms, and then return to *CustomerOrdersForm*. Select the New button, and then press F4 to show its properties. Change the *Text* property to Edit. Double-click the Edit button to open its click event handler code. Remove the generated code, and replace it with the following lines of code:

```
MyPocketPCDemo.OrderEditViewDialog orderEditViewDialog =
 MyPocketPCDemo.OrderEditViewDialog.Instance(this.customer_OrderBindingSource);

orderEditViewDialog.ShowDialog();
```

This code displays the *OrderEditViewDialog* form when the user clicks Edit. Now open the code for the OrderEditViewDialog.cs file (by right-clicking the file in Solution Explorer and then choosing View Code). Add the following line of code to the class constructor, beneath the call to *InitializeComponent*:

```
this.Closing +=
  new System.ComponentModel.CancelEventHandler(this.OrdersEditViewDialog_Closing);
```

This line of code sets up an event handler that fires when the form closes to flush all the values from the user interface (UI) controls back into the *DataSet*. The event handler is part of the code in Listing 13-5 that you should now add to the OrderEditViewDialog.cs file.

LISTING 13-5 Singleton method that returns an instance of the *OrderEditViewDialog* class

```
private static OrderEditViewDialog _instance = null;

public static OrderEditViewDialog Instance(System.Windows.Forms.BindingSource
bindingSource)
{
  Cursor.Current = Cursors.WaitCursor;
  if (_instance == null)
  {
    _instance = new MyPocketPCDemo.OrderEditViewDialog();
    _instance.orderBindingSource.DataSource = bindingSource;
  }
  _instance.AutoScrollPosition = new Point(0, 0);
  _instance.orderBindingSource.Position = bindingSource.Position;
  Cursor.Current = Cursors.Default;
  return _instance;
}

private void OrdersEditViewDialog_Closing(object sender, CancelEventArgs e)
{
  this.orderBindingSource.EndEdit();
}
```

At this point, you have created a data-bound grid form for a SQL Server Compact 3.5 database. The completed UI for the *CustomerOrdersForm* form should look similar to Figure 13-29.

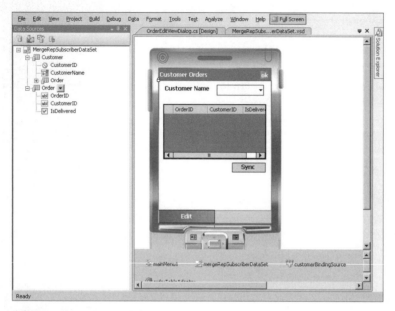

FIGURE 13-29 UI layout of the sample Pocket PC application

Programmatic Synchronization

Now we need to code the application's synchronization functionality in *CustomerOrdersForm*. This will require slight modifications to the form's code that was generated by Visual Studio, integration of the code that was generated by the SQL Server Compact 3.5 Subscription Wizard earlier in this chapter (the code you saved in your favorite editor), and adding a little bit of extra code ourselves. The complete code for the form is shown in Listing 13-6. (Tweaks made to the synchronization code generated by the Subscription Wizard are highlighted in bold.) Refer to Listing 13-6 as we walk through the tasks to implement this code step by step.

 Note As with all the sample code throughout this book, you can download the complete source code for this mobile application from the book's companion Web site. See the Introduction for download details.

LISTING 13-6 Pocket PC application data access and synchronization code behind *CustomerOrdersForm*

```csharp
using System;
using System.Linq;
using System.Collections.Generic;
using System.ComponentModel;
using System.Data;
using System.Drawing;
using System.Text;
using System.Windows.Forms;
using System.Data.SqlServerCe;

namespace MyPocketPCDemo
{
  public partial class CustomerOrdersForm : Form
  {
    public CustomerOrdersForm()
    {
      InitializeComponent();
    }

    private void CustomerOrdersForm_Load(object sender, EventArgs e)
    {
      // Replace code inserted by the wizard with this single line:
      this.FillTables();
    }

    private void FillTables()
    {
      // The location of the .sdf file is as installed on the device.
      const string ConnString =
      @"Data Source=""\Program Files\MyPocketPCDemo\MergeRepSubscriber.
SDF"";Password=""password"";Max Database Size=128;Default Lock Escalation=100;";

      if (MergeRepSubscriberDataSetUtil.DesignerUtil.IsRunTime())
      {
        this.customerTableAdapter.Connection.ConnectionString = ConnString;
        this.orderTableAdapter.Connection.ConnectionString = ConnString;
        this.customerTableAdapter.Fill(this.mergeRepSubscriberDataSet.Customer);
        this.orderTableAdapter.Fill(this.mergeRepSubscriberDataSet.Order);
      }
    }

    private void newMenuItemMenuItem_Click(object sender, EventArgs e)
    {
      MyPocketPCDemo.OrderEditViewDialog orderEditViewDialog =
       MyPocketPCDemo.OrderEditViewDialog.Instance
        (this.customer_OrderBindingSource);

      orderEditViewDialog.ShowDialog();
    }
```

```
      private void btnSync_Click(object sender, EventArgs e)
      {
        this.orderTableAdapter.Update(this.mergeRepSubscriberDataSet.Order);

        SqlCeReplication repl = new SqlCeReplication();

        repl.InternetUrl = @"http://sql08dev/MyWebSync/sqlcesa35.dll";
        repl.Publisher = @"SQL08DEV";
        repl.PublisherDatabase = @"SQL08SampleDB";
        repl.PublisherSecurityMode = SecurityType.DBAuthentication;
        repl.PublisherLogin = @"SubscriberAccount";
        repl.PublisherPassword = @"account";
        repl.Publication = @"MyPublication";
        repl.Subscriber = @"OrderDeliverySubscription";
        repl.SubscriberConnectionString = @"Data Source=""\Program Files\MyPocketPCDemo\
MergeRepSubscriber.sdf"";Password=""password"";Max Database Size=128;Default Lock
Escalation =100;";
        try
        {
          // repl.AddSubscription(AddOption.ExistingDatabase);
          repl.Synchronize();
          this.FillTables();
        }
        catch (SqlCeException ex)
        {
          MessageBox.Show(ex.ToString());
        }
      }
    }
  }
```

Right-click anywhere on the design surface of *CustomerOrdersForm*, and then choose
View Code to open the code window for the form. First we need to bring in the
System.Data.SqlServerCe namespace by adding the following *using* statement to the
collection of *using* statements that are already in place at the top of the code:

```
using System.Data.SqlServerCe;
```

The classes in this namespace will enable us to perform replication between the local SQL
Server Compact Subscriber and the remote Publisher. Now scroll down a little to the form's
load event handler named *CustomerOrdersForm_Load*. Notice that Visual Studio has written a few lines of code already that fill the *Customer* and *Order* tables in the *DataSet* from
the embedded compact database when the form loads. We'll actually need to do this
twice—once when the form loads and then again whenever the user synchronizes the local compact database (Subscriber) with the centralized server database (Publisher). We'll
therefore write our own *FillTables* method to populate the *DataSet* from the compact da-

tabase and replace the code in the *Form Load* method with a call into *FillTables*. Then we'll add another call to *FillTables* from our synchronization code in the next step. Modify the *CustomerOrdersForm_Load* and add the *FillTables* method as follows:

```
private void CustomerOrdersForm_Load(object sender, EventArgs e)
{
  // Replace code inserted by the wizard with this single line:
  this.FillTables();
}

private void FillTables()
{
  // The location of the .sdf file is as installed on the device.
  const string ConnString =
   @"Data Source=""\Program Files\MyPocketPCDemo\MergeRepSubscriber.
SDF"";Password=""password"";Max Database Size=128;Default Lock Escalation=100;";

  if (MergeRepSubscriberDataSetUtil.DesignerUtil.IsRunTime())
  {
    this.customerTableAdapter.Connection.ConnectionString = ConnString;
    this.orderTableAdapter.Connection.ConnectionString = ConnString;
    this.customerTableAdapter.Fill(this.mergeRepSubscriberDataSet.Customer);
    this.orderTableAdapter.Fill(this.mergeRepSubscriberDataSet.Order);
  }
}
```

In the sample application, synchronization occurs when the user clicks the *btnSync* button. Open the form in the designer, and then double-click the button to add a click event handler for it. Add one line of code to the event handler that will commit changes made on the form to the local Subscriber database by calling the *Order* table adapter's *Update* method, as shown here:

```
private void btnSync_Click(object sender, EventArgs e)
{
  this.orderTableAdapter.Update(this.mergeRepSubscriberDataSet.Order);
}
```

The *Update* method call is required because if the changes aren't committed to the local Subscriber database, the agent won't find any changes to synchronize. To synchronize those changes with the server database, paste the code generated by the SQL Server Compact 3.5 Subscription Wizard earlier in this chapter (which is still being held in your favorite text editor) into the event handler following the *Update* method call we just added.

After pasting the code, you have to make a few modifications. (These are highlighted in bold in Listing 13-6.) First modify the *SubscriberConnectionString* property by changing the data source to the runtime path of the database on the device itself, which is \Program Files\MyPocketPCDemo\MergeRepSubscriber.sdf. Changing the path is required because the original autogenerated code points to a location on the development machine—not the device itself. The *MergeRepSubscriber* compact database is copied to the device during deployment. The *SubscriberConnectionString* must point to a location on the actual device; otherwise, you will receive "Database not found" errors when you run the application.

To simplify the sample application, hard-code the passwords for the *PublisherPassword* and *SubscriberConnectionString* properties. Find the password placeholder strings "<...>" in the code, and replace them with the respective passwords you set up for the *SubscriberAccount* login (*account*) and the Subscription database (*password*). Of course, in production, you'd prompt the user for connection information or retrieve it from a configuration file.

We still need to apply some final tweaks to the autogenerated code—specifically, in the *try* block. The wizard creates a line of code that's unnecessary in our scenario. It adds a call to the *SqlCeReplication* object's *AddSubscription* method. Calling this method creates a Subscription. You don't need to make this call because the Subscription is already created in the *MergeRepSubscriber* compact database. Comment out this line of code:

```
// repl.AddSubscription(AddOption.ExistingDatabase);
```

As we just mentioned, add another call to *FillTables* right after the call to the *Synchronize* method to refresh the form after synchronization occurs:

```
this.FillTables();
```

Last, change the variable *e* to *ex* in the *catch* block declaration and in the *MessageBox* statement inside the *catch* block. This is necessary because the *e* variable generated by the wizard collides with the *e* variable declared as the *EventArgs* parameter of the button's click event handler. With the code tweaked, we can hook up the *btnSync* button's click event to its code, which was copied from the listing. Select the Sync button on the designer form, and then press F4 to display the Properties window. In the Properties window, click the Events button. The button's events are shown. Next to the Click event, choose the method named *btnSync_ Click* from the list.

We are now ready to deploy the application to an emulator.

Deploying the Mobile Application

Press F5 to display the Deploy dialog box, as shown in Figure 13-30. You have the option to deploy to an actual device or to an emulator. To test this application, choose the USA Windows Mobile 5.0 Pocket PC R2 Emulator option, and then click Deploy.

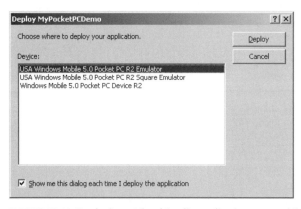

FIGURE 13-30 Deploying a Visual Studio application to a mobile device or emulator

Note For the sample application to work, you need to set up the network on the device emulator. Due to space constraints, we do not describe the steps required to set up networking on the emulator here. Network configuration differs depending on whether you are running inside a virtual machine. One document that describes setting up the emulator in both virtual machine and non-virtual-machine environments is available in the emulator's Help file. Run a Web search, or choose Help, Search and then type **How to: Enable TCP/IP Networking on the Device Emulator**. You can test the network setup on your emulator by opening Pocket Internet Explorer and navigating to the following URL: *http://<YourMachineName>/MyWebSync/sqlcesa35.dll?diag*. If a page appears in the browser, you're all set. If not, networking is not set up properly on your emulator.

Once you have chosen the deployment target, the application runs on the device or emulator. You should observe a couple of things when the application runs. First, only those customers whose orders haven't been delivered are shown in the customer drop-down list. This is by design. Remember, we set up a filter on the Subscription to download only those customers and related order records whose IsDelivered value is zero, so customer data for Jones was not even downloaded to the device. Second, you cannot edit data directly in the grid. Click (or tap) one of the rows in the grid, and then click Edit to edit the row. When you do this, a second form is displayed showing only the single record you selected, as shown in Figure 13-31.

FIGURE 13-31 Data entry form running in device emulator

Here's where all the time and effort you've just put in pays off. Go ahead and select the Is Delivered check box.

Click the OK button in the upper right of the form to close the edit page and return to the application's main page. Now click the Sync button to synchronize the changes made to the record on the device with the Publisher. Remember, this is a pull Subscription. The Subscriber initiates the synchronization process, sending its data changes to the server and then pulling new data down from the Publication. After synchronization has completed, the *DataGrid* is refreshed. Notice that the row(s) you edited no longer appear in the customer drop-down list or the order *DataGrid*—that's the filter at work again.

At this point, you can go back to SQL Server Management Studio and query the records in the *SQL08DevSample* database's *Order* table. When you do, you'll see the order you updated with the new *IsDelivered* value set—pretty cool stuff!

As you've experienced while configuring this sample application, Merge Replication is configured mainly through wizards. For a more programmatic approach, we'll take a look at Sync Services for ADO.NET and SQL Server Change Tracking—brand-new replication technologies for SQL Server 2008.

Sync Services for ADO.NET

Sync Services for ADO.NET is a great technology for building occasionally connected systems. It is tailor-made to synchronize data between data cached on client devices and a centralized server. Sync Services for ADO.NET (or simply Sync Services) provides synchronization capability between ADO.NET-enabled databases. It is based on the familiar ADO.NET development model using providers, adapters, and *DbCommand* objects, and it works in client/server, n-tiered, and service-based architectures.

Sync Services functions through snapshot, download-only, upload-only, or bidirectional synchronization scenarios. Internally, it uses the SQL Server Compact 3.5 database to track information, such as the version number of the last synchronization for a client application. Sync Services manages this database automatically.

Sync Services does not automatically copy schema changes from the server tables to the client tables, although it does provide the ability to manage schema changes through code.

Sync Services for ADO.NET has the following capabilities:

- Synchronization can be performed asynchronously on a separate background thread.

- Sync Services exposes objects and methods for finding conflicting or deleted rows on the server using customized *DbCommand* objects.

- Sync Services can flag important tables as having a higher synchronization priority. Higher-priority tables will be synchronized before less critical tables.

- Security in transit and security at rest. Data transmission can be encrypted using SSL. Data stored on the client device can be secured by encrypting the SQL Server Compact 3.5 database.

An application built using Sync Services always consists of at least two databases—one on the client and one on the server—and application logic employing several classes from the Sync Services API. The client database is a SQL Server Compact 3.5 SP1 database. Sync Services maintains application metadata using this database. Local application data is also cached in the client database. You can have both online and offline tables in the client database.

The server database can be any ADO.NET-capable database—not only SQL Server 2008. This is the central repository where all application data is stored.

Sync Services Object Model

Sync Services provides a rich object model for programming synchronization into an application. Table 13-4 lists the common classes used in an application built with Sync Services.

TABLE 13-4 Commonly Used Sync Services Classes

Class	Description
SyncAgent	Manages synchronization. For each synchronized table, the *SyncAgent* coordinates the execution of the client synchronization provider and server synchronization provider.
SyncStatistics	Synchronization session statistics. Provides information about conflicts, exceptions, synchronization times, and number of changes.
SyncSession	Represents a synchronization session. *SyncSession* objects exist for the lifetime of the session and expose information relative to the session.
SyncAdapter	Synchronization adapter. Provides SQL commands for interacting with the server for a specific table.
SqlCeClientSyncProvider	Client synchronization provider. Primarily responsible for communicating with the client and abstracting the client database away from the synchronization agent.
DbServerSyncProvider	Server synchronization provider. Basically plays the same role as the client synchronization provider, but for the server database.
ServerSyncProviderProxy	Used for n-tier and service-based architectures. The client references this proxy instead of referencing the *DbServerSyncProvider* directly.
SyncTable	Represents a synchronized local table.
SyncGroup	Synchronization group. A collection of related *SyncTable* objects.

SyncAgent and *SyncStatistics*

The *SyncAgent* guides synchronization by looping through each synchronized table, calling the client synchronization provider to synchronize changes at the client and calling the server synchronization provider to synchronize changes at the server.

The *SyncAgent* object's *SessionProgress* event fires during synchronization. You can use this event to track the progress of a synchronization session or to notify the application to refresh cached data after a session is completed.

The *SyncAgent* returns status and error information for each synchronization session in a *SyncStatistics* object, which is returned from a call to the *SyncAgent* object's *Synchronize* method. You can use this object to display status information pertaining to the current synchronization session. By reading the *SyncStatistics* properties, you can capture information such as how many records were uploaded and downloaded, how long it took to complete synchronizing the client and server, and so on.

SyncSession and Session Variables

A *SyncSession* object represents an actual synchronization session and exists for the lifetime of the synchronization event. *SyncSession* objects provide valuable information about the session. A *SyncSession* object has properties for obtaining the client and session ID values and a collection of parameters used by *SyncAdapter* commands for querying data. Table 13-5 lists some of the *SyncSession* object properties.

TABLE 13-5 Partial List of *SyncSession* Object Properties

Property Name	Description
ClientId	A GUID value that identifies the client during synchronization. *ClientID* can be used for conflict detection and to prevent echoing changes back during synchronization. To prevent echoing changes back, you can mark uploaded data as having come from a specific client by using *ClientId*. When changes are downloaded, you can identify the client that changed the data and prevent downloading changes that originated from the client.
SessionId	A GUID value that uniquely identifies the current synchronization session.
SyncParameters	A collection of *SyncParameter* objects. A *SyncParameter* is used to pass values to query parameters—much as a *SqlParameter* object is used in ADO.NET. The parameters can be used in queries to detect conflicts and to filter data for controlling the changes downloaded during synchronization. *SyncParameter* objects get their values during the synchronization process.

Sync Services uses session variables to pass values to query parameters. During synchronization, the Sync Services runtime sets the value of these parameters for you by matching the name of the *SyncParameter* with the name of the query parameter. To facilitate the matching process, the *SyncSession* object provides a number of field constants, listed in Table 13-6, that you can use when naming query parameters and *SyncParameter* objects. Doing so provides a consistent naming convention for common parameters like @ *sync_client_id.*

TABLE 13-6 Partial List of *SyncSession* Field Constants

Field Name	Description
SyncClientId	Returns the string value *sync_client_id*
SyncInitialized	Returns the string value *sync_initialized*
SyncLastReceivedAnchor	Returns the string value *sync_last_received_anchor*
SyncNewReceivedAnchor	Returns the string value *sync_new_received_anchor*
SyncRowCount	Returns the string value *sync_row_count*
SyncSessionId	Returns the string value *sync_session_id*

SyncAdapter

Much in the same way that an ADO.NET *TableAdapter* provides commands for filling and updating a table, a *SyncAdapter* provides commands for synchronizing a table. Each synchronized table has its own *SyncAdapter* object. Each *SyncAdapter* exposes several *DbCommand* properties for specifying queries that are used to select from and apply changes to the server database. Each command can use session variables to pass values to the server queries during synchronization. *SyncAdapter* commands are executed via a *DbServerSyncProvider*. The commands can be specified as stored procedures, parameterized SQL statements, views, functions, and so on.

Client and Server Providers

Sync Services uses providers to interact with specific database implementations. Providers are intended to abstract the database details away from the synchronization agent—just as ADO.NET uses different providers for SQL Server and Oracle databases to provide a common interface to different back ends.

Sync Services includes a client provider for SQL Server Compact 3.5 databases named *SqlCeClientSyncProvider*. A *SqlCeClientSyncProvider* is a class that communicates directly with the client database. It is responsible for storing information about synchronized client tables, retrieving changes from the client since the last synchronization, applying server changes to the client, and detecting data conflicts.

A client provider's server counterpart is the *DbSyncServerProvider* class. Unlike the *SqlCeClientSyncProvider*—which is specific to SQL Server Compact 3.5—this is a generic server-side provider that works with any database. It performs the same duties on the server as the client provider performs on the client. A server provider executes the queries in the *DbCommand* properties of a *SyncAdapter* to retrieve changes from the server table and to apply changes from the client table to a server table.

ServerSyncProviderProxy

As its name implies, a *ServerSyncProviderProxy* is a proxy wrapper for a *DbServerSyncProvider*. Using the proxy on the client allows you to create n-tiered applications. Instead of communicating with a *DbServerSyncProvider* directly, the client communicates with the proxy. In turn, the proxy communicates with a service and the service communicates with the server synchronization provider.

SyncTable and *SyncGroup*

SyncTable objects represent local tables in the client application. *SyncTable* objects expose properties for elements such as the table's name, how the local table is created, and the table's synchronization direction. Multiple *SyncTable* objects can be added to a *SyncGroup*.

Local tables can be created at design time either manually or by using the Visual Studio 2008 Configure Data Synchronization designer or at runtime by using the *SyncTable* object's *CreationOption* property. The *CreationOption* property is an enumeration of type *TableCreateOption* for controlling how local tables are created. Table 13-7 lists the *TableCreationOption* enumeration values.

TABLE 13-7 *TableCreationOption* **Enumeration Values**

Enumeration Value	Description
CreateNewTableOrFail	Create a new local table, or raise an error if a table with the same name already exists.
DropExistingOrCreateNewTable	If the named local table exists, drop and re-create the table. If it does not exist, create the local table.
TruncateExistingOrCreateNewTable	Truncate an existing local table, or create a new table if the named table is not found.
UploadExistingOrCreateNewTable	Upload all rows upon the initial synchronization with the server, or create a new table if the named server table is not found.
UseExistingTableOrFail	Use the existing local table. Raise an exception if a named local table is not found.

Synchronization direction is determined using the *SyncTable* object's *SyncDirection* property, which can be set to *Bidirectional*, *DownloadOnly*, *Snapshot*, or *UploadOnly*.

A *SyncGroup* object is a collection of related tables. The set of tables in a *SyncGroup* is treated as a single unit. Synchronization options are applied to the unit as a whole. Changes to grouped tables are applied at the server as a single transaction. A failure from any change in the group means that all changes are rolled back and will be retried during a subsequent synchronization.

Capturing Changes for Synchronization

Sync Services does not automatically track changes on the server like Merge Replication does. Believe it or not, this is one of the strengths of Sync Services. By not tying its change tracking mechanism to a specific database implementation, you can use any ADO.NET-capable database on the server. The only requirement is that the database must be able to process SQL queries to find changed rows for synchronization or conflicts.

It's nice that Sync Services is database independent, but now you've got some more application functionality to build. You'll need to track changes made to the application's tables in order for synchronization to take place.

You have a couple of options for storing and tracking changes made to data. The first is to create your own custom tracking system. This involves creating or altering table schemas and requires that you create a mechanism, typically involving triggers, to capture metadata when rows are changed—basically lots of extra coding work.

The second option is to use a new feature in SQL Server 2008 called SQL Server Change Tracking. The ability of Sync Services to track changes through queries provides cohesive functionality with Change Tracking.

There are several advantages to using SQL Server Change Tracking, including the following:

- Reduced coding time
- Low impact to performance; minimal overhead to DML operations
- New T-SQL functions for retrieving change information
- Automatic cleanup of tracked changes (can be disabled if desired)

For our sample Sync Services application, we'll use SQL Server Change Tracking.

SQL Server 2008 Change Tracking

The SQL Server 2008 Change Tracking feature maintains information about changes made to tables. It uses a synchronous process to monitor tracked tables for changes made to data through DML statements. An application can then query the data maintained to obtain information about changed rows and the types of changes that occurred.

> **Note** All DML operations, except *TRUNCATE TABLE* and *UPDATETEXT* statements, are tracked by Change Tracking.

Change Tracking does not store the actual values of any changed rows or columns. Nor does it track the number of times a row changes. It records only the bare minimum needed to support synchronization—namely, which rows (and optionally columns) changed and a version number. This lightweight design reduces the performance impact of using Change Tracking.

When a DML statement is executed against a tracked table, SQL Server stores the primary keys of any rows affected by the DML statement. The change information is stored inside internal Change Tracking tables. You can query the *sys.internal_tables* catalog view to obtain a list of the internal tables managed by SQL Server, including those enabled for Change Tracking.

Configuring the Server Database for Change Tracking

To use Change Tracking, you first enable it at the database level and then enable it on any tables whose changes you want to track. Microsoft also recommends that you turn snapshot isolation on for the database before you enable Change Tracking. Using snapshot isolation under these conditions ensures consistent information. Both of these tasks can be performed with two consecutive *ALTER DATABASE* statements, as shown in Listing 13-7.

LISTING 13-7 Enabling Change Tracking on the database

```
ALTER DATABASE SQL08SampleDB
 SET ALLOW_SNAPSHOT_ISOLATION ON
GO

ALTER DATABASE SQL08SampleDB
 SET CHANGE_TRACKING = ON
 (CHANGE_RETENTION = 7 DAYS, AUTO_CLEANUP = ON)
GO
```

The code in Listing 13-7 first turns on snapshot isolation in the *SQL08SampleDB* database (which we created for our Pocket PC application using Merge Replication earlier in this chapter) and then enables Change Tracking on the database. It specifies the change retention option as 7 days and then turns on the auto-cleanup option.

> **Note** Although we do not demonstrate it here, managing and maintaining SQL Server Change Tracking can also be performed through dialog boxes available in SQL Server Management Studio. To access the dialog boxes, display the Properties window for a database or table, and then choose the Change Tracking option.

You specify the length of time that SQL Server retains changes and whether to allow SQL Server to automatically clean up tracked changes by using the *CHANGE_RETENTION* and *AUTO_CLEANUP* options, as shown in Listing 13-7. The retention period units can be specified as days, hours, or minutes. As a rule of thumb, set this to a value at least as long as the longest time period between synchronizations. If it's any less, you could introduce invalid data into the application due to changes made between synchronizations that were cleaned up before the synchronization process occurred.

SQL Server uses a task to remove Change Tracking information that is older than the value specified for the *CHANGE_RETENTION* option. The auto-cleanup option tells SQL Server whether it should run the cleanup task. Setting this value to *False* disables the task and prevents cleanup from occurring. This is helpful in situations where a problem is preventing synchronization from occurring and you don't want SQL Server to remove older data versions until you have resolved the issue.

Enabling Change Tracking on User Tables

Once it is enabled at the database level, you enable Change Tracking on each table you want to have tracked. The only requirement on the target table is that it must have a primary key defined.

> **Note** It is recommended that the primary key in a change tracked table be a *uniqueidentifier* data type. This ensures uniqueness in a distributed environment.

To enable Change Tracking on the *Customer* and *Contact* tables, issue the *ALTER TABLE* statement shown in Listing 13-8.

LISTING 13-8 Enabling Change Tracking on user tables

```
ALTER TABLE Customer
  ENABLE CHANGE_TRACKING WITH (TRACK_COLUMNS_UPDATED = OFF);
GO

ALTER TABLE Contact
  ENABLE CHANGE_TRACKING WITH (TRACK_COLUMNS_UPDATED = OFF);
GO
```

The *TRACK_COLUMNS_UPDATED* option tells SQL Server whether to record information about the columns that changed during an update to a row. When the option is set to *ON*, SQL Server stores extra information about which columns were changed. Using this option, synchronization performance can be improved by downloading only those rows and columns that have changed. However, there is extra overhead of maintaining tracking information for changed columns, so this option is off by default.

Speaking of performance, you might already be wondering about the general performance implications of using SQL Server Change Tracking. Impact on performance will vary depending on several factors, such as the number of columns making up a primary key, the number of rows affected by a DML statement, and the number of statements executed within a transaction. Overall, however, the overhead introduced would be similar to that of maintaining an index on a table.

Managing Tracked Tables and Databases

The *sys.change_tracking_databases* and *sys.change_tracking_tables* catalog views provide information about which databases and tables have Change Tracking enabled and what options have been set. For example, the following query returns a list of databases with Change Tracking enabled:

```
SELECT
  d.name as database_name,
  c.is_auto_cleanup_on,
  c.retention_period,
  c.retention_period_units_desc
FROM
  sys.databases AS d
  INNER JOIN sys.change_tracking_databases AS c on d.database_id = c.database_id
```

The output shows that Change Tracking is enabled on our *SQL08SampleDb* database:

```
database_name  is_auto_cleanup_on retention_period retention_period_units_desc
-------------  ------------------ ---------------- ---------------------------
SQL08SampleDB  1                  7                DAYS

(1 row(s) affected)
```

This query can be used to determine which tables within a specific database have Change Tracking enabled:

```
SELECT
  o.name as table_name,
  c.is_track_columns_updated_on
 FROM
  sys.objects AS o
  INNER JOIN sys.change_tracking_tables AS c ON o.object_id = c.object_id
```

The output shows that Change Tracking is enabled on our *Customer* and *Contact* tables:

```
table_name  is_track_columns_updated_on
-----------  --------------------------
Contact     1
Customer    1

(2 row(s) affected)
```

Disabling Change Tracking

Once Change Tracking is enabled on a table, you can disable it either by using the Table Properties dialog box or with the *ALTER TABLE...DISABLE CHANGE_TRACKING* statement. For example, the following statement stops tracking changes for the *Customer* table:

```
ALTER TABLE Customer DISABLE CHANGE_TRACKING
```

Similarly, you can issue an *ALTER DATABASE* statement to turn off Change Tracking for an entire database. This can be done only after Change Tracking has been disabled in *all* tables. For example, after Change Tracking is disabled for both the *Customer* and *Order* tables, the following statement disables the feature for the *SQL08SampleDb* database:

```
ALTER DATABASE SQL08SampleDB SET CHANGE_TRACKING = OFF
```

Change Tracking Functions

Several new Change Tracking functions in SQL Server 2008 provide vital information for synchronization and give you the ability to determine the current version numbers and retrieve changed rows. Table 13-8 lists several of these functions that we'll use shortly in the sample application; understanding these functions is essential to retrieving tracking information from the database. When writing queries against tracked tables, you'll join the queries to these functions to retrieve changed rows, row version numbers, and system version numbers.

Table 13-8 Commonly Used Change Tracking Functions

Function Name	Description
CHANGE_TRACKING_MIN_VALID_VERSION	Returns oldest valid version number for retrieving changes from a table.
CHANGE_TRACKING_CURRENT_VERSION	Returns a table's current change version number. Used when retrieving changes from a table.
CHANGETABLE (changes)	Returns tracking information for changes made to all data in a table since a specific version. Used for initializing client tables during synchronization.
CHANGETABLE (version)	Returns tracking information for changes made to a specific version of a row. Helpful in detecting row conflicts during synchronization.
WITH CHANGE_TRACKING_CONTEXT	Optional. Use this clause with DML queries to uniquely identify the author of the changed data.

You can use the two functions related to versioning, *CHANGE_TRACKING_MIN_VALID_VERSION* and *CHANGE_TRACKING_CURRENT_VERSION*, for establishing a point in time, referred to as an *anchor*, when changes were made.

The *CHANGETABLE* function is the primary function you'll use with Sync Services. It's versatile enough to return information about changed rows for a table or for a specific recorded data version number. In most cases, the queries including *CHANGETABLE* will be joined to the tracked table.

For example, to retrieve an initial snapshot of customer data, you'd write a query similar to the following:

```
SELECT c.[CustomerId], c.[CustomerName]
  FROM Customer AS c LEFT OUTER JOIN
    CHANGETABLE(CHANGES Customer, 1) AS CT ON CT.[CustomerId] = c.[CustomerId]
```

A query such as this can be used to initialize a table in the local client database with data from the server's table. By specifying a *LEFT OUTER JOIN*, you'll get customer records regardless of whether changes were made to the *Customer* table.

Setting an Anchor Value

SQL Server Change Tracking works by recording changes made to a row according to a moment in time. As mentioned, Sync Services refers to this moment as an anchor. A new anchor value is retrieved during synchronization. The new anchor value and the last anchor value from the previous synchronization become the upper and lower bounds of a range of version numbers. The set of changes to be synchronized are those whose versions fall within the anchor range. To retrieve an anchor value, query the *CHANGE_TRACKING_CURRENT_VERSION* function.

Creating an Application Using Sync Services

To showcase the Sync Services features, we'll use Visual Studio 2008 to create a Windows Forms application named *MySyncServicesDemo*. This application synchronizes data stored locally in a SQL Server Compact 3.5 database with our *Customer* and *Contact* tables in the *SQL08SampleDB* database by using SQL Server Change Tracking, which gives salespeople the ability to view and update customer contact data while away from their office. We'll start out by building it as a typical client/server application. We'll then extend it to an n-tiered model using Windows Communication Foundation (WCF).

> **Note** Our discussion focuses on just the relevant code portions of the sample application, and the code listings are similarly distilled. The complete source code for the fully functional *MySyncServicesDemo* application is available on the book's companion Web site. (See the Introduction for download details.)

The *Customer* and *Contact* tables were created earlier in the SQL Server Compact 3.5 database manually using Visual Studio 2008, when we built our Pocket PC demo with Merge Replication. Remember, you have the option of building tables at design time or programmatically at runtime. The properties of a *SyncTable* object determine whether Sync Services tries to create tables on the client. Creating the tables at runtime is useful for download-only, cache-type scenarios where the tables are used for lookup data. For this example, we've built the tables at design time. The local tables have the same schema as their server counterparts.

The application uses a *DataSet* derived from the two local tables named *LocalCustomerDataset*. We added a relationship between the two tables on the *CustomerID* column. The *TableAdapters* in the *DataSet* have their connection strings configured to use the application's SQL Server Compact 3.5 database.

Each synchronized table in the application uses a set of objects: a *SyncAgent*, a *SqlCeClientSyncProvider*, and a *DbServerSyncProvider*. The *SyncAgent* and client sync provider classes for the *Customer* table are shown in Listing 13-9. In our example, the *MyClientSyncProvider* class is responsible for setting the connection string to the client database. It is also responsible for handling conflicts occurring during synchronization. We'll discuss handling data conflicts later in this chapter.

> **Note** At this point, the application is configured as a client/server application. The *CustomerServerSyncProvider* is the *DbServerSyncProvider* used to communicate with the server. In this example, the client communicates directly with the *CustomerServerSyncProvider* class, which resides on the client. Later, we'll replace this *DbServerSyncProvider* with a *ServerSyncProviderProxy* class and move the *CustomerServerSyncProvider* to a WCF service to model the application as a service-based application.

LISTING 13-9 The *CustomerSyncAgent* class, which inherits from *SyncAgent*, and the *MyClientSyncProvider* class, which inherits from *SqlCeClientSyncProvider*

```
public class CustomerSyncAgent : SyncAgent
{
  public void Initialize()
  {
    this.LocalProvider = new MyClientSyncProvider();
    this.RemoteProvider = new CustomerServerSyncProvider();

    //Add the Customer table: specify a synchronization direction of
    //download only, and that an existing table should be used.
    SyncTable customerSyncTable = new SyncTable("Customer");
    customerSyncTable.CreationOption = TableCreationOption.UseExistingTableOrFail;
    customerSyncTable.SyncDirection = SyncDirection.DownloadOnly;
    this.Configuration.SyncTables.Add(customerSyncTable);
  }
}


public class MyClientSyncProvider : SqlCeClientSyncProvider
{
  public MyClientSyncProvider()
  {
    //Specify a connection string for the local SQL Server Compact database.
    this.ConnectionString = Helper.ClientConnection();
    this.ApplyChangeFailed += new EventHandler<ApplyChangeFailedEventArgs>
      (this.MyClientSyncProvider_ApplyChangeFailed);
  }
}
```

Looking at the *Initialize* method in the *CustomerSyncAgent* class, you can get a better understanding of how a *SyncAgent* drives synchronization. The *Initialize* method creates instances of client and server providers and assigns them to its *LocalProvider* and

RemoteProvider properties, respectively. The queries in these providers will be executed during synchronization. The method also creates a new *SyncTable* for the *Customer* table named *customerSyncTable*.

The *SyncAgent* and *SqlCeClientSyncProvider* classes are rather simple compared with the *DbServerSyncProviders*. Most of the query work is performed in the *DbServerSyncProvider* class using a *SyncAdapter*.

Creating and populating the table is handled by the *SyncAdapter* object's *SelectIncrementalInsertsCommand* property. The query specified is probably the most important query for a Sync Services application. Sync Services retrieves a table schema from the server to create a client table. The schema it gets is based on the columns in the query's *SELECT* list. Whether the table is created is based on the value set for the *SyncTable* object's *CreationOption* property.

In our example, setting the *CreationOption* property to *UseExistingTableOrFail* instructs the *SyncAdapter* not to overwrite the table during the initial synchronization. Earlier, when we were discussing *SyncTable* objects, we mentioned that by default, Sync Services wants to copy the schema and data from the server database to the client during the initial synchronization. Whenever the *CreationOption* property is set to a value other than *UseExistingTableOrFail*, Sync Services will attempt to create the local table on the client.

This capability has its merits, but you should be aware that constraints are not copied to the local database. Also, some data type mapping will occur because of differences in data types between SQL Server Compact databases and "regular" SQL Server edition databases. As a result of the mapping process, some data types might be mismatched.

> **Note** The release version of SQL Server Compact 3.5 available at press time didn't support all of the new SQL Server data types. As a result, a beta version of SQL Server Compact 3.5 SP1 was used for the sample application. You can find the download for SP1 at the following URL: *http://www.microsoft.com/downloads/details.aspx?FamilyID=68539fae-cf03-4c3b-aeda-769cc205fe5f&DisplayLang=en*. Check this book's companion Web site for late-breaking changes.

Because of these and other issues, you might have to edit the table schema through code when Sync Services creates the tables for you. You can do this with the *SqlCeClientSyncProvider*. This class exposes two events, *CreatingSchema* and *SchemaCreated*, which fire before and after table creation. Using these events, you can modify the local table schema during initial synchronization.

Setting the *SyncDirection* property to *DownloadOnly* effectively makes the *Customer* table a read-only copy of the server's *Customer* table. Changes made to the client's *Customer* table will not be uploaded to the server. Sync Services downloads data to the client during the initial synchronization in all cases except when a *SyncTable* object's *SyncDirection* is set to *UploadOnly*. Listing 13-10 shows the stored procedure for the sample application's *customerSyncAdapter*.

LISTING 13-10 Stored procedure for the *SelectIncrementalInsertsCommand* used by the *customerSyncAdapter*

```
CREATE PROCEDURE up_CustomerIncrementalInserts
( @sync_initialized bit,
  @sync_last_received_anchor bigint,
  @sync_client_id_binary varbinary(128),
  @sync_new_received_anchor bigint)

AS

IF @sync_initialized = 0
  SELECT c.[CustomerId], c.[CustomerName]
  FROM Customer c
ELSE
  SELECT c.[CustomerId], c.[CustomerName]
  FROM Customer c JOIN
    CHANGETABLE(CHANGES Customer, @sync_last_received_anchor) CT
    ON CT.[CustomerId] = c.[CustomerId]
  WHERE (CT.SYS_CHANGE_OPERATION = 'I' AND CT.SYS_CHANGE_CREATION_VERSION <= @sync_
new_received_anchor
    AND (CT.SYS_CHANGE_CONTEXT IS NULL OR CT.SYS_CHANGE_CONTEXT <> @sync_client_id_
binary))
```

The stored procedure first checks the *@sync_initialized* parameter. Its value will be zero (false) if the procedure is called during the initial synchronization. In this case, all rows from the *Customer* table are returned to the client. For subsequent synchronizations, *@sync_initialized* will not be zero (true), and only those *Customer* rows that have been inserted (that is, where *CT.SYS_CHANGE_OPERATION = 'I'*) with a version number less than the new anchor value are returned. The *@sync_client_id_binary* parameter is used to prevent changes uploaded by the client from echoing back to the client during the same synchronization.

Initial Synchronization

Several events occur during the initial synchronization of a client table. The table is first created (optionally) and then populated, and a unique id value is assigned to the client database. The query in the *SelectIncrementalInsertsCommand* property is used not only to create and populate a table during the initial synchronization but also to apply incremental inserts for tables whose *SyncDirection* property is *DownloadOnly* or *Bidirectional* during subsequent synchronizations.

After the client table is populated, a unique value is assigned to the client database. This value is a GUID and is available using the *SyncSession* object's *ClientId* property. The *ClientId* is passed to queries to indentify the originator of changes made to data. In the stored procedure in Listing 13-10, the *@sync_client_id_binary* parameter gets its value from the

SyncClientIdBinary property. *SyncClientIdBinary* is a binary value representing the *ClientId* value.

The *ClientId* is useful for identifying which client made the changes to the server data. It also helps to prevent echoing changes back to the client in bidirectional scenarios. During synchronization, changes are uploaded from the client to the server before downloading changes to the client. Without the client being uniquely identifying, the changes are uploaded to the server and then needlessly downloaded back to the client during the synchronization session.

Uploading Changes

Three command properties set the queries for uploading changes from the client to the server. The *InsertCommand*, *UpdateCommand*, and *DeleteCommand* properties are the commands used to apply *INSERT, UPDATE,* and *DELETE* operations from the client to the server. You need to set these properties only for tables specified as *UploadOnly* or *Bidirectional*.

The *Customer* table in the sample application is *DownloadOnly*. However, the *Contact* table is *Bidirectional*. Changes made on the client to *Contact* data are uploaded to the server using the three queries in Listing 13-11.

LISTING 13-11 Stored procedures used to update the server with client changes

```
CREATE PROCEDURE up_ContactInserts
( @sync_row_count int OUTPUT,
  @sync_client_id_binary varbinary(128),
  @ContactId uniqueidentifier,
  @CustomerId int,
  @ContactName nvarchar(100),
  @ContactPhone nvarchar(100),
  @ContactEmail nvarchar(100))
AS
WITH CHANGE_TRACKING_CONTEXT (@sync_client_id_binary)
INSERT INTO Contact ([ContactId], [CustomerId], [ContactName], [ContactPhone],
[ContactEmail])
VALUES (@ContactId, @CustomerId, @ContactName, @ContactPhone, @ContactEmail);

SET @sync_row_count = @@rowcount;
GO

CREATE PROCEDURE up_ContactUpdates
( @sync_last_received_anchor bigint,
  @sync_client_id_binary varbinary(128),
  @sync_row_count int OUTPUT,
  @ContactId uniqueidentifier,
  @ContactName nvarchar(100),
  @ContactPhone nvarchar(100),
  @ContactEmail nvarchar(100))
AS
```

```
WITH CHANGE_TRACKING_CONTEXT (@sync_client_id_binary)
UPDATE Contact
SET [ContactName] = @ContactName,
  [ContactPhone] = @ContactPhone,
  [ContactEmail] = @ContactEmail
FROM Contact c
  JOIN CHANGETABLE(VERSION Contact, ([ContactId]), (@ContactId)) CT
  ON CT.[ContactId] = c.[ContactId]
WHERE (CT.SYS_CHANGE_VERSION IS NULL OR CT.SYS_CHANGE_VERSION <= @sync_last_received_
anchor
OR (CT.SYS_CHANGE_CONTEXT IS NOT NULL AND CT.SYS_CHANGE_CONTEXT = @sync_client_id_
binary));

SET @sync_row_count = @@rowcount;
GO

CREATE PROCEDURE up_ContactDeletes
( @sync_row_count int OUTPUT,
  @sync_client_id_binary varbinary(128),
  @ContactId uniqueidentifier,
  @sync_last_received_anchor int)
AS
WITH CHANGE_TRACKING_CONTEXT (@sync_client_id_binary)
DELETE Contact FROM Contact c
  JOIN CHANGETABLE(VERSION Contact, ([ContactId]), (@ContactId)) CT
  ON CT.[ContactId] = c.[ContactId]
WHERE (CT.SYS_CHANGE_VERSION IS NULL OR CT.SYS_CHANGE_VERSION <= @sync_last_received_
anchor
OR (CT.SYS_CHANGE_CONTEXT IS NOT NULL AND CT.SYS_CHANGE_CONTEXT = @sync_client_id_
binary));

SET @sync_row_count = @@rowcount;
GO
```

The *WITH CHANGE_TRACKING_CONTEXT* clause used in these queries tracks which client made the changes that are applied at the server. The client passes the *@sync_client_id_binary* session variable into the stored procedure for the *CHANGE_TRACKING_CONTEXT* statement. The client ID value is stored in the Change Tracking table, which enables the application to track the context under which a change was made.

Downloading Changes

Listing 13-10 showed the stored procedure the example application uses for the *SelectIncrementalInsertsCommand* property that retrieves inserted data from a server table. Two other command properties are used for retrieving incremental server updates and deletes. The *SelectIncrementalUpdatesCommand* and *SelectIncrementalDeletesCommand* properties retrieve updated and deleted rows from the server and apply them to the client. You need to set these properties only for tables specified as *DownloadOnly* or *Bidirectional*. Listing 13-12 shows the *customerSyncAdapter* object's queries for these properties.

LISTING 13-12 Queries used for *SelectIncrementalUpdatesCommand* and *SelectIncrementalDeletesCommand*

```
CREATE PROCEDURE up_CustomerIncrementalUpdates
( @sync_initialized bit,
  @sync_last_received_anchor bigint,
  @sync_client_id_binary varbinary(128),
  @sync_new_received_anchor bigint)
AS
IF @sync_initialized > 0
BEGIN
  SELECT c.[CustomerId], c.[CustomerName]
  FROM Customer c JOIN
    CHANGETABLE(CHANGES Customer, @sync_last_received_anchor) CT
    ON CT.[CustomerId] = c.[CustomerId]
  WHERE (CT.SYS_CHANGE_OPERATION = 'U' AND CT.SYS_CHANGE_VERSION <= @sync_new_
received_anchor
    AND (CT.SYS_CHANGE_CONTEXT IS NULL OR CT.SYS_CHANGE_CONTEXT <> @sync_client_id_
binary));
END
GO

CREATE PROCEDURE up_CustomerIncrementalDeletes
( @sync_initialized bit,
  @sync_last_received_anchor bigint,
  @sync_client_id_binary varbinary(128),
  @sync_new_received_anchor bigint)
AS
IF @sync_initialized > 0
BEGIN
  SELECT CT.[CustomerId]
  FROM CHANGETABLE(CHANGES Customer, @sync_last_received_anchor) CT
  WHERE (CT.SYS_CHANGE_OPERATION = 'D' AND CT.SYS_CHANGE_VERSION <= @sync_new_
received_anchor
    AND (CT.SYS_CHANGE_CONTEXT IS NULL OR CT.SYS_CHANGE_CONTEXT <> @sync_client_id_
binary));
END
GO
```

Each of the queries uses the *CT.SYS_CHANGE_OPERATION* column to find specific changes. For deletes, the query looks for values of *D*; for updates, it looks for *U*; and for inserts, it looks for *I* (as you saw earlier in Listing 13-10).

Detecting and Resolving Data Conflicts

Data conflicts can occur in any synchronization scenario where changes are supported at both client and server. Imagine someone deleting a row in a server table and that same row being updated offline in the client. When the client tries to synchronize its changes, a conflict occurs because the row no longer exists on the server.

Ideally, your application should avoid conflicts altogether by using the *ClientId* property to filter data so that only particular rows are updated by a given client. Designing your application to avoid conflicts has an added benefit of increasing performance by reducing network traffic. In situations where you can't avoid possible data conflicts, Sync Services provides features for detecting and resolving errors and conflicts.

> **Note** Sync Services treats errors that occur during synchronization as conflicts.

Conflicts can occur on either the server or the client, and they can occur during insert, update, or delete operations. Sync Services detects six types of conflicts; Table 13-9 describes the six types of conflicts available in the *ConflictType* enumeration.

TABLE 13-9 Types of Conflicts Detected by Sync Services

Conflict Type	Description
ClientDeleteServerUpdate	This conflict occurs when the server updates a row that the client has deleted.
ClientInsertServerInsert	Known as a primary key collision. This type occurs when both the client and the server try to insert a row with the same primary key.
ClientUpdateServerDelete	This conflict occurs when the client updates a row that the server has deleted.
ClientUpdateServerUpdate	This conflict occurs when the client and server update the same row.
ErrorsOccurred	This conflict occurs when an error prevents row synchronization from occurring.
Unknown	Used by *DbServerSyncProvider* only if the server can't classify the conflict type. *SqlCeClientSyncProvider* doesn't use this type because it can classify all types.

Depending on whether a conflict occurs on upload or download, an event is raised in the *DbServerSyncProvider* or *SqlCeClientSyncProvider*, respectively. The *DbServerSyncProvider* object's *ApplyChangeFailed* event is raised when an upload conflict occurs. It works in conjunction with the *SelectConflictUpdatedRowsCommand* and *SelectConflictDeletedRowsCommand* properties to select rows in conflict. The stored procedures in Listing 13-13 are used in the sample application to select rows when a conflict occurs.

LISTING 13-13 Queries used by the sample application's *DbServerSyncProvider* to detect synchronization conflicts with the *Contact* table

```
CREATE PROCEDURE up_GetContactUpdateConflicts
  (@ContactId uniqueidentifier)
AS
SELECT c.[ContactId], c.[ContactName],
  CT.SYS_CHANGE_CONTEXT, CT.SYS_CHANGE_VERSION
FROM Contact c JOIN CHANGETABLE(VERSION Contact, ([ContactId]), (@ContactId)) CT
  ON CT.[ContactId] = c.[ContactId];
GO

CREATE PROCEDURE up_GetContactDeleteConflicts
  (@ContactId uniqueidentifier,
   @sync_last_received_anchor bigint)
AS
SELECT CT.[ContactId],
  CT.SYS_CHANGE_CONTEXT, CT.SYS_CHANGE_VERSION
FROM CHANGETABLE(CHANGES Contact, @sync_last_received_anchor) CT
WHERE (CT.[ContactId] = @ContactId AND CT.SYS_CHANGE_OPERATION = 'D');
GO
```

If the conflict occurs during download, Sync Services selects the offending rows for you via the *SqlCeClientSyncProvider* object's *ApplyChangeFailed* event.

The *ApplyChangeFailed* event's *EventArgs* parameter provides information about the conflict and possible resolutions. The idea is that you can control what happens when a conflict arises. Possible resolution options are "server changes win," "client changes win," and so on. Listing 13-14 shows the sample application's *ApplyChangeFailed* event handler. In a production application, you'd add code to this event handler to resolve data conflicts according to your business logic.

> **Note** After resolving conflicts, you must revalidate any business rules. This can be done using the *ApplyingChanges* event of the *DbServerSyncProvider* class.

LISTING 13-14 Testing for various conflict types in the *ApplyChangeFailed* event of the *MyClientSyncProvider* class

```
private void MyClientSyncProvider_ApplyChangeFailed(object sender,
ApplyChangeFailedEventArgs e)
{
  // add logic to handle conflicts here
  switch (e.Conflict.ConflictType)
  {
    case ConflictType.ClientDeleteServerUpdate:
      break;
    case ConflictType.ClientInsertServerInsert:
      break;
```

```
      case ConflictType.ClientUpdateServerDelete:
        break;
      case ConflictType.ClientUpdateServerUpdate:
        break;
      case ConflictType.ErrorsOccurred:
        break;
      case ConflictType.Unknown:
        break;
    }
  }
```

The *ApplyChangeFailedEventArgs* object exposes properties for resolving conflicts. You can determine the conflict type using its *ConflictType* property. Based on the type, you might want to take certain actions, such as continuing with synchronization or retrying the update. Use the property to apply an action. The *Action* property can be set to one of the *ApplyAction* enumeration values, as follows:

- **Continue**   Ignore error and continue.

- **RetryApplyingRow**   Retry the update. If you choose this option, you must fix the offending data prior to retrying; otherwise, the exception will be raised again.

- **RetryWithForceWrite**   Retry and force the update to take place. Use the @*sync_force_write* parameter on the server to force the update to take place on the server.

You can investigate the offending data using the *Context* property, which returns a *SyncContext* object that exposes a *DataSet* of changes involved in the current synchronization session. This data is a copy of the actual data. Changing the data in the *Context* property does not change the rows involved in the current synchronization session.

The *SqlCeClientSyncProvider* class exposes a property named *ConflictResolver*. You can use the *ConflictResolver* property to resolve conflicts on the client. The *ConflictResolver* property can be set to one of the *ResolveAction* enumeration values, as follows:

- **ClientWins**   Equivalent to setting the *ApplyAction* property to *Continue*.

- **ServerWins**   Equivalent to setting the *ApplyAction* property to *RetryWithForceWrite*.

- **FireEvent**   Fires the *ApplyChangeFailed* event on the client.

If you do not resolve conflicts and errors within the session in which they occur, the offending rows are not synchronized again unless a future update to the rows occurs. In some instances, you might need to update rows to get them to resynchronize.

Putting It All Together

We've discussed many of the Sync Services features; now let's see how it all works in the sample application. When *Form1* loads, it initializes both the *customerSyncAdapter* and the *contactSyncAdapter* objects. It also adds event handlers for each of those *SyncAdapter* objects' *SessionProgress* events. Last, it fills the *Customer* and *Contact* tables in the *LocalCustomerDataSet*. The *Form1_Load* event is shown in Listing 13-15.

LISTING 13-15 The *MySyncServicesDemo Form1_Load* event

```
private void Form1_Load(object sender, EventArgs e)
{
  this._customerSyncAgent = new CustomerSyncAgent();
  this._customerSyncAgent.SessionProgress += new EventHandler<SessionProgressEventArgs
>(this.OnCustomerSyncAgentSessionProgress);

  this._customerSyncAgent.Initialize();

  this._contactSyncAgent = new ContactSyncAgent();
  this._contactSyncAgent.SessionProgress += new EventHandler<SessionProgressEventArgs>
(this.OnContactSyncAgentSessionProgress);

  this._contactSyncAgent.Initialize();

  // Fill LocalCustomerDataSet with customer and contact data from local database
  this.contactTableAdapter.Fill(this.LocalCustomerDataSet.Contact);
  this.customerTableAdapter.Fill(this.LocalCustomerDataSet.Customer);
}
```

The local SQL Server Compact 3.5 database is empty when the application runs for the first time. Clicking the Refresh Customer button starts the *Customer* table's initial synchronization by calling the *customerSyncAdapter* object's *Synchronize* method. When the synchronization is completed, the *SyncStatistics* object returned by the call is used to display the session's status information.

During this initial synchronization, the local *Customer* table is populated with data from the server's *Customer* table. The query defined in the *customerSyncAdapter* object's *SelectIncrementalInsertsCommand* property is executed to retrieve customer data. The form tracks synchronization progress using the event handler for the *SessionProgress* event, as shown in Listing 13-16.

LISTING 13-16 Event handler for the *customerSyncAgent SessionProgress* event

```
private void OnCustomerSyncAgentSessionProgress(object sender, SessionProgressEventArgs
e)
{
  // once synchronization is complete, requery the local database
  // to refresh the controls
  if (e.PercentCompleted == 100)
  {
    this.customerTableAdapter.Fill(this.LocalCustomerDataSet.Customer);
  }
}
```

Using the event handler, *Form1* reloads the *Customer* table by calling the *customerTableAdapter* object's *Fill* method. Congratulations, you've just synchronized your first table using Sync Services! Now let's go a step further and actually upload data changed on the client to the server.

The synchronization process for the *Contact* table is roughly the same as that for the *Customer* table. The biggest difference is that the *Contact* table supports bidirectional synchronization. Select the customer named Johnson, and then click the New Contact button to add a new contact. By default, the application creates a contact record for Customer Contact1. Click the Save button to save the contact to the local database.

At this point, if you stopped and restarted the application, Customer Contact1 would continue to appear as one of Johnson's contacts. However, if you queried the *Contact* table in the *SQL08SampleDB* database, you would not see any contacts, because the data has not yet been synchronized. Click the form's Sync Contacts button to upload the new contact to the server. The button's click event handler calls the *contactSyncAdapter* object's *Synchronize* method. Just as before, you'll see a message box displaying statistics when the synchronization is complete. Go back to the *SQL08SampleDB* database and requery the *Contact* table. This time, you'll see a record for Customer Contact1.

Now it's time to really start having some fun with Sync Services. Experiment by adding rows directly to or removing rows directly from the *Customer* or *Contact* server tables and then synchronizing the client. You should also try editing or deleting contact data on the client and synchronizing the changes with the server. Be sure to save your changes on the client before synchronizing with the server. By exercising the application, you'll get a feel for how Sync Services behaves in different scenarios.

Going N-Tier

The sample application we've discussed so far is a client/server application. While a client/server application is a great tool for demonstrating some Sync Services features, it's not very practical. In a production environment, the application logic will not all reside on the client; it will be separated across tiers, with some code on the client and some code on the server.

Sync Services is designed for n-tiered and service-based architectures. In this section, we're going to convert the client application to communicate with a WCF service. You'll really appreciate the flexibility of Sync Services after you see how quickly this can be achieved with just a few simple steps.

Note A detailed discussion of WCF is beyond the scope of this chapter. We'll focus on how to set up Sync Services in a service-based architecture and leave the WCF details to other resources—for example, *http://msdn.microsoft.com/en-us/netframework/aa663324.aspx* or *Programming WCF Services* by Juval Lowy (O'Reilly, 2007).

The example WCF service project included in the sample solution is named
MySyncServicesWcfService. This project is a WCF Service Library configured to run under IIS. It contains several classes, many of which should look familiar, including the
CustomerServerSyncProvider and the *ServerHelper* classes. They are exact copies of the classes
used in the *MySyncServicesDemo* project. The *ServerHelper* class is a utility class containing
common methods. The *MyCustomerService* and *ISyncService* classes are new and are used to
describe the service and service contract.

ISyncService is an interface that defines our service contract. *MyCustomerService* is a service
class that implements *ISyncService*. The code for both is shown in Listing 13-17.

LISTING 13-17 The *ISyncService* interface and *MyCustomerService* class

```
[ServiceContract]
public interface ISyncService
{
  [OperationContract]
  SyncContext ApplyChanges(SyncGroupMetadata groupMetadata, DataSet dataSet,
SyncSession syncSession);

  [OperationContract]
  SyncContext GetChanges(SyncGroupMetadata groupMetadata, SyncSession syncSession);

  [OperationContract]
  SyncSchema GetSchema(Collection<string> tableNames, SyncSession syncSession);

  [OperationContract]
  SyncServerInfo GetServerInfo(SyncSession syncSession);
}

public class MyCustomerService : ISyncService
{
  private CustomerServiceProvider _serverSyncProvider;

  public MyCustomerService()
  {
    this._serverSyncProvider = new CustomerServiceProvider();
  }

  public virtual SyncContext ApplyChanges(SyncGroupMetadata groupMetadata, DataSet
dataSet, SyncSession syncSession) {
    return this._serverSyncProvider.ApplyChanges(groupMetadata, dataSet, syncSession);
  }

  public virtual SyncContext GetChanges(SyncGroupMetadata groupMetadata, SyncSession
syncSession) {
    return this._serverSyncProvider.GetChanges(groupMetadata, syncSession);
  }
```

```
    public virtual SyncSchema GetSchema(Collection<string> tableNames, SyncSession
  syncSession) {
      return this._serverSyncProvider.GetSchema(tableNames, syncSession);
    }

    public virtual SyncServerInfo GetServerInfo(SyncSession syncSession) {
      return this._serverSyncProvider.GetServerInfo(syncSession);
    }
  }
```

With the service set up, we create a reference to the service named *SyncServiceReference1* in the *MySyncServicesDemo* project. Do this by right-clicking the References node under the *MySyncServicesDemo* project and then choosing Add Service Reference from the shortcut menu. From there, browse to and select the service named *MyCustomerService*. Then repeat the same process to add a service reference for the *MyContactService* service.

> **Note** You might have to build and deploy the *MySyncServicesWcfService* WCF project before you can add a service reference in your *MySyncServicesDemo* project.

The service references add proxy objects to the client application. Sync Services uses these proxy objects to makes calls to the services.

Enabling Service-Based Synchronization

Once the service reference is set up, it is now just a matter of telling the *customerSyncAgent* on the client to use the service proxy class instead of the local *CustomerServerSyncProvider* class. This is where you do have to do a little work. In the *MySyncServicesDemo* project, you would edit the *Initialize* method in the *CustomerSyncAgent* class and replace the one line of code that sets the *RemoteProvider* property with the two lines of code shown in Listing 13-18.

LISTING 13-18 Communicating with the server using a proxy instead of directly with a *DbServerSyncProvider*

```
SyncServiceReference1.SyncServiceClient remoteCustomer =
 new MySyncServicesDemo.SyncServiceReference1.SyncServiceClient();

this.RemoteProvider = new ServerSyncProviderProxy(remoteCustomer);
```

Believe it or not, that's all you need to do. Restart the application, change a record in the server's *Customer* table, and then click the Refresh Customer button. Your changes will be downloaded to the client using the WCF service.

Stop the application, repeat the editing process for the *ContactSyncAgent* class, and you're all done. The replacement code for the *Initialize* method is shown here:

```
ContactServiceReference.SyncServiceClient remoteContact =
  new MySyncServicesDemo.ContactServiceReference.SyncServiceClient();

this.RemoteProvider = new ServerSyncProviderProxy(remoteContact);
```

Additional Considerations

Beyond programming Sync Services, there are a few topics you should be aware of when designing and developing applications that use this technology. We conclude this chapter with a brief discussion of these topics, which include using the Visual Studio 2008 Configure Data Synchronization dialog box to build a local data store, using the *SqlSyncAdapterBuilder* class to create *SyncAdapter* objects at runtime, and data type and security considerations.

Using the Designer to Create a Local Data Cache

To really learn and understand Sync Services for ADO.NET and SQL Server Change Tracking, we described the gritty details involved with setting up and programming an application using Sync Services purely by hand. An alternative approach is to use Visual Studio 2008 to build the objects and base code for you. By adding a *LocalDatabaseCache* item to your project, Visual Studio will display the Configure Data Synchronization dialog box, shown in Figure 13-32, which creates the necessary synchronization classes and adds them to your project.

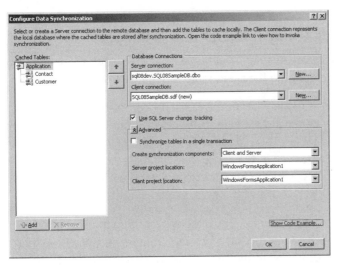

FIGURE 13-32 The Configure Data Synchronization dialog box

You have the option of choosing whether to use SQL Server Change Tracking. In most cases, you'd select this option. However, if your server database is not SQL Server 2008, clear the check box, and the dialog box will build custom Change Tracking tables in your server database, as shown in Figure 13-33. The generated scripts add columns to tracked tables and also create new tables for tracking deleted rows.

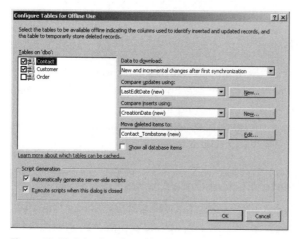

Figure 13-33 Selecting the tables for synchronization and options for generating scripts

Using the Configure Data Synchronization dialog box, you can set up an application very quickly and without having to know many of the details of Sync Services. You could use the tables and classes created as a starting point for extending the application for bidirectional synchronization.

Building Commands Using *SqlSyncAdapterBuilder*

Sync Services provides a *SqlSyncAdapterBuilder* object, which creates a *SyncAdapter* and the necessary queries for synchronizing the client table with the SQL Server database at runtime.

The *SqlSyncAdapterBuilder* is modeled after the ADO.NET command builder object. The builder creates the proper command statements based on information you provide about one or more synchronized tables. This is a useful feature, although it has some drawbacks— you are limited to using SQL Server as the server-side database, some performance overhead is added, and you compromise security because the builder uses inline SQL instead of stored procedures.

Specifying commands manually has a few advantages over using the *SqlSyncAdapterBuilder*. First, you can use stored procedures instead of inline T-SQL. Second, you have more control over the types of changes uploaded to the server. For example, if you don't want to upload deletes to the server but you are using bidirectional synchronization, you simply omit the command for the *DeleteCommand* property. Third, you can use any non–SQL Server database on the server.

> **Note** You should use the *SqlSyncAdapterBuilder* primarily for learning and proof-of-concept purposes. For production applications, you should specify commands that use stored procedures wherever possible for performance and security reasons.

If you decide to use a *SqlSyncAdapterBuilder*, be sure to set the *SyncTable* object's *SyncDirection* property appropriately. The *SyncDirection* determines which commands the *SqlSyncAdapterBuilder* will create for the *SyncAdapter*.

In cases where your *SyncTable*'s direction is *UploadOnly* or *Snapshot*, you don't need to do anything other than call the *SqlSyncAdapterBuilder* object's *ToSyncAdapter* method, as shown in Listing 13-19.

LISTING 13-19 Creating a *SyncAdapter* using the *SqlSyncAdapterBuilder* class

```
SqlSyncAdapterBulder customerBuilder = new SqlSyncAdapterBuilder(serverConnection);
customerBuilder.TableName = "Customer";
customerBuilder.SyncDirection = SyncDirection.UploadOnly;
SyncAdapter customerSyncAdapter = customerBuilder.ToSyncAdapter();
customerSyncAdapter.TableName = "Customer";
this.SyncAdapters.Add(customerSyncAdapter);
```

For tables whose sync direction is *DownloadOnly* or *Bidirectional*, you'll need to set additional properties so that the *SqlSyncAdapterBuilder* can generate the proper commands. A short list of the properties includes *CreationTrackingColumn*, *UpdateTrackingColumn*, *TombstoneDataColumns*, and *CreationOriginatorIdColumn*.

> **More Info** To learn more about how to use these properties with the *SqlSyncAdapterBuilder*, see *http://msdn.microsoft.com/en-us/library/microsoft.synchronization.data.server.sqlsyncadapter-builder_properties.aspx*.

Data Type Considerations

For the most part, you don't have to be concerned about handling data types for Sync Services applications. Here are a few issues you might encounter if your application has special data type requirements:

- Sync Services maps data types between SQL Server Compact 3.5 and SQL Server databases during synchronization. See SQL Server Books Online for more mapping details. If your application has different mapping requirements, you can use the *SyncSchemaColumn* object to map the types.

- Data from *timestamp* columns is not copied to the client from the server.

- For *uniqueidentifier* columns qualified with the *ROWGUIDCOL* attribute, the *ROWGUIDCOL* attribute is not applied in the client database when Sync Services creates the table. Only the data is copied. You can use the events in a *SqlCeSyncClientProvider* to set the *ROWGUIDCOL* attribute on the local table.

- Identity columns are copied to the client from the server, but on the client, the seed is always 0 and the increment is always 1.

- Data in computed columns is copied to a client database, but the computed column expression is not.

Security Considerations

You should be conscious of the fact that client devices might contain sensitive data. Here are some steps you can take to ensure that information doesn't fall into the wrong hands if a user's device is lost or stolen:

- Don't hard-code connection user names and passwords in the application or config files. This technique is useful only for demos and sample code. In practice, *always* prompt the user for connection information on application startup.

- Use stored procedures, and grant access to tables only through the stored procedures. Do not allow direct access to the server tables.

- Lock down servers and services to limit the surface area of attack. Turn off all services not being used by the application.

- SQL Server Compact 3.5 supports encrypting the data stored in the local database. Use this encryption whenever possible.

Summary

You have many decisions to make when building your occasionally connected system. Choosing between Merge Replication and Sync Services for ADO.NET is only the beginning. Merge Replication is the database administrator's tool, providing quick setup and configuration with its myriad wizards and dialog boxes but limited choices in terms of platform and topology. Sync Services for ADO.NET is a developer's dream: total control with a robust object model and lots of interesting possibilities for building occasionally connected client/server or service-based applications.

In this chapter, we explored the development of occasionally connected systems for SQL Server Compact 3.5 using both Merge Replication and Sync Services for ADO.NET coupled with SQL Server 2008 Change Tracking. You saw how to build applications for Windows and Pocket PCs that work in both offline and online modes and that synchronize changes with the server using these replication technologies. With the fundamentals covered in this chapter, you now have the ability to extend your business systems with all sorts of exciting new "occasionally connected" capabilities.

Part IV
Business Intelligence

In this part:

Chapter 14	Data Warehousing	563
Chapter 15	Basic OLAP	611
Chapter 16	Advanced OLAP	639
Chapter 17	OLAP Queries, Tools, and Application Development	717
Chapter 18	Expanding Your Business Intelligence with Data Mining	793
Chapter 19	Reporting Services	879

Chapter 14
Data Warehousing

—Mark Frawley

This chapter is all about data warehousing. If you've been avoiding this topic—dismissing it perhaps as being too advanced, esoteric, or abstract to be applicable—this chapter will help you cast those excuses aside and embrace data warehousing. The practical advice and guidance we give will empower you and your end users to glean more useful information and intelligence from your data. We will begin with an explanation of exactly what data warehousing is and why you should care about it, and then we'll show how to take advantage of specific Microsoft SQL Server 2008 data warehousing features.

Data Warehousing Defined

You're in good company if you wonder exactly what is meant by *data warehousing*—and indeed you might even wonder whether it has any *precise* meaning at all. The term has existed for almost two decades, and you might have seen a variety of definitions. Here is ours:

Data warehousing is both a vision of and a methodological approach toward organizing and managing enterprise data for the purpose of providing a trustworthy, consistent, integrated, and comprehensive data foundation for an enterprise's data-driven requirements and applications, both tactical and strategic.

Why does our definition not include any technical references? Well, that's just the point! While technology *is* essential to actually realizing the vision, data warehousing is not—or should not be—fundamentally about technology. It is about laying the data foundation needed to run an enterprise. *Run* as in making informed decisions. And *enterprise* rather than *business* because data warehousing is equally relevant whether the work is for-profit, not-for-profit, or in the public sector (a subtle distinction resulting from the unfortunate fact that the word *business* is embedded in the term *business intelligence*, or BI)—and, increasingly, whether the entity is small, medium, or large. Compared with what was true in the past, Microsoft's data warehousing–related offerings under the SQL Server product umbrella have made it particularly feasible for data warehousing goals to be attainable by small and medium-size enterprises. Of course, Microsoft continues to deliver industrial-strength data warehousing performance for the largest enterprises—especially with the 2008 release of SQL Server.

The Importance of Data Warehousing

Today, data warehousing in some form has become a *given,* a *must,* for running an enterprise of any significant size. At its best, it enables actual competitive advantage, but even when focused more tactically or departmentally, it is now considered essential to being competitive—as basic and essential as the general ledger or payroll system. While it is often difficult to quantify the benefits of data warehousing in terms of return on investment (ROI), no one these days seriously questions its value and necessity. As a database developer, you are likely to be involved with data warehousing in one way or another—if not directly, at least in interfacing to a data warehouse. So it's important for you to understand what data warehousing is all about.

Developing a data warehouse is in some ways a very different undertaking from traditional online transactional processing (OLTP) database development, with which you are probably more familiar. Two of the most notable differences are that data warehousing essentially emphasizes *data* and its relationships—as opposed to the emphasis on *process* found in the typical OLTP application—and that hard experience by practitioners has evolved specialized ways of modeling data that are particularly useful in achieving the goals of data warehousing.

Even if your role is primarily technical, you will be able to do a much better job of building or interfacing to a data warehouse if you know something about these differences from OLTP and the reasons for them. This will also help you appreciate the perspective of decision makers who rely on accurate data storage and analysis (see the next chapter), which will be very likely different from that of typical OLTP application stakeholders.

Data warehousing is an essential foundation for what has come to be known as business intelligence (BI). We'll learn more about the close relationship between data warehousing and BI later in this chapter, but for now, appreciate that they are *not* synonymous. At the same time, in keeping with our earlier observation, mentally substitute *enterprise* when you hear *business.*

The remainder of this chapter consists of five sections that build upon one another as we progress through our treatment of data warehousing. Instead of immediately focusing on technical details and step-by-step procedures in SQL Server 2008, we review the history leading up to why data warehousing is today a distinct practice and how SQL Server 2008 represents an excellent data warehousing platform.

The first section, "What Preceded Data Warehousing," focuses on the origins of data warehousing to help you appreciate why data warehousing emerged as a distinct practice responding to industry issues. The second section, "Data Warehouse Design," describes the two principal approaches to data warehouse design. The third section, "What Data Warehousing

Is Not," considers various terms often confused with data warehousing and gives them distinct definitions. The fourth section, "Practical Advice About Data Warehousing," alerts you to various common but nonobvious issues that you might encounter when building a data warehouse. Last, the fifth section, "SQL Server 2008 and Data Warehousing," discusses SQL Server 2008–specific details as they relate to data warehousing.

With this ambitious agenda to cover in just a single chapter, we will not actually tell you much about "how" to build the perfect data warehouse—dozens of entire books are available for that. Rather, what we aim to provide is a unique combination of background, clarification of terms, identification of tricky spots, and finally some technical details about the specific data warehousing platform offered by SQL Server 2008.

Data vs. Information

At the risk of sounding pedantic, fully appreciating why data warehousing is valuable requires drawing the distinction between *data* and *information*. Data consists of recorded, characterized "facts"—for example, sale amounts initiated by customer A at store B on date C, paid for with credit card D. These facts are the amounts of the sale (numbers), while the characteristics give these numbers meaning or context. This is the sort of transactional data typically captured by an operational application.

Such characterized facts are essential, but *information* involves interpreting facts, identifying the relationships between them, and finding the more abstract "meaning" (if it exists) implied by them. Each characteristic, such as customer, store, date, and so on, could serve as a predicate in a query. For example, what is the pattern of sales vs. store for this customer? Or what stores have the highest sales by date? Of course, there are countless others. These sorts of questions are *higher order*, or *value adding*, because their answers enable informed decision making for the future, as opposed to mere question answering of the sort that a customer service representative might do from the facts themselves (for example, when answering the question, "what is this charge on my statement that I don't recognize?").

This might not seem an important distinction, but historically, it often simply wasn't technically feasible to assemble the available data in a form suitable for informed decision making. Often, what passed for that instead was instinct and educated guesswork. In contrast, data warehousing emphasizes organizing, standardizing, and formatting facts in such a way as to enable deriving such "information" from them. Building on that, BI is then concerned with defining, extracting, delivering, and acting on that information.

What Preceded Data Warehousing

Depending on your experience, you might remember the term *electronic data processing*, also known as EDP or DP, which was used to describe the use of computers in enterprise applications for much of the 55+ years of computing history. Over the last 15 to 20 years, the term has morphed into today's *information technology*, commonly referred to simply as IT. Although unintentional, the timing of the change and the implication of the two terms could also stand for "pre–data warehousing" and "post–data warehousing."

Until the early to mid-1990s (when the client/server architectural paradigm reached its peak), the application of computers to enterprise needs had a strong emphasis on streamlining or automating manual clerical processes and relatively simple, repetitive high-volume tasks such as billing, payroll, inventory, and maintaining the general ledger (GL). Such applications were obvious initial targets for the application of computers in the business environment for at least three reasons:

- Their repetitive, highly constrained nature (making them relatively easy to model and suitable for automation)

- The presumed cost savings associated with that automation

- The technical feasibility given the state of the art at the time

Early input and output formats were very crude. For a long time, batch-mode processing—based on input via punched cards and output on green-bar lined printer paper—was the norm. Eventually, the state of the art advanced to allow interactive activities (giving us the now quaint and superfluous but persistent adjective *online*). Still, the application of computers to the enterprise remained largely driven by the aforementioned factors. A natural consequence was that each DP-targeted application was closely aligned with the operational process it supported, and marginally if at all with other processes. DP was about recording the basic facts of enterprise transactions while ensuring data integrity and then summarizing the results in fixed reports. The well-known term *online transaction processing* (OLTP) developed as a label for all of this.

Electronic data processing was an apt description of what computers and their users were doing during the pre–data warehousing period—processing data as transactions electronically (as opposed to manually)—and also what they were frequently *not* doing—turning data into information (as previously defined).

While this focus in many cases addressed operational needs adequately, it also led to a host of issues that impeded extracting a higher level of value from the data being collected. Data warehousing evolved, among other things, as a way of addressing these impediments. Let's explore how.

Lack of Integration Across the Enterprise

The emphasis on operational processes inevitably created nonintegrated, stand-alone applications. From both enterprise and technical perspectives, each application defined essential entities as it saw fit—not just the entities unique to itself but also those "master data" entities such as customers and products that exist across the enterprise. There was typically no common understanding of what was meant by these key entities, so each application kept its own version, leading to lots of data duplication.

With this state of affairs, it was difficult or impossible to create a meaningful enterprise-wide view of just about anything. When attempted, such views were necessarily at a high level of summarization, time-consuming, and expensive to create and therefore were created only infrequently. Enterprise decision making, especially at the operational and tactical level, still depended greatly on intuition, experience, and instinct. It often simply wasn't possible to base decisions on hard, accurate, up-to-date information. Late in the pre–data warehousing age, there were attempts to address this in the form of applications known as executive information systems (EIS) and decision support systems (DSS). These were generally ineffective because relative to their cost, they didn't deliver enough value to their small, high-level audience.

Management Reporting and the GL

The one application that typically *was* enterprise-wide was the general ledger (GL). Every other major application concerned with financial information (which was many, if not most applications) had to feed accounting entries to the GL. As a result, the GL often was the single point of integration between applications because it existed and had those connections already. Also, it was accepted as an enterprise-wide single version of "the truth" by its very nature. For these reasons, most early attempts at enterprise-wide reporting were driven from the GL.

There was value in this, but there were grave limitations as well. A GL is not well suited to "management reporting," except possibly at the highest aggregated levels, such as annual report line items. Management reporting is mostly focused on measurements of enterprise performance at much lower levels, levels which are irrelevant to the concerns of a GL—such as the profitability of specific customers. Yet once the GL became the single point of integration and thereby the source of management reporting, it started getting abused. All sorts of accounts and subledgers to support detailed management reporting proliferated in the GL, and modifications to the GL interface of source systems were made to feed them. Over time, this situation had a tendency to collapse under its own maintenance weight, especially when the GL chart of accounts needed to be restructured in the event of a merger. One of the impetuses of data warehousing was to address all this by providing a separate, appropriate environment for management reporting.

Little or No Standardized Reference Data

Closely related to lack of integration, there typically existed no single, agreed-upon "system of record" for key or master referential data across the enterprise, such as customer and product. Problems that stemmed from this included incomplete and inaccurate data, duplicated data entry (and resultant errors), and wasted effort synchronizing multiple versions from different applications. Most important of all was the inability to derive, except possibly at great effort, a consistent, comprehensive, and up-to-date view of the enterprise. In addition to these obvious consequences were some less obvious ones—for example, the embarrassment of severing a relationship with a customer who is unprofitable in one region but is overall very profitable, because you could not see the "big picture" of all your relationships with the customer across all regions, products, and organizational units.

To be sure, these problems and the reasons behind them were well recognized by the DP department and by the operational level of the enterprise almost from the beginning, and this led to attempts to create "master file" versions of the most important referentials—typically, customers, rates, products, and the organizational hierarchy. But technical limitations, political turf battles, and a lack of recognition at senior management levels of the costs of this fragmentation generally kept such efforts suboptimal.

Lack of History

Operational applications (let's call them "OpApps") by their very nature tend to neither require nor maintain historical data going back very far—often not more than a year or two. There are exceptions of course, such as an application that manages mortgage loans at a bank or life insurance at an insurer. These are certainly operational in nature and must also retain historical activity going back even decades perhaps. But in most cases, OpApps maintain a minimum of history in order to optimize their OLTP performance and minimize storage cost, and because there is simply no requirement to do more.

In any case, within the same enterprise, OpApps differ in the length of history maintained, its periodicity (that is, hourly, daily, weekly, monthly, and so on), and the way changes in referential data over time are handled (that is, whether a history of changes is maintained, and if so, on which attributes, and how many versions; for example, is the history of marital status or address of a customer maintained). These differences make integrating the historical data of multiple OpApps difficult, to say the least.

Data Not Optimized for Analysis

There are more significant differences between OpApps and analytical applications ("AApps," for short). As described so far, OpApps—especially in the pre–data warehousing era—were and still are concerned mainly with reliably recording the facts of current transactions. They have limited concern with past history or with other OpApps, which is why they came to be referred to as "islands of automation."

In contrast, AApps are concerned with "digesting" OpApp data to provide actionable insights, predictions, and an apples-to-apples view of the entire enterprise. Sometimes such applications even combine internal and external data, such as benchmarks regarding competitors, providing a view of how the enterprise looks in a larger context. Achieving these goals requires solving all kinds of problems that OpApps do not need to be concerned with. In addition to these general differences, here are some more specific ones:

- Given their uses, OpApps are physically optimized for insert, update, and delete operations, while AApps require read or query optimization.

- The amount of data required to answer a typical OpApps query is quite small, while the amount required to answer a typical AApp query can be huge. Imagine the amount of atomic data that must be digested to answer a query such as "Who were the top 5 customers by purchases for 2007, and what were the top 5 products purchased by each of them?"

- Among the various OpApps that must be integrated for an enterprise-wide view, there are many impediments to integration, in addition to those mentioned earlier. Here are a few:

  - Entities that mean the same thing but that are named differently

  - Entities that mean different things but that are named the same

  - Different encodings of the same thing (for example, country codes)

  - Different scale and precision of measures

  - Different lengths of descriptive text for the same thing

  - Different conventions for the primary key of the same entity

  - "Smart keys"—where information is encoded in primary keys

As a Result...

- Creating any particular view of enterprise data, especially one integrated across multiple applications, was a very technical undertaking that only the DP staff could perform. Usually, there was a large backlog of requests for such views or reports.

- Many such requests (the fulfillment of which might have helped run the enterprise better) never materialized in the first place. That was because users knew that by the time the DP department could fulfill them, it would be too late to meet the business opportunity.

- Each request that was fulfilled was usually implemented through a new report or extract, even if its requirements varied only slightly from an existing one. Given the technology of the time, even something as simple (as we would consider it today) as aggregating the data at a different level—say, quarterly rather than monthly—resulted in a new report. Further, even when a report already existed that could fulfill a request, there was typically no way to know that because no effective metadata was maintained about existing reports—and so a new one would be created.

- Every report or extract would become permanently enshrined in the system infrastructure, forever. There was often no way to track who was using what report for what purpose (if it was being used at all), so once a report was running, it was easier and safer to just keep supporting it.

- Eventually, there were extracts of extracts—one "report" would become the source for another. Keeping track of the dependencies became difficult if not impossible.

It should be obvious how all this represented a huge maintenance nightmare. But up through the early 1990s, this situation was all too common in the average "DP shop," and it just kept getting worse. It became increasingly evident that this was a crisis in the making, and what we today call data warehousing was born in response.

In fairness, it should be noted that there *were* efforts to build what effectively were data warehouses long before the term was coined. But in those days, such efforts essentially re-invented the wheel each time. They could not benefit from what is available today now that techniques have matured and become codified and, thanks to the advent of the Internet, shared. It is also true that hardware advances in the form of drastically lower storage costs and fantastically improved CPU capacities have had a profound impact on the practice of data warehousing and are essential to its viability today.

Data Warehouse Design

The preceding discussion gives you an idea of the issues that data warehousing evolved to address. In this section, we only scratch the surface of design considerations in bringing a data warehouse into existence and hope that will whet your appetite to learn more. Fortunately, it has never been easier to learn more about data warehousing than it is today.

> **Note** The value of data warehousing was not always widely accepted. In its early days, it was viewed suspiciously and considered to be just a fad or an expensive waste of time by many IT practitioners. At best it was thought of as "nice to have" and something that only the largest, best funded, and mostly for-profit enterprises could consider. Fortunately, none of this is true any longer.

Building a data warehouse requires addressing a myriad of technical *and* nontechnical issues, including the following:

- Determination of enterprise goals and objectives to be served by the data warehouse and gaining organizational buy-in for them.

- Identification of the various audiences for the data and their varying requirements.

- Addressing of latency requirements with the appropriate data architecture.

- Extract, transform, and load (ETL)—the process and tools by which data is extracted from source OpApps, cleaned and otherwise transformed as needed, and then loaded into the data warehouse. SQL Server Integration Services (SSIS) is Microsoft's primary ETL tool for data warehousing.

- Design of entitlement, backup, mobility, scalability, delivery, and training schemes.

- Methods of end-user access to the information, including the distinction often made between reporting and analysis. The tools and products for this usually receive a disproportionate amount of attention in a data warehousing project because they are so visible.

- The embedding of an organizational ethos that the data warehouse will constantly evolve with the ever-changing needs it supports. The effort is never "done."

The primary goal of any data warehouse is to integrate data from disparate sources into a centralized store (at least logically speaking), in a form that can be used across the enterprise for decision support by all who need it. Merely dumping all the data from various standalone applications into a common database is not the sort of integration we mean. Rather, a data warehouse requires a schema of some sort to which all the data brought in is made to conform. The data also needs to be "clean"—meaning that all the different ways of representing the "same" thing in the various source systems have been converted to a single consistent form. Both of these tasks are ETL responsibilities, as previously mentioned.

Based on what we've said so far, the 35,000-foot view of a data warehouse is shown in Figure 14-1.

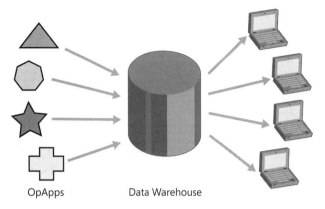

FIGURE 14-1 The generic data warehouse architecture

With this background in place, we can now consider the two predominant data warehousing architectures guiding practice today.

The Top-Down Approach of Inmon

William Inmon is recognized as "the father of data warehousing," having invented the term in 1990. The data warehousing features he characterized can seem self-evident today, but no one had codified them previously as he did. According to his definition, the essential characteristics of data in a data warehouse are as follows:

- **Subject-oriented**   Major entities are common across multiple OpApps. Customer, Product, Shipment, and Account are typical subject areas.

- **Integrated**   Data sources are consistent with one another along common themes.

- **Nonvolatile**   Data, once loaded, is usually never changed (updated or deleted).

- **Time-variant**   Time is part of the key to everything—"as it was at this point in time," also known as "history," is preserved.

These features enable the previously stated goals of any data warehouse.

While an oversimplification, the Inmon style of data warehousing presumes that an enterprise data model has been or will be created—one that identifies all the "subject-oriented" entities common across multiple OpApps, the required numeric measures, the required detail level of each, and the relationships between them. It is posited that the logical data model representing this within the data warehouse is a normalized relational model of the sort associated with OLTP applications. Inmon refers to this as the "enterprise data warehouse" and to the data as being "architected." The emphasis is on a centralized, normalized data store.

Since the typical complexity of a normalized model does not lend itself to direct query from ease of use and performance perspectives, this architecture also posits various *datamarts*, which are additional derived databases whose structure is optimized for query, and which generally contain only aggregated data derived from the data warehouse. The key point is that their architecture is secondary and separate from the data warehouse proper. A refinement of Figure 14-1 that represents Inmon's datamart concept is shown Figure 14-2.

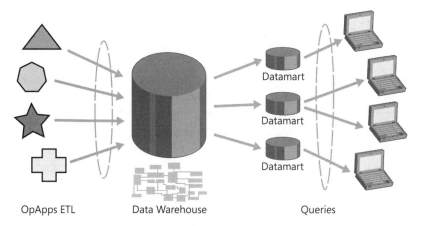

FIGURE 14-2 An Inmon-inspired data warehouse

Because this approach generally insists that a large-scale model already exists or will be created before construction of the data warehouse begins, it is usually characterized as *top-down*.

Inmon has written several books elaborating the principles and refinements of this architecture, and along with Claudia Imhoff (a long-term associate), he has elucidated an even larger architecture, the Corporate Information Factory (CIF), of which data warehousing is only a part. Space constraints preclude us from delving into further detail about the Inmon and CIF approaches. We do want to make two points before moving on, however.

The first you are probably already thinking—that requiring the existence or creation of an enterprise data model is impractical in many organizations. It *has* been successfully done, typically in larger enterprises, but many would find it impossible to justify the time and expense required to develop the model (with nothing to show at the end but documentation). No doubt when it *can* be done, it lays a very powerful foundation for informational applications, but in many cases, it is not feasible.

The second point is that many find this approach relatively abstract—useful in articulating high-level architecture but less helpful with practical details during actual development. The next approach to data warehousing that we'll discuss, at the other end of the design spectrum, evolved to address both these realities.

The Bottom-Up Approach of Kimball

From the mid 1990s to the present, Ralph Kimball has publicized an alternative to the Inmon approach to data warehousing, the heart of which he called the *Dimensional Model*. If the Inmon approach can be called top-down, Kimball's is definitely bottom-up, although both advocate a step-by-step approach. Just as Inmon articulated and formalized concepts that were already in use by practitioners, Kimball codified several practices already in use but lacking an integrative vision.

The first is the Dimensional Model, held to represent the most elegant tradeoffs between end-user intelligibility, ease of use, good performance for both predefined and ad hoc queries, and easy extensibility. The second is the idea of building the data warehouse incrementally, something most enterprises find much more palatable than the all-at-once, "big bang" approach implied by Inmon's architecture. A key part of this is the concept of "conformed dimensions" (which we'll define in a moment) to ensure that each new incremental data warehouse development could be integrated with what was already built, as opposed to each effort becoming the next-generation "island of automation," or as it is usually called today, "stovepipe," application. Third, Kimball emphasizes implementation practicality, with very specific advice on a host of data design issues advanced through his books, Web site, regular seminars, and training offerings.

Many indeed seem to find this approach desirable, as evidenced by the fact that most data analysis tools on the market today, including Microsoft SQL Server Analysis Services (which we cover in Chapters 15 through 18), have a definite affinity for the Dimensional Model. For this reason, as well as because it is less abstract, we will devote the rest of this section to an overview of this approach.

> **Important** Inmon and Kimball are by far the best-known data warehousing pundits. For better or worse, because their approaches are often seen as so different, each has developed a "camp" of supporters who criticize each others' views of data warehousing best practices with sometimes religious zeal. Nonetheless, both share an emphasis on adhering to an architecture for the data warehousing design and on a step-by-step approach to design and construction. Most data warehousing projects in fact combine elements of the two approaches, which is as it should be, because each has excellent ideas to contribute. This is why it is prudent for you to be aware of them both.

This section does not purport to teach the Kimball approach. Space permits us merely to expose you to a few key concepts associated with it. This should make your further investigations easier and more effective.

Terminology

You should be aware of several useful data warehousing terms that—while closely associated with (if not always originated by) Kimball and the Dimensional Model—have come to be more broadly understood due to their representation in many tools (especially OLAP tools). You'll see most of these terms again in the chapters that cover SQL Server Analysis Services (Chapters 15 through 18).

- **Measure**   A typically numeric value of interest in reporting and analysis, such as price, balance, or inventory. As stored in a data warehouse, the relevant measures are defined by the industry of the enterprise and come from the OpApps that are its data sources. A measure is also characterized by *grain*, defined later in this list.

- **Dimension**   The heart of the Dimensional Model, a dimension is variously described as an "axis of analysis" or a "what" qualifier. A dimension helps qualify a measure and give it context (discussed in the next section). In a query, a dimension can be part of the query result and/or part of the query constraints. The most fundamental dimension is *Time*, essential in almost any context. Others are industry-specific but typically include at a minimum *Customer*, *Product*, and *Geography*. Dimensions are typically recognized as referential or master data entities. A dimension is a collection of related values called *members*—for example, *2008* might be a member of the *Time* dimension and *John Smith* a member of the *Customer* dimension. In a Dimensional Model, the dimensions are considered to be independent of one another, even if they really are not. For example, *Customer* and *Product* are not independent, since not every customer buys every product, but by modeling each as a dimension, we treat them as if they are independent because doing so simplifies the conceptual model on which queries are based. Few if any dimensions have zero correlation with any other dimensions.

- **Hierarchy**   A particular parent-child organization of members within a dimension. Each distinct set of parents is called a *level* of the hierarchy. For example, a *Time* dimension might have levels named *Year* and *Month*. The *Year* level might have members like *2007* and *2008*, while the *Month* level might have members like *Jan 2007* and *Jan 2008*, with parent members at the *Year* level of *2007* and *2008*. Hierarchies occur naturally in a wide range of applications and are nothing more than a way of grouping members for summarization. A hierarchy reflects the fact that different members of the same dimension represent different levels of detail.

- **Dimension table**   A relational table containing (typically) one row per member of the dimension (depending on what form of history, if any, is maintained in the dimension). A dimension table usually has a minimum of two columns, one representing the key or identifier that uniquely defines members of the dimension and another giving a descriptive name for the member.

- **Fact table**   A relational table that functions, from a data modeling perspective, as an associative entity between various dimensions. It contains one or more measure columns, and key columns of all related dimensions. It is populated (by ETL) in such a way that the measure values are completely described by the related dimensional keys. A fact table is also characterized by its *grain* (defined later in this list), and all measures in the same fact table (should) have the same grain.

- **Star schema**   Based on what an Entity Relationship (E/R) diagram of a fact table and its related dimension tables look like, this has become a generic term for that pattern (discussed later in this section).

- **Grain**   A characteristic of a measure that is defined in terms of its related dimensions. Grain has two properties: first, precisely those dimensions that define the context of the measure; second, for each such dimension, the *level* within a hierarchy from the dimension that defines the level of detail of the measure. These two properties together define the measure's grain. For example, if all measures in a fact table pertain to values of the *Month* level of the *Year-Month* hierarchy of the *Time* dimension, the *Time* grain of that fact table is *Month*. The overall grain of the fact table, referred to as its *granularity*, is defined by such characteristics for all its dimensions.

- **Conformed dimension**   A dimension, as previously defined, that has been designed and built in such a way that each star schema that includes the dimension can be meaningfully joined (logically) on such dimension. From a practical perspective, this means that all occurrences of such dimension in various fact tables mean the same thing—each includes exactly the same members, and each member has exactly the same meaning in relation to the facts whose context it helps define. Kimball refers to this state of affairs as the "Bus Architecture."

  It is not the case that each fact table using the dimension must use it at the same level (if it has a hierarchy). For example, if one fact table is at the *Year* level of the *Time* dimension and another is at the *Month* level, data from the two can still be meaningfully combined—it is simply necessary to aggregate the *Month* data to the level of *Year* first. Without conformed dimensions, various star schemas cannot be meaningfully combined along their common dimensions—in which case, the incremental approach to building up the data warehouse is not possible. Creating conformed dimensions is probably the most difficult part of the Dimensional Model approach, and where it most intersects with the Inmon approach—it is here that organizational agreement about which dimensions can be conformed, and what they will mean, must be secured. This is also where a lack of needed data (that is, at the required grain) in source OpApps will become apparent.

Note   While the term *conformed dimension* concentrates on dimensions, the grain of the measures to be given context by such dimensions is equally important. To define conformed dimensions, there must exist measure definitions whose grain in the proposed conformed dimensions is the same in all existing or contemplated fact tables.

Context and the Star Schema

As mentioned earlier, dimensions provide the context of a measure. Figure 14-3 depicts an imaginary conversation that demonstrates how context is needed to make sense of data.

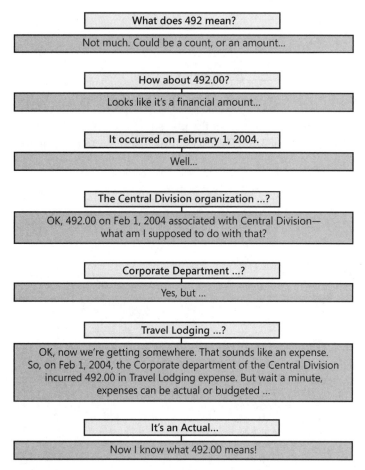

FIGURE 14-3 Determining the context of a measure

> **Note** Actually, do we really now know everything necessary to give 492.00 complete context? Not unless we make a further assumption. Can you guess what? Of course—what *currency* is this in?

Now let's diagram this conversation, as shown in Figure 14-4.

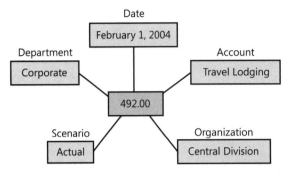

Date
February 1, 2004

Department
Corporate

Account
Travel Lodging

492.00

Scenario
Actual

Organization
Central Division

FIGURE 14-4 A representation of what we know about 492.00 (currency is assumed)

We can examine an actual implementation of the preceding example. Run the code shown in Listing 14-1 against the *AdventureWorksDW2008* sample database to retrieve our exact case.

LISTING 14-1 Querying *AdventureWorksDW2008* for the value of a particular measure

```
USE AdventureWorksDW2008
GO

SELECT
  dd.FullDateAlternateKey,
  do.OrganizationName,
  ddg.DepartmentGroupName,
  da.AccountDescription,
  ds.ScenarioName,
  ff.Amount
FROM
  FactFinance ff
  INNER JOIN DimDate AS dd
   ON ff.DateKey = dd.DateKey
  INNER JOIN DimOrganization AS do
   ON ff.OrganizationKey = do.OrganizationKey
  INNER JOIN DimDepartmentGroup AS ddg
   ON ff.DepartmentGroupKey = ddg.DepartmentGroupKey
  INNER JOIN DimScenario AS ds
   ON ff.ScenarioKey = ds.ScenarioKey
  INNER JOIN DimAccount AS da
   ON ff.AccountKey = da.AccountKey
WHERE
  dd.FullDateAlternateKey = '2/1/2004' AND
  do.OrganizationName = 'Central Division' AND
  ddg.DepartmentGroupName = 'Corporate' AND
  da.AccountDescription = 'Travel Lodging' AND
  ds.scenarioName = 'Actual'
```

Note The sample *AdventureWorksDW2008* database implements a schema that illustrates a Kimball-inspired data warehouse. Refer to this book's Introduction for instructions on locating and downloading this sample database.

From this query and the E/R diagram that represents the tables involved, we can see in Figure 14-5 what is meant by a star schema.

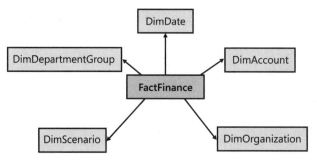

FIGURE 14-5 A star schema from *AdventureWorksDW2008*

Surrogate Keys

The *surrogate key* concept is not original to Kimball or the Dimensional Model, but it is something they strongly advocate. A surrogate key is a system-assigned, typically integer, primary key to a table. In SQL Server, the surrogate key would typically be an identity column, although sometimes a particular architecture might find it preferable to have a central *key generator* that gives out surrogate keys as needed. Surrogate keys have two important characteristics, as follows:

- They have no embedded encodings—that is, they are not "smart" keys. This makes them immune to changes in the source data that would plague nonsurrogate primary keys. One reasonable exception to this is the surrogate key of the *Time* dimension, where making the surrogate integer key smart by representing *YYYYMMDD* (when applicable to the grain of the fact tables) can make partitioning the fact tables much easier.

- As integers, they are the most efficient possible primary keys, both from performance and storage perspectives.

This concludes our brief review of the Kimball approach to data warehousing. You are strongly encouraged to consult the references at the end of this section, as well as appropriate Web searches, for a great deal more information. We'll close here with Figure 14-6, which illustrates what a data warehouse built to Kimball principles looks like. An important aspect to observe in this figure is that the data warehouse *is* the collection of star schemas—there are no separate datamarts, as in the Inmon approach. (And by the way, in an Inmon data warehouse, there is no objection to the datamarts following the Kimball architecture.) Although not shown in this figure, it is assumed that the various star schemas are not *disjoint*, meaning that wherever they share a functional dimension such as *Customer* or *Product*, they have been constructed in such a way as to actually share a single version of the dimension. When this is done, the data in the various star schemas can be validly combined along the common dimensions—a property derived from them having been constructed to be "conformable," in the parlance of the Dimensional Model.

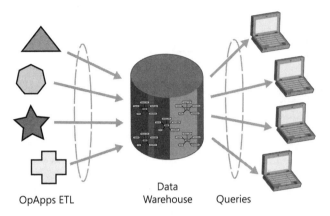

OpApps ETL   Data   Queries
                   Warehouse

FIGURE 14-6 A Kimball-oriented data warehouse

What Data Warehousing Is Not

Much confusion exists in the literature and among practitioners because many terms are regularly conflated with data warehousing, even now when the maturity of the field should preclude this. A charitable view is that this was at least understandable in the past when the field was evolving rapidly in theory, practice, and product. But today, there ought to be more clarity, precision, and common understanding. In furtherance of this, we feel it is worth asserting that there are worthwhile distinctions still represented by certain overused and misused terms. This section provides a brief summary of some of these terms.

OLAP

The term *online analytical processing*, or OLAP, was coined by Dr. E. F. Codd (the originator of the relational model) in 1994 to distinguish a set of properties that analytical applications should satisfy (in contrast with his famous 1985 publication of "12 Rules" that a relational database management system should satisfy; see *http://en.wikipedia.org/wiki/Codd's_12_rules*). The term was intended to draw distinctions between the at-the-time well-known properties of OLTP applications and the less-well-defined properties of analytical applications. It is probably most valuable simply for emphasizing that such a distinction should be made. Today the term can be understood also as referring to a response to the limitations of spreadsheet-based approaches. While not strictly part of the definition, as a practical matter, cube-based technology is now usually associated with OLAP.

> **Note** As with data warehousing, there were OLAP-like efforts long before the term OLAP was coined that were recognizable precursors, going back to the 1960s.

An OLAP application often, although not of necessity, draws its data from some form of star schema. The various OLAP tools on the market today form a spectrum in the degree to which they require a recognizable star schema as their data source. At one end, some tools can deliver OLAP functionality, with relatively simple calculations, from just about any data source with any organization, while at the other end are tools that can use only *cubes* (a data structure designed to facilitate fast analysis, further described in Chapter 15) as their data source (and hopefully can fully exploit their power). A data warehouse is very helpful as the source anywhere on this spectrum and is a virtual necessity on the cube-oriented end of it.

> **More Info** The Fast Analysis of Shared Multidimensional Information (FASMI) test is a more precise, alternative definition of the properties that the term OLAP aspired to distinguish, developed by the authors of *The OLAP Report*. For a detailed definition of FASMI, as well as links to a wealth of other excellent OLAP information (much of it free), see *http://www.olapreport.com/fasmi.htm*.

In the context of SQL Server, Analysis Services is Microsoft's full-featured OLAP engine; it is covered in detail in Chapters 15 through 18.

Data Mining

The traditional way of extracting information from data requires a skilled analyst with a deep understanding of the enterprise who formulates ad hoc queries, the answers to which he or she think would be interesting—for example, "What was the impact of last month's sales promotion on sales?" or "Which stores in the top 10 by sales this year were also in the top 10 by sales last year?" In effect, the analyst forms hypotheses of cause and effect and then tests them against the data. To be effective, this rather hit-or-miss style of information discovery requires tools that permit easily formulating the queries and fast response so that the analyst can maintain his or her train of thought. OLAP technology is ideally suited for this.

In contrast, data mining is an approach in which correlations that might exist in a data set are automatically "discovered" using specialized data models and statistical algorithms. Because it is automated, it is more thorough in finding correlations, and it is unaffected by the prejudices and blind spots that an analyst would have using an ad hoc approach. The analyst still needs to evaluate each correlation found to determine whether it is meaningful or merely correlative, however.

In principle, data mining does not require a data warehouse for its source data. However, a well-crafted data warehouse with clean data could be an ideal source. The intended analysis and the allowable latency also affect whether a data warehouse as an analysis source is feasible. For example, in detecting credit card fraud, is the data warehouse updated often enough to be useful?

Starting with SQL Server 2000, Microsoft has invested much effort in giving SQL Server Analysis Services data mining capabilities that are much easier for relative nonspecialists to use than what has previously been available on the market. These capabilities are covered in detail in Chapter 18.

Business Intelligence

The term *business intelligence* (BI), coined by analyst Howard Dressner in 1989, has turned out to be quite popular. Today it is applied in so many contexts that you would be right to wonder whether it distinguishes anything anymore. Some argue that it doesn't, but we think that it still does. It *is* unfortunate that the *business* in BI obscures the fact that BI can be valuable in any enterprise, not just the for-profit ones implied by the *B*. So as suggested earlier, think *enterprise* intelligence when you hear *business* intelligence.

The most important thing to be clear about is that BI, properly understood, is not about any particular technology—although its implementation certainly depends on technology. BI is fundamentally a management approach and philosophy. Like most good ideas, its basic premise sounds so obvious when stated that it hardly seems worth noting: management decisions should be based on facts, not on educated guesswork, politics, or other subjective bases. Of course, management of an enterprise has always been based at some level on objective information—accounting being the most elemental form. But in the past, such objective measures, especially at the enterprise level, were at a summary level, produced infrequently (if periodically), rigidly structured, and incapable of easily revealing the detail from which they were derived.

BI aims to change all this by ensuring that information is accurate, reliable, updated as frequently as necessary, and readily accessible to whoever needs it, regardless of their level in the organization. One focus of BI *is* on the technologies required to achieve these goals, which generally include some form of data warehouse—hence the association. But the technology focus, especially on user interfaces (UIs), tends to receive disproportionate attention. An equally important focus should be on the vision of fact-based decision making that is supported by senior management and influences the way the enterprise will be run.

Initially, BI often faced significant resistance in the enterprise. If knowledge is power, losing control of knowledge feels like (and often is) losing power. BI threatened this with its emphasis on making information available to a much broader audience. Fortunately by now, the value of BI is recognized in most enterprises.

Last, we must mention that historically, many BI projects and their supporting data warehouse implementations have overpromised and underdelivered, giving BI a bad reputation for being expensive and risky. As a result, some are beginning to rethink the necessity of creating a data warehouse to support BI and instead are using existing reports and other existing data sources directly as BI sources. While this approach has its appeal, only time will tell whether it becomes an important theme in BI implementation.

Dashboards and Scorecards

The terms *dashboard* and *scorecard* are often used synonymously. They both represent information graphically, summarizing it with various elements showing relative magnitudes, trends, and other meaningful relationships. But they are not synonymous.

Dashboards

A dashboard, like its automobile namesake, displays measures without the context of related goals. It has a "just the facts" tactical orientation and is updated as often as necessary for the (typically) operational process that it supports. It is more generic than a proper scorecard in that it can display anything (including a scorecard). Figure 14-7 shows a typical dashboard.

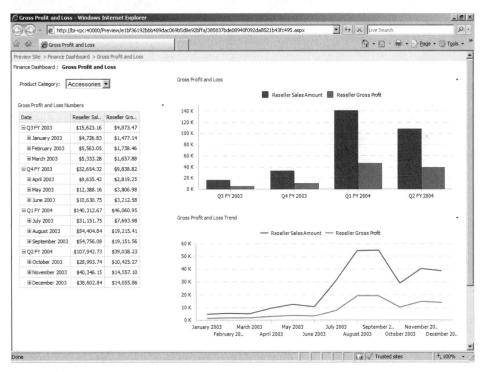

FIGURE 14-7 A typical dashboard

Scorecards

A scorecard displays base measures in the context of related goals, objectives, or target measures and provides at-a-glance visual cues as to whether each such base measure is lagging, achieving, or surpassing its goal measure. Obviously, therefore, a scorecard is not possible unless such goal measures exist in addition to the base measures. A strategy must be devised for such goal measures to exist. It follows that a scorecard is strategic, whereas a dashboard is tactical and operational.

The term *key performance indicator* (KPI) is closely associated with scorecards. The traffic light and trend indicators in Figure 14-8 are KPIs. A KPI encapsulates a measure, a related goal measure, a calculation about the relationship of the two, and a graphic that expresses a "good or bad" indication based on the calculation.

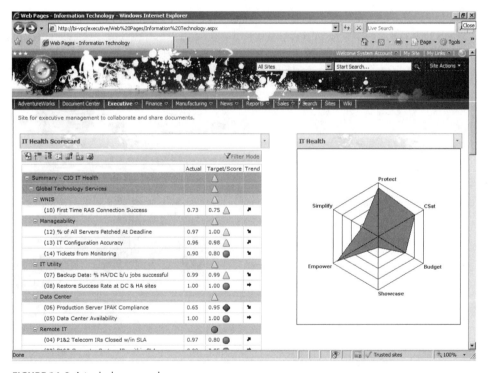

FIGURE 14-8 A typical scorecard

Goal measures are usually not defined at lower levels of detail. Consider the difference in grain between *Actual* and *Plan* measures—the former derive from individual transactions, while the latter are created at a much more summarized level, at least in the *Time* dimension. For this reason, scorecards tend to report at a more summarized level than dashboards, which is consistent with their strategic vs. tactical orientation. This in turn also means that changes occur more slowly, so scorecards are usually refreshed less often than dashboards. In a financial scorecard like the one shown in Figure 14-8, an *Actual* vs. *Plan* KPI exhibits all these principles and is seen as a traffic light in the *Plan* columns. Notice the *Trend* indicator, which is also a KPI that uses some calculation between prior-period *Actual* and *Plan* values.

Since SQL Server 2005, Analysis Services provides KPI objects that can be stored in cubes. They can be consumed and displayed by Microsoft Office Excel 2007, Microsoft Office SharePoint Server, and Microsoft Performance Point, each of which also allows creating and storing KPIs within its respective environment.

> **More Info** See Chapter 16 for advanced OLAP coverage that includes KPIs.

Performance Management

Performance management is a relatively recent term that is a particular flavor of BI but rates its own discussion because of its currency in the literature and market today as a distinct entity. Performance management implies BI—but the converse is not true, because BI is the more general term. As noted earlier, BI's techniques can be focused in many different directions. Performance management is a specific application of BI. It is first about establishing organizational goals and objectives and ways of measuring progress toward meeting them—often using BI techniques to help determine what those goals and measures should be. Once these goals are established, it is then about gathering past, current, and projected performance, explicitly measuring these against the established goals, and widely disseminating how well goals are being met. This is usually achieved in the form of scorecards, which are again facilitated by BI tools and techniques.

The Balanced Scorecard (BSC) is a well-known example of performance management that predates the term. It is worth becoming familiar with the BSC approach, not least because it can help you better understand the factors driving enterprise strategy, and how to ensure that the strategy is enacted.

> **More Info** Start by reading the seminal book that originated the term: *The Balanced Scorecard: Translating Strategy into Action*, by Robert S. Kaplan and David P. Norton (Harvard Business School Press, 1996).

Practical Advice About Data Warehousing

A data warehousing effort requires both theory and discovery. Although the theory associated with building a data warehouse could be considered a rather well understood topic today, practical experience still has much to offer. In this section, we'll look at a few of the data warehousing best practices that we have found most valuable.

Anticipating and Rewarding Operational Process Change

It is almost certain that a data warehousing effort will identify data elements and relationships essential to realizing the enterprise goals that are not currently captured in the operational processes. It is also likely that those who would be most directly affected in their day-to-day work by addressing this will feel that they have nothing to gain by doing so, and often something to lose. For example, an enterprise goal might be to capture which sales groups should get credit, and in what proportion, for working together to make a sale happen—the better to apportion the bonus pool of the sales force. Enabling this requires capturing information about which sales groups were involved at the time the sales transaction is recorded. This is information that is likely not currently available in the workflow of the back-office staff who record the transaction, and moreover, even if it is (or is made to be), the extra time it would take them to record it will reduce the number of transactions they can process per hour. They will most likely resist, given the impact on their productivity, unless this effort is officially recognized and proper incentives are put in place to motivate their cooperation.

Rewarding Giving Up Control

As suggested earlier in this chapter in the section "Business Intelligence," a successful data warehousing/BI effort often requires those who have traditionally been in control of key data to relinquish that control in the interest of the greater good. Any organizational change effort will threaten those who perceive themselves the losers in some way (often correctly), and it is only natural for them to resist the change. If the enterprise recognizes this and provides positive motivators to take this risk, the chances of success are increased. How feasible this is, of course, depends greatly on the organizational culture. The BSC approach can be particularly valuable in this regard.

A Prototype Might Not Work to Sell the Vision

Building a prototype or proof of concept (POC) for a data warehousing/BI approach is often recommended as a way to achieve buy-in from important stakeholders. It is easy to assume that a representative POC will do the trick. By *representative*, we mean that the important technical capabilities are demonstrated as feasible (such as whether particular relationships can be modeled successfully), even if this is illustrated with fictitious data such as the *AdventureWorksDW2008* database.

What you might not realize until it is too late is that stakeholders can find it difficult to appreciate such an approach, particularly when the POC is not based on measures they recognize or the values used are not realistic. If you hear people in your audience calling out "Hey, that number isn't right!" while you are demonstrating the POC, that's exactly what's happening. Logically, in a POC, it might not matter whether the data is accurate, but once your stakeholders lose interest or faith, it can be very difficult to regain. Focusing on such issues is also a favored tactic of those who oppose the data warehouse for whatever reason.

For a POC to have the best chance of success, it should be as realistic and as attuned to the work of the stakeholders who will be judging it as possible. This often runs counter to the idea that a POC requires a minimal investment, which is exactly why we are making this point. The data warehousing project can get shot down before it even gets off the ground with an ill-conceived POC.

Surrogate Key Issues

The value of using integer surrogate keys in a data warehouse was discussed earlier in this chapter in the section "Data Warehouse Design." But their use is not without issues, as described here:

- In general, surrogate keys should not be "smart"—that is, they should not have any significant meaning encoded in their values. However, an exception might be worth considering for the *Time* dimension. At the physical level, there can be value in the *Time* surrogate key taking the form *YYYYMMDD, YYYYMM,* or *YYYYWW* (where *Y, M, D,* and *W* are year, month, day, and week values), all of which are easily represented as an integer. Two reasons justify this violation of the normal best practice. First, if the *Time* surrogate key column is the first in the composite primary key of the fact table (as it usually should be) and the primary key has a clustered index, the fact data will be optimally organized for the *Time* constraint of the typical query—which is usually either a point in time or a range. Second, such a smart *Time* key will make it much easier to implement and maintain physical partitioning of the *Time* dimension at the relational database level.

- Surrogate keys can be generated in several ways, two principal ones being *IDENTITY* columns or a row-by-row assignment facility—for example, *SELECT MAX(Id) + 1*—using appropriate locking mechanisms. Regardless of the method, complications can arise in the typical multienvironment setting—that is, development, quality assurance (QA), and production. Assume that at the start of a development cycle, your development environment is refreshed from production. Then you also copy over ETL input files from production and run the ETL process in development (perhaps as part of a parallel test). Depending on how surrogate keys are assigned, there can be a good chance that the same data (from a business key perspective) is assigned different surrogate keys in development and production. This can greatly complicate reconciliation between the two.

Currency Conversion Issues

Particularly in larger, multinational enterprises, financial applications usually require currency conversion in order to compare similar items (apples to apples). Be aware that this is a subject fraught with business rule and design conundrums. Since SQL Server 2005, Analysis Services has provided features that can make implementation of currency conversion calculations in the cube easier.

But this does not address the issues we want to highlight here, which relate to the tension between designing for ad hoc, not-known-in-advance queries and *needing* to know something, possibly a lot, about likely queries, if a suitable design is to be derived. Issues around currency conversion illustrate this particularly well. There are no "right" answers to the following questions, but you would do well to consider all of them if currency conversion is in any way a part of your business perspective:

- What flexibility is required? Will there be one master currency in which all comparisons are expressed, several standard currencies, or in any existing currency?

- Closely related to the preceding questions, does it make sense to precalculate and store converted amounts, or must this be done on the fly?

   As with all rates and ratios, care must be taken where aggregation is involved to force the currency conversion to be at the appropriate leaf level of detail, followed by aggregation to the required summary level. The capabilities of your OLAP tool influence this greatly.

- Are converted amounts to be at the rate in effect at their original point in time only, or should amounts also be convertible based on the rates at any point in time?

- At what rates should future values (for example, *Budget*) be converted: the rates in effect when the budget is finalized, never after to be adjusted? Or should current rates be used, adjusting the projections every period? Must you be able to distinguish how much of a variance between *Actual* and *Budget* is due to currency conversion vs. changes in the *Budget* measure itself?

The design driven by answers to these business questions has profound effects on both the questions that can be answered later and the technical complexity required.

Events vs. Snapshots

There are two complementary approaches to data warehouse logical design: the event-driven approach and the snapshot approach. Both involve tradeoffs in complexity and in the sort of inquiries they can support.

On the one hand, it can be argued that everything of analytical interest in an enterprise can be represented as an *event*. Events are items like a payment or an order being received or a shipment getting delivered. Events by definition occur asynchronously at points in time. In principle at least, if all relevant events can be identified and captured, it is possible to deduce the state of affairs at any point in time, as well as how that state came to be. For some informational applications, this is critical. Constructing the point in time from events can, however, be exceedingly complex.

On the other hand, a snapshot-based approach does not record events at all. Instead, it simply periodically records the aggregate effect of events. Answering queries about the points in time where snapshots were taken is obviously much easier than it would be with a purely event-based approach, where the state at the point in time would need to be reconstructed.

These approaches sometimes need to be combined. For example, with an *Account* entity, often the only thing of interest is the account balance at periodic points in time, such as month-end. On the other hand, it is also imperative to be able to query each and every event (debit or credit) that affected the balance since the previous snapshot.

Events and snapshots have considerations in addition to which functional questions they support. There is the question of what the source system can provide in terms of either events or snapshots, which has an impact on how much work must be done in the data warehouse ETL to create one or the other. Also, a snapshot approach that takes a snapshot of everything, regardless of how much or little has changed since the last snapshot can lead to data proliferation and can be inefficient compared with an event-based approach when changes are relatively few—although this can be addressed with techniques such as Change Data Capture, detailed later in this chapter.

It is well worth spending considerable time during the design phase thinking through the implications of both approaches before determining the best choices for your requirements.

SQL Server 2008 and Data Warehousing

Earlier versions of SQL Server had new features related to data warehousing, most notably Analysis Services, Reporting Services, and in SQL Server 2005, certain features of SQL Server Integration Services such as the Slowly Changing Dimensions task. But these earlier versions had very little at the level of the relational engine specifically targeting the particular needs of data warehousing. SQL Server 2008 delivers new features that squarely target data warehousing, particularly in relation to making very large databases more manageable and cost effective. This section will review the most important of the data warehousing–oriented enhancements in SQL Server 2008, starting with the Transact-SQL (T-SQL) enhancements aimed at working with data warehousing.

T-SQL *MERGE* Statement

The *MERGE* statement is covered in more depth in Chapter 2 and is applicable to many more scenarios than data warehousing. We cover it here too because it is also very relevant to data warehousing, specifically in the ETL context.

The *MERGE* statement provides what's commonly referred to as *upsert*—meaning *update* the row if it already exists; otherwise, *insert* it. But there is more as well. *MERGE* requires a target table, which is joined in some relationship to a source table. The source table contains the data to be merged or synchronized with the target table. The *MERGE* statement supports up to three types of clauses defining the row-by-row action to be taken on the target table based on how it compares with the source table:

- **WHEN MATCHED**   The row exists in both merge and target tables (performs an inner join and allows *UPDATE* or *DELETE*).

- **WHEN NOT MATCHED BY TARGET**   The row exists in the source table but not the target table (performs a left outer join and allows *INSERT*).

- **WHEN NOT MATCHED BY SOURCE**   The row exists in the target table but not the source table (performs a right outer join and allows *UPDATE* or *DELETE*).

> **More Info**   Each merge clause can also state constraints in addition to the implied join, such as another condition comparing column values between source and target. However, there are some very particular rules governing the use of multiple merge clauses and their various combinations. We cover those in the full treatment given to the new *MERGE* statement in Chapter 2.

In the data warehousing context, the *MERGE* statement is particularly suited to the maintenance of the dimension tables of star schemas. It is also very helpful in maintaining Type 1 slowly changing dimensions (SCDs), where changes simply overlay existing values, and Type 2 SCDs, where *MERGE* can do part of the job (a separate *INSERT* operation is still needed when an existing row is updated, to create the new version of it.) See the section entitled "Data Warehouse Design" earlier in this chapter for more details. (A full treatment of SCDs is beyond the scope of this chapter.)

In SQL Server 2008 Integration Services, *MERGE* can streamline and simplify the insert/update pattern that would be required under SQL Server 2005 Integration Services. Previously, the decision to insert or update in SQL Server 2005 Integration Services had to be based on a lookup of the source row using a Lookup task that was loaded with the target rows and two output data flows based on the failure or success of the lookup: one doing inserts and one doing updates against the target. With *MERGE*, the Lookup task is no longer needed, which simplifies the Integration Services package and avoids the performance, memory, and deadlock issues that can arise with the Lookup task if the target table is large.

Syntactically, *MERGE* requires two joinable tables or table-equivalents. (The target must be either a table or an updatable view; the source can be any table-equivalent.) For Integration Services, this means that the source table must exist or must be created in the package (as a temporary table, common table expression [CTE], or other equivalent).

The code in Listing 14-2 shows a series of representative T-SQL expressions using *MERGE* against the *AdventureWorksDW2008* database. Run each statement by hand as directed by the comments, followed by running the *MERGE* statement at the end. Note that *GeographyKey* is an identity column in *DimGeography*, so the column list must be explicit in the *INSERT* statement in the *MERGE* statement's *WHEN NOT MATCHED BY TARGET* clause. Also note that the ending semicolon is required to terminate the *MERGE* statement.

More Info All the data manipulation language (DML) statements in T-SQL (*INSERT, UPDATE, DELETE,* and *MERGE*) support an *OUTPUT* clause, which can be quite useful for archiving changed data. In addition, the new INSERT OVER DML feature in SQL Server 2008 enhances the *OUTPUT* clause with filtering capabilities. See Chapter 2 for details of the *OUTPUT* clause and INSERT OVER DML.

LISTING 14-2 Using *MERGE* for a data warehousing update

```
USE AdventureWorksDW2008
GO

-- Make a copy of the table.
SELECT * INTO DimGeographyTest FROM DimGeography

-- Create "Changes" table as another copy of same data.
SELECT * INTO Changes FROM DimGeography

-- If you now run the MERGE statement below, no changes will be reported. Note
-- the condition on the UPDATE clause, which prevents unnecessary updates.

-- Now force some UPDATES (53):

UPDATE Changes
 SET SalesTerritoryKey = 11
 WHERE SalesTerritoryKey = 10

-- Now running MERGE reports 53 updates.

-- Now force DELETES (empty table will effectively delete every row in
-- DimGeographyTest):

DELETE Changes

-- Now running MERGE will delete all 653 rows in DimGeographyTest.

-- Testing INSERT is left as an exercise for the reader.

-- MERGE statement:

MERGE DimGeographyTest AS dg
 USING (SELECT * FROM Changes) AS c
 ON dg.GeographyKey = c.GeographyKey
 WHEN MATCHED and dg.SalesTerritoryKey <> c.SalesTerritoryKey THEN
  UPDATE SET dg.SalesTerritoryKey = c.SalesTerritoryKey
 WHEN NOT MATCHED BY TARGET THEN
  INSERT (City, StateProvinceCode, StateProvinceName,
          CountryRegionCode, EnglishCountryRegionName,
          SpanishCountryRegionName, FrenchCountryRegionName,
          PostalCode, SalesTerritoryKey)
```

```
    VALUES (c.City, c.StateProvinceCode, c.StateProvinceName,
            c.CountryRegionCode, c.EnglishCountryRegionName,
            c.SpanishCountryRegionName, c.FrenchCountryRegionName,
            c.PostalCode, c.SalesTerritoryKey)
WHEN NOT MATCHED BY SOURCE THEN
  DELETE
OUTPUT $action, INSERTED.*, DELETED.*;
```

The deletion possibilities of *MERGE* would be rare in a data warehousing scenario except in single-instance fixes of erroneous data, but it is worth knowing about for that purpose alone. In general, beware of using *DELETE* with *MERGE*. If your source table is inadvertently empty (as it is eventually in our example), *MERGE* with a *WHEN NOT MATCHED BY SOURCE* clause specifying *DELETE* could unintentionally delete every row in the target (depending on what other conditions were in the *WHEN NOT MATCHED BY SOURCE* clause).

Change Data Capture

Like one use of *MERGE*, the new Change Data Capture (CDC) feature in SQL Server 2008 targets the ETL component of data warehousing. CDC is available only in the Enterprise edition of SQL Server 2008 (and of course, the functionally equivalent Developer and Evaluation editions).

> **Note** SQL Server 2008 provides a number of change tracking features—each one tailored for a specific purpose. In particular, CDC addresses data warehousing, SQL Server Audit addresses security (see Chapter 5), and SQL Server Change Tracking targets synchronization of occasionally connected systems and mobile devices using ADO.NET Sync Services (see Chapter 13).

CDC is designed to efficiently capture and record relevant changes in the context of a data warehouse. Traditionally, detecting changes in an OpApp table that need to be applied to a data warehouse has required relatively brute force methods such as the following:

- For updates, using the *CHECKSUM* function as a shortcut to detecting inequality of columns between source and target rows (SQL Server only), or comparing time stamps.

- For inserts, outer-joining source and target rows and testing for *NULL* on the target.

- For inserts and updates, implementing triggers on the source table to detect changes and take appropriate action against the target, or performing a lookup (perhaps using an Integration Services Lookup task) to compare source against target and then driving the update or insert by the success or failure of the lookup.

- For inserts and updates, using the *OUTPUT* clause (SQL Server 2005 and 2008) or INSERT OVER DML (SQL Server 2008 only), which we cover in Chapter 2.

The CDC feature introduced in SQL Server 2008 provides a valuable new way of laying the groundwork for maintaining changing data in a data warehouse. Without resorting to triggers or other custom code, it allows capturing changes that occur to a table into a separate SQL Server Change Tracking table (the *change table*). This table can then be queried by an ETL process to incrementally update the data warehouse as appropriate. Querying the change table rather than the tracked table itself means that the ETL process does not affect the performance of applications that work with the transactional tables of your database in any way. CDC is driven by a SQL Server Agent job that recognizes changes by monitoring the SQL Server transaction log. This provides much better performance than using triggers, especially in bulk load scenarios typical in a data warehouse—and there's no code to write or maintain with CDC. The tradeoff is somewhat more latency, which in a data warehouse is often perfectly acceptable. Figure 14-9 depicts a high-level view of CDC architecture using an illustration taken from SQL Server Books Online.

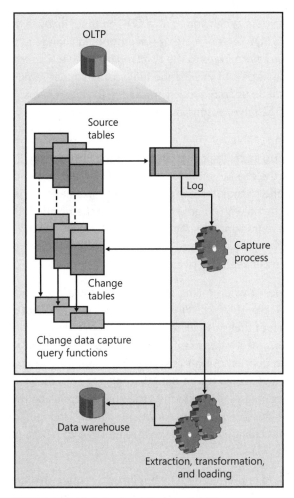

FIGURE 14-9 High-level architecture of CDC

Several new system stored procedures and table-valued functions (TVFs) are provided to enable, monitor, and consume SQL Server Change Tracking output. To begin, you execute the *sp_cdc_enable_db* procedure to enable CDC on the current database. (You must be in the *sysadmin* role to do this.) When you run this procedure, a new *cdc* user, *cdc* schema, and *CDC_admin* role are created. These names are hard-coded, so in the event that you already have a user or schema named *cdc*, you will need to rename it before using CDC.

Once the database is CDC-enabled, you enable CDC on a given table by executing *sp_cdc_enable_table*. (You must be in the *db_owner* role to do this.) When you do that, several objects are created in the *cdc* schema: a change table and at least one (but possibly two) TVFs. Let's look at each of these objects in turn.

When CDC is enabled on a table, SQL Server creates a change table in the *cdc* schema corresponding to the table on which CDC is being enabled. The change table will be populated with change data automatically by CDC and is assigned a name based on both the schema and the table being tracked. For example, when you enable CDC on the *Employee* table in the *dbo* schema (as we'll do shortly), SQL Server creates a corresponding change table named *cdc.dbo_Employee_CT* that will record all changes to the *dbo.Employee* table. The schema of the tracked table (*dbo* in this case) is part of the change table name so that same-named tables from different schemas can all be unambiguously tracked in the *cdc* schema. It is also possible to explicitly name the change table, as long as it's unique in the database.

The ETL process will query this change table for change data in order to populate your data warehouse, but it will not normally do so by selecting directly from it. Instead, the ETL process will call a special TVF to query the change table for you. This TVF is also created for you by SQL Server automatically when the change table is created, and—like the change table—the TVF is also created in the *cdc* schema with a name based on the schema and table name of the tracked table. So again, if we're tracking the *dbo.Employee* table, SQL Server creates a TVF named *cdc.fn_cdc_get_all_changes_dbo_Employee* that accepts parameters to select all changes that occur to *dbo.Employee* between any two desired points in time.

If you specify *@supports_net_changes=1* when calling *sp_cdc_enable_table*, a second TVF is created for the change table as well. Like the first TVF, this one allows you to select changes between any two points in time, except that this TVF returns just the *net* (final) changes that occurred during that time frame. This means, for example, that if a row was added and then deleted within the time frame being queried using this second TVF, data for that row would not be returned—whereas the first TVF would return data that reflects both the insert and the delete. This second TVF is named in a similar fashion as the first, except using the word *net* instead of *all*. For *dbo.Employee*, this TVF is named *cdc.fn_cdc_get_net_changes_dbo_Employee*. Note that querying for net changes requires the tracked table to have a primary key or unique index.

Neither of these TVFs accept start and end times directly but instead require the range to be expressed as log sequence numbers (LSNs) by first calling *sys.fn_cdc_map_time_to_lsn*. So to query between two points in time, you call *sys.fn_cdc_map_time_to_lsn* twice—once for the start time and once for the end time—and then use the LSN values returned by this function as input values to the TVFs for querying change data. This might seem unnecessarily cumbersome, but in fact has good reason related to supporting two change tables on the same table, one feeding the production systems and another supporting ongoing development.

> **Tip** The start and end times this function is called with are not required to fall within the range of time actually represented in the log. If either time falls outside the boundaries in the log, the function "does the right thing": it returns the earliest existing LSN if the specified start time is prior to the earliest LSN, and it returns the latest existing LSN if the specified end time is after the latest LSN. This will be implicitly illustrated shortly in Listing 14-3 for both start and end times.

The *sp_cdc_enable_table* stored procedure has several optional parameters that give you a lot of flexibility. You can, among other options, specify your own name for the change table, a role that a user must belong to in order to query changes (if not in *sysadmin* or *db_owner*), which columns of the table should be tracked (you don't need to track all of them), the filegroup on which to create the change table, and whether the *SWITCH_PARTITION* option of *ALTER TABLE* can be executed against the tracked table (which has very important implications). Consult SQL Server Books Online for more details of *sp_cdc_enable_table* parameters.

When you no longer require CDC on a particular table, you can call the *sp_cdc_disable_table* stored procedure on the table. This procedure drops the change table and the TVFs and updates the system metadata to reflect that the table is no longer tracked. When you no longer require CDC on the database, call the *sp_cdc_disable_db* stored procedure to completely disable CDC for the entire database.

> **Important** You should be aware of several considerations before dropping a database on which CDC has been enabled. To drop a CDC-enabled database, you must either stop SQL Server Agent or first disable CDC by running *sp_cdc_disable_db* on the database to be dropped. If you take the former approach, the SQL Server Agent jobs will be deleted automatically when SQL Server Agent is next started upon detecting that the database the jobs were associated with is no longer present. Of course, SQL Server Change Tracking for other databases running on the server instance will also be suspended while SQL Server Agent is stopped. The latter approach is the preferred method, since it does not interfere with other CDC-enabled databases and will remove all CDC artifacts related to the database being dropped.

The change table records all changes to the requested columns, including intermediate states (per DML statement) between two points in time. Note that CDC supports sparse columns (covered later in this section) but not sparse column sets. Each change table row also includes five metadata columns of great value for change-consuming processes to determine what type of change (insert, update, or delete) each row represents and to group and order all changes belonging to the same transaction. One item it *cannot* capture is who made the change, which is why it is not ideal for maintaining audit trails. For that, you can use SQL Server Audit, which will track and record which users are performing data modifications as well as any other activity of interest. (We cover SQL Server Audit in Chapter 5.)

As we mentioned earlier, CDC relies on SQL Server Agent for automating the capture process. The first time *sp_cdc_enable_table* is executed on any table in a database, SQL Server also creates two SQL Server Agent jobs for that database. The first is a change-capture job, which performs the actual transaction log monitoring to apply changes on the tracked table to the corresponding change table. The second is a cleanup job, which deletes rows from change tables after a configurable interval (three days, by default) and removes all CDC artifacts if the tracked table is dropped. Therefore, SQL Server Agent must be running the first time this procedure is run to CDC-enable a table on any database in the server instance. Subsequently, if SQL Server Agent stops running, changes to tracked tables will accumulate in the transaction log but not be applied to the change tables until SQL Server Agent is restarted.

CDC can at first appear rather cumbersome to use, but it is well thought out in terms of its configuration flexibility and support for various scenarios. Some of these might not be immediately obvious—for example, what happens if a tracked table is dropped, or its structure changed, after CDC is enabled on it? We lack the space to delve into these essential aspects, but you'll find comprehensive details in SQL Server Books Online. The code in Listing 14-3 shows a complete example of using CDC.

LISTING 14-3 Using Change Data Capture

```
-- Create test database
CREATE DATABASE CDCDemo
GO

USE CDCDemo
GO

-- Enable CDC on the database
EXEC sp_cdc_enable_db

-- Show CDC-enabled databases
SELECT name, is_cdc_enabled FROM sys.databases

-- View the new "cdc" user and schema
SELECT * FROM sys.schemas WHERE name = 'cdc'
SELECT * FROM sys.database_principals WHERE name = 'cdc'

-- Create Employee table
CREATE TABLE Employee(
  EmployeeId    int NOT NULL PRIMARY KEY,
  EmployeeName  varchar(100) NOT NULL,
  EmailAddress  varchar(200) NOT NULL)

-- Enable CDC on the table (SQL Server Agent *should* be running when you run this)
```

```
EXEC sp_cdc_enable_table
 @source_schema = N'dbo',
 @source_name = N'Employee',
 @role_name = N'CDC_admin',
 @capture_instance = N'dbo_Employee',
 @supports_net_changes = 1

-- Show CDC-enabled tables
SELECT name, is_tracked_by_cdc FROM sys.tables

-- Insert some employees...
INSERT INTO Employee VALUES(1, 'John Smith', 'john.smith@ourcorp.com')
INSERT INTO Employee VALUES(2, 'Dan Park', 'dan.park@ourcorp.com')
INSERT INTO Employee VALUES(3, 'Jay Hamlin', 'jay.hamlin@ourcorp.com')
INSERT INTO Employee VALUES(4, 'Jeff Hay', 'jeff.hay@ourcorp.com')

-- Select them from the table and the change capture table
SELECT * FROM Employee
SELECT * FROM cdc.dbo_employee_ct

-- Delete Jeff
DELETE Employee WHERE EmployeeId = 4

-- Results from Delete
SELECT * FROM Employee
SELECT * FROM cdc.dbo_employee_ct
-- (Note: result of DELETE may take several seconds to show up in CT table)

-- Update Dan and Jay
UPDATE Employee SET EmployeeName = 'Dan P. Park' WHERE EmployeeId = 2
UPDATE Employee SET EmployeeName = 'Jay K. Hamlin' WHERE EmployeeId = 3

-- Results from update
SELECT * FROM Employee
SELECT * FROM cdc.dbo_employee_ct       -- See note above

-- Give the CDC job a chance to initialize before accessing the TVFs
WAITFOR DELAY '00:00:20'

-- To access change data, use the CDC TVFs, not the change tables directly
DECLARE @begin_time datetime
DECLARE @end_time datetime
DECLARE @from_lsn binary(10)
DECLARE @to_lsn binary(10)
SET @begin_time = GETDATE() - 1
SET @end_time = GETDATE()

-- Map the time interval to a CDC LSN range
SELECT @from_lsn =
 sys.fn_cdc_map_time_to_lsn('smallest greater than or equal', @begin_time)

SELECT @to_lsn =
 sys.fn_cdc_map_time_to_lsn('largest less than or equal', @end_time)

SELECT @begin_time AS BeginTime, @end_time AS EndTime
```

```
SELECT @from_lsn AS FromLSN, @to_lsn AS ToLSN

-- Return the changes occurring within the query window.

-- First, all changes that occurred...
SELECT *
 FROM cdc.fn_cdc_get_all_changes_dbo_employee(@from_lsn, @to_lsn, N'all')

-- Then, net changes, that is, final state...
SELECT *
 FROM cdc.fn_cdc_get_net_changes_dbo_employee(@from_lsn, @to_lsn, N'all')
```

Let's examine this code closely. After creating our sample database *CDCDemo*, we enable CDC on that database by calling *EXEC sp_cdc_enable_db*. The next several *SELECT* queries demonstrate how to retrieve various kinds of CDC-related information. The first *SELECT* query shows how the *is_cdc_enabled* column in *sys.databases* returns true (*1*) or false (*0*), making it easy to find out which databases are CDC-enabled and which aren't. The next two *SELECT* queries show how the new *cdc* schema and user can be found in *sys.schemas* and *sys. database_principals*.

The code then proceeds to create the *Employee* table, which has only three columns to keep our example simple. CDC is then enabled on the *Employee* table by calling *EXEC sp_cdc_enable_table* and passing parameters that identify the *Employee* table in the *dbo* schema for change capture. (Remember that SQL Server Agent must be running at this point.) The next *SELECT* statement shows how to query the *is_tracked_by_cdc* column in *sys.tables* to find out which tables are CDC-enabled and which aren't.

Recall that enabling CDC on the *Employee* table creates a TVF for retrieving all changes made to the table between any two points in time. Recall too that by specifying *@supports_net_changes = 1*, this also creates a second TVF for retrieving only the *net* changes made between any two points in time. The difference between *all* changes and *net* changes will be very clear in a moment, when we call both of these TVFs and compare their results. But first the code performs a mix of *INSERT*, *UPDATE*, and *DELETE* operations against the *Employee* table to simulate database activity and engage the capture process. In Listing 14-3, these operations are accompanied by *SELECT* statements that query the change table *cdc.dbo_employee_ct*. This is done purely to demonstrate that change data for the *Employee* table is being captured to the change table. However, you should normally not query the change tables directly in this manner and should instead use the generated TVFs to extract change information about the *Employee* table, as demonstrated by the rest of the code.

Our code then executes a *WAITFOR* statement to pause for 20 seconds before calling the TVFs, in order to give the SQL Server Agent change capture job a chance to initialize. This is a one-time latency only; it does *not* represent the normal latency for CDC-tracked changes to be recorded, which is on the order of 2 to 3 seconds. Without this delay, or if SQL Server

Agent is not running when you call the TVFs, you will receive a rather misleading error message that unfortunately does not describe the actual problem.

To call either of the generated TVFs, you need to provide a value range that defines the window of time during which you want change data returned. As already explained, this range is expressed using LSN values, which you can obtain by calling *sys.fn_cdc_map_time_to_lsn* and passing in the desired start and end points in time. So first we establish a time range for the past 24 hours, which we obtain by assigning *GETDATE() – 1* and *GETDATE()* to the start and end time variables. Then we call *sys.fn_cdc_map_time_to_lsn* on the start and end time variables to obtain the LSN values corresponding to the last 24 hours. (Note that the starting LSN gets adjusted automatically to compensate for the fact that there are no LSNs from 24 hours ago, as does the ending LSN, since there might not be any from a moment ago either.) We then issue two *SELECT* statements so that we can view the time and LSN range values, an example of which is shown here:

```
BeginTime               EndTime
----------------------- -----------------------
2008-07-08 23:42:55.567 2008-07-09 23:42:55.567

(1 row(s) affected)

FromLSN                ToLSN
---------------------- ----------------------
0x0000001A0000001E0039 0x00000020000000A50001

(1 row(s) affected)
```

Equipped with the LSN range values, we issue two more *SELECT* statements. (These are the last two statements in Listing 14-3.) The first statement queries the range against the *all* changes TVF, and the second statement queries the range against the *net* changes TVF. Comparing the results of these two queries clearly illustrates the difference between the TVFs, as shown here:

```
__$start_lsn            __$seqval              __$operation __$update_mask EmployeeId
EmployeeName      EmailAddress
---------------------- ---------------------- ------------ -------------- ---------- -------
---------- ------------------------
0x0000001E0000007C0013 0x0000001E0000007C0012 2            0x07           1          John
Smith      john.smith@ourcorp.com
0x0000001E000000800003 0x0000001E000000800002 2            0x07           2          Dan
Park       dan.park@ourcorp.com
0x0000001E000000810003 0x0000001E000000810002 2            0x07           3          Jay
Hamlin     jay.hamlin@ourcorp.com
0x0000001E000000820003 0x0000001E000000820002 2            0x07           4          Jeff
Hay        jeff.hay@ourcorp.com
0x0000001E000000850004 0x0000001E000000850002 1            0x07           4          Jeff
Hay        jeff.hay@ourcorp.com
0x0000001E000001AC0004 0x0000001E000001AC0002 4            0x02           2          Dan P.
Park       dan.park@ourcorp.com
0x0000001E000001AE0004 0x0000001E000001AE0002 4            0x02           3          Jay K.
```

Hamlin   jay.hamlin@ourcorp.com

(7 row(s) affected)

__$start_lsn	__$operation	__$update_mask	EmployeeId	EmployeeName	EmailAddress
0x0000001E0000007C0013	2	NULL	1	John Smith	john.smith@ourcorp.com
0x0000001E000001AC0004	2	NULL	2	Dan P. Park	steven.jones@ourcorp.com
0x0000001E000001AE0004	2	NULL	3	Jay K. Hamlin	jay.hamlin@ourcorp.com

(3 row(s) affected)

The first result set includes all the information about all changes made during the specified LSN range, including all interim changes. Thus, the information returned from the first *all* changes TVF shows every stage of change, or seven changes in total. In our scenario, John was inserted once and then never changed. So only his insert (__$operation value 2) is shown. Dan and Jay were inserted (__$operation value 2) and updated (__$operation value 4), so both changes (insert and update) are returned for each of them. Jeff, on the other hand, was deleted (__$operation value 1) after being inserted, so both changes (insert and delete) are returned for Jeff.

The second result set includes only the *final* changes made during the specified LSN range. So for the same LSN range, we receive only three change records from the second *net* changes TVF, each of which provides the final column values in the specified LSN range. John appears only once as in the previous query, since he was inserted only once and never modified or deleted within the LSN range. However, although Dan and Jay were inserted and updated, they each appear only once (with their final values for the LSN range), and not twice as in the previous query. And since Jeff was inserted and deleted within the window of time specified by the LSN range, no change data for Jeff is returned at all by the *net* changes TVF.

Partitioned Table Parallelism

In SQL Server, a *partitioned table* is a table whose physical storage is divided horizontally (that is, as subsets of rows) into multiple filegroups (invisibly to queries and DML) for the purpose of improved manageability and isolation of various kinds of otherwise potentially conflicting access. For example, different partitions of the same table can have different backup and compression strategies and indexes, each optimized to the use of the partition. Given the large size of many data warehouses, this flexibility can be invaluable.

The typical (although by no means required) partition key is *Time*, since that is so often the natural horizontal dividing line. Partitioning by *Time* allows, for example, "old" data to be indexed more lightly than current, more frequently accessed data. Old data can also be backed up and deleted without affecting simultaneous queries against more recent data. Partitioning is an important tool of physical implementation, particularly when building a very large data warehouse.

Another potential benefit of well-designed partitioning is more efficient query plans. Queries specifying the partitioning key that involve only a single partition benefit from having less data to traverse (and potentially more optimized indexes if the partition is for newer data). In addition, when SQL Server is running on multiple-core or multiple-CPU hardware and configured appropriately, multiple worker threads are available and can achieve parallelism in processing a query by assigning multiple threads to it.

> **Note** For maximum partitioning benefit, it is crucial to physically isolate each partition of a table from each of the others. In practice, this means that each filegroup of each partition should be on a different physical disk and, in extreme cases, even on a different disk controller. In general, however, this book does not explain the mechanics of partitioned tables, which are well covered in SQL Server Books Online.

Thread Management

SQL Server 2005 optimized parallelism for queries involving only a single partition, by allocating all available threads to the one partition. However, on a multipartition query, performance could suffer badly because then only one thread is allocated per partition—leading to some parallelism for the query as a whole but none per partition. The result was that queries varying only slightly in their partitioning key constraint could exhibit vastly different degrees of performance.

The new Partitioned Table Parallelism feature in SQL Server 2008 directly addresses this shortcoming by allocating all available threads to a multipartition query in round-robin fashion. The result is that each partition, as well as the query as a whole, achieves some degree of parallelism. This is automatic when applicable. The best gains will be achieved when the number of threads (that is, cores or CPUs) is significantly larger than the number of partitions on the table. The difference between SQL Server 2005 and 2008 in thread allocation for multipartition queries is illustrated in Figure 14-10. Under the latter in this example, three times as many threads per partition operate on the Feb YTD query, and with all else being equal, this should translate to a 200 percent performance improvement.

SQL Server 2005

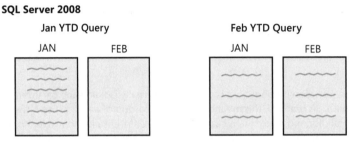

SQL Server 2008

FIGURE 14-10 The difference between SQL Server 2005 and 2008 in how threads are allocated to multipartition queries

> **Note** Partitioned Table Parallelism is available only in the Enterprise edition of SQL Server 2008.

Lock Escalation

Another important feature of Partitioned Table Parallelism relates to table locking behavior. Previously, when deciding whether to elevate to a table-level lock on a partitioned table, the database engine did not take into account whether concurrent statements against the same table were each accessing a different partition. When they were, each was logically independent and there would be no reason for one to block another. But by not recognizing this and escalating one of the statements to a table lock, the database engine could unnecessarily block the remaining statements, in the process also enhancing the possibility of deadlocks among them. In SQL Server 2008, the default behavior on a partitioned table behaves as before, but Partitioned Table Parallelism enables a new *ALTER TABLE* option, which directs the database engine to use partition-level lock escalation, instead of table-level, on a partitioned table. The syntax is shown here:

```
ALTER TABLE MyTable SET (LOCK_ESCALATION = <option>)
```

The *LOCK_ESCALATION* option can be specified as *TABLE, AUTO,* or *DISABLE*. The default is *TABLE,* which means that only table-level lock escalation will occur. If you specify *AUTO,* you get partition-level locking on partitioned tables, table-level otherwise. With *DISABLE,* no lock escalation will occur (in most cases).

Star-Join Query Optimization

Star-Join Query Optimization is an important new feature in SQL Server 2008 (again, available in Enterprise edition only) in the context of data warehouse–oriented performance enhancements, but it does not lend itself to deep explanation in a book like this because it does not offer any user-adjustable properties and its operation is largely buried within the database engine. The good news is that you need not do anything to get the benefit of it when applicable.

As noted earlier, the star schema is a common physical data model in Kimball-style data warehousing architectures. Queries against such a physical model are typically characterized by a central fact table joined to multiple dimension tables, each on single-column equijoins (joins based on equality), where the fact table has much higher cardinality than the dimension tables (more rows in the fact table as compared with the dimension table), and the constraints of the query are all on the dimension tables—a pattern now known as a *star-join.* Since this pattern is common across a large range of data warehousing scenarios, it became apparent that a query optimizer that could recognize such a pattern could potentially produce more efficient query plans than otherwise.

Here's the basic idea. Eliminate as many candidate rows from the fact table as early as possible in the query-resolution pipeline, since the fact table typically has by far the highest cardinality of the tables involved. In practice, this means determining the candidate join keys from the dimension tables first (taking advantage of the winnowing effect of the constraints typically on them) and then using this information to eliminate candidate rows from the fact table ahead of, and more efficiently than, the actual join process further down the pipeline would. The heuristics—or in other words the rules by which the optimizer recognizes a star-join query—are important to the effectiveness of this strategy.

Such mechanisms are complex and, for our purposes, largely opaque. SQL Server 2005 introduced some star-join optimization based on these principles, but SQL Server 2008 extends the degree to which it can recognize and optimize this pattern. Microsoft benchmarks assert that the degree of performance improvement on typical data warehouse queries at which this feature is targeted can range from 10% to 30%. The SQL Server 2008 enhancements in this area also include more detailed information in query plans, which help the designer to understand when or if this feature is being applied to particular queries.

> **Note** This enhancement will be of most value when a significant part of the SQL Server work-load involves ad hoc SQL queries against a star schema. If your architecture directs most ad hoc queries to an OLAP cube, it will be of lesser, if any, benefit, unless your cube is hosted by SQL Server Analysis Services and uses the Relational OLAP (ROLAP) or Hybrid OLAP (HOLAP) storage mode (since in these cases a significant number of cube queries might become SQL star schema queries).

Space considerations preclude us from discussing this feature in more detail here. To learn more, we recommend that you visit the links provided at the end of this section.

SPARSE Columns

Not all practitioners are happy with *NULL* values in a relational database schema, but for better or worse, they are widely used in practice. Without engaging that debate, some will rationalize allowing nullable columns when physically modeling a type (for example, *Product*) that has many subtypes that have few attributes in common and many attributes unique to each subtype. It can be convenient, despite going against the grain of normalization, to physically model this situation as a single table with a column for every attribute across all subtypes. In such a case, each attribute column must be nullable and will be sparse—that is, containing *NULL* in a high percentage of cases. It would be beneficial if the storage for such sparsely populated nullable columns were optimized, particularly in the data warehousing context, given the often large database sizes involved.

In versions earlier than SQL Server 2008, storing *NULL* values was not optimized—it required storage for every *NULL* occurrence. SQL Server 2008 introduces the notion of the *SPARSE* column, a nullable column whose storage is optimized for *NULL* values—at the cost of increased storage overhead for non-*NULL* values. With this option enabled, occurrences of *NULL* use no storage. (Note that this is also true when SQL Server Data Compression, detailed in the next section, is used—although the two are not equivalent.) The density of a column's *NULL* values required to achieve a 40 percent space saving using the *SPARSE* attribute, the nominal space saving value as reported by SQL Server Books Online, depends on the column's data type and ranges from 42 percent for 38-digit high-precision numeric types to 98 percent for *bit*. The *SPARSE* attribute in particular benefits Microsoft Office SharePoint Server, which by its generic and end-user-driven nature is a particular case of the preceding scenario—needing to store many user-defined attributes that are sparse by nature.

A few data types cannot be *SPARSE*, and there are other, potentially significant, restrictions on using *SPARSE* columns—for example, they cannot have default values or rules or be part of a clustered index or unique primary key index. SQL Server Books Online provides full details.

This feature is enabled by decorating column definitions in your *CREATE TABLE* and *ALTER TABLE* statements with the new *SPARSE* attribute. Obviously, the column must also be declared *NULL*. Listing 14-4 shows an example of usage.

LISTING 14-4 Declaring *SPARSE* columns

```
CREATE TABLE SparseTest
(ID        int IDENTITY(1,1),
 LastName varchar(50) SPARSE NULL,
 Salary   decimal(9,2) NULL)
GO

ALTER TABLE SparseTest
 ALTER COLUMN Salary decimal(9,2) SPARSE
GO
```

SQL Server 2008 introduces two other new features that have a relationship to the *SPARSE* feature but do not depend on it. The first is the *column set*, an optionally declared set of specified columns on a table that, once declared, associates an *xml* column with the table as metadata (that is, no additional storage is used). This column represents the specified columns as an XML document and allows querying *and* updating of the columns as a group using XQuery and XML DML (which we cover in depth in Chapter 6). The individual columns can still be referenced in the usual way, but the column set representation can be a more convenient method when a table has a large number of columns and might provide performance improvements in some cases. *SPARSE* columns relate to column sets in that a column set cannot be added to an existing table already containing any *SPARSE* columns, and if *SPARSE* columns are later added to a table with a column set, they automatically become part of the column set.

The second new feature is the *filtered index*. A filtered index is an optimized nonclustered index whose declaration includes a *WHERE* clause that restricts the values included in the index to those specified. This can have wide-ranging implications for index maintenance, index storage, and query plan optimization. This feature is most useful when the query patterns against the table are well understood and they naturally relate to distinct subsets of rows. *SPARSE* columns are good candidates to participate in a filtered index because they represent distinct, well-defined subsets (rows with *NULL*s in the columns and rows with non-*NULL*s). For more details of both these features, which involve considerable complexity in their own right, see SQL Server Books Online.

A final benefit of *SPARSE* columns is that, by their nature, they can reduce the size of large backups, potentially more so than any of the new compression features we cover in the next section.

Data Compression and Backup Compression

Data compression and backup compression are long-awaited enhancements to SQL Server—not surprisingly, also available only in the Enterprise edition (with one exception, as we'll see when we discuss backup compression). They are of benefit in all scenarios, but especially for large data warehouses. Many factors cause a data warehouse to grow at least linearly with time: the desire to facilitate trend analyses, personalization, and data mining; the fact that most data warehouses increase the number of data sources included over time; and last that multiple copies of the data warehouse often exist for redundancy and development and QA purposes. SQL Server 2008 provides both data compression, targeting the database itself, and backup compression, targeting the backup/restore process.

As the size of the data warehouse increases, it affects the cost and complexity of maintaining the online version and of taking backups of it. SQL Server 2008 Data Compression provides many benefits. It aids online query performance by increasing the number of rows stored per page, lessening disk I/O and saving costs in disk space. It improves performance for a given amount of memory, as more rows can be held in memory at the same time. It can benefit the backup/restore process by minimizing the I/O and therefore time and media required, since less physical data needs to be transferred. Last, replication and mirroring scenarios can also benefit for all the same reasons.

Data Compression

SQL Server 2005 made a start at targeting data compression concerns with both its table-level *vardecimal* storage format (in Service Pack 2 for the Enterprise edition) and its ability to use NTFS file system file compression on SQL Server read-only secondary data files (or all files, including log files, if the database is read-only).

These enhancements remain supported in SQL Server 2008, although use of the *vardecimal* option is deprecated and use of NTFS compression for SQL Server data files is mostly not rec-ommended. Instead, SQL Server 2008 goes considerably beyond these earlier enhancements in the features it provides for data compression.

The most basic form of data compression uses a storage format that eliminates unneeded precision in fixed-length data types—that is, representing each value in a column with the minimal number of bits necessary. For example, any value of 255 or less stored in an integer data type could be stored in one byte instead of four (neglecting some slight overhead). SQL Server 2005 provided such compression or variable-length storage only for the *decimal* and *numeric* data types, but SQL Server 2008 provides it for *all* formerly fixed-length data types (including *decimal* and *numeric*). Note that what is changing is storage format, not data type, so the semantics of each data type remain the same to T-SQL queries as well as applications.

Data compression comes in two forms: *row compression* (RC) and *page compression* (PC). RC is another name for the variable-length storage approach just detailed. With RC, all oc-currences of *0* (zero) and *NULL* consume no space. RC is not effective for variable-length data types (they are already effectively compressed), for some shorter data types (where the overhead of compression outweighs the benefit), and for some other data types for technical reasons.

> **Note** To summarize, RC does *not* apply to *tinyint, smalldatetime, date, time, varchar, text, nvar-char, ntext, varbinary, image, cursor, sql_variant, uniqueidentifier, table, xml,* and user-defined types (UDTs).

PC is a superset of RC and provides potentially greater overall compression than RC alone, at the cost of greater CPU overhead. Where RC is concerned with compressing scale and precision on each individual row-column value, PC is concerned with compressing redundancy across all the rows and their columns on a particular page. PC can be used with all the same database objects as RC. It applies three steps to the enabled object, in the order indicated:

1. RC to the leaf level of a table and to all levels of an index.

2. PC—on each page, for each column of each row on that the page, any common prefixes among all values stored in that column (if any) are identified and tokenized. Each such prefix value is stored once in the new Compression Information (CI) section of the page (by column), and values in each column are replaced with short encoded values that identify the prefix and how much of it applies (as a prefix to the remainder of the value).

3. Dictionary compression—on each page, repeating values from any column in any row on the page are identified and stored in the CI area, and the values are replaced with a pointer to the repeated value. This can further compress the results of the first two steps.

As data is added to a PC-enabled object, these operations are initiated only when a page becomes full. If PC is enabled on an existing object containing data, that object must be rebuilt, a potentially expensive operation.

The code in Listing 14-5 shows an example of creating a table enabled for PC.

LISTING 14-5 Enabling PC on a table

```
CREATE TABLE RowCompressionDemo
 (FirstName char(10),
  LastName  char(30),
  Salary    decimal(8,2))
 WITH (DATA_COMPRESSION = PAGE)
```

SQL Server 2008 provides a system stored procedure associated with both forms of compression aptly named *sp_estimate_data_compression_savings*, which can be used to evaluate whether compression is worth applying to a given object. It can be run for a given uncompressed table, index, or partition to estimate the size it would be, using both RC and PC. It can also do the reverse; reporting the size a compressed object would be if uncompressed. This procedure works by sampling the data of the indicated object into a temporary store and running the indicated compression or decompression on it. It is possible for it to report a larger size for compressed than uncompressed data, which indicates clearly that the nature of the data is such that the storage overhead associated with compression outweighs any benefit.

Of course, these forms of compression require more CPU cycles to use than would otherwise be required, both when writing (compressing) and reading (decompressing) data. Each represents a tradeoff between saving space (disk and memory) and increasing CPU use. In addition, the effectiveness of any compression scheme is sensitive to the data type and statistical distribution of the values being compressed. For example, compression of an *int* column (4 bytes) in which most values do not exceed 255 (which fit in 1 byte) would exhibit much more benefit from RC than if the values were evenly distributed or if the column were already declared as a *tinyint* (1 byte). For these reasons, as well as the fine grain of data types that this feature allows to be individually tuned for compression, it is advisable to experiment with the various compression options to determine the optimal combination of settings.

Data compression must be enabled—it is disabled by default. It can be enabled on an entire table (which applies to all of its partitions), on individual partitions of a table, on individual indexes of a table, on individual index partitions, and on the clustered index of an indexed view. These features, together with the separately selectable options of row or page compression, give the database administrator great flexibility in tuning the use of compression to achieve the best tradeoffs.

Data compression is enabled by *CREATE TABLE* (as shown earlier) and *CREATE INDEX* statements, and also by *ALTER TABLE* and *ALTER INDEX*. Note that SQL Server Data Compression is *not* automatically enabled on existing or subsequently created nonclustered indexes of a table on which data compression is enabled—each such index must be separately and explicitly enabled. The one exception to this is that a clustered index does inherit the compression setting of its table.

Last but not least, an uncompressed table can be rebuilt with either form of compression via the new *ALTER TABLE...REBUILD WITH (DATA_COMPRESSION=xxx)* statement, where *xxx* is either *ROW* or *PAGE*. As the compression process is CPU intensive, it lends itself to parallelism, and SQL Server 2008 can take advantage of the availability of multiple CPUs. The *REBUILD* clause therefore supports a *MAXDOP* option to control how many CPUs are allocated to the process.

Backup Compression

SQL Server Backup Compression is a new option with the *BACKUP* statement. Although only the Enterprise edition can create a compressed backup, any edition can restore one.

Compared with data compression, backup compression is extremely coarse grained. It is either enabled or it isn't for the entire backup—there are no options to tune the compression, and the compression methods are opaque. Nevertheless, it is a welcome enhancement since no earlier version of SQL Server provided any form of backup compression, forcing practitioners to compress backups in a separate step with other, non–SQL Server, utilities.

The option is disabled by default, but the default can be changed via server-level configuration or overridden in the *BACKUP* statement. It should be noted that an *uncompressed* 2008 backup operation (both create and restore) can benefit when SQL Server Data Compression has been used on a significant scale in the database being backed up, as a direct result of reduced I/O. If data compression *has* been used, backup compression will likely provide a smaller (possibly much smaller) space-saving benefit, and because of the additional CPU overhead, backup/restore time might perform worse than without backup compression. This feature is therefore most valuable when the database being backed up has not had significant data compression applied—your own experimentation is warranted.

> **Note** Compressed and uncompressed backups cannot be mixed in a backup media set.

As a simple example of the potential efficiency of backup compression, compare the size and time required to back up and restore the *AdventureWorksDW2008* database, as shown in Listing 14-6. The *CHECKPOINT* and *DBCC DROPCLEANBUFFERS* statements are used to ensure that all cache buffers are empty so that one test does not misleadingly improve the performance of the next. Create the directory C:\Backups prior to running the following code.

LISTING 14-6 Comparing the time and size between compressed and uncompressed backups

```
CHECKPOINT
DBCC DROPCLEANBUFFERS
BACKUP DATABASE AdventureWorksDW2008 TO DISK='C:\Backups\AWDWUncompressed.bak'
-- 10.661 sec, 71 Mb

CHECKPOINT
DBCC DROPCLEANBUFFERS
BACKUP DATABASE AdventureWorksDW2008 TO DISK='C:\Backups\AWDWCompressed.bak'
 WITH COMPRESSION
-- 6.408 sec, 13 Mb

CHECKPOINT
DBCC DROPCLEANBUFFERS
RESTORE DATABASE AWDWUncompressed FROM DISK = 'C:\Backups\AWDWUncompressed.bak'
 WITH MOVE 'AdventureWorksDW2008_Data' TO 'C:\Backups\AWDWUncompressed.mdf',
      MOVE 'AdventureWorksDW2008_Log' TO 'C:\Backups\AWDWUncompressed.ldf'
-- 9.363 sec

CHECKPOINT
DBCC DROPCLEANBUFFERS
RESTORE DATABASE AWDWCompressed FROM DISK = 'C:\Backups\AWDWCompressed.bak'
 WITH MOVE 'AdventureWorksDW2008_Data' TO 'C:\Backups\AWDWCompressed.mdf',
      MOVE 'AdventureWorksDW2008_Log' TO 'C:\Backups\AWDWCompressed.ldf';
-- 6.101 sec
```

In this example, you can see that there is much more improvement in the backup (compression) stage than the restore stage, but in both cases, performance for the compressed backup is superior to the uncompressed backup. This is due to the reduction in I/O required for processing the smaller (compressed) backup file. Of course, experiments are warranted in your particular scenario to determine exactly what improvements you will see for yourself.

Learning More

We've made several references to SQL Server Books Online for more detailed information about many of the new data warehousing features in SQL Server 2008. In addition, you can learn more about all of these SQL Server 2008 data warehousing–oriented features by visiting the following links:

- *http://msdn.microsoft.com/en-us/library/cc278097(SQL.100).aspx#_Toc185095880*

- *http://technet.microsoft.com/en-us/magazine/cc434693(TechNet.10).aspx*

These links were valid as of press time, but if they don't work, you can perform a Web search on "SQL Server 2008 data warehouse enhancements."

We can also recommend these additional resources to learn more about the recommended practices of data warehousing:

- *Building the Data Warehouse*, 4th ed., W. H. Inmon (Wiley, 2005)

- *The Data Warehouse Toolkit: The Complete Guide to Dimensional Modeling*, 2nd ed., Ralph Kimball and Margy Ross (Wiley, 2002), and *The Data Warehouse Lifecycle Toolkit*, Ralph Kimball et al. (Wiley, 2008)

- The Data Warehousing Institute, *http://www.tdwi.org/TDWI*

Summary

Data warehousing has become a key component of any enterprise-wide data architecture and is no longer only practical for the largest enterprises. Data warehousing developed as a response to the many impediments to creating actionable information from the data collected by operational applications, impediments that only gradually became recognized as significantly undermining the potential of computers to help turn data into information. The issues existed not only because of historical technical limitations but also because of fundamental differences in optimum design between operational and informational applications.

A data warehouse provides the foundation for many data-driven applications. SQL Server 2008 provides a full-featured, powerful, and cost-effective platform on which to build a data warehouse. You've seen how SQL Server 2008 is particularly targeted to data warehousing issues and provides a number of long-awaited features in that sphere. In addition, Microsoft also offers a wide range of integrated and complementary technology, including Microsoft Office SharePoint, Microsoft Performance Point, and the 2007 Microsoft Office system, which enable you to build informational applications on top of your SQL Server data warehouse foundation.

Chapter 15
Basic OLAP

—Andrew Brust

This chapter and the three that follow it focus heavily on Analysis Services, the core business intelligence (BI) component of Microsoft SQL Server 2008. SQL Server has had BI capabilities since the release of OLAP Services with SQL Server 7.0 in 1999. You might think that with such a significant history of BI components in the product, most SQL Server professionals would be well-versed in the technology.

However, as you probably know, this is not the case at all. For many SQL Server customers, the BI capabilities of the product have been lying dormant, not well understood, and somewhat shrouded in mystery. To be certain, the core SQL Server relational database product is separate from Analysis Services, and it is quite feasible to be an expert in the former while being completely unschooled in the latter.

Wherefore BI?

To be frank, an organization that merely collects and manages its data, and perhaps reviews that data regularly through basic and ad hoc reports, is losing out almost completely on the strategic value and the information that the data holds. Moreover, taking advantage of the basic features of Analysis Services isn't that hard, and the concepts aren't all that difficult for relational database experts to grasp.

If you look carefully at the entire suite of features and components in SQL Server 2005 and 2008 as compared with SQL Server 2000, you'll find that the biggest advances have come from the BI side. Don't get us wrong: relational database features such as the Service Broker, native XML support, and the SQL Common Language Runtime (CLR) programming model are important in their own right. But their importance must be understood in the context of *incremental* change in a relational database engine that was already mature, sophisticated, scalable, and well understood by the market.

The advances in Analysis Services, meanwhile, are much more groundbreaking. The release of SQL Server 2005 Analysis Services marked the product's crossover into mainstream ease of use, programmability, interoperability, and integration with the rest of SQL Server and its toolset. SQL Server 2008 Analysis Services has added "fit and finish" to the 2005 version to make SQL Server BI even more beginner-friendly and, at the same time, powerful for advanced users. Because of this, we feel strongly that coverage of Analysis Services in this book is of paramount importance. And by extension, we feel that every SQL Server professional should have at least a basic understanding of this portion of the SQL Server product.

We also firmly believe that understanding Analysis Services is totally within reach for anyone proficient in the relational side of SQL Server. Our goal is to provide coverage of Analysis Services that is approachable, practical, and fun. This chapter provides a relatively brief introduction to online analytical processing (OLAP). When you finish this chapter, you'll be ready to build OLAP cubes, and you'll likely realize substantial benefits from doing so. You don't have to read any of the next three chapters before starting, and we encourage you to strike out on your own after reading this chapter and taste the victory of your new OLAP knowledge.

Once these practical achievements galvanize your interest in the technology (and, we presume, your self-confidence in being able to learn more about it), you will likely want to move on to Chapter 16, where we cover several advanced OLAP features, including those new to SQL Server 2008. Chapter 16 is much longer than this chapter, but you can read it in pieces and immediately put what you've read about to use. When you finish Chapter 16, you'll be able to build extremely sophisticated OLAP cubes.

You can stop there if you want, but as a developer, you'll probably want to go on to Chapter 17, where we cover a variety of software development techniques you can use to integrate OLAP functionality into your own applications. You'll learn how to build OLAP-enabled user interfaces (UIs) with Microsoft Office Excel and Excel Services. You'll also learn how to use a number of application programming interfaces (APIs)/object models, including ADO MD.NET, XML for Analysis (XMLA), and Analysis Management Objects (AMO). You'll even discover how to use Analysis Services' own CLR programming model to build server-side code in .NET languages. Chapter 17, like Chapter 16, is long, but it can be read and applied gradually.

Again, you can stop there if you want, but you'll probably want to move on to Chapter 18, where we cover Analysis Services' data mining capabilities. Data mining features were first introduced in the SQL Server 2000 version of Analysis Services, but they matured and solidified in SQL Server 2005 to a very significant degree and have been improved further in SQL Server 2008. In many ways, data mining development and design are easier to grasp than OLAP. Therefore, we cover the entirety of data mining in a single, albeit long, chapter. Many of the programming techniques discussed in Chapter 17 will be reprised in Chapter 18, allowing our coverage of them to be concise. Like Chapters 16 and 17, Chapter 18 lends itself well to gradual reading and application. We think you'll be impressed by the power of the product as you read Chapter 18.

OLAP 101

Let's begin our exploration of Analysis Services with a "quick hit" introduction to OLAP. In this chapter, you'll learn the fundamentals of OLAP, including general OLAP concepts and the basics of how to build, maintain, and query OLAP cubes in Microsoft SQL Server 2008. Specifically, we'll cover the following topics:

- Definitions of several terms, including cubes, measures, dimensions, attributes, hierarchies, levels, members, and axes

- Data warehousing concepts and the motivation behind so-called star and snowflake schemas

- The basics of Microsoft Visual Studio Analysis Services projects, such as data sources, data source views, the cube and dimension designers, and various wizards

- Querying cubes in the cube designer's Browser tab

As we just mentioned, SQL Server first brought OLAP functionality to us in version 7.0 with OLAP Services, a product that was essentially separate from, although bundled with, SQL Server proper. SQL Server 2000 Analysis Services included better OLAP functionality and new data mining capabilities but offered only slightly better integration with the SQL Server relational database. Analysis Services in SQL Server 2005 brought huge improvements in functionality over its predecessor, much better integration into the product, an architectural "rethink," and impressive ease-of-use features. In SQL Server 2008, Analysis Services gains new designers, streamlined wizards, and real-time Best Practice Alerts (BPAs) that further increase the product's power while lowering the barriers to entry for new users to build well-designed cubes. In this chapter, we'll begin to cover the sum total of the features introduced in Analysis Services 2005 and 2008, but let's start with some basic concepts first.

OLAP, which is an acronym for the rather vague moniker *online analytical processing*, can be thought of as database technology optimized for drill-down analysis. That's it! Forget all the confusing explanations you might have heard—there's really no magic here, and it need not be confusing. OLAP allows users to perform drill-down queries incredibly quickly and does so in two ways:

- OLAP cubes store so much data that in many cases, both the high-level rollups and the mid-level and low-level drilled-down figures needed for any given query are already calculated and need only be output.

- Even calculations that need to be done on the fly can be performed quickly because an OLAP engine is optimized for this task and doesn't need to concern itself with the complex tasks of a relational database, such as managing indexes, performing joins, or (except in specific circumstances) dealing with updates and concurrency. OLAP cubes essentially contain data at the lowest drilled-down levels, calculate some or all of the higher-level aggregations when a cube is built, and calculate the others at query time by aggregating the lower-level numbers already in the cube.

The result is a technology that lets users do an incredible amount of exploration through their data, allowing them to entertain a number of ad hoc, "what-if" scenarios without worrying about the time and resources it would take a relational engine to satisfy the same queries. If users don't have to be afraid to ask their questions, they'll ask a lot more of them, gain useful insight into their data, make better business decisions, and get a much higher return on investment on the relational systems that supply the cubes' data in the first place.

OLAP Vocabulary

A *cube*, which is the OLAP equivalent of a table in a relational database, consists of *measures*, which are the numeric data that users will analyze (for example, sales amount), and *dimensions*, which are the categories that the measures will be drilled down by (for example, time, geography, shipper, or promotion). Dimensions can be hierarchical. For example, a geography dimension would likely be hierarchical and might consist of country, state/province, city, and postal code *levels*. The individual countries, states, and so on are called the *members* of their respective levels. Such a scheme allows users to break down sales by country, then drill down on a specific country (good to do if that country's sales are particularly high or low), then on a specific state or province within that country, then on specific cities in that state or province, to specific postal codes in one or more of those cities. (This might allow a user to pinpoint quickly why a particular country's sales are so high or low.)

This all seems elementary and unsophisticated, doesn't it? Are you disillusioned? Don't be. Let's up the ante a bit. Imagine a spreadsheet where the columns contain the set of countries in which a company operates, the rows contain each of the four quarters of the last fiscal year, and each cell contains a sales figure for each corresponding combination of country and fiscal quarter. Imagine further that users can drill down on any quarter (to reveal the three months within it) and/or any country to reveal the sales numbers for those cross sections of the cube. Imagine that the spreadsheet is replicated numerous times, once for each salesperson's sales data, where each of these spreadsheets offers the same drill-down capabilities, returning the specific results implied by the drill-down, quickly and easily.

This entire set of spreadsheets can be returned by an OLAP engine with one fairly simple query. Still not impressed? Imagine each of the sales numbers in each spreadsheet appearing next to the corresponding year-ago figure and that, even with this enhancement, the whole interactive drill-down report can *still* be produced with a single query. Hopefully, we've caught your attention and have given you some insight into the power and business value of OLAP.

Dimensions, Axes, Stars, and Snowflakes

Let's go back to some definitions. Because OLAP cubes and even OLAP query result sets can contain data along multiple physical dimensions, not just rows and columns, the term *multidimensional* is often used to refer to OLAP databases. In fact, the language you use to query SQL Server OLAP cubes is called MDX (which stands for *multidimensional expression language*). The object models used to write OLAP applications are called ADO MD (the Component Object Model [COM]–based object model) and ADO MD.NET (its .NET managed equivalent); in both cases, the *MD* stands for *multidimensional*. Thinking tangibly about multidimensional data can be visually and logically challenging. Be prepared for this so that you are not discouraged along the way; meanwhile, we'll do our best to get you through it.

OLAP cubes are created from a collection of special tables in a relational database: *fact tables* and *dimension tables*. To illustrate what's in each of these, imagine a simple cube containing unit sales, total sales, and discount as its only measures and shipper and geography as its only dimensions. Imagine that the shipper dimension is flat—that is, nonhierarchical—and that the geography dimension is hierarchical, with its lowest level being postal code. The fact table then needs to contain the sales data attributable to each shipper in each postal code. Each row contains a postal code in one column, a key for a shipper in a second column, and the corresponding measures data in additional columns. Each possible combination of postal code and shipper corresponds to a separate row in the fact table (except for postal codes where specific shippers were not responsible for any sales).

We also need dimension tables. Let's start with a dimension table for the shipper. This is simply a lookup table containing the shipper ID and name in separate columns. You can see how joining the fact table to this table on shipper ID will allow us to get the shipper's name for each shipper/postal code fact data row.

Because geography is hierarchical, the relationship between the fact table and the geography dimension table is more complex. The geography dimension's information can be captured in a single denormalized table that corresponds to each unique postal code with its corresponding city, state/province, and country, or you can have separate, normalized lookup tables for each level in the hierarchy. (You can also have a combination of semi-denormalized tables, each combining a couple of hierarchical levels.) See Figure 15-1 for a sample representation of the data in a fact table and the two denormalized dimension tables. Notice that the fact table contains only measure data and foreign keys to the lowest level of each of the two dimensions.

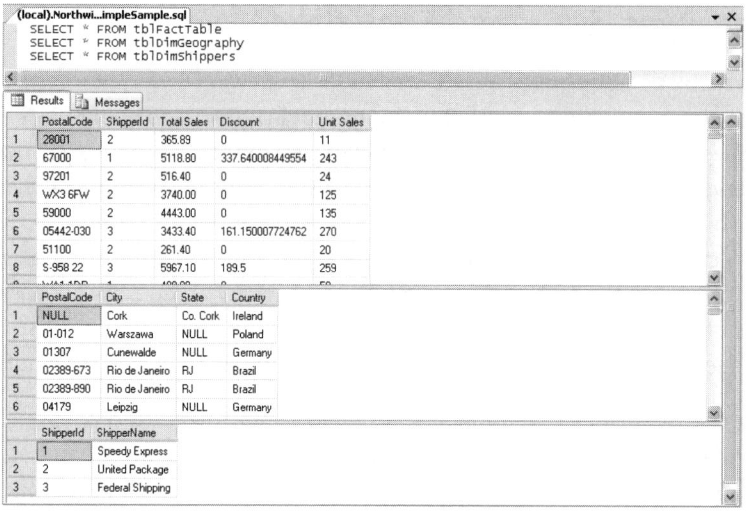

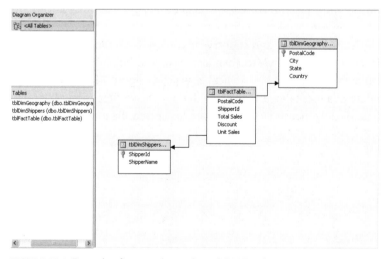

FIGURE 15-1 The data and structure of the two hypothetical dimension tables and a simple fact table that references them

Once the cube is built, the normalized or denormalized basis of its dimensions matters very little, so your choice at cube design time is essentially one of convenience. In the case of fully denormalized dimension tables, the schema ends up consisting of a fact table in the center with "spokes" branching out to each dimension table, as shown in Figure 15-2. The geometry of this type of schema suggests a star, so it is often referred to as a *star schema*. (Although this schema contains only two dimension tables, you can begin to see where the name star schema comes from.) Dimensions that involve multiple tables somewhat weaken the star analogy because the spokes have multiple nodes. Dimensions with multiple tables are therefore more commonly referred to as having a *snowflake schema* (a snowflake essentially resembling a more geometrically complex version of a star).

FIGURE 15-2 Example of a star schema–based OLAP cube

Typically, databases with star/snowflake schemas are created by taking normalized databases and running scripts, stored procedures, or extract, transform, and load (ETL) processes on them to create the transformed fact tables and dimension tables. These tables can be created in a new stand-alone database, and they in effect form the basis of a data warehouse or datamart. As such, they can serve as excellent data sources for running relational reports as well. Given that these tables have some degree of denormalization, they are easy to create reports against, and because they're in a separate database, or at least exist as separate tables in the main database, allowing users to run reports from them poses no strain on the production online transaction processing (OLTP) tables. If you find the physical transformation of the data inconvenient, remember that both fact and dimension "tables" can actually be views.

Building Your First Cube

Now that you can imagine the design and implementation of fact tables and dimension tables, how do you go about creating a cube? Let's go over the steps required to do this now.

Preparing Star Schema Objects

For the purposes of this chapter, rather than using the sample data warehouse and cubes based on the *AdventureWorks2008* sample database for Analysis Services, we'd like to create our own from scratch. This gives us a chance to try things out on our own. For this example, we'll use the older *Northwind* SQL Server sample database since it has no precreated cube set. The Management Studio solution in the sample code for this chapter, available on the book's companion Web site, contains several SQL scripts that create a fact table and several views suitable for use as dimension tables from the *Northwind* database.

> **Note** If you don't have the *Northwind* database, you can quickly and easily download it from Microsoft. Instructions for downloading *Northwind* can be found in the Introduction at the beginning of this book.

With the *Northwind* database installed on your server, run each script in the Chapter15 Management Studio project, *except* the Time.sql script, against the *Northwind* database. (The order of execution of the scripts is insignificant.)

> **Important** The Time.sql script should be run only if you will *not* be creating this chapter's Analysis Services project, database, and cube manually. If instead you want to open the fully created *Chapter15* Visual Studio project supplied with this chapter's sample code and deploy the *Chapter15* database directly from it, you *should* run the Time.sql script first. Running the script will create a populated table named *Time*.

Once these steps are complete, your copy of *Northwind* should contain a new table named *tblFact*, which will serve as the fact table, and the following views, which will serve as the dimension tables: *vwEmployees*, *vwGeography*, *vwProducts*, *vwShippers*, and *vwSuppliers*. Each of these tables and views is created by its namesake SQL script. Once these tables and views are in place, you can proceed to design, build, and query your cube.

A Tool by Any Other Name

You're ready to build your cube now, and in order to do so, you'll need special design tools. Under SQL Server 2000 Analysis Services, cubes were designed and managed in a tool called Analysis Manager, a Microsoft Management Console (MMC) snap-in that was, in effect, the Analysis Services analog to SQL Server Enterprise Manager. Back in the late 1990s, MMC snap-ins were a popular vehicle for management and design tools. These days, Visual Studio, with its rich extensibility APIs, is a more popular choice.

The SQL Business Intelligence team decided to use Visual Studio (specifically, Visual Studio 2008, in the case of SQL Server 2008) as the host for a number of BI-related designers, including those for Reporting Services, Integration Services, and most pertinent to this chapter, Analysis Services. It turns out, as you'll see in the next chapter, that SQL Server Management Studio can also be used as a management tool for Analysis Services databases; however, the Analysis Services *designers* are hosted inside Visual Studio.

Although most of you reading this book will have a copy of Visual Studio 2008 at your disposal, not all developers and administrators working with Analysis Services will. Microsoft realized this, of course, and knew that they needed a workable solution to the problem. In effect, Microsoft needed a way to ship the bare-bones Visual Studio integrated development environment (IDE) with SQL Server so that the various designers and project types supported by the SQL Server BI components that use Visual Studio could be created and manipulated by users who do not have a license for the Visual Studio product itself.

When you install the BI components of SQL Server on a machine that does not have Visual Studio 2008 installed, the SQL Server installer will place just such a scaled-down version of Visual Studio on the target machine; if a copy of Visual Studio 2008 is already installed on the machine, the BI designers will use it instead.

> **Note** The Express editions of Visual Studio are not sufficient to accommodate the various SQL Server BI designers. Machines with any of the Visual Studio Express edition products installed but that lack higher Visual Studio 2008 editions are treated by SQL Server identically to machines that have no Visual Studio 2008 editions on them at all.

So far, all of this seems reasonable, but there is one detail of nomenclature that can make this a bit confusing. The SQL Server 2008 installer will create a shortcut to Visual Studio on your machine (either the bare-bones copy it might have installed or the existing copy you otherwise already had). This shortcut's name is not Microsoft Visual Studio 2008 but SQL Server Business Intelligence Development Studio.

It is important to realize that this shortcut actually points to Visual Studio, be it the bare-bones version or the full product, and that there really is *no such thing* as Business Intelligence Development Studio. You might find this name useful to identify the bare-bones version of the Visual Studio IDE (and the BI designers) we have just discussed, but that explanation becomes inaccurate when you realize that the shortcut labeled SQL Server Business Intelligence Development Studio actually links to the *full* Visual Studio product on machines that have it.

To make things perfectly clear, in this book we will refer to the host environment of the Analysis Services and other BI designers as *Visual Studio*. We make this point for more than just clarifying nomenclature. The real reason it is important to refer to the BI designers as being hosted in Visual Studio and not in Business Intelligence Development Studio is to make clear that a single Visual Studio solution can indeed contain a *mix* of SQL Server BI project types and more conventional Visual Studio .NET application project types.

For example, a single Visual Studio 2008 solution could contain an Analysis Services project, a Reporting Services project, *and* various C# or Microsoft Visual Basic .NET projects, including a Windows Forms application, a Class Library project, and/or an ASP.NET Web site. This fact will allow us to maintain the standard used in other chapters in this book of having a single Management Studio solution and a single Visual Studio solution contain *all* the sample code for a given chapter. This will be especially pertinent in Chapter 18, the sample code for which includes a Visual Studio solution containing one of each of the five BI and .NET project types just mentioned.

Creating the Project

With our understanding of the toolset and its proper name now established, it's time to create an Analysis Services project and design our cube. Start Visual Studio, and then select File, New, Project. In the New Project dialog box, select Business Intelligence Projects from the Project Types tree view on the left, and select Analysis Services Project from the Templates pane on the right. Type **Chapter15** as your project name, with a file path that works conveniently for you. (Figure 15-3 shows how the dialog box should appear.) You're now ready to click OK and create your project.

You'll notice that your new project is empty, unlike most other projects in Visual Studio where a default object is created and opened for you. In Analysis Services projects, you start from scratch. The best things to add right away are a data source and a data source view. Create a new data source by right-clicking the Data Sources folder in Solution Explorer and then selecting New Data Source from the shortcut menu to display the Data Source Wizard.

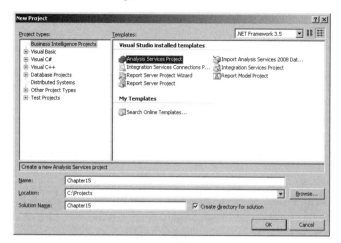

FIGURE 15-3 Creating a new Analysis Services project in the Visual Studio New Project dialog box

Click Next on the wizard's Welcome page to advance to the Select How To Define The Connection page. Click the New button to display the Connection Manager dialog box. For the Provider, specify Native OLE DB\SQL Server Native Client 10.0. For the Server Name, enter the name of your server (and a backslash and instance name, if any), supply your login credentials (Windows Authentication is likely your best choice here), and select Northwind as the database name. The dialog box should appear similarly to what's shown in Figure 15-4.

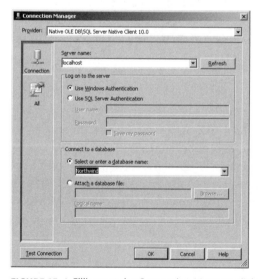

FIGURE 15-4 Filling out the Connection Manager dialog box to create an Analysis Services project data source

Note Make certain that the identity under which Analysis Services is running has read access to the *Northwind* database. If Analysis Services is running under Local System, you should be fine. If not, you'll need to add the account that Analysis Services runs under as a user to *Northwind*.

Click OK to close the Connection Manager dialog box. Back in the Data Source Wizard, click Next to advance to the Impersonation Information page, where you should select the Inherit option (that is, the last option in the list) and then click Next again. On the Completing The Wizard page, accept the default name of the data source (Northwind), and then click Finish.

Adding a Data Source View

What we've done so far is akin to creating a database connection; we still need to specify what objects from the *Northwind* database we want to use in order to build our cube. To specify this information, we need to add a data source view to our project. To do this, right-click the Data Source Views folder in Solution Explorer and select New Data Source View from the shortcut menu. This displays the Data Source View Wizard.

Click Next on the Welcome page, and click Next again on the Select A Data Source page, making sure that the *Northwind* data source you just created is selected. On the Select Tables And Views page, select (that is, move from the Available Objects list to the Included Objects list) the table *tblFact* (tables are listed first in the Included Objects list) and the views *vwEmployees*, *vwGeography*, *vwProducts*, *vwShippers*, and *vwSuppliers* (which appear toward the bottom of the Included Objects list). Figure 15-5 shows how the lists should appear at this point.

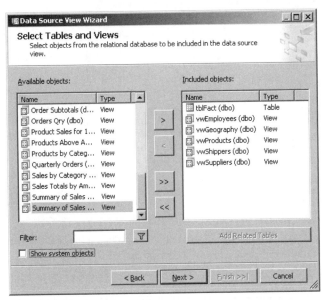

FIGURE 15-5 Selecting fact and dimension tables for your cube

When you're building data source views, don't panic if you're not sure which tables to select. You can bring back this page later as the stand-alone Add/Remove Tables dialog box in the data source view designer when you've finished with the wizard. We'll explain later in this chapter how to do that.

You can type a wildcard filter expression in the Filter text box to limit the tables and views that appear in the Available Objects list. For example, try typing **vw** and then either pressing the Enter key on your keyboard or clicking the funnel icon button to the right of the text box. This will filter the list to display only tables and views that begin with the letters *vw*.

Once you've moved at least one table into the Included Objects list, you can select a table (or multiple tables) and click the Add Related Tables button to instantly select all tables related to it (or them).

> **Tip** This can be a great shortcut: if you include the fact table first and then click Add Related Tables, you can often move over all the dimension tables at once, depending on the design of your star schema database. Because we're using views for our dimension tables, this shortcut will not work in our particular case.

When you've finished selecting your tables, click Next. On the Complete The Wizard page, accept the default name Northwind assigned to your data source view, and then click Finish. After a brief pause, the wizard disappears, and your data source view automatically opens in its designer. The tables in the data source view might need to be manually arranged so that they are all visible simultaneously with the fact table in the center, as shown in Figure 15-6.

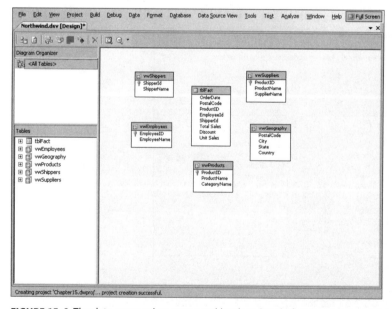

FIGURE 15-6 The data source view generated by the wizard after some layout tidying has been done

The designer is divided into three panes: on the upper left is the Diagram Organizer pane, on the bottom left is the Tables pane, and on the right is the diagram layout pane. The All Tables diagram that is displayed in the diagram layout pane shows all the tables you selected in the wizard. It is possible to add diagrams to the data source view that contain only a subset of the tables/views in the data source view by selecting Data Source View, New Diagram, by right-clicking within the Diagram Organizer pane and selecting New Diagram from the short-cut menu, or by clicking the New Diagram toolbar button (third from left). After taking any of these three actions, you can type a diagram name and then drag tables and views from the Tables pane onto the design surface in the diagram layout pane. If you accidentally drag a table or view that you don't want into the diagram, simply right-click it in the diagram layout pane and choose the Hide Table shortcut menu option, or select the table in the diagram layout pane and select Data Source View, Hide Table from the menu.

The set of tables and views that the data source view is based on, which you first specified in the Select Tables And Views page of the Data Source View Wizard, can be altered within the data source view designer. You can do so through the Add/Remove Tables dialog box, which can be displayed by selecting Data Source View, Add/Remove Tables, by right-clicking in the diagram layout pane and selecting Add/Remove Tables on the shortcut menu, or by clicking the Add/Remove Objects toolbar button (on the far left).

By default, all foreign key constraint relationships between tables are shown in the diagrams as the tables they relate to are added to a diagram. In our case, no predeclared constraint relationships exist, so you must add relationships to the data source view diagram yourself. To do so, just click in the foreign key column in *tblFact* and then drag the mouse pointer to connect to the corresponding column in the corresponding dimension table.

For example, you can click the *EmployeeId* field in *tblFact* (to highlight it) and then drag the mouse to the *EmployeeId* field in *vwEmployees*. Release the mouse button, and you should see an arrow-headed line joining the fact table to the view. Double-click the relationship association you just made (or single-click it and select Data Source View, Edit Relationship, or right-click it and select the Edit Relationship shortcut menu option) to display the Edit Relationship dialog box, shown in Figure 15-7, where you can edit the properties of this relationship and confirm that you joined the correct columns.

The Edit Relationship dialog box is essentially a property sheet for the relationship between the fact table and the employee dimension "table" (which is actually the view named *vwEmployees*). A modified version of this dialog box, the Specify Relationship dialog box, can be used to create relationships if the drag-and-drop method does not appeal to you. You can display the Specify Relationship dialog box by selecting Data Source View, New Relationship, by right-clicking in the diagram pane and selecting the New Relationship shortcut menu option, or by clicking the New Relationship toolbar button (fourth from right).

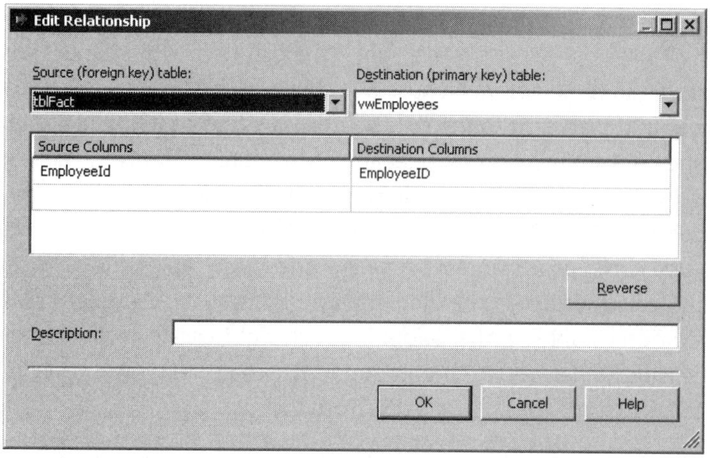

FIGURE 15-7 The Edit Relationship dialog box

For our cube, we need to build relationships between *tblFact* and each of the dimension tables (views). Build the additional relationships listed in the following table, and then save your changes. (See the text following the table for special instructions on the relationship to *vwGeography*.)

Source Table	Source Column	Destination Table	Destination Column
tblFact	*ProductId*	*vwProducts*	*ProductId*
tblFact	*PostalCode*	*vwGeography*	*PostalCode*
tblFact	*ProductId*	*vwSuppliers*	*ProductId*
tblFact	*ShipperId*	*vwShippers*	*ShipperId*

You'll notice that for *vwGeography*, a primary key does not exist, and the designer will ask whether you'd like to define a "logical" primary key. The designer asks this question because no column in this view is a primary key in the physical table it is derived from. Select Yes.

The data source view designer allows you to add and remove tables, relationships, and so-called named queries to and from diagrams. Named queries are much like database views, but they are persisted in your data source view and not in the star schema database. Right-clicking on a particular table, either in the diagram layout pane or in the Tables list, allows you to add a named calculation. This is essentially like adding a calculated field in a view, but again it is persisted in the data source view rather than in the source database. You can also browse the data within any table in your data source view and perform PivotTable, Chart, and PivotChart analysis on it by right-clicking it (again, in the diagram layout pane or the Tables list) and selecting Explore Data from the shortcut menu or by selecting Data Source View, Explore Data.

The data source view designer toolbar's Find Table button (second from right), the Data Source View, Find Table main menu option, and the Find Table option on the diagram layout pane's shortcut menu all allow you to locate and select a specific table by choosing it from a list in the Find Table dialog box. (Merely selecting a table in the Tables pane achieves the same purpose, so this feature is somewhat superfluous.) The Zoom toolbar button and its associated drop-down button (on the far right) allow you to zoom in and out in the diagram. The Refresh Data Source View toolbar button (second from the left), the Data Source View, Refresh main menu option, and the Refresh option on the diagram pane's shortcut menu let you refresh the data source view—this is a great way to update the schemas of all of a data source view's tables if they've been modified in the source database, without having to delete the data source view (or even specific tables within it) and rebuild it (or add the tables back).

Creating a Cube with the Cube Wizard

Once you've finished perfecting your data source view, close it and save your changes. You're now ready to build your cube! To do this, select Project, New Cube, or right-click the Cubes folder in Solution Explorer and then select the New Cube option from the shortcut menu to display the Cube Wizard.

On the Welcome page, click Next to advance to the Select Creation Method page. For our purposes, you'll want to select the Use Existing Tables option (which should be selected by default). Click Next to move to the Select Measure Group Tables page. Confirm that the data source you created before (Northwind) is selected in the Data Source View drop-down list, and select the tblFact check box in the Measure Group Tables checked list box (at another time, you might want to use the Suggest button if you're unsure of which table is your fact table), and then click Next again.

On the Select Measures page, you are asked to create your measures and measure groups. By default, one measure for each numeric field in your fact table or tables that is not a foreign key to a dimension table is listed here, and a default measure (named *Tbl Fact Count*, in our case), based on the row count, will be listed as well. The field-based measures will have the same name as the field names on which they are based, with spaces inserted where "intercap" characters exist in the field names. (For example, a field named *UnitPrice* will create a measure with the default name *Unit Price*.)

You can edit measure (or measure group) names by setting the focus on the tree view node containing the name (by using the mouse or the keyboard) and then either pressing the F2 key or clicking the node a second time (but not double-clicking it). (You can also right-click the node.) Individual measures can also be deselected, preventing them from being added to the cube. For our example, clear the Tbl Fact Count option because we will not need it.

One measure group is created for each fact table you specified on the Select Measure Group Tables page. For our example, change the name of the single measure group detected from *tblFact* by editing the tblFact node and typing in **Main**. When you've finished configuring your measures and measure groups, click Next.

On the Select New Dimensions page, all default dimensions are listed (one per dimension table). Indented under each dimension is the name of the table or view from which it will be created. As with measures, you can deselect any dimension to prevent it from being created. You do so by clearing the check box next to the dimension or its indented dimension table. (Clearing either results in clearing both.) You can change the dimension name using the same procedure described earlier for measures. Use one of these techniques to remove the *Vw* prefix from a dimension name—for example, rename the Vw Products dimension **Products**—and make sure that you do likewise for each remaining dimension.

When you've finished configuring your dimensions, click Next. On the Completing The Wizard page, you can type a name more to your liking than the default (for this example, name the cube **Sales**). The Cube Wizard should appear as shown in Figure 15-8.

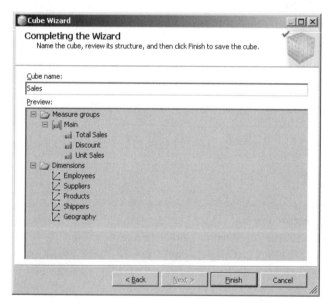

FIGURE 15-8 The Completing The Wizard page of the Cube Wizard

Using the Cube Designer

Click Finish. When the Cube Wizard finishes processing, your cube design will be generated and opened, placing you on the Cube Structure tab of the cube designer, as shown in Figure 15-9.

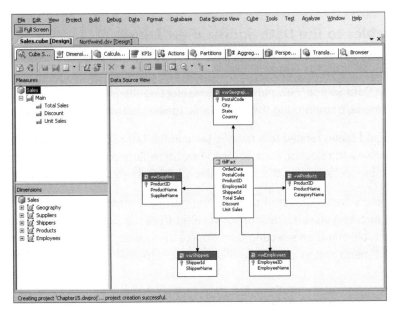

FIGURE 15-9 The Cube Structure tab of the cube designer

The cube designer has an array of tabs across the top, and the Cube Structure tab is divided into three panes: Measures on the upper left, Dimensions on the lower left, and Data Source View on the right. This Data Source View pane depicts what may be a subset of the tables in the data source view upon which the cube is based: it contains only the tables and views selected in the Cube Wizard when we identified our measure group table and dimensions.

By default, the Measures pane contains a tree view with the cube name at the root, measure groups appearing as the root's children, and individual measures listed as children of their measure groups. You can change the tree view to a grid view by selecting Cube, Show Measures In, by right-clicking in the Measures pane and then selecting Show Measures In on the shortcut menu, or by clicking the Show Measures Grid/Show Measures Tree toolbar drop-down button (fifth from the left).

Measure groups and individual measures can be added, deleted, renamed, or moved up and down through options on the main menu, shortcut menus, and toolbar. Even the cube itself can be renamed in this way. In the grid view, only measures are listed; measure groups can be manipulated only in the tree view. The measure's data type and aggregate function can be modified in the grid view. These and other properties can also be edited through the Properties window. (We'll cover advanced property settings in more detail in the next chapter.)

Adding Tables to the Data Source View Pane

You can add any other table to the Data Source View pane that might be present in the base data source view simply by selecting Data Source View, Show Tables, by right-clicking in the Data Source View pane and then selecting the Show Tables option from the shortcut menu, or by clicking the Show Table toolbar button (fifth from right).

You can also add tables related to a specific table in the Data Source View pane by clicking the table and selecting Data Source View, Show Related Tables or by right-clicking the table and selecting the Show Related Tables shortcut menu option.

Some cubes use a great number of tables. If the view becomes cluttered with tables, to get a clearer picture, you can hide individual tables from the Data Source View pane by selecting the table and then selecting Data Source View, Hide Table, choosing the Hide Table shortcut menu option, or clicking the Hide Table toolbar button (fourth from right).

You can revert to showing only tables actually used for measure groups and dimensions by using the Show Only Used Tables shortcut menu option in the Data Source View pane or by selecting Data Source View, Show Only Used Tables. You can also show all tables by using the Show All Tables shortcut menu option in the Data Source View pane or by selecting Data Source View, Show All Tables.

These actions have no effect on the base data source view itself because the Data Source View pane is simply a convenient filtered diagram based on the cube's underlying data source view.

Note The New Linked Object option on the Cube menu, the New Linked Object shortcut menu option (available in the Measures and Dimensions panes), and the New Linked Object toolbar button (seventh from left) allow you to link or import measures, dimensions, and other objects from other cubes into the one you're editing. Although we won't cover linked objects in this book, they are a useful tool to help you avoid building new physical cubes when you want to combine elements of other cubes (including those in other Analysis Services databases and even on other servers). You might want to review SQL Server Books Online for more information about this feature.

The cube designer is the primary tool for designing and building cubes; the Cube Wizard simply provides a front end to the designer to help get you started. If you want to add new measures to the cube after running the wizard, you can easily do so within the designer. Simply select Cube, New Measure from the main menu, click the New Measure option on the Measures pane's shortcut menus, or click the New Measure toolbar button (third from left) to display the New Measure dialog box, shown in Figure 15-10.

FIGURE 15-10 The New Measure dialog box, which allows you to add measures to your cube even after the Cube Wizard has completed its work

From the Source Column list box that occupies most of the dialog box, you can select the fact table field from which you want to derive your measure and then click OK to create the measure. Only non-foreign-key numeric fields are displayed by default; the Show All Columns check box below the Source Column list box allows you to display (and select) other fields.

You can also add measure groups if fact tables exist that have not yet been assigned to an existing measure group. This is a more advanced scenario that we will not cover in this book.

The Dimensions pane on the Cube Structure tab allows you to inspect and maintain dimensions, attributes, and hierarchies. It features a tree view of the dimensional structure of your cube, with the cube as the root node and dimensions listed as the cube's children. Under each dimension is an Attributes folder under which are listed the dimension's attributes; its hierarchies, if any, are listed before the Attributes folder. You can edit a dimension's name, delete the dimension, or move it up or down within the full list of dimensions. You can also add a new cube dimension or edit an existing dimension in the dimension designer.

Using the Dimension Wizard

To open the Dimension Wizard and create a dimension (which we'll need to do because we haven't yet created a time dimension), choose Project, New Dimension from the main menu or right-click the Dimensions folder in the Solution Explorer window and then choose New Dimension from the shortcut menu. Either of these actions displays the Dimension Wizard, shown in Figure 15-11.

FIGURE 15-11 The Dimension Wizard, which allows you to define a new dimension in your Analysis Services database

On the Welcome page of the Dimension Wizard, click Next. On the Select Creation Method page, click the Generate A Time Table In The Data Source option, and then click Next. On the Define Time Periods page, type **July 4, 1996** in the First Calendar Day date picker control and **May 6, 1998** in the Last Calendar Day time picker control, and then confirm that Sunday is selected in the First Day Of The Week drop-down list. In the Time Periods checked list box, confirm that the Date time period is already selected; manually select the Year, Quarter, and Month check boxes; and then click Next. On the Select Calendars page, make sure that the Regular Calendar check box is selected, and then click Next. Confirm that the Completing The Wizard page appears as shown in Figure 15-12. (You'll need to scroll down through the Preview tree view or resize the Dimension Wizard to view all the details shown.) Do *not* click the Finish button yet.

Before we continue, let's review what we're doing in our use of the Dimension Wizard. First, we are creating a *Time* dimension with attributes for *Year*, *Quarter*, *Month*, and *Date*, and we are creating a hierarchy consisting of those attributes in that order. (We'll cover hierarchies in more detail in the next section.) We are also creating attributes, like *Day Of Quarter*, that will provide us with more novel information should we need it. But we're doing one more thing that's very important: we are creating the table that will underlie this dimension and populating it with data. To complete this task correctly and immediately, select the Generate Schema Now check box on the lower left in the Completing The Wizard Page, and *now* click the Finish button.

FIGURE 15-12 The Completing The Wizard page of the Dimension Wizard for our new *Time* dimension

The Schema Generation Wizard will now appear. Click Next on the Welcome page. On the Specify Target page, select the Use Existing Data Source View option to use the Northwind data source view, click Next on this and all remaining pages, and then click Finish. The Schema Generation Progress dialog box should now appear; allow the schema generation process to complete by waiting until the message "Generation Completed Successfully" is displayed in green text in the dialog box's status bar and its Close button is enabled.

Tip If you attempt to build the *Time* dimension a second time, the Schema Generation dialog box will appear instead of the Schema Generation Wizard. In all likelihood, the options displayed in the dialog box will be correct and you can click OK, bypassing the wizard steps described earlier. If you prefer, you can instead click the Change Options button to enter the Schema Generation Wizard.

Note You might notice several warning messages appear in the Schema Generation Progress dialog box; these messages are normal and simply explain that no tables were generated for the other dimensions or for the cube itself, since they are based on tables that already exist.

Click the Close button, and the dimension designer for your new *Time* dimension will appear. Close the dimension designer window by clicking its close box or by pressing Ctrl+F4. When prompted to save changes, click the Save button. Back in the cube designer, you'll notice that the new *Time* dimension does not appear. That's because you've added it to the Analysis Services database but not to the cube itself. Before we can add the dimension to the cube, we need to make sure that its underlying dimension table has been properly added to our data source view.

Open or activate the *Northwind* data source view in the data source view designer. You should see the new *Time* table appear, but you should also notice that it is not properly related to the fact table. Remedy this by clicking and dragging on the *OrderDate* column in the *tblFact* table and dropping it on the *PK_Date* column in the *Time* table. Now save the change made to the data source view.

Back in the cube designer, select Cube, Add Cube Dimension, click the Add Cube Dimension toolbar button (sixth from left), or select the Add Cube Dimension option on the Dimensions pane's shortcut menu to add the new *Time* dimension to the cube. Do this by selecting the Time dimension from the Select Dimension list box in the resulting Add Cube Dimension dialog box and then clicking the OK button. When you return to the cube designer, you should notice that the *Time* dimension has been added to the Dimensions pane's tree view and that the *Time* table has been added to the Data Source View pane (although you might need to adjust the layout/placement of the table to make the schema easily readable—use the Arrange Tables option on the Data Source View pane's shortcut menu to do this most easily).

For the new *Time* dimension, or any of the others, if you drill down, you'll see that the first child node is a clickable link that opens the dimension designer and allows you to edit that dimension. In addition to the link button, you can open the dimension designer by selecting a dimension in the Dimensions pane and choosing Cube, Edit Dimension or choosing the Edit Dimension option from its shortcut menu. Use one of these techniques to open the *Geography* dimension in the dimension designer now.

Using the Dimension Designer

The dimension designer, like the cube designer, has tabs across the top and a three-pane view in the rest of the window. Within the Dimension Structure tab, the Attributes pane is on the left, the Hierarchies pane is in the center, and the Data Source View pane is on the right.

Attributes can be displayed in a tree, list, or grid view. Cycle through the views by choosing Dimension, Show Attributes In from the main menu or by choosing the Show Attributes In option from the Attributes pane's shortcut menus. You can also click the View Attributes As button's associated drop-down button (third button from the left on the dimension designer's toolbar). Note that when you enter the list or grid views, the Hierarchies pane pivots from the center to the upper left and the Attributes pane shifts to the lower left. Certain properties for attributes are available in the grid view, but all properties are accessible through the Properties window regardless of which view you're in. We'll discuss the Properties window in further detail later.

Note that only *Postal Code* is listed in the Attributes pane, but that the *City*, *State*, and *Country* dimension table columns appear in the Data Source View pane. To create attributes from those three columns, simply drag each one from the Data Source View pane to the Attributes pane.

The dimension designer makes it easy to create hierarchies from the universe of a dimension's attributes. Let's create a hierarchy for the *Geography* dimension now so that we can later query our cube data hierarchically by country, then state or province, then city, and then postal code. Start by dragging the *Country* attribute from the Attributes pane to the Hierarchies pane. (You can also right-click the *Country* attribute and select the Start New Hierarchy option from its shortcut menu, or left-click the *Country* attribute and select Dimension, Start New Hierarchy.) This will create a new hierarchy with the default name of *Hierarchy* in its own rectangular block in the Hierarchies pane, with the *Country* attribute as the hierarchy's top (and only) level.

You can drag additional attributes onto this block to create additional levels (or select the hierarchy and then either right-click an attribute and select Create Level from the shortcut menu or left-click an attribute and select the Create Level option from the Dimension menu). You can reorder the levels within the hierarchy by using drag-and-drop, and you can delete and rename attributes and hierarchies in a manner similar to other UI scenarios already described.

Using any of the techniques just discussed, add the *State*, *City*, and *Postal Code* attributes as the second, third, and fourth levels of the new hierarchy (leaving *Country* as the first level). Once you've added all the levels, rename the second level from *State* to *State-Province* and rename the hierarchy itself to *Country - State-Province - City - Postal Code*, and then save your changes. (Click OK when prompted to save the *Sales* cube also.) The completed hierarchy design is shown in Figure 15-13. You can safely ignore the squiggles and yellow exclamation point for now. We will explain these in more detail in the next chapter.

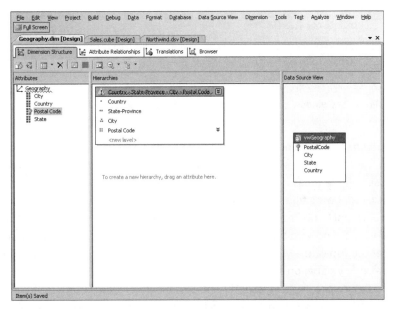

FIGURE 15-13 The dimension designer, with our *Geography* dimension, including its new hierarchy, fully designed and configured

The dimension designer has three other tabs: Attribute Relationships, Translations, and Browser. We'll cover the Attribute Relationships and Translations tabs in the next chapter. You can use the Browser tab to examine all of the dimension's levels and each level's members in a tree view, but only after the cube has been processed (a step we'll take you through shortly).

Working with the Properties Window and Solution Explorer

Some of the settings we've discussed, as well as others we'll discuss in the next chapter, can be set through the Properties window. To see how this works, return to the cube designer's Cube Structure tab, click any measure in the Measures pane, and then look at the Properties window. (Press F4 or choose View, Properties Window if the Properties window is not visible.) To make the Properties window easier to view, assuming that it's docked, double-click its title bar to undock it (you can double-click its title bar again to redock it), center it within your screen, and resize it so that its columns are wide and many rows are displayed without the need to scroll. Your Properties window should now look similar to Figure 15-14.

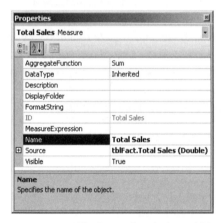

FIGURE 15-14 The Properties window, which allows advanced manipulation of measures, dimensions, cubes, and other objects

Notice that *AggregateFunction* and *DataType* are visible and editable, as are several other properties. Click the drop-down arrow in the upper-right corner of the Properties window, and you should see all the measures in your cube displayed in the drop-down list. Double-click the Properties window's title bar again to dock it, and then select a dimension in the Dimensions pane. Undock the Properties window a second time, and you'll see that this dimension's properties are now editable and that all dimensions in your cube are listed in the drop-down list at the top of the window. This technique works for virtually any class of object in your cube, in any pane, on any tab of the cube designer (except the Calculations and Browser tabs) or dimension designer. Experiment with this technique in different parts of the designers so that you can appreciate the breadth of power the Properties window has in the cube editing process.

Before we move on to processing and querying our cube, you should know that you can manipulate high-level objects such as data sources, data source views, dimensions, and the cube itself by opening them from the Solution Explorer window. For example, to edit a dimension in the dimension designer, instead of clicking its link in the Dimensions pane of the cube designer, you can double-click its node in the Dimensions folder of your project in the Solution Explorer window. Try this to see how easily it works. Also, if you right-click any editable object in the Solution Explorer window and then choose View Code, you'll see that the basis for each object is a simple XML file. Imagine the cube design/generation possibilities this raises for third-party and custom-developed UIs.

> **Note** The particular XML schema used by the designers is an established standard called XML for Analysis, or XMLA for short. We will examine the structure and use of XMLA in more depth in the next three chapters, especially in Chapter 17. We will also cover how the various Analysis Services APIs use XMLA "behind the scenes."

Processing the Cube

You can process the entire cube by selecting Database, Process or Cube, Process, or by clicking the Process button (second from left) on the cube designer's toolbar. Processing the cube or database automatically processes any pending changes to dimensions they might contain.

Processing your cube requires that your Analysis Services project be built and deployed. When you choose to process your cube (do this now), if it hasn't already been built and deployed (which ours has not), you'll be notified that these steps are necessary and asked whether you'd like them to be performed before processing. Click Yes. (Alternatively, you could first execute the Build and Deploy options from the Build branch of the main menu.)

> **Note** You might notice several warnings in the Error List window as you deploy your changes. These are due to Best Practice Alerts (BPAs), a feature that we will discuss in Chapter 16. These are warnings only (not errors) and will not interfere with the build or deploy processes, so you can safely ignore them for now.

You can watch the progress of the build and deploy operations in the Deployment Progress window. Once these steps are complete, you'll be prompted with the Process Cube—*<cubename>* (or Process Database) dialog box. The Remove, Impact Analysis, and Change Settings buttons in this dialog box provide precise control over how your cube is processed. We encourage you to explore the use of these tools in SQL Server Books Online. For the work we will do in this book, it is sufficient simply to click Run. This will process the cube and display the Process Progress dialog box. Once the processing has completed, click Close in both dialog boxes and your cube should be ready to query!

Running Queries

In Chapter 17, we'll cover how to write .NET code to query your cube in your own applications. For now, we'll just use the Browser tab within the cube designer to run some quick queries. Click the Browser tab now—it's the last one. This cube browser is really just an administrative tool and limited to result sets with two axes. It is similar in functionality to the Office Excel PivotTable tool and actually uses the PivotTable control from version 11 of Office Web Components.

Once the browser loads, drill down on the Measures node and then on the Main measure group node in the tree view on the upper left. Drag the *Total Sales* measure into the Drop Totals Or Detail Fields Here area of the output region. Next, drag the *Year* attribute of the *Time* dimension (drill down on the dimension to display its attributes) onto the Drop Row Fields Here area. You'll now see total sales by year from the *Northwind* database dispalyed. Now drill down on the *Geography* dimension. Drag the entire *Country – State-Province – City – Postal Code* hierarchy onto the Drop Column Fields Here area. You should now see the same data but further correlated (on the columns axis) by the *Country* level in the *Geography* dimension's hierarchy, as shown in Figure 15-15. You can drill down on any country to see its data broken down further by state/province, and you can drill down even further to individual cities or postal codes. Notice how quickly the drill-downs are completed.

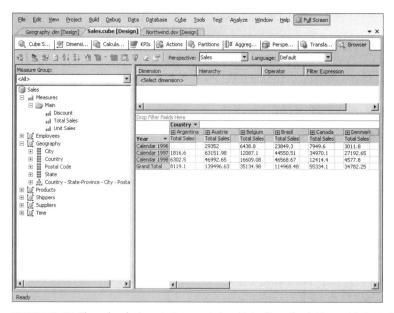

FIGURE 15-15 The cube designer's Browser tab, which allows for fairly sophisticated querying of OLAP cubes

You can now drag even more dimensions onto either axis, optionally removing the old dimensions first. Putting two dimensions on one axis allows you to drill down on one dimension to reveal members of the other. It's a convenient way of projecting multiple logical axes onto a single physical axis. Executing queries that *truly* project onto three or more axes is possible, but not in the Browser tab of the cube designer.

You can also add filters to the query. You do this by dragging an attribute or hierarchy onto the Drop Filter Fields Here area and then clicking the drop-down arrow next to the attribute or hierarchy's name and selecting or deselecting specific members to be counted or ignored in the data below. You can create expression-based filters in the area directly above the Drop Filter Fields Here area. Here you can enter simple conditional or complex MDX expressions for filtering the data below. We'll cover the creation of MDX expressions in the next chapter.

Other Microsoft and third-party query and editing tools let you do even more in the way of queries, and you can also build your own applications that exceed the Browser tab's functionality. But considering that we're on our first OLAP chapter in this book, we've already done a lot.

Summary

We've covered quite a bit in this chapter. You've learned the basic premise and vocabulary of OLAP, including all the principles necessary to understand how to design a star/snowflake schema data warehouse/datamart and a cube based on it. In addition to all this theory, you've learned the practical skills of creating an Analysis Services project in Visual Studio and adding a data source, a data source view, a cube, and a time dimension to your project. You've learned how to create and maintain measures and dimensions and how to process and query a cube.

In this one chapter alone, you have learned to use the Data Source Wizard, Data Source View Wizard, Cube Wizard, and Dimension Wizard as well as the cube designer (Cube Structure and Browser tabs) and dimension designer (Dimension Structure and Browser tabs). You now have enough knowledge to build basic but highly useful OLAP cubes on your transactional data. In the next two chapters, we'll investigate how to implement more advanced features in your cubes and then how to use Office Excel and Excel Services to query them or write .NET code to build OLAP querying functionality into your applications.

Chapter 16
Advanced OLAP

—Andrew Brust

In the previous chapter, you learned the basic concepts and vocabulary of online analytical processing (OLAP) and learned how to create your own cube, based on the *Northwind* database. Building a cube from scratch gives you an understanding of OLAP that would be hard to acquire by merely studying the *Adventure Works* sample cube supplied with Microsoft SQL Server 2008. After going through Chapter 15's process of creating a fact table and dimension tables and then designing, creating, and querying a cube in the cube browser, you should have a sense of the relative ease and power of using OLAP. As a result, you should be able to dispense with the trepidation that many people experience when they approach OLAP.

Most of the features we covered in Chapter 15 were, in fact, available not only in SQL Server 2005 Analysis Services but also in SQL Server 2000 Analysis Services. The ability to create a dimensional version of your database using a fact table and several dimension tables and then perform fast drill-down queries on it has been around for quite a while. In fact, it's been possible to do this since the introduction of SQL Server 7.0 OLAP Services. But make no mistake: the user-friendliness first introduced in the Analysis Services 2005 environment brought marked benefits over Analysis Services 2000; further improvements to features and designers in Analysis Services 2008 have made things better still.

Analysis Services 2005 also introduced, and Analysis Services 2008 extends, a variety of new OLAP features that have and will continue to revolutionize the business intelligence (BI) market. These features make cubes easier to build, query, and keep up-to-date. They enable cubes to track information that is much more relevant to business users than was possible with earlier releases of the product. In this chapter, we'll cover some of these features.

More Info This book's sample code includes two Microsoft Visual Studio solutions: Chapter16Begin.sln and Chapter16End.sln (both in this chapter's VS folder). Chapter16Begin.sln is essentially a clone of the Visual Studio sample code provided with Chapter 15, but with the project and databases renamed *Chapter16*. If you want to follow along with the steps described in this chapter, you should open Chapter16Begin.sln and do your work within it. Chapter16End.sln contains all enhancements from this chapter already implemented. Use this code if you do not want to implement this chapter's steps manually, or if you need to "borrow" from, or look at, the finished version of the project. A SQL Server Management Studio solution with the SQL and multidimensional expression language (MDX) scripts required or referenced in this chapter is available as Chapter16.smsssln in this chapter's SSMS folder.

What We'll Cover in This Chapter

Covering all of the Analysis Services OLAP features would require an entire book. We believe strongly that all database developers should be well acquainted with a subset of those features, however, and at least be aware of the others. So in this chapter, we will extend our *Northwind* cube to take advantage of many of these features.

Specifically, we will extend our cube to use a parent/child dimension, fact dimensions, role-playing dimensions, advanced property settings for measures and dimensions (including attribute relationships), member grouping (discretization), display folders, calculated members, a named set, actions, a key performance indicator (KPI), a perspective, and a translation, and we'll also look at how security roles work. In the next chapter, we'll show you how to "expose" many of these features in your own applications using ADO MD.NET and other OLAP application programming interfaces (APIs).

We will also discuss partitioning, storage options, aggregation design, and proactive caching. The last of these features was perhaps the biggest breakthrough introduced in Analysis Services 2005 and continues to be important in Analysis Services 2008. It's hard to do it justice in just a portion of a chapter, but we'll make you comfortable with the concepts involved.

> **Note** Some concepts and features that we will not cover here, but that you might want to explore on your own, include linked objects, ragged (unbalanced) hierarchies, advanced processing options, MDX templates in the cube designer, multiple fact tables (along with referenced and many-to-many dimensions), and the Analysis Services designers' Add Business Intelligence feature.

MDX in Context

At various points in this chapter, we will cover Analysis Services features that require the entry of expressions written in multidimensional expression language (MDX). This poses a challenge because we provide only the most basic introduction to MDX in this book, and that material is in the next chapter. However, the MDX code we will use in this chapter should be easy to understand in context, given the OLAP conceptual coverage we provide and your own background as a developer. That said, we will provide more top-down MDX coverage in Chapter 17. After reading that chapter, you might want to refer back to the MDX code in this chapter to deepen your understanding of the examples provided here.

And Now a Word from Our Sponsor...

The Books Online documentation supplied with SQL Server 2008, including its Analysis Services component, is excellent. This book is meant to complement the Books Online material by easing you into things more comfortably and providing alternative examples to reinforce certain concepts. Likewise, our use of the *Northwind* database in our OLAP chapters is meant to augment, rather than compete with, the *AdventureWorksDW2008* samples supplied with SQL Server 2008.

We strongly recommend that you also study the *Adventure Works DW 2008* sample Analysis Services database and that you go through the Analysis Services tutorial provided in Books Online. The tutorial provides impressive depth and breadth of coverage, and the *Adventure Works* sample cube goes even further, covering virtually every feature of Analysis Services OLAP.

> **Note** You'll find the Analysis Services tutorial by navigating within Books Online or in Visual Studio help as follows: in the Contents pane, under SQL Server Books Online, select the SQL Server Tutorials node. (You can skip to this page directly from the Windows Start menu by selecting Microsoft SQL Server 2008, Documentation And Tutorials, SQL Server Tutorials.) Next, in the help page itself, scroll down to the Analysis Services—Multidimensional Data heading, and then click the Designing And Implementing: Tutorials (Analysis Services—Multidimensional Data) link below it. Last, in the resulting page, click the SQL Server Analysis Services Tutorial link.

Meanwhile, we recommend that you read this chapter first because it can help you get productive quickly. The Books Online tutorial and sample cube are more top-down and formal, so they will make more sense after you've read the discussion of advanced OLAP features in this chapter. We'll start that discussion by focusing on how to use the advanced dimension and measure features in Analysis Services 2008.

Advanced Dimensions and Measures

In the previous chapter, you learned how to use the Cube Wizard to build several dimensions for our *Northwind Sales* cube. The Cube Wizard offers the convenience of building several dimensions at once, but it does not provide access to all the features you can build into your dimensions.

You also learned in Chapter 15 how to go beyond the Cube Wizard and build your own hierarchy. (We did this by building a *Country - State-Province - City - Postal Code* hierarchy in the *Geography* dimension using the dimension designer.) But that was only a start—we could have done a lot more with that dimension and the others. Let's now refine what we have built.

Keys and Names

We'll start with the *Shippers* dimension. Recall that this dimension is flat (nonhierarchical); therefore, little refinement should be necessary. Meanwhile, this dimension's attribute displays shipper IDs rather than shipper names. We should remedy this right away. We're not doing this just to be elegant—by discussing how to clean this up, we will introduce some important concepts related to dimension attributes.

Open the *Shippers* dimension in the dimension designer. You'll notice that one attribute— *Shipper Id*—is defined for this dimension. You'll also notice that the *ShipperName* column is available in the Data Source View pane of the dimension designer. While it might be tempting to drag that column over to create an additional attribute from it, it turns out that this is not necessary. We can effectively combine the two columns *vwShippers. ShipperId* and *vwShippers.ShipperName* into a single attribute.

Select the *Shipper Id* attribute and make sure that the Properties window is visible. (If it is not, press F4 to show it or select View, Properties Window.) Look at the value settings for the attribute's *KeyColumns* and *NameColumn* properties; they are set to *vwShippers.ShipperId* and *(none)*, respectively. Look also at the *OrderBy* property, and you will see that the members of this attribute are configured to be sorted by their IDs. This dimension attribute is about halfway toward being what we need; its name needs to be changed to *Shipper Name*, its *NameColumn* needs to be changed to *vwShippers.ShipperName*, and its *OrderBy* property needs to be changed from *Id* to *Name*.

To rename the *Shipper Id* attribute, you can modify its *Name* property in the Properties window or you can right-click the attribute and then choose Rename on the shortcut menu (or select the attribute and press F2) and then edit the name in place. Type **Shipper Name** for the new name.

After renaming the attribute, select the *NameColumn* property and then click the ellipsis button. In the resulting Name Column dialog box, select ShipperName from the Source Column list box, as shown in Figure 16-1, and then click OK.

FIGURE 16-1 Selecting a specific column for the *ShipperName* attribute's *NameColumn* property in the Name Column dialog box

Now simply change the value of the *OrderBy* property from *Key* to *Name*, and we've almost finished adjusting our attribute. But before continuing, right-click the newly renamed *Shipper Name* attribute. On the shortcut menu's Set Attribute Usage submenu (an alternative interface to the attribute's *Usage* property), confirm that you see a check mark next to the Key option.

We've finished our attribute work, so now it's time to deploy our changes to the server and then use the dimension designer's Browser tab to make sure everything looks right. Click the Start Debugging button on Visual Studio's main toolbar (not on the dimension designer's toolbar), select Debug, Start Debugging, or press F5 on your keyboard to save your changes and deploy them to the server.

> **Important** You should follow this same procedure throughout this chapter each time we ask you to save and deploy your changes, unless otherwise instructed.

When deployment and processing has completed, click the dimension designer's Browser tab (you may be placed there automatically, after deployment). Drill down on the All (root) node of the tab's tree view control; your screen should appear as shown in Figure 16-2.

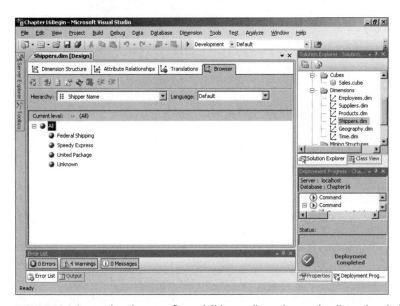

FIGURE 16-2 Inspecting the reconfigured *Shippers* dimension on the dimension designer's Browser tab

Changing the *All* Member

To neaten things up completely, let's change the name of the *Shippers* dimension's *All* member to *All Shippers*. To do this, return to the Dimension Structure tab of the dimension designer, select the root node in the Attributes tree view (that is, select the node representing the dimension itself), and in the Properties window, change the value of the *AttributeAllMemberName* property to **All Shippers**.

Save and deploy your changes. Then return to the *Shippers* dimension designer's Browser tab. Since the structure of the dimension and the cube has changed, the connection between the browser and the dimension is no longer valid. Reestablish this connection by clicking the Reconnect button (second from the left) on the designer's toolbar, choosing Dimension, Reconnect, or by clicking the Reconnect hyperlink in the yellow error panel at the bottom of the designer, as shown in Figure 16-3.

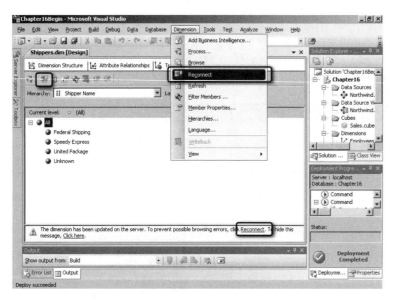

FIGURE 16-3 The dimension browser as it appears when a reconnect is necessary

You should see Shipper Name appear as the default (and only) hierarchy in the Hierarchy drop-down list (on the Browser tab) and an All Shippers node appear in the browser's tree view instead of the All node that appeared previously. If you drill down on All Shippers, you should see the three shipper names and an Unknown member, sorted alphabetically.

> **Note** At some point, you might want to clean up the *Employees* dimension using an approach similar to the one we just took with *Shippers*. The *Geography* dimension was refined in Chapter 15, the *Time* dimension does not need any cleanup, and we will tidy the *Products* dimension shortly using a technique that can be applied equally well to the *Suppliers* dimension. (Note that we will add a new employee-based dimension in the next section, but we will not be cleaning up the original *Employees* dimension.)

Adding a Named Query to a Data Source View

Now let's look at improving some of the other dimensions in the cube and creating a few new dimensions in the process. Let's start by looking at the *Employees* dimension. Open it by double-clicking its node in Solution Explorer. In the Data Source View pane of the dimension designer, take a look at the various fields in *vwEmployees*, the dimension "table" on which it's based. As with the *Shippers* dimension, only two fields—a key and a name—appear in the view. Meanwhile, several other fields are available in the original table, one of which will be useful to add: the *ReportsTo* column. This column contains the ID of the employee's supervisor and thus serves as a self-join foreign key. Using this column will allow us to make a new employee-based parent/child dimension.

To start using the *ReportsTo* column, we could simply modify *vwEmployees* back in the relational database and refresh our data source view. Another approach would be to create a named query in the data source view itself. A named query, in essence, is a view, but creating one does not modify the relational database. Named queries can be a life saver if you have read-only access to the database. In our case, we created a view in the first place, so it would stand to reason that we could modify it subsequently. However, let's create a named query instead, just to see how it's done.

Start by opening the *Northwind* data source view by double-clicking its node in the Solution Explorer window. In the diagram pane, right-click an empty spot, and then choose New Named Query on the shortcut menu to open the Create Named Query dialog box. This dialog box is essentially a container for the same SQL query designer found in SQL Server Management Studio, along with a customized toolbar, text boxes for a name and description, and a drop-down list of data sources. Name the query **Employees**, and insert the following query text in the SQL pane (the multiline text box at the bottom) of the query editor:

```
SELECT EmployeeID, LastName + ', ' + FirstName AS EmployeeName, ReportsTo FROM Employees
```

Click in one of the other panes to force them to update. The dialog box should now appear exactly as shown in Figure 16-4. Click OK, and then save the changes made to the data source view.

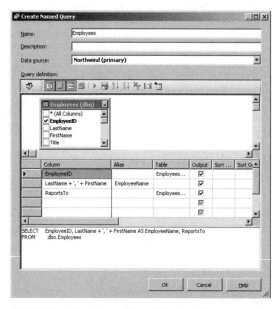

FIGURE 16-4 The Create Named Query dialog box

Before we can use this named query to create a new employee-based dimension, we need to create two relationships on it: one to codify the self-join from the *ReportsTo* column to the *EmployeeId* column and another from the *EmployeeId* column of *tblFact* to the like-named column in the named query. To do this, start by right-clicking the *EmployeeId* column of the *Employees* named query and choosing the Set Logical Primary Key shortcut menu option (or left-click the column and select Data Source View, Set Logical Primary Key). Next create the relationship between the fact table and the named query and the self-join just discussed by using the drag-and-drop procedure described in the previous chapter, by selecting Data Source View, New Relationship, or by selecting the New Relationship option on any of the various shortcut menus in the Diagram pane or the Tables pane. You can also use the New Relationship button (fourth from the right) on the data source view designer's toolbar. When you've finished, your data source view should appear as shown in Figure 16-5. Save your changes before proceeding.

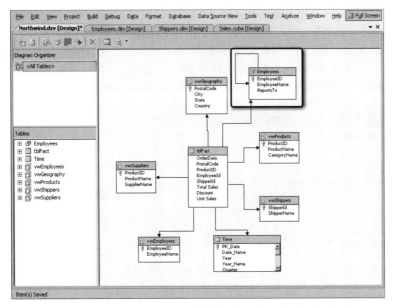

FIGURE 16-5 Our data source view, modified to include and join the *Employees* named query

Parent/Child Dimensions

Before we create a new employee-based dimension, right-click the *Employees* named query in the data source view designer, and then choose Explore Data. Examine the data shown. You will see that Suyama, King, and Dodsworth report to Buchanan, and that Buchanan and all other employees report to Fuller. Our task will be to create a special dimension that represents these relationships, in a hierarchy, without transforming the structure of the dimension table itself. To do this, you invoke the Dimension Wizard.

> **Tip** As you saw in Chapter 15, adding a new dimension to a cube is a two-step process: you must first create a database dimension and then add it to the cube. To create the database dimension, you must use the Dimension Wizard. You can open the wizard by choosing the New Dimension option on the Dimensions node shortcut menu in the Solution Explorer window or by choosing Project, New Dimension.
>
> You add an existing database dimension to a cube by using the Add Cube Dimension dialog box, which you display by choosing Cube, Add Cube Dimension; this option is available when the cube designer is open and its Cube Structure or Dimension Usage tab is active. You can also select the Add Cube Dimension option on the shortcut menu in the Cube Structure tab's Dimensions pane or on the Dimension Usage tab.

Click Next on the Welcome page, and then click Next again to accept the default selection on the Select Creation Method page. On the Specify Source Information page, select the Employees named query from the Main Table drop-down list, accept the default selection of EmployeeId as the key column, and then select EmployeeName from the Name Column drop-down list, as shown in Figure 16-6.

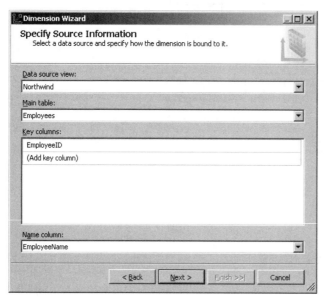

FIGURE 16-6 The Specify Source Information page of the Dimension Wizard

Click Next to advance to the Select Dimension Attributes page, and make sure that the check boxes next to the *Employee Id* and *ReportsTo* columns are both selected. Change the name of the *Employee Id* attribute to **Employee Name**. Click Next to advance to the Completing The Wizard page. Type **Org Chart** as the name of the new dimension, and then click Finish. The new dimension should now open in the dimension designer; otherwise, open it.

The *Org Chart* dimension now contains an attribute named *Employee Name* that displays values from the *EmployeeName* column and is keyed on the *EmployeeId* column. This attribute will serve as the child level of our parent/child dimension.

Notice that the *Reports To* attribute's usage is already set to Parent. You can check this from the attribute's shortcut menu (by selecting the Set Attribute Usage option and verifying the check mark next to Parent) or from the Properties window (by verifying that the Usage property is set to Parent). But we still need a little refinement: select the *NameColumn* property of the *Reports To* attribute, click the ellipsis button, select EmployeeName in the Name Column dialog box (from the Source Column list box), and then click OK. This ensures that, like the *Employee Name* attribute, *Reports To* will be properly configured to display the employee's name and be keyed on the employee's ID (stored in the *ReportsTo* column). To add a finishing touch, set the attribute's *OrderBy* property to *Name*.

Save and deploy your changes, and then click the dimension designer's Browser tab (if you are not placed there automatically). Make sure that Reports To is selected in the Hierarchy drop-down list, and then drill down on each member in the tree view below it. You should see the entire reporting hierarchy properly displayed and the collection of employees at each level sorted alphabetically, as shown in Figure 16-7.

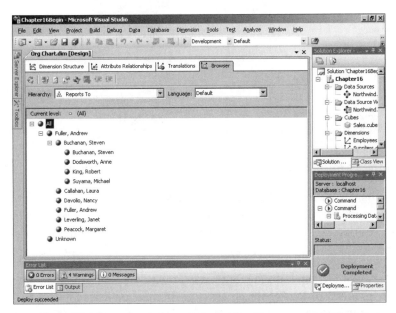

FIGURE 16-7 The dimension designer Browser tab with our parent/child attribute selected

The dimension browser confirms that our parent/child attribute has been correctly configured, for the most part. Note that Fuller and Buchanan are shown as reporting to themselves. We will address this anomaly shortly.

> **Note** Notice that there is no stand-alone *Employee Name* attribute hierarchy. This is because the attribute's *AttributeHierarchyVisible* property is set to *False*. This keeps the attribute in the dimension's structure—which it must be because it is the key attribute—but hides the attribute from client applications.

Now select the first Fuller, Andrew node in the Browser tab's tree view, and notice the name Level 02 listed next to the Current Level label just above the tree view, as shown in Figure 16-8.

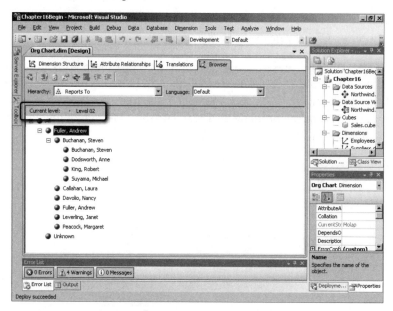

FIGURE 16-8 The dimension designer Browser tab with generic level name highlighted

Click the first Buchanan, Steven node and then the Dodsworth, Anne node, and notice that their levels are named Level 03 and Level 04, respectively. These level names are generated by Analysis Services because the hierarchy is generated automatically and was not explicitly designed by you.

We can change these level names on the Dimension Structure tab by simply using the *NamingTemplate* property of the *Reports To* attribute. In the Properties window, click the property's ellipsis button to display the Level Naming Template dialog box. Complete the dialog box as shown in Figure 16-9, and then click OK.

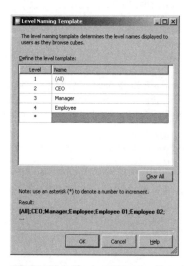

FIGURE 16-9 The Level Naming Template dialog box

The Level Naming Template dialog box allows entry of custom level names for parent/child attributes/hierarchies. By supplying names for levels 2, 3, and 4, we will override the Analysis Services–generated names Level 02, Level 03, and Level 04. Last, to prevent employees with direct reports from being listed twice, set the *MembersWithData* property to *NonLeafDataHidden*.

Save and deploy your changes, and confirm on the Browser tab that the hierarchy is now structured properly and that its levels are intelligently named. (You will need to reconnect for the change to appear.) With these changes confirmed, add the *Org Chart* dimension to the *Sales* cube by using the Add Cube Dimension dialog box in the cube designer, and then save and deploy your changes once more. Now query the new *Org Chart.Reports To* hierarchy and any measure of your choice on the cube's Browser tab (reconnecting first if necessary).

Drill down through the levels to see that you can now query the cube data by *CEO*, *Manager*, and *Employee*. You might also notice that the some of the level totals exceed the sum of their members; this is because we have hidden all data associated with the nonleaf members of the hierarchy. Setting the *Reports To* attribute's *MembersWithData* property back to *NonLeafDataVisible* would eliminate the totaling problem, but it would cause Fuller and Buchanan to be listed twice, as you saw earlier.

Member Grouping

Our next stop is the *Products* dimension. Start with renaming the *Product Id* attribute by typing in **Product Name** as its *Name* property's value, setting its *NameColumn* property to *vwProducts.ProductName* and its *OrderBy* property to *Name*. Next create an attribute from the *CategoryName* column in *vwProducts*, and then create a hierarchy named **Category - Product** using the *Category Name* and *Product Name* attributes, in that order, as its levels. (See the section "Using the Dimension Designer" in Chapter 15 for an attribute and hierarchy creation refresher.) Save and deploy your changes, and on the dimension designer's Browser tab, select Product Name from the Hierarchy drop-down list. Drill down on the *All* member, and you will see that the number of products is rather large. Using the *Category - Product* hierarchy makes the product list more manageable, but you might not always want to break up products along category lines.

One solution to this problem is to use an Analysis Services feature called member grouping, or *discretization*. Essentially, this feature groups members of a particular attribute by creating a new attribute/level "above" it. Each member of the new level ends up containing a specific number of child members from the original attribute.

To implement member grouping for the *Products* dimension, return to the Dimension Structure tab. Drag the *ProductName* column from the Data Source View pane to the Attributes pane, and change its name from the default *Product Name 1* to **Product Group**. Next set this new attribute's *DiscretizationBucketCount* property to *10* and its

DiscretizationMethod property to *Automatic*. This creates 10 discrete parent members that can be used in a new hierarchy along with the *Product Name* attribute. Create a new hierarchy by dragging the *Product Group* attribute into the Hierarchies pane, and then drag the *Product Name* attribute underneath it into the new hierarchy. Name the new hierarchy **Group - Product**, and then save and deploy your changes.

Use the new hierarchy in the cube browser (reconnecting first) to drill down on *Unit Sales* by *Product Group* (using the *Group - Product* hierarchy rather than the *Product Group* attribute). When sales in a particular group look especially high or low, drill down on that group to see which product or products are responsible for the high or low sales. You'll find that looking through the limited number of members in the *Product Group* level is much easier than looking through the entire product list to find outlier data.

User Table Time Dimensions, Attribute Relationships, Best Practice Alerts, and Dimension/Attribute Typing

In Chapter 15, we showed you how to build a time dimension based on a server-generated physical time dimension table (*Time*) that was added to the *Northwind* database. Later in this chapter, we'll show you how to build a time dimension based on a server-generated pseudo-table that does not manifest itself as a physical table at all. In this section, however, we're going to show you how to build a dimension based on an existing table in the database.

User Table Time Dimensions

Basing a time dimension on your own table that's already in the database is a fairly typical task in OLAP cube design but one that, to be honest, is a bit harder to do in Analysis Services 2008 than it was in 2005. In this section, we'll show you how to build such a dimension. And while we're doing so, we'll take the opportunity to explain how to use the *Type* property of dimensions and attributes.

In Chapter 15, when we created a time dimension using a server-generated table, properties were set for us automatically. When using our own table, we'll need to set properties ourselves, and this will provide a good opportunity to explain how they work. Creating our new time dimension will also let us explore two features new to Analysis Services 2008: Best Practice Alerts (BPAs) and the dimension designer's new Attribute Relationships pane. And later in this chapter, when we explore translations, we'll come back to this dimension and make some modifications to it.

To get started, go ahead and run both the tblTime.sql and the tblFact.sql scripts (in that order) in the Management Studio solution included with the sample code for this project. After the scripts are run, a new time dimension table, *tblTime*, will be added to the *Northwind* database, and the structure of *tblFact* will be modified. Return to Visual Studio, add *tblTime* to our data source view, refresh it so that the changes to *tblFact* are added, and then relate *tblFact* to *tblTime* via the *TimeKey* column in both tables. Click Yes when prompted to create a logical primary key, and then save your changes. Open the Dimension Wizard using one of the options already discussed for creating a new dimension.

Click Next on the Welcome page, and then on the Select Creation Method page, confirm that the Use An Existing Table option is selected and click Next again. On the Specify Source Information page, confirm that Northwind is selected in the Data Source View drop-down list, select tblTime in the Main Table drop-down list, and confirm that *TimeKey* is listed as the only column in the Key Columns list. In the Name Column drop-down list, select OrderDate, and then click Next. On the Select Dimension Attributes page, make certain that the left-column check boxes for all attributes except *Month Number* are selected. (The check boxes *are* enabled, even though they appear to be grayed out.)

Change the name of the *Time Key* attribute to **Order Date** (by editing the cell in which the name is displayed). In the Attribute Type column, click in the cell for the *Order Date* attribute, and then click the drop-down arrow. In the resulting pop-up window, drill down on Date and then Calendar, and then select its Date child node (the second one in the list, immediately below the Day Of Year node). Now perform similar actions to set the attribute type to Month for the *Month* attribute, Quarter for the *Quarter* attribute and Year for the *Year* attribute. The wizard should now appear as shown in Figure 16-10.

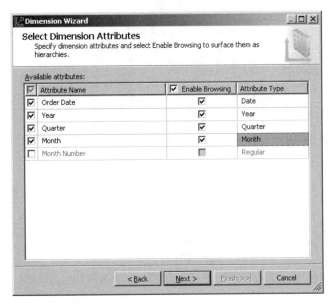

FIGURE 16-10 The Select Dimension Attributes page of the Dimension Wizard

Click Next. On the Completing The Wizard page, name the new dimension **TimeIntl** (we will add translations to this dimension, so we will consider it to be "international"), and then click Finish; the new dimension will open in the dimension designer.

Dimension/Attribute Typing

Before we continue configuring elements in the *TimeIntl* dimension, let's review what's been built. First click on each of the four attributes and view the value of the *Type* property in the Properties window. Notice the values displayed for *Date*, *Months*, *Quarters*, and *Years* rather than *Date*, *Month*, *Quarter*, and *Year*. This is simply because some property values are represented differently in the Dimension Wizard than they are in the Properties window. Now click the TimeIntl root node, and notice that its *Type* property is set to *Time*. Click that property in the Properties window, and then click the drop-down arrow in its value column. Notice the rich list of choices. Normally, you would need to set a dimension's *Type* property explicitly. However, because of the attribute types we selected, the wizard deduced that our dimension needed to be of type *Time*.

Best Practice Alerts

Notice the "squiggly" line under the TimeIntl node in the Attributes pane, representing what appears to be an error. If you hover your mouse pointer over the node, you'll see the following message displayed in a tooltip: "Create hierarchies in non-parent child dimensions." This message is what's known as a BPA and is shown in Figure 16-11.

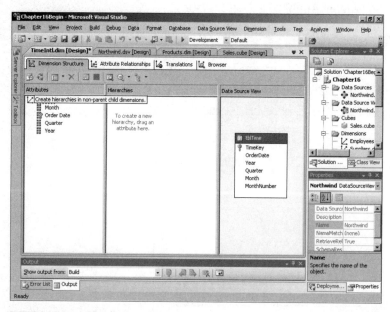

FIGURE 16-11 A BPA displayed in a tooltip.

BPAs are based on a knowledge base of Analysis Services design rules; these rules are applied in real time by the designer as it examines the structure of the Analysis Services database objects you create.

Explore this a little further by changing the *Type* property of the dimension to *Regular*; notice that squiggles now appear under each attribute, in addition to the dimension. Look at the BPA tooltip for the *Month* attribute, and you'll see the following message displayed: "The attribute type is set to 'Months,' which is not compatible with the 'Regular' dimension type." You'll see similar messages for each of the other attributes. Change the *Type* property for the dimension back to *Time*, and after a brief pause, you'll see all the squiggles disappear from under each of the attributes.

The squiggle under the dimension itself is still present, of course. We'll take corrective action to eliminate it shortly, but first, let's make some other changes. Run the tblMonthNames.sql script in the Management Studio solution; this adds the table *tblMonthNames*, which actually contains friendly names for both months and quarters, in both English and Spanish, to the *Northwind* database. We'll use the English name content as the name columns for our *Month* and *Quarter* attributes now; later we'll create a translation that references the Spanish content as well.

Add the table to our data source view. Next create a relationship between *tblTime* and *tblMonthName* on their common *MonthNumber* column. (Click Yes to create the logical primary key when prompted.) Save your changes, and if prompted to save changes to the *TimeIntl* dimension also, click OK. Return to the dimension designer for *TimeIntl*, and add *tblMonthNames* to the Data Source View pane by using its Show Tables shortcut menu option or by selecting Data Source View, Show Tables. (After the table is added, notice that the color of its title bar is a lighter blue than that of *tblTime*; this is because no column in *tblMonthNames* is used as a key column for any attribute.) Last, change the *NameColumn* properties for the *Month* and *Quarter* attributes to *tblMonthNames.EnglishMonthName* and *tblMonthNames.EnglishQuarterName*, respectively.

With our attributes now properly defined and typed, save and deploy your changes, and then view the results in the Browser tab. Examine each attribute hierarchy, drilling down on the *All* member each time. Notice that for the *Months* and *Quarters* attributes, the values repeat; that's because we have data for multiple years in *tblTime*. If you browse *tblTime*'s data, you'll see that the actual values in the *Quarter* and *Month* columns use unique values like *1996Q3* and *1996M 7*. *tblMonthNames* translates these to *Q3* and *July*, respectively. The latter names will make sense within the context of a hierarchy; the former ones will allow the hierarchy to be defined, by avoiding the duplication of key values.

From here, our work is easy. Go back to the Dimension Structure tab of the dimension designer and define a new hierarchy named *Year - Quarter - Month - Order Date*, based on the like-named attributes, in that order. Notice the squiggle under the hierarchy's name and the message displayed: "Attribute relationships do not exist between one or more levels of this hierarchy. This may result in decreased query performance."

What this BPA is telling us is that if a "natural hierarchy" exists between the attributes in our user hierarchy, we should tell Analysis Services. A natural hierarchy is one where a proper one-to-many relationship exists between levels, which is certainly the case with this dimension.

Telling Analysis Services that a natural hierarchy exists aids in the creation of aggregations— why sum up all dates in a year to aggregate it when you could instead add up its four quarters?

> **Important** While you might think that the natural hierarchy should be implied because of the user hierarchy, realize that it's possible, and desirable in some cases, to create hierarchies involving many-to-many relationships. For example, in a product dimension, you might want to create a hierarchy with color as the top level and product category as the second. Given that most product categories would likely by represented in multiple colors, these levels do not form a natural hierarchy, but the user hierarchy is still useful as a drill path.

Attribute Relationships

Specifying the existence of a natural hierarchy is done in the Attribute Relationships tab of the dimension designer. Switch to that tab now, and notice that, by default, Analysis Services only intuits that the key attribute is subsidiary to the other three. In effect, the designer is telling us, "I know that years, quarters, and months each consist of various order dates, but I have no idea what the relationship is between those non-order date attributes."

We can easily specify the relationships— for example, to specify that quarters consist of months, click the oval representing the *Month* attribute in the Diagram (top) pane, hold down the mouse button, and then drag this oval to the oval representing the *Quarter* attribute. Then do the same for *Quarter* and *Year*. If necessary, neaten up the layout of the diagram by using the Arrange Shapes toolbar button (third from right), by selecting Dimension, Arrange Shapes, or by selecting the Arrange Shapes shortcut menu option. The Attribute Relationships tab should appear as shown in Figure 16-12.

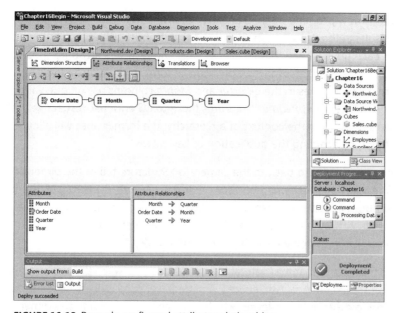

FIGURE 16-12 Properly configured attribute relationships.

> **Tip** There are two types of attribute relationships: those representing natural hierarchies and those representing nonhierarchical relationships. For nonhierarchical relationships, the target attribute appears *within* the source attribute rather than being connected to it by an arrow. The *Promotion* dimension of the *Adventure Works DW 2008* sample Analysis Services database demonstrates this nicely. If you open that dimension and view the Attributes Relationship tab, you will see that there are seven attribute relationships, only two of which are hierarchical.

We have now created three attribute relationships. They are represented by the arrows in the Diagram pane and by the three items listed in the Attribute Relationships pane on the lower right; clicking on one will highlight its counterpart in the other pane. You can double-click one of the diagram arrows, or you can select a relationship and then select Dimension, Edit Attribute Relationship or the Edit Attribute Relationship shortcut menu option in either pane to edit the relationship in the Edit Attribute Relationship dialog box.

Do that now for any one of the relationships, and change the selection in the Relationship Type drop-down list to Rigid (Will Not Change Over Time) and then click OK. Back in the dimension designer, notice that the arrows representing the relationship you just edited are now thicker. Notice also in the Properties window that the *RelationshipType* property's value reflects the change you just made. Now use either the Edit Attribute Relationship dialog box or the Properties window to set the other two relationships' types to *Rigid* as well. Sometimes, hierarchies change over time; in the case of a time dimension, that's certainly not the case.

Return to the Dimension Structure tab, and you should see that the BPA for the hierarchy has now been removed. You will also notice a drop-down arrow to the right of each of the *Quarter*, *Month*, and *Order Date* levels of our user hierarchy. Click any of those drop-down arrows to review the attribute relationships we just created.

You'll notice, however, that an alert for the dimension is still there. Hover the mouse pointer over the squiggle, and you'll see the following alert message in the tooltip: "Avoid visible attribute hierarchies for attributes used as levels in user-defined hierarchies." In other words: "Why have each attribute available for drill-down purposes when they are all represented in the hierarchy you just created? Just make the hierarchy visible and hide the attributes."

One thing to remember here is that BPAs are not always gospel, and arguably, this is one case where the alert does not necessarily make sense. We absolutely might want, for example, to drill down directly by month while, perhaps, filtering by year. The second thing to realize is that BPAs are just warnings; they are not truly errors. In fact, you'll see each alert listed as a warning in Visual Studio's Error List window. You'll need to choose Build, Build Chapter16 to update the list. Once you do, you'll see that the build succeeds (proving the warning to be nonfatal) and that the BPA is listed, as shown in Figure 16-13.

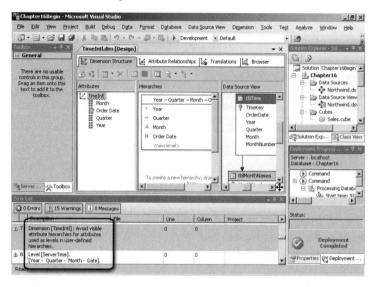

FIGURE 16-13 BPA messages in the Error List window listed after a successful build

We are left with the following options with regard to this BPA:

- Ignore the warning (which we've been doing all along for other parts of our Analysis Services databases).

- Address the issue to remove the warning.

- Dismiss the warning for this occurrence of it.

- Dismiss the warning globally (that is, prevent this particular best practice from being evaluated in this database).

If you right-click the warning in the Error List window and select the Dismiss shortcut menu option, the Dismiss Warning dialog box will appear, allowing you to dismiss this single instance of the warning and advising you how to dismiss it globally. For now, click Cancel so as *not* to dismiss the warning.

Let's resolve the warning first and then look at how to dismiss it globally. To resolve the warning, in the Dimension Structure tab of the dimension designer, simply select all four attributes (hold down the Ctrl key and click each one), and then change their collective *AttributeHierarchyVisible* property in the Properties window to *False*. Notice that the alert has been resolved (the squiggle disappears). Now change the property back to *True* for all four attributes and notice that the squiggle returns. We really prefer to keep the attributes visible, not just here but in other dimensions as well, so let's dismiss the warning globally.

To do so, you'll need to open the database editor. You can get to this designer by right-clicking the Chapter16 project node (it's the immediate child of the Solution root node) in the Solution Explorer window and then selecting its Edit Database shortcut menu option. You can also simply select Database, Edit Database. In the editor, select the Warnings tab. In the Design Warning Rules list, you'll see five main categories of warning displayed. Drill down on the Dimension Design category; in the Importance column, you'll see that the various warnings are categorized as High, Medium, or Low. Scroll to the first warning listed as Low, and you'll see that it's the one we want to dismiss globally. Clear its check box; the database editor should now appear as shown in Figure 16-14.

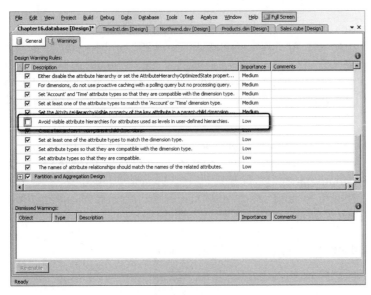

FIGURE 16-14 Dismissing a BPA warning globally in the database designer

Close the database editor, save your changes, and return to the Dimension Structure tab of the dimension designer for *TimeIntl*; notice that the alert has been cleared.

> **Note** We've shown you here how to resolve specific BPAs in the *TimeIntl* dimension, but obviously, others remain elsewhere in our project. It is beyond the scope of this chapter and this book to guide you through resolving all of the alerts. However, we encourage you to review the rest of the BPA messages; even if you don't focus on resolving them all, you will nonetheless learn much about proper design of cubes that perform well.

Save your changes to the dimension. We've almost finished, but remember that we have merely defined a new database dimension and have not yet added it to our *Sales* cube. To do so, open the cube in its designer, and on the Cube Structure tab, add the new *TimeIntl* dimension using any of the Add Cube Dimension options discussed earlier.

Now save and deploy all changes. On the Browser tab of the cube designer, drag the *Total Sales* measure to the Drop Totals Or Detail Fields Here area and drag the *Year - Quarter - Month - Order Date* hierarchy of the *TimeIntl* dimension to the Drop Row Fields Here area. Drill down through the hierarchy to see how it works.

Server Time Dimensions

As we built our original *Northwind Sales* cube in the previous chapter, you might have thought that building a special dimension table for the *Time* dimension was a bit wasteful. After all, the concept of time is fairly universal, and there's a limited set of possible attributes and hierarchies that might be needed, any of which could be easily keyed off a date field in the fact table rather than an arbitrary time key.

In Analysis Services 2000, the concept of a date column–derived time dimension was very basic and easily implemented. Analysis Services 2005 and 2008 enhanced this facility, but its use is slightly less obvious. The new implementation of such time dimensions is based on a server-generated pseudo-dimension table and an array of predefined attributes and hierarchies. In fact, this type of time dimension is implemented by creating a special dimension type called a *server time dimension*.

Let's add a server time dimension to our cube. Simply open the Dimension Wizard, and on the Select Creation Method page, select the Generate A Time Table On The Server option. On the Define Time Periods page, specify January 1, 1996, and June 30, 1998, as the first and last calendar days, respectively, and select Year, Quarter, Month, and Date from the Time Periods list box, as shown in Figure 16-15.

FIGURE 16-15 The Define Time Periods page of the Dimension Wizard

Accept the defaults for all other settings, name your new dimension **ServerTime**, and then click Finish. Add the dimension to your cube as described earlier, and then click the cube designer's Dimension Usage tab. This tab is where you configure dimensions that typically are not based on conventional relationships between fact and dimension tables.

Click in the cell at the intersection of the *ServerTime* dimension row and the *Main* measure group column, and then click the cell's ellipsis button. (The cell to click will be represented by a gray rectangle to the right of the *ServerTime* dimension cell.) In the Define Relationship dialog box, specify a Regular relationship, Date as the Granularity Attribute, and OrderDate as the Measure Group Column, as shown in Figure 16-16.

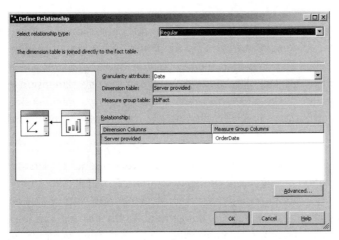

FIGURE 16-16 The Define Relationship dialog box, configured for a server time dimension

Notice the Server Provided designation under the Dimension Columns header; this indicates that the dimension table is server generated and therefore does not require you to specify a dimension column. Click OK, and notice that the cell on the Dimension Usage tab now reads *Date*, indicating the granularity attribute of the server time dimension. Save and deploy your changes, and then inspect them in the cube browser (reconnecting first, as necessary).

> **Note** If you drill down on the *Time* or *ServerTime* dimension in the cube browser's metadata tree view, you will see that both dimensions offer an array of default attributes. If you open the *ServerTime* dimension in the dimension designer, you will see an even larger array of columns (from which new attributes can be created) in the Dimension Structure tab's Time Periods pane.

Fact Dimensions

One hallmark of Analysis Services is its ability to adapt to your database's structure rather than making you perform extract, transform and load (ETL) gymnastics to satisfy Analysis Services' requirements. Suppose, for example, that you want to create a dimension out of data that is stored in your fact table. With Analysis Services 2000, you would have to duplicate that data within the database and then relate that data back to your fact table to use it as a dimension. The current version of Analysis Services, on the other hand, is much less rigid: you simply specify that your dimension data is in your fact table, and Analysis Services will accommodate you.

For example, the *Orders* table in the *Northwind* database contains geographic information pertaining to the shipping location that can be constructed into a useful dimension. Our current *Geography* dimension, derived from data in the *Customers* table, was easy to construct. But it is less obvious how to use fields such as *ShipCountry* and *ShipRegion* from our fact table (and derived from the *Northwind* database's *Orders* table) as levels in a new dimension.

It might be less obvious how, but it is still feasible to build this dimension with Analysis Services 2008. Create a new dimension named *Ship Geography*, making sure to identify *tblFact* as the dimension table, *Ship Region* as the key column, and *Ship Country* as the only additional attribute column. (Deselect all related tables.) Open the new dimension in its designer if it is not already open; create a user hierarchy named *Country - Region* using the *Ship Country* and *Ship Region* attributes, in order, as its levels; and then add the new dimension to your cube.

Before you can save and deploy your changes, a little more work is required. First set the dimension's *ErrorConfiguration.KeyDuplicate* property to *IgnoreError*. Next you must explicitly tell Analysis Services that your new dimension is a fact dimension. You do this on the Dimension Usage tab of the cube designer. The adjustment is rather simple. On the tab, locate the cell where the *Ship Geography* dimension row intersects the *Main* measure group column. The *Ship Region* field name is displayed in that cell. Everything appears to be normal, but an adjustment is indeed necessary.

Click within the *Ship Region* cell, and you should see an ellipsis button appear (as shown in Figure 16-17).

FIGURE 16-17 The Dimension Usage tab with the ellipsis button for the Ship Geography dimension/Main measure group cell highlighted

Because *Ship Geography* is a fact dimension, you'll need to override its default usage and tell Analysis Services to establish a fact relationship as its basis. Click the ellipsis button to open the Define Relationship dialog box, change the relationship type from Regular to Fact, as shown in Figure 16-18, and then click OK.

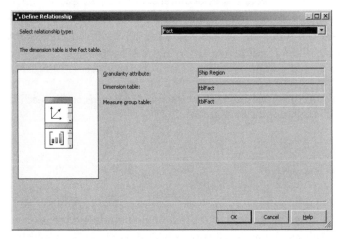

FIGURE 16-18 The Define Relationship dialog box with the Fact relationship type selected

Back on the Dimension Usage tab of the cube designer, notice that the special fact dimension icon now appears in the dimension's cell, as shown in Figure 16-19.

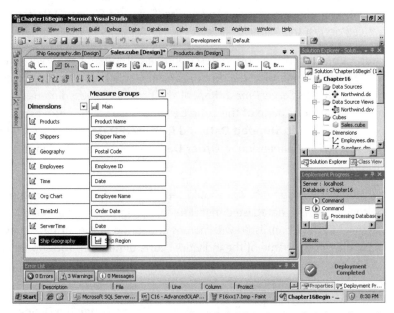

FIGURE 16-19 The Dimension Usage tab with the Ship Geography's fact dimension icon highlighted

Save and deploy your changes. On the Browser tab of the cube designer, reconnect if necessary, and you should be able to drill down on any measure by the *Ship Country* or *Ship Region* attribute or through the hierarchy that includes both. As you do so, consider how quickly you were able to create this dimension, add it to your cube, and start using it. No ETL is required, and you don't need to create a special dimension table, a view, or even a named query. This kind of flexibility—what we might call a *casual* ability to enhance a cube—simply didn't exist in Analysis Services 2000. That Analysis Services 2005 introduced it and Analysis Services 2008 continues to offer it is a true revolution in the BI space.

> **Caution** Each measure group in a cube can have at most one fact dimension, and each fact dimension can be related to only one measure group.

Role-Playing Dimensions

Fact dimensions are not the only specialized type of dimension; there are many others. One of these, *role-playing dimensions*, allows you to reuse a single database dimension as multiple distinct cube dimensions. This can be especially useful with time dimensions, which usually have identical structures.

Our *tblFact* table now contains three date fields: *OrderDate* (which was there all along), *RequiredDate*, and *ShippedDate*. Wouldn't it be nice if we could reuse our *ServerTime* dimension twice more, relating the new "instances" to *RequiredDate* and *ShippedDate*, respectively? As it turns out, we can do just that.

Simply use the Add Cube Dimension option described earlier, select the *ServerTime* dimension in the Add Cube Dimension dialog box, and then click OK. You should see your new dimension added as *ServerTime 1*. Repeat the process to add dimension *ServerTime 2*. In the Dimensions pane of the cube designer's Cube Structure tab, rename *ServerTime 1* and *ServerTime 2* to **Shipped Date** and **Required Date**, respectively, and last, rename the original *ServerTime* dimension to **Order Date** to better identify it in relation to these new dimensions.

Now move to the Dimension Usage tab. You should see all three of the cube dimensions that are based on the *ServerTime* database dimension, including the original *ServerTime* dimension (now renamed *Order Date*), listed with names appearing in the format *ServerTime* (*cubedim*), where *cubedim* is the name of the individual cube dimension. You should also see that the cells at which the two new dimensions intersect with the Main measure group are gray and empty.

Click in one of the empty cells, and then click the ellipsis button to open the Define Relationship dialog box. Select Regular from the Select Relationship Type drop-down list, select Date from the Granularity Attribute drop-down list, and select the appropriate fact table date column (*ShippedDate* or *RequiredDate*, depending on which cube dimension you selected) under Measure Group Columns. These settings explicitly tell Analysis Services the foreign key in the fact table on which to join the server time pseudo-dimension table. Click OK, repeat this process for the remaining unconfigured dimension, save and deploy your changes, and then examine the changes in the cube browser.

In Analysis Services 2000, each distinct time dimension required its own dimension table (or at least its own view). As with fact dimensions, Analysis Services handles data retrieval for you so that no ETL tasks, views, or named queries are required to implement the three different time dimensions. As you might have surmised, role-playing dimensions are so named because they allow a single database dimension to play the "role" of multiple distinct cube dimensions by linking to different columns in the measure group (fact table). This is similar to using the same table more than once in a SQL query and assigning it an alias: the various role-playing dimensions in the cube are essentially aliases of the one physical database dimension.

Advanced Measures

With all this work on our dimensions, we shouldn't forget measures. Shortly, we'll discuss how to create measures that are completely calculated by our cube, but for now, let's just concentrate on tidying up the measures we have.

Measure Formatting

As you browsed the cube, you might have noticed that the dollar amounts stored in the measures are displayed as raw numbers and are not formatted as currency data. This can make the data difficult to read, but the problem is easily solved.

Open the *Sales* cube in the cube designer, click the Cube Structure tab, and select the *Total Sales* measure in the Measures pane. Then, in the Properties window, set the *FormatString* property to *Currency* and do the same for the other two measures. Notice the other formatting options available for use when you design cubes in the future. Analysis Services makes it easy to implement flexible server-side formatting of all your measures. In the next chapter, you'll see how easy it is to display formatted measure values in your applications.

Special Aggregates

The Properties window lets you do more than simply format your measures; it also lets you alter their formulaic definitions. The *AggregateFunction* property allows you to create measures whose aggregations are not simple sums.

For example, in addition to our *Total Sales* measure, we might want to have a measure that reflects average total sales for a given dimensional slice. Adding such a measure to our cube is easy. On the Cube Structure tab of the cube designer, click the New Measure toolbar button (third from the left), select Cube, New Measure, or select the New Measure option on the Measures pane's shortcut menu. In the resulting New Measure dialog box, select Average Over Time from the Usage drop-down list, select the Total Sales item in the Source Column list box, and then click OK.

You'll see the new measure appear as Total Sales – Main. Using its shortcut menu, the F2 key, or the *Name* property in the Properties window, rename it to **Avg Total Sales**. In the Properties window, notice that the *AggregateFunction* property is set to *AverageOfChildren*; this is the result of selecting the Average Over Time option in the New Measure dialog box. As you did with the other measures, set the *FormatString* property of this new measure to *Currency*.

> **Note** Clicking the drop-down arrow in the *AggregateFunction* property value cell reveals numerous other aggregate functions that you can select for your measures. The *MeasureExpression* property allows you to enter an MDX expression that will determine the value of the leaf levels of your dimensions before the aggregate function is applied. You'll learn more about MDX expressions in the next chapter.

Display Folders

When your cube has a large number of measures, you might want to group related ones together, something Analysis Services lets you do with display folders. By simply entering a folder name into a measure's *DisplayFolder* property, you can segregate related sets of measures. The cube browser, embedded in the cube designer and in Management Studio, offers direct support for display folders, as does Excel 2007. In the next chapter, we will cover how to support display folders in your own applications.

Once the display folder name is entered in the Properties window, it morphs into a drop-down list item. You can then easily assign the same display folder name to other measures in your cube without having to type it from scratch and risk entering it inconsistently. Type the name **Non-Sum** as the *DisplayFolder* property value for the *Avg Total Sales* measure you previously created, and type **Sum** as the *DisplayFolder* property value for the *Total Sales* measure. Now select one of the remaining measures, and notice that both Sum and Non-Sum appear in its *DisplayFolder* property drop-down list. Select Sum, and do likewise for the remaining measure.

Save and deploy your changes, and then click the cube designer's Browser tab (unless you're placed there automatically). Reconnect and then browse your cube. The original three measures should appear under the Sum display folder, and the *Avg Total Sales* measure should appear under the Non-Sum display folder (both within the Main measure group). When browsed, each measure's data should be formatted as currency values.

> **Important** User hierarchies within dimensions also have a *DisplayFolder* property that you can use in the same way as outlined here for measures. You can enter folder names using a file path–like syntax (for example, *parent folder**child folder*), allowing you to create display folder hierarchies.

Calculations

There's a lot more to explore than these measure and dimension features. For instance, Analysis Services allows you to store calculated MDX expressions on the server that you can use in your queries. You can reference custom-built sets by name, create calculated measures or dimension attribute members, and more. The Calculations tab of the cube designer provides a nice user interface (UI) for specifying named sets and calculated members, without requiring you to hand-code the MDX yourself. You can view the generated MDX if you're curious or if you want to learn more MDX through reverse engineering.

> **Note** As mentioned, we'll examine MDX more carefully in the next chapter. If the syntax or expression content is confusing to you now, don't worry too much because it will become clearer later on.

Imagine that the Northwind Trading Company has defined Albuquerque, New Mexico; Boise, Idaho; and Kirkland, Washington, as test markets and often needs to view the sales in those three markets. By creating a named set containing those three cities, we can provide users with an easy way to query data for just those test markets. We might also want to see net sales rather than having to look at the *Total Sales* and *Discount* measures separately. By creating a calculated member defined as the difference between *Total Sales* and *Discount*, we can have an easy way to look at net sales without needing to embed that data in the fact table or embed expressions in our queries.

We might also want to define an additional calculated member that specifies our net sales growth for any time period, by comparing the period's net sales with that of the previous period and looking at the growth percentage (positive or negative) between the two. As you will see shortly, the Analysis Services calculations facility and MDX make this pretty easy.

Calculated Members

Let's start by creating the calculated measures we just described. Click the cube designer's Calculations tab, shown in Figure 16-20.

> **Note** Because the calculated *members* created in this chapter belong to the *Measures* hierarchy, they can also be called calculated *measures*. Therefore, the terms *calculated member* and *calculated measure* are used interchangeably.

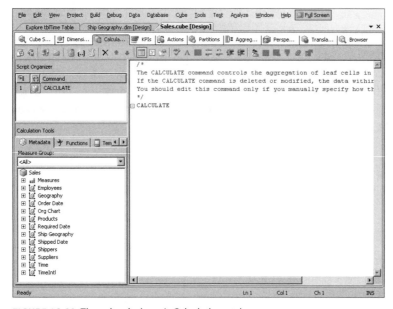

FIGURE 16-20 The cube designer's Calculations tab

A single calculation is already defined; leave that intact because the correct calculation of any new entries will depend on it. Next click the New Calculated Member button (fifth from the left) on the designer's toolbar (or select Cube, New Calculated Member or the New Calculated Member option on the Script Organizer pane's shortcut menu). This action adds a new calculated member to the cube, which you must now configure.

The main area of the designer window displays a form prompting you for various parameters of the calculated member, as shown in Figure 16-21.

Type **[Adjusted Sales]** for the Name field (all calculated member names with embedded spaces must be contained within square brackets), confirm that Measures is selected in the Parent Hierarchy drop-down list, and enter the following MDX expression in the Expression text area:

```
[Measures].[Total Sales] - [Measures].[Discount]
```

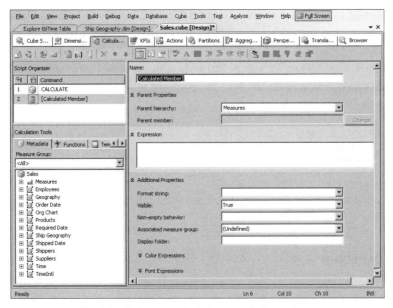

FIGURE 16-21 The cube designer's Calculations tab, in form view

Next select "Currency" in the Format String drop-down list. Select Main in the Associated Measure Group drop-down list, and then type **Sum** in the Display Folder text box. The completed calculated member form for *[Adjusted Sales]* is shown in Figure 16-22.

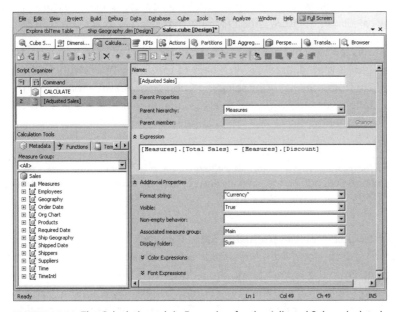

FIGURE 16-22 The Calculation tab in Form view for the *Adjusted Sales* calculated member

You have just defined a calculated measure named *Adjusted Sales*, which is the difference between the values for the measures *Total Sales* and *Discount*. To see the MDX code that the designer generated, simply click the Script View toolbar button (12th button from the left) or select Cube, Show Calculations In, Script. Starting on the second line of the exposed MDX script (excluding comments), you should see the following MDX code, which represents the calculated measure you just created:

```
CREATE MEMBER CURRENTCUBE.[Measures].[Adjusted Sales]
 AS [Measures].[Total Sales] - [Measures].[Discount],
FORMAT_STRING = "Currency",
VISIBLE = 1 ,  DISPLAY_FOLDER = 'Sum' ,  ASSOCIATED_MEASURE_GROUP = 'Main'  ;
```

As you can see, each field in the designer simply prompts you for a different clause of the MDX *CREATE MEMBER* command.

Complex Expressions

Calculation expressions can certainly be more complex than simple arithmetic formulas. The MDX query language is extremely rich and expressive, allowing you to embed powerful declarative analytic functionality within calculations. Although an in-depth look at MDX is beyond the scope of this chapter, let's build one more calculation and, in the process, sample the power of MDX.

First save and deploy your changes (this time by choosing Build, Deploy Chapter16) so that *[Adjusted Sales]* can be used within the expression for a new calculated measure (that is, we will create a *new* calculated measure with a formula that references *[Adjusted Sales]*).

Click the Calculations tab's Reconnect toolbar button (third from the left) to refresh the Calculation Tools pane's Metadata tab. Switch back to form view by clicking the Form View toolbar button (11th from the left) or by selecting Cube, Show Calculations In, Form. In the Script Organizer pane, select the *[Adjusted Sales]* calculated member you just created and add a new calculated member.

 Tip New calculations are always inserted after the one selected. Selecting the *[Adjusted Sales]* calculated member before adding the new one ensures that the latter will be added at the bottom of the list (and thus at the end of the script).

Name the new calculated member **[Adjusted Sales Growth]**, and then select Measures from the Parent Hierarchy drop-down list if not already selected. Skip past the Expression field, and select "Percent" from the Format String drop-down list. Select Main from the Associated Measure Group drop-down list, and then type **Sum** in the Display Folder text box. Now place your cursor back in the Expression text area. The MDX expression for this calculation will be more complex than the last, so let's take it step by step.

First enter the following text:

```
CASE
    WHEN
```

Be sure to type a single space after the *WHEN* keyword. This allows you to insert code immediately afterward and ensures that a space will exist between the *WHEN* keyword and the inserted code.

Using Calculation Tools

The next section of code is prone to typographical errors if typed manually, so we will take advantage of the Calculations Tools pane to continue entering our MDX expression. You can think of the Calculations Tools pane and its Metadata, Functions, and Templates tabs as a sort of drag-and-drop IntelliSense feature: you can actually drag your cube's objects, MDX function call prototypes, or entire code templates into the Expression area, and code corresponding to the item you have dragged will be inserted for you.

> **Important** The Calculation Tools pane is a coder's tool. Therefore, it is visible and usable not only when the cube designer's Calculations tab is in form view but also when it is in script view.

If the Metadata tab is not already selected within the Calculation Tools pane, click it to make it active. Next, drill down on the *Order Date* dimension and locate the *Year - Quarter - Month - Date* hierarchy, which should appear as the dimension node's last child node. Drag and drop this hierarchy object into the Expression area, positioning it at the end of the second line, one space to the right of the *WHEN* keyword. Your expression text should now appear as follows:

```
CASE
    WHEN [Order Date].[Year -  Quarter -  Month -  Date]
```

If the code does not appear exactly as shown here, you can manually edit it to make it so.

You will continue by using a mixture of drag-and-drop and manual typing techniques, developing the MDX expression to contain the following code. (Don't type it just yet.)

```
CASE
    WHEN [Order Date].[Year -  Quarter -  Month -  Date].CURRENTMEMBER.LEVEL.
ORDINAL = 0 THEN
        NULL
    WHEN ISEMPTY(([Order Date].[Year -  Quarter -  Month -  Date].PREVMEMBER, [Measures].
[Adjusted Sales])) THEN
        "EMPTY"
    ELSE
        [Measures].[Adjusted Sales]/
        ([Order Date].[Year -  Quarter -  Month -  Date].PREVMEMBER, [Measures].
[Adjusted Sales]) - 1
END
```

In a moment, we'll discuss what this expression actually calculates; we'll first discuss whether and how to use the items on the various tabs of the Calculation Tools pane to build out parts of the code.

The *CURRENTMEMBER* and *PREVMEMBER* properties can be found in, and dragged from, the Navigation branch of the Functions tab's tree view. Doing so might be more trouble than it's worth, however. You might find it easier to use the List Members or Complete Word shortcut menu options from within the expression edit region. You can also use the like-named options available by selecting Edit, IntelliSense. You might find the Ctrl+J (for List members), Ctrl+Space, or Alt+Right Arrow (for Complete Word) keyboard shortcuts even more convenient as you gain experience.

The *LEVEL* and *ORDINAL* property keywords can be found under the Metadata node of the Functions tab (not the Metadata tab). They can also be dragged and dropped, but again, doing so offers little in the way of productivity increases and requires manual replacement of the generated <<*Member*>> and <<*Level*>> prefixes. Sometimes it's best to use the Calculation Tools pane simply as a reference tool to remind yourself of MDX syntax; at other times, the drag-and-drop functionality can be useful. Typically, complex expressions involving long dimension, hierarchy, and/or level and member names are better dragged than typed.

> **Note** The items on the Templates tab of the Calculation Tools pane offer skeletal versions of long code constructs and give you a great head start for digging deeper into MDX. Items from this tab must, by their very nature, be dragged and dropped.

You will find that the *[Measures].[Adjusted Sales]* item can be dragged and dropped from the Metadata tab; simply expand the Measures node at the top of the Metadata tab's tree view and then expand its Main and Sum subnodes, and then drag and drop the Adjusted Sales node into the Expression text area.

Regardless of how you compose the expression code, you should perform a syntax check on it when you've finished. To do so, click the Check Syntax toolbar button (13th from the right, with a spell check icon) or select Cube, Check Syntax. A message box should appear with the message "The syntax check was successful." If not, check the formula text or open the Chapter16End Visual Studio Analysis Services solution included in the sample code for this chapter, open the *Sales* cube in the cube designer, click the Calculations tab, select the *[Adjusted Sales Growth]* calculated member, and copy and paste the expression text from there.

Deciphering the Code

Now let's discuss how the calculation expression we just entered actually works. The easiest way to understand the expression is to start at the bottom and work your way up. Start by looking at the formula within the *ELSE* clause of the expression, shown here:

```
[Measures].[Adjusted Sales]/
        ([Order Date].[Year -  Quarter -  Month -  Date].PREVMEMBER,
        [Measures].[Adjusted Sales]) - 1
```

The parenthetical part of this formula calculates the *Adjusted Sales* measure's value for the previous period within the *Year - Quarter - Month - Date* hierarchy of the *Order Date* dimension. *Adjusted Sales* for the *current* period is then divided by this number, and last the number *1* is subtracted from the quotient. The resulting value is the period-over-period growth for the *Adjusted Sales* calculated measure.

The previous and current "periods" that the expression references are determined by the context set by the query calling this function. For example, if the expression is calculated for a member of the *Year* level, the expression will record annual growth in *Adjusted Sales*. If it is calculated for a member of the *Quarter* level, the expression will return quarter-over-quarter growth, and so on. You'll see shortly how you can use this calculated member in the cube browser to see *Adjusted Sales* growth at several levels of the *Order Date* dimension's *Year - Quarter - Month - Date* hierarchy.

Once you understand the formula in the *ELSE* clause, the rest of the expression is easy because it deals just with invalid comparison scenarios. Moving upward through the code, if the expression is evaluated for the very first period in its level (for example, January 1996 in the *Month* level), *PREVMEMBER* will be empty and the formula will return the hard-coded string *EMPTY*. If the period passed to the formula is at level 0 of the hierarchy (that is, the *All* member), the formula will return *NULL* because the *All* member by definition can have no predecessor.

Named Sets

Before we deploy and test these new calculations, let's add a named set that references the three test-market cities we mentioned earlier. This is quite easy to do. Simply make sure that the *[Adjusted Sales Growth]* calculated member is selected in the Script Organizer pane of the cube designer's Calculations tab, and then add a new named set using the New Named Set button on Calculation tab's toolbar (sixth button from the left) or the like-named option on the Script Organizer's shortcut menu or on the Cube branch of the main menu. Name the set **[Test Markets]**, and enter the following text in the Expression area:

```
{[Geography].[City].&[Albuquerque], [Geography].[City].&[Boise],
[Geography].[City].&[Kirkland]}
```

Tip You might find it easiest to compose the expression by typing the curly braces ({}), commas, and spaces yourself and generating the rest of the code by dragging and dropping the appropriate members of the *City* attribute of the *Geography* dimension from the Metadata tab of the Calculation Tools pane. Specifically, you would need to expand the Sales\Geography\ City\Members\All node and then drag and drop each of the three cities from the alphabetically sorted list to the appropriate insertion points in the Expression text box.

Using drag-and-drop techniques to specify members of a set results in rather formal syntax usage in the generated code—namely, the use of the ampersand (&) character and the square brackets ([]) around each name, which are technically not necessary. The brackets are superfluous because none of the names contains embedded spaces. The ampersand character is used to reference a member key rather than a member name. In our case, the name and the key are one and the same and the names are unique, so the ampersand is not strictly required. You might want to leave the brackets and ampersands in the expression code so that subsequent name changes involving the use of embedded spaces or member keys can be accommodated without requiring major changes.

More on Script View

Save your changes now, but before deploying them, switch back to script view to look at the entire set of generated code. Notice that each calculation you entered, as well as the *CALCULATE* script command that was there initially, simply forms successive sections of a single MDX script. These snippets of code appear within that script in the same order in which they appear in the Script Organizer pane displayed in form view.

Script view does not contain .NET code, but the dichotomy between form view and script view provides the same experience as working in form (design) view and code view in a .NET project in Visual Studio. There is no concept in MDX of events or "code behind," but the dynamic of designer-generated code is very much in effect, and changes in one view necessarily affect the other.

Furthermore, the code editor supports many of the same features as the code editor in .NET projects: blocks of code can be expanded or contracted; word completion, member listing, and real-time "squiggle" syntax error prompting are supported; parameter information is supplied in tooltips when you use MDX functions; and you can enter comments using either of the Transact-SQL (T-SQL) comment syntax patterns (/*comment*/ and --comment) or the C style (//comment). Comments entered in script view make your MDX code more readable and do not prevent form view from rendering properly.

Tip Even when you're *not* in script view, the Expression text region in form view supports many of the features just described.

Debug Mode

The similarities with .NET projects do not end there; they extend to the entire debugging experience. You can set and clear breakpoints, and you can select Debug, Step Over when a breakpoint is hit. This brings up an important point: until now, we have spoken of selecting Debug, Start Debugging and selecting the Start Debugging toolbar button as being equivalent to deploying the project to an Analysis Services server and processing the cube. In fact, that's not quite true. Selecting Build, Deploy *projectname* does perform that task (which is why we instructed you to use that technique before), but the Start Debugging toolbar/menu options deploy the project *and* step into your cube's calculation script if the cube designer is open and the Calculations tab is selected when the Start Debugging option is executed.

Try this yourself by clicking the Start Debugging toolbar button or selecting Debug, Start Debugging with the Calculations tab open. After the project is built and deployed, Visual Studio places you in script view mode (even if you were in form view mode when you selected the Start Debugging option), and then the whole integrated development environment (IDE) goes into debug mode, just as it would for a .NET project. The Debug toolbar becomes visible, the Debug menu becomes fully enabled, and a special Debug pane opens on the Calculations tab.

The Debug pane provides a Pivot Table tab (onto which you can drag and drop objects from the Metadata tab) and four interactive MDX tabs for diagnostic querying. The Calculations tab debug mode is shown in Figure 16-23.

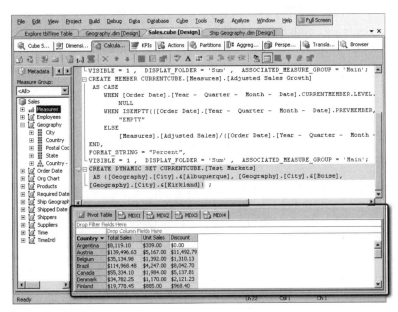

FIGURE 16-23 The Calculations tab in debug mode, with the Debug pane highlighted

Note, and consider the power of, stepping through an MDX script. This option can save you hours of tedious debugging, tabbing back and forth between Visual Studio and SQL Server Management Studio.

Back to the Browser

Before we conclude our discussion of calculations, let's actually cover how to use them. If you're still in debug mode, select Debug, Stop Debugging or click the Stop Debugging button on the Debug toolbar (third from the left, with a VCR stop button icon); you can also use the Shift+F5 keyboard shortcut. Click the cube designer's Browser tab and reconnect. In the metadata tree view, drill down on the Measures node, followed by its child node for the Main measure group and then its child node for the Sum display folder. Drill down also on the Geography node. These actions will reveal your calculated measures and named set as children.

Now construct a query using your new calculations by performing the following steps:

1. Drag the *Order Date* dimension's *Year* - *Quarter* - *Month* - *Date* hierarchy to the Row Fields area.

2. Drag the *Adjusted Sales* and *Adjusted Sales Growth* calculated members to the Detail Fields area. (Be sure to drop *Adjusted Sales Growth* to the right of *Adjusted Sales*.)

3. Drag the *Test Markets* named set to the filter pane (*not* to the Drop Filter Fields Here area of the Pivot Table pane).

4. In the Row Fields area, drill down on the Calendar 1997 node and then on the Quarter 1, 1997, node.

The results of these drag-and-drop steps are displayed in Figure 16-24.

Notice that the *Adjusted Sales Growth* figure is *EMPTY* for Calendar 1996 because there is no previous period from which to calculate growth. For other cells, you should see the proper growth figures (some of them negative) based on the *Adjusted Sales* number compared with its previous period.

The data displayed is filtered to reflect sales for only our three test markets. If you want to see data for the entire cube, right-click the named set's line in the Filter pane and choose Delete from the shortcut menu (or select it and press the Delete key). You might want to then drill down on one of the displayed month's nodes in the Pivot Table pane to reveal the day-to-day *Adjusted Sales Growth* data. (Doing this while the *Test Markets* named set filter was in effect would have displayed many empty cells.)

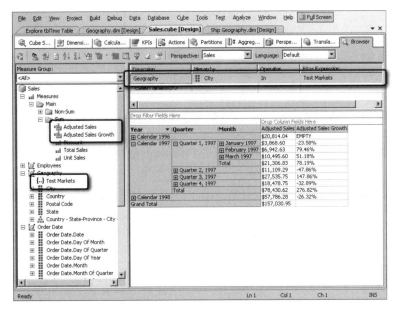

FIGURE 16-24 The cube browser with calculated measures and named set highlighted

Key Performance Indicators

Measures and dimensions define what a cube can show you, giving you insight into, for example, your business's performance, your site's Web traffic, or your clinical experiment's findings. You can run an MDX query and look at a measure's value over some slice of your cube, and because you're familiar with its measures and dimensions, you can decide whether the values meet, exceed, or fall short of your goals or your expectations. With the help of key performance indicators (KPIs) in Analysis Services, you can embed those goal criteria in the cube rather than evaluate it in your head or in your application.

KPIs consist simply of a set of MDX expressions, stored on the server, that return numeric values indicating the performance of a measure, a calculated measure, or a calculated expression over a slice of the cube and/or the relative performance of that value over a period of time. KPIs are associated with certain predefined icon sets, providing a visualization tool (even if a crude one) over your measures and an easy way for your users to get up to speed quickly on what the measures data is telling you.

Pay attention here because this is the stuff that's currently hot in the market: KPIs enable what are known in the BI and business performance management (BPM) worlds as *score-cards*, and they lend themselves extremely well to full BI dashboard implementations. If you incorporate what you learn from this chapter with the programming techniques we'll cover in the next chapter, you'll have what it takes to build scorecard and dashboard applications with relative ease.

> **Note** The Monitoring And Analytics component of the Microsoft PerformancePoint Server product, which works in tandem with Analysis Services, provides a Microsoft Office SharePoint–based platform for delivering dashboards, scorecards, and KPI data to end users.

Let's set up a KPI and then look at it in the special KPI browser view. Unfortunately, the cube's Browser tab will not display or allow querying of KPIs, but after building and browsing our KPI, we'll address this shortcoming. We'll do so by making a short detour over to SQL Server Management Studio, where we will query our KPI values using that application's MDX Query window.

Click the KPIs tab of the cube designer, and then click the New KPI toolbar button (fifth from the left) or choose Cube, New KPI. You should see a new KPI open in form view, which is quite similar to the Calculations tab's form view. The main, right-hand, area of the tab contains a field-oriented form for defining your KPI. A Calculation Tools pane, identical to that of the Calculations tab, appears at the lower left, and a KPI Organizer pane, similar to the Calculations tab's Script Organizer pane, appears at the upper left.

The form fields for a KPI include its name, the measure group it is associated with, and MDX expressions for the value to be tracked and a "goal" value for it. The KPI value and goal value are purely numeric indicators that alone offer little extra value over measures and calculated members.

KPI Visualization: Status and Trend

Extra value *is* provided, however, by MDX expressions for the KPI's *status* and its *trend*. The status expression returns a value, typically between –1 and +1, indicating the relative health of the KPI value; the trend expression returns a value, usually in the same range, indicating the increase or decrease in value relative to a prior period of time. Along with the expressions themselves, you can also select associated indicator graphics (icon sets).

A status value of +1 conveys a "good" or "on target" state of affairs for whatever the KPI is meant to monitor. A value of –1 is a "bad" or "off target" value, and a value of 0 is "neutral" or "slightly off target." Trend values of +1, 0, and –1 represent an increase, no change, or a decrease in KPI value over time. The icon sets selected for your status and trend expressions contain several icons, each corresponding to a different discrete value returned by the expression.

At a minimum, these icons support the values –1, 0, and 1. For example, a Traffic Light graphic displays a red, yellow, or green light. Others, such as a Gauge graphic, accommodate intermediate values, typically –.5 and +.5, which we might associate with "substandard" and "fair," respectively. These intermediate values (and the icons to which they correspond) are relevant only for status; trend, by definition (by the Analysis Services definition, anyway), is always positive, negative, or neutral.

A Concrete KPI

This is all rather abstract, but it will become clear once we've a built a KPI and put it to use. Our KPI will be based on our *Avg Total Sales* measure. Configure the KPI you just added as follows:

1. Set the Name to **Average Total Sales KPI** (no square brackets necessary).

2. Select Main for Associated Measure Group.

3. Set the Value Expression to **[Measures].[Avg Total Sales]**. (You might want to drag the Measures\Main\Non-Sum\Avg Total Sales node from the Metadata tab of the Calculation Tools pane to the Value Expression area rather than typing this manually.)

4. Set the Goal Expression to **1500**.

5. Set the Status Indicator graphic to **Gauge** if it has not been done already.

6. Enter the MDX code in Listing 16-1 in the Status Expression area. (You might want to drag items from the KPI folder of the Functions tab in the Calculation Tools pane to complete this step more easily.)

LISTING 16-1 Status expression MDX code for Average Total Sales KPI

```
CASE
    WHEN KPIVALUE("Average Total Sales KPI") / KPIGOAL("Average Total Sales KPI")
>= .95 THEN
        1
    WHEN KPIVALUE("Average Total Sales KPI") / KPIGOAL("Average Total Sales KPI")
<  .95
    AND
    KPIVALUE("Average Total Sales KPI") / KPIGOAL("Average Total Sales KPI") >=
.85 THEN
        0
    ELSE
        -1
END
```

The MDX expression in Listing 16-1 determines actual average sales as a percentage of the Goal ($1,500) and maps as positive (+1) values that are 95 percent and up. Average sales greater or equal to 85 percent and less than 95 percent of goal are neutral (0), and those below 85 percent are negative (–1).

7. Set the Trend Indicator to Standard Arrow if it has not been done already.

8. Set the Trend Expression to the contents of Listing 16-2 (using drag and drop from the Calculation Tools pane as appropriate).

LISTING 16-2 Trend MDX expression code for Average Total Sales KPI

```
CASE
    WHEN ISEMPTY(( [Measures].[Avg Total Sales],
    [Order Date].[Year -  Quarter -  Month -  Date].PREVMEMBER)) THEN
        NULL
    WHEN [Measures].[Avg Total Sales] < ([Measures].[Avg Total Sales],
    [Order Date].[Year -  Quarter -  Month -  Date].PREVMEMBER) THEN
        -1
    WHEN [Measures].[Avg Total Sales] = ([Measures].[Avg Total Sales],
    [Order Date].[Year -  Quarter -  Month -  Date].PREVMEMBER) THEN
        0
    ELSE
        1
END
```

The MDX expression in Listing 16-2 uses the PREVMEMBER property of our *Order Date* dimension's hierarchy to compare Adjusted Sales Growth for the period and level for which the KPI is being evaluated and compares it with the previous period's value. If the previous period's value is lower, growth is positive and the trend expression returns the value +1; if the value is higher, growth is negative and the value –1 is returned. If the two values are equal, growth is flat and the value 0 is returned.

Note In reality, comparing the difference between the two periods' values and returning 0 for a range of values from slightly below 0 to slightly above 0 might be a better determinant of flat growth, but for the purposes of this exercise, we'll stick with a difference of precisely 0.

Click the drop-down arrow next to the Additional Properties header to expand that section of the form. We won't enter values for all the fields here, but it's important to know the available options. Display folders for KPIs work similarly to the way they do for measures, calculations, and hierarchies, allowing you to group KPIs by category. You can enter multiple folder names, thus allowing your KPIs to appear under more than one folder if you separate them with a semicolon.

A parent KPI allows you to organize your KPIs hierarchically and establishes a calculation relationship whereby the parent KPI's value is determined by that of its children. The relative contribution of each child KPI's value to that of its parent is determined by the value entered in the Weight field. In the Current Time Member field, you can specify an exclusive time period within which the KPI is valid. You must specify a member of a time dimension defined for the measure group with which the KPI is associated.

Note When you enter values for a KPI's fields, remember that the Value Expression, Goal Expression, Status Expression, Trend Expression, Weight, and Current Time Member field values are full-fledged MDX expressions, supporting all MDX language constructs, word completion, member listing, "squiggle" syntax error prompting, and entry of comments.

Last, the Description field allows you to document your KPI by storing a descriptive string of text about it in the cube itself. This text is retrievable by client applications, which, again, makes it easier for users to browse your cube. Go ahead and type **Monitors health of average total sales** in the Description field for our KPI and leave the other fields in the Additional Properties section blank.

Now that we have completed the definition of our KPI, it's time to test it, but our testing method will be different than for other elements in our cube. We'll cover those differences in a minute, but first save and deploy your changes and make sure that you do so while the KPIs tab is visible.

Testing KPIs in Browser View

After the deployment, notice that the KPI tab has switched from form view to browser view. The Browser View toolbar button (second from the right) is now selected, and form fields have disappeared, giving way to a new window. In the upper pane of this window, you can specify a slice of your cube for which to view the KPI data; the lower pane displays your KPI data. This data includes the value for the current slice, the goal value, graphical depictions of the status and trend values, and the weight value. An information icon also appears; you can hover your mouse pointer over it to display the KPI's description in a tooltip.

The KPI browser view provides an easy way for you to view KPI values for specific dimensional subsections (slices) of your cube. However, by default, the browser displays aggregated KPI data for the entire cube, which is almost meaningless. Narrowing down that scope requires making specific selections in the filter pane. For example, we can look at the KPI data for Brazil in the fourth quarter of 1996 by making the selections listed in the following table in the filter pane. (You might need to first reconnect in order to be allowed to make these selections.)

Dimension	Hierarchy	Operator	Filter Expression
Order Date	Year - Quarter - Month - Date	Equal	{Quarter 4, 1996}
Geography	Country	Equal	{Brazil}

For Filter Expression, you must click the drop-down arrow at the right edge of the column. Then, in the dimension browser pop-up window, drill down to the member you're interested in, select its check box, and then click OK. The necessary selection state for the *{Quarter 4, 1996}* member of the *Order Date* dimension is shown in Figure 16-25.

After you specify your cube slice, click away from the selected cell in the filter expression table (for example, click anywhere in the lower pane) to force the new KPI data to load and display.

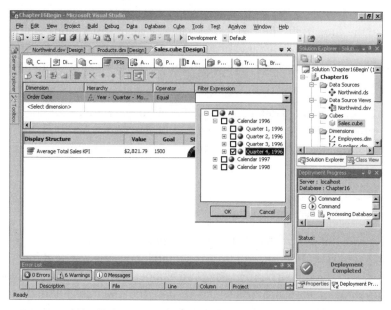

FIGURE 16-25 The KPI browser with the Filter Expression member selection pop-up window displayed

Interpreting Results and Modifying the Slicer

When you've completed the preceding steps, the KPI browser view should appear as shown in Figure 16-26.

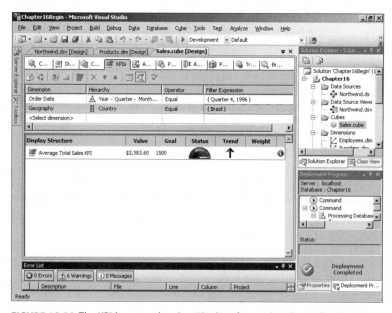

FIGURE 16-26 The KPI browser showing KPI data for a cube slice defined as Quarter 4, 1996, in Brazil

Notice that the Value column displays $3583.60, which is well above goal. Accordingly, the Status column's graphic displays a needle to the right (indicating a status value of +1). The Trend column's graphic displays an up arrow, indicating that the KPI's value here is higher than it is for the third quarter of 1996. You can confirm that yourself by changing the filter value.

Now try changing the country to *UK* (remember to clear the Brazil option before clicking OK), with the Time period still at *{Quarter 4, 1996}*. You should see the KPI value decrease to $1082.23 and the Status column graphic indicate poor status (with the needle to the left), which is correct given that this value is less than 85 percent of goal ($1,500), although the Trend graphic column indicates an increase over the previous quarter. Next change the *Order Date* filter expression to *{Calendar 1997}* and the *Geography* filter expression to *{Brazil, Canada}*. (Again, remember to *clear* the old filter member option—UK—before clicking OK.) You should see the KPI value increase to $1420.01 and the Status column graphic indicate a moderate but not exceptionally good status (with the needle pointing straight up), which is correct given that this value is about 94.7 percent of goal and our "neutral" range (the status formula value 0) is greater than or equal to 85 percent and less than 95 percent. The Trend graphic column displays a down arrow, indicating a decrease over calendar 1996.

KPI Queries in Management Studio

At this point, you should have a sense of the effectiveness of KPIs and the relative ease with which you can create them. The graphics might seem simplistic at first, but they make the data in your cube much more digestible and easier to understand.

To convey KPI data to your end users, however, you must use something other than the KPI browser, which is simply a technologist's tool. For example, access to KPIs from the cube browser might be more helpful. (The cube browser might also seem to be a technologist's tool, but it is actually the Excel PivotTable component, which is available to users through the 2003 versions of Office Web Components.)

Unfortunately, KPIs are *not* available in the cube browser, so you must use a different end-user technology. To this end, we'll now explore how to write simple MDX queries that return KPI data. In the next chapter, we'll explain how to build your own UI around KPIs by generating and executing these queries. For now, we'll simply design and execute these queries interactively, and we'll do so not in Visual Studio but in Management Studio itself.

Management Studio Does BI

So far, we've used Management Studio mostly as a tool to manage relational databases. Management Studio is the successor to Enterprise Manager and Query Analyzer from SQL Server 2000, but it is also the successor to Analysis Manager and the MDX Sample Application, the Analysis Services 2000 management tools.

Using Management Studio, you can create and edit MDX queries for OLAP cubes, Data Mining Extensions (DMX) queries for data mining models (which we'll cover in Chapter 18), and XML for Analysis (XMLA) scripts that you can use to create, modify, and drop virtually any Analysis Services object, as well as to execute embedded MDX and DMX queries. Management Studio also supports the creation and maintenance of Analysis Services Scripts projects, which can contain a combination of MDX, DMX, and XMLA queries/scripts. You can combine Analysis Services Scripts projects and SQL Server Scripts projects into a single solution to manage the entire universe of objects in your BI/data warehouse systems.

To see how all of this works, open Management Studio, and make sure that the Registered Servers and Object Explorer windows are visible. If they're not, select View, Registered Servers and View, Object Explorer in Management Studio. Now click the Analysis Services button on the Registered Servers window's toolbar (second from the left, with a cube icon), and then double-click the tree view node representing your server. (If it's not there, add it.) A node representing your Analysis Services server, as well as Databases and Assemblies child nodes, should now be displayed in the Object Explorer window. Expand the Databases node, and all databases on your Analysis Services server should be displayed, as shown in Figure 16-27.

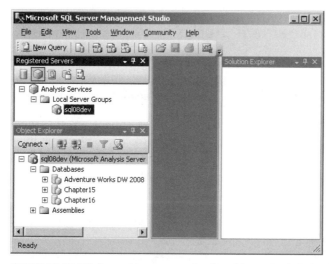

FIGURE 16-27 SQL Server Management Studio, with our Analysis Services server displayed in the Registered Servers and Object Explorer windows

The MDX Query Window

Select the Chapter16 node, and click the New Query button (the far-left button) on the Standard toolbar. An MDX query window appears. On the left, the window has a tools pane, consisting of a drop-down list of cubes in the database; a Metadata tab that lists the measures, dimensions, *and* KPIs in the selected cube, with a drop-down list of measure groups to filter the metadata displayed in the tree; and a Functions tab (equivalent to the one you've seen on the Calculations and KPIs tabs of the cube designer in Visual Studio). On the right side of the MDX query window is an MDX editor that supports color coding, squiggle syntax error prompting, and interspersing of comments and code. Member listing and word completion are available by selecting Edit, IntelliSense or via keyboard shortcuts.

Making MDX Queries

Clicking the New Query button is only one of several ways to open an MDX query window in Management Studio. For example, you can click the Analysis Services MDX Query button (third from the left) on the Standard toolbar or select File, New, Analysis Services MDX Query.

Either action opens the Connect To Analysis Services dialog box, where you specify your Analysis Services server and database names. To specify the database name, click the Options button, click the Connection Properties tab that becomes visible, and select or type the database name in the Connect To Database drop-down list. Then click Connect.

You can avoid the entire Connect To Analysis Services dialog box step by using the New Query toolbar button when a specific Analysis Services database is selected in the Object Explorer window, because the connection and database are implied. Another shortcut is to select New Query, MDX from the database node's shortcut menu in the Object Explorer window.

You can change the connection parameters for an open MDX query window by choosing the Connection, Change Connection option from its shortcut menu, by selecting Query, Connection, Change Connection, or by clicking the Change Connection button (second from the left) on the SQL Server Analysis Services Editors toolbar. The server and database you are currently connected to are displayed in the query window's status bar and in the Properties window when the query window is active. The current database is also displayed in (and changeable from) the SQL Server Analysis Services Editors toolbar (in the drop-down list between the Change Connection and Execute buttons).

If you expand the KPIs node on the Metadata tab, you should see a single node for our new KPI; if you expand that node, you should see one child node each for the KPI's value, goal, status, and trend, as shown in Figure 16-28.

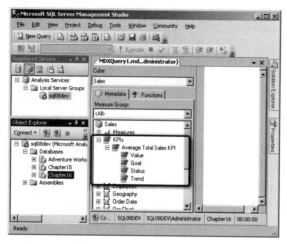

FIGURE 16-28 The Management Studio MDX query window with our sample cube loaded and its KPI displayed on the Metadata tab

You can drag and drop any of these child nodes into the query editor to generate expressions that can be used in an MDX *SELECT* statement. Using a combination of manual typing and drag-and-drop from the Metadata tab, enter the MDX code in Listing 16-3 in the editor pane of the MDX query window. (The query is in the file KPIQuery.mdx in the Management Studio solution included with the sample code.)

LISTING 16-3 An MDX query suitable for execution from Management Studio

```
SELECT
 {
 KPIValue("Average Total Sales KPI"),
 KPIGoal("Average Total Sales KPI"),
 KPIStatus("Average Total Sales KPI"),
 KPITrend("Average Total Sales KPI")
 }
 ON COLUMNS
FROM [Sales]
WHERE
 (
 [Order Date].[Year -  Quarter -  Month -  Date].[Year].&[1997-01-01T00:00:00],
 {[Geography].[Country].&[Brazil],
 [Geography].[Country].&[Canada]}
 )
```

Tip In Listing 16-3, the rather obscure expression involving the *[Order Date]* dimension (in the *WHERE* clause) actually represents the Calendar 1997 member of that dimension. Using drag-and-drop from the Metadata tab, you can avoid manually typing that entire expression.

The query selects the *Average Total Sales KPI* value, goal, status, and trend for data in 1997 from sales to Brazil and Canada (the same slicer data retrieved by our most recent KPI browser view query). You can run a syntax check on the query by choosing Query, Parse, by clicking the Parse button (sixth from the right, with the check mark icon) on the SQL Analysis Services Editors toolbar, or by using the Ctrl+F5 keyboard shortcut. A Results pane appears with a Messages tab, on which the following output should be displayed:

```
Parsing the query ...
Obtained object of type: Microsoft.AnalysisServices.AdomdClient.CellSet
Parsing complete
```

Assuming that you have passed your syntax check, go ahead and execute the query. You will find an Execute option on the query editor's shortcut menu, the Query branch of the menu, or the SQL Server Analysis Services Editors toolbar. You can also press the F5 key or press Ctrl+E to execute the MDX query.

> **Tip** As with the Management Studio Database Engine Query (SQL query) window, the MDX query window executes as a query whatever text is selected, or it executes the entire editor's contents if no text is selected within it. The Parse option behaves this way as well. You should therefore make sure that no text (or all text) is selected in the MDX query editor when you parse or execute your query.

After you execute your query, the result is displayed on a new Results tab in the Results pane of the MDX query editor and should look similar to Figure 16-29.

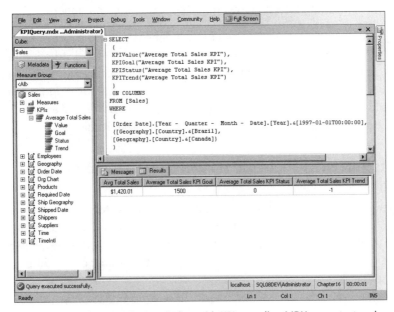

FIGURE 16-29 The MDX Query window with KPI-revealing MDX query text and results shown

Compare the output with the KPI browser view of the cube designer back in our Analysis Services project in Visual Studio, and you will see that they are essentially the same. One obvious exception is that the status and trend values are displayed numerically rather than graphically. In your own application, you can write code to execute this MDX query and render the KPI status and trend data graphically through conditional interpretation of the KPI values.

If you run the query for calendar 1998, you will see that the KPI value rises to $1787.37 and that the KPI trend formula correctly returns the value 1. The trend returned for calendar 1996 is *(null)*, which is correct because we have no data in the cube for what would be the previous period (calendar 1995).

Other BI Tricks in Management Studio

We still need to discuss adding actions, perspectives, translations, and roles to our cube, and how to manage cube storage and aggregation design. Before we do so, however, let's examine what other OLAP-related tasks we can accomplish in Management Studio.

To start with, expand the Chapter16 database's node in the Object Explorer window. You should see child nodes appear for the database's data sources, data source views, cubes, dimensions, mining structures, roles, and assemblies. These are, of course, the same high-level nodes that appear in the Solution Explorer window for an Analysis Services project in Visual Studio. Although Management Studio does not offer full design control over these elements, you can enumerate each of them and view their properties in multipage property sheets by right-clicking any of them and selecting the Properties shortcut menu option.

By using the objects' shortcut menus, you can browse dimensions and cubes in Management Studio just as if you were in Visual Studio (just as you can browse mining structures and mining models, which we'll cover in Chapter 18). You can also process objects and add and configure partitions and aggregation designs. We will cover partitions and aggregation designs shortly, but we mention these options now so that you know they are available in both Management Studio and the Analysis Services designers in Visual Studio.

XMLA Scripts in Management Studio and Visual Studio Analysis Services Projects

You can also generate XMLA scripts for objects by using their shortcut menus. By generating scripts for individual objects, or entire Analysis Services databases, you can easily migrate your databases to other servers. You can then transmit the scripts to other developers and/or keep them in source control by organizing the scripts within Management Studio Analysis Services Scripts projects.

> **Tip** Management Studio offers source control integration through the Source Control\Plug-in Selection tree view item in its Options dialog box. (Choose Tools, Options.)

To get a feel for what XMLA scripts look like, drill down to the *Products* dimension in the Object Explorer window, right-click it, and choose Script Dimension As, CREATE To, New Query Editor Window from the shortcut menu. The XMLA script for the dimension appears in a new XMLA query window. Notice that each facet of the dimension is meticulously described within the various XML elements in the body of the document.

Now return to our Visual Studio Analysis Services project, and drill down to and select the Products.dim dimension node in the Solution Explorer window. Right-click this node and select the View Code option from its shortcut menu, or choose View, Code. You'll see that nearly the same XML content is displayed. This similarity reveals that the Visual Studio Analysis Services project designers are merely graphical user interfaces (GUIs) to the XMLA scripts that are necessary to create the objects on an Analysis Services server. When you deploy your project from Visual Studio, you are essentially executing the scripts generated by the designers. XMLA scripts can also be executed in Management Studio; to do so, you simply use one of the Execute menu or toolbar options from within the XMLA query editor window.

Actions

You might have noticed a pattern emerging in our study of calculations and KPIs: Analysis Services allows you to store a variety of elements in your cube that you could, if called upon to do so, create within your own application or queries. Think about it: your calculations simply represent a collection of commands that make up an MDX script, and each of your KPIs is, in effect, a collection of MDX expressions and literal values (description, status graphic name, trend graphic name) that you could store and evaluate on the client side.

But by that logic, views, functions, and stored procedures in relational databases could be handled by your applications as well. Of course, we use those server-side facilities because DBAs can design, secure, and provide them to a range of applications and users. Similarly, Analysis Services offers calculations and KPIs to put their management and security in the hands of DBAs and to make them available to anyone consuming your Analysis Services databases.

We will now quickly cover actions, which are yet another server-side, MDX-based object type.

Actions Simply Defined

You can think of actions as context-sensitive external commands. In other words, actions allow you to store an MDX-based template that evaluates to a command string of one form or another. Actions are associated with objects in your cube, whether they be structural objects—such as measures, attributes, hierarchies, levels, or their members—or actual cells in the cube. The types of commands range from drillthrough queries that extract a cell's under-lying data from the relational database to URLs that embed a value to SQL or command-line strings that can also embed a value. You can even create an action that passes a value as a parameter to a Reporting Services report.

Actions are defined on the Actions tab of the cube designer, and they appear in the cube browser on shortcut menus. From your own applications, you can enumerate actions and compute their values through programmatic techniques we will discuss in the next chapter.

Designing Actions

The cube designer's Actions tab, like its Calculations and KPIs tabs, consists of an Organizer pane (Actions Organizer, in this case), a Calculation Tools pane, and a form that you must complete in order to fully describe the action you are creating or editing. Unlike the Calculations and KPIs tabs, however, the Actions tab has only a form view; there is no script view or browser view. By now you should be familiar with the meaning and mechanics of editing the fields in form view, so we can proceed with creating a couple of actions without a lot of background discussion.

Start creating a drillthrough action by selecting Cube, New Drillthrough Action or by clicking the New Drillthrough Action button (fourth from the right) on the Actions tab's toolbar. Type **Total Sales Drillthrough** in the Name field (no brackets necessary), select Main from the Measure Group Members drop-down list, leave the Condition field blank, and in a new row in the Drillthrough Columns grid, select Measures in the Dimensions column and Total Sales in the Return Columns column. (You can do the latter by clicking the drop-down arrow, select-ing the Total Sales item's check box in the pop-up window, and then clicking its OK button.) The form should appear as shown in Figure 16-30.

This creates an action that allows you to right-click any cell in the cube browser and see in a pop-up window the *Total Sales* data for each row in the fact table that underlies it.

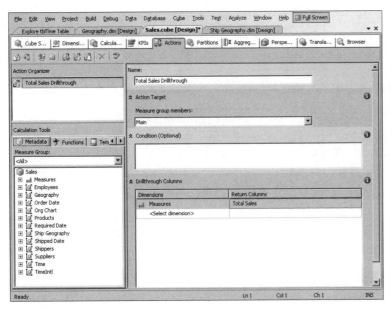

FIGURE 16-30 The cube designer's Actions tab, with a drillthrough action fully configured

Next add a (regular) action by selecting the Cube, New Action option or by clicking the New Action button (fifth from the left) on the Actions tab's toolbar. Type **Live Search** in the Name field, select Level Members from the Target Type drop-down list (if it is not already selected), and select Geography.Country - State-Province - City - Postal Code.City in the Target Object drop-down list. (Click the drop-down arrow, drill down to and select the appropriate node in the dimension browser pop-up window, and then click OK.) Leave the condition expression blank, select URL from the Type drop-down list (if it is not already selected) in the Action Content section, and enter the following in the Action Expression field:

```
"http://search.live.com/results.aspx?q=" + [Geography].[City].CURRENTMEMBER.NAME
```

The form should appear as shown in Figure 16-31.

This action generates a URL that navigates to the Live Search Web site and performs a search on the selected city's name. By right-clicking any city in the row or column headers in the cube designer's Browser tab, you can select the action from the shortcut menu and navigate to the corresponding URL in Windows Internet Explorer.

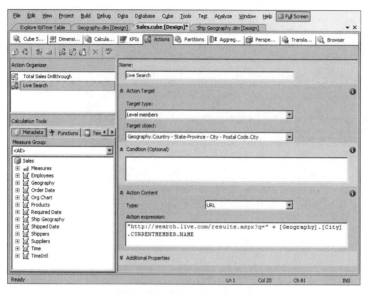

FIGURE 16-31 The cube designer's Actions tab, this time showing a fully configured URL action

Testing Actions

You can test your actions by saving and deploying your changes and then selecting the Browser tab of the cube designer. Drag the *Total Sales* measure to the detail fields area, and drag the *Country - State-Province - City - Postal Code* hierarchy of the *Geography* dimension to the row fields area. Right-click any cell in the data area, and then choose Total Sales Drillthrough from the shortcut menu to view the drillthrough query results for that cell in a pop-up window, as shown in Figure 16-32.

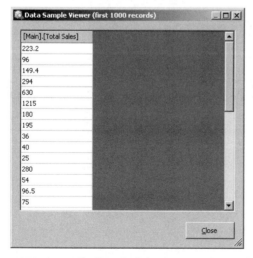

FIGURE 16-32 The Data Sample Viewer window, opened from a drillthrough action on a cell in the cube browser

Drill down to and right-click any city in the row header area, and then choose Live Search from the shortcut menu, as shown in Figure 16-33, to view Live Search results for that city's name in Internet Explorer.

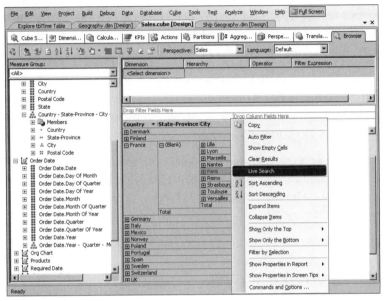

FIGURE 16-33 URL actions appear as shortcut menu options on their target objects (level members, in this case) in the cube browser.

> **Tip** Changing your action to use a different search engine is easy. For example, change the literal portion of the Action Expression from *"http://search.live.com/results.aspx?q="* to *"http://www.google.com/search?q="* to use Google instead of Live Search. (You might, of course, also want to change the action's name.) You will find that Google handles the actions gracefully, even when the city name contains an accented character. At press time, Live Search drops the accented characters altogether, making for less than useful results on some city names.

Experiment with the other action types and consider using actions extensively in your cubes. OLAP is all about drill-down analysis, and what better drill-down functionality is there than providing your users with detailed information about cube data from other applications, databases, and the Web?

Partitions, Storage Settings, and Proactive Caching

Cubes are great, and having all that BI data in one place is convenient, but sometimes parts of your cube will have different demands placed on them than other parts. Analysis Services partitions allow you to slice your cube physically and use specific storage and aggregation settings that are appropriate to each subset of your cube's data and the unique demands placed on it.

For example, if users rarely need data older than a certain date, you might store that data on a slower (cheaper) disk, process it much less frequently, and perhaps precalculate many fewer aggregations for it than you would for recent data. Likewise, since only extremely recent data typically needs to be reprocessed, putting it in its own, smaller, partition will speed reprocessing time and thus lower the latency of your cube's data. Beyond time-based partitioning, you might also or instead want to partition along product lines, geography, or any combination of dimensional criteria. Partitions allow you to do just that.

Analysis Services partitions allow you to define their content (or "source") by specifying a fact table that the partition should be based on or a SQL query that selects only a subset of the rows from a fact table. You can then configure various aspects of the partition's processing and storage as well as its aggregation design.

Every cube consists of at least one partition (or, to be more precise, at least one partition per measure group), so you need to be familiar with partition configuration even if you don't want to "partition" your cube (in the ordinary sense of the word). In fact, we will concentrate on a single-partition scenario using our *Northwind Sales* cube for the remainder of this section.

Editing and Creating Partitions

If you click the Partitions tab of the cube designer, you will find that a partition (named *Tbl Fact*) for the *Sales* cube has already been defined. The existing partition is built on our fact table, *tblFact*, without any filtering query defined for row selection. Storage and processing locations are set to the Analysis Services defaults; you can modify them in the Partition Type Selection dialog box, shown in Figure 16-34, by selecting the partition's row in the designer's grid and then selecting the *StorageLocation* property in the Properties window and clicking the ellipsis button in its value column.

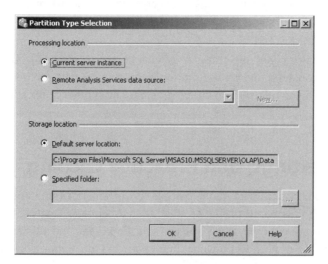

FIGURE 16-34 The Partition Type Selection dialog box

You can modify partition content by clicking in the partition's row in the Source column of the designer's grid and clicking its ellipsis button or by selecting the partition's *Source* property in the Properties window and clicking the ellipsis button in its Value column, as shown in Figure 16-35.

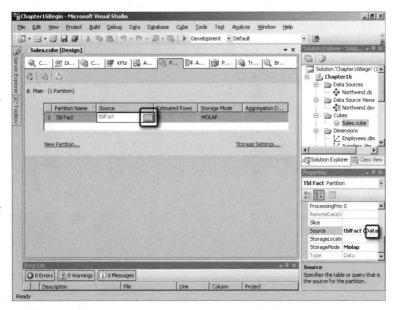

FIGURE 16-35 The cube designer Partitions tab, with the Partition Source dialog box ellipsis buttons highlighted

Either approach opens the Partition Source dialog box in table binding view, as shown in Figure 16-36.

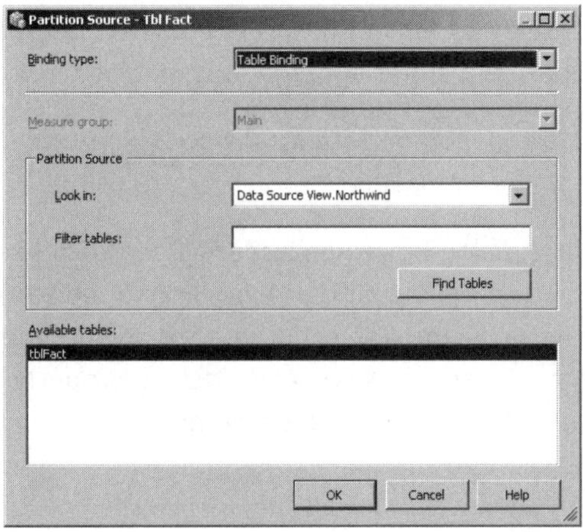

FIGURE 16-36 The Partition Source dialog box in table binding view

Select the Query Binding option from the Binding Type drop-down list to display the query binding view. The table binding view lets you define your partition based on the contents of an entire fact table, whereas the query binding view allows you to specify a SQL query that might select only a subset of rows. When you've finished examining these options, click the dialog box's Cancel button because we don't want to modify our partition's source.

> **Note** You might also be interested in exploring the Partition Wizard, which provides an alternative interface for setting many of the properties mentioned here—but only for new partitions. You can do so by clicking the New Partition toolbar button (second from the left), by clicking the New Partition link, by selecting Cube, New Partition, or by selecting the New Partition shortcut menu option.
>
> You will not be able to fully explore each wizard page unless you delete the existing partition, thus freeing up the fact table to be used in a new partition. If you do this, be sure you close the cube designer after you delete the existing partition and then *discard* your changes. This will ensure that the existing partition is *not* actually deleted from the cube.

In addition to these partition properties, you can also modify storage settings, including those affecting proactive caching, as we'll discuss next.

Partition Storage Options

In the SQL Server 7.0 OLAP Services and SQL Server 2000 Analysis Services days, there were three types of storage: Multidimensional OLAP (MOLAP), Relational OLAP (ROLAP), and Hybrid OLAP (HOLAP). With MOLAP (the default), all fact and aggregation data is stored in the Analysis Services multidimensional store, which provides the fastest query response times. ROLAP, in which facts stay in the relational database's fact table and aggregations are stored in special relational tables of their own, provides for faster cube processing times (for obvious reasons) but slower query response times. HOLAP, a sort of compromise option, keeps the fact data in the relational database but stores aggregations multidimensionally.

Partition storage is configured via the Partition Storage Settings dialog box, shown in Figure 16-37.

You can open the Partition Storage Settings dialog box when a specific partition is selected by clicking the Storage Settings toolbar button (on the far right), by clicking the Storage Settings link, by selecting Cube, Storage Settings, or by selecting the Storage Settings shortcut menu option. You can also select the partition's *ProactiveCaching* property in the Properties window and then click the ellipsis button in its Value column.

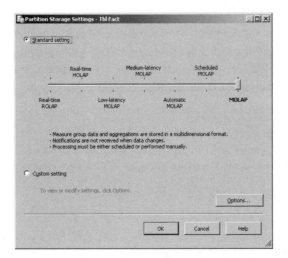

FIGURE 16-37 The Partition Storage Settings dialog box

The fact that partition storage options are simply configured through a dialog box can be misleading. The Partition Storage Settings dialog box actually offers an enormously rich set of options that can take a while to fully appreciate. The dialog box is also, in effect, a dashboard for controlling what is a very important feature of Analysis Services: proactive caching.

Proactive Caching

MOLAP, ROLAP, and HOLAP did not go away in Analysis Services 2005 and 2008, but their limitations are mitigated by the proactive caching feature. For example, proactive caching allows you to use ROLAP as your underlying storage medium (which ensures faster processing time and thus accommodates real-time, or near-real-time, OLAP) but instructs Analysis Services to cache (that is, copy) your cube in the MOLAP medium (for better query performance).

You choose how often the cache is flushed. Depending on your cache settings, the MOLAP copy can be immediately invalidated when certain changes to the underlying data warehouse are made. In this case, queries are fulfilled against the base ROLAP content; the MOLAP version is reprocessed in the background, and then it's swapped back in when processing is complete. You can also configure settings in such a way that the outdated ("stale") MOLAP data continues to be used while updated MOLAP data is being rebuilt and processed. This enhances performance (because MOLAP storage continues to be used) but decreases freshness of data.

As you can see in the Partition Storage Settings dialog box, proactive caching allows for a "spectrum" of seven standard settings, ranging from Real-Time ROLAP on the left to pure, noncached MOLAP on the right. All but the last option set a degree of caching and automatic processing of your partition. As you move the slider between the settings, you see new text appear in the dialog box, below the slider control, with a high-level description of the current setting.

> **Note** You can also modify a partition's storage settings by editing the individual child properties of the *ProactiveCaching* property. However, these properties are available for editing only *after* you've selected a setting from the Partition Storage Settings dialog box, which provides a much friendlier UI at any time.

For an even more detailed view of these settings, click the Options button, which displays the Storage Options dialog box, shown in Figure 16-38.

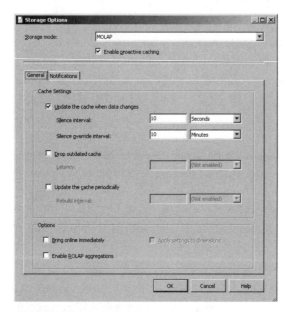

FIGURE 16-38 The Storage Options dialog box

On the General tab of the Storage Options dialog box, you can view the specific cache update and latency intervals. The Notifications tab lets you specify particular tables or SQL queries to monitor for data changes. You get a huge amount of granular control in this dialog box. Take your time getting acquainted with it. These tuning options let you strike the perfect balance between performance, freshness of data, and real-time availability of data. If you find the correct settings mix here, your investment might pay huge dividends in terms of performance.

If you modify any of the preconfigured settings in the Storage Options dialog box, you automatically shift from using one of the seven standard settings to using a custom setting (unless you happen to configure the individual settings to match exactly one of the other six standard settings). Try it yourself and see: change one of the settings slightly, and then click OK. When you return to the Partition Storage Settings dialog box, you'll see that the Custom Setting option, rather than the Standard Setting option, is selected and the slider control is disabled.

> **Note** You can also configure storage settings at the cube, database dimension, and measure group level rather than at the partition level. You can edit cube-level or measure-group-level settings in the cube designer: just select a cube or measure group node on a tab that has one (for example, the cube and measure group root nodes of the Measures tree view on the Cube Structure tab), and then click the ellipsis button in the Value column of the *ProactiveCaching* property in the Properties window. You can similarly configure dimension storage options through the Properties window, but in the dimension designer rather than in the cube designer.

It is impossible to do justice to the proactive caching feature in a book that does not focus exclusively on BI. What's more, you can leave these settings at their default values and still work productively with Analysis Services cubes. But we have attempted to convey a simple overview of what these settings control and how they work.

Additional Features and Tips

Our coverage of partitions and proactive caching would not be complete without mentioning a few miscellaneous points and features that are worthy of your further exploration, as time permits.

First, a word on writeback (write-enabled) measure groups and dimensions. Analysis Services permits users to modify their view of the contents of measure groups. With the Partitions tab selected in the cube designer, choose Cube, Writeback Settings or choose the Writeback Settings shortcut menu option available by right-clicking the partition name to open the Enable Writeback dialog box, where you can specify the data source and table for writeback storage.

In Analysis Services 2005 (and earlier), writeback data had to be stored in relational writeback tables, thus creating a ROLAP partition for the data. In Analysis Services 2008, that option is still available, but there is an additional option, also configured in the Enable Writeback dialog box, to store writeback data in a MOLAP partition, thus avoiding the mutually exclusive choice between writeback functionality and the better performance of MOLAP over ROLAP.

> **Note** Only measure groups that do not contain special aggregates (that is, aggregates other than *SUM*) can be writeback-enabled. Our measure group, because it contains the non-sum-based *Avg Total Sales* measure, cannot be writeback-enabled. However, the *Sales_Quotas* partition in the *Sales Targets* measure group of the *Adventure Works* cube in the *Adventure Works DW 2008* Analysis Services sample database can accommodate writeback, should you want to test it.

You can also write-enable dimensions, thus allowing client applications to update their contents, by simply setting the dimension's *WriteEnabled* property to *True* through the Properties window in the dimension designer.

And one last tip: In Management Studio, you can create partitions and change storage/proactive caching settings at the dimension, partition, and cube level. Management Studio's property sheets let you modify these settings so that you don't have to use Visual Studio to change them after deploying your cube. You can also modify a measure group's writeback settings via its Writeback Options shortcut menu option (or the Enable/Disable Writeback shortcut menu options of its Writeback child node, under which writeback partitions are enumerated).

Aggregations

Aggregation designs specify which precalculated aggregations are stored in your cube. In Analysis Services 2005, there were two types of aggregation designs: algorithmic and usage-based, both of which were created on the Partitions tab of the cube designer. In Analysis Services 2008, configuration of aggregations has changed. First, aggregation designs are now created on the new Aggregations tab. Second, in addition to algorithmic and usage-based aggregation designs, it is now possible to create aggregations manually or to modify designs that are algorithmic or usage-based. We'll briefly describe the creation of each of these three types here. To get started, click the Aggregations tab of the cube designer for our *Sales* cube.

Algorithmic Aggregation Design

You create algorithmic aggregation designs using the Aggregation Design Wizard, which you can open by clicking the Design Aggregations toolbar button (on the far left), by selecting Cube, Design Aggregations, or by selecting the Design Aggregations shortcut menu option. This wizard generates aggregations based on algorithmic determination of which aggregations are most likely to be useful to query performance.

Let's build an aggregation design for our single partition. Start by opening the Aggregation Design Wizard using any of the techniques described earlier. On the Welcome page, click Next. The Review Aggregation Usage page appears. This page lists all attributes in the cube and, for each of them, allows you to specify whether the attribute should be included in all aggregations (by selecting Full), in no aggregations (by selecting None), merely evaluated for inclusion (by selecting Unrestricted) or should be treated in the default manner determined by the aggregation design algorithm (by selecting Default). Leave the Default selection for all attributes, and click Next to advance to the Specify Object Counts page.

> **Tip** The Aggregation Usage page is merely an alternative UI to setting a *CubeAttribute*'s *AggregationUsage* property, available via the Properties window when an individual attribute is selected in the cube designer. The property value assigned in the Properties window will be displayed in the Aggregation Design Wizard and vice versa.

In order to design aggregations, the wizard must know, for the cube and the partition, how many rows each measure group contains and how many members each attribute contains. This can be determined by allowing the wizard to count the rows and members it finds in the cube and partition (by clicking the Count button), or you can supply these counts manually, by entering counts in the grid. (You'll need to drill down on a dimension to enter the counts for its attributes.) The manual method might be preferable for extremely large cubes/partitions where the attribute cardinality is already known. However, our cube is not large, so simply click Count, and when counting has completed, click Next.

While the Analysis Services aggregation design algorithm determines which aggregations will be beneficial, it doesn't strictly specify how many of them will actually be built. You can control the volume of aggregation creation on the wizard's Set Aggregation Options page. This page lets you limit the number of aggregations created as a function of disk space or percentage performance gain. Alternatively, you can manually start building the aggregations and manually end the process—in this case, the aggregations are limited by processing time rather than by disk cost or performance gain.

For our small cube and partition, accept the default Design Aggregations Until selection of Estimated Storage Reaches (and the accompanying setting of 100 MB), and then click Start. Wait until aggregation generation is complete, and then click Next. On the Completing The Wizard page, type **Main** in the Name text box, select the Deploy And Process Now option, and then click Finish. When prompted by the Process Partition dialog box, click Run to perform the cube processing, and then click Close through the various dialog boxes when processing completes. Now click the Partitions tab, and notice that the value of *Main* appears in the Aggregation Design column of the grid; click back on the Aggregations tab, and notice that the value *Tbl Fact* (the name of our partition) appears in the Partitions column.

Usage-Based Aggregation Design

Algorithmic aggregation design can be a great boost to performance, but no algorithm can completely predict which aggregations will be most useful in the context of your specific user query habits and tendencies. The good news is that usage-based aggregation designs do just that: they generate aggregations that will best optimize queries recorded on the Analysis Services query logs. Usage-based aggregation designs are created using the Usage-Based Optimization Wizard (UBO Wizard), which can be opened by clicking the Usage Based Optimization toolbar button (second from the left), by selecting Cube, Usage Based Optimization, or by selecting the Usage Based Optimization shortcut menu option.

The UBO Wizard will generate aggregation designs based on query log criteria start date, end date, list of users, and percentage of most frequent queries. To use the UBO Wizard, query logging must be enabled for your server; this is configured in the server's property sheet in SQL Server Management Studio.

Manual Aggregation Design (and Modification)

New to Analysis Services 2008 is the ability to create aggregations manually or edit them. Entire aggregation *designs* can be created, or *individual aggregations* can be added to, deleted from, or modified within existing aggregation designs. After new aggregation designs are created, they can be assigned to specific partitions.

> **Caution** For the vast majority of readers, manual aggregation design is most likely a feature that need not, indeed *should not*, be used. The algorithmic and usage-based aggregation strategies are quite sophisticated and likely safer to use than manual design. That said, understanding manual aggregation design is helpful in having a better understanding of how algorithmic and usage-based aggregation strategies work and gives you the know-how necessary to view the aggregation designs these strategies generate.

Manual Aggregation Design is accessible by activating the Aggregations tab's Advanced view. Do this by clicking the Advanced View toolbar button (fifth from left) or by selecting Cube, Show Aggregations In, Advanced View.

> **Tip** If you close the cube designer and then reopen it later and click the Aggregations tab, you will be placed back in Standard view. To return to Standard view without closing and reopening the designer, simply click the Standard View toolbar button (fourth from left) or select Cube, Show Aggregations In, Standard View.

To view the contents of our existing aggregation design, enter the Advanced view (using either technique just described), and then select the *Main* aggregation design from the Aggregation Design drop-down list. Next, drill down on each and every dimension. (You'll avoid a lot of scrolling during this process if you drill down on the last dimension and then move upward.)

When you've finished, you'll be able to see the details for each of the aggregations in our aggregation design (generated by the Aggregation Design Wizard). The Sorting and Range drop-down lists configure how the aggregations are sorted and which group of them is displayed. The aggregations appear in labeled columns with headers *A0, A1, A2,* and so on. The attributes included in an aggregation are represented by corresponding check marks down the aggregation's column in the grid. This is all shown in Figure 16-39.

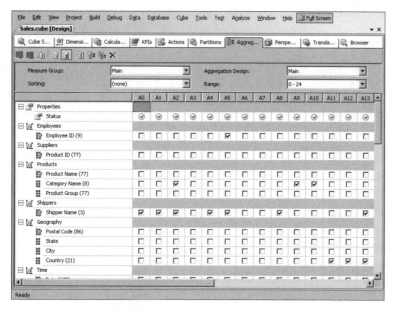

FIGURE 16-39 The Advanced view of the cube designer's Aggregations tab

> **Tip** The column header designations (*A0, A1, A2,* and so on) do *not* constitute IDs for the individual aggregations—they are column labels only. A specific aggregation's name and ID can be seen in the Properties window by clicking anywhere within the aggregation's column. The *Name* and optional *Description* properties are both editable.

The inclusion or exclusion of any attribute in a particular aggregation is editable: just select or clear the corresponding check box. You can also add a new (blank) aggregation or delete an existing aggregation using the New Aggregation or Delete toolbar button (third from the right and far right, respectively) or the New Aggregation or Delete shortcut menu option. There is a Cube, New Aggregation main menu option, but no corresponding main menu option to delete an aggregation.

A single aggregation can also be copied. You can do this as follows: First select the aggregation you want to copy by clicking anywhere within its column other than the column's header. (Clicking in the Properties or Status row or that of any dimension allows the aggregation to be selected without changing the inclusion/exclusion state of any attribute.) Next click the

Copy Aggregation toolbar button (second from the right), select Cube, Copy Aggregation, or select the Copy Aggregation shortcut menu option. This will copy the selected aggregation and insert it into the grid at the leftmost column position displayed at the time; the other displayed aggregations will each shift one column to the right. From there, you can modify the newly inserted aggregation to make it unique.

Aggregation Design Management

An aggregation design can be created by clicking the New Aggregation Design toolbar button (fourth from the right) or by selecting Cube, New Aggregation Design. Clicking either opens the New Aggregation Design dialog box, which allows you to name the new aggregation design and specify whether it will be created empty or copied from an existing one. After you click OK, the new aggregation design can be edited as described earlier, just like any other.

You can assign an aggregation design to one or more partitions by clicking the Assign Aggregation Design toolbar button (third from the left), by selecting Cube, Assign Aggregation Design, or by clicking in the Standard view grid cell at the intersection of the aggregation design's row and the Partitions column (at the far right) and then clicking the ellipsis button. Each of these actions displays the Assign Aggregation Design dialog box, shown in Figure 16-40, which lets you select an aggregation design and then select all the partitions to which you want to assign it. You can also use this technique to *remove* an aggregation design assignment from one or more partitions by selecting (None) from the Aggregation Designs drop-down list and selecting the appropriate partitions.

FIGURE 16-40 The Assign Aggregation Design dialog box

An entire aggregation design can be deleted using the Delete toolbar button (on the far right) or shortcut menu option. If you want to delete a design and you're in the Aggregation tab's Advanced view, make sure that the aggregation design, and not an individual aggregation, is selected before deleting. You can do this by making a selection in the Aggregation Design drop-down list.

Aggregation Design and Management Studio

In Management Studio, you can create algorithmic and usage-based aggregation designs, and you can assign aggregation designs as well. These capabilities are available through the Design Aggregations, Usage Based Optimization, and Assign Aggregation Design shortcut menu options on a specific partition's node (or its parent Partitions node) in the Object Explorer window. The Assign Aggregation Design option is also available from the shortcut menu of a specific aggregation design node or its parent Aggregation Designs node.

Perspectives

As we mentioned earlier, one hallmark of Analysis Services post-version-2000 is its flexibility and accommodating nature. For example, the ability to have drillthrough actions, role-playing dimensions, and multiple fact tables allows you to use a single cube for a multitude of multidimensional *and* relational queries. With Analysis Services 2000, each fact table required its own cube, role-playing dimensions did not exist, drillthrough functionality was much more limited, and the lack of proactive caching meant that cube data could not be as fresh as is sometimes necessary.

This notion of a single cube acting as a one-stop shop for all your dimensional data gives rise to an Analysis Services 2005/2008 concept called the *unified dimensional model* (UDM). The UDM paradigm advocates softening the distinction between OLAP and relational data and promotes an outlook, if you will, that a cube is more than just a cube. The UDM philosophy sees a properly built Analysis Services cube as a comprehensive repository for all aggregated and fact-level data.

That's all well and good, but the UDM paradigm causes an issue of its own: if you jam too much stuff into a single cube, many of your users might become overwhelmed by the content of that cube and therefore find it less useful. For this reason, Analysis Services 2005 introduced, and Analysis Services 2008 continues to provide, the ability to create *perspectives* within your cubes.

Perspectives are simply filtered views of a cube's content. You define a perspective by picking a set of specific measure groups (or specific measures), dimensions (or individual attributes and hierarchies), KPIs, actions, and calculations for the perspective and assigning it a name. Client applications treat perspectives as if they were separate physical cubes. You can, for example, combine sales, inventory, and human resources information into a single cube and then publish each category of data as a separate perspective. This gives you the simplicity and power of the UDM paradigm without dispensing with the ability to deploy components of your dimensional data as discrete units that appear as cubes in their own right.

Creating a perspective is easy. Simply click the Perspectives tab of the cube designer, and then click the New Perspective toolbar button (third from the left), select Cube, New Perspective, or select the New Perspective shortcut menu option. Any of these actions creates a new column in the Perspective tab's grid. From there, you enter the name of your perspective and then select all of the cube objects you want to include. For now, create a new perspective named **Product Info** and assign it the entire *Main* measure group, the *Products* and *Suppliers* dimensions, the *Average Total Sales KPI* KPI, the *Total Sales Drillthrough* action, and the two calculated measures (*Adjusted Sales* and *Adjusted Sales Growth*).

Save and deploy your changes. In the cube browser, first reconnect, and then notice that the Perspective drop-down list now contains two items: Sales (the physical cube) and Product Info (the perspective we just created). Select Product Info from the drop-down list, and notice that in the metadata tree view, only the cube's measures (including the two calculated measures) and the two dimensions we selected when defining the perspective are listed, as shown in Figure 16-41.

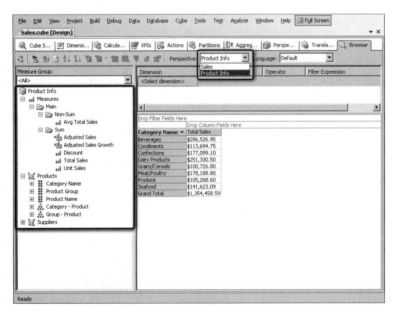

FIGURE 16-41 The cube browser with the *Product Info* perspective selected and highlighted

Notice also that the calculated measures are both listed under the Sum display folder because they were configured this way in the *Sales* cube.

In Management Studio, the Object Explorer window enumerates only the physical cubes in an Analysis Services database. However, the MDX query window lists the perspectives in the Cubes drop-down list (and because the *Product Info* perspective precedes the *Sales* cube alphabetically, the former will be selected by default). The Metadata tab lists just the measures (including calculated measures), dimensions, and KPIs, if any, that belong to the selected perspective or cube, as shown in Figure 16-42.

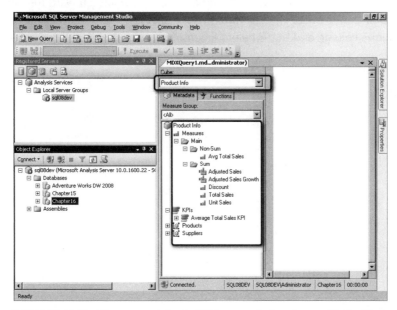

FIGURE 16-42 The Management Studio MDX query window shown with the *Product Info* perspective selected and highlighted

Perspectives provide an audience-targeted experience for your cubes, and they do so through server-side configuration, easing the burden on application developers. This notion of a *server-enforced* customized view of a cube can be extended. For example, language localization of the names of your cube's objects and the cube's contents can be governed on the server as well. You can accomplish this by creating Analysis Services *translations*. Also, enforcement, in the true sense of the word, is made possible by creating security *roles* that include declaratively specified membership and cube object-level permissions. The remaining sections of this chapter will cover translations and roles.

Translations

Much as you do with perspectives, you define translations on their own tab in the cube designer, in a grid containing distinct rows for each object in the cube, with each translation occupying its own column in the grid. Rather than soliciting a name and providing check boxes next to each object, however, the Translations tab solicits a language and culture and provides an editable cell for the translated name of each object.

For our exercise, click the Translations tab, and then click the New Translation toolbar button (third from the left), select Cube, New Translation, or select the New Translation shortcut menu option. Select Spanish (Spain) in the Select Language dialog box, and then click OK. A translation should contain localized strings for each object in the cube, but we will translate just the *TimeIntl* dimension (the table-based one that we defined toward the beginning of this chapter) for this exercise. Type **Tiempo** in the cell at the intersection of the Spanish (Spain) translation's column and the TimeIntl dimension row, as shown in Figure 16-43.

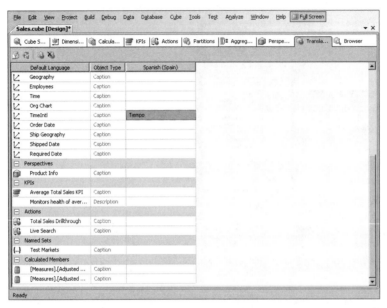

FIGURE 16-43 The Translations tab with the *TimeIntl* dimension translation entry for Spanish (Spain)

Our work on the cube designer's Translations tab is finished, but our work in defining the translation is not. We still need to define translated names for each attribute and hierarchy, and we need to explore how to provide translations for members within the attributes. To define this translation information, open the *TimeIntl* dimension in the dimension designer, click *its* Translations tab, and then add a new translation (using any of the options discussed for adding the cube's translation). As in the cube designer, select Spanish (Spain) in the Select Language dialog box, and then click OK. Now enter the Spanish strings in the following table for the dimension, its attributes, and its hierarchy.

Object	Translated Name
Time (dimension)	**Tiempo**
Year (attribute)	**Año**
Quarter (attribute)	**Trimestre**
Month (attribute)	**Mes**
Order Date (attribute)	**Fecha de la Orden**
Year - Quarter - Month - Order Date (hierarchy)	**Año - Cuarto - Mes - Fecha de la Orden**

Tip To type the ñ in año, hold down the Alt key while entering the number 164 on your keyboard's numeric keypad. If you're using a laptop, be sure to enter NumLock mode, hold down the Alt key and type the digits 1, 6, and 4 using the appropriate letter keys mapped to the numeric keypad, and then exit NumLock mode. You can also use the Character Map utility found in Start, All Programs, Accessories, System Tools.

Tip Translation strings entered for attributes are automatically copied into the cells of any corresponding user hierarchy levels. You can manually overwrite these default level translations if you want.

We have entered a translated name for each attribute but have not yet specified the translated names for the *members* of the *Month* or *Quarter* attribute. Member names are not static; they are derived from data in the dimension table, so their translated names must be data-driven as well. We must, in effect, inform Analysis Services that the Spanish translation should use the *tblMonthNames.SpanishMonthName* column for the *Month* attribute in place of the *EnglishMonthName* column. We must do likewise to plug in the *tblMonthNames. SpanishQuarterName* column for the *Quarter* attribute in place of the *EnglishQuarterName* column.

Doing so is quite easy: Simply click in the Mes attribute's cell (not the Mes hierarchy level cell) in the Translations tab grid, and then click the ellipsis button that becomes visible to open the Attribute Data Translation dialog box. In the Translation Columns tree view, select the *SpanishMonthName* column, as shown in Figure 16-44.

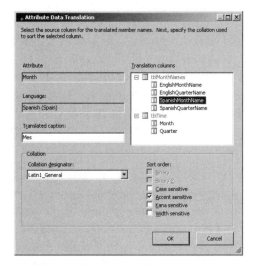

FIGURE 16-44 Configuring Mes members in the Attribute Data Translation dialog box

Now click OK. A special table icon will appear at the left side of the Mes cell, as shown in Figure 16-45

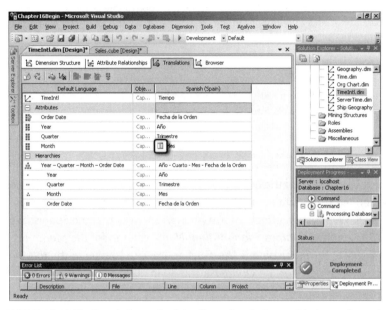

FIGURE 16-45 The Translations tab of the dimension designer with the attribute data translation icon highlighted.

Do likewise for the Trimestre cell (indicating *SpanishQuarterName* as the translation column). Save and deploy your changes, and then check them on the Browser tab of the dimension designer. (We'll also do this in the cube browser shortly.) Select Spanish (Spain) from the Languages drop-down list, and then click the drop-down arrow for the Hierarchy list. Before making a selection, notice that each attribute and hierarchy appears with its translated name. Select the *Año - Cuarto - Mes - Fecha de la Orden* hierarchy, and then drill down to the Month (Mes) level in the browser tree view. Notice that each month name appears in Spanish and that the months are sorted chronologically. The Quarter names have substituted a *T* (for *trimestre*) in place of the *Q* that is present when viewing the hierarchy in English. Change Language back to *Default* to see each of the hierarchy, level, month, and quarter names change to their corresponding names in English.

Now open the cube designer, and then select the Browser tab. Reconnect, select Sales from the Perspectives drop-down list, and once again, select Spanish (Spain) from the Languages drop-down list. In the metadata tree view, notice that the *TimeIntl* dimension's name changes to *Tiempo*. Drill down on the dimension to reveal that all of the attribute names are displayed in Spanish. Drill down on the Año - Cuarto - Mes - Fecha de la Orden node and its child nodes to reveal that all member nodes are displayed in Spanish as well. Using the *Año - Cuarto - Mes - Fecha de la Orden* hierarchy in the query grid will demonstrate equally well that the Spanish names we've created are displayed in place of their English counterparts. All of this is illustrated in Figure 16-46.

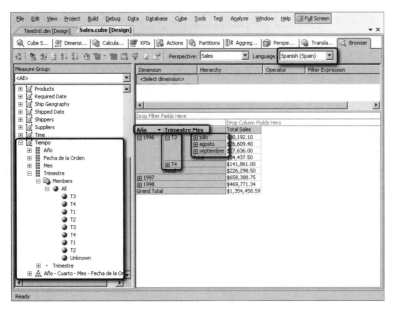

FIGURE 16-46 The cube browser, with the Language set to Spanish (Spain) and translated objects highlighted

Notice that the *Total Sales* measure is displayed in the query grid in English because we provided no translation for it.

Another, perhaps better, way to test translations is by changing your workstation's local language and country settings. To do this, close Visual Studio, and then select the Regional And Language Options applet from the Windows Control Panel. Change the Standards And Formats setting on the Regional Options tab (or, for Windows Vista and Windows Server 2008, the Current Format setting on the Formats tab) to Spanish (Spain), and then click Apply. Restart Visual Studio (and reopen your project), and then open the cube designer Browser tab (for the *Sales* cube). With Language set to Default—*not* to Spanish (Spain)—you should see the *TimeIntl* dimension appear as *Tiempo* and its child objects appear in Spanish as well.

This same technique will force the Metadata tab in the Management Studio MDX query window to display the dimension and its child objects in Spanish—in fact, this technique is the only way to do so. (To see this change, you must open a new MDX query window if one was open when you changed your workstation's regional settings, but you should not need to restart Management Studio itself.) When you've finished experimenting, go back to the Regional And Language Options applet, switch back to your normal language and culture setting, and then click OK. Close and reopen the Management Studio MDX query window, as well as Visual Studio and your Analysis Services project, and everything should return to English.

Roles

Perspectives and translations allow specific groups of users to see customized views of your cubes, but only real security settings can prevent users from seeing specific items in your physical cubes. By defining one or more roles in your Analysis Services project, you can restrict the access that specific users or groups have to certain data sources, cubes, dimensions, attributes, members, and even individual cube cells in your Analysis Services database.

You can block access to objects completely or limit users' permissions to read-only access; you can also control whether users in the role can process the entire database, specific cubes, and/or specific dimensions. Last, you can assign administrator rights within the database to certain roles, and you can grant read access to the definitions of the entire database, its data sources, or dimensions. (You can assign many of these permissions for data mining models and structures as well.)

The basics of the role designer are fairly simple to learn. You add a new role to your project by clicking the New Role option on the Roles node's shortcut menu in the Solution Explorer window or by choosing Project, New Role. Your role will be assigned a default name (both at the object level and at the file name level), which you should change by using the Properties window or the Rename option on the role node's shortcut menu in the Solution Explorer window.

The role designer consists of several tabs where you define permissions for various Analysis Services objects. The General tab allows you to enter a description for the role and assign its database-level permissions: Full Control (Administrator), Process, and/or Read Definition. The Membership tab lets you specify which users and groups belong to the role. You use the tab's Add button to specify the role's membership by using a standard Windows Select Users Or Groups dialog box.

The remaining tabs allow you to configure specific permissions for your database's data sources, cubes, cells, dimensions, dimension data (attribute members), and mining structures. You can also test your role, using a sort of simulated impersonation, via the Cell Data tab's Test Cube Security hyperlink.

To test this feature for yourself, add a role to our cube and name it **NAmericaNoOrderDate** (because it will limit the *Geography* dimension to enumerate only North American countries and will hide all attributes of the *Order Date* dimension). On the General tab, enter a description if you want, and leave all check boxes cleared. (We do not want to assign any database-level permissions to this role.) You can assign specific users and/or groups to this role on the Membership tab, but this is not strictly necessary because we will be testing this role only through the Test Cube Security facility (covered shortly). It is also unnecessary to make any adjustments on the Data Sources tab.

Skip to the Cell Data tab, and note that the Cube drop-down list is empty. To address this, select the Cubes tab, and then set the Access level for the *Sales* cube to Read, as shown in Figure 16-47.

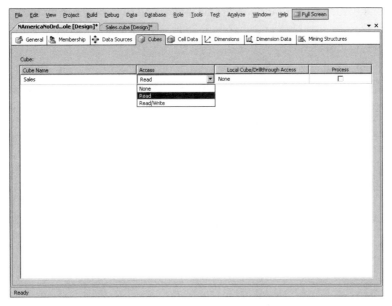

FIGURE 16-47 The Cubes tab of the role designer, showing Access for the *Sales* cube being set to Read

Reselect the Cell Data tab, shown in Figure 16-48, and notice that the *Sales* cube is now listed in the Cube drop-down list. Select it, and then click the Dimension Data tab.

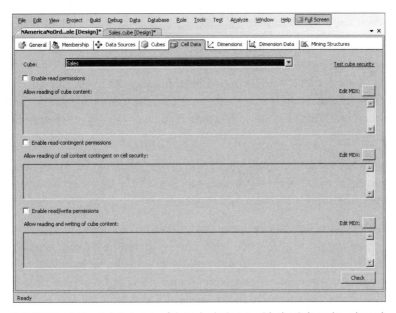

FIGURE 16-48 The Cell Data tab of the role designer, with the *Sales* cube selected

From the Dimension drop-down list, select the *Geography* dimension of the *Sales* cube (not the *Geography* dimension of the *Chapter16* database). From the Attribute Hierarchy drop-down list, select the *Country* attribute. Click the Deselect All Members option to clear the check boxes next to each country, and then manually select the check boxes next to Canada, Mexico, and USA, as shown in Figure 16-49.

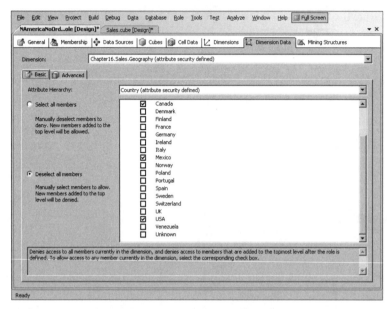

FIGURE 16-49 The Basic tab within the Dimension Data tab of the role designer, with attribute-level security for the *Sales* cube's *Geography.Country* attribute highlighted

Select the *Sales.Order Date* dimension (again, be sure to scroll down through the dimension list past the database dimensions to the cube dimensions), and then for *each* of its attributes (10 in all) click the Deselect All Members option button and do not manually select any members. Click the Advanced tab, and note that it is possible to specify allowed (or denied) members by entering MDX expressions rather than manually selecting (or deselecting) each member on the Basic tab.

Save and deploy your changes, and then click back on the Cell Data tab, where you'll notice that a set of three check boxes and MDX expressions is available to enable read, read contingent, and read/write permissions for the cells in the cube.

Click the Test Cube Security link on the upper right. (If you're prompted to deploy your changes again, agree to this.) A new window will open within Visual Studio containing the cube browser that is connected to the database under a simulated login emulating that of members of the role. (An information icon and descriptive text at the top of the window remind you of these details.) In the metadata tree view, drill down on the *Members* node for the *Country - State-Province - City - Postal Code* hierarchy of the *Geography* dimension and everything under the *Order Date* dimension. *Canada, Mexico,* and *USA* are the only members that appear for *Geography.Country - State-Province - City - Postal Code.Country,* and no members appear under any of the *Order Date* attributes or its hierarchy, as partially shown in Figure 16-50.

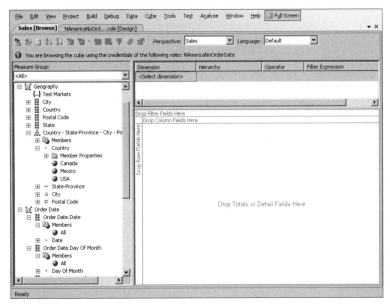

FIGURE 16-50 The cube browser as launched by the Test Cube Security link on the role designer's Cell Data tab

Summary

The Analysis Services OLAP feature set is impressive. Numerous dimension types, powerful calculations, KPIs, perspectives, translations, and proactive caching make it far easier to build cubes and make those cubes more powerful and more relevant to business users than was possible before Analysis Services 2005. Under Analysis Services 2008, these features are made more accessible and manageable through such designer innovations as BPAs, the Attribute Relationships tab in the dimension designer, and the Aggregations tab in the cube designer.

You now know how to build sophisticated cubes. In the next chapter, we'll show you how to develop applications that query cubes by using Microsoft Office Excel 2007 and Excel Services, ADO MD.NET, XML for Analysis (XMLA), and Analysis Management Objects (AMO). We'll also show you how to create server-side logic using the .NET Common Language Runtime (CLR) integration in Analysis Services.

Chapter 17
OLAP Queries, Tools, and Application Development

—*Andrew Brust*

The previous two chapters introduced you to the basic and more advanced online analytical processing (OLAP) features in Microsoft SQL Server Analysis Services 2008. The feature set is a combination of groundbreaking capabilities introduced in Analysis Services 2005 and elegant enhancements new to 2008; other features are merely carryovers from earlier versions of the product, but even those are now more accessible. If you were planning to use the various available OLAP tools against your cubes, including the cube browser we worked with in each of the last two chapters, you'd be all set.

But the reality is that OLAP is most useful when its capabilities are integrated into end-user applications rather than delivered through special tools. So how *do* you connect to cubes from Microsoft Office Excel or work OLAP queries into your .NET applications? What are the programming tools and application programming interfaces (APIs)? What are the user interface (UI) techniques? And how does the multidimensional expression language (MDX) work, anyway?

In this chapter, we'll give you the answers to these questions and more. Whether you want to query your cube from Excel or write .NET code that queries your cube and its metadata, this chapter has it covered. We'll show you how to connect Excel PivotTables to your cubes, introduce you to the MDX query language, and discuss the use of XML for Analysis (XMLA) as the native API in Analysis Services. We'll show you how to program to XMLA directly and how to use ADO MD.NET (ADO.NET Multidimensional) and Analysis Management Objects (AMO) to build full-featured OLAP UI applications in managed (.NET) code. We'll even show you how to write .NET code that runs on your Analysis Services server (which is similar to the SQL CLR programming we covered in Chapter 3).

This might seem like a lot for one chapter, but as you'll see, all of these tools lie along a single continuum and build on each other. As you learn about each successive tool, your knowledge and understanding of the others will be enhanced.

About the Sample Code

The sample code for this chapter (available on the book's companion Web site) bears some explanation. It includes .NET code, MDX and XMLA scripts, a stand-alone HTML page, and even Excel workbook files. The Chapter17 sample code folder consists of four subfolders named Excel, FrontPage-IE, SSMS, and VS. The Excel folder contains two files (PivotTableChart.xlsx for Excel 2007 and PivotTableChart.xls for Excel 2003), each containing a PivotTable and linked chart, on separate tabs. The former file also contains tabs demonstrating scorecard creation and the use of in-cell *CUBE* formulas. The FrontPage-IE folder contains the file OWC.htm, which in turn contains Excel *PivotTable* and *ChartSpace* controls (both supplied by Microsoft Office Web Components). The SSMS folder contains the solution file Chapter17.ssmssln, which in turn contains three separate Analysis Services projects (*MDX Demos*, *XMLA Demos*, and *CLR Demos*). The VS folder contains the solution file Chapter17.sln, which in turn contains a Windows Forms project (*Chapter17*), a Microsoft ASP.NET project (*Chapter17Web*), a Class Library project (*Chapter17AdomdServer*), and a Microsoft Visual Studio Tools for Office project (*Chapter17AddIn*). The Visual Studio Tools for Office add-in code will not be covered in depth here, but we will provide an overview description of it later in this chapter.

The Excel 2003 file (in the Excel folder), the stand-alone HTML file (in the FrontPage-IE folder), and code in the Windows Forms and ASP.NET projects (under the VS folder) using the Office Web Components are all carried over from the previous edition of this book. This chapter will not cover this particular sample code content, but the code is nonetheless provided for those readers who need to develop for an Excel 2003 environment. For the benefit of those readers, the counterpart to this chapter from the previous edition of this book (where the content appeared as Chapter 19) is also available on this book's companion Web site. This older version of the chapter contains detailed documentation on the Excel 2003–related and Office Web Component–related content.

Throughout this chapter, we will examine development techniques using our code samples. You can build the samples from scratch or simply follow along using the sample spreadsheet and code. Almost all of the samples are ready to run (provided that the database built in the previous chapter is available as *Chapter16* on your *localhost* Analysis Services server). The MDX scripts in the *CLR Demos* project will run once the assembly in the *Chapter17AdomdServer* project is deployed to your Analysis Services server.

As we explain techniques in this chapter, we will reference the components of the sample code that best implement them. Some figures in this chapter are from the sample Windows Forms application and Management Studio scripts. In certain cases, the sample code explores techniques that go even deeper into the topics than does the chapter text. If you can, go through all the code carefully; you'll find it to be a valuable reference.

Using Excel

The number one OLAP client in the world today is Excel. For IT organizations, the ubiquity of Microsoft Office—and the resulting simplicity of deployment and low cost—make Excel quite popular. For users, the familiarity of the spreadsheet interface makes Excel a highly requested UI paradigm.

As a result, Microsoft made certain that Excel 2007 PivotTables and charts provided support for virtually every Analysis Services 2005 (and thus 2008) feature, including multiple measure groups, key performance indicators (KPIs), dimension attributes (as distinct from user hierarchies), actions, named sets, and more. In addition, Microsoft added several functions to the Excel formula language to allow querying of cubes from within non-PivotTable regions of a spreadsheet and made connecting to Analysis Services cubes much easier than in earlier versions.

Moreover, with the addition of Excel Services—essentially an interface for viewing Excel content via Microsoft Office SharePoint—Microsoft has enabled Excel 2007 as an authoring tool for powerful Web dashboards. This means that mastery of the OLAP capabilities in Excel 2007 enables you to create both desktop and Web presentation layers for your Analysis Services cubes. Additionally, because the Excel PivotTable and chart interfaces (on the desktop) feature drag-and-drop field lists, you (and your users) can use these tools to query your cubes without any knowledge of MDX.

All of the aforementioned capabilities are available without any programming whatsoever. And for those who are eager to exploit Excel's business intelligence (BI) know-how in a custom development environment, Visual Studio Tools for Office allows you to create Excel 2007 add-ins that feature programmatic manipulation of the Excel OLAP features combined with other .NET code.

In this section, we'll cover how to use Excel as a full-fledged OLAP client, both from the desktop and from the Web browser (using Excel Services). After that, we'll cover programming OLAP from .NET using various APIs. We will also briefly discuss the Visual Studio Tools for Office project included with this chapter's sample code. That code implements an Excel 2007 add-in combining the API programming discussed in this chapter with automation of intrinsic Excel BI capabilities. We will discuss those capabilities right now.

Connecting to Analysis Services

Before we venture into the more advanced BI capabilities of Excel 2007, let's cover the basics: how to connect PivotTables and charts to your cubes from within an Excel spreadsheet. To begin, you'll need to start Excel 2007 and then select the Data tab on the Ribbon (typically the fifth tab from the left). Next click the From Other Sources drop-down menu button (in the Get External Data group, the fourth button from the left), and notice that the second option in the drop-down menu is From Analysis Services, as shown in Figure 17-1.

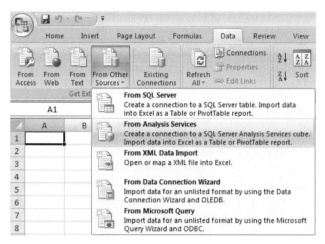

FIGURE 17-1 Connecting PivotTables and charts to your cubes from within an Excel 2007 spreadsheet

Note If you're running at a low resolution or have the Excel window sized small enough, the Get External Data group will not appear directly. Instead, a Get External Data *button* will appear (at the far left of the Data tab) that you'll need to click. This will display the group in a drop-down Ribbon panel; you can then click the From Other Sources menu button and select the From Analysis Services option from there.

Select the From Analysis Service option; the Data Connection Wizard will appear. In the Connect To Database Server page, type the name of your server (which might be **localhost** or simply **"."**), confirm that the Use Windows Authentication option button is selected, and then click Next.

In the Select Database And Table Page ("table" here really means "cube"), you'll find a drop-down list of all databases on the server. Select our *Chapter16* database, and you should see listed in the grid below it the *Sales* cube and *Product Info* perspective (and notice that in the Type column of the grid, Excel distinguishes between cubes and perspectives). Make sure that the Connect To A Specific Cube Or Table check box is selected, and then select the *Sales* cube, as shown in Figure 17-2.

Click Next to advance to the Save Data Connection File And Finish page. On this page, you provide a file name and location in which to save the connection information you have just supplied. The default file name follows the pattern *server database cube*.odc (for example, localhost Chapter16 Sales.odc) and the default location for the file is the My Data Sources folder within the current user's Documents or My Documents folder (depending on which version of Microsoft Windows is used). You can change the default file name by typing a new one, and you can change the default save location by clicking the Browse button and navigating to a different folder.

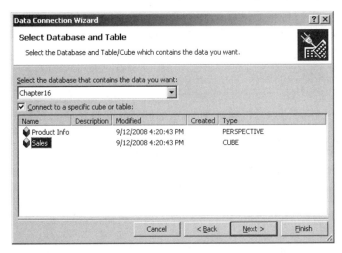

FIGURE 17-2 The Select Database And Table page of the Excel Data Connection Wizard

The file saved by this wizard page is an Office Data Connection file (hence the .odc extension). Naming it carefully and storing it in a location you can remember allows you to reuse it the next time you want to connect to the database and cube that the .odc file points to. (We'll show you how to do that shortly.) The other reason the .odc file is important is that in order to publish your Excel BI content to SharePoint, the file must be copied to a SharePoint connection library and the spreadsheet must be modified to use that copy. (We'll cover how to do this shortly as well.)

Complete the Save Data Connection File And Finish wizard page, as shown in Figure 17-3.

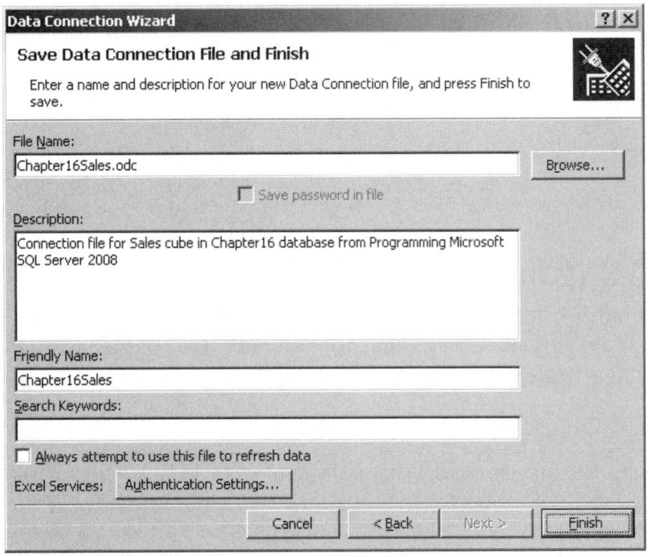

FIGURE 17-3 The Save Data Connection File And Finish page of the Excel Data Connection Wizard

Notice the changes to the File Name and Friendly Name fields. The Description field is optional, but go ahead and fill it out as shown anyway. Do not change the default save location, and leave the Search Keywords field blank.

When you've finished, click Finish, and the Import Data dialog box will appear. The first set of option buttons lets you select whether you want to create a connection (.odc) file only, a connection file and a PivotTable, or both of those plus a chart. Assuming that you elect to create a PivotTable (with or without a chart), the second set of option buttons lets you indicate whether you want to insert the new PivotTable in a specific existing worksheet or a new one, and at what cell location. The Properties button displays the Connection Properties dialog box, which allows you to modify the connection's properties, including its connection string.

Accept the default settings, and then click OK. You'll see a blank PivotTable on the left of your screen and a PivotTable Field List window (either floating or docked) on the right, containing all of the measures (within their display folders), KPIs, and dimensions (and their attributes, hierarchies, and named sets) in the enhanced *Sales* cube we created in Chapter 16, as shown in Figure 17-4.

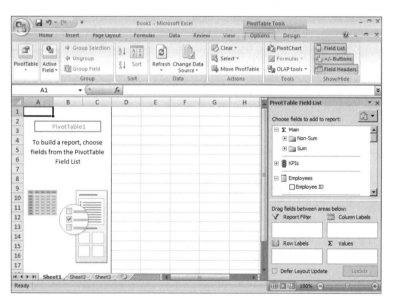

FIGURE 17-4 An empty PivotTable in a new Excel spreadsheet with objects from our *Chapter16* database displayed in the PivotTable Field List window

The PivotTable tab of the file PivotTableChart.xlsx, supplied with this chapter's sample code, contains a fully built-out PivotTable bound to the *Sales* cube of our *Chapter16* database.

> **Note** If our cube had more than one measure group, a drop-down list of the groups would appear at the top of the PivotTable Field List task pane. Try connecting to the *Adventure Works* sample cube to see this for yourself. Notice that even in our case, our sole measure group (*Main*) is shown as the first parent node in the task pane's tree view, with a Greek letter sigma icon to its left.

Before we start to populate the PivotTable, let's make sure that the connection file we created is indeed available. To test this fully, shut down Excel completely (do not save any changes to the workbook), and then restart. Next click the Existing Connections button in the Get External Data group of the Data tab on the Excel Ribbon.

> **Note** As before, depending on your resolution and the size of your Excel window, the Get External Data group might not appear directly. Follow the previous directions to make it appear. A similar procedure might be needed for other Excel Ribbon navigation procedures described in this chapter. We will assume that you will keep this in mind and we will not point it out each time.

After you click this button, the Existing Connections dialog box appears, as shown in Figure 17-5.

FIGURE 17-5 The Existing Connections dialog box

Notice that the connection we created is listed in the Connection Files On This Computer section of the dialog box. Select the connection and click Open, or just double-click it, and the Import Data dialog box appears as it did before. Click OK, and we'll once again be placed in an empty PivotTable with all of the *Sales* cube contents in the PivotTable Field List task pane, as was shown earlier in Figure 17-4. Consider that because our .odc file was created and waiting for us, after opening Excel, it took only five clicks (including the one required to activate the Data tab of the Excel Ribbon) and no typing to get to this point.

Building the PivotTable

If the PivotTable interface and environment you're now in seems familiar, it should: the cube browser hosted by both SQL Server Management Studio and the Visual Studio Analysis Services project cube designer uses a modified version of the Excel 2003 PivotTable.

Obviously, the look and feel has been changed significantly for Excel 2007, but the same general UI workflow applies.

Let's look more closely at the PivotTable Field List shown in Figure 17-4. First, notice that the top half of the task pane contains a tree view indicating the available fields and the bottom half contains the areas we can place the fields. If you click the drop-down button at the upper-right of the task pane, you can choose to show just one or the other of these field input sections or change the layout of how the two sections are presented together.

Within the available fields tree view, notice the different top-level-node icons for measure groups, KPIs, and dimensions. Within the *Main* measure group node, drill down on each of our two display folders to display our six measures (including our two calculated measures). Drill down on the KPIs node to see the node for our *Average Total Sales KPI* key performance indicator, and drill down on its node to see separate nodes for its value, goal, status, and trend. Under the *Geography* dimension's node, drill down on the node for our *Country - State-Province - City - Postal Code* hierarchy to reveal nodes for its levels; drill down on the Other Fields node to reveal nodes for each of the dimension's attributes; and drill down on the Sets node to reveal a node for our *Test Markets* named set.

Notice that most of the leaf-level nodes have check boxes next to them. Those are there so that you can easily include the corresponding objects in your PivotTable. Try this now by checking (in order) the nodes for the *Total Sales* measure, the *Country - State-Province - City - Postal Code* hierarchy of the *Geography* dimension, and the *Reports To* attribute–parent/ child hierarchy of the *Org Chart* dimension.

If you look at the PivotTable, you'll notice that both dimensions have been projected onto the rows axis and that the columns axis is empty. To fix this, look at the field areas of the PivotTable Field List pane (located in the bottom half of the Pivot Table Field List pane, by default). Notice that there is a 2-by-2 display of list boxes that can be used to configure the contents of the Report Filter, Row Labels, Column Labels, and Values areas. Notice also that both dimensions appear in the Row Labels list. To move the *Reports To* attribute to the columns axis of the PivotTable, simply drag its list item from the Row Labels list to the Column Labels list. After doing so, drill down on the Fuller, Andrew column header in the PivotTable. The results should appear as shown in Figure 17-6.

In addition to selecting items from the PivotTable Field List by selecting their check boxes, you can instead drag and drop them from the available fields tree control to any of the four field area lists. However, unlike in the cube browser in Visual Studio and Management Studio, you cannot drag items directly onto the PivotTable itself. Multiple items can be "stacked" in the same area, and you can remove items by dragging them out of the list they are in and dropping them outside the physical boundaries of the areas section of the Pivot Table Field List pane. Once items are in a particular area list, you can click their drop-down arrows (in the area list) to display a shortcut menu that allows you to move them, delete them, or alter their settings.

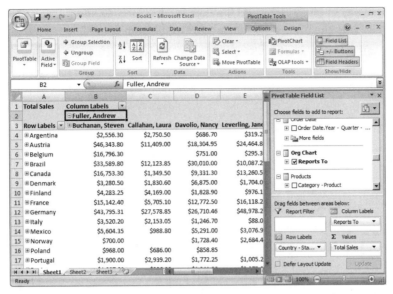

FIGURE 17-6 A populated PivotTable querying our *Sales* cube built in Chapter 16.

Exploring PivotTable Data

From within the available fields tree view, you can click the drop-down arrow to the right of any hierarchy, level, or attribute name to reveal a list of members, any of which you can select or deselect, as shown in Figure 17-7.

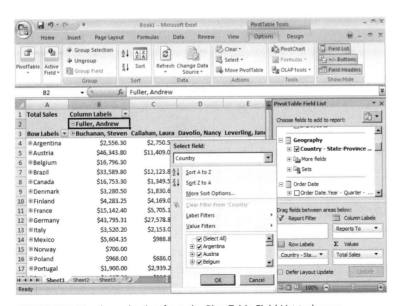

FIGURE 17-7 Member selection from the PivotTable Field List task pane

You can also drag any of these items into the Report Filter list area and then display the member list by clicking the drop-down arrow next to the item in the filter area of the PivotTable itself, as shown in Figure 17-8.

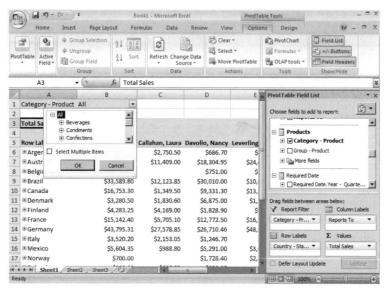

FIGURE 17-8 Member selection from the PivotTable's filter area

Again, these features are similar to features offered by the cube browser. In fact, dragging items into the Report Filter list and making selections in its member list from the filter area allows you to use this area within the PivotTable as you would use the cube browser's Filter Fields area.

To expand a nonleaf member in the PivotTable's Row or Column Labels areas, simply click its plus (+) icon or double-click the label. To collapse a nonleaf member, click its minus (–) icon or double-click the label again. Numerous other expand/collapse options are available from the Expand/Collapse option on the member's shortcut menu.

Hovering over any cell in the data area of the PivotTable will display a multiple-row tooltip. The tooltip will remind you of the particular measure displayed, as well as its value, and the member values for the particular row and column the cell is in.

Any actions defined in the cube are available from shortcut menus. For example, right-click any data cell and select Additional Actions, Total Sales Drillthrough to execute the drillthrough action we built in Chapter 16. Or in the row labels, drill down to a city, and then right-click it and select Additional Actions, Live Search to execute the URL action we created. (When you've finished, collapse the city's parent nodes again so that only countries are displayed on the PivotTable's rows axis.)

One interesting thing about drillthrough actions is that Excel doesn't really need them in order to perform a drillthrough for you. In fact, you can double-click any cell in the PivotTable's data area (or choose the Show Details option from the cell's shortcut menu) to get its drillthrough detail. Try it and see—you'll notice that such a generic drillthrough will display all measure group columns whereas executing a drillthrough action will display only the columns that were included when that action was designed.

Name the current tab PivotTable so that we can build other content elsewhere and find our way back. To do so, right-click the Sheet1 tab, and then select the Rename option from the shortcut menu (or just double-click the tab). You can now type **PivotTable** in the tab's name area. Click outside the tab (or press the Enter key) to retain the changed name.

Scorecards

As mentioned earlier, Excel 2007 ends up being a very capable client for building dashboards, and these can include scorecards using Analysis Services KPIs. To see this for yourself, select the tab named Sheet2, rename the tab to **Scorecard**, and then click the Existing Connections button in the Get External Data group of the Ribbon's Data tab. Select Chapter16Sales from the Connections In This Workbook (top) section of the Existing Connections dialog box and click Open, and then click OK in the Import Data dialog box. In the PivotTable Field List's available fields tree view, expand the KPIs node and then the node for *Average Total Sales KPI*. Now select the check boxes for the Value, Status, and Trend nodes. Scroll down (if necessary) to the *Order Date* dimension's node, and select the check box for its *Year - Quarter - Month - Date* hierarchy. If necessary, drag the latter selection from the Column Labels list to the Row Labels list. In the PivotTable, expand the Calendar 1996 node and its child Quarter 3, 1996 node. The results should be as shown in Figure 17-9.

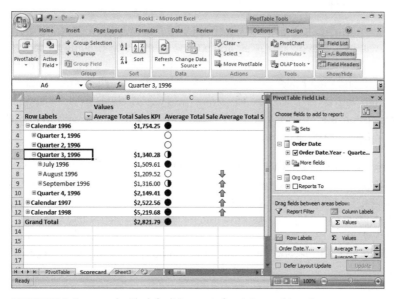

FIGURE 17-9 Scorecard with default icon sets for status and trend

You'll notice that the status and trend indicator graphics configured when *Average Total Sales KPI* was defined in the previous chapter are not the ones that Excel 2007 displays; however, we can change the indicators, for both the KPI's status and trend, by using the Excel 2007 Conditional Formatting feature. Select the column C header so that the entire column is selected, and then click the Home tab on the Excel Ribbon. Click the Conditional Formatting drop-down menu button (in the Styles group), and then select its Icon Sets option to display a graphical pop-up menu, as shown in Figure 17-10.

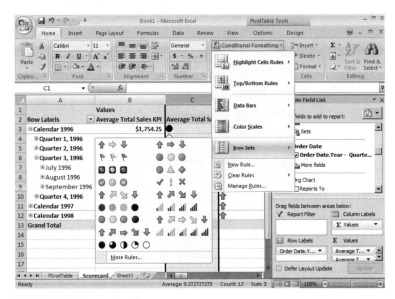

FIGURE 17-10 Icon set options

As you pass your mouse pointer over each icon set in the menu, you'll see both a preview of the selection within the PivotTable itself and a large tooltip that provides a name and description for the selection. If you move the mouse pointer from the Icon Sets option to the Color Scales option and then hover over its subsidiary choices, you'll see that your KPI status can be represented with a cell background color in addition to the icon visualization. Return to the Icon Sets option, and then select the 3 Traffic Lights (Unrimmed) option (usually the second option in the second column, as is shown in Figure 17-10).

In the PivotTable, you should see that the old black-and-white icon set has been replaced with a nice green/yellow/red traffic light icon scheme to represent the status values. The icons appear at the left edge of each cell; you'll notice that the status values also appear, at the right edge. To leave the icons but hide the values, once again select the Conditional Formatting drop-down button and then click the Manage Rules option from its menu. This displays the Conditional Formatting Rules Manager dialog box, as shown in Figure 17-11.

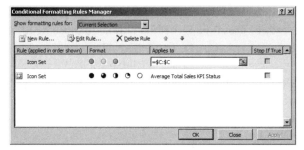

FIGURE 17-11 The Conditional Formatting Rules Manager dialog box

In this dialog box, double-click the row corresponding to the three-color traffic light icon set we just selected, or select it and click Edit Rule on the toolbar. This displays the Edit Formatting Rule dialog box; select the Show Icon Only check box (in the lower right) and click OK, and then click OK again to close the Conditional Formatting Rules Manager dialog box. Your status column should now display the icons only, and the status value should be hidden. Now select the column D header so that the entire trend column is selected, change its icon set to the 3 Arrows (Colored) selection (first option in the first column on the Icon Sets menu), and then edit the column's rule, as you did for the Status column, to hide the trend value and show only the icon. Your scorecard should now appear as shown in Figure 17-12.

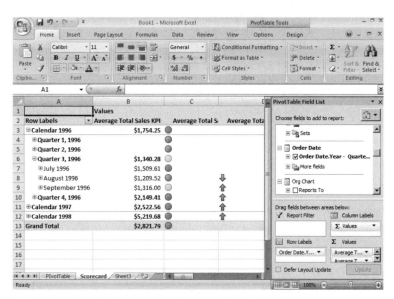

FIGURE 17-12 Finished scorecard with colored icon sets selected

Creating and Configuring Charts

We've now created a very helpful PivotTable and scorecard, and we're getting close to having what we need to export everything to Excel Services to build a nice dashboard view of the

Northwind database's sales data. But one item we're still missing is a chart view of the data. Luckily, Excel makes it uncannily easy to present a PivotTable's data graphically. To see this for yourself, return to the tab/sheet of our workbook we named PivotTable, and click in any cell of the actual PivotTable within the sheet. Now click the PivotTable Tools/Options tab of the Excel Ribbon, and then click the PivotChart button in the Tools group. This displays the Insert Chart dialog box, shown in Figure 17-13.

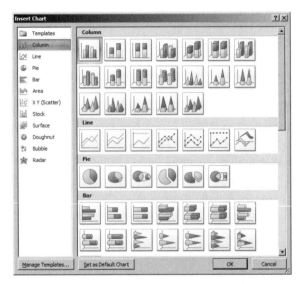

FIGURE 17-13 The Insert Chart dialog box

By default, the Clustered Column chart type is selected; change this to Stacked Column (the selection immediately to the right of Clustered Column), and then click OK. This inserts a chart as an embedded object within the PivotTable tab/sheet and automatically displays four new PivotChart Tools tabs on the Ribbon, with the first of those tabs—Design—activated. To move the new chart to its own sheet, click the Move Chart button (on the far right of the PivotChart Tools/Design Ribbon tab) to display the Move Chart dialog box.

Select the New Sheet option, change the default name to **PivotChart,** and then click OK. The chart should now appear on its own tab, with the PivotChart Filter Pane displayed, either floating or docked next to the PivotTable Field List task pane.

Notice that in the PivotChart Tools/Design tab on the Ribbon, to the left of the Move Chart button, is a Chart Styles gallery. At the very right edge of the gallery are up and down scroll buttons and a More button beneath them. Click the More button to display the entire gallery in a pop-up window, as shown in Figure 17-14.

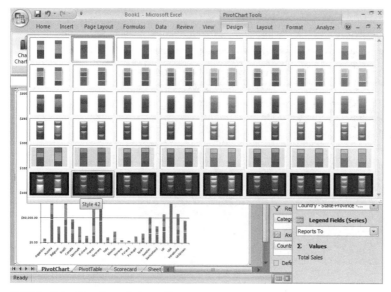

FIGURE 17-14 The Chart Styles gallery

If you hover your mouse pointer over the black background/multicolored foreground option (appearing in Figure 17-14 in the gallery's last row, second column), you'll see a tooltip that displays the message "Style 42." Click that option. Last, to reduce the number of bars displayed in the chart, open the PivotChart Filter Pane's Axis Fields (Country - State-Province - City - Postal Code) drop-down list. In the resulting pop-up dialog box, clear the Select All check box at the top, and then manually select the check boxes for Canada, Mexico, and USA; then click OK. The result should be as shown in Figure 17-15 (in which we have intentionally closed all task panes and minimized the Ribbon so as to maximize the screen area for the chart).

The PivotChart tab of the PivotTableChart.xlsx file, supplied with this chapter's sample code, contains a complete 3-D stacked column chart linked to the PivotTable on the file's PivotTable tab.

PivotTables and PivotCharts are linked in terms of their filtering and expand/collapse settings. If you flip back to the PivotTable tab after having made these changes to the chart, you will see the filtering changes reflected in the PivotTable. If you drill down on Canada in the PivotTable and then return to the PivotChart tab, you'll see that the expansion has occurred there as well. Experiment a bit more, and you'll discover that the converse is true as well.

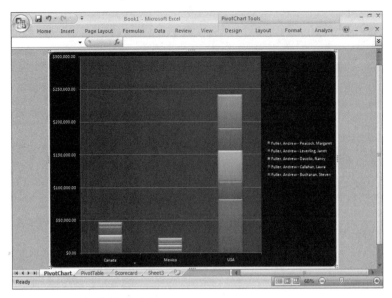

FIGURE 17-15 The finished chart

In-Formula Querying of Cubes

PivotTables make able OLAP clients; virtually all the capabilities of the cube browser are avail-able within them. Those features, combined with the ubiquity of Excel, make Excel a tempt-ing deployment vehicle for your OLAP needs. But with Excel 2007 comes an intriguing, new feature: the ability to bring OLAP data into spreadsheet cells without using PivotTables at all.

Before moving on, you might want, through drag and drop, to reorder the tabs so that the PivotChart tab is positioned in the middle of the PivotTable and Scorecard tabs. After, click the last, still empty tab, and change its label from Sheet3 to **Cell Formulas**.

On this tab, we will use no PivotTables or charts at all, but will instead query our cubes through the use of cell formulas. To see what we mean, click in any cell and type an equals sign (=) followed by the letters **c**, **u**, and **b**. An IntelliSense pop-up list appears, listing seven important new formula functions, as shown in Figure 17-16.

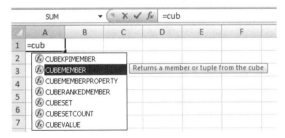

FIGURE 17-16 IntelliSense pop-up list of *CUBE* functions

Notice that as you select each of the seven options, a tooltip appears, displaying a description of the function. As it turns out, two of these seven functions are all that we need to start taking advantage of this new capability in Excel. Those two functions, *CUBEMEMBER* and *CUBEVALUE*, return a dimensional member and a cell value from a cube. Select CUBEMEMBER (the second function in the list), and then press Tab. An IntelliSense syntax tooltip will appear, as shown in Figure 17-17.

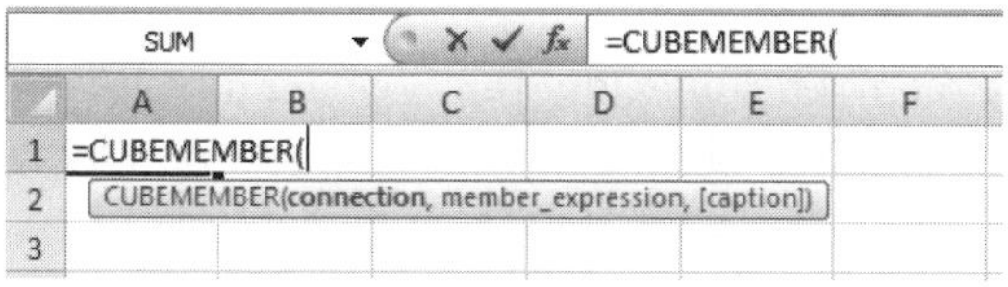

FIGURE 17-17 Syntax IntelliSense tooltip for the *CUBEMEMBER* function

The syntax for these functions can be a little daunting to the uninitiated. That's especially true of function parameters like the *member_expression* parameter of the *CUBEMEMBER* function. Although we're in Excel, this parameter actually expects a short MDX expression string! No worries. Excel arms us with two weapons to make creation of *CUBE* function formulas easy: the Convert To Formulas feature and very good IntelliSense support made available as expressions are entered. Let's look at each of these helper facilities now.

The Convert To Formulas Option

We'll start with Convert To Formulas, because it's quite easy to use and explain. First press Esc to back out of the in-cell formula entry you began. Next click back on the PivotTable tab, and then click within the PivotTable itself. Now select the PivotTable Tools/Options tab of the Excel Ribbon, and then click the OLAP Tools menu button in the Tools group (second from the right). From the drop-down menu, select the Convert To Formulas option. Now watch the magic: the entire PivotTable is converted to conventional spreadsheet cells populated with *CUBEVALUE* and *CUBEMEMBER* functions. Click any of the cells and look at the formula bar to see examples of how these formulas can be composed. Notice the reference to our Chapter16Sales data connection and, in the data area cell formulas, the various cell references that, in turn, point to specific members of the *Geography* and *Org Chart* dimensions. This is a very impressive feature of Excel 2007.

Excel Does IntelliSense

Now let's explore how to create these formulas ourselves, with the help of IntelliSense. First, select Undo (by pressing Ctrl+Z, if you want) to restore the PivotTable back into the sheet. Then navigate back to the Cell Formulas sheet, to cell A1, and then type the word **Country**. Move to cell A2, and again type an equals sign (=) followed by the letters **c**, **u**, and **b**; then select CUBEMEMBER in the drop-down list and press Tab.

The tooltip shows the *connection* parameter in bold, indicating that we need to enter the name of a connection. The problem is that we don't want to type the name manually, and no list of existing connections is shown. To fix this, simply type a double quotation mark ("). A list of connections will then appear. Since we have only one connection in our workbook, the list will contain only a single option, already highlighted (our Chapter16Sales connection—notice that the description we entered for it appears in the tooltip). Simply press Tab to select the connection, and then type a closing double quotation mark, a comma, and a space.

The tooltip is now prompting us for a member expression. This is where things can appear to get tricky, but they're actually not too difficult if you know what to do. Start by typing a double quotation mark again (that's almost always the thing to do if a list of options is not present and you want one to appear), and a pop-up list of the *Sales* cube's dimensions will appear.

Select *[Geography]* (again, by clicking it and pressing Tab), and then type a period (.) to see a list of attributes and hierarchies. Select *[Geography].[Country]*, and then type another period. A list pops up with *[Geography].[Country].[All]* as its only option. Select it (even though the *All* member is ultimately not what we're after), and type one more period. Now a pop-up list of countries (that is, members of the *Country* attribute) should appear, as shown in Figure 17-18!

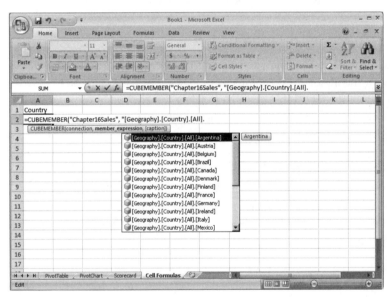

FIGURE 17-18 IntelliSense pop-up list of *Country* attribute members for the *Geography* dimension

Select *[Geography].[Country].[All].[Canada]*, type a closing double quotation mark and a close parenthesis, and then press Enter.

The word *Canada* will now appear in cell A2. That might have seemed like a lot of work just to insert the name of a country, but there will be a payoff, we promise. As a next step, copy the formula in cell A2 to A3 and A4. Then edit the formulas in the two copies to reference Mexico and USA, instead of Canada. Notice that IntelliSense will help you edit an MDX expression, not just create one.

Move to cell B1, and type the label **Total Sales**. Move to cell B2, and begin the entry of a *CUBEVALUE* formula, using roughly the same procedure we used to enter the *CUBEMEMBER* formula previously. Enter the connection name as you did before, and begin entering the MDX expression. When the list of dimensions appears, select *[Measures]*, type a period, select *[Measures].[Total Sales]*, and then type closing quotation marks, a comma, and a space.

> **Note** In MDX, the measures in a cube are actually considered to be members of a special dimension, itself named *Measures*. That is why, within MDX expressions, we select our measures from the list of dimensions provided by the *CUBEVALUE* function's IntelliSense list. We discuss this in greater detail later in this chapter.

The interesting thing about the *CUBEVALUE* function is that it can accept a theoretically infinite number of member expressions. In our case, we want to enter one more so that we can get the total sales specifically for Canada. Doing this is now very simple, because instead of needing to specify the member expression for Canada again, we can simply reference cell A2. To do this, just click cell A2. You should see its cell address added to the formula in the formula bar, as shown in Figure 17-19.

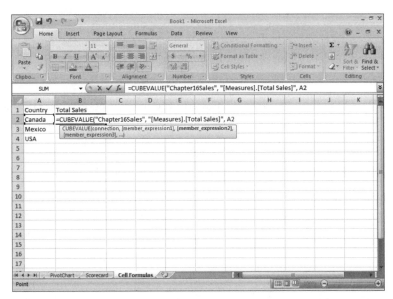

FIGURE 17-19 Inserting a cell reference into the *CUBEVALUE* function by clicking on a cell

Now type a close parenthesis and press Enter. You might see a series of pound signs (#) or the text *#GETTING DATA* briefly appear in cell B2, and then a value of *$55,334.10* will be displayed. That value *is* the total sales in Canada over the whole cube, and Excel just queried Analysis Services, in real time, to fetch and display that number.

If that's not impressive enough for you, try this: click in cell B2, and then grab the cell's handle (the thick square dot at the bottom right of the cell) and drag it down to cover cells B3 and B4. You should see the total sales for Mexico and the USA appear in those two cells. Imagine if you had a long list of countries, rather than just two—this is a great feature and shows how the marriage of OLAP functionality with cell formulas and cell references makes for a very powerful combination.

Table Formatting

Now select all eight populated cells from A1 to B4. Select the Home tab on the Excel Ribbon, and then click the Format As Table menu button in the Styles group. Select Table Style Medium 3 (typically in the fourth row, third column). Notice that our data is now formatted as an Excel table and that we can now filter and sort columns. Next, select cells B2:B4, rese-lect the Home tab of the Excel Ribbon, click the Conditional Formatting menu button (in the Styles group), select the Data Bars option, and select the Blue Data Bar (first) option from the submenu. You have now added a sort of in-cell histogram to better visualize the data presented in the table.

Filtering with Named Cells

Move your cursor to cell A7, type the label **Calendar Year**, and then press Enter. Move to cell B7, and type **1996**. Press Enter, and name the cell (cell B7, that is) **Calendar_Year**. You can either type this name in Excel's name box (under the Ribbon, to the left of the formula bar) or you can use the Name A Range option from the cell's shortcut menu.

Now go back and edit the formula in cell B2. Position your cursor after the A2 cell reference and before the close parenthesis. Type a comma and a space, and then add the following formula for the new member expression:

```
CONCATENATE("[Order Date].[Year].[All].[Calendar ", Calendar_Year, "]")
```

Notice the embedded space at the end of the first string. Now press Enter, and you should see all three data cells' values update to display the *Total Sales* measure values for their corresponding countries, in calendar 1996. Finish by reformatting cells B2:B4 to display values as currency.

 Tip If for some reason cells B3 and B4 do not update, copy the formula in cell B2 to them both.

Change the value in cell B8 to **1997**, and you'll see the cell values above it update again. Your finished table should appear as shown in Figure 17-20.

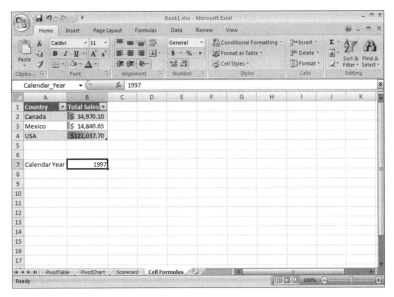

FIGURE 17-20 Finished cell formula sheet with table formatting and calendar year filter

Let's review what we've done and built so that you understand it before we export these various Excel-based BI content assets to SharePoint using Excel Services. First we added a Country column header and cell formulas below it that enumerated three members of the *Country* attribute in the *Geography* dimension. In the adjacent column to the right, we added a Total Sales column header and formulas to query the *Total Sales* measure values for each of the countries we enumerated in the first column. The second set of formulas referenced the first, in order to specify the slice of the cube by which they were constrained.

Next we added table formatting and data bars to our content. And we finished by editing the formulas in the Total Sales column to also be constrained by a particular calendar year, whose value we placed in a single-cell range named *Calendar_Year*. When we edited our *Total Sales* formulas to be constrained by the value in this cell, we did so by referencing the range name assigned to it.

Visual Studio Tools for Office and Excel Add-Ins

One of the most exciting things about the Excel 2007 features we have discussed so far is that they are all programmable. By using Visual Studio Tools for Office technology in Visual Studio 2008, you can create an add-in for Excel that creates PivotTables, charts, scorecards, and even in-cell formulas—all through code. Moreover, you can combine these techniques with the use of ADO MD.NET and AMO (covered later in this chapter) and, as a result, use Excel 2007 as a rich BI application development platform.

Included in the sample code for this chapter is a Visual Studio Tools for Office Excel 2007 add-in project, *Chapter17AddIn*, that demonstrates the programmatic creation of a

PivotTable, a chart, and in-cell formulas against the *Chapter16* database. The add-in inserts a new OLAP tab on the Excel Ribbon and also creates an OLAP Tools task pane. The task pane has drop-down lists that enumerate the dimensions and measures in the cube as well as the attributes of the dimension you select. This allows for the creation of cell formulas completely through code, for each member of the attribute you select. The code can determine all members, as well as populate the drop-down lists, by using ADO MD.NET to read the cube's metadata, using techniques we will discuss later in this chapter.

While scope and space limitations prevent us from discussing the Visual Studio Tools for Office programming techniques and the sample add-in's code, we would still encourage you to review the code and the Ribbon layout at design time. You can run, use, and debug the add-in simply by selecting the add-in project in the Solution Explorer window in Visual Studio and then either pressing F5, or selecting Debug, Start Debugging, or clicking the Start Debugging toolbar button.

Excel Services

The cell formula content was created on a fourth tab in our spreadsheet and joins a PivotTable, chart, and scorecard (which is actually another PivotTable) we had already created. Together, these four assets can be combined into a very helpful dashboard view. Save your changes to the workbook, and now let's use Excel Services to build that dashboard.

> **Note** Excel Services is available to users with an Enterprise Client Access License (Enterprise CAL) to Microsoft Office SharePoint Server 2007. Assuming that you are properly licensed and have appropriate access to a SharePoint server with Excel Services, a connection library, and a report library all properly configured, the steps in this section will work. If you're not a SharePoint Server Enterprise CAL licensee, you might want to read through this section anyway to learn about the capabilities the product offers. Understanding that you might not be able to follow along with each step from here, we'll provide sufficient screen shots to show you what to expect once you're in a properly configured SharePoint Server 2007 environment.

As we mentioned earlier, before we can publish our content to SharePoint via Excel Services, we must move our data connection to a SharePoint connection library. There are several ways of doing this, the most obvious being to navigate to the connection library in the browser and then use the SharePoint UI to upload the .odc file from our My Data Sources folder. The problem is that in addition to uploading a copy of the connection file, we also need to change our spreadsheet to use that copy once it's uploaded. Excel provides us with a way to do both steps together.

Edit the current workbook connection's properties. Start in the Data tab of the Ribbon, click the Connections button in the Connections group, confirm that the Chapter16Sales connection is selected, and then click the Properties button. This will display the Connection Properties dialog box, where you should select the Definition tab and then click Export Connection File (toward the bottom right). A File Save dialog box will appear; from here, you must navigate into your SharePoint connection library and then save the .odc file there, as shown in Figure 17-21.

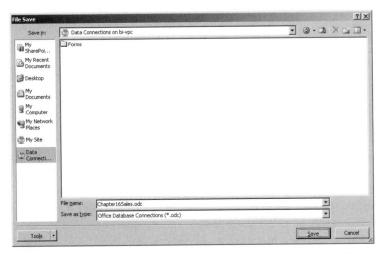

FIGURE 17-21 Saving an .odc connection file to a SharePoint connection library

Once the connection file is saved in the connection library, we need to configure our workbook to use that copy, rather than the one on our local drive. This way, when we publish the workbook's contents to SharePoint and users browse the data, they will be referencing a data connection that is stored on the server and therefore available to them.

To convert our workbook's connection reference, we need to remove the local version and then add the connection library version. If you haven't done so yet, click Save and you'll be returned to the Workbook Connections dialog box. Confirm that the local version of Chapter16Sales is selected, and then click Remove. A message box will appear; click OK, despite its dire warning message. Now click Add, navigate to the connection library and your connection file, and then click Open. Last, click Close in the Workbook Connections dialog box, and save your changes.

Now that the workbook's connection has been migrated to our SharePoint connection library, we're ready to publish our content to Excel Services. Start by clicking the Microsoft Office Button (that is, the round Microsoft Office logo in the upper-left corner of the Excel window), and then select Publish, Excel Services from the menu. These actions will display what *looks* to be a simple Save As dialog box. Look closely, however, and you'll notice a special Excel Services Options button toward the bottom right, just above the Save button, as shown in Figure 17-22.

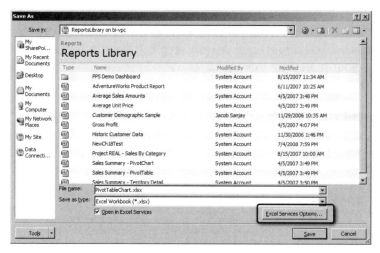

FIGURE 17-22 Publishing to Excel Services via the Save As dialog box using the Excel Services Options button

Click that button to display the Excel Services Options dialog box. This dialog box is where we specify what we want published and how. A drop-down list offers us the simple choices of what to publish: Entire Workbook, Sheets (that is, specific sheets within the workbook), or Items In The Workbook. Select the last of these options, and then select each of our objects except the *Calendar_Year* named range. The dialog box should now appear as shown in Figure 17-23.

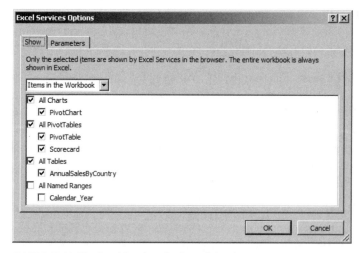

FIGURE 17-23 The Excel Services Options dialog box

Note The object names you see for the table and PivotTables might differ—we assigned these names to our objects using the PivotTable Name and Table Name text boxes in the PivotTable Tools/Options and Table Tools/Design tabs of the Ribbon.

Notice that each of our objects appears as a checkable item: our two PivotTables (one of which is our scorecard), our chart, our table (which contains our cell formula content), and our named range.

We have selected each of these items except the named range. The range will be used, but in a specific capacity to parameterize the data in our table. Select the Parameters tab of the dialog box, and then click its Add button. This displays the Add Parameters dialog box, in which you should see our named range listed, as shown in Figure 17-24.

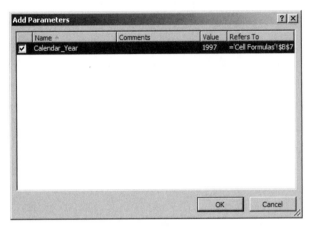

FIGURE 17-24 The Add Parameters dialog box

Select its check box, and then click OK. Our named range should now appear in the Parameters tab, shown in Figure 17-25, which will enable Excel Services to render a special task pane to solicit its value.

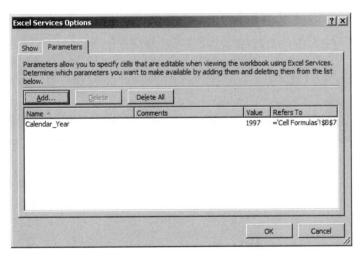

FIGURE 17-25 The Parameters tab of the Excel Services Options dialog box, with our *Calendar_Year* named range configured to expose a parameter

Click OK to close the Excel Services Options dialog box. Back in the Save As dialog box, make sure that the Open In Excel Services check box is selected, navigate to the desired report library, and then click Save. This action will save the workbook into the Report Library and then open a sort of test harness browser page where you can view each of the four items we've just published. Figure 17-26 shows this page displaying our PivotTable.

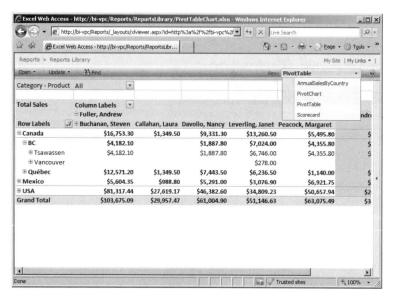

FIGURE 17-26 Excel Services PivotTable browser test page with drop-down list of published spreadsheet items

If we navigate to the Report Library in the browser, we'll see our workbook listed in it and we'll be able to click it at any time to display the same test page that appeared when we published the content from Excel. However, that page is most certainly not ready for end users. What we need for that audience is a special dashboard page containing four instances of the Excel Web Access Web Part. The Dashboard Page option on the New menu within the Report Library will get us about halfway: it creates a new Web Part page with two instances of the Excel Web Access Web Part, plus a few other Web Parts that we won't need.

The steps required to add two more instances of the Web Part and point the resulting four instances to the four items we've published are longer than space here allows us to cover. Rest assured, if you have some basic SharePoint skills, the procedure is relatively straightforward. (If you're not fluent in SharePoint Web Part insertion, see *http://office.microsoft.com/en-us/sharepointserver/HA011605831033.aspx*.) The result is shown in Figure 17-27.

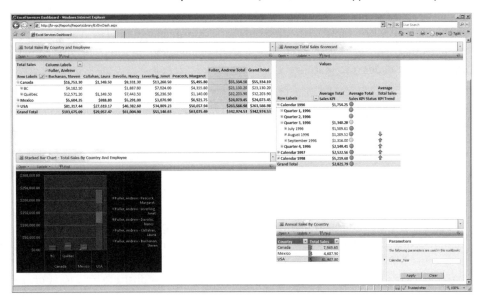

FIGURE 17-27 Excel Services dashboard page featuring all four published items

Note that the PivotTable content is fully interactive: nodes can be expanded or collapsed, and the data can be refreshed at any time. Toolbar buttons allow either a snapshot or an editable copy to be opened in the full Excel 2007 client application, if it is installed on the local machine. The cell formula content is interactive as well. A task pane appears by default in which the *Calendar_Year* value can be entered, and an Apply button can then be clicked to refresh the cells to reflect the new value.

The combination of the Excel 2007 BI capabilities and Excel Services makes for a remarkably capable platform for building presentation layers for your cubes. You can supplement this with Reporting Services reports, as well as other Microsoft products such as ProClarity briefing book pages and PerformancePoint dashboard content. Because *all* of these products display their content in SharePoint, you can merge content from any combination of them in the same dashboard page. The value derived from doing so is extremely high. Meanwhile, Excel 2007 and Excel Services provide immense value on their own, as you've seen.

Beyond Excel: Custom OLAP Development with .NET

We've covered in great detail how to use Excel and Excel Services as powerful presentation tools for your cubes. These UI tools are serious options, given the ubiquity of, and business users' familiarity with, Microsoft Office. Moreover, using Excel enables you to create compelling UIs with minimal programming.

Although the Excel option lets you avoid the need for much programming, it also precludes the granular control that a more programmatic approach would offer. The Excel option also requires that the 2007 Microsoft Office system be installed on the user's machine if you want to offer the full desktop feature set.

If you want fine-grained control over the query, you might want to move beyond the Excel approach. And if you're a .NET developer and want to use your ADO.NET and/or data binding skills in the context of an OLAP application, you'll absolutely want to know how to program against Analysis Services directly.

MDX and Analysis Services APIs

In short, if you want to build highly customized OLAP applications, you'll almost definitely want to learn some basic multidimensional expression language (MDX) and understand how to execute MDX queries using ADO MD.NET (the Multidimensional ADO.NET data provider). We will discuss both of these technologies shortly and demonstrate how to apply them to Windows Forms applications.

As we cover MDX and ADO MD.NET, we will explain how to use SQL Server Management Studio as an MDX client. We will also investigate how to execute XML for Analysis (XMLA) queries from Management Studio. XMLA can be used as both a data manipulation language (DML) and a data definition language (DDL) facility from Management Studio. ADO MD.NET acts as a wrapper around the DML side of XMLA. Another managed object model that we will cover, Analysis Management Objects (AMO), acts as a wrapper over XMLA's DDL functionality. We will examine programmatic use of XMLA in your code and how to expose "raw" XMLA responses from ADO MD.NET.

To complete our coverage of OLAP development, we will show you how to take advantage of the CLR server-side programming features in Analysis Services. As we do this, you'll see how your client-side OLAP development skills can be migrated to the server to develop sophisticated logic that extends the innate capabilities of MDX from the client.

Moving to MDX

Whether you're programming on the client or the server, using ADO MD.NET, or just working with SQL Server Management Studio, you'll need at least a working knowledge of MDX. MDX is an extremely rich language, the complexity of which we can merely sample in this chapter. Luckily, using MDX for simple queries is itself simple and will be somewhat familiar to those with a grounding in SQL. A practical prototype of an MDX query is as follows:

```
SELECT [column members] ON COLUMNS,
       [row members] ON ROWS
FROM [cubename]
WHERE [measure]
```

This "schematic" code glosses over the details of specifying row and column members and oversimplifies the real purpose of the *WHERE* clause, but we will remedy these shortcomings soon. Let's start by looking at an actual query that selects from the *Sales* cube from our *Chapter16* database, showing *Total Sales* broken down by the *Shipper Name* attribute of the *Shippers* dimension (on the *COLUMNS* axis) and *Year* attribute of the *Time* dimension (on the *ROWS* axis):

```
SELECT  Shippers.[Shipper Name].MEMBERS ON COLUMNS,
        Time.Year.MEMBERS ON ROWS
FROM    Sales
WHERE   Measures.[Total Sales]
```

Before we go any further in our discussion of this query or of MDX itself, let's discuss the use of SQL Server Management Studio as a top-notch tool for running, designing, and learning how to write MDX queries.

Management Studio as an MDX Client

In Chapter 16, we looked at Management Studio's capabilities for managing Analysis Services databases, and we provided brief coverage of its MDX and XMLA Query window capabilities. We will now explore the MDX Query window's capabilities more fully.

As mentioned in Chapter 16, SQL Server 2005 introduced Management Studio as a replacement not only for SQL Enterprise Manager and SQL Query Analyzer but also for the SQL Server 2000 Analysis Services tools: Analysis Manager and the MDX Sample Application. The MDX Sample Application, shown in Figure 17-28, allows for execution of ad hoc MDX queries and saving and retrieving them to and from text files, and it includes a simple UI that allows for drag-and-drop visual composition of these queries. It's a useful tool, although it is completely separate from the other SQL Server 2000 tools, and it is provided, as its name implies, as a sample application (including its Visual Basic 6.0 source code) more than as a production-quality tool.

As you saw in the previous chapter, Management Studio includes the functionality of the MDX Sample Application by providing MDX Query windows that work almost identically to its SQL Query windows. MDX query functionality is thus integrated with the rest of the Management Studio feature set, and Management Studio even provides some extra features, including IntelliSense. Analysis Services script projects, which can include MDX queries, can be created within Management Studio, allowing you to create solutions consisting of both Analysis Services and (relational) SQL Server projects with scripts for related cubes and tables.

Caution Although both the MDX Sample Application and Management Studio use the .mdx file name extension for their respective MDX query files, the two file formats are not compatible. The MDX Sample Application stores multiple queries per file and separates them using a quote delimiter scheme. Management Studio stores MDX query text without any additional formatting, much as it does with SQL text in .sql files.

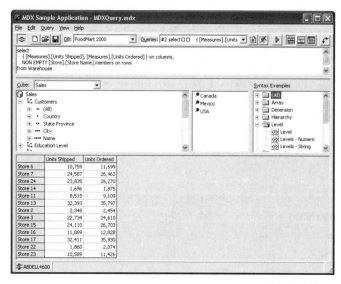

FIGURE 17-28 The MDX Sample Application (supplied with SQL Server 2000 Analysis Services)

The sample code for this chapter includes a SQL Server Management Studio solution, which can be opened via the file Chapter17\SSMS\Chapter17.ssmssln. The solution contains three Analysis Services projects, one of which (Chapter17\SSMS\MDX Demos\1. MDX Demos.ssmsasproj) consists of separate .mdx files for each query presented in the chapter, including the one discussed previously. Open the solution now, and double-click the SimpleQuery.mdx query file to open the query in Management Studio. Click the Execute button on the SQL Server Analysis Services Editors toolbar (or use the keyboard, main menu, or shortcut menu equivalent) to see the results of the MDX query displayed in a grid on the Results tab, as shown in Figure 17-29.

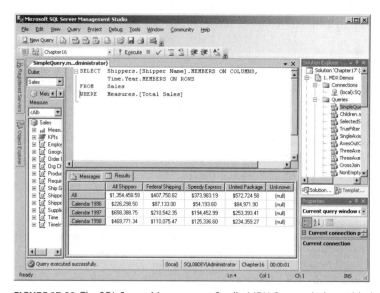

FIGURE 17-29 The SQL Server Management Studio MDX Query window, with the Results tab visible

Rich MDX Support

Besides being a convenient text editor for writing and testing your queries, Management Studio includes many features that make the creation of MDX queries easy for people who are new to MDX. In Chapter 16, we briefly covered the MDX Query window tools pane and the MDX IntelliSense features provided by Management Studio. Let's explore Management Studio's MDX feature set in more depth now.

Making the Connection

First you should understand the various ways to open a new query. We covered some of these in Chapter 16 but include them here again for review and for thoroughness. These include the File, New, Analysis Services MDX Query menu option, and the toolbar button of the same name (third from the left) on the Standard toolbar. Either option opens a new MDX Query window but first presents the Connect To Analysis Services dialog box, which requires you to connect or cancel before it places you in the MDX editor. Much like its Connect To Database Engine "cousin," this dialog box requires you to provide a server/instance name and allows you to enter optional connection properties by clicking the Options button and supplying information (such as the database to connect to) on the Connection Properties tab that appears.

To avoid the Connect To Analysis Services dialog box and go directly into an MDX Query window, select an Analysis Services server in the Registered Servers or Object Explorer window, and then click the New Query button (first on the left) on the Standard toolbar. To view Analysis Services servers in the Registered Servers window, you must click the Analysis Services button (second from the left, with the cube icon) on the window's toolbar.

Other ways of "speed dialing" into the MDX Query window include double-clicking an Analysis Services connection in the Solution Explorer window, right-clicking a connection there and choosing New Query, right-clicking an Analysis Services server node in the Registered Servers window and choosing New Query from the shortcut menu, and right-clicking an Analysis Services server or database node in the Object Explorer window and choosing New Query, MDX. When you use the last of these techniques with a database node, your MDX Query window will select that database by default. Clicking the New Query toolbar button or selecting File, New, Query With Current Connection while a database node is selected in the Object Explorer window will have the same effect.

Once an MDX Query window is open, you can change the connection information by clicking the Change Connection button (second from the left) on the SQL Server Analysis Services Editors toolbar or by choosing either the Query, Connection, Change Connection menu option or the Connection, Change Connection shortcut menu option. Any of these techniques opens the Connect To Analysis Services dialog box. If you did not connect successfully to begin with, you can accomplish the same thing by clicking the Connect button (far left) on the SQL Server Analysis Services Editors toolbar or by choosing either the Query, Connection, Connect menu option or the Connection, Connect shortcut menu option.

Once connected, you can use a different database on the same server by selecting that database from the Available Databases drop-down list (just to the right of the Change Connection button) on the SQL Server Analysis Services Editors toolbar. You can intentionally return your MDX Query window to a disconnected state by choosing Query, Connection, Disconnect (or by choosing Connection, Disconnect from the MDX Query window's shortcut menu).

After you open the MDX Query window and connect to the appropriate server and database, the Tools pane (the section to the left of the MDX edit region) will become enabled, its drop-down list of available cubes/perspectives will populate, and metadata for the selected cube/perspective (and measure group, if any) will be displayed in the Metadata tab's tree view.

Building a Query

With all this in mind, open a new MDX Query window, making sure that you are connected to the *Sales* cube of the *Chapter16* database. In this window, we will create a new query, similar to the previous one, but rather than typing it from scratch, we will use features of Management Studio to help us compose our MDX code.

One excellent way to learn MDX is through the use of the MDX templates supplied with Management Studio. To see these, you must show Template Explorer if it's not shown already. Choose View, Template Explorer, or press Ctrl+Alt+T. Next, click the Analysis Services button (second from the left or right) on the Template Explorer window's toolbar to display the Analysis Services templates. Drill down on the MDX node and then on its child Expressions and Queries nodes to display all available MDX templates, as shown in Figure 17-30.

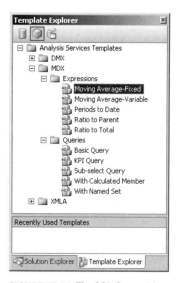

FIGURE 17-30 The SQL Server Management Studio Template Explorer, with Analysis Services MDX templates displayed

In all, SQL Server Management Studio includes 10 MDX templates to help you learn the language. Because we're writing simple queries, we'll start with the Basic Query template. Drag and drop the Basic Query node (under the Queries parent node) into the open MDX window, and then press the Left Arrow or Home key on your keyboard to deselect the MDX template text. Notice that the skeletal MDX provided is similar to the "schematic" MDX query we discussed earlier, as shown here:

```
-- ============================================
-- Basic MDX Query
-- ============================================

Select <row_axis, mdx_set,> on Columns,
      <column_axis, mdx_set,> on Rows

From <from_clause, mdx_name,>
Where <where_clause, mdx_set,>
```

> **Important** Management Studio's Basic Query MDX template erroneously places a *row_axis* placeholder in the *on Columns* clause and a *column_axis* placeholder in the *on Rows* clause. It should, of course, use the reverse arrangement. Nevertheless, if you follow our directions carefully, the query you will generate will be correct.

With this skeletal code in place, our next task is to fill out all the parameterized clauses that appear as angle-bracketed text. Choose Query, Specify Values For Template Parameters or click the Specify Values For Template Parameters button (far right) on the SQL Server Analysis Services Editors toolbar to open the Specify Values For Template Parameters dialog box, shown in Figure 17-31.

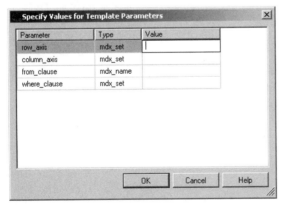

FIGURE 17-31 The Specify Values For Template Parameters dialog box in SQL Server Management Studio

This dialog box offers a single UI for specifying all query specifics, but it is designed for programmers who are already sufficiently experienced with MDX syntax such that typing the clauses without assistance is feasible and preferable. We are still getting acquainted with

MDX, so we'll supply the parameterized clauses through different means. For now, click Cancel to close the dialog box.

We will supply the four requested clauses (*ON ROWS, ON COLUMNS, FROM,* and *WHERE*) one at a time. Let's start with *row_axis*: Select the entire *<row_axis, mdx_set,>* angle-bracketed clause and press the Delete key. Next, in the metadata tree view, drill down on the *Geography* dimension node, and then drag its *Country* attribute child node into the MDX edit region, dropping it just to the left of the *on Columns* portion of the command (leaving a space to the right of the drop position). Press the Right Arrow key to deselect the dropped text. Next, type a period (.). Your query text should now appear as follows:

```
Select [Geography].[Country]. on Columns,
      <column_axis, mdx_set,> on Rows

From <from_clause, mdx_name,>
Where <where_clause, mdx_set,>
```

With the cursor just to the right of the period you typed, choose Edit, IntelliSense, List Members or press Ctrl+J. An IntelliSense pop-up list should appear; type **members** (including the letter *s*), and the keyword *MEMBERS* should become selected. Press Enter or Tab to insert the entire word into your code.

Repeat this process for the *column_axis* clause, but this time use the *Beverages* member of the *Category - Product* hierarchy of the *Products* dimension as the base of the expression (that is, drill down to the Products\Category - Product\Members\All\Beverages node and drag it into the MDX editor). Next, after typing a period as you did for the *row_axis* clause, click on the Functions tab in the Tools pane, drill down to the Navigation\CHILDREN node, and drag it to the right of the period in the editor. After you drop the text, delete the *<<Member>>*. text (including the period) immediately to the left of the *CHILDREN* keyword.

Remove the bracketed *from_clause* text from the query, and then click the Metadata tab and drag the Sales (root) node to the cursor position. Finish by removing the *where_clause* parameter and dragging the Measures\Main\Sum\Total Sales node to take its place. Your query should appear as follows. (If not, you can find it in the sample file Children.mdx.)

```
Select   [Geography].[Country].MEMBERS on Columns,
         [Products].[Category - Product].[Category Name].&[Beverages].CHILDREN on Rows
From     [Sales]
Where    [Measures].[Total Sales]
```

Execute the query. Figure 17-32 shows a partial view of the results you should receive.

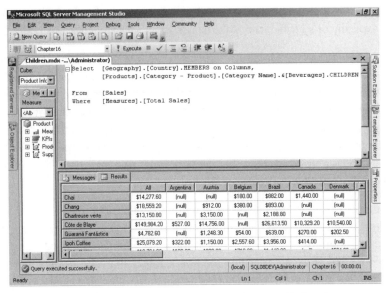

FIGURE 17-32 Our fully configured MDX query, with results displayed

Beyond Syntax

Although we have written only two queries so far, we have covered quite a lot. You've learned the basic MDX syntax and the use of the MDX Query window. You've learned how to use the Registered Servers and Object Explorer windows with Analysis Services servers, including several shortcuts for opening MDX Query windows against specific connections and databases. As we looked at the MDX Query window, you learned how to use the Template Explorer window, MDX IntelliSense, and the Metadata and Functions tabs in the Tools pane to design your MDX queries step by step. However, despite having exposed you to the mechanics of MDX and the MDX features in Management Studio, we haven't really discussed the language itself in much depth. Let's remedy that now by focusing on some important MDX concepts.

Let's start with our first query. Notice that both the *ON COLUMNS* and *ON ROWS* clauses use a dot-separated syntax to specify the dimension and attribute. The name of our measure, *Total Sales*, is enclosed within square brackets—this is required syntax for any name that contains one or more embedded spaces. Names without embedded spaces can also be enclosed in square brackets, although we did not do so in this query. As you saw in the previous chapter, however, use of squared brackets for nonspaced names is encouraged.

Immediately following the attribute names in the *ON COLUMNS* and *ON ROWS* clauses, we used the MDX function keyword *MEMBERS* to request that each individual member of the *Country* attribute be included as a column. Axis specifiers (that is, the expressions preceding the *ON ROWS* or *ON COLUMNS* keywords) must always indicate a *set* (that is, a collection of items belonging to one or a combination of attributes or hierarchy levels). These items must either be listed explicitly or specified through the use of an MDX function, such as *MEMBERS*.

The proper MDX name for an item in a set is *tuple*. A tuple, whose more formal syntax we will describe shortly, specifies a member in *every dimension* in the cube. In practice, however, a tuple need not explicitly specify members for more than one or perhaps a few dimensions. That's because each tuple implicitly references the default member of each dimension when a specific member is not given, and in most cases, the default member is the *[All]* member. So even if we identify a tuple by, say, a shipper name and nothing else, that tuple will refer to the subset of the cube for that shipper in the *Shippers* dimension and the *[All]* member (that is, the entirety) of all other dimensions.

We must tell you now that this rather theoretical definition of a tuple makes sense to very few people at first. At this point, you need simply to acknowledge it and file it away for later—when you've had more OLAP experience, it will make more sense. In practice, you can think of sets as consisting of simply specified members, rather than cryptically defined tuples. To illustrate the set concept more directly, here is a variation on our first query in which we use an explicit set specifier for the *COLUMNS* axis:

```
SELECT  {[Speedy Express], [Federal Shipping]} ON COLUMNS,
        Time.Year.MEMBERS ON ROWS
FROM    Sales
WHERE   Measures.[Total Sales]
```

This query (contained in the file SelectedShippers.mdx) allows us to request a limited, specific set of *Shippers* attribute members rather than having to show them all. Each shipper is technically a tuple, but you can feel free to think of each one as a member for now.

As you can see, explicitly specifying even members can be a bit tedious, and the syntax requirements are quite stringent. That's why functions such as *MEMBERS* can be extremely useful—they allow you to specify large sets with relatively little typing and few curly braces. But OLAP developers do not live by the *MEMBERS* function alone! MDX contains a dizzying array of other set-generating functions.

For example, you can use the MDX keyword *CHILDREN* to list all of the child members of a specified node in a hierarchy. To understand how this works, refer back to our second query (in Children.mdx). The *ROWS* axis shows products in the Beverages category (the children of the *Beverages* member of the *Category Name* level of the *Category – Product* hierarchy of the *Products* dimension).

Grasping the *WHERE* Clause

Now let's discuss the *WHERE* clause of this query in more detail. We have been using the *WHERE* clause thus far as a mechanism to specify the measure we want to see in our result set. This is a valid and typical use of the *WHERE* clause in an MDX query, but it obfuscates the real purpose of the clause: to specify for the query a filter condition for each and every dimension in the cube.

On initial inspection, this seems counterintuitive on a number of fronts. For example, our *WHERE* clause specified our desired *measure*, but it did not seem to specify any type of filter or filter condition, nor anything relating to *dimensions*. But it turns out that, technically speaking, our *WHERE* clause does indeed supply a dimension filter. Understanding why this is the case requires an appreciation of how MDX views measures and how it uses the default members of a dimension.

Simply put, MDX considers your cube to consist of dimensions and data only. Rather than viewing measures as distinct entities within your cube, it considers each measure to be a member of a flat hierarchy of a single dimension named *Measures*. For this reason, the expression *[Measures].[Total Sales]* in the *WHERE* clause *is* a filter condition: in effect, you are telling the MDX engine to limit the query to analysis of the *[Total Sales]* member of the *Measures* "dimension." For all other dimensions in the cube, no filter condition is specified, so the MDX query applies the default member (*[All]*) and returns the entire contents of all the actual dimensions.

If you want to place a filter that seems more "real" in your query, you can do so by adding to the *WHERE* clause. For example, to limit our first query to sales of products in the *Condiments* category, you would change the preceding query to the following (which can be found in the script file TrueFilter.mdx):

```
SELECT  Shippers.[Shipper Name].MEMBERS ON COLUMNS,
        Time.Year.MEMBERS ON ROWS
FROM    Sales
WHERE   (Measures.[Total Sales],
          Products.[Category Name].Condiments)
```

Notice that the filtering condition on the *Products* dimension is concatenated to the existing condition on the *Measures* "dimension" with a comma delimiter and that the entire *WHERE* clause expression is enclosed in parentheses.

The parentheses are required for any tuple that is specified through two or more explicitly named members. Because in this case we are specifying a tuple with two members (*Measures.[Total Sales]* and *Products.[Category Name].Condiments*), we must supply them in a comma-delimited list and enclose the list in parentheses. The tuple in our *WHERE* clause is the subset of the cube consisting of *[Total Sales]* data for products within the *Condiments* product category and the entirety of all other dimensions in the cube. The rest of our query then breaks down this subset of the cube by shipper name and calendar year.

Note It is important to remember that the *WHERE* expression in the preceding query (which contained the simple expression *Measures.[Total Sales]*) was also a tuple in its own right. Even though it appeared to be a simple member specifier, its implicit reference to the *[All]* member of each dimension in the cube qualified it to be every bit as much a tuple expression as the more complex one used just now.

The Power of Axes

Let's take a step back and discuss the concept of *axes*. The queries we've looked at thus far have all returned results over two axes—namely, *ROWS* and *COLUMNS*. Such two-dimensional result sets are convenient and often sufficient, but MDX can handle many more than two axes. Although the first five axes have names, you can also refer to them by number.

For example, consider the following query (which can be found in the file SingleAxis.mdx) that returns data along a single, numbered axis:

```
SELECT  Geography.Country.MEMBERS ON 0
FROM    Sales
WHERE   Measures.[Total Sales]
```

Here we are specifying only a columns axis, using its axis number. Axis 0 is the *COLUMNS* axis, and axis 1 is the *ROWS* axis. Note that no gaps are allowed in the axis sequence, so a single-axis query must use the *COLUMNS* axis and not the *ROWS* axis. Axes can, however, be listed out of sequence, as in the following query (which can be found in the file AxesOutOfSequence.mdx) that returns data on two axes but specifies the *ROWS* axis before the *COLUMNS* axis and does not use a *WHERE* clause:

```
SELECT  Products.[Category - Product].[Category Name].Beverages.CHILDREN ON 1,
        Measures.MEMBERS ON 0
FROM    Sales
```

This query asks for the members of the *Measures* "dimension" to be listed along the *COLUMNS* axis, thus allowing us not to use a *WHERE* clause that would normally specify our selected measure.

What about queries with more than two axes? MDX permits queries to return a theoretically boundless number of axes (although available resources on the server and client hardware will impose some limit). You can name three axes in addition to the *COLUMNS* and *ROWS* axes. The axes' names after *ROWS* are, in axis order, *PAGES*, *SECTIONS*, and *CHAPTERS*. These correspond numerically to axes 2, 3, and 4 (with—again—*COLUMNS* and *ROWS* being 0 and 1, respectively). The names of these higher axes convey what it means to bring back data on more than two axes: although it is difficult to imagine seeing data presented on more than two axes at once, it is relatively easy to imagine a series of two-axis result sets spread over several pages, sections, and chapters of a book.

Another way to think through axis management is to imagine an Excel workbook. In Excel, data is always shown on one spreadsheet at a time, and each sheet has both columns and rows. But one workbook can contain multiple tabs (pages), several workbooks can be contained in a folder (section), and a collection of folders can be contained in a parent folder (chapter). You can easily imagine more "axes" by understanding that multiple drives can be managed by a single server, multiple servers can belong to a single farm, and so on. You can thus imagine writing queries with more axes than the five named ones.

With this understanding of the use of multiple axes, the following query (which can be found in the file ThreeAxes.mdx) should now seem quite sensible:

```
SELECT  Shippers.[Shipper Name].MEMBERS ON COLUMNS,
        Geography.Country.MEMBERS ON ROWS,
        Time.Year.MEMBERS ON PAGES
FROM    Sales
WHERE   (Measures.[Total Sales],
          Products.[Category Name].Condiments)
```

When executed, the query returns total sales for all products in the *Condiments* category, broken down into shippers and countries on the *COLUMNS* and *ROWS* axes, with the data for each distinct calendar year on a separate page.

However, if you execute this query in SQL Server Management Studio, the Results tab will be empty and the following text will be returned on the Messages tab of the Results pane:

```
Executing the query ...
Obtained object of type: Microsoft.AnalysisServices.AdomdClient.CellSet
Formatting.
Results cannot be displayed for cellsets with more than two axes.
Execution complete
```

The second line of this message indicates that the query is valid and executed without error. However, the fourth line indicates that queries returning data over more than two axes cannot be displayed in the SQL Server Management Studio MDX Query window.

> **Note** Although we won't cover XMLA queries until later in this chapter, you might want to open and execute the query in the file ThreeAxes.xmla. This file contains the same MDX query as does ThreeAxes.mdx, but it will execute without error because data is returned as XML rather than in a grid. If you scroll down toward the bottom of the XML returned on the Results tab, you will see the individual values for each cell on all three axes. How you can read and process this XML will become clear by the end of the chapter.

CROSSJOIN and DRILLDOWNMEMBER

So how *can* we process queries that return three or more axes? Shortly, we'll explore how to execute MDX queries in .NET code and discuss programmatic approaches to this challenge. For now, however, you can rewrite your query as follows:

```
SELECT  Shippers.[Shipper Name].MEMBERS ON COLUMNS,
        CROSSJOIN([Time].[Year].MEMBERS,
                   Geography.Country.MEMBERS) ON ROWS
FROM    Sales
WHERE   (Measures.[Total Sales],
          Products.[Category Name].Condiments)
```

The query (which can be found in the file CrossJoin.mdx) uses the MDX *CROSSJOIN* function to "stack" or "flatten" the members of *Time.Year* and *Geography.Country* together on
the *ROWS* axis. This has the effect of creating a result set where each row "header" has two
members within it: a year and a country.

> **Note** In our crossjoin query, data is returned by year and then country. If the order of the sets in
> the *CROSSJOIN* function had been reversed, the data would have been returned by country and
> then year.

If you review the results data, you will see that the second row in the 1996 section of our result set (and the 25th row overall), which contains total sales data for all condiments sold in
Argentina in 1996, contains nothing but *NULL*s. This indicates that no condiment products
were sold in Argentina in 1996; likewise, the last column (for the *Unknown* product member)
consists of empty cells for all rows. MDX makes it easy to suppress these empty axis members
with the use of the *NONEMPTYCROSSJOIN* and *NONEMPTY* functions. To see this in action,
modify the query as follows. (This version can be found in the file NonEmpty.mdx.)

```
SELECT  NONEMPTY(Shippers.[Shipper Name].MEMBERS) ON COLUMNS,
        NONEMPTYCROSSJOIN(Time.Year.MEMBERS, Geography.Country.MEMBERS) ON ROWS
FROM    Sales
WHERE   (Measures.[Total Sales],
          Products.[Category Name].Condiments)
```

When you execute the query, the column and rows that were completely populated with
*NULL*s will be gone, and you will find the results much easier to read.

We can't hope to cover the comprehensive set of hierarchy-oriented functions in MDX, but
we can give you a taste by showing another query (which can be found in the file
DrillDownMember.mdx). This query returns the same data as the preceding query but also
returns the state/province–level data for Canada and the United States:

```
SELECT  NONEMPTY(Shippers.[Shipper Name].MEMBERS) ON COLUMNS,
        NONEMPTYCROSSJOIN(Time.Year.MEMBERS,
        DRILLDOWNMEMBER(Geography.[Country - State-Province - City - Postal Code].Country.
MEMBERS, {CANADA, USA})) ON ROWS
FROM    Sales
WHERE   (Measures.[Total Sales],
          Products.[Category Name].Condiments)
```

Notice the use of the *DRILLDOWNMEMBER* function to obtain the *[Total Sales]* data for
the states and provinces in the USA and Canada in addition to the country data. The
DRILLDOWNMEMBER function accepts two sets and returns the union of the first with the
children of any of its members contained in the second.

KPIs, Calculated Members, and Named Sets

We're almost done with the theoretical side of MDX, and you now have a good sense of its power (although we still have plenty to explain about how to execute MDX queries programmatically). But all the queries we've examined so far take advantage of only the simple components of our cube—specifically, dimensions and measures. Let's not forget, however, that in the previous chapter, we implemented some more complex Analysis Services features, including the definition of calculated members, named sets, and key performance indicators (KPIs). The question is, how can we use these from MDX?

First let's start with KPIs. Recall that a KPI, when applied to a slice of our cube, generates a value, a goal, a status, and a trend (the latter two usually returning a value between –1 and +1, inclusive). Recall also that MDX functions exist for returning all four of these values. The following query (which can be found in the script file AverageTotalSalesKPI.mdx) returns all four values for the KPI we created in the previous chapter (*Average Total Sales KPI*). It does so for each calendar year for which the cube holds sales data in the United Kingdom.

```
SELECT  {KPIValue("Average Total Sales KPI"),
         KPIGoal("Average Total Sales KPI"),
         KPIStatus("Average Total Sales KPI"),
         KPITrend("Average Total Sales KPI")} ON COLUMNS,
         [Order Date].[Year - Quarter - Month - Date].Year.MEMBERS ON ROWS
FROM    Sales
WHERE   Geography.Country.UK
```

MDX cannot tell us the status and trend graphics we configured the KPI to use, but we can retrieve that information from the ADO MD.NET *Kpi* object, which we will focus on later in this chapter.

What about calculated members and named sets? The beauty of calculated members is that they can be referenced from an MDX query as if they were physically part of the cube, rather than calculated. You can use named sets as substitutes for explicitly stated sets, such as the one we examined earlier in the SelectedShippers.mdx query. All of this is much easier to understand when viewed in a query such as the following one (which can be found in NamedSetCalcMember.mdx):

```
SELECT  Time.[Year - Quarter - Month - Date].Year.MEMBERS ON COLUMNS,
         [Test Markets] ON ROWS
FROM    Sales
WHERE   Measures.[Adjusted Sales]
```

This query returns values for the *[Adjusted Sales]* calculated measure, broken down by calendar year on the *COLUMNS* axis and by the three cities in our *[Test Markets]* named set on the *ROWS* axis.

The next query (which can be found in AdjustedGrowthByState.mdx), demonstrates how to query a calculated measure whose formula is based on a time series comparison. In this case, we are querying our *[Adjusted Sales Growth]* calculated measure, which measures year-on-year sales growth as a percentage. This calculated measure requires that the *Order Date* dimension, on which its formula is based, be used in one of the axis specifiers, which it is.

```
SELECT  [Order Date].[Year].MEMBERS ON COLUMNS,
        [Geography].[Country - State-Province - City - Postal Code].[Country].USA.
CHILDREN ON ROWS
        FROM Sales
        WHERE Measures.[Adjusted Sales Growth]
```

This query shows the growth numbers, for all years for which the cube holds data on the *COLUMNS* axis, broken down by individual states in the USA on the *ROWS* axis.

At this point, we've studied enough MDX, and it's time to start learning how to put it to use. Keep in mind that we've covered how to take advantage of a number of advanced cube features, including KPIs and calculations (named sets and calculated members). We haven't covered drillthrough-based or URL-based actions, even though these are all based on stored MDX expressions. We will cover these shortly; having some basic API knowledge under your belt first will make this easier. So let's set aside writing queries for now and learn how to put them to work in our applications.

OLAP Development with ADO MD.NET

Think about everything we've covered in the last two chapters and up to this point in this chapter. You've learned how to design a cube from scratch and extend it with calculations, KPIs, actions, and perspectives. You've also learned how to query the cube using Excel PivotTables, charts, and cell formulas, both in Excel 2007 itself and from SharePoint and Excel Services. And we just covered in great detail how to use MDX to query your cube in a variety of ways in SQL Server Management Studio, giving you extremely precise control over what results are returned.

What we haven't yet covered is how to execute MDX queries from within your own applications and display the results. It will be important to know how to execute queries that return data over two axes and display results quickly. It will also be important to understand how to execute more complex queries—those with three or more axes—and examine the results programmatically so that members of the third and higher axes can be enumerated in your own custom UIs.

Since the introduction of SQL Server Analysis Services 2005, this kind of programming became almost as easy as data access programming against relational databases. That's because Microsoft created an ADO.NET managed data provider called ADO MD.NET, for use against Analysis Services databases. In fact, ADO MD.NET was introduced in May 2004 for use with SQL Server Analysis Services 2000, but using it with that version of the product was tricky. ADO MD.NET is implemented as a wrapper around XML for Analysis (XMLA), which (as we saw in action in the previous chapter) is the native protocol of Analysis Services and has been since version 2005. Analysis Services 2000 did not use XMLA natively (it instead used a protocol called PivotTable Service, or PTS—not to be confused with Excel PivotTables), so using ADO MD.NET against Analysis Services 2000 required the installation of an XMLA wrapper (the XMLA software development kit [SDK]) around PTS.

Using Your ADO.NET Skills

One of the great things about ADO MD.NET is that you can treat it like any other ADO.NET provider—using *Connection, Command, DataReader, DataAdapter, DataTable*, and *DataSet* objects to execute MDX queries and handle the results. But you can also use a wide array of OLAP-specific objects to explore a cube's metadata and carefully crawl through result sets (including those with more than two axes) axis by axis and cell by cell.

These OLAP-specific objects are essentially clones of the objects available in the old ADO MD object model (initially introduced with OLAP Services in SQL Server 7.0), which was effectively the native API for OLAP programming with SQL Server 2000 Analysis Services. ADO MD was a Component Object Model (COM)–based wrapper around OLE DB for OLAP (much as ADO was a COM wrapper around OLE DB). ADO MD.NET is thus the "fusion" of ADO MD and ADO. NET, and it is based on XMLA.

To use ADO MD.NET in your applications, simply set a reference to the *Microsoft. AnalysisServices.AdomdClient* managed assembly, which is listed on the .NET tab of the Visual Studio Add Reference dialog box. If you are working on a PC that has the older ADO MD.NET providers for SQL Server 2000 or 2005 Analysis Services installed, be sure to select the new version (version 10.0), as shown in Figure 17-33. Once you set the reference, use the namespace of the same name in your code.

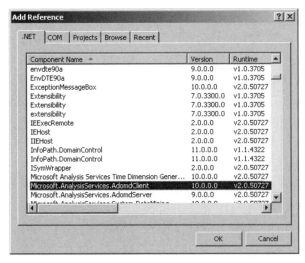

FIGURE 17-33 The Add Reference dialog box in Visual Studio, with the .NET tab active and the ADO MD.NET assembly (Microsoft.AnalysisServices.AdomdClient) selected

You now have direct access to all objects in the ADO MD.NET library, including *AdomdConnection, AdomdCommand,* and *AdomdDataAdapter.* Connection strings for the *AdomdConnection* simply require *Data Source* and *Initial Catalog* specifiers; the *CommandText* property of the *AdomdCommand* can then be set to any MDX query and can be used to return an *AdomdDataReader* (or, using the *AdomdDataAdapter.Fill* method, a *DataTable* or *DataSet*).

Beyond this standard ADO.NET functionality, you can also use the special *AdomdCommand. ExecuteCellSet* method to get back an OLAP-specific result set object called a *CellSet.* Under "classic" ADO MD, *CellSet* objects were the only OLAP result set vehicle available. Although *CellSet* objects are not as convenient to work with as *DataReader, DataTable,* and *DataSet* objects, they have *Axes* and *Cells* collections and thus allow for better programmatic manipulation of MDX result sets, especially when more than two axes are returned.

In addition to *CellSet* objects, ADO MD.NET offers other unique objects that make OLAP-oriented programming easier. ADO MD.NET makes it relatively easy to create .NET code that connects to OLAP cubes and then explores their metadata, executes MDX queries, and displays the results. We'll now show you how to use ADO MD.NET to write code that queries both a cube's data and its metadata.

Executing MDX Queries

Let's start on the data side. The following code connects to the *Chapter16* database on a *localhost* Analysis Services host, executes a simple MDX query against the *Sales* cube, and then binds the results to a *DataGridView* control called *dgvResults*:

```
AdomdConnection conn = new AdomdConnection("DataSource=localhost;Initial " +
  "Catalog=Chapter16");
AdomdDataAdapter da = new AdomdDataAdapter("SELECT Shippers.[Shipper Name].MEMBERS ON " +
  "COLUMNS, Time.Year.MEMBERS ON ROWS FROM Sales WHERE Measures.[Total Sales]", conn);
DataTable dt = new DataTable();
da.Fill(dt);
dgvResults.DataSource = dt;
```

Code similar to this can be found in the function *ExecMDX* in the form *frmAPIs* in the sample code's Windows Forms project, *Chapter17.* Note that the preceding code will work only if the following *using* directive has been placed at the top of the class file:

```
using Microsoft.AnalysisServices.AdomdClient;
```

In case you weren't counting, we connected to, queried, and displayed results using just five lines of code, not including the *using* directive. Granted, we took advantage of the *AdomdDataAdpater* object's ability to accept an MDX command string in its constructor and thus create an *AdomdCommand* object on our behalf. But the point still stands: writing .NET OLAP code doesn't have to be hard.

Working with More Than Two Axes

Now let's consider a harder case: a query with three axes. In this case, we'll need to explicitly declare and initialize *AdomdConnection* and *AdomdCommand* objects, and we'll bring the results back as a *CellSet* object. We'll insert each member of the *PAGES* axis in a *ComboBox* control named *cboPages*, and we'll display all the rows and columns of the selected page (and their data) in a *ListView* control named *lvwResults* (the *View* property of which must be set to *Details*).

To start with, here's the code that declares and initializes our *AdomdConnection* and *AdomdCommand* objects:

```
AdomdConnection conn = new AdomdConnection("Data Source=localhost;Initial " +
  "Catalog=Chapter16");
AdomdCommand cmd = new AdomdCommand("SELECT Shippers.[Shipper Name].MEMBERS " +
  "ON COLUMNS, Geography.Country.MEMBERS ON ROWS, Time.Year.MEMBERS ON PAGES " +
  "FROM Sales WHERE (Measures.[Total Sales], " +
  "Products.[Category Name].Condiments)", conn);
```

Next the code grabs the results of the three-axis MDX query in an ADO MD.NET *CellSet* (assuming that *cs*, an object of type *CellSet*, has already been declared at the class level), as shown here:

```
conn.Open();
cs = cmd.ExecuteCellSet();
conn.Close();
```

Once we have the *CellSet*, we can iterate through axis 2 (the *PAGES* axis) and populate our *ComboBox* control with the name of each page, as shown here:

```
foreach (Position p in cs.Axes[2].Positions)
{
    cboPages.Items.Add(p.Members[0].Caption);
}
```

In almost the same fashion, we can loop through the axis 0 (*COLUMNS* axis) positions and add an item to the *ListView* object's *Columns* collection for each position on the axis (first adding a blank "dummy" column to accommodate the row headers that will appear), as follows:

```
lvwResults.Columns.Add(String.Empty);
foreach (Position p in cs.Axes[0].Positions)
{
    lvwResults.Columns.Add(p.Members[0].Caption);
}
```

Next we'll preselect *PAGE 0* by setting the *SelectedIndex* property of *cboPages*:

```
cboPages.SelectedIndex = 0;
```

In the *SelectedIndexChanged* event handler of *cboPages*, we'll add a new item to the *ListView* control for each position in axis 1 (the *ROWS* axis), setting its text to the caption of the *ROW* axis. We'll then add one *SubItem* to that *ListViewItem* for every column, fetching the *FormattedValue* of the corresponding cell, as shown here:

```
lvwResults.Items.Clear();
foreach (Position p in cs.Axes[1].Positions)
{
    ListViewItem newItem = lvwResults.Items.Add(p.Members[0].Caption);
    for (int i = 0; i < cs.Axes[0].Positions.Count; i++)
    {
        newItem.SubItems.Add(cs.Cells[i, newItem.Index,
        cboPages.SelectedIndex].FormattedValue);
    }
}
```

Notice that we fetch the correct cell using a three-level coordinate, in the (column, row, page) format, where the column is determined by the inner loop's counter value (the position in axis 0, the *COLUMNS* axis), the row is determined by the new *ListViewItem* object's index, and the page is determined by the *SelectedIndex* of *cboPages*.

Code that implements these techniques can be found in the *AdomdCommand.ExecuteCellSet* region in the source code of form *frmAPIs* in the sample code's Windows Forms project, *Chapter17*. Figure 17-34 shows the OLAP APIs form after that code has been executed.

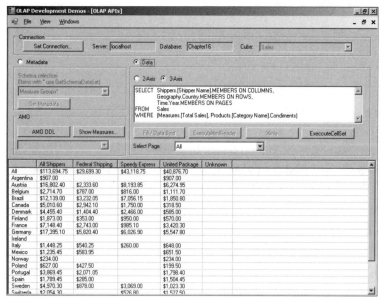

FIGURE 17-34 The sample application's OLAP APIs form, with a three-axis query executed and the *Time.Year* = *All PAGES* axis member displayed

Working with *CellSet* objects is harder than working with *DataReader*, *DataTable*, or *DataSet* objects, but the results are often better. Because we grab the *Caption* property of each axis position/member, our column and row headers are more user-friendly than the unique name-based column and row headers returned in *DataReader*, *DataTable*, and *DataSet* objects. Our data presentation is more user-friendly as well because we're displaying the data fetched from the *FormattedValue* property of each cell (and recall that in Chapter 16 we configured each of our measures to use currency formatting).

> **Note** The API programming techniques we cover in this chapter can be used in ASP.NET as well as Windows Forms applications. However, ASP.NET data binding does not work well with MDX result sets (be they in the form of *AdomdDataReader*, *DataTable*, or *DataSet* objects). Therefore, you might want to limit your ASP.NET/ADO MD.NET development to the programmatic manipulation of *CellSet* objects as we've done here.

Cell References: Coordinate-Based vs. Ordinal

Speaking of cells, they are typically referenced from a *CellSet* object's *Cells* collection by coordinate reference. For two-axis queries, we use a (column, row) coordinate format; for three-axis coordinates, we use a (column, row, page) format. (The coordinate reference is determined by axis order.) But you can also reference cells ordinally, by supplying a single value as the index into the *Cells* collection. For a two-axis *CellSet*, the ordinal value is calculated as follows:

```
row number * column count + column number
```

Therefore, *Cells[5, 2]* in a *CellSet* with 10 columns can be also be referenced as *Cells[25]* (because 2 × 10 + 5 = 25). For a three-axis *CellSet*, the formula is as follows:

```
(page number * row count * column count) + (row number * column count) + (column number)
```

Cells[5, 2, 3] in a *CellSet* with 20 rows and 10 columns can also be referenced as *Cells[625]* (because 3 × 20 × 10 + 2 × 10 + 5 = 625). Understanding the formula for fetching cells ordinally allows you to write code that generically fetches cell values from a CellSet of any number of axes.

Cracking the Metadata

If you know how to fetch MDX result sets as *DataReader*, *DataTable*, *DataSet*, and *CellSet* objects, you can build applications that can query virtually any cube and return the results. Of course, to build these applications, you must have full knowledge of the cube's structure and embed the MDX queries into your application code. This tends to be how we write relational applications, but it does not always work well for OLAP applications.

The whole point of OLAP is to allow users to explore their data. Just as Excel PivotTables and charts offer a PivotTable Field List window where users can change their queries on the fly, your own applications might benefit from offering users a list of measures, dimensions (and their attributes and hierarchies), and KPIs. You might even want to create a high-powered UI that presents the measure groups, display folders, and other advanced metadata derived from features you used when designing your cube.

We will now discuss three distinct methods for fetching metadata in your cubes: two that use ADO MD.NET and one that uses Analysis Management Objects (AMO). Although we don't have room here to provide explicit examples of enumerating every possible piece of metadata, we will provide representative code examples, and you can refer to the sample code provided with this chapter for several more.

Getting Metadata from ADO MD.NET

The ADO MD.NET object model provides access to a full list of your database's cubes and much of their metadata. This is possible because the *AdomdConnection* object contains a *Cubes* collection whose child members, in turn, contain *Kpis*, *NamedSets*, *Measures*, and *Dimensions* collections. Each object in these collections contains important details. For example, each *Kpi* object in the *Kpis* collection has *StatusGraphic* and *TrendGraphic* properties that specify which graphics were selected when the KPI was designed. Combining this information with the data returned by the MDX *KPIStatus* and *KPITrend* functions allows you to present a rich UI for the KPI data in your cube.

Each *Dimension* object has a *Hierarchies* and an *AttributeHierarchies* collection (the latter containing attributes). *Hierarchy* objects have a *Levels* collection, and *Level* objects have a *GetMembers* method that returns a collection of *Member* objects. To get a sense of how this works, consider the following code. It opens a connection to our *Chapter16* Analysis Services database and then populates *cboMeasures* (a *ComboBox* control) with a list of all measures (including our two calculated measures) in the *Sales* cube:

```
AdomdConnection conn = new AdomdConnection("Data Source=localhost;Initial " +
  "Catalog=Chapter16");
conn.Open();
CubeDef cube = conn.Cubes["Sales"];
foreach (Measure m in cube.Measures)
{
    cboMeasures.Items.Add(m.Caption);
}
conn.Close();
```

Code that implements a similar technique can be found in the *Measures* region (within the *Metadata via ADO MD.NET* region) in the source code of form *frmAPIs* in the sample code's Windows Forms project, *Chapter17*.

> **Note** As with the previous example (and later code examples in this chapter), the preceding code will work only if the *Microsoft.AnalysisServices.AdomdClient* namespace is properly referenced in a *using* statement.

Schema *DataSet* Objects

The ADO MD.NET object model itself does not contain collections or objects for measure groups, calculated members, or actions. Instead, you can enumerate these objects by using the *AdomdConnection* object's *GetSchemaDataSet* method, which returns a one-table *DataSet* containing detailed metadata. The method has several overloads, the simplest of which accepts an enumerated constant indicating the type of metadata desired and a special restriction array used to filter the metadata returned.

For example, you can use *GetSchemaDataSet* to get a list of measure groups quite easily. The following five lines of code fetch a *DataSet* containing detailed metadata information for all measure groups in the *Sales* cube in the *Chapter16* database and then display the metadata in *dgvResults*, a *DataGridView* control:

```
AdomdConnection conn = new AdomdConnection("Data Source=localhost;Initial " +
  "Catalog=Chapter16");
conn.Open();
DataSet ds = conn.GetSchemaDataSet(AdomdSchemaGuid.MeasureGroups, new
  object[] { "", "", "Sales" });
dgvResults.DataSource = ds.Tables[0];
conn.Close();
```

Code that implements a similar technique can be found in the *Measure Groups* region (within the *Metadata via ADO MD.NET* region) in the source code of form *frmAPIs* in the sample code's Windows Forms project, *Chapter17*.

When you view the contents of the schema *DataSet* in the *DataGridView* control, you should take note of a few important things. First, notice that the third column (column 2, named *CUBE_NAME*) contains the cube name; this is precisely why we placed our desired cube name (*"Sales"*) in the third element in the inline array passed to *GetSchemaDataSet*. The structure of a restriction array aligns with the columns in the schema *DataSet* table that it filters. Had we not specified a cube name in the restrictions array, all measure groups in the entire database would have been returned. The partial results of such an unfiltered query are shown in Figure 17-35.

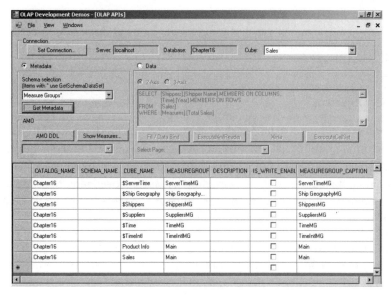

FIGURE 17-35 Unfiltered *MeasureGroups* schema *DataSet* bound to, and displayed in, a *DataGridView* control

Notice that the seventh and final column (column 6, named *MEASUREGROUP_CAPTION*) contains the display name of the measure group. You can therefore use the following code to populate a *ComboBox* control named *cboMeasureGroups* with the measure groups in the cube:

```
foreach (DataRow dr in ds.Tables[0].Rows)
{
    cboMeasureGroups.Items.Add(dr["MEASUREGROUP_CAPTION"]);
}
```

In addition to fetching measure groups, you can use schema *DataSet* objects to fetch lists of databases, calculated members, and actions (using the enumerated constants *AdomdSchemaGuid.Catalogs*, *AdomdSchemaGuid.Members*, and *AdomdSchemaGuid. Actions*) from a server. In fact, you can use schema *DataSet* objects to discover much of the same metadata that can be fetched from the ADO MD.NET object model itself. Just bear in mind that when you use ADO MD.NET, certain metadata can be fetched *only* using *GetSchemaDataSet*.

Executing Actions Using Schema *DataSet* Objects

GetSchemaDataSet technically returns only metadata, but sometimes this metadata is useful for more than determining a cube's structure and contents. Specifically, if you want your application to support any actions you created when you designed your cube, *GetSchemaDataSet* is indispensable. Recall that in Chapter 16 we created a URL action that performs a Live Search on cities and a drillthrough action to show fact data underlying cells in the cube.

The target of our URL action is the members of the *City* level of the *Country - State-Province - City - Postal Code* hierarchy of the *Geography* dimension; the target of our drillthrough is the individual cells in our cube. To get specific URLs or drillthrough result sets, we can use the *AdomdSchemaGuid.Actions* enumerated constant and then apply our knowledge of the actions' targets to the restriction arrays. Doing this will return specific schema *DataSet* objects, with tables that contain a text column named *Content*. This column will contain a fully computed URL for the URL action and an MDX query containing the special *DRILLTHROUGH* command for the drillthrough action.

The following code determines the value generated by the URL action for the city of Vancouver and then navigates to that URL using a *WebBrowser* control:

```
object[] Restrictions = new object[7];
Restrictions[2] = "Sales";
Restrictions[5] = "Geography.[Country - State-Province - City - Postal Code].City.
Vancouver";
Restrictions[6] = MDACTION_COORDINATE_MEMBER;

DataTable results = conn.GetSchemaDataSet(AdomdSchemaGuid.Actions,
 Restrictions).Tables[0];
dgvResults.DataSource = results;
MessageBox.Show("Content = " + results.Rows[0]["Content"].ToString() + "\nClick OK to " +
 "navigate to action URL");

wbrMain.Navigate(results.Rows[0]["Content"].ToString());
```

This code assumes the following:

- As before, that *conn* is a valid, opened *AdomdConnection* object pointing to our *Chapter16* database

- That *dgvResults* is a *DataGridView* control and *wbrMain* is a *WebBrowser* control

- *MDACTION_COORDINATE_MEMBER* has already been defined with its documented value of 4

Code that implements this technique can be found in the *Actions - URL* region (within the *Metadata via ADO MD.NET* region) in the source code of form *frmAPIs* in the sample code's Windows Forms project, *Chapter17*.

The values we store in the restrictions array ensure that the schema *DataSet* returns only actions for the *Geography.[Country - State-Province - City - Postal Code].City.Vancouver* level member of the *Sales* cube. We know that only one action has been defined for this member, so we can assume that row 0 of the *DataTable* object *results* contains that action info and that its *Content* column contains the specific URL for Vancouver (*http://search.live. com/results.aspx?q=Vancouver*). The URL is displayed in a message box; when the user clicks OK, the resulting page is displayed in the *WebBrowser* control.

The next snippet of code works similarly, but instead of retrieving a URL, it retrieves and executes a special MDX query whose results are the drillthough data for the slice of the cube defined by sales of products in the *Beverages* category in Vancouver:

```
object[] Restrictions = new object[7];
Restrictions[2] = "Sales";
Restrictions[5] = "(Geography.[Country - State-Province - City - Postal Code].City.
Vancouver, Products.[Category Name].Beverages)";
Restrictions[6] = MDACTION_COORDINATE_CELL;

DataTable results = conn.GetSchemaDataSet(AdomdSchemaGuid.Actions,
 Restrictions).Tables[0];
dgvResults.DataSource = results;
MessageBox.Show("Content = " + results.Rows[0]["Content"].ToString() +
 "\nClick OK to See Drillthrough Data");

txtMDX.Text = results.Rows[0]["Content"].ToString();
ExecMDX(conn);
```

The code assumes that *MDACTION_COORDINATE_CELL* has already been defined with its documented value of 6. It then fetches an entire MDX query from the *Content* column of the *DataTable* object *results*, inserts that MDX text into the *txtMDX TextBox* control, and calls the sample code's *ExecMDX* void function (mentioned earlier) to execute the query. Drillthrough queries happen to return tabular result sets rather than multidimensional ones. Because *ExecMDX* uses an *AdomdDataAdapter* to execute the query, the tabular result set is handled gracefully and is easily bound to the *DataGridView* control in our application. Code that implements this technique can be found in the *Actions - Drillthrough* region (within the *Metadata via ADO MD.NET* region) in the source code of form *frmAPIs* in the sample code's Windows Forms project, *Chapter17*.

The drillthrough query, which is displayed in a message box before being executed, deserves some discussion before we move on. Here's the text of the query:

```
DRILLTHROUGH
Select  (Geography.[Country - State-Province - City - Postal Code].City.Vancouver,
 Products.[Category Name].Beverages)  on 0
From [Sales]
RETURN [Main].[Total Sales]
```

If you want, you can enter the *DRILLTHROUGH* query text in an MDX query window in SQL Server Management Studio and execute it there. (The query can be found in, and executed from, the file Drillthrough.mdx in the *MDX Demos* project in the Chapter17.ssmssln sample code solution.)

Notice that the query has three parts:

- A *SELECT* query that consists of a single axis specifier that returns *exactly* one cell

- The *DRILLTHROUGH* keyword (at the beginning)

- A *RETURN* clause that indicates the measure(s) whose underlying fact data should be returned (at the end)

As long as you follow these syntax rules, you can execute your own ad hoc drillthrough queries whenever you want, from your own applications or from Management Studio.

As you can see, drillthroughs are just special MDX queries; drillthrough actions do *not* have to be defined in order for drillthrough queries to be performed. Drillthrough actions generate *DRILLTHROUGH* MDX queries for you and let you define on the server which specific columns should be returned, but they are a convenience only and are not strictly necessary.

The combination of MDX and ADO MD.NET provides everything you need to create full-featured OLAP applications. But two other APIs can augment the baseline functionality provided by ADO MD.NET. We'll continue by examining another of these APIs.

Using Analysis Management Objects

If you're left feeling frustrated that ADO MD.NET relies so heavily on schema *DataSet* objects because its native object model does not provide a full picture of Analysis Services databases, you might be interested in learning about its cousin, Analysis Management Objects (AMO). AMO allows you to discover all metadata and to modify and create Analysis Services objects as well. You can use it by simply setting a reference to its assembly, Microsoft.AnalysisServices.dll.

> **Caution** The Microsoft.AnalysisServices.dll assembly does *not* appear on the .NET tab of the Add Reference dialog box in Visual Studio. You must use the Browse tab and reference the file directly. By default, the assembly is installed in the C:\Program Files\Microsoft SQL Server\100\ SDK\Assemblies (or C:\Program Files (x86)\Microsoft SQL Server\100\SDK\Assemblies on 64-bit machines) folder on your development PC.

Once you add the reference, you can import the AMO namespace into your code by using the following line of code at the top of your source code file:

```
using Microsoft.AnalysisServices;
```

The AMO library is rich with objects and methods that enable you to do virtually anything against an Analysis Services database that you can do within SQL Server Management Studio or the Analysis Services designers in Visual Studio. We cannot even begin to cover the full set of capabilities of AMO, but we'll present a few examples.

The following code populates a *ComboBox* control named *cboCatalogs* with a list of all databases on the localhost Analysis Services server:

```
Server s = new Server();
s.Connect("Data Source=localhost");
foreach (Database d in s.Databases)
{
    cboCatalogs.Items.Add(d.Name);
}
```

The following additional code adds a new (empty) database named *NewDatabase*:

```
Database dbNew = new Database("NewDatabase");
s.Databases.Add(dbNew);
dbNew.Update();
```

The code in Listing 17-1 is a bit more elaborate. It adds a new dimension named *NewDim*, with the attribute *NewAttr*, to the *Adventure Works* cube in the *Adventure Works DW 2008* database. Notice that many of the properties manipulated are the same ones that appear in the Visual Studio Properties window when a dimension or an attribute object is selected in one of the Analysis Services designers.

LISTING 17-1 Creating objects with AMO

```
// Create new dimension object NewDim:
Dimension dimNew;
dimNew = s.Databases.GetByName("Adventure Works " +
  "DW 2008").Dimensions.Add("NewDim");
dimNew.Type = DimensionType.Regular;
dimNew.UnknownMember = UnknownMemberBehavior.Visible;
dimNew.AttributeAllMemberName = "All";
dimNew.Source = new DataSourceViewBinding("Adventure Works DW");
dimNew.StorageMode = DimensionStorageMode.Molap;

// Create new dimension attribute NewAttr:
DimensionAttribute atrNew = new DimensionAttribute("NewAttr");
atrNew.KeyColumns.Add(new DataItem("dbo_DimPromotion",
  "EnglishPromotionCategory", System.Data.OleDb.OleDbType.WChar, 50));
atrNew.Usage = AttributeUsage.Key;
atrNew.OrderBy = OrderBy.Name;
atrNew.ID = "EnglishPromotionCategory";
atrNew.Type = AttributeType.Regular;

// Add the new attribute to the dimension:
dimNew.Attributes.Add(atrNew);
dimNew.Update();
```

You might want to remove the new database and the dimension (from the *Adventure Works* cube) in SQL Server Management Studio after you execute the code in Listing 17-1 and the snippet preceding it. These objects were meant to be temporary, for illustrative purposes—we won't use the new objects any further.

These examples, although brief, should give you a sense of the power and the inner workings of AMO. Through AMO object properties and child collections, you can configure virtually every facet of an Analysis Services database. This includes not only major objects such as dimensions and measures and more esoteric ones such as scripts and translations, but also specific configuration settings for proactive caching, partitioning, and security roles.

Note Space limitations prevent us from discussing in detail the code that executes after you click the Show Measures button in *frmAPIs* in the *Chapter17* Windows Forms application. But take a look at the code contained in the *btnMeasureDetails_Click, lstMeasureGroups_ SelectedIndexChanged*, and *lstDisplayFolders_SelectedIndexChanged* event handlers in the *AMO* source code region for an example of how to use AMO to handle measure groups and display folders.

While the *AdomdClient.Measure* object does have a *DisplayFolder* property, you must use *GetSchemaDataSet* with *AdomdSchemaGuid.Measures* to determine what measure group a given measure belongs to. In contrast, The AMO *Measure* object has a *Parent* property that provides this information right from the object model. This allows you to write code that iterates through a collection to determine the parent measure group of each measure, and avoids the need to extract that information from a *DataTable*.

XMLA at Your (Analysis) Service

Together, ADO MD.NET and AMO provide an almost overwhelmingly rich array of programming interfaces. Nothing is hidden: anything that Management Studio and Visual Studio can do against Analysis Services databases and cubes, you can do, too, by using these two libraries. But it's important to understand that underlying each of these libraries is nothing but XMLA.

In the previous chapter, you saw how the Analysis Services designers were, effectively, sophisticated UIs for generating XMLA scripts. You also saw how SQL Server Management Studio innately supports the generation of XMLA scripts for virtually any Analysis Services entity and provides a dedicated XMLA query window for executing those scripts.

We'd like to take some time now to explore XMLA a bit further, by showing you how to use it from Management Studio for more than DDL scripts, how to use XMLA programmatically, and how you can expose "raw" XMLA results from ADO MD.NET. This will provide you with only a high-level understanding of how XMLA works, but we think it's still extremely important. If you understand how to work with XMLA, you can potentially control Analysis Services from virtually any environment or platform that supports XML and Web services. Even if you do not plan to leave the .NET environment, understanding XMLA means understanding the native protocol of Analysis Services, and that has plenty of value in itself.

An API of Many Faces

You can understand XMLA from at least three different vantage points. First, you can see XMLA as a simple, programmable API. The core XMLA Web Service provides just two methods: *Discover* (used to fetch metadata information from the server) and *Execute* (typically used to execute MDX queries and fetch the results). These methods accept and return information in the form of XML documents, which can be parsed or transformed to process or display the results.

Although XMLA can be used as a true Web Service (and before the SQL Server 2005 release of Analysis Services, it had to be), its elevation to native API status changes the ways in which we might use it a bit. On the .NET platform, XMLA works over TCP/IP rather than HTTP, and a thin, managed assembly provides an API with certain enhancements over that provided by a Web reference proxy class. Specifically, if you want to use XMLA, you can set a reference to the Microsoft.AnalysisServices.Xmla library. Then you simply instantiate a *Microsoft.AnalysisServices.Xmla.XmlaClient* object to start writing XMLA code.

> **Important** Adding a reference to Microsoft.AnalysisServices.Xmla can be a bit tricky with Analysis Services 2008. The assembly is not listed on the .NET tab of the Add Reference dialog box in Visual Studio and cannot be found through the Browse tab either. The assembly *is,* however, in the global assembly cache (GAC) and can be extracted from the GAC to a physical folder and *then* referenced through the Browse tab. The sample code's Windows Forms project, *Chapter17,* already contains a reference created through this procedure and the Chapter17\ VS\Chapter17\bin\Debug folder contains a physical copy of the file Microsoft.AnalysisServices. XMLA.DLL.

Before we look at an XMLA coding example, we will explore the second way to use XMLA: through the XMLA Query window in SQL Server Management Studio. You got a glimpse of how this works in Chapter 16, but we will explore that facility further here. As you will see, it is possible to create scripts that query your OLAP cubes as well as scripts that can create cubes, modify their structure, or perform an array of management tasks on them.

Last, you can use ADO MD.NET to access the underlying XML payload returned by XMLA when MDX queries are executed. You get XML-formatted results from your MDX queries without having to submit your MDX queries in XML format or deal directly with XMLA as an API.

Using XMLA from SQL Server Management Studio

We'll start our tour of XMLA in the XMLA Query window in Management Studio. The best way to understand XMLA is to use it in conjunction with the Template Explorer window because the built-in XMLA templates give you an excellent jump-start on understanding the syntax and variety of possible XMLA queries.

Start by opening a new XMLA Query window against the *Chapter16* database. (You can use the same techniques you use to open an MDX Query window: just select the XMLA option, where available, in place of the MDX option, from all relevant menus.) Show the Template Explorer window if it is not visible, click the Analysis Server button (second from the left) on the window's toolbar, and drill down on the XMLA node in the tree view. Drill down further on each of the three child nodes (Management, Schema Rowsets, and Server Status) to reveal the various XMLA templates available.

Using *<Discover>* for Metadata and Status Information

To see how easy it is to perform XMLA queries, drag the Sessions node (the third-to-last node under Server Status) from the Template Explorer window into the XMLA Query window. Move the cursor left to deselect the text. You should see the following text in the window:

```
<Discover xmlns="urn:schemas-microsoft-com:xml-analysis">
  <RequestType>DISCOVER_SESSIONS</RequestType>
  <Restrictions>
    <RestrictionList>
    </RestrictionList>
  </Restrictions>
  <Properties>
    <PropertyList>
    </PropertyList>
  </Properties>
</Discover>
```

The parent *<Discover>* element indicates that we will be calling the XMLA Web service's *Discover* method (rather than its *Execute* method). You can think of the *<RequestType>* and *<Restrictions>* elements in much the same way that you think of the *GetSchemaDataSet*'s enumerated constant and restrictions array. The former is set to *DISCOVER_SESSIONS*, and the latter is empty; this will result in a complete list of all active sessions for the server.

The *<Properties>* child element is required for all XMLA commands. Usually this element/ parameter will contain connection and formatting information. But because we already supplied server-level connection information when the XMLA window was opened, all default settings are acceptable to us and we will leave this element empty.

To see the XML-formatted results of this command, press F5 or Ctrl+E (or use the various Execute toolbar or menu commands). The results might look bewildering at first, but the XML results are easier to interpret if you scroll past the *<xsd:schema>* element to the first *<row>* element. That element's content and format should look similar to the following:

```
<row>
  <SESSION_ID>E2CF368A-DACE-4EC4-BED1-2969BCD6DEEE</SESSION_ID>
  <SESSION_SPID>2024</SESSION_SPID>
  <SESSION_CONNECTION_ID>2</SESSION_CONNECTION_ID>
  <SESSION_USER_NAME>MYDOMAIN\UserName</SESSION_USER_NAME>
  <SESSION_CURRENT_DATABASE>Chapter16</SESSION_CURRENT_DATABASE>
  <SESSION_USED_MEMORY>2</SESSION_USED_MEMORY>
  <SESSION_START_TIME>2008-07-09T20:42:45</SESSION_START_TIME>
  <SESSION_ELAPSED_TIME_MS>502893</SESSION_ELAPSED_TIME_MS>
  <SESSION_LAST_COMMAND_START_TIME>2008-07-09T20:50:48</SESSION_LAST_COMMAND_START_TIME>
  <SESSION_LAST_COMMAND_END_TIME>2008-07-09T20:50:48</SESSION_LAST_COMMAND_END_TIME>
  <SESSION_LAST_COMMAND_ELAPSED_TIME_MS>0</SESSION_LAST_COMMAND_ELAPSED_TIME_MS>
  <SESSION_IDLE_TIME_MS>19277</SESSION_IDLE_TIME_MS>
  <SESSION_CPU_TIME_MS>20</SESSION_CPU_TIME_MS>
  <SESSION_LAST_COMMAND>DISCOVER_PROPERTIES</SESSION_LAST_COMMAND>
  <SESSION_LAST_COMMAND_CPU_TIME_MS>0</SESSION_LAST_COMMAND_CPU_TIME_MS>
  <SESSION_STATUS>0</SESSION_STATUS>
```

```
      <SESSION_READS>8</SESSION_READS>
      <SESSION_WRITES>0</SESSION_WRITES>
      <SESSION_READ_KB>6</SESSION_READ_KB>
      <SESSION_WRITE_KB>0</SESSION_WRITE_KB>
      <SESSION_COMMAND_COUNT>6</SESSION_COMMAND_COUNT>
    </row>
```

XMLA supports two response formats, tabular and multidimensional. Typically, as in this case, the *Discover* method returns tabular-formatted results, with each row contained in a separate *<row>* element and each column contained in its own named child element. The *Execute* method, which we will examine shortly, typically uses the multidimensional format for its response content.

Tip The tabular XMLA response format is nearly identical to the XML format used by the ADO. NET *DataTable* object, which is used, in turn, by the *DataSet* object's *ReadXml* and *WriteXml* methods. Therefore, when you use XMLA programmatically, you can tweak the tabular response content slightly and convert it to an ADO.NET *DataTable*, which is suitable for binding to Windows Forms or ASP.NET controls.

Note The content of the *<SESSION_USER_NAME>* element in the XML snippet just shown has been obfuscated to *MYDOMAIN\UserName*; actual results would present the real domain name and user name of the user logged into the session.

Using *<Execute>* for DDL Tasks

Let's try another query. This time, we'll use XMLA to perform an administrative task—processing the *Adventure Works* cube in the *Adventure Works DW 2008* database:

```
<Execute xmlns="urn:schemas-microsoft-com:xml-analysis">
  <Command>
    <Process xmlns="http://schemas.microsoft.com/analysisservices/2003/engine">
      <Type>ProcessFull</Type>
      <Object>
        <DatabaseID>Adventure Works DW 2008</DatabaseID>
        <CubeID>Adventure Works</CubeID>
      </Object>
    </Process>
  </Command>
  <Properties />
</Execute>
```

Notice that this command is contained in an *<Execute>* element instead of the *<Discover>* element used in our last query. That's because this query performs an action. The *<Execute>* element contains a child *<Command>* element and an empty *<Properties>* child element, as with the last query. Within the *<Command>* element, the *<Process>* child element (and its child *<Type>* and *<Object>* elements) tells Analysis Services to run a full process against the *Adventure Works* cube in the *Adventure Works DW 2008* database.

> **Important** XMLA, as it turns out, works with IDs rather than names, and the two do not always match. To determine the ID of a cube, right-click it in the Object Explorer window in Management Studio, and then choose Properties from the shortcut menu. The cube's ID will appear in the second row of the General page in the Cube Properties dialog box.

Press F5 to run the process task. During processing, you will see the "Executing query..." message and animated icon appear in the XMLA Query window's status bar and various status information on the Messages tab of the Results pane. When the processing is complete, the Results tab will appear, displaying a standard "empty" XMLA message indicating that the process terminated successfully, as shown here:

```
<return xmlns="urn:schemas-microsoft-com:xml-analysis">
  <root xmlns="urn:schemas-microsoft-com:xml-analysis:empty" />
</return>
```

It might seem counterintuitive for an empty response to indicate success, but consider that a failed process will always return an error message on the Messages tab. For example, if you were to intentionally change the *<CubeID>* element's content from *Adventure Works* to *Adventure Works DW* and reexecute the query, you would see the following text on the Messages tab:

```
Executing the query ...
Errors in the metadata manager. Either the cube with the ID of 'Adventure Works DW' does not
exist in the database with the ID of 'Adventure Works DW 2008', or the user does not have
permissions to access the object.
Execution complete
```

Using *<Execute>* to Run MDX Queries

To round out your understanding of XMLA, you must appreciate that XMLA can also be used to execute MDX queries. It is a bit ironic that we are pointing this out *after* discussing XMLA's DDL scripting capabilities, because XMLA was originally designed primarily for MDX query execution (and metadata discovery). As such, XMLA easily accommodates the notion of cell sets containing axes, positions, and a collection of cells. Each of these entities is neatly packaged in the multidimensional-formatted XML response payload.

Under most circumstances, you would let ADO MD.NET process this XML document and populate a *CellSet* (or *DataSet*, *DataTable*, or *DataReader*) object with its contents, but you can use the Management Studio XMLA window to examine the XML content directly. This is relatively easy to do because the XML content, although somewhat complex, is quite readable if you have an understanding of OLAP, MDX, and cell sets.

For example, to run a simple query against the *Sales* cube in our *Chapter16* database, consider the following script (which can be found in the QueryCubeChapter16.xmla file in the *XMLA Demos* project in the sample code Management Studio solution):

```
<Execute xmlns="urn:schemas-microsoft-com:xml-analysis">
  <Command>
    <Statement>
      SELECT  Shippers.[Shipper Name].MEMBERS ON COLUMNS,
              Time.Year.MEMBERS ON ROWS
      FROM    Sales
      WHERE   Measures.[Total Sales]
    </Statement>
  </Command>
  <Properties/>
</Execute>
```

Notice that we once again use *<Execute>* as our parent tag, indicating that we are calling XMLA's *Execute* method. The *<Execute>* element, as before, contains *<Command>* and *<Properties>* subelements. This time, the *<Command>* element consists merely of a *<Statement>* element whose value is the MDX command we want to execute.

Execute the query now to fetch the multidimensional response. You will see that a large XML response is returned. To make this XML easier to read, copy and paste it into a new XMLA Query window. This will allow you to expand and contract elements within the XML using the outline nodes in the left margin of the XMLA editor.

Now contract the *xs:schema* node in the *return/root* element (it begins on the third line of the document), and then contract the *OlapInfo/CubeInfo* element two lines below it. Go down one line more and examine the *AxesInfo* element. Notice that each axis, as well as the "Slicer" axis (which represents the MDX command's *WHERE* clause), is described. Now contract the *OlapInfo* node (on the fourth displayed line of the document) and examine the *Axes* node immediately below it, looking at each *<Axis>* node within it. Notice that each tuple and member is enumerated, complete with *Caption*, *UniqueName* (*<UName>* element), and other property values.

For example, the entire *COLUMNS* axis (axis 0) is described in the XML response payload as follows, with one tuple per shipper (and one each for the *All* and *Unknown* members):

```
<Axis name="Axis0">
  <Tuples>
    <Tuple>
      <Member Hierarchy="[Shippers].[Shipper Name]">
        <UName>[Shippers].[Shipper Name].[All Shippers]</UName>
        <Caption>All Shippers</Caption>
        <LName>[Shippers].[Shipper Name].[(All)]</LName>
        <LNum>0</LNum>
        <DisplayInfo>65540</DisplayInfo>
      </Member>
    </Tuple>
```

```
    <Tuple>
      <Member Hierarchy="[Shippers].[Shipper Name]">
        <UName>[Shippers].[Shipper Name].&amp;[3]</UName>
        <Caption>Federal Shipping</Caption>
        <LName>[Shippers].[Shipper Name].[Shipper Name]</LName>
        <LNum>1</LNum>
        <DisplayInfo>0</DisplayInfo>
      </Member>
    </Tuple>
    <Tuple>
      <Member Hierarchy="[Shippers].[Shipper Name]">
        <UName>[Shippers].[Shipper Name].&amp;[1]</UName>
        <Caption>Speedy Express</Caption>
        <LName>[Shippers].[Shipper Name].[Shipper Name]</LName>
        <LNum>1</LNum>
        <DisplayInfo>131072</DisplayInfo>
      </Member>
    </Tuple>
    <Tuple>
      <Member Hierarchy="[Shippers].[Shipper Name]">
        <UName>[Shippers].[Shipper Name].&amp;[2]</UName>
        <Caption>United Package</Caption>
        <LName>[Shippers].[Shipper Name].[Shipper Name]</LName>
        <LNum>1</LNum>
        <DisplayInfo>131072</DisplayInfo>
      </Member>
    </Tuple>
    <Tuple>
      <Member Hierarchy="[Shippers].[Shipper Name]">
        <UName>[Shippers].[Shipper Name].[All Shippers].UNKNOWNMEMBER</UName>
        <Caption>Unknown</Caption>
        <LName>[Shippers].[Shipper Name].[Shipper Name]</LName>
        <LNum>1</LNum>
        <DisplayInfo>131072</DisplayInfo>
      </Member>
    </Tuple>
  </Tuples>
</Axis>
```

For the Slicer axis, notice that the *Measures* tuple/member has a *UniqueName* of *[Measures].*
[Total Sales], which squares with the *WHERE* clause in our MDX query, as follows:

```
<Axis name="SlicerAxis">
  <Tuples>
    <Tuple>
      <Member Hierarchy="[Measures]">
        <UName>[Measures].[Total Sales]</UName>
        <Caption>Total Sales</Caption>
        <LName>[Measures].[MeasuresLevel]</LName>
        <LNum>0</LNum>
        <DisplayInfo>0</DisplayInfo>
      </Member>
        ...
```

Now contract the *Axes* node and examine the *CellData* node immediately following it. Notice that each cell's *Value* and *FormattedValue* (*<FmtValue>* element) is provided, and that the cells are identified by the ordinal address we discussed earlier:

```
<CellData>
  <Cell CellOrdinal="0">
    <Value xsi:type="xsd:double">1.35445859E6</Value>
    <FmtValue>$1,354,458.59</FmtValue>
  </Cell>
  <Cell CellOrdinal="1">
    <Value xsi:type="xsd:double">4.0775082000000006E5</Value>
    <FmtValue>$407,750.82</FmtValue>
  </Cell>
  ...
```

Calling *Execute* Programmatically from .NET

With this understanding of XMLA's encoding of *CellSet* objects, you can imagine how it would be possible to create an Extensible Stylesheet Language (XSL) stylesheet that transforms the data into a human-readable HTML page. In fact, Microsoft has created just such a stylesheet. It is named Xamd.xsl, and it is distributed as part of a sample application in the XMLA 1.1 SDK (which you can download for free from *http://www.microsoft.com/downloads/details.aspx?familyid=7564a3fd-4729-4b09-9ee7-5e71140186ee&displaylang=en*, and which is actually designed for SQL Server 2000). You can use the stylesheet to transform any two-axis XML cell set into well-formed HTML, with the results displayed in a table.

You can thus execute MDX queries via XMLA directly from .NET applications (using *Microsoft.AnalysisServices.Xmla*, as discussed earlier). You can then use the stylesheet, some *System.Xml* code, and a *WebBrowser* control to display the results. To do so, you'll first need to make sure that you include the following namespaces in your code:

```
using System.Xml;
using System.Xml.Xsl;
using System.IO;
```

Once the namespaces are properly imported, you can use the code in Listing 17-2 (taken from the *Xmla* source code region in *frmAPIs* in the sample code's *Chapter17* Windows Forms application), which performs the XSL transformation for the MDX query we just discussed. This code assumes that the variable *ConnectionString* contains a valid Analysis Services connection string pointing to the server with the *Chapter16* database, that the *TextBox* control *txtMDX* contains the MDX query text to be executed, and that a *WebBrowser* control named *wbrMain* is available to display the HTML results.

LISTING 17-2 Executing MDX queries with XMLA

```csharp
// XMLA:
Microsoft.AnalysisServices.Xmla.XmlaClient xmlac = new
 Microsoft.AnalysisServices.Xmla.XmlaClient();

// System.Xml:
XslCompiledTransform xslCellSetTable = new XslCompiledTransform();
XmlTextWriter xtwCellSetTable = new XmlTextWriter(Path.GetFullPath(".") +
 "\\Execute.htm", null);
XmlDocument xdcResults = new XmlDocument();

string command = "<Statement>" + txtMDX.Text + "</Statement>";
string properties = "<PropertyList>" +
                    "   <Catalog>Chapter16</Catalog>" +
                    "</PropertyList>";
string results;

try
{
    // Load the stylesheet:
    xslCellSetTable.Load(Path.GetFullPath(".") + "\\xamd.xsl");

    // Fetch the XML into a string:
    xmlac.Connect(ConnectionString);
    xmlac.Execute(command, properties, out results, false, true);

    // Load the XML text into an XmlDocument:
    xdcResults.LoadXml(results);

    // Strip off the outer <return> tag (which the stylesheet is not expecting):
    xdcResults.LoadXml(xdcResults.FirstChild.InnerXml);

    // Transform the XML to an HTML file:
    xslCellSetTable.Transform(xdcResults, xtwCellSetTable);

    // Close XmlTextWriter:
    xtwCellSetTable.Close();

    // Display generated HTML file in the WebBrowser control:
    wbrMain.Navigate(Path.GetFullPath(".") + "\\Execute.htm");
}

catch (Exception ex)
{
    MessageBox.Show(ex.Message);
}

finally
{
    // Close the connection:
    xmlac.Disconnect();
}
```

Notice that the *XmlaClient* object has an *Execute* method that accepts XML strings identical to the contents of the *<Command>* and *<Properties>* child elements of the *<Execute>* element supplied in Management Studio's XMLA Query window. The results are assigned to a third string argument. The last two arguments are Booleans of relatively little importance in this case.

Once the *Execute* method call is complete and the XML result string has been assigned to the *string* variable *results*, the code simply loads it into an *XmlDocument* object, applies the stylesheet transformation, and dumps the resultant HTML to a file named Execute.htm. The code then displays the file's contents in a *WebBrowser* control. Your results should look similar to those depicted in Figure 17-36.

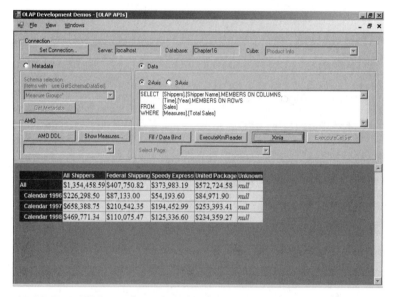

FIGURE 17-36 HTML-transformed results of an MDX query run via the XMLA *Execute* command

Manipulating XMLA Response Content from ADO MD.NET

In addition to using the stylesheet in conjunction with low-level XMLA coding, you can also use it with ADO MD.NET. That is because the *AdomdCommand* object has an *ExecuteXmlReader* method that directly returns the XMLA response payload generated when an *AdomdCommand* object's MDX query is executed. So by combining the *ExecuteXmlReader* method and code similar to that in Listing 17-2, the results can once again be displayed as HTML in a *WebBrowser* control.

Sample code for this technique is provided in Listing 17-3 (taken from the *AdomdCommand. ExecuteXmlReader* source code region in the form *frmAPIs* in the sample code's *Chapter17* Windows Forms application). This code makes the same assumptions as Listing 17-2.

LISTING 17-3 Using *ExecuteXmlReader*

```
// ADO MD.NET:
AdomdConnection conXML = new AdomdConnection(ConnectionString);
AdomdCommand comXML = new AdomdCommand(txtMDX.Text, conXML);

// System.Xml:
XslCompiledTransform xslCellSetTable = new XslCompiledTransform();
XmlTextWriter xtwCellSetTable = new XmlTextWriter(Path.GetFullPath(".") +
 "\\Execute.htm", null);

try
{
   // Open the connection:
   conXML.Open();

   // Load the stylesheet:
   xslCellSetTable.Load(Path.GetFullPath(".") + "\\xamd.xsl");

   // Fetch and transform the XML to an HTML file:
   xslCellSetTable.Transform(comXML.ExecuteXmlReader(), xtwCellSetTable);

   // Close the XmlTextWriter:
   xtwCellSetTable.Close();

   // Display generated HTML file in the WebBrowser control:
   wbrMain.Navigate(Path.GetFullPath(".") + "\\Execute.htm");
}

catch (Exception ex)
{
   MessageBox.Show(ex.Message);
}

finally
{
   // Close the connection:
   conXML.Close();
}
```

For the code in Listing 17-3 to compile properly, the following namespace inclusions must be properly inserted at the top of your source code file:

```
using Microsoft.AnalysisServices.AdomdClient;
using System.Xml;
using System.Xml.Xsl;
using System.IO;
```

Analysis Services CLR Support: Server-Side ADO MD.NET

Our last stop on this tour through various OLAP programming models brings us back to the server itself. That's because, as it turns out, SQL Server Analysis Services supports a programming model very similar to the SQL CLR programming we discussed in Chapter 3. In the Analysis Services CLR model, you can load .NET assemblies onto your Analysis Services server and call their functions programmatically from ADO MD.NET or XMLA, or manually from Management Studio's MDX Query window or XMLA Query window.

> **Important** Unlike SQL CLR integration, Analysis Services CLR support is on by default. In fact, it cannot be disabled. However, only users with administrative permissions on the Analysis Services server or database can load CLR assemblies. This contrasts significantly with the SQL CLR feature, which can be made available to nonadministrative users but is disabled by default and must be turned on using T-SQL or Policy-Based Management (PBM), which we cover in Chapter 4.

Visual Studio offers no project templates for server-side Analysis Services programming, and the programming model does not use code attributes, but the CLR support in Analysis Services is similar to, and about as easy as, SQL CLR programming. In Analysis Services, such functions are referred to as *managed stored procedures*.

Managed stored procedures can execute without returning anything, or they can act as functions that return values or objects. Although these function-like stored procedures can return scalar values, they will typically return and/or accept MDX entities such as tuples, sets, and expressions. This is made possible through the use of the *Microsoft.AnalysisServices. AdomdServer* namespace, which includes definitions for these types and for special builder objects used to create some of them.

> **Note** Managed stored procedures can also be used for data mining tasks and can execute and return result sets from DMX prediction queries. We provide an example of such a managed stored procedure at the end of Chapter 18.

Writing Managed Stored Procedure Code

You can start writing Analysis Services managed stored procedures simply by creating a Class Library project in Visual Studio 2008 and setting a reference to the *Microsoft.AnalysisServices. AdomdServer* library. Then you simply add the following *using* statement at the top of a C# class file:

```
using Microsoft.AnalysisServices.AdomdServer;
```

You're now ready to write your first managed stored procedure.

> **Important** The *Microsoft.AnalysisServices.AdomdServer* library's version stamp is displayed on the .NET tab of the Visual Studio 2008 Add Reference dialog box as 9.0.0.0, seemingly indicating that it is a component of SQL Server 2005, rather than 2008. However, navigating to the actual assembly file (msmgdsrv.dll) and viewing its properties reveals that the assembly has a version stamp starting with 10.0. Therefore, do not be alarmed by the 9.0 version stamp displayed within Visual Studio.

The code in Listing 17-4 (taken from SQL Server Books Online and found in the file StoredProcedures.cs in the *Chapter17AdomdServer* Class Library project in the sample code) implements a CLR function that accepts an *AdomdServer.Set* object and a filter expression (as a string) and then returns a subset of that set containing just the tuples that meet the filter condition.

LISTING 17-4 CLR function *FilterSet*

```
public Set FilterSet(Set set, string filterExpression)
{
    Expression expr = new Expression(filterExpression);
    SetBuilder resultSetBuilder = new SetBuilder();
    foreach (Tuple tuple in set)
    {
        if ((bool)(expr.Calculate(tuple)))
            resultSetBuilder.Add(tuple);
    }
    return resultSetBuilder.ToSet();
}
```

Notice the use of the *Set*, *Expression*, and *SetBuilder* objects for typing one of the function's parameters, its return type, and its variables, and notice the *Tuple* object for the controlling variable within the *foreach* loop. A string containing the MDX expression we want to use is passed to the *Expression* object's constructor. From there, the *Expression* object's *Calculate* method is used to test whether each tuple in the passed-in set meets the filter condition; if it does, the code adds the tuple to the *SetBuilder* object's internal collection via its *Add* method. Last, the *SetBuilder* object's *ToSet* method is used to generate the *Set* object returned by the function.

Once the assembly is compiled and loaded into your database, you can call the *FilterSet* function from an MDX query as if it were part of the MDX language itself.

Loading the Assembly

To load an assembly using Management Studio, first right-click the Assemblies node under your Analysis Services server in Object Explorer and choose New Assembly, as shown in Figure 17-37.

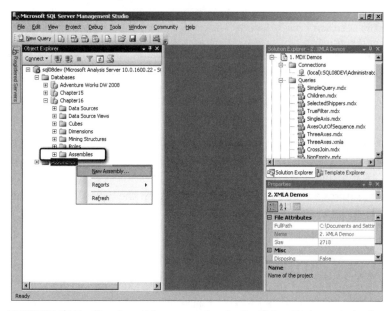

FIGURE 17-37 The New Assembly menu option for the Object Explorer window's server Assemblies node, with the *Chapter16* database's own Assemblies node highlighted

The Register Server Assembly dialog box opens, as shown in Figure 17-38.

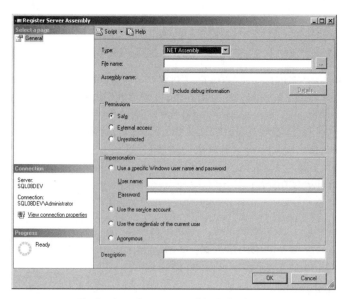

FIGURE 17-38 The Register Server Assembly dialog box in Management Studio

Confirm that .NET Assembly is selected in the Type drop-down list, and then enter the full path to your assembly in the File Name text box or click the ellipsis button to the right of the text box to specify the assembly through a standard File Open dialog box.

Tip You can also add assemblies to individual databases rather than to the server as a whole. The procedure is identical except for one difference: Rather than right-clicking your *server's* Assemblies child node, you right-click the Assemblies child node belonging to a specific *database* (highlighted in Figure 17-37). The Register Database Assembly dialog box will appear instead of the Register Server Assembly dialog box. The two dialog boxes are identical except for their names.

By default, a "friendly" name is generated for your assembly in the Assembly Name text box. This name will be identical to the file name of your assembly, minus the .dll extension. You can change this to any name you want, but you must remember it because you will need to use it when you call any of the assembly functions from MDX. If you want to debug your assembly, select the Include Debug Information check box. We will provide full details on debugging server-side managed code shortly.

As with SQL CLR assemblies, you can assign the assembly any of three permission sets: *Safe* (the default), *External Access*, or *Unrestricted* (similar in concept to the SQL CLR *Unsafe* permission set). You can also set the impersonation technique used by the assembly. Options here include specifying a particular account, using the service account, and impersonating the current user, the anonymous user, or an Analysis Services–defined default. The Impersonation setting is pertinent only when you select the *External Access* or *Unrestricted* permission set because the *Safe* permission set does not grant access to resources outside of Analysis Services, making specific account permissions mostly inconsequential.

After you have specified your assembly's type, file name, friendly name, debug information option, permission set, and impersonation mode, click the OK button and the assembly will be permanently loaded (unless you later delete it, of course). Functions within the assembly are now callable using the naming convention *AssemblyName.FullClassName.FunctionName*, where *AssemblyName* is the assembly's friendly name, *FullClassName* is the fully namespace-qualified name of the class in which your function is defined, and *FunctionName* is the name of your function.

Tip You can also load database-level assemblies by adding them to Analysis Services projects in Visual Studio. Right-click the Assemblies node in the Visual Studio Solution Explorer window, and then choose New Assembly Reference from the shortcut menu to display the Add Reference dialog box, where you can add one or more assemblies to your project. After you add an assembly, you can change its friendly name, permission set, impersonation mode, and description via the Properties window. Once the project is deployed, the assembly will be physically loaded into the database on the server.

Calling Managed Code from MDX

Calling your function from a query is easy. For example, the following MDX code (which can be found in the FilterSet.mdx file in the *CLR Demos* project in the sample code's SSMS solution) uses the *FilterSet* function we just created in a query against the *Chapter16* database:

```
SELECT Chapter17AdomdServer.Chapter17AdomdServer.StoredProcedures.FilterSet(Shippers.
[Shipper Name].MEMBERS, "[Shipper Name].CurrentMember.Name < 'U'") ON COLUMNS,
    Time.Year.MEMBERS ON ROWS
FROM Sales
WHERE Measures.[Total Sales]
```

You can execute this query from your own application (using ADO MD.NET or XMLA), a Management Studio MDX Query window, or an XMLA Query window (if the query is embedded in the appropriate XML stream). Regardless of the method you use, the query should yield the results shown in the following table.

	All Shippers	Federal Shipping	Speedy Express
All	$1,354,458.59	$407,750.82	$373,983.19
Calendar 1996	$226,298.50	$87,133.00	$54,193.60
Calendar 1997	$658,388.75	$210,542.35	$194,452.99
Calendar 1998	$469,771.34	$110,075.47	$125,336.60

Notice that the set we submitted to the *FilterSet* function is *Shippers.[Shipper Name]. MEMBERS*; the MDX expression passed is *[Shipper Name].CurrentMember.Name < 'U'*; and the resultant filtered set becomes our query's *ON COLUMNS* expression. The result is that only shippers beginning with a letter that comes before *U* in the alphabet appear across the columns axis (which means that United Package and the *Unknown* members are skipped).

Debugging Server-Side Managed Code

There is no project type for Analysis Services assemblies, so Visual Studio has no innate awareness of them, but it is still possible to debug your .NET code running in Analysis Services databases. To do so, choose Debug, Attach To Process in Visual Studio 2008 to open the Attach To Process dialog box, shown in Figure 17-39.

Select the Show Processes From All Users check box in the lower left of the dialog box, and then select the msmdsrv.exe process in the Available Processes list box. The string "Managed code" should appear in the (grayed out) Attach To text box. (It might be one item in a comma-delimited list.) If not, click the Select button to the right, select the Debug These Code Types option and the Managed check box in the Select Code Type dialog box, as shown in Figure 17-40, and then click OK.

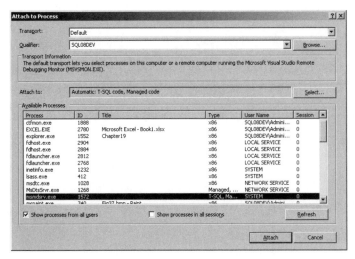

FIGURE 17-39 The Attach To Process dialog box in Visual Studio

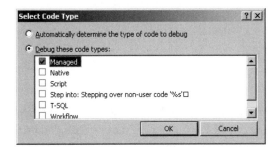

FIGURE 17-40 The Select Code Type dialog box

Note The next time you open the Attach To Process dialog box, the Show Processes From All Users check box should be selected by default. Also, when the msmdsrv.exe process is selected, "Managed code" should appear in the Attach To text box without requiring you to use the Select Code Type dialog box again.

In the Attach To Process dialog box, click the Attach button to start the Visual Studio debugger. You can now set breakpoints in your code, which will be hit whenever the CLR code is called from an MDX query, whether it is run from other .NET code or from an MDX Query window or XMLA Query window in SQL Server Management Studio. To test this, set a breakpoint in the first line of code in the *FilterSet* function, return to Management Studio, and reexecute the previous MDX query. You will hit your breakpoint and have full access to the Visual Studio debugging tools, including the Locals window and expression visualizers, as shown in Figure 17-41.

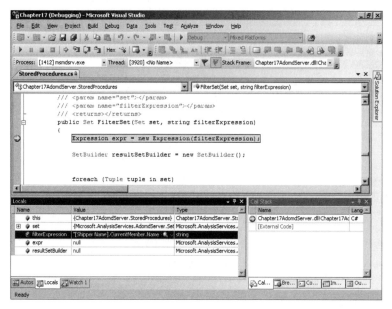

FIGURE 17-41 Visual Studio in Debugging mode, with Analysis Services CLR stored procedure source code being traced

Void Functions

You can also create *void* functions (*Subs* in Visual Basic) that perform various actions and do not return data. Typically, such functions use AMO to perform various data definition tasks, including creating a new database and processing a cube. By combining AMO with a special context connection string, you can create DDL stored procedures that run in the context of the connection you've already established. For example, start by inserting the following namespace code at the top of a class file:

```
using Microsoft.AnalysisServices;
using Microsoft.AnalysisServices.AdomdServer;
```

Then use the code in Listing 17-5 (adapted from one of our initial AMO examples) to implement a stored procedure that creates a new database named *NewDatabase* on the currently connected server. (The code in Listing 17-5 can be found in the source code file StoredProcedures.cs in the *Chapter17AdomdServer* Class Library project in the sample code.)

LISTING 17-5 Server-side AMO

```
public void CreateNewDB()
{
    Server s = new Server();
    s.Connect("*");
    Database dbNew = new Database("NewDatabase");
    s.Databases.Add(dbNew);
    dbNew.Update();
    s.Disconnect();
}
```

Notice the use of a context connection string ("*"), which ensures that AMO connects to the server on which the assembly has been loaded.

The stored procedure shown will execute properly only if the assembly containing it is assigned *Unrestricted* permissions. This is because AMO is not callable from partially trusted callers, and only assemblies with the *Unrestricted* permission set have full trust. If you didn't assign the *Unrestricted* permission set to the *Chapter17AdomdServer* assembly, do so now through the Permission Set property in the Assembly Properties dialog box, by double-clicking the assembly in the Management Studio Object Explorer window or right-clicking it and selecting the Properties option from its shortcut menu.

Void functions are executed using the special MDX *CALL* command rather than the *SELECT* command. So, to call the stored procedure shown in Listing 17-5, you would use the following MDX code:

```
CALL Chapter17AdomdServer.Chapter17AdomdServer.StoredProcedures.CreateNewDB();
```

Try executing the preceding command from Management Studio (by simply opening the file CLR-DDL.mdx from the CLR Demos project and executing it), then right-click your server's Databases node in the Object Explorer window, choose Refresh from the shortcut menu, and then expand the node (if necessary). You should see a NewDatabase node appear; you might want to delete it after completing this test.

Result Set–Returning Functions

Although you should not think of Analysis Services managed stored procedures as being *designed* to return result sets, it is in fact possible to return tabular results sets from them, in the form of *AdomdClient.AdomdDataReader* or *System.Data.DataTable* objects. For example, the code in Listing 17-6 (also found in StoredProcedures.cs) implements a CLR stored procedure that returns a simple two-column, two-row result set.

LISTING 17-6 Returning a *DataTable*

```
public System.Data.DataTable GetDataTable()
{
    System.Data.DataTable dt = new System.Data.DataTable();
    dt.Columns.Add("ID", typeof(int));
    dt.Columns.Add("Name", typeof(string));

    object[] row = new object[2];

    row[0] = 1;
    row[1] = "Andrew";
    dt.Rows.Add(row);

    row[0] = 2;
    row[1] = "Steve";
    dt.Rows.Add(row);

    return dt;
}
```

When called with the following MDX command (found in GetDataTable.mdx), the code in Listing 17-6 returns the result set shown in the table following the command.

```
CALL Chapter17AdomdServer.Chapter17AdomdServer.StoredProcedures.GetDataTable();
```

ID	Name
1	Andrew
2	Steve

This example is trivial, but the ability to return result sets can indeed be helpful. You can, for example, use actual ADO.NET code to return data from a SQL Server relational database based on input values from a passed MDX set.

Mixing Client and Server to Return Flattened Cell Sets

Unlike with SQL CLR programming, you will typically *not* use the ADO MD.NET *client* library (*AdomdClient*) in your server-side code; instead, you'll use the *AdomdServer* library in server-side programming, as it replicates most *AdomdClient* objects. However, if you want your stored procedure to return data from an MDX query (for example, as an *AdomdDataReader*), you *must* use client-side ADO MD.NET (*AdomdClient*) objects in your stored procedure. This is illustrated in Listing 17-7 (also found in StoredProcedures.cs).

LISTING 17-7 Returning a *DataReader*

```
public Microsoft.AnalysisServices.AdomdClient.AdomdDataReader GetDataClient()
{
   Microsoft.AnalysisServices.AdomdClient.AdomdConnection conContext = new
      Microsoft.AnalysisServices.AdomdClient.AdomdConnection("data source=" +
      Context.CurrentServerID + ";initial catalog=" +
      Context.CurrentDatabaseName);
   Microsoft.AnalysisServices.AdomdClient.AdomdCommand comContext = new
      Microsoft.AnalysisServices.AdomdClient.AdomdCommand("SELECT " +
      "Shippers.[Shipper Name].MEMBERS ON COLUMNS, Time.Year.MEMBERS ON ROWS " +
      "FROM Sales WHERE Measures.[Total Sales]", conContext);
   conContext.Open();
   try
   {
      return comContext.ExecuteReader();
   }
   catch
   {
      return null;
   }
}
```

Notice the use of the *Context* object's *CurrentServerId* and *CurrentDatabaseName* properties to build the context-sensitive connection string. When this code is called with the following MDX query (found in GetDataClient.mdx), it yields the results shown in the table following the query.

```
CALL Chapter17AdomdServer.Chapter17AdomdServer.StoredProcedures.GetDataClient()
```

[Time].[Year].[Year].[MEMBER_CAPTION]	[Shippers].[Shipper Name].[All Shippers]	[Shippers].[Shipper Name].&[3]	[Shippers].[Shipper Name].&[1]	[Shippers].[Shipper Name].&[2]	[Shippers].[Shipper Name].[All Shippers].UNKNOWNMEMBER
	1354458.59	407750.82	373983.19	572724.58	
Calendar 1996	226298.5	87133	54193.6	84971.9	
Calendar 1997	658388.75	210542.35	194452.99	253393.41	
Calendar 1998	469771.34	110075.47	125336.6	234359.27	

The integrity of using the *AdomdClient* assembly from server-side code is dubious. You should use this technique only as a last resort, when MDX queries cannot be executed from the calling application (for whatever reason). The scenarios for creating (flattened) cell set–returning stored procedures are thus limited, but the possibility is nonetheless intriguing.

Analysis Services CLR features are at least as compelling as, if not more compelling than, the SQL CLR functionality offered in SQL Server relational databases. They extend the capabilities of MDX, add easy-to-use DDL commands, provide end-to-end debugging, and serve as a unifying environment for ADO MD.NET, AMO, ADO.NET, and mainstream .NET Framework programming.

Summary

This chapter has covered extensive ground. You've learned how to use PivotTables, charts, and cell formulas from Excel 2007 and Excel Services to build compelling dashboards for your OLAP cubes. Also, by learning a small subset of the MDX query language, you learned how to use the MDX Query window in SQL Server Management Studio to query your cubes more precisely than you can with Excel.

You've seen how to apply your MDX knowledge programmatically by using ADO MD.NET and how to get detailed metadata and perform numerous DDL tasks with AMO. You learned how both libraries provide façades around XMLA, and you learned how to use XMLA directly, from the XMLA Query window in Management Studio and in code via *Microsoft. AnalysisServices.Xmla*, as well as through ADO MD.NET. Last, you saw how to use many of these technologies on the server via Analysis Services support for CLR assemblies, including full debugging support in Visual Studio.

Microsoft's OLAP platform is not only powerful and feature-rich, but it is also highly programmable. This developer-friendly approach is a hallmark of Microsoft technologies and is an important part of what has driven Analysis Services' dominant position in the business intelligence market.

Chapter 18
Expanding Your Business Intelligence with Data Mining

—Elsie Pan

The data mining component of Microsoft SQL Server Analysis Services is an intensely compelling feature. It allows developers, even those with no previous data mining experience, to integrate data mining into applications quickly and effectively. The Mining Model Wizard guides you through the choice of inputs and outputs for the models, abstracting much of the complexity of the algorithms. At the same time, several algorithm parameters are exposed, allowing more advanced users to tweak the models by changing parameter values from their specified defaults.

 Note Some of the terms introduced here might be new to you. Rest assured that they will be explained thoroughly over the course of the chapter.

Why Mine Your Data?

The ability of businesses to gather and store data has increased exponentially over the past 30 years. Organizations are increasingly building data mining into their business analysis strategies because data mining offers powerful tools for detecting critical patterns within vast (and usually growing) stores of available data. For example, customer service organizations can identify peak calling hours and schedule staff work hours accordingly. Retail companies can better understand which products are selling well in different geographic regions and can optimize their supply chains in response. Food service companies can observe which perishable food products might spoil before being used and therefore arrange for later deliveries. And clinical medical data can be analyzed to determine demographic factors (such as age, gender, and ethnicity) that might be associated with treatment side effects or reduced treatment effectiveness.

In short, data mining is becoming a key step on the path from business data to business knowledge. Data mining helps you act on your data rather than just maintain it. Figure 18-1 depicts the components of a fully developed data mining infrastructure and the members of the Microsoft business intelligence (BI) "stack" that comprise each of these components.

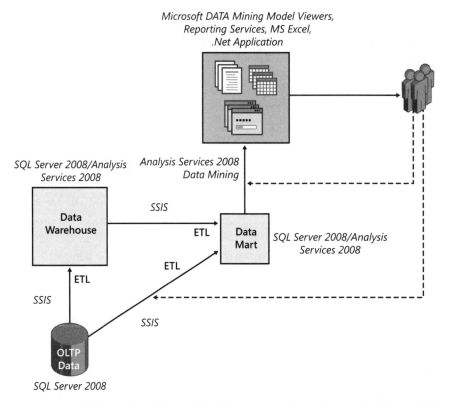

FIGURE 18-1 A fully developed data mining infrastructure using tools from the Microsoft BI "stack"

Let's discuss these components a little bit. Most data mining processes start with raw data, most likely from a conventional, relational online transaction processing (OLTP) system. Typically, the data used for data mining projects has not been collected explicitly for the purpose of mining—instead, it has been collected during the normal course of business.

Next comes the arduous task of cleaning and transforming the data so that it is in a state suitable for analysis. This is the extract, transform, and load (ETL) step, where you can bring together data from multiple systems into a single data warehouse. Next you create a task-driven or content-driven data mart for the specific data analysis task at hand. This is the data to be mined. Figure 18-1 shows two possible paths to the data mart from your OLTP data: a route through a data warehouse and a direct route, in which you forego the creation of a data warehouse. Either way, SQL Server Integration Services can get you there. Integration Services offers a complete tool set for extracting data from source systems, manipulating the data into a format suitable for mining, and saving the data into a data warehouse or data mart.

 More Info   Chapter 14 discusses the topic of data warehousing, and you can learn more about Integration Services at *http://msdn.microsoft.com/en-us/library/ms141026.aspx*.

Using Analysis Services, you can explore and mine your data. The results of the data mining are presented in reports and charts. Business users can then draw new knowledge from the analyses.

Two feedback loops are depicted in Figure 18-1. The feedback loop to the ETL step represents the use of data mining for data validation. By identifying typical data patterns, data mining helps find data anomalies that can be addressed as part of the ETL step. This helps reduce the noise in the data, which in turn improves the quality of analyses based on that data. The feedback loop to the data mining step represents the iterative nature of data mining. Data mining is most effective at generating business knowledge when it is performed as an iterative process. The results from a mining model can be used to refine the analysis population included in the data mart or to tweak the parameters used to estimate a model.

Most important, data mining is a business-driven task. It is commonly defined as the process of finding useful relationships and patterns in large data sets. The relationships and patterns are useful only to the extent that they address a business problem. Some additional examples of business tasks accomplished using data mining include product recommendations or cross-selling, targeted mailing campaigns, fraud detection, customer profiling, forecasting, and data validation. The business task at hand determines the data mining algorithm used. Figure 18-2 shows some common business tasks and the mining algorithms in Analysis Services that are most appropriate for performing each task.

Algorithm Matrix

	Cross-Selling	Targeted Mailing	Fraud Detection	Customer Profiling	Forecasting	Data Validation
Association Rules	✔					
Clustering		✔	✔	✔		✔
Decision Trees		✔		✔		
Linear Regression				✔		
Logistic Regression				✔		
Naïve Bayes		✔		✔		
Neural Nets				✔		
Sequence Clustering				✔		
Time Series					✔	

FIGURE 18-2 The algorithm matrix, showing appropriate mining model algorithms for some common business problems

In his book *Business @ the Speed of Thought,* Bill Gates writes, "The greatest value of data mining will be to help companies determine the right products to build and the right way to price them." The companies that can best determine the "right products" and "right price" will be the companies that can best identify their most likely customers and understand the buying habits of those customers. The power of Analysis Services is that it makes that kind of advanced data mining functionality easily accessible. The tight integration of Analysis Services components with the more traditional database components in Microsoft SQL Server 2008 and the widely used Microsoft Office suite makes data mining available as a natural extension of any BI solution.

A Statistics Refresher

This chapter does not assume in-depth knowledge of statistics, so here are definitions for some basic statistical terms used in the chapter. To get more complete definitions, you can conduct a simple Web search.

- **Mean**   More commonly referred to as "average." The mean is the sum of observed values divided by the count of observations.

- **Median**   The middle value of a set of numbers. Half the numbers in a set have a value greater than the median, and half the numbers have a value less than the median.

- **Standard deviation**   A measure of the dispersion in the data. Specifically, the standard deviation measures how spread out the data values are from the mean.

- **Range**   The difference between the smallest and largest value in a data set.

- **Distribution**   The array of values observed for a particular attribute in your data. Data distributions can often be usefully depicted using histograms or pie charts.

- **Continuous data**   Data whose possible set of values is not countable. Examples are height and age—the more precisely these are measured, the more possible values exist. For example, we are all aging at every fraction of a second.

- **Discrete data**   Data whose values are isolated points or whose possible set of values is countable. Examples are country of residence or marital status. (Data that is continuous can be "discretized" by grouping the possible values into sets. For example, age is continuous but can be discretized by creating groupings such as "Younger than 21," "Age 21 through 50," and "Over 50.")

SQL Server 2008 Data Mining Enhancements

SQL Server 2008 improves on its predecessor in a number of areas, including ease of use, feature richness, sophistication of client tools, and programmability. Several routine data mining tasks have now been built into the data mining component of SQL Server 2008, including the creation of holdout test sets, training and testing mining models on subsets of data, and cross validation of models. Whereas in SQL Server 2005 the creation of holdout test sets had to be done outside the data mining tool, SQL Server 2008 incorporates the creation of a test set within the Data Mining Wizard. The holdout test set is then available when testing and comparing the accuracy of all the mining models in the structure. If a mining model is trained on a specific subset of the data, the same filter can be applied to the test set when it comes time to assess the performance of the model. A Cross Validation tab has been added to the existing Lift Chart and Classification Matrix tabs of the Data Mining Designer Mining Accuracy Chart view. Cross validation of mining models can now be accomplished by specifying a handful of parameters on the Cross Validation tab and then clicking a button to retrieve the results.

Drillthrough functionality has been improved to allow for more flexibility when investigating characteristics of cases used for training and testing. Whereas in SQL Server 2005 only columns included in a mining model were available when drilling through to case details, in SQL Server 2008, any column included in the mining structure can be displayed in the drillthrough. This is useful when you want to see additional information about the drillthrough that isn't relevant to estimating the mining model. For example, it's difficult to imagine a situation where you would want to include identifying information, such as name or ID, about a case in a mining model; however, such identifying information is commonly desired when drilling through to case details.

The Time Series algorithm used in SQL Server Analysis Services 2008 has been enhanced. Most notably, it is now possible to train models using the Autoregressive Integrated Moving Average (ARIMA) algorithm. Previously, the Microsoft Time Series algorithm implemented only the Autoregressive Tree with Cross Prediction (ARTxp) algorithm. By default, Analysis Services takes a weighted approach to the estimation, but it is also possible to specify the weighting of the approaches, including setting the weight to zero for one of the algorithms so that only one or the other algorithm is used. This allows flexibility in specifying whether estimates should be optimized for short-term or long-term predictions.

The data mining add-ins for Microsoft Office Excel 2007 have been updated to reflect the new features in Analysis Services 2008. Better yet, it's now possible to document your mining structures and models using the Data Mining Client add-in for Excel.

We'll point out these new features as we encounter them in the following sections.

Getting Started

Now that you are fired up to mine your data, how do you get started building mining models and using them in your applications? This chapter shows you, by using an example of a customer profitability analysis using the Adventure Works data warehouse sample database, *AdventureWorksDW2008*, that is available for SQL Server 2008. We will create a new Analysis Services database with mining models based on the data and then use scripts that extend the model and query its content.

> **More Info**   Sample databases are no longer included in SQL Server 2008. Instead, they are available from CodePlex (*http://www.CodePlex.com/SqlServerSamples*). The Introduction to this book gives directions on how to download the Adventure Works data warehouse database used in this chapter.

Building on the model and scripts, we'll create sample Microsoft Windows Forms and Microsoft ASP.NET applications that embed similar querying functionality. We'll also load a managed assembly onto the server that implements a data mining query stored procedure, and we'll perform data mining queries by using XML for Analysis (XMLA). Last, we'll go over the data mining add-ins for Excel 2007. Let's start by reviewing the steps required to create a data mining project.

Preparing Your Source Data

The *AdventureWorksDW2008* sample database is a dimensional database with a subset of the data from the normalized OLTP *AdventureWorks2008* sample database. As you might already know, Adventure Works is a fictional bicycle manufacturing company that sells to wholesale customers as well as individual Web customers. Detailed demographic data is available for the individual customers, including income, marital status, number of children, and home ownership. In addition, because the data warehouse is built from a relational database containing data from a transactional order system, it includes detailed data on the buying behavior of customers. This data includes customer tenure, number of products purchased, "recency" of last purchase, types of products purchased, and so on. We want to use this wealth of data to discover detailed information about the customers.

First we'll run the query shown in Listing 18-1, which uses the *NTILE* ranking function that was introduced in SQL Server 2005.

> **More Info**   We cover *NTILE* and the other ranking functions in Chapter 2.

LISTING 18-1 Using the *NTILE* function to analyze data

```
USE AdventureWorksDW2008
GO

SELECT
  count(*) AS NumCustomers
  ,Quartile
  ,min(TotalProfit) AS MinQuartileProfit
  ,max(TotalProfit) AS MaxQuartileProfit
  ,sum(TotalProfit) AS SumQuartileProfit
FROM (SELECT
        Customerkey
        ,ntile(4) OVER(ORDER BY TotalProfit DESC) AS Quartile
        ,TotalProfit
      FROM (SELECT
              Customerkey
              ,sum(SalesAmount)-sum(TotalProductCost) AS TotalProfit
            FROM FactInternetSales
            GROUP BY customerkey) AS c) AS q
GROUP BY Quartile
ORDER BY Quartile
COMPUTE sum(sum(TotalProfit))
GO
```

The query returns the following results:

```
NumCustomers Quartile MinQuartileProfit MaxQuartileProfit SumQuartileProfit
------------ -------- ----------------- ----------------- -----------------
4621         1        1077.4324         5273.81           9149434.8261
4621         2        156.2055          1077.4324         2608879.4859
4621         3        26.4672           156.1322          251766.6393
4621         4        1.4335            26.4672           70802.6937
 sum
--------------------
12080883.645
```

You can see that 25 percent of the customers (Quartile 1) are generating 75 percent of the profit ($9,149,435 divided by $12,080,884 equals 0.757). Who are these customers? Do the high-profit customers fit a certain demographic profile? If so, we could design advertising campaigns geared toward those customers. Or do the customers exhibit certain buying behaviors? Can those high-profit-yielding behaviors be encouraged among more customers? We can use data mining to answer these questions and more.

To start, run the four SQL scripts included in the *Chapter18SQL* project of the SQL Server Management Studio solution included with this chapter's sample code on the book's companion Web site. Execute the four scripts in order: vProfitability.sql, vCustomerProfitability.sql, vCustomerPurchases.sql, and vMonthlyProfit.sql. The scripts add these four views to the *AdventureWorksDW2008* database: *vProfitability*, *vCustomerProfitability*, *vCustomerPurchases*, and *vMonthlyProfit*. The *vCustomerProfitability*, *vCustomerPurchases*, and *vMonthlyProfit* views will be the basis of the mining models we create in this chapter. The *vCustomerProfitability* view has one row for each customer and includes demographic data and summary data about each customer's buying behavior. The *vCustomerPurchases* view has one row per line item for every customer order in the database. The *vMonthlyProfit* view has one row per month from January 2001 through June 2004 along with the total profit per month for each of the Adventure Works regions: North America, Europe, and Pacific. *vProfitability* has one row per customer purchase. The profit associated with each customer purchase is calculated in this view. The view is referenced by *vCustomerProfitability* and *vMonthlyProfit*. *vProfitability* is not referenced directly by any code in this chapter. It is used to simplify the definition of the *vCustomerProfitability* and *vMonthlyProfit* views.

Creating an Analysis Services Project

With our source views created, we are ready to create an Analysis Services project (and database) that will contain our mining models. Typically at this point, we would take our source data and divide it into training and test sets. Previously, we might have done this using the Percentage Sampling Data Flow transformation task in Integration Services. In Analysis Services 2008, however, dividing the source data into training and test sets is now incorporated as a step in the Data Mining Wizard, so we can jump right into creating our Analysis Services project.

> **More Info** A data mining project typically has separate samples for training (building) and test-ing the mining models. Testing the accuracy of a mining model with a sample other than the one on which the model was trained guards against tailoring the model too much to the particular data you have at hand. After all, the true value of data mining lies in how well you can apply the model to new data, not in how well the model tells you about what has already happened.

1. In Microsoft Visual Studio, choose New, Project from the File menu.

2. In the Add New Project dialog box, select the Business Intelligence Projects project type and the Analysis Services Project template. Name the project **Chapter18**. By de-fault, this will also create a solution named *Chapter18*. Figure 18-3 shows the completed dialog box.

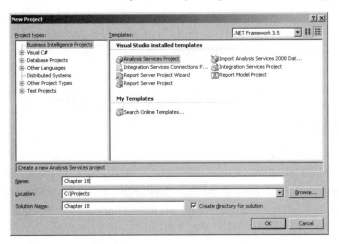

FIGURE 18-3 The New Project dialog box for an Analysis Services project

3. Click OK, and your project will be created.

   As with our cube-containing Analysis Services projects and databases in Chapters 15 and 16, we must define a data source and a data source view in this project.

4. Right-click the Data Sources node in Solution Explorer, and then select New Data Source to open the Data Source Wizard. Click Next and then New to display the Connection Manager dialog box.

5. Specify your provider (.NET Providers or SqlClient Data Provider), server (the local SQL Server instance on which the *AdventureWorksDW2008* database exists), any logon credentials, and the database itself (*AdventureWorksDW2008*). Figure 18-4 shows a completed dialog box. When you have finished, click OK to close the dialog box.

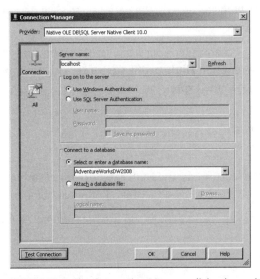

FIGURE 18-4 The Connection Manager dialog box, with the SQL Native Client Provider selected

6. Back in the Data Source Wizard, click Next. On the Impersonation Information page, select the Inherit option (the last one in the list), and then click Next again. Name the data source **AdventureWorksDW2008**, and then click Finish.

Using the Data Mining Wizard and Data Mining Structure Designer

As mentioned in Chapter 15, adding a data source to the solution is akin to creating a database connection. We still need to create a data source view to specify the objects from the *AdventureWorksDW2008* database that we want to use to create our mining models. To do this, right-click the Data Source Views node in Solution Explorer, and then select New Data Source View from the shortcut menu to open the Data Source View Wizard.

Click Next on the Welcome page, and then click Next again on the Select A Data Source page, making sure that the *AdventureWorksDW2008* data source you just created is selected. On the Select Tables And Views page, move the *vCustomerProfitability* view from the Available Objects list to the Included Objects list. You might need to scroll to the bottom of the Available Objects list in order to see the view because the tables are listed before views in the list. Click Next, name your data source view **CustomerProfitability**, and then click Finish.

For the customer profitability analysis, we want to determine the common characteristics of high-profit and low-profit customers. To do this, we must add a calculated column to our data source view that defines "high profit." We don't want to store this in our database because it is a definition specific to the analysis we are doing.

To create a calculated column in the data source view, take the following steps:

1. Right-click the *vCustomerProfitability* view on the data source view design tab, and then choose New Named Calculation.

2. In the Named Calculation dialog box, give your named calculation the name **ProfitCategory**, type the description **High-profit customers in the top quartile of profit**, and type the following in the Expression box:

```
CASE
  WHEN Profit > 1077 THEN 'High'
  ELSE 'Low'
END
```

This creates two categories of customers: the High category for customers in the top quartile of profit amounts and the Low category for all other customers.

3. Click OK. You will see your newly created column in the data source view with a calculator icon to the left of it.

Now we'll browse the data within the data source view:

1. Right-click vCustomerProfitability, and then choose Explore Data. The Data Explorer window opens. Scroll to the rightmost column of the table. You will see the named calculation you just created. It will look no different from any other column of your table.

   You can choose to view either the top *x* rows in your table or a random sample of *x* rows from your table. (The value of *x* is configurable.) By default, the Data Explorer window shows data for the top 5000 rows in your data source. (The exact meaning of "top" will vary, depending on how the data is sorted in your table.)

2. To change this default, click the Sampling Options button (the one with the properties icon) in the upper-right corner of the window. This opens the Data Exploration Options dialog box.

3. Click the Random Sample option, leaving the Sample Count at 5000, and then click OK.

4. To implement this configuration change and see the data for your random sample of records from *vCustomerProfitability*, you must refresh the data. To do so, click the Resample Data button (the one with the refresh icon) in the upper-right corner of the Data Explorer window.

Using the other tabs in the Data Explorer window, you can create PivotTables and charts or simple data distribution charts. To use the distribution chart feature, follow these steps:

1. Click the Chart tab.

   By default, column charts are displayed for a subset of the columns in your data source view. You can click anywhere on the drop-down control at the top of the window to modify the view to display charts for any combination of columns from your table.

2. Select the *ProfitCategory* column from the drop-down list, and either press Enter or click the Chart tab (or click anywhere in the chart area) to close the column list. A column chart for Profit Category should appear alongside the other charts.

3. You can change the chart type to a (horizontal) bar chart or a pie chart. To change your column charts to pie charts, click the pie chart button in the upper-left corner of the Data Explorer window, or right-click a blank area of the chart and then choose Pie Chart. Figure 18-5 shows pie charts of several customer characteristics.

   You can see details about the data represented by a particular item on the Chart tab by hovering the mouse pointer over the item. For example, hovering over a pie slice shows you the count and percentage of records that are represented by that slice (as shown in Figure 18-5).

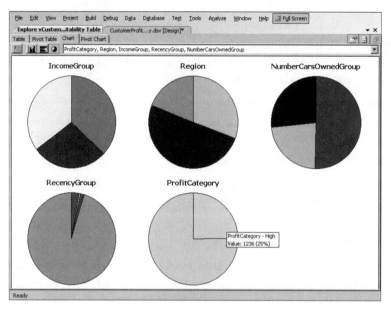

FIGURE 18-5 The Chart tab of the Data Explorer window, which allows you to see how your data is distributed

Data Explorer allows you to see the distribution of your data quickly and easily without writing a single line of code. This can be useful during the startup phase of your data mining project, before any models have been created.

Creating a Mining Structure

Mining models in Analysis Services are contained within *mining structures*. A mining structure consists of a subset of columns from your data source view and one or more mining models that use the columns. The content type of each column is set separately by the mining model—for each mining model in your mining structure, you specify whether the column is a key, an input, or a predictable column. (We'll discuss the content types in more detail later.)

Because you can also indicate that a column in the structure should be ignored for a particular mining model, you can conceivably have two mining models within the same structure that do not share any input or predictable columns. But it makes more sense to group, under the same structure, mining models that answer the same business question and that have some commonality in columns from your data source view. This is because mining models created within the same structure can be compared using the Mining Accuracy Chart functionality of Analysis Services, which we will examine shortly. Furthermore, mining models that share a structure are processed in parallel, with a single pass through the data.

Getting back to our data mining goals, we want to know whether particular characteristics or buying behaviors can help us predict who the high-profit customers are. We also want to cluster customers according to their demographic characteristics and buying behaviors. To that end, we will use the Data Mining Editor in Visual Studio to create a mining structure with models that use the Clustering, Decision Tree, and Naïve Bayes algorithms. (Later we will discuss how each of these algorithms works, how they differ from each other, and their appropriate use for specific prediction scenarios.)

Creating a Mining Model

To create the initial mining model, follow these steps:

1. Right-click the Mining Structures node in Solution Explorer, and then choose New Mining Structure to open the Mining Structure Wizard.

2. On the Welcome page, click Next.

3. On the Select The Definition Method page, select From Existing Relational Database Or Data Warehouse, and then click Next.

4. On the Create The Data Mining Structure page, you can select a data mining technique for your initial mining model, or you can choose to create a mining structure with no mining models. (In the 2005 version of Analysis Services, the wizard required you to specify an initial mining model when the mining structure was created.) After the mining structure is created, you can add mining models to the structure. Select Microsoft Clustering from the drop-down list, and then click Next.

5. On the Select Data Source View page, select the data source view that you created earlier, and then click Next.

6. On the Specify Table Types page, you will see vCustomerProfitability from your data source view along with check boxes for specifying the table type. Select the Case check box next to vCustomerProfitability, and then click Next.

Tables for Mining Models

Analysis Services has two types of tables for use in mining models: *case tables* and *nested tables*. Every mining structure must have a case table. Simply put, the case table defines the entities to be analyzed for your mining model. In the customer profitability analysis, the basic unit of analysis is the customer; therefore, we will define *vCustomerProfitability*, which has one row per customer, as the case table. Nested tables are used to provide additional detail about your cases. Not every mining structure will have a nested table. For now, our mining structure will have only a case table. Later in this chapter, we will extend the profitability models by including the types of purchases customers made. We will do that using a nested table.

7. On the Specify The Training Data page, you will see a list of all the columns in your case table. To the right of each column is a set of three check boxes for specifying whether each column is a Key, an Input, or a Predictable column in your model, as shown in Figure 18-6.

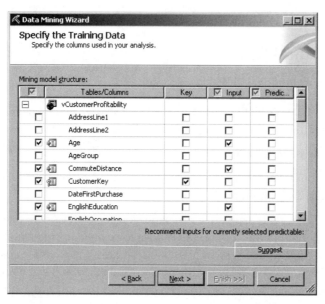

FIGURE 18-6 The Data Mining Wizard Specify The Training Data page

The Key column uniquely identifies each record in your case table. Input columns form the basis on which data pattern discoveries are made, whether they be descriptive or predictive patterns. For example, the clustering algorithm creates clusters based on the values of the input columns. The Decision Trees algorithm decides tree splits based on how well the values of an input column predict a particular outcome.

Predictive and Descriptive Mining Models

From a technical standpoint, marking a column as predictable means that it can be selected from the model in a Data Mining Extensions (DMX) prediction query. (We'll discuss prediction queries in greater detail later in this chapter.) This is true of the predictable columns in any mining model, even those that do not have prediction as a goal. This definition doesn't really convey what predictable columns are for. For a common-sense definition, we need to distinguish between *predictive* and *descriptive* mining models.

Predictive mining models are designed to forecast (predict) the value of their predictable columns. For descriptive mining models, predicted columns have a technical usage, and that usage varies. In a clustering model, input columns are used to determine the clusters. Selecting only the Predict check box for a column means that the column will not be used to determine the clusters; however, including the column as a predictable column in the model allows you to view its distribution within each cluster and compare its distribution across clusters after the model has been processed.

8. Back on the Specify The Training Data page, select *CustomerKey* as the Key column of your case table and select the Input check box for the following columns: *Age, CommuteDistance, EnglishEducation, Gender, HasKidsAtHome, IncomeGroup, IsCarOwner, IsHomeOwner, IsNewCustomer, MaritalStatus, NumProdGroup, RecencyGroup*, and *Region*.

9. Select the Predict check box for the *ProfitCategory* column, and then click Next.

10. On the Specify Columns' Data Type And Content page, click Detect.

This forces Analysis Services to determine whether your input and predictable columns are discrete (categorical) or continuous. You can also modify the content and data type by clicking in the cell and selecting the type from the drop-down list that appears, as shown in Figure 18-7.

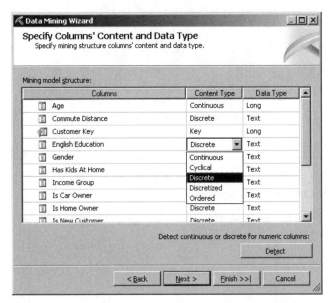

FIGURE 18-7 Content and data types of columns specified at the mining structure level in the Data Mining Wizard

11. Verify that the content type is Continuous for the *Age* column, Key for the *CustomerKey* column, and Discrete for all other columns, and then click Next.

12. This brings us to the new Split Data Into Training And Test Sets page. Before SQL Server 2008, training and test sets would have been created prior to creating the Analysis Services project using a tool such as the Percentage Sampling Data Flow transformation task in Integration Services. Now, dividing the source data into training and test sets is incorporated as a step in the Data Mining Wizard. By default, the percentage of test cases is set at 30. This means that 70 percent of your records would be used to train the mining models, and 30 percent would be used to test the models. Set the maximum number of test cases to 5000. This means that 30 percent of the sample, up to 5000 cases, will be used for the test set. The Create Testing Set page should be configured as shown in Figure 18-8. Click Next.

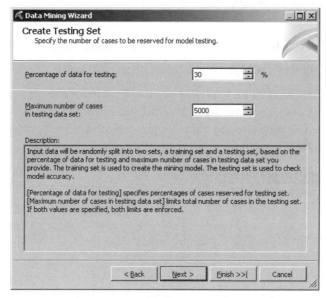

FIGURE 18-8 Splitting the data into training and test sets, now part of the Data Mining Wizard

13. Name the mining structure **CustomerProfitCategory** and the mining model **CustomerProfitCategory_CL**, and then click Finish.

This brings us to the Mining Structure tab of the data mining structure designer, as shown in Figure 18-9.

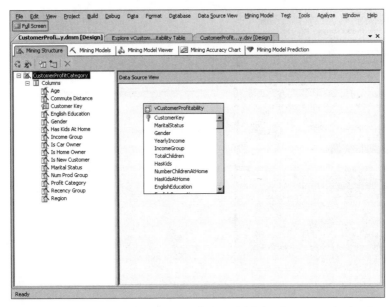

FIGURE 18-9 The data mining structure designer's Mining Structure tab, showing the columns in the mining structure

The left pane of the tab contains a tree view display of our mining structure. From here, you can add and delete columns and nested tables by using the tab's toolbar or by right-clicking anywhere in the tree view pane (on the left) and selecting options from the shortcut menu. The Data Source View pane (on the right) allows you to explore and edit the data source view.

Important   To match the results shown in the figures, you must set the parameters for splitting the sample exactly as specified in the text. Analysis Services splits the source data into training and test sets *randomly*. If a different holdout seed is specified, or if a different number or percentage of test cases is requested, the results of the mining models will not be identical because a different set of cases would have been used to train the models. Of course if the models are robust, the nature of the results should be similar across different random samples—they just won't be an exact match with the examples you see here.

14. For your results to match those shown in the screen shots, the seed used to generate the random training and test sets must be the same as that used for the example in this book. Locate the *HoldoutSeed* property in the Visual Studio Properties pane for the mining structure, and set the value to 1, as shown in Figure 18-10.

FIGURE 18-10 The *HoldoutSeed* property set in the Visual Studio Properties pane of the mining structure

Editing and Adding Mining Models

With your mining structure and first mining model created, you are ready to create additional models within the structure. On the Mining Models tab of the data mining structure designer, you can view the definition of your mining model, as shown in Figure 18-11. You will see the columns in your mining structure configured according to the choices you previously made for how those columns should be used in your clustering model.

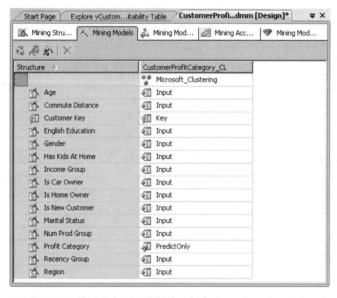

FIGURE 18-11 The Mining Model tab, which shows how the mining structure columns are used in each mining model

Editing a Mining Model

You can also edit the definition of your mining model from the Mining Model tab. Profit Category is specified as a PredictOnly column in the mining model. We want to change the usage type from PredictOnly to Predict. To edit column usage, take these steps:

1. On the Mining Models tab of the data mining structure designer, click the cell next to Profit Category.

2. In the drop-down list that appears, change the column usage to Predict, as shown in Figure 18-12.

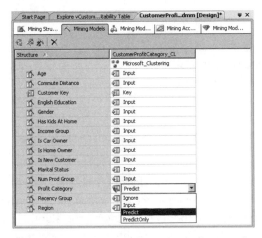

FIGURE 18-12 Clicking a cell next to a column to change its usage in a mining model

Changing the column usage from PredictOnly to Predict allows the customer profit category to be a factor in how the clusters are determined, and not just a descriptive characteristic analyzed after the fact.

Adding a Mining Model

By default, the Microsoft Clustering algorithm creates 10 clusters from your training data. As a thoughtful data analyst, you might be concerned that users will have trouble grasping the nuances of the differences in so many clusters. You might therefore want to create a second clustering model that segments your customers into only five clusters. To do that, follow these steps:

1. Right-click anywhere on the Mining Models tab, and then choose New Mining Model.

2. In the New Mining Model dialog box, type **CustomerProfitCategory_CL5** in the Model Name text box, select Microsoft Clustering from the Algorithm Name drop-down list, and then click OK. A new mining model is added to the right of the existing model.

3. To change the number of clusters created from 10 to 5, right-click the *CustomerProfit Category_CL5* column header or any of its column cells, and then choose Set Algorithm Parameters.

4. In the Algorithm Parameters dialog box that appears, shown in Figure 18-13, you can set algorithm parameters that are specific to the selected mining model.

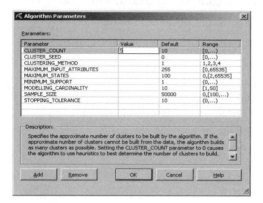

FIGURE 18-13 The Algorithm Parameters dialog box for a Microsoft Clustering model

This can be a bit perplexing at first because the designers abstract much of the complexity of data mining through their user interface (UI) and wizards. Meanwhile, the dialog box allows you to fine tune your model by changing the algorithm parameters from their specific defaults. Click the various parameters in the parameter list, and review the descriptions in the Description area below.

5 When you've finished exploring the parameters, click the cell at the intersection of the *CLUSTER_COUNT* row and the Value column, type 5, and then click OK.

Adding a Model That Uses a Different Algorithm

We now have two clustering models in our mining structure. To validate the accuracy of one model in a mining structure, it is often helpful to create an additional model using a different algorithm. We'll add a new model using the Decision Trees algorithm. This can be done with surprisingly little effort:

1. Right-click anywhere on the Mining Models tab, and then choose New Mining Model.

2. In the New Mining Model dialog box, name your model **CustomerProfitCategory_DT**, select the Decision Trees algorithm (it should be selected by default), and then click OK.

The *CustomerProfitCategory_DT* model appears to the right of the existing clustering models with the same columns and usage.

Changing Column Usage

Adding the model is helpful, but it would be even better if we could use it to predict the number of products people buy (in addition to the predicting profit category). To change the column usage for *NumProductGroup* in the *CustomerProfitCategory_DT* mining model, click the cell corresponding to *NumProductGroup* under *CustomerProfitCategory_DT*, and then select Predict from the drop-down list. By setting the content type of *both* the *ProfitCategory* and the *NumProdGroup* variables to Predict, we are allowing each to be an input in the decision tree of the other. If we had instead set the content type of the *NumProdGroup* to PredictOnly, the number of products purchased would not be a factor in creating the *ProfitCategory* decision tree—that is, the number of products purchased would not be considered in the splits of the *ProfitCategory* tree.

> **More Info** *Splits* are the branches at each node of a decision tree. Each node of a decision tree represents a subset of the population. This subset is characterized by the parentage of the node. Splits at each node are determined by identifying the input characteristic by which the distribution of the predicted variable differs most for the subset defined at that node. When the distribution of the predicted variable at a node does not vary significantly by any input characteristic, there are no further splits, and the branch ends. A node from which there are no splits is referred to as a *leaf*.

Mining Models and Data Types

Let's continue building our mining structure by adding another model, this time using the Naïve Bayes algorithm:

1. Right-click the *CustomerProfitCategory_CL* model, and then choose New Mining Model.

2. Name your model **CustomerProfitCategory_NB**, select the Naïve Bayes algorithm, and then click OK.

   A message box will appear explaining that the *Age* column will be ignored because the Naïve Bayes algorithm does not support working with continuous columns. Click Yes. Notice that the content type for the *Age* column is set to *Ignore*, the content type for the *NumProd* column is set to *Input*, and the content type for the *ProfitCategory* column is set to *Predict*. For this model, we want to predict only *ProfitCategory*, so no content type modifications are necessary.

> **Important** Because we created the Naïve Bayes model by right-clicking the *CustomerProfitCategory_CL* model and choosing New Mining Model, the *CustomerProfitCategory_CL* content type settings were used in the new model, making *ProfitCategory* the only predicted column. Had we instead right-clicked the *CustomerProfitCategory_DT* model and chosen New Mining Model, that model's content type settings would have been used, and *NumProdGroup*, in addition to *ProfitCategory*, would have been a predicted column.

We mentioned earlier that age is ignored in the Naïve Bayes model because age is a continuous variable. If age is a significant determinant of whether a customer is a high-profit or low-profit customer, the Naïve Bayes model will appear to perform worse than other models where age is included. Therefore, we want to include at least some indication of age in the Naïve Bayes model. To do that, we must add a "discretized" version of the age column to our mining structure and include it in our Naïve Bayes model.

1. Previously, mining structure columns could be added only from the Mining Structure tab. In Analysis Services 2008, a column can be added to the structure from the Mining Models tab. Right-click anywhere in the Structure column on the Mining Models tab, and then choose Add A Column.

2. In the Select A Column dialog box, shown in Figure 18-14, select the *AgeGroup* column in the Source Column list, and then click OK to add *AgeGroup* to the mining structure.

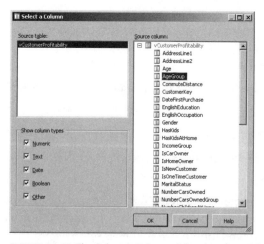

FIGURE 18-14 The Select A Column dialog box for adding a column to your mining structure

> **Note** The *AgeGroup* column in *vCustomerProfitability* categorizes customers into groups such as "Under 30," "Age 30 through 35," and "Age 36 through 45" by using a *CASE* statement. Analysis Services also has a column content type called "discretized" that can be used to categorize a continuous attribute. A discussion of this functionality is beyond the scope of this chapter, but you can read more about it by searching on "discretization" in SQL Server Books Online.

3. You will see that *AgeGroup* appears in the mining structure, although its usage is set to Ignore in all of the defined models. To include it in the Naïve Bayes model, click in the cell corresponding to the *AgeGroup* column under the Naïve Bayes model, and then change the usage to Input.

Filtering a Mining Model

Often you might want to estimate a mining model for only a particular subset of data or to estimate models separately based on a particular characteristic. For example, suppose that we are planning to launch an ad campaign restricted to customers in North America. In order to design the campaign most effectively, we want to gain a better understanding of the high-profit customers in North America, and because of this, we want to estimate a mining model only for our North American customers. Let's see how filtered mining models, new in SQL Server 2008, enable us to do that:

1. Right-click the *CustomerProfitCategory_DT* mining model, and then choose New Mining Model. In the Add New Model dialog box, name the model **CustomerProfitCategory_ DT_NorthAmerica**, verify that the Algorithm Name selected is Microsoft Decision Trees, and then click OK.

2. In the properties pane, select CustomerProfitCategory_DT_NorthAmerica from the drop-down list, and locate the Filter property for this mining model. Click in the empty cell corresponding to the Filter property to reveal the ellipsis button, and then click the button to display the Model Filter dialog box.

3. Select Region from the Mining Structure Column drop-down list, and then type **North America** in the value cell. The completed dialog box is shown in Figure 18-15. Click OK. The *CustomerProfitCategory_DT_NorthAmerica* model will be trained using only records where the Region is North America.

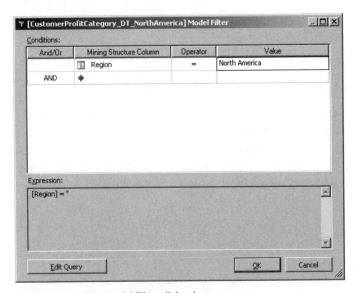

FIGURE 18-15 The Model Filter dialog box

The benefit of filtered mining models in SQL Server 2008 is most apparent when you consider the situation where you want to estimate separate mining models for many different groups. For example, it could be that region is not simply a determinant of customer profitability, but rather the determinants of customer profitability differ across regions. In that case, you would want to estimate separate mining models by region. SQL Server 2008 makes this easy. Whereas in SQL Server 2005 you would have to add a separate table, view, or named query to your data source view and create a separate mining structure for each region, in SQL Server 2008, you simply have to configure the filter property for each mining model. The filtered mining models can all reside in a single data mining structure.

Your Mining Models tab should appear as shown in Figure 18-16.

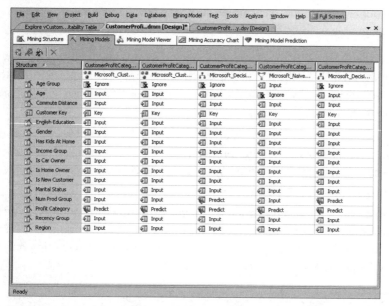

FIGURE 18-16 A mining structure with several mining models

Deploying and Processing Data Mining Objects

We have done a good bit of work already, having defined a mining structure with several mining models. We are almost ready to view and query the models, but we must first deploy and process the Analysis Services database that contains them. We can deploy the database and process the mining models in a single step by choosing the Start Debugging command from the Debug menu, clicking the Start Debugging (play) toolbar button, or pressing the F5 key.

Caution The Visual Studio solution included with this chapter's sample code is configured so that the Start Debugging toolbar options and menu commands will *not* automatically deploy the *Chapter18* Analysis Services project. We took this precaution to keep you from unwittingly deploying the database when debugging the Windows Forms and ASP.NET client applications included in the same solution. If you are working with the sample code and want to deploy the Analysis Services database and process its mining models, simply right-click the Chapter18 project node in Solution Explorer, and then choose the Deploy command.

Deployment and processing might take several minutes. You can monitor deployment progress in the Deployment Progress window, which appears by default as a docked window in the lower-right corner of Visual Studio when you start the deployment. If the Deployment Progress window is not visible, you can show it by choosing Show Deployment Progress from the View menu or by right-clicking the project node and choosing Show Deployment Progress in Solution Explorer.

It is easiest to monitor the progress of the deployment and processing of your mining structure and models by undocking the Deployment Progress window and enlarging it to a convenient size.

Tip The easiest way to undock the Deployment Progress window is to double-click its title bar. You can redock it after processing has completed by double-clicking the title bar a second time. This avoids the tedious drag-and-drop procedure for undocking and redocking the window.

After deployment, Visual Studio displays the Process Progress window while the data mining objects are processed. Figure 18-17 shows the Process Progress window for a successfully deployed and processed Analysis Services project.

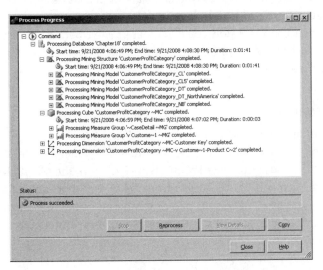

FIGURE 18-17 The Process Progress window after a successful deploying and processing the data mining objects

Caution If you encounter processing errors indicating that columns of your data source do not exist, you might need to change the impersonation information of the data source in your Analysis Services project. To do this, double-click the data source node under the Data Sources node in Solution Explorer, click the Impersonation Information tab, and then select an appropriate user. During development, you can select the Use The Service Account option. Before deploying the database and mining models to production, however, you should select a specific user account with the appropriate rights.

After the initial deployment of the Analysis Services database, you can process mining models without deploying the database. To process all the mining models within a structure, choose Process Mining Structure And All Models from the Mining Model menu. To process a single model in a mining structure, select the model on the Mining Models tab, and then choose Process Model from the Mining Model menu. Both the Process Mining Structure And All Models command and the Process Model command are also available from each model's shortcut menu on the Mining Models tab and from the two leftmost buttons on that tab's toolbar.

Viewing Mining Models

Analysis Services provides algorithm-specific mining model viewers within Visual Studio Analysis Services projects (and in SQL Server Management Studio—more on that later) that greatly ease the otherwise daunting task of interpreting a model's contents, observed patterns, and correlations. The visualization tools provided by the viewers thus make data mining accessible to a larger audience than do traditional data mining products.

Take clustering, for example, which is used to create subsets (clusters) of your data that share common characteristics. Imagine trying to digest the implications of a clustering model with 10 customer clusters defined on 8, 10, or 12 characteristics. How would you figure out the identifying characteristics of each cluster? How could you determine whether the resulting clusters are similar or dissimilar? The Microsoft Cluster Viewer makes it extremely easy to answer such questions. Let's see how.

Using the Cluster Viewer

After you have deployed and processed all of the mining models in the *CustomerProfitCategory* mining structure, you will be brought to the Mining Model Viewer tab. If it's not already selected, choose CustomerProfitCategory_CL from the Mining Model drop-down list. Then choose Microsoft Cluster Viewer from the Viewer drop-down list. The Cluster Viewer offers four ways to view the results of a clustering model: Cluster Diagram, Cluster Profiles, Cluster Characteristics, and Cluster Discrimination. A separate tab is provided for each of these visualization tools.

Cluster Diagram

The Cluster Diagram tab of the Cluster Viewer displays a diagram in which each "bubble" represents a cluster from the model. The cluster diagram uses color coding to indicate data density: the darker the bubble, the more records that cluster contains. You control the actual variable and value indicated by the shading by using the Shading Variable and State drop-down lists; you can select any input or predictable column. For example, if you select ProfitCategory from the Shading Variable drop-down list and select High from the State drop-down list, the diagram will configure itself so that darker clusters contain a greater number of high-profit customers relative to lighter ones, as shown in Figure 18-18.

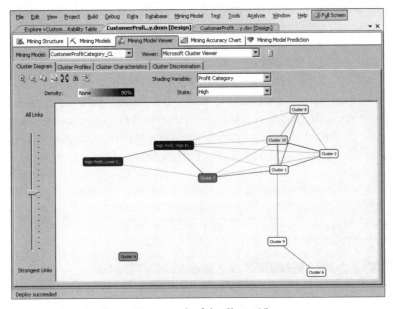

FIGURE 18-18 The Cluster Diagram tab of the Cluster Viewer

> **Note** The cluster numbers you see should match those described in the chapter text and figures. There is, however, some inherent randomness in how the Microsoft Clustering algorithm determines the clusters, and this might cause your numbering to differ from the numbering seen in the text and the figures. Even if your exact cluster numbers differ, you should still see the qualitative results described in the text.

The darkest bubbles are 3, 5, and 7—these are the clusters with a relatively large concentration of high-profit customers. Hovering the mouse pointer over a cluster displays the exact percentage of customers in that cluster who are in the high-profit category. Now select IncomeGroup from the Shading Variable drop-down list and select High from the State drop-down list. The clusters 7, 8, and 3 should now be the darkest bubbles. Select IsCarOwner from the Shading Variable drop-down list and N from the State drop-down list. The darkest clusters should now be 4, 6, and 5.

By examining the cluster characteristics in this manner, we can assign more meaningful names to the clusters. You can rename a cluster by right-clicking the cluster in the diagram and choosing Rename. In fact, let's do that now. Right-click cluster 3 and rename it **High Profit, High Income, Car Owner**, and then right-click cluster 5 and rename it **High Profit, Lower Income, Less Likely Car Owner**.

The clusters are arranged in the diagram according to their similarity. The shorter and darker the line connecting the bubbles, the more similar the clusters. By default, all links are shown in the diagram. By using the slider to the left of the diagram, you can remove weaker links and identify which clusters are the most similar.

Cluster Profiles

The Cluster Profiles tab, shown in Figure 18-19, displays the distribution of input and predictable variables for each customer cluster and for the entire population of customers. This tab is particularly useful for getting an overall picture of the clusters created by the mining model. Using the cluster profiles, you can easily compare attributes across clusters and analyze cluster attributes relative to the model's full data population.

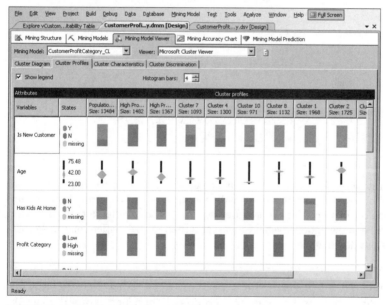

FIGURE 18-19 The Cluster Profiles tab of the Cluster Viewer

The distribution of discrete attributes is shown using a colored bar. By default, the Cluster Profiles tab shows the four most common categories in the population with all others grouped into a fifth category. You can change the number of categories by increasing or decreasing the number in the Histogram Bars text box. Go to the row showing the *IncomeGroup* attribute, and then scroll to the right to see how the distribution of *IncomeGroup* varies across the clusters. Compare the histogram bar between the population *High Profit, High Income, Car Owner* and *High Profit, Lower Income, Less Likely Car Owner* clusters. (You might need to click the Refresh Viewer Content button at the top of the Mining Model Viewer tab in order to see the new names of your clusters.) The histogram bar for the population is divided into three relatively equal segments because the population has relatively equal numbers of customers in the high, moderate, and low income groups. In contrast, the High Income segment of the histogram bar for the *High Profit, High Income, Car Owner* cluster is larger than the other income segments for that cluster because it has relatively more customers that are in the High Income group. The High Income segment of the histogram bar for the *High Profit, Lower Income, Less Likely Car Owner* cluster is virtually indiscernible. If you hover your mouse pointer over the histogram bar, however, you can see that the High Income segment comprises 0.3 percent of the bar.

The distribution of continuous characteristics is shown using a bar and diamond chart. Go to the row showing the age attribute. The black bar represents the range of ages in the cluster, with the median age at the midpoint of the bar. The midpoint of the diamond represents the average age of the customers in the cluster. The standard deviation (a statistical measure of how spread out the data is) of age for the cluster is indicated by the size of the diamond. Compare the diamond chart between the population and the *High Profit, High Income, Car Owner* and *High Profit, Lower Income, Less Likely Car Owner* clusters. The higher and flatter diamond for the *High Profit, High Income, Car Owner* cluster indicates that customers in that cluster are relatively older than customers in the total population and that the age variation in the cluster is less than customers in the total population. You can hover the mouse pointer over the diamond chart to see the precise average age and standard deviation represented by the chart.

By default, the cluster characteristics are shown alphabetically from top to bottom. Locate the cluster you renamed *High Profit, High Income, Car Owner*, and click its column heading. The cluster attributes will be reordered according to the characteristics that most differentiate it from the total population. Click the cluster you renamed *High Profit, Lower Income, Less Likely Car Owner* to see how the order of the characteristics changes.

Initially, clusters are ordered by size from left to right. You can change the order of the clusters by dragging and dropping clusters to the desired location. Figure 18-19 shows the cluster attributes ordered by importance for the *High Profit, High Income, Car Owner* cluster and the clusters ordered by percentage of customers in the high-profit category.

Cluster Characteristics

The Cluster Characteristics tab lets you examine the attributes of a particular cluster. By default, attributes for the model's entire data population are shown. To see the attributes of a particular cluster instead, you can select one from the Cluster drop-down list. For example, if you select the *High Profit, High Income, Car Owner* cluster, the attributes will be reordered according to probability that they appear in that cluster, as shown in Figure 18-20.

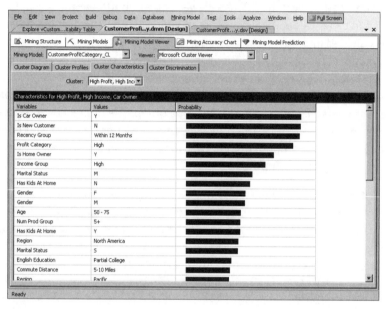

FIGURE 18-20 The Cluster Characteristics tab of the Cluster Viewer

The attribute with the highest probability in this cluster is that of being a car owner—in other words, there is a 96 percent chance that a customer in this cluster is a car owner.

Cluster Discrimination

The Cluster Discrimination tab is most useful for comparing two clusters and understanding what most distinguishes them. Select High Profit, High Income, Car Owner from the Cluster 1 drop-down list and High Profit, Lower Income, Less Likely Car Owner from the Cluster 2 drop-down list. The attributes that are most important in differentiating the two clusters are shown by order of importance. A bar indicates the cluster in which you are more likely to find the particular attribute, and the size of the bar indicates the importance of the attribute. As you can see from Figure 18-21, the two most important distinguishing attributes of the selected clusters are the high-income and low-income groups.

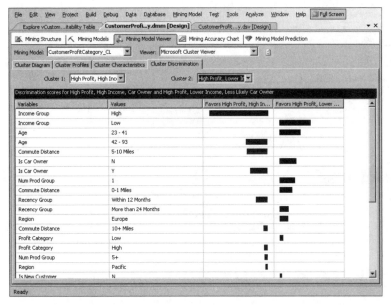

FIGURE 18-21 The Cluster Discrimination tab of the Cluster Viewer

We've covered the Cluster Viewer and its constituent tabs in depth, but don't forget that we have mining models in our mining structure that use the Decision Trees and Naïve Bayes algorithms rather than the Clustering algorithm. We need to also understand how to use the Microsoft Tree Viewer and the Naïve Bayes Viewer—the respective viewers for these models.

Using the Tree Viewer

To view the results of the Decision Trees model, select CustomerProfitCategory_DT from the Mining Model drop-down list. This will display the Microsoft Tree Viewer. The Tree Viewer offers two views of the results from the model estimation: a decision tree and a dependency network view. A separate tree is created for each predictable variable in the decision tree view. You can select the tree to view using the Tree drop-down list. In our model, we have two trees, one for predicting customer profitability and one for predicting the number of products purchased.

Decision Tree

Select ProfitCategory from the Tree drop-down list to reveal the tree for that variable. The Tree Viewer provides a sideways view of a decision tree with the root node at the far left. Decision trees branch, or split, at each node according to the attribute that is most important for determining the predictable column at that node. By inference, this means that the first split shown from the root All node is the most important characteristic for determining the profitability of a customer. As shown in Figure 18-22, the first split in the *ProfitCategory* tree is premised on whether the customer is a new customer.

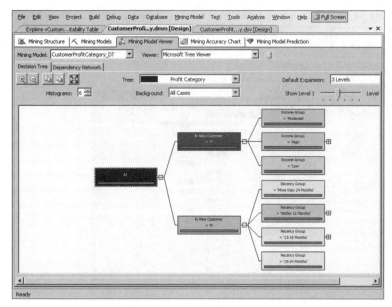

FIGURE 18-22 The Decision Tree tab of the Tree Viewer

The Tree Viewer shows a bar chart of the *ProfitCategory* at each node of the tree and uses the background shading of a node to indicate the concentration of cases in that node. By default, the shading of the tree nodes indicates the percentage of the population at that node. The shading is controlled by the selection in the Background drop-down list, where you can select a specific value for the *ProfitCategory* variable instead of the entire population. If the predictable variable is continuous rather than discrete, there will be a diamond chart in each node of the tree indicating the mean, median, standard deviation, and range of the predictable variable.

By default, up to three levels of the tree are shown. You can change the default by using the Default Expansion drop-down list. A change here changes the default for *all* decision trees viewed in the structure. To view more levels for the tree without changing the default, use the Level slider or expand individual branches of a tree by clicking the plus sign at the branch's node. A node with no plus sign is a leaf node, which means that it has no child branches and therefore cannot be expanded. Branches end when there are no remaining input attributes that help determine the value of the predictable variable at that node. The length of various branches in the tree varies because they are data dependent.

Dependency Network

The Dependency Network tab for the *CustomerProfitCategory_DT* model is shown in Figure 18-23. Each bubble in the dependency network represents a predictable variable or an attribute that determined a split in the decision tree for a predictable variable. Arrows connecting the attributes indicate the direction of the relationship between the variables.

An arrow *to* an attribute indicates that it is predicted, and an arrow *from* an attribute indicates that it is a predictor. The double-headed arrow connecting Profit Category and Num Prod Group indicates that they predict each other—each splits a node in the decision tree of the other. If we had set the usage type of each of these variables to PredictOnly or Input rather than Predict, we would not have been able to make this observation.

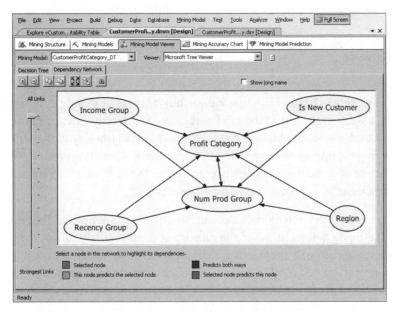

FIGURE 18-23 The Dependency Network tab of the Tree Viewer

Click Profit Category. This activates color coding, as described in the legend below the dependency network, to indicate whether an attribute predicts, or is predicted by, Profit Category. The slider to the left of the dependency network allows you to filter out all but the strongest links between variables. If you move the slider to the bottom, you will see that the strongest predictor of Profit Category is whether the customer is new. Slowly move the slider up. The next bubble to become reddish-orange is Recency Group; this means that the recentness of the last purchase is the second most important predictor of customer profitability after whether the customer is new.

Now move the slider back to the bottom, and click Num Prod Group. The color coding now shows the predictors of that variable instead of Profit Category. Even though no predictors are colored, you can move the slider up slowly and see that the first bubble to become pink is Profit Category, revealing that the most important determinant of the number of products purchased is the profitability of the customer.

Using the Naïve Bayes Viewer

We have yet to view our Naïve Bayes model. To do so, simply select CustomerProfitCategory_ NB from the Mining Model drop-down list, displaying the Naïve Bayes Viewer. The viewer has four tabs: Dependency Network, Attribute Profiles, Attribute Characteristics, and Attribute Discrimination. Our experience with the Cluster Viewer and Tree Viewer will serve us well here because we have encountered slightly different versions of all four of these tabs in those two viewers.

Dependency Network

The Dependency Network tab of the Naïve Bayes Viewer looks and works the same way as the Dependency Network tab of the Tree Viewer, but it arrives at slightly different conclusions. As before, a slider to the left of the tab filters out all but the strongest determining characteristics of customer profitability. If you move the slider all the way to the bottom and then slowly move it up, you will see that according to the Naïve Bayes model, the most important predictors of customer profitability are whether the customer is a new customer, followed by the number of products the customer purchased.

This differs from the decision tree model's determination of customer profit. That model suggests that after being a new customer, the recency of the last purchase was the most important predictor of customer profitability. This underscores an important point: even though the viewers for the two models use the same visualization technique, each one uses a different algorithm and might indicate slightly different conclusions.

Attribute Profiles, Attribute Characteristics, and Attribute Discrimination

The Attribute Profiles, Attribute Characteristics, and Attribute Discrimination tabs of the Naïve Bayes Viewer are functionally equivalent to the Cluster Profiles, Cluster Characteristics, and Cluster Discrimination tabs of the Cluster Viewer. However, instead of allowing a comparison of the distribution of input attributes across *clusters,* they allow a comparison of the distribution of input attributes across distinct values of the predicted column—in our case, the *Profit Category* column.

Click the Attribute Profiles tab, and then select the Low profit group. As shown in Figure 18-24, according to our Naïve Bayes model, the most important characteristics for predicting whether a customer is a low-profit customer are whether the person is a new customer, the number of products purchased, and the region.

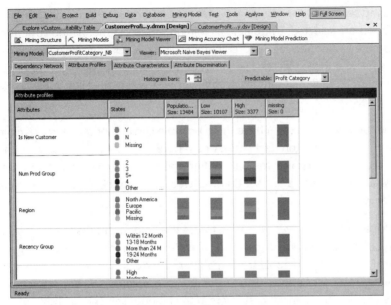

FIGURE 18-24 The Attribute Profiles tab of the Naïve Bayes Viewer

Validating and Comparing Mining Models

We have processed the mining models and analyzed their predictive contents, which, although similar, are not identical. Although it is easy to conclude that being a longtime customer is an important determinant of customer profitability, the models differ somewhat in their conclusions about which other customer characteristics or buying behaviors are important indicators of profitability. Given these differences, how can you determine which of these secondary predictions are correct? You can do so by using the data mining structure designer's built-in "lift charts," classification matrix, and new cross-validation facilities, which make it easy to validate the relative accuracy of the mining models in your mining structure and compare their predictive ability.

Click the Mining Accuracy Chart view. You will be on the Input Selection tab, which has three sections. In the top section, you specify the models, predictable columns, and predictable column values from which lift charts, classification matrices, and cross validation will be performed. In the middle section, you specify the data set that should be used to test your mining models. In the bottom section, you can specify filters for the data set you chose in the middle section.

Starting at the top section of the tab, ensure that the Synchronize Prediction Columns and Values check boxes are selected. By default, all mining models in the mining structure are selected, and no state is specified for the predictable column. Click any cell in the Predict Value column of the grid, and then select the High option from the drop-down list that appears. Because Synchronize Prediction Columns And Values is selected, the High value is selected for all of the models.

In the middle section of the tab, you have three possible choices for the test set: mining model test cases, mining structure test cases, or a different data set. Previously, in Analysis Services 2005, there was no choice: the only option was to specify a different data set. Typically, this would have been a test set that was created using the Random Sampling Task in Integration Services.

In Analysis Services 2008, we have the option to use the holdout set that we created when the mining structure was created; furthermore, if any mining models have filters specified, we can instruct Analysis Services to apply the same filter to the holdout set. To do so, select the Use Mining Model Test Cases option. The *CustomerProfitCategory_DT_NorthAmerica* model will be tested using North American customers in the holdout set. The full holdout set will be used to test all other models in the structure.

Verify that your selections match those shown in Figure 18-25.

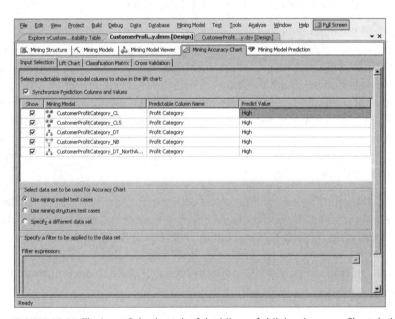

FIGURE 18-25 The Input Selection tab of the Microsoft Mining Accuracy Chart designer.

Now click the Lift Chart tab. After the chart has finished loading, make sure that the Lift Chart option is selected in the Chart Type drop-down list. The result, which compares how well each mining model predicts high-profit customers, is shown in Figure 18-26.

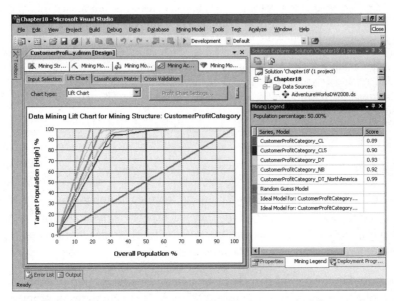

FIGURE 18-26 A lift chart comparing models of customer profitability

The x-axis of the lift chart shows the percentage of the overall population, and the y-axis shows the percentage of the population that is high profit. Recall that we defined high-profit customers as those in the top quartile of customers. In an ideal model, one in which you can predict perfectly who the high-profit customers are, you need to look at only 25 percent of the overall population to identify 100 percent of the high-profit customers. Using the Mining Legend to the right, locate the line representing the ideal model for the overall population on the lift chart. (This is the ideal for models that do not filter the population—for example, *CustomerProfitCategory_CL*.) Notice that it hits the top of the chart at the 25-percent mark along the x-axis. The straight diagonal line in the figure represents random guessing. By randomly guessing, you would need to look at 100 percent of the overall population to iden-tify 100 percent of the high-profit customers. The mining models are an improvement over random guessing; the decision tree model (the one with the highest score as indicated in the Mining Legend) is the most accurate model for the overall population, followed by the Naïve Bayes model. The decision tree model we specified is better able to predict profitability for North American customers than for the overall population.

> **Note** The Mining Accuracy view also offers the capability to perform cross validation. Cross validation is a common method for testing the robustness of your mining models. When you perform cross validation, the data source is partitioned into a specified number of subsamples, or *folds*. Each fold is used as a holdout set with which to test models that are trained from the complement of the holdout set. Accuracy metrics are generated for each trained and tested model. Results of mining models trained using different random samples of the data must be consistent in order for any model to be considered reliable. The built-in cross-validation functionality of the data mining module is new to SQL Server 2008 and vastly simplifies the cross-validation process for data mining developers. A detailed discussion of the cross-validation functionality is beyond the scope of this book. See SQL Server Books Online for details on how to use the Cross Validation tab and interpret the results.

Nested Tables

Nested tables are perhaps one of the most confusing features of Analysis Services data mining. Once you understand them, however, they will likely become an integral component of your data mining toolset. Nested tables allow you to include transactional data in your mining models *without* changing your data structure.

For example, suppose that we want to include data about the *types* of products customers bought in our profitability analysis. Adventure Works sells four categories of products: bikes, clothing, accessories, and components. What kinds of products do the high-profit customers buy? Are bike buyers high-profit customers? What about clothing, accessory, or component buyers? Although we could add four new columns to the case table to flag the types of products a customer bought, what if Adventure Works later decided to sell 10 categories of products? Or what if we want to know whether particular *models* of bikes (of which there are 50) predict profitability? Adding distinct columns to our case table for each of these values would clearly be inefficient, both in terms of storage for the case table and the ETL work needed to build it. Nested tables eliminate these inefficiencies, allowing you to leave intact the transactional data's existing structure.

To understand this a little better in the context of the mining structure and models we've built so far, let's look at the create statement for the *vCustomerPurchases* view shown in Listing 18-2.

LISTING 18-2 A view with transaction data

```
CREATE VIEW [dbo].[vCustomerPurchases]
AS
SELECT
   f.SalesOrderNumber
   ,f.SalesOrderLineNumber
   ,f.CustomerKey
   ,d.FullDateAlternateKey
   ,pc.EnglishProductCategoryName AS ProductCategory
   ,psc.EnglishProductSubcategoryName AS ProductSubcategory
   ,isnull(p.[ModelName], p.[EnglishProductName]) AS [Model]
```

```
  ,f.OrderQuantity
  ,Row_Number ( ) OVER (
    Partition BY f.CustomerKey
    ORDER BY d.FullDateAlternateKey, f.SalesOrderLineNumber)
  AS PurchaseSequence
FROM [dbo].[FactInternetSales] AS f
INNER JOIN dbo.dimProduct AS p
ON f.ProductKey = p.ProductKey
INNER JOIN dbo.dimProductSubCategory AS psc
ON p.ProductSubCategoryKey = psc.ProductSubcategoryKey
INNER JOIN dbo.dimProductCategory AS pc
ON psc.ProductCategoryKey = pc.ProductCategoryKey
INNER JOIN dbo.dimDate AS d
ON f.OrderDateKey = d.DateKey
```

The view is constructed with a simple *SELECT* statement from the fact table with a join to a few dimension tables to pick up product names and product categories. (We'll discuss the *PurchaseSequence* column, which uses the T-SQL *ROW_NUMBER* ranking function, in the next section.)

Table 18-1 shows customer attributes along with transactional data about customer purchases. Suppose that we want to identify Melvin as an accessory buyer and Jennifer as both a bike buyer and an accessory buyer in our mining models, without explicitly adding Bike Buyer and Accessory Buyer attributes to our customer profile data (which in our analysis comes from *vCustomerProfitability*). Adding the transactional data (in this case, *vCustomerPurchases*) as a nested table to the mining structure will do the trick.

TABLE 18-1 Nested Data

| | | | | | Customer Purchases | | |
CustKey	Name	Profit	Gender	Income Group	Product Category	Product Name	Seq
11580	Melvin	Low	M	Low	Accessories	Sport-100 Helmet, Blue	1
11036	Jennifer	Low	F	Moderate	Bikes	Mountain-200 Silver, 46	1
					Accessories	Sport-100 Helmet, Black	2
11376	Lance	Low	M	Moderate	Clothing	Half-Finger Gloves, M	1
					Clothing	Short-Sleeve Classic Jersey, M	2
11136	Brianna	High	F	Moderate	Bikes	Mountain-200 Black, 38	1
					Accessories	Fender Set, Mountain	2
					Clothing	Classic Vest, M	3

To use *vCustomerPurchases* as a nested table in our mining structure, we must first add it to our data source view:

1. Double-click *CustomerProfitability.dsv* in Solution Explorer to display it in the data source view designer.

2. Click the Add/Remove Objects toolbar button (first from the left), right-click the designer window and choose Add/Remove Tables, or choose Add/Remove Tables from the Data Source View menu. Any of these three actions opens the Add/Remove Tables dialog box.

3. Locate *vCustomerPurchases* in the Available Objects list, move it to the Included Objects list, and then click OK.

4. To complete our data source view changes, we must establish the relationship between *vCustomerPurchases* and *vCustomerProfitability*. Click the *CustomerKey* column in *vCustomerPurchases*, and then drag it into the *CustomerKey* column in *vCustomerProfitability*.

5. Save your changes. The data source view designer should appear as shown in Figure 18-27.

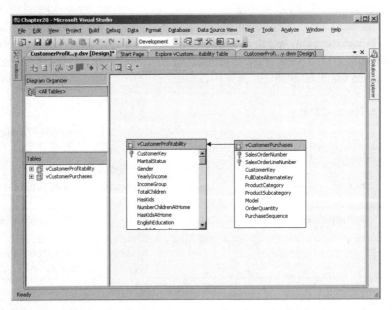

FIGURE 18-27 Transactional data on customer purchases in the data source view, which will be used as the source table for a nested table in the mining model

6. Back in the data mining structure designer, click the Mining Structure tab.

7. Locate, but do not click, the Add A Mining Structure Nested Table Column toolbar button (fourth from the left).

   Note the term "nested table column." Analysis Services considers the nested *table* to be an additional *column* in the mining structure—that is, it considers it to be a *column* that has a "data type" of *table*.

> **Note** In keeping with the Analysis Services mapping of nested tables to a special "data type" of table, note that in Table 18-1 we portrayed *vCustomerPurchases* as just another customer attribute (albeit a hierarchical one), along with *Profit*, *Gender*, and *Income Group*. We did this because we knew we would use *vCustomerPurchases* as a nested table column.

8. Click the Add A Mining Structure Nested Table Column toolbar button. This displays the Select A Nested Table Key Column dialog box.

   Determining the key of a nested table can be counterintuitive initially; your first instinct might be to select *CustomerKey*, *SalesOrderNumber*, or a combination of *SalesOrderNumber* and *SalesOrderLineItem* as the nested table key. In fact, none of these is an appropriate key for the nested table.

   When you specify a column as the nested table key column, the distinct values in that column become usable attributes in your mining model. As such, the correct key for the nested table in this scenario is *ProductCategory*, which has the possible values *Bike*, *Clothing*, and *Accessory*.

9. Select vCustomerPurchases from the Nested Table list, and then select ProductCategory from the Source Column list. Click OK.

   As you will see after we modify and process the mining models, selecting ProductCategory as the nested table key column adds attributes such as *vCustomerPurchases(Bike)* and *vCustomerPurchases(Clothing)* to our mining models.

   Notice that the nested table has been added to the mining structure tree view as a column of the *CustomerProfitCategory* structure (appearing with the name *v Customer Purchases*). Unlike other columns in the mining structure, it has a plus sign next to it.

10. Click the plus sign (+) to expand the table. Now expand the columns of the nested table. The Mining Structure tab will appear as shown in Figure 18-28.

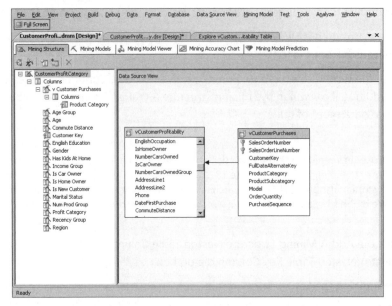

FIGURE 18-28 A mining structure with a nested table column

When you add new columns to an existing mining structure, they will by default be ignored by existing mining models. Therefore, you must specify the usage of the new columns in the models where you want to include them:

1. Click the Mining Models tab, and then click the cell corresponding to the intersection of the *v Customer Purchases* column (the "parent" row) and the *CustomerProfitCategory_ CL* model.

2. Click the drop-down arrow in the cell to view the entries in the drop-down list, and then select Input. Click the plus sign (+) next to *v Customer Purchases*. You will see a new row for the Product Category child column, which is set to Key.

3. Repeat the process of changing the usage for *v Customer Purchase* from Ignore to Input for each of the other mining models in the structure. Notice that each time you change the usage for *v Customer Purchase*, the usage for Product Category is automatically changed from Ignore to Key. Afterward, the Mining Models tab should appear as shown in Figure 18-29.

4. Deploy and process your mining models. This might take several minutes. When processing is complete, click the Mining Model Viewer tab.

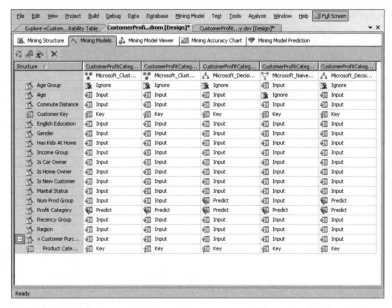

FIGURE 18-29 Mining models in a mining structure with a nested table column

5. Click the Cluster Diagram tab of the *CustomerProfitCategory_CL5* model (the model with five clusters). Using the Shading Variable drop-down list (note the three variables that correspond to product category), change the shading variable to *v Customer Purchases(Bikes)*. In the State drop-down list, the two possible states of the variable are Existing and Missing. If the Bikes key exists in the nested table, the customer is a bike buyer; if the Bikes key is missing, the customer is not a bike buyer. Select Existing.

6. Take note of Cluster 1 and Cluster 4, which have the highest concentration of bike buyers. Change the shading variable to Is New Customer, and select the Y state. Cluster 4 has more new customers than Cluster 1. Change the shading variable to Profit Category, select the High state, and note that the two clusters with the highest concentration of bike buyers also have the highest concentration of high-profit customers.

Figure 18-30 compares the five clusters on the Cluster Profiles tab. When the key of a nested table column is included in a mining model, the distinct values found in the key column form the basis of existence attributes that are used to train the mining model. The value of the key column represented by the existence attribute is shown in parentheses after the nested table column name. Cluster 1 has a markedly higher proportion of bike buyers than other clusters, with Cluster 4 coming in second. The proportion of clothing buyers is similar across all clusters.

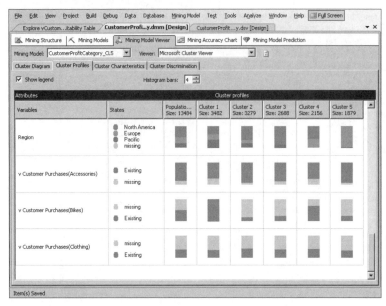

FIGURE 18-30 Viewing the results of a mining model that includes nested table column input

Use the mining model viewers to explore other mining models. Take note of the input attributes added to the models as a result of adding the nested table to the models. Close the project and exit Visual Studio.

Using Data Mining Extensions

So far in this chapter, you've seen how to use the data structure designer within Visual Studio to create, train, and view mining models. Now you'll see how to use SQL Data Mining Extensions (DMX) to do those same tasks. DMX is an extension to the SQL language for creating and working with data mining models in Analysis Services.

As with conventional SQL, DMX has two categories of statements: data definition language (DDL) statements and data manipulation language (DML) statements. DDL statements are used to create mining structures and models. DML statements are used to train, browse, and predict using mining models.

It is true that you can avoid writing DDL queries in DMX by using the Analysis Services designers. It is also true that DML prediction queries (which we will explore a bit later in this chapter) in DMX can be autogenerated using those tools. But as with relational databases, it is better not to completely rely on tools when a powerful, declarative language is available to perform these same tasks. We will now cover writing DMX code to add a mining model to an existing mining structure, create and train sequence clustering and association rules models, and perform prediction queries against trained mining models.

Data Mining Modeling Using DMX

DMX can be used to create, modify, and train the same mining structures and models as those created using the Data Mining Wizard and modified using the Data Mining Designer:

1. In SQL Server Management Studio, open the Object Explorer window if is not visible. If your Analysis Services server does not already appear in Object Explorer, add a connection to it using the Connect drop-down list or the corresponding toolbar button.

2. Drill down on the Databases node and then the node for Chapter18, our sample database. Notice that Object Explorer provides a dedicated node for mining structures. Drill down on the Mining Structures node, and verify that you can see a node for *CustomerProfitCategory*, our mining structure. Drill down on this node, and then drill down further on its child Mining Models node to verify that nodes appear for each of the five models we created previously.

3. Click the Analysis Services DMX Query button (the fourth button from the left) on the Management Studio SQL Server Analysis Services Editors toolbar.

   After you work through the Connect To Analysis Services dialog box, a special query window will open in which you can execute DMX statements. Much like the multidimensional expression language (MDX) query window—which in its Tools pane lists cubes, dimensions, measures, and MDX functions—the DMX query window has a Tools pane containing a drop-down list of all models in the database (for all mining structures), a Metadata tab that lists all columns in the currently selected model, and a Functions tab that lists DMX functions. In addition, Template Explorer offers a number of DMX query templates. (Template Explorer will be discussed later.)

4. For this chapter, we will review the code in several DMX scripts, contained in the *Chapter18DMX* project, belonging to the Management Studio sample code solution Chapter18.smsssln. Double-click the Chapter18.smsssln file from Windows Explorer. Doing so will open the sample solution in SQL Server Management Studio. Next, open the first five script files in the project (the five topmost scripts in Solution Explorer under the Queries node within the *Chapter18DMX* project). Your Management Studio environment should appear similar to that shown in Figure 18-31.

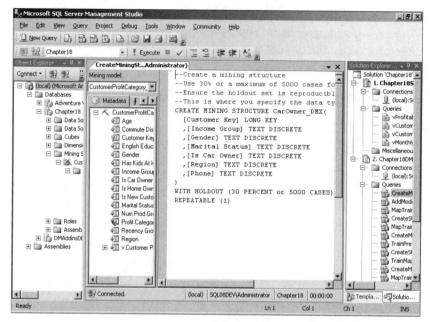

FIGURE 18-31 SQL Server Management Studio with a DMX query window open

Using DMX, you can either create a mining structure and then add a mining model to it or create a mining structure and a model in a single step. The scripts CreateMiningStructure. dmx, AddModelWithDrillthrough.dmx, and MapTrain.dmx, respectively, show how to create a mining structure, add a mining model to the structure, and process the model. The scripts CreateStructureAndModel.dmx and MapTrainOneStep.dmx show how to create a mining structure and model in one step and then process the structure and model.

Why would you bother running three scripts when it seems that you could do the same work using two? To begin with, you might want to create a mining structure that supports many models, where each model will use only a subset of the columns in the structure. The columns defined in the mining structure form the domain of columns from which you can choose to build your individual mining models. But creating a mining structure and model in one step forces the structure and the model to share a set of columns.

The simplest form of the *CREATE MINING STRUCTURE* statement is as follows:

```
CREATE MINING STRUCTURE <structure>
(
    <column name> <data type> <content type>
)
```

You must specify a name for the mining structure and define the columns for the structure. For each column in the mining structure, you provide a column name, the data type of the column (for example, *Text* or *Long*), and the content type of the column (*Key*, *Continuous*, or *Discrete*). Here is an example of a simple *CREATE MINING STRUCTURE* statement:

```
CREATE MINING STRUCTURE CarOwner_DMX( [Customer Key] LONG KEY ,[Income Group] TEXT
DISCRETE ,[Gender] TEXT DISCRETE ,[Marital Status] TEXT DISCRETE ,[Is Car Owner] TEXT
DISCRETE ,[Region] TEXT DISCRETE ,[Phone] TEXT DISCRETE )
```

Take note of the *Phone* column. This will be important when we discuss mining model drillthrough shortly.

Another reason for using separate DMX statements for creating mining structures and models is to take advantage of the new SQL Server 2008 functionality for creating holdout test sets from within Analysis Services. Support for creating holdout test sets is available only in the *CREATE MINING STRUCTURE* statement, not in the *CREATE MINING MODEL* statement, which as you'll see later is used to create a mining structure and model in a single step. The parameters for the holdout set are specified when the mining structure is created as follows:

```
CREATE MINING STRUCTURE <structure> (    <column name> <data type> <content type> ) WITH
HOLDOUT (<holdout specifier>)REPEATABLE(<holdout seed>)
```

As with the Data Mining Wizard in Visual Studio, the holdout set can be specified as a percentage of cases, maximum number of cases, or both. If the holdout set should be reproducible, a holdout seed should be specified.

An example of a *CREATE MINING STRUCTURE* statement with a 30 percent or 5000 case holdout set and a random seed of one is given in the CreateMiningStructure.dmx script. Open the script, and then follow these steps:

1. Click the Execute toolbar button or shortcut menu command, choose Execute from the Query menu, or press F5 or Ctrl+E. You should see a message saying that the execution is complete, and the status bar in the lower-left corner of the query window should indicate that the query executed successfully.

2. Go to the Chapter18 database node in Object Browser, and refresh its Mining Structures node by using the Refresh command on its shortcut menu. You should see the *CarOwner_DMX* structure you just created. Expand the structure, and you will see a Mining Models node indented beneath it. If you expand that node, you will discover that it is empty; this is because the mining structure does not have any mining models associated with it yet.

To add a mining model to an existing mining structure, you use an *ALTER MINING STRUCTURE* statement with an *ADD MINING MODEL* clause. Let's take a look at a simple form of the statement:

```
ALTER MINING STRUCTURE <structure>
 ADD MINING MODEL <model>(
   <column name> [<prediction>]
 )
 USING <algorithm> [(<parameter list>)] [WITH DRILLTHROUGH]
```

The script AddModelWithDrillthrough.dmx gives a specific example of an *ALTER MINING STRUCTURE* statement:

```
ALTER MINING STRUCTURE CarOwner_DMX
 ADD MINING MODEL CarOwner_DT(
   [Customer Key]
  ,[Income Group]
  ,[Gender]
  ,[Marital Status]
  ,[Is Car Owner] PREDICT
  ,[Region]
  )
 USING Microsoft_Decision_Trees WITH DRILLTHROUGH
```

This example adds a Decision Trees model for predicting car ownership to the mining structure. Notice that the column list for the mining structure specifies the data type and content type for the columns. The data type and content type of columns are common among all the mining models that are part of the same mining structure. In contrast, column usage is model specific. Column usage—whether the column is an input column or a predictable column—is specified in the mining model column list. By default, the columns are input columns; therefore, you need to identify only the columns that are predictable. In the example, the *[Is Car Owner]* column is marked as a predictable column because we want to use the Decision Trees algorithm to predict car ownership. You will notice that *Phone*, which was defined in the mining structure, is not specified in the mining model: a phone number is a piece of identifying information—it isn't something we want to use to predict whether someone is a car owner. Creating the mining structure and model separately allows the structure to have identifying columns that aren't used in the mining model. You'll see in a moment how that can be useful. Let's continue the example.

1. Execute the query.

2. Refresh and expand the Mining Models node below the *CarOwner_DMX* mining structure node. You should see the *CarOwner_DT* model. Right-click the model, and then choose Browse. You will receive an error message stating that the model must be processed. Right-click the model in Object Browser, and then choose Process.

3. In the Process Mining Model dialog box, click OK. You will see an error message similar to that shown in Figure 18-32.

This error message appears because Analysis Services does not know the source data for the mining structure. So far, all we have done is specify some column names in a mining structure and model—there has been no mention of the source of the data for the structure or model. Binding the columns of a mining structure to data is done using an *INSERT INTO* DMX statement. Here is a simple form of the statement:

```
INSERT INTO MINING STRUCTURE <structure> (
  <mining structure columns>
)
 OPENQUERY(<named datasource>, <query syntax>)
```

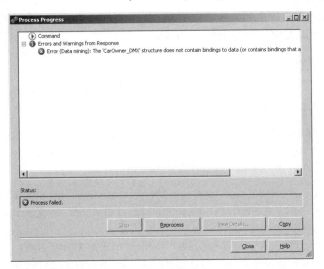

FIGURE 18-32 The error message that appears when you try to process a mining structure for which column bindings have not been specified

To run your own *INSERT INTO* query, close the error message and the Process Mining Model dialog box. Close the empty viewer window, and then open the DMX script file MapTrain.dmx by double-clicking its node in Solution Explorer. An example of an *INSERT INTO* statement to bind data columns to the columns is contained in the script:

```
INSERT INTO CarOwner_DMX(
   [Customer Key]
  ,[Income Group]
  ,[Gender]
  ,[Marital Status]
  ,[Is Car Owner]
  ,[Region]

  ,[Phone]
)
 OPENQUERY(
  [AdventureWorksDW2008],
  'SELECT
     CustomerKey
    ,IncomeGroup
    ,Gender
    ,MaritalStatus
    ,IsCarOwner
    ,Region
    ,Phone
    FROM AdventureWorksDW2008.dbo.vCustomerProfitability'
 )
```

The column list consists of the columns that were specified in the *CREATE MINING STRUCTURE* statement. The named data source was defined in the Analysis Services database—in our case, *[AdventureWorksDW2008]*. Our data source is a SQL Server database, so the code within the *OPENQUERY* expression is actually a Transact-SQL (T-SQL) statement.

To continue with the example:

1. Execute the script. The statement binds the mining structure columns and processes the mining model.

2. Go back to the Object Browser window, right-click the *CarOwner_DT* model's node, and then choose Browse. This displays the Tree Viewer in a new document window. The Tree Viewer is identical to the one you used in Visual Studio.

3. Right-click a node of the decision tree, and then choose Drill Through. The drillthrough feature was enabled by the *WITH DRILLTHROUGH* clause that we specified in the script AddModelWithDrillthrough.dmx. You have the choice to drill through to Model Columns Only or to Model And Structure Columns. In SQL Server 2005, you did not have a choice: it was possible only to drill through to the columns in the mining model. Select Model And Structure Columns. This brings back the rows from *vCustomerProfitability* that belong to the node that was right-clicked, including the phone numbers of the customers.

4. Close the viewer window and any open DMX Query windows.

Moving on, let's explore how to create a mining structure and model in one step. We do so by specifying the column name, data type, content type, and usage in the column list, as follows:

```
CREATE MINING MODEL <model>(
  <column name> <data type> <Content Type> [<prediction>]
)
 USING <algorithm> [(<parameter list>)] [WITH DRILLTHROUGH]
```

The DMX code in CreateStructureAndModel.dmx is an example of this statement:

```
CREATE MINING MODEL CarOwner_DT_OneStep(
   [Customer Key] LONG KEY
  ,[Income Group] TEXT DISCRETE
  ,[Gender] TEXT DISCRETE
  ,[Marital Status] TEXT DISCRETE
  ,[Is Car Owner] TEXT DISCRETE PREDICT
  ,[Region] TEXT DISCRETE
)
 USING Microsoft_Decision_Trees WITH DRILLTHROUGH
```

Because the structure and model are created in one step, we omit the *Phone* column since we do not want to use it as either an input or a predictable column in our mining model.

Take these steps next:

1. Execute the query, and then refresh the Mining Structures node in the Object Explorer window. You should see a new node for a structure with the name *CarOwner_DT_ OneStep_Structure*. Analysis Services appends the *Structure* suffix to the name specified in the *CREATE MINING MODEL* statement in order to distinguish the mining structure from the mining model.

2. Expand the structure's node and then its child mining models node. You should see the *CarOwner_DT_OneStep* model; this model and its parent structure were created by the single DMX statement.

3. Open and execute the script MapTrainOneStep.dmx to process the *CarOwner_DMX* model. Here's the DMX code from the MapTrainOneStep.dmx script:

```
INSERT INTO CarOwner_DT_OneStep(
    [Customer Key]
    ,[Income Group]
    ,[Gender]
    ,[Marital Status]
    ,[Is Car Owner]
    ,[Region]
)
 OPENQUERY(
  [AdventureWorksDW2008],
  'SELECT
    CustomerKey
    ,IncomeGroup
    ,Gender
    ,MaritalStatus
    ,IsCarOwner
    ,Region
   FROM AdventureWorksDW2008.dbo.vCustomerProfitability'
 )
```

This query is similar to the query in MapTrain.dmx, which was used to process the *CarOwner_DMX* mining structure. In MapTrain.dmx, a mining *structure* was specified in the *INSERT INTO* statement; the DMX code in MapTrainOneStep.dmx specifies a mining *model*. Specifying a mining model in the *INSERT INTO* DMX statement processes that particular mining model. Specifying a mining structure in the statement processes the mining structure and all of the models in that structure. The mining structure we created has only one mining model, so the result is the same regardless of whether we specify the structure or the model.

4. Browse the *CarOwner_DT_OneStep* model if you want, and then close the viewer and all open DMX Query windows.

DMX statements for creating and processing mining models with nested tables are slightly more complex than for models without nested tables. As mentioned in the previous section, Analysis Services views a nested table as a column; it is a column with a "data type" of table.

The concept of a nested table being a "column" is confusing. The concept becomes more clear, however, when you consider DMX statements that create mining structures and models that, in turn, use nested tables. Here is the syntax for adding a mining model that uses a nested table to an existing mining structure:

```
ALTER MINING STRUCTURE <structure>
 ADD MINING MODEL <model>(
  <column name>  [<prediction>],
  <table name> [<prediction>] (
    <column name>  [<prediction>]
  )
 )
 USING <algorithm> [(<parameter list>)] [WITH DRILLTHROUGH]
```

An example of adding a mining model with a nested table is shown in the CreateModelWithNestedTable.dmx script file:

```
ALTER MINING STRUCTURE CustomerProfitCategory
 ADD MINING MODEL ProductBuyer_DT(
   [Customer Key]
  ,[Age]
  ,[Commute Distance]
  ,[English Education]
  ,[Gender]
  ,[Income Group]
  ,[Is Car Owner]
  ,[Region]
  ,[v Customer Purchases] PREDICT
    (
      [Product Category]
    )
 )
 USING Microsoft_Decision_Trees
```

CreateModelWithNestedTable.dmx adds a decision tree model—for predicting the category of products that customers buy—to the *CustomerProfitCategory* mining structure that we created with the Mining Model designer earlier in this chapter. Let's add that to our solution now.

1. Run the CreateModelWithNestedTable.dmx script, and then check that the *ProductBuyer_DT* model was added to the mining structure in Object Browser.

2. Right-click the model, and then choose Browse. You will receive an error message stating that you cannot browse the model until it has been processed. Close the error message and the empty model browser window.

3. To fix the problem, run the DMX code in the script file TrainPreMapped.dmx. This query provides an example of using the *INSERT INTO* statement to process a mining model when the column bindings for the structure have already been defined:

```
INSERT INTO ProductBuyer_DT
```

The *CustomerProfitCategory* structure was defined using the data mining structure designer. When you create a structure using this designer, you select columns from your data source view for the structure; the mining structure columns are bound to the source data at that time. When the mining structure columns are already bound to the source data, the DMX statement to process the model is very simple:

```
INSERT INTO <model>
```

4. After you run TrainPreMapped.dmx, go back to Object Browser. Right-click the *ProductBuyer_DT* model in the *CustomerProfitCategory* structure, and then choose Browse. This time the Tree Viewer appears with no error messages.

5. Use the viewer to explore the model. The model predicts whether customers are bike buyers, accessory buyers, or clothing buyers. Figure 18-33 shows the Dependency Network tab for the model.

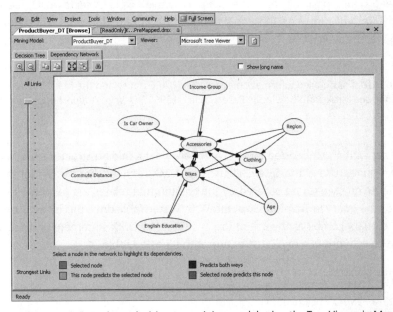

FIGURE 18-33 Browsing a decision tree mining model using the Tree Viewer in Management Studio

The query in CreateStructureWithNestedTable.dmx creates a mining structure and model that uses the Association Rules algorithm to predict the bundles of products customers have purchased:

```
CREATE MINING MODEL PurchaseAssociations(
    [Customer Key] LONG KEY
   ,[Customer Purchases] TABLE PREDICT
    (
      [Product Subcategory] TEXT KEY
    )
)
 USING Microsoft_Association_Rules
```

The Association Rules algorithm is used to find combinations of items that frequently occur together. The most common application of the Association Rules algorithm is in market-basket analysis. By understanding the bundles of products that customers have purchased, you can make recommendations for future purchases.

The script file TrainMapStructureWithNestedTable.dmx contains code that shows how to bind the columns of a mining structure that has a nested table to source data. The source query that specifies the columns from the source data to map to the mining structure columns uses the *SHAPE* clause. At its simplest, the *SHAPE* clause takes the following form:

```
SHAPE {<parent table query>}
APPEND ({ <nested table query> }
    RELATE <master column> TO <child column>)
        AS <nested table column name>
```

The *SHAPE* clause, originally added to support ActiveX Data Objects (ADO) hierarchical (or "shaped") *RecordSet* objects, lets you combine data from multiple *SELECT* statements into a single hierarchical result set (a result set with an embedded table).

> **More Info** For detailed information about the *SHAPE* clause and the MSDataShape OLE DB provider, see Microsoft Knowledge Base article Q189657, at *http://support.microsoft.com/kb/q189657*.

A result set with an embedded table is precisely what a mining structure with a nested table column requires. Use of the *SHAPE* clause with DMX requires that the parent table query and nested table query each be ordered by the column that relates the parent table to the nested table. For the query in TrainMapStructureWithNestedTable.dmx, this is the *CustomerKey* column. The query combines the use of the *INSERT INTO* DMX statement and the *SHAPE* clause to bind the columns in a mining structure with a nested table.

Here is the generalized form for such queries:

```
INSERT INTO MINING STRUCTURE <structure> (
  <mining structure column> | [SKIP],
  <nested table> (
    <nested table column> | [SKIP]
  )
)
SHAPE {<parent table query>}
APPEND ({ <child table query> }
    RELATE <parent column> TO <child column>)
        AS <nested table column name>
```

The actual code from TrainMapStructureWithNestedTable.dmx is as follows:

```
INSERT INTO PurchaseAssociations(
  [Customer Key]
  ,[Customer Purchases]
    (
      SKIP
      ,[Product Subcategory]
    )
)
SHAPE{
  OPENQUERY([AdventureWorksDW2008],
    'SELECT CustomerKey
     FROM AdventureWorksDW2008.dbo.vCustomerProfitability
     ORDER BY CustomerKey')
  }
APPEND ({
  OPENQUERY([AdventureWorksDW2008],
    'SELECT CustomerKey, ProductSubcategory
     FROM AdventureWorksDW2008.dbo.vCustomerPurchases
     ORDER BY CustomerKey'
)}
RELATE CustomerKey TO CustomerKey) AS CustomerPurchases
```

The mining structure columns specified in the *INSERT INTO* clause of TrainMapStructureWithNestedTable.dmx are the structure's column names. The column list after the *INSERT INTO* clause uses the column names with the spaces—these are the names that were specified in the *CREATE MINING MODEL* statement. (Note that the ordinal position of the columns in the list corresponds to the columns returned by the source data query, which in this case is the result set returned by the *SHAPE* clause and it's *APPEND* and *RELATE* clauses.) If the source data query returns columns that are not required by the mining model, you must use the *SKIP* keyword to indicate that the column should be skipped.

The query in TrainMapStructureWithNestedTable.dmx skips the *CustomerKey* column from the child table query. You are required to include the column that relates the child (nested) table to the parent table in the parent and child table queries. Both the parent table query and the child table queries in TrainMapStructureWithNestedTable.dmx select the *CustomerKey* column; however, the *[Customer Key]* column appears only once in the mining structure. Therefore, you must use the *SKIP* keyword to skip the *CustomerKey* column for the nested table.

Run CreateStructureWithNestedTable.dmx, followed by TrainMapStructureWithNestedTable.dmx, and then explore the *PurchaseAssociation* model by right-clicking its node in the Object Browser window and choosing Browse.

The queries in the script files CreateModelCustomClusterCount.dmx and MapTrainSkipColumns.dmx together provide another example of using DMX to create a mining model with a nested table and then binding its structure to the source data.

CreateModelCustomClusterCount.dmx creates a mining structure with a clustering sequence mining model, as shown here:

```
CREATE MINING MODEL PurchaseSequence(
   [Customer Key] LONG KEY
  ,[Profit] LONG CONTINUOUS
  ,[Income Group] TEXT DISCRETE
  ,[Customer Purchases] TABLE
    (
       [Purchase Sequence] LONG KEY SEQUENCE
      ,[Product Subcategory] TEXT DISCRETE PREDICT
    )
)
 USING Microsoft_Sequence_Clustering (Cluster_Count = 0)
```

With the Clustering Sequence algorithm, not only are the combinations of items frequently occurring together of interest, but also the order in which they occur is of interest. In our example, the model clusters customers according to the sequence of the product subcategory of their purchases. The model sets the *Cluster_Count* parameter of the algorithm to 0. This has the effect of forcing Analysis Services to determine the optimal number of clusters to create. By default, the algorithm creates 10 clusters. Execute the queries in CreateModelCustomClusterCount.dmx and MapTrainSkipColumns.dmx, in order, and then browse the model using the Cluster Viewer.

Data Mining Predictions Using DMX

DMX is a powerful tool for mining structure and mining model DDL queries, but you can also use it to write what are arguably data mining's most valuable asset: prediction queries. The next six DMX script files in the *Chapter18DMX* project provide examples of such prediction queries. Using special DMX prediction functions, you can apply the results from data patterns discovered by your mining models to new data.

> **Note** In practice, data mining prediction queries would be written against a new sample of data to which you wanted apply your data mining discoveries. For simplicity, the following data mining prediction queries are written using the same *AdventureWorksDW2008* database that was used to train and test the mining models.

The basic format of a prediction query is as follows:

```
SELECT <select expression list>
 FROM <model>
 PREDICTION JOIN
 <source data query>
 ON <join mapping list>
```

For specific queries, replace *<model>* with the mining model on which you want to base the query predictions and replace *<source data query>* with the data to which you want to apply the prediction. Often you will replace *<source data query>* with an *OPENQUERY* statement similar to those used in the *SELECT INTO* DMX modeling statements for binding the data mining columns to the source data. You can replace *<select expression>* with any combination of columns returned in the source data query, predictable columns from the mining model, and DMX prediction functions that return a column of data, including a nested table column. Replace *<join mapping list>* with the column mapping between the source data and the input columns of the mining model. The LeastLikelyCar.dmx script contains the following code:

```
SELECT TOP 250
  t.FirstName
  ,t.LastName
  ,t.Phone
  ,PredictProbability([Is Car Owner],'N') AS ProbNotCarOwner
FROM CarOwner_DT
PREDICTION JOIN
OPENQUERY([AdventureWorksDW2008],
  'SELECT
    c.FirstName
    ,c.LastName
    ,tc.*
  FROM vCustomerProfitability tc
  INNER JOIN dimCustomer c
  ON tc.CustomerKey = c.CustomerKey')
AS t
ON t.Gender = CarOwner_DT.Gender AND
   t.IncomeGroup = CarOwner_dt.[Income Group] AND
   t.MaritalStatus = CarOwner_dt.[Marital Status] AND
   t.Region = CarOwner_dt.Region
ORDER BY PredictProbability([Is Car Owner],'N') DESC
```

By using the *TOP* and *ORDER BY* clauses supported by DMX, the query returns the names and phone numbers of the 250 people in *vCustomerProfitability* who are least likely to own a car according to the *CarOwner_DT* decision trees mining model we created earlier. The query uses the *PredictProbability* function, which takes two arguments: a predictable column from the mining model and a specified value for the column. The function returns the probability of not owning a car, as predicted by the *CarOwner_DT* model.

Execute the query, and you'll see that the 250 customers least likely to own a car all have a 78-percent probability of not owning a car. The *CarOwner_DT* model predicts car ownership based on gender, income group, marital status, and region. Many customers in the database will have the same values for those characteristics. Customers who share a characteristic that is important for determining car ownership will have the same predicted probability of owning a car. To see the next-highest probability of not owning a car, try selecting a larger number of customers, say, the *TOP 1250*.

When the column names in the model and the source data query are the same, DMX allows the use of a *NATURAL PREDICTION JOIN*. When you use a *NATURAL PREDICTION JOIN*, you do not have to specify an *ON* clause for the prediction query. Analysis Services joins the model and source data based on column names. The script file NaturalPredictionJoin.dmx provides a simple example:

```
SELECT TOP 250
   t.FirstName
   ,t.LastName
   ,t.Phone
   ,PredictProbability([Is Car Owner],'N') AS ProbNotCarOwner
 FROM CarOwner_DT
 NATURAL PREDICTION JOIN
 OPENQUERY(
  [AdventureWorksDW2008],
   'SELECT
     c.FirstName
     ,c.LastName
     ,tc.Phone
     ,tc.Gender
     ,tc.IncomeGroup AS [Income Group]
     ,tc.MaritalStatus AS [Marital Status]
     ,tc.Region
  FROM vCustomerProfitability tc
  INNER JOIN dimCustomer c
  ON tc.CustomerKey = c.CustomerKey')
AS t
ORDER BY PredictProbability([Is Car Owner],'N') DESC
```

Run the query in NaturalPredictionJoin.dmx, and verify that the results are the same as for LeastLikelyCar.dmx.

To be considered a match by the *NATURAL PREDICTION JOIN*, the names in the model and source data query must be identical. If the source data query does not have a column with a name identical to that of an input column, no error message is returned; instead, Analysis Services makes the prediction based on the columns for which matches *are* found. The query in NaturalPredictionJoinMissingMappings.dmx does not alias the column names in the source data query to match the names from the mining model, as shown here:

```
SELECT TOP 250
   t.FirstName
   ,t.LastName
   ,t.Phone
   ,PredictProbability([Is Car Owner],'N') AS ProbNotCarOwner
FROM CarOwner_DT
NATURAL PREDICTION JOIN
OPENQUERY([Adventure Works DW],
   'SELECT
     c.FirstName
     ,c.LastName
     ,tc.Phone
```

```
      ,tc.Gender
      ,tc.IncomeGroup
      ,tc.MaritalStatus
      ,tc.Region
   FROM vCustomerProfitability tc
   INNER JOIN dimCustomer c
   ON tc.CustomerKey = c.CustomerKey')
AS t
ORDER BY PredictProbability([Is Car Owner],'N') DESC
```

In this query, the prediction is made based only on columns in which there is
an exact match in the name (*Gender* and *Region*, in this case). Run the script file
NaturalPredictionJoinMissingMappings.dmx, and notice how the results of the statement in it
differ from those of the previous two predictions.

When the model has a nested table column, the queries are slightly more complex but have
the same basic structure of joining a data mining model with source data and specifying the
mapping of the source data columns to the input columns of the mining model. The complexity of the query comes primarily in the source data query. The query must return a result
set with an embedded table column. As you will recall from the DMX modeling statements
we looked at earlier, this is done using the *SHAPE* clause.

MostLikelyCluster4.dmx provides an example of a DMX prediction query using a model with
a nested table column:

```
SELECT TOP 250
    t.FirstName
    ,t.LastName
    ,t.Profit
    ,ClusterProbability('Cluster 4') AS ProbCluster4
FROM CustomerProfitCategory_CL5
PREDICTION JOIN
SHAPE {
  OPENQUERY([AdventureWorksDW2008],
    'SELECT
      c.FirstName
      ,c.LastName
      ,tc.*
    FROM vCustomerProfitability tc
    INNER JOIN dimCustomer c
    ON tc.CustomerKey = c.CustomerKey
    WHERE tc.IsNewCustomer = ''Y''

    ORDER BY tc.CustomerKey'
  )
}
APPEND({
  OPENQUERY([AdventureWorksDW2008],
    'SELECT
      CustomerKey
      ,ProductCategory
    FROM vCustomerPurchases
```

```
     ORDER BY CustomerKey'
  )}
  RELATE CustomerKey TO CustomerKey)
    AS PurchaseCategory
AS t
ON t.Age = CustomerProfitCategory_CL5.Age AND
  t.CommuteDistance = CustomerProfitCategory_CL5.[Commute Distance] AND
  t.EnglishEducation = CustomerProfitCategory_CL5.[English Education] AND
  t.Gender = CustomerProfitCategory_CL5.Gender AND
  t.HasKidsAtHome = CustomerProfitCategory_CL5.[Has Kids At Home] AND
  t.IncomeGroup = CustomerProfitCategory_CL5.[Income Group] AND
  t.IsCarOwner = CustomerProfitCategory_CL5.[Is Car Owner] AND
  t.IsHomeOwner = CustomerProfitCategory_CL5.[Is Home Owner] AND
  t.IsNewCustomer = CustomerProfitCategory_CL5.[Is New Customer] AND
  t.MaritalStatus = CustomerProfitCategory_CL5.[Marital Status] AND
  t.NumProdGroup = CustomerProfitCategory_CL5.[Num Prod Group] AND
  t.RecencyGroup = CustomerProfitCategory_CL5.[Recency Group] AND
  t.Region = CustomerProfitCategory_CL5.Region AND
  t.PurchaseCategory.ProductCategory =
    CustomerProfitCategory_CL5.[v Customer Purchases].[Product Category]
ORDER BY ClusterProbability('Cluster 4') DESC
```

This query uses the *CustomerProfitCategory_CL5* clustering mining model to predict the probability that a new customer will be in Cluster 4—this is the cluster with a relatively high concentration of high-profit customers, some of whom are likely to be new customers.

We are interested in new customers who are likely to be in this cluster because we'd like to keep them as customers. The preceding query returns a list of customers, including the dollar profit amount generated from each customer and the probability that the customer is in Cluster 4. Execute the query; a portion of the result set returned by the query is shown in Figure 18-34.

FirstName	LastName	Profit	ProbCluster4
Seth	Wood	618.48	1
Alexandra	Price	629.9777	1
Connor	Roberts	429.3139	1
Jenna	Gonzalez	618.48	1
Sebastian	Peterson	429.3139	1
Tiffany	Huang	440.8116	1
Jade	Brooks	635.5572	1
Kelly	Russell	429.3139	1
Evan	Sanchez	629.9777	1
Warren	Xu	904.1998	1
Kristi	Carlson	665.0091	1
Marcus	Parker	418.2293	1
Ian	Thomas	407.4102	1
Sarah	Taylor	236.0914	1
Juan	Suarez	618.48	1
Isabella	Taylor	423.0539	1
Mary	Wright	638.0549	1
Christina	Cox	444.6446	1
Xavier	Stewart	418.2293	1

FIGURE 18-34 The results of a DMX prediction query

The query uses the *ClusterProbability* prediction function, which takes a specific cluster as an argument and returns the probability that the input record belongs to the specified cluster.

You can also return a (nested) table column in a *SELECT* statement. For example, the clustering algorithm supports the use of the *PredictHistogram* function with a clustering column argument. This returns a table column with the predicted probability of each record in the result set being in each cluster. This is illustrated in the query in script file Cluster5ProbabilityDist.dmx:

```
SELECT TOP 250
   t.FirstName
  ,t.LastName
  ,t.Profit
  ,Cluster()
  ,PredictHistogram(Cluster())
FROM CustomerProfitCategory_CL5
PREDICTION JOIN
SHAPE {
  OpenQuery([AdventureWorksDW2008],
    'SELECT
       c.FirstName
      ,c.LastName
      ,tc.*
    FROM vCustomerProfitability tc
    INNER JOIN dimCustomer c
    ON tc.CustomerKey = c.CustomerKey
    ORDER BY   tc.CustomerKey'
  )
}
APPEND({
  OPENQUERY([AdventureWorksDW2008],
    'SELECT
       CustomerKey
      ,ProductCategory
    FROM vCustomerPurchases
    ORDER BY CustomerKey'
  )}
  RELATE CustomerKey To CustomerKey)
    AS PurchaseCategory
AS t
ON t.Age = CustomerProfitCategory_CL5.Age AND
  t.CommuteDistance = CustomerProfitCategory_CL5.[Commute Distance] AND
  t.EnglishEducation = CustomerProfitCategory_CL5.[English Education] AND
  t.Gender = CustomerProfitCategory_CL5.Gender AND
  t.HasKidsAtHome = CustomerProfitCategory_CL5.[Has Kids At Home] AND
  t.IncomeGroup = CustomerProfitCategory_CL5.[Income Group] AND
  t.IsCarOwner = CustomerProfitCategory_CL5.[Is Car Owner] AND
  t.IsHomeOwner = CustomerProfitCategory_CL5.[Is Home Owner] AND
  t.IsNewCustomer = CustomerProfitCategory_CL5.[Is New Customer] AND
  t.MaritalStatus = CustomerProfitCategory_CL5.[Marital Status] AND
  t.NumProdGroup = CustomerProfitCategory_CL5.[Num Prod Group] AND
  t.RecencyGroup = CustomerProfitCategory_CL5.[Recency Group] AND
  t.Region = CustomerProfitCategory_CL5.Region AND
  t.PurchaseCategory.ProductCategory =
    CustomerProfitCategory_CL5.[v Customer Purchases].[Product Category]
```

Execute the query to see how SQL Server Management Studio handles nested tables. You will notice that each cell of the predicted cluster histogram column (the last one) has a plus sign (+). Click one of them to expand the nested table for its row. The result will appear as shown in Figure 18-35. For example, Ruben Torres has a 99-percent probability of being in Cluster 1 and less than a 1-percent probability of being in Cluster 4.

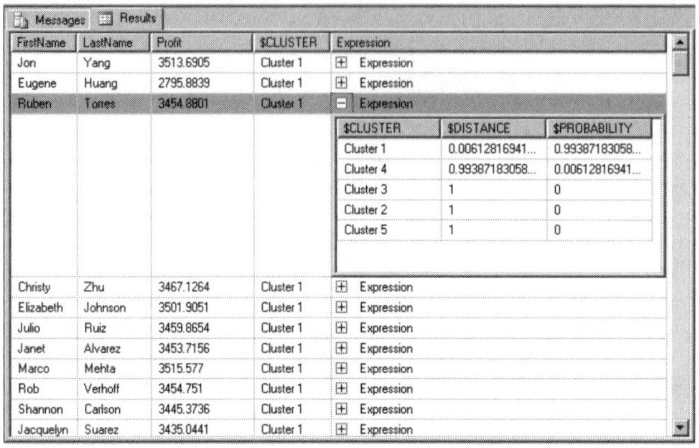

FirstName	LastName	Profit	$CLUSTER	Expression		
Jon	Yang	3513.6905	Cluster 1	⊞ Expression		
Eugene	Huang	2795.8839	Cluster 1	⊞ Expression		
Ruben	Torres	3454.8801	Cluster 1	⊟ Expression		
				$CLUSTER	$DISTANCE	$PROBABILITY
				Cluster 1	0.00612816941...	0.99387183058...
				Cluster 4	0.99387183058...	0.00612816941...
				Cluster 3	1	0
				Cluster 2	1	0
				Cluster 5	1	0
Christy	Zhu	3467.1264	Cluster 1	⊞ Expression		
Elizabeth	Johnson	3501.9051	Cluster 1	⊞ Expression		
Julio	Ruiz	3459.8654	Cluster 1	⊞ Expression		
Janet	Alvarez	3453.7156	Cluster 1	⊞ Expression		
Marco	Mehta	3515.577	Cluster 1	⊞ Expression		
Rob	Verhoff	3454.751	Cluster 1	⊞ Expression		
Shannon	Carlson	3445.3736	Cluster 1	⊞ Expression		
Jacquelyn	Suarez	3435.0441	Cluster 1	⊞ Expression		

FIGURE 18-35 A DMX query result with a nested table column

The results from a query with a nested table column are rich and interesting but might be difficult for many applications to manipulate. To address this concern, DMX has a *FLATTENED* keyword that allows you to return the nested table column within a nonhierarchical re-sult set, even while using the *SHAPE* clause to obtain the nested data. The query in the script file Cluster5ProbabilityDistFlattened.dmx returns almost the same result as that in Cluster5ProbabilityDist.dmx, except that it uses the *FLATTENED* keyword to return a nonhi-erarchical result set. It also specifies that the top 1250 records should be returned instead of the top 250. Each row in the nonflattened result set has an equivalent five rows (one for each segment of the histogram) in the flattened result set. Therefore, to see the same data, we have to request five times the number of records as before:

```
SELECT FLATTENED TOP 1250
    t.FirstName
   ,t.LastName
   ,t.Profit
   ,ClusterProbability()
   ,PredictHistogram(Cluster())
FROM CustomerProfitCategory_CL5
PREDICTION JOIN
SHAPE {
  OpenQuery([AdventureWorksDW2008],
    'SELECT
        c.FirstName
       ,c.LastName
       ,tc.*
    FROM vCustomerProfitability tc
    INNER JOIN dimCustomer c
```

```
    ON tc.CustomerKey = c.CustomerKey
    ORDER BY    tc.CustomerKey'
  )
}
APPEND({
  OPENQUERY([AdventureWorksDW2008],
    'SELECT
       CustomerKey
      ,ProductCategory
    FROM      vCustomerPurchases
    ORDER BY CustomerKey'
  )}
  RELATE CustomerKey To CustomerKey)
    AS PurchaseCategory
AS t
ON t.Age = CustomerProfitCategory_CL5.Age AND
  t.CommuteDistance = CustomerProfitCategory_CL5.[Commute Distance] AND
  t.EnglishEducation = CustomerProfitCategory_CL5.[English Education] AND
  t.Gender = CustomerProfitCategory_CL5.Gender AND
  t.HasKidsAtHome = CustomerProfitCategory_CL5.[Has Kids At Home] AND
  t.IncomeGroup = CustomerProfitCategory_CL5.[Income Group] AND
  t.IsCarOwner = CustomerProfitCategory_CL5.[Is Car Owner] AND
  t.IsHomeOwner = CustomerProfitCategory_CL5.[Is Home Owner] AND
  t.IsNewCustomer = CustomerProfitCategory_CL5.[Is New Customer] AND
  t.MaritalStatus = CustomerProfitCategory_CL5.[Marital Status] AND
  t.NumProdGroup = CustomerProfitCategory_CL5.[Num Prod Group] AND
  t.RecencyGroup = CustomerProfitCategory_CL5.[Recency Group] AND
  t.Region = CustomerProfitCategory_CL5.Region AND
  t.PurchaseCategory.ProductCategory =
    CustomerProfitCategory_CL5.[v Customer Purchases].[Product Category]
```

Execute the query; the results should appear as shown in Figure 18-36. Each column of the nested table now appears as a column of the parent table. The values in the nontable columns of the parent table are now repeated for each row of the nested table. It is important to realize that this flattened view of the nested table's columns is a perfectly valid view of the data, given that the nested table is itself considered a column of its parent.

FirstName	LastName	Profit	Expression	Expression.$CLUSTER	Expression.$DISTANCE	Expression.$PROBABILITY
Jon	Yang	3513.6905	0.88167858...	Cluster 1	0.118321418143098	0.881678581856902
Jon	Yang	3513.6905	0.88167858...	Cluster 4	0.881678581856902	0.118321418143098
Jon	Yang	3513.6905	0.88167858...	Cluster 3	1	0
Jon	Yang	3513.6905	0.88167858...	Cluster 2	1	0
Jon	Yang	3513.6905	0.88167858...	Cluster 5	1	0
Eugene	Huang	2795.8839	0.99861576...	Cluster 1	0.00138423353037342	0.998615766469627
Eugene	Huang	2795.8839	0.99861576...	Cluster 4	0.998615766469627	0.00138423353037336
Eugene	Huang	2795.8839	0.99861576...	Cluster 3	1	0
Eugene	Huang	2795.8839	0.99861576...	Cluster 2	1	0
Eugene	Huang	2795.8839	0.99861576...	Cluster 5	1	0
Ruben	Torres	3454.8801	0.99387183...	Cluster 1	0.0061281694174573	0.993871830582543
Ruben	Torres	3454.8801	0.99387183...	Cluster 4	0.993871830582543	0.0061281694174573
Ruben	Torres	3454.8801	0.99387183...	Cluster 3	1	0
Ruben	Torres	3454.8801	0.99387183...	Cluster 2	1	0
Ruben	Torres	3454.8801	0.99387183...	Cluster 5	1	0
Christy	Zhu	3467.1264	1	Cluster 1	0	1
Christy	Zhu	3467.1264	1	Cluster 2	1	0
Christy	Zhu	3467.1264	1	Cluster 3	1	0
Christy	Zhu	3467.1264	1	Cluster 4	1	0

FIGURE 18-36 A DMX query result with a flattened table column

DMX Templates

Management Studio offers templates for writing DMX queries. To see the templates, choose View, Template Explorer in Management Studio. By default, SQL templates are shown. Click the Analysis Server button on the Template Explorer toolbar (the middle button, with the cube icon) to display a tree view of the Analysis Services Templates. Expand the DMX node to see the DMX templates. The Template Explorer window with the tree view of DMX templates is shown in Figure 18-37.

FIGURE 18-37 Template Explorer in Management Studio

Analysis Services offers templates for three types of DMX statements: Model Content, Model Management, and Prediction Queries. Under the Model Content node, you can find templates for writing queries to return metadata about your mining models (essentially the same information presented by the viewer controls, but without the visualizations). Under the Model Management node are templates for writing queries to create and train mining models, such as the ones we wrote earlier. Under the Prediction Queries node are templates for writing prediction queries. The templates provide a boilerplate for writing some of the most common DMX queries and are a time-saving alternative to writing queries from scratch.

Data Mining Applied

You might be wondering why we have an entire chapter devoted to OLAP application development and only a single chapter for data mining overall. Analysis Services data mining is no less programmable than OLAP, and although Analysis Services data mining can sometimes be more straightforward than OLAP development, for the most part, the two are comparable in complexity.

Then again, data mining development *is* different from OLAP programming. To start with, data mining queries are typically not drilldown-oriented, making Excel PivotTables far less compelling as a presentation development tool. On the other hand, the model content browsers available in Visual Studio and SQL Server Management Studio are available to developers as Windows Forms controls, and building on that visualization programmability, the data mining team at Microsoft has also included sample code that implements a few of those browsers as ASP.NET server controls. Browsing models from within your applications using these controls is important and merits discussion.

But what about executing prediction queries and presenting the results? What about running DML statements in DMX programmatically? What about server-side stored procedures? Or management tasks against your databases, mining structures, and mining models? Why doesn't this plethora of topics merit another chapter? The reason is that what you learned in Chapter 17 about OLAP application programming interface (API) programming gives you almost all the skills necessary to do high-powered data mining development.

Whether it be ADO MD.NET, Analysis Management Objects (AMO), or XMLA used programmatically or from Management Studio, virtually everything you've learned in the context of OLAP cubes works with Analysis Services data mining models. This is true for both client-side development and managed code running on the server. In fact, you can easily create stored procedures that execute DMX prediction queries and return result sets to the client, and you can do so without using the *AdomdClient* library and without granting the assembly Unrestricted permissions.

> **Note** It is also possible to present the results of DMX content and prediction queries using Reporting Services. Just as Reporting Services supports SQL for relational databases and MDX for OLAP databases, it supports DMX for data mining models. While the creation of a data mining model report is not covered in this chapter, the solution file for the chapter includes a Report Server project that uses a DMX prediction query to create a classification matrix report.

In this final section of the chapter, we will provide a few applied examples of using model content browser controls and *AdomdClient* code in both Windows Forms and ASP.NET 2.0 and later environments. We'll also show you how easy it is to create a server-side stored procedure that executes a DMX prediction query and returns the results and an XMLA query that does likewise. We'll finish up by showing you how to take advantage of the data mining add-ins for Excel 2007.

Data Mining and API Programming

As we just said, ADO MD.NET provides full support for data mining. This is true on the metadata side as well as on the query side. For example, the *AdomdConnection* object has both a *MiningStructures* and a *MiningModels* collection. Each member of the *MiningStructures* collection has its own *MiningModels* collection as well. The *MiningModel* object also has a *Parent* property pointing back to the *MiningStructure* object that contains it. This flexibility in the ADO MD.NET object model allows your code to browse the models in a database as a flat database-wide collection or through the hierarchical collection of structures and models. The *MiningModel* object also contains an *Algorithm* property and an *Attributes* collection, allowing you to determine programmatically the input and predictable columns in a model and the algorithmic context in which they are used.

Using the Windows Forms Model Content Browser Controls

One really good application of all of this metadata is to provide an interface where users can select a model and display its contents in the appropriate content browser control. This, in effect, provides much of the same functionality that SQL Server Management Studio provides via its Object Explorer window and the Browse shortcut menu command, but without requiring users to install and use Management Studio itself.

If you have Management Studio installed on your machine, the controls are already there—you set a reference to the Microsoft.AnalysisServices.Viewers.dll assembly, which by default is installed in the C:\Program Files\Microsoft Visual Studio 9.0\Common7\IDE\PrivateAssemblies folder. In order for your application to compile and execute properly, you will also need to set references to the following assemblies (all found in the aforementioned folder): Microsoft.AnalysisServices.Controls, Microsoft.AnalysisServices.Graphing, Microsoft.AnalysisServices.OleDbDM, and Microsoft.DataWarehouse. In addition, you will need to set a reference to the Microsoft.DataWarehouse.Interfaces library, which can be found on the .NET tab of the Add Reference dialog box.

Using the controls is easy; simply drag one onto a form and then set its *ConnectionString* and *MiningModelName* properties through the Visual Studio Properties window or in code (making sure that the algorithm of the model you specify matches the viewer type you selected from the Toolbox). The controls use OLE DB, so make sure that the *ConnectionString* value you assign includes the clause *"Provider=MSOLAP.4;"* in addition to *Data Source* and *Initial Catalog* clauses. Then all you do is call the *LoadViewerData* method on the control, passing *null* as the required parameter value. The following three lines of code show how to do this, assuming that *viewer* is an instance of one of the viewer controls, that *connectionString* contains an ADO MD.NET–compliant connection string (specifying *Data Source* and *Initial Catalog*) as its value, and that *cboMiningModels* is a *ComboBox* control containing a list of mining models on the server, with one having been selected by the user:

```
viewer.ConnectionString = "Provider=MSOLAP.4;" + connectionString;
viewer.MiningModelName = cboMiningModels.Text;
viewer.LoadViewerData(null);
```

The Visual Studio sample solution provided with this chapter on the book's companion Web site includes a Windows Forms project named *Chapter18WinClient*.

> **Important** Make certain that all assembly references in the *Chapter18WinClient* project are valid before proceeding. If warning icons appear next to any references, delete them and add them back manually through the .NET tab or Browse tab of the Visual Studio Add Reference dialog box.

The *Chapter18WinClient* project includes a multiple-document interface (MDI) child form named *frmModelViewer* (file name DMMViewerDemo.cs) that allows the user to specify a server, database, and model to view and then displays the model's content in the appropriate viewer control type. Rather than using a control created at design time, before it executes the code shown earlier, the code in the form declares *objViewer* as type *Microsoft.AnalysisServices. Viewers.MiningModelViewerControl* (the class from which each viewer control inherits). It then assigns a new instance of the appropriate algorithm-specific viewer type to that variable, based on the *Algorithm* property of the selected *MiningModel* object. Last, it adds the object to the form's *Controls* collection and sizes, positions, and anchors it within the form.

The form lets the user click a Show Databases button after specifying a server. The button's *Click* event handler opens an *AdomdConnection* to the server and retrieves a *DataSet* containing the schema with all of the catalogs (databases) on the server, which it uses to populate a *ComboBox* control. Here's a simplified version of that code, in which *txtServer* is a *TextBox* control containing the server name, and *cboCatalogs* is the target *ComboBox* control:

```
AdomdConnection conn = new AdomdConnection("Data Source=" + this.txtServer.Text);
conn.Open();
foreach (DataRow dr in conn.GetSchemaDataSet(AdomdSchemaGuid.Catalogs,
  null).Tables[0].Rows)
{
  this.cboCatalogs.Items.Add((string)dr[0]);
}
conn.Close();
```

Notice that only a *Data Source* clause, and not an *Initial Catalog* clause, is supplied in the connection string. We need server-level information only, so this is sufficient.

When the user makes a selection from *cboCatalogs*, the code fetches a list of, and populates a *ComboBox* control with, names of all the models belonging to the selected database. Here's a simplified version of that code (with *cboMiningModels* as the target *ComboBox*):

```
connectionString =
  "Data Source=" + this.txtServer.Text + ";Initial Catalog=" + this.cboCatalogs.Text;
AdomdConnection conn = new AdomdConnection(connectionString);
conn.Open();
foreach (MiningModel mm in conn.MiningModels)
```

```
{
  this.cboMiningModels.Items.Add(mm.Name);
}
conn.Close();
```

As soon as a model is selected from *cboMiningModels*, the code that instantiates a viewer control and connects it to a specific model can be executed.

Executing Prediction Queries with ADO MD.NET

The programming techniques we have explored so far are fairly straightforward, but executing prediction queries is even easier. In Chapter 17, you learned that you can use the ADO MD.NET *AdomdCommand* and *AdomdDataAdapter* objects to execute MDX queries and return flattened result sets in the form of an *AdomdDataReader* or a *DataSet/DataTable*. Similarly, you can use them to execute DMX prediction queries and return their result sets in tabular form. The following code, a simplified version of the code in the *Chapter18WinClient* project's form *frmDMXAdHoc* (file name DMXAdHoc.cs), executes a DMX query, retrieves the results as a *DataTable*, and then binds the *DataTable* to *dgvResults* (a *DataGridView* control):

```
AdomdConnection conn = new AdomdConnection
  ("Data Source=" + this.txtServer.Text + ";Initial Catalog=" + this.cboCatalogs.Text);
AdomdCommand cmd = new AdomdCommand(this.txtQuery.Text, conn);
AdomdDataAdapter da = new AdomdDataAdapter(cmd);
DataTable dt = new DataTable();
da.Fill(dt);
this.dgvResults.DataSource = dt;
```

In the code, *txtServer* and *cboCatalogs* are equivalent to their namesakes in the form *frmModelViewer* (discussed previously), and *txtQuery* is a multiline *TextBox* control containing the DMX query.

Note that *frmDMXAdHoc* is functionally equivalent to the Management Studio DMX window. This means that almost all of the DMX prediction queries in the sample code's Management Studio project can be run from this form. (Even the comments can be left in the query text.) One exception is that the code will not properly handle result sets with nested columns (such as the one in Cluster5ProbabilityDist.dmx); be sure to use the *FLATTENED* keyword to avoid this problem (as was done in Cluster5ProbabilityDistFlattened.dmx).

Model Content Queries

Other DMX query types can be handled by the ADO MD code used in the viewer in *frmDMXAdHoc*. For example, each of the DML queries in the sample code's Management Studio project can be executed in the form. However, none of these returns any data, and it would be more reasonable to run them using the *AdomdCommand* object's

ExecuteNonQuery method. Last, model content queries (which we briefly discussed earlier in the context of DMX templates) can be executed as well. For example, the following query returns textual information about the *CustomerProfitCategory_CL* clustering model:

```
SELECT NODE_CAPTION, NODE_DESCRIPTION, NODE_PROBABILITY
 FROM [CustomerProfitCategory_CL].CONTENT
```

This query can be run from a DMX Query window in Management Studio or from *frmDMXAdHoc* in *Chapter18WinClient*. (Try it and see.) The content data in text form is much less elegant than the visualization of that data, but its programmatic use is intriguing. Your application could, for example, query the model in advance, learn of certain patterns by parsing the *NODE_DESCRIPTION* column, and then execute predictive business logic upon entry of new data.

ADO MD.NET and ASP.NET

Most of what we've covered so far in the context of Windows Forms development can be implemented similarly in ASP.NET. The *Chapter18WebClient* (which is included with the sample code's Visual Studio solution on the book's companion Web site) shows an example of how to code an ASP.NET equivalent of *Chapter18WinClient*. The model content viewers must be handled in a different way from their Windows Forms counterparts (as we will discuss shortly). However, the execution of DMX queries is dealt with in much the same way as shown previously.

For example, you can populate a *GridView* control named *gvResults* with the nonhierarchical results of a DMX query, as follows:

```
AdomdConnection conn = new AdomdConnection
  ("Data Source=" + this.txtServer.Text + ";Initial Catalog=" + this.ddlCatalogs.Text);
AdomdCommand cmd = new AdomdCommand(this.txtQuery.Text, conn);
AdomdDataAdapter da = new AdomdDataAdapter(cmd);
DataTable dt = new DataTable();
da.Fill(dt);
this.gvResults.DataSource = dt;
this.gvResults.DataBind();
```

In this snippet (which is a simplified version of the code on the DMXAdHoc.aspx page in the *Chapter18WebClient* application), *ddlCatalogs* is an ASP.NET *DropDownList* control containing a list of the databases on the server whose name is specified in the *TextBox* control *txtServer*. This code is strikingly similar to its Windows Forms equivalent and is just as versatile at handling DMX queries.

Using the Data Mining Web Controls

It's good to know that DMX querying can be handled much the same way in an ASP.NET application as in Windows Forms, but what about the visualization of model content? The content viewer controls are designed for the Windows Forms environment, so we can't use them in an ASP.NET application. However, Microsoft provides sample .NET code that implements Asynchronous JavaScript and XML (AJAX) versions of the Cluster, Naïve Bayes, and Decision Trees viewers as ASP.NET server controls. Specifically, the Cluster/Attribute Characteristics and Cluster/Attribute Discrimination tabs of the Cluster and Naïve Bayes viewers and the Decision Tree tab of the Tree Viewer are implemented. This means that only certain models can be browsed and only certain views of those models are possible.

Although they provide only a subset of the functionality supplied by the Windows Forms controls, these ASP.NET components are still extremely helpful, especially given the reach of the Internet and the Web. However, these controls are provided as sample code only and are therefore a little harder to use in your applications than their Windows Forms equivalents.

You can install or view the source code for the controls; it is available in the form of a C# class library project as part of the Microsoft SQL Server 2008 Samples. The samples are no longer shipped with the product. Instead, they are now available from CodePlex (*http://www. CodePlex.com/SqlServerSamples*) as described in the Documentation and Tutorials information included with SQL Server 2008. From the CodePlex Web site, you can either browse the source code for the samples or install them. If you choose to install the samples, the installer places the Visual Studio source code for the controls, by default, in the folder C:\Program Files\Microsoft SQL Server\100\Samples\Analysis Services\DataMining\Data Mining Web Controls. If you open the WebControls.sln solution file in that folder and build the project, you can reference the generated assembly in an ASP.NET Web site in Visual Studio and add the three viewer controls to the Visual Studio Toolbox window.

You can use the controls by placing them on a Web form and setting their *Server*, *Database*, and *Model* properties, each of which is string-typed, and store or return the name of an Analysis Services server, database, and mining model whose content you want to display. As an alternative to assigning values to the *Server* and *Database* properties, you can create an *OleDbConnection* object, connect it to a specific Analysis Services database, and then assign it to the control's *Connection* property.

The Tree Viewer has a *ViewType* property that you must set to one of two enumerated constants: *Tree* or *NodeDetails*. If you set it to *Tree*, you must also set the *TargetTree* property to the name of a predictable column contained in the mining model. If you set it to *NodeDetails*, you must set the *TargetNode* property to a specific node in the decision tree.

The Naïve Bayes and Cluster Viewer controls both feature a *ViewerMode* property that also must be set to one of two enumerated constants, *Discrimination* or *Characteristics*, depending on the functionality of the tab of the Windows Forms viewers you want to duplicate.

> **More Info** See this chapter's sample code on the book's companion Web site for more details on using the ASP.NET viewer controls. The *Chapter18WebClient* application implements certain complex handling, the discussion of which is beyond the scope of this chapter. For example, each viewer is wrapped as an ASP.NET user control to aid in the ability to refresh the viewers with new model content at run time.

Developing Managed Stored Procedures

Applying your OLAP development skills to data mining doesn't end with ADO MD.NET on the client; you can use the *AdomdServer* library to execute server-side DMX prediction or content queries and return the results. For example, Listing 18-3 provides all the code necessary to implement a server-side version of the prediction query in the LeastLikelyCar.dmx Management Studio script covered earlier.

LISTING 18-3 Using *AdomdServer* for DMX queries

```
using System;
using System.Data;
using Microsoft.AnalysisServices.AdomdServer;

namespace Chapter18ServerAssembly
{
    public class StoredProcedures
    {
        public DataTable GetData()
        {
            DataTable dt = new System.Data.DataTable();
            dt.Columns.Add("FirstName", typeof(string));
            dt.Columns.Add("LastName", typeof(string));
            dt.Columns.Add("Phone", typeof(string));
            dt.Columns.Add("ProbNotCarOwner", typeof(double));

            object[] row = new object[4];

            AdomdCommand comContext = new AdomdCommand("SELECT TOP 250 t.FirstName,t.
LastName,t.Phone,PredictProbability([Is Car Owner],'N') AS ProbNotCarOwner
FROM CarOwner_DT PREDICTION JOIN OPENQUERY([AdventureWorksDW2008],'SELECT
c.FirstName,c.LastName,tc.* FROM vCustomerProfitability tc INNER JOIN dimCustomer
c ON tc.CustomerKey = c.CustomerKey') AS t ON t.Gender = CarOwner_DT.Gender AND
t.IncomeGroup = CarOwner_dt.[Income Group] AND t.MaritalStatus = CarOwner_dt.[Marital
Status] AND t.Region = CarOwner_dt.Region ORDER BY PredictProbability([Is Car
Owner],'N') DESC");
```

```
        try
        {
            AdomdDataReader dr = comContext.ExecuteReader();
            while (dr.Read())
            {
                row[0] = dr[0];
                row[1] = dr[1];
                row[2] = dr[2];
                row[3] = dr[3];
                dt.Rows.Add(row);
            }
            dr.Close();
            return dt;
        }
        catch
        {
            return null;
        }
    }
}
}
```

Although it is not possible to execute an MDX query using *AdomdServer*, it is permissible to execute a DMX query. In the case of this stored procedure, we simply create the *AdomdServer.AdomdCommand* object *comContext*, passing the DMX query to its constructor. We make sure to type the function as returning a *DataTable*, and we populate a local *DataTable* variable with the contents of an *AdomdDataReader*. The latter is obtained by calling the *comContext* object's *ExecuteReader* method. As with the managed code in Chapter 17, there is no need to explicitly create a connection to execute this query—it implicitly uses the connection in whose context the code is called.

The code in Listing 18-3 is taken from the Class Library project *Chapter18ServerAssembly* in the sample code's Visual Studio solution. This project can be built and deployed to the *Chapter18* database (using the techniques discussed in Chapter 17 for deploying managed assemblies). When deploying the assembly, you should assign it ExternalAccess permissions; assigning it Unrestricted permissions is not necessary, and assigning it Safe permissions will prevent the DMX query from executing and returning data properly.

Once deployed, the stored procedure can be called using the following DMX code:

```
CALL Chapter18ServerAssembly.Chapter18ServerAssembly.StoredProcedures.GetData()
```

This query can be run in a SQL Server Management Studio DMX Query window (it is contained in the Management Studio project script ManagedCode.dmx) or in the *Chapter18WinClient* and *Chapter18WebClient* applications. If the code were more complex, you would perhaps want to debug it; you could do so by using exactly the same technique described in Chapter 17 (by attaching the Visual Studio debugger to the Analysis Services process).

Keep in mind that your stored procedures can also execute DDL queries using DMX (by using the *AdomdCommand* object's *ExecuteNonQuery* method) or perform administrative or DDL tasks using AMO. The AMO *Database* object contains a *MiningStructures* collection, each member of which contains its own *MiningModels* collection. The AMO *MiningStructure* and *MiningModel* objects each have an array of properties, methods, and child objects that are useful for performing any number of administrative or DDL tasks against your mining structures and models.

XMLA and Data Mining

To round off our coverage of data mining development and how it compares with OLAP development, it is important to mention that XMLA can be used for all data mining tasks, including execution of a DMX query (of any type) or the scripted creation of objects. As with OLAP objects, you can right-click a mining structure or model in the Management Studio Object Explorer window and choose Script Mining Structure As (or Script Mining Model As) to generate an XMLA script for its creation, deletion, or alteration. Similarly, you can use the View Code option from the Solution Explorer window in Visual Studio on a mining structure in an Analysis Services project to reveal the XMLA script that will be executed to deploy that mining structure to the server.

As a quick example, the following query (contained in LeastLikelyCar.xmla in the Management Studio sample solution) runs the same DMX query contained in LeastLikelyCar. dmx and retrieves the result as XML:

```
<Execute xmlns="urn:schemas-microsoft-com:xml-analysis">
  <Command>
    <Statement>
      SELECT   TOP 250 t.FirstName, t.LastName, t.Phone,
               PredictProbability([Is Car Owner],'N') AS ProbNotCarOwner
      FROM           CarOwner_DT
      PREDICTION JOIN
        OPENQUERY([AdventureWorksDW2008],
        'SELECT c.FirstName,c.LastName,tc.*
         FROM    vCustomerProfitability tc
          INNER JOIN dimCustomer c ON tc.CustomerKey = c.CustomerKey')
        AS t
        ON t.Gender = CarOwner_DT.Gender AND
          t.IncomeGroup = CarOwner_dt.[Income Group] AND
          t.MaritalStatus = CarOwner_dt.[Marital Status] AND
          t.Region = CarOwner_dt.Region
      ORDER BY PredictProbability([Is Car Owner],'N') DESC
    </Statement>
  </Command>
  <Properties>
    <PropertyList>
      <Catalog>Chapter18</Catalog>
    </PropertyList>
  </Properties>
</Execute>
```

Notice that the structure of the query is virtually identical to the XMLA script QueryCubeChapter17.xmla from Chapter 17. The only differences are the change in database name within the *<Catalog>* tags and the replacement of an MDX query with a DMX query.

Unlike QueryCubeChapter17.xmla, however, this query returns its XML data using a very straightforward schema. Here's an excerpt from the response stream:

```
<return xmlns="urn:schemas-microsoft-com:xml-analysis">
  <root xmlns="urn:schemas-microsoft-com:xml-analysis:rowset" xmlns:xsi="http://www.
w3.org/2001/XMLSchema-instance" xmlns:xsd="http://www.w3.org/2001/XMLSchema">
    <xsd:schema ...>
      :
    </xsd:schema>
    <row>
      <FirstName>Gerald</FirstName>
      <LastName>Moreno</LastName>
      <Phone>1 (11) 500 555-0189</Phone>
      <ProbNotCarOwner>7.795216741405082E-1</ProbNotCarOwner>
    </row>
    <row>
      <FirstName>Erick</FirstName>
      <LastName>Fernandez</LastName>
      <Phone>1 (11) 500 555-0117</Phone>
      <ProbNotCarOwner>7.795216741405082E-1</ProbNotCarOwner>
    </row>
    <row>
      <FirstName>Alisha</FirstName>
      <LastName>Nath</LastName>
      <Phone>1 (11) 500 555-0173</Phone>
      <ProbNotCarOwner>7.795216741405082E-1</ProbNotCarOwner>
    </row>
      :
  </root>
</return>
```

Because the schema differs so radically from the OLAP/multidimensional schema we studied in Chapter 17, the Extensible Stylesheet Language (XSL) stylesheet we discussed in that chapter is of no use to us for the tabular result sets returned by DMX queries. However, the tabular schema is so transparent that it can be easily parsed using various objects in the .NET *System.Xml* namespace or using a simple XSL stylesheet of your own creation.

Before closing this chapter, let's finish our tour of application-level data mining techniques with a look at the data mining–specific functionality available with Excel 2007.

Data Mining Add-ins for Excel 2007

Data mining add-ins for Excel 2007 are available as a free download from Microsoft. These add-ins allow users to take advantage of the power of the data mining engine of Analysis Services from a tool that the average office worker is probably intimately familiar with.

> **More Info**   At the time of this book's writing, the SQL Server 2005 Data Mining Add-ins for
> 2007 Microsoft Office system were available for download from *http://www.microsoft.com/*
> *sql/technologies/dm/addins.mspx*, and the SQL Server 2008 Data Mining Add-ins for 2007
> Office system were available for download from *http://www.microsoft.com/downloads/details.*
> *aspx?FamilyID=896a493a-2502-4795-94ae-e00632ba6de7&DisplayLang=en*. Follow the instruc-
> tions on the download page for installing the add-ins.
>
> Even if you do not have 2007 Office system, you can still experiment with the add-ins by
> downloading a free trial version. The trial version, as well as a complete list of prerequisites
> for the add-ins, is available from Microsoft at *http://office.microsoft.com/en-us/products/*
> *HA101741481033.aspx*.

The add-in for Excel 2007 comes in two flavors: Table Analysis Tools and the Data Mining
Client. The default installation of the add-ins installs only the Table Analysis Tools. The Data
Mining Client must be explicitly selected during the installation. The data mining add-ins
for 2007 Office system also include a component for use with Microsoft Office Visio 2007.
(Discussion of the Visio add-in is beyond the scope of this chapter.) Figure 18-38 shows the
Excel 2007 Ribbon for the Table Analysis Tools add-in. Figure 18-39 shows the Excel 2007
Ribbon for the Data Mining Client add-in for comparison.

FIGURE 18-38 The Microsoft Office Excel 2007 Ribbon for the Table Analysis Tools add-in

FIGURE 18-39 The Microsoft Office Excel 2007 Ribbon for the Data Mining Client add-in

The Table Analysis Tools add-in has menu choices on the Ribbon that are task oriented: the
user chooses the task, and the add-in chooses the algorithm used to complete the task. It
is not possible to explicitly specify which algorithm to use for the data mining task from the
Table Analysis Tools. Although each task on the Table Analysis Tools Ribbon implies a data
mining task, the user isn't shown that level of detail. Thus, for example, a user need know
only that categories should be detected from the data, not that the Microsoft Clustering algorithm should be used to detect those categories. The Table Analysis Tools add-in can be
used to mine only data that is in an Excel table. Mining models are created as Session Mining
models; the mining model is unavailable after the connection is closed (that is, afer the Excel
workbook is closed).

Tip You won't see the Table Analysis Tools Ribbon unless you have an Excel table in your workbook and the cursor is in a cell that is within an Excel table.

In contrast, the Data Mining Client Ribbon—while more friendly and familiar to the average Office user than Visual Studio—is more technical than the Table Analysis Tools Ribbon. Items on the Ribbon are organized into groups based on the different steps in the data mining project life cyle: Data Preparation, Data Modeling, Accuracy And Validation, Model Usage, and Management. Furthermore, using the Advanced option in the Data Modeling group, the user is able to specify the algorithm that should be used to complete the data mining task at hand. The Explore Data and Clean Data tasks in the Data Preparation group can be applied only to data in an Excel table in the workbook; however, all other tasks can be applied to any external data for which a data source connection can be made from Analysis Services. Mining models can be created as Session Mining models, or they can be saved on the server so that they can be shared with other users and applied to new data.

In the remainder of this section, we will walk through the steps to estimate a profit forecasting model using the Table Analysis Tools, add a profit forecasting model to the database using the Data Mining Client add-in, and browse and generate documentation for the data mining structures and models created in this chapter.

Creating a Model Using the Table Analysis Tools

After installing the data mining add-ins, start Excel 2007. You will see that Data Mining (a new toolbar button) has been added to the rightmost position on the Quick Launch toolbar. You might be left wondering whether something has gone awry with the installation of the Table Analysis Tools add-in. While clicking Data Mining on the Quick Launch menu displays the Data Mining Client Ribbon shown earlier in Figure 18-39, there doesn't appear to be any way to get to the Table Analysis Tools Ribbon shown in Figure 18-38. This is because the Table Analysis Tools add-in can be used only against data in an Excel table, as mentioned earlier. So in order to see the Table Analysis Tools on the Quick Launch menu, we must create an Excel table in our workbook.

Table Analysis Tools Add-in Data Source

We are going to use the data from the *vMonthlyProfit* view that was created at the start of this chapter.

Tip As an alternative to running a SQL query to retrieve the data for analysis, you can use the MonthlyProfit.xlsx file provided as part of the downloads for this chapter. MonthlyProfit.xlsx already has the data from *vMonthlyProfit* in an Excel table ready for use with the Table Analysis Tools add-in.

1. Open Management Studio, and then execute the following SQL statement in the context of the *AdventureWorksDW2008* database:

```
SELECT * FROM dbo.vMonthlyProfit
```

2. Copy the result set into Excel, leaving one row at the top for column headings. Type the headings **MonthYear**, **North America**, **Europe**, and **Pacific** for each of the four columns of data. Highlight the cells with the header and data, and then select Format As Table from the Styles group of the Home Ribbon. Select a style for your table from the available options. Rename your worksheet **Monthly Profit**. Your Excel worksheet should appear similar to Figure 18-40.

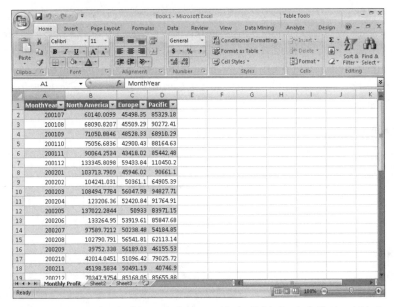

FIGURE 18-40 An Excel table ready for use with the Table Analysis Tools add-in for Excel 2007

3. Click any cell in the table. Now you will see Table Analysis Tools on the Quick Launch menu.

Establishing an Analysis Services Connection

The data mining add-ins rely on the data mining engine of Analysis Services to train the mining models. The data mining algorithms are not added or available in Excel itself. As such, the first step to using the data mining add-ins is to establish an Analysis Services connection.

> **Important** Both the Table Analysis Tools add-in and the Data Mining Client add-in for Excel require a connection to a SQL Server Analysis Services database. At first glance, this is counterintuitive, particularly for the Table Analysis Tools add-in, which allows analysis only of data in Excel tables. A connection to an Analysis Services database is required because the training of the mining models—the detection of patterns in the data—is not performed on the client machine but is done using the data mining engine of Analysis Services.

1. Click Analyze under Table Tools to expose the Table Analysis Tools Ribbon. Click the <No Connection> icon in the Connection group. This will display the Analysis Services Connections dialog box.

2. Because we have not yet established any connections to Analysis Services from Excel, the list of available connections is empty. Click New, enter the name of the server where you have created your mining models, select the database containing your models from the Catalog drop-down list, and then click OK. You will now see your newly established connection identified as the Current Connection. Your dialog box should look similar to Figure 18-41.

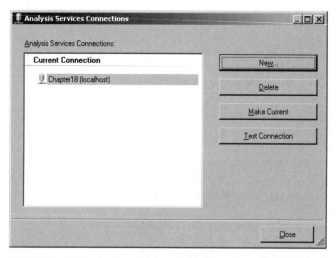

FIGURE 18-41 The Analysis Services Connections dialog box for the data mining add-ins for Excel 2007

3. Test the connection, and then click Close. Instead of <No Connection> you will now see the friendly name of the current connection, which by default is the name of the Catalog followed by the server name in parentheses

Forecasting Using the Table Analysis Tools Add-in

We are now ready to start mining our data from Excel:

1. Scroll to the bottom of the Excel table. Data is available only through June 2004. We want to forecast monthly profit through the end of the year—that is, through December 2004.

2. Click the Forecast task on the Table Analysis Tools Analyze Ribbon. Verify that North America, Europe, and Pacific are selected. Change the Number Of Time Units To Forecast to 6. Select MonthYear from the Time Stamp drop-down list. Click the Periodicity Of Data drop-down list to see the options available: Hourly, Weekly, Monthly, Quarterly, and Yearly. After reviewing the available options, make sure that the original default value of <Detect Automatically> is selected.

> **Note** The Forecast task uses the Microsoft Time Series algorithm to forecast future values of a series based on the historical values of the series. If there is a repeating pattern to the series, you can specify this using the data periodicity parameter. For example, if profit follows an annual pattern, you would choose Yearly from the drop-down list. If you are not certain of the periodicity of the data, you can ask the data mining engine of Analysis Services to detect the periodicity of the data automatically.

Your selections should match those shown in Figure 18-42.

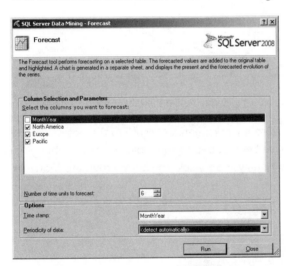

FIGURE 18-42 Configuration of a forecast using the Table Analysis Tools add-in

3. Click Run. Excel will connect to the Analysis Services server specified in the current connection to train the mining model. After a brief wait, the profit prediction results for the next six months are displayed in a chart in a new worksheet titled Forecasting Report, as shown in Figure 18-43. The forecasted values are differentiated from the actual values by a dotted line.

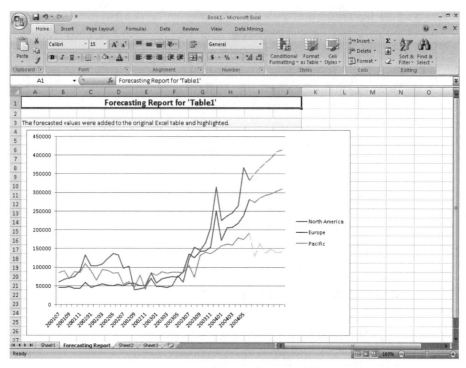

FIGURE 18-43 A forecasting report generated using the Table Analysis Tools add-in for Excel 2007

4. Go back to the Monthly Profit worksheet, and scroll to the bottom of the table. You will see that six new rows have been added to the table. From the table, you can see the exact profit predicted by Analysis Services. The added rows are shown in Figure 18-44.

	MonthYear	North America	Europe	Pacific	E
25	200306	60345.6706	88619.76	86085.28	
26	200307	122199.1829	134912.2	105003.7	
27	200308	153890.7311	126003.4	73509.97	
28	200309	145489.9409	143074.8	132010.5	
29	200310	164882.3533	143978.9	140255.8	
30	200311	206307.8689	153145.6	137105.9	
31	200312	314353.6096	251089.2	146366.4	
32	200401	224900.5372	172393.5	157665	
33	200402	236870.9645	205394.8	162651.4	
34	200403	245800.3068	207235.2	159898.8	
35	200404	264724.3516	217953.6	179565.4	
36	200405	366520.4541	238798.7	174655	
37	200406	332513.9333	282130.4	191656.6	
38		351493.1954	273117.6	129154	
39		365684.5263	286437.3	163150	
40		379524.4629	292433.2	138134.5	
41		392965.1193	295769	149100.6	
42		409364.1068	303299.8	139390.4	
43		413566.9739	311019.2	141488	
44					
45					

FIGURE 18-44 Rows with forecasted data added to the Excel table

5. Close the Excel file, optionally saving it.

As noted at the beginning of this section, the Table Analysis Tools add-in uses Session Mining models. While the predictions from the mining model just created (that is, the six forecasted values) will be saved in the Excel file along with the generated chart, the mining model itself is discarded. It would not be possible to go back and request additional months of forecasted values without retraining the model.

Creating a Model Using the Data Mining Client

Now we will train a similar forecasting model, this time using the Data Mining Client add-in, and save the model to our existing Analysis Services database:

1. Start Excel 2007. Click Data Mining on the Quick Launch menu. Notice that the current connection specified in the Connection group has been defaulted from our previous analysis.

2. Hover the mouse pointer over the Forecast task from the Data Modeling group. The tooltip states that the Microsoft Time Series algorithm will be used to forecast future values of data.

3. Click the Forecast task. This will open the Forecast Wizard, very similar to the one we just used with the Table Analysis Tools add-in.

4. On the Welcome page, click Next. This will bring us to the Select Source Data dialog box.

Data Mining Client Add-in Data Sources

When using the Data Mining Client add-in, we need to specify the data to use for the forecast as a step in the wizard. In contrast, when we used the Table Analysis Tools add-in, the Forecast Wizard was launched while the cursor was in an Excel table, indicating the table as the source for the forecast.

1. In the Select Source Data dialog box, select External Data Source, and then click the Data Source icon next to the text box. This will display the Data Sources Query Editor dialog box, where you will see a drop-down list with all of the data sources available in your current Analysis Services connection. Note that from this dialog box, you can also create a new data source connection by clicking the New Data Source button next to the Server Data Source drop-down list. The only *new* data sources that can be created from the wizard are SQL Server Native Client connections; however, any data source, including connections to non-SQL sources, that has been created in the Analysis Services database will be available to Excel via the drop-down list.

2. Verify that the *AdventureWorksDW2008* data source created earlier in this chapter is selected in the Server Data Source drop-down list. Then look for *vMonthlyProfit* in the list of Available Tables And Columns. Double-click *vMonthlyProfit*. The columns from the view will be added to the Columns In Query box, and a SQL query returning the columns of the view will be specified in the Query box below. Your dialog box should appear similar to the one shown in Figure 18-45.

FIGURE 18-45 The Data Source Query Editor dialog box from the Data Mining Client add-in

3. Click OK to close the dialog box, and then back in the Forecast Wizard, click Next.

Forecasting Using the Data Mining Client Add-in

This brings us to the configuration page for the forecasting model:

1. In the Forecasting Wizard, ensure that MonthYear is selected in the Time Stamp drop-down list. Clear MonthYear in the Input Columns list, leaving North America, Europe, and Pacific selected; we will predict monthly profit separately for each of the three regions. The completed dialog box is shown in Figure 18-46.

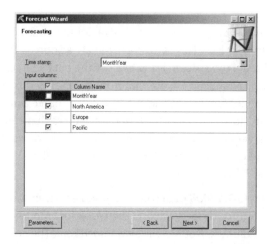

FIGURE 18-46 Configuration of a forecast using the Data Mining Client add-in

2. You will notice that, unlike the dialog box for the Table Analysis Tools shown earlier in Figure 18-42, the periodicity of the data is not overtly specified in this dialog box. In fact, the periodicity of the data can be specified when using the Data Mining Client add-in, along with a host of additional parameters not available from the Table Analysis Tools. Click the Parameters button in the dialog box. This opens a window with the algorithm parameters—exactly the same set of algorithm parameters as would be available from Visual Studio. (Recall the Algorithm Parameters dialog box for the Microsoft Clustering model discussed earlier in this chapter and shown in Figure 18-13).

3. The periodicity of the data is specified via the *Periodicity_Hint* parameter. You might need to scroll down to see this parameter. Unlike the simple set of friendly selections, such as Hourly and Weekly, that were available in the Table Analysis Tools dialog box, the *Periodicity_Hint* parameter is less friendly but more flexible. You must specify a positive integer to indicate the periodicity of the data. For example, to indicate a yearly repeating pattern for data that is stored on a monthly level, you would set the *Periodicity_Hint* value to {12}. Rather than being restricted to the periodicity implied by the selections of Hourly, Weekly, Monthly, Quarterly, or Yearly, any positive integer can be specified. Therefore, if it is known that the data follows a repeating pattern every six months, it is possible to specify {6} in the periodicity hint, whereas there would be no way to indicate this using one of the predefined options in the Table Analysis Tools Forecast Wizard. Specifying an incorrect hint can negatively affect the model estimation; therefore, use care when specifying a periodicity. When in doubt, use the default option, which allows Analysis Services to detect the periodicity in the data. Click Cancel to close the Parameter dialog box and use the default specification.

> **Note** Analysis Services 2005 used the Autoregressive Tree with Cross Prediction (ARTxp) algorithm to estimate time-series models. This is an algorithm written by the Microsoft Research team specifically for the Data Mining module of Analysis Services. The algorithm is optimized for predicting the next value for the series. In our example, this would be the profit for July 2004. For Analysis Services 2008, the widely used and well-understood Autoregressive Integrated Moving Average (ARIMA) algorithm was added to Data Mining module. This algorithm is optimized for forecasts further into the future. By default, the Microsoft Time Series algorithm uses a blend of the two algorithms, weighting the ARTxp algorithm predictions more heavily for short-term predictions and the ARIMA algorithm predictions more heavily for long-term predictions. By setting the *PREDICTION_SMOOTHING* parameter of the Time Series algorithm, you can have complete control over which algorithm is used for estimating the time-series model, including using only the ARTxp algorithm (*PREDICTION_SMOOTHING = 0*) or only the ARIMA algorithm (*PREDICTION_SMOOTHING = 1*).

4. Back in the Forecast Wizard, enter **MonthlyProfit** for the Structure Name and **MonthlyProfit_TS** for the Model Name. Verify that the Temporary Model check box is not selected; we will save the mining model in the Analysis Services database specified by our current connection. Click Finish. Excel will connect to the server and train the

model. When the estimation is complete, the Microsoft Time Series Viewer window will appear.

5. From this window, you can specify the number of time periods to predict by changing the Prediction Steps value, or you can click the Copy To Excel button and generate a forecasting chart report similar to the one created by the Table Analysis Tools Forecasting task. You can also see the equations estimated by the algorithm by clicking the Model tab of the viewer.

> **Tip** If you are curious about how the add-ins create, train, and use the mining models, you can actually see the combination of XMLA and DMX commands executed by the Excel add-ins. Simply click the Trace option in the Connection group of the Data Mining Client Ribbon.

6. When you have finished exploring the model, exit Excel.

Browsing Mining Models

Unlike the session mining models generated by the Table Analysis Tools add-in, mining models saved to the server using the Data Mining Client can be browsed at a later date.

1. Start Excel once again. Select Data Mining from the Quick Launch toolbar, and then click Browse in the Model Usage group of the Ribbon. This will open the dialog box shown in Figure 18-47, with the complete list of mining structures and models created in this chapter, including the mining model created using the Data Mining Client add-in.

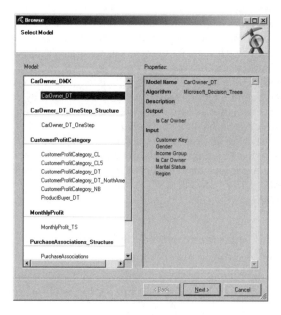

FIGURE 18-47 A list of mining structures and models on the server as seen from the Browse task of the Model Usage group of the Data Mining Client add-in

2. Select the *MonthlyProfit_TS* model, and then click Next. The Time Series Viewer is opened in a new window, and it is possible to interact with the model, just as we did when it was created.

Data Mining Documentation

Using the Data Mining Client add-in, it is easy to document the mining structures and models on your server. Simply click the Document Model task in the Model Usage group of the Data Mining Client Ribbon. Follow the steps in the wizard to generate either summary or detail documentation. Summary documentation includes the mining structure and model names and when the model was last processed. Detail documentation includes details about the column usage and algorithm parameters used by the mining models.

This chapter only scratches the surface of the data mining functionality offered by the data mining add-ins for 2007 Microsoft Office system. In fact, it would be almost possible to avoid using Visual Studio and SQL Server Management Studio entirely and exclusively use the Excel add-ins to complete your data mining tasks. The only caveats are these: the Analysis Services database to which you want to save your mining structures and models must already exist (that is, Analysis Services databases cannot be created using the Excel add-ins), and you cannot create any mining models that require a nested table column. Better yet, the add-ins greatly simplify certain applications of data mining such as filling in missing data and identifying anomalous values in your data. Take the time to explore the various tasks on the Quick Launch menus, and you will be rewarded with the knowledge of a highly functional, easy-to-use tools not only for mining your data, but also for applying your data mining.

Summary

SQL Server Analysis Services 2008 offers a complete tool set for a data mining solution. This chapter has introduced you to these tools and their many uses, from creating random samples to presenting the results in a custom application for business users. You were introduced to the Data Mining Wizard, which guides you through the creation of a mining structure and mining model. You saw how to add and edit mining models, including how to tweak algorithm parameters, from the Mining Models tab of the data mining structure designer.

You browsed the results of several mining models using Microsoft's mining model viewers. Several viewers are provided for each algorithm, allowing you to analyze the results from different perspectives. And you created a lift chart for comparing the performance of different models.

In a brief introduction to DMX, you saw how to use the DMX query language to perform the very same kinds of tasks that you did using the Data Mining Wizard. You then saw how to apply your DMX knowledge programmatically using the development tools you learned in the context of OLAP cubes. As you saw in this chapter, ADO MD.NET provides full support for data mining, and you can easily embed the powerful mining model viewers into a customer application. You also saw how to take advantage of the data mining engine of Analysis Services directly from Excel.

As with the Microsoft OLAP platform, the data mining component of Analysis Services is distinguished by its ease of use and high degree of programmability. The additions made to the data mining component in SQL Server 2008 position Microsoft squarely among the top business intelligence solution providers.

Chapter 19
Reporting Services

—Elsie Pan and Jeff Bolton

Microsoft SQL Server 2008 Reporting Services is a comprehensive server-based reporting solution that supports the full reporting life cycle—from creating and managing reports to securing and delivering reports for end users. In this chapter, we'll examine each phase of that cycle as we walk through a number of real-world reporting scenarios. By the end of this chapter, you will have learned all the fundamentals needed—and more—to effectively take advantage of Reporting Services in SQL Server 2008.

In addition to SQL Server relational databases, Reporting Services supports the creation of reports against a wide variety of data sources, including Analysis Services databases, Oracle, and DB2. In fact, any data source for which an OLE-DB provider or Open Database Connectivity (ODBC) driver is available can be used in a report. It is also possible to combine data from multiple sources into a single report by using multiple data sets and multiple data regions in the report. By using report expressions, developers can control the formatting and visibility of individual report elements. With report parameters and actions, it is possible to create dynamic reports that allow end users to decide the direction and depth of the data analysis. Custom behavior can also be applied to reports by embedding Microsoft Visual Basic .NET script code into the report or by referencing a .NET assembly to call managed code classes and methods written in any .NET language.

After the reports are built, they must be deployed to the report server. This can be accomplished using Microsoft Visual Studio 2008, the Report Manager Web-based user interface (UI), or a command-line tool. We will examine and compare each of these deployment methods when we discuss deployment in detail. Reports that have been deployed to a report server are immediately available to your users. In addition to the Web-based interface for serving reports provided out-of-the box with Reporting Services, you can also render reports from within any .NET application using the *ReportViewer* control. Reporting Services also exposes two Web Services (also referred to as SOAP endpoints) for use in managing and generating reports.

Since Reporting Services is an enterprise-level reporting solution, security and reliability of both the data and the system is paramount. A brief overview of the configuration tool, which has been greatly improved in SQL Server 2008 Reporting Services, is provided to help you understand some of the reliability and security built into Reporting Services. To improve performance and availability, Reporting Services supports the delivery of a report to a user in response to either an event or a schedule. Securing the reports and data is accomplished with a robust system of both site-level security and object-level security with a complete set of configurable roles and tasks. Last, to improve integration and provide a consistent enterprise reporting platform, Reporting Services easily integrates with Microsoft Office SharePoint.

With this basic frame of reference established, we're ready now to dive into Reporting Services! The life of every report begins with the Report Designer, and that's where we'll start. First we'll design several reports that demonstrate many powerful Reporting Services features. We'll then turn our attention to report delivery, which (as we've already briefly described) entails deployment, security, application development, and integration.

Using the Report Designer

The Report Designer is the SQL Server report development tool targeted toward developers. Using the Report Designer, developers can create flexible reports with sophisticated formatting and a high degree of user interactivity. Reports that are graphically composed using the Report Designer are saved in a special XML dialect called report definition language (RDL). These RDL files are, in turn, deployed to a Reporting Services server and rendered to users that request them. The Report Designer is a component of the Business Intelligence Developer Studio, and hence a component of Visual Studio. This tool has been significantly enhanced for Reporting Services 2008.

> **Note** From Visual Studio 2005, you can publish only to a SQL Server 2005 Reporting Services report server. From Visual Studio 2008, you can publish only to a SQL Server 2008 Reporting Services report server. To upgrade 2005 reports to 2008, simply open the report design file (.rdl file) in Visual Studio 2008. An upgrade prompt dialog box will open to confirm that you want to upgrade the report to the 2008 RDL schema. Once a report has been upgraded, you must use the 2008 version of the Report Designer to edit the reports; there is no going back.

Superficially, the Report Designer interface has been reorganized since the 2005 version of the product. Figure 19-1 shows the Report Designer interface in Visual Studio 2008. The functionality formerly provided using the Data tab in Visual Studio 2005 has been moved to the Report Data pane, which appears docked on the left of the screen—outside the designer window itself. Creation and configuration of report parameters and images is also now done from the Report Data pane. A new Grouping pane has been added to the bottom of the Design tab to allow for a more intuitive drag-and-drop experience when creating and configuring groups.

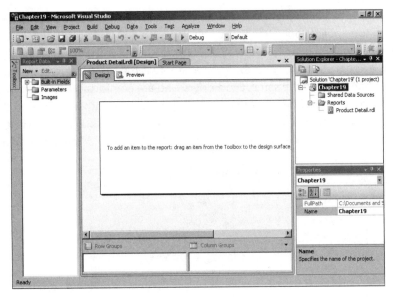

FIGURE 19-1 The new Report Designer in Visual Studio 2008

Functionally, the code base for report data regions has been rewritten and extended to allow for significantly more flexible table and matrix designs and more sophisticated and option-rich charts. Previously, different code bases were used for each of the list, table, and matrix data regions; this resulted in a sometimes inconsistent user experience when configuring each type of data region. The code base for the data regions has now been unified in Reporting Services 2008. In fact, lists, tables, and matrices are all now really based on the new *tablix* region with a list, table, or matrix template. So while you continue to choose list, table, and matrix data regions from the report toolbox, under the covers you are creating a tablix data region.

The unification of the code base not only promotes a consistent user experience when configuring each data region, but it also offers new flexibility in the creation of data regions. For example, it is now possible to add a fixed column or fixed row to a matrix and to specify which data columns should have subtotals included rather than being forced to include subtotals for all or none of the data columns in the matrix. Specific examples demonstrating the increased flexibility of the tablix data region are provided later in this chapter.

In 2007, Microsoft acquired the Dundas Data Visualization product, and as a result, the charting functionality available out of the box from Reporting Services is greatly improved. On a basic level, there is now support for dual-axis charts, something that was sorely missing from earlier versions of the Report Designer. Users requiring more arcane charting capabilities will be happy to discover that stepped line, pyramid, Gantt, and a whole host of other chart types are now available out of the box from Reporting Services. See the Reporting Services documentation in SQL Server Books Online for a complete list of available chart types.

Following the release of SQL Server 2008, the Report Designer will also be available as a stand-alone desktop application with a Ribbon UI similar to 2007 Microsoft Office system products. The interface is shown in Figure 19-2. The code base for the stand-alone Report Designer and the Report designer hosted in Visual Studio is the same; therefore, the dialog boxes and capabilities are the same. Developers who are comfortable working in Visual Studio and who want to combine Reporting Services projects with other projects in the same solution will prefer working in Visual Studio, whereas the familiar Office-like interface of the stand-alone application will make report design accessible to a whole new group of users.

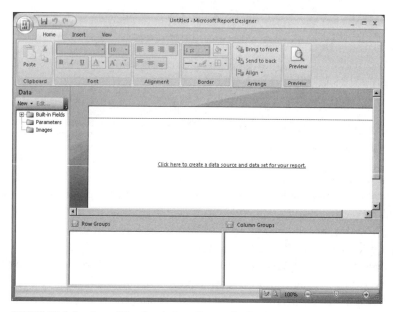

FIGURE 19-2 Preview of the stand-alone Report Designer

Note This chapter uses the sample Adventure Works data warehouse database and Analysis Services database. Sample databases are no longer shipped with SQL Server 2008—they must be downloaded from the CodePlex Web site. See this book's Introduction for instructions on obtaining and installing the sample databases.

We will now walk through the creation of several reports. In the process, we will demonstrate the reporting capabilities of the Report Designer in Visual Studio 2008 and highlight the enhancements added with the 2008 release of the product.

Creating a Basic Report

We'll start with a very basic report showing the products that are sold to customers over the Internet by the fictitious Adventure Works bicycle company. We will create and format this report completely from scratch in order to gain an understanding of the elements that go into a report. Later in this chapter, we will create a report using the Report Wizard, which guides you through the process with a series of dialog boxes and handles many formatting tasks for you automatically.

To get started, we will first create a Visual Studio project and solution for our report designs. Start Visual Studio 2008, and then select New, Project from the File menu. Select the Business Intelligence project type and the Report Server Project template. Name your project **Chapter19**. By default, a *Chapter19* solution will also be created. Right-click the Reports node in Solution Explorer, and then select Add, New Item from the shortcut menu. Select the Report template, name the report **Product Detail.rdl**, and then click Add. This will open the Report Designer interface. You should be looking at a view similar to that shown earlier in Figure 19-1.

> **Note** If the Report Data pane is not visible in the Report Designer, you can show it by selecting Report Data from the View menu.

Report Data Sets

If you are familiar with Report Designer in Visual Studio 2005, you will notice that the Data tab is missing from the new Report Designer in Visual Studio 2008. As we mentioned earlier, the functionality previously provided by the Data tab has been relocated to the Report Data pane, which is by default docked on the left in Visual Studio. Previously, the data pane in the design view merely listed fields available for use in the report, and it was necessary to toggle back and forth between the Data and Layout tabs in order to see the query source for the data sets. Now all information about the report's data sources and data sets is easily accessible in the Report Data pane without ever losing sight of your report design.

The first step to creating a report is to specify the data set for the report. Click the New button in the Report Data pane, and then select Dataset. Name the report data set **ProductDetail**. We need to specify the data source for the data set. Since this is our first report, we don't yet have any report data sources defined. Click the New button next to the Data Source drop-down list. This will open the Data Source Properties dialog box.

Name the data source **AdventureWorksDW2008**. You have a choice of whether to create an embedded data source or a shared data source. The connection information for an embedded data source is stored as part of the RDL in the report file and is accessible only to the report in which it is defined. Creating a shared data source, in contrast, creates a separate file with the data connection information. A shared data source is accessible to any reports created in the same report project. Shared data sources are deployed separately from reports and, once deployed, are available to any reports deployed to the same report server. For our report, we will create a shared data source.

Select the Use Shared Data Source Reference option, and then click New. In the Shared Data Source Properties dialog box, name the data source **AdventureWorksDW2008**, verify that Microsoft SQL Server is selected as the data source type, and then click the Edit button to the right of the Connection String text box.

In the Connection Properties dialog box, enter the name of the server on which the *AdventureWorksDW2008* sample database is stored and provide your login credentials to that server. Select AdventureWorksDW2008 from the Select Or Enter A Database Name drop-down list. (You can then also optionally click the Test Connection button to confirm that the connection is valid.) Then click OK to close the Connection Properties dialog box. Click OK again to close the Shared Data Source Properties dialog box. Last, back in the Data Source Properties dialog box, select the AdventureWorksDW2008 option from the Use Shared Data Source Reference drop-down list, and then click OK to return to the Dataset Properties dialog box.

In the Dataset Properties dialog box, AdventureWorksDW2008 should now be selected as the Data Source. Make sure that the Query Type option is set to Text, and then type the following code into the window (or click the Import button and open the SelectProductDetail.sql file from the chapter's source code available on the book's companion Web site):

```
SELECT
  p.ProductKey,
  pc.EnglishProductCategoryName,
  ps.EnglishProductSubcategoryName,
  p.EnglishProductName,
  p.EnglishDescription,
  p.StandardCost,
  p.ListPrice
FROM dbo.DimProduct AS p
  INNER JOIN dbo.DimProductSubcategory AS ps
  ON p.ProductSubcategoryKey = ps.ProductSubcategoryKey
  INNER JOIN dbo.DimProductCategory AS pc
  ON ps.ProductCategoryKey = pc.ProductCategoryKey
```

This query returns a list of products from *DimProduct* along with the product subcategory and category from *DimProductSubcategory* and *DimProductCategory*. The Dataset Properties dialog box should now appear similar to Figure 19-3.

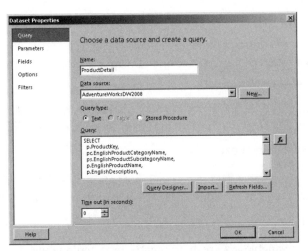

FIGURE 19-3 The completed Dataset Properties dialog box

After you have entered the query in the query window, click OK. The Dataset Properties window will close, and you will now see the *AdventureWorksDW2008* data source along with a new data set in the Report Data pane. Below the data set name, you will see the fields that were specified in the query. These fields are now available to be displayed in the report. Because the data source was created as a shared data source, you will also see a new Report Data Source (.rds file) created under the Shared Data Sources node in Solution Explorer.

> **Tip** The Report Designer allows you to import queries from SQL scripts (.sql files) or other reports (.rdl files). Simply click the Import button in the Query Designer, and then browse to a SQL script or report file. If a report file is selected, the designer will show a list of the data sets defined in the selected report, along with the associated query for the data set. This makes it easy to share queries between reports, or to copy a query from an existing report that is similar to the desired query and then modify that query as needed. Ideally, stored procedures would be used, both from a query performance and reusability standpoint; however, in cases where a stored procedure is not available, the import functionality is a handy way to quickly reuse queries from one report to another.

You have successfully defined a shared data source and a data set for the report and are now ready to begin designing the report.

Adding a Data Region

Data from data sets is displayed in reports using data regions. The choice of data region determines the layout or visualization of the data shown in the report. There are two types of data regions in Reporting Services 2008:

- **Tablix** New data region introduced in Reporting Services 2008. Allows fixed or variable rows and columns in any combination with grouping on rows, columns, or both.

- **Chart** Graphical representation of data.

As we started describing earlier, the tablix data region in Reporting Services 2008 is the general form of these three data regions previously available in Reporting Services 2005:

- **List** Freeform layout of data.

- **Table** Fixed columns and variable rows with grouping supported on rows. The number of rows is based on the number of records in the data set.

- **Matrix** Variable columns and variable rows with grouping supported on both rows and columns. Similar to PivotTables and crosstab layouts. The number of columns and rows depends on the number of unique values of the field by which the columns or rows are grouped.

In Reporting Services 2008, it is easy to change between the table and matrix data region types or to end up with a hybrid tablix type. Technically, it is also possible to change between a list and table or list and matrix, but in practice, this might take a bit more work if the data fields are not already arranged in a gridlike format in the list. The main point is that choosing a data region from the toolbox merely specifies a starting point for the layout—there is great flexibility to add row and column groups as you develop the report.

For this report, we will display the product data in a table (the columns of the report will be fixed, but the rows will be variable). The report will show four fixed columns: product name, product description, standard cost, and list price. The number of rows in the report will equal the total number of products returned by the query.

Select a Table item from the toolbox, and then drag it to the report's design surface. (If you do not see the toolbox, first select Toolbox on the View menu.) After dropping the table onto the design surface, reposition it so that the upper-left corner of the table is flush with the upper-left corner of the design surface. You can do this by selecting the table and dragging it to the upper-left corner. Blue snap-to guidelines will appear to indicate that the top and left sides of the table are aligned with the top and left sides of the design surface. Alternatively, go to the Properties window of the table, find the Location property, and set both Left and Top to zero inches.

To display data from the *ProductDetail* data set in the table, drag and drop fields from the data set onto the Data row of the table. For our sample report, select *EnglishProductName* from the Report Data pane and drag it to the leftmost column of the table. You can also use the new smart tags in the table cells to select a field from the data set. Hover the mouse pointer over the middle cell in the Data row of the table. A smart tag will appear in the upper-right corner of the cell. Click the smart tag, and a list of available fields will be displayed. Select *EnglishDescription* from the list. Either drag and drop *StandardCost* to the rightmost cell of the Data row or use the smart tag to select *StandardCost*. Add *ListPrice* to the table by selecting the field from the Report Data pane and dragging it to the right border of the table. A blue snap-to line will appear on the right border of the table. Drop the field using the blue line as a guide. A fourth column will be added to the table to show the list price. When you've completed adding all four fields to the report, the design surface should appear similar to Figure 19-4.

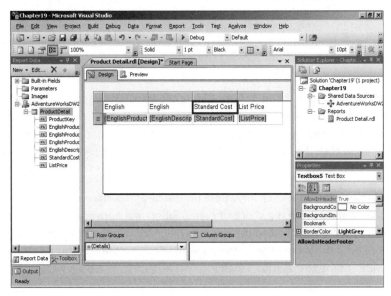

FIGURE 19-4 The Design view for the Product Detail report

Previewing the Report

Click the Preview tab. The report is generated and displayed as it will appear to users. Using the Preview tab is a handy way to check the report formatting and functionality during the development process without having to actually deploy the report.

Applying Report Formatting

You have successfully created your first report—but aesthetically, the report does not look very good. The text is wrapped within the cells. The column heading is not distinguished from the data rows, and moreover, the column heading appears only on the first page of the report. In other words, this is quite a "boring" report—one with a "wow" factor of zero. Let's work on changing that by enhancing the report's appearance.

Adding a Page Header

First, let's add a title to the report. Click the Design tab to return to the report's design surface. Then right-click anywhere on the page area of the design surface and select Insert, Page Header from the shortcut menu. A page header will be added to the design surface. Right-click anywhere in the page header, and then select Insert, Textbox from the shortcut menu. Select and drag the text box so that the top-left corner of the box is aligned with the top-left corner of the page header. Double-click the text box to activate the cursor inside the text box, and then type **Product Detail**.

> **Tip** To select a report item such as a text box or a cell in a table, click it once. Then, to modify the text within the text box or cell, double-click the text box or cell.

With the text box selected, use the text formatting toolbar just above the design surface to change the text to 14pt, bold, with a foreground color of SteelBlue. If you don't see the color you want on the Background Color configuration menu of the Formatting toolbar, click the More Colors link. Now click the Preview tab. The report title is wrapped, which is something we want to fix.

Go back to the Design tab. Right-click anywhere on the design surface outside the page area, and then select View, Ruler from the shortcut menu. Rulers will appear along the top and left side of the design surface. You can use the rulers to help size items on the design surface. Select the text box with the report title in the page header. Use the handles on the text box to expand the width of the text box to 3 inches.

Using Built-in Fields (Globals)

Next we will add page numbers to the report. In the Report Data pane, expand the Built-In Fields node. The list of available global report variables is displayed. Locate the *Page Number* field. Drag and drop it to the page header just below the title text box. If necessary, adjust the location of the newly added text box, using the blue snap-to guidelines, so that it is flush with the bottom of the title text box. Preview the report and verify that the page numbers have been added, and then return to the Design tab.

If you look at the list of built-in fields, you will notice that *Report Name* is also available as a built-in field. Replace the hard-coded report name you typed with the built-in field by dragging and dropping the field from the Report Data pane to the text box with the title. The text in the text box is replaced with the built-in field. Now, if you change the name of your report file, the title of the report will automatically change to match.

Writing Report Expressions

To edit the page number text so that it displays *Page x of y*, right-click the text box that has the *&PageNumber* field, and then select Expression from the shortcut menu. This will display the Expression Editor dialog box. Notice that in the Expression Editor, the *&PageNumber* field is written as *Globals!PageNumber* because the page number is a member of the *Globals* collection. Change the report expression to include the total pages using another member of the *Globals* collection, as follows:

```
="Page " & Globals!PageNumber & " of " & Globals!TotalPages
```

Report expressions must always be preceded by an equals sign (=) and are always written in Visual Basic. The preceding code is a simple yet typical example of using a report expression to combine static text with built-in report fields in the *Globals* collection to make the text in a page header dynamic. Expressions are fundamental to the development of dynamic and full-featured reports. The bottom pane of the Expression Editor dialog box provides assistance in building expressions. Take some time to explore the collections and functions available for building expressions. More examples demonstrating the use of report expressions are given later in this chapter.

> **Tip** The Expression Editor can be launched anywhere you see the Expression button (identified with an *fx* icon) or the Expression option on a shortcut menu or in a drop-down list. Expressions allow property values to be determined dynamically rather than being set to a constant value. Conditional formatting in Reporting Services is implemented through the use of report expressions.

Click OK to save the report expression and close the Expression Editor dialog box. Back on the design surface, you will see that the text box now shows *<<Expr>>*. This is the Report Designer's way of telling you that the text box is using an expression.

Formatting the Data Region

Click a cell in the table so that the gray column and row handles are visible, as shown in Figure 19-5. Select the row with the column headings by clicking the row handle for the top row. This selects the entire top row of the table. Use the Formatting toolbar to change the text to bold font, the foreground color to White, and the background color to SteelBlue.

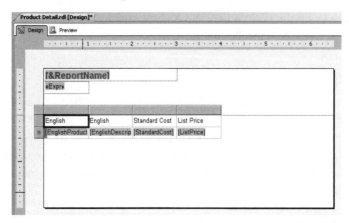

FIGURE 19-5 The Design view showing a Table data region with the row and column handles visible

Double-click the English Product Name header, and change the text to **Product Name**. Now double-click the English Description header and change its text to **Description**. Expand the column widths by clicking and dragging the line between the gray column handles to the right. For more precise control of column widths, select a table column by clicking a gray column handle, locate the width property in the Properties pane, and then type a specific value for the width.

> **Tip** The Properties pane provides easy access to the properties of the currently selected report item. If the Properties pane is not visible, you can show it by selecting Properties from the View menu. The drop-down list at the top of the Properties pane specifies the currently selected report item. When multiple items are selected on the report design surface, the properties common to the selected items are shown in the Properties pane. It is then possible to modify the property for all the selected items at the same time by setting the property value in the Properties pane.

Click the Preview tab to preview the report. Check the formatting, and return to the Design tab to make adjustments as needed.

Adding a Report Group

Our report now shows one row for each product. But there are hundreds of products, and we want to help users to navigate the list of products. We can do this by adding a row group to the report.

Right-click the *(Details)* group in the Row Groups box of the Grouping pane, and then select Add Group, Parent Group from the shortcut menu. In the Tablix Group dialog box, select *EnglishProductSubCategoryName* from the Group By drop-down list. A column is automatically added to the table on the design surface. Double-click the column header for the newly added *English Product Sub Category Name* column, and then change the column heading to **Product Subcategory**. Preview the report. You will see that the products are now grouped by subcategory within the report.

Now repeat the same process, this time adding *EnglishProductCategoryName* as a parent group to the *EnglishProductSubCategoryName* group. Double-click the column header of the newly added column in the table on the design surface, and change the text to **Product Category**.

Next we'll widen the columns for the product category and subcategory. Select each column, one at a time, by clicking the gray column handles at the top of the table. In the properties pane, locate the Size property. Expand the Size property to expose the Width and Height properties. Change the Width property to 2 inches. Your design surface should appear similar to Figure 19-6.

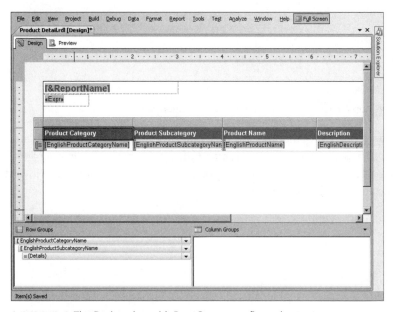

FIGURE 19-6 The Design view with Row Groups configured

Preview the report. Notice that products are now grouped first by category and then by subcategory within category.

Specifying a Sort Order

By default, row groups are sorted by the grouping field. The report is still difficult to navigate because the products are not yet sorted in a meaningful way within each subcategory grouping. To correct this, click the down arrow to the right of the *(Details)* group in the Grouping pane, and then select Group Properties. In the navigation list on the left in the Group Properties dialog box, select the Sorting page. Click Add, select ListPrice from the drop-down list, and change the Order to Z To A (that is, descending sequence to show products with the highest price listed first, within each subcategory). Click Add again, and then select EnglishProductName from the second drop-down list, leaving the Order as A To Z (ascending). Your selections should match Figure 19-7. Click OK to save your selections and close the dialog box.

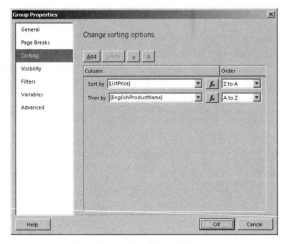

FIGURE 19-7 The Group Properties dialog box with sorting options specified

Preview the report, and verify that the sort order matches the choices we just made. The rows should be sorted alphabetically by *Product Category* and then by *Product Sub Category*. Within each subcategory, the rows should be sorted in descending (highest to lowest) order by *List Price* and then by *Product Name*.

Click the Save All button on the toolbar to save the solution and project files before proceeding.

Working with Parameters

Most likely, our end users will not want to see all the products at once. Using parameters, we can give our users more control over what data is (or isn't) provided by the report.

Reports have two types of parameters: *query parameters* and *report parameters*. Query parameters are used in the data set query, such as input parameters passed to stored procedures or variables specified in a parameterized Transact-SQL (T-SQL) statement. Query parameters are processed by the server hosting the data source.

The first step to creating a query parameter is to modify the query for the data set by adding a parameterized *WHERE* clause to filter the results returned by the query. Right-click the *ProductDetail* data set beneath the *AdventureWorksDW2008* data source in the Report Data pane, and then select Query. Change the query text in the Query Designer window to include a parameterized *WHERE* clause. Either import the ParameterizedSelectProductDetail. sql script from the chapter's sample code, or simply append the *WHERE* clause highlighted in bold here:

```
SELECT
  p.ProductKey,
  pc.EnglishProductCategoryName,
  ps.EnglishProductSubcategoryName,
  p.EnglishProductName,
  p.EnglishDescription,
  p.StandardCost,
  p.ListPrice
 FROM dbo.DimProduct AS p
  INNER JOIN dbo.DimProductSubcategory AS ps
   ON p.ProductSubcategoryKey = ps.ProductSubcategoryKey
  INNER JOIN dbo.DimProductCategory AS pc
   ON ps.ProductCategoryKey = pc.ProductCategoryKey
 WHERE pc.EnglishProductCategoryName = @ProductCategory
```

Note The number of rows in a data set can also be restricted by specifying a filter on the data set. The essential difference between query parameters and filters is that parameters are applied before the data is returned to the report, whereas filters are applied after the data is returned to the report. Moreover, filters can be applied only to columns that are returned in the data set, whereas query parameters can filter on columns that aren't returned in the data set, provided they are valid columns in the query context. For performance reasons, it is recommended to use parameters instead of filters whenever possible. This will reduce the number of records in the query result set and consequently will reduce the number of records returned to the report data set across the network. Furthermore, the database will likely have indexes to allow for quicker searches based on parameter values, whereas post-query filters do not enjoy similar optimization benefits.

Click OK to close the Query Designer window. Next, expand the Parameters node in the Report Data pane. Notice that a new report parameter named *ProductCategory* has been automatically added as a direct result of having just modified the query to include this parameter in the *WHERE* clause. Now right-click the *ProductDetail* data set again, select Dataset Properties, and then select Parameters from the navigation list on the left. Verify that the *[@ProductCategory]* report parameter name has been mapped to the *@ProductCategory* query parameter value. Report parameters are indicated with an @ symbol and enclosed in brackets in the Report Designer. Then click OK to close the Dataset Properties dialog box.

Now click the Preview tab to run the new parameterized version of the report. Instead of immediately displaying the report as before, SQL Server now displays a prompt at the top of the report for Product Category. We must provide a value for the Product Category parameter and then click View Report to invoke the query using the parameter value we provided. To test our current report, type **Bikes** in the text box, and then click View Report. The report should now show only Bikes.

As you've seen, when you create a query parameter by using a variable in your data set query, a corresponding report parameter is automatically created under the Parameters node of the Report Data pane. Report parameters are processed by the report server and are exposed to end users. Query parameters are configured from the Parameters pane of the Dataset Editor dialog box. In our example, we accepted the default mapping of the *@ProductCategory* query parameter to the *[@ProductCategory]* report parameter. In the next section, you'll see how report parameters are configured using the Report Parameter Editor.

Configuring Report Parameters

We've successfully added a parameter to our report: users simply have to enter a *Product Category* to get a report detailing that product category. What about users who are not familiar with the categories of products sold by Adventure Works? We want to make things even easier for those users. Instead of a text box, which requires the user to know the exact category name (and spell it correctly), we want to provide a drop-down list of available product categories so that users need only choose the category they want to see from a prepopulated list.

It's very easy to add this functionality. First we will create a data set that returns the list of product categories. Right-click the *AdventureWorksDW2008* data source in the Report Data pane, and then select Add Dataset. Alternatively, you can click New and then select Dataset from the menu at the top of the Report Data pane. Name the data set **ProductCategories**. The data source should default to *AdventureWorksDW2008*. Type the following code in the query pane or click Import and import the SelectProductCategories.sql query from the chapter's sample code, and then click OK:

```
SELECT EnglishProductCategoryName
 FROM dbo.DimProductCategory
 ORDER BY EnglishProductCategoryName
```

Right-click the *ProductCategory* parameter beneath the Parameters node in the Report Data pane, and then select Parameter Properties. Select the Available Values page from the navigation menu on the left, and then select the Get Values From A Query option. Three drop-down lists will appear. Select ProductCategories from the Dataset drop-down list. Select EnglishProductCategoryName from both the Value Field and Label Field drop-down lists, but don't click OK just yet. Figure 19-8 shows the completed Available Values properties page for the *ProductCategory* report parameter.

Note In the simple examples contained in this chapter, we specify the descriptive name as both the value and the label of the report parameters. In practice, the value will often be mapped to an abbreviated code or ID, depending on what is expected by the query parameter, with the descriptive name used only for the label. The label is the text that users will see in the parameter drop-down lists when the report is run.

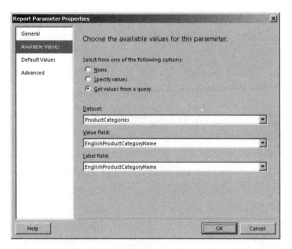

FIGURE 19-8 The Report Parameter Properties dialog box for the *ProductCategory* report parameter

You might have noticed that after the parameter was added to the report, the report was initially blank when it was previewed. That's because no product category value was provided for the parameter. We don't want users to be presented with a blank report, so we'll change this behavior by specifying a default product category for the parameter. To do that, select the Default Values page from the navigation menu on the left. In the Default Values dialog box, select the Specify Values option, click the Add button, and then type **Bikes** in the dialog box that appears. Figure 19-9 shows the completed Default Values properties page for the *ProductCategory* report parameter. Click OK to close the Report Parameter Properties dialog box.

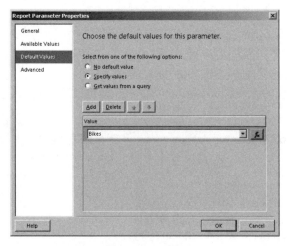

FIGURE 19-9 The default value setting for the *ProductCategory* report parameter

Preview the report. The parameter is now configured as a drop-down list instead of a text box, and the report for Bikes is shown by default. Click the drop-down list for the parameter to see the different product categories. Select any category, and then preview the report again to verify that the report is based on the product category selection from the drop-down list.

Cascading Parameters

Cascading parameters are helpful when users want to filter by several parameters and there is a hierarchical relationship or dependency between the parameters. For example, suppose that the user wants to filter products even further, say, down to the subcategory level. We could simply proceed using our newly acquired knowledge and just add a second query parameter for the subcategory field to our *ProductDetail* data set. Users would then have the ability to filter by subcategory; however, this is a somewhat naïve approach, since we would not be preventing users from inadvertently specifying invalid combinations of products and subcategories. For a more intuitive user experience, we will make use of the relationship between product categories and subcategories and implement cascading parameters to guide users in their parameter selection.

Cascading parameters are implemented by adding query parameters to the data set used to populate the available values list for the parameter. Start by creating a new data set that returns the valid values for the product subcategory. Right-click the *AdventureWorksDW2008* data source in the Report Data pane, and then select Add Dataset. Name the data set **ProductSubCategories**, and type the following query in the Query box (or click Import and load the SelectProductSubCategories.sql query from the chapter's sample code):

```
SELECT ps.EnglishProductSubcategoryName
 FROM dbo.dimProductSubcategory AS ps
  INNER JOIN dbo.dimProductCategory AS pc
   ON ps.ProductCategoryKey = pc.ProductCategoryKey
 WHERE pc.EnglishProductCategoryName = @ProductCategory
 ORDER BY ps.EnglishProductSubcategoryName
```

In the navigation list on the left, click Parameters, and then verify that the *[@ProductCategory]* report parameter value is mapped to the *@ProductCategory* query parameter name. Click OK.

Before we can see our cascading parameters in action, we need to modify our report data set query so that it expects the subcategory parameter. Right-click the *ProductDetail* data set in the Report Data pane, and then select Query. Modify the *WHERE* clause of the query as follows:

```
WHERE (pc.EnglishProductCategoryName = @ProductCategory)
  AND (ps.EnglishProductSubcategoryName = @ProductSubcategory)
```

Click OK. You should now see a *ProductSubcategory* parameter under the Parameters node in the Report Data pane. Right-click the *ProductSubcategory* parameter, and then select Parameter Properties. On the Available Values page, select the Get Values From A Query option, and then choose the *ProductSubcategories* data set from the drop-down list. Select *EnglishProductSubcategoryName* in both the Value Field and Label Field drop-down lists. On the Default Values pane, select the Specify Values option. Click Add, and then type **Mountain Bikes** in the Values text box. Click OK to save your selections and close the dialog box.

Now preview the report. Verify that the report has defaulted to show only Mountain Bikes. Click the *Product Subcategory* parameter drop-down list to verify that only bike subcategories are in the list. Change the *Product Category* parameter to Clothing, and then click again on the *Product Subcategory* parameter drop-down list. Now verify that the options in the drop-down list have changed to reflect Clothing subcategories.

On the File menu, select Save All to save the solution and project files to this point.

Writing Custom Report Code

Earlier in this chapter, we used a report expression to add dynamic text to the header of the report. The available Visual Basic functions are sufficient for most report expressions you will need to write. Sometimes, however, you might find yourself in need of a function that is not available. In those instances, it is possible to write custom functions to use with your report. These custom functions can be embedded Visual Basic .NET script code in the report or in a .NET assembly referenced by the report. We'll now design a new report and embed custom code inside of it that can be called by any expression in the report.

We'll create and add an *Order Detail* report to our solution, and we'll write custom code to alternate the background color of the rows in the report in order to make the report more readable. This time, we will use the Report Wizard to create the report, rather than building it from scratch as we did for our first report. Right-click the Reports folder in Solution Explorer, and then select Add New Report from the shortcut menu to launch the Report Wizard.

The Report Wizard has several built-in report templates to allow you to quickly get up and running with Reporting Services. Now that you've created your first report manually in the Report Designer, you've gained an understanding of the elements that comprise a report. With that knowledge under our belts, we'll use the Report Wizard to rapidly create our Order Detail report.

Click Next on the Welcome page. On the Select The Data Source page, make sure that the *AdventureWorksDW2008* shared data source is selected, and then click Next.

Type the following code in the Query string text box (or click the Query Builder button and then click Import to load the SelectOrderDetail.sql query from the chapter's sample code):

```
SELECT
  d.FullDateAlternateKey,
  fs.SalesOrderNumber,
  g.EnglishCountryRegionName,
  g.StateProvinceName,
  p.EnglishProductName,
  fs.SalesAmount
 FROM dbo.FactInternetSales AS fs
  INNER JOIN dbo.dimDate AS d
   ON fs.OrderDateKey= d.DateKey
  INNER JOIN dbo.dimProduct AS p
   ON fs.ProductKey = p.ProductKey
  INNER JOIN dbo.DimProductSubcategory AS ps
   ON p.ProductSubcategoryKey = ps.ProductSubcategoryKey
  INNER JOIN dbo.DimProductCategory AS pc
   ON ps.ProductCategoryKey = pc.ProductCategoryKey
  INNER JOIN dbo.dimCustomer AS c
   ON fs.CustomerKey = c.CustomerKey
  INNER JOIN dbo.DimGeography AS g
   ON c.GeographyKey = g.GeographyKey
 WHERE g.EnglishCountryRegionName = @Country
   AND g.StateProvinceName = @State
   AND d.CalendarYear = @CalendarYear
   AND d.CalendarQuarter = @CalendarQuarter
 ORDER BY d.FullDateAlternateKey, fs.SalesOrderNumber, p.EnglishProductName
```

Click Next. Keep the default Tabular Report Type selection, and then click Next.

Add all the Available Fields to the Details section, and then click Next. Choose a Table Style, and then click Next. Name the report **Order Detail**, and then click Finish. You will see the Design view for the report. Having built our first report manually from scratch, you can now appreciate how quickly and easily you can build a report with the help of the Report Wizard. Once the wizard generates the report, you then customize and extend it no differently than if you had gotten to the same "starting point" without using the wizard.

Now click the Preview tab to run the report. There are four report parameters (*Country*, *State*, *Calendar Year*, and *Calendar Quarter*), corresponding to the four query parameters in the *WHERE* clause of the *SELECT* statement we specified. Provide values for these parameters as follows: type **Canada** for Country, **British Columbia** for State, **2002** for Calendar Year, and **1** for Calendar Quarter. Then click View Report.

We have successfully created a detail report; however, it is difficult to read. We need to apply some formatting to the date and sales amount columns, and we would also like to shade the background of each alternate row.

First we'll adjust the date formatting. On the Design tab, right-click the *[FullDateAlternateKey]* cell, and then select Text Box Properties from the shortcut menu. Select the Number page from the navigation list on the left in the Text Box Properties dialog box. In the Category list, select Date. Now you can select any date format you want from the Type list. For our report, keep the default date format and just click OK. Then left-align the date by clicking the Align Left button on the Formatting page.

Next we'll format the sales amount. Right-click the *[SalesAmount]* cell, and then select Text Box Properties. Select the Number page from the navigation list on the left. In the Category list, select Currency. Then select the Use 1000 Separator (,) check box to display commas in the *SalesAmount* values, and click OK.

In order to alternately shade the rows, we need to write a custom function. Right-click anywhere on the design surface outside the report page area, and then select Report Properties from the shortcut menu. Review the various report properties pages in the navigation list on the left. For example, note that the report printed page size is set from this Properties dialog box. The References page allows you to reference external custom .NET assemblies and classes. In our case, we want to embed a custom function directly in the report. To do this, select the Code page in the navigation list on the left, and then type the following code in the Custom code text box:

```
Private rowColor1 As Boolean
Function ChangeColor(ByVal color1 As String, _
    ByVal color2 As String, ByVal change As Boolean) As String

  If change Then rowColor1 = Not rowColor1
  If rowColor1 Then
    Return color1
  Else
    Return color2
  End If

End Function
```

Click OK to close the Report Properties dialog box.

Next we will use our newly created function to set the background color of the data rows in the table. Right-click the *[FullDateAlternateKey]* cell, and then select Text Box Properties. Select the Fill page from the navigation list on the left. Click the Expression button (identified with an *fx* icon) to set the expression for *BackgroundColor*. Type the following code in the Expression dialog box:

```
=Code.ChangeColor("White", "Gainsboro", True)
```

Click OK to close the Expression dialog box. Back in the Textbox Properties dialog box, click OK again to close the dialog box. Next, set the background color for all other data cells in the table. Hold down the Shift key while clicking to select multiple text boxes at once. Locate the

BackgroundColor property in the Visual Studio Properties window. Select the Expression link from the drop-down list. Type the following code in the Expression dialog box:

```
=Code.ChangeColor("White", "Gainsboro", False)
```

Click OK, and then preview the report, making the same parameter specifications as before. Your report should appear similar to Figure 19-10.

FIGURE 19-10 A report formatted using a custom function

Click the Save All button on the toolbar to save the solution and project files to this point.

Creating an OLAP Report

Reporting Services supports the creation of reports from an Analysis Services data source. Queries against an Analysis Services data source must be written in multidimensional expression language (MDX). There's good news and bad news about writing MDX for Analysis Services data sets in Reporting Services. First the bad news: Reporting Services requires the data set returned by the query to be flattened. Furthermore, measures—and only measures—can be returned on the columns of the query. These restrictions can make it difficult to write the MDX query for a report. The good news is that Reporting Services provides a graphical query designer for MDX.

> **Note** This section uses the sample *AdventureWorksDW2008* Analysis Services database.
> Sample databases are no longer shipped with SQL Server 2008—they must be downloaded
> from CodePlex. To follow along with the example in this section, you will need to download
> the Analysis Services database project for *AdventureWorks DW 2008*, open the project in Visual
> Studio, and then process the database (right-click the database in Solution Explorer, and then
> select Process from the shortcut menu). See this book's Introduction for instructions on obtaining
> and installing the sample databases.

To get started, we will add a new shared data source pointing to the *Adventure Works DW
2008* Analysis Services database. This is the Analysis Services sample database created using
the *AdventureWorksDW2008* relational database as its source. Right-click the Shared Data
Sources node in Solution Explorer, and then select Add New Data Source. Name the data
source **AdventureWorksCube**, and then select Microsoft SQL Server Analysis Services from
the Type drop-down list. Click the Edit button. In the Connection Properties dialog box, specify the name of the server that has the sample database (or *localhost*, if it's running on your
local machine). Select Adventure Works DW 2008 from the Database Name drop-down list.
Test the connection. Click OK two times to close the Connection Properties and Shared Data
Source Properties dialog boxes.

Next add a report to the solution. Right-click the Reports folder in Solution Explorer, and
then select Add, New Item. Select the Report template, name the report **Sales Summary by
Region and Date.rdl**, and then click Add.

In the Report Data pane, select New and Dataset. Name the data set **SalesSummary**. Click
the New button for the Data Source. In the Data Source Properties dialog box, name the
report data source **AdventureWorksCube**, and then select the Use Shared Data Source
Reference option. Select AdventureWorksCube from the drop-down list, and then click OK.
Back in the Dataset Properties dialog box, click the Query Designer button. This will load the
graphical MDX Query Designer.

Using the Graphical MDX Query Designer

The graphical MDX Query Designer is a drag-and-drop interface for building MDX statements. First verify that the *Adventure Works* cube is selected. The Metadata pane on the left
in the designer shows the cube measures and dimensions in a tree list view. We will create a
report to show sales amounts by region and time.

With the *Adventure Works* cube selected, select Internet Sales from the Measure Group
drop-down list. Expand the Customer node in the Metadata pane, and then expand the
Customer Geography node. Drag the *Country* level to the Query pane as indicated in the designer. Next drag the *State-Province* level to the Query pane. We also want to show the sales
amounts by date. Expand the Date node and then the Calendar node in the Metadata pane.
Finally, expand the Date.Calendar node. Drag the *Calendar Year* and *Calendar Quarter* levels

to the Query pane. Now expand the Measures node, and drag the *Internet Sales Amount* and *Internet Order Quantity* measures to the Query pane.

> **Tip** If you plan to show multiple levels of a user-defined hierarchy in a report, it is better to drag the desired levels from the user defined hierarchy, rather than using the individual attribute hierarchies. Reporting Services builds the MDX query by creating a crossjoin of all members of each hierarchy that is in the Query pane. When levels of a hierarchy are used, Reporting Services requests all members (*AllMembers*) of the lowest level of the hierarchy requested. The parent-age of the members is automatically returned in the query. Therefore, by using *Country* and *State-Province* from the *Customer Geography* hierarchy, a crossjoin is eliminated as compared with using the *Country* and *State-Province* attribute hierarchies of the *Customer* dimension. Use both methods and compare the MDX statements to see the difference.

Last, we will add parameters to the MDX query. This is done using the filtering pane just above the query pane. We will add parameters for the year and customer country. When you click inside the cells in the filtering pane, drop-down lists will be enabled. In the filtering pane, make the drop-down list selections shown in the following table.

Dimension	Hierarchy	Operator	Filter Expression	Parameter Selection
Date	Date.Calendar Year	Range (Inclusive)	:	Both checked
Customer	Country	Equals		Checked

Figure 19-11 shows the completed Query Designer window.

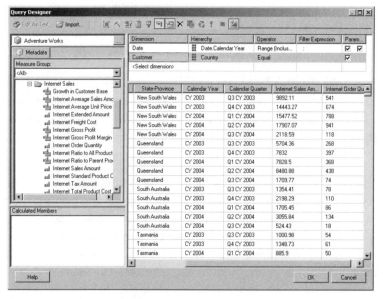

FIGURE 19-11 The completed MDX Query Designer window for the *SalesSummary* data set

To see the MDX generated by the graphical query designer, click the Design Mode button on the toolbar (the rightmost button on the toolbar) at the top of the Query Designer window. Clicking the Design Mode button toggles you back and forth between the graphical design mode and text mode. In the next section, we will modify a query using the text mode. For now, click the Design Mode button once again to return to the graphical design mode.

Click OK to close the Query Designer window. Click OK once again to close the Dataset Properties dialog box. You will be faced with the now familiar Report Design tab. Expand the Parameters node in the Report Data pane, and notice that three report parameters have been created. The report parameters correspond to each of the query parameters. Because we specified the year parameter to be a range, Reporting Services was smart enough to generate two parameters, one for the start of the year range and one for the end of the year range.

Preview the report. The report has three parameter prompts, each with a selection list. Click the drop-down list for the *From Date.Calendar Year* parameter; the list is populated with a list of years. Recall that for the *Product Detail* report, we created data sets with the available values for the *Product Category* and *Product Subcategory* report parameters. These data sets were then specified as the source of available values when we configured the report parameters. In this case, we haven't explicitly created any data sets with the available values for the calendar year, yet the parameter drop-down list is populated with the list of available values. How did this happen? Return to the Design tab for the report so that we can have a closer look at the report parameters added by the Report Designer.

Right-click the FromDateCalendarYear node under the Parameters node in the Report Data pane, and then select the Parameter Properties shortcut menu option. When the Report Parameter Properties dialog box appears, select the Available Values option. The Get Values From A Query option is selected. The available values are sourced from a data set named *FromDateCalendarYear*. We did not create this data set; however, it turns out that Reporting Services automatically creates data sets for the available values for the report parameters corresponding to the query parameters for an online analytical processing (OLAP) report! We just haven't noticed them yet because they're hidden by default.

Click Cancel to close the Parameter Properties dialog box. Right-click the *AdventureWorksCube* data source, select Show Hidden Datasets from the shortcut menu, and notice now that three additional data sets appear under the AdventureWorksCube node. When query parameters are specified using the graphical MDX Query Designer, Reporting Services automatically creates data sets to populate the available values lists corresponding to the parameters. As mentioned, these data sets are hidden by default. Once the data sets are exposed, you can edit their properties from the Report Data pane as you would any other report data set.

When we previewed the report, no default values were specified for the parameters, and the report parameters used default prompts assigned automatically by Reporting Services. Let's change this to make our report more user-friendly.

Right-click the SalesSummary node in the Report Data pane, and then select Query from the shortcut menu. Hover the mouse pointer over the button on the Query Designer toolbar with the @ symbol (the fifth button from the right). The tooltip reads *Query Parameters*, but it is disabled. Click the rightmost button on the toolbar to toggle to text mode. The MDX query generated by the graphical MDX Query Designer is displayed, and the Query Parameters button is now enabled.

Click the Query Parameters button to display the Query Parameters dialog box. Click the Default cell corresponding to the *FromDateCalendarYear* parameter. This will activate a drop-down list in the cell. The drop-down list has a tree view control showing the available values for the parameter. Select CY2001, and then click OK. Repeat the process for the *ToDateCalendarYear* and *CustomerCountry* parameters, selecting CY2003 for the *ToDateCalendarYear* default and both Australia and Canada for the *CustomerCountry* default. Click OK to save the defaults and close the Query Parameters dialog box. Then click OK to close the Query Designer.

Next we will customize the parameter prompts. Right-click the FromDateCalendarYear node under the Parameters node and select Property Parameters again. On the General page, change the Prompt to **From Year**. On the Default Values pane, verify that the default value is set to *[Date].[Calendar Year].&[2001]*. Instead of using the Parameters dialog box in the Query Designer, we could have typed the default in the Default Values here in the Report Parameter Properties dialog box. However, that would require us to know the unique member name of the default member we want, because the Value field used for the Available Values list is set to the unique member names. Click OK to save the new prompt.

Follow the same steps to change the prompts for *ToDateCalendarYear* and *CustomerCountry* to values that are more user-friendly.

Writing MDX Queries in Text Mode

The graphical MDX Query Designer is great for quickly creating a report against an Analysis Services data source without requiring any knowledge of MDX. The MDX generated by the query designer, however, might not be optimal—both in terms of desired behavior and performance. Text mode allows you to modify the designer-generated MDX statement if needed, or to write your own from scratch without using the designer at all.

It is easy to configure parameters for an OLAP report. We simply had to select the Parameters check box in the MDX Query Designer filter pane, and Reporting Services automatically generated report parameters and data sets with available values for the parameters.

You might not always like the available values data sets generated for your report parameters by Reporting Services.

You might have noticed that an All Periods option was available in the From Year and To Year parameter drop-down lists. By default, the available values data set for a report parameter generated by Reporting Services includes the *all* member of the attribute hierarchy for which the filter is created. This is not always desirable. Preview the *Order Summary* report and change the From Year parameter selection to All Periods. An error will appear in the Report pane stating that the query execution failed because All Periods is not a valid endpoint in a date range. We therefore want to remove the All Periods option from the available values lists for the From Year and To Year parameters. We can do that by modifying the MDX for the available values data sets. Return to the Design tab of the report.

Right-click the FromDateCalendarYear node in the Report Data pane, and then select Query. This opens the Query Designer with the MDX query for the data set. Click the exclamation point button (the *run* command) on the toolbar to execute the query. Note that the *All Periods* member is returned. Change *[Date].[Calendar Year].AllMembers* to **[Date].[Calendar Year].[All Periods].Children** in the text, and execute the query once again. Now the *All Periods* member is gone, just as we wanted. (This is because the *All Periods* member is returned by *AllMembers* but not by *Children*.) Figure 19-12 shows the modified query and results in the Query Designer.

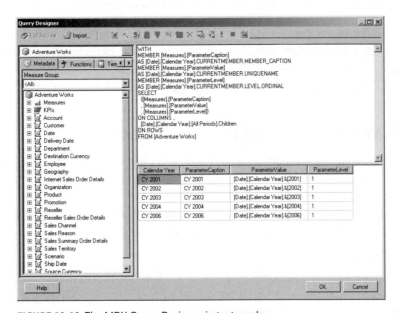

FIGURE 19-12 The MDX Query Designer in text mode

Click OK to close the Query Designer. Follow the same steps to remove the *all* member from the *ToDateCalendarYear* data set.

> **Note** You might have noticed that throughout this chapter, all of the MDX queries viewed in text mode have measures and only measures on the columns. This is not a coincidence. Reporting Services requires flattened data sets returned from MDX queries with measures and only measures on the columns. MDX statements that return dimension members or tuples (a collection of dimension axis members) on the columns will result in an error.

We also do not want the *all* member option to appear in the drop-down list for the *Country* parameter. When we configured the *Country* parameter as a multiple-selection parameter, Reporting Services automatically added a Select All option to the available values list. The All Customers option is redundant with the Select All option.

To remove the All Customers option from the *Country* parameter drop-down list, take the same steps as for the time period drop-down lists, except change *[Customer].[Country]. AllMembers* to **[Customer].[Country].[All Customers].Children** in the MDX statement.

Preview the report. Verify that the *all* member options are no longer available in the drop-down lists.

We've used the text mode of the MDX Query Designer to modify the MDX generated by Reporting Services. As mentioned, text mode can also be used to write MDX queries from scratch. Writing queries from scratch is necessary when reporting needs extend beyond what can be achieved by using the drag-and-drop interface of the graphical Query Designer.

Here is where the distinction between reports built from relational SQL Server data sources and Analysis Services data sources ends. From this point forward, designing a report based on an MDX query is exactly the same as designing a report based a T-SQL query since both types of queries produce the same type of data set that you report against.

Creating a Report with a Matrix Data Region

Matrix data regions are a natural starting point for creating reports against Analysis Services databases. Matrix data regions resemble PivotTables in that data is grouped along columns as well as rows. The exact number of columns and rows displayed in the matrix depends on the number of distinct data values that exist in the fields by which columns and rows are grouped. As is often the case, the matrix data region is best understood through an applied example.

Start by dragging a matrix data region from the toolbox onto the report design surface. Align the matrix with the top-left corner of the design surface either by dragging it to the corner using the blue snap-to guidelines or by setting the *Left* and *Top* properties to zero inches beneath the *Location* property of the matrix data region in the Properties pane.

Now we will configure the column groups. Drag the *Calendar_Year* field from the SalesSummary node to the matrix cell containing the word *Columns*. Next drag the *Calendar_Quarter* field under the *Calendar_Year* field in the matrix. Release the field when you see the blue guideline appear to the bottom of the cell containing the *Calendar_Year* field; this way, a row will automatically be created for the quarter. Notice that the Column Groups in the Grouping pane reflects your selections.

Next configure the row groups. Drag the *Country* field from under the *SalesSummary* data set node onto the matrix cell containing the word *Rows*. Next drag the *State_Province* field from the *SalesSummary* data set to the right of the *Country* field. Remember that fields are indicated in the design surface in brackets. Release the *State_Province* field when you see the blue guideline appear to the right of the cell containing the *Country* field; this way, a column will automatically be created for the *State_Province* field.

Now drag the *Internet_Sales_Amount* field from the Report Data pane onto the matrix cell containing the word *Data*. By default, Reporting Services sums the values in the Data cells.

Now that you've gotten some experience creating reports, you know that the report, as is, will not look very good. To fix that, make the following formatting changes to the report. (We walked through the detailed steps for carrying out these changes earlier in this chapter.)

1. Change the Fill BackgroundColor property of the top two matrix rows to SteelBlue.

2. Change the Font Color of the top two matrix rows to White and the Font Weight to Bold.

3. Widen the State Province column to 1.5 inches.

4. Change the Number formatting of the data cell to Currency (C0 if you are setting the Format property value in the Properties pane).

5. Add a report header to display the report name. Specify the report name using the built-in *ReportName* field so that the header will change to reflect the correct name of the report if the name changes. Format the font of the Report Name as SteelBlue, 14pt, Bold.

6. Minimize the white space in the report header, and make sure that the text box for the report name is wide enough to accommodate the text without wrapping.

When you have finished, your report design surface should appear similar to Figure 19-13.

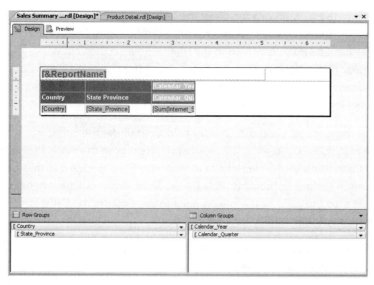

FIGURE 19-13 The completed Design view for the *Sales Summary by Region and Date* report

Preview the report. The matrix report allows users to quickly compare sales amounts by quarter over quarter or between state-provinces. Similar to PivotTables and crosstabs, data is grouped along both rows and columns. As mentioned, the number of rows will depend on the number of distinct state-provinces in the data set, and the number of columns will depend on the number of distinct quarters in the data set.

Click the Save All button on the toolbar to save the files to this point.

Adding Subtotals and Totals

It is often useful to show subtotals and totals in a matrix report. Currently, the report gives the sales amount for a given quarter and specific state-province. Most likely, users would also like to know the total sales amount for the country or for the year, or the total sales amount for a quarter across all countries. Click the Design tab to return to the design surface, if you are not already there.

Subtotals and totals are added to a matrix data region from a shortcut menu on the group cell. To add state-province subtotals, right-click the cell containing the *[State_Province]* field, and then select Add Total. Unlike earlier versions of the Report Designer where subtotals and totals were always placed after the group, the Report Designer in Visual Studio 2008 offers a choice of whether to place the subtotal row before or after the group. Select After. Preview the report. Take note of the Total row added after the list of state-provinces for each country.

Go back to the Design tab, and repeat the process of adding totals for the *[Country]*, *[Calendar_Quarter]*, and *[Calendar_Year]* groups. Preview the report once again. As a result of adding the Total for *[Country]*, the bottom row of numbers now shows the total across all countries. As a result of adding the Total for *[Calendar_Year]*, the rightmost column of numbers now shows the total across all quarters. Because totals were also added to *[Calendar_ Quarter]*, columns of subtotals by year are shown as well.

The matrix on the design surface now has an abundance of cells, each containing the expression *[Sum(Internet_Sales_Amount)]*. Although the expression is the same in each cell, the scope of each expression is different. Clicking a cell in the matrix activates yellow brackets that indicate the scope of the aggregation. Click the upper-left cell containing the *[Sum(Internet_Sales_Amount)]* expression. This is the original data cell of the matrix before we added any totals. Yellow brackets appear above the *Calendar_Quarter* column header and to the left of the *State_Province* row header. This indicates that the sum is within a calendar quarter and state-province. Click the cell immediately below. The yellow brackets are now on the Country row header. This cell represents the subtotal for each country within a calendar quarter. Now click the bottom-right sum expression in the matrix. No yellow brackets are activated. This is the cell representing the grand total. It is the sum of Internet sales amounts over all countries and all calendar years.

We have successfully added subtotals and totals to the report. The totals are useful, but the report is now more difficult to digest with all the additional numbers being shown. We'd like to change that by applying formatting to distinguish the subtotal and total rows in the report.

Adding subtotals and totals to a matrix data region in Reporting Services has always been easy—but formatting them has not. Users familiar with the Report Designer in Visual Studio 2005 will remember the notorious green triangle. In the old Report Designer, subtotal cells were formatted by clicking a small green triangle in the upper-right corner of the cell containing the subtotal label. Clicking the green triangle would expose the properties of the subtotal cell in the Properties pane. Now, formatting the subtotal cells is easy because doing so is just like formatting any other cell in the matrix.

First we'll add bold formatting to the grand total across all countries and make the background yellow. Select the bottom row of the matrix by clicking the gray row handle for the row. Use the Formatting toolbar to make the font bold and set the background color to yellow. Alternatively, set the *FontWeight* property to Bold and the *BackgroundColor* property to Yellow in the Properties pane.

Next, format the country subtotals. Select the middle row of sum expressions. Use the Formatting toolbar or the Properties pane to make the font bold and set the background color to Light Blue. Figure 19-14 shows the formatted matrix.

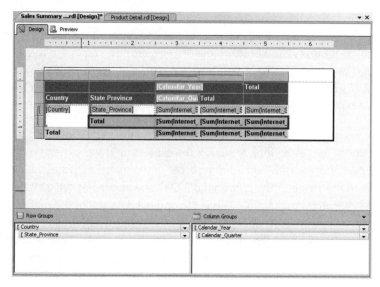

FIGURE 19-14 A matrix data region with formatted totals

Preview the report. With our MDX query and some simple formatting, we have created a report that displays a lot of information yet is highly digestible.

Tablix Explained

Everything we've shown so far could have been done using the Report Designer in Visual Studio 2005—albeit more tediously, particularly with respect to the formatting of subtotals. In this section, we are going to modify our matrix report in a way that wasn't possible before SQL Server 2008 Reporting Services.

We've already mentioned several times that both the table and matrix data regions used in the examples so far are in fact *tablix* data regions. As you might have noticed earlier, when we right-click either a table or matrix data region, the shortcut menu shows a list of menu items beneath a Tablix Properties heading. Up to this point, we haven't taken advantage of the flexibility introduced with the tablix data region with the commands on the Tablix Properties shortcut menu.

Adding Groups

As is often the case, increased flexibility means more options, but having more options can be confusing. From a cell in a data region, there are up to 16 options for extending the data region. The range of options is shown in Table 19-1.

TABLE 19-1 Options for Extending a Tablix Data Region

Add Column Group	Parent Group
	Child Group
	Adjacent Left
	Adjacent Right
Add Row Group	Parent Group
	Child Group
	Adjacent Above
	Adjacent Below
Insert Column	Inside Group Left
	Inside Group Right
	Outside Group Left
	Outside Group Right
Insert Row	Inside Group Above
	Inside Group Below
	Outside Group Above
	Outside Group Below

These 16 options in fact represent five effective options:

- Adding a parent group

- Adding a child group

- Adding an adjacent group

- Adding a fixed column or row inside the group

- Adding a fixed column or row outside the group

Whether a new group, column, or row is added to the left, right, above, or below is mere formatting. What is important to understand are the differences between adding groups and fixed columns or rows; adding parent, child, and adjacent groups; and adding fixed columns or rows inside or outside the group. Options that are not applicable in the cell context are disabled or not shown on the shortcut menu. In the case of inserting a fixed column or row, if the cell is not in a group, the available option is to insert left, right, above, or below without the distinction of whether the insert should happen inside or outside the group.

Parent and Child Groups

Effectively, the only option available in Visual Studio 2005 was to add parent and child groups to tables and matrices. Adding parent and child groups creates a nesting of groups. In the matrix example, the *State_Province* group is a child group of the *Country* group. Records are first grouped by *Country* (the parent group), and within country by *State-Province* (the child group). In the grouping pane, parent groups appear above child groups. So looking at the Column Groups, we can easily identify the *Calendar_Year* group as the parent and the *Calendar_Quarter* group as the child.

Adjacent Groups

Adding adjacent groups opens the possibility of showing parallel dynamic groups. For example, suppose that we wanted to show quarterly sales not only by region, but also grouped by product category in the same matrix. This was not possible in Visual Studio 2005, but now can be accomplished with a few simple steps:

1. Right-click the *SalesSummary* data set in the Report Data pane, and then select Query.

2. In the Query Editor, drag the *Category* attribute hierarchy from the *Product* dimension to the query window to the left of the *Country* column. Click OK to save your changes, and then close the Query Editor window.

3. Right-click the *[Country]* text box in the data region on the design surface, and then select Add Group, Row Group, Adjacent Below from the shortcut menu. Alternatively, click the drop-down arrow for the Country row group in the Grouping pane, and then select Add Group, Adjacent After.

4. In the Tablix Group dialog box, select the *[Category]* field from the drop-down list. Click OK. On the design surface, a row will be added to the data region, and in the Grouping pane, a new group will appear.

5. Click the drop-down arrow for the newly added group in the Grouping pane, and then select Group Properties. Change the name from *Group1* to **ProductCategory**.

6. Copy the sum expressions from the State-Province row into the cells below corresponding to the newly added *[Category]* group row. Change the background color of the blue cells in the *[Category]* group row to No Color.

Your design surface should appear similar to Figure 19-15.

Preview the report. You will see three rows added below Canada: one row corresponding to each of the categories of products sold by Adventure Works. Quarterly sales amounts by geography and by product are displayed seamlessly in a single report.

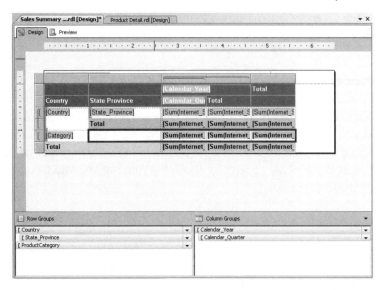

FIGURE 19-15 A matrix report with parent and child groups and an adjacent row group

Adding Fixed Columns and Rows

It's also possible to add fixed columns and rows to the data region. Fixed columns and rows differ from column and row groups in that the number columns or rows added does not vary depending on the data. When we added the *ProductCategory* group to the data region, three rows were added the resulting report, one for each product category in the data set. If Adventure Works began selling an additional category of products, four rows would automatically be shown in the resulting report without any change required to the report design. In contrast, when a fixed column or row is added, only a single column or row is added.

Adding Inside a Group

When a column or row is added inside a group, it will have the scope of that group. For example, suppose that we want to display the order quantities side by side with the sales amount but that we care about order quantities only by quarter and not by year. We can display the order quantities for each quarter by adding a column inside the *Calendar_Quarter* group. Right-click the *[Calendar_Quarter]* text box, and then select Insert Column, Inside Group Left from the shortcut menu. A new column is added within the *Calendar_Quarter* group in the data region. Drag *Internet_Order_Quantity* from under the *SalesSummary* node in the Report Data pane to the newly created column. The cells in the new column will each be populated with *[Sum(Internet_Order_Quantity)]*. Preview the report. You will see a single column added to each *Calendar_Quarter* group in the report showing the order quantity for the quarter. The order quantity and sales amount columns do not have headings. Let's change that.

Go back to the Design tab. Right-click the *[Calendar_Quarter]* text box, and then select Insert Row, Inside Group Below from the shortcut menu. A new row is added to the table. Right-click the cell immediately below the *[Calendar_Quarter]* text box, and then select Split Cells. Type **Quantity** in the left text box and **Amount** in the right text box. Because we are showing only subtotals and totals for amounts, we also want to clarify the label for the Total columns: type **Amount** in the newly added row above the subtotal and totals. Figure 19-16 shows the completed design surface.

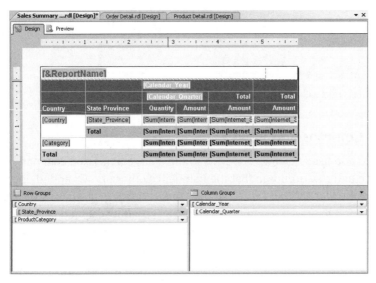

FIGURE 19-16 A matrix report with fixed columns and rows added

Make any formatting changes you want to the report. In Figure 19-16, for aesthetic reasons, additional formatting adjustments have been made such as reducing column widths and centering some column headings. When you are satisfied with your changes, click the Save All button on the toolbar to save the files to this point.

Adding Outside a Group

When a column or row is added outside a group, it will have the scope of the parent group— or of no groups, if no parent group exists. Right-click the *[Calendar_Year]* text box, and then select Insert Column Outside Group Left from the shortcut menu. A new column is added outside and to the left of the *Calendar_Year* group in the data region. We can tell that the column is outside the *Calendar_Year* group because it does not share the *[Calendar_Year]* header, and also, when we click a cell in the column, the yellow grouping indicator for the *Calendar_Year* group is not activated.

In our current example, we will not add a column outside the *Calendar_Year* group. Go back to the Design tab, and then click the Undo button on the toolbar or press Ctrl+Z, or right-click a cell in the newly added column and select Delete Columns from the shortcut menu.

Click the Save All button on the toolbar to save the files to this point.

Adding a Chart Data Region

Charting capabilities in Reporting Services have been greatly improved with SQL Server 2008 as a direct result of Microsoft acquiring the Dundas Data Visualization components in 2007. The Report Designer allows for multiple data regions to be displayed in a single report. This is particularly handy for showing a data grid and chart together in a report, giving users two different ways to view the same data. We are now going to add a trend chart showing quarterly sales amount to the *Sales Summary by Region and Date* report.

Return to the Design tab if you are not already on it. Start by expanding the report body so that there is some white space below the existing matrix: when you hover the mouse pointer over the bottom edge of the report body, the cursor will change to a double-headed vertical arrow indicating that the bottom edge can be dragged downward.

Next, drag a chart item from the toolbox to the white space below the matrix. Take a minute to review the available chart types, and then select the first line chart type within the Line charts row in the Chart Type dialog box (the leftmost line chart with the Line tooltip). Click OK. Position the chart so that it is flush left with the report body and just below the matrix. Expand the chart so that it is 7 inches wide and 3.5 inches high either by dragging the chart borders on the design surface or by setting the Width and Height properties under Size in the Properties pane.

Configure the chart data by dragging and dropping fields from the Report Data pane to the chart region. Double-click the chart. Chart handles will be exposed for data, category, and series fields. Drag *Internet_Sales_Amount* and *Internet_Order_Quantity* from the Report Data pane to the data handle. Drag *Calendar_Quarter* to the category handle, and *Country* to the series handle.

Preview the report. If necessary, scroll down to view the chart. As with tables and matrices that are added to reports, we need to apply some formatting to the chart to make it look better. To begin, the chart should have a title, and the axes should be labeled; furthermore, the chart is compressed to the left because the legend is taking up space on the right. An even bigger problem is that even though the legend shows four items, only two lines appear on the chart—the lines corresponding to the sales amount. Because sales amount and order quantity are of different orders of magnitude, showing them together on a single chart using a single value axis is of little practical use. We are going to address all of these issues. Return to the Design tab.

In Visual Studio 2005, all aspects of formatting chart elements, including assigning a chart title and axis labels, could be completed only through the use of dialog boxes and properties, In Visual Studio 2008, formatting charts is much more intuitive. Whereas in Visual Studio 2005, the chart data region on the design surface was merely a placeholder for the chart, in Visual Studio 2008, the chart region on the design surface more fully represents the chart item, and chart elements can be configured interactively directly on the chart region. Let's see how.

First we will add a chart title and label the chart axes. Double-click Chart Title on the chart data region. This will activate the chart handles and reveal the borders of the text box for the chart title. Double-click Chart Title again to make the text box editable. Change the title to **Sales Amount And Order Quantity Trend**. Double-click the Axis Title for the x-axis (the horizontal axis). Label the axis **Quarter**. Double-click the Axis Title for the y-axis (the vertical axis). Label the axis **Sales Amount**.

Next we will add a secondary y-axis for the Order Quantity values. Dual-axis charts are now native to Reporting Services; previously, a dual-axis chart could be created only with the Dundas add-in for Reporting Services. Right-click the Order Quantity data item in the data handle, and then select Series Properties from the shortcut menu. Select the Axes And Chart Area page from the navigation list on the left in the dialog box. Change the Value axis option from Primary to Secondary. Click OK to save your changes and close the dialog box. Note that a secondary y-axis has been added to the right side of the chart region. Double-click the Axis Title, and then change the text to **Order Quantity**.

Move the legend from the right side of the chart to the below the chart by dragging the legend from the right side of the chart region to the bottom of the chart region. Alternatively, right-click the legend or any white space in the chart region, and then use the Legend Properties dialog box to change the position of the legend. (Because each part of the chart region is representative of the actual item in the chart, it might take a few tries to click a spot that has a shortcut menu with the Legend Properties option.)

Last, we will edit the legend text to make the chart more aesthetically pleasing. Right-click the Sales Amount data item in the data handle, and then select Series Properties from the shortcut menu. Select the Legend pane from the navigation list on the left in the dialog box. Click the Expression button for the Custom legend text. Type the following expression in the Expression Editor text box:

```
=Fields!Country.Value & " Sales Amount"
```

Click OK to save the change and close the dialog box. Repeat the process for the Order Quantity data item, and type the following text in the Expression Editor text box:

```
=Fields!Country.Value & " Order Quantity"
```

Figure 19-17 shows the formatted chart region in the Report Designer.

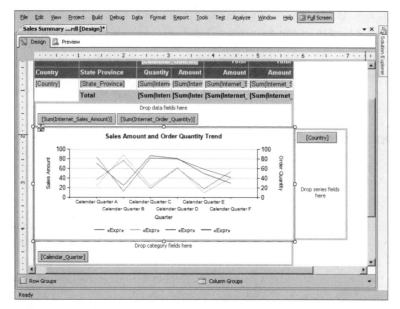

FIGURE 19-17 A formatted chart data region

Preview the report. Four lines now appear in the chart. Change the date range selection or the country selection. The selections are reflected in both the grid and the chart. Click the Save All button to save the files to this point.

Making a Report Interactive

Reporting Services offers numerous possibilities for allowing the user to interact with rendered reports. We've already seen the power of parameters that allow users to choose the data they want to see in reports. Sometimes, however, it's not just the content of the report that we want to let users control, but also the depth to which they can analyze the data. Allowing users to show and hide columns in reports, launch Web pages, or drill through to related reports are some of the ways you can empower users to drive their data analysis.

Toggling Row Visibility

Our simple *Order Summary by Region and Date* report has become a bit unwieldy after adding subtotals, groups, and columns to it. We want to present users with a simple overview when they initially view the report. We will do this by hiding the quarter columns and adding a toggle to the year columns to allow users to drill down to the quarter as desired.

Return to Design view. Click the drop-down arrow corresponding to the *Calendar_Quarter* group in the Grouping pane, and then select Group Properties. Select the Visibility page from the navigation list on the left in the dialog box. Select the Hide option for When The

Report Is Initially Run. Check the Display Can Be Toggled By This Report Item option, and then select Calendar_Year from the drop-down list. Click OK to close the dialog box.

Preview the report. You'll see that the quarter columns are now hidden, and that a plus sign appears next to each year. Click a plus sign next to a year to display the quarter columns for just that year.

Adding Report Actions

Reporting Services allows for three kinds of actions to be configured when users click a tablix cell: Go To URL, Go To Bookmark, and Go To Report. We will add a Go To Report action to our order summary report.

We will allow users to drill through to (that is, open) the *Order Detail* report we created earlier in this chapter from this summary report. Because the *Order Detail* report requires parameters, we need to map values from the selection made by the user clicking the summary report to the *Order Detail* report parameters. Return to Design view. Right-click the cell at the intersection of the *Calendar_Quarter* and *State_Province* groups, and then select Text Box Properties from the shortcut menu. Select the Action page from the navigation list on the left in the Text Box Properties dialog box. Then select the Go To Report option and select *Order Detail* from the Select A Report From The List drop-down list. Click the Add button. Select Country from the Name drop-down list and [Country] from the Value drop-down list. Click Add again. In the second row, select State from the Name drop-down list and [State_Province] from the Value drop-down list.

An expression needs to be written for the *CalendarYear* and *CalendarQuarter* parameters since the member names do not match the values required by the query for the *Order Detail* report. Specifically, the query expects just the year and quarter number. *[Calendar_Year]* is formatted as CY *yyyy* and *[Calendar_Quarter]* is formatted as Q*q* CY *yyyy* in the summary report. The extra characters need to be stripped before passing the value to the *Order Detail* report. This is easy to do using the Visual Basic substring functions *Right* and *Mid*. Type the expressions shown in the following table for the *CalendarQuarter* and *CalendarYear* parameter values.

Name	Value Expression
CalendarYear	*=Right(Fields!Calendar_Year.Value, 4)*
CalendarQuarter	*=Mid(Fields!Calendar_Quarter.Value, 2, 1)*

Figure 19-18 shows the completed dialog box after adding the Go To Report action. Click OK to save your selections and close the dialog box.

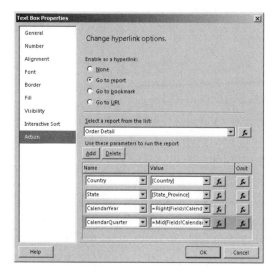

FIGURE 19-18 The completed Text Box Properties dialog box for a Go To Report action

Preview the report. Expand the column showing *CY 2002*, and then hover the mouse pointer over a cell showing the sales amount for a specific quarter and province. The cursor will change to a hand indicating that the cell is clickable. Click the cell. The *Order Detail* report will be displayed showing the orders for the selected quarter and province from the summary report. To return to the summary report, click the left-pointing arrow on the report toolbar.

Click the Save All button on the toolbar to save the files to this point.

Delivering Reports

Now that you've learned how to create different types of useful reports, the remainder of this chapter will show how to deliver those reports to your users.

Deploying to the Report Server

After you've built some reports and tested them in our development environment, it's time to make them available for all users. Deployment involves uploading your report RDL files from the development environment to a report server where all users can access them. There are three ways to deploy reports: directly from within Visual Studio, by using a script and command-line utility, or from within the Report Manager Web interface. We will explore all three approaches next.

> **Note** The ability to deploy reports via SQL Server Management Studio has been removed in SQL Server 2008.

Deploying Reports Using Visual Studio 2008

The simplest way to deploy reports and data sources is right from within Visual Studio. An entire report project or just one individual report can be deployed. To deploy an entire project, select Deploy from the Build menu, or right-click the project in Solution Explorer and select Deploy.

The target locations for reports deployed using Visual Studio are established by setting project properties in the Properties pane. (If the Properties pane is hidden, you can display it by selecting Properties from the Project menu.) Table 19-2 describes the project properties related to deployment.

TABLE 19-2 Visual Studio Deployment Properties

Property	Description
OverwriteDataSources	If true, causes the deployment to overwrite existing data sources.
TargetDataSourceFolder	This is the location where the data sources are deployed. A blank value will cause the data sources to be deployed to the location specified by the *TargetReportFolder* property (that is, the same location where reports are deployed). Values are entered without being prefixed by the absolute URL address (that is, they are relative to the absolute path specified by *TargetServerURL*)—for example, *SampleReports/DataSources*.
TargetReportFolder	This is the location where the reports are deployed. Values are entered without being prefixed by the absolute URL address (that is, they are relative to the absolute path specified by *TargetServerURL*)—for example, *SampleReports/Reports*.
TargetServerURL	The absolute URL of the server on which the reports are to be deployed. Locations specified by *TargetDataSourceFolder* and *TargetReportFolder* are relative to this URL—for example, *ttp://servername/reportserver*.

> **Note** When deploying to a SharePoint-integrated site (discussed later in this chapter), all location values must be entered as absolute URLs. For example, the TargetReportFolder property might be set to http://servername/site/subsite/reports when deploying to a SharePoint-integrated site.

Using Report Manager

An alternative method of deploying reports to the Web site is to use the Report Manager interface. Report Manager is accessed by browsing the URL *http://servername/reports*. The menu items that appear are different between users and administrators. An administrator gets additional items to allow for site settings, maintenance of security, and organizing and uploading reports. Figure 19-19 shows the default administrator view.

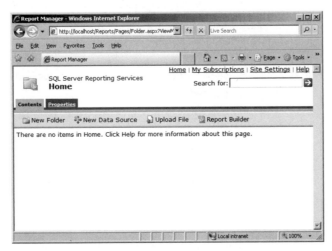

FIGURE 19-19 Report Manager administrator browser sample

The buttons on the toolbar that are used for deploying reports are described in Table 19-3.

TABLE 19-3 REPORT MANAGER TOOLBAR BUTTONS

Button	Functionality
New Folder	Use this button to create a folder within the current folder.
New Data Source	Use this button to create a new data source in the current folder. For information about creating data sources, see the discussion earlier in this chapter.
Upload File	Use this button to upload an item to the current folder. Typically, RDL files are uploaded, but resources can also be uploaded using this button.

To deploy a new report to a new folder, follow these steps:

1. On the Home page of Report Manager, click New Folder. In the Name field, type **Sample Reports**, and then click OK.

> **Note** Newly added items are denoted with a !New icon in Report Manager.

2. Click the Sample Reports folder, and then click New Data Source on the toolbar. In the New Data Source window, enter the values in the following table, and then click OK.

Field	Value
Name	AdventureWorksCube
Data Source Type	Microsoft SQL Server Analysis Services
Connection String	Data Source=localhost;Initial Catalog="Adventure Works DW 2008"
Connect Using	Windows Integrated Security

3. After the window refreshes, click New Data Source again. Enter the values in the following table, and then click OK to deploy the second data source.

Field	Value
Name	AdventureWorksDW2008
Data Source Type	Microsoft SQL Server
Connection String	Data Source=localhost;Initial Catalog=AdventureWorksDW2008
Connect Using	Windows Integrated Security

4. Click Upload File on the toolbar. Click the Browse button, and then navigate to the location of the Reporting Services project we created earlier. Select the Sales Summary by Region and Date.rdl file, click Open, and then click OK.

The final result should look like Figure 19-20.

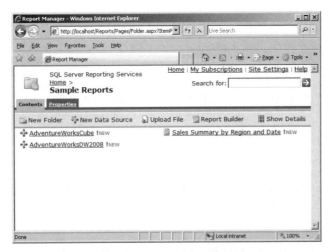

FIGURE 19-20 Report Manager after deploying the report

Tip To edit existing items, click Show Details on the toolbar, and then click the Edit button next to the item you want to change. To delete existing items, click Show Details, select the check boxes next to the items you want to delete, and then click the Delete button.

Using the Command Line

When it comes to implementing an automated deployment process, neither of the preceding deployment methods can be used. In today's corporate environments, deployments must be scriptable and reproducible. This requirement precludes the interactive use of Visual Studio to deploy a project or upload files to a Web site. The *rs* command-line utility (rs.exe) is provided specifically for this purpose. With this utility, you can programmatically administer a report server using Visual Basic .NET scripts stored in .rss text files. In addition to deploying reports, these scripts can be used to perform any action against the Reporting Services Web Services. (The Reporting Services Web Services expose the full functionality of Reporting Services to the developer and are discussed later in this chapter in the section "Administering Reporting Services.")

The syntax for the *rs* utility is:

```
rs {-?} [-iinput_file=] [-sserverURL] {-uusername} {-ppassword} {-ltime_out} {-bbatchmode}
{-vglobalvars=} {-eendpoint} {-ttrace}
```

More Info Thorough coverage of the *rs* utility is beyond the scope of this chapter. Refer to SQL Server Books Online for a complete description of this utility.

A Reporting Services script has the following characteristics:

- It is written in Microsoft Visual Basic .NET.

- It contains a *Main* procedure that is the entry point to the script when the script file is run.

- It uses the *rs* module-level variable to perform any of the Web Service operations that are available in the Web Service libraries. The script environment automatically connects to the report server, creates the Web proxy class, and generates the module-level *rs* reference variable to the Web Service proxy object.

- It can access the *System.Web.Services*, *System.Web.Services.Protocols*, *System.Xml*, and *System.IO* .NET Framework namespaces, which are made available by the scripting environment.

- Global variables are set from the command line using the syntax of *−v variable=value.* Multiple global values can be passed using this method. Two global variables, *server-Name* and *databaseName*, would be set with the following parameters to the *rs* utility:

```
-v serverName=localhost -v databaseName="Adventure Works DW 2008"
```

Most of the Web Service operations that are related to the task of deploying reports are listed in Table 19-4.

> **Note** Although the Web Service endpoint names end with *2005* and *2006,* these are actually the endpoints used for SQL Server 2008 Reporting Services.

TABLE 19-4 Web Services Operations for Deploying Reports

Operation	Description
rs.Credentials	Sets the credentials used by the Web Service. Must be set to an object of type *System.Net.NetworkCredential.* For example: `rs.Credentials = System.Net.CredentialCache.DefaultCredentials`
rs.CreateFolder	Creates a folder on the report server. Both the folder name and parent folder are specified as strings. An array of *ReportingService2005.Property* objects can also be specified to set any properties on the folder. For example: `rs.CreateFolder(folderName, folderParent, Nothing)`
rs.GetProperties	Returns the value of one or more properties of an item. As arguments, the operation takes the full path to the item and an array of *ReportingService2005.Property* objects for which you want the values. For example: `rs.GetProperties(folderParent & folderName, props)`
rs.CreateDataSource	Creates a data source on the ReportServer. The data source name and parent path are specified as strings, and a Boolean value specifies whether to overwrite an existing data source. The definition of the data source is specified by creating a variable of type *ReportingService2005.DataSourceDefinition* and setting the appropriate properties for the new data source. An array of *ReportingService2005.Property* objects can also be specified to set any properties on the data source. For example: `rs.CreateDataSource(dsName, parentPath, True, definition, Nothing)`
rs.CreateReport	Creates a report on the report server. The report name and parent path are specified as strings, and a Boolean value specifies whether to overwrite an existing data source. The report's RDL content is specified as a byte array, which is typically loaded by reading an .rdl file from a source location. An array of *ReportingService2005.Property* objects can also be specified to set any properties on the data source. For example: `rs.CreateReport(reportName, parentPath, True, definition, Nothing)`

Listing 19-1 shows the complete script to deploy two additional reports and redeploy one of the data sources to the same folder we previously created interactively using Report Manager. It accomplishes these tasks by interacting with the Reporting Services Web Service members shown in Table 19-4 and highlighted in bold in Listing 19-1. In addition to interacting with the Web Service, the code uses several standard .NET objects to output status information, read a file from the disk, and implement exception handling.

LISTING 19-1 The DeployReports.rss script, which deploys a sample folder, data source, and reports

```
Dim definition As [Byte]() = Nothing
Dim warnings As Warning() = Nothing
Dim filePath As String = "./"

Public Sub Main()
  rs.Credentials = System.Net.CredentialCache.DefaultCredentials

  'Create the root folders
  CreateFolder("Sample Reports", "/")

  'Create the shared data sources for Sample Reports folder
  CreateSQLDataSource("/Sample Reports", "AdventureWorksDW2008", serverName,
databaseName, "", "")
  PublishReport("Order Detail", "Order Detail", "/Sample Reports")
  PublishReport("Product Detail", "Product Detail", "/Sample Reports")
End Sub

Public Sub CreateFolder(ByVal folderName As String, ByVal folderParent As String)
  If DoesFolderExist(folderName, folderParent) = False Then
    Try
      rs.CreateFolder(folderName, folderParent, Nothing)
      Console.WriteLine("Parent folder created: {0}", folderName)
    Catch e As Exception
      Console.WriteLine(e.Message)
    End Try
  Else
    Console.WriteLine("Folder {0} already exists.", folderParent & folderName)
  End If
End Sub

Public Function DoesFolderExist(ByVal folderName As String, ByVal folderParent As
String) as Boolean
  ' Create the property to retrieve.
  Dim retrieveProp As New [Property]()
  retrieveProp.Name = "Description"
  Dim props(0) As [Property]
  props(0) = retrieveProp
```

```
  Try
    Dim properties As [Property]() = rs.GetProperties(folderParent & folderName,
props)
    DoesFolderExist = True
  Catch e As SoapException
    DoesFolderExist = False
  End Try
End Function

Public Sub CreateSQLDataSource(ByVal parentPath as String, ByVal dsName As String,
ByVal serverName As String, ByVal catalogName As String, ByVal userName As String,
ByVal password As String)
  Console.WriteLine("CreateSQLDataSource: Name:{0}; Server:{1}; Catalog:{2};
User:{3};", dsName, serverName, catalogName, userName)

  Dim strConnection as String
  strConnection = "Data Source=" & serverName & ";Initial Catalog=" & catalogName

  CreateDataSource(parentPath, dsName, strConnection, "SQL", userName, password, True)
End Sub

Public Sub CreateOLAPDataSource(ByVal parentPath as String, ByVal dsName As String,
ByVal serverName As String, ByVal catalogName As String, ByVal userName As String,
ByVal password As String)
  Console.WriteLine("CreateOLAPDataSource: Name:{0}; Server:{1}; Catalog:{2};",
dsName, serverName, catalogName)

  Dim strConnection as String
  strConnection = "Data Source=" & serverName & ";Initial Catalog=" & catalogName

  CreateDataSource(parentPath, dsName, strConnection, "OLEDB-MD", userName, password,
True)
End Sub

Public Sub CreateDataSource(ByVal parentPath as String, ByVal dsName As String, ByVal
strConnection As String, ByVal strExtension As String, ByVal userName As String, ByVal
password As String, ByVal windowsCredentials As Boolean)
  'Define the data source definition.
  Dim definition As New DataSourceDefinition()

  If username = "" Then
    definition.CredentialRetrieval = CredentialRetrievalEnum.Integrated
  Else
    definition.CredentialRetrieval = CredentialRetrievalEnum.Store
    definition.Username = userName
    definition.Password = password
  End If
  definition.WindowsCredentials = windowsCredentials

  definition.ConnectString = strConnection
  definition.Enabled = True
  definition.EnabledSpecified = True
  definition.Extension = strExtension
  definition.ImpersonateUser = False
```

```
    definition.ImpersonateUserSpecified = True
    definition.Prompt = Nothing

  Try
    rs.CreateDataSource(dsName, parentPath, True, definition, Nothing)
    Console.WriteLine("Datasource: {0} created successfully with no warnings", dsName)

  Catch e As Exception
    Console.WriteLine(e.Message)
  End Try
End Sub

Public Sub PublishReport(ByVal reportFile As String, ByVal reportName As String, ByVal
parentPath as String)
  If reportName = "" Then
    reportName = reportFile
  End If

  Dim definition As [Byte]() = Nothing
  Dim warnings As Warning() = Nothing

  Try
    Dim stream As FileStream = File.OpenRead(filePath + reportFile + ".rdl")
    definition = New [Byte](stream.Length-1) {}
    stream.Read(definition, 0, CInt(stream.Length))
    stream.Close()
  Catch e As IOException
    Console.WriteLine(e.Message)
  End Try

  Try
    warnings = rs.CreateReport(reportName, parentPath, True, definition, Nothing)

    If Not (warnings Is Nothing) Then
      Dim warning As Warning
      For Each warning In warnings
        Console.WriteLine(warning.Message)
      Next warning
    Else
      Console.WriteLine("Report: {0} published successfully with no warnings",
reportName)
    End If
  Catch e As Exception
    Console.WriteLine(e.Message)
  End Try
End Sub
```

To execute a deployment script, open a command prompt, and then navigate to the directory where the .rss file is located. For example, to execute the DeployReports.rss script shown in Listing 19-1 against the *AdventureWorksDW2008* Analysis Server database on the local server, execute the following command:

```
rs -i DeployReports.rss -s http://localhost/reportserver -v serverName=localhost -v
databaseName="Adventure Works DW 2008"
```

> **Note** The *rs* executable file is located in \Program Files\Microsoft SQL Server\100\Tools\Binn by default. This directory should be in your search path. If the command fails to execute, either correct the search path or qualify the command with the *rs* executable path and try again.

Accessing Reports Programmatically

Frequently, the requirements for presenting the reports to end users are complex and beyond the scope of the off-the-shelf presentation tools. Fortunately, we have the ability to write custom code for users to access our reports. The supported report delivery programming methods are outlined in Table 19-5.

TABLE 19-5 Supported Report Delivery Programming Methods

Method	Description
ReportViewer control	The report viewer controls allow the programmer to embed a report directly into any Microsoft ASP.NET Web page or .NET Microsoft Windows Forms desktop application.
SharePoint integration	By configuring Reporting Services to run in SharePoint-integrated mode, the reports and other artifacts are published to a SharePoint library. These reports can then be used anywhere in a SharePoint-based reporting solution. A more thorough discussion of the topic is provided later in this chapter.
URL access	This allows almost any application to render a report. There are query parameters that allow the caller to pass in values for parameters and to specify the desired format. The base URL is *http://servername/ reportserver*.
XML Web Service	This allows any application capable of calling XML Web Services the ability to render reports as well as administer the report server.

Using URL Access for Report Viewing

URL access is a very convenient option for integrating report viewing into your applications, especially for non-.NET applications that cannot make use of the *ReportViewer* controls. For example, if you are developing applications using classic Active Server Pages (ASP), URL access can be used to embed links to reports in your Web pages. The report server is accessible using URL requests. The complete list of available parameters is long and reflects the full set of features available in Reporting Services. Refer to "Integrating Reporting Services Using URL Access" in SQL Server Books Online for the complete list. Here's an example of a URL that generates a report as a Word document:

http://localhost/ReportServer/Pages/ReportViewer.aspx?/Sample%20Reports/Sales%20 Summary%20by%20Region%20and%20Date&rs:Command=Render&rs:format=WORD

Table 19-6 lists and explains the meaning of each part of this URL

TABLE 19-6 URL Syntax for Delivering Reports as Word 2007 Documents

Syntax	Description
http://localhost/ReportServer/Pages/ReportViewer.aspx?	The URL for the report server and path to the *ReportViewer* Web page.
/Sample%20Reports/Sales%20Summary%20by%20Region%20 and%20Date	The complete path of the report to be rendered. Spaces in either the folder or report must be replaced with *%20*.
&rs:Command=Render	This parameter instructs the report server to render the report.
&rs:format=WORD	This parameter instructs the report server to render the report as a Microsoft Office Word document, The ability to render a report as a Word document is a new feature in Reporting Services 2008.

Using the *ReportViewer* Controls

To easily integrate reporting with custom .NET applications, Microsoft provides the *ReportViewer* control. Two versions are provided, one for Windows Forms applications and the other for Web Forms applications. Each version of the control supports processing in either remote mode or local mode.

In remote processing mode, the control is configured to render a report that you've deployed to a report server instance that handles all the data retrieval and query processing. In local processing mode, the control uses a local report definition against locally processed data, with several limitations and reduced functionality. This mode does not require a SQL Server license or a report server because it's your own client application that's in charge of querying the data source(s) to acquire the report data.

Let's create a Windows Forms client application that uses the *ReportViewer* control in remote processing mode to display the *Sales Summary by Region and Date* report we created earlier in this chapter.

To create the application, complete the following steps from within Visual Studio:

1. Create a new Microsoft Visual C# Windows Form Application project named *ReportViewerDemo*.

2. From the Reporting tab in the toolbox, drag and drop a *MicrosoftReportViewer* control onto *Form1*. A *ReportViewer* control named *reportViewer1* is added to the form.

3. On the control's smart tag menu that automatically appears, click Dock In Parent Container.

4. In the Properties pane, set the control's *ProcessingMode* property to *Remote*.

5. To connect the control to the server, set its *ReportPath* and *ReportServerURL* properties to */Sample Reports/Sales Summary by Region and Date* and *http://localhost/ reportserver*, respectively. (These properties are nested beneath *ServerReport* in the Properties pane.)

6. Press F5 to run the application. The Windows Form should display the *Sales Summary by Region and Date* report inside the embedded *ReportViewer* control, similar to Figure 19-21.

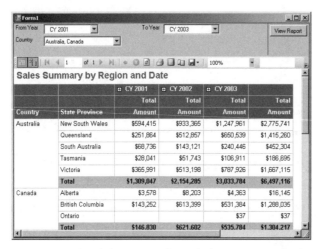

FIGURE 19-21 Rendering a report in a Windows Forms application using the *ReportViewer* control

The ASP.NET version of the *ReportViewer* control used in a Web application is implemented in a very similar manner. However, due to the differences between Windows Forms and ASP. NET Web applications, there are some differences between the two. First, the Web version of the control uses HTML formatting for displaying a report, while the Windows Forms version uses a Graphics Device Interface (GDI). This might result in slight presentation differences due to the inexact nature of HTML rendering. A second difference relates to printing. A Windows Forms application uses the print functionality of the user's machine, but a Web Forms application uses an ActiveX control for printing. Last, the Web version of the control has minimum browser requirements. To ensure that the fullest set of functionality is available to the user, Internet Explorer 6.0 or later with scripting enabled is required.

Scripting Report Generation Using SQL Server Integration Services

You can also use SQL Server Integration Services to generate reports. Our next example demonstrates how to use Integration Services to script a task that interacts with the report server using the Web Services it exposes. This task calls the Reporting Services Web Services to archive a report by generating its output as an Adobe Acrobat Portable Document Format (PDF) file to a destination directory.

In earlier versions of SQL Server, Integration Services Script Tasks could be written only in Visual Basic .NET (a limitation that notably still exists for Reporting Services tasks, as we saw with the *rs* utility). In SQL Server 2008, you can now write Integration Services Script Tasks in C# as well. Follow these steps to implement our Integration Services Script Task in C#:

1. Start Visual Studio 2008, and select File, New Project.

2. Select Business Intelligence Projects from Project Types on the left, and then select the Integration Services Project template.

3. Name the project **SSIS**, and then click OK. Visual Studio automatically generates an empty package named Package.dtsx in the project and opens the package.

4. From the toolbox, drag and drop a Script Task to the Control Flow tab. The package should now look similar to Figure 19-22.

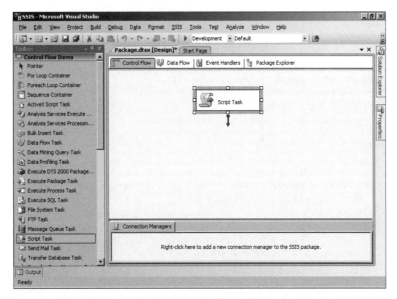

FIGURE 19-22 Integration Services project after adding the Script Task

5. Double-click the Script Task to open its Properties window. Ensure that the *ScriptLanguage* property is set to Microsoft Visual C# 2008. Click the Edit Script button to open the Integration Services Script Task editor. A file named ScriptMain.cs is automatically created and opened in a new Visual Studio editor. This file contains the code to be executed by the Script Task.

6. In Project Explorer, right-click the References node, and then select Add Web Reference.

7. Set the URL to **http://<*servername*>:80/reportserver/ReportService2005. asmx?wsdl**. (This is the location of the management Web Service; replace <*servername*> with the name of your report server.) Then click Go.

8. Set the Web reference name to **ReportManagementProxy**, and then click Add Reference.

9. Repeat the same process to add a second Web reference to URL *http://<servername>:80/reportserver/ReportExecution2005.asmx?wsdl* named *ReportExecutionProxy*. (This is the location of the execution Web Service; again, replace <*servername*> with the name of your report server.)

10. Ensure that the settings for the Web references are correct. To do this, double-click *Settings.settings* beneath the Properties node in Project Explorer, and then verify that the *Value* for each of the entries reflects the two Web Service URLs specified in the preceding steps.

11. Return to the ScriptMain.cs tab, and replace the *Main* function with the code in Listing 19-2. An explanation of the key elements in the code is provided following this list.

LISTING 19-2 Integration Services Script Task code

```
public void Main()
{
  int status = (int)ScriptResults.Success;
  bool refire = false;
  string errMsg = string.Empty;
  string url = "http://localhost/reportserver";

  try
  {
    // Get a reference to the SSRS management service
    ReportManagementProxy.ReportingService2005 mgtSvc =
     GetManagementServiceReference(url);
    if (mgtSvc == null)
    {
      errMsg = "Failed to create instance of SSRS management Web Service";
      status = (int)ScriptResults.Failure;
    }
    else
    {
      // Get a reference to the SSRS execution service
      ReportExecutionProxy.ReportExecutionService execSvc =
       GetExecutionServiceReference(url);
      if (execSvc == null)
      {
        errMsg = "Failed to create instance of SSRS execution Web Service";
        status = (int)ScriptResults.Failure;
      }
      else
      {
```

```
        if (ArchiveReport(mgtSvc, execSvc, "/",
            "Sales Summary by Region and Date", ref errMsg) !=
          (int)ScriptResults.Success)
            Dts.Events.FireInformation(2010, "", errMsg, "", 0, ref refire);
      }
    }
  }
  catch (Exception ex)
  {
    errMsg = ex.Source + ": " + ex.Message;
    status = (int)ScriptResults.Failure;
  }

  Dts.Events.FireInformation(2010, "", errMsg, "", 0, ref refire);
  Dts.TaskResult = status;
}

private ReportManagementProxy.ReportingService2005
 GetManagementServiceReference(string url)
{
  ReportManagementProxy.ReportingService2005 mgtSvc =
   new ReportManagementProxy.ReportingService2005();

  mgtSvc.Url = url + "/ReportService2005.asmx";
  mgtSvc.Timeout = 60000; //60 seconds
  mgtSvc.Credentials = System.Net.CredentialCache.DefaultCredentials;

  System.Net.WebProxy wp = System.Net.WebProxy.GetDefaultProxy();
  mgtSvc.Proxy = wp;

  return mgtSvc;
}

private ReportExecutionProxy.ReportExecutionService
 GetExecutionServiceReference(string url)
{
  ReportExecutionProxy.ReportExecutionService execSvc =
   new ReportExecutionProxy.ReportExecutionService();

  execSvc.Url = url + "/ReportExecution2005.asmx";
  execSvc.Timeout = 900000; //15 minutes
  execSvc.Credentials = System.Net.CredentialCache.DefaultCredentials;

  System.Net.WebProxy wp = System.Net.WebProxy.GetDefaultProxy();
  execSvc.Proxy = wp;

  return execSvc;
}

private int ArchiveReport(
 ReportManagementProxy.ReportingService2005 mgtSvc,
 ReportExecutionProxy.ReportExecutionService execSvc,
 string path,
 string report,
```

```csharp
      ref string errMsg)
{
  int status = (int)ScriptResults.Success;
  bool refire = false;

  try
  {
    string destPath = "C:\\ReportOutput\\";
    Dts.Events.FireInformation(2010, "", "Archiving reports from server " +
mgtSvc.Url, "", 0, ref refire);

    System.IO.DirectoryInfo di = new System.IO.DirectoryInfo(destPath);
    if (!di.Exists)
    {
      di.Create();
    }

    foreach(ReportManagementProxy.CatalogItem item
     in mgtSvc.ListChildren(path, true))
    {
      try
      {
        if ((item.Name == report) &&
            (item.Type == ReportManagementProxy.ItemTypeEnum.Report) &&
            (!item.Hidden))
        {
          // Format can be XML, NULL, CSV, IMAGE, PDF, HTML4.0,
          //  HTML3.2, MHTML, EXCEL, and HTMLOWC
          string destExtension = "pdf";
          string destFormat = "PDF";

          string destFile = destPath + item.Name + destExtension;

          System.IO.FileInfo fi = new System.IO.FileInfo(destFile);
          if (!fi.Exists)
          {
            if (GenerateReport(execSvc, item, destFile, destFormat) !=
              (int)ScriptResults.Success)
              status = (int)ScriptResults.Failure;
          }
        }
      }
      catch (Exception ex)
      {
        errMsg = ex.Message;
        status = (int)ScriptResults.Failure;
      }
    }
  }
  catch (Exception ex)
  {
    errMsg = ex.Message;
    status = (int)ScriptResults.Failure;
  }
```

```csharp
    return status;
}

private int GenerateReport(
 ReportExecutionProxy.ReportExecutionService execSvc,
 ReportManagementProxy.CatalogItem item,
 string destFile,
 string format)
{
  int status = (int)ScriptResults.Success;
  bool refire = false;
  try
  {
    string historyid = null;

    ReportExecutionProxy.ExecutionInfo ei =
     execSvc.LoadReport(item.Path, historyid);

    string deviceInfo = null;
    byte[] results;
    string encoding = string.Empty;
    string mimetype = string.Empty;
    string extension = string.Empty;
    ReportExecutionProxy.Warning[] warnings = null;
    string[] streamIDs = null;

    results = execSvc.Render(format, deviceInfo,
     out extension, out mimetype, out encoding, out warnings, out streamIDs);

    if (results != null)
    {
      System.IO.FileStream stream =
       System.IO.File.Create(destFile, results.Length);
      stream.Write(results, 0, results.Length);
      stream.Close();
    }

    Dts.Events.FireInformation(2010, "",
      "Successfully archived report " + item.Name + " to " + destFile,
      "", 0, ref refire);
  }
  catch (Exception ex)
  {
    status = (int)ScriptResults.Failure;
    Dts.Events.FireInformation(2010, "",
      "ERROR: While archiving report " + item.Name + ": " + ex.Message,
      "", 0, ref refire);
  }

  return status;
}
```

12. Save the code and close the Integration Services Script Task editor, and then return to the Script Task Editor dialog box and click OK.

13. In the Solution Explorer panel of Visual Studio, right-click Package1.dtsx, and then select Execute Package to run our Integration Services Script Task.

Let's examine the code in Listing 19-2. The default entry point to the code is the *Main* method. Two Web Service proxies are first created—one for the management service and the other for the execution service—with these two lines of code:

```
ReportManagementProxy.ReportingService2005 mgtSvc = GetManagementServiceReference(url);
    :
ReportExecutionProxy.ReportExecutionService execSvc = GetExecutionServiceReference(url);
```

Each of these snippets of code calls a method farther down in the script that instantiates the appropriate Web Service proxy and sets its URL, time-out, credentials, and proxy properties. (The proxy is an object that is accessible to our code that interacts directly with the Web Service behind the scenes.) We then call the *ArchiveReport* method and pass it the two Web Service proxies, the path on the report server containing the report to be archived and the report name, as follows:

```
if (ArchiveReport(mgtSvc, execSvc, "/", "Sales Summary by Region and Date" ref errMsg) !=
(int)ScriptResults.Success)
```

The *Main* method finishes by setting *Dts.TaskResult* to indicate either success or failure of the task.

The *ArchiveReport* method begins by checking whether the output directory (hard-coded as C:\ReportOutput\ in this example) exists and creates it if it doesn't. Next the *ListChildren* method of the management Web Service is called in a *foreach* loop to enumerate all the items in the specified source path (passed in as the root '/' directory in this example) on the report server. Following a check to see whether the item is actually the report we are looking for (*Sales Summary by Region and Date*), we generate the report by calling the execution Web Service, with this line of code:

```
if (GenerateReport(execSvc, item, destFile, destFormat) != (int)ScriptResults.Success)
```

The *GenerateReport* method does the actual work of generating the output. First it loads the report item by calling the *LoadReport* method of the execution Web Service, as follows:

```
ReportExecutionProxy.ExecutionInfo ei = execSvc.LoadReport(item.Path, historyid);
```

The actual rendering of the report is accomplished with the *Render* method of the execution Web Service, as follows:

```
results = execSvc.Render(format, deviceInfo,
  out extension, out mimetype, out encoding, out warnings, out streamIDs);
```

The *Render* method returns a byte array representing the report output in PDF format (as specified by the *format* parameter, which was set to *'PDF'* in the *ArchiveReport* method), which is then written to disk using a *FileStream* object.

Administering Reporting Services

SQL Server 2008 provides several tools for accomplishing Reporting Services administrative tasks. In this section, we'll examine Reporting Services administration using Reporting Services Configuration Manager, the Reporting Services Web Services, Report Manager, and SQL Server Management Studio.

Using Reporting Services Configuration Manager

The configuration of a Reporting Services installation is accomplished with the Reporting Services Configuration Manager tool. In a typical installation, the Reporting Services Configuration Manager tool is located in the All Programs, Microsoft SQL Server 2008, Configuration Tools folder in the Windows Start menu. When Reporting Services is installed, the default option is to perform a Files-Only installation. When the installation is complete, the report server cannot be used until configuration is completed using Reporting Services Configuration Manager. SQL Server 2008 introduces two new options for installation: one for a default native mode installation and one for a default SharePoint-integrated mode installation. (SharePoint integration is discussed in more detail in a moment.) If the server was installed using either of the default configuration options, this tool can be used to verify the settings and make changes. Figure 19-23 shows Reporting Services Configuration Manager.

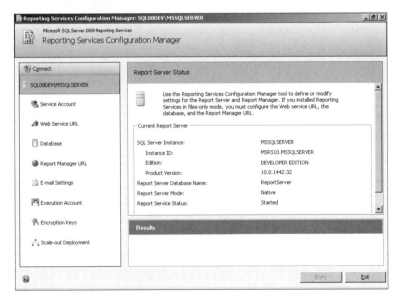

FIGURE 19-23 Reporting Services Configuration Manager

Table 19-7 lists the tasks that can be accomplished with Reporting Services Configuration Manager.

TABLE 19-7 Reporting Services Configuration Manager Tasks

Setting	Description
Service Account	The report server service account is initially configured during setup, but you can update the password or use a different account here.
Web Service URL	The report server is an ASP.NET application accessed through a URL. The report server URL provides access to the SOAP endpoints of the report server. Either a single URL or multiple URLs may be configured for each application.
Database	The report server requires a SQL Server database for internal storage. You can use the tool to create and configure a connection to the report server database, or you can select an existing report server.
Report Manager URL	Report Manager is an ASP.NET application accessed through a URL. The Report Manager URL is used to open Report Manager. Either a single URL or multiple URLs can be configured for each application.
E-Mail Settings	Reporting Services includes the ability to deliver reports or report processing notification to an electronic mailbox using Simple Mail Transfer Protocol (SMTP). You can use the tool to specify which SMTP server and address to use for e-mail delivery.
Execution Account	This account is used for remote connections during scheduled operations or when user credentials are not available.
Encryption Keys	Functionality is provided to back up, restore, or replace the symmetric key that is used to encrypt stored connection strings and credentials. You must have a backup of the symmetric key if you change the service account or move a report server database to another computer.
Scale-Out Deployment	Reporting Services supports multiple report server instances using a single, shared report server database. The tool is used to connect each report server to the shared report server database.

Accessing the Report Server Web Services

As you've seen in a number of examples up to now, the full functionality of Reporting Services is exposed to a developer by the Web Services it provides. This allows a developer to create custom applications that provide all of the functionality of the Report Manager and SQL Server Management Studio interfaces. Such functionality can range from performing administrative tasks such as security and report maintenance to report presentation to subscription maintenance. We've seen only a small sample of what's possible by calling into the Web Services in Listings 19-1 and 19-2, but you should realize that anything that can be accomplished interactively with the existing user interfaces is possible to accomplish programmatically with the Web Service!

The Web Services provide *endpoints* for managing a report server as well as executing and navigating reports. The name of the management endpoint, used for managing the objects on the server such as reports, data sources, and so on, depends on whether the server is running in SharePoint-integrated mode. On a native mode server (that is, a report server that is not configured for SharePoint integration), the endpoint is *ReportService2005*. For SharePoint-integrated mode, the endpoint is *ReportService2006*. Only one of the endpoints is available on a server, and an error will be returned if the incorrect endpoint is used.

The URL to access the Web Services Description Language (WSDL) for the management endpoint on a native mode report server is

http://<ReportServerName>/ReportServer/ReportService2005.asmx?wsdl

The URL to access the WSDL for the management endpoint on a SharePoint-integrated mode report server is

http://<SharePointServerName>/<SiteName>/_vti_bin/ReportServer/ReportService2006. asmx?wsdl

The name of the execution endpoint, used by developers for customizing report processing and rendering is *ReportExecution2005*. The same execution endpoint is used for both native and SharePoint-integrated mode servers. The URL to access the WSDL for the execution endpoint on a native mode report server is

http://<ReportServerName>/ReportServer/ReportExecution2005.asmx?wsdl

The URL to access the WSDL for the execution endpoint on a SharePoint-integrated mode report server is

http://<SharePointServerName>/<SiteName>/_vti_bin/ReportServer/ReportExecution2005. asmx?wsdl

Last, when a report server is configured for SharePoint-integrated mode and the Reporting Services add-in has been installed, an additional endpoint, *ReportServiceAuthentication*, is created. The *ReportServiceAuthentication* Web Service is used to provide authentication between a report server and a SharePoint Web application configured to use Forms Authentication. The URL to access the authentication endpoint on a SharePoint-integrated mode report server is

http://<SharePointServerName>/<SiteName>/_vti_bin/ReportServer/ ReportServiceAuthentication.asmx

Using Report Manager and Management Studio

Prior to SQL 2008, it was somewhat unclear whether Report Manager or SQL Server Management Studio should be used to accomplish a particular task because there was considerable overlap between those two tools. In this release, some of the overlapping functionality has been removed, and it is much clearer which tool to use: SQL Server Management Studio is used to configure the server process itself as well as define the security roles, and Report Manager is used to configure the site content as well as security for the content.

Creating Subscriptions

Standard subscriptions are created by individual users to deliver a report at either a specified time or when an event occurs. This feature relies on SQL Server Agent, which must be running in order to create subscriptions. The format, delivery method, and any required report parameter values are set by the user. In order to create a subscription, the following security details must be met, as follows:

- The user must be able view the report. A user can create subscriptions only to reports that he or she has permission to view.

- The user must be in a role that includes the Manage Individual Subscriptions task.

- The report must use either no credentials or stored credentials when retrieving data. Reports that use integrated security will fail because the user information for the owner of the subscription is not available during processing.

> **Note** In order for the example to work, the *AdventureWorksCube* data source must be changed to use stored credentials instead of Windows integrated security. This is accomplished by opening the *AdventureWorksCube* data source in Report Manager, selecting Credentials Stored Securely In The Report Server, entering a valid user name and password, selecting Use As Windows Credentials When Connecting To The Data Source, and then clicking Apply. Furthermore, the specified user must be granted access to the *AdventureWorksDW2008* Analysis Services database. This is accomplished in SQL Server Management Studio by creating a role and assigning the Windows user as a member of the role.

Subscriptions are created using Report Manager, which you can open from *http://<servername>/reports*. After selecting a report and viewing it, a Subscriptions tab is available if the Manage Individual Subscriptions task is enabled for that user. (The details of how to enable tasks for a user are discussed later in this chapter in the section "Securing Reports.") Clicking the Subscriptions tab, shown in Figure 19-24, allows you to add new subscriptions and modify or edit existing ones.

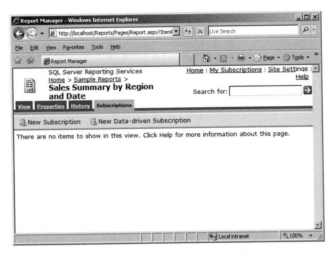

FIGURE 19-24 Report Manager Subscriptions window

Clicking the New Subscription button opens the Subscription Maintenance window. This window is dynamic based on the delivery methods selected and the shared schedules available on the server. For example, when the delivery method is changed to Windows File Share, the UI changes to include fields for file name, path, format, credentials, and overwrite options. To create a subscription for the *Sales Summary by Region and Date* report, follow these steps:

1. Select Windows File Share as the method of delivery. This changes the screen to include the fields required to configure the Windows File Share delivery method.

2. Enter a Universal Naming Convention (UNC) path to a share where the report files are to be delivered, select the format that you want the report delivered in, and enter a set of credentials that have access to the share. Supported formats include XML, CSV, PDF, HTML, MHTML (Web archive), Excel, RPL, TIFF, and Word. The credentials can be either a domain or a local account. In this example, we'll generate a PDF file of the report to the ReportOutput folder on the \\SQL08DEV\ReportOutput share. (Note that the specified path must already exist and be write-accessible to the user account specified by the credentials.) Figure 19-25 shows these settings made in the Subscription Maintenance window.

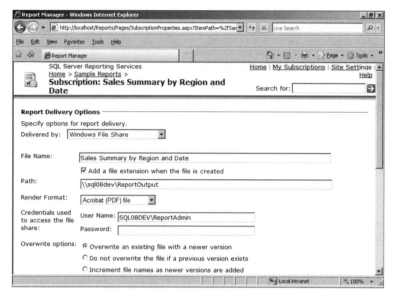

FIGURE 19-25 Subscription Maintenance window

3. Scroll down the page to the Subscription Processing Options section, click the Select Schedule button, change the schedule type to Once, enter a start time of 5 minutes from now, and then click OK.

Warning When you click OK and return to the Subscription Maintenance window, the text that you typed for the password will be cleared. This is due to the browser behavior regarding the password text box, so you will need to type the password again after setting the schedule.

4. Scroll farther down the page to the Report Parameters section. Here you can specify the parameters for the report subscription.

5. Click OK in the Subscription Maintenance window. In about 5 minutes, the report should appear in the path specified.

Using Data-Driven Subscriptions

In addition to standard report subscriptions, there are also data-driven subscriptions. Data-driven subscriptions are used to deliver reports using dynamic subscription data that is retrieved from an external data source at run time. When the subscription is triggered, a query is processed that retrieves current data for the recipients, delivery method, report format, and any required report parameters. Data-driven subscriptions are created or modified using the Create Data-Driven Subscription pages in Report Manager. These pages walk you through each step of creating or modifying a subscription. The query used to retrieve the current data should produce one row for each subscriber, including a valid e-mail address for each recipient, if using the e-mail delivery extension. One delivery is made for each row returned by the query. For example, if the result set has 5,000 rows, the subscription will deliver 5,000 reports.

Since SQL 2008 no longer includes Notification Services, data-driven subscriptions are the recommended way of implementing notification scenarios for reports.

> **Note** Data-driven subscriptions are not supported when the report server is configured for SharePoint-integrated mode (described later in this chapter). Furthermore, data-driven subscriptions are supported only in the Enterprise edition of SQL Server 2008.

A data-driven subscription requires the following:

- The report for which the subscription is defined. (A subscription is always associated with a single report.)

- A single delivery extension used to distribute the report. Options include report server e-mail delivery, file share delivery, the null delivery provider (used for preloading the report cache), or a custom delivery extension.

- A connection string to the data source that contains the subscriber.

- A query that you use to select the dynamic data. This must be specified when you define the subscription.

Caching Reports

In order to improve performance, Reporting Services can cache a copy of a processed report and return that copy when another user opens the same report. A cached instance of a report is based on the intermediate format of a report. The result is significantly less demand on both the report server and the database server, particularly for reports with sophisticated formatting that are based on large or complex queries. The server caches one instance of a report for each unique set of query parameters. The configuration of caching is performed on a report-by-report basis on the Execution page of each report's Properties tab. Figure 19-26 shows 30-minute caching enabled for the *Sales Summary by Region and Date* report.

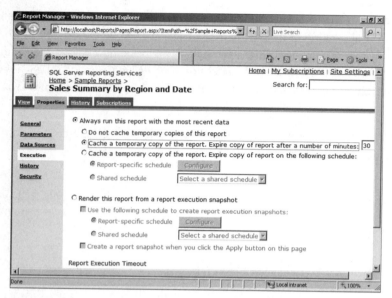

FIGURE 19-26 Report execution settings configured for caching with a 30-minute expiration

> **Important** Not all reports can be cached. If a report includes user-dependent data, prompts users for credentials, or uses Windows authentication, it cannot be cached.

A new version of a cached report is created when a user selects a report after the previously cached copy has expired. A report's expiration can be set either in minutes or at a scheduled time, depending on how and when the underlying data is updated. A schedule can be either shared or report specific. The shared schedules are configured using SQL Server Management Studio.

Securing Reports

Security is one of the top concerns of businesses today, and Reporting Services has been designed to ensure that your data is both secure and reliable. Reporting Services uses a flexible role-based security model to ensure that users can see only the data or artifacts that they have permission to access. Security is configured using both SQL Server Management Studio and the Report Manager Web site.

The first level of security is access to the system. This level of security is configured through the Site Settings page in Report Manager, as shown in Figure 19-27. By default, only administrators have access to this page (which is displayed by clicking the Site Settings link on the upper-right in Report Manager).

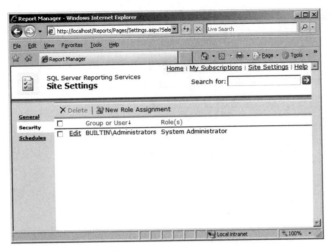

FIGURE 19-27 Site Settings page

To add a new user or group, click New Role Assignment. A screen similar to Figure 19-28 will appear. On this page, enter either a group or user name (including domain), select the role(s) for this user or group, and then click OK. The definition of the roles is maintained from within SQL Server Management Studio.

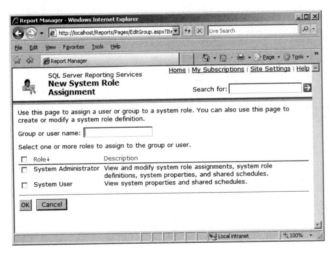

FIGURE 19-28 New System Role Assignment page

The second level of security applies to the individual folders, reports, and other items (such as data sources). This allows you to configure security at a very granular level. Any item can have custom security applied to it, although by default, an item inherits its security from its container object. To access the item security page, select an item, select the Properties tab, and then select the Security menu item. For example, the Sample Reports folder security settings are shown in Figure 19-29.

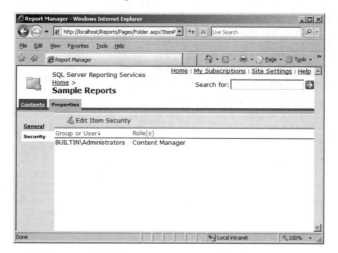

FIGURE 19-29 Viewing item security settings for the Sample Reports folder

In Figure 19-29, notice that the only toolbar option available is Edit Item Security. This indicates that this item is currently using inherited security. Clicking Edit Item Security allows you to change the security settings, after clicking OK to confirm. After you do that, the tool provides additional controls to customize security for this item, as shown in Figure 19-30.

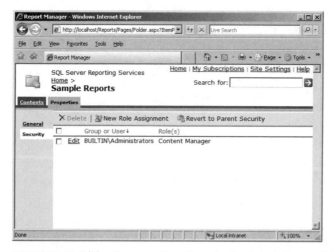

FIGURE 19-30 Editing item security settings for the Sample Reports folder

To add a new user or group, click New Role Assignment. A screen similar to Figure 19-31 will appear. On this page, enter either a group or a user name (including domain), select the role(s) for this user or group, and then click OK. The definition of the roles is maintained from within SQL Server Management Studio.

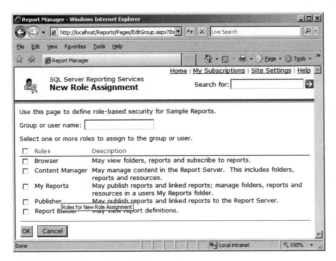

FIGURE 19-31 New Role Assignment page

The details of the roles used in both the site and item security are configured from Object Explorer connected to the report server in SQL Server Management Studio, as shown in Figure 19-32.

FIGURE 19-32 Role maintenance in SQL Server Management Studio Object Explorer

The roles are maintained by right-clicking either the Roles or System Roles folder or a specific role. Figure 19-33 shows an example of a new user role screen.

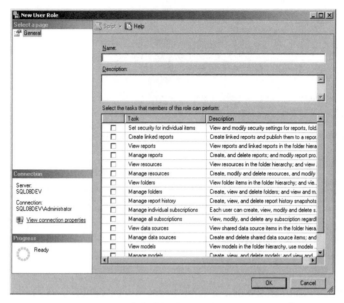

FIGURE 19-33 New user role in SQL Server Management Studio

To create the new role, enter a name and optional description, select the tasks that this role can perform, and then click OK. Table 19-8 summarizes the user role tasks, and Table 19-9 summarizes the system role tasks. The new roles can then be used in the Report Manager Web pages to configure site and item security.

TABLE 19-8 User Role Tasks

Task	Description
Set security for individual items	View and modify security settings for reports, folders, resources, and shared data sources.
Create linked reports	Create linked reports and publish them to a report server folder.
View reports	View reports and linked reports in the folder hierarchy; view report history snapshots and report properties.
Manage reports	Create and delete reports, and modify report properties.
View resources	View resources in the folder hierarchy, and view resource properties.
Manage resources	Create, modify, and delete resources, and modify resource properties.
View folders	View folder items in the folder hierarchy, and view folder properties.
Manage folders	Create, view, and delete folders, and view and modify folder properties.
Manage report history	Create, view, and delete report history snapshots, and modify report history properties.

Task	Description
Manage individual subscriptions	Each user can create, view, modify, and delete subscriptions that he or she owns.
Manage all subscriptions	View, modify, and delete any subscription regardless of who owns the subscription.
View data sources	View shared data source items in the folder hierarchy, and view data source properties.
Manage data sources	Create and delete shared data source items, and modify data source properties.
View models	View models in the folder hierarchy, use models as data sources for a report, and run queries against the model to retrieve data.
Manage models	Create, view, and delete models, and view and modify model properties.
Consume reports	Read report definitions.

Table 19-9 System Role Tasks

Task	Description
Manage roles	Create, view, modify, and delete role definitions.
Manage report server security	View and modify system-wide role assignments.
View report server properties	View properties that apply to the report server.
Manage report server properties	View and modify properties that apply to the report server and to items managed by the report server.
View shared schedules	View a predefined schedule that has been made available for general use.
Manage shared schedules	Create, view, modify, and delete shared schedules used to run reports or refresh a report.
Generate events	Provide an application with the ability to generate events within the report server namespace.
Manage jobs	View and cancel running jobs.
Execute report definitions	Start execution from the report definition without publishing it to a report server.

Integrating with SharePoint

As part of Microsoft's strategy for a unified presentation of data, Reporting Services 2008 supports a tight integration with SharePoint Services 3.0 and SharePoint 2007. When properly configured, this gives the user a single source for all business documents, reports, and dashboards. SharePoint integration allows items to be secured using the same permissions and provider used to secure other business documents on the SharePoint site. The report server continues to provide the report processing, rendering, and delivery of both on-demand reports and scheduled reports.

> **Important** Integration is not supported if the SharePoint Web application is enabled for Anonymous access.

Getting Reporting Services to integrate SharePoint requires steps that must be completed on both the report server and SharePoint server.

To configure the report server, the report server database must be created in SharePoint-integrated mode using the Reporting Services Configuration tool. Normally, the report server database is the sole source for all data including configuration data, report definitions, data sources, subscriptions, and snapshots. In a SharePoint-integrated mode installation, however, the report server database continues to store the configuration data, history, and subscriptions as well as secondary storage for reports and resources, but the primary storage for all report documents and resources is the SharePoint database.

The changes required to the SharePoint server begin with downloading and installing the Microsoft SQL Server 2008 Reporting Services add-in for Microsoft SharePoint Technologies. The download can be found on the Web at

http://www.microsoft.com/DOWNLOADS/details.aspx?familyid=200FD7B5-DB7C-4B8C-A7DC-5EFEE6E19005&displaylang=en.

This installs programs and application pages that are accessed from SharePoint Central Administration to configure the integration. After installation, the feature must be activated and configured to specify settings that determine the connection between the SharePoint server and a report server created in SharePoint-integrated mode. The configuration is done from within the Application Management tab of the SharePoint 3.0 Central Administration tool. For the report server Web Service URL, specify the report server site that you want to use with the current SharePoint site or farm. For authentication mode, you can select either Windows authentication or trusted authentication. Trusted authentication is used when the report server endpoint installed on the SharePoint server sends a header with a security token for an impersonated connection on the report server. During configuration, the service account for the report server instance is granted permissions in the SharePoint configuration and content databases. Additionally, there are configuration options for configuring report history retention, report processing time-out, logging, enabling integrated security, and enabling ad hoc reporting.

A report server running in SharePoint-integrated mode does have several limitations that need to be considered before migrating from native mode. These include the following:

- All report servers connected to a report server database must be the same, either all native mode or SharePoint-integrated mode.

- Since URL addressing is different in SharePoint-integrated mode, custom applications that rely on native-mode-style URL access will not work properly.

- Report Manager is not available to manage a report server instance that is configured for SharePoint integration. Management must be performed from within SharePoint.

- The rs.exe command-line utility is not supported.

- Linked reports are not supported. A linked report is a report server item that provides an access point to an existing report, similar to a program shortcut that you use to run a program or open a file.

- My Reports is not supported. My Reports is a personal workspace available when working in native mode, similar to the My Documents folder in Windows that can be used to store and work with reports that you own.

Summary

This chapter has taken you through the reporting life cycle with SQL Server 2008 Reporting Services. We began by designing reports and the queries that drive those reports using the Report Designer in Visual Studio. After you learned how to create basic reports either from scratch or with the assistance of the Report Wizard, we advanced to build sophisticated OLAP-based reports against an Analysis Services database. Along the way, we touched on other powerful design capabilities, including expressions, formatting, and custom code through embedded script and external .NET assembly references.

Then we covered everything that comes after building the perfect report. Various deployment techniques were described, and we saw how to deliver reports using the *ReportViewer* control in custom .NET applications and using custom script tasks with SQL Server Integration Services. You learned how to administer Reporting Services for configuration, security, caching, and subscriptions, using Reporting Services Configuration Manager, Report Manager, and SQL Server Management Studio. In more than one sense, we've come full circle. Reporting Services empowers you to deliver the data that in turn is empowered by the plethora of programmatic capabilities in SQL Server 2008 that we covered throughout this book.

Index

A

access, cube. *See* roles (OLAP cubes)
access level for FILESTREAM feature, 311, 313
Accordion controls, 432
Accumulate method (aggregate classes), 141
accuracy of date-time values, 62
ACID properties, 449, 450–452
actions (OLAP cubes), 689–693
  designing, 690
  testing, 692
actions, report, 918
ADD MINING MODEL clause, ALTER MINING
    STRUCTURE, 839
adjacent groups, tablix data regions, 912
administering Reporting Services, 937–951
  Report Manager and Management Studio,
    940–949
    caching reports, 943
    data-driven report subscriptions, 942
    securing reports, 944–949
    standard report subscriptions, 940–942
  Reporting Services Configuration Manager,
    937–939
  SharePoint integration, 949–951
ADO MD.NET data provider, 758–769
  cell references, 763
  executing MDX queries, 760
  exploring metadata, 763–769
  fetching metadata in cubes, 764
  prediction queries with, 860
  server-side, 782–792
    calling managed code from MDX, 786
    debugging managed code, 786
    result set–returning functions, 789–792
    void functions, 788
  working with multiple axes, 761–763
  XMLA response content from, manipulating,
    780
AdomdCommand objects, 760
  ExecuteXmlReader method, 780
AdomdConnection objects, 760
  Cubes collection of, 764
  GetSchemaDataSet method, 765
AdomdDataAdapter objects, 760
ADO.NET, 377
  coding, 387–392

connected DataReader objects, 390
typed DataSet objects, 389
untyped DataSet objects, 388–389
validation logic in typed DataSets, 391
  Entity Framework (EF) model. *See* Entity
    Framework (EF) model, ADO.NET
  LINQ, reasons to use, 396–397. *See also* LINQ
  local transactions in, 459–461
  native, why not to use, 396–397
  passing TVPs using, 56
  Sync Services. *See* Sync Services for ADO.NET
  typed DataSet objects, 378–387
    adding validation logic to, 391
    connected use of, 387
    connection string management, 381
    data binding example, 420–424
    TableAdapter Configuration Wizard, 382–385
    TableAdapter objects, 380
    using DataSet designer, 379
ADO.NET Data Services, 377, 411–415
  AJAX client library for, 434
  binding to, 426
ADO.NET Entity Data Model. *See* Entity
    Framework (EF) model, ADO.NET
AFTER trigger, MERGE statement and, 79
aggregates (SQL CLR), 140–145
  managing with Object Explorer, 152
aggregations (OLAP), 700
  algorithmic design, 700
  design management, 704
  Management Studio for, 705
  manual design, 702–704
  special aggregates, 665
  usage-based design, 701
AJAX Control Toolkit, 432
AJAX-enabled Web pages, 367
  for data access, 430–435
    ADO.NET Data Services client, 434
algorithmic aggregation design, 700
All Tables diagram (Analysis Services), 623
alphabetical format for date-time values, 64
ALTER DATABASE statement
  AUDIT SPECIFICATION clause, 221
  SET ENCRYPTION ON clause, 213
ALTER INDEX statement, enabling data
    compression, 608
ALTER MINING STRUCTURE statement, 839

ALTER SERVER AUDIT SPECIFICATION statement, 220
ALTER SERVER AUDIT statement, 217
  WITH AUDIT_GUID option, 218
  WITH ON_FAILURE option, 218
  WITH QUEUE_DELAY option, 217
  WITH STATE option, 218
ALTER SERVICE MASTER KEY REGENERATE statement, 207
ALTER TABLE statement
  CHANGE_TRACKING option, 541
  enabling data compression, 608
  LOCK_ESCALATION option, ALTER TABLE, 603
  AS TYPE, TVPs and, 59
ambient transactions, 476
AMO (Analysis Management Objects), 769–770
Analysis Manager, 618
analysis optimization, lack of, 568
Analysis Services, 611, 618–619. *See also* OLAP
  adding data source views, 621–625
  APIs for custom OLAP development, 744
  BPAs (best practice alerts), 654–656
  Calculation Tools, 671
  CLR support with server-side ADO MD.NET, 782–792
    calling managed code from MDX, 786
    debugging managed code, 786
    result set–returning functions, 789–792
    void functions, 788
  connecting to (Excel), 719–723
  creating projects, 619, 800
  data mining with. *See* data mining
  key performance indicators (KPIs), 677–689
    queries in Management Studio, 683–688
    status and trend expressions, 678
    testing in Browser View, 681–683
  MDX queries, building, 748
  MDX queries, opening, 747
  member grouping, 651
  partitions, 693–700
    editing and creating, 694
    proactive caching, 697–699
  perspectives, 705–707
  proactive caching, 697–699
  processing cubes, 635
  roles, 712–715
  server time dimensions, 660–685
    fact dimensions, 661–664
    role-playing dimensions, 664
  Time Series algorithm, 797
  translations, 707–711
  XMLA queries. *See* XMLA
  XMLA scripts, 688
analytical applications, 568
anchor member, CTE, 18

anchor value, Sync Services, 543
API programming, data mining and, 857
application mobilization. *See* mobile application (example), creating
APPLY operator, T-SQL, 25
area calculations, geospatial data, 355
articles (Merge Replication), 495
ASP.NET
  data binding with, 427–438
    alternatives to GridView controls, 429
    ASP.NET Dynamic Data, 435–438
    using AJAX, 430–435
  data mining and, 861
  ReportViewer controls, 930
ASP.NET Dynamic Data, 435–438
assemblies (SQL CLR)
  deploying, 119, 125–127
  loading (server-side ADO MD.NET), 783
  security, 150
association properties (L2S models), 399
Association Rules algorithm, 846
associations (L2S models), 399
Astoria. *See* ADO.NET Data Services
asymmetric key encryption, 204
atomicity, 451, 452
attack surface, 191
attribute profiles, 826
attribute-based XML, creating, 248
  OPENXML function with, 261
AttributeHierarchies collection (Dimension objects), 764
attributes, dimension. *See* dimensions
attributes, SQL CLR, 117–118
AUDIT_GUID option, ALTER SERVER AUDIT statement, 218
auditing, 216–224
  creating audit objects, 216
  of database events, 221–222
  options for, 217
  querying audit catalog views, 224
  recording audits
    to file system, 219
    to Windows event log, 220
  of server events, 217
  viewing audited events, 222
authentication and authorization, 195–203
  creating client connections, 195
  execution context, 200–203
  guest account, 195
  mobile application synchronization, 513, 518
  password policies, 197
  user-schema separation, 198–200
authorities (SQL Server Data Services), 415
authorization. *See* authentication and authorization

AUTHORIZATION clause, CREATE ASSEMBLY, 125, 127
AUTO mode (FOR XML statement), 248
ELEMENTS keyword, 260
AUTO_CLEANUP option, 539
autocommit transaction mode, 453
automated deployment, 117
axes in MDX queries, 754

B

BACKUP CERTIFICATE statement, 215
backup compression options, 608–610
DECRYPTION BY PASSWORD clause, 215
backup compression with data warehousing, 605, 608–610
BACKUP SERVICE MASTER KEY statement, 207
backup-and-restore applications, creating with SMO, 175–181
backups of certificates, 214
balanced scorecard (BSC), 585
Basic Authentication. See authentication and authorization
batch-scoped transaction mode, 457–459
BEGIN DISTRIBUTED TRANSACTION statement, 472
BEGIN TRANSACTION statement, 462
beginning transactions, defined, 461
BeginTransaction method (SqlConnection), 487
best practice alerts (BPAs), 654–656
BI (business intelligence), 611–612
data mining and. See data mining
key performance indicators (KPIs), 583, 677–689
status and trend expressions, 678
testing in Browser View, 681–683
Management Studio for, 683, 688–689
with PivotTables. See PivotTables in Excel
prototype for, building, 586
bidirectional data synchronization, 494
binary large data. See BLOB data
BinaryReader objects, hierarchyid types with, 306
BinaryWriter objects, hierarchyid types with, 306
binding. See data binding
BindingNavigator component (example), 423, 424
BindingSource component (example), 423, 424
Blend, 439
BLOB data, 307. See also FILESTREAM feature
in databases, 307
in file streams, 309
blocking (transactions), 451
bottom-up approach to data warehousing, 574–580
context and star schema, 577
Star-Join Query Optimization, 603–604

surrogate keys, 579
BPAs (best practice alerts), 654–656
breadth-first index, 296, 298
browsing mining models (Data Mining Client add-in), 876
BSC (balanced scorecard), 585
built-in fields, reports, 888
bulk inserts and updates with TVPs, 48, 49
bulkadmin server role, 193
business intelligence (BI), 582, 611–612
data mining and. See data mining
key performance indicators (KPIs), 583, 677–689
status and trend expressions, 678
testing in Browser View, 681–683
Management Studio for, 683, 688–689
with PivotTables. See PivotTables in Excel
prototype for, building, 586
Business Intelligence Projects, creating new, 619

C

caching, OLAP cubes, 697–699
caching reports, 943
calculated members in MDX queries, 757
Calculation Tools (Analysis Services), 671
calculations. See also aggregations (OLAP)
calculated measures, 668–673
named sets, 673
Script view, 674–676
CALL command (MDX), 789
canonical (element-based) XML, producing, 260
OPENXML function with, 261
cascading parameters, reports, 896
CascadingDropdown controls, 433
CASE construct, GROUPING function, 107
case tables in mining models, 805
CAST function
converting columns to XML, 278–279
extracting from datetime2 data, 64
CATCH block. See TRY and CATCH blocks, T-SQL
CDC (Change Data Capture), 592–600
CellSet objects, 760
cell references, 763
certificates, 204
backing up, 214
creating, 206
Change Data Capture (CDC), 592–600
change tracking for Sync Services, 538–543
changing tracking functions, 542
configuring database for, 538–543
CHANGE_RETENTION option, 539
CHANGE_TRACKING_CURRENT_VERSION function, 542

CHANGE_TRACKING_MIN_VALID_VERSION function, 542

CHANGES keyword, INSERT OVER DML syntax, 94–97

CHANGETABLE function, 542

Chaos isolation level (ADO.NET), 467

CHAPTERS axis (MDX queries), 754

chart data regions in reports, 915–917

charts (Excel), creating from PivotTables, 729

CHECK constraint, XML schemas vs., 239

CheckAllocations method, 182

CheckAllocationsDataOnly method, 182

CheckCatalog method, 182, 183

CHECKPOINT statement, 609

CheckTables methoc, 182

CheckTablesDataOnly method, 182

child groups, tablix data regions, 911

CIF (Corporate Information Factory), 573

Class Library projects, 118
    CLR functions, 134
    CREATE PROCEDURE commands, 128
    deployment, 125
    removing SQL CLR objects, 157
    testing stored procedures, 129

client connections. *See also* occasionally connected systems
    creating, 195
    direct Internet connections, 225
    encrypting, 205

client file I/O streaming, FILESTREAM for, 312

ClientDeleteServerUpdate conflict (synchronization), 550

ClientID property (SyncSession), 535

ClientInsertServerInsert conflict (synchronization), 550

ClientUpdateServerDelete conflict (synchronization), 550

ClientUpdateServerUpdate conflict (synchronization), 550

CLR. *See* SQL CLR feature

cluster characteristics, 822

cluster diagrams, 819

cluster discrimination, 822

cluster profiles, 820

clustering models, 807, 811
    viewing with Cluster Viewer, 818–823
    ViewerMode property, 862

Clustering Sequence algorithm, 848

code attributes, SQL CLR, 117–118

COLLATE statement, xml data type and, 236

collections of XML schemas, 237

column function (sql), 275

column sets, 605

columns
    defined as XML, 235–237
    converting columns to XML, 278–279
    default and constraints, 236
    primary and secondary XML indexes, 244–247
    querying. See XQuery language
    encrypting data within, 206
    FILESTREAM columns, 315–318
    pivoting dynamically, 23
    statements without explicit column lists, TVPs and, 53, 54

COLUMNS axis (MDX queries), 754

<Command> element, XMLA, 774

command-line report deployment, 923–927

comment test function (XML PATH), 257

Commit method (IEnlistmentNotification), 478

commit phase (transactions), 470

committing transactions, defined, 461

Common Language Runtime. *See* SQL CLR feature

common table expressions (CTEs), 14–20
    creating recursive queries with, 18–20
    ranking functions with GROUP BY function, 30–33

communications security, 190. *See also* security

Compact version, SQL Server, 496–497
    binding data to Pocket PC forms, 523

comparing data mining models, 827–829

comparing instances of xml data type, 234, 235

comparison operations in indexed hierarchical tables, 297

compensated transactions, 450

compile errors, statement-level, 41

Complete method (TransactionScope), 476

complex MDX expressions, 670

compression (backup) with data warehousing, 605, 608–610

compression (data) with data warehousing, 605–608

condition (PBM), defined, 184

configuring Report Services, 937–951
    Report Manager and Management Studio, 940–949
        caching reports, 943
        data-driven report subscriptions, 942
        securing reports, 944–949
        standard report subscriptions, 940–942
    Reporting Services Configuration Manager, 937–939
    SharePoint integration, 949–951

ConflictResolver property (SqlCeClientSyncProvider), 552

conflicts, synchronization, 543–552

conformed dimensions (in data warehousing), 576

CONNECT permissions, 196

Connection property (TableAdapter), 381

connection string management (DataSets), 381
connections (client). *See also* occasionally
    connected systems
  creating, 195
  direct Internet connections, 225
  encrypting, 205
ConnectionString property (SqlConnection), 389
consistency (transactions), 451, 452
containers (SQL Server Data Services), 415
context of measures, 575, 576, 577. *See also* star
    schemas
continuous data, defined, 796
Control Toolkit (AJAX), 432
CONVERT function
  converting columns to XML, 278–279
  extracting from datetime2 data, 64
Convert To Formulas option (Excel), 733
coordinate-based cel references, 763
Corporate Information Factory (CIF), 573
correncey conversion issues in data warehousing,
  587
CREATE ASSEMBLY statement, 119, 125
  WITH PERMISSION_SET clause, 126, 127, 152
CREATE CERTIFICATE statement, 215
  ENCRYPTION BY PASSWORD clause, 215
CREATE DATABASE statement
  AUDIT SPECIFICATION clause, 221
  FILEGROUP...CONTAINS FILESTREAM clause, 313
  FOR SERVER AUDIT clause, 222
CREATE FUNCTION statement, 132
  ORDER clause, 135
CREATE INDEX statement, enabling data
  compression, 608
CREATE LOGIN statement, 193, 197
CREATE MASTER KEY statement, 207
CREATE MINING MODEL statement, 839
CREATE MINING STRUCTURE statement, 838
CREATE PROCEDURE statement, EXTERNAL NAME
  clause, 127
CREATE SCHEMA statement, 199
CREATE SERVER AUDIT SPECIFICATION statement,
  220
CREATE SERVER AUDIT statement, 216
  TO APPLICATION_LOG and TO SERVER_LOG
    options, 220
  WITH AUDIT_GUID option, 218
  WITH ON_FAILURE option, 218
  WITH QUEUE_DELAY option, 217
  WITH STATE option, 218
  STATE option, 220
CREATE TABLE statement
  enabling data compression, 608
  ROWGUIDCOL attribute, 315
CREATE TRIGGER statements, 138
CREATE USER statement, 194

CROSS APPLY operator, 25
CROSS JOIN queries, with geospatial data, 347
CROSSJOIN function (MDX), 756
CTEs (common table expressions), 14–20
  creating recursive queries with, 18–20
  ranking functions with GROUP BY function,
    30–33
Cube Designer, 626–629. *See also* cubes, OLAP
CUBE keyword, GROUP BY clause, 104. *See also*
  WITH CUBE operator
Cube Wizard, 625
CUBEMEMBER function (Excel), 733
cubes, OLAP. *See also* OLAP
  actions, 689–693
    designing, 690
    testing, 692
  building, 617–635
    adding data source view, 621–625
    creating project, 619
    with Cube Designer, 626–629
    with Cube Wizard, 625
    preparing star schema objects, 617
    Properties Windows and Solution Explorer,
    634
    using Dimension Designer, 632
    using Dimension Wizard, 629
  defined, 614
  dimensions. *See* dimensions
  Excel with
    connecting PivotTables to cubes, 719
    querying in Excel formulas, 732–737
  measures. *See* measures
  partitions, 693–700
    editing and creating, 694
    proactive caching, 697–699
  perspectives, 705–707
  proactive caching, 697–699
  processing, 635
  roles, 712–715
  server time dimensions, 660–685
    fact dimensions, 661–664
    role-playing dimensions, 664
  translations, 707–711
CUBEVALUE function (Excel), 733, 735
Current property (Transaction), 486
CurrentDatabaseName property (Context), 791
CURRENTMEMBER property (MDX), 674
CurrentServerId property (Context), 791

D

dashboards, 583
data, information vs., 565

data access, 377–418
  ADO.NET. *See* ADO.NET
  LINQ (Language Integrated Query). *See* LINQ
  typed DataSet objects, 378–387
    adding validation logic to, 391
    connected use of, 387
    connection string management, 381
    data binding example, 420–424
    TableAdapter Configuration Wizard, 382–385
    TableAdapter objects, 380
    using DataSet designer, 379
data access infrastructure. *See also* data binding
  ADO.NET Data Services. *See* ADO.NET Data
    Services
  LINQ (Language Integrated Query). *See* LINQ
  models for, 395–411. *See also* ORM
  SQL Server Data Services, 377, 415
data binding, 419–447
  to ADO.NET Data Services, 426
  ASP.NET, 427–438
    alternatives to GridView controls, 429
    ASP.NET Dynamic Data, 435–438
    using AJAX, 430–435
  Silverlight 2.0, 438, 445–446
  Windows Forms, 420–427
  WPF (Windows Presentation Foundation),
    438–445
    lack of design support, 439–514
    XAML for, 441–445
data compression with data warehousing,
  605–608
data conflicts in synchronization, 543–552
data definition language. *See* DDL triggers
data encryption. *See* encryption
data hierarchies. *See* hierarchical data
data mining, 581, 793–878
  applications of, 856
    API programming, 857
    ASP.NET and, 861
    Excel 2007 add-ins, 866–877
    managed stored procedures, 863
    model content queries, 860
    prediction queries with ADO MD.NET, 860
    Web controls, 862
    Windows Forms Model content browser
      controls, 858
    XMLA scripts, 865
  getting started, 798–802
  mining models, 805–816
    adding, 811–813
    changing column usage, 813
    creating new, 805–809
    data types and, 813
    editing, 811
    filtering, 815

  validating and comparing, 827–829
  viewing, 818–826
mining structures, creating, 804
nested tables, 830–836
  DMX statements for, 843, 851
reasons for, 793–796
SQL Server 2008 enhancements, 797
using DMX, 836–856
  for modeling, 837–848
  for predictions, 848–855
  templates, 856
Data Mining Client add-in (Excel 2007), 867,
  873–877
Data Mining Extensions. *See* DMX
Data Mining Structure Designer, 802. *See also*
  data mining
Data Mining Wizard, 802. *See also* data mining
data regions (reports), 886
  chart data regions in reports, 915–917
  formatting, 889
  matrix data regions in reports, 906–910
    subtotals and totals, 908
  tablix data region, 881, 886, 910–915
    extending with groups, 910–912
    fixed columns and rows, adding, 913
    report actions, 918
Data Source View designer, 623–624
Data Source View Wizard, 621–625
Data Source Views
  adding named queries to, 645
  adding tables to, 628
data sources
  adding to Analysis Services projects, 621–625
  for mobile applications, 521–523
  for reports, 883
Data Sources window, 421
data storage, unstructured. *See* FILESTREAM
  feature
data synchronization, 493
  for mobile applications. *See* Web
    Synchronization
data test function (XML PATH), 257
data types
  data mining models, 813
  with Sync Services, 559
data warehousing, 563–610
  defined, 563
  design
    bottom-up approach (Kimball), 574–580
    technical and nontechnical issues, 571
    top-down approach (Inmon), 572–573
  design of, 570–580
  history of shortcomings before, 566–570
  importance of, 564–565
  practical advice on, 585–589

data warehousing (*continued*)
  with SQL Server 2008, 589–610
    Change Data Capture (CDC), 592–600
    data and backup compression, 605–610
    Partitioned Table Parallelism, 600–603
    SPARSE columns, 604–605
    Star-Join Query Optimization, 603–604
data warehousing (*continued*
    T-SQL MERGE statement, 589–592
  what it isn't, 580–585
database encryption key (DEK), 212
database integrity check with SMO, 181
database master keys (DMKs), 206
database roles, logins with, 194
database schemas. *See* schemas, XML
Database task (Reporting Services Configuration
    Manager), 938
database users, 193
  authenticating. *See* authentication and
    authorization
  guest account, 194
  user-schema separation, 198–200
databases
  BLOBs in, 307. *See also* BLOB data; FILESTREAM
    feature
  encrypted, restoring, 215
  encrypting data within, 206
  event auditing, 221–222. *See also* auditing
  FILESTREAM-enabled, creating, 313–315. *See
    also* FILESTREAM feature
data-driven report subscriptions, 942
DataGridView controls (examples), 422, 424
  alternative approaches, 429
  viewing schema DataSet objects, 765
datamarts, 572, 617
DataReader objects, coding with, 390
DataSet, LINQ to. *See* L2S (LINQ to SQL) models
DataSet designer, 379
DataSet objects, typed, 378–387, 424
  adding validation logic to, 391
  coding against, 389
  connected use of, 387
  connection string management, 381
  data binding example, 420–424
  schema DataSet objects, 765–769
  TableAdapter Configuration Wizard, 382–385
  TableAdapter objects, 380
  using DataSet designer, 379
DataSet objects, untyped, 388–389
DataTable objects in typed DataSets, 379
datatime data type, replacing, 59
date and time data types, T-SQL, 59–67
  accuracy, storage, and format, 62–64
  new and changed since SQL Server 2000, 65
  separation of dates and times, 59

time zone awareness, 61–62
date data type, 59
  storage and precision, 60, 62
DATEADD function, 65
DATEDIFF function, 65
DATENAME function, 65, 67
DATEPART function, 65, 67
dateTime data type, 240
datetime2 data type, 59, 60
  storage and precision, 60, 62
datetimeoffset data type, 59, 61–62, 65
  storage and precision, 60, 62
DateTimePicker control (example), 423
db_accessadmin role, 194
db_backupoperator role, 194
db_datareader role, 194
db_datawriter role, 194
db_ddladmin role, 194
db_denydatareader role, 194
db_denydatawriter role, 194
db_owner role, 194
db_securityadmin role, 194
DBCC functions
  DROPCLEANBUFFERS statement, 609
  performing with SMO, 181
dbcreator server role, 193
DBDirect methods, 387
dbo schema, 198
DbServerSyncProvider class, 534
DbSyncServerProvider class, 536
DDL statements, 836. *See also* DMX (Data Mining
    Extensions)
DDL triggers, 43, 136
Debug toolbar (Calculations tab), 675
debugging server-side managed code, 786
Decision Trees model, 806, 812
  DMX statements for, 840
  viewing with Tree Viewer, 823–825
  ViewType property, 862
DECLARE statement, 235
decryption. *See* encryption
DECRYPTION BY PASSWORD clause, BACKUP
    CERTIFICATE statement, 215
Default property (Properties.Settings), 389
DEK (database encryption key), 212
DELETE statements
  bulk deletes with TVPs, 51
  INSERT INTO...SELECT statement around, 90–94
  merges, 79. *See also* MERGE statement
  OUTPUT clause, 90
  TOP parameter in, 26–27
  WAITFOR statement with, 43
DELETED pseudo-table
  merges and, 76, 90
  querying with DML triggers, 137

delivering reports, 919–937
  accessing reports programmatically, 928–937
    ReportViewer controls, 929
    URL access, 928
  deploying to report server, 919–927
    using command line, 923–927
    using Report Manager, 921–923
    using Visual Studio, 920
  scripting report generation with Integration
    Services, 930–937
denial of service, 226
DENSE_RANK function, 34–36
  using with other ranking functions, 36
DENY permission, setting using schemas, 199
dependency networks, 824, 826
deployment
  automated, 117
  of data mining objects, 816
  of mobile applications (example), 530–532
  to report server, 919–927
    using command line, 923–927
    using Report Manager, 921–923
    using Visual Studio, 920
  security, 190. *See also* security
  SQL CLR assembly security, 151
  user-defined aggregates, 142
  user-defined types (UDTs), 149
depth-first indexing, 284, 296, 297
descriptive data mining models, 806
deserialization, with hierarchyid data type, 306
DetailsView control (example), 429
Diagram Organizer pane (Analysis Services), 623
dictionary compression, 607
dictionary-style TVPs, 54
Dimension Designer, 632. *See also* dimensions
  attribute relationships, 656–659
dimension tables
  defined, 575
  in OLAP cubes, 615
  Star-Join Query Optimization, 603–604
Dimension Wizard, 629
  server time dimensions, 660
Dimensional Model (data warehousing), 574–580
  context and star schema, 577
    Star-Join Query Optimization, 603–604
  surrogate keys, 579
dimensions, 614, 626, 641–659. *See also* cubes,
  OLAP
  adding named queries to Data Source Views,
    645
  attribute relationships, 656–659
  attribute typing, 652
  creating with Dimension Wizard, 629
  defined (in data warehousing), 575
  geospatial, 350

key performance indicators (KPIs), 677–689
  queries in Management Studio, 683–688
  status and trend expressions, 678
  testing in Browser View, 681–683
keys and names, 641
member grouping, 651
multidimensional OLAP databases (MOLAP),
  615, 640
parent/child dimensions, 647–651
role-playing, 712–715
server time dimensions, 660–685
  fact dimensions, 661–664
  role-playing dimensions, 664
user table time dimensions, 652
writeback dimensions, 699
direct file I/O streaming, FILESTREAM for, 312
direct Internet connections, 225
dirty reads, 451, 462
  defined, 461
Disabled value (TransactionOption attribute), 473
<Discover> element, XMLA, 773
discrete data, defined, 796
discretization, 651
disk space for audit files, 220
diskadmin server role, 193
Dispose method (TransactionScope), 476
distance calculations, geospatial data, 355, 363
distributed transaction coordinators (DTCs). *See*
  transaction managers (TMs)
distributed transactions, 453, 468–484
  in .NET Framework, 473
  terminology of, 461, 469
distribution, defined, 796
distributors (Merge Replication), 495
  configuring, 499–503
DMKs (database master keys), 206
DML statements, 836. *See also* DMX (Data Mining
  Extensions)
DML triggers, 136–140
DMX (Data Mining Extensions), 836–856
  for modeling, 837–848
  for predictions, 848–855
  query window, 837
  templates, 856
documenting mining structures and models (Excel
  2007), 877
DP (electronic data processing), 566
DRILLDOWNMEMBER function (MDX), 756
drillthrough feature, 842
  with Excel PivotTables, 726
  with schema DataSet objects, 766–769
DTCs (distributed transaction coordinators). *See*
  transaction managers (TMs)
Dundas charting controls, 354
Dundas Data Visualization, 881

duplicates, finding with self-joins vs. CTEs, 16, 282
durability, 451, 452
durable enlistment, 471
Dynamic Data Web Applications, 435
dynamic properties (SQL Server Data Services), 415

E

Edit Relationship dialog box (Analysis Services), 623
editing data mining models, 811
EDP (electronic data processing), 566
EF (Entity Framework) model. *See* Entity Framework (EF) model, ADO.NET
electronic data processing (EDP), 566
element-based (canonical) XML, producing, 260
OPENXML function with, 261
ELEMENTS keyword, FOR XML clause, 260
E-Mail Settings task (Reporting Services Configuration Manager), 938
encryption, 203–210. *See also* Transparent Data Encryption (TDE)
ENCRYPTION BY PASSWORD clause, CREATE CERTIFICATE statement, 215
Encryption Keys task (Reporting Services Configuration Manager), 938
endpoints, 195
enlisting within a transaction, 470, 471–472
enterprise integration, lack of, 567
EnterpriseServices namespace, 473
entities (SQL Server Data Services), 415
Entity Data Model Wizard, 402
Entity Framework (EF) model, ADO.NET, 395–397, 402–405
    adding validation logic to, 410
    data binding, 425
        with ASP.NET, 428
    querying, 406–409
    XML in, 405
EnumAvaiableSqlServers method (SmoApplication), 169
enumerating SQL Server instances, 169
error handling, in T-SQL transactions, 40–42
ErrorsOccurred conflict (synchronization), 550
ETL step of data mining, 794
event log, recording audits to, 220
Event Viewer, 222
EVENTDATA function, 43
EventData property (SqlTriggerContext), 139
event-driven data warehouse design, 588
Excel 2007
    data mining add-ins, 866–877

Data Mining Client add-in (Excel 2007), 867, 873–877
    Table Analysis Tools add-in (Excel 2007), 867–873
OLAP with, 719–743
    building PivotTable interface, 723–724
    connecting to Analysis Services, 719–723
    creating and configuring charts, 729
    Excel Services, 738–743
    exploring PivotTable data, 725–727
    in-formula querying of cubes, 732–737
    scorecards, 727–729
    Visual Studio Tools for, 737
Excel Services, 719, 738–743
exception handling, in T-SQL transactions, 40–42
EXECUTE AS <login> context, 200
EXECUTE AS CALLER context, 200
EXECUTE AS OWNER context, 190
EXECUTE AS SELF context, 200
<Execute> element, XMLA, 774
    calling Execute programmatically from .NET, 778
ExecuteAndSend method (SqlPipe), 121
ExecuteCellSet method (AdomdCommand), 760
ExecuteNonQuery method (SqlCommand), 113
ExecuteReader method (SqlCommand), 121
ExecuteXmlReader method (AdomdCommand), 780
Execution Account task (Reporting Services Configuration Manager), 938
execution context, 200–203
execution modes, SMO, 186
exist method (xml data type), 266, 269
expectations. *See* key performance indicators (KPIs)
EXPLICIT mode (FOR XML statement), 250
EXPLICIT option, 233
explicit transaction mode, 453–456
Express edition, SQL Server 2008, 496–497
Expression Blend, 439
expressions, report, 889
External Access permission set (SQL CLR assemblies), 150, 785
EXTERNAL NAME clause, CREATE PROCEDURE, 127

F

fact dimensions, 661–664
fact tables
    defined, 575
    in OLAP cubes, 615
    Star-Join Query Optimization, 603–604
fanouts, 282

file I/O streaming, FILESTREAM for, 312
file streams, BLOBs in, 309. *See also* BLOB data;
    FILESTREAM feature
file system, recording audits to, 219
FILEGROUP...CONTAINS FILESTREAM clause,
    CREATE DATABASE statement, 313
FILEPATH option, TO FILE clause (CREATE SERVER
    AUDIT), 219
FILESTREAM feature, 307–340
  about, 307, 309
  enabling, 310–318
    creating databases, 313–315
    creating tables with FILESTREAM columns,
    315–318
    for machine, 311–312
    for server instance, 312
  OpenSqlFilestream function, 316, 318–340
    building WPF client, 338
    creating streaming HTTP service, 333–338
    data access, about, 321–331
    file streaming in .NET, 319
  spatial features with (example), 352–373
Fill method (SqlDataAdapter), 389
Fill method (TableAdapter), 423
FillComboWithDatabases method (SMOUtilities),
    173
FillRowMethodName parameter, SqlFunction
    attribute, 134
filtered data mining models, 815
filtered indexes, 605
filtered views of cubes, 705–707
fixed columns and rows, tablix regions, 913
fixed database roles, logins with, 194
fixed server roles, logins with, 193
flat XML output, 248
flat-earth (planar) model, 342. *See also* geometry
    data type
FLATTENED keyword (DMX), 854, 860
FLWOR expressions, 264
for keyword (XQuery), 264
FOR PATH clause (USING XML INDEX), 246
FOR PROPERTY clause (USING XML INDEX), 246
FOR SERVER AUDIT clause
  CREATE DATABASE AUDIT SPECIFICATION
    statement, 222
  CREATE SERVER AUDIT SPECIFICATION
    statement, 220
FOR VALUE clause (USING XML INDEX), 246
FOR XML clause, SELECT statement, 233, 247–263,
    248, 250
  FOR XML AUTO, 248
  FOR XML EXPLICIT, 250
  FOR XML PATH, 255–258
  FOR XML RAW, 248
  element-based (canonical) XML, 260

ELEMENTS keyword, 260
~ FOR XML PATH, 253
inline XSD schemas, 259
ROOT option, 258
TYPE option, 253, 254
XMLSCHEMA option, 259
Force Protocol Encryption option, 206
ForceRollBack method (PreparingEnlistment), 481
forcing encryption, 205
formats for date-time values, 64
formatting measures, 665
formatting reports, 887–890
  subtotals and totals, 909
FormView control, 429
fractional-second precision, 60, 62
FROM clause, CREATE ASSEMBLY, 126
FROM query
  APPLY operator, 25
  PIVOT and UNPIVOT operators, 21–24

G

general ledger (GL), 567
GenerateDBDirectMethods property, 387
geodetic (round-earth) model, 343. *See also*
    geography data type
geography data type, 150, 351
  integrating with Microsoft Virtual Earth,
    364–373
  loading data with Parse method, 346
  Parse method, 346
  spatial reference IDs, 355
  STArea and STLength methods, 355
  STDimension method, 350
  STDistance method, 363
  STIntersection method, 350
  STIntersects method, 347
  ToString method, 349
geometry data type, 150, 345–351
  Parse method, 346
  STDimension method, 350
  STIntersection method, 350
  STIntersects method, 347
  ToString method, 349
geospatial data types, 341–374
  geography data type, 351
    integrating with Microsoft Virtual Earth,
    364–373
    spatial reference IDs, 355
    STArea and STLength methods, 355
    STDistance method, 363
  geometry data type, 345–351
    Parse method, 346
    STDimension method, 350

geospatial data types (*continued*)
    STIntersection method, 350
    STIntersects method, 347
    ToString method, 349
  spatial data types, 344
  spatial models, 342–343
  Well-Known Text (WKT) markup language, 344
GET_FILESTREAM_TRANSACTION_CONTEXT
    function, 318, 327
GetAncestor method (hierarchcal tables), 293–296, 300
GetDescendant method (hierarchcal tables), 286
GetLevel method (hierarchical tables), 284
GetMembers method (Level), 764
GetReparentedValue method (hierarhical tables), 301–303
GetRoot method (hierarchcal tables), 286, 301
GetSchemeDataSet method (AdomdConnection), 765–769
giving up control (data warehousing), 586
GLArgumentException exception, 351
globals, report, 888
goals. *See* key performance indicators (KPIs)
grains (in data warehousing), 576
GRANT permission, setting using schemas, 199
GridView controls, 422, 424
  alternative approaches, 429
  viewing schema DataSet objects, 765
GROUP BY clause, SELECT statement, 97, 99
  ROLLUP and CUBE keywords, 104
GROUP BY function, ranking functions with, 30
GROUPING function, 106
GROUPING SETS operator, T-SQL, 97–109
  NULL values, handling, 105–109
  returning top level only, 103
  rolling up all level combinations, 101
  rolling up by level, 99
  rollup and cube operations together, 103
groups, adding to tablix data regions, 910–912
  fixed columns and rows in, 913
guest user account, 194

H

hacker attacks, types of, 225–227
header on report pages, 888
hierarchical data, 281
  creating hierarchical tables, 283–285
  hierarchyid data type, about, 282
  indexing strategies, 296
  Parse, Read, and Write methods, 305
  populating hierarchies, 285–296
    GetAncestor method, 293–296, 300
    GetDescendant method, 286

    GetLevel method, 284
    GetRoot method, 286, 301
    ToString method, 288–292
  querying hierarchical tables, 299
    indexing strategies and, 296
  reordering nodes, 301
  XML output as, 248
hierarchical queries with CTEs, 18–20
hierarchies
  creating with Dimension Designer, 632
  defined (in data warehousing), 575
  dimension attribute relationships, 656–659
  in OLAP cubes, 614. *See also* cubes, OLAP
Hierarchies collection (Dimension objects), 764
hierarchyid data type, 282. *See also* hierarchical data
  GetAncestor method, 293–296, 300
  GetDescendant method, 286
  GetLevel method, 284
  GetReparentedValue method, 301–303
  GetRoot method, 286, 301
  IsDescendantOf method, 299–301
  Parse method, 305
  Read method, 306
  ToString method, 288–292
  Write method, 306
historical data, lack of, 568
HOLAP (Hybrid OLAP), 688
hosted data services. *See* SQL Server Data Services
HTTP service, FILESTREAM storage as, 333–338
Hybrid OLAP (HOLAP), 688

I

IDENTITY values, 284
IEnlistmentNotification interface, 478
IEnumerable interface, 133
IIS, configuring for Web Synchronization, 514–516
implicit transaction mode, 456
inconsistent state, 451
indexes, XML, 244–247
indexing hierarchical tables, 296
  breadth-first index, 296, 298
  depth-first indexing, 284, 296, 297
  filtered indexes, 605
InDoubt method (IEnlistmentNotification), 478
information vs. data, 565
Init method (aggregate classes), 141
initiating transactions, 470
  enlistment, 470, 471–472
injection attacks, 162, 226
inline XSD schemas, 259
Inmon approach to data warehousing, 572–573
INSERT INTO statements (DMX), 840

INSERT INTO...SELECT statement, 90–94
  SHAPE clause with, 847, 854
INSERT OVER DML syntax (T-SQL), 90–97
  CHANGES keyword, 94–97
  OUTPUT...INTO, extending, 90–94
INSERT statements
  bulk inserts with TVPs, 49
  editing BLOB data, 316
  INSERT INTO...SELECT statement around, 90–94
  merges, 79. *See also* MERGE statement
  OUTPUT clause, 90
  TOP parameter in, 26–27
  WAITFOR statement with, 43
  without explicit column lists, TVPs and, 53
  XML Bulk Load with, 262
INSERTED pseudo-table
  merges and, 76, 90
  querying with DML triggers, 137
INSTEAD OF trigger, MERGE statement and, 79
Integrated Authentication. *See* authentication and
    authorization
integration across enterprise, lack of, 567
Integration Services to script report generation,
    930–937
integrity check with SMO, 181
intelligent observation, 227
IntelliSense technology
  for connection string management, 381
  with Excel, 733
interactive reports, 917–919
Internet connections, direct, 225
intersections, geospatial, 347, 350
IsDescendantOf method (hierarchical tables),
    299–301
ISO8601 format for date-time values, 64
isolation (transactions), 451, 452
isolation levels, 462–468
  in ADO.NET
    Chaos isolation level (ADO.NET), 467
    ReadCommitted isolation level (ADO.NET),
    468
    ReadUncommitted isolation level (ADO.NET),
    467
    RepeatableRead isolation level (ADO.NET),
    468
    Serializable isolation level (ADO.NET), 468
    Snapshot isolation level (ADO.NET), 468
    Unspecified isolation level (ADO.NET), 468
  in SQL Server 2008
    read committed isolation level, 464
    read uncommitted isolation level, 462
    repeatable read isolation level, 464
    serializable isolation level, 465
    snapshot isolation level, 45, 465

J
join method, choosing with MERGE, 78

K
key generators, 579
key performance indicators (KPIs), 583, 677–689
  status and trend expressions, 678
  testing in Browser View, 681–683
keys, dimension, 641
keys, encryption, 204
  creating master key, 211
  Service Master Key (SMK), 206
Kimball approach to data warehousing, 574–580
  context and star schema, 577
    Star-Join Query Optimization, 603–604
  surrogate keys, 579
KPIs (key performance indicators), 583, 677–689
  with MDX (multidimensional expression
    language), 757
  queries in Management Studio, 683–688
  testing in Browser View, 681–683

L
L2S (LINQ to SQL) model, 395–401
  adding validation logic to, 410
  building, 397–401
  data binding, 424
  querying, 406–409
L2S (LINQ to SQL) models
  data binding, 424
    with ASP.NET, 428
Lat property (SqlGeography), 370
lattitudes, obtaining, 351. *See also* geography
    data type
lax validation, XSD support for, 241
length calculations, geospatial data, 355, 363
length for passwords, setting minimum, 197
let keyword (XQuery), 264
Level Naming Template dialog box, 651
LEVEL property (MDX), 672
Levels collection (Hierarchy objects), 764
lift charts, 829
LINQ (Language Integrated Query), 377, 392–395
  LINQ to SQL (L2S) models, 395–401
    adding validation logic to, 410
    building, 397–401
    data binding, 424
    querying, 406–409
  syntax of, 393–395
list data type (XSD), 242

local data caches with Sync Services, 557
Local Security Settings applet (example), 197
local transactions, 452, 453–461
    in ADO.NET, 459–461
    autocommit transaction mode, 453
    batch-scoped transaction mode, 457–459
    explicit transaction mode, 453–456
    implicit transaction mode, 456
    terminology of, 461
lock escalation, 602
LOCK_ESCALATION option, ALTER TABLE, 603
LOG ON clause, CREATE DATABASE statement,
    314
logging. *See also* auditing
LOGINPROPERTY function, 198
logins, 192
    encrypting, 204
    as execution context, 200
    password policies, 197
    permissions. *See* authentication and
        authorization
Long property (SqlGeography), 370
longitudes, obtaining, 351. *See also* geography
    data type

M

management facet (PBM), defined, 184
management reporting, 567
Management Studio
    as MDX client, 744, 745–758
    Reporting Services administration, 940–949
        caching reports, 943
        data-driven report subscriptions, 942
        securing reports, 944–949
        standard report subscriptions, 940–942
    with spatial data, 354
    using XMLA from, 772–778
    viewing audited events with, 223
manual aggregation design, 702–704
mash-up, Virtual Earth (example), 364–373
master key, creating, 211
matrix data regions in reports, 906–910
    subtotals and totals, 908
MAX_ROLLOVER_FILES option, TO FILE clause
    (CREATE SERVER AUDIT), 219
maximum audit file size, 219
MAXRECURSION option, 19
MAXSIZE option, TO FILE clause (CREATE SERVER
    AUDIT), 219
MDX (multidimensional expression language),
    615, 640, 897–900
    actions (OLAP cubes), 689–693
        designing, 690

        testing, 692
    building queries, 748
    calculated members and named sets, 757
    custom OLAP development, 744
    expressions, storing for queries, 667. *See also*
        calculations
    important concepts of, 751–756
    in key performance indicators. *See* KPIs
    KPIs with, 757
    Management Studio for, 684
    OLAP development with ADO MD.NET. *See*
        ADO MD.NET data provider
    opening queries, 747
    queries, writing
        with MDX Query Designer, 901–904
        in text mode, 904–906
        via XMLA. See XMLA
    server-side ADO MD.NET, 782–792
        calling managed code, 786
        debugging managed code, 786
        result set–returning functions, 789–792
        void functions, 788
    SQL Server Management Studio (SSMS) as
        client, 744, 745–758
MDX Query Designer, 901–904
    text mode, 904–906
MDX templates, 748
mean, defined, 796
measures, 614, 625, 627. *See also* cubes, OLAP
    calculated, 668–673
    defined (in data warehousing), 575
    display folders, 666
    formatting, 665
    key performance indicators (KPIs), 677–689
        queries in Management Studio, 683–688
        status and trend expressions, 678
        testing in Browser View, 681–683
    in OLAP cubes, 641–659
    special aggregates, 665
    writeback measure groups, 699
median, defined, 796
member grouping (Analysis Services), 651
MEMBERS function (MDX), 751
Merge Agents, 513
Merge method (aggregate classes), 141, 144
Merge Replication, 492, 494–532
    configuring, 499–520
        configuring distribution, 499–503
        creating publications, 504–512
        verifying subscription, 520
        Web Synchronization. See Web
        Synchronization
    mobile application (example), creating, 520–532
        binding data to Pocket PC forms, 523
        deployment, 530–532

Merge Replication (*continued*)
   programmatic synchronization, 526–530
   setting control properties, 524–526
   setting up data source, 521–523
  occasionally connected application (example),
   496–498
  replication term glossary, 494
  vs. Sync Services for ADO.NET, 492
MERGE statement, 68–90
  in data warehousing, 589–592
  defining merge source and target, 70
  DML behavior, 79–81
  INSERT INTO...SELECT statement around, 90–94
  join method, choosing, 78
  OUTPUT clause, 68, 76, 90
  for table replication, 73
  upsert operations, 81–90
  WHEN MATCHED clause, 71
  WHEN NOT MATCHED BY SOURCE clause, 74
  WHEN NOT MATCHED BY TARGET clause, 72
metadata, 204
Microsoft Clustering algorithm, 811
Microsoft IIS, configuring for Web
   Synchronization, 514–516
Microsoft SQL Server 2008 Reporting Services.
   See Reporting Services
Microsoft Streets & Trips 2008, 351
Microsoft Virtual Earth, 364–373
Microsoft Visual Studio, SMO with, 167–183
  backup and restore applications, 175–181
  interacting through available servers, 169
  programmatic DBCC functions, 181
  retrieving server settings, 171–174
Microsoft.AnalysisServices.AdomdClient assembly,
   759
Microsoft.SqlServer.Server namespace, 121
Microsoft.SqlServer.Types namespace, 283
millisecond accuracy, 60, 62
minimum password length, 197
Mining Accuracy Chart view, 827
mining models, 805–816. *See also* data mining
  adding, 811–813
  changing column usage, 813
  creating new, 805–809
  data types and, 813
  documenting (Data Mining Client add-in), 877
  editing, 811
  filtering, 815
  validating and comparing, 827, 827–829
  viewing, 818–826
mining structures, 804, 808. *See also* data mining
mobile application (example), creating, 520–532.
   See also occasionally connected systems
  binding data to Pocket PC forms, 523
  deployment, 530–532

programmatic synchronization, 526–530
  setting control properties, 524–526
  setting up data source, 521–523
modify method (xml data type), 266, 276–277
MODIFY NAME clause, ALTER SERVER AUDIT
   statement, 217
MOLAP (Multidimensional OLAP), 615, 640, 696
moving hierarchical subtrees, 303
multidimensional expression language. *See* MDX
multidimensional OLAP databases (MOLAP), 615,
   640
multipartition query, 601
multiple-row sets, TVPs with, 48

N

Naïve Bayes algorithm, 813
  ViewerMode property, 862
  viewing with Naïve Bayes Viewer, 826
named queries, adding to Data Source Views, 645
named sets (Analysis Services), 673
  with MDX (multidimensional expression
   language), 757
names, dimension, 641
NativeSqlClient class, 321
NATURAL PREDICTION JOIN (DMX), 850
navigation properties (EF models), 403
nested tables in data mining, 805, 830–836
  DMX statements for, 843, 851
.NET Framework
  calling XMLA Execute programmatically, 778
  code attributes, 117–118
  data access. *See* data access infrastructure
  data binding. *See* data binding
  distributed transactions in, 473
  file streaming in, 319
network connections. *See* client connections
NEWSEQUENTIALID function, 315
node test function (XML PATH), 257
nodes method (xml data type), 266, 275
NONEMPTY function (MDX), 756
NONEMPTYCROSSJOIN function (MDX), 756
nonrepeatable reads, 464
  defined, 461
  preventing, 464
nonvolatile, data warehouses as, 572
NotSupported value (TransactionOption
   attribute), 473
N-tier applications with Sync Services, 554
NTILE functions, 34–36
  using with other ranking functions, 36
NULL values
  in rollup rows, handling, 105
  SPARSE columns, 604–605

numeric format for date-time values, 64
nvarchar(max) data type, 42

O

Object Explorer, SQL CLR types with, 152
occasionally connected systems, 491–560
  components of, 493
  configuring Merge Replication, 499–520
    configuring distribution, 499–503
    creating publications, 504–512
    verifying subscription, 520
    Web Synchronization. See Web
    Synchronization
  creating (example), 496–498
  mobile application (example), creating, 520–532
    binding data to Pocket PC forms, 523
    deployment, 530–532
    programmatic synchronization, 526–530
    setting control properties, 524–526
    setting up data source, 521–523
  Sync Services for ADO.NET, 492, 533–560
    capturing changes for synchronization,
    538–543
    creating applications that use, 543–557
    data type considerations, 559
    local data caches, 557
    vs. Merge Replication, 492
    object model for, 534–537
    security considerations, 560
    SqlSyncAdapterBuilder class, 558
ODBC format for date-time values, 64
.odc files, 721
Office Data Connection files, 721
OLAP (online analytical processing), 580, 611–792
  actions, 689–693
  aggregations, 700
    algorithmic design, 700
    design management, 704
    manual design, 702–704
    usage-based design, 701
  building a cube, 617–635
    adding data source view, 621–625
    creating project, 619
    with Cube Designer, 626–629
    with Cube Wizard, 625
    preparing star schema objects, 617
    Properties Windows and Solution Explorer,
    634
    using Dimension Designer, 632
    using Dimension Wizard, 629
  calculations, 667–676

custom development with .NET, 743–792
  ADO MD.NET. See ADO MD.NET data
  provider
  AMO (Analysis Management Objects),
  769–770
  MDX and Analysis Services APIs, 744
  server-side ADO MD.NET, 782–792
  XMLA for. See XMLA
data mining vs., 856
dimensions in. See dimensions
with Excel, 719–743
  building PivotTable interface, 723–724
  connecting to Analysis Services, 719–723
  creating and configuring charts, 729
  Excel Services, 738–743
  exploring PivotTable data, 725–727
  in-formula querying of cubes, 732–737
  scorecards, 727–729
  Visual Studio Tools for, 737
introduction to, 613–617
key performance indicators (KPIs), 677–689
  queries in Management Studio, 683–688
  status and trend expressions, 678
  testing in Browser View, 681–683
measures in. See measures, in OLAP cubes
partitions, 693–700
  editing and creating, 694
  proactive caching, 697–699
perspectives, 705–707
proactive caching, 697–699
processing cubes, 635
reports, 900–906
  using MDX Query Designer, 901
roles, 712–715
running queries, 636
server time dimensions, 660–685
  fact dimensions, 661–664
  role-playing dimensions, 664
translations, 707–711
On Change execution modes (SMO), 186
ON COLUMNS clause, 751
On Demand execution mode (SMO), 186
ON keyword, MERGE statement, 70
ON PRIMARY clause, CREATE DATABASE
  statement, 314
ON ROWS clause, 751
On Schedule execution mode (SMO), 186
ON_FAILURE option, ALTER SERVER AUDIT
  statement, 218
one-way data synchronization, 493
Open Geospatial Consortium (OGC), 342
OpenGIS Simple Features for SQL standard, 342
OPENROWSET function, 263

OpenSqlFilestream function, 316, 318–340
    building WPF client, 338
    creating streaming HTTP service, 333–338
    file streaming in .NET, 319
    FILESTREAM data access, about, 321–331
OPENXML function, 233
    SQL Server 2008 enhancements, 261–262
operational applications, 568–569
operational process change, anticipating, 586
optimistic concurrency checks, 84
ORDER BY clause, DMX statements, 849
order by keyword (XQuery), 264
ORDER BY statement, ranking functions, 28–30, 36
ORDER clause, CREATE FUNCTION, 135
ordinal cell references, 763
ORDINAL property (MDX), 672
ORM (Object Relational Mapping), 395–411
    ADO.NET Entity Framework. See Entity
        Framework (EF) model, ADO.NET
    L2S (LINQ to SQL) model, 395–401
        adding validation logic to, 410
        building, 397–401
        data binding, 424
        querying, 406–409
OUTER APPLY operator, 25
OUTPUT clause
    INSERT, UPDATE, and DELETE statements, 90
    MERGE statement, 68, 76, 90
        CHANGES keyword with, 94–97
    TVPs and, 59
OUTPUT...INTO clause, extending with INSERT
        OVER DML syntax, 90–94
OVER clause, ORDER BY statement, 29, 36
owner execution context, 190

P

page compression (PC), 606
page header, reports, 888
PAGES axis (MDX queries), 754
parallelism of partitioned tables, 600
parameters in reports, 892–897
    adding to OLAP reports, 902
    cascading parameters, 896
parent groups, tablix data regions, 911
parent/child dimensions, 647–651
parents for subtrees, changing, 303
Parse method
    geometry and geography data types, 346
    hierarchyid data type, 305
partial page updates, 431
PARTITION BY statement, ranking over groups
        with, 37–40

Partitioned Table Parallelism feature, 600–603
    lock escalation, 602
    thread management, 601
partitions in OLAP cubes, 693–700
    editing and creating, 694
    proactive caching, 697–699
passwords. See also authentication and
        authorization
    policies for, 197
    weak, for system administrators, 226
path expressions. See XPath expression
path index (XML), 246
PATH mode (FOR XML statement), 253, 255–258
PBM (policy-based management), 161, 183–188, 191
    defined, 184
PC (page compression), 606
PERCENT option, TOP parameter, 26
PercentComplete event, 178
performance
    audit file disk space, 220
    BLOB data storage, 308, 309. See also
        FILESTREAM feature
    caching reports, 943
    Compact vs. Express edition, 496–497
    data compression methods, 608
    indexing hierarchical tables, 296
    transactions
        reliability, 449
        resource management, 470
performance management, 585
permissions. See also authentication and
        authorization
    execution context, 200–203
    guest account, 195
    setting using schemas, 199
perspectives (OLAP cubes), 705–707
phantom reads
    defined, 461
    preventing, 465
    with read committed isolation level, 464
    with repeatable read isolation level, 465
PIVOT operator (T-SQL), 21–24
    dynamically pivoting columns, 23
PivotCharts, 729
PivotTables in Excel
    building, 723–724
    connecting to cubes, 719
    creating charts from, 729
    exploring data in, 725–727
    in-formula querying of cubes, 732–737
    scorecards, building, 727–729
planar (flat-earth) model, 342. See also geometry
        data type

Pocket PC. *See* mobile application (example), creating
policies for passwords, 197
policy-based [server] management. *See* PBM
populating hierarchies, 285–296
    GetAncestor method, 293–296, 300
    GetDescendant method, 286
    GetLevel method, 284
    GetRoot method, 286, 301
    ToString method, 288–292
preallocating disk space for audit files, 220
precision of date-time values, 60, 62
predictive data mining models, 806
    DMX statements for, 848–855
    prediction queries with ADO MD.NET, 860
Prepare method (IEnlistmentNotification), 478, 481
prepare phase (transactions), 470
Prepared method (PreparingEnlistment), 481
PreparingEnlistment class, 481
PREVMEMBER property (MDX), 674
primary keys, hierarchical tables, 284
primary XML indexes, 244
proactive caching, OLAP cubes, 697–699
processadmin server role, 193
processing data mining objects, 816
processing OLAP cubes, 635
processing-instructiontest function (XML PATH), 257
progress meter, implementing with SMO, 178
promotable single-phase enlistment, 471–472
proof of concept for data warehousing, 586
Properties window (Analysis Services), 634, 665
<Properties> element, XMLA, 773
Properties.Settings objects, 389
property index (XML), 246
Protocols For MSSQLSERVER Properties dialog box, 205
prototypes for data warehousing, 586
PSPE (promotable single-phase enlistment), 471–472
public database role, 194
public server role, 193
publications (Merge Replication), 495
    creating, 504–512
publishers (Merge Replication), 495
    synchronizing database for. *See* Web Synchronization
publishing Excel content at SharePoint. *See* Excel Services

Q

queries
    added to TableAdapter objects, 385
    in ADO.NET, code for, 387–392
        connected DataReader objects, 390
        typed DataSet objects, 389
        untyped DataSet objects, 388–389
        validation logic in typed DataSets, 391
    of audit catalog views, 224
    DMX queries. *See* DMX
    of hierarchical tables, 299
        indexing strategies and, 296
    LINQ, syntax of, 393–395. *See also* LINQ
    MDX queries. *See* MDX
    named, adding to Data Source views, 645
    on OLAP cubes, 636. *See also* OLAP (online analytical processing)
        from Excel formulas, 732–737
    Partitioned Table Parallelism feature, 601
    performance of. *See* performance
    Report Designer, importing into, 885
    Star-Join Query Optimization, 603–604
    of TDE views, 213
    of XML data with XQuery. *See* XQuery language
query method (xml data type), 266, 272–274
Query objects, 385
query parameters (reports), 892
    adding to OLAP reports, 902
    cascading parameters, 896
QUEUE_DELAY option, ALTER SERVER AUDIT statement, 217

R

range, defined, 796
RANK function, 32
    using with other ranking functions, 36
ranking functions, T-SQL, 28–40
    DENSE_RANK and NTILE functions, 34–36
    RANK function, 32
    ROW_NUMBER function, 28–31
    using all together, 36
    windowing functions with, 37–40
RAW mode (FOR XML statement), 248
    ELEMENTS keyword, 260
RC (row compression), 606
RDL (report definition language), 880
    uploading files, 919–927
        using command line, 923–927
        using Report Manager, 921–923
        using Visual Studio, 920
read committed isolation level (SQL Server 2008), 464

read committed snapshot isolation level (SQL
    Server 2008), 466
Read method, hierarchyid data type, 306
read uncommitted isolation level (SQL Server
    2008), 462
ReadCommitted isolation level (ADO.NET), 468
ReadFile function, with BLOB data, 316, 319
READONLY keyword, TVPs and, 59
ReadUncommitted isolation level (ADO.NET), 467
REBUILD WITH clause, ALTER TABLE statement,
    608
recording audits. *See* auditing
RecoveryInformation method
    (PreparingEnlistment), 481
recursive queries with CTEs, 18–20
reference data standardization, lack of, 568
relational databases
    hierarchical tables in. *See* hierarchical data
    SPARSE columns, 604–605
Relational OLAP (ROLAP), 688
reliability, 449. *See also* transactions
remote client file I/O streaming, FILESTREAM for,
    312
reordering nodes in hierarchical tables, 301
reorganizing hierarchical data, 301
reparenting subtrees, 284, 303
repeatable read isolation level (SQL Server 2008),
    464
RepeatableRead isolation level (ADO.NET), 468
replicating tables, MERGE statement for, 73
replication. *See* Merge Replication; Sync Services
    for ADO.NET
report definition language (RDL), 880
    uploading files, 919–927
        using command line, 923–927
        using Report Manager, 921–923
        using Visual Studio, 920
Report Designer, 880–919
    chart data regions, 915–917
    creating reports
        basic reports, 883–887
        interactive reports, 917–919
        OLAP reports, 900–906
    formatting reports, 887–890
        subtotals and totals, 909
    report groups, 890–892
    tablix data region, 881, 886, 910–915
        extending with groups, 910–912
        fixed columns and rows, adding, 913
        report actions, 918
    working with parameters, 892–897
        adding parameters to OLAP reports, 902
        cascading parameters, 896
    writing custom code, 897–900
report groups, 890–892

Report Manager, 940–949
    caching reports, 943
    creating report subscriptions, 940
    data-driven report subscriptions, 942
    deploying reports, 921–923
    securing reports, 944–949
    security of reports, 944
    standard report subscriptions, 940–942
Report Manager URL task (Reporting Services
    Configuration Manager), 938
report parameters, 892, 894
    cascading parameters, 896
Report Server Web Services, 938
Report Wizard, templates in, 897–900
Reporting Services, 879–951
    administering, 937–951
        Report Manager and Management Studio,
        940–949
        Reporting Services Configuration Manager,
        937–939
        SharePoint integration, 949–951
    chart data regions, 915–917
    creating reports
        basic reports, 883–887
        interactive reports, 917–919
        with matrix data regions, 906–910
        OLAP reports, 900–906
    delivering reports, 919–937
        accessing reports programmatically, 928–937
        deploying to report server, 919–927
    formatting reports, 887–890
        subtotals and totals, 909
    report groups, 890–892
    tablix data region, 881, 886, 910–915
        extending with groups, 910–912
        fixed columns and rows, adding, 913
        report actions, 918
    working with parameters, 892–897
        adding parameters to OLAP reports, 902
        cascading parameters, 896
    writing custom code, 897–900
Reporting Services Configuration Manager,
    937–939
ReportViewer controls, 929
<RequestType> element, XMLA, 773
Required value (TransactionOption attribute), 473
RequiresNew value (TransactionOption attribute),
    473
RESERVE_DISK_SPACE option, TO FILE clause
    (CREATE SERVER AUDIT), 220
ResolveAction enumeration, 552
resource managers (RMs), 469
    how to use, 481–484
    performance of, 470
    writing, 477–481

restore applications, creating with SMO, 180
RESTORE SERVER MASTER KEY statement, 207
restoring encrypted databases, 215
<Restrictions> element, XMLA, 773
return keyword (XQuery), 264
REVOKE permission, setting using schemas, 199
RMs. *See* resource managers (RMs)
ROLAP (Relational OLAP), 688
role-playing dimensions, 664
roles (OLAP cubes), 712–715
roles (server), logins with, 193
roles (user). *See* user roles
ROLLBACK command (T-SQL), 486
Rollback method (IEnlistmentNotification), 478
rolling back transactions
    defined, 461
    issued by resource managers, 482
ROLLUP keyword, GROUP BY clause, 104. *See also*
        WITH ROLLUP operator
rollup rows, 99–103
    NULL values in, 105
ROOT option, FOR XML clause, 258
round-earth (geodetic) model, 343. *See also*
        geography data type
row compression (RC), 606
row groups in reports, 890–892
row visibility in reports, 917
ROW_NUMBER function, 28–31
    ORDER BY options, 29–30
    with PARTITION BY statement, 37
    using with other ranking functions, 36
ROWGUIDCOL attribute, CREATE TABLE
        statement, 315
ROWS axis (MDX queries), 754
rs utility, 923–927

S

Safe permission set (SQL CLR assemblies), 150, 785
SafeFileHandle class, 324
Scale-Out Deployment task (Reporting Services
        Configuration Manager), 938
schema DataSet objects, 765–769
    executing actions with, 766–769
Schema Generation Wizard, 631
schemas, separated from users, 198–200
schemas, XML, 237–244
    inline XSD schemas, 259
    lax validation, 241
    SQL Server collections of, 237
    union and list types, 242
    xsl:dateTime enhancements, 240
scorecards, 583–585, 677. *See also* key
        performance indicators (KPIs)

BSC (balanced scorecard), 585
    OLAP with Excel, 727–729
Script Tasks (Integration Services), 930–937
Script view, Analysis Services, 674–676
ScriptManager controls, 367, 431
secondary XML indexes, 244, 246
SECTIONS axis (MDX queries), 754
Secure by Default approach, 190
Secure by Deployment approach, 190
Secure by Design approach, 189
secure communications, 190
security, 189–228
    auditing, 216–224
    authentication and authorization, 195–203
    encryption support, 203–210
        Transparent Data Encryption (TDE), 211–216
    how hackers attack, 225–227
    overview of, 191–195
    reports, 944–949
    SMO and, 162
    SQL CLR assemblies, 150
    Sync Services for ADO.NET, 560
    themes of security framework, 189–191
securityadmin server role, 193
SELECT clause (T-SQL), XQuery and, 273
SELECT INTO statements (DMX), 849
SELECT statement
    FOR XML clause, 233, 247–263, 248, 250
        FOR XML AUTO, 248
        FOR XML EXPLICIT, 250
        FOR XML PATH, 253, 255–258
        FOR XML RAW, 248
        element-based (canonical) XML, 260
        ELEMENTS keyword, 260
        inline XSD schemas, 259
        ROOT option, 258
        TYPE option, 253, 254
        XMLSCHEMA option, 259
    GROUP BY function, 97, 99
    GROUPING SETS operator, 97–109
    merges, 79. *See also* MERGE statement
    TOP parameter, 26–27
    viewing BLOB data (example), 331
    WAITFOR statement with, 43
    without explicit column lists, TVPs and, 54
self-joining, 282
    CTEs and, 16, 282
self-signed certificates, 204
Send method (SqlPipe), 122
Serializable isolation level (ADO.NET), 468
serializable isolation level (SQL Server 2008), 465
serialization, with hierarchyid data type, 306
server event auditing, 217
server instance, FILESTREAM access level for, 312

server logins, 192
  encrypting, 204
  as execution context, 200
  password policies, 197
  permissions. *See* authentication and
    authorization
server management, 161–188
  policy-based management, 183–188
  SMO in Microsoft Visual Studio, 167–183
    creating backup and restore applications,
      175–181
    interacting through available servers, 169
    programmatic DBCC functions, 181
    retrieving server settings, 171–174
Server Management Objects. *See* SMO
server roles, logins with, 193
server time dimensions (OLAP), 660–685
  fact dimensions, 661–664
  role-playing dimensions, 664
serveradmin server role, 193
ServerConnection object, 168
server-side ADO MD.NET, 782–792
  calling managed code from MDX, 786
  debugging managed code, 786
  result set–returning functions, 789–792
  void functions, 788
server-side data access (SQL CLR), 120–125
ServerSyncProviderProxy class, 534, 537
Service Account task (Reporting Services
    Configuration Manager), 938
Service Master Key (SMK), 206
service-based synchronization, 556
services without components, 474
session variables (Sync Services), 535
SessionId property (SyncSession), 535
SET ENCRYPTION ON clause, ALTER DATABASE
    statement, 213
SET TRANSACTION ISOLATION LEVEL statement,
    462
setupadmin server role, 193
SHAPE clause, with DMX statements, 846, 854
SharePoint
  publishing Excel content to. *See* Excel Services
  Reporting Services integration with, 949–951
shred and compose (XML solution), 233
Silverlight 2.0, data binding with, 438, 445–446
single-row operations, TVPs with, 51–54
size, audit file, 219
SKIP keyword, 847
smalldatetime data type, replacing, 59
SMK. *See* Service Master Key
SMO (Server Management Objects), 161–167
  latest features in, 166
  in Microsoft Visual Studio, 167–183

    creating backup and restore applications,
      175–181
    interacting through available servers, 169
    programmatic DBCC functions, 181
    retrieving server settings, 171–174
  namespace map (partial), 162
  SQL-DMO vs., 162–166
Snapshot isolation level (ADO.NET), 468
snapshot isolation level (SQL Server 2008), 45,
    465–467
  SQL Server Change Tracking, 539
snapshot-based data warehouse design, 588
snapshots (Merge Replication), 495
  configuring for mobile application delivery. *See*
    Web Synchronization
snowflake schemas, 616
Solution Explorer (Analysis Services), 634
sort order, report groups, 891
sorting hierarchical data, 301
source data, preparing for mining, 798
source of MERGE statement, 70. *See also* MERGE
    statement
  WHEN NOT MATCHED BY SOURCE clause,
    74–76
sp_addlogin procedure, 197
sp_configure procedure, 191
sp_estimate_data_compression_savings
    procedure, 607
sp_xml_preparedocument procedure, 261
SPARSE columns, 604–605
spatial data types, 344. *See also* geospatial data
    types
spatial models, 342–343
spatial reference IDs (SRIDs), 355
Specify Relationship dialog box (Analysis
    Services), 623
splits, 813
SQL, LINQ and. *See* LINQ (Language Integrated
    Query)
SQL CLR feature, 111–160, 283
  aggregates, 140–145
  assemblies, deploying, 119, 125–127
  best practices, 159
  deployment, 125–131
  enabling CLR integration, 112
  functions, 131–135
  managing types in database, 152–158
  security, 150
  server-side ADO MD.NET, 782–792
    calling managed code from MDX, 786
    debugging managed code, 786
    result set–returning functions, 789–792
    void functions, 788
  stored procedures
    creating (example), 118

SQL CLR feature (*continued*)
    deploying, 127–128
    server-side data access and, 120–125
    testing, 129–131
    usage guidelines, 124
   transactions, 485–488
    example of, 489–490
   triggers, 136–140
   types, 145–150
   Visual Studio/SQL Server integration, 113–118
SQL injection attacks, 162, 226
SQL Server 2000, XML in, 233
SQL Server 2008
   about, 3–5
   Express edition, 496–497
   integration with Visual Studio, 113–118
   XML in. *See* XML
SQL Server 2008 Reporting Services. *See*
   Reporting Services
SQL Server Audit feature. *See* auditing
SQL Server Browser service, 196, 226
SQL Server Change Tracking
   changing tracking functions, 542
   configuring database for, 538–543
SQL Server Compact 3.5, 496–497
SQL Server Configuration Manager tool, 205
   access level for FILESTREAM feature, 311, 313
SQL Server Data Services, 377, 415
SQL Server instances. *See also entries at* server
   connections to, 168
   enumeating available, 169
   settings of, retrieving, 171
SQL Server Integration Services, 930–937
SQL Server logins, 192
   encrypting, 204
   as execution context, 200
   password policies, 197
   permissions. *See* authentication and
    authorization
SQL Server Management Studio (SSMS)
   as MDX client, 744, 745–758
   Reporting Services administration, 940–949
    caching reports, 943
    data-driven report subscriptions, 942
    securing reports, 944–949
    standard report subscriptions, 940–942
   with spatial data, 354
   using XMLA from, 772–778
   viewing audited events with, 223
SQL Server projects, 114–116
SQL Slammer virus, 226
sql:column function, 275
sql:variable function, 276
SqlCeClientSyncProvider class, 534, 536, 552
SqlCommand objects

avoiding creating with SqlDataAdapter, 388,
   389
   preventing SQL injection attacks, 227
SqlConnection objects, 487
   avoiding creating with SqlDataAdapter, 388,
   389
SqlContext class, 121
SqlDataRecord class, 123–124
SqlDbType.Structured enumeration, 56
SQL-DMO (Distributed Management Objects), 161
   SMO (Server Management Objects) vs.,
    162–166
SqlFunction attribute, 131
SqlGeography class, 370
SqlMetaData class, 123–124
SqlPipe class, 121
SqlProcedure attribute (StoredProcedures), 127
SqlSyncAdapterBuilder class, 558
SqlTrigger attribute, 137
SqlUserDefinedAggregate attribute, 141
SqlUserDefinedType attribute, 147
SRIDs (spatial reference IDs), 355
SSL, for mobile application synchronization, 513
SSMS. *See* SQL Server Management Studio
standard deviation, defined, 796
standardized reference data, lack of, 568
star schemas, 576, 577
   preparing to build OLAP cubes, 617
   Star-Join Query Optimization, 603–604
STArea method, geography data type, 355
Star-Join Query Optimization, 603–604
STATE option
   ALTER SERVER AUDIT statement, 218
   CREATE SERVER AUDIT SPECIFICATION
    statement, 220
statement-level recompile errors, 41
static properties (SQL Server Data Services), 415
status expressions, KPI, 678
StatusGraphic property (Kpis collection), 764
STDimension method, geometry and geography
   data types, 350
STDistance method, geography data type, 363
STIntersection method, geometry and geography
   data types, 350
STIntersects method, geometry and geography
   data types, 347
STLength method, geography data type, 355
storage of date-time values, 60, 62
stored procedures
   for data mining, 863
   in EF models, 404–405
   in L2S models, 399–401
   managed (server-side ADO MD.NET)
    calling code from MDX, 782
    debugging, 786

stored procedures (*continued*)
    result set–returning functions, 789
    void functions, 788
    writing code for, 782
  parameters, TableAdapter objects and, 385
  SQL CLR stored procedures
    creating (example), 118
    deploying, 127–128
    managing with Object Explorer, 152
    server-side data access, 120–125
    testing, 129–131
    usage guidelines, 124
  TVPs with. *See* TVPs (table-valued parameters)
storing BLOBs. *See* BLOB data; FILESTREAM
    feature
streamed file access, FILESTREAM for, 312. *See
    also* FILESTREAM feature
  as HTTP service, 333–338
streams, BLOBs in, 309. *See also* BLOB data;
    FILESTREAM feature
Streets & Trips 2008, 351
string formats for date-time values, 64
strings, converting to XML, 278–279
strongly typed DataSet objects. *See* typed
    DataSet objects
structured and unstructured data storage. *See*
    BLOB data; FILESTREAM feature
Structured enumeration (SqlDbType), 56
structures, mining, 804, 808. *See also* data mining
  documenting (Data Mining Client add-in), 877
  validating models in, 812
subject-orientation of data warehouses, 572
subscribers (Merge Replication), 495
  synchronizing database for, 517–519. *See also*
    Web Synchronization
subscriptions, Merge Replication, 495, 520
subscriptions, reports
  data-driven subscriptions, 942
  standard subscriptions, 940–942
subtotals in matrix reports, 908
subtrees, transplanting. *See also* hierarchical data
subtrees, transplanting (reparenting), 303
Supported value (TransactionOption attribute),
    473
surface area for attack, 191
surrogate keys, 579, 587
switching execution context, 203
SWITCHOFFSET function, 66, 67
symmetric key encryption, 204
  Service Master Key (SMK), 206
Sync Services for ADO.NET, 492, 533–560
  capturing changes for synchronization,
    538–543
    changing tracking functions, 542
    configuring database for, 538–543

creating applications that use, 543–557
    data conflicts, handling, 543–552
    N-tier applications, 554–556
    service-based synchronization, 556
  data type considerations, 559
  local data caches, 557
  vs. Merge Replication, 492
  object model for, 534–537
  security considerations, 560
  SqlSyncAdapterBuilder class, 558
SyncAdapter class, 534, 536
SyncAgent class, 534
SyncGroup class, 534, 537
synchronization, 493
  for mobile applications. *See* Web
    Synchronization
SyncInitialized constant, 536
SyncLastReceivedAnchor constant, 536
SyncNewReceivedAnchor constant, 536
SyncParameters property (SyncSession), 535
SyncRowCount constant, 536
SyncSession class, 534, 535
SyncSessionId constant, 536
SyncStatistics class, 534
SyncTable class, 534, 537
syntax errors, TRY/CATCH blocks and, 41
sysadmin server role, 193
sys.certificates view, 212
sys.database_audit_specification_details view, 225
sys.database_audit_specifications view, 225
sys.databases view, 213
SYSDATETIME function, 65
SYSDATETIMEOFFSET function, 65
sys.dm_audit_actions view, 225
sys.dm_audit_class_type_map view, 225
sys.dm_database_encryption_keys view, 214
sys.dm_server_audit_status view, 225
sys.fn_get_audit_file function, 224
sys.server_audit_specification_details view, 225
sys.server_audit_specifications view, 225
sys.server_file_audits view, 225
sys.sql_logins view, 198
system administrator passwords, 226
System.Data.SqlClient namespace, 122, 388
System.EnterpriseServices namespace, 473
System.Transactions namespace, 474, 476
SYSUTCDATETIME function, 65

T

Table Analysis Tools add-in (Excel 2007), 867–873
table columns
  defined as XML, 235–237
    converting columns to XML, 278–279

table columns (*continued*)
    default and constraints, 236
    primary and secondary XML indexes, 244–247
    querying. See XQuery language
    pivoting dynamically, 23
    statements without explicit column lists, TVPs and, 53, 54
table join types, MERGE with, 78
table locking, with Partitioned Table Parallelism, 602
table replication, MERGE statement for (T-SQL), 73
TableAdapter Configuration Wizard, 382–385
TableAdapter objects, 380
    adding queries to, 385
    data binding examples, 423, 424
    GenerateDBDirectMethods property, 387
TableAdapterManager class (example), 424
TableCreationOption enumeration, 537
tables
    adding to Data Source View pane, 628
    for data mining models, 805
    with FILESTREAM columns, 315–318
    hierarchical. See hierarchical data
table-valued functions (TVFs), 132
table-valued parameters (TVPs), 45–59
    bulk inserts and updates, 49
    dictionary-style TVPs, 54
    limitations of, 59
    multiple-row sets, 48
    passing TVPs using ADO.NET, 56
    single rows of data, 51–54
tablix data region, 881, 886, 910–915
    extending with groups, 910–912
    fixed columns and rows, adding, 913
    report actions, 918
target of MERGE statement, 70. See also MERGE statement
    WHEN NOT MATCHED BY TARGET, 72
target type (PBM), defined, 184
TCs (transaction coordinators). See transaction managers (TMs)
TDE. See Transparent Data Encryption
templates
    for DMX queries, 856
    for reports, 897–900
Terminate method (aggregate classes), 141
testing
    actions, 692
    data mining, test sets for, 808
    data web services (ADO.NET), 414
    KPIs (key performance indicators), 681–683
    SQL CLR stored procedures, 120, 129–131
text test function (XML PATH), 257

thread management (data warehousing), 601
time data type, 59
time data types, T-SQL. See date and time data types, T-SQL
time dimensions (OLAP). See dimensions; server time dimensions
Time Series algorithm (Analysis Services), 797
time zone awareness
    T-SQL data types, 61–62, 65
    xsd:dateTime data type, 240
time-variant, data warehouses as, 572
TMs. See transaction managers (TMs)
TO APPLICATION_LOG option, CREATE SERVER AUDIT statement, 220
TO FILE clause, CREATE SERVER AUDIT, 216, 219
TO SECURITY_LOG option, CREATE SERVER AUDIT statement, 220
TODATETIMEOFFSET function, 66
TOP clause
    DMX statements, 849
    MERGE statement and, 79
TOP parameter, T-SQL, 26–27
top-down approach to data warehousing, 572–573
ToString method
    geometry and geography data types, 349
    hierarchyid data type, 288–292
totals in matrix reports, 908
TRACK_COLUMNS_UPDATED option, 540
tracking changes for Sync Services, 538–543
    changing tracking functions, 542
    configuring database for, 538–543
training sets for data mining, 808
transaction abort error, 41
transaction coordinators. See transaction managers (TMs)
transaction managers (TMs), 469
TransactionOption attribute, 473
transactions, 449–490. See also T-SQL
    ACID properties, 449, 450–452
    defined, 450
    distributed transactions, 453, 468–484
        in .NET Framework, 473
        terminology of, 461, 469
    isolation levels. See isolation levels
    local transactions, 452, 453–461
        autocommit transaction mode, 453
        batch-scoped transaction mode, 457–459
        explicit transaction mode, 453–456
        implicit transaction mode, 456
    reliability of, 449
    in SQL CLR (CLR integration), 485–488
        example of, 489–490
    terminology of, 461, 469–470

Transactions namespace, 477
TransactionScope class, 476, 487
    example of, 489–490
translations (OLAP cubes), 707–711
Transparent Data Encryption (TDE), 211–216
    backing up certificates, 214
    enabling, 213
    querying views, 213
    restoring encrypted databases, 215
transplanting subtrees (hierarchical data), 303
tree structures. *See* hierarchical data
Tree Viewer, 823–825
    ViewType property, 862
trend expressions, KPI, 678
TrendGraphic property (Kpis collection), 764
TriggerAction property (TriggerContext), 139
triggers
    DDL triggers, 43, 136
    SQL CLR triggers, 136–140
TRUSTWORTH property, 151
TRY and CATCH blocks, T-SQL, 40–42
T-SQL, 13–111, 111. *See also* transactions
    aggregations, 140
    APPLY operator, 25
    CAST function
        converting columns to XML, 278–279
        extracting from datetime2 data, 64
    common table expressions (CTEs), 14–20
        creating recursive queries with, 18–20
    CONVERT function
        converting columns to XML, 278–279
        extracting from datetime2 data, 64
    date and time data types, 59–67
        accuracy, storage, and format, 62–64
        new and changed since SQL Server 2000, 65
        separation of dates and times, 59
        time zone awareness, 61–62
    DDL triggers, 43
    enhancements in SQL Server 2008, 4
    FILESTREAM access, enabling, 311
    GROUPING SETS operator, 97–109
        NULL values, handling, 105–109
        returning top level only, 103
        rolling up all level combinations, 101
        rolling up by level, 99
        rollup and cube operations together, 103
    INSERT OVER DML syntax, 90–97
        CHANGES keyword, 94–97
        OUTPUT...INTO, extending, 90–94
    MERGE statement, 68–90
        defining merge source and target, 70
        DML behavior, 79–81
        join method, choosing, 78
        OUTPUT clause, 76
        for table replication, 73
        upsert operations, 81–90
        WHEN MATCHED clause, 71
        WHEN NOT MATCHED BY SOURCE clause, 74
        WHEN NOT MATCHED BY TARGET clause, 72
    PIVOT and UNPIVOT operators, 21–24
        dynamically pivoting columns, 23
    ranking functions, 28–40
        DENSE_RANK and NTILE functions, 34–36
        RANK function, 32
        ROW_NUMBER function, 28–31
        using all together, 36
        windowing functions with, 37–40
    shorthand syntax, 109
    SNAPSHOT isolation level, 45, 465–467
        SQL Server Change Tracking, 539
    table-valued parameters (TVPs), 45–59
        bulk inserts and updates, 49
        dictionary-style TVPs, 54
        limitations of, 59
        multiple-row sets, 48
        passing TVPs using ADO.NET, 56
        single rows of data, 51–54
    TOP parameter, 26–27
    triggers, 43, 136
    TRY and CATCH blocks, 40–42
    varchar(max) data type, 42
    WAITFOR statement, 43
    xml data type as variable, 234
tuples, 752, 753
TVFs (table-valued functions), 132
TVPs (table-valued parameters), 45–59
    bulk inserts and updates, 49
    dictionary-style TVPs, 54
    limitations of, 59
    multiple-row sets, 48
    passing TVPs using ADO.NET, 56
    single rows of data, 51–54
two-phase commit transactions, 470. *See also*
    transactions
two-way data synchronization, 494
TYPE option, FOR XML clause, 253, 254
typed DataSet objects, 378–387
    adding validation logic to, 391
    connected use of, 387
    connection string management, 381
    data binding example, 420–424
    TableAdapter Configuration Wizard, 382–385
    TableAdapter objects, 380
    using DataSet designer, 379
types, user-defined, 145–150
    examining and managing in database, 152–158
    managing with Object Explorer, 152

U

UDM (unified domensional model) paradigm, 705
UDTs (user-defined types), 145–150
   examining and managing in database, 152–158
   managing with Object Explorer, 152
UNION ALL operator, recursive queries with CTEs, 18
union data type (XSD), 242
UNION statement, FOR XML EXPLICIT with, 250
Unknown conflict (synchronization), 550
UNLIMITED option (audit file size), 219
UNPIVOT operator (T-SQL), 21–24
   dynamically pivoting columns, 23
UNSAFE ASSEMBLY permission, 151
Unsafe permission set (SQL CLR assemblies), 151, 785
Unspecified isolation level (ADO.NET), 468
unstructured storage, FILESTREAM for. *See* FILESTREAM feature
UPDATE statements
   bulk updates with TVPs, 51
   INSERT INTO...SELECT statement around, 90–94
   merges, 79. *See also* MERGE statement
   OUTPUT clause, 90
   TOP parameter in, 26–27
   WAITFOR statement with, 43
UpdatePanel controls, 431
upsert operations, 79
   MERGE statement (T-SQL) for, 81–90
URL access for viewing reports, 928
usage-based aggregation design, 701
user interface
   for data web services (ADO.NET), 414
   Windows Forms data binding, 421
user roles
   logins with, 194
   for report security, 944–949
user table time dimensions, 652
user-defined aggregates, 140–145
   managing with Object Explorer, 152
user-defined types (UDTs), 145–150
   examining and managing in database, 152–158
   managing with Object Explorer, 152
users, 193
   authenticating. *See* authentication and authorization
   guest account, 194
user-schema separation, 198–200
USING keyword, MERGE statement, 70
USING XML INDEX statement, 247

V

validating data mining models, 827–829
validating mining models, 812
validation logic, adding
   to ORM models, 410
   to typed DataSets, 391
validation of XML. *See* schemas, XML
value index (XML), 246
value method (xml data type), 266, 270
varbinary(max) data type, 42
varchar(max) data type, T-SQL, 42
variable function (sql), 276
vector objects, 344
verifying backups (example application), 178
ViewerMode property (Naïve Bayes and Cluster Viewer controls), 862
viewing data mining models, 818–826
   Cluster Viewer, 818–823
      ViewerMode property, 862
   Naïve Bayes Viewer, 826
   Tree Viewer, 823–825
viewing reports. *See* delivering reports
ViewType property (Tree Viewer), 862
Virtual Earth, 364–373
Visual Studio Analysis Services. *See* Analysis Services
Visual Studio, deploying reports with, 920
Visual Studio Tools for Office, 737
Visual Studio/SQL Server integration, 113–118
visualization of KPIs, 678
void functions in server-side managed code, 788
volatile enlistment, 471

W

W3C XML format for date-time values, 64
WAITFOR statement, T-SQL, 43
Web controls for data mining, 862
Web Service URL task (Reporting Services Configuration Manager), 938
Web services for data. *See* ADO.NET Data Services
Web services operations for deploying reports, 924
Web Services, Report Server, 938
Web Synchronization, 513–519
   configuring IIS for, 514–516
   configuring subscriber database for, 517–519
   programmatic, 526–530
   Sync Services for ADO.NET and, 538–543
      changing tracking functions, 542
      configuring database for, 538–543

Well-Known Text (WKT) markup language, 344
WHEN MATCHED clause, MERGE statement, 71, 78
WHEN NOT MATCHED clause, MERGE statement, 78
WHEN NOT MATCHED BY SOURCE clause, MERGE statement, 74–76, 78
WHEN NOT MATCHED BY TARGET clause, MERGE statement, 72, 78
WHERE clause (MDX queries), 752
WHERE clause (T-SQL), XQuery and, 273
where keyword (XQuery), 264
windowing functions with ranking functions (T-SQL), 37–40
Windows Authentication. *See* authentication and authorization
Windows event log, recording audits to, 220
Windows Forms data binding, 420–427
Windows Forms Model content browser controls, 858
Windows logins, 192
Windows Presentation Foundation (WPF)
  building client, 338
  data binding for, 438–445
    lack of design support, 439–514
    XAML for, 441–445
WITH ALGORITHM clause, CREATE DATABASE ENCRYPTION statement, 212
WITH CHANGE_TRACKING_CONTEXT clause, 542, 548
WITH CUBE operator, 97, 99
WITH DRILLTHOUGH clause, 842
WITH EXECUTE AS CALLER clause, CREATE FUNCTION, 132
WITH PERMISSION_SET clause, CREATE ASSEMBLY, 126, 127, 152
WITH ROLLUP operator, 97, 99
WKT (Well-Known Text) markup language, 344
WPF (Windows Presentation Foundation)
  building client, 338
  data binding for, 438–445
    lack of design support, 439–514
    XAML for, 441–445
Write method, hierarchyid data type, 306
writeback measure groups and dimensions, 699
WriteFile function, with BLOB data, 316, 319
WSDL for report server endpoint, 939

X

XAML (Extensible Application Markup Language), 438
  for WPF data binding, 441–445
XML (Extensible Markup Language), 231
  FOR XML clause, SELECT statement, 233, 247–259
    AUTO keyword, 248
    ELEMENTS keyword, 260
    EXPLICIT keyword, 250
    PATH keyword, 253, 255–258
    RAW keyword, 248
    ROOT option, 258
    TYPE option, 253, 254
    XMLSCHEMA option, 259
  element-based (canonical), producing, 260
  indexes, 244–247
  OPENXML function, 249, 261–262
  querying data using XQuery. *See* XQuery language
  schemas, 237–244
    inline XSD schemas, 259
    lax validation, 241
    SQL Server collections of, 237
    union and list types, 242
    xsl:dateTime enhancements, 240
  in SQL Server 2000, 233
  XML BULK LOAD, 262
  xml type. *See* xml data type
  XQuery. *See* XQuery language
xml data type, 234–247
  inability to compare instances of, 234, 235
  querying. *See* XQuery language
  for table columns, 235–237
    converting columns to XML, 278–279
    default and constraints, 236
  as variable, 234
XML DML language, 276
XMLA (XML for Analysis), 688, 755, 771–781, 863
  as API, 771
  calling Execute from .NET, 778
  data mining and, 865
  manipulating ADO MD.NET response content, 780
  using from SQL Server Management Studio, 772–778
xml.exist method, 266, 269

xml.modify method, 266, 276–277
xml.nodes method, 266, 275
xml.query method, 266, 272–274
XMLSCHEMA option, FOR XML clause, 259
xml.value method, 266, 270
XPath expression, 263
    FOR XML PATH statement, 253, 255–258
XQuery language, 263–279
    converting columns to XML, 278–279
    SQL Server extensions, 275–276
    XML DML language, 276

xml.exist method, 266, 269
xml.modify method, 266, 276–277
xml.nodes method, 266, 275
xml.query method, 266, 272–274
xml.value method, 266, 270
XSD (XML Schema Definition), 237. *See also*
    schemas, XML
    inline schemas, 259
xsd:list data type, 242
xsd:union data type, 242

Resources for SQL Server 2008

Microsoft® SQL Server® 2008 Administrator's Pocket Consultant
William R. Stanek
ISBN 9780735625891

Microsoft SQL Server 2008 Step by Step
Mike Hotek
ISBN 9780735626041

MCTS Self-Paced Training Kit (Exam 70-432) Microsoft SQL Server 2008 Implementation and Maintenance
Mike Hotek
ISBN 9780735626058

Programming Microsoft SQL Server 2008
Leonard Lobel, Andrew J. Brust, Stephen Forte
ISBN 9780735625990

Microsoft SQL Server 2008 T-SQL Fundamentals
Itzik Ben-Gan
ISBN 9780735626010

Smart Business Intelligence Solutions with Microsoft SQL Server 2008
Lynn Langit, Kevin S. Goff, Davide Mauri, Sahil Malik
ISBN 9780735625808

COMING SOON

Microsoft SQL Server 2008 Internals
Kalen Delaney *et al.*
ISBN 9780735626249

Inside Microsoft SQL Server 2008: T-SQL Querying
Itzik Ben-Gan, Lubor Kollar, Dejan Sarka
ISBN 9780735626034

Microsoft SQL Server 2008 Best Practices
Saleem Hakani and Ward Pond
with the Microsoft SQL Server Team
ISBN 9780735626225

Microsoft SQL Server 2008 MDX Step by Step
Bryan C. Smith, C. Ryan Clay, Hitachi Consulting
ISBN 9780735626188

Microsoft SQL Server 2008 Reporting Services Step by Step
Stacia Misner
ISBN 9780735626478

Microsoft SQL Server 2008 Analysis Services Step by Step
Scott Cameron, Hitachi Consulting
ISBN 9780735626201

microsoft.com/mspress

About the Authors

Leonard Lobel is the chief technology officer (CTO) and cofounder of Sleek Technologies, Inc., a New York–based development shop with an early adopter philosophy toward new technologies. He is also a principal consultant at twentysix New York, a Microsoft Gold Certified Partner. Programming since 1979, Lenni specializes in Microsoft-based solutions, with experience that spans a variety of business domains, including publishing, financial, wholesale/retail, health care, and e-commerce. Lenni has served as chief architect and lead developer for various organizations, ranging from small shops to high-profile clients. He is also a consultant, author, trainer, and a frequent speaker at local usergroup meetings, VSLive, SQL PASS, and other industry conferences. He can be reached at *lenni.lobel@sleektech.com* and *lenni.lobel@26ny.com*.

Andrew J. Brust is the chief of new technology at twentysix New York, a Microsoft Gold Certified Partner in New York City, where he leads strategy, evangelism, and business development. Andrew serves as Microsoft regional director for New York and New Jersey, is a Visual Basic MVP, and is a member of Microsoft's Business Intelligence Partner Advisory Council. Andrew has served as track cochair at Tech*Ed North America, is a conference chair for VSLive, and is a highly rated speaker at conferences throughout the United States and internationally. Often quoted in the technology industry press, Andrew has 20 years' experience programming and consulting in the financial, public, small business, and not-for-profit sectors. He can be reached at *andrew.brust@26ny.com*.

Stephen Forte is the chief strategy officer of Telerik, a leading vendor in .NET components. Previously, he was the chief technology officer (CTO) and co-founder of Corzen, Inc., a New York–based provider of online market research data for Wall Street firms. Corzen was acquired by Wanted Technologies (TXV: WAN) in 2007. Stephen is also the Microsoft regional director for the New York Metro region and speaks regularly at industry conferences around the world. He has written several books on application and database development, including coauthoring *Programming SQL Server 2005*. Prior to Corzen, Stephen served as the CTO of Zagat Survey in New York City and also was cofounder and CTO of the New York–based software consulting firm The Aurora Development Group. He is currently an MVP and an INETA speaker and is the comoderator and founder of the NYC .NET Developer User Group. Stephen has an MBA from the City University of New York (Baruch College).

Contributing Authors

Jeff Bolton is a database architect at twentysix New York (*www.26NY.com*), specializing in implementing solutions utilizing all aspects of SQL Server. He has been working with Microsoft SQL Server since 1992. Jeff also has experience as a systems engineer with Microsoft Windows Server products as well as development utilizing many different languages, including C, Microsoft Visual Basic, C#, and PowerBuilder. Prior to joining twentysix New York, Jeff graduated from Rensselaer Polytechnic Institute and worked at a consulting firm specializing in building systems for managing containerized shipping. When not working with databases, Jeff spends most of his time coaching his sons' ice hockey and football teams.

 Paul Delcogliano is a technology director at Optech Systems, Inc., a wholly owned subsidiary of Matrix Financial Solutions. Optech Systems designs and develops the software solutions used by Matrix Financial Solutions to provide automated trading services to its customers. Matrix Financial Solutions is one of the nation's largest providers of products and services for third-party administrators (TPAs), financial advisors, banks, and wealth management professionals. Matrix Financial Solutions, through its wholly owned subsidiaries, serves more than 300 financial institutions by servicing $100 billion in assets on its trading and trust platform.

Paul has been working with the Microsoft .NET Framework since its first public introduction and has been developing Microsoft SQL Server applications even longer. He builds systems for a diverse range of platforms including Microsoft Windows and the Internet. Paul has authored several articles and columns for various trade publications on a variety of topics. He can be reached by e-mail at *pdelco@hotmail.com*. The thoughts and writings in Chapter 13 are solely those of Paul Delcogliano and cannot be attributed to Optech Systems, Inc., or Matrix Financial Solutions, Inc. Paul would like to thank Lenni for offering him the opportunity to write a chapter in this book. It was a great experience and lots of fun. Let's promise never to do it again (wink, wink).

 Mark Frawley is a senior software developer at twentysix New York (*www.26ny.com*) and has been immersed in all aspects of data warehouse design and implementation since 1992, using Microsoft SQL Server and Analysis Services since 2003. With a degree in electrical engineering, Mark's experience spans semiconductor design and fabrication, digital circuit design, assembly language programming for electronic funds transfer, and last his current data-centric business intelligence and data warehousing work. Mark enjoys the perspective that this breadth of experience affords on how things work at every level of a computer and is very glad to have found his way into the endlessly challenging arenas of business intelligence, data warehousing, and OLAP.